Dictionary
of the
Middle Ages

AMERICAN COUNCIL OF LEARNED SOCIETIES

The American Council of Learned Societies, organized in 1919 for the purpose of advancing the study of the humanities and of the humanistic aspects of the social sciences, is a nonprofit federation comprising forty-six national scholarly groups. The Council represents the humanities in the United States in the International Union of Academies, provides fellowships and grants-in-aid, supports research-and-planning conferences and symposia, and sponsors special projects and scholarly publications.

MEMBER ORGANIZATIONS
AMERICAN PHILOSOPHICAL SOCIETY, 1743
AMERICAN ACADEMY OF ARTS AND SCIENCES, 1780
AMERICAN ANTIQUARIAN SOCIETY, 1812
AMERICAN ORIENTAL SOCIETY, 1842
AMERICAN NUMISMATIC SOCIETY, 1858
AMERICAN PHILOLOGICAL ASSOCIATION, 1869
ARCHAEOLOGICAL INSTITUTE OF AMERICA, 1879
SOCIETY OF BIBLICAL LITERATURE, 1880
MODERN LANGUAGE ASSOCIATION OF AMERICA, 1883
AMERICAN HISTORICAL ASSOCIATION, 1884
AMERICAN ECONOMIC ASSOCIATION, 1885
AMERICAN FOLKLORE SOCIETY, 1888
AMERICAN DIALECT SOCIETY, 1889
AMERICAN PSYCHOLOGICAL ASSOCIATION, 1892
ASSOCIATION OF AMERICAN LAW SCHOOLS, 1900
AMERICAN PHILOSOPHICAL ASSOCIATION, 1901
AMERICAN ANTHROPOLOGICAL ASSOCIATION, 1902
AMERICAN POLITICAL SCIENCE ASSOCIATION, 1903
BIBLIOGRAPHICAL SOCIETY OF AMERICA, 1904
ASSOCIATION OF AMERICAN GEOGRAPHERS, 1904
HISPANIC SOCIETY OF AMERICA, 1904
AMERICAN SOCIOLOGICAL ASSOCIATION, 1905
AMERICAN SOCIETY OF INTERNATIONAL LAW, 1906
ORGANIZATION OF AMERICAN HISTORIANS, 1907
AMERICAN ACADEMY OF RELIGION, 1909
COLLEGE ART ASSOCIATION OF AMERICA, 1912
HISTORY OF SCIENCE SOCIETY, 1924
LINGUISTIC SOCIETY OF AMERICA, 1924
MEDIAEVAL ACADEMY OF AMERICA, 1925
AMERICAN MUSICOLOGICAL SOCIETY, 1934
SOCIETY OF ARCHITECTURAL HISTORIANS, 1940
ECONOMIC HISTORY ASSOCIATION, 1940
ASSOCIATION FOR ASIAN STUDIES, 1941
AMERICAN SOCIETY FOR AESTHETICS, 1942
AMERICAN ASSOCIATION FOR THE ADVANCEMENT OF SLAVIC STUDIES, 1948
METAPHYSICAL SOCIETY OF AMERICA, 1950
AMERICAN STUDIES ASSOCIATION, 1950
RENAISSANCE SOCIETY OF AMERICA, 1954
SOCIETY FOR ETHNOMUSICOLOGY, 1955
AMERICAN SOCIETY FOR LEGAL HISTORY, 1956
AMERICAN SOCIETY FOR THEATRE RESEARCH, 1956
SOCIETY FOR THE HISTORY OF TECHNOLOGY, 1958
AMERICAN COMPARATIVE LITERATURE ASSOCIATION, 1960
MIDDLE EAST STUDIES ASSOCIATION OF NORTH AMERICA, 1966
AMERICAN SOCIETY FOR EIGHTEENTH-CENTURY STUDIES, 1969
ASSOCIATION FOR JEWISH STUDIES, 1969

Dictionary of the Middle Ages

JOSEPH R. STRAYER, *EDITOR IN CHIEF*

Volume 5

FAMINE IN THE ISLAMIC WORLD—GROOTE, GEERT

CHARLES SCRIBNER'S SONS
MACMILLAN LIBRARY REFERENCE USA
Simon & Schuster Macmillan
NEW YORK

Simon & Schuster and Prentice Hall International
LONDON · MEXICO CITY · NEW DELHI · SINGAPORE · SYDNEY · TORONTO

Copyright © 1985 American Council of Learned Societies

Library of Congress Cataloging in Publication Data
Main entry under title:

Dictionary of the Middle Ages.

Includes bibliographies and index.
1. Middle Ages—Dictionaries.   I. Strayer,
Joseph Reese, 1904–1987.

D114.D5   1982   909.07   82-5904
ISBN 0-684-16760-3 (v. 1)   ISBN 0-684-18169-X (v. 7)
ISBN 0-684-17022-1 (v. 2)   ISBN 0-684-18274-2 (v. 8)
ISBN 0-684-17023-X (v. 3)   ISBN 0-684-18275-0 (v. 9)
ISBN 0-684-17024-8 (v. 4)   ISBN 0-684-18276-9 (v. 10)
ISBN 0-684-18161-4 (v. 5)   ISBN 0-684-18277-7 (v. 11)
ISBN 0-684-18168-1 (v. 6)   ISBN 0-684-18278-5 (v. 12)

Charles Scribner's Sons
An Imprint of Simon & Schuster Macmillan
1633 Broadway, New York, NY 10019-6785

7 9 11 13 15 17 19   Q/C   20 18 16 14 12 10 8

PRINTED IN THE UNITED STATES OF AMERICA.

The *Dictionary of the Middle Ages* has been produced with
support from the National Endowment for the Humanities.

The paper in this book meets the guidelines for
permanence and durability of the Committee on
Production Guidelines for Book Longevity of the
Council on Library Resources.

Maps prepared by Sylvia Lehrman.

Editorial Board

Advisory Committee

Editorial Staff

Contributors to Volume 5

UMAR F. ABD-ALLĀH
University of Michigan, Ann Arbor
FASTING, ISLAMIC; FRIDAY PRAYER

ROBERT W. ACKERMAN
GRAIL, LEGEND OF

F. R. P. AKEHURST
University of Minnesota
GACE BRULÉ

THEODORE M. ANDERSSON
Stanford University
FÓSTBRŒÐRA SAGA; GÍSLA SAGA SÚRSSONAR; GRÍPISSPÁ

MARIA PILAR APARICIO-LLOPIS
FUERO

MARY-JO ARN
English Institute, Groningen
GROOTE, GEERT

HOWARD I. ARONSON
University of Chicago
GEORGIAN LANGUAGE

JUAN BAUTISTA AVALLE-ARCE
University of California, Santa Barbara
FERNÁN GONZÁLEZ, POEMA DE

TERENCE BAILEY
University of Western Ontario
FRANCO OF COLOGNE; GALLICAN CHANT; GRADUAL

JÁNOS M. BAK
University of British Columbia
GERARD OF CSANÁD, ST.

JOHN W. BALDWIN
Johns Hopkins University
FRANCE: 987–1223

REBECCA A. BALTZER
University of Texas
FLORENCE, BIBLIOTECA MEDICEO-LAURENZIANA, MS PLUTEUS 29.1

CARL F. BARNES, JR.
FLÈCHE; FLEURON; FLUSHWORK; FORMERET; GALLERY; GARGOYLE; GAYRARD, RAYMOND; GÉRARD OF CLAIRVAUX, ST.; GERHARD OF COLOGNE; GOLDEN SECTION

ROBERT BEDROSIAN
GRIGOR AKNERC͟I

JEANETTE M. A. BEER
Purdue University
FET DES ROMAINS, LI; FRENCH LANGUAGE; FRENCH LITERATURE: TRANSLATIONS; GESTA FRANCORUM ET ALIORUM HIEROSOLIMITANORUM

F. BEHRENDS
University of North Carolina, Chapel Hill
FULBERT OF CHARTRES

HUGO BEKKER
Ohio State University
FRIEDRICH VON HAUSEN

DAVID BERGER
Brooklyn College
GALUT

DAVID SANDLER BERKOWITZ
Brandeis University
FORTESCUE, SIR JOHN

LIONEL BIER
FĀRS

IRENE A. BIERMAN
University of California, Los Angeles
FATIMID ART

DALE L. BISHOP
GĀTHĀS

THOMAS N. BISSON
University of California, Berkeley
FRANCE: TO 987

ROBERT J. BLANCH
Northeastern University
GAWAIN AND THE GREEN KNIGHT, SIR

JONATHAN M. BLOOM
Harvard University
FUNDUQ

IMRE BOBA
University of Washington
GREAT (OR OLD) MORAVIA

SÁNDOR BÖKÖNYI
Hungarian Academy of Sciences
FOWL, DOMESTIC; FOWLING

C. E. BOSWORTH
University of Manchester
GAMES, ISLAMIC; GHĀZĀN (KHAN), MAḤMŪD; GHAZNAVIDS; GHURIDS

MICHAEL BRETT
University of London
FĒS

KATHARINE REYNOLDS BROWN
Metropolitan Museum of Art, New York
GEMS AND JEWELRY

ROBERT BROWNING
University of London
GREEK LANGUAGE, BYZANTINE

ix

CONTRIBUTORS TO VOLUME 5

LESLIE BRUBAKER
Wheaton College, Norton, Massachusetts
FIBULA; FINIAL; FLABELLUM; FOLIO; FOUNTAIN OF LIFE; FRANCO-SAXON SCHOOL; FRESCO BUONO; FRESCO SECCO; GEORGE KALLIERGIS; GISLEBERTUS; GLOBUS CRUCIGER; GLYKOPHILOUSA; GOOD SHEPHERD; GOSPELBOOK; GOTHIC, DECORATED; GOTHIC, FLAMBOYANT; GOTHIC, PERPENDICULAR; GOTHIC, RAYONNANT; GRISAILLE

GENE BRUCKER
University of California, Berkeley
FLORENCE

LANCE W. BRUNNER
University of Kentucky
FARCING

BONNIE BUETTNER
Cornell University
GRAF RUDOLF

ANNE HAGOPIAN VAN BUREN
Tufts University
FILLASTRE, GUILLAUME; FOUQUET, JEAN

ALLEN CABANISS
University of Mississippi
FLORUS OF LYONS

ROBERT G. CALKINS
Cornell University
FRANKE, MEISTER; GOTHIC ART: PAINTING AND MANUSCRIPT ILLUMINATION; GOTHIC, INTERNATIONAL STYLE

DANIEL CALLAM
St. Thomas More College
FASTING, CHRISTIAN

JOHN CARSWELL
University of Chicago
GOLDEN HORN WARE

VINCENT H. CASSIDY
University of Akron
GEOGRAPHY AND CARTOGRAPHY, WESTERN EUROPEAN

JAMES E. CATHEY
University of Massachusetts, Amherst
FIMBUL WINTER

MADELINE H. CAVINESS
Tufts University
GLASS, STAINED

GRETEL CHAPMAN
GODEFROID OF HUY; GOZBERTUS

ROBERT J. CHARLESTON
GLASS, WESTERN EUROPEAN

COLIN CHASE
University of Toronto, Centre for Medieval Studies
FRITHEGOD

SIDNEY L. COHEN
Louisiana State University
GOTLAND

LAWRENCE I. CONRAD
American University of Bierut
FARAZDAQ, AL-

PATRICIA L. CONROY
University of Washington
FAROESE BALLADS

JOHN J. CONTRENI
Purdue University
GREGORY OF TOURS, ST.

MADELEINE PELNER COSMAN
City College of New York
FEASTS AND FESTIVALS, EUROPEAN

WILLIAM CRAWFORD
University of Toronto, Centre for Medieval Studies
GESTA APOLLONII

GLYNNIS M. CROPP
Massey University
FOLQUET DE MARSEILLES

BERNARD CULLEN
Queen's University of Belfast
GODFREY OF FONTAINES

FRANCES L. DECKER
FLECK, KONRAD; FLORIS

HELLE DEGNBOL
FLÓRES SAGA OK BLANKIFLÚR

PETER F. DEMBOWSKI
University of Chicago
FROISSART, JEHAN

DON DENNY
University of Maryland
FROMENT, NICOLAS

LUCY DER MANUELIAN
GAWIT^C; GAYIANÉ, CHURCH OF; GELARD; GLAJOR; GOŠAVANK^C

THÉOPHILE DESBONNETS, O.F.M.
FRANCISCAN RITE

WACHTANG DJOBADZE
California State University, Los Angeles
GELAT^{C}I; GEORGIAN ART AND ARCHITECTURE

MARIANNE DJUTH
Ripon College
FAUSTUS OF RIEZ

JERRILYNN DODDS
Columbia University
FIRST ROMANESQUE

DIANE MARIE DOLAN
FLEURY PLAYBOOK

MICHAEL W. DOLS
California State University, Hayward
FAMINE IN THE ISLAMIC WORLD

MARTHA WESTCOTT DRIVER
GLOSS

EDWARD DUDLEY
State University of New York, Buffalo
FLORES, JUAN DE

PATRICIA J. EBERLE
University of Toronto
GOWER, JOHN

JOHN A. EMERSON
University of California, Berkeley
GREGORIAN CHANT

MARCY J. EPSTEIN
Pontifical Institute of Mediaeval Studies, Toronto
FLEXA; GIRAUT DE BORNELH

MICHEL VAN ESBROECK
Société des Bollandistes
GEORGIAN CHURCH AND SAINTS

T. S. FAUNCE
Princeton University
GRÉBAN, ARNOUL

S. C. FERRUOLO
Stanford University
GERALD OF WALES

RUTH H. FIRESTONE
University of Missouri, Columbia
GOLDEMAR

CONTRIBUTORS TO VOLUME 5

JERE FLECK
University of Maryland
GRÍMNISMÁL

JOHN F. FLINN
University of Toronto
GAUTIER D'ARRAS

ROBERTA FRANK
University of Toronto, Centre for Medieval Studies
FLOKKR

JOHN B. FREED
Illinois State University
GERMANY: 843–1137; GERMANY: 1138–1254; GERMANY: STEM DUCHIES; GORZE

EDWARD FRUEH
Columbia University
FARDALFUS ABBAS; FRANCO OF LIÈGE; FRIDUGISUS OF TOURS; GAUFRID (GAUDFRED) MALATERRA; GIBUIN OF LANGRES; GODFREY OF WINCHESTER

KLAUS GAMBER
GLAGOLITIC RITE

STEPHEN GARDNER
Columbia University
GEOFFREY OF NOYERS; GERVASE OF CANTERBURY; GLOUCESTER CATHEDRAL

NINA G. GARSOÏAN
Columbia University
GŌSĀN; GREGORIDS

ADELHEID M. GEALT
Indiana University
FRANCESCO DA RIMINI; FRESCO PAINTING; GADDI, AGNOLO; GADDI, GADDO; GADDI, TADDEO; GANO DA SIENA; GENTILE DA FABRIANO; GERHARDO DI JACOPO STARNINA; GESSO; GIOTTO DI BONDONE; GIOVANNI D'AMBROGIO DA FIRENZE; GIOVANNI DA FIESOLE; GIOVANNI DA MILANO; GIOVANNI (GIOVANNINO) DE' GRASSI; GIOVANNI (NANNI) DI BARTOLO; GIOVANNI DI BENEDETTO DA COMO; GIOVANNI DI PAOLO; GIULIANO DA RIMINI; GIUSTO DE MENABUOI; GOFFREDO DA VITERBO

D. J. GEANAKOPLOS
Yale University
GEMISTOS PLETHON, GEORGIOS

JOSEPH GILL, S.J.
Campion Hall, Oxford
FERRARA-FLORENCE, COUNCIL OF

THOMAS F. GLICK
Boston University
FRUITS AND NUTS

INGEBORG GLIER
Yale University
GERMAN LITERATURE: ALLEGORY

HARRIET GOLDBERG
Villanova University
FORTUNE, OLD SPANISH

PETER B. GOLDEN
Rutgers University
GENGHIS KHAN; GHĀZĪ; GOLDEN HORDE

ROBERT S. GOTTFRIED
Institute for Advanced Study, Princeton
FAMINE IN WESTERN EUROPE

KATHRYN GRAVDAL
Columbia University
GAUCHIER DE DOURDAN

GORDON K. GREENE
Wilfrid Laurier University
FAUVEL, ROMAN DE

RICHARD LEIGHTON GREENE
FORTUNE

JOHN L. GRIGSBY
Washington University, St. Louis
GOLDEN LEGEND

KAAREN GRIMSTAD
University of Minnesota
FREYR; FRIGG; FYLGJA; GEFJON

MARY GRIZZARD
University of New Mexico
FERRER I (THE ELDER), JAIME; GALLEGO, FERNANDO; GONSALVES, NUÑO

AVRAHAM GROSSMAN
Hebrew University of Jerusalem
GERSHOM BEN JUDAH

NATHALIE HANLET
Columbia University
GERHARD OF AUGSBURG; GHISLEBERT OF ST. AMAND; GODZIN OF MAINZ

JACK R. HARLAN
University of Illinois
GRAIN CROPS, WESTERN EUROPEAN

HUBERT HEINEN
University of Texas
GOTTFRIED VON NEIFEN

JOHN BELL HENNEMAN
Princeton University Library
FRANCE: 1314–1497; GABELLE

MICHAEL HERREN
York University
GALL, ST.

ROBERT H. HEWSEN
Glassboro State College
GANJAK; GANJAK OF ATROPATENE; GEORGIA: GEOGRAPHY AND ETHNOLOGY

BENNETT D. HILL
St. Anselm's Abbey
GRANDMONT, ORDER OF

ROBERT HILLENBRAND
University of Edinburgh
GRANADA

MICHAEL J. HODDER
Sotheby Parke Bernet, Inc.
FLAX

RICHARD C. HOFFMANN
York University
FISHPONDS

KATHRYN HUME
Pennsylvania State University
GRETTIS SAGA ÁSMUNDARSONAR

ALFRED L. IVRY
Brandeis University
GAONIC PERIOD

W. T. H. JACKSON
Columbia University
FLODOARD OF RHEIMS; FROMUND OF TEGERNSEE; GERHARD OF SOISSONS; GERMAN LITERATURE: ROMANCE; GODFREY OF RHEIMS; GOTTFRIED VON STRASSBURG

JENNIFER E. JONES
Indiana University
GEOFFROI D'AINAI; GOTHIC, MANUELINE

WILLIAM CHESTER JORDAN
Princeton University
FRANCE: 1223–1328

CONTRIBUTORS TO VOLUME 5

PETER JORGENSEN
University of Georgia
FLÓRES SAGA KONUNGS OK SONA HANS

RICHARD W. KAEUPER
University of Rochester
FELONY; FOREST LAW; FORGERY

TRUDY S. KAWAMI
FĪRŪZĀBĀD

ALEXANDER P. KAZHDAN
Dumbarton Oaks Research Center
GENESIOS, JOSEPH; GEOPONICA; GEORGE OF CYPRUS; GEORGE THE MONK

HANS-ERICH KELLER
Ohio State University
GAIMAR, GEFFREI; GEOFFREY OF MONMOUTH

DOUGLAS KELLY
University of Wisconsin
FRENCH LITERATURE: ROMANCES

THOMAS E. KELLY
Purdue University
GERBERT DE MONTREUIL

RICHARD KIECKHEFER
Northwestern University
FLAGELLANTS

DALE KINNEY
Bryn Mawr College
GATTAPONI, MATTEO; GIACOMO DA CAMPIONE; GIOVANNI DI CECCO

ALAN E. KNIGHT
Pennsylvania University
GARÇON ET L'AVEUGLE

LINDA KOMAROFF
Metropolitan Museum of Art, New York
GHAZNAVID ART AND ARCHITECTURE

MARYANNE KOWALESKI
Fordham University
FOOD TRADES

ANGELIKI LAIOU
Harvard University
FARMERS' LAW

R. WILLIAM LECKIE, JR.
University of Toronto, Centre for Medieval Studies
GILDAS, ST.

RICHARD LEMAY
City University of New York
GERARD OF CREMONA

JOHANNES LEPIKSAAR
FISHERIES, MARINE

ROBERT E. LERNER
Northwestern University
FREE SPIRIT, HERESY OF; FRUTOLF OF MICHELSBERG; GREGORY VII, POPE

JOHN LINDOW
University of California, Berkeley
FENRIS WOLF

LESTER K. LITTLE
Smith College
FRANCIS OF ASSISI, ST.; FRANCISCANS; FRIARS

ROBERT S. LOPEZ
Yale University
GENOA

JAMES F. LYDON
Trinity College Dublin
FITZGERALDS

BRYCE LYON
Brown University
FIEF, MONEY; FLANDERS AND THE LOW COUNTRIES; GHENT; GLANVILLE, RANULF DE

ROBERT D. McCHESNEY
New York University
FARGHĀNĀ (FERGANA)

JAMES W. McKINNON
State University of New York, Buffalo
GALLICAN RITE

DAVID R. McLINTOCK
University of London
GEORGSLIED

GEORGE P. MAJESKA
University of Maryland
FIORAVANTI, ARISTOTELE; GOLOSNIKI

KRIKOR H. MAKSOUDIAN
FRIK; GAGIK I; GAGIK II; GAGIK/ XAČᶜIK-GAGIK; GAGIK OF KARS; GIRK Tᶜ ᵼ Tᶜ OCᶜ; GREGORY THE ILLUMINATOR, ST.; GRIGOR MAGISTROS; GRIGOR II VKAYASĒR

MICHAEL E. MARMURA
University of Toronto
FĀRĀBĪ, AL-; GHAZĀLĪ, AL-

JOAQUÍN MARTÍNEZ-PIZARRO
Oberlin College
GRÍMS SAGA LOĐINKINNA

RALPH WHITNEY MATHISEN
University of South Carolina
FIRMICUS MATERNUS, JULIUS; GERMANUS OF AUXERRE, ST.; GERMANUS OF PARIS, ST.

GUY MERMIER
University of Michigan
FRENCH LITERATURE: DIDACTIC

BRIAN MERRILEES
University of Toronto
FOLIES TRISTAN; FOUKES LE FITZWARIN (FITZ WARYN)

JAN VAN DER MEULEN
Cleveland State University
GOTHIC ARCHITECTURE

JOHN MEYENDORFF
Fordham University
FILIOQUE; GREGORY OF NAZIANZUS, ST.; GREGORY OF NYSSA, ST.; GREGORY PALAMAS

ANNE M. MORGANSTERN
Ohio State University
GEORGES DE LA SONNETTE

MARINA MUNDT
Universitet i Bergen
GǪNGU-HRÓLFS SAGA

PETER MUNZ
Victoria University of Wellington
FREDERICK I BARBAROSSA

JOSEPH FALAKY NAGY
University of California, Los Angeles
FENIAN POETRY

HELMUT NICKEL
Metropolitan Museum of Art, New York
GAMES AND PASTIMES

MARGARET F. NIMS
Pontifical Institute of Mediaeval Studies, Toronto
GEOFFREY OF VINSAUF

THOMAS S. NOONAN
University of Minnesota
FURS, FUR TRADE

CONTRIBUTORS TO VOLUME 5

NICOLAS OIKONOMIDES
Université de Montréal
GEORGE OF PISIDIA

PÁDRAIG P. Ó NÉILL
*University of North Carolina,
Chapel Hill*
GNOMIC LITERATURE

HERMANN PÁLSSON
University of Edinburgh
FORNALDARSÖGUR; GAUTREKS SAGA
KONUNGS

LOUIS B. PASCOE
Fordham University
GERSON, JOHN

CLAUDE J. PEIFER, O.S.B.
St. Bede Abbey
GELASIUS I, POPE; GREGORY I THE
GREAT, POPE

KENNETH PENNINGTON
Syracuse University
GRATIAN

RICHARD PERKINS
University College London
FLÓAMANNA SAGA

CHRISTOPHER PINET
Montana State University
FARCES

VENETIA PORTER
GABRI WARE

JAMES M. POWELL
Syracuse University
FREDERICK II OF THE HOLY ROMAN
EMPIRE, KING OF SICILY

ROGER E. REYNOLDS
*Pontifical Institute of Mediaeval
Studies, Toronto*
FEET, WASHING OF; FURNITURE,
LITURGICAL

TIMOTHY R. ROBERTS
GOTTSCHALK OF ORBAIS

R. H. ROBINS
University of London
GRAMMAR

ORRIN W. ROBINSON
Stanford University
GERMAN LANGUAGE

LINDA ROSE
GEORGE SCHOLARIOS; GERMANOS I;
GIRDLED PATRICIAN; GOLDEN
HORN; GONZÁLEZ DE CLAVIJO,
RUY; GREEK FIRE

RHIMAN A. ROTZ
Indiana University Northwest
GERMAN TOWNS

MARY A. ROUSE
*University of California, Los
Angeles*
FLORILEGIA

STEVEN ROWAN
University of Missouri
GERMANY: ELECTORS; GERMANY:
IMPERIAL KNIGHTS; GERMANY:
PRINCIPALITIES

JAMES R. RUSSELL
Columbia University
GRIGOR NAREKAC̣I, ST.

JOSEPH SADAN
Tel-Aviv University
FURNITURE, ISLAMIC

PAULA SANDERS
Harvard University
FATIMIDS; FEASTS AND FESTIVALS,
ISLAMIC

T. A. SANDQUIST
University of Toronto
FLETA

BARBARA NELSON SARGENT-
BAUR
University of Pittsburgh
FRENCH LITERATURE: LYRIC;
GAUTIER DE COINCI

GEORGE DIMITRI SAWA
FĀRĀBĪ, AL-

PAUL SCHACH
University of Nebraska
FINNBOGA SAGA; FLJÓTSDAELA SAGA

IRFAN SHAHID
Georgetown University
GHASSANIDS

CHARLES R. SHRADER
FOLCWIN OF LOBBES

GIULIO SILANO
GLOSSATORS

LARRY SILVER
Northwestern University
GERHAERT, NIKOLAUS; GRASSER,
ERASMUS

ECKEHARD SIMON
Harvard University
GERMAN LITERATURE: LYRIC

JOSEPH T. SNOW
University of Georgia
GALICIAN-PORTUGUESE POETRY

JAMES SNYDER
Bryn Mawr College
FLEMISH PAINTING; GEERTGEN TOT
SINT JANS; GHENT ALTARPIECE;
GOES, HUGO VAN DER

GABRIELLE M. SPIEGEL
University of Maryland
GRANDES CHRONIQUES DE FRANCE

ALAN M. STAHL
GROAT

RUTH STEINER
Catholic University of America
GLORIA

WESLEY M. STEVENS
University of Winnipeg
FULDA

GERALD STRAUSS
Indiana University
GERMANY: 1254–1493; GERMANY:
IDEA OF EMPIRE

JOSEPH R. STRAYER
Princeton University
FEUDALISM; FIEF; GEORGE OF
TREBIZOND; GILBERT OF POITIERS

RONALD GRIGOR SUNY
University of Michigan
GEORGIA: POLITICAL HISTORY;
GEORGIANS (IBERIANS); GIORGI III

SANDRA CANDEE SUSMAN
GIOVANNI DA CAMPIONE; GIOVANNI
DI BALDUCCIO

DONALD W. SUTHERLAND
University of Iowa
FRANKALMOIN

EDWARD A. SYNAN
*Pontifical Institute of Mediaeval
Studies, Toronto*
FULCHER OF CHARTRES

CONTRIBUTORS TO VOLUME 5

JOSEF SZÖVÉRFFY
Wissenschaftskolleg zu Berlin
GERHOH OF REICHERSBERG

KATHRYN MARIE TALARICO
GALERAN DE BRETAGNE

GEORGE S. TATE
Brigham Young University
GAMLI KANÓKI

PETRUS W. TAX
*University of North Carolina,
Chapel Hill*
FRAU AVA

MICHAEL D. TAYLOR
University of Houston
GIOVANNI PISANO

CHRISTOPHER THACKER
University of Reading
GARDENS, EUROPEAN

PAUL R. THIBAULT
Franklin and Marshall College
GREGORY IX, POPE

JOAN THIRSK
St. Hilda's College, Oxford
FIELD SYSTEMS

J. W. THOMAS
University of Kentucky
FREIDANK

R. W. THOMSON
Harvard University
GEORGIAN LITERATURE

HANS TISCHLER
Indiana University
FRANCONIAN MOTET

M. A. TOLMACHEVA
GEOGRAPHY AND CARTOGRAPHY,
ISLAMIC

MARY C. UHL
GOLIARDS

KARL D. UITTI
Princeton University
FRENCH LITERATURE: TO 1200;
FRENCH LITERATURE: AFTER 1200

CHRYSOGONOUS WADDELL,
O.C.S.O.
Abbey of Gethsemani
GILBERTINE RITE

STEPHEN WAILES
Indiana University
FOLZ, HANS; FRAUENLIST;
FRESSANT, HERMANN

JEANETTE A. WAKIN
Columbia University
FATWĀ

DAVID WHITEHOUSE
Corning Museum
GLASS, ISLAMIC

JOHN WILLIAMS
University of Pittsburgh
FLORENTIUS; FRUCTUOSUS

BRUCIA WITTHOFT
Framingham State College
FRANCESCO DI VALDAMBRINO;
GHIBERTI, LORENZO; GORO DI
GREGORIO

ELISABETH PENDREIGH WORK
FLAMENCA, ROMANCE OF

GEORGIA SOMMERS WRIGHT
GOTHIC ART: SCULPTURE

CHARLES R. YOUNG
Duke University
FORESTS, EUROPEAN

MARK A. ZIER
*Pontifical Institute of Mediaeval
Studies, Toronto*
GREGORY OF RIMINI

RONALD EDWARD ZUPKO
Marquette University
FLORIN; GALLON

Dictionary
of the
Middle Ages

Dictionary of the Middle Ages

FAMINE IN THE ISLAMIC WORLD. Extreme and general scarcity of food was a major factor in the social and economic history of the medieval Islamic world. In the pre-Islamic Near East the evidence for famines (primarily saints' lives) suggests that local food shortages were common, but they were not recorded by the major chroniclers. This neglect of parochial scarcity appears to have persisted throughout the medieval period. The chroniclers devoted their attention to the more dramatic instances of mass hunger and their consequences, although even these sources reflect regional affinities and personal biases. Nevertheless, approximately 186 major episodes of severe food shortages were recorded between 661 and 1500. The bulk of these famines occurred in Egypt, greater Syria, and Iraq; none of them was related to the numerous invasions and military expeditions of the period, such as the succession of Asiatic invasions in the later Middle Ages. It is quite apparent, therefore, that the figure is far too low.

The causes of famine were numerous and the consequences for Islamic society were manifold. The causes were often related to specific conditions in particular regions. The obvious example is Egypt, where famine was customarily the result of an insufficient or erratic Nile inundation. The usual result was crop diminution or failure. The peasants benefited very little, if at all, from the subsequent price increases and, because of a lack of rural reserves, suffered from shortages just as the city dwellers did. In Syria and Iraq the insufficiency of rain and snow was a major contributory factor. In North Africa and Andalusia, as well as in the Middle East, severe food shortages were caused by climatic conditions (such as drought, severe winds, hail, excessive heat or cold), pest infestations (such as rats, worms, and locusts), depredations of armies and bedouin, population movements, and manipulation of grain supplies by governments and merchants. In addition, epidemics among animals caused shortages of meat and dairy products, and hampered the peasants' ability to produce and transport foodstuffs. The impact of these natural and man-made disasters depended on general levels of food production and population. The effects of famine were often dramatic because the peasants, who were the vast majority of the population, normally lived at or below a subsistence level. The threat of starvation was omnipresent. This fear is well reflected in the Koran (Flügel ed., 106:3, 16:13, 2:150), where famine ($j\bar{u}^c$) is mentioned as a punishment for nonbelievers.

From the advent of the Islamic empire, famine periodically afflicted the population and caused many deaths. Very high mortality rates are recorded for Seistan in 836, North Africa in 914–915, Iraq, Syria, and Egypt in 939, Baghdad in 944–945, Nishapur in 1010–1011, and Egypt in 1066–1072, 1201, and 1294–1296. In numerous cases famine contributed to an outbreak of epidemic diseases that took an even more frightening toll of lives.

Such catastrophes disrupted commercial activity, agriculture, and other forms of economic life. Markets and mosques were often closed. Tenements and shops, as well as slaves, were sold cheaply while food costs were, of course, excessive. People deserted their homes in search of food; during rural famines there was usually an influx of population to the cities, where there were food reserves. Thieves and bands of desperate people roamed the cities and countryside in search of food or some commodity that might be exchanged for food. People died in the streets and in the fields; work animals either died or were slaughtered and eaten. Artisans and peasants who survived worked with reduced efficiency and found few customers, while famine curtailed the supply of raw materials for industrial production. Those living on rents or tenants' labor saw their income diminish greatly. Famines also wreaked havoc with governmental revenue receipts and expenditures. Extreme food shortages frequently disrupted normal social and familial relations by death, dislocation, or emi-

1

gration. Abnormal or antisocial behavior was manifested during severe famines: incidents of robbery, sale of children, murder, prostitution, and other criminal or violent acts. Instances of cannibalism can be documented in twenty-two periods of famine in the Islamic world.

The Baghdad physician ᶜAbd al-Laṭīf, who lived in Cairo from 1194 to 1204, provided a graphic description of severe famine in Egypt (*The Eastern Key*, K. H. Zand, J. A. Videan, and I. E. Videan, trans. [1964], 225–255). In 1200 the Nile flood was exceptionally low, the land could not be cultivated and the price of food began to rise. Anticipating a famine, many peasants migrated to the major cities or even out of Egypt. The flood in the following year was still insufficient. Labor and animals were scarce and therefore costly; most villages were not properly irrigated because there was no one to retain the floodwater on the land. Where the land had been adequately inundated, there was no seed. During the sowing season of 1202, there was pestilence. Several peasants might fall dead behind a single plow, and the military landowners had to send out their troops to farm the land. In the cities mass funerals were conducted at the principal mosques, after which funeral processions crowded the roads to the cemeteries, but many corpses lay unburied in homes and gutters. Houses and shops were left vacant, so that rents in Cairo declined to a seventh of their normal level, and the palace ornaments and furnishings were used to fire the ovens. ᶜAbd al-Laṭīf reports that women tried to sell themselves as slaves or prostitutes in order to buy food. Travelers were murdered, and bands of the poor on Roda Island, in the Nile adjacent to Cairo, hunted human beings as a source of food. There were accounts of parents consuming children, physicians consuming patients, and the sale of human flesh. Perpetrators of these crimes were sometimes burned alive, but few of them were apprehended.

The fear and horror induced by these events were frequently channeled into religious activities: communal prayer services for relief, invocation of the saints, and magical practices. Moreover, Sufism may have been given added impetus by the natural disasters that caused famine conditions. Whatever religious explanations may have been proffered for such a scourge, the primary understanding was that it was the result of God's unknowable will. In this context it should be noted that there is virtually no record of millenarian activity, nor is there any clear evidence

that famine was an immediate cause of rural or urban rebellion. In some instances Islamic rulers did work to alleviate food shortages: ᶜAbd al-Raḥmān II distributed wheat to his people in Spain during the famines of 822–823 and 846, and Baybars regulated the sale of wheat in Egypt during the severe famine of 1264 and, along with his officers, supported the destitute for three months.

It is impossible to gauge the psychological impact of the serious famines on the surviving men and women. There is certainly evidence of fear and anxiety, which were especially harmful to individuals who were suffering from malnutrition and social deprivation. Malnutrition is particularly damaging to children, causing diseases such as pellagra and rickets, and lowering resistance to other diseases, such as tuberculosis, diarrheal infections, measles, and diphtheria. Famine can also trigger epidemics: unsanitary food and living conditions in the cities may lead to typhoid and typhus, and a lack of foodstuffs in the countryside may attract plague-infested rodents to human settlements. In addition, malnutrition and stress probably impeded fertility and promoted the use of birth control. In the long run, however, premodern societies were able to repopulate themselves rapidly under favorable circumstances.

Famines were usually the striking symptoms, rather than the causes, of a region's political and economic ill health. The increasing frequency of famines from Spain to Afghanistan from about 1000 appears to coincide, not surprisingly, with unstable and rapacious military dynasties, bedouin encroachments on cultivated land, increased taxation of the agricultural sector, rural depopulation, and the neglect of irrigation systems. The cumulative effect of these factors, together with natural disasters, may be seen in the decayed state of the Middle East in the later Middle Ages.

BIBLIOGRAPHY
The most important study of famine is William F. Tucker, "The Effects of Famine in the Medieval Islamic World" (forthcoming), which includes valuable appendixes; see also his "Natural Disasters and the Peasantry in Mamlūk Egypt," in *Journal of the Economic and Social History of the Orient*, 24 (1981). Also useful are Robert M. Adams, *Land Behind Baghdad* (1965), ch. 8; Eliyahu Ashtor, "An Essay on the Diet of the Various Classes in the Medieval Levant," in Robert Forster and Orest Ranum, eds., *Biology of Man in History* (1975), and *A Social and Economic History of the Near East in the Middle Ages* (1976); T. Bianquis, "Une crise frumentaire dans l'Égypte

fatamide," in *Journal of the Economic and Social History of the Orient*, **23** (1980); Michael W. Dols, *The Black Death in the Middle East* (1977); Thomas F. Glick, *Islamic and Christian Spain in the Early Middle Ages* (1979); Stanley Edward Lane-Poole, *A History of Egypt in the Middle Ages* (1925, repr. 1968); al-Maqrīzī, "Le traité des famines de Maqrīzī," Gaston Wiet, trans., in *Journal of the Economic and Social History of the Orient*, **5** (1962); B. F. Musallam, *Sex and Society in Islam* (1983); S. Sabari, *Mouvements populaires à Bagdad à l'époque ᶜabbaside, IXᵉ–XIᵉ siècles* (1981), 40ff.; Avram L. Udovitch, ed., *The Islamic Middle East, 700–1900* (1981).

MICHAEL W. DOLS

[See also **Agriculture and Nutrition: The Islamic World; Black Death; Nile; Plagues, Islamic World.**]

FAMINE IN WESTERN EUROPE. Famine, along with plague, was the major restraint on population levels throughout the Middle Ages. Because medieval Europe relied so heavily on a monoculture of grains, which were vulnerable to a number of blights and to changes in climate, famine recurred incessantly. Demographically, it was a major stimulus of short-term mortality fluctuations and a secondary stimulus, after pestilence, of longer-term mortality trends. Like pestilence, famine became a fixture of everyday life, art and literature, and the human biological regime.

One of the key factors contributing to medieval famines was the weather. From about 400 to 1500, Europe went through several cycles of climatic change. For the first 350 years it was generally wet and cold; from 750 to 1200 it was relatively mild, with normal levels of precipitation; from 1200 to 1350 it was significantly colder and damper; and from 1350 to 1500 temperatures seem to have moderated but dampness increased. Ultimately, levels of precipitation were more critical in determining harvest bounty than temperatures. In Scandinavia and parts of eastern Europe, cold could be important, and in parts of northwest and north-central Europe, viticulture might cease with temperature drops as small as 1°C. per annum. For most of the continent, however—especially the fertile grain belt running east from southern England, through northern and central France, central Germany, Poland, and the northern fringe of the Ukraine—modest changes in temperature had little bearing on the size of the crop. But excessive wetness made grain rot in the fields,

and it was in this way that climate played a major role in inducing famine.

Medieval agriculture was also famine-prone because it was heavily, in some cases almost exclusively, a monoculture of grain relying too much on wheat. Wheat provided the highest seed-to-plant yield ratios, given medieval agrarian technology, and for a variety of sociocultural reasons it was considered to make the healthiest, best-tasting bread. But when it was not rotated and was planted to the exclusion of other grains, soil exhaustion and a subsequent marked decline in yield ratios could occur. This was particularly true on marginal arable, such as the assarted lands won from the forests and heaths in the twelfth and thirteenth centuries, and when population peaked, as in the mid thirteenth century. Any circumstance or condition that threatened these singular harvests, such as a wheat rust, could bring disaster.

Other major problems included the inadequate European transport system, especially overland, and the poor system of market distribution. These bottlenecks proved particularly severe for towns. Urban centers specialized in nonagricultural production and imported most of their food. Ultimately their size was determined by the quality, quantity, and availability of foodstuffs, which were bulky, perishable, and difficult to move long distances. Most towns therefore tried to secure as much food as possible from their *contados*, the surrounding countryside; but in hard times, when crops failed, townspeople were the first to feel the shortfalls, and securing food supplies became a major preoccupation of municipal governments.

The methods used to assure food supplies varied from town to town. In northern Europe members of the Hanseatic trading confederation stockpiled large quantities of grain in warehouses located in special districts. Netherlandish cities often sent agents to the Baltic hinterlands, northern France, and Germany to buy futures for unsown grains. Italian towns, the largest in Europe, attempted to gain political control over their hinterlands, but some—notably Genoa, Florence, and Venice—were so large that they still had to rely on distant markets to guard against famine. A fourteenth-century grain dealer named Lenzi told the Florentine chronicler Giovanni Villani that the Florentine *contado* produced only 40 percent of the city's grain needs; the rest had to be imported. Landlocked, Florence had perhaps the most acute provisioning problem in Europe and suffered at least thirty famines from 1100 to 1348. In 1328 most of the north Italian wheat crop was destroyed by a rust, and by Easter 1329, Villani claimed, wheat prices had soared by 500 percent. He wrote:

> The famine was felt not only in Florence but throughout Tuscany and a large part of Italy. And so terrible was it that the Perugians, the Sienese, the Lucchese, the Pistoiese and many other townsmen drove from their territory all their beggars because they could not support them. . . . The agitation of the [Florentine] people at the market of San Michele was so great that it was necessary to protect the officials by means of guards fitted out with an axe and block to punish rioters on the spot with the loss of their hands and feet.

Villani also tells of municipal attempts to ameliorate the situation:

> And in the mitigation of this famine the commune of Florence spent in these two years [1328–1329] more than 60,000 gold florins. Finally, it was decided not to go on selling grain in the piazza, but to requisition all the bakers' ovens for the baking of bread in order to sell it on the following morning in three or four shops in every *sesto* [section of the town, which was administratively divided into sixths] at four pennies for the loaf of six ounces. This arrangement successfully tamed the rage of the people since wage earners with eight to twelve pennies could now buy bread on which to live, whereas formerly they had been unable to find the sums necessary to buy a whole bushel of wheat.

At times food was so scarce that even the best efforts of the Florentine patriciate proved unsuccessful. In 1411–1412 famine exacerbated social tensions. A textile worker, Cola di Maestro Piero, is alleged to have said, "These traitorous rulers have taken grain from the poultry and fed it to us; by God, we shall eat the good grain in their houses shortly." Famine proved to be a major social problem in medieval towns, perhaps more so than epidemic disease, since the disenfranchised urban classes felt that food supplies were manipulated by municipal authorities, whereas disease was in the hands of God.

Venice, perhaps medieval Europe's best-governed sovereign entity, dealt with famine in its own unique way. Its maritime power gave it control over much of the Adriatic Sea and its immediate hinterlands, as well as parts of the eastern Mediterranean and the Black Sea, the latter an outlet for much of the southern Russian grain trade. The real key to Venetian success seems to have been a sophisticated delivery system. Here, as in ancient Rome, the oligarchs felt that the regulation of grain prices was necessary to preserve their privileged status. Food prices were ordinarily fixed by competitive bidding rather than monopoly, but when supplies dropped below certain levels, the government stepped in with additional provisions.

Generally, this system worked. In 1268, for example, when no surplus wheat was available in Lombardy or Dalmatia, Venetian ships found supplies in the Crimea and kept wheat prices stable; by comparison, they rose 150 percent in two months in nearby Milan. The Venetian grain commission could also ensure supplies by offering attractive prices to ships carrying surplus food intended for other destinations, and it insisted that all ships from any port in the far-flung Venetian maritime empire must go directly to the mother city, or pay a steep fine.

Venetian food distribution even extended to its foreign policy. In their 1273 war with Bologna, the Venetians triumphed by buying up all the wheat in northern Italy and literally starving the landlocked Bolognese into submission. A similar ploy against the Genoese helped the Venetians win the War of the Chiogga in 1380. Famine was most acute in medieval European towns; only urban centers like Venice, with an elaborate system of supply and distribution, could survive the most serious shortages.

Even in the best of times the medieval diet was spare and based largely on grains. Wheat was eaten everywhere, supplemented by barley and oats in the north and rice in parts of the south. Grains were made into porridge for breakfast, bread for lunch, and gruel for dinner, with ale and beer to drink—an overwhelmingly carbohydrate diet. Meat was of secondary importance for the lower and middling classes and at times even for the aristocracy. Beef was uncommon, and in any case it must have been tough, salty, and stringy. Pork was the principal flesh food, supplemented by mutton, especially in the Mediterranean basin. The availability of meat varied with economic conditions and the price of fodder crops. When population levels were high, most fields had to be reserved for grain production, so that animal proteins could not act as a hedge against crop failure. Olive oil was crucial for cooking and food preparation in the Mediterranean region, a role filled by butter, lard, and fat in the north. Sugar—first from south Asia and later from Iberia and the Spanish Atlantic islands—was a major sweetener in the south, with honey and fruit jams used in northern Europe. Medieval people seem to have had a penchant for sweets, but even in the south those made from sugar were very expensive, and their consumption varied sharply with social class. Legumes, fruits, poultry, eggs, and fish rounded out the diet, but carbohydrates remained the staple food.

Adults can get by on as little as 1,600 calories per day, though at some sacrifice of strength and endurance. Below 1,600 calories, actual death by starvation is rare if fluid intake is sufficient, but the amount of physical activity decreases dramatically and the incidence of debilitating diseases such as tuberculosis and diarrhea increases proportionally. It is difficult to measure medieval caloric intake accurately. In the Tuscan city of Lucca in 765, paupers in the town almshouses were said to prosper on a daily intake of one loaf, two measures of wine, and a dish of legumes. Various monastic dietary regimes suggest that the monks did well on a diet of bread, legumes, wine, and virtually no meat.

By far the best dietary data come from late-medieval Egypt, where peasant standards were fairly close to those of the Christian Mediterranean. In the fourteenth century, peasants barely scraped by on a total caloric intake of 1,598, consisting of 59 grams of protein, 292 grams of carbohydrates, and 19.75 grams of fats. By the fifteenth century, when population pressure had been eased considerably by a century of pestilence and famine, dietary standards had improved greatly. Average intake was up to 1,930 calories, consisting of 82 grams of protein, 294 grams of carbohydrates, and 45.2 of fats. (This compares reasonably well with the mid-twentieth-century standards of India and Italy, where the figures in 1954–1957 were, respectively, 1,880 and 2,550 calories, 50 and 79.9 grams of protein, and 25 and 66 grams of fat.) Despite this late-medieval amelioration, the diet remained overwhelmingly carbohydrate and based on levels of grain production. When weather, locusts, plant diseases, or war disrupted production, the result was often famine.

Famine affected fertility as well as mortality levels. Fertility rates were reduced by the postponement of first marriages until prospects appeared brighter. More directly, food deprivation could result in a condition called famine amenorrhea. A daily diet of less than 700 calories or conditions causing great stress and anxiety can bring about a cessation of the menstrual cycle until caloric intake rises, in some cases causing early menopause. Thus, during famine years death rates rose and fertility dropped, compounding the population problem.

In the early Middle Ages, major national or even regional famines were rather rare, with food shortages occurring mostly within local districts. Population levels in those areas of Europe that had been part of the old Roman Empire were for the most part lower than they had been during the imperial era, and many of the famines that did occur were as much the result of poor transportation and distribution as of actual crop failure and overall food shortages. Among the few major famines were a series that swept the Mediterranean basin in the 360's and in parts of northern and western Europe in the sixth century. Gregory of Tours describes several crises in Burgundy from 530 to 570. In the 550's and 590's food shortfalls drove the Germanic Lombards south into Italy; and in 585 northern and central France, normally one of Europe's most productive areas, experienced widespread famines. In the 570's and 590's the famines coincided with severe flooding and the Lombard excursions to bring agrarian disaster to northern Italian towns. No data survive that might measure quantitatively the impact of any of these famines, but their frequency was sufficient to cause Pope Gregory I to double the amount of alms distributed to paupers in Rome. Further evidence of the troubles comes from the exhumed bones of Lombards that show signs of chronic malnutrition. In general the period 550 to 600 was one of chronic famine, plague, and dislocation.

The ninth century was also a period of chronic famine. Population had grown in many places since the mid eighth century, and in selected areas of northern France population density was as high as it would be in the eighteenth century. Excess rainfall caused famine in 809, 821, and 835 throughout France and Germany. There was actually a crop surplus in 821 in England, but no means by which the grain could be distributed to the famine areas. In 857 famine came for a new and different reason: the northern European rye crop was struck by ergotism. The ergot fungus contained twenty toxins, including the hallucinogen LSD, and caused a disease called St. Anthony's fire. Additional outbreaks of ergotism struck the rye crop throughout the ninth, tenth, eleventh, and twelfth centuries, including one in 1039 that prompted a French lord, Gaston de la Valloire, to build a hospital near Vienne for the sufferers and to dedicate it to St. Anthony. By the mid twelfth century the Antonine Hospitalers, devoted exclusively to easing the sickness of the "burning ones," had established 390 hospitals.

The ninth century opened a 250-year period in which famine was far more frequent and widespread than it had been between 300 and 800. A number of new plant diseases appeared, and Norse, Saracen, and Magyar raiders destroyed fragile food distribution systems. Between 857 and 950 there were at least twenty severe famines, raising mortality rates and depressing fertility rates sufficiently to reverse Europe's century-long population expansion. In the Iberian peninsula in 915 and 929, a rust parasite devastated the entire wheat crop. An Aragonese chronicler wrote: "Life was offered for a loaf, but none would buy it; rank was to be sold for a cake, but none cared for it. . . . Destitution at last reached such a pitch that men began to devour each other and the flesh of a son was preferred to his love." All over Europe there were reports of human flesh for sale during famine years—two-legged mutton, it was called, though one Austrian chronicler claimed that it tasted rather salty, and more like pork.

The number and severity of famines diminished somewhat in the late tenth century but increased again in the early eleventh century. A succession of poor harvests from 1032 to 1036 led to shortages across the entire continent. In France human flesh was for sale in 1032 and 1033. The poor besieged monasteries for food; in 1033 the house of Cluny, in eastern France, dispensed 250 carcasses of salt pork for 16,000 people, and the monks of St. Benoît-sur-Loire fed 600 beggars in a single day. The chronicler Raoul Glauber describes in great detail the butcher stalls at the trade fair of Tournai, in Burgundy, where different grades and varieties of human flesh fetched a wide spectrum of prices.

In 1036 north European harvests improved, but beginning in 1043 they failed for three successive years. By 1045 reports of cannibalism surfaced yet again, along with references to men and women eating soil in order to fill their stomachs. The most likely causes of the famines of the 1030's and 1040's were excessive precipitation and, in some parts of the far north, exceptional cold. The famines brought about at least a decade of chronic malnutrition, which contemporaries called "the penitential scourge." While no data for mortality are available, extrapolation from twentieth-century Indian sources suggests an increase in the death rate from 30 in 1,000 to perhaps 80 in 1,000 or 90 in 1,000 for the worst years between 1030 and 1050.

The famines of the mid eleventh century were a watershed. Political stability began to spread across the continent, and for almost three centuries the European economy blossomed. Climatic conditions were generally favorable for agriculture, and new, prime arable in northwestern Europe was planted. The transportation system, especially that designed to move heavy bulk goods like foodstuffs overland, improved with the development of pack mules, new carts, and a series of transalpine bridges. Population rose steadily, at times approaching increases of 1 percent per annum, but food production generally kept pace. Between 1046 and the early thirteenth century, incidence of famine was irregular and localized, mitigated by higher seed yields and better distribution. The French medievalist Georges Duby goes so far as to claim that there were no major food shortages in the Low Countries and Germany in the twelfth and most of the thirteenth centuries.

In the late thirteenth century, however, conditions began to change once again. The European climate altered: the optimum of dry, warm weather was followed by a century of colder, wetter weather. Population continued the steady rise that had begun in the late tenth century, causing a continuous demand for more foodstuffs. To meet that demand, more and more land was planted. Existing fields were supplemented by newly assarted fields, often of marginal quality; when these were exhausted, pasture and even fallow were forced into use.

Since wheat offered the highest yields throughout most of Europe, it was planted to the exclusion of other grains—short-term gratification at the heavy price of long-term soil exhaustion. Further, with pastures planted and fodder crops cut back, it became virtually impossible to keep animals as a hedge against crop failure; no animals also meant no manure to fertilize the fields. By the early thirteenth century, as population continued to increase, standards of living began to fall. By the mid thirteenth century they had dropped to the subsistence level for much of the populace, and parts of Europe became mired in the throes of a classic Malthusian population/production crisis.

There was a series of local famines in the mid thirteenth century, but full crisis did not arrive until the 1290's, an extremely rainy decade. In the harvest years of 1291, 1292, and 1293, wheat crops in England, France, and Germany reached only about half their levels in the 1280's. The next two harvests produced adequate yields, but in 1297 there was another shortfall, this time in parts of the Mediterranean basin as well as north of the Alps. There are no data available from which European mortality might be estimated, but most experts agree that it was at least 5 percent higher than normal. None of the individual famines of the 1290's struck every corner of the Continent, and northern Germany, the Low Countries, Poland, and the Iberian peninsula seem to have emerged relatively unscathed. Even in England and France, where the effects were most severe, the famines appear to have had minimal psychological impact. Demographic and social patterns underwent few significant changes, and the population/production crisis continued to worsen.

From 1300 to 1380 Europe experienced by far its worst siege of famine. A succession of very wet growing seasons caused a series of crop failures and food shortages that did not entirely end until the Black Death and the subsequent plague outbreaks of the second pandemic substantially reduced Europe's population. In 1304 and 1305 famine struck northern France and Flanders. In 1309 excess rainfall brought about the first pan-European famine in more than 250 years; in France this famine persisted through 1310. The weather continued to be bad; from 1310 to 1319, every year had above-average precipitation, according to dendrochronological evidence.

The rains, the high population, and the heavy dependence on wheat, along with cultivation of much marginal arable, combined to produce the worst decade of famine in European history. The excessive humidity caused trees and bushes to shoot up, rivers to swell, and crops to rot in the fields. In France every harvest from 1308 to 1319 was below the average of the period 1300–1309; in Germany this was the case between 1312 and 1320, and in England from 1313 to 1320. By 1314 even the grain-producing areas of northeastern Europe began to experience shortfalls, and the towns of the Netherlands, southern Germany, and northern Italy had difficulty acquiring food. From England, Holland, France, and central Germany came the first concerted references to widespread hunger and starvation.

The harvest of 1315 was bad, though a little better than those of the preceding five years. Some observers believed that the famine was coming to an end. They were wrong: in 1316 the wheat crops failed once again all across the continent, and conditions became worse than ever. Using 1310 as a base year, wheat prices in the London Cheapside market, after twenty years of inflation, stood at 5s. 7d. per quarter. By July 1316 they were 26s. 8d. in rural areas and 40s. in the Cheap; in the provincial town of Leicester a quarter of wheat sold for the astounding price of 44s. After the disastrous harvest of autumn 1316, wheat prices went up another 75 percent—and England was a grain exporter, with average food prices lower than those on the Continent, where the situation was far worse. In France, beween 1310 and

1314 wheat yields dropped by 50 percent, to four plants per seed. In 1315 yield was 2.5 plants per seed, a ratio that hardly made the toil of planting worthwhile. The chronicler Guillaume de Nangis wrote:

> We saw a large number of both sexes, not only from nearby places but from as much as five leagues away, barefooted, and many even, except for women, in a completely nude state, together with their priests coming in procession at the Church of the Holy Martyrs, their bones bulging out, devoutly carrying bodies of saints and other relics to be adored, hoping to get relief.

The years 1315 to 1317 were the worst for the urban areas of Europe. Netherlandish merchants were unable to buy grain from traditional sources in England, France, and the Baltic hinterlands. Fish prices in Holland rose more than 500 percent, and surplus food stocks, accumulated with great care over a number of years, were all exhausted. In Ypres, Flanders, over 2,800 bodies, approximately 10 percent of the pre-1310 population, were buried from May through October 1316. By 1317 at least 17 to 20 percent of the inhabitants of Ypres had perished, a figure comparable to the mortality suffered by the town a generation later during the Black Death. In Ghent, Bruges, Louvain, and the Dutch towns, mortality from the famines probably ranged between 10 and 15 percent. The great Italian cities, even with their elaborate methods of provisioning and extensive sea power designed to garner imports, may have lost close to 10 percent of their populations. In the German Rhineland, chroniclers tell of the need to post troops at gibbets in Mainz, Cologne, and Strasbourg; ravenous people were rushing the gallows and cutting down and eating the corpses.

These reports of cannibalism might be apocryphal, but there are many more substantial records of the dearness of grain during the great famines. English chroniclers stressed that horsemeat, normally scorned even by the peasants, was too expensive for all but the aristocracy. The rest of the populace was reduced to eating dogs, cats, and "unclean things." In March 1315 a royal proclamation attempted to fix agricultural prices, but in February 1316, according to the *Annales Londonienses*, "the ordinance regarding livestock, fowl, and eggs [was rescinded] because few were found on account of the dearth and lack of victuals." People were determined to pay any price for food.

Added to the general misery was a series of related enteric diseases—probably typhoid fever, dysentery, and diphtheria—that increased the already inflated mortality rates. Heriots (death duties) from rural estates in England in 1316 show an increase to 10 to 12 percent. All social classes were afflicted, and by 1317 normal everyday social life all across Europe began to grind to a halt. Alms collections dried up, and the number of vagabonds and thefts increased markedly. In Kent, England, one-third of all crimes in 1316/1317 involved theft of food, as opposed to just over 6 percent in 1308/1309.

In 1317 and 1318 harvests throughout Europe improved, but a new catastrophe struck: animal murrains. From 1316 to 1321/1322 a series of livestock epidemics devastated what remained of the cattle and oxen populations. The next two years, 1322 and 1323, were a period of respite, but in 1324 and 1325 there came a succession of sheep murrains. Coupled with grain harvest failures in 1321 and 1322, the murrains extended the misery of Europe for another eight years.

The agrarian crisis of 1309–1325 had profound effects on European society and economy. All told, it may have reduced population by 15 to 20 percent, with little opportunity for earlier marriages for females and subsequent higher fertility to compensate for increased mortality. Every grain crop except oats, which thrive in conditions of heavy rainfall and high humidity, produced yields far below average. But crop yields would eventually return to normal: perhaps most crucial and damaging was the depletion of livestock. On Inkpen Manor, Berkshire, England, for example, there were 468 sheep in 1313; by 1317 there were only 137. In 1319–1320, on three Huntingdonshire estates of Ramsey Abbey, also in England, the number of cattle fell from 54 to 6, 47 to 2, and 65 to 9. Recovery, especially in the crucial wool market, was a long time in coming, for many landlords lacked the capital to invest in new breeding stock. In some cases it would be generations before herds reached their pre-fourteenth-century levels.

In the 1310's, as in the 1290's, the famines produced little long-term demographic change. Whatever the reasons, nonfamine fertility levels remained high, and by the 1330's the Malthusian crisis flared up anew. In northern France famine occurred in 1330–1334, 1344, 1349–1351, 1358–1360, 1371, 1373–1374, and 1390, with Paris experiencing additional shortages in 1323 and 1325. In southern France 1329, 1335, 1337, 1343, and 1361 were famine years. All over the kingdom conditions were made worse by the Hundred Years War, fought largely on its territory. In England famine struck in 1335, 1344,

1351, and 1369. Germany and eastern Europe were afflicted in 1346–1350, 1361–1362, and 1374–75, all years of major epidemics as well. Both the Iberian peninsula and the northern Italian cities had major famines in the mid 1330's and the early and late 1340's. In 1347 Sienese paupers, turned out by their own town fathers, appeared at the gates of Florentine almshouses.

The famines discussed to this point were all major regional or pan-European blights, but famine must also be studied on a microeconomic level. Due to the lack of local records for much of the Continent, this cannot be done comprehensively, but because of the confluence of narrative and manorial records, it can be attempted for England. From the seventh century until the great famines of the first third of the fourteenth century, there were forty-two separate famines: two in the seventh century, one in the eighth, one in the ninth, three in the tenth, nine in the eleventh, fourteen in the twelfth, ten in the thirteenth, and two early in the fourteenth century. The most severe were the famines of 665, 793, 976, 1036–1039, 1046, 1110–1111, 1257–1259, 1294, and of course 1309 to 1325; the rest were primarily local and would probably be greater in number, especially in the earlier centuries, if the records were more complete. Nine of the forty-two famines coincided with animal murrains, and at least eight, particularly those from the 1120's to the 1170's, were connected with military actions. Thirty can be connected with climatic aberrations, especially wet weather, the greatest threat to grain crops, and at least seventeen were exacerbated by pestilences. All the major famines coincided with food shortages on the Continent and probably killed in excess of 10 percent of total population.

The inception of the second plague pandemic in 1348, coupled with a moderation in temperature, helped end Europe's subsistence crisis late in the fourteenth century. From 1351 to 1500 there were comparatively few food shortages, as Europe entered an era of depopulation. In Languedoc, for example, there were seven major food crises in the fourteenth century, compared with only three in the fifteenth. Normandy had an identical famine pattern, and in England the only period of severe food shortage in the entire fifteenth century came in 1438–1439, when crop failures were made worse by cold, wet weather and a major plague epidemic. After 1348 pestilence superseded famine as the principal check on population.

Famine in medieval Europe was, as a major catastrophic constraint on population, a crucial element in causing crisis mortality, which in turn regulated long-term demographic movements. Because of insufficient checks on fertility, European population often stood on the brink of subsistence crises, but the principal cause of famine was probably external rather than internal; inclement weather, especially excess precipitation.

Famine was an omnipresent threat that virtually every medieval person experienced at some point in his or her lifetime. With war and pestilence it was one of the banes outlined in the Book of Revelation, a favorite medieval text. Of these three scourges, famine was more important than war but less significant than pestilence, which came more frequently and was usually more deadly and widespread. To this rule there was a single, major exception; between 1285 and 1345, owing to a combination of wet weather, overpopulation, and wheat rusts, the greatest scourge was famine, which recurred about once every five years across the continent.

As was the case with epidemic disease, the late fifteenth century marks a watershed between medieval and modern hunger crises. New wheat fields were opened in eastern Europe and the Atlantic islands. More important, the discovery of America was followed by the introduction from the New World of a number of new plant foods, including corn, tomatoes, beans, and potatoes. Coupled with improvements in land and sea transportation, they brought about a significant rise in the population–food supply ratio. Many more people could be fed before new famines would occur.

BIBLIOGRAPHY

Wilhelm Abel, *Massenarmut und Hungerkrisen im vorindustriellen Europa* (1974), and *Agarkrisen und Agarkonjunktur*, 3rd ed. (1978); Eliyahu Ashtor, "An Essay on the Diet of the Various Classes in the Medieval Levant," in Robert Forster and Orest Ranum, eds., *Biology of Man in History* (1975); Christopher Dyer, "English Diet in the Later Middle Ages," in T. H. Aston, P. R. Coss, Christopher Dyer, and Joan Thirsk, eds., *Social Relations and Ideas: Essays in Honour of R. H. Hilton* (1983); Garnet Carefoot and Edgar Sprott, *Famine on the Wind* (1969); Fritz Curschmann, *Hungersnöte im Mittelalter* (1900); Georges Duby, *Rural Economy and Country Life in the Medieval West*, Cynthia Postan, trans. (1968); Sir Joseph Hutchinson, ed., *Population and Food Supply* (1969); Emmanuel Le Roy Ladurie, *Times of Feast, Times of Famine*, Barbara Bray, trans. (1971), and "Famine Amenorrhoea (Seventeenth–Twentieth Centuries)," in Forster and Ranum, eds., *op. cit.*; Bernard H. Slicher van Bath, *The*

Agrarian History of Western Europe, Olive Ordish, trans. (1964); Reay Tannahill, *Food in History* (1973); Cornelius Walford, *The Famines of the World: Past and Present* (1879, repr. 1970).

Among the numerous studies of local or specific famines, the following are of special importance: Ian Kershaw, "The Great Famine and Agrarian Crisis in England 1315–1322," in *Past and Present*, 59 (1973); Marie-Josèphe Larenaudie, "Les famines en Languedoc aux XIVᵉ et XVᵉ siècles," in *Annales du Midi*, 64 (1952); Henry S. Lucas, "The Great European Famine of 1315, 1316, 1317," in *Speculum*, 5 (1930); Helen Robbins, "A Comparison of the Effects of the Black Death on the Economic Organization of France and England," in *Journal of Political Economy*, 36 (1928); J. Z. Titow, *Winchester Yields* (1972).

A good collection of sources is Dorothea Oschinsky, ed., *Walter of Henley and Other Treatises on Estate Management and Accounting* (1971).

ROBERT S. GOTTFRIED

[See also **Agriculture and Nutrition: The Mediterranean Region; Agriculture and Nutrition: Northern Europe; Black Death; Climatology; Plagues.**]

FAN VAULT. See **Vault.**

FĀRĀBĪ, AL- (Abū Naṣr Muḥammad ibn Muḥammad ibn Tarkhān ibn Awzalagh [Uzlugh?], *ca.* 873–950), a major Islamic philosopher and music theorist. Born in Transoxiana of Turkish ancestry, he studied and taught at Baghdad, where he was associated with Christian scholars who represented a continuation of the tradition of medical and philosophical teaching of Alexandria, a school that moved early in the eighth century to Antioch and then in the ninth to Harrān and Baghdad. One of his teachers was the Nestorian logician Yūhannā ibn Ḥaylān (d. 910). Al-Fārābī, who was keenly interested in the relation between logic and language, also studied Arabic grammar with the noted grammarian Ibn al-Sarrāj (d. 929). For reasons not fully known, al-Fārābī left Baghdad for Syria in 942. Medieval Arabic accounts of his life, particularly concerning this period, vary. He seems to have lived most of the time in relative seclusion in Damascus. He is said to have been sponsored by the Arab prince of Aleppo, Sayf al-Dawla (who came into power in 945), and to have visited Egypt.

While factual information on al-Fārābī's life tends to be elusive, the impact of his writings on the course of Arabic thought is very tangible. It was al-

Fārābī who gave the philosophical venture in medieval Islam—pioneered by al-Kindī (*d. ca.* 873) and al-Rāzī—its direction. The foremost logician of his time, he was the first Muslim to put the study of logic on a firm basis. The Neoplatonic emanative scheme that he developed became a model for the cosmological doctrines of the majority of subsequent Islamic philosophers. He was the originator and major exponent of a Platonized Islamic theory of the state which, again, became very prevalent among the philosophers who succeeded him.

The body of commentary written by al-Fārābī is devoted mostly to Aristotle, particularly to the logical *Organon*. But he also commented on the works of others (for example, Ptolemy and Alexander of Aphrodisias) and wrote critical treatises on such thinkers as Galen, John Philoponus, and al-Rāzī. He wrote a summary of Plato's *Laws* with an introduction and very brief summaries of the dialogues, the latter forming the second part of his trilogy, *Falsafat Aflāṭun wa-Arisṭuṭālīs* (The philosophy of Plato and Aristotle). His own philosophy is developed in such works as *Taḥṣīl al-Saᶜāda* (The attainment of happiness), which forms the first part of the above-mentioned trilogy, *Iḥṣāᵓ al-ᶜulūm* (The enumeration of the sciences), *Kitāb al-milla* (The book of religion), *al-Siyāsa al-madaniyya* (The political regime), and *Arāᵓ ahl al-madīna al-fāḍila* (The opinions of the citizens of the virtuous city).

Neoplatonic emanative ideas are usually given in those works that represent al-Fārābī's own philosophy. In general, his accounts of the philosophy of Plato and Aristotle are remarkably free from Neoplatonic elements. The notable exception is *Kitāb al-jamᶜ bayn raᵓyayy al-Ḥakīmayn Aflāṭun al-ilāhī wa-Arisṭuṭālīs* (The harmonization between the views of the two philosophers, the divine Plato and Aristotle). This work, written in a style all its own, effects a reconciliation between these two philosophers partly by its acceptance of the Neoplatonic *Theology of Aristotle* as a genuine work of Aristotle.

The emanative scheme al-Fārābī formulated is dyadic. From God, a first intelligence emanates. This intelligence undergoes two cognitive acts, an act of knowing God and an act of self-knowledge, each causing respectively the emanation from it of a second intelligence and the outermost sphere of the heavens. The second intelligence repeats the dual cognitive activity, causing the emanation of still another intelligence and the sphere of the fixed stars. This activity is then repeated by the successive intelligences causing the emanation of the spheres of the planets, the sun, the moon, and finally, from the tenth intelligence, the active intellect, the emanation of the world of generation and corruption.

This cosmic order is harmonious and rational. To attain happiness, man must actualize his potentialities and order his life to be in tune with this cosmic harmony. Being a political animal, however, man can only achieve this within a social order. Ideally this social order must itself be "virtuous," a replica of the cosmic rational scheme. A requirement for achieving such an ideal social order is a ruler who is both a philosopher and a prophet, that is, a recipient of the revealed law. Revelation is received from the active intellect by this prophet's imaginative faculty in the form of images that symbolize universal rational knowledge or represent particular instances of it. Hence revelation does not contradict philosophy, but conveys its truth in the language of symbols and concrete particulars which the nonphilosophic multitude can understand. Since people in different regions of the world differ in their languages and symbols, it may well be the case, al-Fārābī maintains, that certain religions differ from each other in their symbols, but not in what is symbolized.

Al-Fārābī discusses the structure of the "virtuous" city, the qualities its leadership must have, and the various types of "nonvirtuous" cities. The majority of these latter are characterized as "ignorant" because their leaders are ignorant of the true nature of happiness. Related to this is al-Fārābī's eschatology, according to which immortality is confined to those souls that have knowledge of what constitutes true happiness. Thus al-Fārābī's political theory is essentially Platonic. Islamic institutions and the role of the Islamic religious sciences are interpreted within a framework that derives ultimately from the *Republic* and the *Laws*.

Islamic philosophers such as Ibn Sīnā (Avicenna), Ibn Bājja (Avempace), Ibn Tufayl (Abubacer), and Ibn Rushd (Averroes) were in different ways al-Fārābī's intellectual and spiritual descendents. His influence on the Jewish Maimonides was also considerable. Some of his works, notably *The Enumeration of the Sciences* and the *Treatise on the Intellect,* were translated into Latin and known to medieval Scholastics and to philosophers of the Italian Renaissance.

BIBLIOGRAPHY

Sources. For editions and translations of al-Fārābī prior to 1962, see Nicholas Rescher, *al-Fārābī: An Annotated*

Bibliography (1962). Al-Fārābī, *Fuṣūl Muntazaᶜa* (Selected aphorisms), Fauzi M. Najjar, ed. (1971); *Kitāb al-Alfāz al-Mustaᶜmala fī al-Manṭiq* (The book of utterances used in logic), Muhsin Mahdi, ed. (1968); *Kitāb al-Milla wa Nuṣūṣ Ukhrā* (The book of religion and related texts), Muhsin Mahdi, ed. (1968); *Kitāb al-Siyāsa al-Madaniyya* (The political regime), Fauzi M. Najjar, ed. (1964); Ralph Lerner and Muhsin Mahdi, eds., *Medieval Political Philosophy: A Source Book* (1963), which includes reliable translations by Muhsin Mahdi and Fauzi Najjar; Muhsin Mahdi, "Alfarabi Against Philoponus," in *Journal of Near Eastern Studies,* 26 (1967), 233–260; Nicholas Rescher, *Al-Fārābī's Short Commentary on Aristotle's Prior Analytics* (1963); F. W. Zimmermann, *Al-Fārābī's Commentary and Short Treatise on Aristotle's De Interpretatione* (1981).

Studies. Thérèse-Anne Druart, "Al-Fārābī's Causation of the Heavenly Bodies," in Parviz Morewedge, ed., *Islamic Philosophy and Mysticism* (1981); Majid Fakhry, *A History of Islamic Philosophy* (1970), 125–147; M. Galston, "A Re-examination of al-Fārābī's Neoplatonism," in *Journal of the History of Philosophy,* 25 (1976); Ibrahim Madkour, *La place d'al-Fārābī dans l'école philosophique musulmane* (1934); Muhsin Mahdi, "Alfarabi," in Leo Strauss and J. Cropsy, eds., *History of Political Philosophy* (1963); Muhsin Mahdi, "Al-Fārābī and the Foundation of Philosophy," in *Islamic Philosophy and Mysticism,* Parviz Morewedge, ed. (1981); Michael E. Marmura, "The Philosopher and Society: Some Medieval Arabic Discussions," in *Arabic Studies Quarterly,* 1 (1979); Fauzi M. Najjar, "Fārābī's Political Philosophy and Shīᶜism," in *Studia Islamica,* 14 (1961); Nicholas Rescher, *Studies in Arabic Logic* (1963), 21–23, 39–54; Leo Strauss, "How Farabi Read Plato's Laws," in *Mélanges Louis Massignon* (1957); Moritz Steinschneider, "Al-Farabi (Alpharabius) des arabischen Philosophen Leban und Schriften," in *Mémoires de l'Académie impériale des sciences de St. Petersbourg,* 4 (1869); Richard Walzer, *Greek Into Arabic* (1962), 18–23, 206–219.

MICHAEL E. MARMURA

AL-FĀRĀBĪ ON MUSIC

In the history of Islam, al-Fārābī is the foremost music scholar. Knowledgeable both in music making and music discourse, he formulated musical theories related to practice; as such, his works constitute a unique document on musical practices from early Islam to the mid tenth century. The thoroughness, accuracy, and lucidity of his music discourse were further enhanced by his multidisciplinary background. His discussion of music philosophy relied on Aristotle's *Posterior Analytics,* and his ideas concerning the use of music for the attainment of happiness relied on political philosophy. His exposition on rhythms was based on grammar, prosody, and Euclidean geometry, whereas his discussion of musical intervals relied on arithmetics.

Of his 160 works, 8 deal with music; only 4 of these have survived. The shortest work, the section on music in *Iḥṣāᵓ al-ᶜulūm* (Classification of the sciences) was known in medieval Europe through several Latin translations. In it, the science of music is defined and then divided into the practical and the theoretical. The latter is divided into five parts: principles and fundamentals; intervals and tone system; application of tone system to instruments; rhythms; composition and ornaments.

His most comprehensive work is the monumental *Kitāb al-mūsīqā al-kabīr* (Grand book of music). As a practitioner al-Fārābī described his own observations and clarified those of previously known competent practitioners, using Greek models of trained logical accuracy so as to give a masterful document on musical theories and practices. (For completeness' sake he also included ancient Greek theories, but clearly set them apart from contemporary practices.) The work comprises two books. Book I is in two parts: part I, "Introduction to the Art of Music," deals with music philosophy and introductory acoustics; part II, "The Art Itself," concerns three arts. The first, "Elements of the Art," deals with acoustics, music intervals, tetrachords, melodic modes, and *īqāᶜ*s (the endings of harmonic phrases). The second art, "Common Musical Instruments," deals with the application of theoretical principles to instruments in practice, as well as the instruments' ranges and capabilities. The third art, "Composition," deals with tables of consonances and dissonances, melodic movement, *īqāᶜ*s, vocal music, performance practice of vocal and instrumental music, and the aim of music. Book II, now lost, was a commentary on the works of preceding writers.

Later al-Fārābī revised the *īqāᶜ* theory in three treatises, two of which have survived: *Kitāb al-īqāᶜāt* (Book of *īqāᶜ*s) and the priceless *Kitāb iḥṣāᵓ al-īqāᶜāt* (Book of classification of *īqāᶜ*s), discovered in Turkey in 1951. In both treatises he clarified the obscurities surrounding the medieval Arabic *īqāᶜ*s: he defined their basic forms, codified rhythmic ornamental techniques, and used a very accurate syllabic notation system for rhythms that allows us now to transcribe the *īqāᶜ*s in their various forms.

Al-Fārābī's comprehensive and systematic approach to the study of music not only illuminates medieval history but also provides a methodology for the study of modern Middle Eastern music.

BIBLIOGRAPHY

For bibliographical information consult Amnon Shiloah, *The Theory of Music in Arabic Writings (ca. 900–1900): Descriptive Catalogue of Manuscripts in Libraries of Europe and the U.S.A.* (1979), 101–108. For the study of the theory of melodic movement see George D. Sawa, "Bridging One Millennium: Melodic Movement in al-Fārābī and Kolinski," in Robert Falck and Timothy Rice, eds., *Cross-cultural Perspectives on Music* (1982). For the theory of performance practice, see George D. Sawa, "Music Performance Practice in the Early ᶜAbbāsid Era: 132 A.H./750 A.D.–320 A.H./922 A.D." (Ph.D. diss., Univ. of Toronto, 1983). For an illustration of al-Fārābī's performance theory using contemporary practices see George D. Sawa, "The Survival of Some Aspects of Medieval Arabic Performance Practice," in *Ethnomusicology*, 25 (1981).

GEORGE DIMITRI SAWA

[See also Iqāᶜ; Kindi, al-; Music, Islamic; Music, Islamic Influence in the West; Philosophy-Theology, Islamic; Rāzī, al-; Rushd, ibn; Sīnā, ibn.]

FARAZDAQ, AL- (literally, "the doughball," *ca.* 640–728 or 730), sobriquet of Abū Firās Tammām ibn Ghālib, a renowned Arab poet of early Islamic times. His unusual name is said to refer to his short, stocky physique.

Al-Farazdaq was born about 640 in Yamāma in eastern Arabia. His family belonged to a prominent sub-clan of the Tamīm tribe, and during the First Civil War (656–661) his father seems to have played a role with the Alids in the Basra area of Iraq. Al-Farazdaq began to show promise as a poet at a young age. He composed panegyrics and epigrams for patrons of his own tribe and worked his way into the literary circles developing in Basra, where he ultimately became very popular.

The life of this poet was a colorful one. Personally he was regarded as a notorious carouser, dissolute and fond of drink, and his verse reveals him as a man of keen wit but limited sensitivity. In his poetry he developed and refined the talent for panegyric and satire that had first raised him to prominence, and at times he could be quite unscrupulous. A blatant opportunist, he furiously satirized former patrons and others by whom he felt himself slighted, and he outraged other poets by plagiarizing their work and ridiculing them in his poems. During his long career,

which took him on frequent travels and gained his verse wide exposure in Syria, Iraq, and Arabia, he made many enemies, who considered him venal and wicked and exaggerated his faults. His bitterest opponent was Jarīr, another great poet of Tamīm; their mutual diatribes continued for years, and their polemic verse *(naqāᵓiḍ)* reached quite abusive levels of insult and obscenity.

Al-Farazdaq was thus a controversial figure, often caught up in serious difficulty that led on several occasions to his imprisonment. He was on fairly good terms with the caliph Muᶜāwiya, but in 669/670 a lampoon he directed against a noble Basran family brought the wrath of the governor, Ziyād ibn Abī Sufyān, down upon him. He fled to Medina, where he was initially welcomed, but his indiscretions eventually inflamed sentiment against him there as well. In 676, however, after Ziyād's death, al-Farazdaq managed to restore himself to favor and was able to return to Basra. He composed panegyrics on ᶜAbd al-Malik, his lieutenant al-Ḥajjāj ibn Yūsuf, and other Umayyad figures, but for a long time found it difficult to gain their patronage. This problem was probably due to his Alid sympathies: he recited some rather inflammatory verse on the 680 massacre of Ḥusayn ibn ᶜAlī and his followers at Karbalā', and during the reign of ᶜAbd al-Malik (685–705), he was imprisoned on the orders of the caliph's son, Hishām, for reciting a moving poem on Ḥusayn's son, ᶜAlī Zayn al-ᶜĀbidīn.

The poet's fortunes improved under al-Walīd (I) ibn ᶜAbd al-Malik (*r.* 705–715) and his brother Sulaymān (*r.* 715–717), both of whom he served as poet laureate of the Umayyad court. After another brief eclipse during the reign of the pious ᶜUmar ibn ᶜAbd al-ᶜAzīz (*r.* 717–720), al-Farazdaq was able to gain the favor of the new caliph, Yazīd (II) ibn ᶜAbd al-Malik by vigorously attacking the rebel leader Yazīd ibn al-Muhallab, whom he had lauded as governor several years earlier. Al-Farazdaq was by then a very old man, but he continued to compose poetry almost to the time of his death.

As one would expect from his biography, al-Farazdaq produced mainly panegyric and satirical verse; bacchic and love themes, oddly enough, hardly appear at all. He avoids unusual meters and contorted structure and rather, in the tradition of the truly great bedouin poets, builds his verse on the strength of his rich vocabulary, broad range of expression, and vivid, energetic style. He was recognized in his own time as a poet of the first rank, and since his poetry was widely circulated by transmitters *(ruwāt)* of the Tamīm tribe, and admired and studied by the learned in Basra, most of it seems to have survived. Though the authenticity of some are now questioned, almost 800 poems or fragments are extant, making the collected verse, or *dīwān,* of al-Farazdaq the largest in all of Arabic poetry.

This verse comprises a record of great importance for our knowledge of early Arabic literature and Islamic history. Al-Farazdaq and his peers were the last of the great bedouin poets, and their poetry reflects values, traditions, and customs that had contributed much to the shaping of Arab society but were now giving way before an emerging Islamic ethical system and influences from the indigenous cultures of the conquered provinces, especially in Iraq. Such poets as al-Farazdaq, Jarīr, and al-Akhṭal, later regarded as the great triad of Umayyad times, also offer contemporary references to important events of their era; in particular, their panegyrics contribute much to our understanding of the self-image of the Umayyad caliphs as rulers of an empire and champions of a new world religion.

BIBLIOGRAPHY

Sources. Al-Farazdaq's *Dīwān* was partially edited and translated by Richard Boucher, *Divan de Férazdak* (1870–1875), with further material in Joseph Hell, *Divan des Farazdak* (1900–1901); the edition by ᶜAbd Allāh Ismāᶜīl al-Sāwī (1936) is the most complete, but mediocre. The *Naqāʾiḍ* of Jarīr and al-Farazdaq was edited by Anthony Ashley Bevan (1905–1912) and translated, though not very readably, by Arthur Wormhoudt as *The Naqaith of Jarir and al-Farazdaq* (1974). For the elegy on ᶜAlī Zayn al-ᶜĀbidīn, see Joseph Hell, "Al-Farazdak's Loblied auf ᶜAlī ibn al-Ḥusain (Zain al-ᶜĀbidīn)," in G. Weil, ed., *Festschrift Eduard Sachau* (1915).

Studies. See the extensive bibliographical details in Fuat Sezgin, *Geschichte des arabischen Schrifttums,* II (1975), 359–363, to which the following should be added: James A. Bellamy, "The Impact of Islam on Early Arabic Poetry," in Alford T. Welch and Pierre Cachia, eds., *Islam: Past Influence and Present Challenge* (1979); Mamdūḥ Ḥaqqī, *Al-Farazdaq* (1976); Khalīl Mardam, *Al-Farazdaq,* Aʾimmat al-adab, V (1939); Reynold A. Nicholson, *A Literary History of the Arabs* (1907), 242–244; Aḥmad al-Shāyib, *Taʾrīkh al-naqāʾid,* 2nd ed. (1954); W. Montgomery Watt, "God's Caliph: Qurʾānic Interpretations and Umayyad Claims," in Clifford Edmund Bosworth, ed., *Iran and Islam: In Memory of the Late Vladimir Minorsky* (1971); Maḥmūd Ghannāwī al-Zuhayrī, *Naqāʾid Jarīr wa-l-Farazdaq: dirāsa adabiyya taʾrīkhyya* (1954).

LAWRENCE I. CONRAD

[See also **Akhṭal, al-; Arabic Poetry; Jarīr; Umayyads.**]

FARCES, short, comic plays averaging 400–500 octosyllabic lines, flourished in France from about 1450 to 1560. Performed first in the marketplace and later at court until Molière's time, usually printed, they influenced Elizabethan drama through John Heywood, who translated several. Thematically similar to the earlier fabliaux, the 150–200 extant farces (the best known being *Maistre Pierre Pathelin*) exploit colloquial language, puns, and slapstick and contain allusions to carnival. Character types include the cuckold, the shrewish wife, the farce lover (often a monk), and the outwitted trickster. The plays often enact popular proverbs and include popular songs. They also reflect the religious tensions of the Reformation and furnish insight into the daily lives of such people as urban tradesmen during the late fifteenth and early sixteenth centuries.

BIBLIOGRAPHY

Barbara C. Bowen, *Les caractéristiques essentielles de la farce française et leur survivance dans les années 1550–1620* (1964); Howard Mayer Brown, *Music in the French Secular Theatre, 1400–1550* (1963); Ian R. Maxwell, *French Farce and John Heywood* (1946, repr. 1976); Christopher Pinet, "Some Reflections on French Farce and the Genre Approach," in *Res publica litterarum,* 2 (1979).

CHRISTOPHER PINET

[See also **Drama, French; Fabliau and Comic Tale.**]

FARCING, the addition of text with music to a preexisting liturgical chant, serving to expand, embellish, and comment on that chant. The practice is analogous to that of troping, and apparently both terms were at times used synonymously. In three respects, however, farcing is generally considered to be a more restricted practice than troping: it is usually limited to less elaborate chants, such as lessons and readings; it is found in the vernacular (Old French, Provençal, and Catalan) as well as in Latin; and it often relies exclusively on centonization (phrases of text and music borrowed from a wide variety of other chants). Whether or not the term was used precisely and consistently in the above sense during the Middle Ages is unclear. Modern scholars such as Arlt, however, have considered the centonate character of farcing basic to the practice. The term farce is found in ordinals and ceremonials and only rarely in the rubrics of service books. Farced pieces, particularly epistles, are found frequently in French, Spanish, and Sicilian manuscripts of the twelfth to fifteenth centuries. Further research is needed to determine the extent of the practice and to define more precisely its relation to troping.

BIBLIOGRAPHY

Wulf Arlt, *Ein Festoffizium des Mittelalters aus Beauvais in seiner liturgischen und musikalischen Bedeutung,* 2 vols. (1970), I.93–95, 105–111, and *passim;* Clemens Blume and Guido M. Dreves, eds., *Analecta hymnica medii aevi,* 55 vols. (1886–1922, repr. 1961), XLIX.167–207; Charles du Cange, "Farsa" and "Farsia," in *Glossarium mediae et infimae Latinitatis,* III (1844), 208; Bruno Stäblein, "Epistel [Katholisch]," in Friedrich Blume, ed., *Die Musik in Geschichte und Gegenwart,* 16 vols. (1949–1979), III.1445–1453, and "Tropus," *ibid.,* XIII.819; Henri Villetard, ed., "Office de Pierre de Corbeil (office de la circoncision) improprement appelé 'Office des fous,'" in *Bibliothèque musicologique,* IV (1907).

LANCE W. BRUNNER

[See also **Centonization; Tropes to the Mass Ordinary; Tropes to the Proper of the Mass.**]

FARDALFUS ABBAS (*d.* 806), of Longobard extraction, was made head of the monastery of St. Denis by Charlemagne and was adviser, friend, and *comites* of the emperor. His extant works are very short poems (*metrica opuscula*).

BIBLIOGRAPHY

The poems are in *Patrologia latina,* XCIX (1851), 823–826. See also Max Manitius, *Geschichte der lateinischen Literatur des Mittelalters,* II (1923, repr. 1976), 811.

EDWARD FRUEH

[See also **Carolingian Latin Poetry.**]

FARGHĀNĀ (FERGANA), a large valley along the upper Jaxartes River (Syr Darya) and a major avenue of international trade and population movements in the Middle Ages. Almost completely enclosed by spurs of the Tien Shan range, Farghānā today is mainly in the Uzbek S.S.R. but in the Middle Ages was one of the eastern marches of the Iranian world. It was traversed by the southern branch of the silk route and was a meeting place for three civilizations: Irano-Muslim, Turco-Mongol, and Han.

Both Chinese and Muslim writers describe Farghānā as densely populated and having a complex economic base of agriculture (cereals, fruits, nuts), stock breeding (horses were exported to China), slave markets (Turks were exported to Iran and Mesopotamia), and mining and metallurgy (gold, silver, iron, lead, copper, coal, ammonium chloride, mercury, and magnetite).

The international character of Farghānā shaped its history. A haven for political refugees and a buffer between Irano-Muslim oasis societies and Turco-Mongol steppe peoples, it preserved a tradition of local autonomy. Within Farghānā an Iranian landlord class, the *dahāqīn* (sing.: *dihqān*), held power in the sixth and seventh centuries while recognizing the regional authority of an *ikhshēdh,* a royal prince. The cities of Farghānā in this period were compact: Kāsān (modern Kasansay), the principal pre-Islamic city, was about one mile in diameter, having walls, a citadel, a central business/residential district, and suburbs (often walled).

At the beginning of the eighth century, Muslim Arabs from the west appeared. Their conquest of Farghānā is usually attributed to Qutayba ibn Muslim, whose campaigns in Transoxiana between 705 and 715 brought Islam to the hitherto Zoroastrian and Buddhist region. Aside from the new religion of Islam, the Arabs had little impact on Farghānā.

In contrast, the movement of steppe peoples from the north and east into Farghānā, beginning about the same time (Qarluq Turks in the early eighth century), had profound political and social effects. Turkish leaders replaced Iranian *dahāqīn;* steppe political ideals institutionalized in the appanage system found a hospitable environment in Farghānā and flourished while the local Irano-Islamic cultural values were, with two notable exceptions, adopted by the steppe invaders. This process of assimilation is typified by the period of the Karakhanid Turks (Ilek Khāns) from about 990 to 1213, during which the appanage state gave rise to a complex political landscape in Farghānā.

The Karakhanids were superseded by the Mongol Qara Khiṭāy in the middle of the twelfth century, but coins from Farghānā show that the Jalāli branch of the Karakhanids continued to govern until the beginning of the thirteenth century under a fiscal arrangement with the Qara Khiṭāy. The latter and their successors, the Mongol Genghisids (1220–1334), broke the earlier pattern of assimilation, attempting to preserve their nomadic traditions while governing urban Farghānā from the steppe. However, by 1334, the Genghisids, represented by the Čaghatay khanate, had reverted to the Karakhanid pattern, adopting Islam and living in the region. In later centuries, under the Barlas Turk Tamerlane and his descendants (1370–1500), the balance between steppe political and military forms and Irano-Islamic culture was firmly established.

BIBLIOGRAPHY

A fundamental source for the history of Farghānā in the pre-Islamic period and up to the mid eighth century is E. Chavannes, *Documents sur les Tou-Kiue (Turcs) occidentaux* (1903), 287–299. For a Chinese description of Farghānā and information on the medieval period generally, see Emil Vasilevich Bretshneider, *Medieval Researches from Eastern Asiatic Sources*, 2 vols. (1910). The descriptions by Muslim geographers of the tenth to fifteenth centuries have been compiled by Guy LeStrange, *The Lands of the Eastern Caliphate* (1905, repr. 1966), 476–480; and W. Barthold, *Turkestan down to the Mongol Invasion*, 3rd ed. (1968), esp. 155–165.

ROBERT D. MCCHESNEY

[See also **Karakhanids; Iran; Mongol Empire.**]

FARMERS' LAW, a Byzantine compilation of laws regulating agrarian relations. It has been variously dated in the late seventh century or the first half of the eighth century. Prevailing opinion attributes it to Justinian II (685–695, 705–711), to whom the full title (Chapters of agrarian law extracted from the volume of Justinian) apparently refers.

The *Farmers' Law* consists of eighty-five chapters and is one of the few sources for the structure of the Byzantine countryside in this period. It shows the existence of a village community *(chorion)*, the bulk of its population consisting not of coloni but of free peasants having freedom of movement and fiscal obligations to the state. Fields and vineyards were private property, unoccupied land belonged to the community, and undivided lands were periodically distributed. The community had collective fiscal responsibility, as is shown by articles 18 and 19, which arrange the fate of the lands and taxes of a person who has left the village. The collective fiscal responsibility of the village community is typical of agrarian relations in the middle Byzantine period.

The *Farmers' Law* shows that a system of polyculture prevailed and that the peasants also owned cattle, which were herded by men hired by the community. After the harvest, fields were opened to pasture. There was differentiation of wealth, as indicated by the fact that some small landowners leased

their lands to others for cultivation, on a share-cropping basis, receiving a tenth of the crops. There were also hired agricultural laborers and slaves. The harsh conditions of rural life are revealed by a list of corporal punishments for stealing or damaging another person's property, as well as heavy fines for destroying agricultural capital.

BIBLIOGRAPHY

Walter Ashburner, "The Farmer's Law," in *Journal of Hellenic Studies,* 30 (1910) and 32 (1912); Franz Dölger, "Ist der Nomos Georgikos ein Gesetz des Kaisers Justinian II?" in *Festschrift für Leopold Wenger,* II (1945), repr. in Dölger's *Paraspora* (1961); Paul Lemerle, "Esquisse pour une histoire agraire de Byzance," in *Revue historique,* 219 (1958); George Ostrogorsky, "La commune rurale byzantine," in *Byzantion,* 32 (1962); M. Ya. Syuzyumov, "Borba za puti razvitia feodalnykh otnoshenii v Vizantii" (The dispute on the development of feudal relations in Byzantium), in *Vizantiskie ocherki* (1961), and "Nekotorye problemy istorii Vizantii" (Some problems of the history of Byzantium), in *Voprosy istorii* (1959).

ANGELIKI LAIOU

[See also **Agriculture and Nutrition, Byzantium; Byzantine Empire: Economic Life and Social Structure; Law, Byzantine.**]

FAROESE BALLADS. At the core of the Faroese ballad corpus is the *kempuvísa* (heroic ballad) typical of West Nordic tradition. Usually containing the word *kvæði* (from Old Norse *kvæði*, "poem" or "song") in their titles, Faroese heroic ballads are very long narrative songs composed in quatrains of the *abcb* type with a four-line refrain at the end of each stanza. Of a character more epic than dramatic, they have as their dominant theme the victory of heroes against overwhelmingly powerful, often supernatural adversaries. Characters and plots alike are highly conventional—young heroes journey to foreign lands to seek a suitable wife, a country to rule, or wrongs to set aright—and are realized to a high degree by means of commonplace stanzas. The longer heroic ballads, generally ranging from 120 to 400 stanzas, can be divided into as many as nine *tættir* (sing.: *táttur*, subballad), each depicting one of a succession of adventures experienced by fathers and sons, in-laws, or sets of brothers.

In the Faroe Islands the performance of ballads as dance songs has persisted to the present day. Until the early twentieth century, the high points of village social life were weekly dances, commonly held on Sunday evenings from Christmas until Lent, as well as the dance fests held in celebration of holy days (the second day of Christmas, New Year's Eve, Epiphany, Shrove Monday, and the feast of St. Olaf), and of weddings and whale hunts. In performing the ballad dance several villagers, usually men, form a chain or ring as one or two of them take the lead in treading leftward the simple steps of the dance and chanting the opening stanzas of the ballad. The dancers often join in the stanzas familiar to them and then lustily take over the chanting of the refrain, while the leaders rest their voices.

Although ballads were doubtless performed in the Faroe Islands during the late Middle Ages, there is no trace of any recorded text until 1639, when a Faroese minister sent a small sampling to the Danish antiquarian Ole Worm. The manuscript was destroyed by fire, and all that remain of the texts are a few quotations in Peder Syv's manuscripts and a passing reference in his edition of Danish ballads, *Et hundrede udvalde danske viser ... Forøgede med det andet hundrede* (1695). The earliest extant texts were recorded in 1781–1782 by Jens Christian Svabo, who recorded fifty-two ballads, having to invent his own orthography in order to do so.

While studying algae in the Faroes during the summer of 1817, a Dane, Hans Christian Lyngbye, recorded a few fragmentary texts, among them "Sjúrðar kvæði," which he showed on his return to Copenhagen to Professor P. E. Müller, who recognized this ballad as a version of the Germanic legend of Sigurd the Dragon Slayer. Given the interest of romantics of the early nineteenth century in antiquities, Müller was prompted to procure additional texts of "Sjúrðar kvæði" from a churchman on Suðuroy (Syderø), thus enabling Lyngbye to publish his find in *Færøiske qvæder om Sigurd Fofnersbane og hans æt* (1822). It was this outside interest in their native traditions that inspired a number of Faroe Islanders to begin collecting their own native ballads in the mid nineteenth century.

In the 1840's the Danish folklorist Svend Grundtvig encouraged a Faroese theology student, Venceslaus Ulricus Hammershaimb, to take up the project of a national ballad collection incorporating all existing manuscript collections and modeled on Grundtvig's own *Danmarks gamle folkeviser*. In 1871, however, Hammershaimb turned the project back to Grundtvig, who, with the aid of Jørgen Bloch, completed a fair copy, *Føroya kvæði: Corpus carminum færoensium,* in fifteen volumes (1876), followed by a sixteenth (1889) and two supplements (1896 and 1905) containing additional texts collected in the 1880's by the Faroese philologist Jakob Jakobsen. Grundtvig and Bloch's compendium, edited by Christian Matras and N. Djurhuus, was published in six volumes (1941–1972). Editions for a popular audience began to appear in the 1880's and 1890's. The earliest recordings of the melodies to Faroese heroic ballads are found in Svabo's notebook from 1775. In 1908 Hjalmar Thuren published an extensive monograph on Faroese ballad music, *Folkesangen paa Færøerne,* containing more than 100 melodies, along with commentary and analysis.

The ballad dance probably reached the Faroes from western Norway sometime during the fourteenth century. Even though fewer than 10 percent of the extant Faroese corpus of heroic ballads have corresponding numbers in the Norwegian corpus, it is clear from the shaping effect of the Norwegian *kjempevise* on Faroese tradition that in the fourteenth through sixteenth centuries many more originally Norwegian heroic ballads were widely sung in the Faroes. The internationalism of Bergen, the administrative center for the islands until 1709, is reflected in the Faroese heroic ballads composed from French and German literary works translated there, such as *Karlamagnús saga* and *Þiðreks saga af Bern,* which render chansons de geste and other forms of narrative that grew up around the figures of Charlemagne and Theodoric the Great. Although a large part of the corpus of Faroese ballads was composed during the Middle Ages, new dance ballads in traditional meters, especially satirical ones about political events or the foibles of given individuals, continued to be composed from written as well as oral sources through the nineteenth century.

Grundtvig and Bloch's compendium contains a total of 236 ballad types, all of which were composed before 1850. In recent years some thirteen ballad types from the nineteenth century or earlier have been collected from oral tradition. In *Corpus carminum færoensium (CCF)* heroic ballads with Nordic motifs are numbers 1–105, but their ordering is somewhat arbitrary. *CCF 1–13* are the ballads published by Venceslaus U. Hammershaimb in the first volume of *Færöiske kvæder* (1851), selected by him as the most important ones dealing with heroic and mythological characters celebrated in Eddic poetry. Best-known of these is "Sjúrðar kvæði" (*CFF 1*) in three *tættir*: (1) "Regin smiður" (Regin the smith), about the death of Sjúrður's father Sigmundur, Sjúrður's youth and acquisition from Regin of the sword Gram, his vengeance on his father's slayers, and his killing of a dragon to win a treasure; (2) "Brynhildar táttur," about how Sjúrður wins Brynhild but, because of a magic potion, forgets her and marries Guðrun, and how Brynhild takes revenge by inciting her new husband Gunnar and his brother Høgni (both Guðrun's brothers) to kill Sjúrður; (3) "Høgna táttur," about Guðrun's marriage to Artala, her successful plan to kill her brothers, and the vengeance of Høgni's son on her and her husband. All three tættir probably had their immediate sources in Norwegian ballads reflecting a combination of Scandinavian and northern German reflexes of this Germanic legend.

CCF 14–32 are the ballads published by Hammershaimb in the second volume of *Færöiske kvæder* (1855); these tell an assortment of stories about heroes and events also known from the medieval Icelandic legendary sagas, family sagas, and sagas of the Norwegian kings. As is apparently suggested by a legend from Sandoy (Sandø) about an Icelandic vellum manuscript rescued by villagers from a foundering ship, the Faroese ballads with close parallels in Icelandic sagas may well have originally been composed from literary sources. This is true, for example, of "Kjartans tættir" (CCF 23), which follows the events of the central part of *Laxdæla saga* very closely, and of "Sigmundar kvæði" (CCF 22), which recapitulates the adventures of the Faroese hero Sigmundur Brestisson as told in *Færeyinga saga.*

The remaining heroic ballads in *Corpus carminum færoensium* (CCF 32–105) are arranged alphabetically by title. While many of these may well be of medieval provenance, others show signs of having been composed during the late eighteenth and early nineteenth centuries. In general, the relatively few heroic ballads composed in couplet stanzas also seem to be of late origin, reflecting the impact on Faroese tradition of the couplet ballads, especially their melodies, in Vedel's and Syv's editions of Danish ballads. CCF 106–113 are ballads about the heroes of legends and romances originating south of Scandinavia. Most important of these is "Karlamagnusar kvæði" (CCF 106), a cycle of ballads about Charlemagne and his champions, with Roland foremost. Most of the ballads in this cycle reflect features of both the Old Norse *Karlamagnús saga* (ca. 1250) and the Danish *Karl Magnus' krønike*

(ca. 1480). Of special interest are "Koralds kvæði" (CCF 111) and "Bevusar tættir" (CCF 112), both of which reveal in their high incidence of alliteration and "unballadlike" rhyme schemes (*aabb*) that they originally were Icelandic *rímur.*

CCF 114–178 are for the most part ballads of mixed thematic content that have been translated and adapted from printed Danish ballads known to Faroese tradition. CCF 179–236 is a mixed group of ballads considered to be of relatively recent composition. A few of these are not ballads at all but have nonetheless been performed in the ballad dance—one such example is "Ljómurnar" ("Rays of light," CCF 220), a religious poem composed by the last Catholic bishop of Iceland.

The bulk of this mixed group, however, consists of satirical ballads (called *tættir*) lampooning the foibles of various residents of the Faroes. The *táttur* is a productive genre today, and it still happens that a hapless villager is lured into the dance, only to discover that the ballad is about him.

BIBLIOGRAPHY

Patricia Conroy, "Oral Composition in Faroese Ballads," in *Jahrbuch für Volksliedforschung,* 25 (1980); Erik Dal, *Nordisk folkeviseforskning siden 1800* (1956), and "Tyske, franske og engelske oversættelser af færøkvæder," in *Fróðskaparrit,* 18 (1970); Otto Holzapfel, *Bibliographie zur mittelalterlichen skandinavischen Volksballade* (1975); Mortan Nolsøe, "Noen betraktninger om forholdet mellom ballade og saga-forelegg," in *Sumlen* (1976), and "The Faroese Heroic Ballad and Its Relations to Other Genres," in *The European Medieval Ballad* (1978); Hjalmar Thuren, *Folkesangen paa Færøerne* (1908).

PATRICIA L. CONROY

[See also **Ballads, Middle English; Brynhild; Dance; Scandinavian Ballads; Sigurd.**]

FÃRS, the Arabicized form of Pãrs, derived from the Greek Persis. This province in southwestern Iran, consisting of high plateau land divided into broad valleys by the southern chains of the Zagros Mountains, extends from Yazd-i Khwast in the north and Furg in the east to the Persian Gulf and its offshore islands in the west and south. Fãrs was the homeland of the two great pre-Islamic Persian dynasties. The vast Achaemenid Empire established by Cyrus (559–530) extended as far as Egypt and Asia Minor when it was overrun by Alexander in the late fourth century B.C. The Persian Empire was reestablished by the kings of the Sasanian dynasty (226–ca. 640), several of whom maintained residences in Fārs while ruling from Ctesiphon in Iraq. The province was divided into five districts (kuras) each named after, and including, an important royal town. This system was retained by the Arabs when they conquered Fārs in 648.

After three centuries of Arab rule, the Persian element reasserted itself with the rise to power of the Buyid dynasty. One of the greatest of its princes, ʿAḍud al-Dawlah, resided in Fārs and fostered Iranian national feeling by stressing continuity with the Sasanian past. After the fall of the Buyids in the 1050's, Fārs was controlled successively by Seljuk, Salghurid, Ilkhanid, Muzaffarid, and Timurid rulers. The prosperity enjoyed by Fārs and its major city, Shīrāz, under the governors sent from Isfahan by the Safavid shahs in the sixteenth and seventeenth centuries ended in the eighteenth century, when the country was devastated by the Afghan wars. Shiraz flourished again briefly when Karim Khan Zand made the city his capital. The death of this beneficent ruler in 1779 initiated a power struggle that eventually brought Fārs under the control of the Qajar kings. The establishment of a permanent capital at Tehran in 1786 relegated Fārs and its major towns irrevocably to provincial status.

BIBLIOGRAPHY

C. E. Bosworth, *The Islamic Dynasties* (1967); Guy LeStrange, *Lands of the Eastern Caliphate* (1966), 248–298; S. M. T. Mastafavī, *The Land of Pārs,* R. Sharp and J. Hopkins, trans. (1978).

LIONEL BIER

[See also **Buyids; Ilkhanids; Iran, History; Iran, Political History; Sasanians; Seljuks; Shiraz; Timurids.**]

FASHION. See **Costume.**

FASTING, CHRISTIAN. Although a fast consists essentially of going without food or drink for a certain time, the term came to be used also of a diet limited in quantity and variety. The early Christians fasted for the two days before Easter and on Wednesdays and Fridays, except during Paschaltide. In Rome the Wednesday fast was moved to Saturday before 400. A fast was broken only in the evening by a frugal meal, usually without wine, meat, or milk products. With time, alterations and additions were made and by 500 the full medieval discipline of fasting was well established. It can be examined conveniently under three headings: sacramental, seasonal, and ascetic fasts.

The custom of not eating or drinking before the reception of the Eucharist was universally observed during the Middle Ages. It was not a penance but a mark of respect for the sacrament. Since morning was the common time for Mass, and Communion was received only a few times during the year, this fast was easily observed.

Fasts were also part of the lengthy process of receiving forgiveness for a serious sin. The severity of the rites of public penance led to their being abandoned in favor of the private confession of sins, which was introduced and propagated by the Irish monks. Severe fasts continued to characterize the new penitential discipline, but they followed rather than preceded the reception of the sacrament of penance. The types and duration of these fasts were prescribed in detail by the popular penitentials that, starting in the sixth century, spread from Ireland throughout Europe.

In the early church catechumens observed a series of fasts before their baptism at Easter. Although the practice of infant baptism gradually eliminated the catechumenate, the fast before Easter continued to be observed as a period of penance for sins committed after baptism.

This custom produced the most important seasonal fast, that of Lent. In the Greek church a meatless fast began eight weeks before Easter; after one week it became more rigorous by the addition of a ban on dairy products. This vegetarian Lenten diet became law for the Eastern churches at the Trullan Synod (692), though relaxations were admitted in particular cases. The Western church also eased the rules of fasting: meat was never allowed, but in some places during the seventh and eighth centuries wine, milk products, fish, and eggs were increasingly permitted at the Lenten meal. Although abstention from them was regarded as a sign of great virtue, the relaxed observance had become widely accepted by the thirteenth century.

While Lent remained the main penitential season, fasts were observed during Advent and on the vigils of major feasts. In time of distress, plague, earthquake, or war, a special fast was often observed. It usually lasted three days and was accompanied by processions and public prayer. The Western church also fasted on ember days and rogation days. In the Eastern church the feasts of Peter and Paul (29 June) and the Assumption of Mary (15 August) were preceded by fourteen days of fasting.

It was recognized that not all Christians should be obliged to fast. Three bases for exemption were allowed by church law: age, infirmity, and necessity. These exceptions came fairly late; in the eleventh century some Latins still prided themselves that the fast was observed universally, in contrast with the Eastern tendency to grant exemptions. Nevertheless, by the thirteenth century dispensations from fasting were granted to all those under twenty-one, to manual laborers, to travelers, to the poor, and to the infirm.

The purpose of ascetic fasts was to subjugate the powers of the flesh and to deliver the mind from distractions. Since meat and wine, even in moderation, were regarded as conducive to sin, some degree of fasting was considered necessary for every Christian. The old connection between fasting and sorrow for sins was reaffirmed in the teaching that fasting was an expiation for sin.

All of these motives inspired monastic fasting. The Rule of St. Benedict (*ca.* 540), the norm for most Western medieval monasteries, prescribed a fast for every day of the year except Sundays and feasts. Only one meal a day was allowed, at 3 P.M., and it was meatless. The Lenten fast was even stricter. In spite of various monastic reforms and the continuing prestige of the Rule, monasteries gradually abandoned full observance of their traditional fasts. Extreme fasts, however, continued to be observed by individual ascetics, whether inside or outside the monasteries.

One monastic relaxation that spread throughout the Western church affected the time of the single meal on fast days. Originally it followed vespers, the monastic evening prayer. By the twelfth century vespers, with its concomitant meal, had been advanced to three in the afternoon. Around 1300 the meal was often allowed at noon, on the basis that fasting was defined as eating only one meal a day, regardless of the time it was taken. Tradition was safeguarded, to some extent, by saying evening prayers in the morning just before the meal. By 1400 it was the universal practice to eat at noon during a fast.

With the meal earlier, a need was felt for nourishment at the end of the day. The opinion developed that taking something at evening, at first only a liquid but later a light collation, did not break the fast because these refreshments were not nourishing

enough to be considered eating. By the fourteenth century this collation had developed substantially, but it was permitted as long as it was not a full meal. Eastern monasticism maintained in principle its primitive rigor.

BIBLIOGRAPHY

Peter Browe, "Die Nuechternheit vor der Messe und Kommunion im Mittelalter," in *Ephemerides liturgicae,* **45** (1931); L. Gougaud, "Some Liturgical and Ascetic Traditions of the Celtic Church," in *Irish Ecclesiastical Record,* 5th ser., **1** (1913); Alexandre Guillaume, *Jeûne et charité dans l'église latine, dès origines au XIIᵉ siècle* (1954), 141–164; Jan Piekoszewski, *Le jeûne eucharistique* (1952), 39–52; Raymond Régamey et al., *Redécouverte du jeûne* (1959), 111–127, 321–327.

DANIEL CALLAM

[See also **Advent; Ember Days; Lent; Penance, Penitentials.**]

FASTING, ISLAMIC. Fasting (Arabic: *ṣiyām, ṣawm*) is frequently practiced in the Islamic religion and constitutes one of its fundamental acts of worship. The fast of Ramadan—the most important Islamic fast—is, according to Islamic belief, one of the "five pillars" of the religion and the only fast that is obligatory on the Muslim community as a whole. Any otherwise voluntary fast becomes obligatory—unless excessively strenuous or otherwise harmful—if a believer undertakes it by way of private vow (*nadhr*). There are, moreover, a number of compulsory acts of atonement (*kaffāra*) for various transgressions of Islamic law that may include different degrees of fasting as optional fulfillments of part or all of the atonement. Thus, fasting is one of the options for atonement for willful violation of the fast of Ramadan, for involuntary manslaughter, for repudiating one's wife according to the pre-Islamic Arab customs of *ẓihār* and *ᶜilāᵓ*, for killing game while in pilgrim's garb, and for breaking an oath. In the case of pilgrimage to Mecca, fasting is an obligatory form of substitute worship for pilgrims who are required to sacrifice animals as part of their pilgrimage but are unable to do so.

Like other types of obligatory worship in Islam, fasting has recommended but purely voluntary variations. It is suggested, for example, that the faithful fast six days in Shawwāl, the month after Ramadan. Nonpilgrims are urged to fast on ᶜArafāt, the ninth day of the twelfth lunar month and the most important day of the pilgrimage, though pilgrims themselves are not supposed to fast this day. Fasting on ᶜĀshūrāʾ, the tenth day of the first lunar month, Muḥarram, is highly recommended and was probably obligatory in the earliest days of Islam, before the institution of the fast of Ramadan, which abrogated it. It is also recommended that fasts be observed during the month of Shaᶜbān (just before Ramadan), on Mondays and Thursdays in general, or three days of each month—especially the so-called "white days," the days of the full moon. By contrast, there are a number of days on which Muslims are directed not to fast—most notably, Fridays and Saturdays in isolation, the days of the two ᶜīd festivals, and the festive days of tashrīq, which follow ᶜīd al-ʾaḍḥā.

Islamic fasting, whether obligatory or voluntary, is always performed in the same general manner with the same broad stipulations and requirements. It begins before the break of dawn—generally about an hour and a half or two hours before sunrise—and ends once the sun has completely set. One fasts by abstaining from all food and drink, from smoking, and from conjugal relations, except at night—all things are allowed during the nights of a fast that are customarily permissible to a Muslim not fasting. It is highly recommended that the fast begin with a morning meal (called al-suḥūr) before the break of dawn and that it be broken as soon as possible after sunset. According to the Koran, one of the chief purposes of fasting is to cultivate the attitude of taqwā—heedfulness of God and the careful observation of his commandments. Consequently, Islam stresses that one deport oneself in an upright and dignified manner while fasting, avoiding vain or abusive thoughts, words, and deeds.

Fasting throughout Ramadan, the ninth lunar month of the Islamic calendar, is required each year of every Muslim who is of age, of sound mind and body, and not in the process of traveling. This fast was instituted in Islamic law early in the Medinan period, probably during the second year after Muḥammad's hegira. The beginning and end of the month are determined by the sighting of the new moon, although other methods of calculation may be used when it is not possible to make a sighting. The first day of Shawwāl, the month immediately following Ramadan, is ᶜīd al-fiṭr, one of the two major festivals of the Islamic religious calendar.

It is never permissible for women to fast during their menstrual periods or the bleeding after childbirth. Women who are pregnant or nursing, and

who fear fasting would cause them to lose their milk or harm the unborn child, are exempted from the fast, as are travelers and the sick. Such persons, however, are required to make up later, when they are able, each day of fasting they miss. The elderly and any others who cannot fast without endangering their health are completely exempted from fasting during Ramadan. Some schools of Islamic law require such persons to feed one poor person for each day of fasting they miss, but other schools only recommend that they do so.

Ramadan should not be confused with the four sacred months [al-ʾashhur al-ḥarām] of the Islamic calendar: Rajab (the seventh), Dhū'l-Qiᶜda (the eleventh), Dhū'l-Ḥijja (the twelfth), and Muḥarram (the first). It is, nevertheless, a month of great sanctity. The Koran associates it with the coming of Koranic revelation, and it is characterized as the month in which God's mercy to humanity is especially generous—just as the coming of the prophet Muḥammad's revelation is regarded as the greatest of God's mercies. The prophet Muḥammad is reported to have taught his followers that anyone who fasts for the month of Ramadan out of sincere belief and in expectation of divine reward will be forgiven all preceding sins, and there are ḥadīth stating that the gates of hell are locked during Ramadan, while the gates of paradise are opened wide.

The prophet Muḥammad urged his followers to exert themselves during Ramadan in worship and good works. Consequently, Muslims make special efforts in this month to recite the Koran and perform supererogatory prayers. Nights are devoted to a special community prayer called ṣalāt al-tarāwīḥ, a prayer much longer than customary. In the course of the month, Muslims often recite in prayer the entire Koran. They occasionally practice iᶜtikāf during Ramadan, a type of worship in which one restricts oneself to the mosque day and night, most commonly during the last half of Ramadan.

Islam teaches that the Night of Destiny, lailat-al-qadr, occurs during Ramadan—a night on which God sends down his decree regarding events of the coming year and that, according to the Koran, is "more excellent than a thousand months." No specific night, however, is designated as the Night of Destiny, although Muslims are encouraged to "seek it" by vigils of prayer and worship during the last ten odd-numbered nights of the month—especially the twenty-seventh night. Having spent the Night of Destiny in worship is believed to be especially propitious; for, since it is more excellent than a thousand months, worshiping that night is like having spent an entire lifetime in worship.

BIBLIOGRAPHY

Maḥmūd ibn ꜥAbd Allāh al-Ālūsī, *Rūḥ al-Maꜥānī fī tafsīr al-Qurꜣān al-ꜥAzīm wa-al-sabꜥ al-mathānī* (1970), 2.56–63; Muḥammad ibn ꜥAbd Allāh ibn al-ꜥArabī, *ꜣAḥkām al-Qurꜣān,* ꜥAlī Muḥammad al-Bijāwī, ed. (1967), 1.74–85; Sayyid Quṭb, *Fī ẓilāl al-Qurꜣān* (1973), 1.168–174; Muḥammad ibn ꜣAḥmad ibn Rushd, *Bidāyat al-mujtahid wa-nihāyat al-muqtaṣid* (1966), 1.206–225, 305–307; Muḥammad ibn ꜥAlī al-Shawkānī, *Fatḥ al-qadīr, al-jāmiꜥ bayna fannay al-riwāyah wa-al-dirāy ah min ꜥilm al-tafsīr* (1964), 1.179–184, and *Nayl al-ꜣawṭār, min ꜣaḥādīth sayyid al-ꜣakhyār: Sharḥ muntaqā-'l-ꜣakhbār* (1973), 4.258–354.

UMAR F. ABD-ALLĀH

[See also **Ramadan.**]

FATE. See Fortune.

FATIMID ART. The Fatimids ruled in North Africa, first from what is now Tunisia and then from Egypt, from 909 to 1171. They were one of three contemporary Muslim dynasties simultaneously making claim to the caliphate, and for a brief time in the tenth and eleventh centuries they were the most economically powerful of the three. They dominated the Mediterranean, eclipsing their Muslim rivals, the Umayyads of Andalusia and the Abbasids of Iraq, as well as the Eastern Christians of Byzantium. As a result, the influence of the Fatimid arts was felt throughout the region, not only in Muslim lands but also in the Christian areas, especially Sicily and southern Italy.

Of the three caliphates, the Fatimids alone were Shiite Muslims, and this affiliation accorded them a particular political-religious ruling position that affected their role as official patrons of the arts. Essentially, as Shiite rulers, the Fatimid caliphs derived their right to rule from a sequence of father-to-son leadership extending back from the ruling caliph to the house of ꜥAlī and his wife, Fāṭima (from whom the dynasty took its name). This genealogical link not only assured the Fatimid caliphs of the special right to rule and guide but also invested them with

special knowledge and the ability to interpret. As minority rulers of a largely Sunni population, therefore, the Fatimids were always at pains to keep the idea of the purity of their genealogically based right to rule before the population and to engage in practices that continuously demonstrated the strength of that right. They used the arts for these purposes.

When the Fatimids conquered Egypt in 969 from their capital of Al-Mahdīya (Mahdia) in Tunisia, they founded the walled city of Al-Qāhirah (Cairo) as a royal administrative center for the caliph and his loyal troops. This walled city served to isolate the Fatimid caliph and to emphasize his position as special ruler. The Sunni population lived outside the walls in Al-Fusṭāṭ, al-ꜥAskar, and al-Qaṭāʾiꜥ, the areas of earlier Muslim settlement. Within the walls of Cairo, the Fatimids built palaces and a congregational mosque, al-Azhar (970), which soon became a teaching institution and center for Fatimid Shiite missionary activity *(daꜥwa)*. In 1125 the mosque of al-Aqmar was also built within the walls; it was the first mosque with its exterior facade aligned to the main city street, while the interior prayer hall was aligned to the Kaaba in Mecca. The facade displays polemical inscriptions and a complex visual program that reflects the Shiite political-religious controversy disrupting the dynasty at the time.

Outside the walls of Cairo the Fatimids began a congregational mosque for the Sunni population at large in 990 (or perhaps 989), which was incorporated within the walls when the capital was expanded between 1087 and 1091. This mosque, which took some twenty years to complete, has been variously named in the sources and finally came to be known as the mosque of al-Ḥākim, after the caliph who ordered its completion in 1003. In 1160 the dynasty began the construction of the mosque of Ṣāliḥ Ṭalaʾiꜥ, which some sources state was intended as a shrine for the head of the Shiite martyr Ḥusayn, though this relic was never placed there. The Fatimids also sponsored the building of a number of *mashhad*s, or funerary monuments, dedicated to members of the house of ꜥAlī or martyrs to the cause of Shiite Islam. The erection of these structures, as well as the mosque of Ṣāliḥ Ṭalaʾiꜥ, seems part of an officially sponsored attempt to focus the attention of the Sunni population on the Alid house and thus on the special ruling position of the Fatimid caliph. In fact, this building program in the environs of Cairo coincided with the succession disputes within the dynasty at the turn of the twelfth century as well

Minaret of the Mosque of al-Ḥākim. Cairo, *ca.* 990–*ca.* 1010. PHOTOGRAPH COURTESY OF S. SOUCEK

Al-Azhar Mosque. Cairo, 970. PHOTOGRAPH BY JEAN MAZENOD

Detail of the painted ceiling of the Palatine Chapel. Palermo, *ca.* 1138. SKIRA VERLAG, GENEVA

Aquamanile in the form of a peacock. Bronze, probably Sicilian, 11th century. MUSÉE DU LOUVRE

Fragment of Kufic calligraphy carved in stone. Great Mosque at Susa, 10th or 11th century. PHOTOGRAPH
COURTESY OF ALEXANDRE PAPADOPOULO

as outside pressures on the dynasty from Sunni forces.

Fatimid minarets have been identified in Luxor, and also in Aswan, where mausoleums are extant from the early Fatimid battles for the Shiite cause in Upper Egypt. The Fatimids made restorations on public monuments within their domain, most notably al-Aqsā mosque in Jerusalem.

In addition to sponsoring the construction of buildings, the Fatimids used Arabic writing on public monuments to emphasize their rule and to highlight the special nature of their position. The floriated kufic style of calligraphy they developed for monumental use was a handsome vehicle for legitimizing Fatimid rule by displaying Koranic verses mentioning the *ahl al-bayt* (people of the house), a key phrase that suggested the house of ᶜAlī. The names of ᶜAlī and Muḥammad were displayed over the Bāb al-Nāṣr (Gate of Victory), one of the main gates into Cairo, on the mosque of al-Aqmar, and on the *mashhad*s.

Fatimid architecture combines Maghribi features with those of Egypt. The monumental entrance built for the mosque of al-Ḥākim reflects Fatimid practice in their previous capital of Al-Mahdīya, and the ways of emphasizing the *qibla* wall with several domes in Fatimid mosques also follow Maghribi models. Fatimid patronage also served as a conduit for features and techniques more common in the eastern Islamic lands to reach the Maghrib, while Armenian craftsmen, brought to fortify the gates of

Cairo in the late eleventh century, introduced Armenian stonemasonry techniques into the Egyptian repertoire.

From what is known of private arts in the Fatimid period, the vocabulary of forms and content, as well as techniques and materials, expresses social and cultural identity with the other medieval Muslim caliphal societies while also conveying a distinctively Fatimid aesthetic. The palaces of rulers and the wealthy are known only through remains in Al-Mahdīya and the Qalᶜa of the Banū Ḥammād in eastern Algeria, since those in Cairo were demolished by later Sunni rulers. Textual references indicate elaborate figural paintings on the palace walls, but these too are unknown except for intimations from fragments of frescoed *muqarnas* in Al-Fusṭāṭ and from the painted ceilings of the mid-twelfth-century Palatine Chapel in Palermo, Sicily. The subject matter of this decoration reflects the urban pastimes of the wealthy, with images of hunters, musicians, dancers, and women in howdahs on camels. Also included is the frontal depiction of a crossed-legged male raising a wine cup in his right hand, a common motif since the ninth century. This repertoire occurs on ivory carvings and pottery as well as in architectural settings.

The Fatimids also used the textile arts to support their rule, not only to the extent that textiles served as capital in the medieval Mediterranean but also as a means of displaying the names and titles of the Fatimid rulers on goods manufactured in state workshops (*ṭirāz*). While these embroidered textiles were given and worn as official court garments, they were also presented as gifts abroad and were collected in the treasuries of European Christian churches.

BIBLIOGRAPHY

In addition to Georges Marçais, "Fāṭimid Art," and J. M. Rogers, "al-Ḳāhira," in the *Encyclopaedia of Islam,* 2nd ed., II (1965) and IV (1978), see Jonathan M. Bloom, "The Mosque of al-Ḥākim in Cairo," in *Muqarnas,* **1** (1983); K. A. C. Creswell, *The Muslim Architecture of Egypt,* I (1952); Oleg Grabar, "Imperial and Urban Art in Islam: The Subject Matter of Fatimid Art," in *Colloque international sur l'histoire du Caire* (1972); Caroline Williams, "The Cult of ᶜAlid Saints in the Faṭimid Monuments of Cairo, Part I: The Mosque of al-Aqmar," in *Muqarnas,* **1** (1983).

                                        IRENE A. BIERMAN

[See also **Cairo; Calligraphy, Islamic; Ceramics, Islamic; Islamic Architecture; Islamic Art; Mosque; Palermo; Shiᶜa; Textiles, Islamic; Ṭirāz.**]

FATIMIDS, the Ismaili Shiite dynasty that ruled North Africa and Egypt from 909 to 1171. Under the Fatimids, Egypt became the center of an empire that included at its peak North Africa, Sicily, Palestine, Syria, the Red Sea coast of Africa, the Yemen, and the Hejaz. Egypt generally flourished under their rule, and it is the Fatimids who must be credited with developing the vast network of commercial relations in both the Mediterranean and the Indian Ocean that determined the economic course of Egypt in the High Middle Ages.

The Fatimids traced their origins to the house of the prophet Muḥammad through ᶜAlī and Fāṭima, the Prophet's daughter, from whom they derived their name. But from the very beginning their genealogy was the subject of bitter dispute. Their enemies, following a common practice of ancient and medieval Arab polemicists, attributed to them Jewish origins, a claim that is totally unfounded. More serious attacks, however, came from the Abbasids, who denied their Alid descent, and from various tenth-century Ismaili heterodoxies that introduced variations into the genealogy. These circumstances, combined with the official leadership's deliberate obfuscation of its true origins—in large part the result of the secret cell organization of the propaganda

mission—has made it nearly impossible to determine their origins with any certainty.

The official Fatimid genealogy that emerged traced the line to Ismāᶜīl, son and designated successor of the imam Jaᶜfar al-Ṣādiq (*d.* 765). In the Ismaili system, unlike that of the Sunnis, the caliph was not elected; rather, he succeeded through the express designation (*naṣṣ*) of his predecessor, which was itself a manifestation of divine will; while the imamate—the religious and spiritual headship of the Ismaili community—passed directly from father to son. Thus, although Jaᶜfar's designated successor Ismāᶜīl had predeceased him, the imamate remained in his line and passed to Ismāᶜīl's son Muḥammad. The founder of the Fatimid dynasty in North Africa, ᶜUbayd Allāh, claimed direct descent from Muḥammad ibn Ismāᶜīl.

The early career of the historical personage of ᶜUbayd Allāh remains something of a mystery, but his career from the time he arrived in North Africa can be established. In 899, ᶜUbayd Allāh assumed leadership of the Ismaili movement in Salamiyya, Syria. Up to this time, the movement had acknowledged Muḥammad ibn Ismāᶜīl as the hidden imam, who had not died but gone into concealment, from which he was to reappear as the messianic figure called al-Qāʾim (the rising) or al-Mahdī (the guide). According to Fatimid doctrine, upon his reappearance the Mahdī would abrogate the law of Islam (called the *ẓāhir,* the apparent or exoteric aspects of religion) and reveal in full the esoteric and inward truths of religion (*bāṭin*). When ᶜUbayd Allāh claimed the imamate for himself, some regarded him as a usurper of the true imam, Muḥammad ibn Ismāᶜīl, and split off from the movement under the leadership of Ḥamdān Qarmaṭ. They became known as the Qarmatians and challenged the Fatimids in North Africa and Egypt into the eleventh century.

ᶜUbayd Allāh was forced to leave Salamiyya and headed west, where an Ismaili missionary, Abū ᶜAbd Allāh al-Shīᶜī had already succeeded in winning over the Kutāma Berbers, who were to become the military mainstay of the inchoate Fatimid state. ᶜUbayd Allāh made his way to Sijilmāsa, where he was held captive until Abū ᶜAbd Allāh rescued him in 910. The two then went to Raqqāda, where ᶜUbayd Allāh assumed the titles of *al-Mahdī* and *Amīr al-Muʾminīn* (commander of the faithful) in a public ceremony that is said to have lasted three days. The ambitious Abū ᶜAbd Allāh and his equally zealous brother soon aroused the suspicions of ᶜUbayd

Allāh, and he had the two assassinated. A bloody revolt followed, and the Kutāma, loyal to Abū ʿAbd Allāh, were subdued only with great difficulty. In spite of these trials, ʿUbayd Allāh managed to retain his position, and in 920 he built a new capital called Mahdia (Al-Mahdiyya) on the coast of what is now Tunisia.

ʿUbayd Allāh's major concern during the years of his reign seems to have been to stabilize his precarious position in North Africa and Sicily and to begin an eastward campaign. Two early expeditions to Egypt ended in failure. In North Africa, the Kharijites posed a constant threat; in Sicily, where the Byzantine presence was firmly established, Fatimid governors were driven out and replaced by a governor elected by the Sicilians, Ibn Qurhub, who immediately declared allegiance to the Abbasid caliph. It was only after a resounding defeat off the coast of Ifrīqiya that the Sicilians surrendered Ibn Qurhub to ʿUbayd Allāh, who had him executed in 916.

Al-Qāʾim began an undistinguished reign of twelve years in 934. His major achievement was the recovery of the Maghrib, lost under ʿUbayd Allāh to the Idrisids. To consolidate his power in North Africa, al-Qāʾim concluded an alliance with the Ṣanhāja Berbers against their rivals in the far west, the Zanāta. But in 943 he faced a Berber rebellion led by the Kharijite insurgent Abū Yazīd, who laid siege to the Fatimid capital in 945. Mahdia, a strong coastal fortress, withstood the assault, and when al-Qāʾim died in 946, the city was once again secure. But it was left to his successor al-Manṣūr to take the final offensive against Abū Yazīd; his crushing defeat of the Kharijites is the sole distinction of his seven-year reign.

After the relatively colorless years of al-Qāʾim and al-Manṣūr, the accession of al-Muʿizz in 953 stands out as the watershed of early Fatimid history. Following three unsuccessful attempts to conquer Egypt (under ʿUbayd Allāh in 913–915 and 919–921 and under al-Qāʾim in 935), the fourth Fatimid campaign, led by the general Jawhar in 969, was successful. Jawhar, a freed slave of Slavic origin living in Sicily, was a brilliant military strategist and a gifted administrator. His prowess, combined with popular discontent in a country ravaged by famine and plague, resulted in one of the most bloodless conquests on record. Fatimid missionaries had been actively propagandizing the Egyptian population with some success, but the passive reception of the Fatimids seems to have more to do with the Egyptian

civilians' disaffection with Ikhshidid rule than with any particular loyalty to the Fatimid cause.

Jawhar entered Fusṭāṭ in July 969 and was received by an embassy of civilian notables. The military regiments of the Ikhshidids, however, refused to accept his terms; the resulting show of arms led very quickly to their defeat. Jawhar laid the foundations of a new palace city, Al-Qāhira (Cairo) on the sandy plain north of Fusṭāṭ. Al-Muʿizz is said to have sketched the plans himself.

The conquest of Egypt and the establishment of a new capital city gave al-Muʿizz a springboard from which to pursue his eastern ambitions. The Azhar mosque, founded in 970, served as the new center of the Fatimid daʿwa, or propaganda mission, which became the third branch of government, in addition to the military and the bureaucracy. This new intellectual center directed a vast network of missionaries who infiltrated eastern territories.

But the real architect of the Fatimid state was Yaʿqūb ibn Killis, a Jewish convert to Islam, who introduced a series of administrative and fiscal reforms so far-reaching that they survived the end of the Fatimid caliphate and persisted throughout the Ayyubid period. Ibn Killis completely restructured the organization of finances, abolishing tax farming and establishing in its stead a highly centralized system of revenue collection. The administration of the state was carried out through the dawāwīn (ministries; sing.: dīwān), of which the foremost was the dīwān al-majlis (dīwān of the council), which seems to have been the forerunner of the dīwān al-amwāl (treasury, comprising fourteen departments) and coexisted along with the dīwān al-inshāʾ (chancery). His extraordinary capabilities were recognized and rewarded by both al-Muʿizz and al-ʿAzīz, and he was the first Fatimid minister to bear the title of wazīr (vizier).

The first task of the new government was to restore order and prosperity to a country that had been wrought by famine and civil unrest. Al-Muʿizz began to restrict access to information about the yearly rise of the Nile in order to prevent speculation and hoarding of grain—a move that is praised by the fifteenth-century historian al-Maqrīzī as the wisest and most praiseworthy act of his reign; he replaced the old, devalued currency of the Ikhshidids with the Fatimid dinar, a highly valued currency, maintaining a standard in excess of 98 percent.

Outside of Egypt, al-Muʿizz met with great success in the holy cities of Mecca and Medina, where a skillful program of propaganda and a liberal distribution of gold achieved recognition for the Fatimids in 970–971; this lasted almost without incident until the reign of al-Mustanṣir. But in Syria, al-Muᶜizz faced the beginnings of the vicissitudes that would characterize the Fatimid presence there throughout their history. The Ikhshidid governor of Damascus had allied himself with the Buyid-supported Qarmatians of Al-Baḥrayn. One of Jawhar's lieutenants, Jaᶜfar ibn Falāḥ, seized Damascus but was killed while doing battle against al-Ḥasan al-Aᶜṣam, the Qarmatian leader, in 971. Al-Ḥasan had the name of al-Muᶜizz cursed in the mosques and set out for Egypt, taking Ramle along the way and finally laying siege to Cairo. Jawhar broke the siege and al-Ḥasan fled, but the Fatimids were able to recover only part of Palestine. When al-Muᶜizz came to Egypt, al-Ḥasan renewed his attack, but his Bedouin troops were bought with Fatimid gold, and he was routed. Fatimid rule was reestablished in Damascus, though the success was short-lived, for soon after, Damascus fell to the Buyid officer Alptekīn, against whom al-Muᶜizz was preparing to march when he died in 975.

Al-ᶜAzīz was determined to carry out his father's plan and sent Jawhar in 976 to attack. But he suffered a humiliating defeat, losing both Ramle and Ascalon in his retreat. In 978, al-ᶜAzīz led an expedition himself and captured Alptekīn, but the Qarmatian insurgents withdrew only after receiving substantial tribute from the Fatimid ruler. In spite of the fact that he soon lost Damascus again, al-ᶜAzīz persisted in his ambition to control southern and central Syria. He turned his attentions now to Aleppo, where three attempts (in 983, 992–933, and 994–995) all ended in failure because of continued unrest in Palestine, intrigue by the Fatimid governors in Damascus, and Byzantine aid to the emir of Aleppo. Nonetheless, the reign of al-ᶜAzīz marks the greatest extent of the Fatimid empire.

Internally, Egypt flourished under the generous hand of al-ᶜAzīz and the superb administration of Ibn Killis. Al-ᶜAzīz introduced fixed rates of pay to the troops and court personnel. He was also the first caliph to bring regiments of Turkish *mamlūk*s into the army, and they eventually supplanted the Berber troops on which the Fatimid empire had been built. By the end of the tenth century, the Berbers had been entirely defeated, but new internal struggles were brewing between the Turks and the black slaves bought in the Sudan. These factional military struggles, which sometimes erupted into open warfare,

would plague the Fatimids to the very end of their rule.

Jews and Christians generally fared well in the tolerant atmosphere of Fatimid Egypt. They were not ghettoized and often lived side by side with Muslims. Not infrequently, they held the highest offices of state: al-ᶜAzīz and al-Ḥāfiẓ each had a Christian vizier; al-Ḥākim had three. Jews and Christians were often in other influential positions as well (for example, the Tustarī brothers under the caliph al-Mustanṣir), and court physicians were almost always non-Muslim. Perhaps the most important role played by Jews, in particular, was in the active Mediterranean and Indian trade, recorded in great detail by the documents of the Cairo Genizah.

Sunnis did not enjoy the same favor as Jews and Christians, however, and policy toward them fluctuated more. There were periods of tolerance, and at one time there were Malikite and Shafiite qadis in addition to the Shiite ones, but this was under the vizier Kutayfāt, himself an Imami rather than an Ismaili Shiite. Nevertheless, it seems that Egypt was not as thoroughly Ismaili under the Fatimids as might be imagined, for the ease with which the country was restored to Sunnism after the installment of Saladin betrays a loose attachment to Shiism on the part of a significant portion of the population.

In foreign relations, the Fatimids continued to have a checkered history in Syria, which was often the site of the Fatimid-Byzantine contest for control. Twice in 998 the Byzantine fleet was defeated and peace proposals were advanced, but a ten-year truce was not signed with the emperor Basil until 1001. In 1009 the caliph al-Ḥākim ordered the destruction of the Church of the Holy Sepulcher, provoking another breach of relations. Aleppo submitted to Fatimid rule in 1015, and a governor was installed, but in the same year, Basil terminated commercial relations between Egypt and the Byzantine provinces.

Relations with Palestine were also troubled. In 1011–1012 the Jarrahid ruler al-Mufarrij revolted, and the following year he proclaimed the *sharīf* of Mecca as an anticaliph, although al-Ḥākim succeeded in bribing al-Mufarrij and his son Ḥasan into abandoning the anticaliph. Generally the Fatimid empire remained intact during his reign and for a short time even extended to Mosul, where in 1010 al-Ḥākim's name was read in the *khuṭba*.

But it is al-Ḥākim himself—the erratic, unpredictable, and thoroughly enigmatic—who fascinated both contemporary chroniclers and modern historians. He introduced a series of strict anti-Sunni measures, numerous laws against Christians and Jews, and a variety of edicts for which no real explanation can be found (for example, he banned the vegetable *mulūkhiyya* [mallow] and twice ordered all the dogs of Cairo to be killed). He also passed a series of harsh measures restricting the activities of women, going so far as to forbid cobblers to make shoes for them lest they venture into the streets. In 1020 he ordered Fustāt burned because of protests and accusations made against him by its inhabitants. His bizarre behavior only increased with age; toward the end of his life, he ordered all the markets to remain open and lighted all night and then took to making nocturnal excursions into the Muqattam hills.

His eccentricities were probably a source of encouragement to a small group who believed him to be an incarnation of Divinity. By 1017 he seems to have been encouraging such notions, advanced by al-Darazī and Hamza. When al-Hakim disappeared in 1021, these extremists declared that he had gone into concealment to test their faith and would some day reemerge. Although their movement faded in Egypt, it remained active in Syria, where it developed into the Druze sect.

Al-Hakim's disappearance remains one of the great unsolved mysteries of Fatimid history. He seemingly vanished while on one of his late-night excursions in the company of two servants, who lost sight of him. After a search of several days, only his bloodied and torn clothes were found. Several explanations were advanced, the most plausible of which seems to be that he was murdered at the behest of his sister, Sitt al-Mulk, who feared that his eccentric behavior would bring the dynasty—and herself—to ruin.

In fact the Fatimids went through a particularly unhappy period after al-Hakim's death. The Jarrahids continued to threaten Fatimid hegemony in Syria and Palestine. The powerful Sitt al-Mulk, regent for the young al-Zāhir, could not restore relations with the Byzantine emperor, who also harbored Syrian aspirations. Negotiations had been reopened unsuccessfully by Sitt al-Mulk in 1023 and by al-Zāhir himself in 1032, when they failed again because of his refusal to accept the condition that Hasan ibn al-Mufarrij be allowed to return to Palestine and resume the possessions he had held during the reign of al-Hakim.

Little else can be said of the reign of al-Zāhir except that it was, in general, a turbulent period, filled with unrest and wrought with famine (as so poignantly chronicled by the contemporary historian al-Musabbihī, who describes the discarded tough stems and leaves of the cauliflower that were the staple of poor Egyptians' diet during this time). Things were to improve little under al-Mustansir, who is outstanding among the Fatimids for both the extraordinary length of his reign (some sixty years) and his extreme incompetence. A succession of low Niles resulted in an intense famine that lasted, off and on, for almost twenty years. In 1054 al-Mustansir was compelled to appeal to the Byzantine emperor for wheat, and in the 1060's the hunger was so intense that people resorted to cannibalism. On top of these natural disasters, the rivalry between the Turkish and Sudanese slave troops erupted into warfare, and the caliph was forced to sell his treasures in order to meet their demands.

In 1073 al-Mustansir appealed to the governor of Acre, a freed slave of Armenian origin, to come to Egypt to restore order. Arriving in 1074, Badr al-Jamālī took the Turkish *mamlūk* troops by surprise and had them all executed. In a matter of months, Badr was the virtual ruler of Egypt, and some degree of order, peace, and prosperity returned.

He assumed leadership of all three branches of government and was awarded the titles *amīr al-juyūsh* (commander of the armies), *hādī al-duᶜāt* (guide of the missionaries), and *wazīr*. It is by the first, however, that he is usually known. Under the energetic Badr, the institution of the vizierate—and the course of Fatimid history—were irrevocably altered. If Ibn Killis was the architect of the first hundred years of Fatimid rule, then Badr shaped its second century.

Up to Badr's time, viziers had been considered as executors of the caliph's will; from the time of Badr's vizierate, they were entrusted with delegated powers. In the first hundred years, the viziers had been bureaucrats, called "viziers of the pen"; in the second century, they were almost exclusively military officials, the so-called "viziers of the sword." They became the actual rulers of Egypt, with only very brief periods in which the caliphs themselves were able to regain any real authority. But the broad powers of the vizierate in the last hundred years of the dynasty did not increase either the stability or the security of the office: viziers were appointed or dismissed at the will of the caliph or the army; they were often banished from the capital in disgrace or imprisoned, only to be released and reappointed. According to Ibn Muyassar, al-Mustansir had no less than two dozen viziers, some of whom were appointed up to three times. Regardless of the insecurities of the of-

27

fice, however, it remains true that after al-Mustanṣir, viziers made or unmade caliphs, and two particularly powerful and ambitious viziers can be credited with provoking the two schisms that ultimately rent the Fatimid state—and the entire Ismaili movement—in half.

However successful Badr al-Jamālī was at restoring order to Egypt, his numerous attempts to recover Syria for the Fatimids all failed. In 1038 a thirty-year treaty had been signed with the Byzantines, initiating a long period of friendship between the two empires, and al-Mustanṣir had granted permission to rebuild the Church of the Holy Sepulcher destroyed by his grandfather, al-Ḥākim. In the same year, the capable Fatimid general Anushtekīn defeated both the Jarrahids and the Kilabis at the battle of al-Uqḥuwāna in Palestine and regained Damascus and Aleppo after defeating the Mirdasids. But the success was short-lived; Aleppo was lost and regained in a succession of victories and defeats until, in 1060, it was lost irrevocably.

For all of its failings, the reign of al-Mustanṣir does boast one success: under the capable direction of al-Muʾayyad fi 'l-Dīn al-Shīrāzī, the Ismaili daʿwa flourished in a period of extraordinary energy and success. Missionaries were active in Iraq, Iran, and even as far as Sind. In Iraq the Turkish emir al-Basāsīrī gained recognition for the Fatimids in Mosul (1057) and, for one year, in Baghdad (1059). In the Yemen, a Fatimid missionary founded the Sulayhid dynasty (1038–1139); the correspondence between the Sulayhid ruler and the Fatimid caliph has been preserved in a remarkable collection.

Nonetheless, the Sunni Seljuks were determined to undermine Fatimid authority not only in the east, but in Syria and the Mediterranean as well. From the mid eleventh century, we can chronicle the steady shrinking of the Fatimid lands, as Aleppo (1070), Jerusalem (1071), and Damascus (1076) were lost. In the west the Zirid al-Muʿizz ibn Bādīs, originally a Fatimid lieutenant in Qayrawān, began to make gestures toward independence; in 1051, he renounced the Fatimids and recognized the Abbasid caliph. His son Tamīm returned temporarily to Fatimid allegiance, but the Norman conquest of Sicily by 1072 permanently ended Fatimid influence in the Muslim West. Thus, by the end of al-Mustanṣir's long reign, all that unquestionably remained of the vast Fatimid empire was Egypt itself, plagued as it was by famine, pestilence, and civil unrest.

Badr al-Jamālī died in 1094 and was succeeded by his son al-Afḍal Shāhanshāh, who was raised to his powerful office by the army only a few months before al-Mustanṣir died. True to the model of dictatorial rule established by his father, al-Afḍal dispossessed the heir-apparent Nizār and installed his own candidate, a younger son of al-Mustanṣir, who was made caliph with the regnal title of al-Mustaʿlī. This act provoked the first of the two schisms that spelled the end of the Fatimid dynasty. Nizār at first fled to Alexandria, where he raised an army to reclaim his rightful position, but he was captured and imprisoned. A group of his partisans, led by the charismatic and ingenious missionary Ḥasan-i Ṣabbāḥ, founder of the Assassins, believed that Nizār had escaped and declared allegiance to him. Known in Egypt as the Nizaris, they waged a veritable campaign of terror against the Mustalian line and assassinated al-Mustaʿlī's successor al-Āmir in 1130.

Al-Afḍal dominated al-Mustaʿlī's short reign of seven years and had at least moderate success in recapturing some lost territory: Tyre in 1097 and Jerusalem in 1098 (lost to the advancing crusaders in the following year, however). On the other hand, the strong ties between the central government in Cairo and the mission in the Yemen continued under the colorful Sulayhid queen Ḥurra. Throughout the period, inspired by a mutual fear of the Seljuk menace, exchanges of embassies between the Fatimids and the Byzantines continued. It remains unclear, however, why al-Afḍal assumed such a passive posture with respect to the crusaders. He never ventured beyond Ascalon when the Franks occupied Palestine in 1101 and later captured both Acre and Tripoli. When al-Mustaʿlī died in 1101, al-Afḍal raised the five-year-old son of the late caliph, al-Āmir, to the caliphate, and the vizier remained in control of the government until he was assassinated in 1121. He was succeeded by al-Maʾmūn ibn al-Baṭāʾihī, whose four years in office were chronicled in great detail by his son. Al-Maʾmūn was imprisoned in 1125 by al-Āmir, who was now an adult and eager to rule directly. Two noteworthy challenges arose during his reign: in 1123 the Lawāta Berbers invaded and were defeated in Alexandria, and throughout, the Nizari insurgents threatened Egypt, sending agents to infiltrate Cairo. In 1122, a public proclamation asserting the legitimacy of the Mustalian succession and his descendants was read, but eight years later al-Āmir himself fell victim to the Assassins, leaving an infant son, al-Ṭayyib, as his heir.

The Nizari schism caused a complete rupture in the relations between Ismaili communities in the East and the Fatimids in Egypt. But even the followers of al-Mustaᶜlī were destined to splinter; another schism followed some forty years later, this time prompted by a different type of succession dispute when ᶜAbd al-Majīd—later the caliph al-Ḥāfiẓ, a cousin of the late al-Āmir—elevated himself from regency to caliphate.

ᶜAbd al-Majīd was named as regent by two army leaders, but the son of al-Afḍal, Abū ᶜAlī Aḥmad ibn al-Afḍal Kutayfāt, overthrew the government on the very day that ᶜAbd al-Majīd assumed the regency, confiscated the palace treasuries, imprisoned the regent, and had the *khuṭba* read in the name of the expected imam of the Twelver Shīᶜa. For over a year, Egypt was officially a Twelver Shiite state, until ᶜAbd al-Majīd arranged for the murder of Kutayfāt and was restored as regent in 1131. As there was no visible heir—the fate of the infant al-Ṭayyib being shrouded in mystery—he soon proclaimed himself imam under the caliphal title of al-Ḥāfiẓ. Opponents of his imamate maintained that al-Ṭayyib had been spirited away to the Yemen, where his supporters awaited his emergence from concealment.

From the time of al-Ḥāfiẓ, conditions in Egypt deteriorated steadily. The last three Fatimid caliphs, al-Ẓāfir, al-Fāʾiz, and al-ᶜĀḍid, were children, and the state was actually governed by several powerful viziers, notably Ṭalāʾiᶜ ibn Ruzzīk, Ibn Maṣal, and Shāwar, with the support of various corps in the fac-tionalized army. A contemporary of these events, ᶜUmāra of the Yemen, remarked that "any man who had received the confidence of his brother betrayed him." After Ṭalāʾiᶜ was assassinated on orders of the young caliph al-ᶜĀḍid's aunt, he was succeeded by his son Ruzzīk. But al-ᶜĀḍid invited Shāwar, the prefect of Upper Egypt, to assume the vizierate. Shā-war took over, only to be betrayed by his own general, Ḍirghām, in 1163. Shāwar took refuge in Aleppo at the court of Nūr al-Dīn, who was only too eager to provide him with military assistance. This he did in the person of Shīrkūh, who went to Egypt with his nephew Saladin and restored Shāwar to the vizierate. But in 1169 Shāwar and Shīrkūh battled; the former was killed, and the vizierate passed to Shīrkūh. He was succeeded in turn by Saladin, who restored order to the country and exterminated the remnants of the Fatimid army. In 1171 the name of the Abbasid caliph was read in the mosques of Cairo; the Fatimid palaces were sacked and the caliphal family taken into custody. The last Fatimid caliph, al-ᶜĀḍid, died only a few days later, and Egypt was officially restored to Sunnism.

BIBLIOGRAPHY

Sources. For a complete bibliography and more details, see Marius Canard's masterful "Fāṭimids," in the *Encyclopaedia of Islam,* 2nd ed., II (1965). Since the publication of

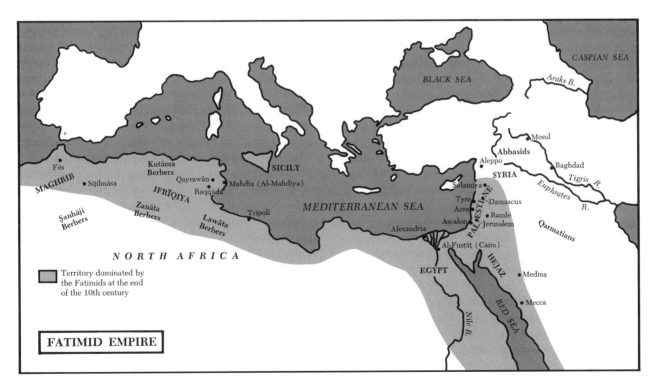

FATIMID EMPIRE

Territory dominated by the Fatimids at the end of the 10th century

that article, new editions of several important sources have been published, including al-Musabbiḥī, *Juzʾ al-arbaʿūn min Akhbār Miṣr*, Ayman Fuʾād Sayyid and Thierry Bianquis, eds. (1978–); Ibn Muyassar, *Choix de passages de la Chronique d'Égypte* (in Arabic), Ayman Fuʾād Sayyid, ed. (1981); and Ibn Ẓāfir, *Akhbār al-duwal al-munqaṭiʿa*, André Ferré, ed. (1972). Another volume of the Musabbiḥī chronicle, including the literary fragments, is expected from the French Institute of Cairo. See also two editions of al-Qāḍī al-Nuʿmān, *Risālat iftitāḥ al-daʿwa*; Farḥāt al-Dashrāwī, ed. (1975), with French summary; and Wadād al-Qāḍī, ed. (1970). Also, al-Maqrīzī's chronicle of the Fatimids, *Ittiʿāẓ al-ḥunafāʾ*, Jamāl al-Dīn al-Shayyāl, ed., 3 vols. (1967).

Studies. A number of useful articles appear in *Colloque international sur l'histoire du Caire* (1972). See also B. J. Beshir, "Fatimid Military Organization," in *Der Islam*, 55 (1978); Thierry Bianquis, "La prise du pouvoir par les fatimides en Égypte," in *Annales islamologiques*, 11 (1972); Claude Cahen, "L'administration financière de l'armée fatimide d'après al-Makhzūmī," in *Journal of the Economic and Social History of the Orient*, 15 (1972); Ayman Fuʾād Sayyid's particularly informative article, "Lumières nouvelles sur quelques sources de l'histoire fatimide en Egypte," in *Annales islamologiques* 13 (1977).

PAULA SANDERS

[See also **Alptigin; Assassins; Badr al-Jamāli; Berbers; Byzantine History; Cairo; Cairo Genizah; Crusades and Crusader States: Near East; Fatimid Art; Ḥākim bi-Amr Allāh, al-; Ifrīqiya; Imam; Ismāʿīliyya; Islamic Architecture; Mustanṣir, al-; Saladin; Sicily, Islamic; Trade, Islamic.**]

FATWĀ, an authoritative opinion on a point of Islamic religious law, given by a qualified legal scholar, or mufti. The institution is called *iftāʾ* or *futyā*. The term *fatwā* (plural: *fatāwā*) applies to responsa arising from practical questions and does not include decisions of the courts or theoretical or literary discussions about the law. From a historical perspective, the *fatwā* represents the guidance of the earliest informal specialists in religious law as well as the decisions of government-appointed jurisconsults in the pre-modern and modern periods. The institution has been compared with the *ius respondendi,* and the *fatwā* itself with the *reponsa prudentium* of Roman law.

With the expansion of the new Islamic state, and the desire of many new Muslims to conduct their lives according to a religious code of behavior, the need was soon felt for individuals who could advise the Muslim community on details arising from ac-

tivities of daily life. In many urban centers, men interested in responding to such questions and concerned with applying religious norms to the whole field of law met together in informal scholarly circles. Since the Koran provided little direct guidance in matters of law, these scholars undertook to evaluate acts and institutions, in specific cases and according to their own reasoned opinions, the surviving law of the former administrations, and customary law, all in the light of general koranic teaching. This informal, nonprofessional guidance continued until the time of Shāfiʿī (*d.* 820), after which the law became increasingly technical, and a class of professional jurists began to appear. In addition, after the first quarter of the eighth century, the provincial governors had responded to the needs of the population for judicial direction by appointing qadis as legal officials responsible for adjudicating disputes, who made their decisions according to the same criteria. While the decisions of the qadis had government backing to the extent that the administration enforced them, the opinions rendered by the scholars were meant to advise and caution Muslims on right behavior and had no binding force beyond the moral influence of the men who gave them.

As specialization increased, the functions of the mufti and qadi, or judge, diverged. The mufti acted as a counselor to private persons, issuing *fatwā*s to those who sought his opinion either for their own instruction or prior to their appearance before a court. Even the qadi consulted a mufti, although he was not bound to accept the mufti's opinion, and the final decision remained in the qadi's hands. The mufti's authority to give *fatwā*s was based on his reputation for knowledge of the law, and individuals were free to seek out any mufti they chose. There was constant need for the mufti's expertise, because Islamic law includes in its subject matter not only those acts and relationships that are normally enforced in the courts, but the whole range of human behavior, including social mores and religious obligations. Furthermore, as the law became even more diverse because of the allowable diversity of opinion among its scholars, and more technical and academic in its form, the mufti became an indispensable figure.

Classical doctrine defines the qualifications required of a mufti to issue a valid *fatwā*. He must be a Muslim and a morally upright person and must have the legal knowledge to rule on unprecedented cases. This meant, ideally, knowledge of the Koran, the traditions of the Prophet (sing.: *ḥadīth*), and the principles governing their relationship, such as abrogation of a tradition by a verse of the Koran or by another tradition, or the particularization of a rule derived from one by the other. The mufti must also know the rules of positive law, the differences of opinion and points of agreement among jurists (an aspect of *ijmā*ᶜ, or consensus), and be skilled in analogical reasoning and other forms of proof. An excellent knowledge of the Arabic language in order to interpret the authoritative sources is also mentioned. These are, in short, the requirements for *ijtihād,* or the ability to reason independently on the basis of the sources. The *mujtahid,* who is the scholar exercising *ijtihād,* may be ranked retrospectively in several grades, the highest being that reached by the founders or eponyms of the schools of law.

By the thirteenth century, however, legal doctrine increasingly took note of reality; *fatwā*s were no longer rendered by *mujtahid*s, but by scholars of lesser accomplishment. Still later, the authors observe that *fatwā*s were given by *muqallid*s, a lower designation indicating a jurist who reports the opinion of an authoritative scholar of a previous generation. The practice was justified on grounds of necessity since it was generally accepted that there were no independent jurists available in their times, and because it was proved by the consensus of the scholars that the practice had been widespread and never renounced.

In spite of the general agreement of these authors that independent reasoning had ceased, the activity of the muftis ensured the continued development of positive law. New circumstances constantly arose, and as actual social practice changed, often moving away from stricter Islamic doctrinal norms that prevailed in earlier times, the muftis gradually adapted many specific legal rulings to new social practice in their *fatwā*s. When the opinions expressed in the *fatwā*s of an individual jurisconsult came to be deemed valid by the consensus of the scholars, they were incorporated into the authoritative handbooks of his school. Further, the presence of muftis as advisers in tribunals supplementary to the qadi's courts, endorsing decisions made particularly in the areas of public and criminal law, contributed to the process of adaptation. Thus over the centuries, the muftis exercised their creative role through their *fatwā*s, and in this way, a theoretically unchangeable body of law was able to evolve imperceptibly.

The activity of the muftis became so important that the *fatwā*s of individuals were collected in separate works, and some achieved great authority as comprehensive manuals of the law alongside the handbooks of the schools. However, like the qadi's decisions (which were not collected), the *fatwā*s were never used as legal precedents, case law having no standing in Islamic law. Many of these compilations date from a later period and are valuable in revealing the issues that were important at the time.

Although the muftis always remained at the service of private persons, they became associated with the judicial organization of the state in varying degrees. Appointments to official positions did not, however, alter the nonbinding nature of their *fatwā*s, nor was their authority diminished. Muftis were assigned to the qadi's court as advisers; they stood among the ranks of magistrates and other officials personally attached to the ruler's retinue and present at his audiences and those of his provincial governors. In particular, the office of the *futyā* acquired a well-defined official status when the Mamluk sultans (1250–1516) created advisory posts for muftis in the principal cities of Egypt and Syria. Furthermore, in Muslim Spain, where the principle of consilium *(shūrā)* prevailed, the muftis were an essential part of the advisory councils. By appointing men responsible to itself, the government tended to give the institution a public character and even claimed the right to control the standards of the profession.

The institution of the *futyā* was subject to a novel development under the Ottoman sultans. In the early Ottoman state, the decision of any mufti was allowed to be decisive when he issued a *fatwā* at the request of the parties to a dispute. But in the interests of orderly administration, the rulers began appointing a few muftis to whom the parties could appeal against the rulings of muftis of lesser rank. By the middle of the fifteenth century, they completed the organization of the judiciary by investing the chief mufti of Istanbul with the title of *shaykh al-islām* and with responsibility for the entire religious hierarchy. All *fatwā*s were now issued in his name, from a special department with a staff of professionals. Muftis in the provinces of the empire received their patents of office from the *shaykh al-islām;* some were simply individuals respected in their local communities, but others were frequently the chief religious and judicial personages in the major cities of Egypt, Syria, and North Africa. At the same time, qadis continued to function in their traditional roles.

In keeping with the constant concern of the Ottoman sultans for applying Islamic law, the *shaykh al-islām* became one of the highest dignitaries of the state and was regularly consulted as to whether an action proposed by the administration conformed to the sacred law. The most distinguished holder of the office was Abu'l-Su^cūd, who was appointed in 1545 and held office for thirty years. Through his *fatwā*s, of which there are several unofficial collections, he exercised an important influence on Ottoman law and administration, incorporating directives of the sultan, and often, local Turkish law and newly introduced customs.

The mufti played an important and unusual role in British India, when beginning in 1772 British magistrates, and later Muslim judges trained in English common law and equity, took the place of the qadis in the courts. They were assisted by muftis, whose function was to advise them of the correct course of action according to strict Islamic doctrine. The *fatwā* thus became a summary of opinion to the magistrate who was not bound to abide by it.

The *fatwā* ceased to be an important instrument in the statement and development of Islamic law during the modern period, when the introduction of comprehensive codifications of Islamic law and secular codes based on European law provided the legal profession and the judiciary of newly created courts with easier access to the law. In general, the mufti no longer plays a role in the courts but may remain part of the judicial hierarchy. In Egypt, for example, the Grand Mufti and especially the Fatwa Committee of Al-Azhar University have been involved in a variety of questions of social reform and religious issues, and even though their rulings are not decisive, they have had an influence far beyond the borders of Egypt.

BIBLIOGRAPHY

Noel J. Coulson, *A History of Islamic Law* (1964), 142–143, 148; Joseph Schacht, *Introduction to Islamic Law* (1964), 73–75; Émile Tyan, *Histoire de l'Organisation judiciaire en pays de l'Islam*, 2nd ed. (1960), 219–236, and "Judicial Organization," in Majid Khadduri and Herbert J. Liebesny, eds., *Law in the Middle East* (1955).

JEANETTE A. WAKIN

[See also **Law, Islamic; Qadi.**]

FAUSTUS OF BYZANTIUM. See P^cawstos Buzand.

FAUSTUS OF RIEZ (*ca.* 410–*ca.* 495), a Semi-Pelagian author in Provence. While still young, he embraced an ascetic life and succeeded St. Maximus as abbot of Lérins in 433, and as bishop of Riez around 458. The Arian ruler Euric exiled him from about 478 until 485 for his opposition to Arianism.

Faustus' major extant works include ten letters and some sermons; *De gratia Dei,* in which he maintains a middle position between the predestinarian teaching of the priest Lucidus and the Pelagian emphasis on free choice; and *De Spiritu Sancto,* in which he argues for the materiality of the human soul.

BIBLIOGRAPHY

Faustus' writings may be found in *Patrologia Latina,* LIII (1847), 681–890, and LVIII (1847), 783–870. See also A. Engelbrecht, "Faustus of Riez," in *Corpus scriptorum ecclesiasticorum Latinorum,* XXI (1891); A. Koch, *Der heilige Faustus, Bischof von Riez* (1895); Gustave Weigl, *Faustus of Riez* (1938).

MARIANNE DJUTH

FAUVEL, ROMAN DE, an early-fourteenth-century satirical allegory on the Christian church and political institutions of the time. Moralistic satires in the form of allegories found favor in the thirteenth century, a time when affairs of state and church were the subject of indignation and criticism. Jean de Meun's *Roman de la Rose* (*ca.* 1275–1280) probably served as a model for the *Roman de Fauvel.*

The original work exists in twelve manuscripts, one of which (Paris, Bibliothèque Nationale, MS fonds fr. 146) is particularly noteworthy because it contains 167 musical interpolations, both monophonic and polyphonic, which are closely integrated into the content of the poem.

The first of the two books constituting the *Roman de Fauvel* (1,226 verses) was completed in 1310. The author, Gervais du Bus, a notary at the French royal chancery, was sufficiently well connected to be able to satirize the troublesome relationships among the various important personages at the French court and the high-placed prelates, including the pope at Avignon. The second book, completed in 1314, continues the allegory, decrying the loss of morality in every facet of French life.

The name *Fauvel* has special significance. It is the masculine form of *Fauvain,* the she-ass or mare that symbolized the evil of the world. In the thirteenth century *Fauvain* referred also to flattery, lying, and deceit through false caresses. There is purpose in Gervais du Bus's use of the masculine *Fauvel:* in the second book Fauvel courts Lady Fortune with the intention of marriage but receives instead Vaine Gloire, with whom he produces innumerable little *fauveaux* who defile the entire world. The name *Fauvel* also serves as an acrostic for six specific vices: Flaterie, Avarice, Vilanie, Variété, Envie, and Lascheté.

The copy of the original work by du Bus was expanded and given copious illustrations in 1316 by Chaillou de Pesstain. This copy (MS fr. 146) is one of the most sumptuous manuscripts of the early fourteenth century. Along with the interpolation of the 167 musical items, there are numerous pictorial representations of scenes in the story, and two major poetic additions. The musical works are widely varied in style, some being monophonic rondeaux and ballades from the previous century, others exhibiting the most current *ars nova* practice, having been written expressly for inclusion in Chaillou's expanded version of the *Roman.* The earliest examples of *ars nova* musical practices, including red notation in two motets, are presented here. Philippe de Vitry, the major *ars nova* musical innovator, was obviously a close colleague of Chaillou, since several of his early works are included among the musical interpolations added in 1316. The musical pieces usually have texts that comment appropriately on the progress of the story where they are inserted. Some texts are so specific and appropriate that they were clearly written specially for this version of the *Roman de Fauvel.* Several of the borrowed works are love songs of the troubadour tradition, sung by Fauvel to Fortune.

The first book, in which Fauvel is flattered by nobles and clerics, including the French king and even the pope, probably remained an underground document as long as Enguerran de Marigny and his colleague Guillaume de Nogaret were in power in France. By 1315 and the completion of the second book, the *Roman* may have surfaced. Nogaret had died, the nobles were organizing to resist taxation by the king, and Marigny was in disgrace over a financial scandal. Philip IV died before the end of 1314, and Marigny was executed in April 1315. However, such a biting commentary must still have remained a private document written for a few of the intelligentsia, probably high clerics. It was likely intended to be read aloud in private circles, the musical interpolations being performed at appropriate places.

BIBLIOGRAPHY

Pierre Aubry, ed., *Le roman de Fauvel* (1907), facsimile of Paris, Bibliothèque Nationale, MS fonds fr. 146; Philipp A. Becker, "Fauvel und Fauvelliana," in *Berichte über die Verhandlungen der Sächsischen Akademie der Wissenschaften zu Leipzig, phil.-hist. Kl.,* **88** (1936); Emile Dahnk, *L'hérésie de Fauvel* (1935); Artur Långfors, *L'histoire de Fauvain* (1914), and *Le roman de Fauvel* (1914–1919); Leo Schrade, ed., *Polyphonic Music of the Fourteenth Century,* I (1956), contains the *Roman de Fauvel* polyphonic repertoire.

GORDON K. GREENE

[See also **Allegory; French Literature: After 1200; French Literature: Romances.**]

FEASTS AND FESTIVALS, EUROPEAN. Activity occupying one-third of a lifetime must be culturally significant. While conditions varied with the country and the century, the medieval Christian calendar generally mandated fifty-two Sundays of enforced leisure plus, from the twelfth century on, at least forty saints' days. To these holidays could be added unlimited local church feasts averaging more than thirty, creating an astonishing 126 or more days per year on which work was not allowed. Englishmen added celebrations of St. Swithin's Day, the weather on which portended fine or failing crops; Canterbury townsfolk honored by holiday not only St. Thomas Becket but also Sts. Alban, Dunstan, Ethelreda, and Edward the Confessor. Universities had their own holidays; fourteenth-century Montpellier's seventy-seven, plus Sundays, totaled 133 yearly festivals. Moreover, many holidays were not limited to twenty-four hours. No matter how hard a person's labors, holidays and festivals prevented existence from being entirely dour and dreary. Traditional costumery, song, dance, divination, drama, feasts, and revelry were as likely accompaniments to holidays as pious prayer, contrition, and acts of penance.

This quantity of church-enforced leisure in western Europe had social and commercial effects. Crops in harvest, buildings under construction, and shiploads of perishables could not be neglected for holiday rest without loss of product or workers' wages. Account ledgers suggest that employers with weekly salaried workers suffered financially when recompensing half a week's labor with full pay. Those paying only for rendered services complained of holiday interference with productivity and profit, and employees lamented lost pay. Ecclesiastics such as John

January. Limbourg brothers, *Les très riches heures du duc de Berry*, 1413–1416. CONDÉ MUSEUM, CHANTILLY

Gerson condemned the multiplicity of required holidays as an unfair burden upon farmers and the laboring poor. Local laws often compromised between clerical demands for holiday leisure dedicated to Christian godliness and contrary ecclesiastical and mercantile insistences that human sustenance was the necessary precursor to contemplating divinity. Some jurisdictions alternated year by year, or month by month, celebration of holidays necessitated by God's calendar and their noncelebration as required by man's.

Forms of festivity also worried critics of holidays. Clerical or civil control over the decorum of celebrations required people's presence in church, chapel, or hall, and some coercion thereafter, lest revelers return from holiday unfit for serious work. While condemnations of celebratory excess may be ascribed to moralistic exaggeration of festal drinking, gambling, and debauchery, nevertheless holiday jubilation might easily deflect attention from piety to sensual pleasure. Furthermore, observant clergymen

visiting church communities, such as thirteenth-century Bishop Eudes of Rouen (Odo Rigaldus), and other church reformers condemned riotous revelments of priests, chaplains, monks, and nuns. As Chaucer asked, if [clerical] gold rusts, what will [the common folk] iron do?

The most startling quality of seasonal holidays and festivals was their reconciliation of Christian custom and earlier pagan fertility rites. Solar solstice observances were rededicated to Christian purpose. Bonfires, originally bone-fires of animals sacrificed to the ancient druidic god Bal or Bel, glorified St. John the Baptist on Midsummer Eve. Such stamping dances as morris dances, Twelfth Night oxhorn rounds, and Maypole dances originated in pagan reminders to winter-slumbering earth spirits to reawaken and assure spring crops and summer abundance. Augustine and Gregory the Great agreed that what Christianity could not eliminate, it must adapt.

This pagan heritage for the games, songs, dances, and foods of calendar festivals (originally not entertainments, but stimulators and propitiators of fertility gods) partially explains their persistence and their identity in form among people of nearly all ages, degrees of education, wealth, and social status. Castle and cottage ceremonies differed in detail but not in basic structure. Merrymaking around a Maypole was ritualistically patterned, whether the shaft was elegant, strung with gold and silken streamers, and crowned with jeweled wreaths, or rude, wrapped with rope and topped by daisies. Knights and carpenters similarly enjoyed Midsummer Eve plays with St. George's customarily terrifying "dragon," either an expensive marvel of machinery with mechanical wings and bellowing smoke, or a homespun dragon-shaped kite held aloft by shepherds' sticks and strings.

The Christian celebrations in western Europe of the tenth through fifteenth centuries necessarily included political fetes such as public honorings of royal crownings, marriages, births, and funerals; war and peace commemorations; kings', queens', and prelates' visitations and progresses; and other festive occasions. Banquets and entertainments upon these occasions were affirmations of power. They introduced classical, historical, and moral allusion in their subtleties and illusion foods, as well as in their pageants, tableaux, farces, and pantomimes. King Charles V of France regaled Emperor Charles IV in 1378 with a grand dinner spectacle simulating the crusaders' capture of Jerusalem in 1099, complete with battling knights scaling ladders beside a turreted castle and a rigged ship on the waters. Indoor or outdoor mock bowers, fountains, and grottoes looked up to theatrical clouds and heavenly gates where classical divinities, epic heroes, or allegorical figures declaimed, chastised, or smiled upon the delighted audience. Horse-drawn cars moved Victory and the Virtues in triumph through archways erected at dramatic vantage points on parade routes.

Banquet courses crafted to stimulate the festive mood were interrupted by huge, edible, allegorical devices, such as the Four Ages of Man, edifying first spirit, then palate. John Russell's fifteenth-century *Boke of Nurture* describes such subtleties: a young man called Sanguinus or Spring, joyously loving, singing, and piping, standing on a cloud; an angry man of war, Colericus or Summer, standing in flames; a tired, sluggish, fat man, wielding a sickle and standing in a river, Fleumaticus or Harvest; and last, feeble, old, envious, sad Melencholicus or Winter, gray-haired and sitting on a hard, cold stone. Refined noblemen performed as rustics or wildmen dressed in grass and straw costumes. In 1393 the infamous Ball of the Flaming Ones, the *bal des ardents,* nearly incinerated King Charles VI of France when an inquisitive torchbearer ignited the antic players. Disasters notwithstanding, such occasional holidays, sometimes for a vast public, sometimes more private, were ornamental to the traditional holiday procession from January to December. Twelve calendar festivals typify that yearly ritual cycle.

A major January holiday was Twelfth Night, the eve of Epiphany. Concluding the twelve days of Christmas, Twelfth Night observances were ritual contests between good and evil. Star-led Magi in dramas outsmarted wicked King Herod to find the marvelous child in his manger. Traditional country actors, called mummers in England, perfomed St. George and the Dragon plays in which the saint overcame an evil knight. Team games such as Oranges and Lemons ended with a tug-of-war between representatives of Winter and Spring. The necessary winner was the triumphant new season.

Food rites also assured a bountiful rebirth of the land after its winter deadness. Wassailing toasts of spiced and herbed ales and wines were drunk and offered to the trees. Wassailing fruit trees in country orchards, or symbolically in a hall, was accompanied by loud, jubilant, stamping dances such as the oxhorn rounds. Revelers capped by "oxhorned" headdresses joyously circled the wassail tree, their earthpounding, ankle-belled feet rhythmically signaling

spring awake. Also derived from rural fertility practices were Twelfth Night fires, rings of twelve small fires set around a larger one in grainfields, originally to stimulate harvests, or recreated indoors by circles of twelve candles centered by a thirteenth; Christianized, these flames represented the twelve days of Christmas or the twelve apostles, and the thirteenth signified the Virgin Mary or Christ. Honored guests at the Twelfth Night high table were the king and queen of the bean. They were selected by their finding the Twelfth Night luck amulet, a bean—in poor farm kitchens a dried vegetable; in castles a precious gold, porcelain, or jeweled favor—baked into the twelfth-cake, otherwise known as kings' cake or *gâteau des rois* or *galette des rois.*

A February feast for St. Valentine's Day paid tribute to Love, seemingly more closely related to the classical Venus and Cupid than to the deeds or deaths of the several second- and third-century Christian saints named Valentine. Love lanterns, hollowed and pierced vegetable candleholders, lit the hall while erotically stimulating love music, often raucous and discordant, called the shivaree, regaled people garbed in love sleeves (stylish arm covers separable from garments for exchange with a beloved) and love jewelry, such as a gold or fabric love knot, symbolizing eternal affection, or a crowned *A,* standing for *amor vincit omnia* (love conquers all). Foods of love were thought to stimulate affection. To these aphrodisiacs were added symbolic edibles such as plum shuttles, oval cakes for "weaving" love into the "fabric" of life, and cherry or pomegranate "heart" cakes for heartfelt emotions.

Diversions included Valentine pairing games such as selections by lot of nonce lovers, required to serve one another in affection—jocularly, not truly—for the day or a year. Divinations revealed true loves or false. Hemp seed thrown over the shoulder fell in a readable pattern. The vitality of sprigs of yarrow, eryngo, and southernwood, known also as lad's-love or boy's-love, signaled durable affection; fading or wilting leaves told of doomed love. Secret love messages were sent in rebus writing and signed "your valentine." A wonderful valentine note exists in the fifteenth-century *Paston Letters.*

Easter Sunday was the central holiday in a seventeen-week cycle calculated to begin nine weeks earlier, on Septuagesima, and to end eight weeks afterward, on Trinity Sunday. Between, such holidays as Quinquagesima, Shrove Tuesday, Ash Wednesday, Mothering Sunday, Carlings (Care) Sunday, Palm Sunday, Maundy Thursday, Good Friday, Rogation

Sunday, Ascension, Pentecost, and Whitmonday were celebrated in the most observant ecclesiastical centers. But considering the potential disruption of agricultural and mercantile enterprise, secular rules often countervailed to emend or ignore parts of the Easter cycle.

The name Easter derived from the pagan goddess of dawn and spring, Eostra or Eostre, and the Easter rituals pertained to the rising of the sun and to the triumph of ascending spring over winter. Christian sermons and liturgies easily adapted these earlier sun sanctifications to lauding the Son's ascent to heaven, revealing the light of understanding and the day of salvation and promising victory over death. Pace-egging was a popular Easter entertainment. From the Hebrew word *pesaḥ*, whence Passover and paschal, hard-boiled pace-eggs were splendidly painted and decorated, exchanged as gifts, rolled in contests, or given in recompense to itinerant mummers or to morris dancers. While the name morris came from the Moorish dancers of Spain, the dances themselves were traditional spring fertility observances, with wooden taps on shoes and belled ankles stamping to insistent music of cymbals, pipes, and tabors, and vigorous leaps for inspiring grain to grow tall, flocks to multiply, and folk to thrive. Mystery plays dramatized Christ's crucifixion and resurrection. Others retold such Old Testament stories as that of Noah and the Flood, which as *The Deluge,* from the English town of Chester, prefigured the Easter themes of rebirth, renewal, and restoration.

An April festival of All Fools' Day sometimes was united with the church holiday the Feast of Fools, as often a January feast, in which the ordered world was portrayed upside down. Festivities were directed by the Lord of Misrule, and boy bishops conducted holy services, whiddershins, in reverse. In Rouen and Beauvais the Feast of Asses was commemorated with playlets on adventures of the biblical prophet Balaam and his wondrous talking donkey. Ennoblings of Folly and ludicrous antics were indirect reaffirmations of order and restraint.

May Day customs, costumes, decorations, dances, and symbolic spring green foods indirectly saluted earlier pagan spirits of trees and woodlands. Most European towns had festive equivalents of the English Maypoles, Maying-round-the-Maypole, crowning the Queen of the May, hoop rolling, and athletic contests, and verdant foods such as peppermint rice, and the lime-glazed gingerbread man called Jack-in-the-Green or Jack-in-the-Bush.

Similarly identifiable pagan vestiges were canon-

All Fools' Day: adults play with toys while children mock them and give them orders. Hans Burgkmair, *Der Weisskunig,* 15th century. METROPOLITAN MUSEUM OF ART, NEW YORK, HARRIS BRISBANE DICK FUND

ized in the June festivals of Midsummer Eve and St. John's Eve. Beltane bonfires from May Day were reconsecrated to St. John, and the plants St.-John's-wort, St.-John's-bread, and St.-John's-fern were used for country divinations. Circular, clockwise pagan sun worship processions were transformed into Christian rogations around churches, marketplaces, and great halls.

July holidays usually honored fruitfulness—and rain. Weather on St. Swithin's Day, named after the ninth-century English bishop of Winchester, was thought to predict wet or drought for forty days thereafter, and therefore the proper time to make sun and star measurements for weather almanacs determining planting, harvesting, and traveling. In August grain harvests and bread were generally celebrated. The geometrically shaped, many-colored, whimsically devised loaves baked on Lammas Day (from the Anglo-Saxon "loaf mass") in England were typical of European ecclesiastical grain blessings and thanks for God's bounty at high summer, before the agricultural year reached its end.

Michaelmas (St. Michael's feast, 29 September) gave its name to the fall season, Michaelmastide, a quarterly rent payment, the autumn term in schools and universities, and important merchandise markets and fairs. Michaelmas was busy season for lawyers and magistrates of the Pie Powder courts (from French *pieds poudres,* dusty feet) adjudicating market larcenies and crimes of the fairs' travelers and merchants. October concluded with Halloween, the eve of All Hallows' or All Saints' Day, honoring all Christian saints, followed by All Souls' Day, solemnized by prayer for the souls of the dead in Purgatory. Summer's end, Samhain in the Celtic calendar (coincident with All Hallows' Eve), was the year's finale; its customs included candle and torchlight processions, apple-bobbing contests, nut-cracking divinations, and the masked "soulers" begging for soul cakes for wandering spirits.

Catherning (Cathern or St. Catherine's Day, 25 November) honored one of the most famous women saints: noble, intelligent, learned Catherine of Alexandria, martyred, according to legend, on a spiked wheel of torture before being beheaded in the fourth century. Patron saint of lawyers, wheelwrights, rope makers, carpenters, and others, she was particularly revered by working women as guide and guardian of lace makers, spinners, unmarried women, and women students. Catherngs were often specifically women's feasts. Commemorating the instrument of her death, Catherine wheels decorated windows, walls, costumes, and jewelry. The serving of Catherine cakes, spike-shaped currant, orange, and caraway biscuits, preceded divertissements with Catherning candle circles, for jumping over or through, and radiant catherine-wheel fireworks.

Christmas Day introduced the twelve winter holy days culminating in Twelfth Night. Called Time of the Twelves, these twelve days in the twelfth month, alluding also to the twelve apostles, required twelve ritual gifts given and got, twelve wassailings to the celebrants' health, and twelve kisses exchanged beneath the Christmas bush (a mistletoe, holly, and evergreen decoration, ornamented with ribbons, small sculptures, and fruits, suspended from the ceiling). Household festivities began only after an entertainer called First Foot or Lucky Bird crossed the symbolic Christmas threshold, allowing good fortune and Christmas joy to be "let in" the dwelling. Christmas also was Time of the Bee. Just as bees produced sweetness and light, by means of honey and beeswax candles, so, according to St. Ambrose, in the hive of life, the church, faithful Christians ceaselessly labored for the sweetness of Christ's teachings and the light of Christian understanding, which qualities were affirmed in Christian customs. Sweet plum pud-

ding, frumenty, posset, honeyed gingerbread Yule dolls, and hot elderberry wine were eaten by the light of the Yule candles and the Yule log blazing on the hearth.

Wassailing with the Milly was a Christmas parade with children singing, collecting gifts, and carrying a small shrine with the Virgin and Child. Other pageantry included a boar's head procession, and a play of the Three Shepherds. Typical was the charming fourteenth-century Christmas playlet from Rouen, incorporating the so-called *Quem quaeritis* Latin trope. Two midwives ask the shepherds "Whom do you seek in the manger, shepherds? Tell us." As they draw back the curtains protecting the Christ child, the shepherds gasp in wonderment and triumphally, worshipfully cry "Alleluia!"

Such dramas, symbolic foods, decorations, ceremonies, and rites of the calendar year occupied more than a third of the lifetime of townsmen, country folk, and castle dwellers. In addition to the usual amateur mummers and morris dancers, professional actors, jugglers, jesters, acrobats, mimes, magicians, minstrels, composers, jongleurs, raconteurs, comedians, puppeteers, ventriloquists, animal trainers, and masters of revels worked their way through the seasons, individually or in troupes, from marketplace to fair to festival. Wealthy houses augmented entertainment by household artists with itinerant acts, the total productions coordinated by a surveyor of ceremonies or professional dance master, often politically powerful and an arbiter of cultural taste. In the yearly round of holidays and festivals, play beautifully balanced life's work.

BIBLIOGRAPHY

Sources. Antoninus of Florence, *Confessionale* (1490); *Cartulaire de l'universite de Montpellier, 1180–1400,* 2 vols. (1890–1912); Henricus de Glorichem, *Tractatus de celebratione festorum* (1477).

Studies. Johannes Butzbach, *Autobiography: A Wandering Scholar of the Fifteenth Century,* R. F. Seybolt and Peter Monroe, trans. (1935); Madeleine Pelner Cosman, *Fabulous Feasts: Medieval Cookery and Ceremony* (1976), and *Medieval Holidays and Festivals: A Calendar of Celebrations* (1981); Knoop Douglas and G. T. Jones, *The Medieval Mason* (1933); John Dowden, *The Church Year and Calendar* (1910); Edith C. Rodgers, *Discussion of Holidays in the Later Middle Ages* (1940); Roy Strong, *Splendour at Court* (1979); Joseph Strutt, *Sports and Pastimes of the People of England* (1810, repr. 1968); Hutton Webster, *Rest Days: A Study in Early Law and Morality* (1916).

MADELEINE PELNER COSMAN

[See also **All Saints' Day; All Souls' Day; Calendars and Reckoning of Time; Christmas; Cookery, European; Easter; Ephiphany, Feast of; Games and Pastimes; Twelve Great Feasts.**]

FEASTS AND FESTIVALS, ISLAMIC. There are only two canonical festivals in the Muslim calendar, *ᶜīd al-fiṭr* (the festival of the breaking of the fast) and *ᶜīd al-aḍḥā* (the festival of sacrificing), popularly called the "minor festival" and the "major festival," respectively. Although two entirely separate festivals, they share a number of common features, of which the most significant is the form of public prayer on these occasions, *ṣalāt al-ᶜīdayn* (the prayer of the two festivals).

The law *(fiqh)* books devote a separate chapter to the regulations for this special communal prayer. Like the Friday prayer, *ṣalāt al-ᶜīdayn* must be led by an imam and is obligatory only for those Muslims living in a city large enough for a *jāmiᶜ* mosque. But there are important differences. The prayer takes place between sunrise and noon, unlike the Friday prayer, which takes place just after noon. There is neither the customary first nor second call to prayer *(adhān, iqāma);* instead, the simple formula *al-ṣalāt jāmiᶜatan* (Come to public prayer) is pronounced just before the beginning of the prayer. The *khuṭba* is delivered after, rather than before, the prayer. On *ᶜīd al-fiṭr* it consists of instructions concerning the alms *(zakāt)* for the festival; on *ᶜīd al-aḍḥā* it concerns the regulations for the sacrifice. Finally, the location is different; the prayer for the festivals takes place at the open-air *muṣallā* rather than in a mosque (except at Mecca, where it is held in the Mosque of the Prophet).

ᶜĪd al-fiṭr is celebrated on 1 Shawwāl, the first day of the month following Ramadan. It has only two obligatory practices: attending the prayer of the festival and paying the alms due on this day, *zakāt* (or *ṣadaqa) al-fiṭr.* The alms donation consists of foodstuffs, given generally to the poor and needy. There is some divergence of opinion regarding the recipients of the *zakāt,* which in practice is often distributed to family and friends. It is obligatory on every free Muslim and must be given on behalf of himself and his dependents. The amount is one *ṣāᶜ* or four *mudd* of wheat, dates, raisins, or barley. There was some question in the early days of Islam about the relation between this *zakāt* and the regular *zakāt,* but the final determination was that both were oblig-

Celebrating *ᶜīd.* Folio 86r of an early-sixteenth-century manuscript of the *Dīwān* of Ḥāfiẓ, *ca.* 1325–1390. FROM A PRIVATE COLLECTION

atory. The day of the *ᶜīd* marks the last day on which this *zakāt* may be paid.

The *ṣalāt* and *zakāt* comprise the obligatory observances of the *ᶜīd,* but numerous popular practices and customs were followed with equal attention to detail. It was customary to wear new clothes, to exchange gifts and visits, and to visit cemeteries. In medieval Egypt the caliph distributed so many gala costumes and robes of honor to court and bureaucratic officials that the festival was known for some years as *ᶜīd al-ḥulal* (the festival of gala costumes).

Worshipers were supposed to go to the *muṣallā*

on foot by one route and return by another. Medieval commentators attributed the custom to the desire to distribute as much of the *zakāt* as possible to different people. Modern anthropologists, however, believe that the underlying reason was magical: the faithful are relieved of their sins on the way to the *muṣallā* and avoided encountering them again by returning on a different path.

The sacrificial feast, *ᶜīd al-aḍḥā* (known also as *ᶜīd al-naḥr* and *ᶜīd al-qurbān*) is celebrated on 10 Dhū'l-Ḥijja, coinciding with the day on which the pilgrims make their sacrificial offerings at Minā. It is one of two occasions on which Muslims sacrifice, the other being the *ᶜaqīqah* offering seven days after the birth of a child. The sacrifice on the day of the feast is considered by the commentators to have been instituted as a commemoration of the near-sacrifice by Abraham of his son, said in Muslim tradition to be Ishmael, not Isaac.

According to most legal schools, the offering of a sacrifice is not an absolute duty, except in fulfillment of a vow, but highly laudable for every free Muslim who is not traveling and possesses sufficient means to provide an animal. The usual offering is a sheep for one person, but a cow or camel may be offered for up to ten. A lawful sacrifice must be an unblemished animal: not blind, lame, too lean, or missing most of the ears or tail. The person doing the sacrificing may distribute the flesh to whomever he pleases, rich or poor (in contrast with the *zakāt al-fiṭr*), but is enjoined to reserve at least a third of the flesh for voluntary alms (*ṣadaqa*).

The sacrifice, which was permitted on the day of the *ᶜīd* as well as on the two (in some cases, three) days following it, took place either at the *muṣallā* or at a *manḥar* (a plaza designated for slaughtering, literally place of sacrificing). Whereas Muslims were enjoined to break their fast on *ᶜīd al-fiṭr* before going to pray, they were exhorted to delay their sacrifice and meal until after the prayer on *ᶜīd al-adḥā*. Although called the "major festival," this *ᶜīd* was often overshadowed by the festivities of *ᶜīd al-fiṭr*, coming after the month of fasting.

The sacrificial feast was just one of several observances associating Muslims across the world with the activities of the hajj. These activities include the farewell to and reception of the pilgrim caravans, the *kiswa*, and the *maḥmal*. The *kiswa* is the covering for the Kaaba and, since the Middle Ages, has been sent by the Egyptian ruler to Mecca with the pilgrim caravan. The *kiswa* was usually paraded through the streets of Cairo and Al-Fustāt for the general popu-

lation to see before being sent to Mecca. From the thirteenth century on, an additional but entirely separate practice was added: the *maḥmal* (or *maḥmil*), an empty, decorated litter, was borne by the camel leading the caravan to Mecca. By some accounts it contained a prayerbook that was exhibited on the return from Mecca. Sending the *maḥmal* became an important statement of political independence by Islamic rulers.

ᶜĀshūrāʾ, celebrated on 10 Muḥarram, is one of several optional fast days. It was originally an obligatory fast, modeled, it seems, on the Jewish Day of Atonement. Later it was superseded by the month of Ramadan for the fast. *ᶜĀshūrāʾ* acquired its greatest significance, however, as the anniversary of the death of the martyr of Ḥusayn at Karbalāʾ. It became a day of mourning for Shiites, who make pilgrimages to Karbalāʾ on that day and put on passion plays, *taᶜzīya*, commemorating the deaths of their martyrs. In Egypt during the reign of the Shiite Fatimids, this day was marked by banquets at court featuring dishes made of lentils (a traditional mourning food) and prayers.

Several nights in the Islamic calendar are particularly significant. *Laylat al-miᶜrāj* (night of the ascension) marks the evening on which Muḥammad is said to have ascended to heaven and returned to earth. It is usually considered to have taken place on 27 Rajab. In some traditions it is associated with the *isrāʾ*, the night journey from Mecca to Jerusalem, when Muḥammad is believed to have been transported to Jerusalem and returned to Mecca in the same night. The festival is celebrated like the birthday of the Prophet, with prayers and recitations of the legend.

On the night of 15 Shaᶜbān, called *laylat al-barāʾa*, the tree of life, on which the names of every living being are written, is shaken. The leaves on which are written the names of those who will die in the coming year fall off the tree. Allah is said to descend to the lowest of the seven heavens, where he summons mortals to forgive them their sins (hence the name *laylat al-barāʾa*, night of quittance). This festival preserves some features of a New Year.

The most important festival of all is *laylat al-qadr* (night of the divine decree), celebrated on 27 Ramadan, commemorating the night on which the Koran was revealed to Muḥammad. The angels are said to descend to convey blessings and, since the gates of heaven are open, prayer is regarded as especially efficacious on this night. It is not absolutely certain that the revelation occurred on 27 Ramadan, but some believe it took place on one of the odd nights of the last ten days of the month. During these ten days the pious follow the custom of *iᶜtikāf*, retreat from the world in a mosque.

On 12 Rabīᶜ I, the birthday of the Prophet (*mawlid al-nabī*) is observed. It was first recorded by al-Maqrīzī for Fatimid Egypt, where three other *mawālīd* were also observed—those of ᶜAlī, Fatima, and the current imam. In the late Fatimid period the birthdays of Ḥasan and Ḥusayn were added, reflecting, it seems, official patronage of a cult of saints in Cairo. These festivals were the occasions for palace ceremonies in which the Fatimid imam sat, veiled, on one of the balconies of his palace, while the three *khuṭabāᵓ* of the mosques of Cairo delivered sermons. These must have been important official celebrations, for al-Afḍal, a powerful and ambitious vizier, abolished them when he took power; they were restored on his death as a symbol of the caliph's renewed independence and authority.

After the end of the Fatimid period, the *mawālīd* seem to have fallen into obscurity until 1207, when al-Malik al-Muẓaffar introduced the *mawlid al-nabī* at Arbalāᵓ. From that time on, it was well established, and the *mawālīd* of many other Islamic prophets and local saints became widely observed popular festivals. As Sufism gained more adherents, the *mawālīd* were layered with Sufi practices, and the *dhikr* (remembrance [of God]) became a familiar feature of the popular celebration. The *mawālīd* were particularly numerous in Egypt, where the celebrations on the birthdays of the saints al-Sayyida Zaynab, al-Sayyida Nafīsa, and Ahmad al-Badawī rivaled the festivities on *mawlid al-nabī*.

Muslims also celebrated Christian festivals with great enthusiasm and energy. In Baghdad the feasts of patron saints were particularly popular; in Cairo, Muslims and Christians often gathered together along the Nile to celebrate *Shaᶜanīn* (Palm Sunday), Easter, and Christmas. Egyptians were especially fond of the Christian *ᶜīd al-ghiṭās* (Epiphany). On this occasion Christians paraded openly with crosses and burning candles (in spite of injunctions against the public display of Christianity and Judaism), and dived into the Nile (hence the name *ᶜīd al-ghiṭās*, festival of diving). Periodically caliphs issued public proclamations prohibiting Christians and Muslims from mixing; but just as often the caliph himself had one of his many riverside pleasure houses (*manāẓir*) readied so that he could observe the festivities.

Three New Year's days were observed: the Persian *naurūz*; the Coptic New Year (also called *nau-*

rūz) in August, coinciding with the annual flooding of the Nile; and the beginning of the Muslim year. The power of the pre-Islamic survivals is evidenced by the elaborate preparations surrounding the celebration of the Persian and Coptic New Years, as compared with the ordinarily austere observance of the beginning of the Muslim year. On both the Persian and Coptic New Years it was customary for people to sprinkle each other with water, a practice reported by both al-Bīrūnī and al-Maqrīzī. In Cairo the Muslim New Year was the occasion for a lavish caliphal procession, involving thousands of mounted soldiers, extravagant costumes, and a magnificent display of wealth. The prefects of Cairo and Fusṭāṭ supervised the decoration of the streets, which were lined by the population in anticipation of the appearance of the caliph in all his splendor.

Equally opulent celebrations accompanied the flooding of the Nile (*wafāᵓ al-nīl*). The caliph went first to the nilometer on Roda Island, in the center of the Nile, to anoint it—a pre-Islamic survival that was given an Islamic veneer by introducing continuous koranic recitation and Muslim prayer into the festivities. Then the caliph proceeded to the dam that had been built at the mouth of the canal at Cairo, where the breaking of the dam occurred and the floodwaters swept into the canal.

Two important festivals—circumcision (*khitān, ṭahāra*) and *ᶜaqīqa*—were not public holidays but family celebrations with a distinctly public aspect. The circumcisions of rulers' sons were often elaborate public ceremonies, when as many as several hundred boys would be circumcised at once. Even among the common people it was not unusual to circumcise several boys at the same time. *ᶜAqīqa* designated the sacrifice on the seventh day after the birth of a child, when the child's hair was shaved and an animal was offered. (The flesh was distributed to the poor, and a small portion was retained for a family meal.) The usual sacrifice was two rams for a boy, one for a girl. Although not an obligatory sacrifice, it was recommended and widely practiced. The name *ᶜaqīqa* was also given to the sacrifice at the end of the hajj, when the pilgrim's hair was cut.

BIBLIOGRAPHY

For general legal regulations of *ᶜīd al-fiṭr* and *ᶜīd al-aḍḥa*, see the chapters in *fiqh* books entitled ṣalāt al-ᶜīdayn, zakāt (or ṣadaqat) al-fiṭr, and uḍḥiyya. A French translation of Shiite *fiqh* is available in Amédée Querry, *Droit musulman: Recueil de lois concernant les musulmans schyites*, I (1872), 91–94, 169–174. For *ḥadīth*, see A.

J. Wensinck, *A Handbook of Early Muhammadan Tradition* (1927, repr. 1960), with voluminous listings under "Festival," "Muṣallā," "Slaughtering," "Victims," and "Zakāt." The articles "ᶜAqīqah," "ᶜIdu'l-Azḥa," and "ᶜIdu'l-Fiṭrin" in T. P. Hughes, *A Dictionary of Islam,* are very useful not only for the details on legal regulations, but also for descriptions of modern Indian celebrations. Georges Henri Bousquet, *Les grandes pratiques rituelles de l'Islam* (1949), gives overviews of both legal requirements and variations in actual practice. On sacrifices in general, see Joseph Chelhod, *Le sacrifice chez les arabes* (1955). For discussions and descriptions of actual practices, see G. E. von Grunebaum, *Muhammadan Festivals* (1951); Edward Lane, *Manners and Customs of the Modern Egyptians* (1963), chs. 24–27; and Adam Mez, *The Renaissance of Islam,* Sallahudin Khuda Bukhsh and D. S. Margouliouth, trans. (1937), ch. 23. In Arabic, al-Bīrūnī, *Chronologie orientalischer Voelker . . . ,* Edward C. Sachau, ed. (1878, repr. 1963), 215–238 (for non-Muslim festivals in Islamic lands), 328–335 (for Islamic festivals), translated by Sachau as *The Chronology of Ancient Nations* (1879); and al-Maqrīzī, *al-Mawāᶜiz wa-al-lᶜtibār fī dhikr al-khiṭaṭ wa-al-āthār* (1853), I.387–391, 432–434, and 451–457. On the history of the *mawālīd,* see J. W. McPherson, *The Moulids of Egypt* (1941). Ignác Goldziher, "Veneration of Saints in Islam," in his *Muslim Studies,* II (1966), is indispensable as background. For the *maḥmal,* consult Jacques Jomier, *Le maḥmal et la caravane égyptienne des pelerins de la Mecque* (1953). On the New Year, see A. J. Wensinck, "Arabic New-Year and the Feast of Tabernacles," in *Verhandelingen der Koninklijke Akademie van Wetenschappen,* n.s. 25 (1925).

PAULA SANDERS

[See also **Birūni, al-; Fasting, Islamic.**]

FEET, WASHING OF, known also ritually as the *pedilavium* or *mandatum,* grew out of pre-Christian hygiene, hospitality, and cultural practice. It was the practice in the Mediterranean world to cleanse the feet of dust and dirt before entering a house, eating, or retiring. In terms of hospitality, the good host saw to it that the feet of his guests were washed. Because it was a demeaning duty, foot washing was often performed by slaves, but as a sign of humility, charity, and honor to the guest, the host might perform the task himself. The domestic practice eventually became a religious ritual, as Old Testament Tabernacle and Jewish synagogue rites show.

The supreme examples of foot washing for the patristic and medieval church was Christ's washing the feet of the apostles during the institution of the Eu-

charist at the Last Supper and his *mandatum* that they should follow his example. In some quarters Christ's act was seen to be the institution of baptism, and hence in several territories in the Western church the ritual of foot washing became an integral part of baptism, following the immersion and pouring and the imposition of chrism. The churches of the East and Rome did not adopt this practice, but the North African church seems to have known the baptismal *pedilavium* until it was dropped in the fourth century, perhaps out of fear that it could be understood as a Donatist practice, a second baptism. In Spain during the fourth century the practice was condemned by the Council of Elvira, but in Milanese, Gallican, and Celtic practice the rite survived. Ambrose considered the baptismal *pedilavium* a sacrament. In Gallican territories Caesarius of Arles spoke of the baptismal *pedilavium* as an expiation of both venial and mortal sins, and the *Missale Gothicum, Missale Gallicanum vetus,* and Bobbio Missal all have rites for baptismal *pedilavium.* Later in Carolingian times the baptismal interrogatories returned to Charlemagne attest to the continued presence of the practice of Frankish territories, and Pope Fabian of the pseudo-Isidorian Decretals speaks of the *pedilavium* as a form of baptism. Finally, in the Stowe Missal with its Celtic rite of baptism, the *pedilavium* plays an integral role.

Beyond its use in baptism, foot washing was an important ritual in the Western church; in early medieval monastic practice it became a ritual accompanied by psalms, prayers, and processions. Owing to the large numbers of guests in monasteries, however, the practice had to be restricted in the early Middle Ages to those persons designated in the Rule of St. Benedict, pilgrims and the poor. By the early ninth century there was a daily *mandatum* for the poor, who might have their feet washed in the refectory or the cloister. This *mandatum pauperum cotidianum,* the practice of which varied according to the time of year and day and the number of persons involved, passed by the eleventh century into chapters of canons. And by the later Middle Ages the custom was extended in some regions to novices.

Besides the *mandatum pauperum* there existed a *mandatum fratrum* of monks. As early as the seventh century this practice is mentioned as taking place on Saturdays and Sundays, and by the early ninth century it was a firm practice in monasteries that later used an ordo following that of Benedict of Aniane or one used at Monte Cassino. And like the *mandatum pauperum,* the *mandatum fratrum* passed into chapters of canons by the eleventh century.

Although the monastic and clerical *mandata* might be held at any time, the chief days for them were the Saturday before Palm Sunday, celebrating the unction of Christ's feet at Bethany, and Maundy Thursday, the day connected not only with the Last Supper but also with baths for the sick, poor, and catechumens after the abstinences of Lent. As early as the seventh century in Spain, it was the practice on Holy Thursday to wash "twenty-two feet" (probably representing the twelve apostles less the traitor Judas), and most of the Western liturgical books thereafter contain *mandatum* ceremonies for Holy Thursday. By the eighth or ninth century the *mandatum* of Holy Thursday had been taken up in the Eastern churches, and with the reception in Rome of the German *Pontificale Romano-Germanicum* in the eleventh century, the *mandatum* became a feature of the Roman rite. It was usually carried out by persons of superior rank—emperors, kings, popes, bishops, priests, and abbots—who humbled themselves before inferiors—lower clerics, monks, or the poor. Associated with the *pedilavium* was the presentation to those whose feet were washed of food, drink, and money, designated as the *mixtum, cena, mandatum,* and Maundy money.

Because of its prominence in the life of Christ, the *pedilavium* came to play a significant role in sacramental theology, clerical spirituality, and artistic expression in the Middle Ages. In sacramental theology Ambrose of Milan argued that the *pedilavium* as a mystery and sanctification not only cleansed the feet on which the venom of Satan had collected, but also washed away *peccata hereditaria* (inherited sins). Later in the twelfth century Bernard of Clairvaux and Ernaud of Bonneval counted the *mandatum* as one of the sacramentals that washed away daily venial sins. In clerical spirituality Christ's example in the *pedilavium* was frequently cited in the Ordinals of Christ to explain the origins of the offices of deacon, who read the Gospel account of the *pedilavium* at the *mandatum,* and of subdeacon, who was responsible for the water at the Eucharist.

The *pedilavium* played a major role both in manuscript illumination, painting, and sculpture, and in music. In medieval visual art, Christ is often portrayed as washing the feet of Peter. In music and poetry the *pedilavium* was the occasion for the deeply moving *Congregavit* or *Ubi caritas* chant. Composed about 800, perhaps at Reichenau as one of the *Caritaslieder,* it was originally sung at the

Caritas in refectorio, the ceremony in which monks were given an extra allotment of wine in gratitude for their prayers for benefactors and departed brethren. In the early manuscripts it was often connected with the *Laudes regiae* or regal lauds in which the emperor or king was wished *multos annos.* By the tenth century the *Ubi caritas* had come to play an appropriate part in the *mandatum,* where, together with other antiphons that often emphasized the historical and sacramental aspects of the *pedilavium,* it could be used to stress the charitable, nonsacramental aspects.

BIBLIOGRAPHY

Ernst H. Kantorowicz, "The Baptism of the Apostles," in *Dumbarton Oaks Papers,* **9–10** (1955–1956); Susan A. Keefe, *Baptismal Instruction in the Carolingian Period: The Manuscript Evidence* (diss., Univ. of Toronto, 1981), 331–338, and "Carolingian Baptismal Expositions: A Handlist of Tracts and Manuscripts," in Uta-Renate Blumenthal, ed., *Carolingian Essays: Andrew W. Mellon Lectures in Early Christian Studies* (1983), 211; Henri Leclercq, "Lavement," in Fernand Cabrol, ed., *Dictionnaire d'archéologie chrétienne et de liturgie,* VIII.2 (1929); A. Malvy, "Lavement des pieds," in *Dictionnaire de théologie catholique,* IX.1 (1926); Roger E. Reynolds, *The Ordinals of Christ from Their Origins to the Twelfth Century* (1978); Thomas Schäfer, *Die Fusswaschung im monastischen Brauchtum und in der lateinischen Liturgie: Liturgiegeschichtliche Untersuchung* (1956).

ROGER E. REYNOLDS

[See also **Baptism; Holy Week.**]

FELIRE OENGUSSO CELI DE. See **Martyrology, Irish.**

FELIX VITA GUTHLACI. See **Guthlac, St.**

FELONY. Felonies were very slow to emerge as a separate class in the practice of medieval English courts; even a distinction between accusations of crime and civil suits can scarcely be dated before the thirteenth century. Reflecting its continental, feudal origins, "felony" at first meant some breach of the feudal bond leading to the forfeiture of a fief to the offended lord; after the king "wasted" to his profit the lands of a convicted felon for a year and a day, the land reverted to the felon's lord. Something of the original emotional impact of the term "felon" would long survive; it was, Frederic Maitland wrote, "as bad a word as you could give to man or thing."

But the label was in time applied to a range of offenses much wider than feudal misdeeds. One factor in this change was the willingness of lords to accept a definition that brought them increased forfeitures. Another was the vigorous work of Henry II (1154–1189) in establishing law and order. A tradition as old as Anglo-Saxon times held that certain offenses placed a man at the king's mercy for life, limb, and property; Henry II established mutilation and forfeiture as penalties for a list of serious crimes including "murder, theft, robbery, or harboring men who do such things" (1166), forgery, and arson (1176). Distrusting the ordeal, Henry II ordered all those accused, even if they passed the ordeal, to abjure the realm if they were notoriously suspect of a base felony. The similarity of punishment for these offenses and for feudal felonies may have made the merging of categories more easily accomplished. Moreover, Henry's work helped to establish a distinction between civil and criminal cases; he provided new writs to initiate civil cases and grand juries to name those guilty of serious crimes.

Yet some future felonies were not included in the list used by grand juries, and many ordinary men still preferred to appeal (that is, charge) their opponents on either civil or criminal charges, indicating their willingness to fight a judicial duel rather than buy a writ at Westminster. Judges were reluctant to place men in peril of life and limb for offenses that seemed minor. By the early thirteenth century every crime prosecuted by appeal, involving potential loss of lands and goods or life and limb, was a felony. Thus legal effects rather than the quality of the crime itself determined which crimes would be felonies. The list included homicide, suicide, wounding and imprisoning (though these offenses were fast falling into the new category of trespass), robbery, larceny, rape, arson, and treason. Punishment, which had at first included mutilation, or even in some cases burning, was increasingly standardized; felons commonly went to the gallows.

BIBLIOGRAPHY

Alan Harding, *A Social History of English Law* (1966); Frederick Pollock and Frederic W. Maitland, *The History of English Law Before the Time of Edward I*, 2nd ed. (1968).

RICHARD W. KAEUPER

[See also **Law, English Common; Law, Procedures of: 1000–1500.**]

FENIAN POETRY. An extensive tradition of Fenian verse—mantic, lyrical, and narrative—can be found in all stages of secular Irish literature as early as the seventh and eighth centuries. Fenian poetry has survived in Gaelic folklore as well. Texts of Fenian *laoithe* (ballads), a genre that is already found in the twelfth-century Irish manuscript known as the Book of Leinster, have been recorded as late as the mid twentieth century from Scottish Gaelic traditional singers. The terms "Fenian" and "Ossianic" refer to the Irish and Scottish Gaelic narrative cycle centered on the hero Finn mac Cumaill and his band of men, the *fían* (singular) or *fían(n)a* (plural). Fenian tales have survived in both prose and verse. While it would be hasty at this stage in our knowledge of the Fenian tradition to postulate the existence of two separate narrative repertoires, certain Fenian stories in literary and oral tradition are usually told in a prose medium, while others are usually told, or alluded to, in the medium of verse.

In the remains of pre-twelfth-century Irish literature, scholars have unearthed a sufficient number of references to Fenian tales and characters to demonstrate convincingly the existence of an archaic body of Fenian narrative with its roots in pre-Christian mythology. Yet there is little extant pre-twelfth-century Fenian literature per se. With the ascendancy of the province of Munster in the eleventh century and the Anglo-Norman invasion in the twelfth, new sociocultural factors and aesthetic influences change the tenor of Irish literature, and the Fenian tradition assumes a larger role in it. It is during this period that the first recension or recensions of the *Acallam na Senórach* (Colloquy of the ancients)—a compendium of Fenian lore—is written. Throughout the rest of the medieval period and into the early modern period of Irish literature (that is, thirteenth to eighteenth centuries), the Fenian cycle grows in literary importance and finally becomes dominant among the heroic cycles. Fenian prose tales and ballads, borrowed from the concurrent oral tradition or at least inspired by it, are written down and become part of the literary tradition. The relation between oral and literary material becomes increasingly complex, as literary versions of Fenian tales and *laoithe* reenter the oral tradition, particularly during the period of the breakdown of Gaelic literary culture in

Ireland and Scotland, from the sixteenth to the nineteenth centuries.

Finn is depicted in medieval Irish literature as a leader (*rígfhénnid*, head of the *fían*), a warrior, and a poet-seer (*fili*). Like King Arthur in the Arthurian tradition, the *rígfhénnid* Finn usually plays a background role in Fenian tales, though one of the longest-lived and best-known of the traditional Fenian stories is the account of Finn's youth. This tale (actually a group of tales) bears a strong resemblance to the *macgnímrada* (boyhood deeds) narratives of the great Ulster hero Cú Chulainn, which are included in the text *Táin Bó Cúailnge* (Cattle-raid of Cúailnge). The *macgnímrada* of Finn also resemble the *enfances* of Perceval and other Arthurian heroes, as well as the youthful adventures of the Norse hero Sigurd.

Besides Finn, there are many other notable members of the *fían* (warring and hunting band) about whom stories are told in the Fenian tradition. Perhaps the most famous of Finn's heroic companions is Oisín (Little Deer), the son of Finn and an otherworldly deer-woman. This son of Finn functions as the "poet laureate" of the *fían* in the many poems attributed to him in both literary and oral tradition. It is from Oisín's name that the designation "Ossianic" derives, by way of the Fenian "translations" of the eighteenth-century Scotsman James Macpherson. According to a medieval tradition that lives on in Fenian folklore, at the conclusion of the Fenian era, when all the other Fenian heroes are dead, Oisín and another famous *fénnid* (member of the *fían*), the fleet-footed Cailte mac Rónáin, go into the otherworld *(síd)* and, like Irish counterparts to Rip Van Winkle, survive into the historical period. In the fifth century the two aged *fénnidi* meet St. Patrick on his missionary tour of Ireland and supply him with information about Finn, Finn's men, and their adventures. Thus it is in the context of the extended conversation between pagan heroes and Christian saint that, according to this widespread Fenian topos, the Fenian *laoithe* attributed to Oisín or Cailte are composed.

Another member of the *fían* who figures prominently in Fenian tradition is the son of Oisín, Oscar (Stranger or Deer-lover), the paradigmatic warrior-hero, whose death in the Battle of Gabair signals the end of the *fían*. Another heroic grandson of Finn is Mac Lugach (Shining Youth), whose youth-tale closely resembles that of his grandfather. There is also the exemplary yet ill-fated youth Diarmaid, whose tragic elopement with the aged Finn's wife Gráinne brings out the dark, vengeful side of the *rígfhénnid*. The sinister Goll (The One-eyed) and his troublemaking brother Conán (Little Hound) are enemies of Finn who form an uneasy alliance with him but finally forsake the *fían*. Also worthy of mention are Fergus Fínbél (Fergus Wine-mouth), the chief poet of the *fían*; Cnú Deróil (Diminutive Nut), the chief musician; and Finn's favorite hunting dogs (his own metamorphosed nephews), Bran (Raven) and Sceolang (Survivor). All of these characters appear frequently in Fenian tales and ballads. There are countless other members of the *fían* mentioned in the tradition, but most of them are hardly more than names to us.

In fact the main character of the Fenian tradition is really the *fían* itself, and the main attraction of the tradition is the way of life that the *fénnid* heroes represent. It is virtually impossible to determine just what the historical counterpart in ancient Irish society to the *fían* of narrative was, if such a counterpart existed at all. As a mythical reality, however, the *fían* derives from Indo-European *männerbund* (male martial organization) ideology, which has been studied by Georges Dumézil and others. As described in early Irish literature, the *fían* (cognate with Latin *venari* [to hunt]) is an initiatory band of warrior-hunters living in the wilderness and operating outside the territorial and behavioral restrictions of the basic social units of ancient Irish society, the *fine* (kin-group) and *túath* ([tribal] kingdom). The *fénnid* is a man (or in some instances a woman) who is put, or puts himself, "beyond the pale." He is either an outlaw without hope of readmittance into society or a youth who, too young to take on adult responsibilities, is undergoing a wilderness rite of passage, in the setting of *fénnidecht* (life in a *fían*).

In the variety of Fenian tales, to some extent categorizable according to their traditional titles, we see reflected the freedom, instability, and danger inherent in the liminal lives led by these "heroes outside the tribe." The *fénnid* heroes are torn between two separate realities: human society, which they serve and protect (the *fían* is, at least officially, in the service of the mythical king of Ireland), and the otherworld, which the *fénnidi* continually confront, living as they do on the margins of social existence. The blend of friendship and hostility which marks Fenian encounters with the otherworld—whether it is in nature, underground, or across the sea—is expressed vividly in the extant *bruidhean* ([supernatural] hostel) tales, wherein Finn and his men are invited to a feast in the otherworld, only to find that they have been lured into a trap from which they can barely escape.

Complementing the humiliation that the trapped *fénnidi* regularly experience in the *bruidhean* tales is the triumph of their being able to penetrate supernatural realms hidden from normal men. In stories of *tóraidheacht* (pursuit) and *eachtra* (adventure), the Fenian heroes are shown drawing out the otherworld: denizens of supernatural realms visit the *fénnidi* to impose difficult tasks on them and lead the *fénnidi* on otherworldly quests, particularly for women. Fenian heroes acquire supernatural lovers and are often themselves the children of otherworldly beings. The many Fenian stories about coming of age in the *fían*, tales about demonstrations of prowess that in some instances lead to tragically premature deaths, are played out on the boundary zone between childhood and adulthood—a zone different from, yet related to that which separates this world from the otherworld. In the story of the Battle of Ventry *(Cath Finntrágha)*, young *fían* heroes prove themselves, sometimes at the cost of their lives, in a cataclysmic battle fought on the shores of Kerry between the *fían* and an otherworldly horde invading Ireland. Such Fenian *Bildungsromane* are undoubtedly generated by the function of initiation that is at the heart of *fénnidecht*, whether real or mythical.

Poetry is not incidental to the Fenian tradition. More than just a medium for the transmission of the tradition, it is in fact one of the central concerns of the Fenian heroes themselves, who, according to literary descriptions of the *fían*, are required to study the art of poetry as part of their initiation into Finn's band. Their leader, Finn, is a poet, and the story of his boyhood climaxes in his acquisition of the supernatural knowledge *(imbas)* that, according to traditional Celtic ideology, generates the institution of poets and poetry. The poet in ancient Irish culture is more than just an artist: he is *the* formulator of the truth—past, present, and future. In the Christian era, the poet *(fili*—etymologically "the one who sees") assumes many of the aspects of the pagan priest, the druid. Thus, the *fili*, as he is depicted in early Irish literature and even contemporary Gaelic folklore, mediates between this world and the otherworld, and he exists, shamanlike, on the boundaries of human life, where he awaits otherworldly inspiration. In his freedom to travel from kingdom to kingdom and in his stereotypical straying from the stric-

tures of conventional behavior, the *fili* of early traditional Irish society and myth closely resembles the *fénnid* of the Fenian tradition—who, not coincidentally, is a *fili* himself, describing his adventures in nature and the otherworld through the medium of verse. Paradoxically, the unorthodox figure of the *fili* serves as the proclaimer and upholder of sociocultural orthodoxy, through the power of poetry in its functions of praise and blame. Similarly, the Fenian heroes live outside society, yet as a community they are a paradigm of social existence; in their capacity as metaphysical border guards, these warrior-poets bravely protect human society. Perhaps the most intriguing message encoded in Fenian myth is that the *fili* and other liminal figures such as the *fénnid* are, at least in theory, closely related, and that their spheres of activities overlap.

The poetry attributed to Finn and the other Fenian heroes, a body of verse that constitutes a significant portion of extant Fenian literature and folklore, varies in meter, style, and content from age to age. In general, however, the poems supposedly composed by the Fenian heroes belong to genres not in the mainstream of the poetic craft *(filidecht)*, at least as it is represented elsewhere in medieval literature. The *fénnid*-poet, an exile from the social realm, does not celebrate kings and nobles, nor is he a recorder of their history. Unlike the traditional *fili*, he does not directly proclaim social truths in their social setting; rather, he is an outsider formulating the puzzling realities of the *fían*, nature, and the otherworld. All of these alternate realities do, though, reflect in their own ways the same social values articulated in the occasional verse of the *fili*.

In the earliest strata of Irish literature (sixth to tenth centuries), there are extant some verses attributed to Finn in his poetic persona as seer. These short, almost indecipherable poems, called *roscada*, are found in non-Fenian literature as well (for example, the *Cattle-Raid of Cúailnge)*, usually in contexts of prophecy or dramatic dialogue. Finn's *roscada*, mantic utterances featuring archaic Irish versification and language, are supposedly composed by this *fili/fénnid* after he acquires supernatural inspiration by chewing his "thumb of knowledge"— his mantic "prop" that he acquires when he burns himself while cooking a salmon of knowledge from the otherworld. In another version of the story of how Finn acquired his poetic ability, the hero chases a food thief to the door of the otherworld, where he slays the thief and gets his finger stuck in the door;

when Finn finally extricates his finger, he puts it in his mouth and begins to chant, according to Gerard Murphy's translation:

> Come to Femen. A judgment!
> A happy blow from a long ever-swift shaft
> increases my dish by a pig;
> it is Finn's ale-drinking at Cúldub's tomb we chant.

The point of this *roscad* is Finn's identifying the previously anonymous otherworldly food thief as a certain Cúldub. Thus here, and in other narrative settings of *roscad* (also known as *retoiric*) composition, Finn is marked as an extraordinary human because, through his poetic vision, he "knows" the otherworld and announces what he knows in a mantic poem.

Most of the later medieval poetry attributed to Finn and the other Fenian heroes, composed in the rhymed stanzaic meters characteristic of medieval Irish verse from the ninth century onwards, continues this distinctly "otherworldly" tone—unlike the typical poetry of praise and blame which it was the task of the *fili* to compose on a day-to-day basis. The many lyrical Fenian poems preserved in the text of the *Colloquy of the Ancients* and elsewhere are more extrasocial than intrasocial in subject matter and mood. Akin to certain kinds of *dindshenchas* (place-name lore) poetry and to "hermit poetry" of the ninth and tenth centuries, these Fenian verses celebrate the haunts of the *fían* in nature and the life of the *fénnidi* on the interface between this world and the otherworld. In a twelfth-century telling of the story of Finn's youth, there is a corrupt text of what the scribe claims is the dissertation of Finn the matriculating *fili*: a poem (probably composed much earlier than the twelfth century) in praise of May Day and summertime. The following verses of the poem are from Carney's translation:

> Lovely season of May! Most noble then is the color
>   of trees;
> blackbirds sing a full lay, when the shaft of day is
>   slender.
> The vigorous harsh cuckoo calls "Welcome to noble
>   Summer";
> subdued is the bitter weather that caused the
>   branching wood to dwindle.

The joyousness of such Fenian nature poetry is balanced out by the wistful longing for the past, for old heroic companions, and for the sylvan life of *fénnidi* expressed in the medieval and early modern poems

attributed to Oisín and Cailte, who engage in sometimes contentious dialogue with the representative of the "new," Patrick.

Perhaps the most distinctive type of Fenian poetry, the Fenian *laoidh*, first appears in the twelfth-century *Book of Leinster*, where we find three such poems. Murphy suggests that the *laoidh*, composed in quatrains of rhymed, usually seven-syllable lines, may have been generated by the same cultural and aesthetic forces that shaped the medieval English and Scandinavian ballad. There are considerable lyrical and elegiac elements in the typical *laoidh*, a genre that, particularly in Scottish Gaelic tradition, is to be found to a limited degree outside the Fenian tradition as well. Unlike most other kinds of Celtic poetry, the Fenian ballad, ranging in length from a few quatrains to scores, usually tells a story, albeit elliptically. Frequently put in the mouths of participants in the action of the tale, *laoithe* proliferate in literary tradition (and presumably oral tradition as well), from the twelfth to the sixteenth centuries. *The Book of the Dean of Lismore*, compiled in Scotland in the early sixteenth century, contains several Fenian *laoithe*, collected from oral and literary sources. Even more are to be found in the early-seventeenth-century Irish manuscript *Duanaire Finn* (The songbook of Finn).

As literature on the page, these *laoithe* lose much of the rhythmical element that marked them in oral performance, in which they were sung or chanted. The meter of the later *laoithe* tends toward the newer or reemerging accentual song meters characteristic of post-seventeenth-century Gaelic verse. A typical Fenian *laoidh* is the "Lay of the Smithy," in which Finn and his men meet a supernatural smith who challenges them to a contest. A version of this lay, in the Irish of the early fifteenth century, is preserved in the *Duanaire Finn:*

> We were on the hill only a short time
> —long will the tale be remembered!—
> when came onto the bright-surfaced plain
> a gigantic warrior on a single foot.
>
> A wonder, the appearance of the warrior;
> we picked up our weapons upon seeing him;
> three arms on him, all of them moving;
> the color of charcoal on his face.
>
> . . . .
>
> Upon coming onto the hill
> he said, having approached us:
> "May the gods bless
> you, O son of Cumall."

"Blessings to you too," said the *fénnid* Finn.
"Who are you, O lone man that I do not know?
Tell us your real name,
O man with clothes of skin."

"Light, son of Sharpening, is my baptismal name;
I have mastered the form of every craft;
and I am the chief of smiths
in the service of the king of Lochlann in Beirbhe [i.e.,
    the otherworld].

To seek a fair race
have I come to you from Beirbhe;
they say you are swift,
O people skilled in craft."

(My translation is based on Murphy's edition.) Finn and his men do, of course, succeed in keeping up with the otherworldly smith, and at the end of the tale they win magical weapons from the devious craftsman. Versions of this lay collected in Scotland from singers tell essentially the same story. But there is sufficient multiformity in motif and language among *laoidh* texts preserved in medieval and early modern literature and collected from oral informants to suggest that oral formulaic composition, as described by Albert Lord, played a vital role in the development and transmission of this narrative verse genre. Further study is needed before we can decide whether the *laoithe* as we have them were composed in an oral, literary, or "transitional" mode.

BIBLIOGRAPHY

James Carney, ed. and trans., "Three Old Irish Accentual Poems," in *Ériu*, **22** (1971); Georges Dumézil, *The Destiny of the Warrior*, Alf Hiltebeitel, trans. (1970); Albert B. Lord, *The Singer of Tales* (1960); Proinsias Mac Cana, "On the Use of the Term *Retoiric*," in *Celtica*, 7 (1966); Eoin MacNeill and Gerard Murphy, eds. and trans., *Duanaire Finn: The Book of the Lays of Fionn*, in Irish Texts Society, VII (1908), XXVIII (1933), and XLIII (1953); Kuno Meyer, *Fianaigecht*, in Royal Irish Academy Todd Lecture Series, XIV (1910); Gerard Murphy, ed. and trans., *Early Irish Lyrics*, rev. ed. (1962), and *The Ossianic Lore and Romantic Tales of Medieval Ireland*, revised by Brian Ó Cuív (1971); Standish Hayes O'Grady, ed. and trans., *Silva Gadelica: A Collection of Tales in Irish*, 2 vols. (1892); Thomas F. O'Rahilly, *Early Irish History and Mythology* (1946); Marie-Louise Sjoestedt-Jonval, *Gods and Heroes of the Celts*, Myles Dillon, trans. (1949); J. E. Caerwyn Williams, "The Court Poet in Medieval Ireland," in *Proceedings of the British Academy*, 57 (1971).

JOSEPH FALAKY NAGY

[See also **Acallam Na Senórach; Ireland, Early History; Irish Literature; Mythology, Celtic; Táin bó Cúailgne.**]

FENRIS WOLF. In Scandinavian mythology the Fenris wolf is an important enemy of the gods. There is some confusion about the name: some passages have the form *Fenrir*, others have *Fenrisúlfr* (wolf of Fenrir); a plural (wolves of Fenrir) also occurs. The meaning of *Fenrir* is unclear.

In the mythology the wolf is bound by the gods with a special fetter (*Snorra edda, Gylfaginning*, 34). Týr pledges the good faith of the gods by placing his hand in the wolf's mouth. When the wolf is unable to escape from the fetter, he bites off Týr's hand. At Ragnarǫk the wolf will break free, kill Odin, and swallow the sun. Odin's young son Viðarr will avenge him, according to *Vafþrúðnismál* 53, by tearing the wolf's jaws apart (in the variant cited in *Gylfaginning*, 51, by stabbing the wolf).

Axel Olrik found the Fenris wolf and the hound Garmr to be variants of a tale type describing a bound beast who breaks free and destroys the world. This type, he said, is typical of Scandinavia, southern Russia, and the Caucasus, and ultimately derives from conceptions of an earthquake monster.

Whatever its origin and cognates, the figure of the Fenris wolf is central to Scandinavian mythology. The wolf is one of three evil beings sired by Loki on the giantess Angrboða; the others are Hel, whom Odin cast down into the world of the dead, where she presides, and the Midgard serpent, whom Odin cast into the sea, where he surrounds the earth (*Gylfaginning*, 34). Thus the wolf has links both to death and to Thor's great adversary. Furthermore, he links Týr, whom he maims, and Odin, whom he kills—two major sovereign figures. By killing the head of the pantheon and swallowing the sun, he points out the connection between the gods, particularly Odin, and the cosmic order (see *Vǫluspá, 5–6*) and consequent disorder of Ragnarǫk. That Odin's great enemy should be a beast of battle is appropriate because of Odin's association with slain warriors. He also keeps two wolves as pets (*Gylfaginning*, 25).

BIBLIOGRAPHY

Ólafur Briem, "Fenrisúlfr," in *Kulturhistoriskt lexikon för nordisk medeltid*, IV (1959); Axel Olrik, *Ragnarök: Die*

Sagen vom Weltuntergang (1922); Jan de Vries, *Altgermanische Religionsgeschichte,* I (1956), 265–267.

JOHN LINDOW

[See also **Eddic Poetry; Scandinavian Mythology; Snorra Edda; Vafþrúðnismal.**]

FERGANA. See **Farghānā.**

FERNÁN GONZÁLEZ, POEMA DE, an anonymous Castilian epic poem, the extant version written around 1250 by a monk of the Benedictine monastery of S. Pedro de Arlanza (in the southeast of the province of Burgos) or by a person related to that monastery. The imperfect fifteenth-century copy of the *Poema* kept at the library of the Escorial (MS B-IV-21) ends at stanza 701. It constitutes an anomalous and extraordinary case in the history of Castilian medieval poetry. MS B-IV-21 is anomalous because it is a *mester de clerecía* that poeticizes an extensive epic narration, a subject matter identified then and now with the *mester de juglaría.* It is extraordinary because it constitutes the most daring thirteenth-century poetic experiment in Castile in that it uses a new meter (the *cuaderna vía,* recently popularized by Gonzalo de Berceo). Its stringent regularity became the ideal pattern (frequently broken, to be sure) for the traditional and well-known irregularities of the Castilian epic.

The *Poema* tells the story of the historic Fernán González, count of Castile from 932 to his death in 970, with liberal poetic and folkloric reworkings of the documentary evidence. The *Poema* is the lone survivor of a series of epic poems that told the early history of autonomous Castile, a "small region" ("Estonçe era Castyella un pequenno rryncon," 170*a*) that occupied roughly the northern half of the present province of Burgos. Its suzerain was the kingdom of León, to the west; on the east it was threatened by the kingdom of Navarre, and on the south by the Moors.

The *Poema* begins with a typical clerical invocation, then tells of the fall of Spain to the Arabs and the beginnings of the *Reconquista.* An erudite and topical *laus Hispaniae* appropriately introduces the origins of Castile. The *Poema* then tells of the folkloric childhood of Fernán González and of his his-

torico-poetic struggles to gain the autonomy of Castile, in which he engages in almost daily contest with the Moors, the Navarrese, and the Leonese. The most famous poetic episode of these struggles is the *venta al gallarín* (a sale in which the price grows daily by geometric progression) by Fernán González to King Sancho I of León of his horse and hawk (*coplas 564–575*), which, because of the accrued interest, in due time assures the autonomy of Castile from León. This episode has been traced back to the sixth-century *Getica* of Jordanes, a history of the Goths. The *Poema,* incomplete at the end in its extant fifteenth-century copy, does not tell of the actual achievement of the autonomy of Castile, but it can be reconstructed by the *crónicas,* in their well-known relationship with epic poetry in medieval Castilian literature. All of the *Poema,* in fact, was prosified in the *Primera crónica general* of Alfonso X (*ca.* 1289). The *Poema* itself depended on a lost epic poem of the *mester de juglaría,* attested by Gonzalo de Berceo and usually identified as the *Cantar de Fernán González,* which enjoyed demonstrable popularity before and after the composition of the *Poema.*

BIBLIOGRAPHY

Juan Bautista Avalle-Arce, *Temas hispánicos medievales* (1974), ch. 2; Alan D. Deyermond, *The Middle Ages,* ch. 2, "The Epic," in R. O. Jones, ed., *A Literary History of Spain,* I (1971); Ramón Menéndez Pidal, *Reliquias de la poesía épica española* (1951), 34–180; Alonso Zamora Vicente, ed., *Poema de Fernán González* (1946).

JUAN BAUTISTA AVALLE-ARCE

[See also **Cuaderna Vía; Mester de Clerecía; Mester de Juglaría; Spanish Epic Poetry; Spanish Literature; Spanish Versification and Poetry.**]

FERNANDO DE ROJAS. See **Celestina, La.**

FERRARA-FLORENCE, COUNCIL OF, the meeting of the Latin and Greek churches to try by free discussion to solve their doctrinal differences and to unite. The council opened in Ferrara on 8 January 1438. The Greeks were represented by Patriarch Joseph II with 20 metropolitans (some as procurators of Alexandria, Antioch, and Jerusalem), Emperor

John VIII, and his retinue—in all about 700 persons. They reached Venice on 8 February 1438, and Ferrara on 4–7 March. Their voyage, maintenance, and return were at the expense of the pope. The council was solemnly inaugurated on 9 April, the emperor stipulating a four-months' delay to await envoys of the Western princes from whom he hoped to obtain military help for Constantinople: only two responded. From 4 June until mid July, committees of ten per side discussed purgatory, without agreement. In thirteen sessions from 8 October to 13 December, the Greeks argued that, since the Council of Ephesus had forbidden any change, even of a syllable, in the Nicene Creed, the addition to it by the Latins of the *Filioque* was illegal. The Latins claimed that the Council of Ephesus forbade change of meaning, not of word. No agreement was reached. Owing to plague, danger from Milanese troops, and lack of money to pay the Greeks, the council was transferred to Florence on 10 January 1439.

In eight sessions at Florence the Greeks held that the Spirit proceeds from the Father only, the Latins that it proceeds from the Father and Son—without agreement. From 24 March to 27 May there were various negotiations. Then the unionists among the Greeks argued that all saints, as inspired by the one Spirit, cannot err in faith; thus, though Latin and Greek saints express themselves differently about the procession, they must believe the same. Therefore, they argued, the faiths of both churches must be substantially the same. Finally, on 8 June, all the Greek prelates except three freely acknowledged the orthodoxy of the Latin faith. Patriarch Joseph died two days later. In the following weeks the Latins presented statements on the Eucharist, papal primacy (these two were also explained in two public sessions), purgatory, and the addition to the Nicene Creed, all of which, with some modifications, were eventually accepted by the Greeks. The decree of union (*Laetentur caeli*), composed of those statements and an introduction, was signed by the Latins and all but two of the Greek prelates on 5 July, and was promulgated the next day.

The Greeks left shortly afterward. Unions with the Armenians (22 November 1439), with the Copts of Egypt (4 February 1439), with certain Syrians (30 August 1444), and with Chaldeans and Maronites of Cyprus (7 August 1445) followed. The council was transferred in September 1443 to Rome, where it ended, probably on the death of Pope Eugenius in February 1447.

The importance of the Council of Ferrara-Florence lies in its definition of doctrine; in the principle it established, followed in subsequent unions, of unity of faith and equality of rite; in its check of the Latin conciliar movement; and in its leaving the problem of church reform unsolved. The union with the Greeks, freely accepted in Florence, was repudiated by most Greeks on the return home of the delegates. The Armenian union lasted until Caffa fell to the Turks in 1475. Caffa was a Black Sea port on the Crimea and a center for Armenians. Those Armenians who went to Rome and accepted union were from Caffa. For the others who were also party to the agreement, exact information is lacking.

BIBLIOGRAPHY

E. Cecconi, *Studi storici sul Concilio di Firenze*, I (1869); *Concilium Florentinum: Documenta et Scriptores*, 11 vols., esp. V, VI, and IX; Deno J. Geanakoplos, "The Council of Florence (1438–1439) and the Problem of Union between the Greek and Latin Churches," in *Byzantine East and Latin West* (1966), 84–111; Joseph Gill, *The Council of Florence* (1959), with ample bibliography, *Personalities of the Council of Florence* (1964), and *Church Union: Rome and Byzantium (1204–1453)* (Variorum Reprints, 1979); Louis Petit, X. A. Sidéridès, Martin Jugie, eds., *Oeuvres complètes de Georges Scholarios*, 8 vols. (1928–1936); Ambrosius Camaldulensis Traversarius, ... *Latinae epistulae*, Laurentian Mehus, ed. (1759).

JOSEPH GILL, S.J.

[See also **Byzantine Church; Church, Latin: 1305 to 1500; Councils, Western (1311–1449)**.]

FERRER BASSA. See **Bassa, Ferrer.**

FERRER I (THE ELDER), JAIME, an International Style painter in Lérida, active during the first four decades of the fifteenth century, who founded a family of artists with the Ferrer name. His best-known painting is the *Last Supper* (Museo de Solsona), which has similarities to Borrassá's style. His son, Jaime Ferrer II (the Younger), also active in Lérida, showed the influence of the Barcelona painter Martorell.

BIBLIOGRAPHY

Chandler R. Post, *A History of Spanish Painting*, 14 vols. (1930–1966): see especially, "The School of Lerida,"

Last Supper. Jaime Ferrer the Elder, first half of the 15th century; now in the Museo Diocesano, Solsona. ORONOZ

VII, pt. 2, 512–545; José Gudiol Ricart, *Pintura gotica* (1955).

MARY GRIZZARD

[See also **Borrassá, Luis; Gothic, International Style; Martorell, Bernardo.**]

FĒS (also Fez; Arabic: Fās), the Muslim capital of northern Morocco, took the place of the old Roman capital, Volubilis, fifty kilometers to the west. It lies in a side valley of the Sebou where the river emerges from the Middle Atlas, at the junction of the route from Tlemcen to Tangier and Córdoba (which passes through the Taza Gap between the Middle Atlas and the Rif), and the route to Salé on the Atlantic coast. The route from Tlemcen, the highway of the Arab conquest of North Africa and Spain, remained arterial, and fundamental to the commercial and political development of Fēs. The city was founded in 789, in the aftermath of the Kharijite revolt of 739, which left northern Morocco independent of the Arab empire and without a central government. The founder, Idrīs ibn ᶜAbd Allah, was a Ḥasanid refugee from the Abbasids in the Middle East, who with the aid of the chief of Walīla (Volubilis) set out to create his own state in opposition to the Abbasids and their representatives in Ifrīqiya. The city he built on the right bank of the stream, however, may have been abandoned after his death in 795. In 809 his son Idrīs II built a city on the left bank with the name of Al-ᶜĀliya (the high city)—a reference to ᶜAlī and the claims of his descendants to the caliphate.

Al-ᶜĀlīya was a royal fortress, with palace and mosque. Outside, a market became the nucleus of a much bigger settlement of immigrants, the most notable of whom came from Córdoba after 814, and from Qayrawān after 825. The Andalusians settled on the right bank, opposite Al-ᶜĀliya, and the Qayrawanians (al-Qarawiyyīn) on the left bank below it. Thus began the division of the city into two unequal parts—the smaller Andalusian bank and the larger Qayrawanian bank, each with its great mosque, the Andalusian and the Qarawiyyīn (Karaouiyine). With this rapid growth, Fēs became the most important city of northern Morocco in the ninth century, though after the death of Idrīs II, in 828, it was no more than one of a number of capitals of princes of the Idrisid dynasty. In the tenth century it was central to the repeated attempts of the Fatimids of Ifrīqiya and the Umayyads of Al-Andalus to extend their dominion over northern Morocco, being variously ruled by Idrisids, Berber chiefs, and governors appointed by the two rival caliphates. The disappearance of both caliphates from the Maghrib in the eleventh century, however, left the city in the hands of Zanāta Berber princes, who were the principal beneficiaries of their conflict.

Fēs was patronized by the Umayyads of Córdoba, who caused the Qarawiyyīn Mosque to be rebuilt in 956 on a scale probably commensurate with the growth of the population. This growth was resumed under the Almoravids, who conquered the city in the 1070's, making it, together with Marrakesh and Tlemcen, one of the three capitals of their empire in North Africa. Walls were built, corresponding roughly to the present *enceinte,* and a new citadel upstream on the left bank. In 1135 the Qarawiyyīn Mosque was enlarged still further, rebuilt in its present form (in Andalusian style) in close association with the Qayṣarīya (central souk). Royal patronage continued under the succeeding dynasty of the Almohads, who built the present walls and rebuilt the Andalusian Mosque at the beginning of the thirteenth century. Fēs was then the residence of an Almohad prince who ruled northern Morocco on behalf of the Almohad caliph. An important route now ran south across the Middle Atlas and the upper Moulouya to Sijilmāsa in the Tafilelt, thus enhancing the crucial position of the city. But its greatest period followed the collapse of the Almohad empire in Spain and North Africa (1212–1269), when it was the capital of the Marinids.

The Marinids were Berbers from the Tafilelt and Moulouya region who captured Fēs from the Almohads in 1248, confirming their hold on the city with the drastic suppression of a revolt in 1254. Distancing themselves from their subjects, in 1276 they began to build a large and heavily fortified palace-city in place of the citadel, and still further upstream. The palace-city, analogous to the Alhambra of Granada, became known as Fās al-Jadīd (New Fēs), while the city itself was called Fās al-Bālī (Old Fēs). Fēs profited from its metropolitan character to grow still further, both within and without the walls, until, by the end of the fifteenth century, suburbs had appeared outside the walls. Even before the fall of Granada in 1492, it probably received immigrants from Al-Andalus. An important Jewish community developed, together with one of converted Jews called Muhājirūn (emigrants), subsequently Bildiyyīn. To the trade of the city was added scholarship, as Fēs became a major center of Islamic learning. The aristocrats of the old town were the *shurafāʾ* (sing. *sharīf*), the "nobles" who claimed descent from the Prophet, and specifically from Idrīs, the founder of the city. By the fourteenth century the cult of Idrīs and the position of the Idrisid *shurafāʾ* were well established.

By neglecting the two great mosques the Marinids attempted to reduce the influence and the ability of the *shurafāʾ* and the scholars to oppose the dynasty. Instead, they created six madrasas or colleges of the sciences, with a seventh at New Fēs, to bring students from all over Morocco and train a more loyal scholarly and clerical elite. These madrasas (al-Ṣaffārīn, 1271; al-Ṣahrīj, 1321; al-Ṣabaʿiyyīn and al-ʿAṭṭārīn, 1323; al-Miṣbāḥiyya, 1346; Bū-ʿInāniya, 1350) are masterpieces of architecture, but during the decline of the dynasty after 1359 they failed to prevent the consolidation of political opposition in Old Fēs. The importance of the Idrisid *shurafāʾ* was finally recognized in 1437, when the body of Idrīs II was miraculously discovered at Fēs and the present shrine was founded, with the participation of the Marinid vizier, Abū Zakariyāʾ al-Waṭṭāsī. When the Wattasids fell from power in 1458, the Marinid sultan ʿAbd al-Ḥaqq turned to the Jews, now installed in a ghetto at New Fēs, and to the Muhājirūn.

In 1465, however, the *shurafāʾ* led a popular rebellion in which ʿAbd al-Ḥaqq was killed. Fēs was then ruled by the leader of the *shurafāʾ*, Muḥammad ibn ʿImrān al-Jūtī, until 1472, when the Wattasids regained power. Fēs continued as the capital, even though the south of Morocco was now independent, and after the fall of Granada in 1492, profited from the arrival of numerous refugees. At the beginning of the sixteenth century, one such refugee, Leo Africanus, who was educated at Fēs, bore witness to its size and prosperity.

BIBLIOGRAPHY

Mercedes Garcia-Arenal, "The Revolution of Fās in 869/1465 and the Death of Sultan ʿAbd al-Ḥaqq al-Marīnī," in *Bulletin of the School of Oriental and African Studies,* **41** (1978); Roger Le Tourneau, *Fes avant le protectorat* (1949), and *Fez in the Age of the Marinides* (1961); Johannes Leo Africanus, *Historie of Africa* (1600); M. Schatzmiller, *L'historiographie merinide* (1982).

MICHAEL BRETT

[See also **Almohads; Almoravids; Berbers; Fatimids; Idrisids; Ifrīqiya; Marinids; Umayyads.**]

FESTIVALS. See **Feasts and Festivals.**

FET DES ROMAINS, LI (The deeds of the Romans), was compiled around 1213, probably in the court of Philip II Augustus, by an anonymous clerical translator. This early example of French prose translation converted into the vernacular all the books of Caesar's *Commentarii de bello gallico* and of Lucan's *Bellum civile,* Suetonius' *Vitae Caesarum* I, and Sallust's *Catilina.* It used, to a lesser degree, Flavius Josephus' *Bellum Judaicum,* Peter Comestor's *Historia,* St. Augustine, Isidore of Seville, and the author's own inventions. The prologue announces the translator's intention to provide a complete history of Rome from Julius Caesar to Domitian, undoubtedly on the model of Suetonius' *Vitae.* Only the life of Caesar survives, and perhaps the remaining emperors were never treated. In the manuscripts the work is variously titled *li Fet des Romains, li Livre de Julius Cesar, li Livre de Cesar,* or *la Grant hystoire Cesar.* A few manuscripts supplement Caesar's biography with continuations from other sources.

The translator followed the Latin histories fairly closely, especially the *Bellum gallicum* (which he did not know to have been written by Caesar, and attributed to "Julius Celsus"). He made no attempt to imitate the varying styles of the sources, but his own prose style shows marked variations (for example, between the sustained explication of the prologue and the epic-inspired battle interpolations introduced to supplement gaps in the material).

Thus, the translator was responsive to the literary tastes of a public that continued to enjoy the chanson de geste, despite the fact that his work had functions beyond amusement. He expressly claims its didactic and moral usefulness—"because from the deeds of the Romans one can learn how to do good and to avoid evil." Undoubtedly Caesar's success in building an empire had a political use also. The translator twice points out similarities of behavior between Julius and his own king, "monseignor Phelipe le roi de France." It is evident that the production of *li Fet des Romains* on the eve of the Battle of Bouvines was a magnificent piece of propaganda for the aspirations of Philip Augustus (as he was later to be called). But the survival of *li Fet des Romains* in more than sixty manuscripts scattered over Europe demonstrates its universal appeal throughout the Middle Ages.

BIBLIOGRAPHY

Jeanette M. A. Beer, *A Medieval Caesar* (1976); Louis-Fernand Flutre, *Li fait des Romains dans les littératures française et italienne du XIIIe au XVIe siècle* (1932); Louis-Fernand Flutre and Kornelis Sneyders de Vogel, eds., *Les fet des Romains* (1938).

JEANETTE M. A. BEER

[See also **French Literature: After 1200; Philip II Augustus; Translations and Translators, French.**]

FEUDALISM is a difficult concept to define. The word "feudal" was first used in the seventeenth century, when the social phenomena it purported to describe either had vanished or were decaying rapidly. It was a pejorative word, applied to almost any privilege or custom that seemed unfair or ridiculous. The English novelist Smollett made fun of it in his *Humphry Clinker* (1771): "Every peculiarity of policy, custom and even temperament is traced to this ori-

gin. . . . I expect to see the use of trunk-hose and buttered ale ascribed to the influence of the feudal system." At the other end of the time scale, no writer in the period in which "feudalism" was supposed to have flourished ever used the word itself.

To be fair to the antiquaries of the seventeenth and eighteenth centuries, they were trying to understand the survival of institutions that were difficult to harmonize with prevailing political theory. Restraints on the power of the sovereign, the possession of public authority by private persons, and peculiar rules about the use and transfer of real estate did not fit with belief in the sovereign state or in the sanctity of private property. Most of these annoying peculiarities seemed to be associated in some way with the medieval institution of the fief (*feodum* in Latin); hence, they were lumped together under the name of feudalism.

This usage was not entirely wrong; the fief did have an important role in the political and social structures of western Europe in the Middle Ages. Other elements of what we call feudalism, however, came into existence before the fief. First was the armed retainer, who was bound to his superior by a private agreement and whose primary loyalty was to a lord who rewarded him with gifts and booty. Such retainers might exist even in a fairly well-organized state such as the late Roman Empire, but they could also exist when there was only the shadow of a state or no state at all. Then there was the fragmentation of political authority. The Roman Empire in the West broke up in the fifth century and was divided into Germanic kingdoms. The kingdoms, in turn, tended to break into smaller units as they were divided among heirs of the ruling familes, and as the county became an important unit of goverment. The process was halted, and even temporarily reversed, by the Frankish kings of the Carolingian family, but it speeded up with new invasions by Muslims, Northmen, and Magyars.

In many places counties crumbled into even smaller units, the castellanies (districts controlled by the lord of a castle). In others the counts kept control of their regions but let most rights of local government pass to the lords of castles. In England and in Germany the king preserved some real authority, although dukes and counts (earls in England) had to be given a considerable amount of local jurisdiction. In general, however, the counts and lords of castles were practically independent rulers of their districts, and they treated their rights of government as private possessions. These rights could be inherited by their sons or given as marriage portions to their daughters. Eventually counties and castellanies could be sold or mortgaged, just as a large ranch might be sold or mortgaged today.

It was at this point that the fief became an essential element in the political pattern. At the lower level the armed retainer had to have arms, armor, a place to live, and some support for his old age. Some of these retainers had small holdings of their own, but these were seldom large enough to meet all their needs. Others were originally companions in their lord's home, or at least lived clustered around his dwelling place; such household knights can be found in the retinues of all important lords throughout the Middle Ages. There were, however, difficulties in such an arrangement. Early castles were not very large; it must have been a nuisance to house and feed numbers of hungry, boisterous, quarrelsome fighting men year after year. Moreover, the young knight (as he was soon to be called) must have wanted to marry and to have a home of his own, an independent income, and some time to spend on his own affairs. The obvious solution was to give him a homestead, with sufficient income to support him and his family. Some of the early homesteads were small, but by the twelfth century such a grant usually took the form of an estate worked by peasants, over whom the holder had the right of ban (command). The peasants paid rent for their land, worked lands reserved for the grantee, and also paid various dues for the use of common utilities such as mills, ovens, winepresses, and markets.

This grant of an estate and the powers that went with it was called a fief, and the holder of a fief was a vassal. Fiefs could be inherited very much as the great lordships were, but they reverted to the donor or his heirs if the vassal failed to do service or to produce a descendant to take his place, or if he betrayed or fought against his lord. The holder of a fief owed military service—unlimited at first, but later reduced to a fixed number of days per year (often forty days). Service was quite often limited to the region in which the lord's castle lay or to expeditions in which the lord took part. The vassal was required to attend the lord's court, which was both a court of justice and an administrative council. He also owed monetary contributions when his lord faced an emergency or a great expense, such as a crusade, ransom, or the knighting of an eldest son or marriage of a daughter (both occasions of very elaborate festivities).

These services were called feudal aids. A powerful lord could also ask for an extraordinary aid if he were involved in any prolonged military operation. Finally, while the vassal's heir inherited his fief, the new tenant had to pay relief, a large sum of money often equal to a year's income, as a sign of the lord's ultimate right to the holding. If the heir was underage, he was a ward of the lord. The lord could take the income from the fief and raise the heir in his household, or he could grant the wardship and income to one of his vassals. If the only heir was a daughter, the lord also decided whom she should marry. This would prevent an enemy from gaining control of the fief, but it was also a source of income. Men would pay large sums to gain the right to marry a rich heiress; heiresses were also known to pay large sums to avoid marriage to a man they disliked.

Thus, at the local level of a count or a lord of an important castle, feudalism was a system of government in which the lord possessed military and administrative power in his district and was aided by vassals who owed him service in his army and in his court. Government had become a private possession. It was regulated by agreements between lords and vassals. This did not mean that local government was completely arbitrary; each district, even each village, had its own customs, which were generally respected. Nevertheless, there are enough complaints by the weaker classes—clergy, minor vassals, and peasants—to suggest that a good many lords tried to increase their power and their income by simple usurpation. They took away grants they had previously made to churches and vassals and demanded increased services and payments from their peasants.

There were obvious disadvantages—psychological, military, and economic—to a system in which the effective unit of government was only the small county or castellany. Such small political units were not entirely self-sufficient. They could not protect themselves against invasion by more powerful neighbors, and they had to import many of their supplies. Wine could not be produced everywhere; grain crops could fail; not every region had its own deposits of iron and copper; even millstones were scarce in many places. The memory of larger units, such as empires and kingdoms, had not entirely faded, and indeed the anointed king still existed. He had prestige, if little power, and it was the king who had, by his appointment of counts, created the families that now claimed hereditary rights of government. Thus it is understandable that a second layer of feudalism existed above the first working layer of the local lord and his vassals.

There has been a long and inconclusive argument as to whether the great lords were from the beginning vassals of the king. The great lords certainly were in theory subordinate to the king and they swore fidelity to him, but fidelity is not homage (the act of becoming the "man" [*homo*] of a superior). Some of the lords were royal officials who became more or less independent, such as the count of Anjou, but others had created their own principalities, such as the duke of Normandy, and were simply seeking official acceptance of their already existing power. In practice the king had little control over them. They might assist him, when they wished; they might attend his court on great occasions; but they did as they pleased in their own lands. Eventually most of the great men did do homage and become vassals of the king. But the vassalage of a duke of Normandy or of a count of Flanders was rather different from that of a simple knight to his lord. It was, as Lemarignier has pointed out, more like a nonaggression pact. The duke or count would not hurt the king if the king would not hurt him. They seldom if ever attended his court; they rarely assisted him in his wars; but through the fiction that the great lordships were fiefs and the great lords vassals, the theoretical unity of the kingdom was preserved. Flanders and Normandy were part of France, though it took several centuries before this had much significance. Nevertheless, the fact that the lords of these principalities were vassals gave the king, in the end, an excuse to confiscate all of Normandy and part of Flanders.

There were, therefore, two levels of feudalism—the working level of the county or large castellany where the vassals owed real service to the lord and were on the whole obedient to him, and the level of the kingdom, where vassalage was symbolic and where the great lords were, at best, allies and not subordinates.

The pattern of feudalism that has just been described developed first and most completely in France; it spilled over into western Germany, parts of Italy and Spain, and—with peculiar results—into England. In Germany the pattern was distorted, east of the Rhine, by the existence of extensive alodial estates, that is, districts held in full ownership by their lords, who therefore owed no service to the king for these lands. Germany also had an open frontier on the east, and lands newly conquered from the Slavs and Balts could not easily be fitted into a feudal pattern. North Italy was at first not unlike France, but the rise of the great trading cities and the

interference of the papacy prevented feudalism from becoming a dominant political force. Naples and Sicily, conquered by Normans, had for several generations a Norman type of feudalism, but the collapse of the Norman kingdom of Sicily attenuated this pattern. In Spain, Catalonia, as part of the Frankish (and, briefly, of the French) kingdom, had feudal institutions, but Spain, like Germany, had an open frontier, and the long struggle with the Moors produced a political pattern unlike that of France.

England, in one sense, exemplified feudalism in its most complete form. Conquered by the duke of Normandy in 1066, the institutions of a duchy were made the institutions of a kingdom. Every foot of land in England was held of the king, either directly by his vassals, or indirectly by the vassals and tenants of the king's vassals. All of England was divided into fiefs. (The chartered towns were not exactly fiefs, but each had a lord, either the king or a man who held the town from the king.) Everyone who held from the king, including bishops and abbots, owed military service, court service, and on occasion financial aid. The whole structure of English government grew out of the court attended by the king's vassals, and that court could give direct orders to any landholder in the realm. France did not have such an integrated system until the end of the twelfth century; Germany and Italy never had it at all.

By contrast, while England was a perfect example of the tenurial side of feudalism, since all land and rights of local government were held from the king, it was a very imperfect example of the fragmentary aspects of feudalism. No English earl (the equivalent of a French count) ever became as independent as the count of Flanders or the duke of Brittany. Even the palatine earls, men who had special privileges because they held exposed border districts such as Durham or Chester, remained obedient to the king. Lesser lords might try to build up their power by carefully arranged marriages, flimsy legal claims, and sporadic acts of violence, but open and sustained private war was impossible. Only in Wales (not yet a part of the kingdom) and in Ireland could adventurous barons hope to establish a semi-independent lordship. Even in these remote areas they were never entirely free from royal supervision.

The English case, however, was only an early example of a trend that affected many parts of western Europe in the twelfth and thirteenth centuries. After all, it was not very profitable or comfortable to be the lord of a small county or castellany. Income from such a holding was not large, and defense against neighbors trying to increase their wealth and power was difficult. Knights were not very eager to come to the aid of their lords. They sought to limit the area in which they would fight and also the number of days of military service they would give. In England, where unpaid service was due for only forty days, English vassals argued strenuously that they were not obliged to serve outside England. In Germany there had to be special rules about accompanying the ruler on his frequent expeditions to Italy.

Another problem arose out of subinfeudation. Take the case of a lord who received a large fief from the king or a duke or a count: he certainly owed service when called. Equally certainly, he would not appear alone, for his dignity required that he be accompanied by a decent retinue. But his common sense required that he leave knights to guard his lands during his absence. How was the balance to be struck? In England and in Normandy the overlord assigned quotas of knights—Richard must bring ten knights when summoned; Gilbert must bring twenty. Elsewhere the obligation was less precise, but nowhere did a superior lord receive all the military service owed by his immediate vassals.

Vassals were quite willing to serve longer, and to bring more knights with them, if they were paid. A great lord could also hire knights or men-at-arms who were not his vassals. Only lords with a fairly large income, however, could use these expedients. The others could obtain help only by calling on a higher lord. If the higher lord was the lord of both the parties to a dispute, he could summon them to his court and impose a settlement. Otherwise he could give military support to his vassal. In either case the vassal became more dependent on his lord and more obedient to orders from his superior.

A variant on this theme was the protection of bishops and abbots who were being annoyed by neighboring lords. Churchmen held vast estates in many parts of western Europe; they frequently had rights of secular administration and justice in these lands. They even had vassals who owed them military service, but seldom enough vassals to fully protect their holdings. A neighboring lord might promise to be the protector of church lands, but often he tried to change his duty of protection into a right of lordship. It was far safer for the church to appeal to a king or a powerful count for protection. It was the duty of these great men to protect the church; it was also to their advantage. If they could force a greedy local lord to renounce unjustified claims, either by an order of their court or by a military operation (often by a combination of the two), they demonstrated that they had authority outside the lands they ruled directly. They were beginning to put an end to the fragmentation of political power that marked the early period of feudalism.

Efficient procedures in the lord's court were just as necessary in ending excessive fragmentation as was increased military power. No overlord, not even a king, could keep an army of occupation in disputed territories year after year. There had to be legal procedures that would persuade the greater part of the military class to accept the solution imposed by the overlord, whether it was confirmation of earlier agreements, division among claimants, or complete denial of the rights of one claimant. These legal procedures were based largely on the concept of *seisin* (possession). The claimant who could show that he had held certain lands and rights of government for a reasonable length of time (the period varied from place to place) had a claim that was hard to dispute.

Proof of ownership was much more difficult to establish. In the first place, in strict feudal theory (such as one finds in the English Domesday Book) no one owned lands or rights of government; he simply held them of some superior. (Even a king might be said to hold his kingdom of God.) Second, very few lay lords had documents to prove their claims. Churchmen did, and sometimes were able to prove their rights by producing charters or copies of charters. But not many laymen had charters before the thirteenth century and charters had been lost; and copies could also be forged or at least heavily interpolated. Proof of *seisin*, by contrast, could be established by witnesses taken almost at random. Everyone in a village knew who had received the rents and services that they owed or who took the fines levied in the local court. Thus in many cases it was easy to establish the facts. The lord would call some of his men together, who would hear the reports and reach a decision. Often the defeated claimant would immediately drop his suit; if not, the lord was justified in calling on his vassals to enforce the decision of the court. After all, it was their decision, since they (or some of them) were the court. The lord, or his deputy, was merely the presiding officer.

Thus out of the fragmentation of early feudalism came reconsolidation. The process was most effective in England, where there had never been real fragmentation, and in France. It was less complete in Germany, where many petty lordships remained virtually indpendent until the time of Napoleon, and in

Italy, where the rise of wealthy and powerful communes created regional urban centers of power. Nevertheless, by 1500 much of western Europe was no longer feudal in the sense of fragmentation of political power. Europe was divided into sovereign states, some quite large, such as the kingdom of France, some quite small, such as the petty German principalities. Large or small, however, the old terms of lord and vassal, fief and rear-fief (a fief granted by a man who already held the land from his lord), had become almost meaningless.

Why, then, was "feudalism" discovered only in the seventeenth and eighteenth centuries? This was because, in the process of consolidation into sovereign states, the fief holders had been allowed to retain certain social and economic privileges. Kings still needed the assistance of the landholding class. They could not have dealt with the petty problems of village communities; they could not have policed vast areas with their tiny standing armies (no army in England, and one of only about 25,000 men in France as late as 1300); they could not have found a sufficient number of administrators in their own domains. Moreover, the kings (or the princes in Germany) were brought up in aristocratic courts. The men they knew, and with whom they felt comfortable, were the nobles. There was no absolute bar against middle-class officials rising to the top, but if they did they were sooner or later ennobled. A noble was, almost always, a landlord. As a landlord, he collected not only rents for the use of his land but also payments for the use of utilities on his land. He often had the right to hold a private court for petty offenses, or, as in England, he would be almost automatically one of the justices in a public court (justice of the peace). In many places he could still require certain unpaid services from his tenants—plowing his land, carrying his produce to market, repairing roads and bridges.

These privileges were remnants of feudalism, but they were only remnants. No peer in England, no count or marquis in France was a completely independent ruler of the lands that paid him rent. But precisely because these remnants of feudalism seemed so useless and so out of place in a Europe where the sovereign state was the basic political entity and the free market the ideal of the economists, the reformers of the eighteenth century began to apply the term "feudalism" to what had become essentially landlordism.

Their mistake has caused endless confusion. Almost every society has had landlords who profited from the labors of their tenants or slaves. Feudal lords were also landlords; they profited from rents and services of their tenants long after they had lost independent political power. The ancient Middle East, the Roman Empire, the American South before the Civil War, even a communist state with collective farms would all fit this definition. By contrast, as recent studies have shown, feudalism in the sense of a prolonged period in which public power is in private hands, in which basic powers of government (justice and defense) are controlled by private contracts, is rare. It was the possession of political power—the right to command—that gave medieval landlords such opportunities to take services and payments from their peasants. Feudalism, in this sense, certainly existed in Japan in the period of the shoguns; it may have existed in nineteenth-century Ethiopia; it certainly did not exist in its fully developed form anywhere else (though protofeudal and semifeudal institutions appeared in a number of decaying polities). It is precisely because fully developed feudalism was so rare that the western European political experience led to an unusual type of state—a state in which the sovereign's powers were limited by law and by private rights, which were the legitimate, if much altered, relics of feudal privileges.

BIBLIOGRAPHY
Marc Bloch, *Feudal Society,* L. A. Manyon, trans. (1961); Constance Bouchard, "The Origins of the French Nobility: A Reassessment," in *American Historical Review,*" 86 (1981); Robert Boutruche, *Seigneurie et féodalité* (1959–); Joseph Calmette, *La société féodale,* 7th ed. (1952); Rushton Coulborn, ed., *Feudalism in History* (1956); Georges Duby, "Un enquête à poursuivre: La noblesse dans la France médiévale," in *Revue historique,* 226 (1961); *La société aux XIe et XIIe siècles dans la région mâconnaise* (1953), and *Hommes et structures du moyen âge* (1973); École française de Rome, *Structures féodales et féodalisme dans l'Occident méditerranéan: X[e]–XIIIe siècles* (1980); Guy Forquin, *Lordship and Feudalism in the Middle Ages,* Iris and A. L. Lytton Sells, trans. (1976); François L. Ganshof, *Feudalism,* Philip Grierson, trans., 3rd ed. (1964), "L'origine des rapports féodo-vassaliques," in *I problemi della civiltà carolingia* (1954), and "Les relations féodo-vassaliques aux temps post-carolingiens," in *I problemi communi dell'Europa post-carolingia* (1955), the latter two published in the Settimane di studio del Centro italiano di studi sull'alto medioevo.

Paul Guilhiermoz, *Essai sur l'origine de la noblesse en France au moyen âge* (1902); Walther Kienast, *Untertaneneid und Treuvorbehalt* (1952); Jean François Lemarignier, "La dislocation du pages," in *Mélanges Halphen* (1951), "Les fidèles du roi de France," in *Recueil Clovis*

Brunel (1955), and "Structures monastiques et structures politiques de la France de la fin du Xᵉ et des débuts du XIᵉ siècles," in *I monachismo nell'alto medievo* (1957); Heinrich Mitteis, *Der Staat des hohen Mittelalters,* 5th ed. (1955); Charles Odegaard, *Vassi and Fideles in the Carolingian Empire* (1945); Charles Petit-Dutaillis, *The Feudal Monarchy in France and England,* E. D. Hunt, trans. (1936); Jean-Pierre Poly and Eric Bournazel, *La mutation féodale* (1980), the best study of feudal origins to date; John H. Round, *Feudal England* (1909); Frank M. Stenton, *The First Century of English Feudalism* (1932); Carl Stephenson, *Mediaeval Feudalism* (1942); Joseph R. Strayer, *Feudalism* (1965); Karl F. Werner, "Untersuchungen zur Frühzeit des französischen Fürstentums (9.–10. Jahrhundert)," in *Die Welt als Geschichte,* **18–20** (1958–1960).

JOSEPH R. STRAYER

[See also **Allod; Ban, Banalité; Benefice, Lay; Castellan; Class Structure, Western; County; Escheat; Fief; Homage; Inheritance, Western European; Knights and Knight Service; Land Tenure, Western European; Political Theory, Western European; Scutage; Seisin, Disseisin.**]

FEZ. See **Fès.**

FIBULA, an ornamental clasp or brooch fastened with a pin restrained by a guard (somewhat like a safety pin), usually used to hold clothing together. The migratory tribes moving across Europe during the third through seventh centuries—for whom fibulae often seem to have had some sort of apotropaic function—developed numerous varieties, usually in precious metals and often encrusted with gems. Round fibulae are simple circular brooches; eagle fibulae, frequently worn in pairs, present the bird with its body en face and its head turned in profile and apparently commemorate the eagle's association with the sun, which was worshiped by the pagan tribes; looped fibulae have a large, semicircular end separated from the tail bar by a projecting curved band (the loop) slightly narrower than the tail.

BIBLIOGRAPHY

Jean Hubert, Jean Porcher, and W. F. Volbach, *Europe in the Dark Ages* (1969), 215–243; Marvin Ross and Philippe Verdier, *Arts of the Migration Period in the Walters Art Gallery* (1961), 15–23.

LESLIE BRUBAKER

[See also **Gems and Jewelry.**]

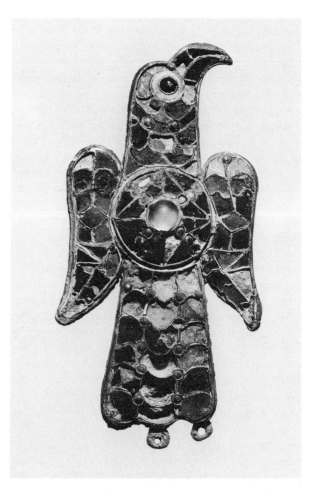

Fibula in the shape of an eagle. Gilded bronze, inlaid with colored stones, 6th century, found in Tierra de Barros, Estremadura. BALTIMORE, WALTERS ART GALLERY

FIEF is probably derived from a Germanic word meaning "cattle" (modern German: *vieh*), and by extension any sort of transferable property (compare in English "cattle" and "chattel"). In the earliest Latin examples the word is spelled *feo, feus, fevum.* Forms with *d,* such as *feudum,* are late. A fief was a grant made to a dependent in return for his support and services. Gradually it came to have much the same meaning as "benefice," and the service to be rendered was made more specific; usually it was military or administrative in nature. It was more convenient for a lord to grant his adherents, such as knights and ministerials, something that would produce a steady income than to support them in his household or to make yearly gifts.

A fief could be any revenue-producing right or property. The obvious and most common grant was that of an estate—a village or part of a village with its peasants, the dues and labor services owed by the peasants, and the produce of the lands worked for the benefit of the lord. There were also intangible rights—the right to hold a court for petty offenses, to take a profit from the local mill or winepress or oven, and often the right to select the village priest. The more important the fief holder was, the more estates he held, and the greater were his rights of government. A lord of middling importance might have several knights under him and wield rights of justice over major crimes, and receive profits from tolls and marketplaces. A lord who was a count or a duke might hold his county or duchy as a fief but in practice could be an almost independent ruler. He could settle disputes among lesser fief holders and even confiscate their estates for failure to give service or for open opposition to his policies.

Fiefs were not originally hereditary grants. They were made for the lifetime of the holder, or for his life and that of a specified descendant (or descendants). There was, however, a strong tendency to favor hereditary succession. A man should hold what his ancestors held, whether it was land or office; the knowledge that a certain fief would be held by a certain family saved trouble and uncertainty. Thus, while on the death of the holder the fief legally reverted to the lord who had granted it, it became customary to regrant the fief to the nearest heir. As a token of the lord's basic right, however, the new holder of the fief paid relief (from *relever,* to pick up again) to the lord. In the High Middle Ages, relief was often equal to a year's income from the fief.

There were not many problems if the heir was a son, grandson, or nephew, though it was not entirely clear whether a grandson descended from a deceased elder son had a stronger claim than his uncle, who would be a younger son but older and more experienced than the grandson. The "wicked uncle" was not just a legend; King John of England ignored the rights of his nephew Arthur (the son of John's elder brother) and eventually was accused of having the young man put to death. Another problem arose when the fief holder had married twice and a son by the second marriage claimed that the first marriage had been invalid.

There were many more problems if the nearest heir was a remote cousin (for there were always other cousins with competing claims) or a daughter. In England and northern France strict male primogeniture was the rule, but this did not prevent a war between Matilda, the daughter of Henry I, and his nephew Stephen, and in the end the daughter gained Normandy and her son became king of England. If, however, daughters were the only heirs, the holdings would be divided equally among them, though the eldest would receive the chief residence and in some areas the whole fief. Even then the daughters' fiefs would be administered by their husbands, though they could descend only to the children of the heiress.

Few families were fortunate enough to produce an unbroken line of male heirs, and there were many disputed successions. Legal and military controversies, however, did not change the rule that fiefs were hereditary; they simply decided who was to inherit the fief. Only in the case of the extinction of a lineage would a fief revert to the heir of the original grantor.

Two unusual types of fief appeared in the later Middle Ages. The first would include a whole kingdom held of the pope, the emperor, or a neighboring king. Thus the kingdom of Sicily was a fief of the papacy, which gave thirteenth-century popes an excuse to intervene, first to protect the rights of the young Frederick II to the kingdom, and later to deprive Frederick and his heirs of the kingdom for disobedience. During the same century England was officially a fief of the papacy, as a result of an agreement that King John had made in ending his quarrel with Innocent III. Reflecting its status as a fief, England paid the pope an annual tribute of 1,000 marks (though it fell into arrears after 1333, and was formally repudiated by parliament in 1366), and the papal legate, as representative of the overlord, had considerable influence during the minority of John's son, Henry III. At the same time, however, England was claiming Scotland as a fief held of the English crown, and this gave Edward I an excuse for deciding who should be king of Scotland during a disputed succession in the 1290's. The German emperors tried to make kings on their eastern borders admit that their realms were held as German fiefs. This tactic had little permanent effect in Hungary except to give an excuse for occasional German intervention in the affairs of the kingdom; but Bohemia, while it was practically independent, was nevertheless part of the empire.

The other unusual type of fief, the money fief, became common only in the twelfth century. It was used primarily as a means of gaining military and diplomatic support; in return for an annual payment, the recipient promised to aid the donor, often with a specific number of men.

The duties of a fief holder, discussed more fully under "Feudalism," were basically to give assistance in war, in government, and in financial emergencies (such as helping to pay the ransom of a lord who had been captured). It was, of course, easier to secure real service from the holder of a small fief than from the ruler of a duchy or a county. This was one reason for the strength of the central government in England, where there were no fiefs as large or as populous as Flanders or Aquitaine. On the Continent, however, the relationship of the holder of a great fief to his nominal superior was at best that of an ally, sometimes that of a more or less friendly neighbor, and frequently that of a competitor for lands and power. Normandy was a fief held of the king of France, but until the end of the twelfth century the most that the king could gain from this relationship was a tenuous nonaggression pact. Yet in the long run, the fact that Normandy was a fief did turn to the king's advantage. When Philip II Augustus of France defeated John, king of England and duke of Normandy, the French ruler could quite legitimately confiscate the fief, for John had not fulfilled his obligations as a fief holder; notably, he had not obeyed a summons to the king's court.

There are other examples: in 1180 the emperor Frederick Barbarossa confiscated the fiefs of the duke of Saxony and Bavaria for failure to give military service, and in 1265 the papacy transferred the kingdom of Sicily from the Hohenstaufen to Charles of Anjou for persistent disobedience and hostility. On the whole, however, such confiscations were rare. The king of France could take Normandy, but in spite of repeated wars he never succeeded in taking Flanders. There was a strong and natural prejudice among the upper classes against dispossessing long-established families from their lordships. The usual result of a quarrel between an overlord and the holder of a great fief was a compromise. The lord would receive some land or money; the fief holder could keep the larger part of his fief. Thus large fiefs tended to retain their identities. Smaller fiefs were less durable; they could be combined, divided among heirs, exchanged, or (by the thirteenth century) sold or seized by an overlord when there were no close heirs. But while there might be changes in the size of a fief or in its relationship to other fiefs, the land and rights associated with it continued to be a social and economic entity. A wealthy lord might hold many districts, each of which had once been a separate fief, but the customs and dues in each district would not be identical.

In northwestern Europe—England, Normandy, northern France, the Low Countries, the Rhineland area—almost all rural lands and the rights associated with landholding were held as fiefs. (Smaller towns could be included in a fief; the larger ones gained some rights of self-government.) In this region the French slogan "nul terre sans seigneur" (no land without a lord) was almost universally true. Farther south, in southern France, Italy, and the Iberian peninsula, there were many alods (lands held in full ownership), but even in this area fiefs were common, and alods were frequently turned into fiefs. In central Europe there were fiefs, but there were also large regions that owed no feudal services. Thus when the duke of Saxony lost his duchy in the thirteenth century, his heirs kept an extensive area around Brunswick that had owed no service to the emperor. Fiefs became even more scarce as one moved east into regions where Baltic, Magyar, and Slavic traditions were strong. In Russia alodial property was the rule. The *pomestye* (land granted in return for service) had some of the characteristics of a fief, but it appeared only in the fourteenth century. While it became more common in the fifteenth and sixteenth centuries, it never had the political and institutional importance of the Western fief.

BIBLIOGRAPHY

Most of the books listed in the bibliography to "Feudalism," above, discuss the fief. For the Russian *pomestye*, see Jerome Blum, *Lord and Peasant in Russia from the Ninth to the Nineteenth Century* (1961). Jean François Lemarignier discusses feudal agreements between lords of approximately equal power in his *Recherches sur l'hommage en marches et les frontières féodales* (1945).

JOSEPH R. STRAYER

[See also **Allod; Benefice, Lay; Feudalism; Inheritance, Western European; John, King of England; Land Tenure, Western European; Seisin, Disseisin; Sicily; Kingdom of.**]

FIEF, MONEY. Unlike the classic fief of land, the money fief (called also the *fief-rente*) usually consisted of an annual sum of money paid by a lord to a vassal in return for homage and fealty, military service (customarily knight service), and various feudal obligations and services. Instead of money there could also be payment in kind, such as grain, wine, chickens, and wood. In general, customary rules of feudal tenure applied to the money fief. The economic revival of Europe in the late tenth and eleventh centuries gave feudal lords and princes the pecuniary resources needed to grant fiefs of money. Appearing first in the late tenth century, money fiefs increased in the eleventh century and again in the twelfth. They reached their highest number, some thousands, in the thirteenth and fourteenth centuries. Then, sharply declining, the money fief disappeared as a feudal institution by the middle of the fifteenth century. Though most prevalent in England, France, the Low Countries, and Rhenish Germany, the money fief existed also in northern Italy, the Norman kingdom of Sicily, and the Latin states of the crusaders. It developed only in areas that had been feudalized, and flourished in those feudal states most affected by the revived money economy.

Feudal lords, traditionally dependent on granting fiefs of land for obtaining military service, could now easily secure additional service by granting money fiefs, limited as to number and value only by the lords' financial resources. The money fief enabled lords who had depleted their landed domains to obtain more vassals and service. During the twelfth, thirteenth, and fourteenth centuries the English and French kings, the counts of Flanders and Champagne, the dukes of Brabant, and Low Country and Rhenish bishops and archbishops obtained a considerable amount of their military service by means of the money fief. John, Edward I, and Edward III of England, and Philip II Augustus and Philip IV the Fair of France constructed military alliances by granting money fiefs to Low Country and German lords.

Money fiefs were also employed as a diplomatic instrument to win the friendship or neutrality of important lords or to obtain valuable information from individuals well placed in Rome or at princely courts. Lords often used agents, themselves remunerated with money fiefs, to act as brokers to secure military and political service from others by promising them money fiefs. Grants of money fiefs also induced lords to make their castles available in time of war, to provide castle guard, or to furnish supplies. Sometimes lords received money fiefs as a bonus if they would do homage for their fiefs of land. Princes would reward favorites and officials with money fiefs, sometimes only until they could provide them with fiefs of land of equal annual value.

Money fiefs were mostly paid in semiannual installments by the principal treasuries, such as the English Exchequer or wardrobe, but could also be paid by local officials directly from specified sources of revenue, such as tolls and customs. In the thir-

teenth and fourteenth centuries, acting on behalf of the grantors, merchants and bankers paid money fiefs. Without landed or geographical limitations, the money fief facilitated and widened feudal relations. The great princes contracted feudal ties with vassals for all sorts of purposes all over western Europe. Grantors often never saw their vassals, who did homage and received investiture of their money fiefs from intermediaries empowered to make the necessary arrangements. In small states such as Flanders, with meager landed resources but ample money derived from trade and industry, money fiefs enabled the counts to obtain military and political service far in excess of what they could have obtained if limited to fiefs of land.

The money fief remained a prominent feudal institution into the fourteenth century, and kept feudalism viable considerably longer than if it had depended solely on land. During the fourteenth and fifteenth centuries the money fief yielded to nonfeudal fees or pensions. It was, in fact, the feudal antecedent of the indenture system, whereby nonfeudal contracts provided for the payment of fees and wages in return for military and political services. The revival of money that made possible the money fief also brought changes in institutions and outlook that eventually resulted in its demise.

BIBLIOGRAPHY

The principal studies on the money fief are Bryce Lyon, "The Money Fief Under the English Kings, 1066–1485," in *English Historical Review,* **66** (1951), "The Feudal Antecedent of the Indenture System," in *Speculum,* **29** (1954), "The *Fief-Rente* in the Low Countries: An Evaluation," in *Revue belge de philologie et d'histoire,* **32** (1954), and *From Fief to Indenture* (1957). See also Michał Sczaniecki, *Essai sur les fiefs-rentes* (1946).

BRYCE LYON

[See also **Feudalism; Fief.**]

FIELD SYSTEMS, a term applied to regular patterns in the distribution of land for agricultural purposes that are accompanied by rules of cultivation and grazing imposed by a community of landholders on its members. "System" might seem to imply the existence of a set of regulations arbitrarily imposed on farming communities, obliging them to lay out their land and use it in a fairly uniform way. In fact, the field systems of different villages prove to be extremely varied when examined in detail. But in general they display many common elements, and it is these that permit classification.

The most widespread in Europe was the common-field system, under which individual landholders held scattered strips of arable land and of meadow, and shared in the collective use of common pasture and waste. Rotations of crops were agreed for the arable fields by the community, but individuals took their crops of hay and grain from their own strips. After harvest all land was grazed in common by the livestock of all landholders. Within this general framework the exact rules laid down by different village communities varied greatly. In England the agreed rotation might be a two-course of crop and fallow (in harsh climates this would mean spring grain only and a fallow); a three-course; or, on fertile soils, a four-course of three crops with one fallow. The grazing of the pastures and herbage in the meadows and arable fields might be allowed without stint, or controlled by specifying exactly how many cattle, sheep, and horses could be grazed by each farmer possessing a holding of a certain size. Regulations are first illustrated in manorial bylaws of the thirteenth century. Many later examples show communities altering the rules, temporarily or permanently, to meet changing conditions. The system was sufficiently flexible to permit clover, sainfoin, turnips, saffron, and vegetables to be grown in common fields in the seventeenth century. Changes in bylaws were agreed in manorial courts, and recorded on court rolls.

Another field system is termed infield-outfield, under which the infield was kept in permanent tillage, while segments of the outfield were selected in turn for temporary cultivation. The system, found in northern England and Scotland, has strong affinities with the rundale system of Ireland. It reflects the influences of abundant land, climatic limitations on the growing of cereals, and small settlements. One of the distinctive characteristics of the East Anglian system was the vesting of grazing rights in manorial lords, not in the community of landholders; thus each lord had a large area of land for his foldcourse, which was grazed and manured by demesne sheep flocks that incorporated the sheep of his tenants. In Kent land was mostly enclosed, but when lands lay in intermingled strips, some might be grazed in common by a few neighbors only. Similarly, common pastures were frequently grazed by a few rather than all. In Wales tenurial and social differences, coupled with climatic and soil constraints, gave rise to a distinctively Celtic system.

In continental countries field systems ranged from the nonintensive, like infield-outfield, to the more intensive common-field system. The relative power of lords and tenants differed in different situations, and this, coupled with the need for agricultural systems to suit the local environment, led to variations in detail in customs of land management. The differing power of lords in relation to tenants is illustrated in the contrast between foldcourse rights in East Anglia and common grazing rights in Midland England. It is implied also in the allocation, or reallocation, of strips by "sun division," which is documented in many places in Scandinavia from the fourteenth century on, and is occasionally found in England and other countries of Europe. Strips allotted by "sun division" show a regular order of intermingling, and are located by reference to the sun's course.

It is now generally accepted that field systems underwent continuous change, and hence their origins occasion lively debate. In the late nineteenth and early twentieth centuries different systems were associated with settlers of different races, the common-field system being labeled Anglo-Saxon in origin, the infield-outfield system Celtic, the Kentish system Jutish, and so forth. Writing in 1938, Charles and Christabel Orwin deemed the scattered strips of the common-field system a practical consequence of cooperative plowing by teams assembled among neighbors, a practice that led them to allocate land equally. The strips distributed good and bad land fairly among landholders, and spread the risks of crop failures. In this explanation, as in the earlier one, it was assumed that field systems came into existence fully fledged with well-formulated rules, from the very beginnings of settlement.

More recently it has been argued that the system evolved gradually, in response to practical farming problems that loomed steadily larger as population increased and land became more subdivided. Subdivision occurred through the partitioning of land among heirs and the buying and selling of pieces. The oldest element in the common-field system was the right of common grazing over pasture, which in England existed in Anglo-Saxon times and was probably immemorial. But rules governing cropping and grazing, organized on a village basis and solidifying into a system, were forced into existence by the increasing complexity of land-holding, difficulties in obtaining access to strips and to water, and shortages of grassland, and thus were a gradual development occurring at different times in different places.

Field systems are better documented for more recent centuries than for early ones, and their similarities in the seventeenth and eighteenth centuries should not be regarded as an immemorial feature. It is more likely that systems were infinitely varied at the start of settlement, but moved toward a general conformity as a result of pooled practical experience. Lawyers exerted a strong influence from the later thirteenth century by enunciating what were probably local expedients as general principles. The convention that no landholder should keep more animals on the common pasture in summer than he could support on his holding in the winter may be one such expedient that, with the help of published law books and the ministrations of professional managers of manorial estates, was established as a general law. Similarly, the notion that landholders were entitled to equal shares of land, measured in both value and extent, is spelled out meticulously in Bracton's *De legibus* (mid thirteenth century) in relation to co-heirs; it may be another principle that gradually evolved under the pressure of land shortages and was then extended to resolve village disputes among landholders in general.

If field systems underwent continuous change until enclosure, documents need to be more carefully scrutinized to reveal the nature of those changes and their explanation. But advancing knowledge of the way prehistoric settlement and institutional patterns shaped landscapes in the Anglo-Saxon period is not yet fully absorbed into the corpus of knowledge on field systems. That corpus must eventually accommodate the possibility that some field systems originated in prehistory and that their beginnings will never be documented.

BIBLIOGRAPHY

Alan R. H. Baker and Robin A. Butlin, eds., *Studies of Field Systems in the British Isles* (1973); Bruce M. S. Campbell, "Population Change and the Genesis of Common-fields on a Norfolk Manor," in *Economic History Review*, 2nd ser., 33 (1980); Robert A. Dodgshon, "The Landholding Foundations of the Open-field System," in *Past and Present*, 67 (1975), and "The Origin of the Two- and Three-Field System in England: A New Perspective," in *Geographia polonica*, 38 (1978); Staffan Helmfrid, ed., *Morphogenesis of the Agrarian Cultural Landscape, Papers of the Vadstena Symposium at the XIXth International Geographical Congress, August 14–20, 1960,* repr. from *Geografiska annaler*, 43 (1961); Charles S. Orwin and Christabel S. Orwin, *The Open Fields*, 3rd ed. (1967); Trevor Rowley, ed., *The Origins of Open Field Agriculture* (1981); Joan Thirsk, "The Common Fields," in *Past and Present*, 29 (1964), with further discussion in 32 (1965) and 33 (1966).

JOAN THIRSK

[See also **Agriculture and Nutrition; Land Tenure, Western European.**]

FIESOLE, ANDREA DA. See **Andrea da Firenze.**

FIESOLE, GIOVANNI DA. See **Giovanni da Fiesole.**

FILIOQUE, word added to the Latin version of the Creed of Nicaea-Constantinople, probably in seventh-century Spain, and gradually accepted throughout the Latin West as a genuine expression of Trinitarian dogma. The *Filioque* affirms the procession of the Holy Spirit "from the Father and the Son" (*a Patre Filioque*), whereas the original Greek text of the Creed defined the Spirit as "proceeding from the Father." Eventually the interpolation became a major issue, contributing to the schism between the Eastern and the Western churches.

A certain difference in interpreting and expressing the Trinitarian doctrine was already apparent in the fourth century, between the Greek Cappadocian fathers (St. Basil, St. Gregory of Nyssa, St. Gregory Nazianzus) on the one hand and St. Augustine of Hippo on the other. The issue, however, was not used in polemics between the two sides before the eighth century. Charlemagne, in his *Libri Carolini* (790), was the first to attack Greek Trinitarian terminology (procession of the Spirit through the Son) and to make the mistaken affirmation that the *Filioque* was part of the original creed. Charlemagne was rebuffed by popes Adrian I and Leo III, who, while accepting the doctrine implied in the *Filioque*, condemned the unilateral interpolation of a creed accepted by the whole church. This did not prevent the continued use of the interpolation in Frankish lands. Greek rebuttal came almost a century later, when Patriarch Photios, in an encyclical to the Eastern patriarchs (867), accused Frankish missionaries in Bulgaria of heresy because they were introducing the interpolated creed. In 879/880 Photios obtained from legates of Pope John VIII a formal disavowal of the *Filioque*. Nevertheless, the interpolated creed was eventually accepted in Rome, at the instance of Emperor Henry II (1014).

For centuries Greek and Latin theologians carried on the debate, which involved both the issue of the procession of the Holy Spirit and the authority of the Roman see, since it had now endorsed the interpolation. The Latins invoked the unity of the divine essence, which, according to them, presupposed that the Father and the Son, being essentially one, were necessarily to be seen together as the one origin (*spirator*) of the Spirit. The Greeks maintained that the Father personally (hypostatically) is the source of the divinity of the Son and the Spirit. They also rejected the right of the Western church alone to interpolate a creed approved by ecumenical councils. The Second Council of Lyons (1274) and the Council of Ferrara-Florence (1439) required that Eastern Christians who entered the communion of Rome accept the *Filioque* doctrine, but neither council was able to heal the schism between the two churches.

BIBLIOGRAPHY

Richard Haugh, *Photius and the Carolingians: The Trinitarian Controversy* (1975); Martin Jugie, *De processione Spiritus Sancti ex fontibus revelationis et secundum Orientales dissidentes* (1936); Vladimir Lossky, "The Procession of the Holy Spirit in the Orthodox Triadology," in *Eastern Churches Quarterly,* 7, suppl. 2 (1948).

JOHN MEYENDORFF

[See also **Councils, Western (869–1274); Councils, Western (1311–1445); Nicene Creed; Photios.**]

FILLASTRE, GUILLAUME (*ca.* 1400–1473), bishop of Verdun, Toul, and then Tournai, statesman, and author. As abbot of St. Bertin, he commissioned a notable altarpiece in 1455. He served Duke Philip the Good of Burgundy as administrator and envoy, and as chancellor of the Order of the Golden Fleece (1460). His last years were spent in transforming his eulogy of the late duke, preached at the 1468 meeting of the order, into his multivolume *Histoire de la toison d'or.*

BIBLIOGRAPHY

Georges Doutrepont, *La littérature française à la cour des ducs de Bourgogne* (1909); "Guillaume Fillastre," in *Souvenirs de la Flandre-Wallonne,* 20 (1880); Joseph Du Teil, *Un amateur d'art au XVe siècle: Guillaume Fillastre*

(1920); and Edith Warren Hoffman, "A Reconstruction and Reinterpretation of Fillastre's Altarpiece of St.-Bertin," in *Art Bulletin,* **60** (1978), with complete bibliography. The last two items both contain errors.

ANNE HAGOPIAN VAN BUREN

[See also **Marmion, Simon.**]

FIMBUL WINTER. In *Vafþrúðnismál* 44–45 the *fimbulvetr* is the final event in Nordic world history, after which two humans, Líf and Lífþrasir, survive by hiding in the woods of Hoddmímir and nourishing themselves on morning dew. From there the future generations of a new world order will proceed. Snorri Sturluson quotes from *Vǫluspá* and *Vafþrúðnismál* in *Gylfaginning* 51, where it is stated in response to a question concerning *ragnarǫk* that the *fimbulvetr* will come with snow from every quarter, great frosts, and sharp winds. The sun will avail nought. Preceding this catastrophic winter, lasting three years with no summers intervening, will be three years of great battles pitting brother against brother for the sake of avarice, and neither father nor son will be spared in manslaughter or family desecration. Following the *fimbulvetr*, Snorri relates, will come the destruction of the world and universe, after which the earth will arise anew.

Much has been made of the similarity between *fimbulvetr* and ancient Persian tradition, whereby Ahura Mazda ensures the protection of species in an enclosure against the raging winters at the end of the world. Various scholars have claimed either that the concept of the *fimbulvetr* reached the north via cultural diffusion from the east, or that the Nordic and Persian traditions derive from a common Indo-European heritage, or, of course, that the myths arose independently.

The notion of a monstrous winter as prelude to the end of the world occurs in documentation transcribed prior to the Old Icelandic material in a letter of about 600 from Pope Gregory the Great to Ethelbert, king of Kent, in which Gregory, in predicting the imminent end of the present world, foresees "changes in the air, and terrors from heaven, and storms contrary to the order of the times" (Bede, *Ecclesiastical History,* 1.32). Of course Christian tradition (for example, Luke 21:11) may have been the original influencing factor here and even in the Icelandic sources, although the arctic conditions would in any case indicate either a Nordic tradition or adaptation of a motif from elsewhere.

BIBLIOGRAPHY

John Stanley Martin, *Ragnarǫk* (1972), 125–127; Folke Ström, "Fimbulvinter," in *Kulturhistorisk leksikon for nordisk middelalder,* IV (1959), 261; *Vafthruthnismol,* in *The Poetic Edda,* Henry Adams Bellows, trans. (1957), 80–81; Snorri Sturluson, *The Prose Edda,* Arthur G. Brodeur, trans. (1960), 77–78; Jan de Vries, *Altgermanische Religionsgeschichte,* II (1957), 441.

JAMES E. CATHEY

[See also **Gylfaginning; Ragnarǫk; Scandinavian Mythology; Vafþrúðnismál.**]

FIN'AMOR. See **Courtly Love.**

FINIAL, the culminating ornament, often an elongated fleur-de-lis form, at the top of a Gothic pinnacle or gable. Finials have no structural function, but usually serve visually to continue, and emphasize, the vertical thrust of the element they crown.

LESLIE BRUBAKER

[See also **Gothic Architecture.**]

FINNBOGA SAGA, probably compiled about 1310, has been preserved in two vellums: in *Mǫðruvallabók* (before 1350) and in a deviant text in *Tómasarbók* (ca. 1550). Although Finnbogi was a historical person—he is mentioned in *Landnámabók* and *Íslendingadrápa*—the first part of his story is a fantasy made up of popular saga and fairy tale *(märchen)* motifs. Abandoned as an infant to die on a heap of stones, Finnbogi is discovered and reared by an old cotter and his wife, who name him Urðarköttr (Stone-heap cat). On his dying day a seafarer named Finnbogi, whom Urðarköttr has saved from a sinking ship, gives his own name to his rescuer. Through superhuman feats abroad Finnbogi earns the epithet "the Strong," which is bestowed on him by Jón, king of Greece. At home, too, Finnbogi's achievements are remarkable, but more realistic. In order to pre-

Gables topped with fleur-de-lys finials. St. Catharine, Oppenheim, exterior from the south, designed 1317. FOTO MARBURG

serve peace and order in the community, he twice has to move to regions more remote from his adversaries.

The relation between *Finnboga saga* and earlier historical works and sagas is complicated by the fact that there are many motival correspondences between them but few verbal ones of the kind that demonstrate direct borrowing. The most intriguing parallels and differences are those between this story and *Vatnsdœla saga.* In *Vatnsdœla* Finnbogi is bested by Þorsteinn goði and his pugnacious brother Jökull. In *Finnboga,* however, Finnbogi is morally and physically far superior to Jökull, who is caricatured as a truculent, clumsy oaf. Some scholars have felt that this contrast reflects preliterary differences in local traditions that developed in the districts of Vatnsdalr and Víðidalr, Finnbogi's original home. The consistent enhancement of Finnbogi in his saga and the corresponding denigration of Jökull, however, suggest authorial intent. In both stories Þorsteinn goði is depicted as an ideal chieftain.

The smooth style of *Finnboga saga* is unique for

its use of unusual words that seem to belong to colloquial rather than to literary language. Another characteristic feature is the combining and doubling of motifs—Finnbogi kills two bears single-handed, for example—and the literal repetition of phrases in similar situations. The use of alliteration, antithesis, and pairs of synonyms, especially at the beginning of the story, is more frequent than in most older sagas but less frequent than in *Vatnsdæla saga*. The author lapses into the first person a number of times, mostly in the final chapters. Although *Finnboga saga* is not a great work of literature, several of the scenes are skillfully and effectively constructed. The author's major purposes in composing this story seem to have been entertainment and the literary rehabilitation of Finnbogi of Víðidalr, who comes off rather badly in the saga of the Vatnsdalr chieftains.

BIBLIOGRAPHY

"Finnboga saga," in Jóhannes Halldórsson, ed., *Íslenzk fornrit*, XIV (1959), lvii–lxix, 251–340; "Finnboga saga ramma," in Guðni Jónsson, ed., *Íslendinga sögur*, XI (1949); Paul Schach, "Character Creation and Transformation in the Icelandic Sagas," in Stephen J. Kaplowitt, ed., *Germanic Studies in Honor of Otto Springer* (1978).

PAUL SCHACH

[See also **Vatnsdæla Saga**.]

FIORAVANTI, ARISTOTELE (*ca.* 1415–*ca.* 1486), Bolognese architect and engineer who arrived in Russia around 1474 after working previously in Hungary and Italy. In Moscow he worked on the rebuilding of the Kremlin, for which he designed and oversaw the construction of the Uspensky (Dormition) Cathedral, completed in 1479. Fioravanti applied Italian Renaissance architectural skills and aesthetic canons to traditional northeast Russian church architecture.

BIBLIOGRAPHY

The basic work on Fioravanti is still V. L. Snegirev, *Aristotel' Fioravanti i perestroika moskovskogo kremlia* (1935), which can be supplemented by *Uspenskii Sobor moskovskogo kremlia* (1971). In English see Hubert Faensen and Vladimir Ivanov, *Early Russian Architecture* (1972), 399–409, 418–420, and plates.

GEORGE P. MAJESKA

[See also **Moscow Kremlin, Art and Architecture**.]

FIRDAUSE. See **Shahnama**.

FIRMICUS MATERNUS, JULIUS (*d.* after 350). A senator of Sicily, Julius Firmicus Maternus initially embarked on a legal career but soon retired to become a writer. Around 334–337 he composed the *Matheseos* in eight books, a defense of astrology and the longest extant Latin work on the topic. Shortly thereafter, however, he became a zealous convert to Christianity. In the mid 340's he wrote a virulent attack on paganism, *On the Error of the Profane Religions,* which was dedicated to the emperors Constantius II and Constans I and exhorted them to stamp out paganism utterly. It is the earliest known Christian appeal for such assistance from the imperial government.

BIBLIOGRAPHY

Matheseos libri VIII, W. Kroll, F. Skutsch, and K. Zeigler, eds., 2 vols. (1897–1913); *De errore profanarum religionum*, K. Zeigler, ed. (1907). See also A. H. M. Jones, J. R. Martindale, and J. Morris, *The Prosopography of the Later Roman Empire*, I, A.D. 260–395 (1971), 567–568; T. Wikström, *In Firmicum Maternum studia critica* (1935).

RALPH WHITNEY MATHISEN

FIRST ROMANESQUE. Primarily used in architecture, this term refers to tenth- and early-eleventh-century buildings that prefigure mature Romanesque design. Puig i Cadafalch pointed out the typological connections between this group of small, southern churches and later Romanesque, citing in particular vaults and pier types. Also recognized was a northern First Romanesque style that fed into later architecture through its ashlar masonry, sculpture, monumentality, and planning. Work by Edson Armi, however, suggests that these typological connections are less significant than the aesthetic systems they accompany, which played a major role in the development of High Romanesque in Burgundy.

BIBLIOGRAPHY

Edson Armi, "Orders and Continuous Orders in Romanesque Architecture," in *Journal of the Society of Architectural Historians*, **34** (1975); José Puig i Cadafalch, *La géographie et les origines du premier art roman*, J. Viellard, trans. (1935), and *Le premier art roman* (1928).

JERRILYNN DODDS

FĪRŪZĀBĀD (ancient Ardešīr-Khurra [Glory of Ardešīr], medieval Gūr) was founded by the first Sasanian king Ardešīr I (*ca.* 224–240) about 100 kilometers (60 miles) south of Shiraz, in a valley approached through a spectacular gorge. This gorge, guarded by a fortress (Qalᶜa-ye Dukhtar), bears a colossal relief of Ardešīr in battle. A large vaulted palace built by Ardešīr, presumably before 224, faces a lake nearby. The town itself has a circular plan bisected by two main streets at right angles. This intersection in the center of the city is marked by a tall tower (*minār*) of unknown purpose, which some authors connect with fire worship, some 30 meters (98.4 feet) high. North of the tower is a masonry platform believed to have been the base of a Zoroastrian fire temple. The town survived the fall of the Sasanian dynasty in 637 and remained important into the tenth century.

BIBLIOGRAPHY

Dietrich Huff, "Zur Rekonstruktion des Termes von Firuzabad," in *Istanbuler Mitteilungen,* **19/20** (1969–1970), and "Der Takht-i Nishin in Firuzabad," in *Archäologischer Anzeiger* (1972); Klaus Schippmann, *Die iranischen Feuerheiligtümer* (1971), 100–122.

TRUDY S. KAWAMI

See also **Ardešīr I; Sasanians.**]

FISHERIES, MARINE

SOURCES

Facts needed for the reconstruction of marine fisheries in the Middle Ages can be obtained from written or pictorial sources and, above all, from archaeozoological studies of fish remains and finds of fishing gear. The most reliable sources are legal and commercial documents in official archives. Some information can also be found in medieval household diaries and cookery books, but the terminology used there is often more culinary than zoological. Interesting information about the fish trade is recorded in court and monastic chronicles, in travelers' reports, and in medieval poetry, particularly in the Icelandic sagas. The surprisingly realistic fish motifs of Hellenistic art—floor mosaics, decorative textiles, and illuminated manuscripts—survived to some extent, especially in the Byzantine areas, but the fish depicted by medieval artists are usually mere conventional symbols. In late-medieval books on natural history, fishes are drawn as didactic caricatures, their features extremely exaggerated. Quite informative about the importance of particular fish species are the heraldic herrings, cods, and hakes on the coats of arms of fish-trading cities and fishmongers' guilds, as well as the fish images on coins, such as the tunas on Byzantine coins.

Fish remains can provide archaeologists with detailed information on the environment of a particular site and its contacts with more remote areas. The hard parts of bony fishes—bones, teeth, scales, and statoliths (earstones)—do not decay easily. Although cartilaginous fishes, such as sharks and rays, lack bones, their teeth, placoid scales, fin spines, and calcified backbone centers can survive, as can their horny egg capsules. The collecting of fish remains was long neglected by archaeologists, and much valuable information was thus lost, but recent studies have led to very rewarding cooperation between zoologists and archaeologists. For example, remains of herring, one of the most economically important species, often have not been recorded at sites where one might have expected them: small, transparent herring bones can easily be overlooked, and they are difficult to collect if coarse sieves are used. Recently, however, the use of magnifying lenses and finer sieves, and the water-sieving of sediment samples, have produced much valuable information on the history of herring fisheries and the ecology of excavated sites. The bones of unsalted herrings are not likely to survive, as the bony substance is very soon dissolved by the oxidized body fats. Therefore, herring bones and those of other fatty fishes (eels, salmonids, scombrids, and flatfishes) tend to be underrepresented in proportion to their original numbers and to the fish taxa having more resistant bones (particularly codfishes).

ECONOMIC ROLE

Since prehistoric times marine fisheries have been an important source of food. The "sea harvest" is much less affected by the seasons, catastrophes of climate, disease, and war than are agriculture, stockkeeping, and hunting. The enormous resources of the marine fisheries—many times greater than freshwater resources—could make up for shortages of other foods at critical moments. Fish filled a nutritional gap in the High and late Middle Ages, when longer fasting periods were ordered by the church and perhaps, in some areas, dictated by the shortage of agricultural products. The fishery products available, however, depended on the natural distribution

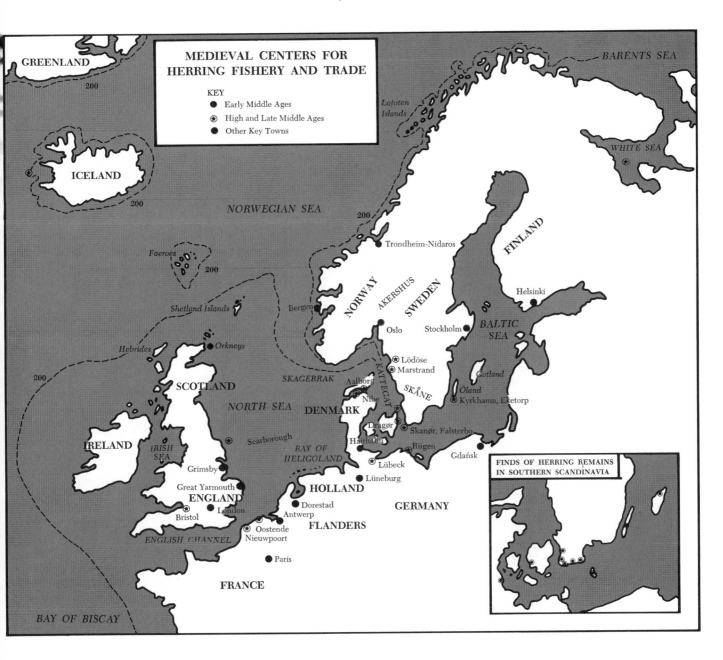

MEDIEVAL CENTERS FOR
HERRING FISHERY AND TRADE

KEY
● Early Middle Ages
⊛ High and Late Middle Ages
● Other Key Towns

FINDS OF HERRING REMAINS
IN SOUTHERN SCANDINAVIA

of fish species, the efficiency of fishing methods and gear, the methods of preserving surplus catches, and the organization of transport from the coasts to inland sites. Of special importance was transfer of local resources from different faunal regions to remote areas of demand by long-range international trading.

FISHING METHODS AND FISHING GEAR

Until the late Middle Ages, marine fisheries could be only as far from the shore as fishermen could wade or dared to navigate their small open boats. Deep-sea resources could be exploited locally only on coastal steeps. In deep water the main fishing gear was the hook, baited or ripping (unbaited hooks with very sharp points that pierce the fish when the line is quickly hauled in), forged of iron or bronze or made of bent wire. Primarily handlines with few hooks were used until the late Middle Ages, when longlines appeared (there is a line with 120 hooks on an inventory list from an Icelandic church in 1482). On sloping shores fish traps and seine nets were originally used. In northern Europe the seines were often made of line bast, but fibers of grass, rushes, hemp, flax, and wool were also used. On tidal beaches, sea hedges *(heia maris)*—devices midway between fish traps and seines—were used.

A means of fishing used by the Phoenicians and practiced around the Mediterranean involved the use of *tonnara* or *madrague,* complicated systems of seines leading migrating shoals of tuna toward a "death chamber" *(camera della morte).* The active encircling of fish with beach seines *(sagenae)* was also very ancient. In the Mediterranean, shoals of pelagic pilchards and anchovies were caught from lampara boats on moonless nights. The fish were attracted by lamps fixed to the boats, then encircled by nets. (This type of fishing is well depicted in Byzantine copies of Greek manuscripts.) The most primitive method of fishing was spearing, used for tuna and swordfish *(Xiphias gladius),* as well as for rays and flatfishes on the sea bottom. In the late Middle Ages finer gill nets were introduced, in the meshes of which fish were entangled. These nets, which greatly improved efficiency in fishing pelagic shoals of herring and mackerel, were floated, drifted, or fixed to the seabed by stakes or anchors (set nets).

An ancient method used in the Mediterranean and the Black Sea was fishing with rafts of rush bundles. Shoals of gray mullets were driven by noisy fishermen toward the rafts, tried to jump over them, fell onto the rafts, got entangled in the rushes, and were picked up. Dolphins *(Coryphaena hippurus)* sought the shadows beneath the rafts and could be caught there. The driving of fish may also have been used in medieval Norway, where it was forbidden to kill a whale that drove shoals of herring shoreward.

METHODS OF PRESERVATION

In northern Europe, during the winter, fish could be transported frozen to markets as far as a thousand kilometers away, whereas in southern Europe inland sites could obtain fresh marine fishes only if situated one or two days' journey away along rivers or roads. Fish smoked in fumes of wood or peat could be preserved for two weeks or more. The smoked fish meat even acquired a delicate flavor. Smoked sea fishes are mentioned in English documents of the late thirteenth century, but apparently the method was much older. According to Olaus Magnus (1555), smoked herrings (bucklings) were shipped from Flanders via Spanish ports to Rome; before smoking they were probably salted.

The most efficient method of preserving fish for extended periods was salting. In southern Europe sea salt was easily produced by evaporation in salinas, a method used since classical times. In northern Europe the salt from seawater had to be obtained by boiling. Local salt of inferior quality was produced by the Norsemen from seaweed ashes (black salt), by the Frisians from the ashes of submerged marine peat, and by the English from tidal shore sand. The pure salt imported from salinas on the Iberian coasts and the Bay of Biscay was very expensive, as was the mineral salt from salt springs in northern Germany.

The wind-drying method, which preserved fish using little or no salt, was developed mainly in Norway and Iceland. It was best suited for codfish, which have lean meat and fats concentrated in the liver. Fish were dried on poles or wooden stands, hence the name stockfish (Spanish: *estocafís;* Italian: *stoccafisso).* In winter the eviscerated fishes could be dried as roundfish (Norwegian: *rundfisk).* In summer they were split in half down to the tail and most of the backbone was removed; these "summer" fish were called rotfish (Norwegian: *råskjaer;* German: *rotscher).*

Codfishes, dried after salting, then decapitated and flattened, were called *Klippfisch.* Fatty fish, such as herring and mackerel, were ill suited for wind drying, unless small and lean; but even large fatty fish could be dried if cut into strips called *rekling.* Halibut strips from nearest the dorsal and anal fins were called *rav.* Fish salted fresh were "green"-salted; salted and smoked herrings were "red"; unsalted herrings were "white." Codfish brought home by the Basques from Newfoundland were called Terra Nova fishes; if salted, Labezdan.

OTHER FISHERY PRODUCTS

Caviar, prepared from unspawned roe from the ovaries of anadromous sturgeons, particularly from the beluga *(Huso huso)* in the Caspian Sea, was a luxurious and very expensive exotic dish. It was said to have been eaten by the Byzantines and was known in France at the beginning of the sixteenth century. At about the same time Olaus Magnus mentions *bottargi* (Italian: *bottarga;* French: *boutargue;* Turkish: *putago),* which was prepared from the salted, pressed, and dried roe of gray mullets and was said to be preserved in wax, like cheese.

If slightly salted fish is kept wet and warm, the meat grows soft or dissolves and it acquires a tasty, sourish flavor. Ancient Greeks and Romans appreciated highly fermented fish sauces called *garum,* usually produced by fermenting fish entrails, blood, and small, cheap fishes (pilchards, anchovies, sand smelts) in an open earthenware pot left in the sun. Around the Mediterranean, factories developed for salting fish and producing *garum*. These expensive sauces, an essential part of classical cooking, were transported in special amphorae as far north as Britain and Norway. Outside formerly Roman areas, "sour" fishes were fermented in Scandinavia. In Iceland the meat of the Greenland shark, poisonous when fresh, was buried in sand to ferment; it could then be eaten as "sour shark" *(skyrhåkarl)*.

Apart from the meat, oil was the most important fish product in medieval northern Europe, where, as lamp fuel and also as food, it replaced the olive oil of the south. Fish oil was mainly produced from the liver of codfish and sharks and from the waste from herring fisheries. In the late Middle Ages the sounds (air bladders) of stockfish were used in England as edible jellies. Olaus Magnus mentions the use of fish glue by Finns. In Iceland the hide of the Greenland shark was used to scour tables and benches.

FISH TRADE

Apart from a very small number of toxic species, practically all sea fish are edible, but a profitable fishery depends mainly on mass fishes, those existing in great abundance. Catches of these provide a surplus that can be traded outside the local consumption area. In northern Europe, because of the rich resources of mass fishes, few other species were systematically harvested for human food. Around the Mediterranean, on the other hand, many other types of fishes, including very small ones, have been used since the classical period.

The long-range Roman trading of luxury fish products in specially designed amphorae had ceased in western Europe by the early Middle Ages. In Byzantine areas it persisted a little longer. In the Near East the shipment of fish (such as tuna and parrot fish) from the Red Sea to Palestine seems to have survived. In the Mediterranean the Venetians are said to have started their extensive trade with salt and fish (probably salted). In addition to more expensive species, they certainly exploited the rich resources of picarels *(Maena sp. sp.)* as cheap food.

In the North Sea the autumnal and winter concentration of herring and cod at the mouth of the English Channel attracted, from the beginning of the Middle Ages, Angles, Gauls, and Belgae. They sold their catches directly to consumers at market ports, of which the most famous was Great Yarmouth (Gernemutha Magna) in East Anglia. In

northern Europe the rich seasonal resources of cod and other codfish had been exploited since prehistoric times on the steep coasts of Finnmark and western Norway; the surplus, frozen or dried, was distributed throughout northern Scandinavia. At the end of the early Middle Ages, the Vikings introduced dried codfish as a foodstuff and tradable commodity in eastern England. The southern Scandinavians at that time exploited local resources of herring that, after salting or smoking, they marketed in Denmark, Skåne, and the Baltic islands.

At the height of the Middle Ages, a class of fishmongers developed, linking producers and distant consumers. English, Flemish, Dutch, and German traders began a long and hard competition for fish markets. At first those of the Hanseatic League were successful and dominated fishing centers of northern and central Europe. With their large ships of the cog type, they were very efficient merchants. They established offices at fish-trading centers and took over commerce from native fishermen. They marketed Norse dried codfish (which they called stockfish or Bergen fish) over the whole of Catholic Europe, and they traded herrings from the Skanör-Falsterbo area of Skåne and from the Bohuslän coast of Skagerrak. For the Hansa, access to the salinas of the Lüneburg area was a great adventure.

In the late Middle Ages the "Icelandic fare" from England began the exploitation of codfish and herring resources near Iceland. The English were soon followed by the Dutch and the Germans of the Hansa. At the very end of the Middle Ages the Basques discovered a rich new source of codfish near Newfoundland, and Terra Nova fish competed with the stockfish of the Hanseatic League. Some time before, the Dutch started offshore fishing for herring in the North Sea, cutting into the fish trade of the Hanseatic league.

MOST IMPORTANT MARINE FISHES

The frigate mackerel *(Auxis thazard)* and the skipjack tuna *(Katsuwonus pelamis)*, both pelagic shoalfish, are summer visitors to the Mediterranean that have been fished with hooks and the *tonnara*s (fish traps) since prehistoric times. Medieval remains of both species have been found in Jordan.

Parrot fishes, of the family *Scaridae,* were highly appreciated by the Romans. Medieval finds of three species and of the kawakawa tuna *(Euthynnus affinis)* have been made in Jordan.

The spurdog *(Squalus acanthias)* has been fished for with hooks since prehistoric times. Finds of clawlike fin spines and cyclospondylic calcifications of vertebral centrums are not uncommon in middens dating from the Middle Stone Age to the late Middle Ages in Denmark and western Sweden.

The porbeagle *(Lamna nasus)* was fished for meat and liver oil, first with hooks, then with baited lines in the mid sixteenth century at Skagerrak. Finds of asterospondylic calcifications of vertebrae have been recorded from the late Middle Ages in Denmark.

Rays *(Raja sp. sp.)* were a popular dish in the Middle Ages. In 1488 the fish stored at Akershus Castle in southern Norway were mainly dried rays. They were harvested in summer at the beginning of the fifteenth century on the coasts of eastern England by fishermen from Scarborough. They were exported dried from Iceland to England in 1476, as well as from Norway to England and Sweden. Finds include an egg capsule of the starry ray *(Raja radiata)* at the Viking city of Haithabu on the southwestern Baltic, and knoblike, spiny placoid scales and flattened asterospondylic calcifications of vertebral centra (mainly of the thornback ray, *R. clavata*) at medieval sites.

Finds of needlefish *(Belone belone)*—which indicate a warmer season—are numerous at Haithabu and not uncommon at late-medieval sites in southwestern England, in Denmark, on the western coast of Sweden, and on the island of Öland.

For the Byzantines, mackerel *(Scomber scombrus)* was a cheap substitute for tuna. Olaus Magnus mentions fishing for mackerel in Oslo Fjord. Because it is a fatty fish, it tends to be underrepresented in digs, but it has been found at Haithabu. Mackerel are quite numerous in medieval layers of Lahebia Cave (southern Kattegat, Sweden) and are recorded in middens from the High and late Middle Ages in England, Denmark, and Sweden. Its presence indicates a warm season.

Turbot *(Scophthalmus maximus)* has been considered a delicacy since classical times. Finds have been made at the inland Carolingian city of Dorestad in the Netherlands (apparently imported smoked or salted fishes), as well as at mid- and late-medieval sites in Denmark and Sweden (western coast, Lahebia Cave, Öland).

Plaice *(Pleuronectes platessa)* and flounder *(Platichthys flesus),* important for local consumption, tend to be underrepresented in finds but are not uncommon on sites from prehistoric to medieval times.

The Danes are said to have fished for hake *(Merluccius merluccius)* in the Irish Sea in the eleventh and twelfth centuries. Olaus Magnus mentions the fishing of *marlucz* by Spaniards and Portuguese who sold their catches in Italy. Finds are recorded from the High and late Middle Ages in Denmark and western Sweden. Rich deposits of cranial bones and vertebrae have been found at the inland city of Lödöse (western Sweden), probably from imported whole salted fishes (perhaps from England). Medieval fishermen from Lahebia Cave caught hake in the southern Kattegat.

Pilchard *(Sardinia pilchardus)* and anchovy *(Engraulis encrasicholis)* have been exploited in quantities since classical times with lampara boats and seine nets. Gray mullets, of the family *Mugilidae,* have also been popular since antiquity and were enjoyed by the Byzantines. They were fished with seines, boats, and fish rafts, and the roe was used for *bottarga.* Medieval remains have been found in Jordan (probably imported from the Red Sea).

Since prehistoric times the bluefin tuna *(Thunnus thynnus)* has been a very important food fish in the Mediterranean and the Black Sea. Large concentrations at the Bosporus were well known to classical writers, and there was intensive tuna fishing near Herakleia Pontike on the Black Sea. The red flesh of the bluefin tuna was much appreciated by the Romans and Byzantines. Remains of large tuna from medieval Borlund (western Norway) indicate local fishing, whereas those from the inland city of Lödöse are probably imported bits of salted tuna meat.

The Greenland shark *(Somniosus microcephalus)* is amply recorded in documents of medieval Norway and Iceland, where it was fished for its liver oil and meat. (A contract dating from 1277 between the king of Norway and the archbishop concerns delivery of shark oil, *hákarla lysi,* for lamp fuel.) From Norway shark oil was exported to England or sold to the Hansa.

The Atlantic herring *(Clupea harengus)* was the most abundantly fished seafood in the North Atlantic, the North Sea, and the Baltic. It had been caught in great numbers since antiquity with handlines, seines, and gill nets. Inshore fishing was most successful at spawning times, which were different for different stocks. The autumn-spawning down-stock herring spawned in the southern North Sea, at the mouth of the English Channel. It was exploited in the early Middle Ages (as documented by a monastery chronicle dated 702), and its main harbor and international market was Great Yarmouth. The peak of Yarmouth trade was reached at the beginning of the High Middle Ages. The French fished herring off the coast of Normandy in the twelfth century, selling their catches in Paris. In the late Middle Ages fish traders from Flanders sold smoked and salted herrings in Spain and Italy.

Bank-stock herrings spawn on the northern banks of the North Sea, which, apart from sites near the Orkneys and eastern Scotland (exploited by Norse colonists), were less accessible to inshore fishermen. Lean younger herrings were caught in summer near eastern England by Scarborough fishermen. In the late Middle Ages the Dutch began a more intensive exploitation of this stock, using boats of the *buyzer* type and new methods of cutting and salting (said to have been introduced by a Fleming named Willem Beukelsz, Beuckels, Beukelzn, or Blökel).

There were vast invasions of skerries and fjords by shoals of herring in autumn and winter: the best-recorded medieval influx was in the fourteenth century. At the end of the thirteenth century, the city of Marstrand was founded as a fishing and marketing center. English, Dutch, and Hansa merchants were involved in the commerce, which peaked in the mid sixteenth century. According to osteometric studies, these invasions were probably caused by excess populations of bank herring, which after spawning visited the Skagerrak to feed.

The sizes of individual herrings decreased toward the brackish Baltic, the rich resources of which have been exploited since prehistoric times. Fishing, salting, and smoking were particularly intensive in the late Middle Ages around the twin cities of Skanör and Falsterbo in Skåne (founded at the end of the twelfth century), reaching a peak in the fourteenth century under the Hanseatic League. Intensive fishing also occurred near Dragør. The Swedes obtained their herring from southern Öland. Well-preserved (salted or smoked) remains have been found at several Viking marketplaces in southern Sweden and on the Baltic islands of Öland and Gotland. There are also rich medieval finds at Lahebia Cave on the southern Kattegat.

The spring-spawning Atlanto-scandic stock has the largest and most numerous herrings in the eastern North Atlantic. Medieval fishing occurred mainly at spawning time, in winter and spring, off the coasts of Iceland and western Norway. After the early fifteenth century, English "Icelandic farers" brought green-salted herrings to western England. Fishing for spring-spawning herring with gill nets was recorded in western Norway in 1410. The large

offshore resources were inaccessible to medieval fishermen. The herrings of Aalborg were reportedly appreciated in northern Europe in the fifteenth century. Dutch merchants provided the herring fishery at Nibe with bay salt in 1517. Rich remains of spring-spawning herring of the southern Baltic have been found at Haithabu. Well preserved, probably salted, the herring obviously were caught in weirs in the nearby Schlei inlet (recorded from the fifteenth century).

The dwarf herring of the north and central Baltic (*Culpea harengus membras*) are both spring- and autumn-spawning stocks. A fishery in southwestern Finland is mentioned in documents from 1488. The White Sea herring (*Culpea pallasi maris-albis*), an Arctic subspecies of the Pacific herring, was first fished in the fourteenth century by monks from a monastery on the Solovetsky Islands.

Shoals of sprat (*Sprattus sprattus*) were intensively fished in the North Sea (*S. s. sprattus*) and the Baltic. Sprats are listed in a fourteenth-century Kentish fishmonger's assortment and in a Northumberland household book of 1512.

Reklings and *rav* of halibut (*Hippoglossus hippoglossus*) were popular as food and trade goods in medieval northern Europe, as recorded in duty taxes from 1316. Intensive fishing around the Lofoten Islands is mentioned in the mid fifteenth century. A few finds of large imported halibut at Haithabu include a perforated vertebra, perhaps worn as a talisman. Middens yielding large halibuts date from the late Middle Ages in Denmark and western Sweden.

The cod (*Gadus morhua*) was, after the Atlantic herring, the most abundant and commercially important mass fish of the North Atlantic, the Barents Sea, the Norwegian Sea, the North Sea, and the Baltic. The Terra Nova stock spawned near Newfoundland and was discovered at the end of the Middle Ages by Basques. A second stock spawned near Iceland and southern Greenland: after the fifteenth century it was exploited not only by Icelanders but also by the English, the Dutch, and the Hansa. A Barents Sea stock spawned near the Lofoten Islands. According to *Egils saga*, the Vikings traded dried cod with England; later, catches were marketed in Trondheim and Bergen, the latter being the Hanseatic League's center for stockfish and Bergen fish. Another stock spawned at the Faeroes; another north of the Hebrides, the Orkneys, and eastern Scotland (exploited since the Norse colonization); another near Grimsby in eastern England (the "morue de Grimsby" of medieval cookery books); another in the Bay of Heligoland; another at the mouth of the English Channel (exploited early by East Anglian, Dutch, Flemish, Norman, and French fishermen); and others in Skagerrak-Øresund and in the Baltic. Local, nonmigratory coastal cod could be fished all year round; the migrating stocks, mainly at spawning time in winter and spring. In northern Norway large shoals of young followed their prey, the capelin *(Mallotus villosus)*, to the coast, where they could be fished in the summer. Cod was caught first with handlines (and perhaps rippers) and, after the fifteenth century, with longlines and special drift nets.

Very durable cod bones usually dominate fish finds from coastal sites in northern Europe and are often greatly overrepresented. They are common from prehistoric to medieval times. Bones of large imported cods are also recorded at inland sites, such as Buchy in Normandy and the city of Skara in western Sweden.

A few caudal vertebrae of imported large saithes *(Pollachius virens)* have been unearthed at Haithabu. In medieval middens of Denmark and western Sweden, saithe bones are much less numerous than those of cod and ling.

Haddock *(Melanogrammus aeglefinus)* devours quantities of herring roe: hence rich finds of haddock can indicate the presence of spawning herring. Archaeologists have located deposits from the High and late Middle Ages in Britain, the Netherlands, Norway, Denmark, and western Sweden. Haddock was imported (probably smoked or salted) to inland sites, such as the Carolingian town of Dorestad and the late-medieval Gudhems nunnery in western Sweden.

A few remains of larger imported lings *(Molva molva)* have been unearthed at Haithabu. Ling are not uncommon at late-medieval Danish and western Swedish sites.

BIBLIOGRAPHY

General. Kulturhistorisk Leksikon for Nordisk Middelalder-Kulturhistoriskt Lexikon för Nordisk Medeltid, ed. by John Danstrup *et al.,* 22 vols. (1956–1978, repr. 1980–).

Sea fishes in medieval literature and art. Zoltan Kádár, *Survivals of Greek Zoological Illuminations in Byzantine Manuscripts* (1978); Olaus Magnus, *Historia de gentibus Septentrionalibus* (1555), and *Historia om De Nordiska Folken,* 4 vols. (1976), Swedish trans. and commentary by John Granlund.

Icelandic sagas. Fínnur Jonsson, ed., "Egils saga Skallagrímssonar," in *Altnordische Saga-Bibliothek,* III (1924).

History of sea fishing and fishing gear. Andres v. Brandt, *Fish Catching Methods of the World* (1964), 191; William Radcliffe, *Fishing from the Earliest Times* (1974).

Fish as food and fish saving. Alan Davidson, *Mediterranean Seafood* (1972); C. Anne Wilson, *Food and Drink in Britain* (1973).

Ichthyology. Alwyne C. Wheeler, in *Fishes of the World: An Illustrated Dictionary* (1979), 366.

Archaeozoology and osteology of sea fishes. Richard W. Casteel, *Fish Remains in Archaeology and Paleo-environmental Studies* (1976); Antje T. Clason and Witske Prummel, "Collecting, Sieving and Archaeozoological Research," in *Journal of Archaeological Science,* 4 (1977); Hanns-Hermann Müller, *Bibliographie zur Archäo-Zoologie und Geschichte der Haustiere* (1971–), annually.

Regional research in archaeozoology and the history of marine fisheries: Denmark. Knud Rosenlund, *Catalogue of Subfossil Danish Vertebrates: Fishes* (1976), with extensive bibliography. *England and Scotland:* Andrew K. G. Jones, "Reconstruction of Fishing Techniques from Assemblages of Fish Bones," in *Fish Osteo-archaeology Meeting, Copenhagen 20th–28th August 1981* (1981); Alwyne C. Wheeler and Andrew Jones, "Fish Remains," in A. Rogerson, ed., *Excavations on Fullers Hill, Great Yarmouth, East Anglian Archaeology, Report,* II (1976), 208–224; Alwyne C. Wheeler, "The Fish Bones from Buckquoy, Orkney," in Anna Ritchie, "Excavation of Pictish and Viking-Age Farmsteads at Buckquoy, Orkney," in *Proceedings of the Society of Antiquaries of Scotland,* 108 (1976–77), 211–214; Alwyne C. Wheeler, "Fish Bone," in Helen Clarke and Alan Carter, ed., *Excavations in Kings Lynn 1963–1970* (1977). *France:* Johannes Lepiksaar, "Restes d'animaux provenant du Grand Besle," in *Meddelanden från Lunds Univ. Historiska Museum, 1968–69* (1969), 85–116. *Germany:* K. Jagow, "Die Heringsfischerei an der deutschen Ostseeküste im Mittelalter," in *Archiv für Fischereigeschichte,* 5 (1915); Johannes Lepiksaar and Dirk Heinrich, "Untersuchungen an Fischresten aus der frühmittelalterlichen Siedlung Haithabu," in *Berichte über die Ausgrabungen in Haithabu,* 10 (1977); Christian Radtke, "Bemerkungen zum mittelalterlichen Fischfang mit Heringszäunen in der Schlei," in *Berichte über die Ausgrabungen in Haithabu,* 10 (1977), 123–140. *Netherlands:* Dick C. Brinkhuizen, "Preliminary Notes on Fish Remains from Archaeological Sites in the Netherlands," in *Palaeohistoria,* 31 (1979); Wilske Prummel, *Early Medieval Dorestad, an Archaeozoological Study* (1980), Dutch with English summary. *Norway:* B. Stoklund, "Bonde og fisker. Litet om det middelalderige sildefiskeri og dets udøvelse," in *Handels og Søfarts-museets årbog 1959* (1959). *Poland:* E. Cieślaka, ed., *Historia Gdańska (tom I do roku 1454), Rybolowstwo* (1978). *Sweden:* Karl A. Andersson, "De stora sillfiskeperioderna på Sveriges Västkust och sillen, som framkallade den," in *Institute of Marine Research Lysekil, Ser. Biol. Report,* 5 (1950); Arne Hallström, "Die Fischknochen," in *Eketorp, Die Fauna* (1979), 422–494; Olof Haslöf, "Västnordiskt kustfiske under medeltiden," in *Nordisk kultur,* 11–12 (1955); Johannes Lepiksaar, "Über die Tjerknochenfunde aus den mittelalter- lichen Siedlungen Südschwedens," in A. T. Clason, ed., *Archaeozoological studies* (1976), 230–239.

JOHANNES LEPIKSAAR

[See also **Trade, European.**]

FISHPONDS. In what they called *vivaria, piscinae, étangs,* stews, or *Teichen,* medieval Europeans kept concentrations of fish for use as food. Intentional human intervention in fish habitat and populations thus distinguishes a fishpond from a fishery (*piscatura*), where people gathered naturally occurring fish, although this intervention ranged from mere artificial confinement or live storage of wild fish and the rearing of captives to the practice of real pisciculture—the use of artificial habitats to control the reproduction of captive fish and to rear their offspring to edible size.

By the seventh century fish had become an important source of protein for the 140 to 160 days each year when meat was prohibited to obedient Christians. Inadequate means of preservation and the high cost of overland transport limited the distribution of sea fish to interior Europe, so the large populations of freshwater fishes were exploited. Live storage and artificial culture compensated for seasonal or local shortages in natural fish populations or difficulties in catching an adequate supply. Although the Romans had a sophisticated luxury fish culture, medieval efforts emphasized different kinds of fish and different techniques for somewhat different ends. Except for the temporary storage of large seasonal catches in some sections around the Mediterranean, saltwater fishponds were little used at this time.

Before the twelfth century information about fishponds is scattered in passing references of considerable ambiguity. Terms and descriptions rarely distinguish among natural and artificial ponds and fish populations, specify the fish varieties, or mention cultural and managerial practices. In many instances and for whole regions this obscurity persisted through the entire Middle Ages.

Water mills often had associated fisheries and *vivaria* were common on great landed establishments, especially monastic but also episcopal and lay. In the sixth-century *Institutiones divinarum et humanorum Lectionum* Cassiodorus tells how his southern Italian monastery, Vivarium, possessed diversions from a nearby river where captured fish were kept

for domestic use. Charlemagne instructed his local stewards to take from the ponds on his estates fish for household consumption, to sell any surplus, and to restock the ponds. By about 1100 King Koloman of Hungary had to restrict monastic ponds to the needs of the brethren. The ubiquitous early medieval fishpond was thus usually intended to support self-sufficient local elite consumption rather than large-scale commerce.

The emergence of advanced fish culture in the Middle Ages seems associated with the spread of the carp (*Cyprinus carpio*) across western Europe, to which it was not native. The domestic carp and its culture are traditionally said to have come to Europe from east Asia during Roman or early medieval times, but Eugene K. Balon has recently shown European carp to be a distinct subspecies descended from naturally occurring wild carp indigenous to the lower and middle Danube. In his opinion, Roman enthusiasts of exotic fishes brought specimens to Italy, and early medieval monks subsequently carried carp north to improve the productivity of their ponds. Historians have not yet systematically tested the two theories against the medieval evidence. Cassiodorus, whose mention of monastic fishponds would have been widely read, elsewhere tells of carp brought from the Danube to grace the table of Theodoric the Ostrogoth. The first medieval citations of the fish, in the Latin epic *Ruodlieb* (written in the mid eleventh century at Tegernsee in Bavaria) and the writings of Hildegard of Bingen (twelfth century) pertain first to the Danubian, and then probably to the Rhenish, watershed. By the thirteenth century the carp was well known as a pond fish in the Atlantic and Mediterranean drainages of western Germany and France. The biology and habits of the carp well suited it to the more developed pisciculture then detectable in some European regions.

In the later Middle Ages better-managed and more productive fishponds served the needs of a larger population that obtained more of its food on the market. This advance had four main technical features: multiple, specialized artificial ponds; regular drainage and cultivation of the pond bottom; human control of the species reared; planned, large-scale harvesting for market sale. These sophisticated enterprises appear in French records starting in the twelfth century and in east-central European documents in the fourteenth century.

Each full-scale fishpond complex had several small ponds for spawning, for nurseries, and for mature fish awaiting sale or consumption, and larger ponds for fattening or overwintering the fish. Water was supplied by diverting a river with a log weir or blocking small streams and overland drainage with an earthen dam. However filled, each pond had a diversion channel to prevent overflowing, a specially deepened area where the fish could be concentrated for easy removal, and a sluice to regulate the water level. Heavy capital costs meant that most large pond complexes belonged to great lords, but lesser men could invest in one or two ponds and manage them in a similar way.

By the early twelfth century operators knew that they could improve production by draining a pond every few years, planting grain in the dried bottom, pasturing animals there, and then reflooding and restocking with fish. They preferred to raise carp or bream (*Abramis brama*), with pike (*Esox lucius*) an intentional by-product fed with surplus fry. Where necessary, carp could be fed artificially on grain. The year's round of activities culminated in later winter and spring, when the ponds containing three- to five-year-olds were lowered to concentrate the fish for harvest and sale, storage, or consumption during Lent. In some Burgundian and Moravian ponds cold-water salmonids were raised. According to one source, the special problems of artificially spawning trout were solved before 1420 by a monk named Pinchon from the abbey of Rheome.

Specialized fishpond enterprises emerged, notably in regions with good access to concentrated inland markets and either impermeable or poorly drained soils. In twelfth-century France monastic and secular lords of the Orléanais, Sologne, Berry, Maine, and Poitou built ponds to gain better returns from wet and forested lands. Their peers in thirteenth-century Forez, Bresse, and Burgundy did likewise, seeking to profit from rising market demand. In Dombes pisciculture was a response to the lack of agricultural labor during the fourteenth and fifteenth centuries. Special domanial officers managed most French ponds; some of their detailed financial accounts are extant, though little studied.

Pisciculture is also well known in Bohemia and Moravia from the mid fourteenth century and in Slovakia, Upper Silesia, and the southwestern part of the Polish kingdom. Large Czech estates employed professional pond masters; Polish ponds more often belonged to small landowners or even peasants.

Knowledge of other regions is less full. Those with abrupt relief, rich natural waters, or a Mediterranean climate—including much of Germany, southern France, Spain, and Italy—relied more on wild or sea fisheries and simple storage ponds. The oft-cited Bolognese agricultural writer, Pietro de Crescenzi (1233–1320), offers only general remarks on the usefulness of stocking ponds with local wild fish. The British Isles and Scandinavia certainly lagged in adopting an advanced pisciculture based on carp. Thirteenth-century English writers on agriculture say little of ponds, and what they say is not always correct. Ponds that were managed with care used the native bream, not carp. The latter species is first recorded in England in the mid fifteenth century, and it remained a recognized novelty well after 1500, when writers still eagerly borrowed advice on its culture from continental authorities.

BIBLIOGRAPHY

Before the mid sixteenth century no known writings were devoted solely or even in large part to fishponds, nor does any one modern study cover the subject on a European scale. The following are useful, however: Euguene K. Balon, *Domestication of the Carp Cyprinus carpio L.* (1974); Jan Dubravius [Jan Skalý z Doubravky], *De piscinis ad Antonium Fuggerum* (1547), repr. in Sbornik filologicky ČSAV, I (1953), trans. as *A New Booke of Good Husbandry* (1599), and repr. in facsimile in J. M. French, ed., *Three Books on Fishing (1599–1659)* (1962); Jules Haime, "La pisciculture, son histoire et ses progrès dans les pays étrangers et en France," in *Revue des deux mondes*, 2nd ser., 6 (1854)—all modern references to Pinchon's artificial spawning of trout can be traced back only to this discussion; Rudolf Hurt, *Dějiny rybnikařství na Moravé a ve Slezsku* (1960); Wilhelm Koch, "Die Geschichte der Binnenfischerei von Mitteleuropa," in Reinhard Demoll *et al.*, eds., *Handbuch der Binnenfischerei Mitteleuropas*, IV (1925), 28–30; John McDonnell, *Exploitation of Inland Fisheries in Early Medieval Yorkshire 1066–1300* (1981); Brian K. Roberts, "Fish Culture in Sixteenth-century Poland," in *Agricultural History Review*, **16** (1968), the only English-language discussion and a brief sketch of comparative data from England; Olbrycht Strumieński, *O sprawie, sypaniu, wymierzaniu i rybnieniu stawów* (1573), repr. 1897); Wojciech Szczygielski, *Z dziejów gospodarki rybnej w Polsce w XVI–XVIII wieku* (1967); Jean Verdon, "Recherches sur la pêche et la pisciculture en occident durant le haut moyen âge," in *Actes du 102ᵉ congrès national des sociétés savantes (Limoges, 1977), Section d'archéologie et d'historie de l'art* (1979).

RICHARD C. HOFFMANN

[See also **Fisheries, Marine.**]

FITZGERALDS. The Anglo-Norman invasion of Ireland in 1169 was led by the sons and grandsons of a remarkable Welshwoman, Nesta the daughter of Rhys ap Tewdwr. Of these Maurice Fitzgerald, her son by Gerald of Windsor, was the most important. He came to Wexford with two ships carrying ten knights, thirty mounted archers, and about one hundred foot. His enterprise was rewarded with a grant of lands in Kildare and Wicklow, and his heirs became barons of Naas. From him were descended the leaders of the two great Geraldine houses of medieval Ireland, those of Kildare and Desmond. His son Gerald, ancestor of the earls of Kildare, received lands centering on Maynooth, as well as Croom in Limerick, and became baron of Offaly, which he acquired through his marriage to Eva de Bermingham. Another son, Thomas, ancestor of the earls of Desmond, acquired Shanid in Limerick, a place afterward referred to in the famous Desmond war cry, "Shanid aboo." Although these two branches of the family were to go their separate ways, the Geraldines as a lineage were still sufficiently homogeneous to be referred to as *Geraldini* in fourteenth-century sources, and later still to claim, falsely, a family connection with the Florentine *Gherardini*. They remained a formidable force in the faction-torn politics of the medieval lordship of Ireland, and the name of Fitzgerald has continued to play a prominent part in Irish politics down to the present day.

A grandson of Maurice I, another Maurice Fitzgerald, became chief governor in 1232 and ruled Ireland for the next thirteen years. He greatly extended his lands, notably into Connacht. This eventually brought the Geraldines into conflict with the great de Burgh family, which resented this intrusion into their sphere of influence across the Shannon. Eventually, after what amounted to a civil war, a compromise was reached: the Geraldines ceded their Connacht lands to de Burgh, and were compensated with lands in Munster and Leinster. With their holdings thus consolidated, they were greatly strengthened in the midlands.

It was John Fitzthomas who sealed this agreement in 1298 as baron of Offaly and who was belted first earl of Kildare in 1316 during the height of the crisis of the Bruce invasion. He was a remarkable man who acquired the largest proportion of the vast estates subsequently held by the Kildare Geraldines. He proved his mettle as a marcher lord, successfully coping with the Irish on the frontiers of his lands. Service with Edward I in Flanders and Scotland not only demonstrated his loyalty and ability as a soldier but also brought him to the notice of the king. This stood him in good stead when he clashed with Wil-

liam de Vescy, lord of Kildare, who became chief governor of Ireland in 1290. The success of Fitzthomas in this struggle, and the failure of the government to suppress him even when he flirted with Irish enemies later in that decade, guaranteed Geraldine ascendancy in the midlands. When Fitzthomas was raised to an earldom in 1316, it confirmed his high rank among the nobility of Ireland. When he died soon afterward, his son Thomas not only inherited the earldom but had the liberty of Kildare restored to him in August 1317, which greatly augmented Geraldine independence. From now on the family fortunes, despite fluctuations occasioned by political crises, continued to flourish. Prominent in the government of the lordship (each earl in turn served at the highest level), married into the great Irish and English noble families, allied with the leading Irish chieftains, with landed wealth exceeding that of any other resident lord, the earls of Kildare remained a dominant force in the life of the medieval lordship.

Without any doubt the greatest of them all was the eighth earl Gerald (appropriately called the "Great Earl"). Under him the so-called Kildare supremacy reached its peak. He governed Ireland, almost continuously, under four kings: Edward IV, Richard III, Henry VII, and Henry VIII. Popularly known as the "all-but-king-of-Ireland," he never attempted to make himself king in name. Nevertheless, through adroit manipulation of office and the patronage which power conferred, he held the government securely in his hand for much of the time. Irish lords paid him a form of "protection money." His Yorkist sympathies led him to support the pretender Lambert Simnel in 1487 and to have him crowned Edward VI of England in Christ Church Cathedral, Dublin. When another pretender, Perkin Warbeck, landed in Ireland in 1491, Kildare's position was at best dubious, even if he had not actively supported this new Yorkist plot. But after his arrest and a famous meeting with Henry VII (when the king is reputed to have made the famous remark, "If all Ireland cannot rule this man, then it is meet that this man should rule all Ireland"), the Great Earl was restored to power and continued to rule Ireland until his death in 1513. His son, Garret Oge, the ninth earl, ably took his place. But when Henry VIII and his powerful ministers of state began to resent Kildare power in Ireland, there began a series of interventions from England that eventually led to the rebellion of Garret's son Thomas (famous as "Silken Thomas"). Ruthlessly crushed, the rebellion enabled the new government to end the dominance of the house of Kildare.

The other main branch of the Geraldines, based on Desmond, had a much more stormy passage through Irish politics. The first earl, belted in 1329, was notorious for his harassment of lands and communities in the south and was believed to have plotted to make himself king of Ireland. There is no real evidence to support this charge, but he certainly engaged in rebellious activity. Despite this, he served as chief governor and died having regained the trust of Edward III. The third earl was famous for his prowess as a poet in Irish and serves to illustrate how gaelicized this earldom had become in the course of the fourteenth century. Nevertheless, the earls continued to serve in office and never seriously wavered in their loyalty to successive kings. During the Lancastrian-Yorkist struggle, Desmond played a key role in securing Ireland for the Yorkist cause and was thanked by Edward IV after his accession. But he became too powerful in the view of the new English monarchy and suffered attainder and execution in 1468. From then on the earls of Desmond held themselves aloof in their lands in the southwest until they became involved in the Yorkist plots at the end of the century. Subsequent treasonable correspondence with the continental enemies of the new Tudor monarchy further alienated the house of Desmond. Rebellion and war ended with Munster in ruins, the earl living in a hovel, and savagery rampant. With the capture and beheading of the earl in 1583, the medieval earldom came to an ignominious end.

BIBLIOGRAPHY

Donough Bryan, *Gerald Fitzgerald: The Great Earl of Kildare* (1933); Art Cosgrove, "The Execution of the Earl of Desmond, 1486," in *Journal of the Kerry Archaeological Society*, 8 (1975); Edmund Curtis, *A History of Medieval Ireland from 1086 to 1513* (1938); Brian Fitzgerald, *The Geraldines, 1169–1601* (1951); Goddard H. Orpen, *Ireland Under the Normans*, 4 vols. (1911–1920, repr. 1968); Annette J. Otway-Ruthven, *A History of Medieval Ireland* (1968); George O. Sayles, "The Vindication of the Earl of Kildare from Treason, 1496," in *Irish Historical Studies,* 7 (1950), and "The Rebellious First Earl of Desmond," in John A. Watt *et al.,* eds., *Medieval Studies Presented to Aubrey Gwynn* (1961), 203–229.

JAMES F. LYDON

[See also **Ireland under English Rule.**]

FLABELLUM (Rhipidion), a liturgical fan described in the fourth-century *Apostolic Constitutions* as made of feathers, parchment, or cloth; it was used to keep insects away from the Eucharist. By the sixth century, the practical use was supplanted by a symbolic one: large circular medallions, usually metal, were held aloft on long staffs by deacons to protect the Eucharist from spiritual contamination. Flabella were often decorated with images of cherubim or seraphim (see illustration for the article "Cherub," vol. 3, p. 298), to recall the winged creatures who support the throne of God and embellished the Ark of the Covenant, and who were equated with the deacons and commemorated in the eucharistic liturgy.

BIBLIOGRAPHY

Kurt Weitzmann, ed., *Age of Spirituality: Late Antique and Early Christian Art, Third to Seventh Century* (1979), 617–618.

LESLIE BRUBAKER

[See also **Apostolic Constitutions; Eucharist.**]

FLAGELLANTS. The use of flagellation as a punishment can be found in early medieval monasticism and penitential discipline. Self-flagellation as a voluntary form of penance, though, became common only in the eleventh century, when it was promoted especially by Peter Damian. It became widespread as a public exercise for the laity in the later Middle Ages, first in Italy and then in northern Europe.

The first widespread flagellant movement arose in 1260 at Perugia, when that town was beset with civil strife and was recovering from famine and plague. In keeping with the Franciscan themes of sharing in Christ's sufferings and doing penance for sin, large numbers of people went in procession through the streets, naked from the waist up, whipping themselves on the shoulders vigorously enough to draw blood. Before the end of the year, the devotion spread to other Italian cities, arousing some opposition but attracting followers from various positions in society. To some extent, the movement spread into northern Europe. It was in Italy, though, that it became solidified in the form of confraternities, controlled by the clergy and devoted to flagellation and other forms of piety.

Flagellation gained importance in northern Europe in the mid fourteenth century, as a means of averting God's wrath and checking the advance of the Black Death. Arising late in 1348 in Austria and perhaps Hungary, the flagellant movement spread to Thuringia and Franconia, where it took on anticlerical overtones. It spread quickly to southwestern Germany, where sources speak of it as disciplined and rigorously ascetic, though dominated by lay leaders. Eventually it reached the Low Countries, where it was usually supervised by the clergy.

In principle, adherents were to proceed from town to town over periods of thirty-three and a half days. When the flagellants entered a town in procession, they would combine their mortification with ritual practices. The chronicler Henry of Herford describes them as proceeding with hymns to a church, where they would disrobe except for a waist-cloth and flagellate themselves. Then they would lie on the ground outside the church in various postures, symbolizing their sins, and ask God's pardon. They resumed their procession and singing, and each time they came to a verse mentioning Christ's passion they would fall to the ground, regardless of mud, thistles, or stones.

The flagellants were frequently blamed for arousing disorder, particularly violence against the clergy and Jews. In October 1349 Clement VI condemned their alleged excesses and forbade public flagellation. While the movement soon dissipated, groups survived secretly in and around Thuringia, where they were prosecuted in the fifteenth century for various beliefs they had developed, particularly their rejection of the church's sacraments.

The fourteenth-century movement is often seen as having proceeded from an orderly and orthodox to a violent and heretical phase. It is more likely that it varied from place to place, depending on religious and social influences.

BIBLIOGRAPHY

John Henderson, "The Flagellant Movement and Flagellant Confraternities in Central Italy, 1260–1400," in *Studies in Church History,* **15** (1978); Richard Kieckhefer, "Radical Tendencies in the Flagellant Movement of the Mid-fourteenth Century," in *Journal of Medieval and Renaissance Studies,* **4** (1974); Gordon Leff, *Heresy in the Later Middle Ages,* 2 vols. (1967).

RICHARD KIECKHEFER

[See also **Black Death; Clement VI, Pope; Heresies, Western European; Peter Damian, St.**]

FLAMENCA, ROMANCE OF, an anonymous thirteenth-century Provençal narrative poem sometimes attributed to the troubadour Bernardet. It is a fragment consisting of 8,096 octosyllabic verses recounting the amorous adventures of the "perfect" lady Flamenca and her ultimately accomplished knight-clerk-lover Guillem in their efforts to circumvent Archimbaut, jealous husband and foolish cuckold. The lovers, well-versed in an art of love derived from their reading of contemporary romances, act according to these literary conventions. The poet humorously manipulates his collage of stock characters and situations against a nonconventional background in which historical reality is suggested by specific dates, places, and people. The satiric clash of *fin amors* with an unidealized world creates a unique fusion of romance, fabliau, and chronicle reminiscent of *Cligés* and *Aucassin et Nicolette*.

BIBLIOGRAPHY

An English translation is Marion E. Porter, ed., *The Romance of Flamenca,* Merton J. Hubert, trans. (1962). See also Charles Grimm, *Étude sur le Roman de Flamenca* (1930); René Nelli, *Le Roman de Flamenca, un art d'aimer occitanien du XIIIᵉ siècle* (1966).

ELISABETH PENDREIGH WORK

[See also **Courtly Love; Provençal Literature.**]

FLANDERS AND THE LOW COUNTRIES. The provinces of West and East Flanders in Belgium and the departments of Pas-de-Calais and Nord in northeastern France comprised in the Middle Ages the county of Flanders, much of which lay between the North Sea and the Schelde River. In the early fifth century when various German tribes occupied the Roman Empire in the West, Flanders was seized by the Franks. From western Flanders near Tournai the Frankish leader Clovis launched his conquest of Gaul and founded the Merovingian kingdom of the Franks that fell to the Carolingians in the middle of the eighth century. By the ninth century Flanders, a military frontier zone, served as a defense against the recurring raids of the Vikings that contributed to the disintegration of the Carolingian Empire after Charlemagne's death in 814. By the third quarter of the ninth century, Flanders was a county held by Baldwin I Iron-arm, whom legend has descending from the forester Lideric, lord of Harelbeke. Baldwin ad-

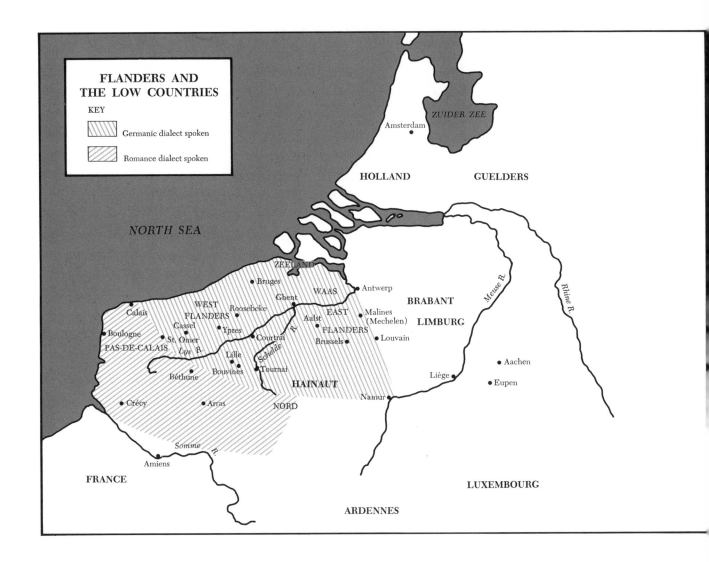

ministered Flanders for the Carolingian king Charles the Bald, who ruled over the western part of the Carolingian lands. In 862 Baldwin, a rude military adventurer, managed to marry Judith, the daughter of Charles, thus securing a tighter grip over a territory that included the flat marshy area at the confluence of the rivers Lys and Schelde, the environs of Bruges, the land of Waas, and some holdings around St. Omer. From this kernel Flanders was to grow.

When Baldwin I died in 879, he was succeeded by his son Baldwin II (879–918), who constructed rudimentary fortresses against the Vikings and forced their retreat from Flanders in 883. Baldwin II married a daughter of King Alfred the Great of England and then acquired most of the possessions that constituted medieval Flanders by expanding his control over lands to the southwest around Arras, Boulogne, Tournai, and St. Omer. In the southern part of this territory people spoke a Romance dialect (French or modern Walloon), while those north of a line extending from Calais to Eupen spoke a Germanic dialect (modern Dutch or Netherlandish, sometimes known as Flemish). This linguistic frontier still exists in modern Belgium and marks the division between the Dutch- and French-speaking inhabitants.

During the tenth century the successors of Baldwin II took more land to the south in what is now France and expanded eastward across the Schelde, ultimately winning the islands of Zeeland, the so-called Vier Ambachten along the Schelde, and the area around Aalst. This territory lay in the old Carolingian state of Lotharingia, ruled by the German

78

emperors. From the reign of Otto the Great (936–973), it had been part of the reconstituted Holy Roman Empire. In 925 the Schelde became the permanent border between the empire and the evolving kingdom of France. The counts of Flanders held the part to the west of the Schelde in fief from the French kings and the part to the east—so-called imperial Flanders—in fief from the German emperors.

With the subsequent weakness of the German rulers, the counts of Flanders became de facto independent rulers over imperial Flanders. They enjoyed almost the same status in the rest of Flanders until the reign of Philip Augustus (1180–1223) because the Capetian kings were likewise too weak to exercise their powers of feudal lordship. Although the counts occasionally did homage to their German and French lords and sporadically rendered military service, in practice they were independent princes who, during the eleventh and twelfth centuries, behaved like the rulers of a miniature kingdom. They were richer and more powerful than the Capetian kings, certainly as powerful as their neighbors the Norman dukes, and were surpassed only by the kings of England.

During the eleventh century there were three exceptionally able counts. Baldwin V (1035–1067) married his daughter to William I, king of England and duke of Normandy, thereby inaugurating a tie with England that, strengthened by the Flemish need for English wool, continued into the fourteenth century. Baldwin V was even chosen guardian of the young French prince, the future King Philip I. Robert the Frisian (1071–1093) established diplomatic relations with the king of Denmark, to whom he married one of his daughters. On a pilgrimage to the Holy Land he passed through Constantinople, was received by the emperor Alexios I Komnenos, and as a friendly gesture later sent a band of knights to Alexios, who had expressed the desire to have some of the Flemish warriors in his entourage. His son, Robert II (1093–1111), was the greatest French prince to participate in the First Crusade, returning with military glory and many holy relics.

The long line of counts descending directly from Baldwin Iron-arm ended when Baldwin VII (1111–1119), the son of Robert II, died without heirs. The countship then passed to Charles the Good (1119–1127), a son of Adèle, daughter of Robert the Frisian. Extremely conscientious and able, Charles dealt effectively with a food shortage resulting from a famine in 1125 and labored to make Flanders a well-administered and peaceful state. But his success bred the resentment of a number of powerful feudal families, including the Erembalds, over their loss of power. The comital chancellor Bertulf, an Erembald, hatched a conspiracy that led to the murder of Charles on 2 March 1127 in his castle-church of St. Donatien at Bruges. An exceptionally realistic account of this murder, the siege and punishment of the conspirators, and the subsequent civil war connected with the struggle over succession comes from Galbert of Bruges, a clerk of the count's administration and an eyewitness to the principal events.

The conspiracy against Charles reveals the success of the counts in reducing feudal disorder and consolidating the organs of government in their hands. By the early twelfth century the county of Flanders was one of the best-governed states of western Europe. A council of leading secular and spiritual aristocrats gave advice and performed some tasks of government while an entourage of more skilled and professional officials performed others. A chancellor assisted by some clerks operated a writing office. He was also head of the treasury, though the actual direction of financial operations was under a chief notary and several chamberlains. The county was divided into financial districts, each headed by a notary who collected revenues, made disbursements, and appeared annually before an auditing session held at Bruges. For defense and administration the county was arranged into castellanies grouped around castles that often became the sites of important urban centers. Over these districts were castellans who held their offices in fief. The counts and their councils and, in addition, the castellans presided over courts of justice. By the time of Charles the Good the counts had converted the Peace and Truce of God, a church-inspired institution, into a comital peace that was rigorously enforced and produced the desired result: peace and security along the roads and waterways and in the developing markets and towns. Breach of this comital peace brought heavy fines and severe physical punishment. Baldwin VII, for example, boiled a fully armed knight in a kettle for stealing two cows from a poor peasant.

Because of its strategic location along the North Sea and around the mouths of such rivers as the Schelde, Meuse, and Rhine, Flanders early became the scene of a brisk economic revival. By the late tenth and early eleventh centuries, both local and long-distance trade gave rise to such towns as Ghent, Ypres, and Bruges. Soon noted as a commercial center to which merchants came from Germany, France, Italy, England, and the Scandinavian area,

Bruges was on its way to becoming the commercial emporium of western Europe during the thirteenth and fourteenth centuries. At Ghent, Ypres, and smaller towns the wool industry began to thrive. The damp, mild climate was most conducive to the production of excellent wool cloth. When the local production of wool was insufficient, these towns began importing English wool. These activities were in the hands of the merchants and artisans who composed the growing bourgeois class in the towns. First acquiring social, economic, and legal privileges, they subsequently gained the right of local self-government during the twelfth century.

In the eleventh and twelfth centuries, the counts and religious establishments reclaimed much land from the sea and swamp by diking and creating polders for agriculture and herds of sheep. The growing towns provided fine markets for agrarian products and became centers of escape for the peasants. By the thirteenth century few serfs remained in Flanders. The economic revival of Flanders contributed to the early decline of feudalism and seigniorialism. During the twelfth century the towns became a major political force with which the counts and feudal aristocracy had to reckon, a development graphically seen during the aftermath of the murder of Count Charles when the towns assumed a leading role in the fighting and negotiations for a successor to the childless count. No candidate could hope for success without urban support, a lesson that the counts of the twelfth century did not forget. Into the early thirteenth century, they cooperated with the urban movement and benefited enormously from the income generated from the expanding commerce and industry. The chief difference between the political and economic development of Flanders and that of northern Italy was that the counts of Flanders never completely lost political control over the great communes.

By the early twelfth century Flanders was the most prominent of the several small states that made up the Low Countries. Like the eastern part of Flanders, these other states lay in Carolingian Lotharingia, theoretically under German lordship but in reality quite independent. Less favored geographically and with less talented leaders, these states lagged behind Flanders politically and economically until the twelfth and thirteenth centuries when their history began to impinge upon that of Flanders, sometimes with significant consequences. The most important of these states was the duchy of Brabant, just east of Flanders, with its towns of Brussels, Louvain, Ma-lines (Mechelen), and Antwerp. Equal to Flanders in area by the late thirteenth century, it was a serious commercial and industrial competitor by the fourteenth century. To the south was the largely agrarian county of Hainaut, which because of its location between Flanders and France and its family connections with the Flemish comital house, played a leading role in Flemish and French history. Along the Meuse lay the smaller county of Namur, controlled for a time in the thirteenth century by Flanders. East of Namur and Brabant was the bishopric of Liège with some busy commercial and industrial towns bordering the Meuse. In the southeast corner, the Ardennes region, was the hilly duchy of Luxembourg, the least developed economically and politically. On the eastern outskirts were the small duchies of Guelders and Limburg. To the north was the county of Holland, which, however, took no significant part in the political or economic history of the Low Countries until the late thirteenth century.

After the murder of Charles, the French king Louis VI interfered for the first time in the affairs of Flanders. As feudal overlord he led a force into Flanders in support of the countship of William Clito of Normandy, the grandson of Matilda and William I of England. This was the first of what were to be frequent French involvements in Flemish politics. Holding the support of the towns for a time by promising them local self-government, William eventually lost to Thierry of Alsace (1128–1168), the son of Gertrude, Robert the Frisian's second daughter and the wife of Count Thierry II of Alsace.

Under Thierry and his son Philip (1168–1191), Flanders reached the peak of its political power. Both counts supported the urban aspirations of the towns and enjoyed good relations with the townsmen. Philip reformed the criminal and fiscal law and introduced a new nonfeudal administrator, the bailiff, who supplanted the feudal castellan and notary. Celebrated for his participation in tournaments and jousts, he went to the Holy Land four times, the last on the Third Crusade during which he died at the siege of Acre in 1191. From one trip he brought back to Bruges a vial of the blood of Christ where today it is annually carried through the streets in the Procession of the Holy Blood. Philip founded numerous *villes neuves*, enlarged Flanders to its greatest area, and even acted as guardian to King Philip Augustus of France during his minority. With Philip's unfortunate death Baldwin VIII (1191–1194) became count by virtue of his descent from Marguerite, Philip's daughter. Already count of Hainaut,

Baldwin now ruled over both counties. Baldwin IX (1194–1202) succeeded his father in 1194, also ruling both counties. He participated in the Fourth Crusade, was elected emperor of the recently established Latin Empire of Constantinople in 1204, and died in captivity among the Bulgarians in 1205.

The crusading and international ambitions of the Flemish counts finally spelled misfortune for Flanders. After the death of Baldwin IX a succession of political problems plagued Flanders for the rest of the Middle Ages. Fatefully, Baldwin died during the reign of France's first great king, Philip Augustus, whose objective was to establish a de facto lordship over all the French fiefs and, if possible, to absorb them into his kingdom. He was remarkably successful. He not only deprived the English kings of most of their French lands but almost made Flanders a French province, and his grand political design was adopted by most of his successors.

Baldwin left only two daughters. Philip Augustus immediately forced a weak regent to turn them over to him to protect, educate, and marry suitably. He married the elder, Joan (countess, 1205–1244), to Ferrand of Portugal, an obscure prince from the Iberian peninsula whom Philip was certain he could control. In Flanders, however, Ferrand soon showed his independence by concluding with King John of England, who hoped to regain his lost French possessions, an alliance abetted by the growing Flemish need of English wool. By 1214 John had built a coalition of Ferrand, the Welf emperor of Germany Otto IV, and some German and Low Country princes, and was prepared to strike. Philip Augustus, meeting the allied army on Flemish soil at Bouvines, won a crushing victory that established French political hegemony on the Continent for the next century.

Ferrand, taken to Paris, was a prisoner until released twelve years later on payment of a huge ransom and territorial concessions. He returned to Flanders the abject, servile vassal of the French king. Luckily for Flanders the young daughter of Joan and Ferrand died before being married to the brother of Philip Augustus. Flanders was thus spared a French count from the royal house.

When Joan died in 1244 she was succeeded by her sister Margaret (1244–1278), whose two marriages further complicated Flemish political history. First marrying Bouchard of Avesnes and producing two sons, she discovered that her marriage was illegal because Bouchard was in holy orders (though the truth of this claim has been disputed). She then married

William of Dampierre and had two more sons, a situation that guaranteed a struggle for the countship after her death. Asked to be mediator, Louis IX of France awarded Hainaut to the Avesnes family and Flanders to the Dampierre, a shrewd move that separated the two counties and ensured a struggle between the two families for the next eighty years.

As count, Guy of Dampierre (1278–1305) inherited problems inconceivable to his predecessors of the twelfth century. Flanders was much weaker and in constant danger of being absorbed by France. French influence was strong with the feudal aristocracy and with many of the patrician townsmen who, seeking more political independence for their towns, repeatedly turned to the French kings for support. To increase their power in the towns, the counts often sided with the common people such as the artisans. The pro-French group was called Leliaerts, after the French symbolic fleur-de-lis, and the anti-French, Clauwaerts, because of their loyalty to the clawed lion of Flanders.

Opportunistic and astute, Philip the Fair (1285–1314) repeatedly intervened for the Leliaerts, forced Guy to stand trial in Paris for feudal disloyalty, and finally imprisoned him after the dissolution of his ill-fated alliance with Edward I of England. By 1300 Flanders was occupied and under French rule. The haughty French officials were hated and massive resistance developed among the urban artisans and rural inhabitants. At dawn in Bruges on 18 May 1302 all but a few of the French soldiers and officials were butchered in the so-called Matins of Bruges. An imposing feudal army then invaded Flanders and was met outside Courtrai on 11 July 1302 by a motley force of 8,000 to 10,000 foot soldiers from the towns and countryside. In the celebrated Battle of the Golden Spurs that ensued, the French were slaughtered. No prisoners were taken. Dead on the battlefield were 68 French lords and 1,100 knights. Seven hundred golden spurs were collected and hung in a church at Courtrai in expression of gratitude for God's help.

This stunning victory, however, did not free Flanders from French interference. Not strong enough and too divided to reap the benefits of victory, it had to fight two more indecisive engagements that resulted in the new count Robert of Béthune (1305–1322) concluding the Peace of Athis in 1305, which condemned Flanders to huge indemnities, surrender of Walloon Flanders, and destruction of key fortresses. All that Flanders gained was a precarious independence. Unable to comprehend such harsh terms after their sacrifices and victory, the mass of the townsmen and peasants were convinced that they had been betrayed by the count and the Leliaerts.

For Flanders, and indeed for western Europe, the fourteenth century was one of catastrophe. Flanders resembled a rudderless ship in rough seas. The counts, fearful of the consequences of disloyalty and increasingly dependent on the French kings, cooperated with them, implementing political, military, and economic policies that were often at odds with the vital interests of Flanders. In this reversal of the traditional positions of their predecessors, they gained some Leliaert support but lost the confidence of the majority of their subjects, especially the numerous artisans in the wool industry. The pro-French stance of Robert's successor Louis of Nevers (1322–1346) at the outset of the Hundred Years War between France and England incurred the wrath of Edward III of England, who imposed embargoes on English wool and restrictions on trade. These actions caused severe economic depression and unemployment leading to social and economic strife and disorder. The guilds fought both among themselves and against the patrician merchants and the counts. Convinced that their misery stemmed from lack of political power, they repeatedly tried to acquire it in both towns and county, a move that pitted them against the counts.

For a time it seemed that comital authority would be destroyed and that Flanders, like northern Italy and the Rhine Valley, would become a land of particularistic and independent communes. Compounding these troubles was the bitter economic and political rivalry between the leading towns. Each fought for supremacy in the wool industry and for political dominance in the county by attempting to impose its will over the surrounding territory and the smaller towns. Bands of urban artisans, angry at the growing wool industry in the countryside, repeatedly marched out and destroyed the looms and wool. The Peace of Athis caused such resentment that Robert of Béthune could not pay the indemnities. An effort by Louis of Nevers to collect money for this purpose sparked a revolt of the peasants in maritime Flanders that lasted from 1324 to 1328. Bruges joined the revolt, which was suppressed only by a French army at Cassel in 1328. With this defeat the hatred for Louis intensified; it was further exacerbated by the outbreak of the Hundred Years War in 1337.

The economic plight of Ghent was such that the merchant Jacques van Artevelde gained control in 1338 and became the leader of opposition to Louis. After negotiations Artevelde finally met Edward III of England at Ghent in 1340. There Edward was proclaimed king of France and assured of Flemish military assistance in return for lifting the embargo on wool. For five years Artevelde virtually controlled Flanders. Edward's inability to honor all his commitments, however, spawned discontent, and in July 1345 Artevelde was killed by a mob. The guild of the weavers temporarily controlled Ghent, with Louis relegated to the role of bystander. Louis died fighting for the French at Crécy in 1346, bequeathing a troubled county to his son Louis of Male (1346–1384).

Shrewder than his father and determined to follow a policy of neutrality toward France and England, Louis of Male concluded a fragile modus vivendi with the towns. But worsened economic conditions and endemic urban strife in the wake of the Black Death (1348–1350) blocked any real reconciliation. The wonder is that Louis survived. In 1369, for the return of Walloon Flanders, Louis agreed that his daughter and heiress Margaret should marry the Burgundian duke Philip the Bold, brother of Charles V of France. Louis managed to cope with the towns until 1379, when a quarrel over a canal between Bruges and Ghent flared into a general rebellion led by the weavers of Ghent. Overwhelmed, Louis fled to France to seek help from Charles VI. At the urging of his uncle, Philip the Bold, Charles sent to Flanders an army that speedily routed the Flemish force on 27 November 1382 at Roosebeke. Found the next day among the slain was the body of the Flemish leader who was, ironically, Philip van Artevelde, the son of Jacques. But no defeat could quench the flame of rebellion, which continued until Louis died. With the help of a French army and the offer of reasonable terms to Ghent, Philip the Bold (1384–1404) ended the resistance and gained recognition as count.

When Flanders went to the ducal house of Burgundy, a new era began for all the Low Countries. Surprisingly, Philip and his successors devoted little time to French Burgundy but concentrated on gaining authority in Flanders and reviving it economically. Rulers over the richest state in the Low Countries, they used it as a springboard for extending their control over all the Low Countries, a goal achieved by the time of Philip the Good (1419–1467). Though part of this larger Burgundian state, Flanders never lost its predominance. Considering it their most valuable possession, the Burgundian dukes spent much time in its cities. With its proud towns tamed and amalgamated into a larger political and economic entity, Flanders became the center of a rich artistic and cultural movement that, patronized by Philip the Good, heralded the achievements of the Renaissance in northern Europe. The paintings of the brothers van Eyck and of Rogier van der Weyden that have immortalized the Flemish merchants and towns are evidence of the political and economic achievements of medieval Flanders. The interesting Burgundian state of the Low Countries created between France and Germany, which Philip ruled and which resembled the old Carolingian kingdom of Lothair, was to succumb to the excessive military and territorial ambition of Philip's son Charles the Rash (1467–1477) and finally to fall to the House of Habsburg.

BIBLIOGRAPHY

There are few reliable works in English on medieval Flanders; the finest are in French and Dutch. Although in need of revision, the best account is still Henri Pirenne, *Histoire de Belgique*, 5th rev. ed. (1929). See also his *Belgian Democracy: Its Early History*, J. V. Saunders, trans. (1915), reprinted as *Early Democracies in the Low Countries* (1963). The most recent comprehensive history is Jan A. van Houtte *et al.*, eds., *Algemene geschiedenis der Nederlanden*, II–III (1950–1951, 2nd ed. 1981), with extensive bibliography. Other works on special topics are Paul Bonenfant, *Philippe le Bon* (1944); Renée Doehaerd, *L'expansion économique belge au moyen âge* (1946); Galbert of Bruges, *The Murder of Charles the Good, Count of Flanders,* James B. Ross, trans. (1960); François L. Ganshof, *La Flandre sous les premiers comtes* (1949), and *La Belgique carolingienne* (1958); Bryce Lyon and Adrian E. Verhulst, *Medieval Finance: A Comparison of Financial Institutions in Northwestern Europe* (1967); Raymond Monier, *Les institutions centrales du comté de Flandre de la fin du IXe siècle à 1384* (1948); Henri Nowé, *La bataille des éperons d'or* (1945); Adrian E. Verhulst, *Histoire du paysage rural en Flandre de l'époque romaine au XVIIIe siècle* (1966); Charles Verlinden, *Les origines de la frontière linguistique en Belgique et la colonisation franque* (1955); Hans van Werveke, *Een vlaamse graaf van Europees formaat: Filips van de Elzas* (1976).

BRYCE LYON

[See also **Baldwin I of Flanders; Baldwin I of the Latin Empire; Bruges; Burgundy, Duchy of; Flemish Painting; France; Ghent; Hundred Years War; Philip II Augustus; Philip IV the Fair; Textiles; Trade, European; Urbanism, Western European; Wool.**]

FLAX, a fibrous plant *(linum usitatissimum)* cultivated since Neolithic times for the fibers running vertically through its stem, which, when processed, may be spun into thread and woven into linen cloth. Products derived from flax in medieval times included tablecloths, sheets, shirts, smocks, towels, napkins, altar cloths, albs, and other liturgical vestments.

The cultivation and manufacture of flax was a laborious process. Flax seed required carefully prepared beds for germination; the seedlings were tended weekly for the first few weeks after sowing, requiring weeding by hand if the young plants were to prosper. Harvest usually occurred in mid June or early July. Unlike other land crops, flax was not reaped; rather, the stems were pulled from the ground by hand. Tied into bundles, the stems were retted (rotted) by being submerged, roots downward, in specially built ponds (characteristic of practice on Cistercian estates) or in stagnant, slow-running streams and rivers. After two weeks the fleshy parts of the stems would have rotted. The sodden bundles were then dried in sheds, or upon the open ground in fair weather. After the bundles had dried, it was fairly easy to crack the stems, freeing the unaffected fibers from the remains of the fleshy skin. After combing the fibers free of all stem material, they could be spun on the spindle and distaff into thread suitable for weaving into linen cloth.

Flax cultivation was, in Roman and medieval times, a highly labor-intensive undertaking. Upon the *latifundia* and state farms of the Roman Empire, labor costs were reduced by reliance on slave labor, and production could, consequently, be large. With the dissolution of these means of agricultural exploitation during the sixth and seventh centuries, large-scale production of linen cloth disappeared. In its place a smaller-scale cottage industry arose, producing limited quantities of what, in a woolen-wearing age, had become a luxury restricted to liturgical and aristocratic uses.

Along with other textiles, the production and quality of linen increased from the twelfth century onward, though linen never ceased to be a luxury item. The chief distinction between the linen industries of the earlier and later Middle Ages lies in the consolidation of linen weaving into urban centers; cottage industry thereafter produced only the raw materials, which were finished (woven and dyed) elsewhere. In Germany, Augsburg and Ulm were important linen weaving towns; in the Low Countries,

Ypres (weaving the "diaper" pattern); in France, Laon (weaving "lawn" finishes) and Valenciennes (weaving what came to be known as "valences").

MICHAEL J. HODDER

[See also **Textiles.**]

Flèche. Amiens Cathedral from the northwest, begun 1220.
PHOTOGRAPH COURTESY OF W. S. STODDARD

FLÈCHE (from French *flèche*, arrow), a slender, sharply pointed spire, composed of timber with a protective sheathing of copper or lead, rising vertically from the ridge of a roof. Flèches may contain bells, but normally they are essentially decorative, employed to break up the horizontality of the roof ridge or to demarcate the intersection of the nave, choir, and transept on cruciform churches.

CARL F. BARNES, JR.

FLECK, KONRAD, the author of a Middle High German *Floire und Blanscheflur* (*ca.* 1220) and possibly of a *Cliges* surviving only in very fragmentary form. He is known to us by name solely through Rudolf von Ems, who mentions him in the catalog of poets contained in his *Alexander* (vv. 3,239–3,248) and his *Willehalm von Orlens* (vv. 2,220–2,223). Of

Fleck himself nothing is known except that, by his own testimony, *Floire und Blanscheflur* was his first work, for which he asks patient indulgence, and that his source was a French text, now lost, by a certain Ruopreht von Orbent (vv. 138–146). The transmission of Fleck's poem is late; the only two complete manuscripts are of poor quality and from the fifteenth century.

The poem, 8,006 lines in length, treats one of the most popular and widespread stories of the Middle Ages, that of the youthful lovers Floris and Blanchefleur, who overcome religious differences, parental objections, separation, physical obstacles, and threats of death by the sheer force of their mutual devotion. Fleck, whose poem is more than twice as long as the French versions, offers a conventional, if tender, retelling of the traditional subject matter, but he greatly expands the length and number of direct dialogue exchanges and devotes particular attention to detail. For example, he tarries lovingly over the descriptions of the *Kopf*, a goblet that was Blanchefleur's purchase price and was elaborately engraved to depict the story of the fall of Troy, and of the tomb constructed by Floris' parents to convince him that his beloved had died.

In language and style Fleck was certainly influenced by Hartmann von Aue and probably by Gottfried von Strassburg; these influences are particularly noticeable in the prologue, which stresses the importance of virtue (*Tugent*) in general and love (*Minne*) in particular, regardless of the suffering necessary for their attainment. Fleck's narrative technique is straightforward and uncomplicated; he seldom interrupts the flow of the narrative with asides to the audience or moralizing generalizations. His work seems to have enjoyed little lasting influence.

BIBLIOGRAPHY

Konrad Fleck, *Flore und Blanscheflur*, Emil Sommer, ed. (1846). Peter Ganz, "Fleck, Konrad," in *Die deutsche Literatur des Mittelalters: Verfasserlexikon*, 2nd ed., II (1980); T. R. Jackson, "Religion and Love in *Flore und Blanscheflur*," in *Oxford German Studies*, 4 (1969).

FRANCES L. DECKER

[See also **Floris; German Literature.**]

FLÉMALLE, MASTER OF. See **Campin, Robert.**

FLEMISH PAINTING. The term "Flemish," with reference to the Belgian provinces of East Flanders and West Flanders, is used somewhat loosely by historians of art. For one thing, the artists considered to be Flemish were, with few exceptions, immigrants born and trained in the northern Netherlands and northwestern France who had settled in the major Flemish commercial centers, Bruges and Ghent, to benefit from the lucrative art market that developed there during the fifteenth century. Second, the preeminence of the art produced in Flanders rapidly influenced the style of painting in neighboring centers in Holland and northern France, and thus work from these areas has come to be called "Flemish" as well. The term "Netherlandish" is more appropriate since it encompasses the provinces of the south (Flanders, Hainaut, Brabant) bordering France as well as those in the north (Holland, North Brabant, Zeeland, and Gelderland). In the fifteenth century political and cultural boundaries divided the Netherlands. The southern portion (modern Belgium) was under Burgundian rule, while the north was governed by Bavarian counts until it was taken over by Burgundy in 1436.

The golden age of Flemish painting was initiated with the acquisition of south Netherlandish provinces by the Burgundian duke, Philip the Bold, who married Margaret of Flanders (daughter of Louis II, count of Flanders) in 1384. Philip, of the French house of Valois, established his ducal court at Dijon; for the many projects he promoted there, especially the decorations of the Carthusian monastery that he founded at Dijon, he called in Netherlandish painters and sculptors. Claus Sluter, from Haarlem, executed the sculptures for the portal of the chapel, the Well of Moses in the cloister, and the tomb of Philip, introducing a robust realism and pictorial drapery style that was to have a lasting influence in Burgundy. The painters and book illuminators he commissioned were also from the north Netherlands. Jean Malouel, his court painter, was from Zutphen near Nijmegen, as were Malouel's nephews, the Limbourg brothers, who also illuminated manuscripts for Charles V and John, duke of Berry (the *Très riches heures* in Chantilly). For the high altar of the monastery Philip commissioned Melchior Broederlam, from Ypres in Flanders, to paint the outer shutters and Jacques de Baerze, also from Flanders, to execute the sculptures on the interior (completed in 1399). Broederlam has been called the first truly Flemish painter, and his works, while representative of the prevailing International style of the fourteenth century, announce the coming of the *ars nova* of the van Eycks and Robert Campin in its exacting technique and in the use of disguised symbolism.

Philip the Bold's son, John the Fearless (*d.* 1419), moved the ducal residence to Flanders and established a flourishing court there; but it was under his son, Philip the Good (*d.* 1467), that Flemish painting established its illustrious reputation throughout the north. In 1425 Philip appointed Jan van Eyck, from Maeseyck in Limburg, who was his *valet de chambre*, as a special court painter exempt from local guild regulations. Van Eyck had formerly worked in the Hague at the court of John of Bavaria. Some believe that he executed the finest miniatures (Hand G) in the *Turin-Milan Hours* while in the Hague, but this is very problematic. After entering the service of Philip the Good, van Eyck settled in Lille and then Bruges, where he served not only as the official court painter but also as a diplomat on a number of missions sponsored by the duke. Van Eyck's paintings are distinguished by a microscopic-telescopic realism and by a profundity of disguised symbolism in which objects have meaning on two or three levels; as everyday objects executed with a precise realism and as symbols of higher religious beliefs. The *Madonna in the Church* (Berlin, Staatliche Museen), in which the Virgin is placed in a very convincing cathedral interior, can also be interpreted as the Madonna *as* the church, the highly detailed interior serving as an attribute of Mary—or, conversely, the Madonna can be seen as the personification of the meaning of the church in society.

Van Eyck's exacting technique was enhanced by the use of clear oil as a matrix for the pigments and by the application of numerous glazes that produce a brilliance and depth of color and light unlike the matte finish of traditional techniques. Jan van Eyck has long been considered the inventor of oil painting, but this is an exaggeration. His most famous work is the Ghent Altarpiece, a polyptych featuring on the interior God the Father flanked by the Virgin and John the Baptist, with side panels of angelic musicians and, on the extremities, nude figures of Adam and Eve. This upper ensemble surmounts a panoramic landscape on five panels, the *Adoration of the Lamb* (Rev. 4, 5, 7). Since its completion the huge altarpiece has been considered the masterpiece of Flemish painting. An inscription on the frame states that the work was begun by "Hubert" and finished by Jan in 1432. It has long been believed that Hubert (recorded in Ghent until his death in 1426) was the elder brother of Jan van Eyck, but there is much controversy over his identity. In recent years Robert Campin (to be identified as the Master of Flémalle), who was older than van Eyck, has been given much credit for the invention of the new Flemish style. Recorded in Tournai as early as 1406, he headed a large atelier in which Rogier van der Weyden was trained. Campin's art displays a combination of the colorful manner of the late Gothic International style and bold experimentation in an earthy realism with heavy, sculptural figures placed in interiors with plunging perspectives and exaggerated lighting effects. His masterpiece, the Mérode Triptych (Cloisters, New York), from about 1425/1430, features a matronly Madonna seated on the floor of a domestic interior filled with household objects executed in exacting detail. St. Joseph appears in the right wing as a hardworking carpenter in a workshop that opens on a colorful view of city streets. Campin's style and subject matter clearly reflect a more bourgeois environment than the elegant richness of van Eyck's aristocratic art.

Campin's most illustrious apprentice, Rogier van der Weyden, received his master's status in the Tournai painters' guild in 1432. By 1435 he had settled in Brussels, where he was appointed city painter and established a large workshop. In 1450 he made a Holy Year pilgrimage to Rome. Rogier's earliest works are clearly indebted to the sculptural style of Campin, but his figures are more delicately posed and are draped in elegant flowing mantles, a hallmark of his style. His Deposition (ca. 1438/1440, now in the Prado) is a masterpiece of Flemish devotional art. Rogier was more concerned with emotional content and expressive figures than with richness of detail and intricate symbolism. For the first time the mourners about Christ's dead body weep real tears, and Mary falls into a swooning posture that echoes Christ's.

Van der Weyden devised a number of new compositional types that were widely copied. One invention featured abridged narratives, resembling staged icons, placed within simulated church portals, as in the Miraflores Altarpiece (now in Berlin). For the Burgundian chancellor Nicolas Rolin he executed a huge polyptych of the Last Judgment at Rolin's hospital in Beaune (ca. 1443/1446), with a broad frieze of figures enthroned just below Christ the Judge, above a shallow ground line on which nude figures quietly emerge from their graves. His last works,

such as the monumental Crucifixion (ca. 1455/1460, now in the Escorial), display a remarkable abstraction, with only two mourners, the Virgin and John the Evangelist, standing beneath the cross placed against a red cloth of honor that seals off any indication of a landscape setting. Rogier had numerous followers, and his influence spread east far beyond the Rhineland. His style represents the second pole, the first being that of van Eyck, between which Flemish painting vacillated during the fifteenth century.

The second generation of painters, active from about 1445 to 1475, is best represented by three artists born and trained in the north Netherlands. Albert van Ouwater and Dirk Bouts were both from Haarlem and formed a school noted for its proclivities in landscape painting. Only one painting by Ouwater is known for certain, however, and that is an interior scene, the Raising of Lazarus (now in Berlin).

An early work by Bouts, the Altarpiece of Mary (now in the Prado), is closely related to Ouwater, and the colorful landscapes behind the narratives of Christ's infancy give some idea of the early Haarlem landscape mode. Bouts moved permanently to Louvain by 1457, and there he led a large workshop. His mature style is represented by the Deposition Triptych (now in Granada), which shows the influence of van Eyck in the richly attired figures and of Rogier van der Weyden in a number of compositional motifs, such as the swooning Virgin in the Deposition panel. His most famous work is the Last Supper Altarpiece (1464/1467, now in St. Pierre, Louvain), commissioned by the Confraternity of the Holy Sacrament. On wings flanking the solemn depiction of the Last Supper are four Old Testament prefigurations of the Eucharist. The Gathering of Manna, also part of the triptych, with puppetlike figures scattered about a deeply receding landscape bathed in a colorful morning light, exemplifies Bouts's treatment of space with various coulisses staggered along a winding road leading to the far distance.

A third painter of this generation, Petrus Christus, is something of a problem. He too came from the north, and his early works show close affinities to those of Ouwater and Bouts. By 1444 he had settled in Bruges. His early paintings, such as the Lamentation (now in Brussels, Musées Royaux des Beaux-Arts), also show the strong influence of van der Weyden, but his mature works, such as the Exeter Madonna (now in Berlin), painted about 1450, often are variations of compositions by van Eyck—so much so, in fact, that many scholars have described Christus as the inheritor of van Eyck's shop in Bruges.

In 1477 Charles the Bold's daughter, Mary of Burgundy, married Maximilian of Austria, and the Burgundian territories became Habsburg domain. This change had little effect on the art, and the style of van Eyck and van der Weyden prevailed during the last decades of the century. Changing patterns of religious devotion, however, brought about innovations in composition and subject matter. Hugo van der Goes represents the temperamental and melancholic genius in Flemish art. After pursuing a career in Ghent, he retired to the monastery of the Red Cloister near Brussels. His melancholy and madness grew, and brought on an illness from which he was not to recover. His early works, the *Fall of Man* and the Lamentation Diptych (*ca.* 1468/1470, now in Vienna, Kunsthistorisches Museum), reveal clearly his dependence on both van Eyck and van der Weyden, but a certain strained drama pervades both compositions.

Hugo's masterpiece, the Portinari Altarpiece (*ca.* 1475/1476, now in the Uffizi, Florence), is a huge work with large figures organized in a monumental fashion in a deep space. The somber blue tonalities and the somewhat erratic balance of the Nativity, together with the eerie expressions of the shepherds who join the circle of delicate angels about Mary and the Child, contribute to a disturbing and melancholic presentation of what is usually a joyous moment. Hugo's last works, such as the *Adoration of the Shepherds* (now in Berlin), display even stronger expressionistic effects.

During the last quarter of the fifteenth century, painting in Haarlem was dominated by Geertgen tot Sint Jans, a young genius who died at the age of twenty-eight. Geertgen, whose art reflects the mystical orientation of the north, worked for the Knights of St. John; about 1485, for their church in Haarlem, he executed a large Crucifixion altarpiece of which only the right panel, the *Lamentation* on the interior and the *Story of the Relics of John the Baptist* on the exterior (now in Vienna), survives. Geertgen not only drew on the earlier traditions of Haarlem landscape but also cleverly adapted motifs from the works of van der Weyden and van der Goes. In addition he introduced new compositional devices, fractional figures in his *Man of Sorrows* (now in Utrecht), and unusual lighting effects in the *Night Nativity* (now in the National Gallery, London), that mark his pictures as masterpieces of mystical devotion. His tender characterizations of the Madonna were widely imitated by the next generation of Dutch painters.

The inheritor of the Bruges tradition, Hans Memlinc, exemplifies the final phase of fifteenth-century painting in Flanders. His demure Madonnas were repeated in a number of placid compositions, many of which were executed for the Hospital of St. John in Bruges, with an engaging mellowness and charm that merited him the title "finest painter in Christianity" by his contemporaries. Memlinc was an inventive narrator as well, and in such works as the *Joys, Sorrows, and Glories of the Virgin* (now in Munich, Alte Pinakothek) and the *Shrine of St. Ursula* (now in Bruges, Memling Museum) he introduced new modes of storytelling that reflect the tastes of the later religious communities.

Gerard David, perhaps trained in Haarlem, settled in 1484 at Bruges, where he tempered his more homey Dutch style with the reserved elegance and monumentality of Memlinc. His Baptism Triptych (1502/1507, now in Bruges, Groeninge Museum) is a splendid example of the quietism and mellowness that characterize the final détente of Netherlandish art at the end of the century.

The enigmatic and eccentric Hieronymus Bosch (*d.* 1516), active in 's Hertogenbosch in north Brabant, presents special problems. His earlier works, such as the *Crucifixion* (now in Brussels, Franchomme Collection) suggest that he had his background in the more traditional Flemish imagery, but by the turn of the century he was producing his own imaginative and often macabre paintings, such as the *Garden of Earthly Delights* (*ca.* 1510, now in the Prado, Madrid), that defy precise interpretation and reflect more the prevailing spirit and pessimism of the early sixteenth century.

BIBLIOGRAPHY
Charles D. Cuttler, *Northern Painting from Pucelle to Bruegel* (1968); Max J. Friedländer, *Early Netherlandish Painting,* Heinz Norden, trans., I–VI (1967–1971); Erwin Panofsky, *Early Netherlandish Painting,* 2 vols. (1953); Leo van Puyvelde, *The Flemish Primitives* (1958); Margaret Whinney, *Early Flemish Painting* (1968).

JAMES SNYDER

[See also **Baerze, Jacques de; Bouts, Dirk; Broederlam, Melchior; Campin, Robert; Christus, Petrus; David, Gerard; Eyck, Jan van and Hubert van; Geertgen tot Sint Jans; Goes, Hugo van der; Limbourg Brothers; Malouel, Jean; Memlinc, Hans; Ouwater, Albert van; Sluter, Claus; Weyden, Rogier van der.**]

FLETA, a Latin treatise on the laws of England written between 1290 and 1300. The author is unknown, but the work has been ascribed to a royal attorney, Matthew Cheker. The title comes from the author's assertion that he wrote while imprisoned in the Fleet. The work, which enjoyed little popularity when it was composed, survives in only a single manuscript and had little influence on later works. *Fleta* was first printed in 1647 with an introduction by John Selden.

Fleta is in the main a derivative work, based primarily on Bracton's *De legibus* and on *De legibus et consuetudinibus regni Angliae,* a treatise attributed to Ranulf de Glanville. However, the work is not merely an epitome of earlier material. Modern scholars value the treatise for the information it provides concerning Parliament, the courts, and the royal household in the late thirteenth century. In addition, the material on husbandry and estate management is useful and supplements other works on these topics. Finally, the author has integrated material drawn from the statutes of Edward I with the purely legal discussions that constitute the bulk of the treatise.

The lack of contemporary interest in *Fleta* is probably explained by the fact that it was written in Latin. *Britton,* an anonymous treatise of similar content written at the same time as *Fleta*—but in French, the language of pleading—enjoyed great popularity with the lawyers of the day.

BIBLIOGRAPHY

Henry G. Richardson and George O. Sayles, eds., *Fleta,* 2 vols. (1953–1972); John Selden, ed., *Fleta* (1647). See also Noel Denholm-Young, "Who Wrote Fleta?" and "Matthew Checker," in *Collected Papers on Medieval Subjects* (1946), 68–85; Dorothea Oschinsky, *Walter of Henley* (1971); John Selden, *Ad Fletam dissertatio,* David Ogg, ed. and trans. (1925).

T. A. SANDQUIST

[See also **Bracton, Henry de; Britton; Glanville, Ranulf de; Law, English Common.**]

FLEURON, specifically, a floral motif, such as a rosette, in the center of each side of the abacus of a Corinthian capital. Generally, the term can apply to any floral motif employed for decoration. Fleurons derive from classical architecture and are especially common in Provençal Romanesque buildings—for instance, at St. Gilles.

CARL F. BARNES, JR.

FLEURY PLAYBOOK (Orléans, Bibliothèque Municipale, MS 201), a manuscript 16.8 by 14.4 centimeters, 251 pages plus one page (numbered 111 bis) and two blank pages (111 ter and 111^4). It contains a collection of religious texts plus the most important extant medieval manuscript collection of Latin plays with music (pp. 176–243). The music is written in *notation cursive* (according to the description of Corbin) on four red lines, nine to thirteen staffs per page. The dramas date from the end of the twelfth or early thirteenth century and were compiled and copied by an unknown scribe. During the fourteenth century the manuscript was housed in the library of St. Benoît-de-Fleury (St. Benoit-sur-Loire), whence its modern name.

The dramas may be divided into two types: those having music that can be traced to a liturgical connection, such as the *Visitatio sepulchri* (Easter drama) and *Ordo ad representandum Herodem;* and the remainder, such as the saint plays, which had a much lesser connection with the liturgy. The dramas are, in order: *Tres filiae, Tres clerici, Iconia Sancti Nicholai, Filius Getronis* (comprising the four St. Nicholas plays), *Ordo ad representandum Herodem,* [*Ordo*] *ad interfectionem puerorum, Visitatio sepulchri, Peregrinus, Conversio Sancti Pauli,* and *Versus de resuscitatione Lazari.*

The origin of the manuscript has been disputed. Solange Corbin suggested that the provenance was the monastery of St. Lomer at Blois, for the following reasons: (1) the manuscript contains a sequence in honor of a patron, St. Lomer (*Launemari patris pii*); (2) there is no proven tradition of dramatic performance at Fleury; and (3) paleographic/neumatic evidence. A study of the neumes suggests a similarity with a few manuscripts originating within an area bounded by Sens, Massay (Cher), and Orléans. However, there is no known musical manuscript by which the exact provenance of the *Fleury Playbook* might be traced.

There is no proven connection between the Easter trope from Fleury in the thirteenth-century manuscript Orléans, Bibliothèque Municipale, MS 129, and the *Fleury Playbook.* Thus, the supposed tradition of liturgical drama at the monastery is questioned by some scholars. Proponents of a Fleury provenance for this manuscript, such as S. K. Rankin, point out that the dramas clearly came from an artistic center where they were reworked and enriched with new material by the compiler/author/ authors, and that they could well have originated in the cultural milieu of St. Benoît-de-Fleury.

BIBLIOGRAPHY

Solange Corbin, "Le Manuscrit 201 d'Orléans: Drames liturgiques dits de Fleury," in *Romania*, 74 (1953); Diane Marie Dolan, "The Notation of Orléans Bibliothèque municipale Ms 201," in *Studia Anselmiana*, 85 (1982); S. K. Rankin, "Les drames du manuscrit 201 de la Bibliothèque municipale d'Orléans," in *Les sources en musicologie* (1981); Karl Young, *The Drama of the Medieval Church*, 2 vols. (1933, repr. 1967).

DIANE MARIE DOLAN

[See also **Drama, Liturgical.**]

FLEXA, an inflection within a phrase of Gregorian psalmody—that is, a deviation from the reciting tone. The *flexa* occurs within the line of chant as a phrase mark to clarify the syntax of the Latin phrase and to allow the singers to breathe. *Flexa* is also an alternative term for the descending two-note ligature in neumatic chant notation *(clivis)*. In early notations it resembles the circumflex (ˆ), while in later square notations the two notes are clearly delineated (⅊).

MARCY J. EPSTEIN

[See also **Musical Notation, Western.**]

FLJÓTSDÆLA SAGA (Story of the people of Fljótsdalr), probably compiled about 1500 in the Eyjafjarðar district of northern Iceland, seems never to have existed as a complete, independent work. In the oldest manuscript (Arnamagnaean MS 551 *c*, quarto) it appears as an extension of an augmented version of *Hrafnkels saga*, but breaks off at the end of chapter 26. In later manuscripts *Hrafnkels saga* has been omitted and the story completed through the addition of the last two-thirds of *Droplaugarsona saga*. For this reason the work is sometimes called "the longer story of Droplaugr's sons" and is often not listed separately in bibliographies. The compiler drew on additional sagas, especially those recorded in *Moðruvallabók* and several dealing with events in eastern Iceland. Evidently *Fljótsdæla saga* was written for the purpose of revitalizing a genre that had died out about 1400. The endeavor found no resonance in the Icelandic community, no doubt because literature of that kind no longer had contemporary relevance. The many transcripts of the story stem from the seventeenth century, when the Scandinavian countries were seeking their historical roots in the Icelandic sagas.

Modeled as it is on *Hrafnkels saga*, the style of *Fljótsdæla* is generally quite good except for the excessive use of similes and alliterative phrases, which is more characteristic of the *fornaldarsögur* than of the *Íslendingasögur*. Another influence of the "stories of ancient times" can be seen in the imaginative expansion of the sources. The uneventful marriage of Droplaugr, for example, is transformed into a vivid rescue from a giant abductor, which is preceded by a prophetic dream that prepares the scene of action in minute detail. In *Droplaugarsona saga* Droplaugr's sons happen to come upon a pagan temple during a blizzard; in *Fljótsdæla saga* this brief passage is expanded into a six-page description of that temple and its destruction by Helgi, Droplaugr's elder son. Although anachronisms are frequent in the *Íslendingasögur*, there are few so blatant as the description of one of the characters reading a story about ancient times, many decades before Icelanders had learned to read and write. The last of the sagas about native heroes sheds light on the composition of older sagas, the sources of which are more difficult to determine, partly because some of them no longer exist.

BIBLIOGRAPHY

Fljótsdæla saga, in *Íslendinga sögur*, X, Guðni Jónsson, ed. (1947), and in *Íslenzk fornrit*, XI, *Austfirðinga sǫgur*, Jón Jóhannesson, ed. (1950).

PAUL SCHACH

[See also **Droplaugarsona Saga; Family Sagas, Icelandic; Hrafnkels Saga.**]

FLÓAMANNA SAGA, an Icelandic family saga, is preserved in two redactions: a fragmentary longer one and a complete shorter one. On the whole the former represents the more original version; the latter, according to Björn Sigfússon, is the result of not always successful abridgment. *Flóamanna saga* is among the most derivative of the family sagas: its borrowings from older literature, particularly older sagas, are numerous. It has negligible value as a historical source.

Chapters 1–9 tell of the hero Þorgils' ancestors and are closely based on the *Sturlubók* redaction of *Landnámabók*. The story of Þorgils' childhood contains episodes reminiscent of *Grettis saga*. In chapters 12–17 Þorgils journeys to Norway to claim ancestral properties; the main source here is *Egils saga*. Back in Iceland, Þorgils embraces Christianity and is persecuted by Thor, his former idol. This theme and Þorgils' saintlike steadfastness in the face of Thor's maliciousness give *Flóamanna saga* an idiosyncratic position within its genre.

Sources drawn on include Oddr Snorrason's and Gunnlaugr Leifsson's sagas of Óláfr Tryggvason, religious writings, and even a borrowing from the Bible. Þorgils is invited by Eiríkr rauði to emigrate to Greenland but is shipwrecked in that country's icy wastes. His wife is murdered by absconding thralls. Not until he has suffered many trials and finally rid himself of Thor's attentions does he reach civilization. The sources for this part of the saga (chapters 20–26) include *Landnámabók*, *Grœnlendinga saga*, and *Eiríks saga rauða*. Distaste for the heathen Eiríkr causes Þorgils to return to Iceland. In the final section (chapters 29–35), in which definite sources are most difficult to pinpoint, Þorgils marries Helga Þóroddsdóttir and renews a feud with the powerful chieftain Ásgrímr. *Flóamanna saga* ends with his death at the age of eighty-five.

The borrowing from the Bible, a rare feature in a family saga, appears just before Þorgils sets sail for Greenland. In a dream Thor leads him onto cliffs overlooking a stormy sea and says: "In such storms you shall suffer unless you become my man." Þorgils' reply—"No! No! Begone, foul fiend!"—corresponds to Christ's *Vade Satana* (see Matt. 4:8–10). When Þorgils finally drives Thor away, he pronounces a curse, and the god, reduced in form to a young razorbill, flies off northward. There is probably influence here from the Icelandic version of Gregory the Great's *Dialogues,* in which St. Benedict puts the Tempter, disguised as a black bird, to flight with the sign of the cross (see *Patrologia latina,* LXVI, 132). The most extraordinary episode in *Flóamanna saga* occurs when the one-time Viking raider Þorgils suckles his motherless infant son. This is probably akin to Christian legends in which milk is marvelously forthcoming or babes are miraculously suckled.

Flóamanna saga contains thirteen dream episodes, several of considerable interest, including the well-known tree-dream motif in which a branching tree represents the progeny of the dreamer. Folktale motifs include two ships that converse about their future fate and, when Þorgils threatens his disobedient wife Helga with chastisement after the example of a cock, a truncated version of Aarne-Thompson, no. 670, "Der tiersprachenkundige Mann und seine neugierige Frau" (The man who knew the language of animals and his inquisitive wife). A curious element is a duel fought inside a large vat *(kerganga).* The longer version preserves what is probably a medieval Icelandic rowing chant.

Flóamanna saga may reasonably be dated to between 1290 and 1350, possibly somewhat later; Richard Perkins (1978) suggests a connection with Lawman Haukr Erlendsson (*d.* 1334) and/or the farm Gaulverjabær in southwest Iceland.

BIBLIOGRAPHY

Richard Perkins, "The Dreams of *Flóamanna saga,*" in *Saga-book,* **19** (1975–1976), and *Flóamannasaga,* Gaulverjabær and Haukr Erlendsson (1978); Björn Sigfússon, "Tvær gerðir Flóamanna sögu," in *Saga, tímarit Sögufélags,* **2** (1958).

RICHARD PERKINS

[See also **Egils Saga Skallagrímssonar; Family Sagas, Icelandic; Grettis Saga Ásmundarsonar; Vinland Sagas.**]

FLODOARD OF RHEIMS (*ca.* 893–966) was born probably in Épernay and was attracted to the school at Rheims by the fame of its director, Hincmar, who had died in the year of his birth. His earliest work was a continuation of the *Annales Bertiniani,* a chronicle of the church at Rheims begun by Hincmar. He continued the work until the year of his death, using written and oral sources.

Flodoard was appointed to head the archives at Rheims and shortly afterward began his great poetical work, *De triumphis Christi sanctorumque Palestinae,* in three books made up of separate poems on Christ, on Mary, and on the apostles and saints. He followed this with a shorter work in two books of various meters on the saints of Antioch, and a third, in fourteen, on Italian saints.

In 936 Flodoard visited Rome, where he no doubt found material for this last work, which contains 302 poems and is a valuable source for church history. Flodoard's account of the miracles at Rheims is not extant, but his *Historia Remensis ecclesiae* is among the most important historical works of the Middle Ages.

BIBLIOGRAPHY

Annales, in Georg H. Pertz, ed., *Monumenta Germaniae historica: Scriptores,* III (1889), 363–407; *Historia Remensis ecclesiae,* Johannes Heller and Georg Waitz, eds., in *Scriptores,* XIII (1881), 405–599; the Latin poems are in *Patrologia latina,* CXXXV (1879), 491–886. See also Max Manitius, *Geschichte der lateinischen Literatur des Mittelalters,* II (1923), 155–166.

W. T. H. JACKSON

[See also **Historiography, Western European; Latin Literature.**]

FLOKKR (flock [of stanzas]), one of two common Old Norse names for an extended *dróttkvætt* praise poem that, in contrast with the *drápa,* had no refrain. The other name was *vísur* (verses), which probably first appeared in the titles of works by the early-eleventh-century skald Sighvatr Þórðarson (for example, *Víkingarvísur, Nesjavísur, Bersǫglisvísur*). There are about a dozen poems extant with names ending in *flokkr,* most apparently dating from the eleventh century—for example, *Liðsmannaflokkr, Úlfsflokkr, Tryggvaflokkr, Magnúsflokkr, Kálfsflokkr, Valþjófsflokkr.* Haldórr ókristni's praise poem for Earl Eiríkr Hákonarson, composed around 1010, was probably the first to use *flokkr* in a title; only eight stanzas of his *Eiríksflokkr* survive. The fragmentary preservation of most of the early praise poems usually makes it difficult to determine whether a particular group of unnamed but related stanzas was composed as a *drápa* or as a *flokkr. Vellekla* is called a *drápa* in the sources, but no refrain has survived.

In the eyes of later centuries, the *flokkr* was a less impressive form than the *drápa.* Thirteenth-century sagas contain anecdotes about skalds who fell out of favor by composing *flokkar* rather than *drápur:* Þórarinn loftunga composed a *flokkr* for Cnut the Great, who ordered him to turn it into a *drápa;* Gunnlaugr reproached Hrafn Ǫnundarson for composing a mere *flokkr* for the Swedish king. The twelfth-century poem *Rekstefja* by Hallar-Steinn innocently

wonders: "Why do people think that only *flokkar* have been composed for Óláfr Tryggvason? Hallfreðr and Bjarni made real *drápur* for him" (stanza 34). The contents of the *flokkr* are sometimes regarded as more episodic than those of the *drápa,* but even in the latter form stanzas rarely dissolve in a fluid, syntactic movement with temporal links and transitions; as in the *flokkr,* they remain a series of discrete, dramatically intense moments and gestures.

BIBLIOGRAPHY

Hans Kuhn, *Das Dróttkvætt* (1983), 209–210; E. O. G. Turville-Petre, *Skaldic Poetry* (1976), xxxix–xl; Jan de Vries, *Altnordische Literaturgeschichte,* 2nd rev. ed., I (1964), 232–233.

ROBERTA FRANK

[See also **Dróttkvætt.**]

FLORENCE, a major city in Tuscany in central Italy, ranked among the greatest urban centers of Europe during the late Middle Ages and the Renaissance. It was founded as a Roman colony sometime in the first century B.C. on the banks of the Arno River. During the imperial period the city became a regional center of modest size. Little is known of its history in these centuries or during the barbarian invasions. A small Christian community existed in the city by the fourth century A.D.; its first noteworthy bishop was St. Zenobius, consecrated by St. Ambrose in 393.

Florence successfully resisted the siege of an Ostrogoth army in 405, but after the sack of Rome in 410 the city was occupied successively by Goths, Byzantine Greeks, and Lombards. These invasions contributed to the economic decline of Italy, which had begun centuries earlier, and to the contraction of trade and industry. The population of Florence declined with that of other urban centers. During the years of Lombard rule (568–774), the city's inhabitants, perhaps no more than a thousand, huddled for protection within their walls, subsisting on the scanty resources that could be extracted from the rural hinterland. In this sparsely populated, predominantly agrarian world, the survival of towns like Florence was due largely to the presence of the bishop and his curia, which provided a bare minimum of organizational skill.

The literary and archaeological record of Florence in the Lombard period is very scanty. Ecclesiastical documents contain sporadic references to bishops; other sources reveal the presence of a Lombard garrison in the town. A Carolingian army destroyed the Lombard kingdom in 774; thereafter, Frankish officials governed Tuscany and Florence, either directly or through their subordinates (*visconti* or *visdomini*). By the mid ninth century a powerful family, the margraves of Tuscany, had become the de facto rulers of the province. The German emperor Otto I (ruled 962–973) appointed the margrave as his vicar in Tuscany. The authority of the margraves survived until the mid twelfth century, when the rise of the communes and the struggle between papacy and empire destroyed that political system.

THE EARLY MEDIEVAL PERIOD

By the mid tenth century signs of demographic and economic revival are visible in extant Tuscan records. Much of the surviving documentation concerns local churches and monasteries, and particularly property transactions, but the sources also contain references to laymen and their affairs: purchases and sales of real estate, pious donations, testaments, judicial disputes. After centuries of stagnation, the population of Florence and her hinterland was growing. The city's inhabitants doubtless included many poor peasants of servile condition, but also men of property who perceived opportunities for improving their status in an expanding urban environment. In Florence, as in other Italian towns in the eleventh century, there developed a small urban elite composed of episcopal officials, judges, notaries, and petty nobles, with holdings and clienteles in the country but already having strong ties to the expanding city. From this elite were recruited, in the next century, the leaders of the Florentine commune.

Most of the evidence for Florentine history in the eleventh century comes from ecclesiastical sources, especially monastic records, which reveal the intimate and intricate ties between lay society and the church. Many secular fortunes were built or enlarged by the seizure or lease of ecclesiastical property. At the same time, new foundations were established by pious laymen such as Margrave Hugo of Tuscany, who lavishly endowed the Florentine Badia. In the city and countryside, new churches and monasteries were built, the most famous being the abbey of S. Miniato, founded by Bishop Hildebrand (*d. ca.* 1024).

From that monastery Giovanni Gualberti (*d.* 1073) led the movement to reform the Florentine church, to expose and expel simoniacs who held ec-

clesiastical office, and to enforce clerical celibacy. After being driven from Florence by his bishop, Gualberti founded his own monastery at Vallombrosa in the hills east of Florence, which became the center of a new monastic order. He led a successful campaign in 1068 to expel the simoniac Florentine bishop, Piero Mezzabarba, and to raise the moral standards of the Florentine clergy. Gualberti's challenge to the Florentine ecclesiastical hierarchy involved the urban populace, which became, for the first time, an active agent in the political and religious life of the city.

The sources reveal few details of the social structure of Florence and nothing about the embryonic associations that were being formed in the late eleventh century. Kinship ties were the strongest social bonds, but there may also have been informal groupings (*vicinanze*) of neighbors who lived in the same parish. Political power was still in the hands of the feudal lord, Countess Matilda, and the great magnate clans that provided the military forces for her armies and controlled the land and castles in the Tuscan countryside. The feudal order of Tuscany was declining in these years, as the manorial system—on which its power was based—distintegrated. Population pressure in the countryside contributed to this process and also to the steady growth of Florence.

Urban expansion in turn stimulated demand for food and raw materials, which resulted in higher prices for these commodities and also higher prices and rents for land. No evidence survives to warrant any conjectures about population, but the existence of thirty-five parish churches in 1070 is an index of significant growth. Records of urban real estate transactions appear more frequently in the sources, as do references to the activities of Florentine merchants. Prior to 1100, that evidence is very sparse; Florence entered slowly and tardily into the larger mercantile economy that maritime cities like Pisa and Genoa had been participating in for a century. In 1113 Florence did contribute to the naval enterprise organized by Pisa to conquer the island of Majorca from a band of Muslim pirates. That involvement indicates the existence of a mercantile community in Florence strong enough to act in its own economic interest.

COMMUNAL ORIGINS

In central Italy the eleventh century was a period of dramatic change, which the documents reflect imperfectly. The impact of those changes is more visible in the twelfth century, when the cities became vital centers of economic and political power. Their emergence as a significant force in Italy was the consequence of long-term demographic and economic growth and the decay of traditional structures of authority. The breakup of the manor, the typical early medieval form of agrarian organization, was already visible in Tuscany by the early twelfth century. The great ecclesiastical and lay estates were disintegrating, and servile labor and customary tenure were being replaced by free labor and contractual tenures, often short-term leases with money rents. The economic and political power of the lay and clerical rural magnates eroded as their estates were fragmented and their vassals (*fedeli*) moved into the towns or established themselves on lands that had formerly been part of the great estates of Tuscany's nobility.

These processes of disintegration were very gradual. A more dramatic blow to the old order was the conflict between empire and papacy over the investiture of ecclesiastical officers by lay rulers. The papacy challenged the authority of the emperor and his subordinates to invest bishops and abbots with their offices and the lands pertaining to them. In Tuscany, Countess Matilda fervently supported the papal cause against the German emperors, but in so doing she undermined her own authority, which derived from imperial power. The main victors in this struggle were the Italian towns, because they exploited the divisions between their temporal and spiritual rulers to establish their political independence.

The origins of the Florentine commune are obscure. Not until 1138 is there a reference to the existence of consuls, the first executives in the embryonic phase of communal government. It is probable that consuls had been chosen for some years before that date by members of the commune, who had taken an oath to act collectively in support of their interests. The fragmentary documentation of communal origins in Florence reveals a structure similar to that of other towns, such as Pisa and Milan, which had earlier created forms of communal government. The consuls were elected periodically by the members of the commune assembled in a *parlamentum,* which could also vote on legislative proposals submitted for its sanction.

The membership of this early commune was restricted to a small group of prominent citizens: landowners in town and country, many of whom had been (or whose ancestors had been) officials in the imperial, comtal, or episcopal administrations of Tuscany. Their social rank was aristocratic; their economic interests, landed; their background and training, military and knightly. They belonged to prominent families with holdings and connections in the city and countryside; within Florence they lived in towers, in tightly knit neighborhoods, surrounded by kinsmen, friends, and clients. Within their ranks, accepted as their social equals, were men with legal training, judges who were well qualified to serve as consuls and in other administrative positions. In this early commune there were few merchants, though their numbers did increase as the city's population and economy expanded. The social distinction between those citizens who belonged to the commune and those who were excluded (retail merchants, artisans, laborers) was maintained in the Florentine army. It was divided between *milites,* who could afford to maintain a horse, and *pedites,* who fought on foot.

Although the evidence for the functioning of this communal government is sketchy, a plausible pattern of development involved a progressive expansion of responsibilities, a broadening of jurisdiction, and a burgeoning self-confidence and audacity exhibited by these officials in their relations with imperial and ecclesiastical authorities. Initially the consuls were preoccupied with settling disputes between members of the commune, with defending their rights against aggressors, and with internal security. Gradually the scope of their activities widened to include the apportionment of taxes, relations with ecclesiastical foundations, and, most significantly, decisions of war and peace.

By the end of the twelfth century the commune had become the dominant political power within the city and was aggressively extending its authority over the territory outside the city walls (*contado*)—sometimes by persuasion and compromise, sometimes by force. Bishops surrendered their civil jurisdiction over their lands without a struggle, as did many nobles and rural communities. Communal armies besieged the castles of the powerful noble clans, the Guidi and the Alberti, to coerce them into submission; and they conquered the neighboring towns of Prato and Fiesole. The commune began to confront and quarrel with its neighbors: Siena, Pistoia, Pisa, Arezzo, Bologna. Like other towns in northern and central Italy, Florence was motivated by economic and military considerations to dominate her hinterland: to insure control over local food supplies and trade routes and over the manpower and resources of the rural population.

For decades after the death of Countess Matilda in 1115, the imperial authority in Tuscany did not constitute a serious obstacle to Florentine expansion. Emperor Henry V (d. 1125) was preoccupied with German affairs, as were his successors; their Tuscan lieutenants, who established a military base at S. Miniato del Tedesco west of Florence, were not able to sustain imperial power in the region. Finally, in the 1150's, the Hohenstaufen emperor Frederick Barbarossa (d. 1190) made a determined effort to restore imperial power in Italy. He fought tenaciously, but ultimately without success, to subdue the Lombard towns led by Milan and supported by the papacy. He also reorganized the imperial administration of Tuscany, appointing officials to collect taxes and administer justice.

In 1187 Florence received a charter from Henry VI, Barbarossa's son and imperial successor, confirming the authority of the commune in the city but limiting its extension in the *contado* to a five-mile radius. Henry VI was a formidable ruler who maintained tight control over his Italian kingdom, but his premature death in 1197 created a power vacuum. Florence joined other Tuscan towns in organizing a league to defend themselves against German rule. She also completed the reconquest of those parts of the *contado* that had been lost and became involved in wars with neighboring Siena and Pistoia. These wars between rival city-states were to be a permanent feature of Tuscan history throughout the thirteenth century.

About 1200, the executive authority of the Florentine commune was transferred from the consulate to the office of podesta. That constitutional change had already occurred in other towns; the shift from a multiple to a single executive was nearly universal in Italian city-states at that time. The podesta was a foreigner, a noble usually chosen from Lombard towns. His term of office was normally fixed at one year. He was the chief magistrate of the city and the head of the judiciary and the police force, both of which he brought with him. In time of war, the podesta led the Florentine army into battle. He was not a dictator; he was required to follow the orders of the legislative councils. The consular regime that had governed the city throughout the twelfth century had been plagued by faction; it was hoped that the podesta would contribute to the pacification of the community, but that expectation was not realized.

GUELPH AND GHIBELLINE

The regime of the podesta in Florence coincided with the intensification of factional conflict between rival magnate families and their supporters in the early thirteenth century. These houses had long been influential in the city's political and military affairs; their towers were symbols of their authority and of their ability to defend themselves. Violent altercations between feuding families, organized into "tower societies," had been common for decades. Chroniclers focused on the murder (1216) of a prominent magnate, Buondelmonte de' Buondelmonti, by his enemies from the Arrighi and Uberti houses as the event that led to the creation of the rival parties, Guelphs and Ghibellines, that became permanent fixtures of communal politics for a century. These parties took on political and ideological colorations, with the Guelph faction supporting the papacy and the Ghibellines favoring Emperor Frederick II. Similar parties were established in other Italian towns, fighting for control of their communities and allying with their counterparts in neighboring cities. The Florentine struggle between Guelph and Ghibelline thus spread to the rest of Tuscany and ultimately to the whole of Italy.

In Florence the Buondelmonti became leaders of the Guelph or papal party; their enemies, the Uberti, joined the imperial Ghibelline faction. In the 1220's and 1230's, these groups jockeyed for advantage in the city and countryside. They collected supporters among other magnate clans and in the ranks of the *popolo;* they competed for control of the communal councils and for the right to select the podesta; they fought pitched battles in the city streets and in their rural domains. The Ghibellines gained a significant advantage over their rivals after 1237, when imperial authority in Tuscany was strengthened by Frederick II's victory over a coalition of Guelph Lombard towns at Cortenuova. The Florentine commune was forced to accept the imperial ratification of its choice of podesta. In 1246 that office was filled by the emperor's illegitimate son, Frederick of Antioch, and in February 1248 the Guelphs abandoned the city to their enemies. Imperial control of Florence ended, however, in December 1250, when a Guelph army defeated a Ghibelline force near Figline, southeast of the city, shortly before Frederick II died in southern Italy. In Florence the citizenry organized a new regime of the *popolo* in which, for the first time in the city's history, merchants, cloth manufacturers, and other guildsmen gained a preponderant role in the commune, excluding most magnates from civic office.

THE APOGEE OF THE MEDIEVAL COMMUNE (1250–1340): THE PRIMO POPOLO

The establishment of the regime of the *primo popolo* was a political act that reflected the economic and social changes occurring in Florence since the late twelfth century. These were years of rapid population growth and urban construction; burgeoning commercial, industrial, and craft activity; and the rise of business and professional groups that were restive under the political domination of the magnate clans. These *popolani* were engaged in a wide range of entrepreneurial activities: real estate, moneylending, trade both local and regional, and the manufacture of cloth, leather goods, and metalwork. Through their professional organizations, the guilds, they developed a sense of their common interests. They formed military associations to guard their neighborhoods in times of civic strife and to join the Florentine army when the city was at war. During the decades of Guelph-Ghibelline rivalry, the *popolo* had gradually increased its numbers, self-confidence, and organizational experience. The crisis of 1250 enabled it to seize power.

The regime of the *popolo* did not abolish the office of podesta but instead added a new executive, the captain of the *popolo,* and a new council of the *popolo* to the commune's institutional structure. To house the captain and his retinue, the commune built a palace that still stands in the center of the city (now called the Bargello). The commune also authorized (1252) the first gold coin of the city, the florin, which became a standard monetary unit in Italy.

Pursuing a vigorous campaign to regain control of those parts of the *contado* that had been lost in the 1240's, the new regime fought wars with Siena and Pisa, cities ruled by Ghibelline parties. Initially the Florentines and their Guelph allies from other Tuscan towns were victorious, but at the battle of Montaperti (September 1260) a Guelph army that included a large Florentine contingent was routed by a Sienese force aided by Florentine Ghibellines and German mercenaries. As a consequence, the Ghibelline party regained control of Florence, expelling the Guelphs and confiscating their property. For seven years, the imperial party maintained a tenuous hold on the city. Then, in the spring of 1267, they abandoned it when an army of exiled Guelphs and French

soldiers appeared before the city walls. Florence was again ruled by the Guelph party.

By the 1260's, the population of Florence was over 50,000; she ranked among the largest and wealthiest cities in Italy. But her Guelph regime depended for survival on papal support and the military power of the French ruler of Naples, Charles of Anjou. Florentine merchants and bankers profited greatly from these links to Naples and Rome. They were particularly active as collectors of papal taxes levied on ecclesiastical offices and property throughout Europe. The ideological ties linking Florentine Guelphs with their allies in Naples and Rome were thus reinforced by economic bonds.

The price that the city paid for her Guelph alliances was some degree of interference in her domestic affairs. Charles of Anjou held the office of podesta in Florence from 1267 to 1282, though he was rarely in the city and normally exercised authority through vicars. This Angevin presence in Florence was strongly favored by Guelph leaders, who lived in fear of reprisals from their Ghibelline enemies. In 1273 Pope Gregory X failed in his efforts to reconcile the two factions. Pope Nicholas III sent his nephew, Cardinal Latino, to Florence in 1279 on a peacemaking mission; he did persuade the Guelph leadership to allow some Ghibelline exiles to return to the city. The guild community of Florence was increasingly troubled by the disorders fomented by the aristocratic factions and resentful of Angevin and papal interference in their government. When in 1282 the Sicilians successfully rebelled against Angevin rule in their island, the Florentine *popolo* took advantage of Charles's weakness to expel his officials. A new regime was established, based on the city's mercantile, industrial, and craft guilds.

Though its institutions and procedures were later modified, the basic features of the guild regime established in 1282 survived for more than 200 years. Civic office was reserved for members of the guilds, initially twelve but later twenty-one. The city was divided into six districts *(sesti),* each represented in the executive magistracy *(priores artium)* by a guildsman. A new group of priors was selected every two months. The majority of the priors came from the largest and wealthiest guilds: the *Calimala* (cloth refiners), *Lana* (woolen cloth manufacturers), *Cambio* (money changers), and *Giudici et notai* (judges and notaries). In addition to exercising general executive authority, the priors were also responsible for formulating legislative proposals that were presented for approval to the two legislative councils of the podesta and the *popolo*. The records of this legislation *(Provvisioni)* and of the deliberations and votes on the proposals *(Libri Fabarum)* have survived; they constitute a valuable source for the political history of the commune after 1282.

The establishment of the guild regime gave political recognition to the growing wealth and power of the commercial, industrial, and craft elements in Florentine society; it represented a defeat for the old political order dominated by the Guelph aristocracy. The cleavage between the guild community and the Guelph magnates was not so wide or permanent as to preclude social and economic contacts—or intermarriage—between these groups. Though the leaders of the guild regime viewed the magnate houses with suspicion, they needed their military skills for the wars then being waged against the neighboring towns of Arezzo and Pisa. In 1293, however, the guild regime, led by a nobleman named Giano della Bella, enacted the Ordinances of Justice, which imposed severe restrictions and penalties on the 150 lineages designated as magnate. Members of these houses could not become priors; they were required to post surety of 2,000 lire that they would keep the peace. Acts of magnate aggression against *popolani* were severely punished, and if convicted magnates were contumacious, their kinsmen could be fined for their crimes. By such draconian measures, the members of the Florentine guild community sought to restrain the violence and lawlessness of the magnates. Though occasionally revised and rarely enforced with rigor, the Ordinances remained a part of the Florentine constitution until their repeal in 1434.

The enactment of the Ordinances of Justice did not signify the permanent triumph of the guild community nor the end of factional strife. The Guelph magnates remained a potent force in communal politics through their control of the Guelph party (with its own statutes, treasury, and militia) and their network of clients and supporters. In 1295 the magnates succeeded in driving their enemy, Giano della Bella, into exile. Despite the Ordinances of Justice, their partisan feuds became more violent and disruptive of civic order. By the late 1290's, the struggle between magnates and *popolo* was overshadowed by the rivalry between two factions headed by the Donati and the Cerchi, powerful magnate clans. Through their identification with feuding groups in the neighboring town of Pistoia, the Donati party became known as the Blacks and the Cerchi as the Whites. Complicating this partisan struggle was the intervention of

Pope Boniface VIII, who supported the Blacks and who hoped to exploit these divisions to gain control of the city.

We know the details of this dramatic struggle between Blacks and Whites from the chronicle of a White partisan, Dino Compagni, and from the writings of the poet Dante Alighieri. In 1301 the White faction under Cerchi leadership had gained control of the commune. Pope Boniface VIII sent a French prince, Charles of Valois, to Florence with a detachment of soldiers, ostensibly to bring peace to the strife-torn city. But Charles, like the pope, was committed to the Blacks, and he allowed their leader, Corso Donati, to return to the city (5 November 1301), even though he was under a communal ban. The triumphant Blacks then wreaked vengeance on their enemies, burning their houses and forcing hundreds to flee. Together with other Whites, Dante, who had held office as prior in 1300, was condemned to death for treason. He found refuge initially in Arezzo, as did a Florentine notary named Francesco di Petracco, father of the poet Petrarch (who was born there in 1304). Communities of exiled Whites were established in many Tuscan towns, joining forces with local Ghibelline parties and seeking revenge for their losses.

The expulsion of the Whites created a permanent danger for the Guelphs in Florence, since these exiles were continually seeking aid from their Ghibelline allies in Tuscany, in Lombardy, and across the Alps. They appealed in vain to the emperor-elect, Albert of Habsburg (*d.* 1308), to invade Italy and reestablish imperial authority there. His successor, Henry VII of Luxembourg, was more sympathetic to their petitions. Henry VII crossed the Alps in October 1310 and received the submission of some (but not all) Italian towns. Florence refused to submit, and the emperor placed the city under the imperial ban. When Henry arrived in Pisa, he was greeted by exiled Florentines and other Tuscan Ghibellines, who urged him to attack the rebellious city. But Henry first traveled to Rome to receive the imperial crown (June 1312), and then came north to besiege Florence. The city resisted Henry's attacks, and he was forced to lift the siege and establish winter quarters at Pisa. After receiving military reinforcements from Germany, the emperor again marched south toward Rome, to recover that city from the army of King Robert of Naples. But near Siena he became ill and died (August 1313); his leaderless army disintegrated; and the Guelph regime of Florence was saved.

Henry VII's legacy to Tuscany was two decades

of bitter conflict between Guelphs and Ghibellines. Florentine control of her western territory was challenged, first by the Ghibelline lord of Pisa, Uguccione della Faggiuola, and then by his successor, Castruccio Castracani, lord of Pisa and Lucca. In 1313 the Guelph leadership of Florence delegated extensive military and political authority to King Robert of Naples for a five-year period, but this Neapolitan connection did not prevent a Florentine army from suffering a major defeat at the hands of Uguccione's troops at Montecatini in August 1315. In September 1325 Castruccio overwhelmed another Florentine army at the battle of Altopascio near Lucca. The desperate Guelph regime turned again to Naples for help. The commune elected King Robert's son, Duke Charles of Calabria, as its lord for a ten-year period. He was made supreme military commander of the army, and he also received the right to appoint the podesta and the priors. The Guelph regime had surrendered most of its authority to a foreign prince, whose physical presence (with a large military retinue) was an indication of his determination to rule the city with a firm hand. Castruccio, however, died of a fever in September 1328, and two months later Charles of Calabria also died.

The Guelph leadership responded to these fortuitous events by promulgating certain institutional reforms designed to stabilize the regime. Most important was the establishment of a fixed procedure for periodic scrutinies of guildsmen, to select those eligible for the priorate and the two collegiate groups, the Sixteen (standard-bearers of the military companies) and the Twelve ("Good Men" who advised the priors on policy and who voted with them on executive decrees and legislative proposals). These electoral reforms contributed to the formation of a stable polity, dominated by the merchants, bankers, industrialists, and lawyers from the leading Guelph families. These men constituted the political elite that governed Florence in the 1330's, when the city was at the height of its wealth, power, and prestige.

A detailed account of the golden age of Florence may be found in the chronicle of Giovanni Villani (d. 1348), who traced the history of his city from its origins to his own time. Villani chose the year 1338 as the zenith of Florence. Her population was then (he estimated) 90,000; she was the fifth largest city in Europe. Villani provided detailed statistics on local food consumption; on the woolen cloth industry (30,000 workers and 70,000 to 80,000 pieces of cloth produced annually); on the number of money changers and the value of gold coins minted every year; on

the number of churches, convents, and hospitals; on the amount of taxes collected by fiscal officials. The chronicler also described the civic building projects that had been launched in his lifetime: the construction of the third wall, the palace of the priors (Palazzo Vecchio) and its piazza, the cathedral, the campanile, the Ponte Vecchio, the great basilicas of the mendicant orders—S. Maria Novella (Dominican) and S. Croce (Franciscan). Within the walls were the fine palaces of the wealthy citizens, many of whom had also built country villas on their estates. While taking pride in this material display of wealth, Villani conceded that the Florentine building mania had become too costly and lavish, sinful in its excesses.

One remarkable statistic in Villani's chronicle is his estimate that one-tenth of the city's population (8,000 to 10,000 youths) were attending schools. The majority of pupils learned only the basic skills of reading, writing, and arithmetic to enable them to gain employment in a mercantile community. A few (Villani's estimate was 500 to 600) studied Latin to prepare for careers as lawyers, notaries, physicians, or churchmen. By the early fourteenth century, Florence had become a major center of learning in Italy. Theology and philosophy were taught in the *studia generale* at S. Maria Novella, while other schools gave instruction in Latin grammar, logic, and rhetoric.

The greatest literary figure of his age, Dante, was a product of this educational environment. Villani commemorated his death in 1321: "On account of the virtues and learning and valor of this citizen, it is appropriate to eulogize him in our chronicle, for all of his noble works that he has left . . . have contributed to the glory and reputation of our city" (*Cronica*, book IX, ch. 136). Dante's peer in the plastic arts was Giotto, described by Villani as "the greatest painter of his time, who surpassed all others in his ability to depict figures and actions naturally" (book XI, ch. 12).

THE ERA OF CRISIS (1340–1382)

A new era of Florentine history began in the 1340's. It was characterized by economic recession, political and social turmoil, and, most dramatically, the decimation of the Tuscan population. An epidemic struck the city in 1340, killing several thousand people, and it was followed by the Black Death in 1348, which may have claimed the lives of 40,000 inhabitants. The population of Florence was thus reduced by one-half in less than a decade, and for the next two centuries it fluctuated around 50,000. The epidemics drastically reduced the city work force, and woolen cloth production declined sharply. The Florentine mercantile and banking community had been shaken by the bankruptcy (in 1343 and 1346) of its two largest units, the Bardi and Peruzzi companies. Despite these adverse conditions, the Florentine economy recovered to some degree in the 1350's, though it never achieved the productivity and prosperity of the early fourteenth century.

These demographic and economic vicissitudes contributed to the turbulence of Florentine politics in these decades. The financial resources of the city had been drained by a lengthy and unsuccessful campaign to conquer Lucca in the 1330's. In September 1342, in an attempt to stave off the bankruptcy of the Bardi and Peruzzi companies, a group of prominent citizens established a permanent lordship (signoria) for a French nobleman, Walter of Brienne, duke of Athens. Walter's rule did not survive long: in August 1343 he was expelled from the city by a coalition of magnates, *popolani,* and artisans. Within weeks of this uprising, a conflict broke out between magnates and *popolani,* resulting in the defeat of the magnates in September 1343.

The regime established in the aftermath of these disorders was broadly representative of the guild community. Power and office was shared by the influential *popolani* families, by upwardly mobile "new men" (merchants, industrialists, lawyers), and by artisans and shopkeepers from the fourteen lower guilds. Magnates had only minimal representation in the regime and were prohibited from holding major offices. Also excluded from the government were thousands of cloth workers and other laborers who did not belong to any guild, as well as the residents of the *contado* and district.

The institutions of this guild regime had evolved gradually since the late thirteenth century. They had become stabilized by 1348 and, with only minor alterations, were to survive until 1530. Executive authority was vested in the nine-man Signoria (one standard-bearer of justice and eight priors), who held office for a two-month period. Assisting and advising the Signoria were two collegiate groups, the Twelve and the Sixteen. These officials promulgated executive decrees and proposed legislation that was submitted for approval (by two-thirds vote) to the two legislative assemblies, the councils of the *Popolo* and the Commune. These councils numbered some 200 to 300 citizens each; their tenure of office varied from four to six months. Before proposing legisla-

tion or making policy decisions, the Signoria frequently requested advice from the colleges and other magistracies, and from prominent citizens. While the Signoria and the colleges possessed wide executive authority, a number of special magistracies staffed by citizens had jurisdiction over specific areas of administration: for example, over grain supplies, the recruitment and pay of mercenaries, and the inspection of treasury records. The administration of territories outside the city was entrusted to citizens (vicars, castellans, podestas). Justice and public security were the responsibility of foreign officials (podesta, captain of the *popolo,* executor of the Ordinances of Justice), who came to Florence with their retinues for six-month periods.

Most civic offices were filled not by direct election but by a process known as a scrutiny. Periodically, all citizens eligible for specific offices would be scrutinized by a special electoral commission, and those receiving a two-thirds majority were declared eligible for that office. Their names were placed into bags *(borse),* and officeholders were selected by lot from the bags. An elaborate system of controls was created to prevent the monopolizing of offices by particular families. This electoral system was designed to maintain a balance of power among parts of the city (which was divided into four quarters, each quarter into four districts or *gonfaloni*), among socioeconomic groups, and among families. But factions did emerge, despite stringent legislation against their formation, and the scrutinies were subject to manipulation by these groups. The most profound division within the regime pitted a cluster of old families, which dominated the Guelph party, against segments of the guild community, which contained a large proportion of "new men" (*gente nuova*). The Guelph party sought to intimidate its opponents by identifying certain citizens as suspected Ghibellines, thus making them ineligible for office.

These internal tensions were a persistently disruptive force in Florentine politics, varying in intensity with changing circumstances. Invariably they became more acute in moments of crisis: during a war, famine, or economic depression. The regime nevertheless survived and maintained control over the city and its subject territory. It was remarkably successful in rebuilding the fabric of society after the Black Death: burying the dead, restoring essential public services, supervising the massive redistribution of property left by plague victims. The Florentine poor, who lived precariously on their earnings in the cloth factories and from menial labor, were a constant threat to public order. In times of famine and unemployment, the commune bought grain to feed the hungry laborers and their families. The authorities also acted swiftly to suppress disorders caused by high grain prices or low wages.

External dangers threatened the commune in the years after the Black Death. In 1343 Florence had lost much of the territory that had been acquired so laboriously in the early fourteenth century. She was vulnerable to attack from military companies that preyed on Tuscan cities, and also by Italian and foreign princes. In 1354–1355 and again in 1368, the Holy Roman Emperor Charles IV crossed the Alps and threatened the city. Florence also fought two wars against the Visconti rulers of Milan, in 1351–1353 and 1369–1370. Pisa and Florence were involved in a bitter conflict over mercantile issues in the 1360's. The cost of fighting these wars rose steadily in these decades, forcing the commune to increase taxes, to impose forced loans frequently, and to expand its fiscal bureaucracy to apportion and collect levies. The tax burden fell most heavily upon the peasantry in the countryside and the disfranchised workers in the city. The urban poor had to pay taxes on their food, at rates that (on many commodities) increased tenfold between the 1290's and the 1370's.

The 1370's were very troubled years for Florence. The economy, and particularly the cloth industry, was depressed, creating widespread unemployment and unrest. Factional discord intensified as the Guelph party and its rivals fought for control of the commune. In 1375 the enemies of the Guelph organization launched a war against the papacy, whose officials in the Papal States were accused of threatening Florentine independence. Many cities in the papal territory rebelled against the church. An infuriated Pope Gregory XI placed Florence under an interdict and in January 1377 returned to Rome from Avignon to lead the struggle against the commune. Guelph partisans in the city intensified their campaign against the Ghibellines, who were held responsible for starting the war against the traditional ally of Florence. Tensions created by these tactics, and by the fiscal and psychological pressures of the war, erupted into violence in June 1378. Led by the standard-bearer of justice, Salvestro de' Medici, the war party passed legislation penalizing leaders of the Guelph party while a mob burned their houses.

Civic peace was restored briefly before disorders again broke out in mid July. Thousands of Florentines, recruited mainly from the ranks of the cloth workers, assembled and marched to the palace of the Signoria and, in an atmosphere of escalating violence, forced the communal government to disband on 22 July. A new regime was established, which included representatives from three new guilds numbering some 13,000 men—dyers, weavers, shirtmakers, menders, and laborers in the cloth industry—who had previously been excluded from the commune.

This regime of the Ciompi, as the cloth workers were called, survived for only six weeks before it was overthrown. During its brief tenure, the city was governed by a special magistracy (balìa), which sought to restore order. To reconcile the diverse socioeconomic groups within the commune, it pursued a cautious policy. Its task was complicated by the disruption of the municipal economy. Many shops, particularly those producing cloth, were closed down, creating unemployment and distress among the workers, whose leaders sought to force the regime to pursue a more radical policy. This agitation aroused the fears of wealthy citizens, guildsmen, artisans, and shopkeepers, who distrusted the motives and objectives of the Ciompi leaders. On 31 August armed guildsmen fought and defeated the cloth workers and their supporters in the Piazza della Signoria. Their leaders were forced into exile, and the guild of cloth workers was disbanded. The most democratic moment in Florentine history had come to a violent and dramatic end.

The Ciompi revolution has been viewed by some historians as a manifestation of urban class conflict in late-medieval Europe, and as a portent of the struggles between industrialists and workers in modern society. Other scholars have interpreted the revolt as an attempt by the cloth workers to join the guild community and to share in its corporate values and privileges. The regime established on 1 September 1378 after the downfall of the Ciompi was based on the guilds of merchants, manufacturers, artisans, and shopkeepers. Its efforts to restore order and stability were hampered by economic difficulties, by threats from abroad, and by deep divisions within the city. Ciompi exiles organized a series of unsuccessful revolts, while Guelph extremists also plotted to overthrow the regime. These conspiracies intensified the fears of the new leadership, which included representatives from prominent families (Strozzi, Alberti, Scali) and also parvenus from the lower ranks of the guild community. Discord among these leaders sparked a political crisis in January 1382, which led to the downfall of the regime and its replacement by a more conservative government in which old

Guelph families regained their former power and status.

THE EARLY RENAISSANCE (1382–1434)

The early years of the post-1382 regime were characterized by an uneasy balance between the old Guelph families, with their aristocratic habits and values, and the guild community, with its popular and corporate orientation. By manipulating the electoral process and organizing vendettas against their rivals, a coalition of Guelph houses gained control of the government by 1393, when their most potent enemies, the Alberti, were exiled. Among the prominent new leaders were Maso degli Albizzi, Rinaldo Gianfigliazzi, Niccolò da Uzzano, and Gino Capponi. Their power was based on their wealth, their family status, and their networks of clients and supporters. They were the most influential figures in a restricted elite, an inner circle of prominent citizens who were continually active in politics. They did not change the constitutional structure, which still allotted a share of offices to lower guildsmen, but they were able to manipulate the system to stay in power and to promote their interests. They were also successful in thwarting numerous plots to overthrow the regime, organized by dissidents within and outside the city.

More threatening to the regime's security than these conspiracies were the wars fought with a series of aggressive Italian rulers. In the 1380's and 1390's, the lord of Milan, Giangaleazzo Visconti, created a powerful state in northern and central Italy, embracing much of Lombardy and, in addition, Perugia, Siena, and Pisa on the southern and western frontiers of Florence. The republic fought three wars with this formidable antagonist, who attempted a siege in the summer of 1402: the city was saved by Giangaleazzo's unexpected death and the dissolution of his army. An equally dangerous enemy was King Ladislaus of Naples, who fought wars with Florence in 1408–1410 and again in 1413–1414. After Ladislaus' death in 1414, Florence enjoyed a decade of peace before being embroiled in a conflict (1423–1428) with Filippo Maria Visconti of Milan. Only an alliance with Venice in December 1425 saved the republic from defeat at the hand of that powerful ruler.

While involved in these debilitating wars, Florence was steadily expanding her control over territory that lay outside her frontiers. In 1384 she purchased Arezzo southeast of Florence; other towns in that region, Montepulciano and Cortona, were occupied in 1390 and 1411. The most important territorial acquisition was Pisa, purchased from her lord in 1405 and reconquered in October 1406 after the city had rebelled against Florentine rule. Fifteen years later, in 1421, Florence bought the coastal town of Livorno south of Pisa. The republic now had direct access to the sea, and in the 1420's she launched her first galley fleet to compete with Genoa and Venice for Mediterranean trade.

Wars and territorial expansion created pressures to expand the bureaucratic structure of the republic. Each new parcel of territory required additional personnel to govern the acquisition: to staff the local courts and to man the fortifications. The costs of these military and diplomatic enterprises rose steadily, forcing Florence to search for new sources of revenue. An expanding fiscal bureaucracy extended its tentacles into every corner of the state and into every sphere of economic activity.

A significant manifestation of this bureaucratic impulse was the institution in 1427 of the *catasto,* a property register, which contained a detailed and comprehensive survey of the human and material resources of Florence and her territory: some 60,000 households and 262,000 souls. Legislation mandating this survey was passed by the government to assure a fair distribution of the tax burden. Each head of a household was required to submit to the *catasto* officials a statement including age of each household member and a catalog of assets, debts, and obligations. The compilation of this mass of data was completed within three years; the results still survive in hundreds of massive tomes in the Florentine archives.

The *catasto* records reveal that the city's population in 1427 was approximately 37,000, and that of the whole territory (11,000 square kilometers), 262,000. These figures reflect the dramatic decline of the city population since the Black Death, reduced by nearly two-thirds in a century. In 1427 the inhabitants of Florence owned property valued at twelve million florins, but the distribution of that wealth was very inequitable. Fourteen percent of the households owned no property, while the richest one percent possessed one-quarter of the city's total wealth. Florentines had also made massive investments in the surrounding territories, totaling some four million florins of real estate in Tuscany. Even though the population of the city included thousands of poor people *(miserabili),* the per capita wealth of Florentine inhabitants (273 florins) was twenty times larger than that of the peasants (13 florins) in the *contado* and district. Wealth from Tuscany's rural areas thus flowed into the city, and specifically into the hands of a small group of rich men who also received income from business investments, real estate, and communal bonds. The richest Florentine in 1427 was Messer Palla di Nofri Strozzi, whose gross assets exceeded 160,000 florins.

THE CULTURE OF THE EARLY RENAISSANCE

The significance of Florence for the history of humanism lies primarily in the precocious receptivity of its ruling elite to the study of the classics. Petrarch, the apostle of humanism (*d.* 1374), came from Florentine stock, though he spent little time in the city. Giovanni Boccaccio, author of the *Decameron,* was an enthusiastic promoter of classical learning. But humanism, as an education system and a program for living, flourished most strongly in Florence after the election of Coluccio Salutati as chancellor of the republic in 1375. Salutati was instrumental in arranging for the appointment of a Greek scholar from Constantinople, Manuel Chrysoloras, to a professorship at the university. He was also the patron of a group of young scholars who became avid students of the languages and literature of ancient Greece and Rome.

The core of humanism was the study of grammar and rhetoric, the art of writing and speaking eloquently. Students of the "humanities" read the works of Cicero, Livy, Vergil, and Seneca and used those authors as models for developing their own values. In Florence those values were civic and social, focused on the problem of leading a moral existence. The essence of the good life was its active character, the engagement of the citizen and businessman, in contrast to the medieval monastic ideal of withdrawal and asceticism. Among the first generation of Florentine humanists, Matteo Palmieri wrote a treatise, "On Civic Life," that praised the involvement of citizens in politics. Leon Battista Alberti described the virtues of family life and, more generally, of social experience in his essay on the family. Leonardo Bruni, who became chancellor of the republic in 1427, wrote a history of Florence, describing her development as a secular dream and eulogizing her commitment to republicanism and liberty.

Florentine humanism thus developed as an educational program and an ideology for the city elite. The values of republican Rome were integrated into her culture, as were the forms of classical monuments, which were much studied by Florentine architects in these years. In 1403 the architect Filippo

Brunelleschi and the sculptor Donatello went to Rome to explore the ruins there. Back in Florence, both artists used their knowledge of classical forms to develop their distinctive "early Renaissance" styles. Donatello's statues of St. Mark (1411–1413) and St. George (1415–1416) were landmarks in the evolution of Renaissance sculpture, combining classicism and realism to create dynamic images in stone. Brunelleschi's first building in the new style was the Foundling Hospital (1421–1424); in these years he was also working on the cupola for the cathedral. Classicism and realism were also fused in the work of Masaccio, the first painter in the new style. His frescoes of the life of St. Peter in S. Maria del Carmine (1427–1428) rank among the greatest monuments of Florentine Renaissance art.

The cultural eminence of Florence had been established in the fourteenth century by the work of Dante, Petrarch, and Boccaccio, and of Giotto and his contemporaries. The achievements of this new generation of scholars and artists further enhanced the city's reputation. As the leading center of humanism Florence attracted the interest of scholars from other cities, particularly those living in Rome. A network of personal contacts and correspondence linked Florentine humanists with their colleagues in other cities in Italy and abroad. Likewise, the achievements of Florentine artists were known and admired outside the city: Donatello's work in Padua had a profound impact on artistic developments in northern Italy. In their more sanguine moments, Florentines viewed their cultural achievements as equaling those of ancient Rome.

THE AGE OF THE MEDICI

The war between Florence and Milan in 1423–1428 was a costly and divisive struggle. The overburdened citizenry became increasingly critical of their political leadership, particularly after a campaign against Lucca failed (1429–1433). Two political factions formed in these years: one headed by a wealthy banker, Cosimo de' Medici; the other, by Rinaldo degli Albizzi. These factions were held together by ties of kinship, friendship, and neighborhood; they were vehicles for obtaining offices and benefits for their adherents. The Albizzi faction was recruited largely from aristocratic clans, while the Medici party contained a substantial number of "new men." In September 1433, Rinaldo degli Albizzi and his allies moved against their rivals, exiling Cosimo and seven kinsmen. A year later, in September 1434, friends of the Medici arranged for their re-

101

turn to Florence and for the banishment of the leaders of the Albizzi faction.

The regime headed by Cosimo de' Medici differed little in structure from its predecessor. The Signoria continued to be chosen in the traditional manner; the legislative councils and civic magistracies functioned as in the past. Greater controls were established over the electoral process to insure that supporters of the Medici would dominate the major offices. Medici wealth, and Cosimo's friendship with princes and prelates throughout Italy, were important assets in promoting the interests of the Medici party. The tight control that Cosimo and his associates exercised over the government was resented by some citizens; civic discontent was particularly widespread in the 1450's. But Cosimo resisted all challenges to his authority, and at the time of his death in 1464 his regime was stable.

In foreign affairs Cosimo's authority was great; he was primarily responsible for a major shift in Florentine diplomacy in the 1440's. He had always been friendly with the Romagnol condottiere, Francesco Sforza; he supported Sforza's efforts to gain control of Milan after the death of Filippo Maria Visconti in 1447. This support alienated Florence's old ally, Venice, and led to a realignment of Italian powers: Florence and Milan against Venice and Naples. Peace between the combatants was finally achieved at Lodi in 1454. It provided a framework for the political stabilization of Italy, which functioned quite effectively until the French invasion of 1494.

When Cosimo died in 1464, his position in Florence was assumed by his son Piero, an intelligent man whose political effectiveness was vitiated by ill health. In 1466 the city experienced a major crisis, as resistance to the Medici crystallized around a group of prominent citizens. With the aid of loyal troops brought into the city, Piero quelled this abortive revolt. When Piero died in 1469, his son Lorenzo, age twenty, became the "first citizen" of Florence and, like his father and grandfather, the unofficial head of the regime.

The most famous member of his illustrious family, Lorenzo de' Medici received a humanist education and achieved a reputation as a poet in the Tuscan vernacular. He was a knowledgeable connoisseur of the arts, though his role as a patron was modest. His political authority was based on the same coalition of prominent families that had supported Cosimo and Piero; it was maintained by his unceasing vigilance in cultivating and rewarding that support. Lorenzo was particularly active in diplomacy, for which he had an exceptional talent. Personally acquainted with the rulers of the major Italian states, he gained their friendship by assiduous attention to their interests.

The major threats to Lorenzo's position in Florence occurred during the first decade of his public career, in the 1470's. The first signs of trouble occurred at Volterra, where the Medici monopoly of alum had aroused local resentment. When Volterra rebelled, a mercenary army in Florentine pay sacked the city; some of the blame for this barbarity attached to Lorenzo. A more serious challenge to Lorenzo's authority was organized by Pope Sixtus IV, who believed that the Medici had thwarted his efforts to gain control over parts of the Papal States. Sixtus gave covert encouragement to a conspiracy, organized in 1478 by a rival Florentine banking house, the Pazzi, to assassinate Lorenzo. Lorenzo survived that plot, but his brother Giuliano was killed; the Pazzi and their henchmen were caught and killed by the mob. The war that then broke out between Florence and the papacy was ended when Lorenzo traveled to Naples (December 1479) to make peace with the pope's ally, King Ferrante. This diplomatic success strengthened Lorenzo's position in Florence; after 1480, his control of the regime was not seriously threatened.

In the 1480's, Lorenzo assumed the role of peacemaker in Italy; he was instrumental in preserving the tenuous balance of power between the major states. In 1482 he sent Florentine troops to aid the marquis of Ferrara, whose state was threatened by Venetian and papal forces. Two years later, the republic supported the king of Naples in his war with Pope Innocent VIII. Lorenzo also acted to preserve the status quo in Romagna, after two of the signori of that province, the lords of Forlì and Faenza, were assassinated in 1488. He maintained close relations with the traditional ally of Florence, the Sforza of Milan, in the person of the flamboyant duke, Lodovico il Moro. He was also on friendly terms with Pope Innocent VIII who, in 1489, granted Lorenzo the coveted prize of a cardinal's hat for his young son Giovanni (later Pope Leo X).

Although the Medici did not maintain a court like those created by Italian princes in Milan, Urbino, Ferrara, and elsewhere, the family palace was a major cultural center in Florence. The view of Lorenzo as a lavish patron of the arts has been discredited by recent scholarship, but he was very knowledgeable about the work of Florentine artists and was often consulted by foreign patrons who wished to employ them. He was also interested in major building schemes, both at home and abroad, though he did not indulge in that expensive pastime. He was personally acquainted with many of the leading intellectuals of his age: the poets Luigi Pulci and Angelo Poliziano (Politian), the philosophers Marsilio Ficino and Giovanni Pico della Mirandola. In the Medici palace and in the villas at Careggi and Poggio a Caiano, these men and their friends gathered to discuss the major intellectual issues of the age.

Florence was the cultural capital of Italy in the late fifteenth century, and her fame had spread beyond the Alps. Artists, among them the young Raphael, came to the city to study the works of her masters dead and living. The latter included the painters Verrocchio, Botticelli, the Pollaiuolo brothers, Filippino Lippi, Ghirlandaio, Leonardo da Vinci, and Michelangelo. The French humanist Lefèvre d'Étaples and the English scholar John Colet visited Florence to converse with Marsilio Ficino, the head of the Platonic Academy. The writings of medieval Scholastic philosophers were studied in the city by the Dominican friar Savonarola and his pupils; so were the works of Greek and Hellenistic philosophers. Pico della Mirandola brought Hebrew and Arabic texts with him to Florence. Paolo dal Pozzo Toscanelli, who died in 1482 at the age of 85, reflects the breadth and variety of this culture. He studied medicine as a young man, and then became interested in mathematics, physics, astrology, astronomy, and geography. He was a friend of Brunelleschi and Alberti, of the philosophers Nicholas of Cusa, Cristoforo Landino, and Ficino. His writings included a treatise on comets, notes on astrology, and a famous letter of 1474 (later copied by Columbus) to the king of Portugal, suggesting the possibility of a westward voyage to the Indies.

Lorenzo de' Medici died in 1492. Two years later, in September 1494, his son Piero was expelled from Florence by a rebellion of the citizenry, prior to the entry of an invading French army under King Charles VIII. The French invasion marked the end of an era of Florentine—and Italian—history. Although a republican regime replaced the government dominated by the Medici, its authority was always weak and tenuous, and eventually (1512) the Medici were restored as the leading family in the city. In the 1530's the republican facade that had masked their power was dismantled, and the principate under Duke Cosimo de' Medici was established in 1537. For two centuries the Medici ruled Florence in an Italy that was dominated by Spanish power.

BIBLIOGRAPHY

Sources. Mario Bernocchi, *Le monete della Repubblica fiorentina,* 4 vols. (1974–1978); Ildefonso di San Luigi, ed., *Delizie degli eruditi toscani,* 24 vols. (1770–1789); Lorenzo de' Medici, *Lettere,* Nicolai Rubinstein, ed., 4 vols. to date (1977–); Walter and Elisabeth Paatz, *Die Kirchen von Florenz,* 6 vols. (1940–1954); Pietro Santini, *Documenti dell'antica costituzione del comune di Firenze,* 2 vols. (1895, 1952); *Statuta populi e communis Florentiae,* 3 vols. (1778–1783); Richard Trexler, *Synodal Law in Florence and Fiesole, 1304–1518* (1971); Armando Verde, *Lo studio fiorentino 1473–1503,* 3 vols. (1973–1977); *Cronica di Giovanni Villani,* F. Dragomanni, ed. (1844–1845).

Studies. Hans Baron, *The Crisis of the Early Italian Renaissance* (1955, 2nd ed. 1966); Marvin B. Becker, *Florence in Transition,* 2 vols. (1967–1968); Alison Brown, *Bartolomeo Scala, 1430–1497, Chancellor of Florence* (1979); Gene Brucker, *The Civic World of Early Renaissance Florence* (1977), *Florentine Politics and Society, 1343–1378* (1962), and *Renaissance Florence* (1969, 2nd ed. 1983); Romolo Caggese, *Firenze dalla decadenza di Roma al risorgimento d'Italia,* 3 vols. (1912–1921); Samuel Cohn, Jr., *The Laboring Classes in Renaissance Florence* (1980); Elio Conti, *La formazione della struttura agraria moderna nel contado fiorentino,* 3 vols. (1965–1966); Robert Davidsohn, *Forschungen zur älteren Geschichte von Florenz,* 4 vols. in 3 (1896–1908), and *Geschichte von Florenz,* 4 vols. (1896–1927), Italian trans. by G. B. Klein, 7 vols. (1956–1965); Alfred J. Doren, *Das Florentiner Zunftwesen vom XIV. bis zum XVI. Jahrhundert* (1898), Italian trans., 2 vols. (1940); Enrico Fiumi, "Fioritura e decadenza dell'economia fiorentina," *Archivio storico italiano,* **115** (1957), **116** (1958), and **117** (1959); Richard A. Goldthwaite, *The Building of Renaissance Florence: An Economic and Social History* (1980), and *Private Wealth in Renaissance Florence* (1968); Guidubaldo Guidi, *Il governo della città-repubblica di Firenze del primo Quattrocento,* 3 vols. (1981); John R. Hale, *Florence and the Medici: The Pattern of Control* (1977); David Herlihy and Christiane Klapsisch-Zuber, *Les toscans et leurs familles* (1978); George A. Holmes, *The Florentine Enlightenment, 1400–50* (1969); Hidetoshi Hoshino, *L'arte della lana in Firenze nel basso medioevo* (1980); Dale Kent, *The Rise of the Medici: Faction in Florence 1426–1434* (1978); Francis W. Kent, *Household and Lineage in Renaissance Florence* (1977); Lauro Martines, *Lawyers and Statecraft in Renaissance Florence* (1968), and *The Social World of the Florentine Humanists, 1390–1460* (1963); Anthony Molho, *Florentine Public Finances in the Early Renaissance, 1400–1433* (1971); John M. Najemy, *Corporatism and Consensus in Florentine Electoral Politics, 1280–1400* (1982); Nicola Ottokar, *Il Commune di Firenze alla fine del dugento* (1926); Johan Plesner, *L'émigration de la campagne à la ville libre de Florence au XIIIe siècle*, F. Gleizal, trans. (1934); Niccolò Rodolico, *I Ciompi* (1945), and *Il popolo minuto ... (1343–1378)* (1899); Charles de la Roncière, *Florence, centre économique au XIVe siècle*, 4 vols. (1976), 2nd ed. 1983); Nicolai Rubinstein, ed., *Florentine Studies* (1968), and *The Government of Florence Under the Medici (1434–1494)* (1966); Gaetano Salvemini, *Magnati e popolani in Firenze dal 1280 al 1295* (1899, 2nd ed. 1960); Armando Sapori, *Studi di storia economica: Secoli XIII, XIV, XV*, 3 vols. (1955–1967); Ferdinand Schevill, *History of Florence* (1936); Feodor Schneider, *Die Reichsverwaltung in Toscana von der Grundung des Langobardenreiches bis zum Ausgang der Staufer (568–1268)* (1914); Randolph Starn, *Contrary Commonwealth: The Theme of Exile in Medieval and Renaissance Italy* (1982); Richard C. Trexler, *Public Life in Renaissance Florence* (1980); Martin Wackernagel, *The World of the Florentine Renaissance Artist: Projects and Patrons, Workshop and Art Market*, Alison Luchs, trans. (1981); Donald Weinstein, *Savonarola and Florence* (1970); Ronald F. Weissman, *Ritual Brotherhood in Renaissance Florence* (1981).

GENE BRUCKER

[See also **Alberti, Leon Battista; Banking, European; Boccaccio, Giovanni; Brunelleschi, Filippo; Bruni, Leonardo; Dante Alighieri; Donatello; Giotto di Bondone; Guelphs and Ghibellines; Italian Literature; Italy, Fourteenth and Fifteenth Centuries; Italy, Rise of Towns; Lombards, Kingdom of; Masaccio, Tommaso Cassai; Matilda of Tuscany; Medici; Milan; Naples; Petrarch (Francesco Petrarca); Pisa; Sforza.**]

FLORENCE-FERRARA, COUNCIL OF. See **Ferrara-Florence, Council of.**

FLORENCE, BIBLIOTECA MEDICEO-LAURENZIANA, MS PLUTEUS 29.1, a thirteenth-century illuminated parchment manuscript, is the largest and most central source of music of the Notre Dame school of Paris (*fl. ca.* 1160–1250). It is also the largest musical source for modal notation. Produced in Paris sometime between 1245 and 1255, the manuscript was not intended as a performing copy but, rather, as a comprehensive collection of all the major types of Latin-texted music that had flourished since the mid twelfth century: organum, clausula, conductus, motet, and rondellus. Although none of the pieces bears attribution in the manu-

script, it is the most important source of the works of Pérotin, several of whose known compositions are prominently placed at the beginning of the volume and at the beginning of the conductus collections. Some of the texts set to music are by Walter of Châtillon and Philip the Chancellor.

F (as it is known in musicological literature) has 476 numbered folios (232 by 157 millimeters) plus the opening unnumbered leaf, the verso of which contains the only full-page miniature. The thirteenth-century roman-numeral foliation goes to folio 355; the continuation to folio 476 is in modern arabic numerals. The original foliation indicates that folios 48–64, 94, 185–200, and 255–256 are now missing, and that lacunae of unknown length occur after folios 398 and 414, since they were not numbered before the loss. The manuscript is divided into eleven fascicles, which range from one to seven gatherings in length; the twenty-seven extant gatherings are unusually large, varying from fourteen to twenty-two folios, but the majority (fifteen) are of sixteen folios. (The missing leaves included at least two complete gatherings, the first of seventeen folios and the second of sixteen.) In fascicles that contain more than one gathering, the subsequent ones invariably start not with a new piece but with the conclusion of a work carried over from the previous folio.

Although his passion for completeness sometimes reveals little regard for the quality of the works he included, the editor/scribe was evidently moved by a true collector's zeal. He began each fascicle with an assembled body of compositions, usually all of the same type and number of voice parts. If his supply of pieces in a particular genre ran short before the end of the allotted space, he was able in several instances to gather more works to fill out the fascicle. In other cases the musical staves on the last few folios of a fascicle were simply left blank. In the first eight fascicles each page contains twelve staves ruled in red ink, an arrangement that provided the maximum flexibility in layout, allowing three lines of music per page for the four-part works, four for the three-voice pieces, and six for the two-voice works. The last three fascicles use a format of ten staves per page, to allow for text under each staff.

Fascicle 1 comprises a single gathering of four-voice works, beginning with Pérotin's two monumental liturgical organa, the Christmas gradual *Viderunt omnes* and the St. Stephen's Day gradual *Sederunt*. They are followed by a single clausula and three nonliturgical conductus, all of which, if not directly by Pérotin himself, certainly stem from his contemporaries. These six works apparently exhausted the compiler's supply of four-voice pieces, for he concluded the fascicle with a single two-voice clausula and a random group of eight three-voice organa and clausulae, leaving the last verso blank.

Fascicle 2 (folios 14–47, originally three gatherings, now missing folios 48–64) contains three-voice liturgical compositions, with some twenty-six Office and Mass organa intermingled in a single series. Nearly all follow the order of the church year, and they include graduals and alleluias for the Mass, responsories for vespers and matins, two processional pieces, and five *Benedicamus Domino* settings. At least three of the Office responsories in this collection could not be used in the Paris liturgy, giving evidence of the scribe's urge to include whatever examples of a type he could obtain. Two of these works (Ludwig's O 37 and O 39) have been identified as coming from Beauvais and Sens, but the third (O 38) has not been localized. The *Benedicamus Domino* settings conclude at the end of folio 44v; the scribe then added five three-voice clausulae, another responsory, and parts of two other works that break off at the bottom of folio 47v, the end of the second gathering. The third and last gathering is entirely missing. But, even incomplete, the fascicle is still the largest extant collection of three-voice organa.

The two gatherings of the third fascicle (folios 65–98) contain a version of Léonin's great book of organum on the antiphonal, or two-voice organa for the Office; vespers and matins responsories, processional pieces, and settings for the *Benedicamus Domino*. The responsories and processional pieces go from Christmas around the year to St. Nicholas Day (6 December), followed by pieces for the common of saints, the Trinity, and the dedication of a church. Then come seven settings for the *Benedicamus Domino* (through folio 88r), after which the scribe again proceeds in piecemeal fashion. The second gathering (folios 81–98) has an irregular structure of 8 + 4 + 1 + (1) + 4 leaves (with folio 94 missing), as if lengthened by several afterthoughts. The scribe added various works that run to the top of folio 93: some *Domino* clausulae, four complete settings for the *Benedicamus Domino,* and three responsories that are a distinct appendix to the collection. The remaining folios have empty staves. Again, several works may not be of Paris use.

Fascicle 4 (folios 99–146) continues Léonin's great book of organum with settings of fifty-nine graduals and alleluias for the Mass, arranged in a liturgical order like that of fascicle 3. The compiler's main

corpus of works took him to the middle of folio 144v; the final piece, which concludes on 145r, is out of liturgical order and was probably not on hand when he first arranged the works for copying. Folios 145v–146v, which complete the three even gatherings of this fascicle, are ruled but blank.

In musical style the two-voice organa in fascicles 3 and 4 tend to be very segmented works; sections are clearly delineated by stereotyped musical formulas or by distinct changes in musical style from one text phrase or word to the next. Any given segment was easily replaced or recomposed, resulting in a pastiche that nonetheless served the artistic purposes of the day. Although exactly what parts of a composition have been reworked is not always clear, the result is that hardly any two-voice organum found in more than one surviving source is note-for-note the same from one copy to another. Some differences may stem from scribal preference; others may be the result of geographical, chronological, or now undeterminable factors.

Another type of musical transfer occurred when sections of different organa that used the same basic chant melody as their foundation were borrowed from one composition to another, resulting in what may be termed polyphonic contrafacting, or using the same music for differently texted works. This procedure, which serves a purpose that is basically utilitarian, is especially frequent in the Office responsories of fascicle 3; the Mass organa of fascicle 4 generally proved more attractive to the kind of recomposition that was probably done for artistic reasons. In any case, it seems simplistic to think that all of this musical/editorial activity represents Pérotin's revisions of Léonin's earlier work; probably it involved at least half a century of changes through transmission by several different compositional and editorial hands.

Recomposition is strikingly exemplified in the 462 two-voice clausulae of fascicle 5, which provide numerous alternative settings for various sections of the organa in fascicles 3 and 4. In a fascicle that covered folios 147–200 (the third gathering, folios 185–200, is missing), the scribe collected several different groups of clausulae. Four of these sets were arranged in liturgical order, while the other two groups were copied at random; the stylistically most recent collection takes pride of place (Ludwig's nos. 1–203). In these usually short pieces the rhythmic modes are displayed in both common and uncommon combinations, and rhythmic architecture is often a clear artistic concern.

The sixth fascicle (folios 201–262, four gatherings) turns to nonliturgical works, and the fifty-nine pieces, with the exception of three motets, are all three-voice conductus. These rhyming, strophic Latin poems are normally devotional but sometimes polemical; the musical settings may be either strophic and syllabic or through-composed and melismatic. Pérotin's *Salvatoris hodie* begins the collection; the main scribe ceased copying at the top of folio 252v, and a later hand has added, in a more mensural notation, two more conductus for which the texts were never written in (folios 252v–254v). The next two leaves are missing, and the rest of the fascicle has empty staves.

The conductus collections continue in fascicles 7 and 10, with two-voice works in the former and monophonic pieces in the latter. Fascicle 7 is an enormous compilation of two-voice conductus, some 130 pieces covering seven gatherings (folios 263–380, with the last six folios blank). This repertory subdivides into several smaller collections and contains some of the longest works in medieval polyphony, running to several hundred measures in transcription. The eighty-three monophonic conductus in fascicle 10 (three gatherings, folios 415–462) contain a significant number of texts by Philip the Chancellor as well as texts that refer to datable events extending from 1181 to 1236. The notation of this collection, however, is especially problematic in rhythmic intent. The music stops on folio 451v.

Two different types of early Latin motets make up fascicles 8 and 9, which separate the two-voice from the monophonic conductus. Each fascicle consists of a single gathering followed by a lacuna of unknown length. Fascicle 8 (folios 381–398) contains twenty-six three-voice conductus-motets, so called because the top two parts are written in score over a single text, like a conductus; the chant tenor follows at the end. Like the clausulae on which most of these motets are based, they are arranged in liturgical order according to their tenor melodies.

The motets in fascicle 9 (folios 399–414) number forty-three, with forty of them being two-voice motets. The other three represent the most advanced type of motet in the manuscript: they are three-voice works that have a different Latin text in each of the upper voices; hence, they are Latin "double" motets as opposed to conductus-motets. They are interspersed at random among the two-voice pieces; in fact, less than half the pieces in this fascicle are in liturgical order. Several of the two-voice motets are based on three-voice clausulae with the top voice

omitted, and several others do not seem to have a clausula source at all, being newly composed as motets. The motet, and especially the three-voice double motet, clearly represents the music of the future in this manuscript.

The last fascicle, number 11, is a single gathering (folios 463–476) containing sixty monophonic Latin rondeaux (rondelli), so called because they all make use of refrains in some way. Although the music stops at the top of folio 471v, fascicle 11 is the largest collection of such pieces to survive.

The full-page miniature and thirteen historiated initials in *F*—one each at the beginning of fascicles 2–11 and three more dividing the long collection of two-voice conductus in fascicle 7—were all done in an atelier active in Paris between about 1235 and 1270. Named by Robert Branner the Johannes Grusch atelier, this shop worked on nearly forty extant manuscripts, mostly Bibles and liturgical books. With few exceptions the standard illustrations developed for such books were made to serve the Florence manuscript as well. Six initials each contain one or more traditional scenes from the life of Christ (folios 14, 65, 99, 201, 299, and 381), though they are not consecutive. Two more show Adam and Eve tasting the forbidden fruit and being expelled from the Garden (folio 263) and Adam and Eve laboring (folio 415). Another initial depicts the Seven Liberal Arts (folio 349), while the remainder seem to have been devised to illustrate words or ideas of the texts (folios 147, 336, 399, and 463), though their relevance is not always obvious or completely accurate. Wholly exceptional in its subject is the frontispiece miniature, the only known illustration of Boethius' division of music into *musica mundana* (world music), *musica humana* (human music), and *musica instrumentalis* (instrumental or sounding music)—a concept familiar to any medieval student of the liberal arts but not to the average lay illuminator.

F belonged to Piero de' Medici by the mid fifteenth century; where it spent the previous two centuries is unknown. The original owner was probably a churchman for whom this manuscript represented something of a luxury book. With its nearly pristine state of preservation and its large number of unique works, it is an indispensable source for knowledge of the music of twelfth- and thirteenth-century Paris.

BIBLIOGRAPHY
Luther Dittmer, ed., *Firenze, Biblioteca Mediceo-Laurenziana, Pluteo 29. I: Facsimile Reproduction of the Manuscript*, 2 vols. (n.d. [1966–1967]). See also Rebecca A.

Baltzer, "Thirteenth-century Illuminated Miniatures and the Date of the Florence Manuscript," in *Journal of the American Musicological Society,* 25 (1972); Robert Branner, "The Johannes Grusch Atelier and the Continental Origins of the William of Devon Painter," in *Art Bulletin,* 54 (1972), and *Manuscript Painting in Paris During the Reign of Saint Louis* (1977), 82–86, 222–223; Friedrich Ludwig, *Repertorium organorum recentioris et motetorum vetustissimi stili,* I.1 (1910, repr. 1964), 57–125, a catalogue raisonné; Gilbert Reaney, ed., *Manuscripts of Polyphonic Music, 11th–Early 14th Century* (1966), brief description, bibliography, and thematic incipits of the polyphonic works in the manuscript.

REBECCA A. BALTZER

[See also **Benedicamus Domino; Clausula; Conductus; Contrafactum; Léonin; Motet; Motet Manuscripts; Music, Western European; Musical Notation, Modal; Notre Dame School; Organum; Pérotin; Rondellus; Walter of Châtillon.**]

FLORENTIUS (*ca.* 920–*ca.* 980), one of the chief scribes and illuminators of Spain. His name appears in manuscripts and charters written at the Castilian monastery of Valeranica between 943 and 978. Among these are the *Moralia in Iob* of 945 (Madrid, Biblioteca Nacional, codex 80) and the densely illustrated Bible of 960 (León, Real Colegiata de San Isidoro de León, codex 2). The inspiration of Carolingian illuminated initials is evident.

BIBLIOGRAPHY

John Williams, *Early Spanish Manuscript Illumination* (1977), 21, 50–60.

JOHN WILLIAMS

[See also **Manuscript Illumination, Western European.**]

FLORES, JUAN DE (*fl.* 1475–1500) is the author of three prose works, *Grisel y Mirabella, Grimalte y Gradissa,* and *Triunfo de Amor.* Nothing certain is known of the author's life except a few details that can be found within the texts themselves. Flores states that he was of Castilian origin, while references are made to the poets Alonso de Córdoba and Pere Torrellas. The last documented record of the latter is in 1475. Typographic evidence indicates that *Grisel y Mirabella* and *Grimalte y Gradissa* were printed in Lérida in 1495, but because of an earlier

reference to *Grimalte* in a Catalan miscellany dated 1486 we know it was composed considerably before the date of printing.

These two works belong to the fifteenth-century genre of the sentimental romance. As in other examples of this genre, Flores' narratives concern unhappy love stories in which either one or both of the lovers die. Suicide, torture, madness, and extreme forms of penance are characteristic of these romances. Both of Flores' romances tell of two sets of lovers caught in situations in which the tragic fate of one pair precipitates the undoing of the other.

In *Grimalte y Gradissa,* the most developed of the two romances, Gradissa requires that her suitor, Grimalte, attempt to resolve the tragic problems of Boccaccio's lovers Fiometa (Fiammetta) and Pamphilo (Panfilo). The work is therefore in part a continuation of Boccaccio's *Elegia di Madonna Fiammetta* (1343–1345) and in part an original story of two Spanish lovers. Flores does not follow the simple autobiographical form of the *Fiammetta* but uses instead the complex *tratado* narrative structure found in Juan Rodríguez' *Siervo libre de amor* and in Diego de San Pedro's *Cárcel de Amor.* Of these three Spanish romances, *Grimalte y Gradissa* is the most realistically told, and Flores is the most successful in integrating the narrator into the plot line.

Grimalte survives in only one copy from the only known printing, but a French translation by Maurice Scéve is known to have had two editions. *Grisel y Mirabella,* more didactic in tone, had several sixteenth-century Spanish editions, and an embellished Italian translation enjoyed further translations into French, German, English, and Polish.

Triunfo de Amor has only recently (in 1977) been rediscovered. It exists in two manuscripts, the best one in the Biblioteca Nacional in Madrid. Like Flores' other works *Triunfo* is concerned with the ancient feminist debate about male and female culpability in matters of love. *Triunfo* belongs to a hybrid genre that combines stylistic features found in medieval debate and allegory traditions.

In all his writings Flores portrays the psychological conflicts of love, often without the excessive concern with honor prevalent in his day. In this way his works mark a stylistic transition toward the more realistic treatment of human passions found in *La Celestina.*

BIBLIOGRAPHY

Juan de Flores, *Triunfo de Amor,* Antonio Gargano, ed. (1981); Juan de Flores, *Grimalte y Gradissa,* Pamela Waley, ed. (1971), see esp. xi–lix; Patricia E. Grieve, "Juan de Flores' Other Work: Technique and Genre of *Triumpho de Amor*," in *Journal of Hispanic Philology*, 5 (1980); Barbara Matulka, *The Novels of Juan de Flores and Their European Diffusion* (1931), for editions of both *Grimalte y Gradissa* and *Grisel y Mirabella.*

EDWARD DUDLEY

[See also **Boccaccio, Giovanni; Celestina, La; Rodríguez del Padrón, Juan; San Pedro, Diego de; Spanish Literature: Sentimental Romances.**]

FLÓRES SAGA KONUNGS OK SONA HANS is a *lygisaga,* a mixture of native folktale and romantic elements, and the style is heavily influenced by that of foreign romances. The saga is preserved in three fifteenth-century vellum manuscripts as well as in some thirty-three paper manuscripts. Motifs commonly found in Scandinavia abound, including an analogue to *Beowulf,* but direct borrowing is likely from *Þiðreks saga, Trójumanna saga, Óláfs saga helga,* the *Speculum regale* (Norwegian: *Konungs skuggsjá*), *Karlamagnús saga,* and the more recent redaction of *Örvar-Odds saga.*

After some literary remarks on saga types in the prologue, including a favorable comment on the *lygisaga,* the narrative relates the story of King Flóres, who sues for the hand of Elína, daughter of King Kastús of Kartagía. Rejected, he kidnaps Elína, who bears him three sons: Félix, Fénix, and Ajax. Kastús recaptures Elína along with her sons, but his ship sinks on its return voyage. After many years Prince Sintram of Féneði sues for the hand of Eléná, Flóres' daughter by his second wife. Rejected, Sintram returns with an army that includes the heroes Únús, Sekúndús, and Tertíús. All four are captured, and they pass their time in captivity by relating their life stories. Sintram was once saved from a dragon by Dietrich of Bern, and the other three were all saved from a shipwreck: Únús was picked up by a ship and later fought a dragon in a cave, Sekúndús was snatched by a vulture and was later helped by a king's daughter to escape from prison, and Tertíús was attacked by a sea ogress before being rescued by five mermaids. Flóres overhears them, recognizes his three sons, effects a reconciliation, and marries his daughter to Sintram.

The same material has been treated in seven late *rímur* versions, all unedited, two from the seventeenth century and five from the nineteenth.

BIBLIOGRAPHY

Finnur Jónsson, *Den oldnorske og oldislandske litteraturs historie,* 2nd ed., III (1924), 111; Åke Lagerholm, ed., *Drei lygisǫgur* (1927); Margaret Schlauch, "Another Analogue of Beowulf," in *Modern Language Notes,* 45 (1930); Bjarni Vilhjálmsson, ed., *Riddarasögur,* V (1961), 63–121.

PETER JORGENSEN

[See also **Fornaldarsögur.**]

FLÓRES SAGA OK BLANKIFLÚR *(FsB)* is an Old Norwegian prose translation of version I (the "aristocratic" version) of the French twelfth-century *roman, Floire et Blancheflor,* and thus it belongs to the group of "translated romances" *(riddarasögur).* This charming love story was translated into many languages in the Middle Ages, and the Norwegian translation should be studied in comparison with the French, as well as the Flemish, English, and German versions. The translation must have been made from an older and more reliable text than those in the surviving Anglo-Norman and continental French manuscripts. Its source was almost certainly Anglo-Norman.

The nature of the manuscript traditions places a number of restrictions on a study of the translation. The Anglo-Norman fragment, which is the French text to which *FsB* shows the greatest similarity, contains only one-third of the *roman.* The Norse tradition consists, as so often in the case of translated romances, almost exclusively of Icelandic texts; and they give an unreliable representation of the orginal Norwegian translation, since one of the main manuscripts is defective and the other contains a radically shortened and often corrupt text. Fortunately, however, a small fragment of a Norwegian manuscript from about 1300–1320 exists; its text seems to be close to, if not identical with, the original translation. Also to be considered is a Swedish poem *Flores och Blanzeflor* (one of the *Eufemiavisor*) which was translated from *FsB* before major corruptions occurred.

It is therefore possible only to hazard guesses as to the content and form of the original *FsB.* In the existing material scholarly elements are cut back, some longer descriptive passages are left out, and allegories are restructured, but on the whole the translator seems to have reproduced the narrative content faithfully. The lyrical element is suppressed, but not the dramatic: the hero's passionate exclamations and laments are retained, and direct speech is sometimes substituted for the indirect speech of the *roman*.

The end of *FsB*, in which Flóres saves his life and honor by fighting a duel, is quite different from the more sentimental conclusion of the *roman,* but at this point in the work the Anglo-Norman text is defective, and only the continental French manuscripts are available, so a number of questions arise. Did the text from which the Norwegian translation was made already contain this form of ending? Or is it the work of the translator? And in that case, is the similarity between the ending of *FsB* and that of version II (the "popular" version) of *Floire et Blancheflor,* in which the hero also duels, just a matter of chance, or might the translator have heard the latter version and found its conclusion more to his taste?

On the basis of the Norwegian fragment, the style of the translation can be characterized as plain "translator's prose" without rhetorical embellishments—that is, unlike the "court style" of the thirteenth-century translated works *Strengleikar* and *Elis saga.* Apart from reflecting a desire simply to retell the story for its own sake, this style may show an attempt to imitate the unostentatious style of the French source.

It is not possible on the basis of style to connect *FsB* with the other translated romances, and it is altogether unnecessary to associate the entire corpus of translations with the cultural efforts of King Hákon Hákonarson (1217–1263). If it is assumed that the translation of *FsB* was commissioned by someone at the Norwegian court, an equally likely patron would be Hákon Magnússon (1299–1319) or his queen, Eufemia—who, it is believed, initiated the subsequent translation of *FsB* into Swedish; it is not unreasonable to assume that the two translations are connected.

BIBLIOGRAPHY

Helle Degnbol, ed., *Flóres saga ok Blankiflúr,* in Editiones Arnamagnæanæ (1984); Eugen Kölbing, ed., *Flóres saga ok Blankiflúr* (1896); Jean-Luc Leclanche, *Contribution à l'étude de la transmission des plus anciennes œuvres romanesques françaises: Un cas privilégié, Floire et Blancheflor,* II (1980), 97–105; Bjarni Vilhjálmsson, ed., *Riddarasögur,* IV (1951), 137–194.

HELLE DEGNBOL

[See also **Eufemiavisor; Floyris; Riddarasögur.**]

FLORILEGIA. A florilegium is a collection of quotations or excerpts selected by its compiler from the works of others. While the term itself is of early modern coinage (from *flos* [flower] and *legere* [to pick out or pick up]), "flower" in the sense of "the best part" of something goes back to antiquity; and by the twelfth century *flores* was one of the commonest terms for "selected extracts," as the titles of many popular collections suggest: *Liber florum, Libri deflorationum, Flores paradysi, Manipulus florum, Florarium, Floretum.*

Surviving medieval florilegia vary greatly in length, in type and formality of structure, and in purpose. Their contents are as diverse as the written tradition from which they derive: for example, extracts from Scripture, the Latin classics, the Latin Aristotle, and—much the most frequent element—the works of patristic and ecclesiastical authors. A reasonably lengthy florilegium ordinarily represents a mixture of sources; but there are also florilegia of the works of a single author, such as the *Flores Bernardi,* and florilegia composed entirely of excerpts from classical, or mixed classical/Christian, poetry. Virtually without exception, though with greatly varying degrees of precision, florilegia cite the sources of their extracts; and a majority of the popular collections—those compiled for public circulation rather than for private use—begin with a compiler's prologue that explains such things as his purpose, his choice of materials, and the structure or arrangement of the collection as a whole.

In the twentieth century, and particularly in its second half, medievalists have become increasingly conscious of the wealth of information to be garnered from a study of florilegia. Such information may be subdivided roughly into three categories:

First, florilegia have traditionally been valued for the texts they contain. A florilegium constitutes a selective record (though not an exhaustive nor even a representative one) of the sources available to its compiler, at a specific time and place, usually in the library of his own house, order, or college. Furthermore, florilegia may preserve snippets of rare works useful to the editors of those texts. This has been the case especially for classical florilegia such as the twelfth-century *Florilegium Gallicum* and *Florilegium Angelicum;* but there are examples as well from patristic/ecclesiastical florilegia, such as extracts from the works of Transmundus of Clairvaux and Valerianus of Cimiez in the thirteenth-century *Flores paradysi.*

Second, florilegia encapsulate the outlooks of the milieus in which they were compiled. For example, it was not chance but specific circumstance that determined that the seventh-century *Liber scintillarum,* a loosely structured collection compiled by Defensor of Ligugé for monastic meditation, found it adequate to cite, as source for an extract, simply "Hilary"—while the alphabetically arranged fourteenth-century *Manipulus florum,* compiled at the Sorbonne by Thomas of Ireland for the use of university-trained preachers, cites precisely: "Hilary, at the beginning of book 10 of his *De Trinitate.*" Variations in structure, content, terminology, even physical appearance are not haphazard but meaningful. The act of relating a florilegium to its immediate context often increases the understanding both of the florilegium and of the milieu itself.

Third, florilegia served as the immediate sources consulted by many medieval writers, over many centuries; and such collections underlie the apparent breadth of learning exhibited by many a well-known literary figure. This fact should be self-evident, given that many florilegia survive in large numbers of copies—for instance, the *Manipulus florum* in some 180 manuscripts, and the *Liber scintillarum* in more than 360—a clear indication that they were useful, and were used. Both historians and editors have now learned to suspect, and often to verify, the use of florilegia in displays of otherwise inexplicable erudition; such investigations provide a truer picture of the available resources and the working methods of a given author.

Books of quotations, common enough in more recent times, were especially popular throughout the Middle Ages. By the very fact of their being ordinary and commonplace, florilegia—more than the exceptional works of outstanding intellect or creative genius—give useful insights into the typical world of the literate populace of the Middle Ages.

BIBLIOGRAPHY

Jacqueline Hamesse, "Les florilèges philosophiques de XIII᷄ au XV᷄ siècle," in *Les genres littéraires dans les sources théologiques et philosophiques médiévales* (1982); Birger Munk Olsen, "Les florilèges d'auteurs classiques," *ibid.;* Henri M. Rochais, "Florilèges spirituels, I, Florilèges latins," in *Dictionnaire de spiritualité ascétique et mystique,* V (1964), 435–460; Mary Ames Rouse and Richard Hunter Rouse, "*Florilegia* of Patristic Texts," in *Les genres littéraires dans les sources théologiques et philosophiques médiévales* (1982).

MARY A. ROUSE

[See also **Anthologies.**]

FLORIN, a Florentine gold coin *(fiorino d'oro)* first struck and issued in 1252. Like the Venetian ducat that appeared in 1284, it consisted of approximately 3.5 grams of pure gold (twenty-four carats). Valued in the beginning at 240 Florentine denarii or common pennies, it had an image of St. John the Baptist on the obverse, and on the reverse a lily. This valuation ratio of 1:240 did not remain constant for very long, and severe fluctuations took place after the fourteenth century.

The florin enjoyed its greatest prestige and circulation from its date of issuance to the end of the fourteenth century, and competed with the ducat, the Byzantine nomisma (*ca.* 4.5 grams), and the Muslim dinar (*ca.* 4.25 grams) throughout the Mediterranean world. Considered one of the "dollars of the Middle Ages" (along with the coins mentioned above) because of its high unitary value, its intrinsic stability in both weight and fineness, and its association with a great economic and cultural metropolis, the florin eventually eclipsed the French gold coinage in international transactions during the later fourteenth century. It also overshadowed in historical and mercantile importance the contemporary Genoese *genovino* and the later fifteenth-century gold issues of the Burgundian dukes and Rhenish princes.

Chiefly an aristocratic coin circulating among the upper classes and in regional and interregional mercantile and financial relations, the florin declined in importance after 1400. Because of lighter-weight issues at the beginning of the fifteenth century, its position as an international unit of currency and as a standard diminished, and it was gradually superseded by the ducat.

RONALD EDWARD ZUPKO

[See also **Dinar; Ducat; Mints and Money, Western European; Nomisma.**]

FLORIS. The story of Floris, the son of the pagan king Fenix, and Blanchefleur, the daughter of a captured Christian pilgrim, is represented in the vernacular literatures of most western European countries. They are raised together at the court of Fenix where their growing affection for each other arouses fears in the king that Floris will marry Blanchefleur, and he resolves to have/her killed. Instead, however, he sends Floris away to school and sells Blanchefleur to merchants traveling to Babylon (that is, Cairo), where she is sold to the emir. Floris' parents construct a magnificent tomb that bears Blanchefleur's name, but Floris' reaction to the news of her death so alarms them that they tell him the truth, whereupon he resolves to find her.

Floris eventually arrives outside Babylon and receives counsel from the bridge warden, Daire, who tells him about the emir's tower of maidens, from among whose dwellers he annually selects a new wife, having the former one killed. Rumor has it that Blanchefleur will be next. To gain admittance to the tower, Daire advises Floris to play chess with the watchman but to keep returning all winnings until the watchman swears him fealty and is thus obligated to assist him. The plan functions as it is supposed to, and the watchman smuggles Floris into the tower in a basket of flowers, which is mistakenly placed in the room of Blanchefleur's friend Claris. She arranges a reunion between the two, who are discovered two weeks later by the emir. He spares their lives until he has consulted his advisers. So impressed are the latter by the young lovers' willingness to die for each other that they convince the emir to pardon them. Floris is knighted, he and Blanchefleur are married, and the emir weds Claris, promising to retain her as his only wife. Soon messengers arrive with news of Fenix' death, and the emir reluctantly consents to the couple's departure. Once home, Floris embraces Christianity and encourages his subjects to do likewise.

Containing elements of both the older heroic and the incipient courtly traditions, the Floris material, in the "aristocratic" version, is characterized by the lack of adventure or knightly combat (the later "popular" version does include such elements), the conflict between pagan and Christian, the absence of a court in the Arthurian mold, and the importance and motivating force of love.

The "aristocratic" French version, summarized above, marks the first appearance of this possibly Oriental tale in European literature around 1160. The "popular" French version was composed by 1200, and for the next century and a half the tale of Floris remained one of the most popular of all romance plots. The fragmentary Rhenish *Floyris* (ca. 1170) was followed by Konrad Fleck's Middle High German *Floire und Blanscheflur* (ca. 1220) and by a Middle Low German version, *Flos unde Blankeflos,* after 1300. There were also versions in English (*Floris and Blancheflour,* before 1250), in Middle Netherlandish (by Diederic van Assenede, ca. 1260), and in Italian (after 1300). A lost Anglo-Norman version seems to

have been the source for the Old Norwegian prose translation *Flóres saga ok Blankiflúr,* made some time around 1300.

BIBLIOGRAPHY

Sources. Diederic van Assenede, *Floris ende Blancefloer,* Hoffmann von Fallersleben, ed. (1836), the Middle Netherlandish version; Konrad Fleck, *Flore und Blanscheflur,* Emil Sommer, ed. (1846), Middle High German; *Floire et Blancheflor,* Jean Luc Leclanche, ed. (1980), French; *Floire et Blancheflor,* Margaret Pelan, ed. (1956), French; *Floire et Blancheflor, seconde version,* Margaret Pelan, ed. (1975), late-twelfth-century French; *Flóres saga ok Blankiflúr,* Eugen Kölbing, ed. (1896), Old Norwegian; *Floris and Blancheflour,* A. B. Taylor, ed. (1927), Middle English; *Flos unde Blankeflos,* Otto Decker, ed. (1913), Middle Low German; *The Romance of Floire and Blanchefleur,* Merton J. Hubert, trans. (1966), from the French; "Trierer Bruchstücke. I: Floyris," in *Zeitschrift für deutsches Altertum,* **21** (1877), fragments in Low Franconian.

Study. J. H. Winkelman, *Die Brückenpächter- und die Turmwächterepisode im 'Trierer Floyris' und in der 'Version Aristocratique' des altfranzösischen Florisromans* (1977)—though there is no bibliography, the latest scholarship is liberally cited in footnotes.

FRANCES L. DECKER

[See also **Fleck, Konrad; Flóres Saga ok Blankiflúr; French Literature: Romances.**]

FLORUS OF LYONS (*ca.* 800–*ca.* 860). The entire life of Florus, deacon of Lyons, was spent in the service of the church in that city. Of unknown parentage, he was reared from infancy in the church. His primary function at Lyons was probably as master of the cathedral school; he is known not only as deacon but also as teacher *(magister).* Florus served four bishops: Leidrad (*d.* 814), Agobard (*d.* 840), Amulo (*d.* 852), and Remigius (*d.* 875).

Studying in the school of Lyons, Florus became a master of Scripture (possibly in its original languages) and a competent student of the Latin classics and prosody, of theology, and of the church fathers, especially Augustine. He seems above all to have been a reliable assistant of his bishops in the scriptorium. Florus was a bitter enemy of Amalarius of Metz, who administered the diocese during the exile of Bishop Agobard in 835–838, and he was particularly responsible for securing the condemnation of Amalarius' works on liturgiology.

Florus was also prominent in the debate over the

morose doctrines of Gottschalk of Orbais. He stalwartly defended the teaching of the Saxon monk against the learned vagaries of John Scottus Eriugena. Like his spiritual father Agobard, Florus distrusted discursive reason and secular philosophy, and demanded biblical texts as evidence for Christian doctrine.

Thirty poems, mainly in dactylic hexameters, flowed from his pen. Fourteen prose works (scriptural exposition, letters, attacks on Amalarius' writings, a martyrology, a sermon, and a theological defense of Gottschalk) have also been preserved. Florus' poetry has many surprising, delightful, and imaginative touches that establish the writer as a serious man of letters. His prose is generally stolid, but full of sharp and bitter invective.

BIBLIOGRAPHY

Most of the poems are in Ernst Dümmler, ed., *Poetae latini aevi carolini,* II (1884), 509–566; most of the prose, in *Patrologia latina,* CXIX (1852), 9–422. See also Allen Cabaniss, "Florus of Lyons," in *Classica et mediaevalia,* **19** (1958), repr. in his *Judith Augusta . . . and Other Essays* (1974), 153–173.

ALLEN CABANISS

[See also **Agobard; Amalarius of Metz; Gottschalk of Orbais.**]

FLUSHWORK, a decorative design or pattern created by setting flush into a wall bricks, tiles, or stones of colors or textures that contrast with the wall itself. The word is most commonly applied to the decorative use of knapped flint in buildings in East Anglia, but applies equally to buildings in various areas of Europe, including Islamic Spain.

CARL F. BARNES, JR.

FLYING BUTTRESS. See Buttress.

FOLCWIN OF LOBBES (*ca.* 935–990) became a monk in 948 at St. Bertin, near Thérouanne. He was abbot of Lobbes from 965 until his death, except for four years (968–972) when the office was usurped by Rather of Liège. Folcwin's writings demonstrate a critical appreciation of documents and oral tradition.

BIBLIOGRAPHY

An edition of Folcwin's history of the abbots of Lobbes is in *Monumenta Germaniae historica, Scriptores,* IV (1841), 52–74; XIII (1881), 606–634; XV, pt. 1 (1888), 423–430; XV, pt. 2 (1887), 832–842. See also Max Manitius, *Geschichte der lateinischen Literatur des Mittelalters,* II (1923), 210–214; J. Warichez, *L'abbaye de Lobbes depuis les origines jusqu'en 1200* (1909), 251–254.

CHARLES R. SHRADER

FOLIES TRISTAN. The *Folie Tristan de Berne* and the *Folie Tristan d'Oxford,* both linked to the Tristan legend, are named for the present locations of their manuscripts. The works probably date from the late twelfth century. The Bern text, which may well have been Norman in origin though copied by a Burgundian scribe, is related to Béroul's version; the Anglo-Norman Oxford text, in part to Béroul but principally to the version by the insular writer Thomas. In both stories Tristan appears at King Mark's court disguised as a fool and is eventually recognized by Isolt.

BIBLIOGRAPHY

Joseph Bédier, *Les deux poèmes de la folie Tristan* (1907); E. Hoepffner, *La Folie Tristan d'Oxford* (1943), and

Flushwork. St. Peter's, Barton-on-Humber, Lincolnshire. PHOTOGRAPH COURTESY OF THE AUTHOR, NEG. 1969-16-36

La Folie Tristan de Berne (1949). See also Mary Dominica Legge, *Anglo-Norman Literature and Its Background* (1963), 121–128.

BRIAN MERRILEES

[See also **Anglo-Norman Literature; Tristan, Roman de.**]

FOLIO, both sides of an individual leaf (page) in a hand-produced book. To distinguish the two sides, the front (the side that falls on the right in an open book) is called the recto; the back, the verso. Hence, folios 1 recto, 1 verso, and 2 recto would translate in a pagination system to pages 1, 2, and 3, respectively.

LESLIE BRUBAKER

FOLKLORE. See Magic and Folklore.

FOLQUET DE MARSEILLES (*d.* 25 December 1231), of Genoese descent, was a wealthy merchant living in Marseilles from at least 1178. His nineteen extant Old Provençal lyrics, written between about 1185 and 1195, reveal his concern for permanent values and spiritual happiness beyond worldly pleasures and courtly love. Around 1200, with his wife and two sons, Folquet entered the Cistercian abbey of Le Thoronet, became its abbot, and, in 1205, bishop of Toulouse. He helped to found the Order of Preachers and to organize the Albigensian Crusade. Folquet made three diplomatic missions to the north of France on behalf of that crusade and may have met the mystic Marie d'Oignies. As merchant, troubadour, and bishop he was celebrated by Dante, Petrarch, and John of Garland.

BIBLIOGRAPHY
Glynnis M. Cropp, "The *Partimen* Between Folquet de Marseille and Tostemps," in W. T. H. Jackson, ed., *The Interpretation of Medieval Lyric Poetry* (1980); R. Lejeune, "L'évêque de Toulouse Folquet de Marseille et la principauté de Liège," in *Mélanges Félix Rousseau: Études sur l'histoire du pays mosan au moyen âge* (1958); Stanisław Stroński, ed., *Le troubadour Folquet de Marseille* (1910).

GLYNNIS M. CROPP

[See also **Provençal Literature: to Twelfth Century.**]

FOLZ, HANS (*ca.* 1435/1440–15 December 1512/16 February 1513). In 1459 the imperial city of Nuremberg granted citizenship to one "Hans, barber-surgeon from Worms." This is undoubtedly the man who identified himself as author in each of his longer poems in couplets, normally in the last line (as, for example, in "Der witzige Landstreicher," line 178: "Spricht Hans Folcz zu Nürmberg barwirer"), and to whom numerous *Meisterlieder* and Shrovetide plays are attributed.

For more than half a century Folz practiced his profession in one of Europe's most prosperous, dynamic, and cultured cities. Nuremberg was, by 1450, home to many men with modern interests in philosophy, law, politics, and literature, but was even more noted for its artisans and businessmen. Konrad Celtis was there crowned poet laureate of the empire by Frederick III in 1487, and a few years later he completed a famous panegyric on Nuremberg. The most notable German artist of the age, Albrecht Dürer, was a native of Nuremberg, and the city also boasted the outstanding printer Anton Koberger.

Folz exemplified this environment in serveral respects. He achieved distinction within his profession, for in 1498 he is listed as a "sworn master," a title given to those men selected by the masters in a particular field to represent their profession before the municipal council. Folz also operated his own printing press between roughly 1479 and 1488—printing, it appears, only his own works. As an author he enjoyed commercial success, to judge from his activity as a publisher, from the fact that several works were pirated or reprinted by others, and from the measure of civic recognition he apparently gained.

Folz, however, stands apart from all innovations in the areas of science, philosophy, and literature that are associated with the Humanism of late-fifteenth-century Germany. The forms and content of his writing are highly traditional. His Shrovetide plays and couplet poetry appealed to popular taste, which was conservative, and his reputation as a "reformer" in the *Meistersang* rests on controversial evidence that, with the most liberal interpretation, shows him concerned merely to gain a certain formal flexibility within the codified art. No critical or questioning tones are perceptible in Folz's many songs and poems on religious subjects. On the contrary, he stigmatizes the followers of John Hus as converts of Judas (in "Judas der Ketzerapostel"), and manifests the anti-Semitism of medieval bourgeois Christianity in "Jüdischer Wucher," "Der falsche

Messias," and "Die Wahrsagebeeren." In his thought and art Folz remained an orthodox man of the Middle Ages.

But for his writing and printing, Folz would be nearly indistinguishable from many other successful tradesmen in Nuremberg around 1500. In reviewing the long and varied canon of his work, it is important to recall that his couplet poems and plays originated within a period of at most two decades, less than half his life in Nuremberg, and the reference to his trade within his literary signature ("Hans Folcz barwirer") points out the centrality of his vocation to his self-esteem. By contrast, his *Meisterlieder* may well have been composed throughout his adult life—there is little firm evidence of chronology—and so notable was his achievement in this poetic and musical art that Hans Sachs, writing in 1515, included Folz among the twelve master practitioners of *Meistersang* in the history of Nuremberg.

Nearly 100 *Meisterlieder* are attributed to Folz, of which many are hundreds of lines long. Following the traditions of this art, which called for meticulous adherence to complex rhyme schemes and to strophic structures in which corresponding lines contained exactly the same number of syllables, Folz wrote in thirteen historical *Töne* and fourteen of his own invention. (Each *Ton* is a unity of poetic structure and melodic setting.) His subjects are mainly religious, though secular narrative material also appears. Of special interest is a group of six 150-line poems treating the traditions and practice of the art (numbers 89–94 in Mayer's edition), which for many years were understood to reflect a conflict between Folz as innovator in *Meistersang* and the conservatives of the Rhenish region, but which may be little more than a subtle polemic against rivals.

Twelve preserved Shrovetide plays (*Fastnachtspiele*) are attributable to Folz, either by virtue of his poetic signature in the text or because of internal evidence. As a group they resemble the rich Nuremberg tradition of Shrovetide entertainments, being crude in subject matter and sacrificing literary subtlety for the sake of impact, but Folz did treat serious subjects in this form (*Die alt und neu ee, Kaiser Constantinus*). His play *Salomon und Markolf,* though composed according to dramaturgical principles far removed from those of modern theater, demonstrates his skill in the adaptation and integration of his materials.

More than 13,000 lines of poems in couplets survive in Folz's name. (The textual attribution of a poem surely by Folz to an unknown "Doctor Günther of Mosspach" ["Judas der Ketzerapostel," line 320] awaits clarification.) Current opinion holds that Folz wrote these pieces, and his Shrovetide plays, with an eye firmly fixed on their commercial appeal; hence the wide range of subjects reflects the tastes and interests of the Nuremberg citizenry. There are twenty comic vignettes (*Mären*) ranging in substance from wordplay to sexual and scatological farce; about a dozen didactic poems on religious, moral, erotic, scientific, and economic subjects; four sacred tales; and three topical poems (for instance, "König Maximilian in Nürnberg"). Although Folz's literary gifts and ambitions were limited, he had a swift and vigorous style. He seems to have written virtually nothing in prose: surviving are a redaction of his poem on plague remedies and a short parody of the almanac (*Reimpaarsprüche,* pp. 429–441).

BIBLIOGRAPHY

Sources. Die Meisterlieder des Hans Folz, August L. Mayer, ed. (1908); *Die Reimpaarsprüche,* Hanns Fischer, ed. (1961); *Fastnachtspiele aus dem fünfzehnten Jahrhundert,* Adelbert vom Keller, ed., in Bibliothek des literarischen Vereins in Stuttgart, XXVIII–XXX, XLVI (1853)—the plays generally attributed to Folz are nos. 1, 7, 20, 39, 43, 44, 51, 60, 105, 106, 112, and 120 in this collection, all in vols. XXVIII–XXIX.

Studies. Herwig Buntz, "'Der Stein des Weisen.' Eine zweite Handschrift des Lehrgedichtes von Hans Folz," in *Zeitschrift für deutsche Philologie,* **94** (1975); Eckehard Catholy, *Das Fastnachtspiel des Spätmittelalters. Gestalt und Funktion* (1961), detailed analysis of *Salomon und Markolf,* 13–138; Hanns Fischer, *Studien zur deutschen Märendichtung,* 2nd ed. (1983), 160–162, 309–314, 397–406; Christoph Petzsch, "Zur sogenannten, Hans Folz zugeschriebenen Meistergesangsreform," in *Beiträge zur Geschichte der deutschen Sprache und Literatur* (Tübingen), **88** (1966–1967).

STEPHEN WAILES

[See also **German Literature: Lyric; Mären; Nuremberg.**]

FONTENAY ABBEY, a Burgundian Cistercian monastery founded on 26 October 1118 by St. Bernard of Clairvaux. The complex was begun in 1139 at the expense of Bishop Everard of Norwich and was consecrated on 21 September 1147. Although it contains some later buildings, such as the refectory, the Fontenay complex is one of the best-preserved

Fontenay Abbey, cloister. 1139–1147. PHOTOGRAPH COURTESY OF W. S. STODDARD

early Cistercian foundations. In its layout and architecture, it most nearly represents the ideal of Cistercian purity in the age of St. Bernard.

BIBLIOGRAPHY

Marcel Aubert, *L'architecture cistercienne en France*, 2nd ed., 2 vols. (1947), I, 157–160; Lucien Bégule, *L'abbaye de Fontenay*, 4th rev. ed. (1957); M.-Anselme Dimier, "Fontenay," in *L'art cistercien, zodiaque la nuit des temps*, XVI (1962).

CARL F. BARNES, JR.

FONTEVRAULT. See Robert d'Arbrissel.

FOOD TRADES. The most important sector of the medieval economy was the trade in victuals. The vast majority of medieval people spent at least 60 to 80 percent of their annual income on food and drink. Both agriculture and commerce reflected this distribution. Agriculture in the Middle Ages was almost wholly concerned with the production of foodstuffs, and the retail sale and purchase of foodstuffs served as the foundation for all village and town markets. At the same time, the wholesale trade in such food products as grain, fish, salt, and wine represented a substantial proportion of all regional and long-distance trade. In an age of subsistence agriculture, when highly variable harvests, poor storage facilities, and inadequate transport made food supply un-predictable, the assurance of a steady stream of food-stuffs was of vital concern to people and their governments. Indeed, the fundamental anxiety over proper food supply meant that the food trades were among the most regulated aspects of medieval life.

EARLY MIDDLE AGES

During the early Middle Ages, because of barbarian invasions, a decrease in town life, and political instability, the food trades, like all organized commerce, dwindled considerably. Large estates and small farms alike generally met the primary subsistence needs of their inhabitants, though great noble households were often forced to move from one estate to another in order to provide for their alimentary needs. Subsistence needs were also met by a type of indirect trade in food through the widespread custom of food rents or payments in kind. Thus peasants could pay all or part of their rent to the lord in wheat, poultry, or eels, while lords could pay for labor services in bread or ale.

Yet evidence of frequent problems of supply, usually in the form of bad harvests, in addition to occasional fluctuations in demand, indicate that the trade in foodstuffs never ceased entirely. Some urban communities, though much reduced in size, did continue, and required a regular source of food provided through trade. The spread of Benedictine monasticism, with its emphasis on meatless days, probably stimulated the trade in fish. Moreover, many of the monastic foundations possessed vast estates that produced substantial agricultural surpluses. Because the subsistence demands of monks tended to be moderate and because they required cash to pay for their clothing and other needs, monastic lords often chose to sell their surplus agricultural products in the local markets.

Problems of storage and transportation frequently hindered the trade in food. The seasonality of food harvests, the lack of refrigeration for perishable produce, the insecurity of travel, the primitive road conditions, and the slow forms of transportation (by packhorse or cart, and occasionally by boat) induced landowners to grow their own food, thereby eliminating the agricultural specialization that would have led to greater profits and increased trade. Lords tried to avoid some of these problems by moving from one estate to another, consuming the produce of each estate in turn. Other lords, especially monastic landowners who could not travel frequently, required their peasants or abbey servants to provide carting services to transport food supplies from distant estates on a regular basis. But such strategies were not always effective when estates were located far apart. As a result many lords arranged to sell the agricultural produce from their estates at local markets, thus stimulating food trade in that region. Some food products, such as wine, wheat, and salted fish, could be traded over longer distances since their storage and transport requirements were more easily met. Evidence exists for long-distance and regional trade in these commodities throughout the early Middle Ages, encouraged in part by the religious demands and luxury tastes of the clergy and nobles.

Food production began to increase in medieval Europe, possibly as early as the eighth century and certainly by the end of the tenth century, in response to the adoption of new agricultural techniques. The widespread use of the heavy plow in northern Europe, the switch to a three-field system of crop rotation, the emphasis on leguminous crops, and the increased reliance on horses, mills, and a variety of agricultural tools all worked to yield a larger surplus of food. Swelling food supplies prompted a growth in population and stimulated economic life, commercial activity, and the expansion of towns. All these factors in turn enhanced the demand for food and thus boosted the food trades tremendously. Other factors, such as rising luxury consumption and changing patterns of taste (which stimulated demand for wine and the more costly varieties of meat and fish) also augmented the victual trades.

The records from the eighth through tenth centuries reflect this upsurge in the food trades. Carolingian capitularies, for example, attempted to control the retail prices of grains, as well as the growing role of middlemen in the sale of cereals and wine. In the ninth century Einhard referred to merchants from Mainz who sold wheat in the city that they had bought in the upper Rhine valley. Other documents of this period mention merchants from Saxony, Frisia, and Rouen who purchased wine and other foodstuffs at the fair of St. Denis in Paris and then exported these goods to England. Grants of market rights by kings and powerful lords become more frequent, as do references to the foundation and growth of towns. By the eleventh century Europe was in the midst of a "Commercial Revolution," characterized by an upsurge in urban life, an improvement in commercial organization and techniques, and a marked expansion of trade. The food trades were an integral part of this expansion, as a result of increased supply from new and larger sources of food, and of increased demand arising from the growing population and multiplication of towns, markets, and fairs.

RURAL FOOD TRADES

As commerce and urban life progressed and became more complex from the eleventh through fifteenth centuries, the impact of trade upon agicultural enterprises grew more dramatic. Cultivated areas expanded in response to growing food demands from a rising population, which increasingly chose to settle in towns or cities. Many regions witnessed a rise in cereal prices, which may have further stimulated agricultural production. Rising luxury consumption also worked through the market to encourage specialized agriculture. Viticulture, particularly around large cities, spread rapidly in response to the demand for wine. Such agricultural specialization in turn stimulated further demand for cereals and promoted exchange between wine- and cereal-producing areas. The needs of the expanding woolen cloth industry prompted increasing reliance on sheep raising in places like England. This emphasis on stock breeding served to bolster the food trades, both because of the meat by-products from stock farming and because of increased labor specialization.

By 1300 even states of moderate size were often geared to production for the market, production frequently aimed at the food trades. Larger estates, such as those of the bishop of Winchester in England, sold one-half of their annual gross demesne product, or an average of 13,000 bushels of grain each year, on the market. Such large-scale cereal production was increasingly affected by price fluctuations, as well as by changes in demand. Indeed, the expansion of grain cultivation slowed in the late thirteenth and early fourteenth centuries, and contracted even more severely after the Black Death, when demand plummeted as a result of the fall in population. With the exception of short-term price rises due to interruptions in supply (caused by such events as flare-ups in the Hundred Years War), grain prices generally fell in the late Middle Ages, providing little incentive to landowners to expand grain production.

Grain prices also fell in response to vast new supplies of inexpensive cereals from eastern Europe. Beginning in the twelfth century, German colonization east of the Elbe River opened up the fertile plains of Prussia and Poland for grain cultivation. With the rise of the Hanseatic League of German cities, commerce developed rapidly in the Baltic region. By the late thirteenth century the Hansa was regularly exporting eastern grain to German, Scandinavian, Flemish, and English ports. The ease and cheapness of water transport on the Baltic Sea and the great rivers also encouraged this trade, as did increased ship capacities in the fourteenth century. These same factors stimulated long-distance grain trade in the Mediterranean as well. Italian merchants imported grains in bulk from places like Sicily and redistributed these cereals throughout the Mediterranean and Atlantic coast areas. These new grain supplies meant that many landowners gave up grain cultivation and switched to more specialized forms of agricultural production, such as stock breeding and viticulture.

Stock farming expanded greatly in Europe from the thirteenth century on. Demand for animal products such as meat, butter, cheese, and wool increased at the same time that profits from stock raising exceeded those to be made from grain cultivation. Historians estimate that the price of animals rose three to four times faster than grain prices after the Black Death. Moreover, the rise in wages at this time adversely affected cultivators more than stock raisers. In response to these market conditions, many owners of estates and even of small farms deliberately extended their livestock enterprises. Marshlands were reclaimed, enclosure of lands was accelerated, vaccaries were set up on the edges of moorland rivers and streams, new sheep, cattle, and dairy structures were built, and purchases of ewes and cows increased. Many of these actions infringed upon arable farming, resulting in heightened tension between flock owners and grain cultivators. Entrepreneurs often exacerbated these tensions by injecting capital and management techniques that made stock farming even more commercialized and profitable. Thus town butchers often appeared in the countryside, advancing money to shepherds in order to build up flocks. Contracts varied, but the shepherd or peasant usually returned the flock to the investor after one to three years, retaining half of its increase for himself.

Burgesses increasingly invested in other agricultural pursuits as well. For example, in the early thirteenth century merchants from Trento in northern Italy speculated in future prices of grain growth in Alpine valleys. In the mid fourteenth century Florentine traders frequently bought up the annual production of cheese on states in Apulia. Merchants also purchased vineyards, olive groves, and fruit orchards in the countryside around towns. Other urban residents leased such areas or bought the right to collect tithes in the form of agricultural produce, which they then sold in town markets. Great profits could

be made from such ventures. A rising standard of living meant that late-medieval people had more disposable income for meat, wine, and other noncereal foodstuffs. Agriculture in the late Middle Ages had become increasingly commercialized and subject to the demands of the urban food markets.

To what extent did individual peasant producers respond to these changing market conditions? This is a difficult question for historians to answer, since evidence on what peasants cultivated and how they disposed of their surplus is sparse. There is some indication that peasant producers followed the lead of large estate owners, especially in the switch from arable to pastoral farming on soils more suitable for the latter. But the timing of such responses to market conditions often lagged behind the response time of larger landowners. Wheat appears to have been the main cash crop of many, if not most, peasants in northern Europe, while elsewhere viticulture, olive cultivation, and stock raising predominated. Most significant is the fact that not only did peasants expend most of their energy on the production of food crops, but they also produced the greater part of the food supply of Europe in the Middle Ages.

The peasant's involvement in the actual trade of foodstuffs is likewise not entirely clear. Many peasants plainly had minimal participation in the food trades; living on the edge of subsistence, they produced only enough food to supply the needs of their own families. The development of the retail food trades in the rural sector was also limited by the prescription for many unfree peasants that they grind their grain and bake their bread in mills and ovens owned by the lord. Furthermore, the lower standard of living in the countryside hindered the expansion of a retail victual trade. Most peasants survived on a monotonous diet of dark bread, pottage, cheese, ale, a few vegetables in season, and occasional meat or fish. All these foods were generally supplied from the peasant's own resources. Rent and wage payments in food continued throughout this period, though they did decline considerably in the later Middle Ages.

From the thirteenth century on, however, the exchange economy increasingly penetrated rural life. The spread of cash rents, wages, and fines, the commutation of labor services, the expansion of labor and agricultural specialization, and the peasants' efforts to meet the growing demands of taxation all point to the monetization of the peasant economy. The sale of the peasants' agricultural surplus represented a substantial proportion of this movement. The peasants' food surplus was traded in a variety

FOOD TRADES

of ways; some sold their surplus to estate owners or middlemen such as cornmongers, who in turn sold these products in larger amounts for greater profits. Other peasants, especially those living near densely settled towns and villages, brought their surplus to market and sold it themselves, sometimes to consumers, more often to middlemen. Eggs, cheese, fruits, vegetables, honey, and live animals were often sold by country producers in towns on market days.

Peasants used their cash profits to purchase goods or services they could not provide themselves. Although these purchases did include some foodstuffs such as bread, ale, and meat, most of their income went for taxes, rents, and manufactured items. By and large peasants still supplied the vast majority of their food requirements from their own agricultural resources. While peasants were crucial in the production and supply of food, town residents represented the more important traders and consumers in the food trades. Towns and town dwellers stimulated the expansion of food trades in the Middle Ages and were almost solely responsible for the development of the organization and techniques of the trade in victuals.

URBAN FOOD TRADES

Medieval towns originated and developed largely as centers for the redistribution of agricultural products, primarily foodstuffs. Unlike rural inhabitants, most townspeople were not involved in the direct agricultural production of food, and hence had to rely on the retail purchase of victuals in order to meet their subsistence needs. Even those practicing a victual trade were so specialized that they were compelled to purchase a large part of their food in the marketplace. As a result, a sizable proportion of town residents, representing anywhere from 30 to 70 percent of all urban occupations, depending on the nature of the town's economy, participated regularly in the sale of foodstuffs.

These urban food traders may generally be divided into four groups. Primary producers, such as fishermen and gardeners, constituted the smallest group. They transported and sold their own food products in the market; their profits and occupational status were never high. A second, and the largest, group of food traders consisted of those working in the food industries, such as bakers, butchers, brewers, cooks, and poulterers. These people usually purchased raw foodstuffs, processed them in some way, and then sold the final food products. Retail sale to the consumer was the norm, but on occasion

the wealthier members of this group, especially the butchers and brewers, sold in bulk. Pure retailers, including hawkers, victuallers, taverners, and innkeepers, represented the third group. Some specialized in the sale of one type of food, such as wine, vegetables, dairy products, or bread, but many sold a wide variety of both foods and other commodities that they had purchased from peasants, food processors, or other middlemen. Their activities were carefully watched by municipal authorities, and as retailers of mostly inexpensive foodstuffs, they had very low profits and occupational status.

The highest profits in the food trades were reaped by the fourth group, the middlemen who sold necessary or expensive foodstuffs in bulk. Such wholesale merchants traded most often in grain, wine, salt, fish, oils, and spices. They regularly participated in long-distance trade and frequently imported nonfood items such as cloth and wool as well. Their substantial profits and commercial involvement placed them among the wealthiest town residents and propelled some to high municipal office and civic power.

The primary concern of any town government reflected the most vital concern of town residents: a steady supply of reasonably priced food. Small towns and villages satisfied most of their food needs by relying on the agricultural produce from nearby fields. Middle-size towns had to depend more on regional trade to supply subsistence requirements, while the larger towns were often forced to rely heavily on long-distance trade, particularly to meet the demand for grain. A medieval town of 3,000 consumed about 1,000 tons of grain each year; that amount of grain required about 4,500 acres of arable land. The proximity of a town to good trade routes on navigable rivers or safe harbors was also crucial in determining its ability to feed its inhabitants. It is quite possible that food supply problems limited the size of many cities and influenced the well-being of town populations.

The provision of an adequate food supply was the subject of many a medieval town council meeting and the motivation for expansion of urban influence over surrounding rural areas. The military conquest and political control of the *contado* by Italian cities from the twelfth century on was largely motivated by the desire of the cities to control agricultural resources. Towns like Florence forbade food retailing in a zone three to six miles around the city, in order to force producers to sell their foodstuffs in the urban market. Indeed, the sale of such products as wine and grain was often prohibited anywhere in the *contado* but the urban market. Stronger towns took even more forceful measures to ensure an abundant food supply—as well as monopolies and profits for their own merchants. For example, in 1234 Venice pushed through a treaty that compelled merchants from Ravenna to sell all their grain and salt at Venice. In 1236 a similar agreement prohibited Ragusa from all trade in the northern Adriatic Sea except for that involving the transport of food to Venice. Venice also claimed monopolies on all grain exports from such regions as the lower Po valley and limited the ability of towns including Bologna to purchase grain in certain agricultural regions.

Few cities could control their food supply as authoritatively as Venice. But towns followed other trading strategies to achieve a similar goal, especially in times of dearth. Port towns often regulated the import and export of foodstuffs in order to ensure a continual flow of victuals. For example, some towns stipulated that every ship's cargo imported into the town must contain a certain proportion of a particular foodstuff, such as wheat. Exports of food could be forbidden, particularly when prices rose above a fixed level, or heavy duties could be placed on such exports in order to discourage them. Many cities possessed communal ships and used tax revenues or public loans to purchase and transport food supplies to the town.

Within town markets, municipal regulations also served to procure a steady and cheap food supply. Food trades were actively encouraged by town guarantees to merchants of safe passage to and security within the marketplace. Well-regulated urban markets and fairs assured traders of fair commercial practices and quick, efficient settlement of disputes. Toll concessions and other trading privileges were frequently offered to traders to attract them to urban markets. Many towns also relaxed traditional prohibitions against trading by noncitizens or nonguildsmen if such outsiders sold victuals.

The concern of towns with food supply was most intense during times of dearth. Periodic bad harvests resulted in widespread famines—in that of 1316, for instance, 10 percent of the population of Ypres died. The price of wheat and bread doubled, tripled, and even quadrupled during such periods, resulting in urban unrest and riots, as well as disease and death. Consequently, town governments took special steps to keep prices down and supply adequate, especially for wheat, rye, and barley, since these formed the basis of subsistence. In Paris during times of scarcity,

the king ordered peasants in the surrounding area to bring all their grain not needed for local consumption or seed to market for sale. Hoarding of grain and flour was forbidden, and maximum cereal prices were established. Other measures included a ban on wholesale trade in grain and strict controls on the time and place of food purchases; markets and granaries were open only in the afternoons. Towns such as Barcelona took additional actions, sending city-owned ships to purchase Baltic grain in Flanders and Sicilian and Sardinian grain in the Mediterranean islands. Such measures were more common in the late Middle Ages as the incidence of famine became more frequent.

Second only to concern for adequate food supply was the preoccupation with reasonable food prices and quality control. Town regulations aimed to protect the consumer, frequently by placing limits on the activities of middlemen. Acceptable retail practices today, like forestalling and regrating, were frowned upon in the Middle Ages, in the belief that they led to monopolies and higher prices. Forestallers resold foodstuffs that they had purchased before the market officially opened or before the producers had a chance to reach the marketplace. In Southampton, for instance, only actual fishermen were permitted to sell fresh fish, and they were required to bring their whole catch to the market, so as to restrict opportunities for the forestaller and regrator. Regrators bought up victuals early in the day, often in bulk, and resold them later, when they were scarce, for a higher price.

Towns often fought a losing battle against such practices. In a thirteenth-century dispute in Oxford, for example, the university so vigorously complained of high food prices that the king tried to fix food prices and limited the number of regrators to thirty-two. But within twenty years of this agreement, the university protested that 100 regrators plied their trade in the town, causing even higher food prices. Town authorities also viewed hucksters or hawkers with suspicion, often charging them with selling poor-quality or stolen food. Towns sought to discourage forestalling, regrating, and hawking because such practices infringed on the privileges of more prosperous merchants, limited sales tax revenues, and led to higher prices and reduced civic control of food quality.

Towns also secured price and quality control through other methods. Outright price controls, especially on wheat, were instituted through the use of assizes. The assizes of bread and ale also checked the quality of these goods through regular inspections and testing by their officials. Municipal authorities appointed or elected market officials such as ale tasters and meat wardens to supervise prices, quality, and hygiene in the marketplace. Large cities such as Florence created municipal departments to pass regulations and repress frauds in the food trades. All towns passed laws that dictated the places where certain foods could be displayed for purchase and the proper weights and measures. These controls enabled town and market officials to restrain some of the worst quality and price offenses while they enforced payment of tolls and taxes on the food trades. All these regulations were backed by a series of fines and punishments administered through the town courts or special market courts, the main business of which was directed at control of the food trades.

Municipal authorities, particularly in large towns, often shared the regulation of the food trades with the guilds. Individual guilds, such as the bakers, butchers, and vintners, not only passed numerous ordinances concerning price and, especially, quality control, but also appointed inspectors and maintained their own courts to enforce guild rules. Yet tension inevitably arose over the degree of power guilds exerted over their own industries, since the basic aim of most guilds was to assert a monopoly over their trade. The situation was further complicated when guilds shared in town government at the same time that they worked to consolidate their monopoly of the food trades.

Their efforts were often limited, however, by the public interest; such monopolies posed an obvious threat to the desire of the town to obtain a flow of good-quality, cheap foodstuffs. Therefore, when the food trade guilds pursued quality-control objectives that coincided with the public interest, their practices were sanctioned. On the other hand, when their objectives worked to raise food prices, town governments stepped in to curtail the guilds' powers. Actually, many guild practices worked both ways. The institution of an apprentice/journeyman/master hierarchy, for instance, gave the guild control over access to the occupation, and also provided a cheap pool of labor from apprentices. Yet such a hierarchy also provided substantial training to novices and operated to assure a disciplined group of professionals.

It is significant that the food trade guilds never attained the power and prominence enjoyed by others, such as those in the textile trades. Part of the reason lies in the retail nature of most of the food trades, as well as the generally low prices of most

food products. But, more important, the food trades were too vital to the public interest to allow them to fall under the control of any one group. As a result, there were always loopholes that restricted the influence of the food trade guilds. These loopholes mainly concerned the supply of food. Country victuallers, for example, were always a source of irritation to London food guilds. The London poulterers and bakers were particularly vocal and active in protecting their interests against outsiders. But the municipal authorities of London often failed to enforce the guild regulations against victuallers from outside the city, since the assurance of a cheap and adequate food supply prevailed above all other considerations.

Towns were also anxious to maintain control over the food trades because they represented an excellent source of tax revenues. City regulations stipulating the exact place food should be sold made it easier to collect taxes on sales. In Venice all fish had to be taken to a certain "tall pole" in the San Marco and Rialto fish markets for payment of duty before they could be sold. Almost all food sales, except that of wheat, were taxed in some way by town officials. Toll collections took place at the gates of the city, on the quay, or at a special tollbooth in the marketplace. In some instances annual flat fees were paid by food sellers, especially bakers and taverners, in lieu of a tax on each sale. Some of these food taxes, such as the gabelle, a salt tax, could be quite substantial and constituted an important element of municipal or even national revenues. Towns also charged rents on stalls, shops, and display places in the marketplace, the butchers' shambles, or the butter cross. The right to collect such stallage fees or food sales taxes could be farmed out to an individual for a fixed fee every year. Unfortunately, while the town or rich merchants benefited financially from such arrangements, victuallers and the poorer consumers suffered because most of the tolls on the food trades were indirect taxes.

The diet of town residents was both more varied and usually more nutritious than that of their rural counterparts. Meat, fish, and wine were consumed in far larger quantities in the towns. These food items, as well as bread, ale, spices, oils, and cereals, were most frequently acquired through retail purchase by the consumer. While bread, ale, and fresh meat and fish were bought daily or weekly, wine, cereals, salted meat or fish, spices, and oils were probably purchased less frequently but in larger quantities, since they could be stored for a longer period. Indeed, more than half of all urban households in the late Middle Ages hoarded relatively large stocks of foodstuffs, especially grain. Such hoarding represented a reaction to the sometimes violent price fluctuations and famines.

It is important to remember that town dwellers often managed to produce much of their food themselves. Many burgess tenements contained vegetable and herb gardens, dovecotes, poultry sheds, and pigsties. As late as 1481, Frankfurt authorities were trying to enforce decrees that pigsties must not be located in front of houses or on public streets. Some town residents also produced their own ale and bread dough. Yet these people still had to purchase the raw materials to make these food products; they bypassed only some of the services offered by the professional food processors.

BREAD AND GRAIN

Bread represented the most vital element of the medieval diet. People spent more of their salaries on either bread or the grain used to make bread than on any other single item. An unmarried male worker in fourteenth-century Florence, for example, spent well over one-third of his monthly income on bread or wheat. Large noble households, such as that of the earl of Leicester in thirteenth-century England, required 300 pounds of grain daily, while an urban household of ten in medieval Genoa purchased some five and a half tons yearly. Grain was clearly an object of constant demand.

National and urban policies reflected the medieval preoccupation with a sustained supply of grain. In towns like Barcelona, which could not depend on the poor grain harvests of its hinterland, the urban authorities regularly purchased large quantities of wheat, mainly from Sicily, and were the most prominent sellers of wheat in the city. Barcelona also took special care to assure transport routes; corsairs who threatened grain shipments were tracked down, and land routes were closely watched. Grain retailing practices also were subject to intense scrutiny. Fines and punishments for the forestalling and regrating of wheat, rye, barley, and oats were substantially higher than those assessed for those same practices with other commodities.

Professional grain sellers may generally be divided into four groups (besides the municipal government, which usually marketed grain only in the larger towns). Grain merchants were wholesale dealers who purchased large quantities of grain, usually from estate owners, and sold it in bulk to other deal-

ers or middlemen. Cornmongers were primarily local dealers, middlemen who purchased grain from producers and sold directly to consumers. Grain regrators usually bought in the open market from peasant producers or cornmongers and sold later in the same market. Unlike cornmongers, regrators did not transport grain and did not travel around the countryside to purchase grain. Grain brokers brought together sellers and buyers—one party was usually a stranger in town—and collected commissions for their services or took part in the deal themselves. In some places the grain broker was a guild or town official, acting as a witness in commercial dealings and watching out for the interests of the guild or town.

While medieval authorities closely regulated the factors affecting the supply of grain, they rarely controlled the price of grains except in instances of dearth, largely because grain prices fluctuated violently in the short term and price controls adversely affected the supply of grain. But in the interest of the consumer, officials did attempt to control the price and quality of bread, the chief grain product. In England this was accomplished through national legislation administered locally in the form of the assize of bread, which fixed the price of a loaf of bread but allowed the weight of the loaf to vary inversely with changes in the price of wheat. Tables were constructed to show how much the weight of a loaf would decrease with every six-pence rise in the price of a bushel of wheat.

The baker's profit was also regulated; his expenses, which included the cost of labor, fuel, light, salt, and yeast, were covered by a fixed allowance added to the price of wheat. His share of the sale of the bread was also limited. Obviously bakers resented these controls, and often complained so loudly that they were losing money that the fixed allowance was raised several times, notably in London. Similar price controls were in effect elsewhere in Europe, although there regulations were usually imposed by local or guild authorities and varied more widely from place to place.

The assize of bread also governed the quality of bread. Bread inspectors, who were bakers themselves or prominent citizens, could fine bakers for selling bread that was badly fermented, mixed, or baked. Dishonest bakers were known to put everything from sand to cobwebs in the bread dough in order to increase their profit. To ensure recognition of quality baking, all bread had to be stamped or sealed (often with a particular pattern of pricks) by its baker. The size of the loaf was also a matter of dispute, since bakers did not like to make loaves smaller than a penny's worth; but consumers wanted even smaller loaves of a half-penny or a farthing. Some town courts were forced to fine bakers to get them to bake the smaller loaves.

While many bakers made and sold their own bread in shops or market stalls, most bakers spent the majority of their time either making dough from grain or flour owned by the consumer, or baking dough supplied by the consumer. Thus many town residents purchased their own grain, paid to have it milled into flour, prepared their own dough, and then brought it to the baker. Others purchased the grain and brought it to the baker, who made it into flour and then into dough, and baked it. Even with this more limited role, bakers were often accused of deliberate price raising, since they owned all of the ovens, or, more commonly, of fraud in the production of dough or bread. One of the more ingenious frauds was perpetrated by several fourteenth-century London bakers, including one named John Brid. John cleverly cut a trapdoor in the bottom of the "moldingborde" upon which customers placed their dough. A servant hid underneath the board, opened the trapdoor, and sliced off some of the customer's dough "piecemeal and bit by bit, frequently collecting great quantities from such dough, falsely, wickedly and maliciously." John used this dough in bread he sold as his own. The London aldermen ordered that John and the other offenders be placed in the pillory with dough hanging around their necks as punishment.

Town authorities and bakers' guilds often acted to limit the potential harm to consumers from the baker's desire for greater profit. In Arras, for example, regulations stipulated both the times and the number of daily bakings. Bread had to be baked in the morning to ensure freshness, while the baking of gateaux was reserved for the afternoon, closer to the time they would be consumed. The Arras regulations also established a guild hierarchy of master, journeyman, apprentice, and boy helper, and ordered that the master had to be a full citizen of the town. Each master could have no more than four journeymen, and only three of them could be out selling bread at any one time. Bakers frequently employed street hawkers, mainly poor women, to help sell their wares in the neighborhoods.

The type of bread a consumer purchased or had made varied with the consumer's income. White bread was the most expensive; in England the finest white bread was called wastel. Simnel bread was made of the same quality flour but sold at a slightly higher price because it was made in a biscuit form and may have been boiled before baking. Cocket bread consisted of a coarser and cheaper grade of wheat, and thus was less costly than wastel or simnel. In London and other large cities, a form of raised white bread, called puff or French bread, was also sold. Brown breads, made from rye, maslin, or greater portions of bran, cost less than white breads and were the most commonly consumed type of bread in medieval Europe. Makers of brown bread also produced the poorest-quality bread, made of beans, peas, or oats and usually referred to as horse bread because it was regularly eaten by horses. Only the very poor depended solely on horse bread for sustenance.

In addition to the three major types of bread (white, brown, and horse), bakers produced a wide variety of pies, tarts, buns, and other baked goods. In the larger towns, bakers of these specialty products frequently formed a separate occupational group or guild. In fact, in some towns, such as London, measures were taken to separate even the white and brown breadmakers in order to keep up the quality of the cheaper breads and thus protect the poor. While penalties were assessed on those trespassing on another group's business, it appears that the regulations were habitually broken.

MEAT

Butchers sold meat salted or fresh, by the piece or on the hoof. Mutton was the most common meat, even among the nobility. The French royal household of Charles VI purchased some 200 sheep each week, and the 35,000 citizens of late medieval Barcelona often consumed more than 70,000 sheep each year. Pork and beef were also popular, followed by veal and lamb. Many people purchased pigs, and less often cattle, on the hoof, then killed and salted them. This procedure usually took place in the autumn, in order to save winter feeding. Other consumers bought their meat fresh in small portions from the local butcher, who also sold animal bones, heads, feet, and offal. Butchers rarely retailed venison or rabbit, expensive items that were most often hunted and consumed by the upper classes. Hares, goats, and fowl were more commonly raised and consumed by the less well-off. Cooks and innkeepers also sold prepared roasts, meat pies, and stews to the public.

The popularity of mutton was due largely to its availability and price; pork was twice as expensive, and beef four times as expensive. Even so, the price of mutton still represented a substantial outlay for the consumer; a laborer in 1373 Poitiers had to use almost five days' salary in order to purchase an average-size sheep. As a result meat was often considered a luxury item except in regions that specialized in livestock farming. It became an increasingly common element in all medieval diets, however, as standards of living rose and urban populations grew in size.

The relative costliness of meat and its growing importance in the diet were reflected in the prominent position of medieval butchers, who represented a solid upper-middle-class element in most towns. Indeed, with the exception of wine, grain or spice merchants, butchers were the most prosperous members of the food trades. Some butchers amassed small fortunes by selling up to 10,000 or more animals in a year, and also by acting as graziers, investing in huge flocks, pasture lands, and slaughterhouses. Other factors also worked to make the butcher's trade a lucrative one: the late-medieval extension of stock breeding; the long-term rise of meat prices, particularly beef prices; and the butcher's involvement in the sale of such meat by-products as tallow, hides, skins, and bristles.

Butchers were among the first groups to form guilds in medieval towns. By the thirteenth and fourteenth centuries they possessed highly developed craft organizations that, along with town authorities, controlled all aspects of the sale of meat. Annually elected or appointed meat inspectors and wardens of the shambles ensured price and quality control, and supervised the slaughter and sale of live animals and meat. Some town councils tried to fix retail prices of certain meats, such as mutton, on a yearly basis, but most authorities confined the fixing of meat prices to times of dearth caused by murrain or harsh weather. Seasonal price and demand fluctuations also had to be taken into consideration; increased supply lowered meat prices in the summer and autumn, while church restrictions on the eating of meat during Lent lessened demand in the spring. Most threatening to reasonable meat prices, however, was the monopoly enjoyed by butchers; in smaller towns they were often accused of conspiring to hold back supplies in order to raise prices.

Meat quality and freshness were of utmost concern to the customer. Many towns prosecuted butchers for selling unsound or fetid meat, notably in warm weather, when meat, particularly pork, deteriorated quickly. York and other cities passed ordinances forbidding butchers to sell fresh meat that had been displayed outside in the sun for more than one day. Frequent complaints were also voiced against the sale of unwholesome animals and "measly" meat, especially from pigs, which were apparently most liable to disease. To limit this offense, butchers could not buy meat from others, nor could they sell any meat that they themselves had not slaughtered. Fraud was also a continual problem. In 1340 London citizens grumbled that butchers often attached the fat of fatty oxen to the meat of lean oxen by means of thread and wooden skewers, then sold the result at a higher price. Other butchers tried to pass off ewes as lamb or sold sheep killed by wolves. Punishments for these infractions ranged from heavy fines to placement of the malefactor in the pillory while the offending meat was burned under his nose.

But the most bothersome problem between butchers and the public concerned the slaughter of animals and the disposal of waste. Whether animals were killed in the streets or yards of butchers' houses, the marketplace or the slaughterhouse, the disposal of blood, entrails, bone, and offal, as well as the continual stench and filth, remained a major issue. Townspeople were well aware of the nuisance and health hazards arising from butchers' activities. Complaints about butchers often coincided with outbreaks of disease or drought, and town court rolls contained weekly fines and warnings for butchers who spilled blood or left rotting entrails in public streets. Large cities like London faced a particularly severe challenge; the city had three different meat markets and several live cattle and sheep markets. In 1358 the "Stokkes" meat market by London Bridge alone contained stalls for seventy-one butchers. Although London, Paris, and other cities forbade the slaughter of animals within the city, the ordinances were never fully enforced. Scalding houses for pigs, geese, and other animals, which had to be located near meat markets, also aggravated the problem. The scalding house in London's Pentecost Lane continually discharged blood, hair, and entrails into both public streets and the Greyfriar's garden. Sundry methods for the disposal of entrails were tried, with varying degrees of success. Rivers were favorite disposal sites; London and Paris butchers often cut up entrails and threw them into the Thames or Seine at a time when the tide would carry the refuse downstream. Other butchers took their waste out of the city to pits specially dug for the disposal of entrails. Cities also contained barrow houses for the disposal of animal waste (so called because the refuse was carried there in barrows). As urban populations and meat consumption rose, these problems accelerated. By the fifteenth century, in London at least, much of the slaughtering and waste disposal took place outside of the city. But the transport problems engendered by the separation of market and processing point served to raise the price of meat even more.

FISH

Fish was a mainstay of the medieval diet, in large part as a result of the ban by the church on meat consumption during all of Lent, as well as on certain feast days and every Friday and Saturday. Saltwater and freshwater fish were sold salted, pickled, dried, smoked, or fresh. Shellfish, such as mussels, cockles, and oysters, cost relatively little and often retailed fresh by the bushel. Most expensive was fresh fish; in late thirteenth-century England, for example, six fresh herring sold for the same price as twenty red or smoked herring. The lowest-priced fish were cheap salted herring and dried stockfish. The latter formed a staple of the diet of the poor and was cured by drying in the cold and sunny air of early spring. While stockfish lasted indefinitely, it had to be beaten and soaked to make it edible. More expensive types of fish, such as ling, whiting, and pollack, could also be dried or wind-cured. Fish preserved with salt were either salted on board ship or immediately upon docking. Some fishermen barreled fish in salt or heavy brine until the end of the voyage, when they took the fish out and dried it.

Freshwater fish from ponds and rivers, such as salmon, pike, and carp, were valued highly. Noble lords jealously guarded their fishing rights in streams and millponds, and towns vigorously defended their interests in local fisheries. Authorities regulated not only the size and shape of nets and implements, but also the season and hours of fishing, in order to assure a continual stock of fish. Once caught, freshwater fish could be sold fresh, or preserved in a variety of ways. Salmon was often pickled and barreled in brine, while eels were sold salted or fresh "on a stick," in groups of a dozen or more.

Fresh fish sold for much more than salted fish because it spoiled so quickly. Fishermen often kept their catch alive in a well in the hold of the boat, until they could reach the town and its market. Fresh fish, unlike preserved fish, could be hawked in the streets because of its perishability, but under no circumstances could it be sold after the second day un-

less it was properly salted. Once it was in the marketplace, fish was subject to regulations like those imposed on the sale of meat. Sales took place in a predetermined location in the market. Saltwater and freshwater fish had to be sold separately, and quality was watched carefully by special officials of the fish market. Fish sellers who disguised the freshness of fish by frequently throwing water on their display were fined, as were those who sold outside the assigned fish market.

Municipal authorities took care to ensure a proper supply of fish to the town, particularly during Lent, when town councils of cities such as Arles and Marseilles designated certain individuals to guarantee adequate fish supplies. Most port towns required fishermen to carry their catch directly to the market after docking. Sales of fish to noncitizens were authorized only after local needs had been satisfied. Ordinances required out-of-town fishmongers to confine their trading to particular hours at specific locations. On the other hand, demand for fish was so great during Lent that London licensed other occupations, such as salters and chandlers, to sell fish. At other times of the year the London fishmongers' guild enjoyed a retail and wholesale monopoly on fish.

Fishmongers, and less frequently fishermen, often belonged to organized guilds, especially in the larger cities. Fishmongers grew wealthy not from retail trade but from their importing and exporting activities in the fish trade. In smaller towns, however, where regular merchants handled the wholesale trade in fish, fishmongers were merely retailers, and possessed little wealth and influence. Fishermen concentrated mainly on actual fishing, although many of them probably retailed fish occasionally. In coastal regions such as Provence, fishermen regularly made contracts with fishmongers who agreed to buy all or part of their catch during a particular season for a fixed price.

Because of the problem of preserving freshness and the slowness of medieval transport, fresh fish was usually marketed retail over a fairly short distance. But salted and dried fish was often sold in bulk and shipped over quite long distances. Towns in southern France imported salted tuna from Spain and Sicily, and salted herring, whiting, and mullet from La Rochelle and Bordeaux. The merchants of the Hanseatic League dominated the Baltic, and to a lesser extent the North Sea, trade in salted fish, most notably herring. English merchants also played a prominent role in this trade, frequently exporting fish to France in exchange for wine. Bergen in Norway, Yarmouth in England, Brielle in Holland, and Lübeck in Germany imported large quantities of herring and served as redistribution points for fish carried inland or reexported along the coast.

WINE, ALE, AND BEER

The trade in wine played an important role in long-distance commerce in the Middle Ages. By the early fourteenth century, wine represented more than 30 percent of English imports and 25 percent of all imports to the Low Countries. The growing demand for wine greatly stimulated commercial viticulture in France, Italy, Spain, Greece, the Mediterranean islands, and parts of Germany. The basis of this demand was the considerable taste of the nobility, higher clergy, and wealthier townspeople for wine. Indeed, the nobles' expenditures on food differed from those of most other people in their greater outlay for wine; it was not unusual for aristocratic households to spend 30 to 40 percent of their budget on wine.

Vintners often organized into guilds and imported wine wholesale in large tuns or casks. In some towns they also monopolized the retail sale of wine, but in general taverners controlled most of the direct sale of wine to the consumer. The retail sale of wine was subject to strict regulations of price, quality, and measure. In 1330 the London authorities, for example, fixed the price of different qualities of wine through the assize of wine; a gallon of the best Gascon wine, for example, could sell for no more than four pence, while a gallon of Rhine wine could retail for no more than eight pence. In the provinces, authorities allowed slightly higher prices in order to cover the costs of transport. But such price ceilings were difficult to enforce, especially during the Hundred Years War, which caused frequent interruptions in supply. Seasonal fluctuations in supply and the rapid deterioration of wines aggravated the situation.

Surveyors of wine, appointed by the local vintners' guild or the town council, implemented not only price controls but also quality standards. Taverners and vintners often tried to increase their profits by adulterating good wine with cheap or spoiled wine. By adding gum, resin, starch, or sugar to weak French or Spanish wines, retailers tried to give these thin wines more body in order to sell them at higher prices. Wine sellers also sold wine dregs colored with fruit juice or even dyestuffs. They were fined and punished like other offenders by being forced to drink their unsound products or having the wine poured over their heads. In many towns, patrons had the right to investigate the tavern's wine cellars, as well as its measures, in order to check the illegal practices of taverners.

While wine was the most popular drink of the upper classes and was consumed even by the less well-off in wine-producing areas, it was too expensive for most residents of northern Europe, where viticulture did not thrive. Ale was the staple drink of the vast majority of those who lived in England, the Low Countries, Scandinavia, northern France, and much of Germany and eastern Europe. Unlike wine, ale was considered a food necessity, not a luxury drink. Malted barley, water, and yeast were the basic ingredients, although herbs and spices such as rosemary, yarrow, nutmeg, and pepper could be added for flavor and preservation. In some areas of Europe, oats or mixed cereals were salted and used for brewing.

Ale spoiled within five days or so, and thus had to be brewed quite frequently. Throughout much of the Middle Ages, particularly in peasant communities, brewing was considered a household activity and most brewers were women. Even many of the commercial brewers in villages and towns were women, who supplemented family income by full- or part-time brewing. Ale was retailed by individual public brewers and by tapsters, taverners, and hucksters, who often purchased their supplies from the commercial brewers. To indicate brewing premises, brewers placed stakes or other signs outside their houses; when they had prepared a fresh batch of ale, they affixed a bush or bunch of ivy to the end of the stake, to indicate that the local ale-tasting officials should come to assess and price the ale.

Because ale was the common drink of so many people, its price and quality were strictly regulated. In England ale, like bread and wine, was subject to an assize dictated by the king and enforced by local officials. The assize of ale fixed the price of ale according to the changing price of grain from which malt was made. For every six-pence rise in the price of a quarter of barley, for example, the amount of ale a penny bought dropped by one-half gallon. Similar regulations were in force elsewhere in Europe by town decree. Ale tasters, who were appointed or elected in every town and village, supervised the quality of ale according to the assize or town decrees. Brewers who used impure water or bad malt, who sold ale before the dregs settled or when it was old and spoiled, or who tried to pass off weak ale as a more expensive grade were fined by the local authorities in the public interest.

Proper measures were also enforced; all vessels had to be stamped or sealed yearly, for a fixed payment. Abuses were frequent, however. Brewers put false bottoms in their measures or used elaborately shaped vessels that held less than the designated amount of ale. Customers also evaded these laws for the sake of their own convenience by bringing unstamped pitchers from home to be filled by the brewer or tapster. Indeed, the brewing laws on price, quality, and measures appear to have been most difficult to enforce. Town courts prosecuted those breaking the assize of ale more frequently than any other food traders. Most brewers found it easier to break the laws and pay the fines, which they and the authorities probably regarded primarily as licensing fees.

Beer, an alcoholic drink made from malt, hops, and water, became increasingly popular in the late Middle Ages, especially in Holland and Germany. The addition of hops to the traditional ale brew acted as a preservative and gave beer a much longer shelf life than ale. As a result, beer brewers could trade their product over longer distances and, unlike ale brewers, who had always retained strong household links, became highly commercialized. Indeed, the mostly male beer brewers quickly organized into guilds, in contrast with the low level of guild organization among the many female ale brewers. Only in larger cities such as Paris, where ale brewing was more trade-oriented and dominated by men, did ale brewers regularly form guilds.

DAIRY PRODUCTS

The retail sale of cheese, butter, milk, and eggs from the countryside often took place in a special hall or covered area in the marketplace called a butter cross. Peasants brought these dairy products into town each week, and frequently sold them directly to the consumer. At other times regrators and hucksters, many of whom were women, dominated the retail sale of these goods. In larger towns cheesemongers acted as middlemen, purchasing supplies from rural producers and estate owners, and selling to urban consumers in a shop or stall in the marketplace.

Cheese in the Middle Ages was made primarily from ewe's milk. But fourteenth-century consumers increasingly exhibited a taste for cow's-milk cheese, a taste that farmers satisfied by switching to specialized dairy farming in suitable agricultural regions. Such transitions to dairy farming also promoted the substitution of butter for lard in the same period. Dairy farming and butter production were especially prominent in Denmark, Sweden, and Norway. The export trade in butter, however, was largely handled by merchants of the Hanseatic League.

While salted butter and cheese did not spoil quickly, and thus could be traded wholesale over fairly long distances, the perishability of milk and eggs generally limited their sale to retail exchange. But eggs were sometimes traded in bulk; a fourteenth-century Norwich man reputedly forestalled so many eggs in the market that he managed to export twenty-eight barrels of them to foreign countries, much to the dismay of local officials. Such large-scale trading in eggs parallels other evidence that raising poultry for eggs was developing into a commercialized specialization in many areas of Europe.

FRUITS AND VEGETABLES

Most households in the Middle Ages had gardens where people grew a large proportion of fruits and vegetables for personal consumption. But commercial gardening thrived in this period as well, particularly in the vicinity of large towns. Most manors and monasteries had fruit orchards in which grew apples, from which a hearty cider was produced, or olives, from which a fine oil was extracted. Also considered fruits were nuts such as almonds and hazelnuts. Fruits and nuts were used in a variety of ways: in desserts and preserves, as the bases of cider, oils, or fruit drinks, or were eaten fresh or dried. The trade in fruits could thus be quite profitable. Much of the retail trade was in the hands of professional gardeners or rural producers, who sold their own products to the consumer in the marketplace. Middlemen occasionally intervened in this trade with bulk purchases from the commercial orchards of large estates. A thriving export trade was also carried on. Dried figs, dates, raisins, and nuts, as well as olive oil, were commonly exported northward from the Mediterranean regions.

Vegetables were less often an item of such trade, since most people grew their own. But townspeople did purchase some vegetables in the market, in particular onions and garlic, which were often exported by sea because they stored better than most vegetables. But the most commonly consumed vegetables—

cabbage, beans, peas, and leeks—if traded at all, were retailed close to where they had been grown. Professional gardeners and peasant producers handled almost all of this trade; merchants and wealthy middlemen rarely participated.

BIBLIOGRAPHY

William James Ashley, *The Bread of Our Forefathers* (1928); Judith Bennett, "The Village Ale-wife: Women and Brewing in Fourteenth-century England," in Barbara Hanawalt, ed., *Women and Work in Pre-industrial Europe* (1985); André Bouton, "L'alimentation dans le Maine aux XVᶜ et XVIᶜ siècles," in France, Comité des travaux historiques et scientifiques, *Bulletin philologique et historique* (1968); Claude Carrère, *Barcelone, centre économique à l'époque des difficultés, 1380–1462*, 2 vols. (1967); Pierre Charbonnier, "L'alimentation d'un seigneur auvergnat au début du XVᶜ siècle," in France, Comité des travaux historiques et scientifiques, *Bulletin philologique et historique* (1968); Hubert Collin, "Les ressources alimentaires en Lorraine pendant la première partie du XIVᶜ siècle," *ibid.*; Madeleine P. Cosman, *Fabulous Feasts: Medieval Cookery and Ceremony* (1976), 67–102; Charles L. Cutting, *Fish Saving: A History of Fish Processing from Ancient to Modern Times* (1955); Philippe Dollinger, *The German Hansa*, D. S. Ault and S. H. Steinberg, trans. (1970); Georges Duby, *Rural Economy and Country Life in the Medieval West*, Cynthia Postan, trans. (1968); G. Espinas, "La corporation des Boulangers-Patissiers d'Arras, 1356," in *Revue d'histoire économique et sociale*, **20** (1932); Frédéric Eyer, "La cervoise et la bière au moyen âge et à la Rennaisance," in France, Comité des travaux historiques et scientifiques, *Bulletin philologique et historique* (1968); Gustave Charles Fagniez, *Études sur l'industrie et la classe industrielle à Paris au XIIIᶜ et au XIVᶜ siècles* (1877); Robert Favreau, "La boucherie en Poitou à la fin du moyen âge," in France, Comité des travaux historiques et scientifiques, *Bulletin philologique et historique* (1968).

Norman S. B. Gras, *The Evolution of the English Corn Market from the Twelfth to Eighteenth Century* (1915, repr. 1967); A. B. Hibbert, "The Economic Policies of Towns," in *Cambridge Economic History of Europe*, III (1963); Margery K. James, *Studies in the Medieval Wine Trade* (1971); Philip E. Jones, *The Butchers of London* (1976); Charles de La Roncière, *Florence, centre économique regional au XIVᶜ siècle*, 5 vols. (1976); Teresa McLean, *Medieval English Gardens* (1980); Michael Prestwich, *York Civic Ordinances, 1301* (1976); Ernest L. Sabine, "Butchering in Mediaeval London," in *Speculum*, **8** (1933); Louis F. Salzman, *English Trade in the Middle Ages* (1931); Gérard Sivéry, "Les profits de l'éleveur et du cultivateur dans le Hainaut à la fin du moyen âge," in *Annales: Économies, sociétés, civilisations*, **31** (1976); Louis Stouff, *Ravitaillement et alimentation en Provence aux XIVᶜ et XVᶜ siècles* (1970); Reay Tannahill, *Food in History* (1973); Sylvia L. Thrupp, "The Grocers of London: A Study of Distributive Trade," in Eileen Edna Power and M. M. Postan, eds., *Studies in English Trade in the Fifteenth Century* (1933), and *A Short History of the Worshipful Company of Bakers of London* (1933); Robert Trow-Smith, *A History of British Livestock Husbandry to 1700* (1957); Cornelius Walford, "Early Laws and Customs in Great Britain Regarding Food," in *Transactions of the Royal Historical Society*, **8** (1880); C. Anne Wilson, *Food and Drink in Britain; from the Stone Age to Recent Times* (1973); Philippe Wolff, "Les bouchers de Toulouse du XIIᶜ au XVᶜ siècle," in *Annales du Midi*, **65** (1953).

M ARYANNE K OWALESKI

[See also **Agriculture and Nutrition; Animals, Food; Brewing; Fisheries, Marine; Fishponds; Fowl, Domestic; Fruits and Nuts; Guilds and Métiers; Hanseatic League; Trade** (various articles).]

FOREST LAW. Accompanying the common law of medieval England, but usually distinct from it, was a special law elaborated ostensibly to provide for royal hunting by protecting certain beasts within the royal forest: red deer, fallow deer, roe deer (until removed from the category by a decision in King's Bench in 1339), and wild boar. This forest law, with a reputation for severity and arbitrariness, did not, as was once thought, create wooded islands of special jurisdiction totally immune from common law. Rather, within all the tracts of royal forest scattered throughout the realm, forest law and administration were, in effect, added to existing common law, which generally continued to operate for all its usual purposes. Forest law was used to prosecute offenders against vert or venison through a system of courts, justices, and officers that came to be essentially independent of the common law. Medieval administrators and some medieval litigants did not distinguish the two systems with exactitude, and a great deal of overlapping occurred, especially in the formation period of the twelfth century; but usually the overlap and the occasional confusion created very little difficulty.

Determining precisely which areas were within the royal forest may have caused more trouble than did overlapping functions. The royal forest was not simply made up of tracts of wooded land but was an extensive game preserve. At its greatest size it covered as much as one-quarter of England, including nonwooded land, villages, and almost the entire county of Essex. Whether any particular tract of land was technically forest might vary over time and depend as well on the point of view taken in the quarrels between the king and his baronial opponents, for the extent of the forest and forest administration were recurrent points of contention. Even within the forest, areas known as parks or chases (the precise meaning of each and the distinction between them were often blurred) created zones for private hunting. Rights of warren, however, had no part in forest law, since warrens were usually outside the forest and were areas where their owners hunted rabbits, not "the beasts of the forest."

Several distinct periods in the history of forest law stand out. The Norman kings created the royal forest as an institution, whatever the precedents of Anglo-Saxon royal woods and hunting preserves. After the troubled reign of Stephen (1135–1154), the Angevin kings, especially Henry II (1154–1189), reestablished a strong forest administration and expanded the forest to its greatest extent. In the thirteenth century the system of forest law and administration reached its height, but the resistance and resentment it provoked made the forest a significant political issue: the Forest Charter of 1217 came to stand with the Magna Carta as a symbol of limitations on royal power. By the early fourteenth century the king could not maintain the royal forest intact, but he felt less need to make the attempt, having created much more efficient sources of revenue in percentage taxes on personal property. By 1327 the crown accepted the major disafforestation long demanded by its subjects. Even more significant was the marked decline in effective administration of the forest law: John Manwood, the author of the first treatise on the royal forest, wrote at the end of the sixteenth century that forest laws were so little used that they "are growen clean out of knowledge in most places in this Land."

Sources for the history of forest law, never adequate, do not permit a systematic analysis of the workings of the law before the thirteenth century. Documents are particularly sparse for the Norman period. Although William the Conqueror began the royal forest, both he and his son William Rufus (1087–1100) seem to have enforced forest laws through shire courts rather than through separate forest courts. By the time of Henry I (1100–1175) there are glimpses of the system that appeared more clearly under Henry II, who claimed to be restoring the situation that had obtained under his grandfather. Even for the reign of Henry II much remains uncertain, since the picture must be reconstructed largely from records made for financial rather than

judicial purposes. The forest eyre—a tour of the king's justices to judge those accused of violating forest law—began in the reign of Henry I and became a more regular and significant institution under Henry II; but totally separate, parallel forest eyres and general eyres cannot be assumed for the twelfth century.

Not all forest offenses were tried in forest eyres, and the justices of the forest might hear pleas unrelated to the forest while on their circuit. Separation and specialization of function appeared more fully only in the thirteenth century, and even then the sheriff continued to play a critical role in forest as well as common law. When the eyre justices came round, the accused were presented either by forest officials or by local people who had witnessed a violation of forest law. Before the justices appeared, an earlier stage of the legal process had already taken place in local forest courts, which can be studied only indirectly: when an accused found pledges for his appearance at the eyre, or when local men took responsibility for the chattels of those who fled rather than appear in court, or when a sheriff pledged to pay the value of farm animals seized within the forest. The final settlement of charges awaited the eyre justices. Ordinarily the guilt or innocence of the accused was determined by the ordeal by cold water, just as in common-law charges brought by presentment juries. Since men of status (again, as in common law) could claim the right to trial by battle, the zeal of a forester or villager to accuse a local knight must not have been keen.

The Assize of Woodstock apparently prescribed the death penalty for a third offense against the king's venison, and under Richard I the assize of 1198 ordered mutilation (blinding and castration) for the killing of deer. In practice, however, fines seem to have been imposed more commonly than these savage punishments. Moreover, it seems that, though less spectacular, offenses against the many restrictions regarding use of forest land were of greater importance than the poaching of deer. Causes for fines were numerous. In addition to fining for forest offenses as such, eyre justices fined townships or individual pledges (standing surety for an accused) for nonappearance, forest officials who failed to produce their rolls, and those who failed to have dogs kept in the forest "lawed" (a euphemism for the crippling of dogs by cutting off three toes on each forefoot to prevent their use in hunting). Certainly the eyre brought in welcome sums of money, though only at irregular intervals. Annual figures on the pipe roll do not record all the king's revenue, but those figures in 1175, a year when justices went out on forest eyre, increased by more than 50 percent over 1168, a year with no forest eyre, and several times revenue increased by more than 10 percent.

The very might of forest law and the revenue it brought help to explain Sidney Painter's assertion that the chief forester, Hugh de Neville, was the most powerful royal official under King John (1199–1216). Until 1229 this chief forester (or chief justice of the forest) commanded the entire corps of foresters and their assistants throughout England, answering only to the king; he heard forest pleas outside of the eyre and sat as a justice during an eyre. After various administrative experiments this vast jurisdiction was permanently divided in 1239, when Henry III established one justice for forests north of the Trent and one for those south of the Trent.

By that time forest law and administration had been fully elaborated, although the charters wrung from John and confirmed by Henry III had established that the king could not run the forests arbitrarily. Since many of the records produced in great quantity by this forest system have survived, the historical picture now comes into much clearer focus. The eyre continued to be the centerpiece of the system, but the work of local officials and local courts was essential. Terms varied, but each forest was supervised by some sort of warden or chief forester who paid the king a fixed rent and made his profit by what additional sums he could collect. Below the warden were foresters (classified as riding or walking), who served as actual gamekeepers. Since they seem frequently to have paid the warden for the job, with its abundant opportunities for remunerative repression of local people, a warden was tempted to appoint a larger number than needed and let them recover their investment by petty corruption. Two other officials were theoretically more independent of the warden. The verderers were elected in county court, presented their roll of all attachments made for forest offenses (paralleling that of the foresters) at the eyre, and were expected to inform the justices of any misconduct by forest officials. Regarders were chosen by the sheriff to conduct the regard and, like the verderers, were to report official misconduct.

The main duty of forest officials was to detect offenders. A vert or venison case might begin dramatically with foresters apprehending the offenders (who occasionally shot foresters as well as deer) or with villagers raising the hue and cry. Just as likely, evidence of an illegal hunt or cutting of timber might lead to a special inquisition at which representatives of four local townships would testify before the foresters and verderers about suspicious hides or antlers or an expanse of ground covered only by tree stumps. In addition to these ad hoc procedures, several local courts met regularly under the direction of foresters and verderers. At the regard, held frequently but not every third year, as formally established, twelve prominent local men gave answers under oath to a series of questions (called the chapters or articles of the regard) that would reveal any assarts (clearings made for agricultural purposes), purprestures (clearings made for buildings), waste (substantial cutting of timber), or primitive industrial enterprises (such as mines or forges) operating within the forest. In short, the regard surveyed damage to vert rather than venison and presented the information at the eyre.

In order to collect the fee called pannage, the crown allowed pigs to feed in the forest; officials called agisters counted the pigs as they entered and collected the money as they left. Farm animals were not allowed to wander into forest land, and some forests had local courts to assess the value of animals discovered and seized by foresters in forbidden areas. In these courts foresters similarly had to assess the value of timber that had been cut illegally, but recovered and sold, so that they could account for it before the justices. The terms used for these courts are confusing: some were called swanimotes (a term used elsewhere for the attachment court and at a later time for the general inquisition), whereas others were termed forest hundreds.

The attachment court, meeting every six weeks, was the most important local court, for in it the multitude of minor offenses against the vert were heard and amerced. (Technically these were cases involving dry saplings worth less than four pence.) In this court as well, all those accused of more serious offenses against the vert or of killing the king's deer had to find pledges for their appearance before the next forest eyre. All individuals attached either in their persons or by pledges were brought before the justices; the sheriff was ordered to arrest the person or seize the property of any defendant who had not given pledges or who failed to appear. If a defendant had no property and could not be found, he would be outlawed at the county court, following standard common-law procedures.

The main function of the justices was as much financial as judicial. In most cases, after the foresters and verderers presented the accused, the justices simply certified the record presented and set the fine. In a few cases the justices made further inquiries or considered a case that the attachment court could not settle; a few other cases came directly to the eyre without going first to the attachment court. The eyre assessed penalties not according to the seriousness of the offense but according to the justices' perception of the transgressor's capacity to pay. From one point of view the practice was humane; from another, purely practical and efficient. Some clerks kept running totals of the money collected as forest pleas were presented to the justices, clearly revealing something of the cast of mind at work in the court. Even the clergy, though produced at the eyre by the bishops and not by forest officials, and excused from finding pledges, nonetheless paid fines just like laymen. Indeed, justices regularly assessed heavier fines on clerics, presumably because they were thought to be able to pay. Similarly, Jews were fined more than Christians. Trespasses against the vert accounted for most fines; the number of venison cases was surprisingly small in most years, and even in large forests the eyre justices might be presented with only a few poachers.

The system was inefficient, or at least irregular, in many ways; but from an administrative point of view it suffered most from the decline of the forest eyre. Across the thirteenth century, paralleling the general eyre, forest eyres visited the counties at lengthening intervals. The justices reached most counties only in 1229, 1255–1256, 1262, 1269–1270, and 1285–1286; in some areas the gap between eyres was much greater. At a forest eyre in Nottingham in 1286, no fewer than 247 men summoned were reported dead; twenty-four years had elapsed since the forest justices had last appeared.

As the eyre ground almost to a halt, the general inquisition took over some of its functions. After the ordinance of 1306 (in which the general inquisition is confusingly called a swanimote), general inquisitions became quite common, at first supplementing, and later replacing, the eyre. An instructive parallel can be drawn between the role assumed by the general inquisition as the forest eyre declined and the role of the general commissions of oyer and terminer, known as trailbastons, after the decline of the general eyre: in each case a more streamlined inquest was substituted for the grander and more cumbersome eyre so that important work could be done.

Although trailbaston flourished, the success of the general forest inquisition is more doubtful. The procedure used in the general inquisition can scarcely be

faulted. According to the 1306 ordinance, forest ministers were to indict—before the foresters, verderers, regarders, agisters, other ministers of the forest, and a jury from the neighborhood—all those who had committed forest offenses within their bailiwick. Any assessment of the efficiency of this method, however, awaits detailed study. Apparently general inquisitions heard relatively few forest pleas.

It is important to distinguish between symptoms and causes. The virtual disappearance of the forest eyre and the possibly halfhearted substitute of the general inquisition mirrors a basic shift in royal administrative policy. Unlike the common law, forest law existed only for the king's benefit and had no arguable basis in common utility. From an early time, quite likely from its inception under William the Conqueror, the forest and forest law existed mainly as a source of revenue of a type typical in more inchoate medieval states: a royal right was maintained and a jurisdiction elaborated so that payments for exemptions could be collected along with a flow of amercements. In post-conquest England the difference was the royal power, which could afforest vast areas of the realm and administer an arbitrary forest law within them. Such a system was not easily dismantled, as the political struggles of the thirteenth century so clearly demonstrated: resistance to reduction of the forest and demands for reform of forest law could easily become a point of honor for so royal a king as Edward I.

Nevertheless, once the revenue produced by the forest system (relative to other sources of income) no longer offset the political opposition it generated, forest law was bound to fade, as it did during the fourteenth and fifteenth centuries. Edward III in 1369 pardoned all forest offenders (except indicted forest officials) in gratitude for the generous parliamentary taxation his subjects had provided. Richard II, in a 1383 statute, showed greater concern for subjects entangled in forest law than for the protection of vert and venison; offending officials faced double indemnity payments—to the damaged party as well as to the crown. A Norman king transported into the fourteenth century would have found such royal pronouncements incomprehensible, until he consulted the Exchequer.

BIBLIOGRAPHY

H. A. Cronne, "The Royal Forest in the Reign of Henry I," in H. A. Cronne *et al.*, eds., *Essays in British and Irish History in Honour of James Eadie Todd* (1949, repr. 1977); Nellie Neilson, "The Forests," in James F. Willard and

William A. Morris, eds., *The English Government at Work, 1327–1336,* I (1940, repr. 1965); F. H. M. Parker, "The Forest Laws and the Death of William Rufus," in *English Historical Review,* 27 (1912); Charles Petit-Dutaillis, "The Forest," in *Studies and Notes Supplementary to Stubbs' Constitutional History,* II, William T. Waugh, trans. (1930); G. J. Turner, ed., *Select Pleas of the Forest* (1901); Elizabeth Cox Wright, "Common Law in Thirteenth-century English Royal Forest," in *Speculum,* 3 (1928); Charles R. Young, "English Royal Forests Under the Angevin Kings," in *Journal of British Studies,* 12 (1972), "The Forest Eyre in England During the Thirteenth Century," in *American Journal of Legal History,* 18 (1974), and *The Royal Forests of Medieval England* (1979).

RICHARD W. KAEUPER

[See also **Forests, European; Hunting, Western European; Oyer and Terminer, Trailbaston.**]

FORESTS, EUROPEAN. Much of Europe was heavily wooded in the fifth century, when various Germanic peoples established their kingdoms in what had been the western part of the Roman Empire. Spain had some important forests, but the other lands bordering the Mediterranean supported only a fragile forest because of unfavorable climate and the destruction of trees in antiquity. Beyond the frontiers of the former Roman Empire, central Europe was heavily wooded throughout the early Middle Ages. For most of Europe the forest cover remained the dominant feature of the landscape until the great wave of clearing in the tenth through twelfth centuries brought agricultural expansion at the expense of the forests.

For the period before the clearings, information about forests is only partial, and the vague outline of forest history has to be gleaned from a variety of sources. There are a few provisions dealing with use of woods in the Germanic law codes; names of forests sometimes appear in narratives written by chroniclers and annalists; and references to woods and forests are found in saints' lives, diplomas, and other Merovingian documents, as well as Carolingian capitularies and polyptychs. The study of place names in connection with maps can reveal a pattern of forest covering or the making of clearings. Other techniques have been borrowed from the sciences: the study of geology applied to soils for determining where forests may have existed, pollen analysis to distinguish areas formerly wooded and patterns of clearing over time, and radiocarbon dating of

wooded areas. Only for England (the Domesday Book of 1086) is there any written source approaching a general description of wooded areas. In addition to its unparalleled information, Domesday Book permits some confirmation of other research methods, for the areas thought to have been wooded on the basis of literary references and place-name studies are almost identical with the areas reported as wooded in the survey.

The sparse population of early medieval Europe lived surrounded by forests. Hunters, gatherers, and stockmen depended on the forests, which also provided material for houses and implements and fuel for cooking and heating. Domestic animals foraged in the woods and undeveloped wastes: indeed in Domesday Book and other literary references the size of a wood was often expressed in terms of the number of pigs that could be supported by feeding on the mast from the trees. Forests were also barriers separating village from village, providing natural boundaries between kingdoms, and marking the outer reaches of church dioceses. Medieval forests were also refuges—first for pagans resisting the spread of Christianity, later for hermits and monks fleeing what the Christian world had become, and always for outlaws and misfits on the fringes of society. For most of the population the forest never lost its aura of mystery, and some people continued to venerate sacred trees or to believe in spirits that lived within the forest depths.

In the latter half of the seventh century, the Merovingian kings began to assert some political control over the use of the forests. Earlier there had been no legal restrictions on hunting, though the Germanic law codes had provisions against the indiscriminate cutting of trees. There is some evidence that landholders followed the kings in attempting to guarantee their own rights over certain woods and to restrict their use by all others. As part of this development, the earliest example of the word "forest" is found in a Merovingian diploma of 648 (or a later one of 697, if the earlier diploma is not authentic), but the concept of the "forest" obviously developed before the word itself.

Scholars do not agree on the etymology of the Latin word for forest (variously *foresta* and *forestis*) or the German word *Forst,* which became assimilated to the Latin, but there is no debate about the institution to which these terms applied. Throughout most of the Middle Ages, a "forest" was an area set apart from other land by special restrictions on hunting and other uses. Several capitularies of Charlemagne are quite unambiguous about this meaning in its full juridical sense. Roman law, with its provisions for protecting property, included compensation for damages to woods but had no penal code nor hunting restrictions like those in the Carolingian forest laws. In fact, the forest in its juridical sense is found only in western Europe as a legacy from the Carolingian Empire; it was unknown to the Byzantines.

Carolingian capitularies show that many royal woods had been made forest, subject to laws, not so much to protect the woods as to preserve wild animals for the king's hunting. Royal officials imitated the king in establishing reserved areas in which hunting by others was forbidden, to the detriment of what had been a common right in earlier centuries. By 817 the great lords were adding so many forests that the king forbade his counts to create new ones without his express authorization. In contrast, the forest in a botanical sense was being diminished somewhat, mainly by monks who founded new religious houses and then cleared the fields needed to support their new communities.

In spite of the restrictions adopted by lay and ecclesiastical lords, the woods remained indispensable to country life. The customary right to have domestic animals in the forest continued, with some regulation or in defiance of prohibitions that were not very effective (as shown by capitularies of the late ninth century). The extension of the legal concept of the forest beyond the royal domain was accomplished by means of the king's ban—the royal prerogative to command and punish—and the further extension of forest regulations by ecclesiastical and lay lords beyond their own domains had some governmental elements that blurred the distinction between public and private.

The Carolingian institution of the forest as an area of special legal jurisdiction survived the Carolingian Empire both in Germany and in France, and it was carried to England by the Norman Conquest. In the eastern part of the Frankish Empire, the forest system continued in the tenth century with least change. The German kings maintained their sovereign prerogative over the forest and authorized territorial princes to establish their own forests. The Saxon and Salian kings gave forests to churches and to the aristocracy, inadvertently contributing to the political power of lords. The concept of a forest granted to magnates by extending the king's ban meant that a forest was no longer connected to a particular piece of land but encompassed any lands placed under the ban. The old customary rights in common, known as the *Markgenossenschaft,* were replaced by the narrower rights of the lords, as authorized by the king, over hunting, clearing land, and other uses that might interfere with the wild game.

The process of decentralizing control over forests continued in Germany in the early eleventh century, as kings gave away royal rights over whole districts, with wood and fields included as parts of the forest. Such aristocratic rights increased with the development of regional political power during the investiture controversy. The movement for clearing lands that opened the mountains of central Germany for economic exploitation also contributed to princely territorial expansion. The Hohenstaufen kings excelled in the process by building their own estates and administering the forests on them by means of their *ministeriales.* Their success might have led to renewed central control over the forests, as happened in France and England, except that the sudden death of Frederick II in 1250, and the subsequent decline of the Hohenstaufens, left Germany with decentralized forests in the control of local lords.

Decentralization of the Carolingian forest came earlier in the western part of the Frankish Empire, with the decline of royal authority in the tenth century. Rights to the forest were given to any lord who had the right to high justice, and these lords spread forest rights even more widely through subinfeudation. Before long the right to establish a forest became a seigneurial right, so that by the eleventh century the king of France had no monopoly over the forest. Moreover, since many peasants still had rights in the forest (collecting firewood, pasturing pigs), the word ceased to mean a protected hunting reserve. A new word, *garenne,* was substituted in French to designate a restricted area for hunting.

Already reduced by gifts to the church and lay lords, the remaining royal forests were blended with the royal domain after the election of Hugh Capet as king in 987. The Capetian kings shared the ban with their counts, and they continued to give away forests to the church and to lay lords. Aristocratic usurpation of forest rights belonging to abbeys left the forests primarily in the control of lay lords and further reduced the number of authorities with an interest in a controlled use of the woods. The *garennes* were multiplied by the lords through exercise of the ban, and the rights formerly enjoyed by the peasants were more and more restricted by seigneurial privilege. Responsibility for the remaining royal

132

forests rested with *prévôts* or *maires* as part of the royal domain. When this diffused responsibility led to administrative neglect, officials called baillis were superimposed to care for waters and forests along with other parts of the royal domain, and finally a separate forest service was established.

In some local areas, such as the duchy of Normandy, the special jurisdiction of the forest remained strong and under the control of the dukes. It was this concept of the ducal forest that the Normans introduced to England after the Conquest. Ironically, Norman England preserved the Carolingian royal forest more faithfully than either Germany or France in the eleventh century. William the Conqueror was fond of hunting, and his enemies charged that while he loved the stags as if he were their father, he ignored the hardships of his human subjects. The forest law under the Norman kings earned a reputation for severity because of its penalties of capital punishment or mutilation for offenses against the king's game. Protection of the forest law covered the "beasts of the forest"—several kinds of deer and the wild boar—and the trees, known as the vert, which provided their habitat. The king had a monopoly over the forest except for grants he might make in the form of "chases," which allowed his barons to control hunting in a specified portion of their lands as private forests; parks, which consisted of enclosed areas for keeping deer; or warrens, where the barons could freely hunt animals other than the "beasts of the forest."

Although a few incidental references in literary sources seem to imply that Anglo-Saxon kings had forests, the concept of the forest in its full juridical sense was imported by the Normans. William I was notorious for creating the New Forest, although his monastic critics exaggerated the destruction of villages caused by its formation. In fact, the royal forest in England differed from those in Germany and France by including entire districts of the countryside, with villages and towns, not just areas covered with trees. In the later twelfth century Henry II, the first of the Angevin kings, continued to expand the boundaries of royal forests until they included more land than at any other time. These forests were administered by special courts on the local level, called attachment courts, and by regular judicial eyres to enforce a forest law separate from the emerging common law. The Assize of the Forest in 1184 provided the basic outline of English forest law and guided the proceedings of the justices in eyre for forest pleas. Thanks to a strong, centralized system of

administration, English royal forests were not as severely affected by the expansion of agriculture as those in France in the twelfth century and in Germany in the mid thirteenth century.

However they were organized in a legal sense, forests and wastelands were essential to the expanding agricultural economy of the Middle Ages. By the twelfth century, clearings and reclamation of wastes had upset the balance between agriculture and forests. The establishment of new villages (*villeneuves*) as one method of developing land meant extensive clearing to provide an agricultural base for the relocated population. The resulting imbalance led to the near destruction of forests in Germany, the reorganization and reemergence of royal authority over forests in France, conflict between the king and his barons over the extent of the royal forests in England, and general conflict between the rights of the lords and the remaining rights of common that peasants had exercised in lands newly brought under the plow.

Another force putting pressure on the forests was the expansion of towns. Wood was necessary to house the increasing urban population and to provide fuel for cooking, heating, and industry. Paris had large forests in the Île-de-France to supply an insatiable demand for lumber. During the interregnum in thirteenth-century Germany, an informal alliance of townsmen and countrymen managed to obtain some rights to the profits of forests that had belonged to the princes.

With this increasing need for land, the forest came to be valued less as a hunting preserve and more as an economic resource. The growth of trade based on cattle and forest products raised the value of uncultivated land, sometimes above that of the arable. By the thirteenth century demand for arable land had resulted in so many clearings that efforts began in France to protect the remaining forest and waste from further uncontrolled development.

The centralized administration of the royal forests of England was less affected by the pressures of expanding agriculture and towns than the decentralized forests in the control of local lords in France and Germany. The Assize of the Forest in 1184 and the system of forest courts, which had stabilized the royal forests, was renewed in 1198, though in practice fines were substituted for punishments by death or mutilation. There is evidence that under King Henry II royal interest in the forests had already shifted from the protection of animals for the king's hunting to the economic profits that could be extracted by an efficient administration. Fines for forest offenses had been regularly collected long before the change was recognized officially by the Forest Charter of 1217.

The pressure to develop new agricultural land in England is reflected in the increased assarting (clearing) in royal forests. Royal policy was to collect fines for any new assarts made in a royal forest without the king's authorization, and then to assess annual rents on the land brought under cultivation. Still, some effort was made to control the assarts in order to protect areas for the king's hunting.

An elaborate forest administration was headed by a chief justice of the forests (an office divided into two jurisdictions for the areas north and south of the Trent after 1238), with foresters or wardens responsible for managing particular forests by means of subordinate foresters and lesser officials. Local men holding land within the county were elected as verderers in the county court to meet regularly with the foresters in attachment courts, which settled minor infractions and prepared cases for royal justices on eyre when they visited the county to hear pleas for other offenses against venison and vert. Other officials, known as regarders, made general inspections of the forests and their officials at regular intervals (formally specified in 1215 as every three years). The key of the operation of the forest administration was the forest eyre, held by royal justices every few years, at which monetary penalties were assessed for all serious trespasses against forest law.

This system of royal forests, with control over all lands within its boundaries—estimated at one-fourth of all the land in England in the thirteenth century—became a political issue between the king and his barons. The barons, restless under the restrictions placed on the use of their own lands that happened to fall within the boundaries of royal forests, sought to have those forests reduced to the limits fixed before the expansion carried out by Henry II. Grievances about the royal forest played a part in the war between the barons and King John, and in 1217 the clauses in Magna Carta relating to the royal forest were incorporated in a separate Forest Charter that became the fundamental legal document on forests, confirmed along with Magna Carta in 1225 and 1297. Although the area included within royal forests changed several times in response to political demands, the long decline of the English royal forest dates from 1327, when substantial disafforestment was granted by a weakened monarchy.

In France the wave of clearings culminated in the twelfth century and provoked a reaction. The king and some of the nobility began to reorganize their forest administrations to resist further encroachment into the wooded areas. Sales of wood helped to call attention to the problem of shrinking forests by emphasizing the value of timber in contrast with the alternative value of crops from newly opened fields. In 1219 an ordinance of Philip II Augustus stipulated that no new usage rights over the forests could be granted by king or noble, a policy that became permanent with its confirmation in an ordinance of 1346. Conflicts between lords and peasant communities over the collective use of uncultivated lands were especially frequent where the population was rapidly increasing, as in Flanders, but the attempt by some lords to curtail use of the forests brought similar conflict to other regions.

The reaction of king and aristocracy to these conditions produced a kind of forest administration that lasted in France throughout the Middle Ages. The basis of this administration was the *gruerie,* which divided forests into different zones, some completely restricted in regard to hunting and other uses. Because the control of forests was only marginally in the hands of the king and was widely distributed among the landholding lords, there developed many regional variations of the *gruerie* system. Lords converted some woods to agricultural use and then established restricted zones to protect the remaining woods from intrusion by peasants or other potential users. In general, the lords followed the royal example in appointing an official to supervise the use of the forest, judge offenses against forest policy, and regulate the cutting of woods, but the variety of names for this official is a reminder of many regional differences within a general pattern: *gruyer* in the Île-de-France, *verdier* in Normandy, *maître-général* in Champagne, and *garde* in Languedoc. These officials rendered an account twice a year for the profits of the forests to the baillis or *prévôts,* who were above them in authority. Among the many subordinate officials with specific duties were the *garenniers,* whose duty it was to protect the hunting within the *garenne.*

In the thirteenth century new royal officials, the *maîtres des forêts,* began to replace the baillis in their jurisdiction over forests. These new officials received the accounts of the *gruyers* and transmitted them to the baillis, who incorporated the figures into their own accounts. The position of the new officials was not formally consolidated in the administration of the forests until Philip VI's fundamental ordinance of 1346. In contrast with the Île-de-France and Champagne, Normandy developed a distinctive practice known as the *tiers et danger:* a tax paid to royal forest officials on each sale of wood by ecclesiastical or lay lords at the rate of one-third and one-tenth (43 percent). Apparently the dukes of Normandy had controlled the sale of wood by requiring a license to sell, and from this practice the Capetian kings after 1204 developed the *tiers et danger* as a tax based on this precedent. This Norman practice took on wider significance in the later thirteenth century, when some references from the reign of Louis IX show the Capetian monarchs beginning to adopt a similar tax for their domains outside of Normandy. The definitive form of the *tiers et danger* was fixed by Louis X in his charter to the Normans in 1315.

Philip VI's ordinance of 1346 formed the basis for all subsequent ordinances concerning the forests until the end of the ancien régime. It provided that the *maîtres* of waters and forests should hold inquiries in all forests and woods, and should supervise sales of wood so that the forest should be maintained perpetually in a good state. It also provided that no new right of usage should be granted in the forests. The *maîtres* served as judges in all cases except for hunting offenses, which continued to be heard by the baillis. There was some ambiguity about whether their sentences could be appealed to the *parlements,* but the ordinance clearly prohibited baillis, *sénéchaux* (seneschals), *prévôts,* or *vicomtes* (viscounts) from considering any matter concerning the waters or forests. This broad grant of authority was divided among four or, at times, five *maîtres* who supervised the king's forests.

In 1360 another official, the *souverain-maître des eaux et forêts,* was superimposed to receive appeals from decisions by the *maîtres.* His principal seat, called the *table de marbre,* was in Paris, and he had jurisdiction over all of France except Normandy, which retained jurisdiction in its own *échiquier.* Six years later the function of receiving profits from forests that had been retained by the baillis was concentrated in the hands of a new official, the *receveur général des eaux et forêts.* The administrative reorganization of the royal forests had broader significance because the lords followed the royal example and set up similar administrations within their important forests. When royal forests were mixed with forests belonging to other lords, royal officials often attempted to assert a broader claim to inspect the operation of the seigneurial forests nearby. Although

the Estates General attempted to restrain the claims of royal officials, the attempt was unsuccessful, and the authority of the king expanded beyond the forests of the royal domain.

In Germany, as in France, clearings eventually transformed the wooded landscape. In some areas it became necessary to prohibit further clearings, but the general pattern in Germany was a transition to an ordered forest economy in which special areas were set aside to grow the best wood possible for use in building. The pressure of clearings and the necessity for controlling the use of woods was felt in Germany in the fourteenth century, almost two centuries later than in France. The earliest references to imperial reforestation in a cutover royal forest are found in documents dating from 1304 and 1309, but such efforts did not become sustained until the fifteenth century.

After the mid fourteenth century the princes and other landed lords extended their authority over forests by restricting hunting in entire districts and by managing the forest economy under the authority of their ban. Forests had become part of the seigneurial domain and were administered by bailiffs, or by a royal forester in lands belonging to the king. The official known as *magister forestarius* or *comes forestarius* gradually took the place of older officials. The administration of forests was made more complex because remaining woods used in common had their own officials, with various names, to administer the customs in effect there. During the fifteenth century the lords succeeded in gaining more control over these common woods, and seigneurial officials tended to supersede those who had supervised the common use of the woods.

The general trend throughout Europe in the fifteenth century was that less attention was given to the problem of administering and protecting the forests. With a diminished population for a century after the Black Death, some land that had been cleared was abandoned, reverted to waste, and then gradually became wooded again. A rough equilibrium between the agricultural need for land and the need for wood and forest products returned. Political events, such as the Hundred Years War and the enfeeblement of the monarchy in France, also contributed to the neglect of the forests. At a more basic level, the economic value of forests to the kings of France and England lessened dramatically with the development of taxes that produced a greater proportion of the royal revenues. Receipts from the royal domain in France for 1483 contributed only one-fiftieth of all royal income, and the royal forests accounted for only a small part of the domain.

In England, where the administration of the royal forest had been the strongest through the centuries, the key institution in overseeing the operation of the forests was the forest eyre, at which the justices collected fines for trespasses against the forest and examined the conduct of forest officials. These eyres became infrequent in the early fourteenth century and ceased after 1368—an indication of monarchial neglect. The forest inquests that replaced the eyres were sporadic and failed to supervise the lower forest courts, which had only the power to prepare cases for the justices and could decide penalties only for minor offenses. The extent of the royal forest had been greatly reduced by disafforestment in 1327, and the enforcement of forest law in the remaining forest was in complete decay by the sixteenth century.

The reasons for the decline of the medieval forest in Germany were somewhat different from those in France and England. It was only in the fourteenth century that the expansion of agriculture produced fundmental change. The peasants continued to be dependent on the woods and attempted to regulate their use; but the belated growth of towns put additional pressure on the forests, as it had in France, and upset the balance between town and countryside. The princes, seeking an opportunity for profits, responded by trying to turn the forests into a monopoly for themselves while overriding the surviving claims of common usage put forth by the peasants. Under the pressure of these contending needs, forests were much reduced in northwestern Germany and a new type of economy, no longer dependent on the interrelationship of field and woods, emerged. Cattle and dairy farming developed in the west, and cultivation of cereal grains became the dominant pattern in the east.

BIBLIOGRAPHY

Michel Bur, "Le défrichement et le partage de la forêt du Mans près de Meaux (1150–1250)," in *Bulletin philologique et historique du Comité des travaux historiques et scientifiques 1963* (1966); H. C. Darby, ed., *Domesday England* (1977); Edouard Decq, "L'administration des eaux et forêts dans le domaine royal en France aux XIVᵉ et XVᵉ siècles," in *Bibliothèque de l'École des chartes,* **84** (1923); Michel Devèze, *Histoire des forêts* (1973); Henri Gilles, "L'administration royale des eaux et forêts en Languedoc au moyen âge," in *Bulletin philologique et historique du Comité des travaux historiques et scientifiques 1963* (1966); Félix Goblet d'Alviella, *Histoire des bois et forêts de Belgique,* I (1927); Charles Higounet, "Les forêts de l'Europe occidentale du Vᵉ au XIᵉ siècle," in *Paysages et villages neufs du moyen âge* (1975); Nellie Neilson, "The Forests," in James F. Willard and William A. Morris, eds., *The English Government at Work, 1327–1336,* I (1940, repr. 1965); Charles Petit-Dutaillis, "The Forest," in *Studies and Notes Supplementary to Stubbs' Constitutional History,* II, William T. Waugh, trans. (1930); Maurice Prou, "La forêt en Angleterre et en France," in *Journal des savants,* n.s. **13** (1915); Albrecht Timm, *Die Waldnutzung in Nordwestdeutschland im Spiegel der Weistümer* (1960); Charles R. Young, *The Royal Forests of Medieval England* (1979).

CHARLES R. YOUNG

[See also **Forest Law.**]

FORGERY may have been practiced by all the literate classes of society throughout the Middle Ages, but it seems to have had particular periods of flourishing when particular practitioners were especially busy. Some forgeries were propaganda: for example, supporters of Philip IV of France in 1302 circulated documents purporting to be an exchange of letters between Pope Boniface VIII and the king, with exaggerated papal claims and a scornful royal rebuttal. The great feudatory Robert III of Artois forged documents to support his claim to the county of Artois on the eve of the Hundred Years War. The most famous medieval forgery was the spurious eighth-century donation by which the late Roman emperor Constantine was made to grant the pope control over Rome and Roman possessions in the West.

The golden age of forgery was the late eleventh and twelfth centuries, and the most successful forgers were monks. As one litigant charged, the documents produced by his opponents at the papal court were forgeries "in parchment and script, thread and bulla [the papal seal]," thus providing a list of the media of the forger's art. Parchment was rubbed to look ancient, or ancient parchment was erased and rewritten; scripts were copied; authentic seals were sliced in half and applied to the threads of the new creation. In England, for example, of 164 extant charters in the name of Edward the Confessor, forty-four are probably spurious and another fifty-six are doubtful. Seventeen of thirty pre-conquest religious houses apparently practiced forgery on a significant scale. The archbishop of Canterbury owes his primacy, and Westminster Abbey its exclusive privilege of being the coronation church of English sovereigns, to skillful forgeries. The deception was common to all of western Europe.

Modern sensibilities may be shocked that monks combined the work of God with the practice of forgery. Two important reasons help to explain their actions. First, in common with most medieval men, monks lacked a developed historical sense. The past was not to them a closed book recording a different world; the members of a religious house that possessed the relics of a saint or a saintly king might act on behalf of this immortal who still "lived" for them. The pious intentions of good men could be fulfilled even after their death. Second, recording good intentions in black ink on parchment was a requirement of the more legalistic world of the twelfth century, as the shift from oral testimony to written record progressed. A king or lord might have made a grant, but he might not have provided a charter, or it might have been lost or damaged by damp or fire; if extant, it might simply fall short of the legal requirements of a new age. The royal chancery, with no better historical sense than the monks, might reject valid oral tradition but accept a "good" fake charter. Moreover, between the absolute poles of the "genuine" and the "spurious" were many more subtle gradations: poor copying, alteration, improvement, bringing up to date. But every forgery shows the tension between a conservative absence of a historical sense and the rapidly developing legal renaissance.

BIBLIOGRAPHY.

C. N. L. Brooke, "Approaches to Medieval Forgery," in his *Medieval Church and Society* (1971); Michael T. Clanchy, *From Memory to Written Record in England, 1066–1307* (1979); Brian Tierney, *The Crisis of Church and State, 1050–1300* (1964), prints the Donation of Constantine and the forged letters of 1302; Thomas F. Tout, *Mediaeval Forgers and Forgeries* (1920).

RICHARD W. KAEUPER

[See also **Decretals, False; Donation of Constantine.**]

FORMERET (from the French *forme,* "window"), an arch or rib placed at the junction of a vault severy and a wall, usually over a window. Formerets may be structural, supporting the edge of the vault, but are employed principally to conceal the junction of the vault and wall and to give definition to the area of the vault severy.

CARL F. BARNES, JR.

FORNALDARSÖGUR. As is the case with certain other labels for literary forms in medieval Iceland, the term *fornaldarsögur* (stories of ancient times) is a legacy from nineteenth-century romanticism, which tended to base its generic divisions on historical rather than critical considerations. It was coined by the Danish scholar Carl C. Rafn (1795–1864), who used it as a blanket title for his three-volume edition of early Icelandic tales, *Fornaldar sögur Norðrlanda* (1829–1830), which have been regarded collectively, with only minor modifications, as a separate saga category ever since. In this context the phrase "ancient times" *(fornöld)* refers to the temporal setting of the stories involved, suggesting not only a distant and dimly remembered Scandinavian past, prior to the settlement of Iceland late in the ninth century, but also a purely imaginary age of legend and myth. Thus the time factor serves to distinguish the *fornaldarsögur* from the *Íslendingasögur* (stories of Icelanders), the *konungasögur* (stories of kings), and other narrative types dealing with the historical period beginning with the discovery of Iceland (*ca.* 870). Taken as a whole, the *fornaldarsögur* present an alien and unfamiliar world, contrasting sharply with the naturalism of stories set in tenth- and eleventh-century Iceland, such as *Bandamanna saga* and *Hrafnkels saga.* On the other hand, the *fornaldarsögur* share so many features with the *lygisögur* (fabulous stories) that it is difficult to draw a definite line between the two groups. In terms of general literary theory, the *fornaldarsögur,* particularly the "adventure tales," probably could best be regarded as secular romances.

The raw materials that went into the making of the *fornaldarsögur* were diverse in origin and kind, and so are the finished products, the tales as they are found in medieval manuscripts. Some of the stuff was gleaned from a fading aristocratic tradition that had its roots in the preliterate culture of pagan Scandinavia; some came from folktales and other primitive forms of storytelling; fragments of ancient lore are found side by side with nuggets of foreign learning; memories of Viking life as it was lived, or thought to have been lived, in the ninth and tenth centuries are mixed with elements from the French romances and other European models. But heterogeneous as the ingredients are, the style and narrative technique are, with certain exceptions, remarkably consistent throughout the corpus.

Setting aside certain minor tales that either deal with provincial rulers in early Norway (*Af Upplendinga konungum, Hversu Nóregr byggðisk, Fundinn Nóregr*) or are set at one level in a legendary situation and at another in historical times (*Norna-Gests þáttr, Tóka þáttr Tókasonar, Þorsteins þáttr bæjarmagns, Helga þáttr Þórissonar*), the *fornaldarsögur* can be divided into two groups: "hero legends" and "adventure tales."

Stories in the first group represent a continuation of an ancient heroic tradition, surviving partly in a poetic form. Some of them have close parallels and analogues in other Germanic languages, both Old English (*Beowulf, Widsith*) and Old and Middle High German (*Das Hildebrandslied, Das Nibelungenlied*), as well as in the heroic poems of the *Poetic Edda*, on which *Völsunga saga* is based, and the *Prose Edda* of Snorri Sturluson. In contrast with the tragic mode of the "hero legends," in which the death of the hero tends to be the predominant element in the narrative, the essential feature of the "adventure tales" is that the hero undertakes a quest, or a series of quests, leading to a happy ending. Another significant difference between the two types is that the principal purpose of the "adventure tales" was not so much to perpetuate the traditional heroic ideal as to create new narrative sequences suitable for entertainment. While the "hero legends" kept open a window on a remote pagan past, the "adventure tales" invited the medieval audience to escape from the harsh realities of its everyday struggle by making imaginary journeys to the world of fantasy and romance.

The "hero legends" among the *fornaldarsögur* include *Völsunga saga, Hervarar saga ok Heiðreks konungs, Ásmundar saga kappabana, Hálfs saga ok Hálfsrekka, Sögubrot af fornkonungum* (part of *Skjöldunga saga*), *Sörla þáttr* (also known as *Heðins þáttr ok Högna*), and the Starkaðr episode in *Gautreks saga*. *Ragnars saga loðbrókar*, describing a ninth-century Danish warrior who led Viking expeditions to England and elsewhere, is presented as a sequel to *Völsunga saga*. A somewhat different account of his life and death is found in the *þáttr af Ragnars sonum*. Like Gunnarr in *Völsunga saga*, Ragnarr suffers the agony of death in a snake pit, but elsewhere in the "hero legends" the protagonist is killed by different means, often at the instigation of someone close to him. Incest, filicide, and other forms of perversion and unnatural cruelty provide some of the tragic ingredients of the "hero legends."

To the "adventure tales," which could also be labeled "Viking romances," belong the following stories about aristocratic warriors: *Bósa saga ok Herrauðs, Egils saga einhenda ok Ásmundar berserkjabana, Friðþjófs saga frækna, Göngu-Hrólfs saga, Hálfdanar saga Brönufóstra, Hjálmþérs saga ok Ölvis, Hrólfs saga Gautrekssonar, Hálfdanar saga Eysteinssonar, Sörla saga sterka, Þorsteins saga Víkingssonar*, and the so-called *Gjafa-Refs þáttr*, which is part of *Gautreks saga*. Like the title heroes of *Hrómundar saga Gripssonar* and *Illuga saga Gríðarfóstra*, Gjafa-Refr comes from a farming background, but he ends up as an earl. The protagonists of the following tales belong to a certain farming family in Halogaland in the north of Norway: *Gríms saga loðinkinna, Ketils saga hœngs, Áns saga bogsveigis*, and *Örvar-Odds saga*; of these, the last-mentioned is the only one in which the hero attains the status of a king. *Yngvars saga víðförla*, which is not included in Rafn's collection but appears in later editions of the *fornaldarsögur*, gives a fanciful description of an expedition to Russia and beyond; the title hero, a Swedish nobleman, was a historical personage who died in 1041. In addition to the secular tales, Rafn's edition of the *fornaldarsögur* includes one sacred romance, *Eiríks saga víðförla*, describing the hero's search for the earthly paradise (the Land of the Living).

The quests in the *fornaldarsögur* can be divided into several categories, depending on the ultimate goal and the nature of the hazards involved. The hero may set out to rescue an abducted princess, to carry out a dangerous mission at the behest of a hostile king, to lead an army against the usurper or a throne, to seek a wife for himself or for a friend, to take revenge for the death of a kinsman or a blood brother, or even to search for the source of a great river. Lust for loot and fame is yet another recurrent motive behind the quest: again and again the hero launches his longship to seek out formidable Vikings; emerging victorious from the encounter, he sails away with a dragon-headed warship as his most precious booty. The obstacles confronting the hero on his perilous journey to the chosen goal include monsters, berserks and other enemies of the social order, the hostile elements of nature, and the lady's reluctance to be wooed. On the completion of his quest, the hero emerges a greater man than before he set out, and in doing so he has proved himself superior to the rest of the cast. In some cases the quest is the result of a solemn vow, which tends to give the story the same kind of formal quality found in the *Íslendingasögur*, in which dreams and predictions may serve to control the ultimate narrative shape. The quest is almost invariably successful, the most notable exception being *Örvar-Odds saga*, the title hero of which fails in one attempt after another to take revenge on a protean, superhuman adversary who is, in the final analysis, an evil spirit and therefore indestructible.

On his quests the hero is usually accompanied by a blood brother, who is either a close friend from boyhood or an erstwhile opponent, in which case a deadly fight between them has resulted in a draw and everlasting friendship. When the blood brothers play an equal part in the course of events, both of them figure in the title role, as is the case in *Bósa saga ok Herrauðs* and *Egils saga einhenda ok Ásmundar berserkjabana*. In *Hjálmþérs saga ok Ölvers*, however, the second title hero plays only a minor role; the third blood brother, Hörðr, has the most important part. It is one of the nontragic features of the "adventure tales" that the bonds of blood brotherhood, friendship, and kinship are properly observed by the hero and those close to him; traitors are always outsiders, typically of a low social status. On the other hand, in the "hero legends" (such as *Völsunga saga*, *Sörla þáttr*, and the Starkaðr episode in *Gautreks saga*), as well as in the *Íslendingasögur* (*Gísla saga Súrssonar*, *Njáls saga*, *Laxdæla saga*, *Vápnfirðinga saga*), a heroic figure may be killed by a blood brother, a trusted friend, or a kinsman. The loyal blood brother usually survives all the hazards on the journey and afterward shares the glory with the hero, but in this respect, as in others, *Örvar-Odds saga* differs from the rest: not only does the hero lose one blood brother after another on his abortive revenge quests, but the presentation of one of them, the tragic Hjálmarr, has a genuine pathos about it, reminiscent of the "hero legends."

Other recurrent character roles include the old wise man, who in some cases acts as foster father to the hero or the heroine, and his counterpart, the evil counselor; the wicked and amorous stepmother, who tries, unsuccessfully, to seduce the hero; the giantess who fights and then befriends the hero, sometimes providing him with a memorable nickname (*Hálfdanar saga Brönufóstra*, *Illuga saga Gríðarfóstra*); the helpful dwarf who is also a master craftsman; the amazon who ultimately abandons her warlike career

to become a wife and mother; the beautiful princess in a typically passive role, abducted by a monster or a ruthless enemy and later rescued by the hero; the oppressive tyrant who usurps a throne and provides the hero with his greatest challenge; and, finally, an assortment of sorcerers, berserks, and other evildoers who keep preventing the hero from reaching his goal. It is with such set pieces that the quest game is played, the essential rules being invariable, though each individual author endeavored to introduce new combinations and variations of the basic patterns.

As in the *Íslendingasögur*, there is usually some anticipatory description of the hero's moral and physical attributes, marking him out from the rest of the cast and serving as a guide to his character. The introduction of the protagonist of *Hrólfs saga Gautrekssonar* may be quoted as an example:

> Hrólfr was unusually tall and strong, and very handsome. He was a man of few words, always honoured his promises, and wasn't over-ambitious. Whenever something was done or spoken against him, he used to pretend he hadn't noticed, but later when it was least expected, he was ruthless in taking his revenge. When people tried to sway his opinion about something that concerned him, he used to pay no attention to begin with, but afterwards, perhaps years later, apparently having thought things out fully, he'd raise it again, no matter whether it was good or bad for him. Once he'd made up his mind, he had to have his way. He was wellliked by everyone, and some people were very fond of him (Pálsson and Edwards [1972], 30).

In contrast, his brother is described in the following terms:

> Ketill was extremely small, boisterous, ambitious, impulsive, and full of drive and grit. He was so tiny he was nicknamed Ketill "Mite" [kregð]. (*ibid.*)

Ketill is well suited to act out a subsidiary role: he sets out on one quest after another, but he cannot complete them without Hrólfr's help, and he keeps egging his slow but resolute brother into hasty action. Hrólfr, on the other hand, typifies the ideal hero, the man who is destined for great things and who, even at an early age, displays what he can and will achieve.

The boyhood deeds of the hero usually redound to his credit, but there is another distinctive type: the male Cinderella, the unpromising youth who suddenly and unexpectedly is transformed into a true warrior. Starkaðr in *Gautreks saga* "was an exceptionally big man, but he was a layabout and slept among the ashes by the fire." Nevertheless, as soon as he is given weapons at the age of twelve (an age when many of the legendary heroes take up arms), he becomes an outstanding fighter, aiding his lord in a series of campaigns and gaining high honors. Another slow developer in the same saga is Refr Rennisson, who ultimately becomes the ruler of an earldom, notwithstanding an inauspicious beginning:

> When he was young Refr used to lie in the kitchen and eat twigs and tree bark. He was an exceptionally big man, but never bothered to wash the filth off his body, nor would he ever give anyone a helping hand. His father was a very thrifty man and took a poor view of his son's shiftless behaviour. So Refr didn't earn his fame by any wisdom or bravery but rather by making himself the laughing-stock of all his sturdy kinsmen. His father thought it unlikely that Refr would ever do anything worthwhile, as was expected at that time of other young men. (Pálsson and Edwards [1968], 37–38)

Other examples of a youthful layabout who later develops into a heroic figure are the title characters of *Göngu-Hrólfs saga, Ketils saga hængs,* and *Áns saga bogsveigis.*

Most of the "adventure tales" are set, partly at least, in Scandinavia, but the hero may wander far from home: north to Lappland and, beyond the White Sea, to Permia; south to the Mediterranean; east across the Baltic to Russia; and west over the North Sea to the British Isles—but never to Iceland. Beyond Europe he may travel south to Ethiopia *(Bláland)* and east to India. The more venturesome heroes make their way to Giantland, the Underworld, and other purely imaginary places, including the uncharted regions of ancestral myth.

What the authors of the *fornaldarsögur* knew about foreign parts was derived largely from reading rather than from travel, and there is a strongly bookish flavor about some of the geographical descriptions—for example, in the following sketch of England in *Göngu-Hrólfs saga:*

> England is the most productive country in Western Europe, because all sorts of metal are worked there, and vines and wheat grow, and a number of different cereals besides. More varieties of cloth and textiles are woven there than in other lands. London is the principal town, and then Canterbury. Besides these are Scarborough, Hastings, Winchester and many towns and cities not mentioned here. (Pálsson and Edwards [1980], 122)

Descriptions of this kind are not necessarily an organic part of the narrative, but they show an interesting aspect of the "adventure tales"; that in spite of the fantastic nature of the stories, their authors were anxious to give some semblance of reality where it suited them to do so. They used this opportunity not only to impart geographical knowledge, and so instruct the public on foreign countries, but also to add to the verisimilitude of the setting. Only one of the tales in Rafn's collection, *Hjálmþérs saga ok Ölvers,* has no reference to Scandinavia. The title heroes of that story belong to an imaginary country called Mannheimar, while other characters are associated with Syria, Boecia, Arabia, and the land of the Saracens *(Serkland).* The geographical setting constitutes one of the significant differences between the "hero legends" and the "adventure tales"; in the former, most of the action is confined to Scandinavia and other Germanic-speaking lands, though occasional scenes may be set in mythical regions.

There often appears to be some correlation between the hero's character and his country of origin. Norwegians are as a rule represented favorably, as are Danes and Götalanders, though the Swedes are often less agreeable. The Russians and the English are usually described with some sympathy, whereas the Irish, the Lapps, and the Permians are savage peoples and closely associated with sorcery and witchcraft.

Locations are stylized and recurrent: the king's hall, the peasant's hut, the harbor on a deserted coast, the clearing in the wood. Beyond the human world the hero may find himself in a shadowy cavern infested with ogres and giants, or at some other inhospitable place in a mythical landscape. Each conventional location tends to mark a stage in the hero's progress from his first excursion into a hostile world to the final scene, which, typically, is set in a banqueting hall where he celebrates his wedding and victories. A good deal of the action is set in a wild forest, at sea, and on the battlefield: the hero is essentially a fighter and a traveler.

With certain exceptions, such as *Ragnars saga loðbrókar, Þáttr af Ragnars sonum,* and *Yngvars saga víðförla,* the *fornaldarsögur* are not set in any particular period, though some of the heroes are linked tenuously with a royal house in Scandinavia or with the original settlers of Iceland by means of genealogies. The stories are set in what may be called the legendary heroic age at one level and, though more vaguely, in the less distant Viking age at another. The hero is a composite character in cultural terms, for some of his features are borrowed from a later and more refined ethos than that of pagan Scandinavia. He is the synthesis of several incongruous elements, combining the heroic ideal as manifested in ancient poetry with the acquisitive Viking type of

Scandinavian expansion and the courtly knight of romance. While the adventurous hero may receive "a fine education as is fitting for princes," excel at jousting and other knightly sports, live in a splendid castle, and treat women with a true sense of chivalry, most of his actions are dictated by a native literary convention. The courtly element is therefore often little more than a mere varnish, a thin veneer barely concealing the essential roughness of the narrative. It is particularly in descriptions of a luxurious material life that the influences of foreign models show through, as in the following depiction of a wedding feast in *Göngu-Hrólfs saga*:

> Now they had their ships unloaded, and they prepared for a magnificent feast with all the best fare that could be got in Denmark or anywhere near. They spared nothing on halls or furnishings or anything that was to be found in Scandinavia. To this banquet they invited burghers and courtiers, counts and earls, dukes and kings, and everyone of any standing. Most of the nobility in Denmark were there and, when all of them had arrived and been shown to their seats, there were courteous young squires and the finest gentlemen to attend on them. All kinds of dishes were served there, spiced with the most precious herbs, and every sort of game and wild fowl, venison from deer and reindeer, pork from the best wild boars, goose, ptarmigan, and peppered peacock. There was no shortage of glorious drink, ale and English mead, and the best of wines, both spiced and claret. And once the wedding and the banquet had begun, all kinds of stringed instruments, harps and fiddles, pipes and psaltery, were to be heard. There was a beating of drums and a blowing of horns, with all variety of pleasant play to cheer the body of man. After that the two young ladies were escorted into the hall with a colorful train and a cluster of splendid women. Two noblemen led by the hand each of the two ladies who were to marry the bridegrooms. Above them, supported on painted poles, was a canopy to conceal their resplendent clothing and elegance until they were seated. When the canopy was taken away, no color, it seemed, could outshine their complexion, their skins, their glossy hair, and all the glowing gold and jewels that they wore. (*ibid.,* 121–122)

But more characteristically and in a different mode, the *fornaldarsögur* contain extended accounts of pitched battles, describing the gory proceedings in vivid detail, blow by blow. While one hero keeps hacking his way through the enemy ranks, "surging forward like a man wading through a torrent," "his arms drenched in blood up to the shoulders," another "piles the corpses of his victims so high around him that the carnage reaches up to

his waist." Even with all this slaughter, victory is by no means a foregone conclusion: the unscrupulous enemy may have the power to raise fallen warriors from the dead and send them, reanimated and invulnerable, back into the fray. The "everlasting battle," described in *Sörla þáttr* and elsewhere, shows that such a nightmarish situation was an element in the heroic tradition. The world of fighting and dying warriors presented in the *fornaldarsögur* is often lacking in the sheer dignity and restraint found in the earlier heroic poetry.

Apart from the "abducted princess" and the "reluctant bride" themes, the *fornaldarsögur* have several other features normally associated with romance. The tragedy of Hjálmarr and Ingibjörg in *Örvar-Odds saga* (also found in *Hervarar saga ok Heiðreks konungs*), who are not allowed to marry and are finally united after death, belongs to a world of romantic sentiment alien to the nature of most of the narrative. The heroine of *Helga þáttr Þórissonar* is a seductress showing unmistakable affinities with those of the romantic ballads. But the outstanding love romance, *Friðþjófs saga frækna*, has a happy ending: after a long separation, during which the heroine is married off to an aging king who guards her virginity, the two lovers become husband and wife. Occasionally a hero falls in love with a girl at first sight; more often marriage is an arranged affair, though afterward "they came to love each other dearly." The typical heroine has a strong sense of honor and integrity, but some of the minor female characters are promiscuous—as for example the farmer's daughter in *Bósa saga ok Herrauðs*.

An antiquarian interest in ancient customs and beliefs pervades some of the *fornaldarsögur,* not only the "hero legends," in which it would be expected, but also the "adventure tales." Descriptions of rituals, such as pagan sacrifices, funerals, drinking contests, duels, and various kinds of competitive sport no longer practiced in the author's time, serve to strengthen the impression that the work is a mirror of a truly pagan ethos. References to the old "Viking laws," as in the following passage in *Örvar-Odds saga,* are probably not based on genuine tradition, but they reveal a nostalgic admiration of a bygone age and convey the notion that the fighting hero is not necessarily a barbarian:

> The first point I want to make is that I and my men refuse to eat raw meat. Plenty of people are in the habit of squeezing a bit of flesh in a piece of cloth and then calling it cooked meat, but in my opinion it's a habit more fit for wolves than men. I never rob merchants or

peasants beyond the odd raid to cover my immediate needs. I never rob women, even when we meet them on the road with plenty of money, and no woman's ever to be brought down to my ship against her own free will. And if she can show she's been taken to the ship against her will, the one who took her, no matter whether he's rich or poor, shall be put to death. (Pálsson and Edwards [1970], 27)

Mythical elements abound. *Sörla þáttr* opens in the world of the gods with an account of Odin, Freyja, and Loki, and the human tragedy that follows is the consequence of a conflict among these pagan deities. Elsewhere, the one-eyed Odin (often disguised as an old man) and the red-bearded Thor make occasional appearances in the world of men, changing the destinies of the characters involved; however, it is only in *Gautreks saga* that the two gods confront each other, as they ordain the destiny of the tragic hero Starkaðr. Thor bears malice toward him, and for every blessing Odin bestows on the hero, Thor counters with a curse.

The old gods are not necessarily treated with due reverence. In *Egils saga einhenda ok Ásmundar berserkjabana,* the giantess Arinnefja, describing how her seventeen sisters used to bully her, relates that she "made a vow to Thor to give him any goat he'd choose to have if he'd even things up between my sisters and me. Thor paid us a visit, and went to bed with my eldest sister and lay with her all night, but my other sisters were so jealous of her that they killed her in the morning. Thor did the same thing to all my sisters, he slept with them all in turn, and they were all killed" (Pálsson and Edwards [1968], 109). In *Völsunga saga,* on the other hand, in which Odin plays an important part, the author follows his pagan source closely enough to present the god with a sense of propriety.

In the world of the *fornaldarsögur,* the ordinary laws of nature can be suspended at will. Powerful sorcerers control the elements and transform themselves and others into any animal form they choose. The hero may be helped by a friendly dwarf or a sympathetic giantess, but his enemies include the living dead, man-eating ogres, and other terrifying monsters belonging to the shadow world of pagan myth or to the fantasies of Christian authors, in either case endowing the narrative with a sense of the horrific and the grotesque.

The stories are mostly in prose, but in a number of them verse and prose alternate, the verse ordinarily being spoken by one of the characters. Of partic-

ular interest are the "autobiographical" poems, delivered by a dying hero (as in *Örvar-Odds saga*) or by a warrior past his prime (as in *Hálfs saga ok Hálfsrekka* and *Gautreks saga*). Some of the poems (such as those in *Hervarar saga ok Heiðreks konungs*) are much older than the rest of the tale, whereas others were probably composed by the saga authors.

Although many of the characters in the *fornaldarsögur* appear to bear the names of real personages, the historical value of these tales taken as a whole is only slight. It would, however, be foolish to dismiss them all as mere figments of the imagination. As one medieval Icelander put it, "most sagas are made out of certain specific materials," and some of the stuff in the *fornaldarsögur,* orally transmitted over many generations, may ultimately be based on fact. The authors of the "adventure tales" can hardly have expected their readers to treat the literary creations as true descriptions of actual events, although they may have hoped that some people, at least, would be taken in. The epilogue to the fictitious *Hrólfs saga Gautrekssonar* opens with a positive statement: "People say this is a true story. Although it's never been committed to vellum, learned men have preserved it in their memories with many of King Hrólfr's exploits not recorded here." The final words, however, indicate the real purpose of the tale: "But whether it's true or not, let those enjoy the story who can, while those who can't had better look for some other amusement" (Pálsson and Edwards [1972], 148). In this connection a passage from the prologue to *Göngu-Hrólfs saga* may be of interest:

Since neither this tale nor anything else can be made to please everyone, nobody need believe any more of it than he wants to believe. All the same, the best and most profitable thing is to listen while a story is being told, to enjoy it and not to be too gloomy: for the fact is that as long as people are enjoying the entertainment, they won't be thinking any evil thoughts. Nor is it a good thing when listeners find fault with a story just because it happens to be uninformative or clumsily told. Nothing so unimportant is ever done perfectly. (Pálsson and Edwards [1980], 28)

In their present form, none of the *fornaldarsögur* can be older than the thirteenth century, many of them evidently belong to the fourteenth, and several were written at an even later date. The earliest documentary reference to tales of this kind is found in *Þorgils saga ok Hafliða* (in *Sturlunga saga*), describing a wedding feast at Reykhólar in western Iceland in 1119, at which a certain Hrólfr of Skálmarnes told a story of his own composition about Hrómundr Gripsson, King Ólafr, Hröngviðr the Viking, and the breaking of Þráinn's grave mound. The author of this source adds that King Sverrir of Norway (d. 1202) found such fabulous stories particularly entertaining. The twelfth-century version of *Hrómundar saga Gripssonar* is not extant in its original form, but a fourteenth-century metrical version *(Griplur)* survives; the *Hrómundar saga Gripssonar* in Rafn's collection is a seventeenth-century prose rendering of that metrical version. Many *fornaldarsögur*, in oral or written form, were known to the Danish writer Saxo Grammaticus, who retold them in his *Gesta Danorum*, in which he pays tribute to the "story treasures" of the Icelanders. Around the middle of the twelfth century, not long before Saxo started collecting materials for his *Gesta*, Earl Rögnvaldr Kali of Orkney (d. 1158) and the Icelandic poet Hallr Þórarinsson jointly composed the poem *Háttalykill*, in which they give brief summaries of the deeds and destinies of legendary kings and heroes.

BIBLIOGRAPHY

Inger M. Boberg, *Motif-Index of Early Icelandic Literature* (1966); Paul Herrmann, trans., *Daenische Heldensagen, nach Saxo Grammaticus* (1925); Anne Holtsmark, "Heroic Poetry and Legendary Sagas," in *Bibliography of Old Norse-Icelandic Studies 1965* (1966); Finnur Jónsson, *Den oldnorske og oldislandske litteraturs historie*, 2nd ed., II and III (1923–1924); Guðni Jónsson, ed., *Fornaldarsögur Norðurlanda*, 4 vols. (1950); Knut Liestøl, *Norske trollvisor og norrøne sogor* (1915); Axel Olrik, *Kilderne til Sakses oldhistorie* (1892–1894), and *The Heroic Legends of Denmark*, Lee M. Hollander, trans. (1919); Hermann Pálsson and Paul Edwards, *Legendary Fiction in Medieval Iceland* (1970); idem, trans., *Gautrek's Saga and Other Medieval Tales* (1968), *Arrow-Odd: A Medieval Novel* (1970), *Hrolf Gautreksson* (1972), and *Göngu-Hrolf's Saga* (1980); Carl C. Rafn, ed., *Fornaldar sǫgur Norðrlanda*, 3 vols. (1829–1830); Helga Reuschel, *Untersuchungen über Stoff und Stil der Fornaldarsaga* (1933); Margaret Schlauch, *Romance in Iceland* (1934); Hermann Schneider, *Germanische Heldensage*, 2 vols. (1928–1934); Einar Ó. Sveinsson, *Verzeichnis isländischer Märchen-Varianten* (1929), *Dating the Icelandic Sagas*, E. O. G. Turville-Petre, trans. (1959), and "Celtic Elements in Icelandic Tradition," in *Béaloideas*, 15 (1959); M. C. van den Toorn, "Über die Ethik in den Fornaldarsagas," in *Acta philologica scandinavica*, 26 (1963); E. O. G. Turville-Petre, *The Heroic Age of Scandinavia* (1951), and *Myth and Religion of the North* (1964). For fuller bibliographical details see *Islandica*, V and XXVI; and *Bibliography of Old Norse-Icelandic Studies* (1963–).

HERMANN PÁLSSON

[See also **Áns Saga Bogsveigis; Ásmundar Saga Kappabana; Beowulf; Bósa Saga ok Herrauðs; Egils Saga Einhenda ok Ásmundar Berserkjabana; Gautreks Saga; Gísla Saga Súrssonar; Göngu-Hrólfs Saga; Gríms Saga Loðinkinna; Hálfdanar Saga Brönufóstra; Hálfdanar Saga Eysteinssonar; Hálfs Saga ok Hálfsrekka; Helga Þáttr Þórissonar; Hervarar Saga ok Heiðreks Konungs; Hildebrandslied; Hjálmþérs Saga ok Ölvis; Hrómundar Saga Gripssonar; Illuga Saga Gríðarfóstra; Ketils Saga Hængs; Laxdœla Saga; Nibelungenlied; Njáls Saga; Örvar-Odds Saga; Ragnars Saga Loðbrókar; Skjöldunga Saga; Sörla Saga Sterka; Þáttr af Ragnars Sonum; Þorsteins Saga Víkingssonar; Vápnfirðinga Saga; Völsunga Saga.**]

FORTESCUE, SIR JOHN (1385/1395–after May 1479), achieved distinction as a lawyer and judge, attained prominence as a political figure under both Lancastrian and Yorkist kings, and won enduring fame as a writer on the English constitution. He was admitted to Lincoln's Inn, probably in 1413 or 1414, and in 1424/1425 he was elected its "gubernator." His appointment in 1430 as serjeant-at-law (a status not attainable until after sixteen years of "general study of the law") necessitated severence of all formal relations with Lincoln's Inn—a small price to pay for identification with the select body of men who had a monopoly of practice before the Court of Common Pleas. For some twenty-five years after 1435 Fortescue received at least seventy commissions of oyer and terminer, assize, jail delivery, and special inquisitions, some of which were more administrative than legal. From 1438 he was appointed a justice of the peace thirty-eight times in some fifteen counties or boroughs. Before Easter term 1441 he received the higher title of king's serjeant, and within the year was designated chief justice of the court of King's Bench. He was knighted before February 1443.

The nineteen years of Fortescue's judicial career are richly reflected in the Year Books (21 Henry VI– 38 Henry VI). His most important constitutional issue was the ruling (1454) in Thorpe's Case that the court had no right to intervene in the alleged breach of parliamentary privilege involved in the arrest of Speaker Thorpe for felonies committed outside Parliament. The decision confirmed the constitutional principle that parliamentary privilege does not extend to immunity from prosecution for felonious activity.

While a law apprentice at Lincoln's Inn, Fortescue became involved in political affairs. Beginning in 1421 he was a member of Parliament for Tavistock and, later, for Totnes and Plymouth. Between 1444 and 1456 he served Parliament as a trier of petitions. In 1455, as political tensions between Lancastrians and Yorkists deteriorated into open warfare, Fortescue and his family cast their lot with the house of Lancaster. In November 1459, following the Lancastrian victory at Ludlow, Fortescue assisted the Coventry Parliament in drafting the attainder of the Yorkists.

In October 1460 the duke of York claimed the throne as Edward IV, and the Lancastrians abandoned London. Fortescue followed Henry VI to the north and was present at the Battle of Towton in March 1461 and at the skirmishes at Ryton and Brauncepeth in June 1461. He joined the royal family at Edinburgh, where he was named lord chancellor and appointed a member of the king's council. Here he wrote several tracts describing kingship as a form of private property infused with a public interest. At this time he probably also composed the *De natura legis naturae*.

In December 1461 the Yorkists took their revenge on Fortescue by a parliamentary act of attainder: thus began ten years of exile. In early 1462 Henry sent Fortescue on a mission to Louis XI of France, and in June Henry's queen Margaret and Louis signed a treaty. In April 1463 Margaret and Prince Edward, accompanied by Fortescue, were relocated in the castle of Koeur, near St. Mihiel in Bar, where Fortescue was kept busy with restoration plots and diplomatic negotiations with Louis. In October 1470 Henry VI was briefly restored to his throne, and Fortescue drew up a program to strengthen the machinery of government. But in May 1471 the Lancastrians were routed at the Battle of Tewkesbury, and Fortescue was taken prisoner.

With the Yorkist victory, his imprisonment, and the death of both his Lancastrian king and the Lancastrian heir to the throne, Fortescue's world collapsed and his view of the legitimate succession underwent a profound change. For him the king was the foundation, the focus, the emblem, and the bond of national unity. Lancastrianism as a lost cause was mere sentimentalism, whereas law and order were a present reality: for the time being, this was the touchstone of legitimacy.

For the Yorkist dynasty, Fortescue was the most eminent of the Lancastrians, and his support and adherence were, in a sense, a legitimization of their claim to the throne. Fortescue's legal status was remedied by the general pardon of October for all offenses committed before 9 July 1471. Shortly thereafter he was appointed a member of Edward IV's council and wrote the tract *Declaracion ... upon Certayn Wrytinges ...*, in which he successfully refuted his earlier succession tracts on behalf of the Lancastrians. In 1474 he was clearly involved in the work of the king's council, and his attainder was reversed no later than February 1475.

Fortescue's *De natura legis naturae* sketches out a rudimentary theory of jurisprudence applicable to England. Virtually unacquainted with the history of law and apparently owing nothing to the influence of Glanville and Bracton, Fortescue combined Roman law and canon law principles—a fusion that sometimes creates problems. For example, it is not clear whether the law of nature is human or divine law, but it is higher than any human law whether custom or statute. Consequently, statute law cannot enact any rule contrary to natural law; statute is, in fact, merely declaratory of law that is already expressed as customary or natural law.

The optimistic tone of *De laudibus* suggests that it was written shortly after the restoration of Henry VI. It was fashioned as a dialogue between Fortescue and Edward, prince of Wales, whose inheritance then seemed more assured than at any time previously. The substance of the work is remarkable, ranging among comparative jurisprudence, political theory, and comparative constitutional law. Though composed in Latin, it was the first work on English law written for the layman.

Fortescue's first principle is the necessity of fundamental law, originating with divine law. The supremacy of law is essential, no matter how its subsidiary sources are defined. Unlike his revered authority, Aristotle, Fortescue could not entertain the viability of a system without law, a *dominium despoticum*. The contemporary alternatives were the *dominium regale*, exemplified by France, and in England the *dominium politicum et regale*, which Fortescue regarded as the superior form of monarchy, one in which the power of the crown was limited by the constitutional necessity of parliamentary assent to taxation and legislation.

After his return from exile, Fortescue wrote *The Governance of England*, his most mature and developed work and the first book written in English on the English constitution. Although the work rested on the basic ideals outlined earlier, its essential emphasis was more programmatic than theoretical. It may have been conceived as a Lancastrian memorandum, but the tone of urgency suggests a Yorkist application. Fortescue had a keen appreciation of the weakness of Lancastrian rule: the unfortunate consequences of unsound royal finances and dependence on the aristocracy. He proposed to reduce the overgrown power of the feudal nobility, and he advised the king to recover those sources of revenue that had been granted away. Also, the crown was to resume control of appointment to office, and no one man should hold too many offices. Since the accumulation of estates accompanied accumulation of offices, restraint in that area did much to change the role of the aristocracy in government. What Fortescue wanted was an appointive officialdom, ruling effectively on behalf of the crown and not in its own class interest.

BIBLIOGRAPHY

Thomas Fortescue, *The Works of Sir John Fortescue,* Lord Clermont, ed., 2 vols. (1869), must not be employed where supplanted by later works, of which two are admirable: C. Plummer, ed., *The Governance of England* (1885), which contains a fine biographical survey, historical background, and bibliographical information; and Stanley B. Chrimes, ed., *De laudibus legum Angliae* (1942), with an excellent biographical and historical account by Chrimes and an outstanding general introduction to Fortescue's place in the history of English law by Harold D. Hazeltine.

Recent historical scholarship has concentrated on Fortescue's work in political theory. The new emphasis began with Charles H. McIlwain, *The Growth of Political Thought in the West* (1932), and has continued (chronologically) with Ernest F. Jacob, "Sir John Fortescue and the Law of Nature," in *Bulletin of the John Rylands Library,* **18** (1934); Stanley B. Chrimes, "Sir John Fortescue and His Theory of Dominion," in *Transactions of the Royal Historical Society,* 4th ser., **17** (1934); Felix Gilbert, "Sir John Fortescue's 'Dominium Regale et Politicum,'" in *Medievalia et humanistica,* **2** (1944); Max A. Shepard, "The Political and Constitutional Theory of Sir John Fortescue," in Carl Wittke, ed., *Essays in History and Political Theory in Honor of Charles Howard McIlwain* (1936, repr. 1967); and Bertie Wilkinson, *Constitutional History of England in the Fifteenth Century (1399–1485)* (1964), with documents.

DAVID SANDLER BERKOWITZ

[See also **Henry VI of England; Wars of the Roses.**]

FORTUNE, an unpredictable and uncontrollable influence on human affairs, was often personified by medieval Europeans as a minor female deity. Dame Fortune was regarded as either a real goddess or a merely allegorical figure comparable to Prudence and Fortitude, the traditional allies of a man or woman who resists Fortune's power. Fortune derived from the Greek concept of *tyche,* meaning "chance," "luck," or "what happens." The Romans paid homage to an assortment of Fortunes, including a Fortune of War *(fortuna belli)* and a Fortune of Women *(fortuna muliebris),* each with special associations, spheres of influence, and customs of worship.

One might think that the rise of Christianity, with its almighty monotheism and its sweeping away of pagan deities, would have ended the career of the minor goddess Fortuna. Indeed, St. Augustine ruled out any qualification of God's omnipotence and total foreknowledge of events. But quite illogically, perhaps because Scripture and theology could not explain all the vicissitudes of human life to ordinary people, Fortune crept back into at least partial acceptance. It is not often noted that Fortune's apparent circumvention of the supposedly fixed laws of causality parallels some of the miracles of Christian saints, who are permitted on special occasions to heal without drugs, stay mill wheels, or even intervene in such trivial matters as the loss or theft of household objects.

It was Boethius, a Christian steeped in classical learning, who ushered Fortune the goddess into the much allegorized intellectual world of the Middle Ages. *The Consolation of Philosophy* established a powerful and haunting conception of Fortune: volatile, unpredictable, and uncontrollable by human agency but subordinate to a higher power, whether the Christian God, the classical Jove, or immutable Fate. She is, in Chaucer's inspired phrase, "executrice of wierdes" (the word "wierdes" is derived from Old English *wyrd* and means "fate"; the modern denotation of "weird" developed later). In a long and eloquent lecture to the imprisoned and condemned Boethius, the lady Philosophy brings forth a chain of reasons for resisting the power of Fortune. Paradoxically, her central argument—that wealth, fame, and high degree are not only transient but also not really worth having—reminds the reader of how great a loss Fortune is able to inflict. In succeeding centuries, the *Consolation* was required reading for students and scholars throughout western Europe, in the original, in translations (notably that of Chaucer into Middle English and that of Jean de Meun into Old French), and in countless imitations, digests, and commentaries.

In *Le roman de la rose* (the part written by Jean de Meun) and the *Remede de fortune* by Guillaume de Machaut, Fortune frustrates the hopes of a lover who is helped by a personified Philosophy, called Reason in the *Roman* and Esperance in the *Remede*. Guillaume de Guilleville, Jean Froissart, Eustache Deschamps, Christine de Pizan, and Charles d'Orléans were among a host of other Old French authors who found a place for Fortune in prose and, especially, in poetry.

In the seventh canto of Dante's *Inferno*, Vergil briefly explains the nature of Fortune to the poet. Dante must, of course, fit her into his Christian scheme of the universe: he makes her God's "general minister and guide," who controls the empty wealth and splendor of the world of men. She is inscrutable, and both swift and powerful within her licensed limits. Though often slandered, she dwells above in bliss, untroubled.

Boccaccio was a more active transmitter of the lore of Fortune than Dante. His *Teseida* is the principal source of Chaucer's Knight's Tale, as his *Filostrato* is of Chaucer's *Troilus*. Boccaccio's uninspired *De casibus virorum illustrium* was translated into French by Laurent de Premierfait as *Des cas des nobles hommes et femmes* (*ca.* 1409), which in turn was used by John Lydgate to compose his *Fall of Princes*. The many explicit references to Fortune in the above works have no logic or consistency: the same "tragedy" is caused by Fortune and sin in one passage, by Fortune alone in another, and by impiety toward the heathen deities or the Christian God in yet another. The process of rising to power and fame and wealth is rarely dealt with: the emphasis is on the downward turn of Fortune's wheel.

Boccaccio was more directly the source for most of the "tragedies" related by Chaucer's Monk's Tale, which are prefaced by the assertion that, when Fortune chooses to desert a person of high degree, there is no stopping her. The knight is perhaps more bluntly disrespectful of Fortune's power than anyone else in medieval literature. He attempts no philosophical refutation of the monk's pessimism but calls for stories of achievement and lasting prosperity. In his attitude toward Fortune the knight stands for the countless unlearned medieval men of action who did not let Fortune's unreliability sap their military courage.

It is surprising that personified Fortune does not appear more often in medieval Latin lyric poetry. She does make one fine appearance in *Carmina burana*, but she found a much more popular form of expression in the humble proverb. Perhaps the most often repeated was *Audaces Fortuna iuvat* (Fortune helps the daring), a favorite motto in heraldry, occurring at least once with the cautious addition *non in omnibus horis* (not always). Others include *Fortuna rerum humanarum domina* (Fortune rules human affairs), *Fortunae status est non stare, sed usque moveri* (Fortune does not stand still, but continually moves), and *Fortuna in homine plus quam consilium valet* (Among men, Fortune is worth more than a plan). There were, of course, vernacular versions of these and other proverbs.

The idea of Fortune was conveyed from Boethius to late-medieval authors by the pedantic and verbose, but much studied, *Anticlaudianus* (1182–1183), a "theological epic" of Alan of Lille. The eighth book opens with a detailed description of the House of Fortune, which became a subject for many writers and illustrators. It sits on a cliff in the midst of the ocean, alternately exposed and submerged by the surging waves. Zephyrus brings flowers to it; Boreas blasts them. There are contrasting trees (green and dry, blooming and bare), a boding owl rather than a nightingale and two streams of water: a sweet one flowing into a bitter flood. The house itself is half palace, half thatched hovel, tottering and open to the elements, an image borrowed by Jean de Meun for *Le roman de la rose*.

The Roman cults depicted Fortune with a cornucopia in her left hand while her right hand rested on an unshipped tiller and rudder, a combined reference to Fortune as the provider and to the risky calling of the mariner. The ubiquitous and ominous wheel of Fortune was a legacy to the Middle Ages from the second book of Boethius' *Consolation*. It took on many styles, from the delicately drawn miniatures of fine manuscripts to the huge rose windows of the cathedrals at Amiens and Basel. Fortune herself is often drawn larger than the human figures, in accordance with medieval convention, to underscore her greater importance. The wheel is frequently absurd in its mechanics: Fortune may propel it with a graceful touch of a spoke or with an awkward-looking crank; each revolution may be swift or require a full lifetime. The wheel characteristically bears on its rim four shelves or "stages" with four human figures. The figure rising on the left is usually labeled *regnabo* (I shall reign), the one at the top is marked *regno*

(I reign) and is often crowned, that descending on the right is *regnavi* (I have reigned), and the writing figure at the lowest point is *sum sine regno* (I have no kingdom). The victim is sometimes depicted as thrown from the wheel by gravity and centrifugal force, and sometimes as crushed under a wheel fit for a heavy cart.

Medieval representations of Fortune emphasize her duality and instability. She often displays two faces, either side-by-side, or back-to-back like Janus; with one black face and one white, or one smiling and one lowering. Sometimes one eye is beaming and one weeping. She may appear blindfolded, like Justice, but without the scale: she is, so to speak, impartial in injustice. Sometimes her head is bald behind but has a long forelock for seizing, like Opportunity. Her clothing may be of changeable colors or sharply divided into dark and bright or rich and beggarly. Occasionally her vivid clothing and bold bearing suggest the prostitute.

Most of the numerous references to Fortune and her wheel are perfunctory and of no descriptive value, but the image is developed at some length by James I of Scotland in *The Kingis Quair,* a poem that may be taken as the concluding appearance of the goddess in British literature before the Renaissance. James, a prisoner like Boethius, sees in a vision the goddess with her wheel before her on the ground. Below this wheel is a pit as deep as hell, into which many of the folk "swarming" on its rim are cast. As he is about to mount the wheel, the dreaming king awakens.

In Italy the Renaissance treatment of Fortune is matured in chapter 25 of Machiavelli's *The Prince.* It is characteristically brief, sharp, and cynical. To accept Fortune as completely in control of human affairs would deny the purpose of the whole work, which is to teach the art of gaining such control. Machiavelli's formula for the obligatory compromise is that Fortune rules one half of men's activities, leaving to their volition the other half "or perhaps a little less." In the brilliant conclusion of the chapter the author reminds the reader that Fortune is a woman, that she therefore welcomes a strong and even violent hand, and that she favors the more aggressive and audacious young men over their more timid elders.

BIBLIOGRAPHY

A. Doren, "Fortuna im Mittelalter und in der Renaissance," in *Bibliothek Warburg: Vorträge 1922–1923,* pt. 1 (1924); Raimond van Marle, *Iconographie de l'art profane du moyen âge et à la renaissance,* 2 vols. (1931–1932), II, 181–195; Howard Rollin Patch, *The Tradition of the Goddess Fortuna in Medieval Philosophy and Literature* (1922), 131–235, *Fortuna in Old French Literature* (1923), and *The Goddess Fortuna in Mediaeval Literature* (1927, repr. 1967); F. P. Pickering, *Literature and Art in the Middle Ages* (1970), 168–222.

RICHARD LEIGHTON GREENE

[See also **Fortune, Old Spanish.**]

FORTUNE, OLD SPANISH. Fortune in medieval Spanish literature is an expression of a need to portray an orderly universe in which even random events follow a logical course of cause and effect. Called Ventura in early texts, her name shifted to Fortuna. In the fifteenth century the meaning of Ventura had contracted to "luck in love," particularly among the Cancionero poets. In the novel *Caballero Zifar (ca.* 1300), a grieving person rages against Ventura for her variability, perversity, and cruelty, and puns on the new name: "Mas con derecho te dizen Fortuna porque nunca eres una" (And rightly they call you Fortune, because you are never constant—Nelson, 289).

Fortune's other names—Dicha or Suerte (luck), Hado (fate), Providencia (divine providence), Sino (astrological destiny)—were ancillary and seldom interchangeable. In *El Cid,* Ventura is subject to God's will, though the usual epic epithet for the hero refers to his birth at a fortunate hour. Ventura is powerless against Hado in strophe 821 of Juan Ruiz's *Libro de buen amor* (1330–1343). In Juan de Mena's *Laberinto de fortuna* (1444), Providence is the poet's guide through Fortune's realm.

Consistent with the alternating cycles of pessimism and optimism characteristic of Hispanic medieval letters, humankind was either helpless in Fortune's grasp or was able to dominate her through effort. Translating from an Arabic text, Petrus Alfonsi (born Moisés Sefardí, 1062) wrote in the *Disciplina clericalis:* "Good fortune will come to you even if you are weak; . . . even though you be strong you will not avoid bad fortune." While the anonymous author of the *Libro de los doze sabios (ca.* 1237) wrote that good fortune belongs to the strong and the daring, an opinion also found in the *Libro de Alexandre (ca.* 1255–1230), Aristotle tells the prince: "Dizen que buen esfuerço vence mala ventura" (They say that good efforts overcome bad luck, 71*a*). In *Fernán González* (1240) Christ is asked to move Fortune's wheel to help free Castile from the Moors (179). Fortunes rise and fall, but human toil and God's help can overcome the Fates in the *Libro de buen amor* (692). In *Diálogo de Bias contra Fortuna* by Iñigo López de Mendoza, Marqués de Santillana, Bias (a Greek sage) wins a debate with Fortuna by declaring finally that in heaven he will escape her ceaseless mischief.

The individual's responsibility for his or her fortune is dramatized in Pero López de Ayala's translation (completed 1422) of Boccaccio's *De casibus virorum illustrium*. Fortuna, vanquished by Poverty, is tied to a post; only those who choose to free her are subject to her power. Alfonso Martínez de Toledo's *Arçipreste de Talavera* (1438) and Fray Martín de Córdoba's *Compendio de la fortuna* (1454) are other Castilian versions. Don Álvaro de Luna, constable of Spain, rose from humble beginnings and died on the public gallows in 1453: by antonomasia, he became the figure of Fortune's victim. Juan de Mena praised him for his ability to tame Fortuna (*El laberinto de fortuna*, 235); but Santillana rejoiced in his fall: "De tu resplandor, o Luna, / Te ha priuado la Fortuna" (Your radiance, O Luna, Fortuna has taken away from you—*Coplas*). Jorge Manrique, writing of his father's death, disparaged Fortune's gifts, but elsewhere he challenged her by asserting his superior strength. On balance, from the twelfth to the fifteenth century, the Christian conviction that Fortune is subject to divine providence and to the exercise of free will prevailed over its pessimistic converse.

BIBLIOGRAPHY

Michèle S. De Cruz-Sáenz, "The Marqués de Santillana's *Coplas* on Don Álvaro de Luna and the *Doctrinal de privados*," in *Hispanic Review*, **49** (1981); Alan D. Deyermond, *A Literary History of Spain: The Middle Ages* (1971), 215–230; Harriet Goldberg, "Fifteenth-century Castilian Versions of Boccaccio's Fortune–Poverty Contest," in *Hispania*, **61** (1978); Otis Howard Green, *Spain and the Western Tradition*, 4 vols. (1964), 2.212–337; Charles L. Nelson, *The Book of the Knight Zifar: A Translation of "El Libro del Cavallero Zifar"* (1983).

HARRIET GOLDBERG

[See also **Fortune; Spanish Literature.**]

FÓSTBRŒÐRA SAGA (Saga of the foster brothers or sworn brothers) tells the story of Þorgeirr Hávarsson and Þormóðr Bersason, the former a re-doubtable warrior and the latter an important skald attached to King Olaf Haraldsson (ruled 1015–1030). As young men they swear a pact committing the one who lives longer to avenge the other. The first part of the saga is devoted largely to Þorgeirr's career, which consists of a series of slayings recorded by his sworn brother in a memorial poem called "Þorgeirsdrápa" (fifteen stanzas of this poem are set down in the saga). He begins his exploits by avenging his father at the age of fifteen, then embarks on a series of seven other, less well-justified slayings. After the fourth such slaying he provokes Þormóðr with an invidious comparison of strength, and the two part ways. After the fifth slaying the narrative turns to Þormóðr long enough to relate two of his romantic entanglements. Before his eighth and last encounter Þorgeirr visits with King Olaf, who foresees his death. Þorgeirr's last killing is finally avenged, and he falls after a memorable stand.

The second part of the saga recounts Þormóðr's vengeance for his sworn brother. He goes to King Olaf's court in Norway, then sails for Greenland to seek out one of Þorgeirr's killers. In a complicated series of maneuvers he succeeds in executing the vengeance and eluding his enemies. He then returns to Norway, where he becomes Olaf's faithful skald and falls by his side in the great battle of Stiklarstaðir (Stiklestad, 1030).

Fóstbrœðra saga survives in six manuscripts with textual importance, sometimes abbreviated, sometimes interpolated, and sometimes combined with the *Saga of Saint Olaf (Óláfs saga helga)*. This transmission creates unusual problems. The saga was long thought to be the earliest of all the family sagas (from around 1200) because a manuscript in relatively classical style (*Hauksbók*) was judged to be closest to the archetype. But it has been argued (and disputed) that the passages from other manuscripts in learned or florid style are original. On the basis of this and other evidence, the Icelandic scholar Jónas Kristjánsson concluded that the saga should be dated in the last decades of the thirteenth century.

Fóstbrœðra saga is not among the more elegant family sagas. The succession of events is constructed less dramatically than in some sagas, there is narrative matter not immediately pertinent to the story, and Þorgeirr's adventures are described along stereotypical lines with a good deal of repetition in motif and wording. Both protagonists are potentially interesting, but their characters and psychologies are not developed to any great extent and there are no arresting minor characters. The most telling feature is found in a few vivid episodes in which the action is described with the laconic and mannered understatement characteristic of saga style. The author's primary source was presumably Þormóðr's verse, of which thirty-five stanzas are cited.

BIBLIOGRAPHY

Sources. Björn K. Þórólfsson and Guðni Jónsson, eds., *Vestfirðinga sögur* (1943), 121–276; a translation is *The Sagas of Kormák and The Sworn Brothers,* Lee M. Hollander, trans. (1949), 83–189.

Studies. Jónas Kristjánsson, *Um Fostbræðrasögu* (1972), with English summary, 311–326; Jacoba M. C. Kroesen, *Over de Compositie der Fóstbrœðra saga* (1962); Klaus von See, "Die Überlieferung der Fóstbrœðra saga," in *Skandinavistik,* **6** (1976).

THEODORE M. ANDERSSON

[See also **Family Sagas, Icelandic.**]

FOUKES LE FITZWARIN (FITZ WARYN), a fourteenth-century Anglo-Norman prose romance, probably derived from an earlier verse account, now lost, of the deeds of the Fitzwarin family, who played an important role in Anglo-Welsh border history. The history of the family is traced from the Conquest to the death of the main hero, Fouke III, around 1256, but much of the text deals with the rebellion of Fouke against King John—whose enmity he had incurred, according to the romance, while still a child—and with his subsequent outlawry.

BIBLIOGRAPHY

E. J. Hathaway, P. T. Ricketts, C. A. Robson, and A. D. Wilshire, eds., *Foukes le Fitz Waryn* (1975).

BRIAN MERRILEES

[See also **Anglo-Norman Literature.**]

FOUNTAIN OF LIFE, an image normally found as a manuscript illumination prefacing the Eusebian canon tables, showing a fountain enclosed in a hexagonal precinct beneath a conical dome supported by eight columns. The fountain represents a baptismal font, and is often flanked by animals (such as the hart) specifically associated with baptism. The image probably refers to the font in the Lateran Baptistery in Rome consecrated by Pope Sixtus III (432–440),

where epigrams equate baptismal rebirth with Christ as the fountain of life. The four rivers of Paradise associated with the fountain of life in the Book of Revelation symbolize the four evangelists, hence the image was appropriate as a frontispiece to the canon tables both for its allusion to the Gospels' authors and for its reference to Christ as redeemer. Though apparently invented in the fifth century, the best examples date from the Carolingian period, where the fountain of life appears in two manuscripts affiliated with Charlemagne: the Godescalc Lectionary made to commemorate the baptism of the emperor's son in Rome at the Lateran in 781, and the Soissons Gospels. The fountain of life was also associated with the Holy Sepulcher, since Christ's death and resurrection were interpreted as the source of salvation. In images with this connotation, well represented by the Ejmiacin Gospels of 989, the fountain is often flanked by cyprus trees and topped by vegetation; curtains or grillwork normally enclose the inner precinct. In some examples, particularly Ethiopian pictures, elements of both visual interpretations coexist.

BIBLIOGRAPHY

Paul A. Underwood, "The Fountain of Life in Manuscripts of the Gospels," in *Dumbarton Oaks Papers,* 5 (1950).

LESLIE BRUBAKER

[See also **Canon Table; Manuscript Illumination.**]

FOUQUET, JEAN (*fl. ca.* 1445–1481), illuminator and painter to Charles VII and Louis XI in Tours. He painted a now-lost portrait of Eugenius IV at Rome about 1445 and a documented copy of Josephus' *Antiquities of the Jews* (Paris, Bibliothèque Nationale). Attributed works include a Boccaccio manuscript (Munich, Staatsbibliothek); the book of hours of Étienne Chevalier (Chantilly, Musée Condé); portraits of Charles VII and Guillaume Junéval des Ursins (Paris, Louvre); and Chevalier's Madonna diptych divided between Berlin (Dahlem Staatliche Museen Preussischer Kulturbesitz) and Antwerp (Koninklijk Museum voor Schone Kunsten). His style combines Italian monumentality and architectural details with a French austerity.

BIBLIOGRAPHY

Claude Schaefer, *Recherches sur l'iconologie et la stylistique de l'art de Jean Fouquet* (1972); Charles Sterling and Claude Schaefer, eds., *The Hours of Étienne Chevalier* (1971), with bibliography—reviewed by Eberhard König in *Zeitschrift für Kunstgeschichte*, 37 (1974), 164–180.

ANNE HAGOPIAN VAN BUREN

[See also **Gothic Art: Painting and Manuscript Illumination**.]

FOWL, DOMESTIC. The fowls, particularly the chicken, were not among the earliest domestic species, and the time and place of their domestication are still rather vague, but by the end of the Middle Ages they were as common as domestic mammals. The secret of the quick advance of fowls is that they utilize fodder much more efficiently than mammals do, thus producing meat much more cheaply. The special position of chickens is strengthened by the fact that a good hen lays its body weight in eggs about six times every year.

The earliest domestication of the chicken took place somewhere in the Indus Valley in the third millennium B.C. The domestic form reached southwest Asia and Egypt in the second half of the second millenium B.C. First it was probably used for fighting and was venerated as the symbol of the rising sun. The Persians and Scythians played an important role in its early distribution, and through them the chicken reached Europe. In the Mediterranean basin the chicken occurred by the second half of the eighth century B.C., and it reached central Europe by 600 B.C. Interestingly, its representations appeared everywhere earlier than its bones. The Celts were most responsible for the spread of the chicken, but the Greeks and Romans were the first to keep it in large numbers and to start its conscious breeding.

In Europe the use of the hen changed: it lost its religious importance and became a simple food animal. The rooster kept its role as a fighter and as a guardian of good against evil and for a time was a symbol of fertility or of sexual vigor. Bones or whole skeletons of chicken are often found in early medieval graves. Eggs, sometimes painted, were not uncommon in the graves; in all probability they were fertility symbols. One such egg, found in an Avar grave, has been reconstructed as weighing 38 to 40 grams, about forty percent smaller than the average modern egg.

The size of chickens underwent striking changes

between the time of domestication and the end of the Middle Ages. The wild form was dwarf. Domestication resulted in a size increase, but even so the chicken remained small, weighing between 1 and 1.5 kilograms up to the period of the Roman Empire. In the latter period, as a result of conscious breeding, the chicken reached the size of a modern Leghorn. After the fall of the Roman Empire, chickens reverted to the size of the pre-Roman era. Their size began to increase only in the fourteenth and fifteenth centuries, with the reappearance of conscious breeding.

The main value of the chicken in the Middle Ages consisted of its production of eggs (most of the hens were killed as adults). According to the anonymous thirteenth-century author of *Hosebanderie*, each hen ought to produce 115 eggs and 7 chickens in a year—quite a high amount, considering the primitive state of animal husbandry at that time. Most of the roosters were made into capons, according to both osteological finds and literary sources.

The time and place of the earliest domestication of the goose are not known, for the wild form lives throughout Europe and much of Asia, and morphological differences between the wild form and early domestic geese are almost nonexistent. The domestic white geese that saved Rome in 390 B.C. were already an ancient breed. In medieval times geese lived in flocks of up to 1,000. According to the *Hosebanderie*, there should be one gander to five geese, and each goose should have five goslings every year. In Hungary in the eleventh and twelfth centuries the serfs had to give tithes of geese to the church and there is an order from the thirteenth century prescribing that the geese delivered to the squires should be white.

The time and place of the first domestication of the duck are similarly obscure. In all probability there were domestic ducks in classical Greece, and they were certainly kept in the Roman Empire, though they were much rarer than geese. Ducks were rare in the Middle Ages too, but their number was increased by the local domestication of the wild European form.

The pigeon was kept domestically in the Roman Empire, and in the Middle Ages it was known all over Europe, mainly bred by the lords of the manors for its meat and manure. The Romans had discovered that it can be used for transmission of messages, and carrier pigeons were widely known in the Middle Ages.

The guinea fowl came to Greece from Africa by the fifth century B.C. Both representations and archaeological finds show that it spread from there to Italy and the Roman colonies in central and western Europe. Later the bird ceased to be kept in Europe until Portuguese explorers rediscovered it on the west coast of Africa and reintroduced it to Europe in the late sixteenth century.

The peacock, of Indian origin, may have been domesticated in the second millennium B.C. It reached Palestine around 1000 B.C. and appeared in Greece, where at first it was regarded as sacred, in the sixth century B.C. In ancient Rome it played an important role; its meat was regarded a delicacy and it was often represented in art. The Romans introduced it to their European colonies. In the Middle Ages the peacock was mainly kept in manors and palaces for its meat and for its "eyed" feathers, which were held in high esteem, particularly by knights.

The turkey is of American origin, which has led to the assumption that it reached Europe in post-Columbian times. However, there is recent evidence of its possible appearance on the European mainland in the tenth through twelfth centuries with the Vikings. Nevertheless, the rapid spread of the bird in Europe occurred in the sixteenth century. In the second half of that century it became so numerous that in Arnstadt, Germany, as many as 150 turkeys were eaten at a wedding. The turkey first appeared on the English Christmas menu in 1585.

BIBLIOGRAPHY

Sándor Bökönyi and D. Jánossy, "Adatok a pulyka Kolumbusz előtti európai előfordulásához" (Data about the occurrence of the turkey in Europe before the time of Columbus), in *Aquila,* 65 (1958); B. Brentjes, "Die Haustierwerdung im Orient," in *Die neue Brehm-Bücherei,* 344 (1965); O.-F. Gandert, "Zur Abstammungs- und Kulturgeschichte des Hausgeflügels, insbesondere des Haushuhnes," in *Beiträge zur Frühgeschichte der Landwirtschaft,* 1 (1953); H. Linder, *Zur Frühgeschichte des Haushuhns im Vorderen Orient* (1979); J. Matolcsi, "Avarkori háziállatok maradványai Gyenesdiáson—Überreste von Haustieren der Awaren in Gyenesdiás," in *Magyar Mezőgazdasági Muzeum Közleményei* (1967–1968); Michael L. Ryder, "Livestock," in Joan Thirsk, ed., *The Agrarian History of England and Wales,* I, *Prehistory* (1981); Friedrich E. Zeuner, *A History of Domesticated Animals* (1963).

SÁNDOR BÖKÖNYI

[See also **Animals, Food.**]

FOWLING comprises both killing and capturing wild birds. With the exception of the northern islands of the Atlantic fowling did not play an important role in the Middle Ages.

The methods of fowling were quite varied. They started with simple seizure, clubbing, use of throwing-sticks, and shooting with bow and arrow, followed by the use of nets, snares, traps, and birdlimes, and ended with the use of decoys and hunting birds such as falcons.

The list of bird species killed and/or captured is rather long. The occurrence or absence of the different species—and thus whether they were hunted or not in a certain region—depends on environmental factors and the aim or aims of hunting.

The environment affects the list of the hunted birds: some species live in a particular region throughout the year and others migrate. In the case of the latter, the season of the kill can be determined. For example, the white-fronted goose lives in northern Europe between April and September, migrates through central Europe between October and March, and winters there or in southeast Europe; its Greenland race winters mainly in Ireland and western Scotland. The eider, velvet scoter, and other northern species are rare winter visitors in central Europe.

There were several aims of fowling. The first would be to complement the diet with wild birds' meat. Periodically all edible species were hunted, even those that would not be eaten now because of their smelly meat. Partridge, pheasant, hazel hen, capercaillie, black grouse, mallard, and white-fronted goose were common. Songbirds—sparrows, yellowhammers, white wagtails, starlings, thrushes, finches—were traditionally hunted in southern Europe. Many kinds of waterfowl were hunted as well: goldeneye, merganser, goosander, eider, velvet scoter, garganey, shelduck, and crane. Among the waterbirds the coot has a special position: its meat (it eats only fish) could be eaten even on fast days. Finally, the great bustard was hunted on the plains of Hungary, the Ukraine, south Russia, and Anatolia.

Second, birds were hunted to secure feathers as raw material. Feathers were used for fletching arrows, for decorating hats and caps, and for filling pillows or blankets. For the first purpose the pinion and tail feathers of eagles, geese, and probably the great bustard were the best. As decoration, the feathers or whole wings of eagles, falcons, great bustards, jays, and others were used. The feathers of the crane were particularly precious. The twelfth-century *Russkaya pravda* mentions cranes captured when young and kept on estates for their feathers. Various duck and goose species were hunted for their fine down.

Third, birds of prey were killed as vermin. Medieval farmers sought to protect their domestic stock by killing sparrow hawks, goshawks, kestrels, red kites, and several species of eagles. The flesh of these birds was probably not eaten.

Fourth, birds were captured for domestication or taming. Young mallards were taken and added to the domesticated stock. The capture of young falcons had another aim: to produce hunting birds. Although falconry started very early—in southwest Asia in the time of Ashurbanipal (668–625 B.C.) and in Egypt not later than 850 B.C.—it reached Europe only in the Middle Ages. It became the privilege of the nobility; according to rank, nobles were permitted to use different falcon species from the gyrfalcons down to the sparrow hawks.

Fifth, birds were hunted for sport. Fowling was reserved for the nobles and forbidden to peasants, which is why hardly any wild bird bones have been found in medieval villages. The quarry of sport hunting was any species, which may explain the occurrence of remains of such species as eagle owls, tawny owls, white storks, buzzards, hoopoes, and great crested grebes in medieval sites.

BIBLIOGRAPHY

G. Clark, "Fowling in Prehistoric Europe," in *Antiquity*, 22 (1948); Kurt Lindner, *Die Jagd im frühen Mittelalter* (1940); H.-M. Piehler, *Knochenfunde von Wildvögeln aus archäologischen Grabungen in Mitteleuropa* (1976); Frederic E. Zeuner, *A History of Domesticated Animals* (1963).

SÁNDOR BÖKÖNYI

[See also **Hunting and Fowling, Western European.**]

FRA ANGELICO. See **Giovanni da Fiesole.**

FRANCE. French history is covered in a series of articles comprising the following: **To 987; 987–1223; 1223–1328;** and **1314–1494.**

FRANCE: TO 987. Medieval France had its origins in the tenth century. It was then that the West Frankish realm formerly dominated by the Carolingians began to assume the natural boundaries of modern France; it was then that the duchy of "the Franks" (Francia) achieved titular primacy among the Frankish principalities; it was then, too, that a form of Romance language derived from Gallo-Roman Latin speech came to resemble the spoken French of later times. None of these changes was abrupt, to be sure. The dukes of France were the protégés and servants of a Frankish dynasty the traditions of which would be proudly appropriated by later kings of France. As early as the first half of the ninth century, Louis the Pious had trouble preserving the political solidarity of his Germanic- and Romance-speaking aristocracies. But it was only after the death of Charles the Fat in 887 that the great men of West Frankland, obliged to elect a king from among themselves, chose Odo (888–898), whose father (Robert the Strong, d. 866) was the progenitor of the Capetian kings of France.

Odo's own achievement was modest. Dominating the lands bordering Neustria, he valiantly defended Paris against the Northmen. He did not insist on his right to the throne in the face of claims for the Carolingian Charles III "the Simple" (893–922, d. 929), who was crowned king of the West Franks after Odo's death in 898. It was during the reigns of the last Carolingian kings—Charles the Simple, his son Louis IV (936–954), his grandson Lothair (954–986), and his great-grandson Louis V (986–987)—that Odo's family secured the preeminence by which it won the throne for good in 987. Odo's brother Robert bided his time, gained the support of magnates who opposed King Charles's pan-Frankish policy in Lorraine, was elected king in 922, but was killed in battle in 923; the throne then passed to his son-in-law, Duke Radulf of Burgundy (923–936). By Robert's time Francia could be spoken of as a coherent territorial and dynastic patrimony that descended to his son Hugh the Great, who died in 956, and then to his grandson Hugh Capet, elected king in 987, from whom a new royal house later took its name.

The ducal lands were an aggregate of counties, protectorates, and titular abbacies, with direct domains surrounding Paris. They were "French" (that is, Frankish) only in the sense that their aristocracies could not better be described as Burgundian, Norman, Aquitainian, or the like. But it was by no means obvious that the dukes of the Franks would prove

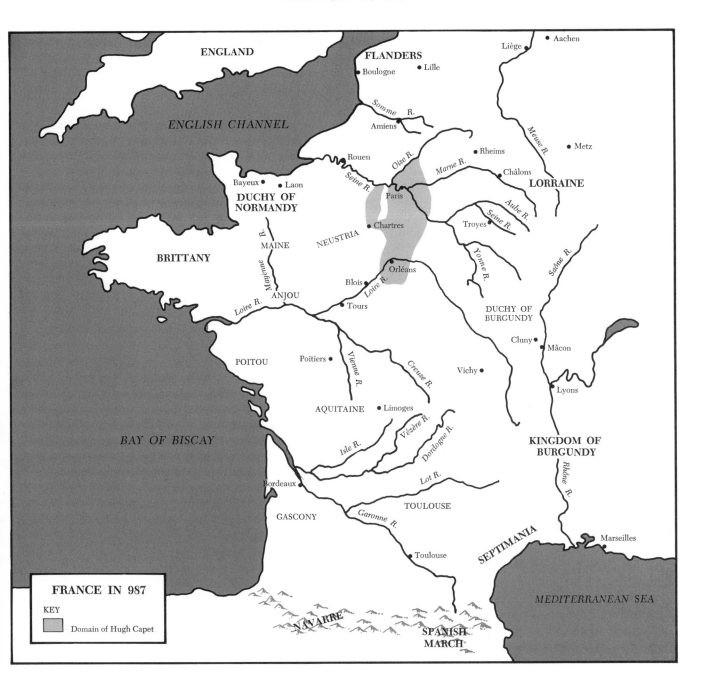

FRANCE IN 987

KEY

Domain of Hugh Capet

dominant among the princes, for the effect of the Carolingian restoration in 898 was to strengthen the position of all the dukes and marcher lords who had served or allied themselves with the old royal house. Not only "France," but also Burgundy, Flanders, Normandy, and Poitou rose to power, and comparable aggregates of lordship were narrowly thwarted in Vermandois and elsewhere. Only in such principalities could peasants and monks find protection

from invaders or pillagers, and the farther they were from northern centers of royal command, the more easily the princes diverted to themselves the fidelity of royal vassals in their lands.

In theory, it is true, nothing had changed. The kings retained fiscal domains and rights of patronage throughout the greater West Frankish realm formerly ruled by Charles the Bald. As late as 985 a count of the Spanish March could think of the king as his lord and defender against the Moors. But the tendency everywhere was for royal rights to devolve to the princes. The process was made easier because most of the princely families (including the Robertians) were related to the Carolingians. As their influence narrowed geographically, the kings were reduced de facto to princely status. Nor did the devolution end there, for by the later tenth century few of the princes effectively controlled their counties and viscounties; and in some regions, such as the Mâconnais, the county itself failed as a burgeoning new class of knights usurped fiscal and judicial powers and built new castles. Not even the monks were immune to the anarchy. In 910 Cluny was founded as a monastery exempt from episcopal supervision, although in other respects the reforms instituted there, and later at Gorze and Brogne, were patterned on Carolingian practice.

The collapse of regalian power was most serious in Burgundy, Aquitaine, and Septimania, where the princes were less successful in disciplining their knights than in defending against external invaders. The more prosperous domains, notably those of the church, were ravaged. Of older institutions, only the episcopate was capable of counteracting the disorder. The bishops worked in several ways. They revived the Carolingian synodal provisions for the protection of the weak, the unarmed, and the clergy, replacing the old royal sanctions with ecclesiastical censures and requiring sworn commitments to the peace by the knights. In this form the Peace of God spread through Aquitaine before 1000. But in some northern regions where the king remained visible, the bishops resisted the Peace as an intrusion on royal power. Purveyors of a Carolingian ideology of theocratic kingship, the bishops remained the natural allies of the old dynasty.

But when Louis V died without an heir, they and the other magnates were faced with a choice between Louis's uncle Charles and Hugh Capet. The latter could claim suzerainty over Normandy, Burgundy, and Aquitaine, as well as ancestors in the kingship. The legitimist Charles stood for an older way that, had it not been for his own vacillations, might have prevailed: as duke of Lorraine he sought to reestablish power over Franks east and west. But such a policy, along with his fidelity to Otto III of Germany, could now be represented as "service to a foreign king." Hugh Capet's election in 987 decisively confirmed the separatism of the West Frankish polity and opened the way to a gradual fusion of

ducal and royal authority from which a kingdom of France was eventually built.

BIBLIOGRAPHY

Sources. Among the chief narratives are Philippe Lauer, ed., *Les annales de Flodoard* (1905); Richer, *Histoire de France (888–995),* Robert Latouche, ed. and trans., 2 vols. (1930–1937). Royal diplomas in the series Chartes et diplômes relatifs à l'histoire de France have been edited by Robert-Henri Bautier, *Recueil des actes d'Eudes* (1967), Jean Dufour, *Recueil des actes de Robert Ier et de Raoul* (1978), Louis Halphen and Ferdinand Lot, *Recueil des actes de Lothaire et de Louis V* (1908), and Philippe Lauer, *Recueil des actes de Louis IV* (1914).

Studies. Jean-François Lemarignier, *Le gouvernement royal aux premiers temps capétiens (987–1108)* (1965); Ferdinand Lot, *Les derniers Carolingiens* (1891); Karl Ferdinand Werner, "Untersuchungen zur Frühzeit des französischen Furstentums (9.–10. Jahrhundert)," in *Die Welt als Geschichte,* **18** (1958), **19** (1959), and **20** (1960), and, with convenient bibliography, "Westfranken-Frankreich unter den Spätkarolingern und frühen Kapetingern (888–1060)," in Theodor Schieder, ed., *Handbuch der europäischen Geschichte,* I (1979).

THOMAS N. BISSON

[See also **Capetian Family Origins; Carolingians and the Carolingian Empire; Merovingians; Peace of God, Truce of God.**]

FRANCE: 987-1223. In 987, despite some signs of consolidation, "France" was little more than a geographic expression for a region consisting of virtually independent principalities over which the king exercised minimal authority. By 1223 the monarchy had taken the first steps toward establishing a strong, unified nation that would enable France to dominate western Europe in the thirteenth century. This remarkable transformation was the achievement of a new dynasty, the Capetians, during the rule of its first seven members: Hugh Capet (987–996), Robert the Pious (996–1031), Henry I (1031–1060), Philip I (1060–1108), Louis VI (1108–1137), Louis VII (1137–1179), and Philip Augustus (1179–1223). Although these regnal dates have traditionally provided historians with a chronological framework within which to consider French history, such divisions of early Capetian history in fact obscure the long-range and more important developments that linked the conscious policies of successive kings. Taking into account these broader movements, four

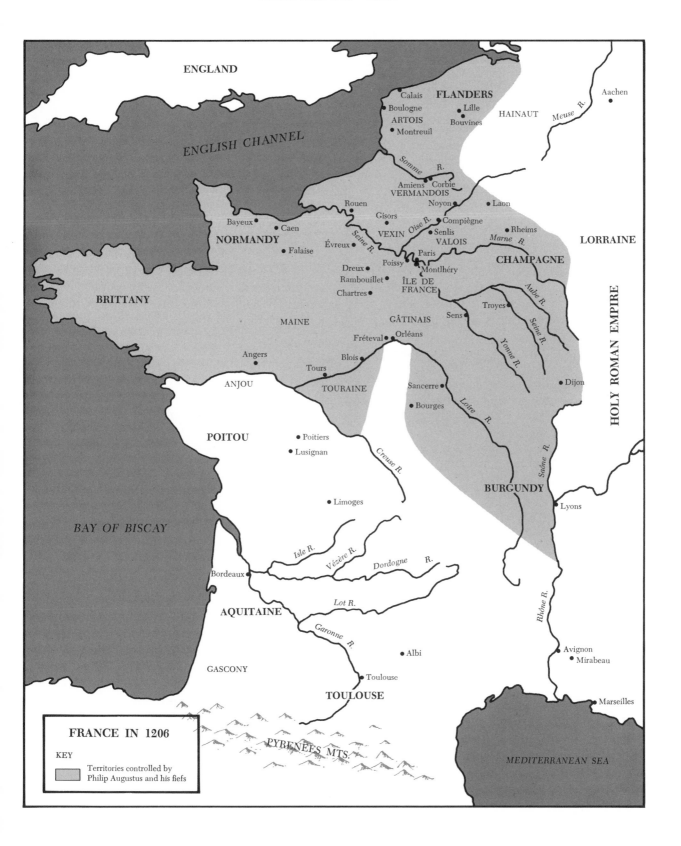

FRANCE IN 1206

KEY

Territories controlled by
Philip Augustus and his fiefs

periods will be distinguished: the continued disintegration of royal authority (987–1070); the regrouping of the royal domain (1070–1149); the competition among the great principalities (1149–1190); and the imposition of royal supremacy (1190–1223). During the first three periods the other great baronies of France underwent a similar process of disintegration, regrouping, and competition. But after the Third Crusade in 1190, Philip Augustus subjected most of northern France to royal authority, thus establishing leadership over the kingdom.

The documents that permit the tracing of these developments were influenced by the underlying political movements. Until 1190 the principal sources for royal history are the chroniclers, all churchmen, who usually (with some notable exceptions) interpreted contemporary events from a regional, nonroyalist point of view. The few royal letters and charters that have survived from this period are preserved in monasteries, cathedrals, and other large churches, thus further saturating the evidence with ecclesiastical bias. After 1190, however, not only did the king commission chroniclers to promote his cause, but new governmental machinery generated documents that were systematically collected in newly established archives and registers. These new collections allow, for the first time, a glimpse into the workings of the French monarchy.

Deriving their name from the sobriquet Capet, meaning "cape" or "coat" and later interpreted as "hat," the Capetians were the third royal dynasty (following the Merovingians and Carolingians) to govern France after the dissolution of Roman authority in the West. On 21 May 987 the last Carolingian king, Louis V, was killed in a hunting accident. Since Louis died young and without direct heirs, the great barons, led by Adalbero, archbishop of Rheims, ignored the claims of surviving Carolingians and, instead, elected Hugh Capet, a descendant of Robert the Strong, duke of the Franks. In June 987 the archbishop anointed and crowned Hugh king at Noyon, thus initiating a dynasty that was to retain the throne without interruption for nearly three and a half centuries. In 987, however, the transition was scarcely noticed, because three times descendants of Robert the Strong (Odo, Robert, and Radulf) had briefly held the throne during the confusion of the preceding century. Thus the Capetians were not newcomers to the throne, and this time they were there to stay.

Yet the new dynasty could not escape the processes of dissolution that had troubled Carolingian

rule and had, in some measure, been responsible for its own rise to the throne. For more than a century Carolingian authority had steadily eroded under pressure from within and without. Although they had espoused the ancient Roman ideal of universal empire, the Carolingians had never possessed the economic and technical resources necessary to unite all of western Europe under one political system. In addition to its internal weakness, the regime received severe blows from a series of external attacks that began in the ninth century. The most serious of these came from the Vikings, whose fleets ravaged the coasts of France and penetrated by river deep into the interior, leaving destruction and disorder in their wake. Unable to meet the Northmen's attacks on all sides, the Carolingian kings responded by creating territorial commands on the borders that regrouped several counties (the old units of local administration) under dukes. For example, Robert the Strong was entrusted with the defense of the Loire region of Angers, Blois, and Tours. As the danger mounted, these commanders increasingly assumed governmental functions normally reserved for the king, such as protecting the population from invasion and regulating internal disputes.

On the borders of France, therefore, emerged the territorial principalities of Burgundy, Flanders, Normandy, Brittany, Aquitaine, and Toulouse, of which Brittany and Flanders were founded on important ethnic groups. The establishment of the duchy of Normandy in the early tenth century illustrates this process; it simply conceded the province to the Viking intruders to separate them from the rest of the Franks. In most cases the rulers of these principalities not only took over governmental functions but also succeeded in perpetuating themselves by asserting a hereditary claim to their office, thus usurping the king's right to appoint his own subordinates. By the middle of the tenth century, political disintegration had reached the heartland of France. Individual counties such as Mâcon, on the border of Burgundy, and Maine and Anjou, toward Normandy, won independence from royal control, further diminishing the scope of royal authority.

As the rulers of these emerging principalities gradually established their hereditary claims, the kingship succumbed to contrary forces. In 877, after the death of Charles the Fat, the great barons forced the Carolingians to submit to election. Thereafter the crown became elective, and thus at the mercy of baronial politics. This accounts for the three brief appearances of the descendants of Robert the Strong, and the final accession of Hugh Capet. Scarcely able to retain their crown during the last century, the Carolingians preserved only one element of their former greatness: their sacred character. With the cooperation of churchmen, they had established the principle that the king be anointed by a priest with holy oil to set him apart from all other laymen. As the *Christus,* the Lord's anointed, the king ruled by God's special grace and was obeyed as his divine representative on earth. In recognition of this ecclesiastical support, the king promised at his coronation not only to do justice but also to defend the Christian faith and the church from its enemies. Royal consecration thus signaled an important alliance forged between the king and the clergy.

Elected to the throne in place of the last Carolingian, Hugh Capet inherited all the weakness of his predecessors. His principal resources consisted of land and men, assets common to all contemporary lords. The land he held directly was called the domain and furnished the basic wealth of the monarchy. It supplied not only agricultural products but also a body of rights attached to the land that were of economic benefit. The men included both those who bore arms in the king's service and the members of the royal entourage who advised the king, aided him in adjudicating disputes in his court, and administered the royal domain. The sole advantage the king enjoyed that was denied other lords was his close ties with churchmen as manifested at his consecration. This consecration made him not only the divinely appointed defender of the church but also the patron of certain bishoprics and abbeys specially designated as regalian. Here lay his principal resources against his competitors, the great barons of the principalities. While these magnates included great churchmen, who as territorial lords in their own right often resisted royal authority, on the whole the prelates normally supported the king in his struggle against the lay princes. The subsequent history of the Capetians was determined by their management of the basic resources of domain, entourage, army, and clergy in their struggle against the great barons.

THE CONTINUED DISINTEGRATION OF ROYAL AUTHORITY (987–1070)

During their first century on the throne, the Capetians were unable to stem the steady erosion of royal power begun under the late Carolingians. Of the four kings who ruled in this period—Hugh Capet, Robert II the Pious, Henry I, and Philip I—only

Robert and Philip have left clear traces of their personalities, because they were able to arouse the interest of clerical chroniclers. Since Robert demonstrated a knowledge of Latin and a taste for theology and liturgy, of which the clergy approved, he was depicted as an agreeable person with soft eyes and fine hair. His grandson Philip, by contrast, who vigorously opposed church reform, was condemned for his corpulence, gluttony, sensuality, and greed. The personalities of Hugh and Henry, deserving of neither praise nor blame, went all but unnoticed.

The weaknesses of the first four Capetians are best represented by the diminutive size and diffuse character of their domain. From the Carolingians they inherited some properties and palaces around Laon, to which they joined their ancestral lands concentrated around three major centers: at Senlis-Compiègne, extending to Laon; at Paris in the Seine basin; and at Orléans in the Loire valley. Outside these areas they could claim only a few scattered lands to the north and in the Loire valley. Rather than a compact territory, the royal domain can best be depicted on a map as clusters of points. Within these clusters the king might possess diverse kinds of properties, such as fields at Poissy, forests at Rambouillet, a palace at Orléans, and a market at Compiègne. Such lands or rights did not remain constant, because the king habitually gave some away, recovered previously lost ones, and acquired new ones. Within these clusters were considerable areas that constituted the domains of neighboring lords. During the first century of Capetian rule, the royal domain experienced further fragmentation of public authority, a process shared by most principalities in France. The largest unit of effective public authority shrank to the size of the local castellany. Possessing a stronghold that could intimidate a small area, the castellan came to exercise public functions once reserved for kings, counts, and dukes: protecting the population, holding court, and collecting revenues. No longer could the territorial prince or count assert authority throughout his principality; he controlled only those areas in which he personally held castles. Local jurisdiction was not only divided among castellans but also among abbeys and other churches that possessed fortified houses. In the royal domain, for example, the first Capetians shared authority and resources with the castellans of Montmorecy and Montlhéry and the abbots of St. Denis. The king's control of his domain became as tenuous as that of other territorial princes.

Despite internal fluctuations and insecurity, the

royal domain retained its outward configuration throughout the first century of Capetian rule and thereby was known as the Île de France, the nucleus or island of the king of France. Minuscule in size compared with the domains of the Carolingians at their height, the Île de France apparently comprised the maximum area that the Capetians were capable of governing directly. When Robert II acquired the duchy of Burgundy in war, he made no attempt to add it to the royal domain. Instead, his son Henry gave it as a fief to his brother Robert, thus initiating the line of Capetian dukes of Burgundy. Since a territory of this size was beyond their means to control, the Capetians preferred to grant it to a family whose loyalty was assured.

Possessing a small domain that was easily crossed in a few days' journey, early Capetian kings performed the primitive tasks of government by means of an itinerant court made up of the king and his entourage. As the royal baggage train perambulated through the domain, the king waged wars, rendered judgments, supervised lands, was seen by his subjects, and, most important, housed and fed himself on his domanial properties. When he arbitrated disputes peacefully in his court, his entourage consisted chiefly of his close counselors; when fighting was required, it was swelled by soldiers who owed him military service. As long as the domain remained small, it was easier to transport the government to the countryside than to require subjects to come to the king. The tent, the packhorse, and the wagon were characteristic features of the royal government.

The petty domanial preoccupations of early Capetian kings transformed the nature of royal charters and documents. Departing from the practice of Carolingian kings, whose charters were drawn up in ornate formulas and attested only by the high officials of the imperial chancery, the Capetians began adding the names of witnesses at the bottoms of their charters. Rather than stately public acts, their charters increasingly assumed the character of private agreements attested by local men. While such charters suggest the decline of royal dignity, they are also valuable sources for historians to ascertain who attended the king's court and to trace the composition of the royal entourage. Until about 1028 the Capetian court was composed largely of bishops, abbots, and counts. After that date, however, the high aristocracy was increasingly joined by local castellans, lower clergy, and even simple knights. More often the prelates and counts came from territories close to the royal domain. This increase in lower social elements and neighboring aristocracy indicates that the king's court was becoming less representative of the kingdom at large and more and more oriented toward local affairs of the domain. By the middle of the eleventh century, King Henry's court could hardly be distinguished from the entourage of any other territorial prince or count.

Outside the narrow confines of the royal domain, the first Capetians had little success in dealing with territorial princes, counts, or other great barons. Hugh Capet's chief opponent was the surviving Carolingian claimant to the throne, Charles, duke of Lorraine. Although Charles was pitifully weak, Hugh required three years to wrest Laon from his hands. Robert II was able to conquer Burgundy only with the aid of the dukes of Normandy. The Capetians' most persistent enemy was the family whose various members held the counties of Vermandois, Troyes, and Blois, lands encircling the Île de France on all sides except the northwest. Against this threatening assembly of neighbors, the Capetians survived only through the help they received from the dukes of Normandy and the counts of Anjou.

With the great churchmen, however, the Capetians enjoyed better relations. The Carolingian legacy of church patronage provided the new dynasty with rights of supervising more than one third of the bishoprics of the entire realm. These regalian sees were located both within and outside the domain, with concentrations to the east and south, principally in the ecclesiastical provinces of Rheims and Sens. In addition, the Capetians exercised patronage over scores of Benedictine abbeys, such as St. Denis and St. Germain-des-Prés around Paris, and Corbie to the north. Royal patronage gave the Capetians the right to enjoy ecclesiastical revenues during vacancies (that is, from the death of one bishop or abbot to the appointment of his successor) and a role in the choosing of new prelates. Like most rulers of their day, French kings were tempted to profit from the latter privilege by committing simony, the sale of church offices outright, usually to the highest bidder. Although dubious from an ecclesiastical point of view, these practices filled royal bishoprics and abbeys with men generally favorable to the king. Because of their special ties to the king, they swore oaths of fealty directly to him, assuming in return the obligations normally owed by vassals. As a royal *fidelis,* for example, Adalbero, archbishop of Rheims, sent troops to Hugh Capet at the siege of Laon. By these special connections with the monarchy, royal bishoprics and abbeys extended the king's sphere of influence and support beyond the royal domain.

Churchmen also cooperated with the early Capetians to perpetuate the new dynasty. When the archbishop of Rheims consecrated Hugh Capet in 987, he declared that the throne was elective, the prevailing practice under the later Carolingians, and the means by which Hugh himself had ascended to the throne. Six months later, however, Hugh asked Adalbero to consecrate his son Robert as well, because he intended to fight the Muslims in Spain and might not survive. The archbishop grumbled that he was not accustomed to create two kings in the same year, but fearing further anarchy if Hugh died, he complied. Thereafter, without exception, each Capetian king until 1223 had his son consecrated before he died. Since unction created a king, the consecration of a designated heir assured the succession of the dynasty. Deciding that the choice should go to the eldest son, Robert the Pious established the principle of primogeniture for the Capetians, and by the twelfth century it was customary for the king to receive his anointing from the archbishop of Rheims.

The triumph of hereditary succession over elective kingship depended not only on ecclesiastical cooperation but also on the unfailing survival of sons, not easy in an age of high infant mortality. For this reason Robert and Philip I married and repudiated a succession of wives, despite vociferous ecclesiastical opposition to divorce. Robert himself was obliged to wed three wives before he obtained the desired heirs. When Philip's first queen produced only one son after twenty years of marriage, the king sought to reinforce this slim guarantee against the future by choosing another wife, who rewarded him with the birth of two additional boys. Powerless against the great barons, the first Capetians were nonetheless potent in producing sons through whom they secured an incontrovertible right to the French throne—the one unqualified achievement of their first century of rule. In contrast with German and English kings, the Capetians did not suffer the disruptive threat of contested successions until the fourteenth century.

THE REGROUPING OF THE ROYAL DOMAIN (1070–1149)

By 1070 Philip I showed signs of attempting to reverse the disintegration of royal authority by rebuilding the royal domain. This task was accomplished chiefly by his son Louis VI, who began it in 1100, before his father's death. Sympathetically de-

scribed by his friend and biographer, Suger, abbot of St. Denis, Louis was an energetic, if enormously corpulent, military commander. His main goals were continued by his son, Louis VII, until the latter's departure on the Second Crusade in 1147.

The rather modest aim of Louis VI, the central figure in this period, was to reinforce the Île de France as the territorial base of the French monarchy. In this task he was inspired by the success of two neighboring principalities, Normandy and Flanders, where public authority had not disintegrated to the same extent as in the royal domain and elsewhere. By 1050 the dukes of Normandy, and to a lesser degree the counts of Flanders, had begun to recover the local jurisdiction other princes had lost to the castellans. In particular they administered their territories by means of local officials who remained responsive to their commands. In a turbulent age their lands enjoyed a greater measure of security and peace than the rest of France. If the Capetians hoped to succeed against their rivals, they needed to pacify their own domain.

Philip I began the task of reconstruction by making some modest additions to the domain in the north through the acquisition of the Vexin and in the south by acquiring the Gâtinais and Bourges. In 1100 his son Louis began to attack the strongholds of local castellans who routinely disturbed the peace of the royal domain. With determination and energy, if not total success, Louis spent the greater part of his life subduing the castles of Hugh du Puiset, the lord of Montlhéry, Thomas de Marles, and other rapacious castellans until the kings of France at last controlled their own lands. Clearest evidence of royal mastery over the Île de France is found in the creation of local officials called *prévôts*, who executed commands, judged suits, and collected revenues for the king. Appearing first in significant numbers at the end of Philip I's reign, they were assigned to concentrations of royal holdings from which they took their titles—for example, the *prévôts* of Poissy and Orléans. Functioning as true royal officers, the *prévôts* were drawn from the same castellan families the Capetians were in the process of subjugating.

At the same time, in order to win the loyalty of the rising number of townsmen brought about by the commercial revival of the twelfth century, Louis VI issued charters of privileges to towns in the royal domain and neighboring lands. Except for the minor acquisitions of Philip I, however, the Capetians' efforts were directed toward strengthening the king's hold on his domain, not enlarging it. When Louis

VII married Eleanor, heiress to the duchy of Aquitaine in 1137, he made no attempt to incorporate that vast southern principality into the royal domain. Like Burgundy, Aquitaine was considered too large to be governed successfully by the primitive domanial administration and was later lost.

The reconstruction of the royal domain was accompanied by the appearance of new figures in the king's central entourage—the household officers. Modeled after the members of the Carolingian court, these officials originally performed domestic tasks. The seneschal provisioned the royal household; the butler procured its drink; the chamberlain supervised the king's bedroom; the constable, his horses; and the chancellor, his chapel. Shortly after their initial appearance, however, they began to assume governmental tasks as well. The chancellor, for example, drew up the royal charters as well as serving the king's religious needs. The subscription lists at the bottoms of these charters chronicle the growing importance of the household officers within the royal entourage. First appearing in 1043, when they are listed haphazardly among numerous castellans and local figures, their attestations began to displace all others by the end of Philip I's reign. By the accession of Louis VII in 1137, household officers alone subscribed royal documents. Henceforth royal charters ceased to reflect the local and diverse character of the king's entourage and became, as in Carolingian times, an instrument of royal authority subscribed only by the king's household officers, testimony to the professionalization of the court staff demanded by a newly strengthened domain.

Like the *prévôts,* the household officers were recruited from the castellan families of the Île-de-France. Although the loss of their castles curbed their action, these families transferred their competition to the royal court. During the reign of Louis VI, the Garlande family successfully monopolized three of the household offices. Its most ambitious member, Stephen of Garlande, was chancellor and seneschal at the same time. In order to regain control over his own court, Louis VI expelled Stephen from his household and was obliged to leave the post of seneschal vacant for a while. Because of his intimacy with the king, Stephen of Garlande had been recognized by contemporary observers as a royal counselor, a position he shared with others at court.

After Stephen's disgrace his preeminent role, although not his multiple offices, was gradually assumed by a young monk named Suger who was elected abbot of St. Denis in 1122, after proving himself a successful manager of the abbey lands. A friend and companion of Louis VI since boyhood, when they had been raised together at St. Denis, Suger had been a frequent visitor to the royal court and a devoted agent of the king in the early years of the reign. When Suger became abbot of St. Denis, the king could draw on the great abbey for services and resources, as he had previously relied on castellan families. When the young Louis VII departed on the Second Crusade in 1147, it was not surprising that he confided the regency to Suger, who had been the foremost counselor of his father's court. Drawing on his administrative experience as head of St. Denis, Suger managed the domain and exercised justice in the king's name until Louis's return from the Holy Land.

During Philip I's reign Capetian reliance on regalian churches was disturbed by a reform party that, under the leadership of Pope Gregory VII, not only campaigned against the gross abuses of simony and clerical marriage but also threatened royal control over appointments to bishoprics and abbacies. In 1077 a papal legate, Hugh of Die, was commissioned to convene church councils throughout France in which bishop after bishop was deposed for having unlawfully purchased his office. Although Philip proved impervious to these reform ideals, Louis VI responded by refraining from blatant simony, although he continued to appoint churchmen whose loyalty to the monarchy was assured. Louis VII followed his father's ways and resorted to strong measures to impose his chancellor, Cadurc, as archbishop of Bourges. Ultimately failing in this case, he nevertheless demonstrated his determination to retain control over ecclesiastical appointments.

Through his skills as a warrior and his tireless efforts, Louis VI reduced the castles of the Île-de-France and pacified the royal domain. At last military master of his own lands, he forced all the castellans and even many simple knights to become his direct vassals. In neighboring counties such as Chartres, on the other hand, he was able only occasionally to attach castellans as vassals, and rarely anyone below that level. Outside the royal domain, Louis's contacts were limited, for the most part, to the rank of count or above. As for the territorial principalities on the periphery, only the great dukes and counts grudgingly acknowledged him as lord.

Nonetheless, by the end of Louis VI's reign, sufficient ties with vassals had been established that the royal counselor Suger was able to devise a theory of feudal hierarchy that placed the king as titular lord over the baronies of all the great dukes and counts. According to the theory, the king bound to himself by feudal oath the great barons, who in turn were lords over the lands of lesser barons and castellans, who finally were lords over the fiefs of simple knights. At the time Suger wrote, this feudal hierarchy was more theoretical than actual, because from a practical standpoint, the only vassals on whom the king could count to respond with effective contingents of knights were those of the royal domain. But the theoretical claims to feudal overlordship were useful in providing Louis VI with an excuse to intervene in Flanders in 1127, after the assassination of the count. Louis VII employed similar justifications to lead his army into the lands of the Blois-Troyes family in 1143 and against Normandy in 1144. These occasions were, however, exceptional, and neither king exercised permanent influence outside the royal domain.

COMPETITION AMONG THE GREAT PRINCIPALITIES (1149–1190)

Louis VII departed on the Second Crusade an energetic soldier like his father. But the disasters encountered during the expedition broke his military spirit and profoundly changed his personality, as was apparent when he returned in 1149. His former combativeness gone, keenly aware of the failure of his crusade, he became susceptible to the influence of churchmen. In addition, one particular failure worried him greatly. Unlike his forebears, he had not yet produced a son to assure the continuation of the dynasty. After his wife, Eleanor of Aquitaine, gave birth to a second daughter, Louis divorced her in 1152 and married two more wives before obtaining the long-desired son, Philip Augustus, born in 1165. Philip's late birth, combined with Louis's failing health, forced the young prince to mount the throne in 1179 at the age of fourteen, exposing his youthful inexperience to court intrigue for the first decade of his reign. Eleanor's divorce naturally removed the vast duchy of Aquitaine from Louis's hands, but since it had never been subjected to royal administration, its loss was not greatly felt. Throughout the period the king's lands remained stable in size. Only a slight increase was realized in 1185, when Philip acquired the Amiénois and parts of Vermandois through inheritance.

In the period between the Second and Third Crusades mounting competition developed among the French territorial principalities. Great lords like the counts of Flanders continued to improve the re-

sources and administration of their lands. The counties of Troyes, Blois, and Sancerre were held by three brothers—Henry I of Troyes, Thibaut V of Blois, Stephen of Sancerre—who allied with one another to form the great fief of Champagne that virtually surrounded Île-de-France. But the most spectacular development of the period was the sudden emergence at the forefront of Henry II of Anjou. The eldest son of the count of Anjou, he inherited the county from his father, and Normandy and the kingdom of England from his mother. No sooner had Louis VII separated from Eleanor of Aquitaine than Henry married her, adding Aquitaine to his lands. By the time of his accession to the English throne in 1154, Henry possessed not only the royal dignity but also the western half of France extending from the English Channel to the Pyrenees. With territories and resources far exceeding those of the French kings, Henry II posed by far the most serious threat the Capetians had yet had to face.

In the past the counts of Anjou had traditionally competed with the counts of Blois for the Touraine in the Loire valley. In this contest Capetians had usually supported Anjou against Blois, their nearest, and thus natural enemy. But the union of Anjou, Normandy, and Aquitaine forced Louis to reverse this policy and seek help from his former foe. In 1160 he married Adèle, sister of the counts of Troyes, Blois, and Sancerre, and forged a new alliance with the house of Champagne. Even the support of Champagne, however, did not appreciably improve Louis's military effectiveness against the Angevins. The best the French king could do was to exploit Angevin family quarrels, as when Henry's sons revolted against him in 1174, in the hopes that such internal conflicts would seriously weaken his formidable rival. Continuing his father's policies, Philip Augustus in 1188 played off the ambitions of Henry's second son, Richard, count of Poitou, against his father; but the maneuver, while temporarily successful, brought little permanent gain. Since Capetian resources remained insufficient for direct confrontation of the great fiefs of Flanders, Champagne, and the newly combined lands of Anjou, Normandy, and Aquitaine, the French king's survival relied on competition among and dissension within the great principalities.

The increased level of baronial activity penetrated even the royal court. For the first time in two generations, counts and territorial princes appeared at royal gatherings as Louis VII laid preparations for the Second Crusade from 1145 to 1147. Upon his return individual counselors within his entourage began to function more as a permanent *conseil* to advise the king regularly. Increasingly, numbers of important barons took their place alongside the crowds of chamberlains, knights, and clerics who frequented the court. Thibaut, count of Blois, was appointed seneschal of the royal household in 1145 and, with his sister Queen Adèle, promoted the interest of the Champagne family. As Louis became enfeebled in his last years, the Champagne clique was challenged at court by Philip, count of Flanders, who initiated negotiations for the marriage of his niece, Isabella of Hainaut, to the young Philip Augustus, hoping by this means to undermine the privileged position exercised by the Champagne family through Queen Adèle.

The coronation of Philip Augustus in November 1179 acted out in its pageantry the baronial rivalry. The count of Flanders bore the king's sword in the procession and presided over the concluding banquet, testimony to his success in insinuating himself at court. The king was anointed and crowned by the archbishop of Rheims, who was none other than a brother of the Champagne counts. The crown was carried by the eldest son of Henry of Anjou, who, with his two brothers, the counts of Poitou and Brittany, surpassed all others in the splendor of their retinue. Abandoned by his ailing father, the young King Philip cut a frail figure beside these displays of baronial might.

Faced with this array of powerful rivals, the Capetians continued to find their most solid support in their traditional alliance with churchmen. Chastened by his disastrous crusade, Louis VII had sought to make amends by espousing the cause of church reform. Refraining from simony, he also abandoned his earlier policy of intervening in ecclesiastical elections to bishoprics and monasteries. Despite this renunciation of royal privilege, cathedrals and abbeys continued to elect candidates who, for the most part, were faithful to the royal cause. In effect, Louis secured more from his espousal of church reform than his grandfather had done from the sale of church offices, because he gained both devoted clergy and the gratitude of the reformers.

Louis further befriended the clergy by providing a refuge for Thomas Becket, archbishop of Canterbury, who had been harried from England by Henry II, and by offering a haven to Pope Alexander III when he was driven from Rome by the antipope Victor IV. Setting up court at Sens, to the south of Paris, the grateful Alexander in 1163 sent Louis a golden rose, a token of his appreciation. Of all Capetian monarchs, Louis rightly received this symbol of devotion to the church, for he had consistently shown himself faithful to its causes and worthy of its respect. Philip Augustus' subsequent dealings with the papacy and his own clergy were never so cordial, but he harvested the ecclesiastical goodwill garnered by his father.

THE IMPOSITION OF ROYAL SUPREMACY (1190–1223)

Philip Augustus' departure on the Third Crusade in 1190 marked, as had his father's leaving on the Second Crusade, a turning point in the development of the French monarchy. Philip's projected absence provided him opportunity to publish an ordinance for the reorganization of the royal administration and to reconstitute the personnel of his entourage. Before departing, the king definitively designated Paris as the capital of his kingdom, surrounding it with a new set of protective walls. Nearby he placed a financial bureau to which *prévôts* were summoned from the domain three times a year to render account of the king's revenues. New royal agents, called baillis, were dispatched throughout the domain to hold monthly courts, called assizes, to which local inhabitants could bring their pleas. The baillis, like the *prévôts,* were called to Paris triannually to report on conditions in the domain and to account for any extraordinary revenues they had collected. In effect, by his ordinance of 1190 Philip Augustus had brought about a fundamental reversal in the flow of government. In place of an itinerant court that reached out into the countryside, the *prévôts* and baillis were increasingly drawn from the countryside to a fixed center at Paris.

The reorganization of governmental machinery was matched by a change in court personnel. The young king had insisted that the great barons accompany him on the crusade to the East, where the rigors of the journey, the heat of the sun, and the danger of battle did not fail to take their toll. He left most of the important barons of his father's generation buried in the sands of Palestine, including the counts of Flanders, Blois, and Troyes. Among the former royal counselors, only the archbishop of Rheims, from the Champagne family, lived on after the crusade, for he had been left behind in Paris as regent.

After the death of Thibaut of Blois, Philip left vacant the household office of seneschal, as he had earlier left the chancellorship vacant. The other household offices were reduced in importance to titular dignities, deprived of any real governmental functions. Their former roles as royal counselors were filled by minor chamberlains, royal knights, and royal clerks, all drawn from lesser ranks. Royal administrators such as Walter the Young, from a loyal family of minor chamberlains; Bartholomew de Roye, from petty knights of Vermandois; and Brother Guérin, from the crusading order of Knights Hospitallers—to take only three examples—were the active figures and important advisers who formed the king's *conseil*. Brother Guérin, in particular, who was made bishop of Senlis in 1213, was the true successor of the archbishop of Rheims as second only to the king within the court. Both Guérin and Bartholomew were young men when Philip chose them, and their participation in royal government outlasted the king's reign.

The new men of the *conseil* no longer relied on the collective memory of a traveling entourage to conduct their business. The new bureaucratic machinery required recordkeeping and archives. Although the chancellor's position remained unfilled, the royal chancery, made up of seven to eight clerks, composed the king's letters and other documents. When Philip lost his baggage, including his documents, in an ambush at Fréteval in 1194, he instructed the chamberlain, Walter the Young, to establish permanent archives at Paris, where all incoming documents were safely preserved.

A decade later the chancery began to compile registers of important outgoing charters and of other information useful for the daily operation of government. By 1190 scribes had already begun to make records of the receipts and expenditures accounted for during the regular visits of the *prévôts* and baillis to Paris, thus initiating financial recordkeeping. Permanent records, combined with other reforms, improved the working of royal government and increased the royal revenues so that an effective army could be kept. In 1194 Philip assessed special levies of men, wagons, and money on the towns and abbeys of the royal domain. By 1202 these exactions were commuted entirely into money and assigned for maintaining a standing army of 2,100 to 2,800 men stationed on the border of the Île-de-France and Normandy. For the first time Capetians possessed both the administrative and the military means to confront the great barons beyond the confines of the domain.

Events of the crusade gave Philip an opportunity to move against two major fiefs, Flanders and the Angevin realm. When Philip of Alsace, count of Flanders, died at the siege of Acre in 1191, Philip used his death as an excuse to return immediately to France to execute a long-prepared plan to acquire the lands that lay between the Île-de-France and Flanders. These consisted of Artois, Vermandois, and Valois, which the counts of Flanders had obtained through strategic marriages. In a series of extremely complicated prior negotiations involving one of his distant cousins, Eleanor, heiress of Vermandois, and his wife Isabella of Hainaut, niece of the count of Flanders, Philip Augustus had raised counter-claims to these territories. The initial phase in acquiring the Amiénois and portions of Vermandois had already taken place in 1185. With the death of the count of Flanders, Philip assumed control of Artois in 1192, and his wife's dowry, together with additional lands in Vermandois. By 1213, when Eleanor of Vermandois died without direct descendants, he received the remainder of Vermandois and Valois as her heir. Through manipulating marriage and family inheritance, therefore, Philip added these extensive and heavily populated lands to the royal domain.

While Philip hurried back to France in 1191, his Angevin competitor, King Richard I, successor to Henry's extensive fiefs on the Continent, remained in Palestine fighting the Muslims until 1192. On his return journey to England from the Holy Land, Richard fell into the hands of the duke of Austria, who turned him over to the German emperor; both were old enemies having scores to settle with the English king. With the connivance of Philip Augustus, Richard's captivity was prolonged until 1194. This unexpected stroke of luck gave Philip a chance to attack the lands of his Angevin rival undisturbed, and to revive the Capetian strategy of playing one Angevin against another. This time he allied with Richard's younger brother John, with whose help in 1193 Philip captured the castle of Gisors, which lay at a strategic point between the Île-de-France and Normandy. Unfortunately for Philip, Richard's return to France in 1194 precipitated John's defection, and Richard's superior finances and army once more overpowered the Capetians and put them on the defensive.

When Richard was killed, in the prime of his life, during a campaign in the Limousin in 1199, Philip Augustus was able to profit from this second stroke of luck by pitting, once again, Angevin against Angevin. In opposition to John, who now sought to succeed his brother, Philip advanced the claims to the throne of John's twelve-year-old nephew, Arthur, count of Brittany. After initial maneuverings, however, in 1200 Philip and John reached an agreement at Le Goulet by which Philip recognized John as Richard's successor in exchange for a large sum of money and the concession of the territory of Évreux, on the Norman border. Momentarily content to bide his time, Philip recognized that John, untried in battle and unstable in political resolve, was not the formidable adversary that his brother and father had been. Philip had only to wait for his new opponent to provide him with an excuse to renew hostilities against the Angevins. That excuse came in the very next year when John, attending to problems in his southern lands, outraged the honor of the powerful Poitevin family of Lusignan by abducting and marrying a woman already promised to Hugh of Lusignan. The Lusignans brought complaint against John to the French king as their feudal suzerain; he summoned John, as duke of Aquitaine, to answer the charges in the royal court. When John obstinately refused to obey Philip's summons, the king's court in solemn session adjudged him forfeit of all his French lands in 1202.

Thus furnished with legal justification, Philip Augustus revived Arthur's claims to the throne and made military preparation to execute the sentence of his court. This time, however, luck favored John, who captured Arthur in a surprise move against the castle of Mirebeau. Arthur disappeared in a Norman prison and was never heard of again. Despite this setback, in 1203 Philip began his drive down the Seine valley into Normandy. When John proved to be incapable of taking decisive measures to defend the duchy, Rouen, its chief city, capitulated to the French in June 1204. By then it was clear that Arthur had been murdered by his uncle, and revulsion against John swept the ranks of the barons, particularly in Brittany and Anjou, which had favored Arthur as Richard's successor. Offering only token resistance, these regions were quickly taken by Philip Augustus, who drove John beyond the Loire valley. Only in Poitou and Aquitaine did John find sufficient support to make a stand. By 1206, therefore, Philip Augustus was in military control of Normandy, Brittany, Anjou, Maine, and Touraine.

Although initially defeated, John had not resigned himself to his continental losses. Rallying his vassals in Poitou and the south, he allied in the north with the counts of Flanders and Boulogne, and with his nephew, Otto of Brunswick, the German emperor, for a two-pronged attack against the Capetian lands.

John's southern thrust from Poitou was met and checked by Prince Louis, Philip's eldest son, at La Roche-au-Moine in 1214. At the same time Philip met the northern coalition on the fields of Bouvines in one of the rare full-scale, pitched battles of the century. When the sun set that day, royal forces had captured the counts of Flanders and Boulogne, and other northern barons, and the German emperor had fled the field. The rout at Bouvines decisively sealed Philip's victory over his Angevin foes and guaranteed the conquest of their northern territories.

Annexations through inheritance and conquests were of little lasting value, however, unless they were integrated into the governmental structure of the realm. Now, some of these acquisitions were joined to the royal domain. Philip Augustus began applying to his new lands the administrative machinery he had fashioned after his return from the crusade. To Amiénois, Artois, and parts of Vermandois, which had passed to the crown by 1192, Philip assigned new prévôts who reported the domanial revenues three times a year at Paris. Teams of two to three baillis circulated throughout Vermandois, performing judicial, financial, and supervisory duties, and they too reported triannually at Paris. When Vermandois was thereby attached firmly to the king's domain, the royal chronicler, Rigord of St. Denis, bestowed on Philip the title of "Augustus," because he had "augmented" the domain.

After its conquest Normandy, with its highly developed administrative system, also was permanently annexed to the domain. This system included an exchequer, which functioned as both a financial and a judicial body, holding sessions at Caen and Falaise; local officials called vicomtes, who collected the regular revenues like their French counterparts, the prévôts; and baillis, who performed duties similar to those of their colleagues in the royal domain, but in Normandy their territories were better defined. Normandy, the former heartland of the Angevin continental territory, became the cherished possession of French kings. With Artois, Vermandois, and Valois, it enlarged the royal domain almost threefold.

Elsewhere, Philip refrained from burdening the royal administration with more territory to govern. The Loire fiefs of Anjou, Maine, and Touraine, which the Angevins had ruled through seneschals, were kept under the same regime. In Anjou, Philip appointed to the post of seneschal William des Roches, the leading baron of the region, who had been responsible for bringing the local nobility into the Capetian camp after the death of Arthur. Assuming charge of the Loire castles, William divided the revenues with the king. Other outlying baronies were offered as fiefs to loyal vassals. In 1212 the turbulent county of Brittany was given through marriage to a royal cousin, Peter of Dreux (Peter Mauclerc). After the capture of the count of Boulogne at Bouvines, his fief was confirmed to Philip Hurepel, the king's second son. Two of the greatest baronies, Troyes and Flanders, also fell into royal guardianship through fortune and military victory during the second half of the reign. In 1201 the count of Troyes died, leaving an unborn heir whose succession was contested. As feudal overlord of a fief claimed by a minor heir, Philip took Troyes under his wardship until the new count's rights could be examined and judged. After the royal court decided in favor of the young count in 1216, the king continued to retain the barony under his tutelage. When Ferrand, count of Flanders, was taken at Bouvines in 1214 and imprisoned as a felonious vassal, his fief reverted to his wife. Philip similarly placed it under royal wardship. The houses of Troyes and Flanders, the two dominant influences at court at the beginning of the reign, were now under royal tutelage. Their subordination, along with the expulsion of the Angevins, eliminated all rivals capable of challenging royal authority in northern France.

The victory at Bouvines brought peace to the royal domain, which remained undisturbed during the closing years of the reign. Only Prince Louis continued to fight outside the royal lands. In an attempt to sustain the momentum of Bouvines, he crossed the Channel and invaded England in 1216, but lack of support from English barons and sharp opposition from the pope brought the expedition to naught. In 1218 Louis journeyed to the south of France to combat the Albigensian heretics, but this enterprise, although it anticipated royal policy of succeeding reigns, similarly failed to accomplish its objectives.

Beyond these two expeditions, Philip used the remaining, uneventful years of his rule to define more clearly his rights as feudal suzerain. In 1201 the royal court had entertained a suit from the Lusignan family against John, then the powerful duke of Aquitaine. When Philip enforced the decision of his court against John by military conquest, and repulsed the counterattack at Bouvines, he confirmed his supreme authority over the feudal structure of France. In effect, he made fact what in the past had been only Suger's theory of feudal hierarchy. The judgment concerning the succession of Troyes in 1216 was an-

other instance of the king's superior feudal authority. At the same time Philip extended his jurisdiction as feudal lord over the lesser fiefs in the royal domain. Following the pattern of the Norman dukes, he instructed his baillis to make inventories of all the fiefs in his domain, which were fully recorded in the royal registers. With this information he could penetrate to the lower levels of the feudal hierarchy, at last regulating and controlling the lesser vassals of northern France.

Bouvines also had an impact on literature, for it prompted members of the royal entourage to exalt the king and publicize his majesty to new audiences. William the Breton, Philip's chaplain and an eyewitness to the victory, was moved to recopy and continue the life of Philip begun by Rigord of St. Denis, which had fallen into oblivion. In William's revision Philip figures as the glorified ideal of a conquering France, no longer merely *Augustus* but *Magnanimus,* a magnificent hero of a powerful nation. Rigord's and William the Breton's lives of Philip were added to Suger's life of Louis VI as part of a developing historiographic tradition carried on by the monks of St. Denis to glorify the deeds of French kings. Rich in resources, powerful in authority, and celebrated in literature, the Capetian kings had succeeded in transforming the fragile institution of kingship bequeathed them by the Carolingians into a strong, active government capable of administering a vastly enlarged realm. Undisputed masters of France by 1223, the Capetians stood on the threshold of asserting supremacy over western Europe.

BIBLIOGRAPHY

Broad surveys of early Capetian history include Robert Fawtier, *The Capetian Kings of France* (1960); Elizabeth Hallam, *Capetian France, 987–1328* (1980); Jean-François Lemarignier, *La France médiévale: Institutions et société* (1970); Ferdinand Lot and Robert Fawtier, *Histoire des institutions françaises au moyen âge,* 3 vols. (1957–1962); Achille Luchaire, *Les premiers Capétiens (987–1137)* and *Louis VII—Philippe Auguste—Louis VIII,* vols. II and III of Ernest Lavisse, ed., *Histoire de France depuis les origines jusqu'à la Révolution* (1901); William M. Newman, *Le domain royal sous les premiers Capétiens (987–1180)* (1937); Charles Petit-Dutaillis, *The Feudal Monarchy in France and England* (1926).

More recent interpretations may be found in John W. Baldwin, "La décennie décisive: Les années 1190–1203 dans le règne de Philippe Auguste," in *Revue historique,* 540 (1981), and *The Government of Philip Augustus: Foundations of French Royal Power in the Middle Ages,* to be published by the University of California Press, Berkeley; Robert-Henri Bautier, ed., *La France de Philippe*

Auguste: Le temps des mutations (1982); Eric Bournazel, *Le gouvernement capétien au XIIe siècle, 1108-1180* (1975); C. Warren Hollister and John W. Baldwin, "The Rise of Administrative Kingship: Henry I and Philip Augustus," in *American Historical Review*, 83 (1978); Jean-François Lemarignier, *Le gouvernement royal aux premiers temps capétiens (987-1108)* (1965); Andrew W. Lewis, *Royal Succession in Capetian France: Studies on Familial Order and the State* (1981); Michel Nortier and John W. Baldwin, "Contributions à l'étude des finances de Philippe Auguste," in *Bibliothèque de l'École des Chartes*, **138** (1980).

The standard regnal studies include Alexander Cartellieri, *Philipp II August, König von Frankreich*, 5 vols. (1889-1919); Augustin Fliche, *Le règne de Philippe Ier, roi de France (1060-1108)* (1912); Ferdinand Lot, *Études sur le règne de Hugues Capet et la fin du Xe siècle*, in Bibliothèque de l'École des hautes études, sciences historiques et philologiques, fasc. CXLVII (1903); Achille Luchaire, *Louis VI le Gros, annales de sa vie et de son règne* (1890); Marcel Pacaut, *Louis VII et son royaume* (1964); Christian Pfister, *Études sur le règne de Robert le Pieux (996-1031)*, in Bibliothèque de L'École des hautes études, sciences historiques et philologiques, fasc. LXIV (1885).

JOHN W. BALDWIN

[See also **Angevins; Aquitaine; Bailli; Becket, Thomas, Saint; Crusades and Crusader States; Eleanor of Aquitaine; Flanders and the Low Countries; Henry I of England; Henry II of England; Louis VI of France; Louis IX of France; Normans and Normandy; Philip II Augustus; Rigord; Seneschal; Suger, Abbot of St. Denis.**]

FRANCE: 1223-1328. When Prince Louis the Lion acceded to the throne in 1223, he became ruler of a country of several million people, the largest political unit in western Europe at the time. But perhaps "unit" is too strong a word. Francia, the historic patrimony of the Capetian rulers, and Vermandois, an acquisition going back over thirty years, were loyal to the dynasty. But Normandy, Anjou, Maine, Touraine, Poitou, Saintonge, the Limousin, and Quercy—the lands "won" from the English kings—varied from a submissiveness imposed by military occupation (Normandy) to occasional violent hostility (Poitou). Other areas in the north and center—such as Champagne, Burgundy, the Mâconnais, and Flanders—were under the immediate control of great feudatories who frequently opposed Capetian policies. Further south, a great struggle was taking shape. The "private" conquerors of Languedoc (the crusaders who had overcome the Albigensians) were unable to control the south. They called upon the Capetians to do the job for them; but the likelihood that this region, stretching from the borders of Gascony to the Rhône River, would ever become thoroughly French in loyalty would not have occurred to any serious thinker.

By 1328, when the death of the last direct Capetian brought an end to the third dynasty of the French monarchs, a country recognizably similar to the modern nation had emerged. There were still trouble spots—the passionate attachment of natives to local institutions and the anomaly of an "English" Gascony are two examples. Nonetheless, a fundamental political victory had been won. France existed. It was talked about and lauded in sermons, such as those of the Dominican preacher, Guillaume de Sauqueville; a man who came from as far away as Languedoc, Guillaume de Nogaret, had said he was willing to die for it; and poets, such as Richier of Rheims, sang its praises with an audacity that has seldom been matched in any place or at any time. How did this fundamental transformation come about? And what were the events, ideas, and structures that give the transformation its context?

The monarchy itself benefited from a number of strong rulers. Louis VIII (1223-1226), though he died young, managed to achieve a decisive military victory in Languedoc over the supporters of the Albigensian heretics. His death led to a rebellion against the crown in the north, for he had chosen his wife, Blanche of Castile, as regent for their young son, Louis IX. Blanche was repugnant to the northern barons because she was both a woman and a "foreigner." She proved herself more than capable, however, and worthy of the trust the dying Louis VIII had placed in her. Careful alliances with certain factions of barons against others, her decision to seek an immediate coronation of her son, and her readiness to take military action when it was necessary mark her as one of the most effective rulers in French history. Repeated violent attempts by the barons to seize power ended in repeated failures. She exercised a dominant influence on French government for the next twenty-five years. Her advisers became the advisers of her son when he came into his own in the 1240's.

Louis IX—St. Louis (1226-1270)—was cut from the same cloth as his mother and father. He was pious without being weak, and by his moral and political leadership he raised the French monarchy to the premier rank in the West. His son and successor, Philip III the Bold (1270-1285), was less able. Philip

FRANCE: 1223–1328

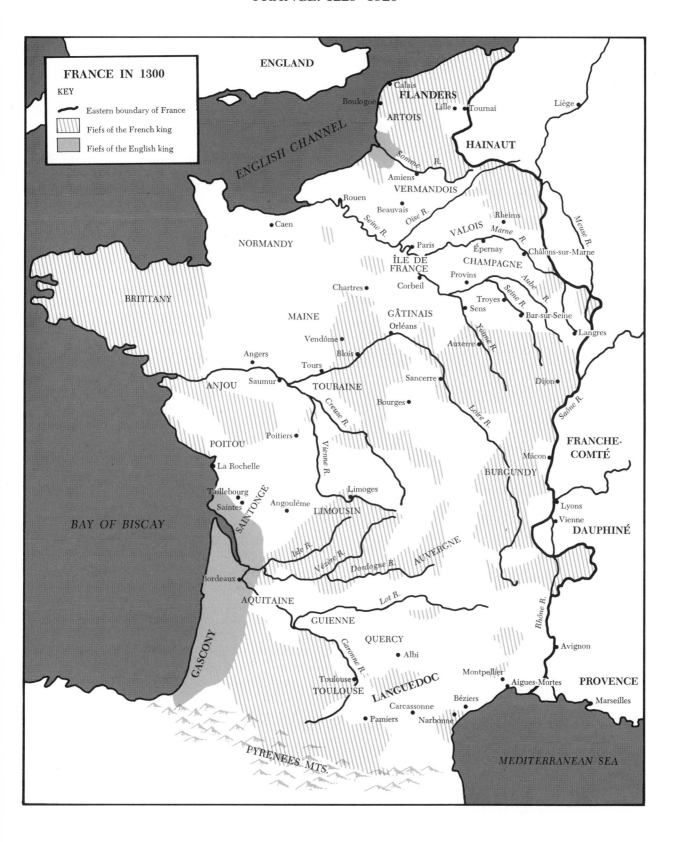

FRANCE IN 1300

KEY

⌇⌇⌇ Eastern boundary of France

⌇⌇⌇ Fiefs of the French king

▨ Fiefs of the English king

ENGLAND

ENGLISH CHANNEL

Calais
Boulogne
FLANDERS
Lille • Tournai
Liège
ARTOIS
HAINAUT

Somme R.
Amiens
VERMANDOIS
Rouen
Beauvais
Oise R.
VALOIS
Rheims
Meuse R.

Caen
Seine R.
Paris
Marne R.
Épernay
Châlons-sur-Marne
NORMANDY
ÎLE DE FRANCE
CHAMPAGNE

BRITTANY
Chartres
Corbeil
Provins
Aube R.
Troyes
Sens
Seine R.
Bar-sur-Seine
Langres
MAINE
GÂTINAIS
Orléans
Vendôme
Blois
Yonne R.
Auxerre
Angers
Tours
Sancerre
Dijon
ANJOU
Saumur
TOURAINE
Bourges
Saône R.
Creuse R.
Loire R.

POITOU
Poitiers
Vienne R.
Mâcon
FRANCHE-COMTÉ
BURGUNDY
La Rochelle
Taillebourg
Limoges
Saintes
SAINTONGE
Angoulême
LIMOUSIN
Lyons
Vienne
BAY OF BISCAY
Isle R.
Vézère R.
AUVERGNE
DAUPHINÉ
Bordeaux
Dordogne R.
GASCONY
AQUITAINE
Lot R.
Rhône R.
GUIENNE
QUERCY
Garonne R.
Albi
Avignon
Montpellier
Toulouse
Aigues-Mortes
PROVENCE
TOULOUSE
LANGUEDOC
Béziers
Carcassonne
Marseilles
Pamiers
Narbonne

PYRENEES MTS.
MEDITERRANEAN SEA

167

was conventionally pious, but he spent far too much time indulging in aristocratic pleasures, such as hunting. Nonetheless, the government created by his forebears was sufficiently sophisticated by the time of his accession to endure the relative indifference he had for administration. The fifteen years of Philip the Bold's reign were not a period of decline but a hiatus in the development of the monarchy.

Philip IV the Fair (1295–1314) was a worthy descendant of the Capetian line. This is judged not from any deep insight into his character, which is obscured by a paucity of pertinent evidence, but from his policies (assuming they were his and not those of his counselors), which were revolutionary in many of their consequences. The personal quality of his sons, the last three direct Capetians, is more difficult to gauge, owing to the brevity of their reigns (1314–1328).

By and large, then, the seven men and one woman who ruled France either as monarchs or as regent from 1223 through 1328 were extremely competent. The exceptions (or possible exceptions) did not rule long enough to have a negative effect on the "progress" of the monarchy. The problems faced by all of them, however, were enormously difficult, so difficult that even a brief interruption in the quality of rulership might have been fatal to the development of central government and the stability of the realm.

First, there was the task of integrating into the kingdom the conquests of Philip II Augustus and his son, the future Louis VIII. The classic example is Normandy, which was allowed to maintain its peculiar institutions, with the exception of the pound sterling as currency, as long as the province remained loyal. This meant that the judicial Exchequer, located at Caen, would continue to serve as the court of last resort in Normandy and that it would continue to apply the law of the Norman custumals. It meant, too, that the financial Exchequer, located at Rouen, would continue to serve as the final auditor of Norman income, obedient to Norman methods and terms of collection. But the men who ran these institutions, from the top nearly to the bottom, were Frenchmen in the narrow sense of that word, men from the Île-de-France and the Gâtinais. (The king of France himself assumed the title duke of Normandy.) Not until the end of the thirteenth century were Normans permitted to serve in the high administration of their own province.

The method was successful, as measured by the only test relevant to the politics of conquest in the thirteenth century: Normandy remained loyal.

Moreover, without a great deal of pressure, certain of its peculiar legal and institutional forms withered away. The jury gave way to the inquest form of judicial inquiry. The writ and action of novel disseisin ceased to be employed in Norman courts by the end of the century. Other institutions and modes of administrative behavior flourished in the province and made the French intensely aware of the inadequacies of their administration elsewhere. Thus, the Norman system of territorial baillis and subordinates was adopted throughout the royal domain. It was Philip Augustus who oversaw this adoption, but the practice was to be repeated by future French kings. The pattern of maintaining local institutions (those, at least, that were not an affront to the royal dignity), of having Frenchmen run them, and of adopting their best features for the whole country was to be used in every major accretion to the royal domain.

The Normandy of the thirteenth century was a rich land. The ducal estates, now in the hands of the French king, were extensive and especially abundant in forest properties. Rights of lordship were strong and the financial advantages that came with such rights were considerable. Taxes on sales of timber (the *tiers* and *danger*) were a particularly valuable addition to the royal income. In total, nearly half of the French royal income by the mid thirteenth century came from Normandy. By the end of the Capetian period, as a result of the continued enlargement of the royal domain, this proportion decreased, but it was always a substantial part of crown revenue.

The Capetians' success with Normandy (and their more limited success with the other Plantagenet fiefs) was not immediately duplicated in their annexation of the south (Languedoc). Louis VIII had inflicted a crushing military defeat on the region, but resistance was not eliminated. The military governors of the south were—perhaps they had to be—ruthless in accomplishing the one task they were supposed to accomplish: even a hint of rebellion led to stiff reprisals and confiscation of property. Many leaders of the opposition, such as the viscount of Béziers, Raymond-Roger Trencavel, chose to bide their time in exile. In 1229, as a result of the Treaty of Paris, the fortunes of the south, from the perspective of native leaders, seemed to be at their lowest ebb. The provisions of that treaty called for the inheritance of the county of Toulouse, the premier principality in the south, by Count Raymond VII's daughter. She was to be married to Alphonse of Poitiers, brother of Louis IX.

For years the settlement of 1229 provided the

basis of royal policy in the south. It was supplemented, of course, by the religious policy of the Dominican inquisitors, seeking out heresy (with its political taint) and strengthening the information-gathering potential of the French government. Royal support for Dominican houses was closely tied to this mission. But no one was misled into thinking that the south would easily succumb to this political and religious pressure. Occasionally there were assassinations accompanied by localized revolts, as in Narbonne in 1237, but the first major confrontation came in 1240, when the rebel Trencavel came out of exile to raise the standard of opposition. In a brutal campaign royal representatives in the south suppressed the rebellion.

Meanwhile, the king's brother Alphonse had reached majority and was to be invested with the county of Poitou as his appanage. (The appanage system was designed to endow cadet princes of the royal family with considerable landed property; its institution was the idea of Louis VIII.) Poitevin barons and other southwesterners and southerners naturally looked upon this event as the beginning of the end of their independence. Again the standard of rebellion was raised, this time doubly dangerous owing to English support. At the end of July 1242, however, at Saintes and Taillebourg, the French under Louis IX inflicted a major and, as it turned out, decisive blow to the rebels and their English allies. The southwest and south now lay open to much more profound penetration by northern culture than ever before.

In late 1244, after nearly two years of meticulously exacting oaths of submission to the settlement of 1229 from the former rebels and working out a truce with the English, the king took the cross. The dangers latent in this policy were averted somewhat by his determination that the leaders of the rebellion join him on the crusade. The crusaders did not take ship until August 1248 and later, but when they did so, it was from a new port, a new symbol of royal preeminence in the south, Aigues-Mortes. The local representatives of royal authority compelled lords who had been in opposition to the king to contribute men and materiel for the construction of the port.

During the crusade problems foreseen by astute people in the royal government did arise, but they were of less consequence than might have been supposed. The English, for example, despite papal remonstrances, were not averse to threatening the lands of the crusading French king. But the English monarch, Henry III, had already lost credibility with

his barons. When the crusade failed in 1250, there was an abortive rising in Languedoc, but it was put down easily by the king's men. Partly, the stability of the south during 1248–1254 was a result of the disastrous events of the early 1240's. Partly, it was the result of the dearth of leadership owing to death (the count of Toulouse, for instance, died in 1249 and his county was taken up by the proctors of Alphonse of Poitiers with minimal difficulty) or to the absence of many native barons on the crusade. But the stability of the south was ensured principally by the *enquêteurs,* investigators sent out to receive and adjudicate complaints against the royal administration. Here, at last, was a vehicle for southern complaints—a very sympathetic vehicle, to judge from the decisions of the investigators.

Contrasting the situation in the south with that in the north is informative. Not all northern barons were eager supporters of an increasingly authoritarian Capetian mode of rulership. Nonetheless, many accepted the new order. In any case, the barons constituted only one element of "public opinion." The communes (administratively independent towns) of the north were devoted to the monarchy and had long looked to it as an ally in their struggles with the feudatories. They gave generous benevolences to the crown on the eve of and during the crusade. Churchmen, it is true, felt abused when the king extracted money from them for the crusade and by his occasional refusals to back them in their own conflicts with the baronage. On the whole, however, they looked upon the king as the protector of their interests and were zealous to elevate his dignity. The peasantry had its grievances, of course—not the least of which was the problem of the requisition of their goods during royal progresses—but in general it had an idealized view of the monarchy. While some elements in Languedoc saw Louis IX's defeat and capture in 1250 as the opportunity for a revolt, in the north the news of the crusaders' fate gave birth to a new "crusade"—the crusade of the shepherds *(pastoureaux)*—intended to rescue the sovereign and redeem the glory of his arms.

In many ways Louis IX's first crusade was indeed a touchstone of the monarchy. The demands put on both the clerical and the lay populations to support the war with a great deal of money and the absence of the monarch from 1248 to 1254, during which time the institutions of the central administration might have collapsed, were real tests for the royal government. In the north as in the south, however, the reforming *enquêteurs,* many of whom were

Franciscan and Dominican friars, defused latent discontent on the eve of the king's expedition.

The temporary defusing of discontent was but the first step in the evocation of real loyalty from the population. The problem, to be sure, was less profound in the north than in the south. Yet even in Languedoc the promise of good government was fulfilled. When Louis IX returned from the crusade in 1254, he began to meet with nobles, prelates, and urban elites in the region and to listen to their complaints. Soon the *enquêteurs* were at work again, making restitution for illegal seizures that had taken place during the Albigensian crusades and the subsequent revolts, seeking out widows and orphans who had been ill-treated under the French regime, giving compensation to those who had suffered as a result of the building of Aigues-Mortes, and removing officials who were guilty of atrocities. The last sixteen years of the reign of Louis IX are a watershed in the history of the south. Fifty years of hostility gave way to decades of loyalty and, as it turned out, still greater opportunities for French penetration. That penetration had the happy result of fostering an awareness in the monarchy of the excellence of the traditional judicial organization in the south, which in turn became the blueprint for modifications in judicial organization throughout the realm.

In the north, where the king spent most of the remainder of his reign, striking developments in government took place. Immediately on his return to Paris in 1254, Louis undertook a systematic inquiry into the quality of local officials, sending out *enquêteurs* and going out himself. Concomitantly he issued a set of regulations, based perhaps on the problems identified by the pre-crusade reports of the *enquêteurs,* designed to improve the administration of the provinces. These regulations focused on the baillis and seneschals. Also in the period 1254–1270 the Parlement of Paris was more carefully organized. This did not lead to the depersonalization of the royal court, however, for Louis was nearly always present at its sessions and often interfered, to the disapproval of the more professional jurists, in its decisions.

During the last part of the reign there was also an attempt to moderate the deleterious effects of the right of hospitality exacted by the monarchy and by ecclesiastics throughout the realm. A new program providing powerful social and economic incentives for the voluntary conversion of the Jews went into effect. Meanwhile, the administration of Paris was subjected to a thoroughgoing reform; and eventu-

ally, in the late 1250's and early 1260's, urban administration at large underwent a thorough scrutiny in an attempt to eliminate corruption and extravagance in government. Indeed, practically no area was left untouched by the reformist king: There was a fundamental reform of the royal coinage; royal charity achieved a new importance; relations with the church (somewhat strained in the 1240's) improved. Behind it all was a restless king, always trying to do as much of the work of government as he possibly could, always looking forward to a new crusade that would succeed, he felt, if he could only show himself to be a decent ruler.

In most of the policies outlined above, the king enjoyed more or less success (though the Eighth Crusade, on which he died, did not live up to his dreams). Nonetheless, this review of the growth of France and the influence of the monarchy should not obscure lingering problems or dangerous peculiarities. The appanage system was potentially dangerous, and only fortune prevented the danger from coming to the surface in the thirteenth century. For example, when Alphonse of Poitiers, who controlled Poitou, Auvergne, and, after 1249, Toulouse, died without heirs in 1271, the inheritance escheated to the crown. Charles of Anjou, another of Louis IX's brothers, maintained only a financial interest in Maine and Anjou, his appanage; he played out his spectacular career largely in Mediterranean politics. Robert I of Artois, still another of the king's brothers, died in 1250 on the Seventh Crusade; during the minority of his son and for some decades thereafter, royal influence was paramount in Artois. Moreover, except for the original grants of appanages, the areas turned over to subsequent cadet princes in the thirteenth century (though not later) tended to be much smaller and less strategic.

The great fiefs posed another problem. Here again, however, luck was on the side of the monarchy in the thirteenth century. Purchase brought the Mâconnais into the royal orbit in 1239. Marriage brought Provence under the friendly dominance of a cadet branch of the dynasty in 1246, and it brought Champagne into the domain by 1285. The Burgundian duke married a daughter of St. Louis; and although this was no assurance of his or his progeny's loyalty, fortunately for the monarchy the Burgundians were the most devoted of the great feudatories through the thirteenth century. Brittany had been forced to accept Capetian suzerainty in the 1230's, when the Breton count, Peter Mauclerc, had supported the unsuccessful efforts of other northern barons to seize power. Brittany remained a feisty region, but no real threat to the crown. Flanders, too, was taught a military lesson by the French under Philip the Fair in the early fourteenth century that led to the recognition of French suzerainty and to the incorporation of the southern part of the county (so-called French Flanders) into the domain.

The widening of the influence of the monarchy went hand in hand, though perhaps unconsciously in the beginning, with a greater precision in defining the territorial extent of France in the thirteenth century. The boundaries of the kingdom became much less complicated. The Treaty of Corbeil (1258) established the Pyrenees as the southern limit (Montpellier remained a possession of the Aragonese monarch but was eventually purchased). The Lyonnais came under French domination in the reign of Philip the Fair. Indeed, the whole eastern rim of lordships began to be drawn more closely into the French orbit during his reign. Under St. Louis barons of this region already looked to the Capetian king as the arbiter of their disputes; by Philip the Fair's time the lawyers involved in central government saw the imposition of such an "appellate" jurisdiction in the king's Parlement as a positive enhancement of the royal sovereignty. Steeped in the Roman law, these lawyers were used to thinking of power in these terms (though it should be noted that the Roman law, as it was interpreted in the Middle Ages, could be as antagonistic to as it was supportive of princely absolutism).

English Gascony alone remained as a major incongruous element in the growth of the kindgom. Here too, however, there was an attempt to absorb the region. For reasons that will always be obscure, Philip the Fair felt compelled in 1294 to go to war with Edward I of England over the question of jurisdiction in Gascony. In 1259 the Treaty of Paris had recognized Gascony as a possession of the English king in return for an unequivocal acknowledgment of his feudal dependency. But the terms of the treaty were not clear enough, nor were the issues involved bland enough, to forestall conflict. That the conflict should have been violent is more difficult to explain. Possibly it was the personality of the French monarch, still young and wanting to make a name for himself, that gave all his policies a somewhat adventurist character. Whatever the case, neither side got anything out of the war—except a quarrel with the papacy.

The issue was taxation for the defense of the realm. Even though the average annual revenues of the French crown had doubled from about 200,000 pounds to more than 400,000 pounds since the mid century, they were insufficient for a prolonged war. The clergy, normally exempt, would have to contribute in an emergency. But could the clergy be taxed without papal permission? Both kings argued for such taxation; the pope, against it. Philip the Fair's strong reaction to this interference, as he saw it, induced Pope Boniface VIII eventually to concede the point. But Philip's reaction went deeper. The papacy had historically called upon the French monarchy when it was in trouble; and the French, in spite of an occasional hesitancy, had usually come to its aid: against England when King John refused to respond to the interdict; against the Albigensian heretics when their reluctance to submit to papal persuasion became manifest; against Emperor Frederick II when he threatened the pope in the 1240's; against the Hohenstaufen when their control of Sicily in the 1250's seemed a challenge to the popes; and against the Aragonese when they upset the situation in Sicily in 1282. But the Aragonese crusade of 1285 (the French response to the last of these crises) was an unmitigated military disaster. Philip had been there; his father had died on the ill-fated expedition; and like the world at large, the young king must have blamed the failure on the papacy and its politics.

Moreover, by the time of the struggle over taxation, the papacy was in the hands of a notorious factionalist. The Capetians had not yet gone so far in 1294 as to glory unrelievedly in the reports of Boniface VIII's degeneracy, but such reports could not have been unknown to them. Had Boniface stolen the papacy from the saintly hermit Celestine V? In contrast with the pope, the French king was elevated by the dynastic myth, fully accepted in the thirteenth century, that he was the heir of Charlemagne, that he was crowned with oil come down from heaven in the mouth of a dove, and that the French dynasty was blessed with a veritable saint, Louis IX. True, the canonization proceedings for Louis were slow, but everyone knew Philip's grandfather was a saint. In 1297, to end the dispute between himself and the French king, Boniface VIII finally brought the canonization process to a successful culmination.

In the royal ideology associated with the reign of Philip the Fair, several elements are found: the French king is the true representative of Jesus Christ on earth; the French king is a wonder-worker, healing the sick by touch; the French people are the chosen people ruled by the most Christian ruler; to die for France is a sublime opportunity. How much of this was believed, it is hard to say, but such sentiments were frequently used to justify some otherwise unjustifiable policies. Again, the most famous involved Boniface VIII, for the pope, having extricated himself from the dispute over taxation but feeling the exhilaration of the first Holy Year, 1300, became less careful, perhaps, in his political relations with the French. The arrest of Bishop Bernard Saisset of Pamiers for treason in 1301 led the pope to make the most extreme statements about the immunity of churchmen and the power of the pope. An insulting war of words began. The Estates were convoked for the first time to witness the monarch's wrath and to be harangued about French excellence and papal depravity. Churchmen were coerced into remonstrating with the pope; they found the coercion tolerable partly because of the pope's reputation and partly because of their own belief in the French monarchy. Finally, Guillaume de Nogaret hit upon a radical solution: arrest the pope and put him on trial. The kidnapping of Boniface at Anagni, his rescue by the populace, his death and the death of his successor, leading eventually to the election of a French archbishop, Bertrand de Got, as Pope Clement V, and the Babylonian Captivity are well known.

This was assuredly the high point of Philip the Fair's reign—if only the extent of his influence and prestige are being assessed. The monarch whose religion, as he saw it, was sounder than the pope's followed his success against Boniface with the expulsion of the Jews in 1306 and the seizure of their chattels. A little later he turned his attention against the Templars in one of the most sordid episodes of Capetian history. Through torture and perjury, "evidence" of Templar complicity in the most repugnant acts was gathered, leading—with the reluctant support of Clement V—to the suppression of the order, the confiscation and redistribution of its property, and the execution of its leaders. Yet the financial benefit of this action to the monarchy seems to have been far less than had been expected.

None of Philip the Fair's efforts would have been successful without a towering sense of his own and his family's moral rectitude. The great shock to this belief was the adultery of his daughters-in-law, a scandal that chastened the prematurely aging king and complicated the succession for his sons' children. Philip did not live to hear the stories of his daughter's adulterous escapades in England, where, as the wife of Edward II, she had been intended to cement peace between the two countries. Philip died in 1314, unsure about the quality of his rulership (if

his deathbed utterances are recorded accurately) and profoundly uncertain whether he had lived up to the model set by St. Louis.

His successors were his three sons, Louis X, Philip V, and Charles IV. They left no acceptable heirs: their daughters were excluded because the accession of any one of them would have meant the elevation of the baronial house of her husband, and their sons died in infancy. These last three Capetians lived under the twin burden of the memory of St. Louis and the memory of Philip the Fair. It was difficult to formulate royal policies consistent with the idealized moral tone of the government of the saint-king while pushing—pushing relentlessly and ruthlessly, if necessary—in the direction of aggrandizing the kingdom in the tradition of their father, Philip the Fair. It was certainly possible in theory to reconcile these two goals. Whatever a holy monarchy attempted might be considered holy in itself. But there were problems with this facile equation. The Capetians had put inordinate demands on their government and people. Opponents were beginning to appear everywhere. Any weakness at the summit portended vociferous criticism somewhere down the political or social hierarchy.

Philip the Fair's reign had ended in a flurry of rebellion, amid demands for charters of liberty, when still another war with the Flemings—and another wave of taxation—loomed. Resistance was strong. Louis X the Quarrelsome (1314–1316) had little time in his brief reign to assuage the popular discontent but did his best to return to the days of St. Louis, repudiating those counselors who were associated with the excesses of his father's last years. When he died, he did so in the grand Capetian manner, making restitution for his injuries and giving such lavish bequests as to threaten the ability of his successor to govern.

Both Philip V the Tall (1316–1322) and Charles IV the Fair (1322–1328) were faced with similar problems: uncertainty over the succession, a need to devise a systematic mode of taxation, and the desire to live up to the traditional moral demands of French kingship. Philip was less successful than Charles (especially portentous was the failure, in 1321, of his plan to use the Estates as an institution for taxation). Charles IV was particularly astute in making do with revenues of an extraordinary nature (seizures of the chattels of the returned Jews and of the profits of Italian bankers, for example). He was also successful in restoring a good deal of the moral image of the monarchy. Even in war—in Guienne and Flanders—

he enjoyed temporary military successes without exciting, by his modest taxation, the rebellious opposition of his subjects. During peaceful interludes he refrained from exacting subsidies, obedient to the principle that when the cause of the subsidy ceases, the subsidy itself must cease. Below the surface, of course, historians can see unresolved major problems; but to the educated or influential Frenchman of 1328, the year of Charles's death, the monarchy strengthened by Philip Augustus, hallowed by Louis IX, and made conscious of its destiny by Philip the Fair, seemed to have weathered the stormiest period in a century with little loss of prestige.

A recurring question in the historiography is whether and to what extent the monarchy thus far described can properly be called feudal. In fact, throughout the period 1223–1328 most of the income of the French monarchy was probably generated from what should not strictly be called feudal sources, such as aids. This does not mean that aids or other feudal sources of revenue were unimportant, or even that "feudal" ought to be taken in so strict a sense (how should the subventions from the towns, which were indifferently known as aids or gifts through most of the century, be categorized?) But these difficulties do raise problems. To look at the issue another way, the feudal army—if by that is meant the service rendered by feudatories—was always second in importance in the thirteenth century to soldiers hired directly. Certainly, then, the military organization of the Capetian polity does not justify the adjective "feudal."

The discussions of justice and sovereignty that characterize the last century of Capetian rule also had no particularly feudal savor. Baronial justice was being eroded by the pretensions of the monarchy to supervise and seize jurisdictions where failure of justice occurred. Feudal notions of justice (allied closely with the idea of private war and the judicial duel) were being steadily undermined by royal legislation. Nascent ideas of sovereignty, of course, began with the feudal notion of suzerainty; but they went far beyond that notion. The reassertion of regalian rights—for example, over coinage—was directly at variance with traditional feudalism and indicates that traditional divisions of authority and power were breaking down.

Some historians see the distinction as one between a first stage of feudalism (the fragmentation of public authority before Philip Augustus) and a second stage of feudalism, the so-called feudal monarchy, the creation of a network of hierarchical relationships culminating in a strong king and the concomitant creation of a "bureaucracy" as a counterweight to particularism. Whether this characterization is accurate has been disputed; and the word "feudalism" has been used in so many other ways than these that some have suggested abandoning the term altogether.

One thing seems clear: to characterize the political entity ruled by the king of the Franks in the thirteenth century as a state is certainly erroneous. Yet again the century is peculiar, for it was precisely in these hundred years that the foundations of the modern state were laid. Moreover, since the French model of state building was for long the dominant model, it seems legitimate to inquire into the institutional history of the thirteenth-century monarchy at some length. Some of the more dramatic features of French governance have already been made clear but need restating: an authoritarian monarchy; the realization that some respect had to be paid to local institutions; an aversion to local people actually running these institutions at the highest levels; and intermittent submission of local officials and local jurisdictions to special investigation.

Never did these methods work perfectly. Difficulties of dialect made some use of natives absolutely essential, for example. Special investigators, such as the mendicant *enquêteurs* of St. Louis, when used often enough or when drawn from a more traditional pool of personnel than the friars, became little more than fiscal officials. Nonetheless, these methods of administration were constantly remembered when government seemed to need revitalization. Again the glue that held the patchwork of jurisdictions together was the appellate system (unnecessary for Normandy, where the king became duke). The idea of the Parlement of Paris as the highest court, specifically the court of highest resort, was insisted upon with vehemence as the century progressed. Every augmentation of appellate jurisdiction was an augmentation of territorial authority, thus of judicial sovereignty, and thus of the authoritarian monarchy.

These aspects of French government were not peculiar to France, but they were emphasized under the Capetians to a degree seldom attained elsewhere in the West. They rested, of course, partly upon more common modes of governance. There were household officials in France, as one example, but the danger such people posed had made itself manifest before 1223, with the result that the household offices under the later Capetians, when they were not simply left vacant, were stripped of nearly all their power. The afforced council, to take another example, was surely a feature of French government, but it never took institutional form until the Estates of 1302; and though there were attempts to use such assemblies in ways made familiar by the Plantagenet use of the English Parliament, the results were quite disappointing for the French before 1328. As might be expected, therefore, local estates, under the careful scrutiny of royal officials, more or less displaced the central assembly. The specialized parts of the council were also slow to develop in France. A separate treasury (*chambre des comptes*) was not fully realized until the late thirteenth century. When it did come into existence, its personnel represented a new, more aggressive, even more authoritarian element in politics and administration. This was the only way they could hope to have influence.

Government in the last century of Capetian rule may therefore be characterized as essentially authoritarian, though by no means arbitrary. There were no parliamentary constraints—in the judicial or the constitutional sense of that word. Every policy and every justification for every policy radiated from the center, from a king (or his advisers speaking in his name) surrounded with an aura of holiness, the defender, according to the propaganda, of all that was best. Fundamental restraints, however, certainly existed: the fear after 1270 of criticism, even of rebellion, for failing to rule in the manner of St. Louis; the need always to take counsel (though not necessarily in an institutional framework like the English Parliament); and the need to be respectful of tradition and local custom.

The events between 1223 and 1328 briefly outlined above did not take place in a social vacuum. The last century of the Capetians saw important developments in many areas of French life, some intimately tied to political developments. In agriculture the fundamental social and juridical development was the gradual emancipation of the peasantry and the strengthening of customary tenure. These changes were encouraged both by rural landlords and by the monarchy, partly as an acknowledgment of the inefficiency of servile labor and partly as a measure for raising revenue, since servile peasants always paid large sums for their manumission. Serfdom did not disappear, but it became much less prevalent in many areas, such as the Sénonais.

Another development the significance of which can hardly be overestimated was the complete displacement of the old Auxerrois wine-growing region, with its mercantile ties to Flanders and England, by the Bordeaux wine-growing district, which was under the control of the English. This development should not be considered in isolation from two other great economic facts: the decline in the importance of the fairs of Champagne and the beginning of a horribly persistent depression perhaps as early as 1285.

The direct influence of the monarchy on economic life was minimal by modern standards, but in at least one area it was profound. The government of Philip the Fair, more than any other, debased the coinage for temporary financial gain, which led to severe inflation in the 1290's and a more modest but still significant increase in prices around 1311. This policy, sometimes regretted by Philip, was considered morally reprehensible by those who cast nostalgic glances back to the sound coinage of St. Louis.

Perhaps the central fact of economic life, however, was the final leveling off of population by 1300 or slightly thereafter. The steady demographic increase since approximately 1100—largely confined to the countryside—was over. Whether France (the population of which is estimated as high as 16 million in 1300) was overpopulated is quite another matter. Marginal land, from which the surplus was dangerously low even in a good year, was certainly under cultivation. But it is probable that this population might have been sustained indefinitely had it not been for a general shift downward in average temperatures by two or so degrees. The shift probably explains, for example, the veritable end of profitable viticulture in England. The famine of 1315–1317 and the consequent decline in population in France to a slightly lower equilibrium have also been associated by some with the shift in the weather cycle.

The change in urban population probably followed the rural curve in general. There were, of course, exceptions. Paris was undoubtedly growing at a faster pace. The best data on population in the city come from the taille lists of the very late thirteenth century and the early fourteenth century. One estimate is that the population of the capital at its maximum reached approximately 200,000. Evidence suggests that other towns experienced more in-migration than out-migration, but there are few signs of spectacular urban growth. Except for the relatively large cities on the Mediterranean littoral (Marseilles and Montpellier, for example), urban population in the range 1,000 to 5,000 was most common.

Social, economic, and political developments in

the towns are more easily documented than demographic shifts. The thirteenth century witnessed the evolution of the communes in the north of France into municipal oligarchies with problems of administration that prompted royal interference at the mid century and ultimately led to the weakening of communal independence and the strengthening of royal power. Paris underwent, in the thirteenth and early fourteenth centuries, a major period of building stimulated largely by the royal government, and a fundamental systematization of mercantile life under the royal *prévôt,* Étienne Boileau, *ca.* 1260. Southern cities and towns—at least those actually in the royal domain—were frequently subjected to direct royal intervention in their affairs, particularly when their loyalty was in question. Finally, a number of new towns, the vast majority of ephemeral importance, came into existence in the course of the century. Perhaps the most significant of these was the port of Aigues-Mortes.

The culture of the thirteenth century was very much a city culture and depended on the vitality of city life for its success. But that success has frequently been characterized and implicitly criticized as synthetic rather than original. In this view the original achievements of the twelfth century were merely being routinized and integrated into the fabric of Christian culture during the next century. The University of Paris was instrumental in this effort. Indeed, the synthesis that occurred in the thirteenth century would have been unthinkable without the flourishing of theological studies at Paris under the mendicant masters, Aquinas and Bonaventure. But education and systematization of knowledge flourished elsewhere as well—at schools and universities in Orléans, Toulouse, and Montpellier, and at the royal court with a man like Vincent of Beauvais (mid thirteenth century).

If, however, it can be said that the thirteenth century was an age of synthesis, and if many names (such as Vincent of Beauvais) and many books (such as the *Summa theologiae*) can be cited in defense of this proposition, nonetheless the very act of synthesis in the period was extraordinarily creative. Nearly every major monument of high culture—literary, liturgical, or architectural—speaks both to the past, as the culmination of clear traditions, and to a promising future: the Sainte Chapelle in Paris, the *Romance of the Rose,* the chronicles of St. Denis, the *Coutumes de Beauvaisis* of Philippe de Beaumanoir.

Underneath the confidence so well expressed by the proliferation of summae, there were peculiarly strident and often conflicting voices raised against this comfortable world. The secular party of the University of Paris had been raising serious questions since the mid century about the validity of the mendicant mode of piety and the propriety of the friars' Aristotelian theology. Criticism of the crusades, especially against Christians, became a major tendency in satirical expression. Indeed, from the critics' point of view, even St. Louis's expeditions were outmoded and a waste of resources.

But most serious, perhaps, was criticism of the Christian life as lived by prelate and layperson alike. In one sense the Cathars were the most radical critics. Even though they were being effectively eliminated by military power and the Inquisition in the thirteenth century, the criticisms they made against worldliness were expressed, sometimes in nearly as radical form, throughout France and gave rise to a search for a new or, rather, a truly primitive spirituality. This helps explain not only the attraction, in many quarters, for the traditional mendicant orders in France, but also the rapid expansion of the beguine movement among French women and what was seen as the dangerous multiplication of less well-organized mendicant orders until their "suppression" by the Second Council of Lyons in 1274. In the early fourteenth century groups of holy men and women in open conflict with ecclesiastical and lay authorities were a persistent and disturbing fact of life.

But, again, just as the first decades of the new century seemed, in political history, to be only a brief interruption in the advance of French rulership, so in most other areas of French life of which there is evidence, the era of the last direct Capetians was characterized by an underlying optimism. There were problems, to be sure, but the history of the past hundred years had shown that problems could be faced—indeed, could be solved. There were a few great verities in the world, a few certainties, such as the glory of France, which would never pass away. Such must have been the feeling of many, perhaps the majority of educated and influential French men and women on the eve of the greatest series of crises Europe had known since the Viking age.

BIBLIOGRAPHY

On the reigns of the French kings. Jean Favier, *Philippe le Bel* (1978); William Jordan, *Louis IX and the Challenge of the Crusade* (1979); Charles-Victor Langlois, *Règne de Philippe III le Hardi* (1887); Paul Lehugeur, *Histoire de Philippe le Long* (1897), and *Philippe le Long, roi de France*

(1931); Charles Petit-Dutaillis, *Étude sur la vie et le règne de Louis VIII* (1894); Jean Richard, *Saint Louis* (1983); Gérard Sivery, *Saint Louis et son siècle* (1983); Joseph R. Strayer, *The Reign of Philip the Fair* (1980).

General histories. Robert Fawtier, *The Capetian Kings of France,* Lionel Butler and R. J. Adam, trans. (1960); Elizabeth Hallam, *Capetian France, 987–1328* (1980); Charles Petit-Dutaillis, *Feudal Monarchy in France and England,* E. Hunt, trans. (1936).

Institutional history. Leon Borrelli de Serres, *Recherches sur divers services publics du XIIIᵉ au XVIIᵉ siècles,* 3 vols. (1895–1909); Léopold Delisle, *Recueil des historiens des Gaules et de la France,* XXIV (1904); James Fesler, "French Field Administration: The Beginnings," in *Comparative Studies in Society and History,* 5 (1962–1963); Arthur Giry, *Manuel de diplomatique* (1894); Henri Hervieu, *Recherches sur les premiers états généraux et les assemblées représentatives pendant la première moitié du XIVᵉ siècle* (1879); Ferdinand Lot and Robert Fawtier, *Histoire des institutions françaises au moyen âge,* 3 vols. (1957–1963); Robert Michel, *L'administration royale dans la sénechaussée de Beaucaire au temps de saint Louis* (1910); James Shennan, *The Parlement of Paris* (1968); Joseph R. Strayer, *The Administration of Normandy Under Saint Louis* (1932, repr. 1971), *Medieval Statecraft and the Perspectives of History,* foreword by Gaines Post (1971), and *Les Gens de justice du Languedoc sous Philippe le Bel* (1970); Henri Waquet, *Le Bailliage de Vermandois aux XIIIᵉ et XIVᵉ siècles* (1919); Charles Wood, *The French Apanages and the Capetian Monarchy, 1224–1328* (1966).

Fiscal matters. Léopold Delisle, "Les Opérations financières des Templiers," in *Mémoires de l'Académie des inscriptions et belles-lettres,* 33 (1889); Jean Favier, *Un Conseiller de Philippe le Bel: Enguerran de Marigny* (1963); John Henneman, *Royal Taxation in Fourteenth Century France: the Development of War Financing, 1322–1356* (1971); Adolphe Landry, *Essai économique sur les mutations des monnaies dans l'ancienne France de Philippe le Bel à Charles VII* (1910); Joseph R. Strayer and Charles Taylor, *Studies in Early French Taxation* (1939).

Local studies. Thomas Bisson, *Assemblies and Representation in Languedoc in the Thirteenth Century* (1964); Edgard Boutaric, *Saint Louis et Alfonse de Poitiers* (1870); Richard Emery, *Heresy and Inquisition in Narbonne* (1941); Joseph Vaissète and Claude de Vic, eds., 2nd ed., A. Molinier, ed., *Histoire générale de Languedoc,* 16 vols. (1872–1904).

Heresy. Jean Guiraud, *Histoire de l'Inquisition au moyen âge,* 2 vols. (1935–1938); Emmanuel Le Roy Ladurie, *Montaillou, village occitan, de 1294 à 1324* (1976); Joseph R. Strayer, *The Albigensian Crusades* (1971); Walter Wakefield, *Heresy, Crusade and Inquisition in Southern France, 1100–1250* (1974).

Urban history. Raymond Cazelles, *Nouvelle histoire de Paris* (1972); Georges Duby, ed., *Histoire de la France urbaine,* II (1980); Charles Petit-Dutaillis, *Les communes françaises* (1947).

Religion. Elie Berger, *Saint Louis et Innocent IV* (1893); Robert Chazan, *Medieval Jewry in Northern France: A Political and Social History* (1973); Richard Emery, *The Friars in Medieval France: A Catalogue of French Mendicant Convents, 1200–1550* (1962); Simon Vigor, *Histoire du differend d'entre le pape Boniface VIII et Philippe le Bel* (1655).

Economic history. Elizabeth Chapin, *Les Villes de foires de Champagne* (1937); Roger Dion, *Histoire de la vigne et du vin en France dès origines au XIXᵉ siècle* (1959); Georges Duby, *Société aux XIᵉ et XIIᵉ siècles dans la region mâconnaise* (1953); Robert Fossier, *La Terre et les hommes en Picardie,* 2 vols. (1968); Georges Duby, ed., *Histoire de la France rurale,* I, *La Formation des campagnes françaises dès origines au XIVᵉ siècle* (1975).

Law. Joseph Declareuil, *Histoire générale du droit français dès origines à 1789* (1925); Franklin Pegues, *The Lawyers of the Last Capetians* (1962); Gaines Post, *Studies in Medieval Legal Thought* (1965).

Royal ceremony and ideology. Marc Bloch, *The Royal Touch: Sacred Monarchy and Scrofula in England and France,* J. E. Anderson, trans. (1973); Ralph Giesey, *The Juristic Basis of Dynastic Right to the French Throne,* in *Transactions of the American Philosophical Society,* n. s. **51,** pt. 5 (1961); Ernst Kantorowicz, *Laudes regiae: A Study in Liturgical Acclamations and Medieval Ruler Worship* (1946), and *The King's Two Bodies: A Study in Medieval Political Theology* (1957); Percy Schramm, *Der König von Frankreich,* 2 vols. (1939).

Feudal monarchy. Thomas Bisson, "The Problem of Feudal Monarchy: Aragon, Catalonia, and France," in *Speculum,* 53 (1978); Elizabeth Brown, "Feudalism: The Tyranny of a Construct," in *American Historical Review,* 79 (1974); Joseph R. Strayer, *On the Medieval Origins of the Modern State* (1970).

WILLIAM CHESTER JORDAN

[See also **Albigensians; Appanages; Aquinas, St. Thomas; Babylonian Captivity; Bailli; Beguines and Beghards; Bonaventure, St.; Brittany; Cathars; Commune; Crusades and Crusader States; Languedoc; Louis IX of France; Normans and Normandy; Parlement, French; Toulouse, City and County.**]

FRANCE: 1314–1494. Political historians associate 1314 with the death of Philip IV of France, but for many contemporaries the most important characteristic of the year may have been the cold, wet weather that caused a crop failure and subsequent famine in Europe.

DEMOGRAPHIC TRENDS

Despite the difficulty of estimating actual population from surviving sources that enumerate house-

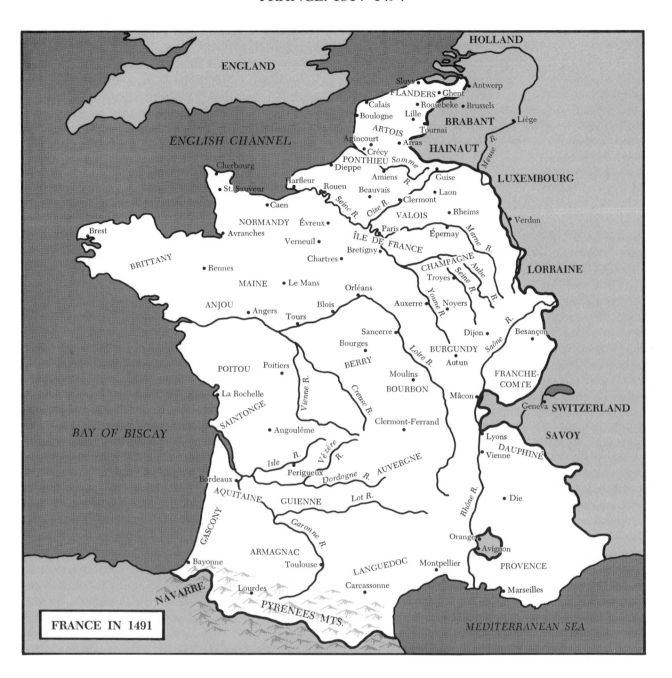

FRANCE IN 1491

holds, it is possible to establish a demographic index and depict the relative populations for certain years. The most successful recent research, based on eastern Normandy, seems to confirm what other local studies have suggested about French demographic trends. The population had been rising slowly for several generations and in 1314 reached its medieval peak, to which can be assigned an index of 100. Production, especially in agriculture, had leveled off well before the population reached this peak. When the crops failed in 1314, a period of rising prices and stagnant production had already left a growing number of people undernourished and barely able to subsist. The severe famine of 1315–1317 led to thousands of deaths in northern France and definitively ended the centuries of medieval demographic growth.

A far more serious demographic disaster, however, occurred in 1348, when the Black Death struck France for the first time. The population index tumbled from about 97 to 70 between 1347 and 1357. The reader must be wary of exaggerated statements about the Black Death, but this first visitation of plague was a genuine disaster in the urban communities it touched. In most rural areas the demographic effect of the plague was indirect. The sharp reduction of urban population meant a diminished demand for agricultural produce, and thus a fall in the peasants' income. In the towns, however, the survivors had more money than before and a greater inclination to spend it. Yet a shortage of artisans accompanied this demand and resulted in rising wages and prices. Unable to pay the higher prices because of the decline in their income, many peasants abandoned their fields and moved to the underpopulated towns, hoping to take advantage of the high wages there. This scenario, repeated after each new epidemic, established a pattern of migration from countryside to town that was given additional impetus by the ravages of war and brigandage in the country. This migration, far more than direct encounters with the plague, accounted for the "deserted villages" of the late Middle Ages.

Recurrences of the plague, notably in 1361 and 1374, attracted less attention from the chroniclers than the epidemic of 1348 and also caused less disruption in the flow of administrative documents. It may be inferred that the adults who had survived the first epidemic had acquired some immunity—psychological as well as physiological—that permitted official life to proceed with less evident dislocation. In the later epidemics a high proportion of the victims were children.

While the urban populations were vulnerable to epidemics, the inhabitants of the countryside were vulnerable to war. The armies of opposing governments were not large and did not inflict heavy casualties on each other in most encounters, but there was a sharp increase in irregular warfare, the great scourge of the peasantry. Civil wars in Normandy and Brittany were especially destructive between 1356 and 1364, while virtually all of France experienced the brigandage of unemployed soldiers, particularly between 1357 and 1370. The towns were physically secure, but their inhabitants were frightened into paying large sums to combat the brigands. Whether they were royal or local taxes or direct bribes to their tormentors, these payments diverted funds from other purposes and were all the more burdensome because the brigands disrupted trade and commerce, the ultimate source of most urban income. The peasants, whose lives and crops were particularly vulnerable to brigandage, received little

protection from the royal army, which in 1359 began to avoid pitched battles with the English invaders. Thereafter the forces of both sides not only lived off the country but also pursued a scorched-earth policy to deny each other vital supplies.

With all these factors at work, the population index continued to fall, and Guy Bois estimates that in eastern Normandy it was no more than 43 in 1380. The fiscal and military history of the period leads to the conclusion that conditions were already improving by that date and that the period of greatest misery may have been the immediate aftermath of the famine and plague of 1374. There seems little doubt that the population actually declined by a greater percentage between 1357 and the mid 1370's than it did in the decade 1347–1357.

The upswing that began in the mid 1370's lasted for nearly forty years and produced an increase of nearly 50 percent in the population index. Both outright war and brigandage subsided in the last quarter of the fourteenth century, and epidemics and crop failures were more local and less severe. The reduced population was better nourished, and for a generation or so the demographic pressure on production subsided.

Toward 1410, however, the factors that had encouraged population growth began to cease operating, while the growth already achieved began to exert new pressure on what remained an essentially stagnant level of production. More frequent crop failures and epidemics, princely civil war, English invasion, and a serious revival of brigandage combined to bring about a new decline in population. The wealthy and populous regions of northwestern France suffered grievously from both the English conquest (the decade after 1415) and the French reconquest (the decade after 1435). Toward the middle of the fifteenth century the population index probably reached its low point for the entire period, dipping below 30 in some places. A substantial recovery followed, but the evidence suggests that the French population in 1494 was only about half that of 1314.

ECONOMIC TRENDS

From the scattered accounts of indirect taxation and other bits of scanty evidence, it appears that prices, wages, and other economic indicators tended to parallel the rise and fall of the demographic index, but only the most cautious statements can be made about wages and prices because the silver currency was subject to extreme fluctuations in this period.

The French money of account was based on the traditional system of pounds, shillings, and pence (*livres, sols,* and *deniers*). Most royal accounts were kept in Parisian pounds, four of which equaled five pounds of the much more widely used Tournois currency. Circulating coins varied in alloy, weight, and official valuation. These variables were combined in a complicated formula called the *pied de monnaie.* The *pied,* divided by four, equaled the number of *livres tournois* minted from one mark of silver that was .958 fine (4,416 grains of silver). Although the *pied,* divided by four, equaled the number of *livres tournois* minted from a mark, the *pied* was always expressed as an ordinal numeral. Thus, when three *livres tournois* were taken from the mark, the money was said to be "on the twelfth *pied.*" If, for instance, the crown struck silver *gros* on the twelfth *pied,* the number of these coins minted from one mark would equal three *livres tournois* in money of account.

The mints were supposed to be self-supporting, so when they had to pay a higher price for silver, the crown felt obliged to raise the *pied.* If the crown wished to make a significant profit from the mints, it might raise the *pied* a great deal more. Raising the *pied* weakened the currency, and generally exerted an inflationary economic impact by increasing the number of coins in circulation. When the crown weakened the currency for its own profit, it was, in effect, levying a concealed tax on those whose wealth was primarily in movable property. Lowering the *pied* strengthened the currency and was regarded as a reform by the moneyed classes though it reduced the money supply. Frequent changes, in whatever direction, came to be widely unpopular and led to a demand for sound money, meaning a relatively stable *pied.*

Aside from complicating the task of interpreting economic data, the changes in the currency were a major political issue in fourteenth-century France. In 1314 the "good money of St. Louis" (based on the twelfth *pied* or three *livres tournois* per mark) was regarded by the public as strong currency, and the government was under attack for having weakened it slightly. Further weakenings began in 1323, but when the silver mark reached six *livres tournois* in 1329, the government reformed the coinage and returned it to the twelfth *pied.* This popular level was maintained with great difficulty for eight years, but some mints had to close because they could not attract silver bullion. After 1337 the currency was se-

riously weakened until 1343, when the mark reached fifteen *livres tournois.* Then the moneyed classes forced a new reform that abruptly strengthened the coinage, restoring the level of three *livres tournois* to the mark. This action created such dislocations as to end forever the nostalgia for the money of St. Louis. The currency crept back to six *livres tournois* per mark, which gradually became the new standard for strong money.

After the Black Death, and especially in the 1350's, the government manipulated the currency incessantly, trying to obtain the largest mint profits while minimizing economic dislocations. Nobody was happy with this policy. Now the subject of bitter debate, the coinage for a time in 1360 was so weak that a mark equaled 100 *livres tournois.* Following an Anglo-French treaty in that year, however, the establishment of regular taxes made it possible to stabilize the silver currency at around six *livres tournois* per mark for about fifty years. Minor weakenings, at wide intervals, to attract bullion to the mints aroused no opposition. Serious new weakenings began around 1410, when France dissolved into civil war, and became acute after 1417. By 1422, in the part of France controlled by Charles VII, the coinage seems to have contained only a tiny amount of silver. Then conditions improved somewhat, but stability was not attained until 1438, by which time "strong money" meant the forty-eighth *pied* (or twelve *livres tournois* per mark of silver). For the rest of the fifteenth century, a very gradual weakening occurred without serious dislocations.

These generalizations neglect the fact that practice sometimes varied from mint to mint. In Normandy, where the inhabitants had long paid a special hearth tax to ensure stable money, and in Languedoc, where the Estates played an active role in granting taxes, the fluctuations of the fourteenth century were much less extreme than elsewhere. After 1420 Anglo-Burgundian France had more monetary stability than Charles VII's lands.

The monetary fluctuations, like the demographic crises, aggravated the severe economic difficulties of the period. The famine of 1315–1317 caused food prices to soar temporarily, but thereafter they slumped and the manorial economy suffered. Large estates abandoned the cultivation of marginal land and in some cases expanded grape production because prices of wine remained higher than those of cereals. The poor harvests of the 1340's doubtless led to undernourishment that made the Black Death more lethal, and slumping agricultural prices recurred in the 1350's. In this period the rural economy was especially vulnerable to the "scissors" effect because industrial goods rose in price, while prices for produce declined.

Despite the destruction of rural capital during the violence of the 1350's and 1360's, the last quarter of the century was marked by a modest economic recovery that paralleled the rising population and stable coinage. Despite a brief but savage reaction against taxation around 1380, the populace generally paid much higher taxes with much less complaint than earlier in the century. Early in the fifteenth century, however, economic conditions began to grow worse, again paralleling the demographic curve. In the next thirty years warfare did severe damage to the rural economy in many parts of the kingdom. The recovery of the mid fifteenth century began with the towns and then spread to the countryside. The rural seigneurs were the last to recoup their losses. Louis XI (1461–1483) was able to levy sharply higher taxes, and French merchants were able to engage in the sort of international ventures once monopolized by the Italians. Louis endeavored to attract back into French territory the trade between the Low Countries and Italy and sponsored the increasingly important fair at Lyons. The French gained new prosperity from silkmaking, printing, and artillery, and Lyons gradually became an important banking center.

CLASSES OF SOCIETY

The fortunes of the French peasantry fluctuated sharply in the fourteenth and fifteenth centuries. Hard hit by undernourishment and "stagflation" at the beginning of the period, they suffered severely from marauding soldiers later on. When these conditions were alleviated in the later fourteenth century, their condition improved. Royal taxation did not yet bear heavily upon them, in part because nobles included their peasant subjects when seeking to claim tax exemption.

Contrary to what historians have usually said, the fourteenth century was not notable for widespread peasant revolts. The *pastoureaux* uprising of 1320 was a brief millenarianist movement confined to the south of France. The *Jacquerie* of 1358 also was very local in character. It lasted only three weeks and was an antinoble movement in which peasants played a relatively minor role. Similarly, several Flemish rebellions and the French rising against taxation in 1379–1383 involved only limited participation by peasants. In general, the declining population left a

demand for labor that proved beneficial to the peasants, while the scourge of war caused their greatest misery. Peasant rebellions did occur during the terrible years from 1410 to 1440. Yet in the later fifteenth century the peasants experienced what one scholar has called a golden age, at a time when they faced an increasing royal fiscal burden.

Although the urban population escaped the worst ravages of war, the townspeople bore the main brunt of both the plague and royal taxation, as well as having to depend on outside sources for their food. The rural immigrants who came to the towns after each epidemic rarely were numerous enough to replace the dead, and generally lacked the skills to be as economically productive. The urban poor were probably more desperate and destitute than their rural counterparts, and their plight was accentuated by the declining resources of lay and ecclesiastical charities. The increasingly restrictive policies of established guilds blocked opportunities for advancement and may have encouraged the growth of rural industry outside the traditional guild structure. It is the artisans, rather than the peasants, who provide the major evidence of social unrest in the fourteenth century.

By the second third of the fifteenth century, traces of reviving urban prosperity can be detected, first among the more fortunate segments of bourgeois society. The tribulations of Italy and Flanders enabled French merchants and bankers to play a greater international economic role. Legal training and royal service remained important throughout the period. The growth of royal financial and judicial institutions did not slacken, and an increasing percentage of the governmental offices were available to people of bourgeois, rather than noble or clerical, origin. Nobles in the fifteenth century benefited mainly from growing fiscal privileges and expanded opportunities for military employment. The growing bureaucracy was the avenue to advancement for the bourgeoisie. By the reign of Louis XI, the more fortunate members of this class were well on their way to becoming a service nobility—the "robe."

The old nobility of feudal origins—the rural seigneurs—experienced periods of success and failure between 1314 and 1494. At the beginning of the period, they were in revolt against royal fiscal policies and suffering from the economic "stagflation." Their continuing economic difficulty is reflected in their strenuous efforts to avoid taxes, restore strong money, raise military salaries, and promote aggressive (rather than defensive) warfare. The French nobles in the fourteenth century seemed overanxious to prove themselves and justify their values and their tactics in military combat. Factional conflict and disenchantment with the Valois monarchy created strains, particularly among the nobility of the north and west. The military disasters of 1346 and 1356, and serious brigandage thereafter, led many people to blame the nobles for the kingdom's misfortunes. From the 1340's to the 1380's the nobles had less success in escaping royal taxation than at any other time in the history of the monarchy.

The embattled nobility turned to the monarchy, which patched up its differences with the northwestern nobles and adopted policies calculated to please the lords: stabilizing the coinage, paying military salaries more regularly, and levying essentially regressive taxes. Toward 1390 the nobles made major breakthroughs in their effort to secure exemption from taxes. Like the rest of French society, they experienced better economic conditions in the later fourteenth century and disastrous economic problems between about 1410 and 1440. Their influence was diluted by the divisions of the princely civil war. They suffered staggering losses at the battle of Agincourt in 1415. The English overran northwestern France, where there was a higher density of nobles than elsewhere. New weakenings of the currency, less regularity in military pay, and the serious destruction of rural capital combined to wreak havoc on noble fortunes. The worst was over by the 1440's, when the crown again stabilized the coinage, reaffirmed the exemption of nobles from taxation, and established a regularly paid army of mounted warriors. Yet the economic recovery of the rural lords did not make real progress until late in the century.

By then, the French clergy was drawn from all social classes, although mainly from the more prosperous ones. Much of the history of the French church is inseparable from that of French politics and foreign affairs, but the economic position of the church most closely paralleled that of the seigneurial class. The economic tribulations of the manors and villages also affected the church, reducing tithes and other kinds of income as well as rural capital. The epidemics of plague were a particular disaster for the clergy, whose losses were high and whose ranks could not be refilled quickly with people of equal caliber. The departure of the pope from Avignon in 1377 and the beginning of the Great Schism a year later created terrible strains among royal policymakers, theologians, and the hierarchy of secular clergy. Periodic withdrawals of obedience to the pope, shift-

ing royal policies, and the growth of conciliar theories gave rise to the various forms of Gallicanism. The University of Paris and the Parlement became increasingly Gallican, favoring considerable autonomy for the French church. The Pragmatic Sanction of Bourges, issued in 1438 by Charles VII, was an expression of this sentiment and was resented in Rome. Louis XI, with characteristic perversity, began his reign by trying to reverse as many of his father's policies as possible. He canceled the Pragmatic Sanction, then restored it, and in 1472 negotiated a concordat with the papacy that paved the way for the more enduring Concordat of Bologna in 1516. Louis XI's concordat was enforced only sporadically, as the king let expediency govern his papal policies.

POLITICAL DEVELOPMENTS

For all its importance in economic and demographic history, the year 1314 is best remembered as the year of Philip the Fair's death. Leagues of nobles and towns were then in rebellion against unpopular taxes for an abortive campaign in Flanders, and the king's daughters-in-law had recently been involved in an adultery scandal. People remembered that the grand master of the Templars, while dying at the stake early in the year, had pronounced a curse on the king and the royal house. The sudden death of the forty-six-year-old king was the culmination of a year of sensational and distressing events.

Louis X (1314–1316) attempted to defuse the political opposition, mainly by issuing charters of reform to various regions. Historians have considered it significant that the French rebels (mostly nobles) did not demand or receive a national Magna Carta, but were content with specific charters addressed to the particular interests of their localities. Regional particularism remained a potent factor in France, placing limitations on the scope of opposition to the crown but also preventing the crown from establishing common, centralized policies or institutions. Despite the expansion of royal power and institutions of government in the preceding reigns, France lacked a sense of "community of the realm." Like his father, Louis X needed money to fight the Flemings and experimented with representative assemblies. Louis did not use the latter merely for propaganda but tried to have them endorse royal taxes. His early death cut short this effort.

Becoming king in a rebellious situation, Louis needed scapegoats to blame for the unpopular actions of the preceding reign: Enguerran de Marigny was the most famous victim. Yet Louis might in any case have reacted against the former regime because the government was becoming divided into opposing factions. Advocates of an aggressive fiscal policy and the innovative use of representative assemblies had been prominent in Philip IV's last years, were associated with the emerging Chamber of Accounts, and enjoyed support from Philip IV's middle son, Philip V, and the latter's mother-in-law, Mahaut of Artois. Most of the greater nobles, along with Louis X, his youngest brother Charles (later Charles IV), and their powerful Valois cousins, supported a more conservative group associated with the Parlement and with the crown's judicial rather than fiscal traditions. These parties, and the various solidarities that composed them, were ill defined, but they cannot be ignored when discussing the troubled years after 1314.

When he died suddenly in 1316, Louis X was survived by a pregnant widow, but for the first time in twelve generations there was no son to succeed the monarch. His brother Philip assumed the regency with the grudging acquiescence of the other princes. It was agreed that if the unborn child were male, he would be king; if not, the crown would pass to Louis X's four-year-old daughter Joan. When the child, John I, died five days after his birth, the regent could claim that the arrangements governing Louis X's succession did not apply to John's. In any case, Philip usurped the throne.

Philip V (1316–1322) was an intelligent man with a keen interest in administration and strong support from like-minded people in the government. Yet he and his mother-in-law were generally unpopular, and his successful coup requires some explanation, especially since the princes had just demonstrated that they had no inherent objection to having a woman on the throne. Joan's tender years and the likelihood that her eventual marriage could be a bitterly divisive issue may have given them second thoughts, and there were lingering doubts about her legitimacy because of her mother's adultery. Philip shrewdly capitalized on such concerns and doubtless argued that a kingdom troubled by tragedy and famine needed the strong leadership of an adult male. Nurtured by generations of male primogeniture and the saintly tradition of Louis IX, the French royal house had an extremely strong sense of legitimacy.

The accession of Philip V carried with it the understanding that his daughters could not inherit the throne, which would pass to his brother Charles if

he had no son. Thus originated the rule that a woman could not occupy the French throne, a rule that remained irreversible as long as the Capetian dynasty produced males who were capable of ruling. The decision proved to be awkward, first because Joan had a strong claim to the important county of Champagne and the kingdom of Navarre, which Louis X had inherited from his mother, and second because it left undiscussed the question of whether a woman might transmit to her son a claim to the throne. Neither of these problems was immediately apparent because Philip V and his brother were young and healthy.

Philip V gradually brought back into power the officials associated with financial innovation and representative assemblies. He experimented greatly with the latter, sometimes convening all three Estates (clergy, barons, townsmen), and sometimes only one or two. He made peace with Flanders, where his son-in-law became count. He tried to systematize the administrative changes operative since the reign of Louis IX, regulating the Parlement, the waters and forests, and the customs service. He undertook to recover alienated portions of the royal domain and buy up nonroyal currencies. The Chamber of Accounts became an officially constituted body. Philip's government was far ahead of its time in proposing a uniform system of weights and measures for the realm.

Some of these projects entailed a substantial short-term cost, and in 1321 Philip V tried to obtain moral and material support from the three Estates in order to complete his reforms. Despite an elaborate series of assemblies, however, the Estates rejected his proposals. Perhaps they were suspicious of the king's advisers or resented pressures to give binding consent in central assemblies; the towns surely wished to avoid setting a dangerous precedent of paying an extraordinary subsidy in peacetime. As he experienced this defeat, Philip contracted a terminal illness. He died unlamented early in 1322 and his brother Charles IV (1322–1328), after assuming the throne, quickly ousted the officials associated with the Chamber of Accounts. His more conservative regime avoided central assemblies, sweeping reforms, and flashy new policies, augmenting revenues by forced loans and weakening the currency.

Charles IV spent most of his reign feuding with his brother-in-law, Edward II of England. The latter was dilatory in rendering to Charles liege homage for Guienne. Then a border incident in Gascony in

1323 triggered the "War of St. Sardos." The French won a quick victory, but a negotiated peace lasted only from the summer of 1325 to that of 1326. Then war flared up again, and Charles and his barons organized an elaborate fiscal and military buildup aimed at conquering Guienne once and for all in the spring of 1327. The past record of Anglo-French military encounters gave this project a high probability of success, but the overthrow of Edward II and the accession of Charles IV's nephew, as Edward III, to the English throne persuaded Charles to give up the project and make peace in March 1327. The problem of Guienne lingered on, and the French soon lost the military supremacy that might have resolved it.

Early in 1328 Charles IV sickened and died, thereby opening the second phase of the royal succession crisis. Charles had no sons, and even before he died, the magnates decided that his first cousin, Philip of Valois, would be regent, becoming king if the pregnant queen did not bear a son. In arranging the Valois succession of 1328, the French had to resolve the two problems left from 1316. Philip VI had no claim at all to Champagne or Navarre; these were supposed to pass to Joan, Louis X's daughter, who was now married to her cousin, Philip of Évreux. Champagne was so strategic that the crown retained it, substituting other lands and revenues for Joan, but managing the matter so badly that she and the Évreux branch of the family bore a grudge against Philip and the Valois.

Joan's son Charles of Navarre (1332–1387), later surnamed "the Bad," inherited this grudge and illustrated the implications of the other question that the Valois succession was meant to resolve: whether a woman, herself excluded from the throne, could transmit a claim to her son. In 1328 the nearest male relative of Charles IV was his nephew, Edward III of England. He was then a teenager dominated by his unpopular mother and (if he was in fact of legitimate birth) he now headed the Plantagenet family, France's ancient enemy. It has been argued persuasively, however, that these considerations were less important to the French magnates than practical politics. Joan of Navarre and all the other granddaughters of Philip IV were descended from more recent kings than was Edward's mother, Isabella. The sons of any of them might advance a claim to the throne in the future if a woman could transmit such a claim. The only certain way to avoid such conflicting claims was to reserve the throne of

France to the male line. Philip VI was in the prime of life, had a healthy son, would bring to the royal domain a sizable appanage, and "looked every inch a king."

Philip could not secure the throne, however, without making promises. He remained beholden to the magnates far more than his predecessors had been. Edward III rendered homage and did not formally claim the French throne for another decade, but a lingering uneasiness about Philip's title is revealed in his own lack of self-assurance and in the willingness of dissident magnates to play off Edward against his Valois cousin.

Philip VI began his reign with a military victory over Flemish rebels in 1328, and by 1331 he had resolved the problem of Edward III's homage short of war. He continued the conservative policies of Charles IV, with whom he had been congenial, but was embarrassed by another old friend, Robert of Artois, who for nearly thirty years had felt wrongly excluded from his inheritance by his aunt, Mahaut, and her heirs, the duchess of Burgundy and the countess of Flanders. Initially influential at Philip's court, Robert sought to acquire Artois. In opposing him, Burgundy and Flanders began to flirt with Edward III, and Philip VI, who could not risk their defection, ruled against Robert. Branded a rebel in 1332, Robert fled to England, hoping to induce Edward to dispute Philip's title. This episode illustrates the way in which the Hundred Years War would differ from earlier Anglo-French conflicts: an alternative dynasty that could succor French dissidents posed a real dilemma for the Valois.

Robert's influential position at the French court now passed to Eudes IV of Burgundy, brother of Queen Joan. Burgundian influence seems to have been resented in northwestern France. One chronicler thought the queen too influential and said that she hated Normans. Burgundians and Auvergnats became increasingly numerous among Philip's advisers, while nobles of the north and west seem to have been under-represented. Some former supporters of Robert of Artois were linked by blood, friendship, or clientage to Joan of Navarre and her husband, Philip of Évreux. The nucleus of an opposition party began to form.

Relations with England steadily deteriorated in the 1330's. Besides the endless jurisdictional and territorial disputes involving Guienne, the French continued their tradition of supporting Scottish resistance to England, while Edward III worked to build up a system of alliances in the Low Countries. After a decade of uneasy peace, France and England went to war again in 1337. The so-called Hundred Years War was actually a series of wars, continuing the succession of Anglo-French conflicts that had begun in 1294. The one significant difference between the wars that preceded 1337 and those that followed was the existence of the Plantagenet claim to the French throne. The English invoked the claim only sporadically, but it enabled them to attract the support of enough anti-Valois magnates to justify the argument that the whole struggle was essentially a civil war between competing factions of French princes. Recent English scholarship permits identification of three twenty-year periods of intense conflict: the Edwardian War of 1340–1360, the Caroline War of 1369–1389, and the Lancastrian War of 1415–1435. The first and third of these were marked by English victories.

Philip VI's major Burgundian adviser after 1332 was Mile de Noyers, an influential noble in the reign of Philip V who returned to prominence with the party associated with the Chamber of Accounts. Until the mid-1340's this party was dominant, and the king's small council was virtually identical with the "sovereigns" of the Chamber of Accounts. These financial experts could not push the French into abandoning their historic hostility to taxation, an attitude that made collection of significant taxes impossible until outright fighting was in progress. The minor skirmishing and many truces that followed 1337 led many taxpayers to doubt that the war was a genuine threat to their vital interests. Always unprepared when truces expired, the French monarch suffered a string of reversals—naval defeat at Sluys in 1340, disputed succession in Brittany after 1341, growing disaffection among the northwestern nobles, major English gains in Gascony in 1345, Edward III's invasion in 1346 and subsequent victory at Crécy, and finally the capture of Calais by Edward in 1347.

At last the magnates and towns began to recognize the gravity of their predicament. Governmental shake-ups occurred, and the Estates General of late 1347 authorized an extremely large tax to finance an effective army. As regional assemblies were determining the form of this tax and arranging for its collection, the Black Death arrived in Europe and disrupted the whole scheme. The timing of the plague made it doubly disastrous for France, and when it had passed, the English retained their earlier momentum.

The second Valois king, John II (1350–1364), had been a leading figure in the government since late 1347. On his accession he launched energetic measures to promote a financial recovery from the effects of the plague, but despite the success of these efforts, his fiscal position remained fragile because much of the realm still resisted paying in times of truce or limited fighting. In northern and western France, assemblies at the bailiwick or regional level granted modest indirect taxes almost annually in return for royal promises of reform. These meetings doubtless increased the confidence and influence of many who would participate in the Estates General when these central assemblies began to meet frequently after 1355. Financial need soon forced John to utilize mint profits, and the frequent mutations of the currency in the 1350's aroused growing opposition.

Criticism of the royal monetary policy and the king's dishonest advisers became part of a much more serious problem—the progressive alienation of important segments of the French nobility, mostly concentrated in the north and west. The opposition, which began under Philip VI, may be traced to several overlapping groups: former supporters of Robert of Artois, those who resented Burgundian influence at court, those with lands or ties in England, those with personal grudges against the king or the men he favored, and opponents of the French-backed candidate for duke of Brittany. With some fiscal concessions and a few timely executions, Philip VI surmounted a brief crisis in 1343, but new rebels kept appearing, such as Godefroi d'Harcourt, lord of St. Sauveur in Normandy. John II made new enemies when he executed his constable, Raoul d'Eu, in 1350. The pro-French faction in Brittany lost adherents steadily.

The center of opposition, however, proved to be the house of Évreux. King of Navarre since 1349, the young Charles the Bad drew his greatest political strength from scattered family possessions in Normandy and the Île-de-France. The new constable, Charles of Spain, was beloved by John II and regarded as a hated enemy by Charles the Bad, who had him murdered in 1354 and then made overtures to the English. He succeeded twice in bullying John II into making favorable new settlements with him, but in April 1356 John lost patience, imprisoned the king of Navarre, and executed four of his prominent Norman supporters. This act further alienated the northwestern nobility, plunged Normandy into civil war, and facilitated a new English assault.

In 1355 Edward, prince of Wales, had marched

out of Bordeaux to ravage Languedoc. In December of the same year the Estates met in Paris, demanded governmental reforms, and promised new taxes for troops. Their financial measures failed completely, both because they bore too heavily on the towns and spared landed fortunes, and because the centralized form of tax and collection machinery offended local sensibilities. The Estates in subsequent meetings substituted less regressive taxes but still failed to produce the promised sum. Centers of opposition like Normandy cannot have produced much money, and new royal manipulations of the currency irritated reformers. Despite such problems, John collected an army and cornered the prince of Wales near Poitiers in September 1356, only to be defeated utterly and taken prisoner by the prince's Anglo-Gascon troops.

The king's capture may well have been the most important single event in late-medieval French history. It had three main results. First, the Estates General, just coming of age as a political institution, fell into the hands of ambitious adventurers whose actions promoted discord between social classes rather than raising money for the king's release. Rather than becoming an indispensable source of funds, the assemblies fatally impaired their future usefulness by antagonizing the crown and aristocracy. Second, the king's capture led to a truce and then a treaty with England, subject to the payment of a large ransom that forced the French to pay high and regular peacetime taxes for the first time. The third consequence of John's capture was that both monarchies soon stopped paying troops, stranding thousands of soldiers on French soil without a livelihood. Their ensuing brigandage not only caused considerable destruction but also affected French attitudes toward taxation. The government had to employ the best soldiers on a permanent basis and use them to punish those who disrupted the peace. This necessary but expensive policy led to the first regular direct taxation in 1363.

These results of John's capture dominated the momentous decade after 1356. The Estates General, largely discarded after the disappointments of 1321, were revived for occasional meetings in the 1340's, but when they met following the battle of Poitiers, it was the fourth such central assembly in less than a year. The Estates were to meet six times more between February 1357 and May 1358, though often with much reduced attendance. At the meeting of October 1356, the dominant figure was Robert le Coq, bishop of Laon, an ambitious supporter of the captive king of Navarre. The disinterested support-

ers of governmental reform were largely eclipsed by his oratory, but the true reformers wielded greater influence at the next assembly, which produced the great reforming ordinance of March 1357. For most of the period of John's captivity, however, the issue of reform was submerged by the special interests of two complex personalities: Charles of Navarre and Etienne Marcel.

Charles the Bad wanted to be released from prison and to postpone the release of John II. Beyond that, it was never clear whether he sought the French throne, or large additional lands, or merely to irritate his Valois cousins. Marcel, his occasional ally, was provost of the merchants of Paris. His jealous hatred of the royal financial officials was shared by many who rightly regarded them as corrupt parvenus, but he seemed especially eager to punish his personal enemies in the government. His desire to free the Parisian region from brigandage may have led him to support Charles of Navarre. Marcel's strong antinoble sentiments were echoed by the upper bourgeoisie of other northern cities and were reflected by the efforts of each succeeding assembly to shift a greater burden of taxation from the towns to the nobility.

Increasingly alienated, the nobles began to boycott the Estates. Their feelings were outraged further in February 1358, when a Parisian mob under Marcel's control murdered two prominent nobles. Four months later the frankly antinoble *Jacquerie* in northern France (which Marcel supported) completed the cleavage between noble and bourgeois critics of the dynasty. John II's youthful son, the dauphin Charles, suffered many indignities in the first months of his father's captivity, but once the nobles became alienated from the bourgeois opposition, he found the means to gain a support from the aristocracy that his father and grandfather had been denied. Charles the Bad, after securing his release, disappointed many of his followers, and the dauphin regained control of Paris when Marcel was murdered in the summer of 1358.

Rejecting an extremely unfavorable treaty in 1359, the dauphin's government avoided battle when Edward III invaded France that fall. In 1360 the English had to settle for the Treaty of Brétigny, which restored to the Plantagenets their former holdings in Aquitaine. With a remarkable fiscal effort, Charles secured the funds needed to obtain his father's release in the autumn. At the end of the year, the crown finally stabilized the currency and imposed the indirect taxes that were to pay the balance of the royal ransom. John II spent just three more years in France, and scholars are divided over whether he or his son really controlled the government. The king's preoccupation with a crusade was not purely frivolous, being dictated by the necessity of finding employment for the vast brigand companies who defeated a royal army in 1362. Already benefiting financially from the taxes for the ransom, the crown obtained a new hearth tax *(fouage)* from the Estates late in 1363 to finance measures against brigandage. At this assembly John II announced his plan to return to England. He had to negotiate outstanding differences with Edward III, now that one of his hostage sons had broken parole, but it was alleged that he also wanted to enjoy the pleasures of the English court.

John's death in England brought to the throne Charles V (1364–1380), a frail and studious prince whose avoidance of martial exploits and survival of the crises of the late 1350's earned him the surname "the Wise." He was also fortunate, having inherited a structure of regular taxation, a stable currency, and a nobility that had been pushed into the arms of the monarchy. At the moment of his accession, Bertrand du Guesclin, a royal commander of growing reputation, crushed the forces of Charles the Bad at Cocherel in Normandy. Charles V exploited his favorable situation with the utmost skill. His energetic brother, Louis of Anjou, went to Languedoc and governed with ruthless efficiency. The new hearth tax maintained an army that curtailed brigandage and served effectively against the English when the war resumed.

Charles V's reign achieved its greatest success between 1368 and 1372. Gascon nobles antagonized by the prince of Wales appealed to the French court in 1368; and after building up a base of support in the southwest, Charles accepted the appeals and broke with England. At the same time he carefully cultivated an important Breton lord, Olivier de Clisson, who abandoned his English-backed duke to join the French side in the renewed conflict. In Languedoc, Louis of Anjou's heavy taxation of the towns raised enough money to keep the brigands employed elsewhere; in 1369 this unorthodox forerunner of the standing army installed a pro-French ruler in Castile and then was turned against the English in Aquitaine. With papal connivance Charles V arranged for the heiress of Flanders to marry his brother, Philip of Burgundy, rather than an English prince. This time it was the French who were prepared for hostilities. They quickly recovered Ponthieu and most

of Aquitaine, and were able to reoccupy Poitou after their Castilian ally crushed the English fleet off La Rochelle in 1372.

Thereafter, the French recovery lost momentum, and Charles V's final years were marked by failures and mistakes in policy that helped to create some of the problems of the next reign. France could not take the English bastions of Calais, Cherbourg, Brest, and Bordeaux. Anti-French sentiment began to revive in Brittany. Flanders was swept by rebellion and social strife, and a rising against harsh taxation forced the recall of Louis of Anjou from Languedoc. Most serious was the failure of French policy toward the papacy, whose long presence at Avignon had been profitable to the Valois. Gregory XI had returned to Italy despite French objections, and the predominantly French college of cardinals quickly repented its choice of Urban VI to succeed him. When they tried to depose Urban and replace him with a French cardinal, Charles V accepted this action with undue haste, despite grave misgivings on the part of the theologians at the University of Paris.

The result was perpetuation of a papal schism that could not have survived if France had supported Urban. The French, moreover, had now made a commitment that no future French government could repudiate without the implicit admission of having been schismatic. After 1378, therefore, France faced limited options in dealing with the papacy: full support for the pope at Avignon, withdrawal of obedience from him, or commitment to the principle of conciliar supremacy.

Charles V's final act was his cancellation of the *fouage,* which had been the main support for the French army but was unpopular with the nobles. The surviving indirect taxes were unpopular in the towns, where riots against these *aides* in the fall of 1380 forced the government of the young Charles VI (1380–1422) to cancel all taxes. One factor in the uprising may have been a general distrust of the regent, Louis of Anjou, who was known for his ruthless fiscal exactions in Languedoc and his potentially costly ambitions in Italy. Philip of Burgundy, his youngest brother, soon engineered the overthrow of Charles V's plan for the regency by having the eleven-year-old Charles VI declared an adult. Supported by another brother, the prodigal Jean, duke of Berry, Philip emerged as the strong man in the ensuing struggle for power. Anjou, whose support for the Avignon pope and opposition to the duke of Brittany were completely opposed to Burgundy's policies, drew support from the former advisers of Charles V (known derisively as the Marmousets) and from the northwestern nobility. These last, who had been drawn back into the royal camp under Charles V, now provided most of the military leaders of the realm, but many came from families that had resented Burgundian influence in the government forty years earlier.

Louis of Anjou's friend Olivier de Clisson was appointed constable in 1380 and, after Louis departed for Italy in 1382, became the leader of the Marmousets. For a few years this group cooperated with Philip of Burgundy, under whose skillful leadership the government salvaged the awkward political situation in Brittany and concluded a new treaty with Duke John IV in 1381. The crown obtained new funds through painful negotiations and in 1382 won a military victory at Roosebeke in Flanders, facilitating Philip's accession to that county in 1384. Restoration of the old indirect taxes in 1382 provoked widespread urban revolts, which the government suppressed. Several plans to invade England miscarried, however, and the regime of the royal uncles acquired a reputation for corruption and greed. Clisson and the Marmousets influenced Charles VI and his brother Louis against their uncles, who were ousted from power in the fall of 1388.

The king ruled with the advice of the Marmousets for about four years, promulgating ordinances of reform, practicing frugality, and in 1389 concluding a truce that ended the latest war with England. In 1392, however, an attempt on Clisson's life led to a punitive expedition against Brittany, during which Charles VI went mad. The uncles quickly regained power, banishing the leading Marmousets. Thereafter, Charles VI suffered from increasingly recurrent insanity. During these "absences" Philip of Burgundy was generally in control of the central government, while in Charles's periods of relative lucidity the king came increasingly under the influence of his brother, Louis of Orléans, who had considerable backing from the military aristocracy and gradually inherited Clisson's mantle as the head of the anti-Burgundian party.

The dukes of Orléans and Burgundy differed on many points of foreign policy, and their rivalry was all the more intense because both princes found themselves increasingly dependent on royal pensions, gifts, and tax receipts from their lands. Many supporters of Orléans had long careers in the royal service, with ties to the old Marmouset party or the military aristocracy. Louis attached some of these key people to his household or granted them pen-

sions. Between 1401 and 1403 the princely feud became a bitter struggle to dominate policy and control the intermittently lucid king. Philip found the followers of Louis too well entrenched to oust. His son, John the Fearless, who became duke of Burgundy in 1404, lacked Philip's prestige and was not liked by the old duke of Berry and the queen.

Beginning in 1405, the crown sharply curtailed Burgundian access to funds from the royal treasury. In 1407 the royal council was virtually purged of Burgundian supporters. In desperation John had his cousin Orléans assassinated, plunging the realm into civil war. John was widely condemned, but without their leader the Orléanists were in disarray, and John enjoyed some popular support, especially in Paris, because he was perceived as a fiscal reformer. The Orléanists came to be led by Bernard VII, count of Armagnac, whose brutal Gascon troops were much dreaded in northern France.

The anti-Burgundian party quickly became known as the Armagnacs, and the civil war dragged on until 1435. By 1415, however, it was submerged in the new Anglo-French conflict, the Lancastrian war. John the Fearless gained in power and influence between 1408 and 1413. The squandering of royal revenues and the proliferation of princely clients in the royal administration had accelerated since 1400, and the evident need for reform enabled John to gain support despite the alliance of almost all the other princes against him. He grew stronger in Paris with the execution of a hated financial officer in 1409 and a purge of Armagnac sympathizers in 1411.

In 1413 the Estates General met for the first time in thirty-two years. The growing English threat seemed to require new taxation, but the assembly demanded reforms that would prevent the money from being wasted. Little was done until a violent uprising led by a butcher named Simon le Coustellier (called Caboche) prompted the drafting of an enormous ordinance of reform with 259 articles. The rebellion discredited John of Burgundy, who had to relinquish Paris. The Armagnacs suppressed the riots and annulled the *Ordonnance cabochienne*. When negotiations with England failed, Henry V invaded France in 1415, taking Harfleur and destroying an essentially Armagnac French army at Agincourt in October.

Agincourt was a major disaster for the nobility of northwestern France, which had been the bulwark of the kingdom's military leadership since its reconciliation with Charles V after 1358. In a few years the English overran the nearly defenseless lands of many old families in Normandy, Maine, and Anjou. The deaths of several royal princes left as leader of the Valois after 1417 the future Charles VII, born in 1403. His legitimacy was later challenged, but not until he made the mistake of antagonizing his mother in 1418. With her support John of Burgundy managed to regain Paris in 1418, seizing the person of the king and promoting a massacre of many Armagnacs, including Count Bernard. John was in no position to stop the rapid English advance, so he opened negotiations with the dauphin Charles, who was in league with the remaining Armagnacs, a motley array of Gascon adventurers and brigand chiefs. Both sides tried to win support by canceling the *aides,* but then had to resume weakening the currency. At a meeting with the dauphin in 1419, John the Fearless was murdered by revenge-seeking Armagnacs.

This act forced into the English camp the entire Burgundian party, led by the new duke, Philip the Good, whose growing authority in the Low Countries was to make him one of Europe's mightiest princes. In 1420 the Treaty of Troyes disinherited the dauphin and declared Henry V of England heir to the French throne. Henry married a daughter of Charles VI; his brother, John of Lancaster, duke of Bedford, married a sister of Philip of Burgundy. The Valois monarchy was saved from possible destruction by the early death of Henry V in 1422, which left his infant son as heir to both realms and gave a valuable reprieve to Charles VII (1422–1461).

Charles, however, was recognized only in parts of central and southern France. This young "king of Bourges" was dominated by quarreling favorites, was denied the once formidable military support of northwestern France, and received only limited taxes from the Estates of mutually jealous regions. Bedford was an energetic English regent, and Burgundy gave him periodic support against Charles. A few old Armagnac zealots were prepared to sabotage any reconciliation with Burgundy, and the other important nobles at Charles's court were suspicious of each other. A serious defeat at Verneuil in 1424 further weakened the Valois cause. The one faction at court that maintained some cohesion throughout the reign was the Angevin branch of the family (Charles having married the sister of Louis III of Anjou). Charles skillfully utilized the awkward blend of support and domination from these in-laws. His best military commanders were Jean de Dunois (bastard son of Louis of Orléans) and Arthur de Richemont (younger son of John IV of Brittany). Richemont became con-

stable in 1425, but his major role in the Valois revival was delayed by his rivalry with another royal adviser, Georges de la Trémoille.

In these circumstances the English continued to advance until Bedford's troops invested Orléans, the key to the Loire valley, in 1428. As the city's fall appeared increasingly probable, Charles VII received a visit from a peasant girl named Joan of Arc, who claimed to have heard saintly voices calling on her to restore Charles to his rightful throne. Her forcefulness and perseverance, far more than her mystical experiences, are what establish Joan today as an extraordinary personality. When experts at court declared that she was free of heresy or sorcery, Charles let her don armor and accompany a final effort to save Orléans. Her presence seems to have had a strong effect on the morale of both sides. The English were defeated and fell back from the Loire. Subsequently Joan was able to conduct Charles to his coronation at Rheims without serious opposition. Captured by the Burgundians in 1430 and executed by the English the next year, Joan of Arc disappeared from the stage almost as suddenly as she had appeared, but the Valois were now delivered from their greatest peril.

The real turning point came in 1435, when Charles purchased the long-delayed peace with Burgundy by the Treaty of Arras, which gave Burgundy a strategic set of fortresses along the Somme that the French could redeem only by making a very heavy payment. The death of Bedford, princely strife at home, and growing recognition of Charles VII further weakened the English, and Richemont took Paris in 1436. The Lancastrian war had given way to what was essentially a mopping up operation. In the next decade the reenactment of much of what Charles V had accomplished in the 1360's completed the institutional groundwork for the modern French state.

In 1436 the Estates restored the *aides.* The crown soon reestablished a strong and stable currency, as it had when the *aides* had originally been levied. The Treaty of Arras left thousands of unemployed troops, whose atrocities led them to be called the *écorcheurs.* To combat them, the Estates in 1439 enacted an apportioned direct tax. This *taille,* like the *fouage* of 1363, was to pay troops to restore order. After putting down the *Praguerie,* a rebellion of princes in 1440, Charles VII made a truce with England in 1444 and sent thousands of brigands on a dangerous expedition against the Swiss. Finally, in 1445, the king made use of his steady taxes to establish the *compagnies d'ordonnance,* a permanent paid force of 9,000 mounted troops. With annual taxes, a stable currency, and a regularly paid army, the French state was firmly established, essentially along lines first sketched out in the 1360's.

The truce of 1444 marked the real end of 150 years of successive Anglo-French conflicts and launched a new chapter of French history, in which a well-financed, militarily strong Valois monarchy spent half a century "gathering in" large blocks of territory that had gained virtual autonomy under hostile princes during the preceding crisis. The first of these were the residual English possessions, Normandy and Guienne, which speedily fell to the French after the truce expired in 1449. There remained Brittany, several southwestern fiefs, the holdings of the houses of Anjou, Bourbon, and Orléans, and especially the extensive Burgundian state. The principal architect of the "gathering in" was Louis XI. This perverse, peculiar, and widely hated king owed as much to good luck as to his own genius. At the very least, it can be said that Charles VII was far more fortunate in his successor than Charles V had been.

Charles VII himself would not have agreed: he and Louis had been estranged for years, and on becoming king in 1461, Louis reversed so many of his father's policies as to provoke a major rebellion in just three years. Louis exacted heavy payments in order to buy back the Somme towns held by Burgundy since 1435. He dismissed his father's major councillors, altered religious policy, and antagonized important interests. The rebellion, misnamed the War of the Public Weal (1464–1465), was led by Charles the Bold, soon to be ruler of the Burgundian state. After an indecisive battle Louis began to detach some princes from the coalition with separate concessions. He purchased peace by returning the Somme towns to Burgundy and giving Normandy to his half brother Charles.

After this inauspicious beginning, Louis resolved to break the power of the princes, but he must not be viewed as antinoble on that account. Since 1445 the *compagnies d'ordonnance* had signaled a new alliance between crown and nobility. Gradually purged of bastards, foreigners, and low-born adventurers, this army offered respectable employment to the nobility. Louis expanded the army and did nothing to hinder the growing exemption of the nobles from royal taxation. The nobility again became a bulwark of the state. Louis XI did ally himself with one prince, the duke of Bourbon, whose brother and

heir, Pierre de Beaujeu, married the king's daughter, Anne.

With Bourbon's help Louis expelled his brother from Normandy in 1466 and then survived a great peril after falling into Burgundian hands in 1468. He fought off a Burgundian attack along the Somme frontier in 1471–1472, bought off the invading English in 1475, and gave encouragement to Burgundy's relentless enemies, the imperial cities of Switzerland and the upper Rhine, at the hands of which Charles the Bold met defeat, and then death, early in 1477. French forces moved quickly to seize ducal Burgundy, and for a time added Artois and the Franche-Comté. The remnant of the Burgundian state, notably Flanders and the imperial Netherlands, remained a bone of contention for centuries between France and the Austrian Habsburgs, to whom it passed through marriage.

Meanwhile, the "gathering in" continued elsewhere, with the sudden demise of Louis XI's brother Charles in 1472, then with the defeat and death of John V of Armagnac in 1473, and finally with the deaths of René and Charles of Anjou in 1480 and 1481, which enabled the crown not only to regain Anjou and Maine but to acquire Provence as well. The Bourbon lands would soon pass to Louis's daughter and son-in-law, while the king tried to ensure the extinction of the house of Orléans by marrying the duke to his younger daughter, Jeanne, whose deformities precluded bearing children.

When Louis XI died, hated and unlamented, in 1483, the kingdom was stronger at home and abroad than it had been for a century. A reaction against his harsh rule quickly developed because Charles VIII was only thirteen. The Estates General of 1484 inveighed against high taxes; and the princes, led by Orléans, Bourbon, and Brittany, engaged in several ineffectual revolts. Anne and Pierre de Beaujeu, who ruled for Charles VIII, surmounted the reaction with considerable skill. They sacrificed a few of Louis XI's most hated officials and reduced taxes drastically, but retained custody of the young king and maintained the achievements of the late reign in all important essentials. They inherited the duke of Bourbon's lands in 1488. In the same year the duke of Brittany died, leaving only daughters. After a considerable struggle over her marriage and inheritance, Anne of Brittany married Charles VIII in 1491. A strategically important and long autonomous fief was thus drawn back into the royal orbit.

The Breton marriage largely completed the great gathering in of lands that had begun in 1449. The territory of the king of France now extended farther than at any time since the early ninth century. The relative size and speed of the acquisitions made necessary certain institutional policies that greatly affected the future of the state: the preservation of local legal traditions and the decentralization of fiscal and judicial bodies. The crown in the early fourteenth century had moved too fast toward centralization. Reformers called for more regional autonomy, and regionalism in fiscal matters was dictated by the military situation in the 1360's. A century later regionalism was well entrenched: princely territories often had their provincial Estates, parlements, courts of aids or accounts, and the like. Charles VII and Louis XI found it prudent to retain these institutions as the territories were annexed by the crown. This decentralization of institutions, which the First Republic and First Empire completely reversed, was in fact an asset to the consolidation and administration of the fifteenth-century state.

By 1494 France was fiscally and militarily sound, no longer threatened by English kings or native princes, and in the process of economic and demographic recovery, when Charles VIII inaugurated a new historical era by invading Italy.

BIBLIOGRAPHY

Jacques d'Avout, *Le meurtre d'Étienne Marcel* (1960); Guy Bois, *Crise du féodalisme* (1981); Raymond Cazelles, *La société politique et la crise de la royauté sous Philippe de Valois* (1958), and "Le parti navarrais jusqu'à la mort d'Étienne Marcel," in *Bulletin philologique et historique* (1960), and "Jean II le Bon: Quel homme? quel roi?" in *Revue historique*, **232** (1974); Philippe Contamine, *Guerre, état, et société à la fin du moyen âge* (1971); S. H. Cuttler, *The Law of Treason and Treason Trials in Later Medieval France* (1981); Roland Delachenal, *Histoire de Charles V*, 5 vols. (1909–1931); Georges Duby, *Rural Economy and Country Life in the Medieval West*, Cynthia Postan, trans. (1968); Étienne Fournial, *Histoire monétaire de l'occident médiéval* (1970); Guy Fourquin, *Les campagnes de la région parisienne à la fin du moyen âge* (1964); John Bell Henneman, "The Military Class and the French Monarchy in the Late Middle Ages," in *American Historical Review*, 83 (1978), and *Royal Taxation in Fourteenth Century France: The Captivity and Ransom of John II, 1356–1370* (1976); Peter Shervey Lewis, *Later Medieval France: The Polity* (1968).

James Russell Major, *Representative Institutions in Renaissance France, 1421–1559* (1960); Michael Nordberg, *Les ducs et la royauté: Études sur la rivalité des ducs d'Or-*

léans et de Bourgogne, 1392–1407 (1964); John Joseph Norman Palmer, *England, France, and Christendom, 1377–1399* (1972); Paul Pelicier, *Étude sur le gouvernement de la dame de Beaujeu* (1882); Edouard Perroy, *The Hundred Years War*, W. B. Wells, trans. (1951); Charles Petit-Dutaillis, *Histoire de France*, Ernest Lavisse, ed., IV (1902), still the best general treatment of fifteenth-century political history, but badly in need of restudy; Richard Vaughan, *Philip the Bold* (1962), and *John the Fearless* (1966); Claude de Vic and J. J. Vaissete, *Histoire générale de Languedoc*, Auguste Molinier *et al.*, eds., new ed., 16 vols. (1872–1904), vols. IX–XII of which are indispensable for the history of southern France in this period.

JOHN BELL HENNEMAN

[See also **Aquitaine; Black Death; Brittany; Burgundy, Duchy of; Cabochien Riots; Charles V of France; Charles VII of France; Charles of Orléans; Edward II of England; Edward III of England; Henry V of England; Hundred Years War; Jacquerie; Joan of Arc, St.; Louis XI; Lyons; Marmousets; Mints and Money, Western European; Normans and Normandy; Pastoureaux; Philip VI of Valois; Pragmatic Sanction of Bourges; Valois Dynasty.**]

FRANCESCO DA RIMINI, painter active in the 1320's–1340's. Influenced by Giotto, he painted a signed fresco cycle previously the former convent of S. Francesco, Bologna, and now in a detached and fragmented state in the Pinacoteca, Bologna. Frescoes depicting scenes from the life of St. Francis, in the refectory of the same convent, are also attributed to him.

BIBLIOGRAPHY

Bernhard Berenson, *Italian Pictures of the Renaissance, Central and North Italian Schools*, 3 vols. (1968); Carlo Volpe, *La pittura riminese del trecento* (1965).

ADELHEID M. GEALT

FRANCESCO DI VALDAMBRINO (*ca.* 1370–1435), Sienese sculptor in wood and stone. He was influenced by Lorenzo Ghiberti and by Jacopo della Quercia, and assisted the latter in executing the tomb of Ilaria del Carretto in Lucca (1406). In 1400 he competed unsuccessfully for the commission to execute doors for the Baptistery in Florence. Francesco's works include various saints for the cathedral of

Siena (now in the Museo dell'Opera) and an Annunciation group in Asciano (Museo di Arte Sacra).

BIBLIOGRAPHY
Pèleo Bacci, *Francesco di Valdambrino* (1936).

BRUCIA WITTHOFT

FRANCIEN. See **French Language.**

FRANCIS OF ASSISI, ST. (*ca.* 1182–1226), founder of the Franciscan Order and probably the most widely admired and venerated saint of the Middle Ages. He was born at Assisi in the central Italian province of Umbria. Even in his own time many regarded his life as conforming more closely than that of any other person to the life of Jesus. His feast day is 4 October.

Francis' parents were Pietro di Bernardone, a wealthy cloth merchant, and Giovanna, called Lady Pica, whose ancestry was partially French. They had their son baptized Giovanni, but it was the nickname Francesco, referring either to his mother's ancestry or his father's business trips to France, that took hold.

In school Francis learned how to read and write, and he acquired the rudiments of arithmetic, poetry, and music. Like many well-to-do young Italians of his time, he developed a taste for Provençal and French songs and knightly legends. Apparently no thought was given to a university education for Francis; instead, he began to learn his father's trade while an adolescent.

Francis was a vivacious, friendly young man, a leader among his peers in the pursuit of carefree revelry. He had romantic dreams of chivalrous adventure and glory. In his early twenties he sought to realize his dreams by joining military expeditions. He fought for Assisi against Perugia, but was taken prisoner and held for a year. After a year of freedom tempered by sickness, he went off in 1205 to fight under Walter of Brienne in the papal cause against an imperial army. At Spoleto he was halted by a voice calling him to a more noble role back in Assisi.

Francis thus entered upon his protracted and agonizing religious conversion. He suffered intense dis-

satisfaction with his life while for a long time not understanding what way he was to take (shedding his inherited identity without being in full control of a new one). He thus became alienated from family, friends, and former ways, seeking instead the company of such social outcasts as lepers and beggars. He worked at repairing dilapidated churches, notably S. Damiano, on the very edge of Assisi, and S. Maria degli Angeli, known as the Portiuncula.

Cloth became an important theme in his conversion. One day Francis took a load of his father's cloth to market; he sold it and then gave away the money it earned him. His father was outraged, and for a while imprisoned him. When at last resigned to his son's rebellion, he had Francis come before the bishop of Assisi to renounce his patrimony formally. Francis complied, but with a theatrical gesture no one expected: he stripped himself naked and handed his clothes to his father.

In such ways Francis gained greater confidence in his new self. Once in 1209 he listened to a reading of Matthew 10, containing Jesus' charge to the apostles to live in poverty and to preach. Francis felt the text addressed to him personally and took its contents as a literal, specific program for his own life.

His conversion over, Francis—always a leader—organized a band of followers into a religious group: they had neither home nor possessions; they worked or begged for food; they lived in caves outside of towns by night and preached the Gospel in town by day. In 1210, when they numbered twelve, they went to Rome, where, after initial hesitation, Pope Innocent III gave formal approval to their way of life and to Francis' statement of their evangelical ideals. This approval marked the beginning of the Order of Lesser Brothers or, more commonly, Friars Minor (from *Ordo Fratrum Minorum*). Francis became a deacon, but was never ordained to the priesthood.

In 1212 a noble girl of Assisi named Clare (Chiara di Favarone) sought to join the company of Francis and his brothers. His response was to help her organize a religious community for women, the Poor Clares, at the church of S. Damiano.

As hundreds of people joined the movement over the next few years, the order spread its activities throughout the Italian peninsula. The first ventures outside of Italy were decided upon and taken in 1217. Earlier, Francis himself had twice started off to bring the Gospel directly to the Muslims, but he was stopped both times, once by bad sailing conditions in the Adriatic and once by bad health in Spain. In

1219 he succeeded in crossing to Egypt, where he preached before the Ayyubid sultan al-Kāmil.

During his absence, some brothers at Bologna accepted the gift of a house, a move that Francis felt compromised his ideals of itinerancy and poverty. The ensuing conflict marked the first major rift between the charismatic, saintly founder and the more mundane priestly organizers faced with the task of managing the order.

Francis continued to be influential in the affairs of the order, especially in the composition of the rule of 1221; yet from then on, he left the direct overseeing of the affairs of the order to others. He withdrew into a lonelier and more mystical life. He was suffering from conjunctivitis and perhaps also malaria. In any case his health was deteriorating and this condition was accelerated by the severity of his ascetic practices.

There was a spontaneity about Francis that attracted people to him when he lived and that has attracted people to his memory ever since. Thomas of Spalato, a cleric who saw Francis preach in the open in Bologna in 1222, described him as ragged in appearance and without training in either theology or oratory. And yet, he reported, Francis won the admiration of the scholars present for his clarity of exposition, moved leaders of bitterly opposed factions to seek reconciliation, and attracted crowds of people who sought to touch him or even tear off a piece of his habit. Among the favorite stories of him are those in which he communicated with birds, fish, wolves, and other animals. His "Canticle of Brother Sun" is an ecological hymn of praise honoring all creatures.

In 1223 Francis celebrated Christmas with his friends by re-creating the manger of Bethlehem. In the year following he underwent an intense mystical experience, from which he emerged bearing the stigmata. Only his close companions knew about the stigmata until after his death, which occurred at the Portiuncula, a chapel on the plain below Assisi. Francis' sanctity was so widely believed that canonization followed within less than two years, and between 1228 and 1230 a basilica was constructed at the north end of the city to house his remains and serve as a focus for his rapidly growing cult.

BIBLIOGRAPHY

All relevant sources are gathered in Marion A. Habig, ed., *St. Francis of Assisi, Writings and Early Biographies: English Omnibus of the Sources for the Life of St. Francis* (1973). See also Edward A. Armstrong, *Saint Francis: Na-ture Mystic, the Derivation and Significance of the Nature Stories in the Franciscan Legend* (1973); Rosalind B. Brooke, "The Lives of St. Francis of Assisi," in T. A. Dorey, ed., *Latin Biography* (1967), 177–198; Rosalind B. Brooke, ed. and trans., *Scripta Leonis, Rufini, et Angeli, sociorum S. Francisci: The Writings of Leo, Rufino, and Angelo, Companions of St. Francis* (1970); Leonard von Matt and Walter Hauser, *St. Francis of Assisi: A Pictorial Biography*, Sebastian Bullough, trans. (1956); Hendrik W. van Os, "St. Francis of Assisi as a Second Christ in Early Italian Painting," in *Simiolus: Netherlands Quarterly for the History of Art*, 7 (1974); Paul Sabatier, *Life of St. Francis*, Louise S. Houghton, trans. (1977).

LESTER K. LITTLE

[See also **Franciscan Rite; Franciscans.**]

FRANCISCAN RITE. Today there is no Franciscan rite properly speaking; it is merged with the modern Roman rite it helped to form and disseminate. In its history it has experienced several periods in which the practice of liturgical prayer, the evolution of legislation, and the elaboration of liturgical books are intermingled.

ORIGINS: 1208/1209

St. Francis evokes the period of origins in his Testament, in which he provides a description of the original liturgical practice: "Officium dicebamus, clerici secundum alios clericos, laici dicebant Paternoster; et satis libenter manebamus in ecclesiis. Et eramus idiotae et subditi omnibus" (We shall say the Office, those who can read shall say it like clerics, those who cannot read shall say the paternoster, and we shall gladly enough remain in the churches. And we shall be simple and subject to all: 18–19). The words *clerici* and *laici* are not used here in the canonical sense; rather, they denote "literates" and "illiterates." As for *idiotae*, it can only mean "simple" or "unpretentious." This passage of the Testament, then, indicates that the friars wished to participate in church prayer; that at the time this prayer was recited only in those churches having books containing the Office and in which clerics were obliged to recite it (for example, because of a benefice); and that those who could read had learned to do so from the Psalter, which most of them knew by heart. Those who were illiterate, and thus unfamiliar with the Psalms, recited the paternoster; according to the adage of the period, "qui non potest psallere debet patere" (who cannot read the hours should recite the

Our Father). The *Legenda trium sociorum* (38) provides an example of the practice described above.

FIRST LEGISLATIVE ELABORATION (1209–1221)

The culmination of the first legislative elaboration was the *Regula non bullata* of 1221. The prescriptions of the third chapter of this rule, which describe the practice of the first decade, can be summed up as follows: all friars shall perform the Divine Office; clerics shall perform the Office according to the custom of the Roman church; the friars and clerics, as well as the members of the laity who can read, shall have at their disposal the books necessary to perform the Office; and those members of the laity who cannot read shall recite an Office composed essentially of the paternoster. It will be noticed that the type of Office assigned depends not on any canonical distinction between laymen and clerics, but on the cultural distinction between the literate and the illiterate. This fact attests that the Franciscan Order, at least in this period, was primarily a fraternity of laymen (in the canonical sense), the greatest number of whom, belonging to the rising (and therefore learned) class, could recite the Office of the clerics.

Sometime between 1160 and 1185, a pope decided to eliminate the old Roman character of the liturgy of the papal chapel. He authorized the chaplains to celebrate the solemn papal liturgy of the "stations" in a simplified form. In order to establish this liturgy as a model for the entire Latin church, Innocent III later codified it in an Ordinal. The expression "secundum consuetudinem clericorum romanae ecclesiae," which is found in the rule of 1221, thus means "after the usage of the chaplains of the curia."

Because Bishop Guido of Assisi and his cathedral chapter had introduced among themselves the Office (but not the missal) of the curia, the practical choice for Francis and his first friars was to adopt the local liturgy.

THE RULE OF 1223

The Roman curia played an important role in drafting the definitive Rule, which was approved in 1223. The style of the Rule, accordingly, is more strictly canonical. The Rule marks three significant changes in liturgical practice. First, it reintroduces the canonical distinction between clerics and laymen, and does not state that laymen are permitted to recite the Office with the clerics. Second, the structure of the laymen's Office is simplified. Third, it is stated that the clerics' Office will be performed "secundum ordinem sanctae romanae ecclesiae"—which, despite the emphatic character of the formula, means "after the fashion of the chaplains of the curia"—and conducted "excepto psalterio," that is, with the Gallican rather than the Roman Psalter. The Rule also uses an obscure expression that touches upon a much discussed topic: "ex quo habere poterunt breviaria," variously translated as "as soon as they can have breviaries," "from which office they might have breviaries," or "in order that they might have breviaries." Probably this links the privilege of performing the Office to possession of the expensive breviary.

FIRST APPEARANCE OF LITURGICAL BOOKS (1230)

Once the Rule was approved, it became necessary to provide the friars with the books required to apply its prescriptions. Continuing the work of Innocent III, Honorius III had published a breviary and a missal suited to the friars' use. In addition, a scriptorium was built at the Portiuncula to produce sufficient numbers of these books. It is convenient to call the breviary and missal adapted by Honorius for the Friars Minor the regula-books. At the chapter of 1230, these breviaries and missals were distributed to the provincials of some twenty provinces (the expression found in the manuscripts of Jordan of Giano concerning this subject—"breviaria et antiphonalia"—doubtless results from a paleographically explicable misreading of "breviaria et missalia"). Fourteen manuscript breviaries and four manuscript missals of this type are known.

THE WORKS OF HAYMO OF FAVERSHAM (1240–1244)

The application of the Rule of 1223 was not accomplished without raising certain questions, an echo of which is audible in the *Expositio quatuor magistrorum* (1241–1242); the regula-books were rendered impractical by their incomprehensible rubrics. Furthermore, the missal that was provided for the solemn Mass did not contain an *ordo missae* for the private Mass that spread in the order despite Francis' discouragement in his *Letter to the Entire Order*. Haymo of Faversham, elected general in 1240, devoted an important part of his activity to the compilation of liturgical books that would remedy these difficulties. He is responsible for an *Ordo missae,* approved at the chapter of Bologna in 1243, that describes the speeches and actions of the private Mass; an *Ordo breviarii* and an *ordo missalis,* "secundum consuetudinem romanae curiae," approved by Innocent IV in June 1243; an *Ordo ad benedicendum mensam* for the entire year, doubtless completed before Haymo's death; and the revision of the *Graduale* that, although previously believed not to have been completed before 1251, was in fact completed in 1244, as was proved by the discovery of a letter of Haymo's successor, Crescentius of Jesi.

THE SUBSEQUENT EVOLUTION

In accordance with the *Ordines* of Haymo, a *Capitularium,* a *Tonale tonorum communium* or *Cantorinus* (1251), and probably a *Martyrologium* (*ca.* 1254) were written. In 1260 there appeared a second edition of the breviary and missal as well as a revised calendar under Bonaventure, who can be considered their editor because of his modifications of them. Also published were the *Ritual for the Last Sacraments* in 1260 and, in 1263, a table, known as *Tabula Parisiensis,* designed to determine the antiphons of the Office during the week before Christmas. The successive general chapters often promulgated liturgical statutes; for the most part, however, these chapters were concerned with modifying details.

It remains to be demonstrated how the expansion of the Franciscan order, facilitated by these liturgical books, favored the diffusion of the liturgy "secundum consuetudinem romanae curiae," thus accomplishing the goal pursued by the papacy of standardizing the liturgy of the Latin church.

BIBLIOGRAPHY
Fundamental works are: Stephen J. P. van Dijk, *The Sources of the Modern Roman Liturgy* (1963), and *Ordinal of the Papal Court from Innocent III to Boniface VIII and Related Documents* (1975); as well as Stephen J. P. van Dijk and J. Hazelden Walker, *The Origins of the Modern Roman Liturgy* (1960). An excellent summary of the problem is Stephen J. P. van Dijk, "Ursprung und Inhalt der franziskanischen Liturgie des 13. Jahrhunderts," in *Franziskanische Studien,* 51 (1969). Descriptions of the MSS include Théophile Desbonnets, "Un témoin de la liturgie franciscaine primitive, Meaux Bibl. Municip. 3," in *Archivum Franciscanum historicum,* 63 (1970), and "Un rituel franciscain de 1458, Dôle, Bibl. Municip. 49," *ibid.,* 65 (1972); and Stephen J. P. van Dijk, "The Breviary of St. Clare," in *Franciscan Studies,* 8 (1948) and 9 (1949), "The Breviary of St. Francis," *ibid.,* 9 (1949), and "Some Manuscripts on the Earliest Franciscan Liturgy," *ibid.,* 14 (1954). Although the works of Stephen J. P. van Dijk have superseded those of almost all his predecessors, it is possible to find material of interest in Giuseppe Abate, "Il primitivo breviario francescano (1224–1227)," in *Miscellanea francescana,* 60 (1960), which must be used in connection with its critique, Stephen J. P. van Dijk, "An Authentic Copy of the Franciscan *Regula Breviary,*" in *Scriptorium,* 16 (1962); and Arsène Le Carou, *Le bréviaire romain et les frères mineurs au XIIIe siècle* (1927).

THÉOPHILE DESBONNETS, O.F.M.

[See also **Francis of Assisi, St.; Franciscans; Innocent III, Pope.**]

FRANCISCANS. The word denotes members of the Franciscan order, established by Francis of Assisi in his native town in Umbria in central Italy, during the years between 1206 and 1210. The official name of the order is Ordo Fratrum Minorum (Order of Friars Minor, O.F.M.).

While Francis' life can be seen as fitting into the context of central Italian urban society in his time, he was nonetheless a truly extraordinary person. Similarly, although the origins of the order he founded should be seen as part of one trend in a tumultuous period of church history, the institution that eventually emerged was remarkably different from the major religious orders of earlier times. The Franciscans were friars, as distinguished from monks. They lived in convents located exclusively in towns: they engaged in an active ministry directed toward town dwellers, both rich and poor; they lived by the ideal of material poverty for themselves as individuals but also maintained that their order, as a corporate body, should be poor.

The order had one of the great success stories of the thirteenth century as well as of the history of religious orders. Within that century it spread to over 1,400 convents, located in all the Latin Christian countries, and its missionaries went to many countries beyond. Its members included several of the most famous and influential figures in both intellectual and ecclesiastical matters during its first three centuries. The most famous of all, always, was Francis himself, probably the most revered saint in Latin Christian history, with the order serving as the chief instrument for the propagation of his cult. Moreover, the order had a greater impact than did any other religious order on the lives of the laity. Whereas other orders tended either to be aloof from society or else to concentrate on influencing elites, the Franciscans had an exceptionally broad appeal and an immeasurably great talent for involving Christian lay people in the religion they professed.

Francis' younger contemporary, Clare, organized a female branch of the order starting in 1212; it received the official approval of Honorius III in 1219 and has been known by such names as the Order of the Sisters of St. Francis, the Order of St. Clare, the Clarisses, or Poor Clares. The Franciscans and the Clarisses constituted, respectively, the First and Second Orders of St. Francis. Francis himself was instrumental in encouraging many lay people to reform their lives while not abandoning entirely their lay status. Such encouragement led eventually to the formation of a Third Order, the Order of Penitence, reserved to lay people, both men and women, who wished to maintain a special tie, even while married and working in society, with the Franciscans. The earliest extant documentation on this lay order dates from around 1280, but there are indications that its foundations go back to 1221.

The Franciscans have endured to the present. Their numerous varieties and branches in modern times seem of impenetrable complexity to an outside observer. Right from the early years of the order, there were disagreements about some of the most fundamental aspects of its nature and program. While the chart of organization for the earliest centuries is not nearly as complicated as it is at present, the controversies and the formation of factions and parties form a central part of the early history of the order. In a history of the Christian religion, the corresponding part would be held by schisms and heresies, and by divisions both theological and ecclesiological. In this article, then, there will be greater emphasis on the earlier period, and the major, recurring theme will be the interpretation of the original ideals of the founder and of his order. This problem of interpretation was apparent already in discussions of poverty and of property ownership during Francis' lifetime; it was paramount in the half century of struggle, 1274–1328, involving the Spiritual Franciscans; and it was still central at the time of the definitive division of the order into two in the year 1517.

FRANCIS AND THE START OF THE ORDER

All of the dates mentioned here that fall prior to 1215 are approximate; it would have been difficult at the time to foresee the immense historical importance of the modest happenings of those years. Francis, born about 1182, was the son of a wealthy cloth merchant. He was a charming, extroverted young man, a leader among his peers. Though literate, he received no university education, for he was supposed to take over his father's business. He had dreams of gaining glory through military exploits, but became ill as he set out on one expedition in about 1205. His conversion was now begun and was to last for three or four years. Slowly he shed his inherited identity and worked out a new one. The latter became focused on a desire to imitate the life of Jesus and the Apostles, and the details on how to do that came from various Gospel texts. The most important of these were Matt. 19:21, "If you wish to go the whole way, go, sell your possessions, and give to the poor"; Luke 9:3, "Take nothing for the journey, neither stick nor pack, neither bread nor money"; and Matt. 16:24, "If anyone wishes to be a follower of mine, he must leave self behind." All three texts consist of injunctions spoken by Jesus, and Francis took them (and many others) as direct, literal commands for the conduct of his life. He rejected his patrimony entirely. He lived an extremely simple life, repairing dilapidated churches and not handling any money whatever. He attracted a few companions, Bernard of Quintavalle, Peter Catani, and Giles of Assisi, and they went about in pairs, in imitation of the Apostles, preaching penance. Francis remained the leader, charismatic just as he had been years before amidst his youthful companions. The numbers grew to the apostolic figure twelve.

With a document that is no longer extant but that apparently consisted mainly of biblical passages such as those cited above, the brothers went off to Rome to seek the approval of the pope for what they were doing and also for this text, which they evidently regarded as their rule. The appearance of these twelve somewhat scrawny characters at the court of Pope Innocent III probably caused some commotion; at least they had considerable difficulty in getting admitted. And yet this sort of group was not wholly unheard of in Rome, a point that allows us to see these earliest Franciscans, however outstanding, as part of a general socioreligious movement of their time.

The Roman church was in a period of grave crisis on several counts. It had not reacted creatively to the rapid development in Europe, but especially in Italy, of an urban society and a commercial, monetary economy over the previous century and a half. More specifically, it had made a weak response at best to the urban laity, which was far more demanding of the clergy than the rural laity had been and continued to be. Urban people were more literate, more curious, and, in particular, more desirous of knowing what message was contained in sacred scripture and of having the word preached by the clergy. Yet this is exactly what the clergy did not do, showing instead more concern about its own rights and privileges. From the middle of the twelfth century the church hierarchy was increasingly in the hands of lawyers. They were defining the status of priests ever more precisely and narrowly, placing special emphasis on such exclusive clerical preserves as the dispensing of sacraments.

Meanwhile, there were developing many spiritual tendencies within Christian society over which the church had no control. Some of these, such as the Cathars, put forth genuine differences of doctrine, while others, such as the Waldensians, had disagreements only about priestly prerogatives. Both types, however, were categorically denounced, declared heretical, and cast aside.

But they did not go away. And Innocent III finally reversed a half century of conservative papal policy when he showed a willingness to examine carefully all such lay initiatives and to encourage those elements within them found to be worthy and doctrinally sound. Thus in 1201 he approved a rule for the Humiliati, who had been condemned by the Council of Verona in 1184. He even allowed them to continue their practice of gathering every Sunday to hear one of their own brothers speak. The qualifications for such a lay preacher were that he be strong in faith, knowledgeable in religion, gifted in speech, and consistent in behavior and speech. The qualifications for what was preached were found in the pope's distinction between preaching doctrine and giving witness to faith and morals. The latter, built of exhortations to observe decent moral behavior and to engage in works of piety, was wholly acceptable; the former, involving discussion of theological issues and of the sacraments of the church, was judged outside their competence and expressly forbidden.

The Poor Men of Lyons had also fallen under anathema at the Council of Verona in 1184. One of their leading spokesmen, Durand of Huesca, led a group of them back into the Catholic fold in 1208. They made a profession of faith to Innocent III and asked his approval for their program of evangelical, antiheretical preaching. Their request was granted and they took the name "Poor Catholics" (*Pauperes catholici*). An Italian offshoot of the Lyons movement was known as the "Poor Lombards" (*Pauperes Lombardi*). A group of these came before Innocent III in 1210 under the leadership of Bernard Prim. They called themselves the "Reconciled Poor" (*Pauperes reconciliati*), and they engaged in manual labor. The pope approved of their preaching, provided it was limited to penitential exhortation.

Enter Francis and his companions. With assistance from the bishop of Assisi, they gained admittance to the papal court in 1209 or more probably 1210. One account says they called themselves the "Lesser Poor" (*Pauperes minores*) and only afterward changed their name to "Lesser Brothers" (*Fratres minores*). In any case, the pope approved of their program, too, including the right to preach moral reform and to give witness to the faith. He asked that they all be tonsured, which had the effect of giving them minor clerical status. Still, that did not make them priests, and indeed Francis, as well as a considerable number of his followers, never did join the priesthood.

From Rome they returned to Umbria. They took temporary shelter in huts and caves outside of towns and then either worked or begged for their food. They preached in towns and there ministered to the poor and downcast, giving special attention to the care of lepers. In the summer they divided up and traveled far afield in the Italian peninsula and then returned to Assisi. Twice Francis tried to preach to the Muslims. In 1212 he sailed out of Ancona but rough seas forced the boat back to port; two years later his trip to Morocco was cut short in Spain by illness. All the while the ranks of the order were expanding rapidly, to several hundred members already in 1215, the year of the Fourth Lateran Council.

At the council there took place a strong reaction against the recent proliferation of religious orders. Anyone wishing to form a new religious group was ordered to settle for following one of the established, approved rules, instead of submitting a new one for approval. It happened that Dominic of Guzman appeared at this council in the company of the bishop of Toulouse; he was seeking approval for the formation of his group of antiheretical preachers, which had already been active in the Toulouse region for a decade. He had the strong backing of the bishop, but as he had no previous approval from Rome, the new legislation applied to him. Eventually the Dominicans adopted the Rule of St. Augustine. Whatever agreement had transpired between Francis and Innocent back in 1210 now served Francis well, for his group was officially considered to have been founded prior to the council.

By 1216 and 1217 the friars were so numerous that during the annual periods of dispersal they reached into nearly every part of Italy. In this connection, momentous decisions were taken at the

May 1217 general chapter meeting at Assisi. Some more formal structure for the order was provided by dividing Italy up into six provinces: Tuscany, Lombardy, the Marches of Ancona, Campania, Apulia, and Calabria. In addition, it was now decided to expand beyond the confines of Italy, and expeditions were planned for Germany, France, Spain, and the Holy Land. Each of these areas was to constitute a province, except France, which was divided into two provinces. Each province was placed under a minister who was in turn responsible to Francis, as head of the order.

The first expeditions outside of Italy fared badly because of faulty linguistic and material preparation. Thus trips to Germany and Hungary failed completely in 1219, but others were successfully undertaken to Germany in 1221 and Hungary in 1228. The settlement in Spain began in 1217, that in France in 1218, and one also in England in 1224.

While these attempts at expansion were going on, Francis turned again to his desire to go convert Muslims. In 1219 he sailed from Ancona for Crete, Cyprus, Acre, and finally Damietta. There in Egypt he got through to the sultan, before whom he preached the Christian religion. The sultan was cordial, even though not convinced. More important, Francis had established a precedent by his clear preference for conversion over the crusade. While he was in Syria, five of his followers suffered martyrdom for their faith in Morocco.

In these years of rapid expansion, practical problems arose in the order and decisions were made by many other people besides Francis. The most notable of these persons was Hugolino, a nephew of Innocent III and a cardinal (as well as the future Gregory IX). Beginning in 1217 Hugolino was the official "protector" of the order, which made him both the chief lobbyist for the order at the papal court and at the same time the pope's representative in the running of the order. Hugolino was instrumental in the early plans for expansion and for provincial organization. When Francis was in Egypt, the brothers in Bologna accepted the gift of a house, a specially attractive gift since Bologna was the leading university city in Italy. Yet Francis upon his return was deeply opposed to this move and went to Bologna to drive the friars physically out of the house. Then Hugolino stepped in and calmly announced that the house belonged to him. The Franciscans thus owned no property; their ideal had not been compromised; and meanwhile they were welcome to make use of the property. This legal fiction, which distinguished between ownership and use, subsequently lay at the center of some of the order's most bitter internal disputes.

Francis was quite ill and was now clearly no longer in full command of the order. He sought to put its affairs in line by naming a successor and by revising the rule. In 1221 he named as his own successor one of his first collaborators, Peter Catani, who, however, died shortly afterward. He then named Brother Elias, who had joined him about ten years before and had been the first provincial minister in the Holy Land. Francis also worked with some companions on a new version of the rule, which was presented to the general chapter meeting in May 1221. It consists of twenty-three chapters and is made up in large part of biblical passages. It claims at the start to be the rule approved by Innocent III and goes by the title "First Rule." Yet it did not meet with general approval and so Francis, now quite withdrawn from the daily administration of the order, devoted much effort to getting an acceptable rule over the next two years.

The people running the order, including Hugolino, favored a more juridical and less spiritual document for a rule. They were more satisfied with the version that came before the general chapter of 1223 and that was subsequently approved by Honorius III. It is known as the "Second Rule" or the *Regula bullata* (approved by papal bull). It is both less strict and less spontaneous than the First Rule: for example, there is no mention of the friars having to travel by foot, or their not taking anything with them when they travel. There were several other such alterations, and they make clear that this rule gained general approval only in spite of the objections of Francis. He had included, for example, a passage saying that a friar could observe this rule literally even if his superiors decreed otherwise, but Honorius III persuaded him to drop it. He had hoped to start and finish the rule by saying that the friars must obey the Holy Gospel, but he lost on that point, too.

Thus the priestly organizers won out and the charismatic founder withdrew more and more from the affairs of the order. At Christmas 1223 he was at Greccio (north of Rome near Rieti) with friends and he had them stage a reenactment of the scene of Jesus' birth at Bethlehem; with this simple act of imitation, the Christmastime veneration of the crèche began. The following summer Francis came close to a reenactment of the Passion as well, for while in a mystical trance at Alverna (*La Verna,* in the mountains above Arezzo), he received the stigmata, the signs of the five wounds of Jesus, on his hands, his feet, and his side.

The last two years were passed in terrible sickness. His final act as concerns the history of the order was his dictating a testament. This document recounts to the brothers his recollection of the earliest days of the order. In it Francis admonished them always to live as strangers and exiles and to refrain from soliciting privileges from the Roman curia. He asked that the testament be always kept with and read with the rule, and that no glosses be made on either of them. Toward the end he was carried to Assisi where, amid touching scenes of farewells, blessings, and prayers, he died on 3 October 1226.

FROM ELIAS TO BONAVENTURE, 1226–1274

Brother Elias took temporary charge of the order until the following May, when John Parenti was elected minister general. Elias, at the urging of Hugolino, now Gregory IX, meanwhile took charge of the construction of a suitable resting place for the remains of Francis, who was widely regarded, even in his lifetime, as a saint. Elias got the land at the north end of town and began raising money for a huge basilica. In July 1228 Gregory IX came to Assisi to bless the foundation of the church and to announce the canonization of Francis. He also commissioned one of the friars, Thomas of Celano, to write a biography of the new saint. With much of the construction complete already in the early part of 1230, the body was transferred to a tomb inside the new church, and the pope decreed that the basilica be regarded as the "head and mother" (caput et mater) of the order.

In the same year, the issue of whether the order could hold any properties and whether friars could ever have secure lodgings came to a head. With the problem of property was in turn tied up the whole problem of study, particularly whether those friars studying in universities could have books and fixed places to stay. The resolution of these issues came in the bull Quo elongati issued by Gregory IX. He observed that the testament of St. Francis could not be binding because Francis drew it up by himself and also because he had no authority to restrict his successors. The pope then glossed the rule in such a way as to justify the order having houses, furniture, and books. These were to be and remain possessions of the donors, with their use reserved to the Franciscans.

Thus interpretations of the words and wishes and actions of St. Francis became the critical bases of authority in the order, which continued to expand rapidly in both the number of converts and the number of convents. Brother Elias was a staunch ally of Gregory IX in this flexible view of the order's constitution; in 1232 he was elected to succeed John Parenti as minister general.

In an attempt to gain better administrative control, Elias subdivided the existing provinces, raising their total number from seventeen to over thirty-two; in Italy the number rose from six to sixteen. Expansion continued on the outer edges of Latin Christendom: Scandinavia and Bohemia were settled in 1232, Poland in 1237, Prussia in 1239. And further afield, during Elias' time missionaries went to such places as Morocco, Tunisia, Syria, Mesopotamia, Georgia, and Armenia.

Elias was well regarded for his active support of theological studies; he had these introduced into every province and he encouraged settlements in more convenient and more stable houses within university towns. He favored improved housing conditions for the friars in general, and he sponsored the construction of churches alongside the convents. With the work on the basilica at Assisi about complete, he commissioned the first part of the fresco decoration in the lower church and he began construction of a new and larger convent immediately behind the basilica.

These were all noteworthy accomplishments (and there were more) and yet the most striking aspect of his reign was the wild, raging storm of controversy that circled about Elias himself and eventually swept him from office. He was a member of the order from shortly after the time it gained papal approval. He was then and he remained always a layman. Obviously he was a close and trusted associate of Francis. And he had many years of experience at conducting the affairs of the order. Yet things went disastrously wrong between 1232 and 1239; and while part of the trouble was the perennial Franciscan problem of strictness as against laxity in interpreting the original ideal, the greater part of it centered on the person of the minister general.

Elias affected a princely manner. The elegance of his living quarters, his table, his retinue, and his horses was blatantly inappropriate for the head of the Franciscans. Elias was autocratic: he tried to rule the order without convoking the general chapter. To exert control in certain provinces, he sent out visitors with powers that included excommunication. Some of these were perceived as spies. Some used their authority to exact funds for the church at Assisi. Some stayed for such long periods that they effectively usurped the powers of those they were supposedly visiting. Finally, Elias displayed a clear preference for laymen over clerics, particularly in the way he made appointments.

The leadership of the opposition not only consisted of clerics but was openly hostile to the lay brothers. Herein lies a strong indication that Elias' favoring of the laity was the key issue. The order was becoming increasingly clericalized, as clerics joined the order, as friars were called on more and more to adopt clerical functions, as competition with the (markedly clerical) Dominicans intensified, and as the church in general became more clericalized. Learning went with clerical status, and the view that many clerics had of lay brothers was simply that they were useless to the order.

Elias can thus be seen as a conservative, resisting the progressive tendencies of many of his confreres. Francis himself had demonstrated considerable ambivalence about learning, having once suggested that a novice divest himself of his learning just as he would leave off any other form of wealth or power. Elias was true to Francis' testament in not seeking privileges in Rome, and yet he was criticized for not doing so, while his successors were in fact quick to send off many such requests to Rome.

The leaders of the opposition were three scholars, Haymo of Faversham, Alexander of Hales, and John of La Rochelle. Robert Grosseteste lent them his support by warning the pope in a letter against the destructiveness of Elias. Delegations from several northern provinces converged on Rome in 1238. Gregory IX heard them, then asked them to return home and to prepare for a general chapter at Rome in the following year.

Elias counted on his friendship with the pope to save him, and indeed the pope held out for long against the plaintiffs. Yet all the complaints did get aired in Rome. Haymo of Faversham gave the final, devastating presentation, with Elias interrupting and insulting him. In what must have been a most dramatic scene, Gregory IX, presiding over the chapter, spoke of his respect for Elias, the friend of St. Francis, and of what a capable minister he was, but then, citing his lack of support in the order, declared him deposed.

Elias was out but the scandal was not over, because he subsequently consorted with the emperor, Frederick II, even when the latter was under a ban of excommunication. Thus Elias himself was excommunicated. Various attempts to heal the breach and quiet the scandal failed; peace came only as Elias lay on his deathbed at Cortona in 1253.

His successor was Albert of Pisa, the first priest to head the order. Albert initiated a series of reforms. Although the text of these is not extant, they were evidently confirmed and then included in the Constitutions of Narbonne passed in 1260. Clearly the main intention in 1239 was to restrain the authority of the minister general; provision was made for meetings of the general chapter every three years and for the election of provincial ministers by provincial chapters.

Albert died within less than one year, to be replaced by Haymo of Faversham. A former master of theology at Paris and delegate of Gregory IX in discussions of reunion with the Greek church, Haymo is credited with a major reform of the Franciscan breviary. He was scrupulous in consulting others in governing the order, and he traveled through Europe visiting the provinces. Much attention was then being devoted to disputed points in the Rule. Still extant is an "Exposition on the Rule" by four masters at Paris: Alexander of Hales, John of La Rochelle, Robert of Bascia, and Eudes Rigaud. They reaffirmed support for *Quo elongati* with its distinction between possession and use, and regarded the testament of Francis as representing only his personal wishes.

After the death of Albert in 1244, the new minister was Crescentius of Iesi (Jesi), a lawyer and a doctor of medicine. The faction known as the Spirituals first emerged in the time of Crescentius. According to the report he made to the general chapter that elected him, there were rebellious friars in the Marches of Ancona where he had been serving as provincial minister. These refused to live in convents but carried on in the original tradition of the homeless, propertyless companions of Francis. Some of these were actual onetime companions of Francis. Some were imbued with the writings of Joachim of Fiore. They claimed to be guided by the Holy Spirit, which thus excused their insubordination to priests or officials of the order. Crescentius had tried to discipline these *Zelanti,* or Spirituals, and in 1244 denounced them before the whole order.

Crescentius put a series of questions to Pope Innocent IV in the hope of getting a further relaxation of the rule than that allowed by Gregory IX. The papal reply, contained in *Ordinem vestrum* of 1245, left the brothers free to ignore precepts of the Gospel not specifically quoted in the rule. Properties occupied and used by the friars were henceforth owned by the papacy. Dealings in money or other worldly matters could be handled through agents.

Crescentius also issued a call to the brothers to write down all they knew of the life and miracles of Francis. A remarkable collection of material came back from the hermitage at Greccio, sent by three of Francis' closest friends: Leo, Rufino, and Angelo. It consisted of stories, "picked as it were from a field of flowers," rather than a continuous narrative. These writings were neither published right away nor lost; they were to surface decades later in works of decidedly Spiritualist leanings. Still, they had some immediate impact on one work at this time, a second biography of Francis by Thomas of Celano, in 1247.

There are accounts of several disciplinary measures against Spirituals by Crescentius, but then his generalship came to a curious end when in 1247 he refused to call a general chapter as he was required to do, and Innocent IV deposed him. Even at this time, while the order's internal troubles continued to brew, John of Piancarpino was leading a Franciscan mission (1245–1247), at Innocent IV's request, to the court of the great khan in Outer Mongolia.

John of Parma came into office in 1247 with broad support, the choice of the ministers but also acceptable to many of the *Zelanti*. He traveled about the provinces, he called and presided over general chapters when supposed to, he observed the rule, and he tried to restore the friars' esteem for Francis' testament; indeed he tried to let some of the more lenient aspects of *Ordinem vestrum* lapse. He could not escape being drawn into a dispute between the friars and the secular masters at the University of Paris, and his participation in the dispute eventually compromised him.

The dispute at first was neither intellectual nor spiritual, but essentially institutional: it concerned the right of access to professorial chairs. Once the friars had gained a strong foothold in the university, the secular masters retaliated with various tactics: strike, expulsion for not participating in the strike, and imposition of a loyalty oath. The friars appealed for papal support and through the pope gained readmittance to the university. John of Parma came to Paris and preached reconciliation but matters had already gone too far. In 1254 the secular masters set out their grievances in a long letter to all scholars and prelates. Innocent IV now turned against the friars, but he shortly thereafter died (and not without the help of the mendicants' prayers, said some). Alex-

ander IV intervened very strongly on the side of the friars and the masters replied by dissolving the university.

The attack turned from the constitutional issue to the whole purpose and existence of the mendicant orders. The appearance of a fervently Joachimite tract, *The Introduction to the Eternal Gospel*, by Gerard of Borgo San Donnino, a reader in theology at the Franciscan convent in Paris, seriously weakened the case of the friars by implicating them in anti-clerical and heretical opinions. John of Parma and his Dominican counterpart tried to impose a tight control on what members of their orders said in public and published, but the real damage had already been done. The seculars' attack, led by William of St. Amour, denounced the friars as false apostles, as precursors of Antichrist, and as dangers to the life of the university and hence also the church.

In 1255 Gerard's book was condemned as heretical, and the pope asked John of Parma to resign. A general chapter convened in Rome early in 1257 where John announced his intention to resign. His confreres at first tried to dissuade him. Once they learned of the papal pressures on him, they acceded to his wish but asked him to nominate his own successor. He turned without hesitation to Bonaventure, a native of Bagnoregio, near Orvieto, and at that time only about forty years old.

Bonaventure took a coherent, moderate line in defining and defending the order. He met the charges about the friars' construction of large, stone convents in cities and their furnishing them with books and furniture by pointing to the demands of the urban ministry and the problems of urban real estate values and fire dangers, besides reiterating the papal distinction between ownership and use. He met the charge about the friars' not working by arguing that all friars work, whether at study, in saying the Divine Office, in collecting alms, in domestic labors, in preaching, or in hearing confessions. He met the charge that the friars had usurped many of the functions of the secular clergy by arguing that their purpose was to support the clergy and to make up for deficiencies in its ministry. And to the charge that the order at present was far different from what it had been in the early days, he replied with evident pleasure by comparing the history of his order to the history of the Christian church, from the earliest times of the humble fishermen.

Within the order he tried to steer a middle course, attacking excessive laxity in regard to the rule and clamping down firmly on Spiritualist tendencies. He had Gerard of Borgo San Donnino tried and condemned to prison for life. He also had John of Parma put on trial, but moderate voices at the papal court intervened on behalf of the deposed but highly respected minister general, who was allowed to live out his life quietly at Greccio.

Bonaventure's first general chapter met at Narbonne in 1260, when he had a set of constitutions passed, most of which can be understood as replies to contemporary complaints. The minimum age for reception into the order was set at eighteen. Greater simplicity in church buildings and appointments was called for. Many regulations against aggressive money collecting were passed. Habits, fasts, discipline, visitations, training of novices, university studies, and the general chapters were all closely regulated. In all, there was a prologue and 255 separate decrees.

The general chapter of Narbonne sought to reform the order's history as well, by promulgating an official biography of St. Francis. Bonaventure was charged with writing it. The resulting work was distributed, one per province, in 1263, while the chapter of 1266 ordered that there be one in each convent. Moreover, all other biographical writings about the founder were to be burned. The intention was to eliminate any kind of Francis different from Bonaventure's moderate, official Francis, to whom the Spirituals or any other dissidents might turn for justification and a model.

Bonaventure traveled widely and also continued to study and write. While he turned down the archbishopric of York, he did accept a cardinal's hat in 1273, the year before his death.

DEFEAT OF THE SPIRITUALS, 1274–1328

The order now entered a period when the basic tension between strict adherence to the poverty and simplicity of Francis and the desire to build upon a firm and enduring material base broke out into open conflict. Among the Clarisses, a similar tension had once existed but without leading to such a conflict. Clare and her companions had wanted to participate fully in the homeless, wandering, apostolic life, but Francis and the other men of his order, plus the men in the hierarchy who concerned themselves with these matters, could not tolerate the notion of religious women living in any way except closed inside a convent. Although Clare secured from Innocent III a "privilege of poverty" for San Damiano, permitting an exceptionally austere way of life and a total lack of ownership for the community, Hugolino

later imposed on them the life of Benedictine nuns. Clare lived in obedience at the little church of San Damiano, on the edge of Assisi, from 1212 to 1253—in obedience but not without resentment. In the year she died, she was still seeking approval from Innocent IV for a rule of her own, based on that of the First Order. After her death, the ministers and popes met little opposition in maintaining a benign, moderately comfortable, propertied life in the Second Order. It grew to have nearly three hundred convents in 1300, located mostly in Italy, France, Spain, and Portugal.

All the mendicants came under attack at the Second Council of Lyons in 1274. The most vehement protests came from Spirituals living in the Marches. Their leaders, including Peter of Macerata and Peter of Fossombrone, were condemned to life imprisonment. Another center of Spiritualist activity was southern France, where in the 1270's Peter John Olivi was preaching and writing. Olivi, a native of Béziers, studied in Paris under some of the order's greatest scholars, including John Peckham, Matthew of Aquasparta, and Bonaventure. He led a life of exemplary simplicity and poverty; he worked for the reform of his order but he was both moderate and obedient; in fact he criticized what he saw as the excesses of the Spirituals.

Olivi was well enough regarded to be appointed to a commission, along with two Franciscan cardinals and two provincial ministers, to prepare a new interpretation of the rule for the pope. The resulting bull, *Exiit qui seminat,* issued by Nicholas III in 1279, followed the moderate line of Bonaventure. On the aggravated issue of poverty, it went beyond the earlier distinction between property and use to distinguish between use in right and use in fact, the former inadmissible, the latter permissible if moderate.

Olivi's fortunes within the order wavered. Accusations of spreading Joachimite heretical views were brought against him in 1282 and again in 1285, leading the order to try to suppress some of his works. But in 1287 Matthew of Aquasparta became minister general and appointed him reader in theology at S. Croce in Florence. There, presumably, he met and taught his most famous disciple, Ubertino of Casale, a friar recently returned from studying in Paris. After a few years, Olivi took a similar post at Montpellier. He lived in peace until his death at Narbonne in 1298, a hero to the Spirituals and a heretic to their opponents, who were known as Conventuals.

The Conventuals took heart from Pope Martin

IV, who in 1283 established the positions known as apostolic syndics or procurators. These were papal appointees charged with overseeing the business affairs of the friars. This measure and related ones were driving some of the Spirituals to seek separation from the order rather than its reform. The first Franciscan pope, Nicholas IV (1288–1292), was particularly harsh in trying to suppress the Spiritualist opposition in the Marches.

The power of the Spirituals was not wholly confined to the fringes of the order, for in 1289 one of their own, Raymond Gaufridi, was elected minister general. Raymond went to the Marches to set free the Spiritualist leaders imprisoned there fifteen years before. These went first to live in Armenia, but the Franciscans in Syria did all in their power to make life difficult for them. They returned to Ancona, where they were also not welcome, and then became involved in the curious episode of Pope Celestine V, who reigned for five months in 1294. Celestine released these men from their vows of obedience to their Franciscan superiors and let them form a separate order called the Poor Hermits of Pope Celestine. Peter of Macerata took the name Liberato, and Peter of Fossombrone became Angelo Clareno. When Boniface VIII ascended the papal throne, he suppressed the Poor Hermits and he deposed Raymond Gaufridi. Liberato, Angelo, and their friends sought refuge on a Greek island, returning to Italy only after Boniface died. Meanwhile the suppression of Spirituals took a savage turn in southern Italy under the direction of the Dominican inquisitor Thomas of Aversa.

In the Holy Land at this time, when Acre fell at last to the Muslims in 1291, the entire community of Clarisses was massacred. A few male Franciscans lost their lives, while the rest escaped to Cyprus. Farther east, the Franciscan missionary John of Montecorvino went to India and then on to China, where he ran a mission from 1293 until his death in 1328. He and his successors, who kept the mission open until 1369, had churches built, baptized children, and trained boys in Latin and in singing the offices. They had the entire New Testament and the psalter translated into Chinese.

The general chapter held at Lyons in 1299, a year after the death of Olivi, ordered all of Olivi's books burned. There followed a roundup of his books and of his followers as well. The Spiritualist message was further propagated, though, by Ubertino of Casale, who taught in Florence and preached throughout Tuscany in the years around 1300. In 1304–1305, he lived in seclusion at Alverna to write his *Arbor vitae crucufixae Iesu.*

Several appeals of the Spirituals to the pope were apparently blocked, so it was only through the pleas of friendly intermediaries that their call for help got through. Arnald of Villanova, a Catalan physician who had kings and prelates among his clients, and who dabbled in Joachimism, was one such person who pleaded with Clement V to end the persecutions of the Spirituals and to heal the divisions in the order. Another was Cardinal Napoleone Orsini, who took Ubertino into his service as a chaplain. In reply to many such requests, Clement set up a commission of inquiry at Avignon. The spokesman for the Conventuals was Gonsalvo of Valboa, the minister general since 1304, while for the Spirituals it was Ubertino. A lively pamphlet war ensued, and some of the tracts are still extant.

In 1310 Clement intervened on behalf of the Spirituals to state openly that many of the criticisms they made of the order appeared to be true. He released the leaders of the Spirituals from obedience to their superiors, placing them instead under the investigating commission itself. The Conventuals pressed hard against any such division of the order, claiming that they were the only genuine Franciscans and that the Spirituals were heretics. Once again Olivi's works were subjected to official scrutiny and some of them found heretical. The settlement reached in 1312, as announced in *Exivi de paradiso,* gave something to both sides, restating many of Ubertino's charges of laxity against the order, while once again glossing the rule as popes since Gregory IX had done. Both the pope and the minister general tried to encourage the reintegration of the opposed parties, but they both died in 1314 and there followed a two-year interregnum in both offices. Chaos again reigned, with secessions, denunciations, punishments, and so on as before.

In 1316 the Franciscans elected a scholar at Paris named Michael of Cesena as their minister general, and the cardinals chose as pope the former chancellor of the kingdom of Naples, who took the name John XXII. Michael took a line that held to the tradition of Bonaventure and the bulls of 1279 and 1312, essentially the side of the Conventuals but with insistence on the need for reform.

In 1317 John XXII turned his attention to the discussion among the friars. He summoned both Ubertino and Angelo Clareno to hear them out. Then he issued a bull, *Quorundam exigit,* in which he reaffirmed the bulls of his predecessors. He ruled that there could no longer be differences of dress in the order (and the attendant claims that some were more austere than others). The officials of the order were to set the standard and all brothers were to obey. He also ruled that, for security and convenience, the friars could store up supplies in granaries and cellars, the amounts to be determined by the officials of the order.

There followed a severe crackdown on those who refused to accept this latest papal ruling. In *Sancta romana* of December 1317, John declared an all-out war on the Spirituals, by whatever name they went (he listed several, including "Fraticelli"). He included all those who had their own convents and leaders, all who refused to obey the duly constituted authorities of the order, and all who claimed to be or derive from the Poor Hermits of Celestine. At Avignon itself, a group of recalcitrants was called before an inquisitor. All but five submitted. One received a sentence of life imprisonment; the other four were burned to death in May 1318.

Angelo Clareno, after a brief period in prison, went to Subiaco to live as a Benedictine monk. There he wrote his *History of the Seven Tribulations of the Order of the Minors* and an *Exposition of the Rule of St. Francis*. The friars threatened to come after him there, so he moved on to Basilicata, where he lived until 1337. Ubertino lived briefly with some Benedictines, then returned to Avignon, stood trial for heresy in 1325, escaped, surfaced briefly a few years later at Como, and otherwise vanished from history. At Narbonne, the Conventuals dug up the bones of Peter John Olivi and defaced his tomb.

With the matter of the Spirituals apparently at an end, the pope then turned against the victorious Conventuals. He brought into question the very basis of their claims about the historical and theological value of poverty. He opened a vast debate on the issue of whether Jesus and the Apostles had possessions. The case for the order was argued by Bonagratia of Bergamo.

Bonagratia and his colleagues referred repeatedly to *Exiit qui seminat* of 1279, a bull that did more than favor their order. It put forth a whole doctrine of the absolute poverty of Jesus and the Apostles as justification for the poverty practiced by the Franciscans; moreover, it closed with an admonition against disputing or altering its contents, which were inviolable, on pain of excommunication. A curious irony to derive from this debate between the order and the pope was that the order was in the position of arguing on behalf of papal infallibility. The bull

of Nicholas III in 1279 had stimulated Peter John Olivi to write about, and in favor of, papal infallibility in 1280. Now the Franciscans were holding to that very line in their dispute with the pope.

In March 1322, John XXII struck down those clauses of *Exiit qui seminat* limiting further discussion, for, he argued, that bull contained many disputable points. In May the order solemnly declared that Jesus and the Apostles possessed nothing and that such an assertion was not only not heretical but true and catholic. The papal reply of December 1322 broke down utterly the distinction between ownership and use. All ownership of things given to the friars and used by them was henceforth turned over to the order. The Franciscans could no longer claim not to be proprietors. The final touch was for the pope to declare, as he did in *Cum inter nonnullos* of November 1323, that to teach that Jesus and the Apostles did not have lawful possessions—a position he thought readily refuted by biblical evidence—is heretical.

The Franciscan leadership reacted cautiously. Michael of Cesena made no open move against the pope. But in a time of severely strained relations with the emperor, Louis of Bavaria, John XXII suspected Michael of collaboration with the emperor and had him detained at Avignon in 1328. His fellow prisoners included such other Franciscan notables as Bonagratia of Bergamo and William of Ockham.

Louis subsequently had himself crowned at Rome. The Franciscan general chapter received orders from the pope to depose Michael of Cesena and to elect another minister general. Emperor Louis declared Pope John a heretic and deposed him, placing a Franciscan named Peter of Corbaro in his stead as pope under the name of Nicholas V. The Franciscans went ahead by reelecting Michael, who, with imperial help, escaped along with his confreres first to Pisa and then to Munich.

The Spirituals had been driven from the order; the doctrine of the absolute poverty of Jesus and the Apostles had been declared heretical; Hugolino's distinction between use and ownership had been quashed; the Franciscans were now a propertied order; and after more than a century of special papal protection for the order, its leaders were now estranged from the papacy.

TRIUMPH OF THE OBSERVANTS, 1329–1517

John XXII excommunicated Michael of Cesena but managed to regain his hold on the order by securing the election to the minister generalship of one of his friends, named Gerald Odo, who served from 1329 to 1342. In 1336, Pope Benedict XII, a former Cistercian monk, promulgated a set of constitutions for the friars that tried to make them over into monks, but his efforts were strongly resisted. There were several attempts at altering the statutes of the order; those passed at Assisi in 1354, notable for allowing considerable latitude in the handling of money, were to remain in effect for a century and a half.

The tendencies toward austerity and laxity that had so bitterly divided the order from the early days right on into the reign of John XXII were not long in returning. Scattered groups of Spirituals turned up from time to time, usually designated as Fraticelli. They were hunted down as heretics by the Inquisition. Starting in 1334, John of Valle responded to the laxity prevalent in the order by establishing a hermitage at Brugliano, high up in the hills that divide the Marches from Umbria. John was probably a follower of Ubertino, and his idea was to live by a closer observance of the rule. His successor, Gentile of Spoleto, obtained from Clement VI in 1350 an exemption from obedience to superiors in the order, so once again there seemed to be the makings of a separate way for those in search of a more rigorous adherence to the rule. But just five years later Gentile and his fellow friar-hermits were accused of holding to the ideas of the Spirituals and as a result were compelled to disband.

They did of course hold to and perpetuate Spiritualist ideas. One way of doing this was to read and disseminate the Spiritualist writings about Francis produced during the turbulent reign of John XXII. Two of the better known of these were the *Mirror of Perfection* and the *Acts of St. Francis,* both based on the recollections reported in the 1240's by Brothers Leo, Ruffino, and Angelo and preserved through the book burnings of the 1260's and later.

The *Mirror of Perfection* is important for reviving those earlier recollections but also for two particularly significant original passages. One is the opening chapter, which tells of a group of ministers of the order going to Francis at the time of his redrafting of the rule in 1221. They go to express their fear that he would write something too difficult for them and to suggest that he write something for himself alone. Francis thereupon turns to the sky and converses with Jesus, within full hearing of the ministers. Jesus says emphatically that he himself and not Francis was the author of the rule, that he wants it observed literally and without any commen-

taries, and that those too weak to follow it should get out of the order.

The other new passage in the *Mirror* is Francis' description of the ideal friar, made up of the specially praiseworthy virtues of each of his original companions. The last of the virtuous models was a friar who never lived in any place for more than one month.

During the third quarter of the fourteenth century, the *Acts of St. Francis* was partly paraphrased and partly translated into the Tuscan dialect; the result was a work that has had a widespread success through the centuries under the title of *Fioretti* or *Little Flowers.* It opens with a chapter on the original twelve companions of St. Francis, and its first sentence asserts that the glorious St. Francis, in all the acts of his life, conformed to the blessed Christ. "For just as Christ, at the start of his preaching, called twelve Apostles to reject the things of this world and to follow him in poverty and in the other virtues, so St. Francis, at the start of the foundation of his order, chose twelve companions who would embrace the most complete poverty." The theme of Francis' conformity to Christ, here given its first, fully elaborated expression, has origins in many earlier texts, most notably Bonaventure's discussion of Francis' similarity with Christ, Francis' transformation into Christ, and Francis' conformity with Christ.

Yet another fresh start was made by the latter-day Spiritualists, again at Brugliano, in 1368, and within a decade this time there existed a network of ten such hermitages. By 1390 Paul of Trinci, as head of Brugliano, had authority over twenty-one other houses as well. In that same year, the first house with this rigorous tendency was organized in France, at Mirebeau near Poitiers. Expansion was also taking place into Spain and Portugal at this time.

The great events of the century had their impact on the order. The Black Death of 1348 and after hit cities particularly hard and, with special severity, clerics who ministered to lay people within cities. Some convents were difficult to staff adequately and the general quality of the order, both intellectual and spiritual—as the quality of the entire clergy—apparently declined in the second half of the fourteenth century. The image of the friar in Chaucer, to cite only one of many sources, testifies to this decline. Then at the time of the Great Schism, there were first two and then three sets of administrative officers for the order, all in all an unedifying spectacle.

The houses associated with Brugliano numbered

about twenty-five in 1400; their members were coming to be called Friars Minor of the Observance, or simply Observants, the reference being to their special regard for the rule of the order. The fortunes of the Observance were greatly enhanced by the arrival of four exceptional persons: Bernardino of Siena in 1402, John of Capistrano in 1415, Albert of Sarteano in 1415, and James of the Marches in 1416.

Bernardino joined the Franciscans in the hope of finding an austere religious life, but was disappointed by the ease and comfort of the convent at Siena. But when he switched to the Observance he found what he was after, and he became one of its greatest propagandists. He was ordained and commissioned as a preacher, which was his principal vocation. One of his most powerful themes, and one that helps historians establish the long-range ties between the Spirituals and the Observants, is that of *Franciscus alter Christus*, Francis as the Second Christ. His immediate source was the *Book of the Conformity of the Life of St. Francis to the Life of the Lord Jesus*, written around the year 1390 by Bartholomew of Pisa. This book contained a lengthy theological elaboration of the theme of Francis' conformity to Christ found in the *Acts of St. Francis* and the *Little Flowers*. Bernardino also quoted directly from the *Arbor vitae* of Ubertino of Casale. Bernardino's influence in turn helped to propagate the iconographic theme of *Franciscus alter Christus* in fifteenth-century Italian painting.

John of Capistrano was trained in the law and served as a judge prior to his conversion to the religious life, while Albert of Sarteano was a noted biblical scholar. James of the Marches studied law and tried out the Carthusian order briefly before joining the Franciscans. Together with Bernardino, these men are regarded as the "four pillars of the Observance."

The differences between the Conventuals and the Observants were aired at the Council of Constance in 1415 because of a petition brought by the latter. The Council granted them the right and responsibility to elect a vicar for each province and a vicar general of the order, who would serve under the minister general with special responsibility for the houses following the Observance. Thus was a division made that was to stand for a century and that prefigured the separation of a century later. Bernardino was eventually chosen vicar for the Observant Friars in Tuscany and Umbria.

In 1428 Martin V restored the distinction between ownership and use, thus making the order

theoretically propertyless once again. Then he convened a reform meeting at Assisi in 1430. He had John of Capistrano draw up the reform proposal, which called on the Conventuals to abandon several of their basic positions and come over to the Observance. They were all rather quick to agree, and even to take oaths to support the reforms, but just a few days after the dissolution of the meeting, several thought better of what had happened and asked the pope to be released from their vows. One of these was William of Casale, the new minister general, who within three months obtained a bull revoking all the recent reforms.

The Observants now had no reason to hope for union within a reformed order, and so concerned themselves with their own needs and interests. They sought and obtained from Eugenius IV the right to elect two vicars general, one for Italy and one for the provinces outside of Italy. This tendency was further advanced by the bull *Ut sacra* in January 1446, which confirmed that they elect their own vicars and allowed them to hold their own chapters and to legislate for themselves. Within the context of a still united order, the independence of the two main wings or factions had gone about as far as it could go. Over the next few years the Conventuals tried hard to get this effective separation annulled, but to no avail.

An important advocate of the Observant cause in this period was Aeneas Silvius, bishop of Siena and the future Pius II. In 1455 he wrote on their behalf about the decline of the Conventuals from the obvious intentions of St. Francis and his companions, and he commented on how their houses at present were falling into ruin while the Observants were establishing new convents all the time.

There were still other attempts at reunion, notably under Callistus III in 1456 and Julius II in 1506, but they found both sides too deeply dug into their respective positions to be able to move. Meanwhile, as Aeneas Silvius had noticed, the Conventuals stagnated while the Observants grew. The Observants themselves included several splinter groups, but taken together they became the larger of the two main groups within the order at some point in the years shortly before or after 1500. Moreover, their influence had made a clear mark upon the Second Order, which had gone into a serious decline in the late fourteenth century but then revived, largely in response to the preaching of Bernardino and his contemporaries.

Pope Leo X sought to resolve for all time the

problem of disunity. He appointed a study commission and then summoned all factions to Rome. His solution, expressed in the bull *Ite et vos* of May 1517, was to recognize in effect the primacy of the Observants. They were to elect a leader from their ranks who would take the title "minister general of the whole order of Friars Minor," and who was to keep the seal of the order. Perhaps Leo X hoped that the Conventuals would accept this new arrangement, but they did not and the pope acquiesced in their becoming an independent religious order, with the right to elect their own leader, henceforth called the "master general." The long struggle to maintain unity had collapsed with this definitive split of the Franciscans into two separate orders.

The latter part of this history has been accorded less space and given in less detail than the earlier because it becomes both wearily repetitious and progressively less important. The internal disputes of the Franciscans in the thirteenth century touched the most sensitive spiritual questions of that time. The Franciscan order was then at the cutting edge of the spiritual life in the Latin church, and the direction taken by the order was a matter of importance for every constituency in that church. By comparison, the internal disputes in the fifteenth century, no matter how intense the passions they aroused, remained essentially domestic quarrels. The very vocation or purpose of the order had changed over time. After the first century, no challenge of the stature of either the urban apostolate or early Scholastic theology again engaged its members' energies or stimulated the creativity as these initial challenges had. Still, toward the close of the fifteenth century a major assignment awaited the friars, as the Portuguese and Spanish explorers opened up whole continents where the Christian Gospel was unknown.

BIBLIOGRAPHY

Rosalind B. Brooke, *Early Franciscan Government: Elias to Bonaventure* (1959); Rosalind B. Brooke, ed. and trans., *Scripta Leonis, Rufini, et Angeli, sociorum S. Francisci: The Writings of Leo, Rufino, and Angelo, Companions of St. Francis* (1970); Decima L. Douie, *The Nature and Effect of the Heresy of the Fraticelli* (1932); John B. Freed, *The Friars and German Society in the Thirteenth Century* (1977); Marion A. Habig, ed., *St. Francis of Assisi, Writings and Early Biographies: English Omnibus of the Sources for the Life of St. Francis* (1973); Malcolm D. Lambert, *Franciscan Poverty: The Doctrine of the Absolute Poverty of Christ and the Apostles in the Franciscan Order, 1210–1323* (1961); Michel Lollat, ed., *Études sur l'histoire de la pauvreté* (1974); John Moorman, *A History of the Franciscan Order: From its Origins to the Year 1517* (1968); Hendrik W. van Os, "St. Francis of Assisi as a Second Christ in Early Italian Painting," in *Simiolus: Netherlands Quarterly for the History of Art*, 7 (1974); Williell R. Thomson, *Friars in the Cathedral: the First Franciscan Bishops, 1226–1261* (1974); Brian Tierney, *Origins of Papal Infallibility, 1150–1350* (1972).

LESTER K. LITTLE

[See also **Alexander of Hales; Assisi, San Francesco; Bacon, Roger; Bernardino of Siena, St.; Bonaventure, St.; Celestine V, Pope; Eudes Rigaud; Friars; Gregory IX, Pope; Grosseteste, Robert; Heresies, Western European; Innocent III, Pope; Joachim of Fiore; John of Capistrano, St.; John XXII, Pope; Matthew of Aquasparta; Mendicant Orders; Missions and Missionaries, Christian; Ockham, William of; Olivi, Peter John; Paris, University of; Peckham, John; Pius II; William of Casale.**]

FRANCO OF COLOGNE (*fl. ca.* 1250), music theorist. Very little is known of Franco's life. Although one of the manuscripts of the *Ars cantus mensurabilis*, his most important and perhaps his only genuine treatise, refers to a Franco of Paris, the German origin of its author and his association with Cologne are confirmed in an earlier copy and by other medieval theorists. References by writers who were mainly concerned with Parisian polyphony—such as Johannes of Liège, who lived from about 1260 to after 1330, and the English Anonymous (Coussemaker's Anonymous IV), who must have lived about the same time—and the importance of Franco in the development of the notation used for the music disseminated from Paris do, however, suggest that he had some contact with that city, perhaps even a career in what was then the musical center of Europe. It is also recorded that he was a *magister* (the degree given, perhaps, by the University of Paris), that he was a papal chaplain, and that he served as preceptor at the Hospital (founded 1263) of the Knights of St. John of Jerusalem in Cologne.

Franco mentions only Boethius, Gregory the Great, and Guido of Arezzo as sources, acknowledgments that are obviously pro forma and intended to show his reverence for plainsong. But when he turns to measured music, and speaks of including things "well said by others" and "correcting their errors," he makes it clear that he based his work on current practices, and perhaps even on other treatises. Nevertheless, the general and rapid acceptance of his terminology and ideas attests to their force and originality. Among those who made commentaries or digests of Franco's work were Johannes of Liège, Marchettus of Padua, Jerome of Moravia (who attributes the *Ars cantus mensurabilis* to a John of Burgundy), and Simon Tunstede.

Franconian notation employs the old note shapes (the square, Gothic versions of the late Middle Ages), but in a new way. The old figures—virga, punctum, liquescent, and the rest—were used originally to show whether notes were higher or lower than those preceding or following, or to indicate nuances of performance; and for the most part such distinctions had been made redundant by the introduction of the musical staff and by the later singing style of plainchant, which admitted few subtleties. The new mensural notation assigned to the old neumes new meanings. But since the conservatism of the age forbade new figures, and there were not sufficient signs for them to be given explicit values, many of Franco's note forms are ambivalent, their meaning decided only by context. The "difficult" nature of early mensural notation may be as much owing to another kind of conservatism, the medieval predilection for "secret" arts restricted to the initiated, as it was to lack of invention. Before the introduction of printing there was little reason to make musical notation widely accessible.

The forms and styles mentioned by Franco (rondellus, cantilena, conductus, organum, discant, motet, copula, hocket) were all current in the first part of the thirteenth century and earlier, and this has been taken by some to indicate a date early in the century for the *Ars cantus mensurabilis*. But this is by no means proved. Franco may have restricted himself to well-known pieces; perhaps he acted, in this respect, like most other music theorists and ignored the newest tendencies. In any case, his treatise is concerned only with the triple meters of the earliest (explicitly) rhythmic polyphony. Franco's notation treats the division of notes into two equal parts as exceptional, and makes no provision whatever for music in duple time—even though there is good evidence for the partition of the breve into two equal semibreves and even for widespread use of duple rhythm by the middle of the thirteenth century. But if the musical examples and musical practice of the treatise might suggest an early date, what appear to be quotations from the writings of Magister Lambertus and the St. Emmeram Anonymous, both writing about 1279, indicate a date later in the century. It need hardly be said, however, that such

verbal correspondences might be owing to the influence of an unknown writer cited by all three. A date in the middle of the century for the *Ars cantus mensurabilis* is, at the moment, the best guess.

Although the most important part of Franco's treatise is its explanation of the rules of mensural notation, it also contains valuable information on other matters: the rhythmic modes (the theoretical basis of the earlier rhythmic notation), musical prosody, the characteristics, terminology, and performance practice of the current forms and styles, and the theoretical status of the consonances and dissonances.

Another treatise, *Compendium discantus,* which begins "Ego Franco de Colonia," is found in a single fourteenth-century manuscript. It includes rules for voice leading in two-part discant and a discussion of consonance and dissonance. The evidence for (or against) Franco's authorship is inconclusive.

BIBLIOGRAPHY

The *Ars cantus mensurabilis* and the *Compendium discantus* are edited by Edmond de Coussemaker in *Scriptorum de musica medii aevi, n.s.* I (1864), 117–136, 154–156. An English translation of the *Ars cantus mensurabilis* is included by William O. Strunk in *Source Readings in Music History* (1950), 139–159. For further information and bibliography, see Andrew Hughes, "Franco of Cologne," in *The New Grove Dictionary of Music and Musicians* (1980).

TERENCE BAILEY

[See also **Anonymous IV; Ars Antiqua; Ars Nova; Mensural Notation.**]

FRANCO OF LIÈGE (*d.* 1064), a Dominican monk. His extant work is *De quadratura circuli,* in six books, which considers several problems concerning the circle.

BIBLIOGRAPHY

See *Patrologia latina,* CXLIII (1853), 1373–1376; Constantin Winterberg, ed., *Abhandlungen zur Geschichte der Mathematik,* IV (1882), 137–183.

EDWARD FRUEH

FRANCO-PROVENÇAL. See French Language.

Franco-Saxon School: initial to the Book of Genesis from the Second Bible of Charles the Bald. From the Monastery of St. Amand, 870–873. BIBLIOTHÈQUE NATIONALE, MS FONDS LATIN 2, fol. 11r

FRANCO-SAXON SCHOOL, a distinctive group of illuminated manuscripts produced in northeast France, especially associated with the monastery of St. Amand, from the late Carolingian period through the tenth century. The school is characterized by its emphasis on ornamental, nonrepresentational decoration, though a few manuscripts—such as the Gospels of Francis II of the second half of the ninth century—incorporate the human figure. The style relies on traditional insular interlace and initial patterns that have, however, been submitted to rigidly symmetrical and geometrical treatment. One of the finest examples is the Second Bible of Charles the Bald produced at St. Amand during the 870's (Paris, Bibliothèque Nationale, MS fonds lat. 2).

BIBLIOGRAPHY
André Boutemy, "Le style franco-saxon, style de Saint-Amand: Sources inutilisées," in *Scriptorium,* **3** (1949);

Florentine Mütherich and Joachim E. Gaehde, *Carolingian Painting* (1976).

LESLIE BRUBAKER

[See also **Manuscript Illumination: Western European.**]

FRANCONIAN MOTET. The motet evolved as a new species of music in the twelfth century. Most early motets consisted of a basic structural voice part (tenor), derived from Gregorian chant and arranged in one of several short rhythmic patterns, and of one to three newly composed parts sung to a Latin liturgical poem in a related but different metric rhythm. Soon after 1200 the motet turned prevailingly to secular texts, often French and influenced by the contemporary trouvère poetry. Now the tenor was played instrumentally, and each of the additional voices, called respectively motetus, triplum, and quadruplum, received a separate text, each normally differently phrased and often very contrasting—for instance, pitting a Latin religious text against a French love poem. Such works are termed, respectively, two-part, double, and triple motets, and the texts cover a wide range: liturgical, religious, social, and political subjects; pastourelles; love poems; moral criticism.

During this early phase of motet composition, only a few poets and no composers can be identified. In double and triple motets the rhythmic-melodic character of the upper parts—which often cross the tenor—is very similar, though their phrases are usually of different length. They all follow, from beginning to end, one or another of six modes, patterned rhythms that express the metric properties of the poetic texts—chiefly iambs, trochees, and dactyls. These modal patterns are all expressed by relatively simple long and short note values, known as *longa* and *brevis.*

In the mid thirteenth century an important new style emerged, connected with the name of Franco of Cologne. Although not a single composition can be identified as his, brief excerpts from motets that appear in his highly influential treatise on music, *Ars cantus mensurabilis,* exemplify the new style. This treatise was written, it seems, about 1260–1270, toward the end of Franco's long career as teacher and composer at Paris. In two fifteenth-century copies of his treatise, Franco is said to have been a papal chamberlain and a preceptor at the hospital of the Knights of St. John of Jerusalem at Cologne.

The Franconian motet was built on the early motet. It is normally a double motet and often employs a tenor and motetus from the early repertory, to which a new triplum is added, often replacing an older triplum. These new tripla introduce two new features. First, the six rhythmic modes are intermingled; as Franco explains it, all of them can be reduced to simple ternary units. (Indeed, throughout the late twelfth century and the thirteenth century basic ternary units reigned supreme in music and were recognized for centuries thereafter as "perfect," binary units being called "imperfect.") As a result Franconian tripla employ a freer, more varied rhythm. Second, whereas formerly the text syllables employed only the longs and breves of the six modal patterns, Franconian tripla introduce syllabified subdivisions of the breve value, dividing it sometimes into two, sometimes three, semibreves. Thereby the poetic meter gradually lost musical expression. In addition, in order to give clear enunciation to these short syllables, the overall tempo of the music had to slow.

In the last decades of the century the breve became further subdivided, into four to nine more or less equal semibreves, all carrying syllables. The composer connected with this development was Pierre de la Croix (Petrus de Cruce) of Amiens. His innovation led to further slowing of the basic tempo and to a felt need to control such groups of four or more short notes rhythmically. This need in turn led to the adoption of new methods of musical notation in the early fourteenth century, those of the *ars nova*. Pierre's innovation correlates with a complete disregard for poetic meter, rhyme, and accent in the modernistic music of the time. It should be added that both within France, where these developments primarily occurred, and especially elsewhere—in England, Spain, and Germany—more conservative motets of several styles continued to be enjoyed around 1300.

The largest and most representative collection of thirteenth-century motets, the Montpellier Codex (Faculté de Médecine, H 196), contains eight separate gatherings or fascicles, the last two of which contain a substantial number of motets of these various types. Among them are forty of the Franconian style, three of which are works of the trouvère Adam de la Halle, and seven Petronian pieces. Several of these works and some additional Franconian and Petronian motets also appear in three other major collections—the Bamberg (Staatliche Bibliothek, Lit. 115 [Ed. IV. 6]) and Turin (Biblioteca Reale, vari 42)

manuscripts and the *Roman de Fauvel* (Paris, Bibliothèque Nationale, MS fonds français 146)—and in several smaller or fragmentary manuscripts.

BIBLIOGRAPHY

Ernst Apfel, *Anlage und Struktur der Motetten im Codex Montpellier* (1970); Pierre Aubry, *Cent motets du XIIIe siècle publiés d'après manuscrit Ed. IV. 6 de Bamberg*, 3 vols. (1908); Friedrich Blume, ed., *Die Musik in Geschichte und Gegenwart*, 14 vols. (1949–1968), I.1201–1206, VI.1248–1252, IX.642; Yvonne Rokseth, *Polyphonies du XIIIe siècle, le manuscrit H 196 de la Faculté de Médecine de Montpellier*, 4 vols. (1935–1939), IV.77–94; Hans Tischler, "Intellectual Trends in Thirteenth-century Paris as Reflected in the Texts of Motets," in *Music Review*, 29 (1968), and *The Montpellier Codex*, 3 vols. (1978).

HANS TISCHLER

[See also **Ars Nova; Franco of Cologne; Motet; Motet Manuscripts; Tenor.**]

FRANKALMOIN (free alms). Where they prevailed, feudal notions of the later Middle Ages required that lands and tenements must be held of a lord. In the twelfth century and after, this concept was strong enough in England, Scotland, and parts of France (especially Normandy) to be imposed even when property was donated to churches. Given freely for God's sake, the property was not held for military service, at rent, or upon any of the other continuing obligations that usually lent meaning to feudal tenure. So it was said to be held "in alms," "free alms" or frankalmoin, "pure alms," or "perpetual alms." The donor could expect prayers to be offered for him in the grateful church. If men must conceive of a service due to the lord from the tenure, they could suppose that these prayers constituted "spiritual service."

Frankalmoin was held only by churches, never by clergy or anyone else in a personal capacity. But by no means was everything that belonged to churches held in this way, for churches could always acquire and hold, or be treated as holding, by other tenures. In England especially, the bishops and greater abbeys held the bulk of their lands by knight's service.

In Normandy and Scotland the church holding property in frankalmoin owed nothing to the immediate lord, neither secular service nor feudal incidents nor even homage and fealty. In Normandy a simple acknowledgment of lordship was made, and if the property had been the foundation gift of a new church, then it followed that the lord was the patron of the church. In England the tenure was equally free of homage and fealty and feudal incidents, but it was quite common for the donor to stipulate some secular service, perhaps an annual rent. If the gift was essentially in charity and for the prayers of the church, or was taken to be so, that was enough to make the tenure frankalmoin. But in both England and France property held in frankalmoin lay under feudal obligations to the superior lords of the donor. However freely he might grant with respect to himself, the donor had no power to give away their rights. If the land owed the service of one knight to the donor's lord while the donor had it, the service remained due from the land as frankalmoin held of the donor by the church. At most, the superior lords might be persuaded to release their claims, or the donor might "defend and acquit" the land by himself performing this forinsec (outside) service. In Scotland frankalmoin tended in practice to escape all duties to all superior lords.

In France and Scotland it was early established that lands held in frankalmoin were under the jurisdiction of the church courts and not of secular courts, and this immunity remained throughout the Middle Ages and long after. In England such a privilege was recognized in and around the 1160's, though the exemption from secular jurisdiction was not complete and it remains uncertain how far it went. It did not last long. About 1200, without controversy that can now be discerned, the regular procedures of the king's court were made generally available for litigation about interests in frankalmoin and the church courts were excluded from the business. Ecclesiastical jurisdiction survived only for churchyards, the precincts of monasteries, and cemeteries.

BIBLIOGRAPHY

Paul Cauwès, "Aumône," in *La grande encyclopédie,* IV.679–681; Audrey W. Douglas, "Frankalmoin and Jurisdictional Immunity: Maitland Revisited," in *Speculum,* 53 (1978), and "Tenure *in elemosina*: Origins and Establishment in Twelfth-century England," in *American Journal of Legal History,* **24** (1980); Elisabeth G. Kimball, "Tenure in Frank Almoign and Secular Services," in *English Historical Review,* **43** (1928); Charles Mortet, "Féodalité," in *La grande encyclopédie,* XVII.210–211; Frederick Pollock and Frederic W. Maitland, *The History of English Law,* 2nd ed. (1898), I.240–251.

DONALD W. SUTHERLAND

[See also **Land Tenure, Western European.**]

FRANKE, MEISTER, a German painter active in Hamburg in the first quarter of the fifteenth century. Probably trained in Paris in the circle of the Boucicaut Master, he introduced the courtly International Gothic style to Germany, particularly in his Martyrdom of St. Barbara triptych (Helsinki, Suomen Kansallismuseo) and St. Thomas Altar (Hamburg, Kunsthalle).

BIBLIOGRAPHY

Charles D. Cuttler, *Northern Painting from Pucelle to Bruegel* (1968); Bella Martens, *Meister Franke* (1929); Thomas Puttfarken, *Meister Franke und die Kunst um 1400* (1969); Alfred Strange, *Deutsche Malerei der Gotik,* III, *Norddeutschland in der Zeit von 1400 bis 1450* (1938).

ROBERT G. CALKINS

[See also **Boucicaut Master; Gothic: International Style.**]

FRANKISH STATES IN GREECE. See **Latin Principalities and Frankish States in Greece.**

FRATER. See **Refectory.**

FRAU AVA, the first known female author in German literature. She names herself at the end of her last poem, and this name is normally identified with an *Ava inclusa,* a recluse whose death is recorded for the year 1127 in the annals of the Austrian monastery of Melk (on the Danube) and in some other annals.

She is the author of four poems in rhymed couplets of short lines (or, according to Friedrich Maurer, in long lines with interior rhyme): *Johannes* (446 short lines); *Leben Jesu* (2,418 short lines, 2269–2418 containing a special poem about the seven gifts of the Holy Spirit); *Der Antichrist* (118 short lines); and *Jüngstes Gericht* (406 short lines).

The four works form a structured whole, almost a cycle. *Johannes* presents the transition from the Old Testament to the New; *Leben Jesu* follows as the exemplary beginning of the New Testament in Christ, in which Christ's divinity and his mission of salvation are strongly emphasized. Emanating from Pentecost and from Christ's command to spread the

Gospel is the poem about the seven gifts of the Holy Spirit, which are connected with another septenary, and seven of the nine Beatitudes from the Sermon on the Mount, with groups of three or four virtues, proprieties, or elements. In *Der Antichrist* the author deals briefly with the short reign of the Antichrist at the end of time, during which many Christians will be tempted and fall into eternal punishment, and many others will overcome in the last battle. *Jüngstes Gericht* depicts the fifteen signs of the Last Judgment, then the day of final judgment itself, with the separation of the blessed from the devil and his host, and with *jubileus,* a year of rejoicing, followed by all the joys of life eternal. Thus the four poems represent a short but informative history of Christian salvation.

Ava's main source and guide for her abbreviated and selective narration very probably was a book containing the liturgical pericopes. She appears to have been quite learned and well read, enriching the biblical accounts with materials from biblical exegesis and other theological and religious sources; she also uses Latin phrases and technical terms quite frequently. It follows that Ava's reading or listening public must have been quite educated; among the first to come to mind are lay brothers in Benedictine monasteries, whose required participation in many liturgical services would profit greatly from basic meditative materials in the vernacular and in poetic form.

The style of the poems is compact and straightforward, often vivid, with much direct discourse and dialogue, but with little rhetorical adornment. Religious instruction was apparently Ava's primary purpose.

Ava's work has been preserved in two manuscripts: Vorau, Stiftsbibliothek, codex 276, folios 115va–125ra (end of the twelfth century, without *Johannes;* after folio 116 a folio is missing: *Leben Jesu,* Tines 405–668); and (now lost) Görlitz, Bibliothek der Oberlausitzischen Gesellschaft der Wissenschaften, codex 10, folios 1ra–24rb (fourteenth century, all four poems, illustrated).

Whether these poems were written in stanzas (of different length) of older long lines or in the more modern rhymed couplets with short, four-beat lines has become an issue and a cause of extended scholarly discussion, especially since Friedrich Maurer, the chief proponent of the long-line theory, published most of the texts in his monumental *Die religiösen Dichtungen des 11. und 12. Jahrhunderts* in long lines.

BIBLIOGRAPHY

Friedrich Maurer, ed., *Die Dichtungen der Frau Ava* (1966), in Altdeutsche Textbibliothek, LXVI, and *Die Dichtungen der Frau Ava,* in his *Die religiösen Dichtungen des 11. und 12. Jahrhunderts,* 3 vols. (1964–1970), II.381–513; Edgar Papp, "Ava," in *Die deutsche Literatur des Mittelalters. Verfasserlexikon* (1978), 560–565; Peter K. Stein, "Stil, Struktur, historischer Ort und Funktion. Literarhistorische Beobachtungen und methodologische Überlegungen zu den Dichtungen der Frau Ava," in *Festschrift für Adalbert Schmidt,* Gerlinde Weiss, ed. (1976).

On the controversy over long versus short lines, see Friedrich Maurer, *Die religiösen Dichtungen,* 1.1–60 and 3.viii–xxxi; Werner Schröder, "Noch einmal zu Friedrich Maurers Neuedition der deutschen religiösen Dichtungen des 11. and 12. Jahrhunderts," in *Beiträge zur Geschichte der deutschen Sprache und Literatur,* **93** (1971).

PETRUS W. TAX

FRAUENLIST. Preserved in two fourteenth-century manuscripts, this *Märe* of 618 lines in the preferred manuscript is divided compositionally into two unequal parts: the first (lines 1–548) tells of the seduction of a beautiful and well-born woman by a poor but virtuous student; the second presents the jealousy of her husband, who sees the student leaving her chamber on three occasions, and shows how she appeases him.

The plot is one frequently found in medieval comic tales—adultery and the outwitting of a suspicious cuckold. In this regard "Frauenlist" is remarkable only for its triviality. It has little narrative substance: the lady consents simply because she feels like doing so, the husband is involved in schematic episodes without detail, and his wife "proves" that he cannot believe what he sees by pointing out that images in a tub of water are not the "real" things they seem to be.

The stylistic and rhetorical sophistication of "Frauenlist" contrasts strongly with its banal plot. The scholar is described as a paradigm of virtue; his extraordinary devotion to ladies and concern for moral behavior are painted with elegant strokes, largely in interior monologue. The lady is plainspoken and rude, as well as slow-witted. When a conversation with her heart allays her scruples, she welcomes the young zealot of virtue, "who would rather have let himself be murdered than commit the least immorality," to her bed.

"Frauenlist" is a sophisticated parody of such conventions as the riotous behavior of students and the gentility of noblewomen. It makes humorous use of those notions of "proper" behavior in love that underlie the *De amore* of Andreas Capellanus.

BIBLIOGRAPHY

The text is available in *Neues Gesamtabenteuer*, I, Heinrich Niewöhner, ed., 2nd ed., rev. by Werner Simon *et al.* (1967), 87–95. See also Hanns Fischer, *Studien zur deutschen Märendichtung* (1968, 2nd ed. 1983); Stephen L. Wailes, "Students as Lovers in the German Fabliau," in *Medium Aevum*, **46** (1977).

STEPHEN WAILES

[See also **Capellanus, Andreas; Mären.**]

FRAUENLOB. See **Heinrich von Meissen.**

FRECHULF (FREUCHULPH) (*fl. ca.* 825–852), bishop of Lisieux, was a friend of Hrabanus Maurus, with whom he may have been a pupil of Alcuin's. As bishop, he composed a universal *Historia* in two parts, the first work of its kind that emphasized narrative rather than chronology. The first part, in seven books, runs from the Creation to the Incarnation and is dedicated to Helisachar, abbot of St. Riquier; the second part, in five books, continues to the times of Gregory the Great and is dedicated to the empress Judith, for whose son, Charles the Bald, Frechulf prepared an edition of Vegetius' *De re militari.* The *Historia*, basically ecclesiastical in interests, draws upon a large collection of sources and enjoyed considerable repute in the Middle Ages.

BIBLIOGRAPHY

Frechulf's *Historia* is in *Patrologia latina*, CVI (1864), 917–1258; his letters in *Monumenta Germaniae historica, Epistolae*, V (1899), 317–320 and 618–619. See also W. Goez, "Zur Weltchronik des Bischofs Frechulf von Lisieux," in *Festgabe für P. Kirn* (1961); C. F. Natunewickz, "Freculfus of Lisieux, His Chronicle and a Mont St. Michel Manuscript," in *Sacris eruditi*, **17** (1966).

EDITORIAL STAFF

[See also **Hrabanus Maurus.**]

FREDEGARIUS (*fl.* seventh century), modern name for an anonymous Frank who, toward 660, composed a four-book *Chronicle*, a major historical work for its century. The first book, running from the Creation, is drawn from the *Chronicle* of St. Hyppolitus, but includes the original account of the Trojan descent of the Franks; the second book is extracted from the *Chronicle* of St. Jerome as continued by Hydatius (or Idacius), but with legendary additions about Theodoric the Ostrogoth, Justinian, and others; the third is a condensation of books 2–6 of Gregory of Tours's *Histories,* also with additions; and the fourth is an original narrative of events from 584 to about 641, with allusions to the 650's. Its place of origin may be Burgundy or the vicinity of Metz. In the eighth century, the four-book core was augmented by successive continuations, to 734, 751, and 768, which "provide us with the first official record of the doings of the Carolingians" (Wallace-Hadrill). The special flavor of the Latin of Fredegarius and his continuators has attracted much scholarly attention.

BIBLIOGRAPHY

Fredegarii et aliorum chronica, Bruno Krusch, ed., in *Monumenta Germaniae historica, Scriptores rerum Merovingicarum*, II (1888). See also J. M. Wallace-Hadrill, *The Fourth Book of the Chronicle of Fredegar with Its Continuations* (1960); Walter Goffart, "The Fredegar Problem Reconsidered," in *Speculum*, **38** (1963).

EDITORIAL STAFF

[See also **Historiography, Western European.**]

FREDERICK I BARBAROSSA (*ca.* 1122–1190) was elected king of Germany in 1152. With Germany at the brink of civil war, the election of Frederick, a member of the Hohenstaufen family, promised peace because, through his mother, he was related to the rival Welf faction. Promises to his Welf cousin Henry the Lion appeared to assure peace.

As king, Frederick endeavored to follow in the footsteps of his predecessor, Conrad III. He agreed in 1153 to assist Pope Eugenius III against Arnold of Brescia, in return for an imperial coronation in Rome. The degree of civic resistance in Rome to papal rule turned his first Italian expedition into a nightmare. Although he was crowned in Rome on 18 June 1155, he was forced to return to Germany without aiding the current pope, Adrian IV.

On his return to Germany, Frederick enlisted the services of Rainald of Dassel, an unscrupulous but shrewd and worldly cleric. With Rainald's help Frederick decided on a totally new plan of action. He abandoned the papal alliance and issued an edict that would compensate his Hohenstaufen cousin Henry II Jasomirgott for ceding Bavaria to his Welf cousin Henry the Lion by making the former a territorial ruler in the East Mark of Austria (*Privilegium minus,* 1156). For himself he sought to build a territorial kingdom that would include his own duchy of Swabia, Burgundy around the upper Rhône, and Lombardy in northern Italy. In Swabia and Alsace he met no resistance. He gained Burgundy through his marriage to Beatrice, heiress of the county of Burgundy. In June 1158 he set out for Italy to receive the homage of the city-republics. The chances of an accommodation with the republics seemed good, as he was willing to guarantee peace in return for homage.

Unfortunately for Frederick, Pope Adrian died in 1159 and a growing party among the cardinals, anxious to advance papal influence and monarchical rule over the clergy of Christendom, took control. Prompted by Rainald, Frederick rashly alienated that party by opposing the newly chosen Alexander III and by supporting an antipope, Victor IV. A schism resulted. Alexander gained wide support because Victor, owing his election to imperial intrigues, was branded a "simonist." Alexander encouraged sufficient resistance in the Lombard towns to make the enactment of the decrees of the Diet of Roncaglia (November 1158), which had assured urban self-government (provided the elected consuls were confirmed by the emperor), impossible. With the schism resistance flared up, and Frederick, manipulated by Rainald, was drawn into a direct military confrontation that led to the destruction of Milan (in March 1162.) This made the realization of the original plan for the peaceful incorporation of Lombardy into Frederick's territorial kingdom impossible, and thus prevented the formation of a central European "state." Faced by total lack of cooperation in Lombardy, Frederick had to place the cities under German commissars whose rapacity hardened a resistance soon to be fanned and supported by the exiled Alexander III.

Frederick's original plan to found a central European kingdom became increasingly utopian. The king of France remained adamant in his support of Alexander, and a promise of support from Henry II of England proved ephemeral. In a last desperate effort Frederick set out for Rome, whither Alexander III had returned. Rome was conquered in 1167, but Alexander escaped.

The growing schism in the church diverted Frederick from his original territorial plan, and the last popular support in Lombardy was alienated by the misconduct of the German squires. Years of indecision were punctuated by halfhearted attempts to seek an understanding with Alexander III, who, encouraged by Frederick's ill luck in the field and by growing support for papal efforts to build up an administratively efficient curia, held out for a complete surrender. In 1174–1175 Frederick tried one more military effort against the Lombard League, and suffered a defeat at Legnano on 29 May 1176. Although the military situation was not desperate, Frederick finally decided to scrap his plan for a central European kingdom. He made peace with Alexander (Venice, July–August 1177) and effected a truce (eventually confirmed as the Peace of Constance in 1183) with the Lombard League.

According to the *Privilegium minus,* the German princes, especially Henry the Lion, duke of both Saxony and Bavaria, would have been allowed to transform their dominions into territorial sovereignties just as Frederick was planning to lay the foundations of a similar sovereignty in Swabia, Burgundy, and Lombardy. Now Frederick completely changed his course. Sizing up the social pressures in Germany correctly, he accepted that feudal tenures had multiplied and that a truly feudal suzerainty would be all he could hope for. The independent state of Henry the Lion, the growth of which he had countenanced for nearly twenty-five years, was the one obstacle. He therefore summoned the princes of Germany to a campaign against Henry, promising them an open and explicit recognition of their feudal status. Henry the Lion, confident in his own territorial strength in Saxony, tried to resist such "feudalization." Declared an outlaw and deprived of his lands, he had to flee. Thus, in the process of destroying Henry's independent power in Saxony, Frederick consolidated the feudalization of Germany. Confident in the success of his third plan, he held a major court and festival in Mainz at Pentecost of 1184, benevolently surveying his newly confirmed position as a feudal king. Swimming with the tide, he had at last obtained peace.

In the meantime news had arrived from the Holy Land that the Latin Kingdom of Jerusalem was nearing collapse. Frederick, who had always taken his position as emperor very literally, vowed, although sixty-six years old, to organize the Third Crusade (spring 1188). In May 1189 he led a large army down the Danube toward Constantinople and then across Asia Minor. After laborious progress, he was drowned while leading a small advance party across the river "Saleph" (modern Gök Su) on 10 June.

BIBLIOGRAPHY

Marshall W. Baldwin, *Alexander III and the 12th Century* (1968); G. Ellis, trans., *Boso's Life of Pope Alexander III,* with intro. by Peter Munz (1973); Karl Hampe, *Germany Under the Salian and Hohenstaufen Emperors,* Ralph Bennett, trans. (1973); Heinrich Mitteis, *The State in the Middle Ages,* H. F. Orton, trans. (1975); Peter Munz, *Frederick Barbarossa* (1969); Marcel Pacaut, *Frederick Barbarossa,* A. J. Pomerans, trans. (1970).

PETER MUNZ

[See also **Adrian IV, Pope; Alexander III, Pope; Germany: 1137–1254; Henry the Lion; Holy Roman Empire; Lombard League; Rainald of Dassel.**]

FREDERICK II OF THE HOLY ROMAN EMPIRE, KING OF SICILY (26 December 1194–13 December 1250), was born at Jesi in the march of Ancona. His father was Emperor Henry VI, from the German house of Hohenstaufen, and his mother was Constance of Sicily, daughter of King Roger II. Named Frederick Roger after his two grandfathers, he seemed destined to unite the claims of both houses in his own person, but the deaths of his parents before his fourth birthday led to the succession of his uncle, Philip of Swabia, in Germany and to a long period of anarchy in the kingdom of Sicily. The effort of Constance to ensure the throne for her son by entrusting him to Pope Innocent III was opposed by Markward of Anweiler, who claimed to represent the interests of Henry VI, and by some of the nobles of the kingdom. Although Markward died in 1202, it was not until 1206 that forces loyal to the regency gained control of Palermo and not until 1209 that Innocent, by arranging a marriage between Frederick and Constance of Aragon, was able to provide security for the young king.

During this same period the conflict over the German throne between Philip of Swabia and Otto of Brunswick, leader of the Welfs, was resolved in 1208 by the murder of Philip in a private quarrel. But Otto's election to the German crown and his subsequent imperial coronation as Otto IV did not bring the result anticipated by the papacy. Despite warnings from Innocent III, Otto made clear his intention

of pursuing the policies of Henry VI in Italy. Innocent excommunicated Otto and, at the suggestion of Philip Augustus of France, supported the election of Frederick II by a group of German princes. Frederick accepted and, with support from the papacy, the Genoese, and the bishop of Constance, was able to enter Germany. Bolstered by an alliance with France, he soon gained broad support. Philip Augustus defeated Otto at Bouvines on 27 July 1214, and in the following year Frederick was crowned at Aachen. At the same time he vowed to go on crusade.

During the next few years Frederick worked to consolidate his position in Germany, relying heavily on the ecclesiastical princes. After he had secured the election of his son, Henry, as German king, he descended to Rome and was crowned emperor by Pope Honorius III on 22 November 1220. There he renewed his crusade vow and promulgated a series of laws supporting the liberties of the church and enacting imperial penalties against heresy. As soon as he had reentered the Kingdom of Sicily, he issued the Assizes of Capua, aimed at restoring the rights lost to the monarchy during the "Time of Trouble." He defeated the rebellious magnates of the kingdom, limited the influence of the maritime cities of northern Italy, and suppressed a revolt of the Muslims of Sicily. In 1224 Frederick founded the University of Naples, the first state university of the Middle Ages. However, his pursuit of his Italian interests and his failure to fulfill his crusade vow—especially after the defeat of the crusade army at Damietta in 1221—undermined his previous good relations with the church. Frederick's wife Constance died in 1222 and in 1225 Honorius III arranged a marriage between Frederick and Isabella (or Yolanda) of Brienne, heiress of the Kingdom of Jerusalem, and reached agreements with Frederick regarding his leadership of a new crusade. But tensions with the church continued over the issue of prolonged vacancies in the episcopal sees of the Kingdom of Sicily. Soon after, Honorius died; the cardinals immediately elected Cardinal Hugolino of Ostia, long a friend of Frederick and a strong supporter of the new mendicant orders, as Pope Gregory IX (1227–1241).

During the summer of 1227, crusaders gathered at Brindisi, but fever struck the army. Nevertheless, Frederick departed, only to fall sick and return. Gregory rejected his explanations and, in accordance with the agreement of 1225, excommunicated him. Despite his excommunication and the small force at his disposal, Frederick again departed, and by 18 February 1229 he had concluded an agreement with the Sultan al-Malik al-Kāmil of Egypt for the return of Jerusalem and a ten-year truce. This agreement was essentially the same as the one rejected by the crusaders at Damietta. Frederick's defiance deepened the rift with the papacy. Gregory began to negotiate with dissidents in Germany, and Rainald of Spoleto, the imperial vicar in Italy, invaded the march of Ancona and his old duchy of Spoleto. Gregory raised an army and drove the imperial forces deep into the Kingdom of Sicily, but Frederick quickly returned and defeated the papal army. The Treaty of Ceprano (1230) was basically a return to the status quo, but left Frederick free to pursue his previous course in Italy.

The promulgation of *Liber Augustalis* (Constitutions of Melfi) in 1231 revealed Frederick's intention to centralize and bureaucratize his kingdom as a remedy to the centrifugal forces that threatened its peace and security. These laws made apparent, too, the importance of the Kingdom of Sicily in Frederick's vision of empire. In Sicily, his power did not suffer the checks that it did in Germany, to which he looked chiefly for support for his Italian policies. His son Henry, on the other hand, attempted to pursue a strong imperial policy against the German princes, but they rebelled and forced concessions (1231) that Frederick had to confirm. He compelled Henry to take an oath of obedience, and when, just four years later, Henry broke that oath, Frederick, with papal support, sent his son a prisoner to the Kingdom of Sicily. He then summoned the princes and tried to restore some of the lost status of the monarchy. But his mind was chiefly on Italy and on the support he needed to bring the Lombards into line with his imperial program. It was this preoccupation that aroused the concern of the Roman Curia.

Bolstered by his success in Germany, Frederick began to move against his Italian enemies. After taking Mantua in September 1237, he defeated the Lombard army near Cremona in November. Numerous cities surrendered and Milan was prepared to negotiate, but Frederick made the mistake of showing his implacability and thus strengthened the resolve of his remaining opponents. Gregory threw his support to the Lombards, excommunicated Frederick (March 1239), and helped to form a new coalition. He also summoned a general council to meet in Rome at Easter of 1241, but a Pisan fleet captured many of the prelates. As the conflict worsened, Gregory died (August 1241). It was two years before the cardinals were able to resolve their differences and elect Cardinal Sinibaldo Fieschi as Innocent IV.

The new pope, a famous canon lawyer, was under great pressure from some cardinals to pursue a vigorous anti-Hohenstaufen policy, but there were also strong efforts by King Louis IX of France and the German princes to bring about peace. Although papal forces made some gains in the papal state, the presence of Frederick near Rome threatened the security of the papacy. Innocent left Rome on 28 June 1244 and went to Lyons, to which he summoned a council. The First Council of Lyons (opened 26 June 1245) dealt mostly with the status of Frederick, who was once more excommunicated. Innocent also relieved his subjects of their oaths of loyalty and deposed him. Although Frederick's representatives tried to defend him, it was to no avail. Frederick decided to go to Lyons, but news of the fall of Parma to Guelph exiles turned him back. On 18 February 1248 he suffered a major defeat. There were other reverses, including the treason of some of his closest supporters. His natural son, King Enzio of Sardinia, was imprisoned by the Bolognese in May 1249. Still, Frederick's position remained strong. His commanders continued to menace northern Italy. But at the end of November 1250, he fell ill, and, on 13 December, died at Castel Fiorentino, near Lucera, in his beloved Apulia.

Frederick was, as his contemporary Fra Salimbene noted, an extraordinary person. His court was a center of culture where translations were made from Arabic and Greek, and where vernacular poetry was written. He himself composed a work on hunting with falcons *(De arte venandi cum avibus)* that revealed the scientific bent of his mind. He played a direct role in the making of the first western European public health code. He was friends with some of the leading scholars of his time and queried Muslim thinkers on philosophical questions. No wonder his contemporaries saw him as one who changed his world.

BIBLIOGRAPHY

Ernst Kantorowicz, *Frederick the Second,* E. O. Lorimer, trans. (1931, repr. 1957); James M. Powell, trans., *The Liber Augustalis or Constitutions of Melfi* (1971); Hans M. Schaller, *Kaiser Friedrich II, Verwandler der Welt* (1964); Thomas C. Van Cleve, *The Emperor Frederick II of Hohenstaufen* (1972).

JAMES M. POWELL

[See also **Germany, 1137–1254; Gregory IX, Pope; Hohenstaufen Dynasty; Holy Roman Empire; Innocent IV, Pope; Italy and the Empire; Salimbene; Sicily, Kingdom of.**]

FREE SPIRIT, HERESY OF, a name often given to heterodox European mysticism of the later Middle Ages. It is misleading, however, insofar as it suggests that there was a well-defined Free Spirit belief system. In fact there was no body of doctrine common to all Free Spirits because there was no organized sect of that name. Instead, Free Spirits were mystics of different persuasions who appeared in different times and places and were related primarily by the circumstance that their mysticism was regarded as dangerous or unsound by ecclesiastical authorities.

Unlike modern scholars, late-medieval church officials often operated on the assumption that there was an organized Free Spirit heresy. The most influential official description of the "heresy" was the decree *Ad nostrum,* drafted in 1312 by the Council of Vienne and formally promulgated as part of canon law in 1317. It listed eight errors of "an abominable sect of malignant men commonly known as beghards and faithless women commonly known as beguines in the kingdom of Germany," central among which were the tenets that (1) "Man can attain such a degree of perfection in the present life that he is thoroughly incapable of sin and can no longer advance in grace"; that (3) "Those who are in such a state of perfection and liberty of the spirit are not subject to human obedience or to any laws of the Church"; that (4) "Man can reach the same final blessedness in the present life as in the eternal life"; and that (5) "The soul does not need the light of glory to be elevated to the vision and enjoyment of God." In other words, the prelates of Vienne proclaimed that heretics of the Free Spirit were German beghards and beguines who subscribed to radical mysticism and antinomianism.

Recent scholarship, however, asks whether the evidence of *Ad nostrum* does not distort rather than aid the overall understanding of the Free Spirit phenomenon. In particular, modern scholars question whether Free Spirits were always German beghards and beguines and whether their mysticism was as radical and antinomian as the fathers of Vienne thought.

The evidence for the existence of Free Spirits before 1312 is very sparse. The earliest forerunners of the heresy are often considered to be the Amalricians, followers of the Parisian theologian Amalric of Bène, who died around 1206 after being forced to recant certain theological errors. It is not known exactly what Amalric taught, but it is known that fourteen of his leading disciples were arrested in and around Paris in 1210 for teaching extreme pantheism and antinomianism. Allegedly the Amalricians believed that God is everywhere and that consequently man can be suffused with God and have godlike potentialities. According to the hostile sources (the only evidence), they believed that they themselves were already spiritually perfect, and that within five years "all men will be spirituals so that each will be able to say 'I am the Holy Spirit.'" When that happened, there would no longer be any need for the sacraments. Supposedly the Amalricians also stated that the spiritually perfect were sinless, and therefore could even fornicate freely.

There definitely were no direct connections between the Amalricians and subsequent Free Spirits because the Amalrician sect did not long outlast the roundup of 1210 (the last known Amalricians were heard of in Amiens in 1212 and Troyes around 1221), whereas the earliest known Free Spirits appeared half a century later. Furthermore, later Free Spirits rarely espoused full pantheism and most of them differed from the Amalricians in believing that identification with God would not come about as the result of a new historical dispensation but, rather, would be attained by individuals who strove for spiritual perfection through their own efforts. Nonetheless, the Amalricians foreshadowed the Free Spirits insofar as they taught that individuals could become godlike and attain complete spiritual freedom.

Other forerunners of the Free Spirit heresy were the German Ortliebians, followers of Ortlieb of Strasbourg, who was condemned for heresy by Pope Innocent III sometime in the first or second decade of the thirteenth century. According to Albertus Magnus, Ortlieb taught that men should abstain from externals and follow the spirit within them. That is all that is known of Ortlieb's own doctrines, but there are more detailed reports about the beliefs of his followers. These reports describe a very eclectic heresy that drew on Waldensian evangelicalism and Cathar rigorism, but also proclaimed that the sectaries themselves were equivalent to the Father, the Son, and the Holy Spirit. The belief in their own deification made the Ortliebians resemble the Amalricians, but they differed from the Amalricians in avoiding antinomianism. For the Ortliebians asceticism rather than license was the consequence of spiritual perfection: indeed, they were so dedicated to fasting and continence that some historians have taken them to be a German branch of the Cathars (although this view is not widely accepted).

The reports about the Ortliebians say nothing about where they existed, how large their numbers were, or how long their sect survived. In all probability the sect died out by the middle of the thirteenth century at the latest, because no sources mention it after that time. Although the Ortliebians agreed with later Free Spirits about the possibility of human deification, their insistence on fasting and continence even for the "perfect," as well as many other aspects of their doctrine, were not repeated by later heterodox mystics.

The earliest evidence that is usually classified as describing an unquestionable manifestation of the Free Spirit heresy is a *determinatio* (a set of theological rulings) written by Albertus Magnus around 1273. It ascribed to men and women living in the Ries (a district of Swabia) mystical and antinomian errors ("man is able to become God"; "a sin is not a sin") that were afterward taken to be the essence of Free Spirit thought. Later scribes added a heading to Albertus' *determinatio* that stated that it pertained to a heresy of the "New Spirit," but Albertus himself made no reference to any organized sect, and there is no way of knowing whether the heretics of the Ries had any unified organization or survived to merge with subsequent Free Spirits. Albertus' *determinatio* is most valuable in displaying for the first time a Free Spirit pattern of thought and in showing that the beliefs of the Ries heretics were closely related to those of contemporary orthodox German nuns and beguines, such as Mechthild von Magdeburg, who exulted in ecstatic mystical union.

The clearest example of the close relationship between the heresy of the Free Spirit and orthodox mysticism is the case of Marguerite Porete, the first Free Spirit who can be identified by name. Marguerite spread mystical teachings in the first decade of the fourteenth century in the diocese of Cambrai and environs, and was burned for heresy at Paris in 1310. Her book, the *Mirouer des simples ames,* has survived in its original Old French version as well as in medieval Latin, Italian, and English translations. There is no doubt that it was considered fundamentally orthodox by many medieval readers: in one transmission it was ascribed to the orthodox Flemish mystic Ruusbroec, and it was translated from English into Latin in 1491 by the orthodox English Carthusian Richard Methley. Even in the twentieth century (in 1927) an English edition was published with the *nihil obstat* and *imprimatur* to attest doctrinal orthodoxy before it was discovered that the

author was really Marguerite Porete. At present there is scholarly disagreement about the extent of heresy in the *Mirouer,* but it is clear that the most daring passages in the treatise arose from bold reformulations of earlier orthodox forms of mysticism and piety.

Between 1305 and 1307, while Marguerite Porete was circulating her ideas in northern France, in Umbria the Franciscan Ubertino da Casale was combating adherents of "the Spirit of Liberty," led by Bentivenga of Gubbio. It is virtually certain, however, that Bentivenga, who was finally imprisoned by inquisitorial authorities in 1307, knew nothing of Marguerite and vice versa. Further concern with Free Spirits in Italy is displayed in a bull issued by Pope Clement V in April 1311, which attacked a new sect of the Free Spirit in the area of Spoleto and elsewhere. Unfortunately, practically nothing is known about the composition of ideas of this alleged sect, and the entire subject of later Italian Free Spirits remains to be studied more carefully. (Further research on possible Italian Free Spirit cases would have to consider, at a minimum, the trial of Franciscan Spirituals at Tivoli in 1334, the trial of Paolo Zoppo at Rieti in 1334, and the trial of Giacomo Ristolassio at Chieri in 1395.)

Although authorities in France and Italy were concerned about Free Spirits shortly before the convening of the Council of Vienne, it appears almost certain that the council's decree *Ad nostrum* was the work of German representatives, for the decree refers exclusively to heretics in Germany. There is no information about the details, but most likely the leading German prelate who pressed for legislation against heretical German beghards and beguines was the archbishop of Cologne, Henry of Virneburg. His synodal decree of 1306 against beghards demonstrates his prior concern on the subject. That decree is the first known text to charge German beghards with espousing mystical and antinomian errors: according to it, beghards in the diocese of Cologne said that whoever was moved by the Spirit of God was not under the law and was without sin.

Presumably Henry of Virneburg was still trying to combat the same heretical beghards six years later at Vienne. John of Zurich, bishop of Strasbourg, may have supported him, for it is known that John acted against heretical beghards in his diocese in 1317, before the formal promulgation of *Ad nostrum.* There is, furthermore, no question that the Rhineland was a center of mystical heterodoxy in the first half of the fourteenth century, but it is nonetheless noteworthy that provincial councils of Trier and Mainz legislated against beghards and beguines in 1310 without mentioning mystical or antinomian errors.

After the promulgation of *Ad nostrum* in 1317, numerous trials of alleged heretics of the Free Spirit occurred throughout the century, primarily in German-speaking areas. The protocols of some of these trials survive, but they must be used with great caution because they show that alleged heretics were often led by the use of inquisitorial formularies to repeat errors listed in *Ad nostrum* or statements made by other heretics, rather than being allowed to speak for themselves. Among alleged heretics of the Free Spirit brought to trial in the fourteenth century were Walter "the Hollander" of Cologne (*ca.* 1326), John and Albert of Brünn (between 1335 and 1350), Herman Kuchener (tried at Würzburg, 1342), Constantine of Arnhem (tried at Erfurt, 1350), Berthold von Rohrbach (tried at Speyer, 1356), John Hartmann of Ossmannstedt (tried at Erfurt, 1367), Conrad Kannler (tried at Eichstätt, 1381), Bartholomew of Dordrecht (tried at Utrecht, 1382), Martin of Mainz (tried at Cologne, 1393), and Nicholas of Basel (tried at Vienna between 1393 and 1397).

Some of these men were beghards (John and Albert of Brünn, John Hartmann); others were not (Constantine of Arnhem, Conrad Kannler, and the Augustinian friar Bartholomew of Dordrecht). Although all were charged with extreme antinomian mysticism, their actual beliefs were very diverse. John Hartmann, for example, confessed to believing that man could obtain final beatitude on earth without need for the light of glory, whereas Conrad Kannler said that blessedness could be obtained on earth only as "through a glass darkly," and that the soul needs the light of glory to be elevated to God.

Groups of beghards and beguines were also prosecuted throughout the fourteenth century in centers as far removed from each other as Strasbourg, Schweidnitz (Silesia), Metz, Magdeburg, Mühlhausen, and Cologne, but not always on the ground that they subscribed to mystical errors. Rather, beghards, and particularly beguines, were often subject to prosecution and harassment because of official opposition to their semiregular way of life. In Strasbourg, for example, beguines prosecuted in 1374 were not charged with upholding any doctrinal errors but, rather, with adhering to a semiregular and mendicant pattern of living, in alleged contravention of canon law. Thus it is clear that Free Spirits were not

always beghards and beguines, and that beghards and beguines—even those prosecuted for heresy—were not always Free Spirits.

In the fifteenth century trials for mystical heresy in continental Europe became increasingly rare, and by the last quarter of the century they had ceased. The outstanding cases were those of William of Lübeck (1402), William of Hildernissen (considered to be one of the "Men of Intelligence," tried at Cambrai, 1411), Werner of Ulm (1434), Magdalena Walpotin (tried at Regensburg, 1434), Hans Becker (tried at Mainz, 1458), and the Wirsberger brothers from western Bohemia (1466–1467). Probably none of these alleged heretics was a beghard or beguine; certainly they had no organizational relationships to one another. Some scholars see a Free Spirit influence on the Hussite movement in the cases of the Picards (1418) and the Adamites (1421), but this thesis appears difficult to sustain. Certainly the heresy of the Free Spirit had no influence on any aspect of the Protestant Reformation, for it completely disappeared in the later fifteenth century.

The best sources for understanding the beliefs of the heretics of the Free Spirit are their own extant writings. Foremost among these are Marguerite Porete's *Mirouer* and the fourteenth-century mystical tract *Schwester Katrei,* a fictional dialogue between Meister Eckhart and Sister Catherine, a beguine in search of mystical illumination. There are other surviving fourteenth-century Free Spirit writings, including some short German texts and sermons spuriously attributed to Meister Eckhart (who clearly had a marked influence on some German Free Spirits), a Dutch tract called *Meester Eggaert en de onbekende leek* (Meister Eckhart and the unknown layman), and extracts from heretical Rhineland texts made in the first half of the fifteenth century by the theologian Henry of Kamp.

These sources show that Free Spirits usually sought to lead an uncompromisingly moral and holy life, often in imitation of the "apostolic poverty" of the Gospels. In the *Mirouer des simples ames,* for example, the first two steps on the path to mystic union are said to be observing the Ten Commandments and following the counsels of evangelical perfection as typified by the life of Christ. Similarly, in *Schwester Katrei* Catherine first obeys the Ten Commandments and then leads an uncompromisingly mendicant existence, forsaking all her relatives and giving up all her possessions.

Unflinching pursuit of the apostolic life was expected to lead ultimately to full spiritual abnegation, and consequently to a state of union with God. Although hostile accounts insist that Free Spirits emphasized the role of nature over grace in the mystical union, and boasted of antinomian consequences of their supposed deification, there is hardly any clear affirmation of such beliefs in authentic Free Spirit sources. Marguerite Porete's *Mirouer,* for example, attributes a central role to divine power and glory in its account of the soul's deification, and although it has the transformed soul "taking leave of the virtues," it goes on to explain that after the mystical transformation, the soul really becomes the mistress of the virtues and, accordingly, never acts in conflict with them.

Free Spirit texts do appear to express heretical views more clearly on three points: the possibility of total deification for humanity in the present life; the possibility that this deification could be lasting rather than momentary; the possibility of circumventing sacramental intermediaries in the mystical way. The clearest statement of total deification is made by Sister Catherine when she exultantly exclaims to Meister Eckhart: "Rejoice with me, I have become God." The fact that her deification is more than momentary is shown when she then retreats into a corner of a church and lies there for three days, in a complete trance. The circumvention of sacramental authorities is more implicit than explicit in the Free Spirit sources, but Marguerite Porete does say that the liberated soul "does not seek God by penance or by any sacrament of the Holy Church."

If Free Spirits clearly stepped beyond the bounds of strict orthodoxy in such expressions, they nonetheless were very closely related to orthodox fourteenth-century mystics. Orthodox mystics such as Eckhart, Suso, Tauler, and Ruusbroec were on occasion taken for Free Spirits, and many Free Spirits probably arrived at their positions by misunderstanding or pushing to the limits the doctrines of orthodox mystical teachers, above all Meister Eckhart. The fact that Tauler, Suso, and Ruusbroec sharply repudiated the Free Spirits only serves to show that they felt an urgent need to preserve their reputations.

It is entirely mistaken to think of the late-medieval heretics of the Free Spirit as forerunners of modernity as exemplified in revolutionary protest movements. The only aspect of their thought that might possibly be viewed as "progressive" is their confidence in the spiritual potentialities of the laity and of women: laymen, they thought, could become divine without the aid of priests, and a simple woman like Sister Catherine could attain divinity and then reverse roles with her learned male adviser, Meister Eckhart, by offering him spiritual instruction. But Free Spirits by no means aimed to change society; by seeking abnegation and mystical union they hoped, rather, to depart from society. Hardly any of them expressed eschatological views, and none were revolutionary millenarians. For want of evidence, it is difficult to generalize about their social background, but it seems that Free Spirits were seldom, if ever, members of the lowest orders of society. Certainly they were not motivated by the hope for material or social benefits, but by the religious and emotional search for inward peace and the sense of perfection. As such they were extreme representatives of the widespread late-medieval search for godliness.

BIBLIOGRAPHY

Edmund Colledge and Romana Guarnieri, "The Glosses by 'M. N.' and Richard Methley to the 'Mirror of Simple Souls,'" in *Archivio italiano per la storia della pietà,* 5 (1968); Marilyn Doiron, "Margaret Porete: 'The Mirror of Simple Souls,' a Middle English Translation," *ibid.;* Martin Erbstösser, *Sozialreligiöse Strömungen im späten Mittelalter* (1970), 84–119, 160–163; Romana Guarnieri, "Il movimento del Libero Spirito," in *Archivio italiano per la storia della pietà,* 4 (1965); Herbert Grundmann, *Religiöse Bewegungen im Mittelalter,* 2nd ed. (1961), 355–438 and 524–538, "Ketzerverhöre des Spätmittelalters als quellenkritisches Problem," in *Deutsches Archiv für Erforschung des Mittelalters,* 21 (1965), and *Bibliographie zur Ketzergeschichte des Mittelalters (1900–1966)* (1967), 60–63; Robert E. Lerner, "The Image of Mixed Liquids in Late Medieval Mystical Thought," in *Church History,* 40 (1971), and *The Heresy of the Free Spirit in the Later Middle Ages* (1972); Eleanor McLaughlin, "The Heresy of the Free Spirit and Late Medieval Mysticism," in *Medievalia et humanistica,* n.s. 4 (1973); Jean Orcibal, "Le 'Miroir des simples âmes' et la 'secte' du Libre Esprit," in *Revue de l'histoire des religions,* 176 (1969); Alexander Patschovsky, "Strassburger Beginenverfolgungen im 14. Jahrhundert," in *Deutsches Archiv für Erforschung des Mittelalters,* 30 (1974); Kurt Ruh, "'Le Miroir des simples âmes' der Marguerite Porete," in *Verbum et signum: Beiträge zur mediävistischen Bedeutungsforschung,* II (1975); Walter L. Wakefield and Austin P. Evans, *Heresies of the High Middle Ages* (1969), 258–263, on the Amalricians.

R<small>OBERT</small> E. L<small>ERNER</small>

[See also **Amalric of Bène; Beguines and Beghards; Eckhart, Meister; Heresies, Western European; Hussites; Mechtild von Magdeburg; Mysticism; Ruusbroec and His Associates; Suso (Seuse), H[e]inrich; Tauler, Johannes.**]

FREIDANK. Little is known of the life of the gnomic poet who called himself Freidank. A document written about 1297 refers to him as "Frydanckus vagus," implying that he was either a wanderer or a classless member of society; a record, dated 1233, of the Cistercian abbey in Kaisheim tells of the death of a "Fridancus magister," who was probably the poet; and a passage in Rudolf von Ems's *Alexander* (*ca.* 1235) speaks of him in the past tense. The designation *magister* in the chronicle and the title *meister* that Rudolf gives him indicate that the poet was not a member of the nobility. Freidank's writings provide further biographical information: he knew Latin, but apparently was not a cleric; he accompanied Emperor Frederick II on the crusade of 1228–1229; and he may have visited Rome.

Freidank's single extant work is a collection of verse aphorisms, some 4,800 lines in all, to which he gave the title *Bescheidenheit* (discernment or wisdom). Most of the poems consist of a single rhymed couplet in tetrameter, a much smaller number are made up of two such couplets, and a few have three or more. The lack of consistency among the various manuscripts with respect to the arrangement of the sayings suggests that the author did not put them into any particular order, but merely recorded them as they were composed. He draws from the Bible, Latin encyclopedic and patristic works, fables, and the large store of folk adages of the time, and addresses his wisdom to everyone, regardless of class. He treats religious, moral, political, and social questions, as well as matters of practical common sense.

Although *Bescheidenheit* is primarily concerned with universal and timeless problems of everyday life, it also deals with conditions peculiar to its own period. The poet bitterly attacks the avarice and corruption of the papal court, the selling of indulgences, and all efforts to expand the secular authority of the church at the expense of the emperor, whom he considers the guardian of order and justice. He is even more vehement in his criticism of the stewardship of the higher nobility and the growth of power of the ruling princes. Perhaps the most enlightened aphorisms are the ones that condemn a double standard for men and women and those that, in surprisingly democratic language, stress the basic equality of all people. *Bescheidenheit* is characterized by piety, practicality, and concreteness of expression. Its general tone, despite frequent censure of sin and folly, is optimistic, for Freidank sets attainable goals for humanity and believes in the possibility of gaining both earthly happiness and God's favor.

The large number of manuscripts and fragments of *Bescheidenheit* (131) indicates that it was widely read. It exerted a significant influence on medieval didactic verse and probably also, through many sixteenth-century printings, on that of the early modern period.

BIBLIOGRAPHY

A catalog of the *Bescheidenheit* MSS and an extensive bibliography are in Berndt Jäger, *"Durch reimen gute lere geben": Untersuchungen zu Überlieferung und Rezeption Freidanks im Spätmittelalter* (1978). Significant works that Jäger does not list are Hermann Gumbel, "Brants *Narrenschiff* und Freidanks *Bescheidenheit*," in his *Beiträge zur Geistes- und Kulturgeschichte der Oberrheinlande* (1938); Friedrich Neumann, "Was sagt Freidank über Gott?" in Werner Besch et al., eds., *Studien zur deutschen Literatur und Sprache des Mittelalters* (1974), and "Freidank," in Kurt Ruh et al., eds., *Die deutsche Literatur des Mittelalters: Verfasserlexikon,* II (1980); Leslie Seiffert, *Wortfeldtheorie und Strukturalismus* (1968); Bruno F. Steinbruckner, "Über Freidank," in *Monatshefte,* **60** (1968).

J. W. Thomas

[See also **Gnomic Literature.**]

FRENCH LANGUAGE

EXTERNAL HISTORY

The first documentary evidence for the existence of the French language as a separate entity is found in the historian Nithard's *De dissensionibus filiorum Ludovici Pii.* There he writes that in 842 two grandsons of Charlemagne, Louis the German and Charles the Bald, contracted an alliance against their brother Lothair by swearing public oaths (the *Serments de Strasbourg* or *Strasbourg Oaths*) in the vernacular languages of their two armies. Thus, the German leader Louis swore his oath in *lingua romana* in order to be intelligible to his brother's army; the French leader Charles used the *teudisca lingua;* then each army swore allegiance in its own vernacular. Politically the *Strasbourg Oaths* signaled the disintegration of Charlemagne's empire. Linguistically they are tangible evidence of a situation that had probably obtained for at least one and one-half centuries: the existence of distinct and mutually incomprehensible languages throughout what had once been the Roman Empire.

Obviously such linguistic divergence could not have happened instantaneously. Thus, to posit an arbitrary date, or even century, when the crystallization of Latin into French took place would be to misrepresent a long and gradual process in which the *Strasbourg Oaths* were merely a historical milestone.

The Roman conquest of southeastern Gaul around 120 B.C. and of northern Gaul by 51 B.C. substituted the spoken or "Vulgar" Latin of the Roman Empire for the Celtic language. This Vulgar Latin was predominantly a language of soldiers, settlers, and traders, and its initial lines of development were similar throughout the life of the empire. The Vulgar Latin period of Romance (sometimes called Proto-Romance) extends from the time of the Roman invasions of Gaul to around A.D. 500. Sources of information about the language of the Vulgar Latin period are: the remarks of Latin grammarians in the third-century *Appendix Probi* and the fifth-century *Ars Consentii* and *De barbarismis et metaplasmis;* the usage of contemporary writers in such works as the *Peregrinatio Aetheriae;* the intentional colloquialisms of church sermons, especially of St. Jerome and St. Augustine; the orthography of inscriptions and Greek transliterations; and the phonetic renderings of Latin words that were borrowed by other languages. These direct sources, when combined with the evidence provided by the subsequent development of the Romance languages, have made possible a surprisingly detailed reconstruction of Vulgar Latin.

The only important non-Roman influence upon this period (apart from the Celtic language, which survived for several centuries in isolated, rural areas of Gaul) was Greek. Latin had for centuries drawn upon the scholarly vocabulary of Greek, and in the Vulgar Latin period ecclesiastical terms were an important addition to the learned borrowings from Greek into Latin. Popular Greek words were also introduced from the thriving Greek maritime community of Massilia (Marseilles) and its colonies (Agde, Antibes, Monaco, and Nice).

In the fifth to the ninth centuries (the Gallo-Roman period) distinctions between Gallo-Romance and other variants of Romance defined themselves more clearly. Without the pressures of a centralized political system and without the restraining influences of Latin literary tradition, local speech variants developed freely. There was an inevitable, although lesser, differentiation also between the dialects of northern and southern Gaul because of the differing degree of Romanization in those areas. Generally speaking, the south remained more conservative

than the north in its preservation of the Roman sound system and of Roman speech habits. Another source of local variation was the succession of invaders who occupied and then settled permanently in certain areas of Gaul. The most important of these were the Visigoths, the Burgundians, and, above all, the Franks, for whom Gaul was renamed "France" (Francia).

Neither the Merovingian nor the Carolingian dynasties succeeded, however, in reimposing the concept of an enduring and unified empire for any length of time. Charlemagne had, by the time of his death in 814, built a fragile "Romania" in the west, but the rivalries of his three grandsons, formalized in the *Strasbourg Oaths,* were sufficient to bring about its disintegration. This parceling-out of the empire had linguistic implications for the future development of the French language, since it effectively blocked the development of Gallo-Romance in Louis the German's "Francia orientalis" (the foundation of the future Germany).

Charlemagne's efforts to bring about a renaissance of literary Latin were similarly short-lived. Written Latin, which had continued through the centuries as the official language of church and state in Gaul, was by the eighth century seriously debased. (The literary Latin of these centuries is, in fact, usually labeled "Low Latin.") The Carolingian dynasty's reforms in grammar, orthography, and handwriting eventually resulted in the accentuation of divergences between the spoken and written languages because the "purification" of Latin could only be a return to the traditions of Classical Latin. It was not surprising that around the seventh century the clergy began to produce "glosses" of early Latin texts. These annotations explained problematic words that had disappeared from current usage. For example, the *Reichenau Glossary (ca.* 800) was a collection of glosses to the Vulgate. It explained thousands of words from Old and New Testaments by listing more familiar equivalents in the vernacular. Thus *caseum* was glossed as *formaticum* (*fromage* in later French), *umo* as *terra* (later *terre*), and *oves* as *berbices* (later *brebis*). Latin charters, letters, inscriptions, and writers' colloquialisms are other important sources of linguistic information for the Gallo-Roman period.

The Old French period is usually considered to extend from the ninth to the fifteenth century. Regional divergence characterized the early centuries of the period. It was customary in the Middle Ages to distinguish between the languages of northern and southern France, the *langue d'oïl* and the *langue d'oc* (so named because of their characteristic forms of the word for "yes"). As Dante said in his *De vulgari eloquentia*, "nam alii *oc*, alii *si*, alii vero dicunt *oil*" (some say *oc*, some *sì*, and some *oil*), referring to southern French, Italian, and northern French, respectively.

There was further differentiation within those broad categories, causing Roger Bacon to observe in the thirteenth century: "Even dialects of the same tongue vary among different groups, as is clear from the Gallic language, which varies in many details among Gauls and Normans and Burgundians. Words properly spoken in the Picard tongue would horrify Burgundians, still more so nearby Gauls" (*Opus majus* 3.1). Catalan, Gascon, Limousin, and Provençal were seen as major dialects in the *langue d'oc*. Within the area of the *langue d'oïl* there were noticeable resemblances between the Picard-Walloon dialects of the northeast, between Lorrain and Champenois in the east, between Angevin, Poitevin, and Saintongeais in the west, and between Burgundian and Franc-Comtois in the southeast. Norman (northwest France) and Anglo-Norman were obviously related—the Norman dialect was imported to England after the Norman Conquest of 1066, and French remained the official language of England until 1362, when Edward III first sought to impose the use of English on the law courts. The central dialect of the Île-de-France, Francien, was destined to supersede all other dialects in France during the Old French period because of the geographical accessibility of Paris, that city's political importance as the seat of the Capetian monarchy, and the intellectual dominance of its university (which received its charter from the pope in 1231).

Conquests outside France enhanced the prestige of the French language generally during the Old French period. The Norman conquests of Sicily and south Italy between 1016 and 1075, of England in 1066, the crusades, including the Albigensian Crusade, the Italian wars (1494–1514), and the Concordat of Bologna (1515) were all instrumental in promoting French abroad. The language's role as the diplomatic vernacular of Europe enriched the lexicon with hundreds of exotic borrowings from all sources: Arabic, Dutch, English, German, Greek, Italian, Persian, and Slavic.

Toward the end of the period the French language was obviously encroaching on all the traditional domains of Latin. Translations (especially of the Bible), the invention of printing, and continuing foreign enterprises all contributed to the potential of the language. In 1539 Francis I finally imposed the use of the vernacular in the procedures of the law courts. His decree of Villers-Cotterets ensured that "all decrees and proceedings, any other acts, and deeds in law or belonging thereto, be pronounced, registered, and delivered to the parties concerned in the maternal language and not otherwise." From that date both Latin and the regional dialects were effectively banished from the judicial courts. French was at last the official vehicle of communication. It would soon displace Latin in all other contexts.

Surviving texts from the early centuries of the Old French period are surprisingly few in number: the *Strasbourg Oaths* (842) and *La séquence de Ste. Eulalie* (*ca.* 880) from the ninth century; French notes (northeastern dialect) on a Latin sermon about *Jonah,* a Provençalized *Passion du Christ* and *Vie de St. Léger,* and a Provençal *Boecis* from the end of the tenth century; the Provençal *Chanson de Ste. Foi d'Agen,* six versions of *La vie de St. Alexis* (written *ca.* 1050), the *Pèlerinage de Charlemagne* and *Chanson de Roland* from the eleventh century. Beginning in the twelfth century, however, a rich and varied literature developed in the French language.

THE SOUND SYSTEM

Symbols. The phonetic alphabet employed here is that given by M. K. Pope in *From Latin to Modern French.* The following sound symbols are used in this section:

Vowel quantity is denoted by ‾ (long) and ˘ (short).

[a]	as in Modern French *patte*
[ę]	as in Modern French *fête*
[e]	as in Modern French *fée*
[ẹ]	as in Modern German *Gabe*
[i̥]	as in Modern French *pli*
[ǫ]	as in Modern French *bosse*
[ọ]	as in Modern French *sot*
[u̯]	as in Modern French *coup*
[ü]	as in Modern French *plus*

Nasalization is denoted by the tilde ~; it should be noted that at certain stages in Old French *all* vowels and diphthongs were assimilated toward nasal consonants. However, since the section on nasalization below deals only with end products of the process, only the following symbols appear:

[ę̃]	as in Modern French *faim*
[ã]	as in Modern French *an*
[ǫ̃]	as in Modern French *on*
[ö̃]	as in Modern French *un*

The following consonant symbols are used:

[ð] as in Modern English *then*
[j] as in Modern French *yeux*
[ʎ] as in Modern Italian *figlio*
[ŋ] as in Modern French *agneau*
[ł] as in Modern English *old*
[ǥ] as in Modern French patois *gaie*
[ʄ] as in Modern French patois *qui*
[tš] as in Modern English *chin*
[dž] as in Modern English *gin*

When necessary, an acute accent is used to denote stress, as in *virtútem.* > denotes "becomes," as in *portare > porter.*

Evolution. The language of the Roman conquerors, Vulgar (spoken) Latin, had many phonetic features that distinguished it from Classical Latin. Between the first and fifth centuries quantitative distinctions between vowels disappeared in favor of a differentiation by stress accent. Thus, certain sounds merged in the new vowel system: Long and short *a* (*ā, ǎ*), long *e* and short *i* (*ē, ǐ*), long *o* and short *u* (*ō, ǔ*) merged into [a], [ẹ], and [ọ] respectively. Short *e* and *o* (*ě, ǒ*) became the open vowels [ę] and [ǫ]. Long *i* and *u* persisted as [ị] and [ụ]. The latter subsequently palatalized to [ü]. The diphthong *ae* became the open vowel [ę]; *oe* became the close [ẹ]; and *au* survived in certain circumstances, while reducing in others to [ǫ] or [ọ].

It was the position of the stress accent in a word that determined its development into French. In general, syllables that had been emphasized in the quantitative system of Classical Latin continued to be emphasized by the expiratory accent. The following pattern can be seen: in two-syllable words, stress was placed on the first syllable, as in *rósa*, which developed into *rose;* in words of several syllables, stress fell upon the penultimate syllable if its vowel had been long (as in *virtútem*, which developed into *vertu*) but on the antepenultimate if the penultimate had been a short vowel (as in *árbŏrem*, which developed into *arbre*). Changes of stress occurred, however, in certain circumstances, notably with the juxtaposed vowels *íe, ío, éo*, which became *ié, ió, eó*, and in proparoxytones containing a short vowel plus a plosive plus *r* (as in *pálpebras*, which eventually became *palpébras* [OF *palpieres*], though compare earlier *paupres*).

When vowels were in a stressed position and were free (that is, followed by only one consonant or by *pr, br, dr, tr, gr, pl,* or *bl*), they tended to lengthen and often to diphthongize as well. Development of the tonic free vowels was as follows:

portáre > porter	*sóror > suer*
mel > miel	*flórem > fleur*
víta > vie	*múrem > mur*

Blocked vowels (those followed by two or more consonants except the combination of plosive plus *l* and *r*) remained relatively stable in tonic (stressed) position:

partem > part	*fortem > fort*
terram > terre	*ursum* [ọ] *> ours* [ụ]
missam [ę] *> messe*	*nullum > nul* [ü]
villam > ville	

Unstressed (atonic) vowels, on the other hand, were usually weakened or lost, such as the second *i* in *víridum* (French: *vert*), the second *o* in *collocáre* (French: *colchier*), and the final *u* of *múrum* (French: *mur*).

Certain consonants were also vulnerable. Final *m* had disappeared except in monosyllables as early as the Vulgar Latin period. By the sixth century most consonants except *s* (maintained in Gaul as a flexion distinguishing subject and object cases) had been lost when in a weak position (when they preceded another consonant or were unsupported in final position), for example, *ruptam > route*. Intervocalic voiceless consonants were voiced around the sixth century and were subsequently lost, for instance *t > d >* [ð] in *nativum >* [*nadif*] *>* [*naðif*] *> naïf*.

The same fate befell certain functional words when they received little or no sentence stress. One of the changes that distinguished French from Latin was, in fact, the growing importance of group stress. By its influence monosyllabic pronouns might, for example, be linked proclitically with a subsequent, and enclitically with a preceding, tonic syllable: thus, *qu'elle* (*que elle*) by proclisis; *se jel puis faire* (*se je le puis faire*) by enclisis.

There were other speech habits besides expiratory stress that modified early French substantially. There was a particularly strong tendency in Gaul toward palatalization, whether by isolative change, such as the transformation of [ụ] to [ü] in Gallo-Roman, or by combinative change, such as the raising of [a] to [ẹ] (which was later reduced to [ę]) by assimilation toward the palatal [u], as in *fatutum* [fẹü].

By the third century velar plosives (*k* and *g*) before a front vowel (*e* and *i*) had moved forward. The initial [kẹ] of *cervum*, for example, became [ʄ], and then, by stages, [ts], and in the thirteenth century [s]. Similarly the initial *g* of *gentem* became [ǥ], then [dž], then [ž]. The medieval pronunciation of these groups is still audible in English borrowings from Old French, such as the doublet *gentle-genteel.*

Velar *k* and *g* palatalized in many regions when those sounds preceded *a*, as in the development of *carum* to *chier* (with initial [tš]), and *gaudium* to *joi* (with initial [dž]). Such palatalization was a characteristic feature of certain central dialects, notably Francien, but did not affect such northern dialects as Norman and Picard, or the dialects of the south.

Velars palatalized to a yod before a consonant: *factum* > *fait.* The combination of *n* or *l* plus yod produced the new palatal sounds [ŋ] and [ɟ]: *agnellum* > *agneau* [ŋ], *filia* > *fille* [ɟ].

After several centuries of intensive palatalization, to which all nonpalatal consonants may have been susceptible at some stage, a gradual depalatalization began—in some cases even before the ninth century. Frequently palatal sounds freed an *i* before their disappearance, thus providing a source of new diphthongs to the French language.

Another source of diphthongs was the vocalization of *l* before another consonant, a process that was probably completed by the tenth century. By vocalization the *au* diphthong, which had been reduced to *o* by the end of the eighth century, was restored to the language. By the influence of vocalizing *l*, French acquired the following diphthongs or triphthongs:

[a] + [ɫ] > [aʊ̯]	*caballos*	> *chevaux*
[ɛ] + [ɫ] > [ɛaʊ̯]	*bellos*	> *beaux*
[e] + [ɫ] > [eʊ̯]	*capillos*	> *cheveux*
[ɔ] + [ɫ] > [ɔʊ̯]	*colpum*	> *coup*
[o] + [ɫ] > [oʊ̯] > [ʊ̯]	*fulgurem*	> *foudre*

By the process of labialization, labials sometimes exerted influence upon neighboring vowels or consonants, rounding front vowels (*casipula* > *chasuble*), for example.

Another assimilatory process, nasalization, became particularly strong in Gaul around the ninth century. Beginning with *a* and *e* (low vowels are more easily assimilated toward nasal consonants than high vowels), the nasal consonants [m], [n], and [ŋ] nasalized preceding vowels. All tonic vowels nasalized, whether free or blocked. Nasalization occurred under the influence even of intervocalic nasal consonants, as in *amare* > [ãmɛr]. (In the following list only the end product is given, though several stages often preceded it.)

ă + nasal blocked, tonic or protonic > [ã]: *camera* > *chambre*

ă tonic + final nasal free > [ɛ̃]: *famem* > *faim*

ĕ + nasal blocked, tonic or protonic > [ã]: *pendere* > *pendre*

ĕ tonic + final nasal free > [ɛ̃]: *bene* > *bien*

ē, ĭ + nasal blocked, tonic or protonic > [ã]: *subinde* > *souvent*

ē, ĭ tonic + final nasal free [ɛ̃]: *Remos* > *Reims*

ī + nasal blocked, tonic or protonic > [ɛ̃]: *principem* > *prince*

ī tonic + final nasal free > [ɛ̃]: *vinum* > *vin*

ŏ, ŭ + nasal blocked, tonic or protonic > [ɔ̃]: *contra* > *contre*

ŏ, ŭ tonic + final nasal free > [ɔ̃]: *bonum* > *bon*

ū + nasal blocked, tonic or protonic > [õ]: *lunaediem* > *lundi*

ū tonic + final nasal free > [õ]: *unum* > *un.*

The process of nasalization reversed itself in later Middle French, beginning with the vowels [i] and [ü], the high vowels that had been the last to nasalize.

ORTHOGRAPHY

The orthographical symbols by which the sound system of medieval French was represented were inherited from Latin. Nevertheless, medieval orthography was, broadly speaking, phonetic, and was certainly more successful in that regard than modern orthography. Of course the early scribes encountered many problems as they attempted to render the new sounds of the French vernacular. In the following excerpt from the *Strasbourg Oaths,* for example, the Latin-trained scribe has resorted to *a, e,* and *o* indiscriminately to denote the sound [ɛ̦] of *fradre, Karlo,* and *nulla:* "Si Lodhuvigs sagrament, que son fradre Karlo jurat, conservat, et Karlus meos sendra de suo part lo fraint, si io returnar non l'int pois, ne io ne neuls cui eo returnar int pois, in nulla ajudha contra Lodhuwig nun li iv er." In the above excerpt it should also be noted that *i* has been added to certain vowels to denote the palatal element of an agglutinated diphthong *(pois),* that *h* (which had disappeared as a phoneme from the Vulgar Latin sound system several centuries before) is used successfully to render the transitional sound [ð], which developed from the dental *t* intervocalic.

The Germanic invasions were responsible for the reintroduction of aspirate *h* as a phoneme and for the importation of a bilabial *w* to the French sound system. In some areas that were little affected by the invasions, initial *h* was ignored by scribes as a superfluous graphy (for example, the Provençal *elme* and the Francien *heaume*). *W* was used as a graphy for that bilabial in certain northern dialects, but it was rendered as *gu* in those central regions where its pronunciation necessitated an accompanying aspiration (for instance, *wisa* was rendered in Francien as *guise*).

Despite all inconsistencies, traditionalisms, and regionalisms, medieval French orthography was more successful in rendering each phoneme of the language than any later orthographical system— French was not yet weighted down with the heavily latinized accretions of Middle French, nor with the rigidly traditional conventions that the invention of printing would impose.

MORPHOLOGY AND SYNTAX

Phonetic erosion of Latin flexions and the effacement of many phonetic distinctions that had been crucial to Latin declension and conjugation had profound effects upon the morphology and syntax of the French language. *S* survived as a flexion in common parlance, reinforced by the conservatizing influence of the schools in Gaul. A simplified flexion system for nouns and adjectives, in which the complex case system of Classical Latin had been reduced to a subject and an object case, was thus maintained until the late Middle Ages. The maintaining of some case distinction allowed variability in the order of words, and medieval French was in this regard intermediate between the flexibility of Classical Latin and the rigidity of Modern French. Masculine nouns were of two types: those derived from the Latin second-declension *-us* type and those derived from the other masculines.

Masculine Nouns I

	Singular	Plural
Subject	*murs*	*mur*
Oblique	*mur*	*murs*

Masculine Nouns II

	Singular	Plural
Subject	*pere*	*pere*
Oblique	*pere*	*peres*

Similarly, the two types of feminine nouns in French derived from the first-declension Latin *-a* type and from the third-declension feminines.

Feminine Nouns I

	Singular	Plural
Subject	*fille*	*filles*
Oblique	*fille*	*filles*

Feminine Nouns II

	Singular	Plural
Subject	*flor(s)*	*flors*
Oblique	*flor*	*flors*

There was, in addition, an anomalous group of nouns whose development was affected by the fact that their subject and object cases in Latin had contained different numbers of syllables. This differing number of syllables between the cases induced a variable development, and thence a changing form of stem in French:

Imparisyllabic Nouns

Singular

Subject	*(látro)*	*lerre*
Oblique	*(latrónem)*	*larron*

Plural

Subject	*(latrónes)*	*larron*
Oblique	*(latrónes)*	*larrons*

A small group of indeclinables existed in French, deriving from Latin nouns whose stem ended in *-s* and thus allowed no distinction between subject and oblique cases. In the above system the five declensions of Latin were reduced to three, because the fourth declension had merged with the second, and the fifth with the first. Neuter nouns of the second and fourth declensions merged with the masculine second-declension *-us* type, but a few neuter nouns that were frequently used in their *-a* plural form as collectives merged with the feminine declension as in *mirabilia* > *merveille* and *folia* > *feuille*.

Adjectives showed a similar two-case system and a similar remodeling of the Latin declensions:

Adjectives I

Singular

	Masc.	Fem.
Subject	*bons*	*bone*
Oblique	*bon*	*bone*

Plural

	Masc.	Fem.
Subject	*bon*	*bones*
Oblique	*bons*	*bones*

Adjectives II

(When there was no *-s* in the masculine nominative of the Latin.)

Singular

	Masc.	Fem.
Subject	*tendre*	*tendre*
Oblique	*tendre*	*tendre*

Plural

	Masc.	Fem.
Subject	*tendre*	*tendres*
Oblique	*tendres*	*tendres*

Adjectives III

(When there was one common form for masculine and feminine in Latin.)

Singular

	Masc.	Fem.
Subject	*granz*	*grant*
Oblique	*grant*	*grant*

Plural

	Masc.	Fem.
Subject	*grant*	*granz*
Oblique	*granz*	*granz*

There was a small group of imparisyllabic adjectives derived from the Latin comparatives.

Imparisyllabic Adjectives

Singular

	Masc.	Fem.
Subject	*graindre*	*graindre*
Oblique	*graignor*	*graignor*

Plural

	Masc.	Fem.
Subject	*graignor*	*graignors*
Oblique	*graignors*	*graignors*

The simple two-case system outlined above started to disintegrate with the gradual loss of the flexional -s, beginning in the twelfth century. The analytic tendencies of French—its use of explicit modifying and determining words and an increasingly fixed word order—continued to develop correspondingly to meet the needs for clarity. The disintegration of the case system was faster in Anglo-Norman, in which it was completed by around 1200, than in central French, in which the oblique form was generalized only by the end of the fourteenth century.

A significant development in the Romance trend from synthesis to analysis had been the creation of the definite article. In the Vulgar Latin period the demonstrative *ille* had been persistently used to particularize the noun it preceded, and even in the early Old French period this demonstrative function persisted to some extent. The definite article was not yet an automatic adjunct of the noun; and indeed, certain nouns (such as proper names, abstract nouns, or individual entities) apparently required no further particularization and were not accompanied by it: for example, *Dieu, Sarrazinois, amor, ciel, terre.*

The Definite Article

	Singular		Plural	
	Masc.	Fem.	Masc.	Fem.
Subject	*li*	*la*	*li*	*les*
Oblique	*lo, le*	*la*	*les*	*les*

The indefinite article (from Latin *unus* which was already used occasionally by post-classical writers for *quidam*) did not become regularized in its French function of singling out an unspecified object from a group until much later. Furthermore, its plural forms continued to be used until the sixteenth century for pairs or for collective groups of objects: *unes botes, uns grans dens.*

The Indefinite Article

	Singular		Plural	
	Masc.	Fem.	Masc.	Fem.
Subject	*uns*	*une*	*un*	*unes*
Oblique	*un*	*une*	*uns*	*unes*

The forms of the personal pronouns were also derived from Latin—with, however, a dual development of stressed and unstressed forms (Table 1).

In early Old French the personal pronouns were not yet automatic concomitants of the verb. They were used for emphasis, clarification (for instance, to

Table 1. Personal Pronouns

First Person

	Stressed	Unstressed
Sing. Subject	*gie > je*	*jo je*
Sing. Oblique	*mei > moi*	*me*
Plural Subject	*nos > nous*	*nos > nous*
Plural Oblique	*nos > nous*	*nos > nous*

Second Person

	Stressed	Unstressed
Sing. Subject	*tu*	*tu*
Sing. Oblique	*tei > toi*	*te*
Plural Subject	*vos > vous*	*vos > vous*
Plural Oblique	*vos > vous*	*vos > vous*

Third Person

	Masc.	Fem.	Masc.	Fem.
Sing. Subject	*il*	*ele*	*il*	*ele*
Sing. Oblique	*lui*	*li*	*lo > le*	*la*
Sing. Dative	*lui*	*li*	*li*	*li*
Plural Subject	*il*	*eles*	*il*	*eles*
Plural Oblique	*els > eus*	*eles*	*les*	*les*
Plural Dative	*lor > leur*	*lor>leur*	*lor >lour*	*lor>lour*

Reflexive Pronoun

sei > soi   *se*

226

Table 2. Possessive Pronouns

First Person

	Stressed		Unstressed	
	Masc.	Fem.	Masc.	Fem.
Sing. Subject	miens	meie	mes	ma
Sing. Oblique	mien	meie	mon	ma
Plural Subject	mien	meies	mi	mes
Plural Oblique	miens	meies	mes	mes

Second Person

	Masc.	Fem.	Masc.	Fem.
Sing. Subject	tuens	toe	tes	ta
Sing. Oblique	tuen	toe	ton	ta
Plural Subject	tuen	toes	ti	tes
Plural Oblique	tuens	toes	tes	tes

Third Person

	Masc.	Fem.	Masc.	Fem.
Sing. Subject	suens	soe	ses	sa
Sing. Oblique	suen	soe	son	sa
Plural Subject	suen	soes	si	ses
Plural Oblique	suens	soes	ses	ses

First Person

	Masc.	Fem.	Masc.	Fem.
Sing. Subject	nostre	nostre	nostre	nostre
Sing. Oblique	nostre	nostre	nostre	nostre
Plural Subject	nostre	nostres	nostre	noz
Plural Oblique	nostres	nostres	noz	noz

Second Person

	Masc.	Fem.	Masc.	Fem.
Sing. Subject	vostre	vostre	vostre	vostre
Sing. Oblique	vostre	vostre	vostre	vostre
Plural Subject	vostre	vostres	vostre	voz
Plural Oblique	vostres	vostres	voz	voz

Third Person

	Masc.	Fem.	Masc.	Fem.
Sing. Subject	lor	lor	lour	lour
Sing. Oblique	lor	lor	lour	lour
Plural Subject	lor	lor	lour	lour
Plural Oblique	lor	lor	lour	lour

signal changes in subject), and euphony (for instance, if the sentence in which they occurred would otherwise have begun with an unstressed monosyllable). The table of pronouns (Table 1) shows several inter-

Table 3. Demonstrative Pronouns

Icil (later *cil*)

	Masc.	Fem.	Neut.
Sing. Subject	(i)cil	(i)cele	(i)cel
Sing. Oblique	(i)cel, (i)celui	(i)cele, (i)celi	(i)cel
Plural Subject	(i)cil	(i)celes	
Plural Oblique	(i)cels > iceus	(i)celes	

Icist (later *cist*)

	Masc.	Fem.	Neut.
Sing. Subject	(i)cist	(i)ceste	(i)cest
Sing. Oblique	(i)cest, (i)cestui	(i)ceste, (i)cesti	(i)cest
Plural Subject	(i)cist	(i)cestes > (i)cez	
Plural Oblique	(i)cez	(i)cestes > (i)cez	

changes of forms: the dative plural *lor* was originally a genitive *(illorum)*, the singular datives *li* and *lui* served also as singular oblique stressed forms for both masculine and feminine, and the feminine plural oblique form (derived from *illas*) was generalized to serve as both subject and oblique case.

Possessive pronouns showed the same dual development of stressed and unstressed forms (Table 2). The Classical Latin demonstrative pronouns *iste* and *ille* (the former denoting what is nearby, and the latter what is remote) were reinforced in Vulgar Latin by the addition of the demonstrative adverb *ecce*. This gave a dual set of medieval French demonstrative pronouns that could be used either substantivally or adjectivally (Table 3). The distinction between relative and interrogative pronouns with their many classical Latin forms was early lost, and even the forms given in Table 4 were frequently replaced by a multipurpose *que*.

The Classical Latin verb system was substantially modified by the following changes: deponent verbs were lost (their passive form having early been transformed into the active voice); the inflected passive was replaced by a new composite passive; auxiliaries served increasingly as flexions; and the conjugations were confused. Of the indicative, active-voice tense forms, the present, imperfect, perfect, and pluperfect survived (the latter only in isolated examples in such

Table 4. Relative and Interrogative Pronouns

	Relative Masc.-Fem.	Interrogative Masc.-Fem	Relative-interrogative Neut.	
			Stressed	Unstressed
Subject	qui	qui	quei quoi	que
Oblique	cui, qui, que	cui, qui	quei quoi	que

Table 5. Present Tense

Chanter	Partir	Fenir	Valeir	Beivre
chant	part	fenis	vail	beif
chantes	parz	fenis	vals	beis
chante	part	fenist	valt	beit
chantons	partons	fenissons	valons	bevons
chantez	partez	fenissez	valez	bevez
chantent	partent	fenissent	valent	beivent

early texts as the *Eulalie* and *La vie de St. Alexis*). Five different forms of the present tense of medieval French are given in Table 5.

As for the imperfect tense, the *-ebam* ending was regularized over most of Gaul, giving a single set of endings, as in:

partir

parteie	partiiens
parteies	partiiez
parteit	parteient

The *-abam* ending, however, yielded the following endings in Norman, Anglo-Norman, and western dialects:

chanter

chantoe	chantiiens
chantoes	chantiiez
chantout	chantoent

Past-definite verbs in medieval French continued the three different types of Latin perfects: "weak" (in which the stress fell uniformly on the flexion), "strong" (in which the stress alternated between the stem and the flexion), and "reduplicated," or weak, perfects (which in Vulgar Latin were constructed upon the reduplicated perfect of *dare*) (Table 6).

In addition to the imperfect and perfect (that is, past-definite) forms already discussed, two new composite past tenses—perfect and pluperfect—arose in Vulgar Latin and continued into French. In origin, these were a composite of the present and imperfect tenses: *habeo* with an adjectival past participle—for instance, *habeo litteras scriptas* (I have the letters written)—and had been used as such as early as Plautus' time. Their composite nature remained visible throughout medieval French, since their past participles customarily agreed with the accompanying direct object: *jo ai les letres escrites* (compare the Modern French *j'ai écrit les lettres*).

An analytic future tense displaced the Latin synthetic future. It comprised an infinitive plus contracted forms of the present indicative of *habeo*—for example, *chanter-ai, chanter-as, chanter-a, chanter-ons, chanter-ez, chanter-ont*.

A new "conditional" tense comprising infinitive plus contracted forms of the imperfect tense of *habeo* (such as *chanter-eie, chanter-eies, chanter-eit, chanter-iiens, chanter-iiez, chanter-eient*) had no

Table 6. Past Definite

	Weak		Weak reduplicated	
	Chanter	*Dormir*	*Vendir* (from the Vulgar Latin)	
	chantai	dormi	vendi	vendedi
	chantas	dormis	vendis	vendedisti
	chanta	dormi	vendiét	vendedit
	chantames	dormimes	vendimes	vendedimus
	chantastes	dormistes	vendistes	vendedistis
	chanterent	dormirent	vendiérent	vendederunt

Strong

-i type	*-si* type	*-ui* type
Venir	*Dire*	*Paroir*
vin (from *veni*)	dis (from *dixi*)	parui (from *parui*)
venis	desis	parus
vint	dist	parut
venimes	desimes	parumes
venistes	desistes	parustes
vindrent	disrent	parurent

Note: The *fen-ir* type derived from a Vulgar Latin inchoative form with the verbal suffix *-iscere*.

Table 7. Subjunctive

Present

Chanter (-are type)	Partir
chant (Latin -em)	parte (Latin -iam)
chanz	partes
chant	parte
chantons	partons
chantez	partez
chantent	partent

Past

Chanter	Partir	Pareir
chantasse	partisse	parusse
chantasses	partisses	parusses
chantast	partist	parust
chantissons	partissons	parussons
chantisseiz	partisseiz	parusseiz
chantassent	partissent	parissent

equivalent in Latin. It would eventually displace the subjunctive in some of the functions of the latter, notably in the apodosis of conditional sentences.

The subjunctive mood, however, remained vital throughout the medieval period. The pluperfect forms of the Latin subjunctive served as a multipurpose past subjunctive for phonetic reasons. The distinctive -iss infix preserved it, whereas the imperfect and perfect forms had become indistinguishable from each other and, it might be noted, from the infinitive and from the future perfect indicative. The present subjunctive had two types of endings: -e, -es, -e(t) developed from the Latin -(j)am, -(j)as, -(j)at, while those Latin -are verbs which required no supporting e in their development showed different endings until the twelfth century, when they began to be assimilated to the others (Table 7).

A new composite perfect subjunctive, derived from the present subjunctive of habeo and a past participle, was also available and became increasingly common in later French.

The imperative mood survived, although its future forms disappeared. Thus, the singular imperative of chanter was chante (Latin: canta), and of faire was fai (Latin: fac) and, in the thirteenth century, fais. The plural forms were identical with those of the second person plural, present indicative.

The various types of the Latin infinitive did not remain equally strong in their transition to French. The -er (-are) type was the most stable, dominating all others. The -ir (-ire) type also survived and was augmented by inchoatives as well as by other acces-

sions. The other two infinitive endings of medieval French were -eir (> -oir) and -re. Since there were no clear distinctions now to separate one Latin conjugation from another, many transfers between infinitive types took place—for instance, sapĕre developed into saveir, but ridēre became rire.

The same interchange was frequent among the past participles. Apart from -atum, which was relatively unaffected by the confusion, all the types of participles were subject to some remodeling, as in quaesitum > quaesu > quis; pensum > penditu > pente; perditum > perdutu > perdu. -Etum forms were lost.

The present participle survived in the subject and object cases, which were declined like the masculine form of the adjective granz (see above under Adjectives III). The Latin gerund survived into Vulgar Latin in only one form, -ando, which because of its similarity with the endings of the present participle, merged with the latter.

VOCABULARY

Latin was not the only source of vocabulary for medieval French. Despite their cultural overthrow, the Celts, who had arrived in Gaul in successive waves between 900 and 600 B.C., provided some 200 words to Vulgar Latin. A few of these may have originated even further back, among the Ligurians and Iberians. For instance, place-names ending in suffixes derived from -acus, -asca, -ascum, -oscus, -osca, -oscum were Ligurian in origin; and the word artigue was probably Iberian. Many Celtic borrowings were topographical: borne, combe, lande, greve. Many were toponymic: Paris from the Latin name for its inhabitants the Parisii, Rheims (Remi), Amiens (Ambiani), Angers (Andecavi), Beauvais (Bellovaci), Cahors (Cadurci), Nantes (Namnetes), Poitiers (Pictavi), Soissons (Suessiones), Tours (Turnones), Trèves (Treviri), Troyes (Tricasses); the suffixes -briga, -dunum, and -durum (all meaning a fortified settlement) and -acum (the property of).

Names of domestic and rural objects reflected Celtic daily life: braie (britches), broche (spit), bresche (honeycomb), charpentier (carpenter), charrue (plow), chemise (shirt), landier (firedog), veautre (hunting dog), boisseau (bushel), tonneau (barrel), suie (soot), if (yew), bouleau (birch), chêne (oak), vassal (vassal), truand (vagrant). Very few abstract words survived: rêche (rough), bler (dappled gray), dur (thick), and the substantive brif (strength).

Another pre-Roman source of vocabulary was the Greek language. From about 600 B.C. Greek mariners had interested themselves in the southern coast of "Gaul" and, over several centuries, had founded the colony of Massalia (Marseilles), then Monaco, Nice, Antibes, Agde, and other trading ports. Many Greek words were later absorbed into Latin and, predictably, more of them survived in the dialects of the south than in the north. Some of the Greek words adapted at that period were *pierre (petra), corde (khordē),* and the dialectal *caliourno* (a mooring rope from *kalōs*) and *brountar* (thunder, from *brontaō*), and various other navigational, meteorological, architectural, and other technical terms.

The Germanic borrowings into Vulgar Latin were at first sporadic. *Framea* (spear) is found in Tacitus, and Pliny used *ganta* (wild goose) and *sapo* (soap). These were isolated loanwords from a culture that at the time seemed of negligible importance. Before the fifth century Germanic borrowings into the spoken language probably numbered no more than 100 words, many of them military: *herberge* (literally, army shelter), *marche* (frontier territory), *heaume* (helmet), *éperon* (spur), *guerre* (war), *trêve* (truce). Other miscellaneous borrowings came from the daily life of the German soldiers: *bâtir* (build), *rôtir* (roast), *soupe* (soup), *blond* (blonde), *blanc* (white).

From the fifth century on, successive tribal migrations moved through Gaul—the Vandals, Alani, and Swabians one after the other terrorized the romanized settlements of Gaul. The Visigoths, who arrived around 412, had a slight influence upon place-names because they had assumed the role of defending the Roman frontier. Their contribution is exemplified by place-names in the Pyrenees: *Adervielle, Estarvielle, Loudenvielle,* and *Loudervielle.* Their influence upon northern Gaul was minimal since that territory was occupied by the Franks (already known to Caesar and Tacitus), who had defeated the Visigoths at Vouillé in 507. Of lesser importance linguistically were the Burgundians and the Alamani. The former were soon assimilated to Roman culture, and the latter withdrew to the Alpine regions.

The Roman defeat at Soissons by the Salian Franks in 486 marked the beginning of a new direction in Gaul. Frankish settlement of this new land, which they called *Neustria,* and the successful alliance of invading Franks with Gallo-Roman inhabitants brought a wealth of new Germanic borrowings to the language. Symbolically, *Frantia* displaced *Gallia* to give, eventually, the name *France* to the region. War terminology was dominant among the

borrowings: *hanste* and *espiet* (two types of spear), *gonfanon* (battle standard), *broigne* (cuirass), *dart* (spear), *hache* (ax), and *ban* (ban or military levy). But there were also many more general terms: *franc* (free), *alleu* (property), *seneschal* (seneschal), *bru* (daughter-in-law), *haïr* (hate), *honnir* (shame), *orgueil* (pride), *bleu* (blue), *isnel* (swift), *bois* (wood), *jardin* (garden), *osier* (willow), *houx* (holly), *bacon* (bacon), *aune* (ell), *danse* (dance), *estampir* (stamp, dance). In the formation of new words the Frankish suffix *-ing* was responsible for the Old French *-enc,* as in *paisenc* (pleasant) and *Loherenc* (Lorrain); *-hart* and *-wald* supplied the frequently used *-ard* and *-aud* suffixes, as in *viellard, bastart, coart, badaud,* and *salaud.*

The Old French prefixes *for-* and *mes-* seem to have acquired their derogatory connotations from the Frankish *ver-* and *miss-,* as in the verbs *se forfaire* (to act wrongly) and *mesfaire* (to misbehave).

Frankish influence upon the language was primarily lexical, but Frankish speech habits seem to have been influential in diphthongization; the reduction, or suppression, of unstressed vowels; the reintroduction of the phoneme *h;* and the introduction of a Germanic *w* that was variously rendered according to region.

The Gallo-Roman period of the language was influenced by other varieties of Germanic borrowings. North German migration brought Norse invaders to France and, with them, place-names and nautical terms: *Le Torp (thorp =* village), *Bolbec (beck =* stream), *Yvetot (toft =* hut), *Normand, cingler, équiper, guinder, vague, crique, tillac, hune, bitte, étrave, étambot, guindas.*

Anglo-Saxon provided a few words: *bâteau* (from *bat*), *bouline, flotte, rade, varech,* and the points of the compass.

Arabic contributed scores of cultural items, many of them indirectly through the translation of Arabic works into Low Latin, or through Spanish and Italian. Alchemical terms *(alchimie, elixir),* military terms *(auferrant, genet, barbacane),* scientific terms *(zénith, nadir, nuque, algèbre),* social and administrative terms *(algalife, amirafle, amiral, annuable),* and a wide miscellany of other loanwords demonstrate the exotic and varied contribution of the Arabs to European civilization.

Borrowings from the other Romance languages into French were sparse until the later Middle Ages, with the exception of Provençal, which provided many lexical items: *aigle, aigrette, auberge, bar-*

rique, bécasse, brague, cabane, câble, cadastre, cadeau, cadet, caisse, cap, cembel, donnei, donneier, escalier, fadaise, figue, fleute, gabel, gai, garer, goujat, langouste, mistral, notuner, palefrenier, radeau, rôder, rossignol, solaz, tenzon, tocsin, tose, velos, viguier, viole.

Written Latin and, via Latin, Greek were important sources of learned words throughout the Middle Ages. The continuing influence of the church, whose clerics interpreted and translated ecclesiastical terminology for their lay congregations, brought scores of borrowings into the vernacular. Some were adopted so early that they show all the sound changes undergone by the Vulgar Latin base language—for instance, *parabolare* (preach) became *parler*. Others were borrowed later, or were so little used that they continued as "learnedisms": *angele, virgene, esperit.* One of the earliest texts, the *Eulalie,* shows a complex mixture of Latinisms (*anima, in, Christus),* learned borrowings (*empedementz, element, christiien),* and popular developments *(diaule).* Unfortunately, the scribe's latinizing orthography adds to the learned appearance of the text, and makes it difficult to distinguish among the three categories.

Translations, sermons, legal documents, lapidaries, and other learned and semilearned texts all added to the stock of late Greek and Latin borrowings, of which the following list provides a few examples: *menestier, criminel, heriter, scorpion, embolisme, allegorie, argument, disputacion, praticien, anatomie, chapitre, trinitet, stratagème, sympathie, symptôme, rhomboïde.* Frequently a Latin or Greek word was borrowed early, then reborrowed in a form that was closer to the original, thus creating doublets: *ange* and *angele, vierge* and *virgene.*

DIALECTS

It is obvious even in the first latinized texts that there was no single standardized form of the French language in the Gallo-Roman period, nor through most of the Middle Ages. An overall distinction was made, certainly, between the two "languages" of the north and south of Gaul, the *langue d'oïl* and the *langue d'oc.* The dividing line between the two ran from Bordeaux via Lussac and Montluçon to the south border of Isère. And it is now customary to categorize as "Franco-Provençal" the language of certain intermediate regions that contained features of both the *langue d'oïl* and the *langue d'oc.*

The main variants of the *langue d'oïl* were Francien (in the Île-de-France), Norman (in the northwest), Anglo-Norman (in England), Picard and Walloon (in the northeast), Lorrain and Champenois (in the east), Burgundian and Franc-Comtois (in the southeast), and Poitevin, Saintongeais, and Angevin (in the west). Of these, Picard, Norman, and Anglo-Norman provided the strongest challenge to Francien as a literary language. The ultimate triumph of the Francien dialect was, however, due to political, legal, social, and geographical advantages rather than to its early literary achievements.

THE USE OF THE FRENCH LANGUAGE

Despite the fact that Latin remained the main vehicle for learned writing and discourse in the Middle Ages, Old French was the most prestigious of the European vernaculars. Brunetto Latini chose to write his thesaurus *Li livres dou tresor* (1262–1266) in French because, he said, French was the most "delitable" (delightful) and "plus commune a toutes gens" (universal) language. Marco Polo made the same choice and dictated his travelogues in French (*ca.* 1297) for reasons of prestige and easy access. From 1066 until the fourteenth century French was the official and literary language of the English aristocracy. And within France it encroached increasingly upon the domains of Latin until, in 1539, it was officially imposed even in the law courts by the Ordinance of Villers-Cotterets. With that royal imposition of one standardized form of the language over the whole of France, the French language was recognized as an official entity.

BIBLIOGRAPHY

Édouard Bourciez, *Éléments de linguistique romane,* 4th ed. (1956); Arsène Darmesteter, *A Historical French Grammar,* Alphonse Hartog, trans. (1934); W. D. Elcock, *The Romance Languages,* rev. ed. (1975); Alfred Ewert, *The French Language* (1933); Lucien Foulet, *Petite syntaxe de l'ancien français,* 3rd ed. (1970); Robert A. Hall, Jr., *External History of the Romance Languages* (1974); Mildred K. Pope, *From Latin to Modern French,* 2nd ed. (1934, repr. 1956); Rebecca Posner, *The Romance Languages* (1966); Gerhard Rohlfs, ed., *From Vulgar Latin to Old French,* Vincent Almazan and Lillian McCarthy, trans. (1970); Walther von Wartburg, *Évolution et structure de la langue française,* 10th ed. (1971); Philippe Wolff, *Western Languages, A.D. 100–1500,* Frances Partridge, trans. (1971).

JEANETTE M. A. BEER

[See also **French Literature; Latin Language; Strasbourg Oaths; Vulgar Latin.**]

FRENCH LITERATURE. The history of French literature is covered in a series of articles, in two parts. First, there are two surveys, **French Literature: To 1200** and **French Literature: After 1200.** Second, there are shorter articles devoted to specific genres: **French Literature: Didactic; French Literature: Lyric; French Literature: Romances;** and **French Literature: Translations.**

FRENCH LITERATURE: TO 1200

THE LANGUAGE

Any attempt to define what has come to be known as Old French, the remarkably standardized and yet greatly varied literary vernacular that had established itself in what is now called northern France by the middle of the twelfth century, is fraught with problems. From one perspective there is no single language that may be tagged "Old French." There are, or were, merely a group of more or less closely related spoken Gallo-Romance dialects known collectively as manifestations of *langue d'oïl* (language of *oïl* [= *oui,* yes])—a designation found in Dante's *De vulgari eloquentia* (*ca.* 1303). These dialects (including Picard, Walloon, [Anglo-] Norman, Champenois, Lorrainese, and especially Francien, the spoken tongue of Île-de-France and Paris) must be contrasted with the non-Romance languages of bordering areas (Breton to the west in Brittany; English and surviving Celtic languages in the British Isles; Flemish to the north in what is now extreme northern France and western Belgium; various Germanic dialects to the east including areas of Lorraine and Alsace).

To the south, beyond the Loire, the *oïl* dialects give way to two other sets of Gallo-Romance dialects. The first is Franco-Provençal, a hybrid group spoken in an area virtually impossible to circumscribe precisely but, *grosso modo,* corresponding to lands east of Lyons, south of Burgundy, parts of the Dauphiné, and regions of Romance-speaking Switzerland. The second group, from which the *oïl* family must also be distinguished, is that known as Provençal or Occitan (compare Dante's *lingua oc* [*oc,* yes]), which during the Middle Ages developed a major literary tradition of its own. By the close of the twelfth century, the two genuinely important literary vernaculars on Gallo-Romance territory were *oïl,* or "French," and *oc,* the "Old Provençal" koine.

As spoken dialects, the various forms of *oïl* differed substantially among themselves. Thus, for example, before *a* the initial Latin *k-* sound underwent palatalization in Francien to *č* (Modern French *š*): *caballus > cheval.* This shift did not occur in Picard (Latin *causa >* Francien *chose,* Picard *cose*). Meanwhile the Latin *ty* (*ky*) was palatalized in Francien to *ts* and in Picard to *tš*: Latin *captĭare >* Francien *chacier* (Modern French *chasser*), Picard, *cachier.* This *oïl* doublet passed into English, giving the modern "chase" and "catch." In their purely spoken form, then, the *oïl* dialects may each be said to represent the radically transformed vulgar, or spoken, Latin utilized by the inhabitants of a given northern Gallo-Romance geographic area. If, as has been averred, *oïl* territory came to differ linguistically from the *oc* area because of heavy Germanic (mainly Frankish) influence and pressure, local conditions contributed to an even greater fragmentation of the emerging Romance vernacular(s).

Conversely, no dialect or geopolitical entity remained in complete isolation—cultural, political, or commercial—from the others. From the eighth to well into the tenth century, northern France was part of what came to be known as the Carolingian Empire; goods were exchanged, and words were borrowed and lent. Thus, although in west-central *oïl* territory the diphthongization of the stressed Latin *-ē-* to *ei > oi* was restrained by the presence of a nasal (for instance, *pœna > pēna > peine* [not *poine*]), such was not the case to the east, as in Champagne (Latin *avēna > avoine,* oats). *Avoine,* not *aveine,* prevailed in French, very possibly because oats were grown largely in the east; when they were sold in Paris, the eastern form of the word, accompanying the product, entered Francien and, eventually, French. Furthermore, the extraordinary variety in Modern English (Cockney, Dublin, Brooklyn, Alabama versions) reveals that mutual comprehensibility can occur within an extreme range of phonic divergency.

As the several Romance vernaculars diverged increasingly from one another, they became more and more distinct from the earlier spoken Latin that had been their common parent. The Latin spoken in the various lands of the Roman Empire had never been completely homogeneous, but such homogeneity as had obtained during the time of Pax Romana eventually succumbed to the creation of genuinely new vernaculars whose speakers encountered ever greater difficulty in understanding the parent tongue, which in literate form and in ecclesiastic usage remained indispensable to western European religious, legal, political, and cultural intercourse.

During the seventh and eighth centuries a very modified form of Latin came into existence as a kind of low-grade lingua franca, a heavily vernacularized "Latin" that had, to a large extent, lost its connection with the stylized, albeit Christianized, Latin of late antiquity, and that was utilized in church correspondence, notarial documents, and the like. But even this "corrupt" Latin could hardly be understood by the illiterate majority. Thus, as the standard of written Latin declined, the gap between Latin and the vernacular widened. Nowhere was this state of affairs more pronounced than in *oïl* territory, where the Romance vernaculars were farthest from their Latin ancestor.

The corruption of written Latin and the radical vernacularization of the *oïl* dialects led, during the reigns of Pepin and Charlemagne, to two extraordinarily important linguistic developments. The first of these was the purpose, and the consequence, of what has been named the Carolingian renaissance. Fostered by Charlemagne and, significantly, achieved to a very large degree by scholars of other than Romance origins (Irishmen, Englishmen, Germans), this "renaissance" brought about a major renewal of learning and the restitution in the court and monasteries of a "pure" literary Latin purged of many lexical vulgarisms and based, grammatically and syntactically, on the correct style of admired Latin authors. Thus, Einhard's *Vita Karoli* (*ca.* 830), a biography of Charlemagne, constitutes a stylistic imitation of Suetonius' *Lives of the Caesars*. Also—a fact of incalculable importance—the Carolingian scholars copied and preserved the texts of these authors.

For men whose own vernacular was, instead of Romance, Anglo-Saxon or Frankish, Latin was by definition a learned language. Thus, their teachings and their example contributed immensely to their neighboring—mainly *oïl*—Gallo-Romance contemporaries' grasping that Latin was also a learned language for them. But once the notion of a pure Latinity had been restored (ideally as well as by example), the gap between Latin and the Romance vernacular could only appear even more unbridgeable. The second of the two important linguistic developments resulted, then, from the official recognition of this de facto state.

It might be wondered why eighth- or ninth-century scholar-writers were concerned with these matters. The answer lies in the age-old preoccupation of

the Christian ministry to bring the word of God to the people. At times this preoccupation had resulted in a relaxing of previously accepted literary standards, as when Augustine proclaimed that "it is better for grammarians to chastise [us priests] than for the people not to understand us." In the early ninth century, however, it led to the official position that the vernacular henceforth ought to be utilized in the sermon or homily, so that the faithful might come to participate more intimately and meaningfully in the Holy Sacrifice. This position was promulgated at the Council of Tours (813), which stated that henceforth homilies would be said "in rusticam romanam linguam aut theotiscam" (in the folk romance, or in the Germanic, tongue). What no doubt had already been a prevailing practice in Germanic-speaking countries (and also, by this time, probably in *oï* territory) became an officially established policy in Western Christendom. Thus, by the close of Charlemagne's reign, the door was opened to the written use of the vernacular in the Romance domain, and the conditions for a revitalized, though specialized and "medieval," literary Latin were also established. Meanwhile, given the literary bent of the Carolingian renaissance (especially its concern for ancient authors and their texts), what might be described as the medieval relationship of imitation/creation with regard to classical antiquity and the new literary vernacular was instituted.

The first authentically Romance documents—at least those that have survived—were composed in *oïl*. From the ninth century two such documents—one in prose, one in verse—have been preserved. Neither is in Francien, the prototype of Old (and Modern) French.

The *Strasbourg Oaths* (*Serments de Strasbourg*) date from 842; the manuscript in which they have been preserved, a copy of Nithard's Latin chronicle, is usually dated about 1000. In this text Louis the German swears in "Old *oïl*," before the Romance-speaking soldiers of his brother Charles the Bald, that he will undertake no activity against Charles—an oath repeated in Germanic by Charles. After their respective lords speak, the two groups of soldiers swear—the first in Romance, the second in Germanic—not to aid their king should he break his vow. The heavily Latinized Romance texts cannot authoritatively be assigned to any specific dialect, though they clearly were spoken by men from *oïl* territory.

The *Séquence de Ste. Eulalie* (*ca.* 880) is the first genuinely literary work in "Old *oïl*" to have survived; it corresponds exactly to the didactic spirit of the Council of Tours in that it "translates," or adapts, a Latin poem by Prudentius (fourth century) into an assonanced twenty-nine-line song commemorating the persecution and martyrdom of an early-fourth-century Spanish girl at the hands of the "pagan king" Emperor Maximian. This work was designed to be sung during Mass on the saint's day, after the alleluia and before the Gospel. Linguistically, the text displays several Picard characteristics, probably having been composed near Valenciennes, an area not too distant from Flemish-speaking territory and close to Wallonia.

A third vernacular text, a fragment dating from the tenth century, was also composed in this border area, most likely at St. Amand-les-Eaux. A direct response to the injunctions of the Council of Tours, it is couched in a mixture of *oïl* and Latin, deals with the biblical story of Jonah, and, in the opinion of specialists, constitutes a priest's sermon notes on that subject.

Two later poems, both preserved in an eleventh-century manuscript discovered at Clermont-Ferrand and consequently known as the "Clermont poems," are usually dated at about the end of the tenth century; their titles are generally given in French: *La passion du Christ* and *La vie de saint Léger*. Both are written in stanzas containing two assonanced couplets. Based on the Gospels, the *Passion* (516 verses) recounts the story of Christ's trial, crucifixion, resurrection, and ascension; the *St. Léger* (240 verses) narrates the martyrdom of its protagonist (which took place in 679–680). Replete with Latinisms and the kind of literary learning found in much subsequent Old French hagiography and other narrative, the two poems are linguistically quite mysterious: *oïl* and *oc* forms coexist side by side. Modern scholarly opinion seems to hold that, like *Eulalie* and the Jonah fragment, they were originally composed in the Picard-Walloon region and were subsequently "Occitanized" in the surviving Clermont copy. This linguistic hybridization, occurring before the rise of Francien as the dominant *oïl* dialect, suggests the existence in the tenth and eleventh centuries of an intense monastic commerce between northern and southern Gallo-Romance territory, with the possibility of a shared desire among vernacular writers to develop a pan-Gallo-Romance literary koine or *scripta* according to the dictates of the Council of Tours.

However, such a *scripta* was fated not to be: the literary standards of *oc* and *oïl* took ever more sep-arate paths until the fourteenth century, when, largely as a result of political conditions, *oïl*, now become Old French, began its steady encroachment upon *oc* territory, eventually destroying and replacing it as the region's principal vernacular vehicle of culture.

Just as the beginnings of a vernacular Gallo-Romance literature may be dated to the Council of Tours, so the impetus for Old French can be dated as coinciding with the establishment, in 987, of the Capetian dynasty. Linguistically, *oc* differed more substantially from *oïl* than the various *oïl* dialects differed from one another, but (in my opinion) linguistically external reasons—geopolitical reasons—must be adduced in order to account for the utter failure of such linguistico-literary attempts at hybridization as the Clermont poems, and for the "creation" of Old French during the eleventh and twelfth centuries.

The accession of Hugh Capet, son of the powerful Count Hugh of Paris, to the throne of France not only consummated the ever-widening rift between an emerging "France" and the increasingly Germanic Carolingian Empire but also placed the geographic and political center of "France" squarely in Paris, at the very heart of *oïl* territory. It also defined the main lines of what would become the constant concerns of "French" policy for several centuries; to acquire and defend "French" legitimacy (in regard to the Carolingian Empire, especially); to identify that legitimacy with the claims of the house of Capet; to "recover," on behalf of the "French" crown, those areas—largely Gallo-Romance-speaking—having masters (and, at times, peoples) who showed something less than eagerness to declare fealty to the crown; and to lead in the seemingly never-ending struggles against the Normans (and later against the English). These goals required the creation of as strong and as centralized a state as possible. The Capetians hardly achieved their purposes overnight, but they sowed the seed for the eventual predominance and centrality of Paris—and of its language, Francien (French)—in Gallo-Romance life and culture. The Capetian dynasty, in effect, invented the characteristically French linking of political expansionism with cultural and linguistic expansionism, as well as the equally typical French idea that what is peculiarly French is also, almost by definition, universal (or at least should be so understood). The linguistic and literary consequences of these policies and values can hardly be overestimated.

Although its date of composition is in dispute—

held by some to be as early as about 1050, by others to be at the start of the twelfth century—the *Life of St. Alexis* is the first surviving truly Old French poem. As well as can be ascertained, it was composed in an essentially Francien dialect with admixtures of Norman—and thus is linguistically distinct from its Occitanian contemporary, *The Song of St. Fides (Ste. Foy)*. The protagonist of this work is identified both as Roman ("universal" in the Christian sense) and as one of "our ancestors" from the "good days of yore," when authentic "faith, justice, and love" reigned. This poem of 125 stanzas, each containing five assonanced decasyllabic lines, symbolizes the close connection then prevailing between the church of "France" and the fledgling monarchy, both of which were centered at the abbey of St. Denis (of which Hugh Capet had been titular abbot), near Paris.

Alexis is a monastic poem—it renders a Latin *vita* into the vernacular—that celebrates what can be described only as a form of Christian hero: the saint, whose love and miraculous behavior help bring the blessings of God upon his people. This "people," as defined by the language of the text, is the community of those who understand the French language—a community viewed both specifically in terms of language and universally (as descendants of the Romans). Moreover, this language is not monolithic. Although it fundamentally corresponds to the spoken dialect of the Île-de-France, it is not limited to that dialect; it assimilates words and (potentially, at least) structural features of related vernaculars as well as of Latin, and in turn it can allow itself to be assimilated to some degree by other dialects. The fact that the earliest surviving manuscripts of *Alexis,* having been copied in England, present numerous Anglo-Norman traits is a case in point and constitutes yet another proof of the assimilatory power of Old French.

Evidence that, by the close of the eleventh century, *oïl*-speaking clerics were conscious of the separateness of their dialect from *oc*—that, in effect, two vernacular *scripta* coexisted on Gallo-Romance territory—may be adduced from the sole surviving copy of the Old Provençal *Song of St. Fides*. This indisputably *oc* text was copied, at the abbey of Fleury (St. Benoît-sur-Loire), near Orléans (in *oïl* territory), by a scribe apparently not at home in the *oc* language. However, instead of this resulting in a hybrid text like those of the Clermont poems, a second *clerc* carefully corrected his predecessor's "mistakes," and "restored" an authentic—and pure—*oc*

linguistic character to the text, much as late-nineteenth-century philologists would do in editing the Picardized manuscripts of Chrétien de Troyes (who was from Champagne). By about 1100, then, the erstwhile pan-Gallo-Romance ideal (or possible solution) had given way to the equally flexible, but ever more distinct, French-based koine of *oïl* and its Occitan counterpart.

Thus, Old French, in evolving into a written language, developed certain characteristics—a certain dynamism—that it would retain at least until the time of Rabelais. Based on the speech of the Paris area, it would freely give to, as well as take from, those other languages with which it came into contact, one important result of this process being that Old French texts surviving in two or more manuscripts usually bear the linguistic marks of the areas in which they were copied while retaining their fundamental, and very literary, "Frenchness." Meanwhile, what was "French" would continue to enrich itself and grow. This written koine aggregates and controls the numerous Picard, Francien, and Champagne dialect traits present in codices containing works by Chrétien de Troyes, as well as in the extant manuscripts of his predecessor, the Norman Wace. "Pure" Francien, in the dialect sense, is thus much less a reality than a kind of ideal—an ideal that, when put into practice, becomes the language of France and of French culture. Just as the *dulce France* of the *Song of Roland* is simultaneously the French (Capetian) kingdom of about 1100 and the vision of a united, imperial Western Christendom, so "Old French" is the Francien of Paris and the *oïl* dialects, tempered with Latin and borrowings from elsewhere and hammered, through literary and political means, into one of the most extraordinary and influential of vernacular expressive instruments.

There is a rich legacy of medieval testimonies to the preeminence of French offered by Frenchmen and foreigners alike: the statement of a writer living in late-twelfth-century Norman England that her name is Marie and "si suis de France" (I am from [Île-de-]France); Conon de Béthune's sadness (*ca.* 1180) that his Artois accent has been mocked by the French-speaking court; Jean de Meun's proud boast (*ca.* 1275) that he will sing out the doctrines of Love at the crossroads and in the schools "selon le langage de France" (in the language of France); Brunetto Latini's choice to write his encyclopedic *Livres dou tresor* (late 1260's) in French, partly because "la parleüre [of France] est plus delitable et plus commune a toutes gens" ([its] speech is the most pleasurable and the most common to all peoples).

Before the end of the thirteenth century the use of French had, of course, expanded far beyond the borders of the French and English kingdoms; it was carried by crusaders to the Middle East and by Norman and Angevin lords to southern Italy and Sicily; it was well known in German and Scandinavian courts. Even during the fifteenth century—a period of relative retrenchment—François Villon, in his famous ballade to the ladies of Paris (*Testament* [*ca.* 1461]), felt able to assert that "il n'est bon bec que de Paris" (only Paris talk is of good quality).

The Old French example not only helped provide a standard for other emerging literary vernaculars (its influence on English can scarcely be overstated), it also provoked strong, nationalistic counterreactions. By the end of the fourteenth century French was replaced by English at Oxford and at the royal court. Dante's Illustrious Vernacular (literary Italian) was designed to do what *oïl* and *oc* had done, only better. Similar processes of imitation and resistance took place in Germany and Spain. However, it was not until the end of the Middle Ages that French and French literature became a net importer of words and forms belonging, above all, to neighboring Romance languages, especially Italian, and at least temporarily gave up their rank as the universal model for the European vernaculars and their literatures.

EARLY NARRATIVE (CA. 1050–1150)

From the time of its inception Old French literature was celebrated for its preeminence in narrative. The *St. Fides* poet (*ca.* 1030–1070) declares his intention to treat his "Spanish material" *a lei francesca* (in the French manner)—that is, according to procedures utilized by his *oïl* contemporaries, poets who sang the lives of the saints and the feats of epic heroes. Some two and a half centuries later, Dante (*De vulgari eloquentia*) would proclaim that *oc* was the language best suited for lyric song, while *oïl* held clear primacy in narrative. The earliest Old French narrative is entirely dominated by hagiography and the chanson de geste; "romance"-type storytelling would not come into its own until toward the middle of the twelfth century. (On the other hand, relatively few Old French lyrics survive from before the last third of the twelfth century, when the influence of Provençal models began to make itself strongly felt.)

The saint's life and the epic share a number of important attributes. They both purport to serve,

through poetic means, a truth that is viewed as being located outside of their textual organization. This truth is historical; in the case of the hagiographic work, it is the ideal truth of the saintly Christian who succeeds in achieving an almost perfect imitation of Christ and who, in this success, shows himself, or herself, capable of performing miracles that are of great consequence to the community. The saint's existence bears witness to the power of faith, even—perhaps especially—when the saint is faced with the certainty of suffering or of martyrdom. In his witness the saint acts as an intermediary between the faithful and God. The saint, in turn, is witnessed by the person or persons who will eventually tell his story, authentically and "truthfully." The saint's story/history constitutes, therefore, the record of those who, in different times and places (and in different languages), have nurtured the saint's cult. The saint's existence is consequently inseparable from the texts that celebrate that existence. These texts make up the sum of the saint's legend and, obviously, vary considerably over time and space in their accounts of his existence. The saint's efficacy as holy person is what matters, not the kind of "objective" anecdotal accuracy preferred by modern historians; and that efficacy can be measured only by the specific community to which the saint's story is being related and for which his pertinence is being demonstrated. A Latin saint's life, designed to be read by learned clerics, is by its very nature different from the vernacular poem-song concerning the same saintly person but destined to be addressed to a nonlearned audience—at times as different as a written scenario is from a completed motion picture. Yet, both Latin *vita* and Old French *vie* are, by definition, equally "true."

Similar historicity pervades the early chanson de geste. However, the origins of this genre are shrouded in mystery. Since many deal with events represented as having taken place in the eighth and ninth centuries—Carolingian times—and since no manuscript of any surviving chanson antedates the twelfth century, scholars have sought to account for the time differential. In the case of the *Song of Roland,* for example, Roland's death (at the hands of Basque Christians, not Muslims) occurred in 778; MS Digby 23 (Bodleian Library, Oxford), usually considered the best version of the *Roland* tradition, is most often dated in the second quarter of the twelfth century. This text, in turn, is said to reflect a version of the *Roland* story-poem that was put together during the closing decades of the eleventh century. (Matters are further complicated by the fact that *Roland* has survived in a number of rather widely differing manuscripts.)

In contrast with most Old French hagiography, there is seldom an identifiable, written (Latin) book standing as the direct source of a given chanson de geste. Whereas the vernacular *Life of St. Alexis* constitutes, in effect, a translation-adaptation of a Latin *vita* (or of several Latin antecedents)—the process of learned transmission and of vernacularization is easily documented—bookishness of this sort does not characterize the chansons de geste. Legends concerning Roland, Olivier, Ganelon, and their peers have to be pieced together from a great variety of documents and monuments spanning some three centuries. These facts have led many scholars—especially the romantics and their late-nineteenth-century successors—to posit the existence of essentially oral traditions concerning, for instance, Roland or Count Guillaume and originating in the eighth or ninth centuries. These orally transmitted traditions took the shape of songs—balladlike narratives—that told, and celebrated, the exploits of past heroes in their struggles (mainly) with pagan ("Saracen") enemies in Spain, the south of France, and elsewhere. Only much later, and over time, did these primitive epic building blocks "evolve" into the chansons de geste that were eventually copied down in twelfth-century manuscripts. According to the romantics, the Old French chanson de geste constitutes a spontaneous, collective, and "popular" recasting, into the Old French vernacular, of Germanic poetic and spiritual values.

These romantic-inspired theories came under serious attack during the opening decades of the twentieth century. For Joseph Bédier, the antitraditionalist par excellence, the chanson de geste was purely and simply the invention of the late eleventh and twelfth centuries. It was born of two closely related phenomena—a fervent crusading spirit (*gesta Dei per francos)* that caught the French imagination during the second half of the eleventh century, and a newly developing practice of mass pilgrimages to holy places (Rome, Santiago de Compostela, the Holy Land)—and was nurtured by monastic sanctuaries located along the pilgrimage routes. As previously monasteries had fostered the cults of saints associated with their establishments (St. Martin at Tours; St. James the Apostle at Santiago; Sts. Peter and Paul at Rome), so they began to exploit such legendary associations with the heroes of yore as they could more or less legitimately claim (Roland's tomb at Blaye; the tomb of Girart de Roussillon at Pothières, on the route to Vézelay). These legendary connections were developed, then, very consciously and deliberately—not "spontaneously"—by clerics desirous of responding to, and even fomenting, the religious and crusading fervor of those to whom they gave sanctuary on their journeys. Local heroic legends (more or less coherent, more or less plausible) were pressed into service, reelaborated, and made to exalt a new French (and universalist) "national" self-consciousness. The use of these new compositions was not restricted to the sanctuaries, however. They were also sung at courts, in towns and villages, in public places. It is reported that a version of the *Roland* was sung on the occasion of the Norman victory over the Saxon king Harold, at Hastings in 1066.

The Bédierist and romantic views concerning the origins of the chansons de geste would seem to be irreconcilable. Either there existed an oral tradition of Merovingian and Carolingian narrative ballads that culminated in the twelfth-century chansons de geste or there did not. If it did exist, however, Bédier and his followers are surely correct in expressing astonishment at the extraordinary paucity of documentation for its existence during the "three centuries of silence." By the same token, it is hard to believe that in all respects the creation of the Old French chanson de geste happened ex nihilo at the end of the eleventh century. It would appear, rather, that neither of the two views is absolutely—monolithically—right, that no single theory accounts in all respects for the origin of the chansons de geste.

To put the matter another way, even to inquire into—to posit—a single origin of so complex a cultural and historical phenomenon is to put the problem inadequately. It makes far better sense to understand the late-eleventh-century flowering of the chanson de geste as belonging to, and partaking of, the processes of Old French vernacular composition—processes beginning with saints' lives and originally corresponding to the policies set down at the Council of Tours—that accompanied the eleventh-century stabilization of the Francien-centered Capetian monarchy in its alliance with ecclesiastical centers such as St. Denis. The chanson de geste applies procedures already noted in hagiography to the partly popular, partly learned traditions inherited, at least to some extent, from the Carolingian era and constantly refashioned since then in order to give expression to the spiritual and military—French, Christian, and universalist—values contained in the ideology of crusades and of pilgrimages. Whereas hagiography celebrates the saint as hero, the chanson de geste, at its most perfect, celebrates the ideal feudal system in which king and knight unite in harmony to defend the faith and Christian order against attacks from both outside and within. The *dulce France* of the *Song of Roland* is simultaneously the entirety of (Carolingian) Christendom and the new, expansionist French kingdom of 1050–1100. Roland is a "French" knight in a fashion very analogous to the way Alexis, the Roman saint, incarnates "our ancestors."

Both the *Life of St. Alexis* and the *Song of Roland* formally link their eleventh- and twelfth-century public with the period of the events they recount. This is achieved both explicitly and implicitly. Thus, the *Alexis* narrator informs us, the holy protagonist of his poem lived when "faith, justice, and love" prevailed, whereas, nowadays the world has become "old and weak"; by remembering the saint and praying for his intercession, we may learn to profit from his example and prepare ourselves for salvation. Similarly, in the Oxford *Roland*, Charlemagne is described (at the start) as "king, our great emperor," who "has been seven whole years in Spain." Through plays on verb tenses (artfully "confused" presents, preterits, imperfects, and present perfects) what takes place in the past is related both as past and as present action. Historical fact merges with present-day relevance. The story of Roland's betrayal and of his victory and death is recounted as though it were a chapter in an eternal, ongoing "history of immortal Charlemagne" in which we too, like the knight Thierry (who avenges the dead Roland), are, or will be, called upon to play a role.

The *Life of St. Alexis* survives in seven twelfth-century manuscripts; scholars disagree as to the exact provenance and date of the original poem. Most specialists hold that the manuscripts are copies, and that the lost original was composed on the Continent, probably in Normandy, in the mid eleventh century, though other scholars argue a later (early twelfth century) date and an English location. The Alexis legend is composite, one branch harking back to fifth-century Syria (and redacted in Syriac), the other, now known as the Greco-Latin version, being introduced to the Latin West at Rome during the late tenth century. The Old French texts are adaptations of this (Greco-) Latin tradition.

The story (as reported in MS *L*), in brief, tells of a noble, childless couple who live in early Christian Rome and whose prayers for a child are granted by God. A son is born; he is baptized Alexis. The boy is educated and placed in the emperor's service. A marriage to a noble Roman maiden is arranged, but on their wedding night Alexis, after telling his bride of the frailty of human love, commends her to God and departs from his father's house. A ship transports him to Syria, where he commences a life of anonymous charity and poverty. Back in Rome, Alexis' father, mother, and bride lament their loss. Eventually their servants find Alexis in Edessa, but do not recognize him: he has been transformed by his ascetic life. Alexis spends seventeen years in the service of his Lord until, one day, he is miraculously identified as the "man of God." Shunning the honors that would befall him were he to remain in Syria, Alexis returns to Rome, where he begs shelter in his father's house; his family does not recognize him. He spends seventeen years under the staircase, suffering humiliation at the hands of the servants. Sensing that he is about to die, he writes down the story of his life on parchment. A voice is heard in Rome telling the citizens, including the pope and the two emperors, to seek out the "man of God." This man, of course, is Alexis, whose mortal remains are found in his father's house. Alexis' parchment, released by his dead hand to the pope, is read; everybody grieves until the pope instructs all to rejoice that a holy man has lived among them. When Alexis' father, mother, and bride eventually die, their souls join his in heaven, where their "joy is great." (This last episode is not included in MS *A;* nor does it appear in the Latin prose *Vita,* the principal source for the Old French version.)

This sober tale corresponds in all respects to what may be called the "saintly paradigm," the set of components and motifs that are found in one form or another in all hagiographic compositions and that reflect the concept of *imitatio Christi.* Thus, the saint's meaningfulness starts with his death; his life is but a foreshadowing of the power he gains upon dying. His birth is surrounded by unusual—even miraculous—circumstances. The saint's chastity on earth is counterpart to his charitable potency after death. The saint is firmly identified with a specific community of believers, here the "universal capital" of Christendom, Rome. He is not "understood" by his family, who find his devotion to God a source of cruelty to them. His story is adequately witnessed; in this case it derives from his own writing. Similarly, the Old French text, though idiosyncratic, provides an entirely coherent and recognizable version of the Alexis legend. Such departures as it effects from its Latin source(s) constitute part and parcel of a systematic transformation. The *Vita* is a text designed for learned clerics; the *Vie* is a vernacular poem. Consequently, the *Vie* depicts more explicitly the relevance of Alexis' asceticism and of his holy powers. The characters of the father, the mother, and especially the bride are carefully, even dramatically, developed. The presence and the authority of the clerkly narrator are emphasized: it is he, as continuing witness to the legend and as active participant in the telling of the story, who guarantees its truth and its meaning. He is a kind of officiant in a ritual that culminates in his calling the audience to prayer. Considerable use is made of direct speech *(oratio recta)* and even of dialogue. Certain structural parallelisms and antitheses are made to carry more weight in the *Vie* than in the *Vita*. Thus, Alexis' "joy" in heaven, in the company of his bride, resolves the matter of her (and his own) pain at having, in life, to forsake the (ephemeral) pleasure of conjugal love; this eternal joy justifies, in a concrete way, Alexis' leaving his bride earlier—an act that might be otherwise interpreted as excessively cruel or inhumane. (Later Old French and other vernacular versions of the *Life* are even more explicit in this regard.)

Many studies have documented the extraordinary level of literary training evinced by the *Alexis* poet. He was a highly educated man, fully versed in the arts of writing and possessed of a good classical background. His predilection for, and knowledge of, numerology has also been noted. From the standpoint of medieval literary history three issues bear mentioning at this juncture: (1) the composition of the *Alexis* constitutes an act at once of poetic and religious devotion (it reflects, on a superior level, the injunctions of the Council of Tours); (2) the *Alexis* testifies to the high regard in which what might be tagged "clerkly witness" was held, both as theme (Alexis was his own clerkly witness, and as such was indispensable to the process of his own story) and as activity: the clerk's duty is to do what the *Alexis* clerk-narrator did; (3) the activity of clerkly witness as evidenced in, and by, the vernacular *Alexis* is essentially creative: translation and recasting involve creativity. To these three issues may be added another, related point: the overwhelming emphasis placed by early Old French hagiography on saints who were not local, on holy men and women like Alexis, Nicholas, and Mary the Egyptian who flourished in the early days of Christianity and who have no specific connection (as did Fides with Occitania) with France. (There is, surprisingly, no twelfth-cen-

tury Life of St. Martin of Tours.) The universalism of Old French hagiography is remarkable; it is linked to the stress placed by that literature on clerkliness. The faithful are brought to venerate these ancient saints through the miracle of clerkliness—of literary art and learning—not because these saints belong naturally to the people of France. This same universalism influenced the analogously universalist "Frenchness" of a large number of chansons de geste whose protagonists, though "local," were not narrowly French.

There are twenty-five or so surviving early French hagiographic narratives. It should be noted, however, that Old French hagiography in no way represents a static genre. For the reasons just summarized it underwent all manner of adjustments and transformations, reflecting changes in literary tastes and values as well as certain devotional emphases. Thus, Wace's *Vie de St. Nicolas (ca.* 1150) utilizes forms and procedures we associated with courtly romance narrative (such as formal and personalized prologue; octosyllabic rhyming couplets; naming of a patron); this text, like most early *romans,* was clearly destined for an aristocratic (Anglo-) Norman public. The extraordinary popularity of the St. Mary the Egyptian legend (a dozen surviving Old French redactions spanning the period 1180–1260) testifies to the increasingly important Marian cult of that time. Moreover, several such texts provide interesting examples of the late-twelfth- and thirteenth-century tendency to blend narrative and lyric modes: the poet-narrator of these works derives his authority from Mary's witness, the clerk Zozimas, who knew and, in a real sense, loved her.

Equally interesting is the *Vie de saint Thomas* (1174), by Guernes de Pont-Ste.-Maxence, devoted to the recently martyred (1170) Thomas Becket. This lengthy poem—more than 6,000 lines—is, like the *Alexis,* written in five-line stanzas; however, these stanzas are rhymed and utilize the newly devised alexandrine line. Guernes consciously applies the tonality and form of vernacular hagiography to a contemporary subject; his sources were two Latin *vitae* composed by eyewitnesses to Thomas' murder as well as interviews he conducted with former associates of the archbishop. Guernes causes Thomas' life to fit within the bounds of the hagiographic paradigm as this paradigm had been used to depict the values incarnated by the ancient saints (for instance, Thomas' mother dreams of her son's future glory while he is still in her womb, a frequent hagiographic motif), thereby creating a saint by sheer poetic or literary association. Even more significant in this regard, perhaps, is Guernes's self-conscious stress of his literary craft and pure French language: "Mis langages est bons, car en France sui nex" (My language is good, for I was born in [Île-de-]France, v. 6,165). It is as though the author's diction and art justify, and impart truth to, his polemical and creative enterprise.

In each of the above cases the goals of hagiographic composition—above all the sense of historical truth this kind of writing seeks to convey—are served by transforming the modes of such composition. Old French saints' lives are necessarily protean in their formal variety. Yet, even when hagiographic requirements led on occasion to so major a transformation as the breaking up of the narrative frame (for instance, Jean Bodel's text concerning St. Nicholas [ca. 1200] is a play, not a narrative), what consistently remains central to the enterprise is the notion of authentic clerkly witness, the clerk's placing his learning and his art at the service of his, and his public's, faith. Saintly witness—the saint's imitation of Christ—is inextricably linked to clerkly witness and to the power of poetic art. Literary and artistic experimentation—a genuine, and sometimes radical, dynamism—thus goes hand in hand with the desire to preserve intact an unchanging value. It is important to remember that Old French literature started precisely on this note and that this fact is dominant throughout the first two centuries of its history.

Similar generic dynamism characterizes the ninety or so surviving chansons de geste. Composed for the most part in monorhymed, assonanced laisses of varying length, and in decasyllabic verse lines (of two hemistichs, respectively comprising a minimum of four and six syllables, the fourth being the last stressed syllable before the caesura and the last counted syllable being the sixth following the caesura), these poems usually fall into one of three major categories: the geste du roi (such as the Song of Roland), celebrating the exploits of the king-emperor and his loyal knights in their wars against the infidel; the rebellious barons: tales of noble vassals who, justly or unjustly, find themselves obliged to take up arms against the king (for instance, the octosyllabic Gormond et Isembard and Raoul de Cambrai); and the cycle of William of Orange, sometimes known as that of Garin de Monglane (William's ancestor), in which the protagonist—usually William and/or a member of his family—bears arms on behalf of a weak king, either against the Saracens or against the king's own (unworthy, traitorous) bar-

ons. A fourth group of poems, called the crusade cycle, deals not with remote Carolingian matters but with late-eleventh- and twelfth-century expeditions to the Holy Land; the Chanson d'Antioche (ca. 1140) epitomizes the genre, the popularity of which, renewed in the thirteenth century, came increasingly to be based on the figure of Godefroi de Bouillon and led to a vast fourteenth-century recasting.

The fact that these poems were sung from memory by professional entertainers (jongleurs), who accompanied themselves on a stringed instrument called a vielle before audiences of widely differing social strata and sophistication (at noble courts, public squares, crossroads, places of pilgrimage), had much to do with their particular poetic character. Textual variation in the performance was rather more the rule than the exception, with the jongleur more or less free to lengthen or to shorten the laisses, as well as to repeat them in parallel groups (laisses similaires) differing only slightly (in vocabulary, in assonance) from one another. Thus, a single event can be retold in consecutive laisses, making it seem that it "takes place" several times; or an event may be "broken into" by another event and then resumed later, creating an antilinear, almost cubistic, narrative effect. The hemistich structure of the verse line encouraged the use of stock formulas (two per line) that also permitted variation. The text of a given chanson de geste is less, then, the canonic book than a repository of poetic possibilities to be utilized by the jongleur in his performance. Consequently, as the manuscripts have come down to us, given "poems" frequently exist in multiple versions. In some cases (such as the Song of William, which survives in a single late-twelfth-century manuscript) originally "independent" poems are grafted onto one another, creating a new poem. On other occasions the popularity of a given epic figure brings about, by a sort of spin-off, poems devoted to that figure's ancestors, nephew, or successors. More or less coherent legends proliferate and cycles come into being. An interesting and illustrative case in point is William of Orange. Although originally known as William "Curvednose" (al corb nés), he eventually was identified as "Shortnose" (al cort nés); in all likelihood this development was due to the misreading of corb as cort. This misreading caused the poet of the Couronnement de Louis (ca. 1140) to include an entire episode explaining how the tip of William's nose had been sliced off. Analogously, the death at Roncevaux of Roland, Archbishop Turpin, and the peers of dulce France provokes Guiteclin, the pagan Saxon king, to wage war on the (presumably) enfeebled Charlemagne in Jean Bodel's *Song of the Saxons* (*ca.* 1198); Baudouin, another of Charlemagne's nephews, takes Roland's place and saves the day, only to die later in battle.

Given the extraordinary open-endedness of the chanson de geste form, it is hardly surprising that, as tastes and values changed over time, certain poems eventually incorporated traits and novelties not found in earlier specimens of the genre. Bodel's *Saxons* contains an important amorous subplot, linked with the well-known theme of the beautiful Saracen princess converted to Christianity (such as Bramimonde in *Roland*) who marries a Christian hero (such as *William*'s Guiborc), but is also replete with the kind of courtly gallantry found in much romance-type narrative. Consonantal rhyme is not uncommon in later chansons de geste nor is the twelve-syllable verse line (alexandrine), pioneered by the mid-twelfth-century *Roman d'Alexandre*.

This open-endedness and the generic dynamism of the chanson de geste, as well as matters pertaining to its "historicity," have caused the despair of modern scholars seeking to pinpoint dates, textual relationships, and generic characteristics in regard to the origins, specifications, and composition-diffusion of the poems. Categories like "popular," "learned," "oral," and "bookish," though indispensable, do not suffice to circumscribe the immense variety or the complex reality of the genre. No generalization quite fits all the material.

Jean Bodel's self-conscious learnedness is related to, but of a different order from, the clerkliness of the poet(s) who composed the *Roland*. The boisterousness—even the raucousness—epitomizing much of the behavior of characters in the William of Orange poems, frequently downright funny, has its counterpart in the starkly virile world of *Roland* and of *Gormond et Isembard* (indeed, scenes like that of Vivien's death in *Aliscans* are as tragically poignant as any in *Roland*), but the mixed tonality—humor and pathos—is distinct. (Thus, in response to his wife's fears that he will dally with the beautiful ladies at the royal court, William vows never to change his shirt; he will reek so that no lady will want to approach him!) Yet, perhaps paradoxically, such variety of tone strengthens the essential unity of the chanson de geste rather than detracting from it. The power and the glory of Charlemagne and his twelve peers, not to mention the esteem and affection in which they were held by the twelfth-century French public, must have been very securely estab-

lished for the anonymous author of the *Pèlerinage de Charlemagne* (*ca.* 1145) to utilize their drunken boasts in order to poke fun at the relic cults and relic commerce of his day. (Compelled to accomplish their boasts in a day, the heroes do so only with the aid of relics they have brought back from the Holy Land.)

A system of ideals and values—some already alluded to—lies at the heart of the chanson de geste, permitting—even engendering—the variety and open-endedness. Honor, prowess, service to Christendom (and to the king and/or emperor at its head), justice, reward for fidelity (and punishment for treason), holy war against the Muslim (or Norman or Saxon) infidel, extraordinary feats of strength in battle (it is not unusual for a paladin to split asunder his opponent, as well as his horse, with one mighty sword stroke!)—all these find their way into chansons de geste, the ultimate motto of which is *gesta Dei per francos* (the deeds [and will] of God accomplished by Frenchmen). When the sovereign vacillates or is weak, it is up to a noble vassal (like William) both to protect him and, frequently, to carry on the fight in his stead. Christian knights (like Roland and Olivier) choose freely to serve Charlemagne, to be the instruments of his will (and, thereby, of the will of God), whereas, as the Oxford *Roland* demonstrates, their pagan adversaries are the servants of false gods and are addicted to purely material things. A Saracen potentate offers his men "gold, land, and women" provided they fight well; when they lose, the pagans destroy the statues they have raised of their gods, "Appolin, Muhumet, and Tervagan." In contrast, Charlemagne speaks to his forces of God's love and promise of salvation.

The crusading spirit of the late eleventh and twelfth centuries pervades the chansons de geste. Their political dimension is fundamental. Thus, in the *Roland*, Capetian France is identified with the empire of Charlemagne—the entirety of Western Christendom—at the same time that the French kingdom retains its own particularity. In this sense poems like the *Roland* and *Aliscans*—even Bodel's *Saxons*—are profound works of propaganda, designed to give transcendental legitimacy and purpose to "France." The "pagans" constitute an "anti-France," a materialist, pseudo-feudal people for whom personal interest prevails over true righteousness: "The pagans are in error [*unt tort*], the Christians are righteous [*unt dreit*]." Unlike that of Charlemagne, their regime is one of abject tryanny. Yet, as individual men and women, pagans are at least potentially virtuous: witness the not unusual conversion of Saracen ladies, or the common formula applied to worthy pagan warriors: "God! what a fine baron, if only he were a Christian!"

Just as "France" and "Christendom" (or empire) are at once coterminous and distinct from one another, so the temporality of the *Roland* and many congeners fuses Carolingian times with the eleventh- and twelfth-century "present." Charlemagne is both "the king" and "our emperor." This temporal "confusion" proved to be very fertile. Epic tales purporting to relate events dating from, say, the ninth century on numerous occasions actually dealt with contemporary (twelfth-century) matters: one thinks of the implicit commentary on the relics trade offered by the *Pèlerinage de Charlemagne,* or of the *Couronnement de Louis,* which tells of the coronation of Charlemagne's son Louis, depicted as a weak monarch, but may also refer to the crowning of the eleven-year-old Louis VII at the instigation of his father in 1131.

The double-edged temporality of the chanson de geste made the genre an ideal vehicle for the expression of the dissensions, betrayals, and even civil wars that affected the real body politic (no matter how idealized) or a rapidly secularizing French monarchy. Many poems present an arbitrary, unjust, or possibly unfit king, who persecutes his feudal vassals or in other ways fails to live up to the ideal incarnated by the Charlemagne of the *Roland.* Similarly, renegades like Isembard carry on the tradition best exemplified by the traitor Ganelon, whose personal vanity and desire for revenge impel him to betray the high cause of service to king and faith, to *dulce France.* Conversely, Roland's tragic, though victorious, death in the mountain pass of Roncevaux leads not only to Charlemagne's terrible vengeance on the Moors of Spain but also to Ganelon's trial, judgment, and execution, and to the consequent emergence of Thierry. This unknown knight, described as "thin, slight, dark-haired," successfully overcomes Ganelon's puissant defender, thus enabling Charlemagne's will—Ganelon's punishment—to be achieved by Roland's "replacement," a kind of French Everyman. Charlemagne's defense of Christendom is consequently (and brilliantly) explained as an ongoing, eternal process in which all are summoned to take part. Never will Charlemagne—or anyone else—be allowed to rest until "Saracenism" in the world and in individual souls is entirely rooted out.

The chansons de geste constitute, then, a poetic exploration, both characteristically French and universalist (they were often imitated and even translated into other European vernaculars), of the heroic ideal envisaged as pertaining to an entire people's identity: the French people, all Christendom. This identity is simultaneously constant, and yet contingent upon the facts of history: the past and the here-and-now are both situated within the Christian scheme of the history of human salvation. (Indeed, Charlemagne frequently is made to resemble an Old Testament patriarch.) This historical "factuality," in all the variety of its presentation, has little to do with the "anecdotal accuracy" of modern historians. Rather, it reposes, like the "biography" of medieval hagiography, upon a mythopoetic conception. The "Saracens" of the *Song of Roland* or of *William* are no more—and no less—"real" than the Indians of Hollywood Westerns. (This irreality is not due to twelfth-century "naiveté"; the cultural relativism of modern anthropology was simply not a concern of the St. Denis-inspired clerks and poets.) The "Saracens" are merely stock literary figures or, when depicted by a poem of genius like the *Roland,* contribute to a deeper understanding of *Chrestientet.*

Binary oppositions of various sorts predominate structurally in chansons de geste: good and evil; prowess and wisdom (Roland's *prouesse,* Olivier's *sagesse*); Christian versus Saracen; king and vassal. They extend even to the poems' form: the two hemistichs of each verse line; line and laisse; laisse and poem; present and past tenses. Hyperboles abound: individual knights hold off vast enemy armies. The world of the chanson is permeated with the supernatural and the preternatural: angels appear in order to give advice and comfort; devils remove dead pagans to hell; dreams reveal things to come. Among the conventions, the uncle-nephew relationship is paramount; adversaries exchange insults before combat; pagans—even Saxons!—are at times "black as pitch"; the setting, whether Spain or Normandy, usually includes pines and olive trees, and often (another duality) steep hills and deep valleys. It has been frequently—although somewhat inexactly—stated that women play but a minor role in chansons de geste. It is true that the Old French epic ambiance is essentially masculine and that relationships of the heart do not occur with any frequency until late in the twelfth century, perhaps in response to the rise of romance-style narrative. Nevertheless, though they appear only briefly, Aude (Roland's fiancée and Olivier's sister) and Bramimonde are of considerable importance to the economy of the Oxford *Roland*; and Guiborc is absolutely essential to the William of

Orange poems. Many other texts confirm that women are by no means absent from the epic tradition.

Like hagiography and other medieval genres, the chanson de geste underwent numerous permutations over the centuries: Rabelais's *Gargantua* and *Pantagruel* are latter-day descendants of the tradition. In addition, Old French epic themes were taken up by other European vernaculars—in Italy, Spain, Germany, and Norway—that emphasized, particularly in Spain, their own developing (and at times anti-French) national values. The crusade cycle found a renewed and splendid expression during the late Renaissance in the works of Torquato Tasso, which inspired numerous admirers and imitators. Chanson de geste elements are found in many other generic contexts, such as a *roman antique* like *Thèbes* (*ca.* 1170) and Bodel's *Jeu de saint Nicolas* (*ca.* 1200). By the close of the twelfth century, with the emergence of prose and a new kind of interest in history, the old stories were retold in chronicle form—both in Latin and in the vulgar—and led to the enterprise known as the *Grandes chroniques de France*. In numerous respects Joinville's early-fourteenth-century *Life of St. Louis,* one of the authentic masterpieces of medieval literature, constitutes a recasting of the chanson de geste (as well as of the hagiographic) spirit. Villon's haunting refrain "Où est le preux Charlemagne?" (Where is our brave Charlemagne?) proves that, as late as 1460, the *matière de France* was still deemed suitable for evoking a powerful poetic nostalgia for heroic times past.

ROMANCE NARRATIVE, COURTLINESS, AND LYRIC (1150–1200)

The first surviving Old French narratives known as "romances" (from Latin *romanĭce,* in the vernacular; OF *romanz*) date from the third quarter of the twelfth century. Of these the earliest are the *romans antiques* (romances of antiquity), which consist of translations or adaptations of Latin texts. The *Roman de Thèbes* was based on Statius' *Thebaid;* the equally anonymous *Roman d'Énéas* (*ca.* 1155) is a transposition of Vergil's *Aeneid;* the *Roman de Troie* (*ca.* 1165), by Benoît de Ste. Maure, retells, in more than 30,000 lines, the story of the fall of Troy, as recounted by two "eyewitnesses," Dares and Dictys, whose versions of the tale survived in Latin. Two shorter romance texts derived directly from Ovid, *Pyramus et Tisbé* (*ca.* 1165–1170) and *Narcisus* (*ca.* 1165). All these works are poems composed in octosyllabic rhyming couplets *(rimes plates).* (One of the oldest romance cycles is that devoted to the story of Alexander the Great. Some 105 octosyllabic lines of an early-twelfth-century Franco-Provençal *Roman d'Alexandre* predate versions written in decasyllabic and, later, in twelve-syllable—"alexandrine"—lines.)

Learnedness—in Old French called *clergie* (clerkliness)—is systematically built into these romance texts. The poets were proud to show off their literary training, their command of Latin, and their ability to utilize, in the vernacular, the poetic devices employed by the great authors (*auctores,* authorities) of the past. Their self-conscious learnedness reflects, as well, the fact that they directed their efforts to an aristocratic public of presumably refined tastes. The *Thèbes* romancer specifically declares in his prologue that his audience is made up of "clerks" and "knights," that a peasant listening to his work being read would be no more appropriate than a jackass attending a harp concert. Another mid-twelfth-century romancer, the Norman Wace, bluntly states that he is "speaking to rich and powerful people, who have revenues and money, for books are made for such people" (*Roman de Rou,* Andresen ed., vv. 163ff.). These attitudes are a far cry from the socially much less distinctive chansons de geste.

Alongside learnedness, those who composed the romances of antiquity stressed the moral obligations of clerks: their light must not be hidden under a bushel. Without writing, important matters would have been forgotten; human beings would live like animals; the way names change would not be understood. Clerks must preserve these things. Statements of this sort permeate romances, especially in exordiums, where clerks explain and justify their activity. Yet, in romances, what serves to link the clerk's public and his subject matter tends to separate poet and *matière* in a fashion not found in texts like *Alexis* and *Roland.* The hagiographic and epic poet-narrators intervened between tale and public, often self-consciously, but they fully belonged to both. Such is not the case in romance. Although the romancer is indispensable to his material and to his audience, he may not be entirely identified with either. His identity resides more completely in his craft: it is he who "speaks well," and whose good speech is to be valued in and for itself. The locus of meaning, in romance, lies not quite so much in what ostensibly is being said as in how it is said and in the fact that a certain kind of saying is going on. A "history" quite different from the history found in saints' lives and in epic is at issue.

Early romance is associated with the Norman-Angevin kingdom, which, by the time of Henry II's coronation (1154) and because of his marriage to Eleanor of Aquitaine (1152), comprised not only England but also vast stretches of territory located on the Continent. This powerful empire constituted the greatest political rival of the kingdom of France. In England, of course, the governing classes spoke French; from the date of the Norman Conquest (1066) England had become an important French literary center. Men of letters and scholars, like their chivalric counterparts in the noble families, came and went freely across the Channel; Englishmen studied at the great cathedral schools on the Continent (such as Chartres), and manuscripts in French were copied, or even composed, at English places of learning (such as St. Albans and Canterbury).

A principal concern of the Norman kings and of the aristocracy that maintained Norman-Angevin power in England as well as across the Channel was the establishment and defense of their political legitimacy, both in regard to the kings of France, whose titular vassals they were, and with respect to the recently defeated Saxons. Scholars and writers were pressed into service in order to justify—even to exalt—the Conquest. The myth of the Trojan origin of Britain was born: that the Britons descended from Brutus, Aeneas' great-grandson, a hero of Trojan lineage. The line of British kings, of whom the legendary Arthur was the most splendid, was broken by Saxon usurpers who were later vanquished by the Normans. The conquest of 1066 could therefore be seen as the restoration of British legitimacy. In a very real sense Henry II could be viewed as a latter-day Arthur or as his restorer and genuine heir.

Meanwhile, narrative poems glorifying Arthur and the British "past" (the Trojans, the foundation of Rome, the early British kings) stood in opposition to the chansons de geste praising Charlemagne and the house of France: Arthur became the Norman-Angevin counterpart of Charlemagne. (Small wonder, then, that about 1198, the authentically French poet Jean Bodel protested that, in reality, it was Charlemagne who had conquered the Saxons, the *matière* of the house of France—the chansons de geste—being "noble" and "true," whereas the *matière de Bretagne*—the Arthurian material—was but "vain and pleasant.") In consolidating their power in Britain, the Normans affected to make common cause with the once-defeated Celtic populations against the hated Saxons. The earliest romances of antiquity—*Énéas, Troie, Thèbes*—thus are part and parcel of a "historical" reevaluation that interpreted, or purported to interpret, Norman-Angevin legitimacy in terms of the transfer or movement of power (*translatio*) from Troy to Rome to Britain. Analogously, the authors of these poems, the *clercs*, in translating Vergil, Dares and Dictys, and Statius participated in a process of transfer, the *translatio studii*, through which what Bodel called the "wise content" of the *matière de Rome* was vernacularized and brought up to date.

How thoroughly these learned myths were actually believed by those who professed them is a matter of considerable doubt. It is widely held today that a key Latin text like the *History of the Kings of Britain*, by Geoffrey of Monmouth (*ca.* 1140), which was "translated" in romance form by Wace (*Roman de Brut* [*ca.* 1135]), was not taken all that seriously, even in England. Once again it may be said that the main appeal of these stories lay in the art with which they were composed and in the prodigious imagination they deploy (uniting elements of classical learning, fabulous Celtic lore, and hagiographic and chansons de geste reminiscences). Romancers tended to maintain a clear distance between themselves and their subject matter. Thus when, in the *Brut*, Wace tells of Arthur's retirement to Avalon so that he might be cured of his mortal wounds, he notes that the Bretons expect him to return to them one day; but, he adds, this "doubtful" matter is not for him, *Maistre* Wace, to decide: "For all time men will wonder whether he is dead or alive" (Arnold ed., vv. 13,238ff.). By and large, then, these "historical" concerns constitute a pretext for the flowering of romance rather than a truly forceful or generative cause.

With romance there occurs a new fusion of literary learning and the courtly ethic. Romance narrative becomes an area of speculation and meditation, both on poetic technique and on arms and love—that is, on civilization as the twelfth century understood it. By recounting the horrors of the Theban wars in all their gruesome fratricidal implications, the *Roman de Thèbes* comments most pertinently on civil war, something surely not far from the realities of the third quarter of the twelfth century, and later, when Henry II and his sons quarreled among themselves.

Clergie and "knightliness" (*chevalerie*) become the two points on which the axis of romance turns: *chevalerie*—noble arms and love—provides the ostensible subject matter while *clergie*, its counterpart, works upon this material, transforming it into texts that have themselves as their center of gravity. Romance narratives offer numerous points of comparison with Gothic cathedrals: rigorously structured, they are nevertheless extraordinarily open-ended, lending themselves to recastings, to new deployments of conventions, to amplification and abbreviation. Cathedrals and romances also share an inherent nobility, though both permit the incorporation of elements (the presence of gargoyles in cathedrals; the treatment of adultery or gory battle scenes in romances). Like Gothic cathedrals, romances tend to be very complex; their basically simple design encompasses the possibility of almost inexhaustible ramifications, which are usually held together by principles of analogy (comparisons and metaphors, in the case of romance). Thus, in the *Roman d'Énéas*, the protagonist's "progression" from the tragically passionate Dido, through the defeated (and killed) *bellatrix* Camilla (a potential danger to him), to eventual love and marriage with Lavinia duplicates the paradigm of cosmic choice faced by Paris as he selected Venus (and her gift) over Juno and Minerva; at the same time, this progress undoes historically the disruptions provoked by Paris' action: Rome will come to replace Troy; order is restored through *translatio.*

It is within this framework rather than in terms of an a priori doctrine that the "courtliness" of much romance narrative must be understood. To be sure, *courtoisie* is an ideal of behavior associated with the aristocracy and it does possess many attributes of a code. (Thus, a knight who meets a lady alone in an isolated place must scrupulously respect her; however, if she is accompanied and the knight defeats her escort, he may do his will with her.) Bravery, kindness to others (especially the weak), service to lord and lady, selflessness, hatred of all evil—these are the characteristics of the good knight, who is also, of course, handsome and usually well spoken. Through his service to others and his intrepidity he merits the esteem of others and the love of his *dame.*

At his noblest and most interesting, the knight is invested with a sense of mission (for instance, Énéas' founding of a New Troy or Perceval's seeking to learn the mystery of the Grail castle and the bleeding lance). This sense of mission prompts the knight to undertake a series of adventures, or quests, during which he proves his worth and earns renown. The ideal courtly lady, always marvelously beautiful, exists primarily to be worthy of the knight's love and service—indeed, to inspire them. She may or may not be married: Chrétien's Lancelot loves, and is loved by, Guenevere, the wife of King Arthur; Énéas first loves Dido, a widow who had sworn fidelity to her deceased husband, before he falls in love with, and marries, the maid Lavinia. The ideal of courtliness is itself frequently a theme in romances; characters often comment positively or negatively on other characters' *courtoisie.* Lancelot's nobility is called into question (wrongly) after he consents to ride in an infamous cart; Lavinia's mother accuses Énéas of pederasty. At times the narrators, like that of Chrétien's *Chevalier au Lion* (*ca.* 1180), contrast the "true courtliness" of Arthurian times with the baseness of their own day.

One begins to understand, then, how the courtly ideal—the basic pattern—led, in romances, to all manner of variations. Perceval at first behaves loutishly, but he has an innate courtliness that he will develop to a state of genuine profundity. Although Lancelot is an adulterer, it is he, rather than the cuckolded Arthur (or the superficial Gauvain), who engages the reader's sympathy. Yet, by no means can it be affirmed that Chrétien de Troyes, in telling Lancelot's story, approves of, or celebrates, adultery. The romance system of patterns and variations projects, even feeds on, a many-faceted reality in which viewpoints and perspectives—the events themselves and the commentaries upon them—predominate over sheer facts and ideology. The fact that Marie de France's Guigemar loves a beautiful married woman makes him out to be a fornicator and her, an adulteress. However, that fact and its accompanying ideological judgment are essentially irrelevant; what is important is that the lady is unhappily married (a conventional *malmariée* figure of romance and courtly lyric) and therefore deserving of pity, whereas Guigemar, a handsome and brave knight, whose love was desired by many ladies and maidens (and refused by him), had been unjustly accused of homosexual tendencies. Furthermore, the lovers endure much suffering before they can finally be together. They are, so to speak, justified in Marie's charming story. Once again, this is not to say that Marie is preaching adultery and fornication. The world of books and the "real world" are not identical. In another of her short narratives (lais) she describes how the deceitful and criminal conduct of an adulterous pair leads to their horrible death.

"Courtliness" thus contributes to a romance's being a fictional speculation concerned with appearances and realities. This concern outweighs doctrine for its own sake. What was earlier referred to as the main subject matter of romance, arms and love, becomes in romance narrative something complex and conducive both to analysis and to interpretation. Romances are at once highly entertaining (at their best) and essentially intellectual—a sophisticated game, sometimes profound (as in the case of Marie de France and Chrétien de Troyes), frequently moving, and at still other times delightfully amusing. In certain instances they combine all these characteristics. Enjoyment of them depends on a willingness to accept the world of their conventions and the self-referential system of their dazzlingly varied permutation.

Next to the corpus of texts dealing with the court of King Arthur and his brilliant entourage, the most influential romance narratives of twelfth-century France tell the tragic story of Tristan and Iseut. Despite the painstaking detective work of generations of scholars, the origins of this story remain shrouded in mystery. Celtic, particularly Irish, folklore certainly constitutes an important source, but as with the Arthurian material, what the French and Anglo-Norman romancers did with their sources is of primary concern here. No set of texts more aptly illustrates the problematic nature of romance than the surviving, often fragmentary, Old French *Tristan* poems. No legend ever knew greater popularity or more varied treatment than that of Tristan and Iseut; the second half of the twelfth century, it may fairly be said, was obsessed with their story.

No "complete" Old French version of the *Tristan* has survived. Whether such a version (or its putative Celtic antecedent) ever existed is a matter of great controversy. However, there are texts, like *Chievrefeuil* (The honeysuckle), a lai by Marie de France, and the *Folies Tristan* (Tristan's madness) that are at once complete (though brief) and presume an audience familiar with a coherent *Tristan* legend. Also, at a greater remove from the *Tristan* story proper, there are romances (for instance, virtually all five extant romances of Chrétien de Troyes [*ca.* 1170–1190]) that make constant reference to *Tristan* motifs; indeed, Chrétien's *Cligès* so depends on *Tristan* that it has been described as an anti- or hyper-*Tristan*. It is assumed, consequently, that Chrétien's audience, at the court of Champagne, must have known the story well. (In the prologue to *Cligès*, Chrétien claims to have been the author of a now lost romance entitled "King Mark and the Blond Iseut.")

Such romances as those of Chrétien and many others, in addition to numerous references in lyric poems, thus constitute what may be called the de-

rived and interrelated textual corpus within which the *Tristan* legend functioned. Given the immense popularity of that legend, it is surprising that no "complete" version of it has survived. On the other hand, given the successful manner in which Chrétien's romances refer to a legendary system of the *Tristan*, utilizing it intertextually, it might be conjectured that there was perhaps no need for a "complete" version in poem form, that the reconstruction of the "entire story" by Joseph Bédier in 1902–1905 corresponds not to an actual poem but rather to a legendary construct from which surviving poems and fragments drew and to which they contributed. In its own way *Cligès* may be viewed as partaking of this construct just as authentically and thoroughly as the *Folies* and *Chievrefeuil*. Each extant *Tristan* poem exists in regard to the legendary construct—the sum total of story possibilities—as each Old French romance exists in regard to the totality of the Old French romance corpus.

Two extensive fragments of longer poems devoted explicitly to Tristan and Iseut have survived. One of these (more than 3,000 lines in various manuscripts), usually dated in the third quarter of the twelfth century, is attributable to a single author, Thomas, and provides a "courtly" version of the story. The other, of close to 4,500 lines, is ascribed to a certain Béroul, though the surviving text may well have been the work of two poets. Scholars believe this romance to have been composed, presumably on the basis of a lost "common version," in the closing decade of the century. It is said to represent an earlier, "primitive" (noncourtly) state of the tradition. (A Middle High German poem, by Eilhart von Oberg [*ca.* 1190], reflects this same tradition, whereas that of Gottfried von Strassburg [*ca.* 1210], an undisputed masterpiece, carries on the courtly manner of Thomas.) A lengthy Old French prose version of the *Tristan*, compiled between about 1220 and 1240, was the forerunner of numerous *Tristan* texts in other European vernaculars.

Reduced to its barest outlines, the (reconstructed) story of Tristan and Iseut tells of the orphaned nephew of King Mark of Cornwall who, while escorting his uncle's intended bride across the Irish Sea to her wedding, inadvertently drinks with her a love potion intended for Iseut and her future spouse. The two fall desperately in love and consummate their passion before arriving in Cornwall. Nevertheless, the marriage of Iseut and Mark takes place, with Brangein, Iseut's serving maid (who had given the potion to the lovers), assuming her mistress' place on the wedding night. The love of Tristan and Iseut continues, in stealth and deception. They are found out, however, by Mark's evil courtiers, who, jealous of Tristan's prowess and favor at court, denounce them to the king. The lovers manage temporarily to thwart the plots hatched against them, but finally they are apprehended and sentenced to death. They escape to the forest of Morrois. Iseut longs to return to the court and is eventually able to do so, but Tristan is exiled. He repairs to Brittany, where he serves the duke and, because of her name, marries the duke's daughter, Iseut of the White Hands. The marriage remains unconsummated; Tristan cannot forget his true love. He and Kaherdin, his brother-in-law, go to Cornwall, where, thanks to disguises, Tristan is reunited with Iseut. His presence is discovered, and he is forced once again to flee to Brittany. He is severely wounded in battle; only Iseut, who has done so twice before, can cure him. Tristan summons her. If she is on board, the ship will display a white sail; if she is not, a black sail. Too ill to see for himself, Tristan asks his wife to tell him the sail's color. Jealous of Iseut, she lies, informing him that it is black. Tristan dies of despair; Iseut arrives, only to expire upon her beloved's body. Mark learns the truth of the potion, and has the lovers buried side by side.

This, then, is a story of love and death, a drama of fatality; in none of the versions can Iseut's, or especially Tristan's, nobility be placed in doubt. Nor is Mark an unsympathetic figure; he desperately wants to give the lovers the benefit of the doubt, despite the charges brought against them by the jealous barons. (One of these, incidentally, in Béroul is called "Ganelon," the archetypal name of the traitor; it is he, therefore, not Tristan, who is characterized as the betrayer.) The three main characters are all, in a sense, victims of destiny. Mark cannot permit the disruption of his royal authority by allowing the lovers free rein. Iseut is incapable of renouncing her queenly status no matter how much she loves Tristan; she is content so long as she can enjoy her love—at court. Tristan is torn between his duty to King Mark and his passion for Iseut. As a result this peerless *chevalier*—this bravest of all knights, who is also a poet and a matchless singer—must resort to ruse, lawlessness, and deception at every turn. He is forced to be an outlaw. His fellow knights (and even Mark) are nevertheless depicted as much inferior to him.

The story is one of great pathos. It is also—and Chrétien de Troyes, for one, saw it this way—shock-

ing, particularly if the reader gives in to the temptation of considering it as something other than a book, a romance. For, after all, Mark's evil dwarf and the felonious barons are, "objectively" speaking, right in their denunciations of the lovers. How the story is told is, consequently, of primary importance. For the courtly Thomas the effects of the potion remain until the lovers' death. The potion, and it alone, is responsible for what happens. Purely moral questions, then, do not need to be addressed. Thomas therefore can focus not only on the facts of his narrative but also, and above all, on the utilization of these facts in order to probe into his characters' souls: their drama as they live it through to the tragic end. As artifice, the potion permits this stance. Thomas seeks to have his reader understand how his noble personages come to grips with their tragedy. He explores their nobility and such other matters as fidelity, loyalty, jealousy, and friendship (as well as their opposites)—in short, human virtues and vices. He depicts suffering with consummate skill. His narrator is omniscient, fully in control of what the text says.

Béroul's text operates quite differently. It stresses the tragedy itself, in almost supernatural terms; his characters, including the narrator, do little more than play out the roles assigned to them. This is underscored by the fact that the effects of the potion are dissipated by the time the lovers decide, with the help of the hermit Ogrin, to return to Mark's court. They choose this commendable course of action, and convince the holy hermit of the correctness of their motives. However, remaining the prisoners of their past actions (and love), they are unable (and unwilling) to forswear their passion. Ogrin (and perhaps God) is duped: the tragedy, daringly presented as a kind of negative salvation, will run its course. The lovers merely promise to do their best to behave as though they were no longer in love; naturally they do not succeed. Béroul's narrator adopts the position of an astounded and deeply moved witness to their history; his text is replete with the formulas and interjections associated with hagiographic narrative and chansons de geste. His Tristan and Iseut appear to participate in a design as cosmic as, say, that of Alexis or Roland. Ironically, then, the "romanceness" of the work resides in its being couched, unlike Thomas' poem, in explicitly nonromance terms. Its powerful poetry depends on its being formally apprehended as not self-referential, as not essentially "literary," but as "true" history—although, as Chrétien's *Cligès* reminds us, this is really the purest kind of romance. There is nothing primitive in this representation of the "common" or "primitive" version of the story of Tristan and Iseut.

Even this brief comparison of Thomas and Béroul provides an excellent example of the sophistication achieved by twelfth-century French romance narrative, as well as with a good illustration of the kinds of permutation—of formal play—that characterize both the genre and the various *matières* within it. The inventiveness displayed in the surviving texts of the *Tristan* cycle is quite extraordinary. By the start of the final quarter of the century, thanks to the romances of antiquity (as well as to Wace) and the earlier *Tristan* experiments, the Old French vernacular was in full possession of its most remarkable narrative instrument. The stage is set for Marie de France and Chrétien, and for their numerous epigones and successors.

Next to nothing is known of the biography of either Marie or Chrétien. The Marie to whom the collection of short romances called the *Lais* (ca. 1170?) is attributed may or may not be the same Marie de France mentioned in the prologue to a volume of *Fables*. She also may or may not have been the author of the *Espurgatoire saint Patrice* (early 1200's?). Scholars have long debated these matters. Here consideration will be given only to the Marie who names herself in verse 3 of *Guigemar,* the first of her twelve lais, and who, in the general prologue to that collection, dedicates her work to a "noble king," presumably Henry II of England. It is usually stated that she was born in continental France but lived in England, where she frequented the royal court, flourishing during the final third of the twelfth century.

As for Chrétien de Troyes, references to himself and to his work in the prologues and epilogues of the five romances of certain attribution indicate that he lived and wrote for at least twenty years at the court of Count Henri and Countess Marie (daughter of Eleanor of Aquitaine by her first husband, Louis VII of France), from perhaps the late 1160's to the 1180's, when he may well have entered the service of Philip of Alsace, Count of Flanders. He alludes to himself as "Crestïens de Troies," in verse 9 of his first extant romance, *Érec et Énide* (ca. 1170); elsewhere he says simply "Crestïens." The prologue to *Cligès* reveals that Chrétien, in addition to writing *Érec,* had translated Ovid (*Ars amandi,* perhaps the *Remedia amoris,* several tales from the *Metamorphoses*) and composed a *Tristan* poem; with the exception of the Ovidian *Philomela,* preserved in a late-

thirteenth-century redaction, these works have been lost. From about 1178 to 1181 Chrétien wrote his *Chevalier de la Charrette* or *Lancelot* (The knight of the cart), which he dedicated to Countess Marie, who had given him its theme. Perhaps simultaneously he composed the *Chevalier au Lion* or *Yvain* (The knight of the lion). The *Conte du Graal* or *Perceval* (The story of the Grail), which he left unfinished, was dedicated to Philip of Alsace, who died in 1191.

Both Chrétien and Marie were thoroughly familiar with the Latin *auctores* studied in the schools and with the vernacular romance tradition. They may properly be tagged "second-generation romancers." Both, moreover, exerted considerable influence on subsequent writers. In Germany, for instance, Wolfram von Eschenbach adapted Chrétien's *Graal* (referring to him as *meister Christjân von Troys*), and Hartmann von Aue "translated" both *Érec* and *Yvain.* Nine of Marie's *Lais* were rendered into Old Norse during the thirteenth century. The romances of Chrétien and the works of the *Perceval* continuators led to the monumental Vulgate *Prose Lancelot* (ca. 1220–1260).

With Marie and Chrétien *clergie* becomes more self-conscious than ever before; it also reflects, both on its own account and in regard to its audience, a new, even more refined sensibility (and irony) than one finds in earlier romance. (This refinement of sensibility is also found in the contemporary courtly lyric, which, following Occitanian models, began to flourish during the final quarter of the century in *oïl* territory.) Indeed, we "know" Marie and Chrétien far better as artists than as human beings. References to craftsmanship in their works are much more explicit and detailed than what they say of their lives. It is as though they identify themselves entirely with their craft—with, quite literally, their mastery and their specific poetic voice. Just as the courtly lover, in his lyric song, views himself exclusively in terms of his love, so Marie and Chrétien are clerkly actors, participating fully in the enterprise of *clergie.*

Chivalry, in the sense of knightliness or prowess, is not the predominant theme of Marie's *Lais;* these texts offer, rather, a set of meditations on love—that is, on the personal desires of individual knights and, especially, ladies who live, more often than not, in a society that is hostile to them. *Les deux amants* (The two lovers) tells the pathetic story of a youth and the princess he loves; their marriage is thwarted by the girl's jealous father, and the young people die. *Équitan* recounts the betrayal by his wife and by his king of a noble and loyal seneschal; their plan to murder him (in a tub of scalding water) leads to their own, thoroughly merited, demise. *Éliduc* deals with the Tristan-like dilemma of a man who forsakes his first wife (and love) in order to marry another, but with the difference that Éliduc's first wife generously gives way to the second; the husband is depicted as weak and vacillating, unlike the utterly faithful Tristan. Several of Marie's *Lais* make important use of Celtic motifs of magic and the supernatural: the wondrous boat and talking white hind of *Guigemar,* the fairy-mistress of *Lanval,* the werewolf figure in *Bisclavret* (a nobleman, who is also a werewolf, is betrayed by his wife and rendered unable, until the end of the story, to resume his human shape). Lyric imagery is often put to narrative use, as in *Laüstic* (The night-ingale), in which the beautiful songbird, killed by the lady's jealous husband, symbolizes her (unconsum-mated) love for a knight; the bird, as in much Old Provençal poetry, stands for art (or song) and love, fusing the two.

These marvelous tales, both immensely varied and very skillfully contrived, form what many scholars believe is a highly coherent, well-wrought set of texts. The general prologue outlines Marie's inten-tions and also constitutes one of the rare twelfth-century articulations of literary theory in the vernac-ular. Marie begins, in true romance fashion, with a declaration that God-given eloquence must never re-main hidden: great good can bloom only when it is heard. Verses 9–27 evoke the ancients, who, accord-ing to Priscian, intentionally wrote obscurely so that those who would come after them might "gloss," and thereby complete, the meaning of what they said ("de lur sen le surplus mettre"). In this way subtlety and sharpness of mind would be maintained, and works would continue to be produced that would protect one from vice and sorrow. Marie stresses here the great moral value of writing (and of the kind of entertainment she will exemplify in the *Lais*), focusing on literature as continuous process. Because of the example of the ancients, she states, she bethought herself of composing a "good story" *(bone estoire)* and "translating from Latin into the vernacular." However, the romancers of antiquity have already done this; she instead will put into rhymed form the (Breton) lais (narrative songs?) she has heard and, with this hard work, gain fame for herself as well as preserve the memory of the adven-tures they recount (vv. 28–42). In short, Marie will be like the ancients and will also resemble her im-mediate vernacular predecessors, but she will carve

out her own special literary—and personal—terri-tory. In so doing, she will serve the purposes, moral and other, to which "eloquence" should be put. The "adventures"—the events and experiences of olden times, the things-that-had-to-come-to-pass—will be saved from oblivion.

These declarations reflect extraordinary self-as-surance and a genuine belief in the value of the lit-erary enterprise. Marie speaks proudly on behalf of the Old French romance narrative. Anchored in the wisdom and in the practices of the ancients, her work is nevertheless resolutely "modern" and, one must conclude, in harmony with the sensibilities of the aristocratic audience she is addressing.

Similar focus on "modernity" and on the proce-dures of romance informs the work of Chrétien de Troyes. In describing the transfer of *clergie* and *chevalerie* from Greece to Rome, and then to France (*Cligès,* vv. 28–42), Chrétien notes that the heyday of Greece and Rome is over; but, he proclaims, may *clergie* never leave France! And in the prologue to *Érec et Énide,* he states that he has taken a simple (and formless) "adventure story" and "derived" *(tret)* from it a "molt bele conjointure" (a very beautiful putting-together), a unity and form that will enable his *estoire* to live in readers' memories as long as Christendom. "France," then, the erstwhile *dulce France* of Roland's prowess, is the locus of both *chevalerie* and *clergie.* However, the emphasis is placed on the latter, for in *Cligès* none of the action, which ranges virtually all over Europe, takes place in France. Yet France is the place where the ro-mance, as text, was "found" (in a library at Beauvais) and composed. France is where the *translatio studii* has come to fruition, where Chrétien exercises his artistry (the work of *bele conjointure* in his first ro-mance) in order, as he puts it in the prologue to his last poem, the *Conte du Graal,* to "rhyme the best story ever told in a royal court."

Interestingly enough, Chrétien's subject matter is scarcely French at all. Each of his romances relates to the court of King Arthur and the knights of the Round Table. A legendary "Britain" (and "Brittany") as well as, in *Cligès,* Constantinople and Germany, provides the geography of his oeuvre. The time and the place are ostensibly those of *courtoisie*—arms and love—as this courtliness, within the context of romance, had come to be associated with the marvels and the splendor of the Arthurian world. Yet, Chré-tien displays no true nostalgia for the times of Ar-thur; they constitute, for him, merely the building blocks of a characteristically and self-consciously

French fictional romance world. Indeed, Chrétien's King Arthur is frequently depicted as a fool: he is a bumbling cuckold in *Lancelot,* the ultimate cause for the (temporary) breakup of a good marriage in *Yvain,* a curiously weak and ineffectual monarch in *Perceval.* Arthur's nephew, Gauvain, whose "official" status is that of the best of all knights, plays the role of a superficial *mondain* in these three texts, and is easily surpassed, when it comes to dealing with real problems, by their protagonists. In fact, if Arthur's court is the reference point of courtly value (*chevalerie*), then, it might be concluded, Chrétien deliberately subverts such value—in favor, perhaps, of a *clergie* to which he systematically opposes *chevalerie.*

Matters, however, are not so simple. Like Marie, who utilized the "adventures" of the old Breton lais to her own purposes, Chrétien took the trappings of the Arthurian "myth" (as first vernacularized and augmented by Wace, with whose *romans* he was very familiar) as a place of invention—in medieval terms, as a point of departure for a number of elaborations (these would be called "amplifications" in medieval literary theory). Just as Wace, not the "learned source" provided him by Geoffrey of Monmouth, had been the first to mention and describe the Round Table, so Chrétien was the first to deal with the loves of Lancelot and Guenevere, or with the mysterious and "spiritual" Grail. Also, when it suits his purposes, Chrétien utilizes a full panoply of Celtic legends and folklore, such as fairies, magic balms, and supernatural fountains. (These accoutrements are by no means window dressing; they affect the tonality of the romances and often help further the plot.)

An authentic virtuoso, Chrétien also incorporates techniques, themes, and motifs borrowed, always to some precise effect, from the romancers of antiquity and from Latin poets like Vergil and Ovid. His texts are replete with examples of favorite twelfth-century poetic embellishments gleaned from antiquity and taught in the schools: literary etymologies, chiasmus, similes, and other such devices. Stories related to Arthur and his court do, then, provide Chrétien with the wherewithal to display and to celebrate his clerkly prowess. This display, however, is not entirely gratuitous, nor is the romance entertainment, for its own sake, Chrétien's sole purpose.

That Chrétien's King Arthur is often shown to be a fool does not necessarily mean that Chrétien is attempting to unmask or condemn "Arthurianism" in the way, for instance, the *Roland* rejects "Saracen-

ism." Chrétien's moral concerns are of a different order. His undermining of his *matière* and his concomitant celebration of *clergie* permit him to shift the terrain of his romances from their superficial subjects to matters of greater significance. Chrétien takes the basic romance principle of self-referentiality and variability (as exemplified by the *Énéas* "translation" or by the *Tristan* of Thomas or Béroul) to more complex levels of sophistication. If Marie de France is the perfect miniaturist, Chrétien is an architect, working on the grand scale.

More than any other romancer of his time, Chrétien operates within the framework of elaborate textual reference. For instance, for him Ovid is no mere "source"; what Chrétien "borrows" from Ovid is integrated into his own purposes, and the very fact of borrowing is designed to be meaningful. That is, everything that has to do with literary processes, as they were understood in his century, is rendered poetically significant. This is *clergie* carried to the ultimate. Arthur's foolishness, like the Celtic faerie, is a device of meaning in *Lancelot,* not a denunciation of a myth in which few people really believed. Chrétien's *clergie* institutes what might be called the "myth of poetry," according to which poetic discourse is, in and of itself, meaningful to the highest degree (more so, perhaps, than the discourse of logic, which, in Chrétien's day, already had begun to usurp the privileged position held by the liberal study of letters).

Chrétien's oeuvre operates intertextually: his poems derive from, respond to, and act with respect to other poems (or systems of text). They function, in essence, mythopoetically: as representing, even incarnating, the "myth of poetry." Following upon the learned traditions associated with such fifth-century Latin practitioners of mythopoesis as Martianus Capella and Macrobius, whose works stood at the very center of Chartrian thought and expression, Chrétien's vernacular romances brought to the French language the profound notion that the bookishness of books, when properly understood, furnishes the means to apprehend the worldliness of the world. Thus, Chrétien's texts repeatedly comment intertextually on the bookishness of the vernacular *Tristan* story. The tragic union and disunion of Tristan and Iseut constitutes, along with Martianus Capella's *De nuptiis Mercurii et Philologiae* and Wace's *Brut,* the backdrop for what will be the universally important marriage in harmony and love of *Érec et Énide.* The forest of Morrois exile will be replicated, and reversed, by Yvain's forest madness after he learns of his wife's entirely justified disgust with him. By submitting to the mythopoetic process Chrétien's readers learn more of such matters as the union of man and woman, authentic chivalric conduct, and even, as in the case of *Perceval,* of the dimensions of spiritual profundity without which their lives remain empty and barren. Except for *Perceval,* Chrétien's romances are not especially religious, yet in their emphasis upon poetic creativity, they authentically mirror the complexity and the wonder of the Creation, just as the Gothic cathedral does.

Although song as such—an indispensable ingredient of early vernacular hagiography and chanson de geste—is largely absent from Chrétien's romances, motifs of singing—of lyric form, of music, of harmony—are present everywhere. The night of love, followed by an inevitable separation, of Lancelot and Guenevere has the shape of a medieval dawn song *(alba).* Harmony—*bele conjointure*—characterizes not only the text but also the marriage of Érec and Énide. The red-and-white motif of *Perceval* reflects typical lyric imagery of the beloved's colors, as well as that of the Song of Songs and its twelfth-century manifestations. The pure courtliness of Chrétien's diction owes much, as does that of Marie, to the refined courtly lyric of the Provençal troubadours (Chrétien himself composed *oïl* lyrics in the troubadour vein). In romance, then, the song accompanying earlier Old French narrative performance becomes a poetic or literary means; it is subverted to a type of text that was destined to be read (usually aloud). It is therefore perhaps not sheer coincidence that at the same time romance narrative came into favor among the aristocracy, a new love lyric style, imitated from the Provençal and in its own way as courtly as the narratives of Chrétien and Marie, rose to the fore in Old French, merging with, and largely replacing, the indigenous lyric tradition. Begun in the final quarter of the twelfth century, this new style would undergo significant transformations, but would prove sufficiently vigorous to last until the close of the Middle Ages.

The courtly trouvère lyric was formed on Occitanian models, the importation of which was doubtless promoted by Eleanor of Aquitaine's entourage when this great lady of the Midi married, first, Louis VII of France and, subsequently, Henry II of England. Though many forms (including the crusade song, *jeu parti,* aubade, sirvente) were cultivated, the *grand chant courtois,* or courtly love song, predominated. Until well into the thirteenth century, the other genres were, at best, ancillary to it.

The courtly lyric comprises both words and music. The love poem, sung by the poet or by a performer impersonating him, tells of his love for a lady and, usually, of the difficulties he must face. It is thus ostensibly autobiographical, even confessional. The lover is noble, either by birth or by intrinsic merit (or both); the lady is the focus of all his thoughts. The song, in effect, symbolizes this love experience. The craft that has entered into its composition is emblematic of the lover's worth. The act of lyric composition is consequently—on a verbal and musical level—very much analogous to acts of chivalric service, such as Lancelot's total subjugation of himself to Guenevere's service. The structure of this kind of lyric may be likened to an equilateral triangle comprising three identifiable and, to a considerable degree, interchangeable "angles": (1) the lyric "ego" (the poet who composes and who loves); (2) the love experience itself (what the poem is "about," its subject matter); (3) the craft or art that the poem displays. The poet's self, his language and music, and his love (experience) are all coterminous.

One of the most famous late-twelfth-century courtly lyrics is "Mout me semont Amours que je m'envoise" (Love enjoins me greatly that I be gay), by the noble lord Conon de Béthune. The poem illustrates admirably what has just been explained. Conon, a Picard, whose accent has been mocked by the queen and the court (their Francien dialect, they think, is socially superior to his provincialism), feels that they have acted in an uncourtly manner; this shames him and prompts him to prefer not to sing because his language is inextricably tied to his sense of self. The court has disobeyed the rules of courtly deportment in making fun of his (presumed) infringement of the rules of good French. But, by God! he will tell his lady of his love for her (compose this lyric) anyway, because such "are the rules" *(tel cont li usage);* if he be "outrageous" in writing this poem *(trover),* his lady must not blame him, but rather Love, who causes him to speak outrageously *(qui me faite dire outrage).* His Picard accent ought not to be held against him, since he was not born in Île-de-France. Furthermore, despite his accent, his speech is quite understandable to Frenchmen.

Conon thus illustrates the "lyric triangle": self, language, and love are conjoined and identified both with one another and with the traditional obstacles (usually "others") that the poet-lover must surmount if he is to express, and perhaps obtain, his love. Moreover, his emphasis on rules *(usages)* in language as well as in behavior—his seeing courtliness as a verbal-behavior code—along with his stress of his own singularity (his Picard speech, the uniqueness of his love) can be seen as articulating the main conditions that seem, in general, to have governed the courtly lyric. For as "individualistic," or ego-centered, as this kind of poetry was, it was also, and equally, as "conventional" and as "intertextual" as courtly romance. Unlike the romantics and later poets of the nineteenth and twentieth centuries, for whom "originality" and "uniqueness" consisted in a refusal to work within defined and accepted conventions, the trouvère lyricists found genuine authenticity precisely in the conventions that regulated their art.

As in the case of the courtly romancer whose narrative text existed as part of an intertextual system, so the ego-song-love configuration in effect situates the personal identity, the craft, and the experience of the great lord like Conon or Thibaut de Champagne (or, for that matter, of men of presumably humbler origins like Chrétien and Gace Brulé) into a framework that is at once meaningful (because it is general, because each song participates in The Song) and particular: Spring is the time of renewal, of love; birdsong is naturally equivalent to the lover's *chant;* both are "sweet and heartrending" *(doux et piteux);* musical tropes play upon—reiterate or subvert—verbal tropes. Lack of space precludes listing here more of even the most common lyric conventions. It should be said, however, that the *grand chant courtois,* like its Provençal counterpart, possessed a strong stanzaic structure built on rhyme patterns. Considerable variety was possible. The above-quoted "Mout me semont Amours" comprises three stanzas of seven decasyllabic lines apiece, rhyming, respectively, *ababbba, babaaab, cdcdddc.* (The rhymes of stanzas I and II are in *-oise* and *-ois,* the Old French suffix *-ois* [from the Latin *-ēnse*] often serving, like the English *-ese,* to indicate various types of language—for instance, *françois* (French) or *gelinois* (hen talk). The rhyme words thus reinforce the theme of language.) The order of the stanzas in given poems frequently varies from manuscript to manuscript.

Thanks to the lyric, song remained an essential part of the late-twelfth-century courtly literary experience. Also, it was through the lyric that the non-scholar—the *chevalier* and not invariably the *clerc*—could participate directly and actively in the articulation of *courtoisie,* with sophistication and with feeling. It is tempting to see in the courtly lyric a certain defense against the establishment of a me-

dieval literary mandarinate. The Old Provençal lyric was of incomparably greater intrinsic importance than the collective work of the northern trouvères, but the historicocultural achievement of the latter must not be underestimated. In many instances they were, so to speak, Lancelots singing to, and of, their own Gueneveres. This represents a broadening of the possibilities open to Old French literature; its consequences for the future of that literature would be considerable.

CONCLUSION

In the preceding pages much more has necessarily been left out than included. The sheer abundance—quantity and quality—of these early centuries of Old French literature is overwhelming. I have focused on narrative, to the partial exclusion or minimizing of other genres because, even in medieval times, Old French was usually accorded preeminence in narrative. But even so, I have been unable to do more than hint at the variety and complexity of Old French storytelling. I have had to forgo even mentioning such important texts as *Floire et Blancheflor* (ca. 1170–1180) or authors such as Chrétien's rival, Gautier d'Arras, a superb romancer. Also unmentioned is the primitive tradition of didactic and scientific works in the vernacular (for instance, the *Bestiary* and the *Lapidary* of Philippe de Thaon, a mid-twelfth-century Anglo-Norman). Perhaps even more serious is the omission of a report on the indigenous lyric: the sewing songs *(chansons de toile)* and the pastourelles, or knight-and-shepherdess poems, which are of sociological, as well as of literary, interest.

Nevertheless, I hope to have conveyed at least a sense of the dignity accorded literature during the first four centuries of the establishment of the Old French language as a major cultural vehicle and, perhaps, a few keys to an understanding of its dynamics—for instance, the unbookish mythopoetic vision of the *Roland* transmogrified, by Chrétien de Troyes and his antecedents, into self-conscious and specifically bookish mythopoeses. A mere catalog of dates and titles would not have sufficed to demonstrate these things.

Literarily speaking, the single most important feature of the Old French experience is its tendency to generate new modes—even new genres—from previously extant forms, Latin and vernacular. The old is recombined into the new. Nowhere is this more apparent than in the process by which hagiography and chanson de geste—the two original, performed narrative genres—combined certain of their characteristics with aspects of church liturgy and given practices of amplifying upon the Mass (first in Latin, subsequently in the vulgar) to engender, by the end of the twelfth century, a promising Old French theater. The Anglo-Norman *Jeu d'Adam* (Play of Adam), usually dated during the final third of the century, is a case in point. It comprises three sections: the Fall, the Murder of Abel, and—here the text is truncated—prophets announcing the coming of Christ. A clerkly work (stage directions are given in Latin) and based on the Bible, it depicts, with dialogue, scenery, and costumes, the immense story of the fall from grace and the hope of salvation. The characters are carefully delineated. Satan, disguised as a serpent and seducing Eve, gains her confidence by flattering her; he then tells her of the great powers she will obtain by eating of the forbidden fruit. To which she replies, "What does it taste like?" Just as the narrative saint's life brought home to the people the marvelous truth of the saint's imitation of Christ, so this *Jeu* relates the human *geste*, human history as Christians, in a manner calling upon men to participate in the drama as spectators and actors. The theater is reborn.

Bits of prose—legal texts, fragments of biblical translation, some sermons—predate the close of the twelfth century. However, it is at that point, and at the start of the thirteenth, that prose begins to come into its own. Chronicles, recastings of works written originally in verse, apologies, and historical compositions in prose flourish. It is claimed by many of these early *prosateurs* that verse is intrinsically mendacious, that only in prose can one tell the truth, what really happened. This is criticism, in fact, like that of Jean Bodel concerning the "vain and pleasant" matter of Britain, of what has been tagged the "self-referentiality" of romance. A kind of crisis of literature occurs, then, in the years around 1200. By that date, when Old French had completed the development of strong traditions in virtually every area of literary activity—verse and prose, narrative and lyric, didactic literature and entertainment, history and theater—new defenses and illustrations of the value and power of poetry became necessary.

BIBLIOGRAPHY

Dictionaries and grammars. E. Einhorn, *Old French: A Concise Handbook* (1974); Frédéric Godefroy, *Dictionnaire de l'ancienne langue française, et de tous ses dialectes du IXe au XVe siècle*, 10 vols. (1881–1902), and *Lexique de l'ancien français* (1901, repr. 1976); E. Huguet, *Dictionnaire de la langue française du XVIe siècle* (1925–1967); Eduard Schwan and Dietrich Behrens, *Grammaire de l'ancien français*, French trans. by Oscar Bloch (1923); Adolf Tobler and Erhard Lommatzsch, *Altfranzösisches Wörterbuch* (1925–).

General anthologies (in Old French). Karl Bartsch and Leo Weise, *Chrestomathie de l'ancien français, VIIIe–XVe siècles*, 12th ed. (1968); Albert Henry, *Chrestomathie de la littérature en ancien français* (1953); Paul Studer and E. G. R. Waters, eds., *Historical French Reader, Medieval Period* (1924).

Bibliographies. Robert Bossuat, *Manuel bibliographique de la littérature française du moyen âge* (1951; 12 supplements, 1955, 1961); *Bulletin bibliographique de la Société internationale arthurienne* (published yearly); U. T. Holmes, ed., *The Middle Ages* (1947), in D. C. Cabeen, ed., *A Critical Bibliography of French Literature.*

Studies. Robert Bossuat, *Le moyen âge* (1955); William Calin, *A Muse for Heroes: Nine Centuries of the Epic in France* (1983); Roger Dragonetti, *La technique poétique des trouvères dans la chanson courtoise; contribution à l'étude de la rhétorique médiévale* (1960); Edmond Faral, *Les arts poétiques du XIIe et du XIIIe siècle: Recherches et documents sur la technique littéraire du moyen âge* (1925, repr. 1971); John Fox, *The Middle Ages* (1974), in P. Charret, ed., *A Literary History of France*; Grace Frank, *The Medieval French Drama* (1954); *Histoire littéraire de la France*, vols. 1–41 (1865–1981); K. D. Uitti, *Story, Myth and Celebration: Old French Narrative Poetry, 1050–1200* (1973); Eugène Vinaver, *The Rise of Romance* (1971); Paul Zumthor, *Langue et technique poétiques à l'époque romance (XIe–XIIIe)* (1963).

Texts and translations. Marie de France: Robert Hanning and Joan Ferrante, trans., *The Lais of Marie de France* (1978); Jean Rychner, ed., *Les Lais de Marie de France* (1981). Life of St. Alexis: Carl Odenkirchen, ed. and trans., *The Life of Saint Alexius in the Old French Version* (1978); Gaston Paris, ed., *La Vie de saint Alexis* (1872, 1967). Song of Roland: Joseph Bédier, ed. and trans., *La Chanson de Roland* (1922, 1960); Dorothy Sayers, trans., *The Song of Roland* (1957). *The William of Orange Cycle:* Joan Ferrante, ed. and trans., *Guillaume d'Orange: Four Twelfth-century Epics* (1974); Duncan McMillan, ed., *La Chanson de Guillaume*, 2 vols. (1949–1950). Tristan and Iseut: Joseph Bédier, *Le Roman de Tristan et Iseut* (1900, repr. 1946), a modern French reconstruction; Hilaire Belloc, trans. of Bédier, *The Romance of Tristan and Iseut* (1946); Béroul, *Le Roman de Tristan*, Ernest Muret, ed., revised by L.-M. Defourques (1947); Janet Caulkins and Guy Mermier, trans. of Béroul, *Tristan and Iseult* (1967); Ernest Hoepffner, ed., *La Folie Tristan de Berne* (1934), and *La Folie Tristan d'Oxford* (1943); Bartina Wind, ed., *Les fragments du roman de Tristan* (Thomas) (1960). Chrétien de Troyes: Wendelin Foerster's earlier editions of Chrétien's romances (as well as Alfons Hilka's edition of the *Graal*) have not been superseded by the editions listed below; however, these are more readily accessible at present. *Les Romans de Chrétien de Troyes édités d'après la copie de Guiot*, in Classiques Français du Moyen Âge: LXXX, Mario Roques, ed., *Érec et Énide*; LXXXIV, Alexandre Micha, ed., *Cligès*; LXXXVI, Mario Roques, ed., *Le Chevalier de la Charrette (Lancelot)*; LXXXIX, Mario Roques, ed., *Le Chevalier au Lion (Yvain)*; C and CIII, Felix Lecoy, ed., *Le Conte du Graal (Perceval)*, 2 vols.; William Roach, ed., *Le Roman de Perceval; ou Le Conte du Graal* (1956).

Also in English are Richard Axton and John Stevens, trans., *Medieval French Plays (Le jeu d'Adam, La seinte resureccion, Le jeu de Saint Nicholas, Courtois d'Arras, Le miracle de Théophile, Le garçon et l'aveugle, Le jeu de la feuillée, Le jeu de Robin et de Marion)* (1971); W. W. Comfort, trans., *Arthurian Romances: Chrétien de Troyes* (1931), all the romances except the *Graal*; Frederick Golden, trans., *Lyrics of the Troubadours and Trouvères, an Anthology and a History* (1973), original language and English versions; Robert Linker, *The Story of the Grail (Perceval)* (1952); Albert Pauphilet, ed., *Jeux et sapience du moyen âge (Le jeu d'Adam, le jeu de Saint Nicolas, Courtois d'Arras, Le miracle de Théophile, Le jeu de Robin et Marion, Le dit de l'herberie, La passion du Palatinus, Maistre Pierre Pathelin, La farce du povre Jouhan)* (1951).

KARL D. UITTI

[See also **Anglo-Norman Literature; Arthurian Literature; Assonance; Aubade; Benoît de Sainte-Maure; Béroul; Bodel, Jean; Chanson d'Antioche; Chansons de Geste; Chansons de Malmariée; Chansons de Toile; Chrétien de Troyes; Conon de Béthune; Courtly Love; Espurgatoire St. Patrice; Eulalie, La Séquence de Ste.; Floris; Folies Tristan; Hagiography; Lai, Lay; Laisse; Latini, Brunetto; Marie de France; Matter of Britain, Matter of France, Matter of Rome; Provençal Language; Roland, Song of; Strasbourg Oaths; Thibaut de Champagne; Tristan; Troubadour, Trouvère, Trovadores.**]

FRENCH LITERATURE: AFTER 1200. During the early thirteenth century, the French kingdom had attained political and cultural preeminence in west European Christendom. In 1214 King Philip II Augustus defeated the imperial forces of Otto IV at Bouvines; a year earlier, at Muret, Simon de Montfort had routed the armies of the count of Toulouse and King Peter II of Aragon in a contest that initiated the inexorable incorporation of the Midi into the territories effectively controlled by the French crown. French—and Capetian—supremacy seemed assured; and French monarchs were among the leaders of the international crusading movement.

During the same period Paris became the undisputed intellectual center of Western Christendom,

with the founding there, about 1208, of the university whose greatness and authority, especially in the fields of logic and theology, would be universally recognized during the reign of Louis IX (1226–1270). Masters and students flocked to Paris from all over Europe.

By the close of the thirteenth century, when it was becoming increasingly clear that the accomplishments of Philip Augustus and his immediate successors were in danger of being undone, astute observers looked back on the time of St. Louis with nostalgia. For them the period seemed a golden age. Consequently, it makes sense to devote the first, and lengthiest, section of the present essay to the thirteenth century, the *grand siècle* of the French Middle Ages, in literature as in other fields.

With the extinction of the direct Capetian line in 1328 and the accession of Philip VI of Valois, a new and largely disastrous period of French history began: the Hundred Years War (1337–1453), with its weakening of the monarchy and other established institutions, frequent economic devastation, the Black Death, and repeated military defeat. Also, intellectual primacy and vigor passed, during this time, from France to the prosperous and more "modern" city-states of "renascent" Italy.

Many influential historians—scholars mainly concerned with defining the "Renaissance"—have viewed the fourteenth and fifteenth centuries in France as a time of virtually unmitigated decay, the "waning" of the Middle Ages. This judgment, based on outmoded metaphors of "decadence," is far too one-sided to be of undisputed value. It is better to study these centuries on their own terms in order to understand the vital continuities between the *grand siècle* and what followed; the extraordinarily high level of intellectual speculation and poetic experimentation that took place during these difficult times; and the degree to which the fourteenth and fifteenth centuries helped shape the character of the French (and north European) revival of letters and learning after 1500. We now realize that poets like Machaut (also the greatest musician of his time), Froissart, Christine de Pizan, and Villon are by no means to be dismissed lightly as mere epigones; nor can such prose masters as Froissart, Antoine de la Sale, and Comines be ignored. Finally, it should not be forgotten that after the defeat at Agincourt (1415) France experienced a period of remarkable national resurgence, symbolized in the person of Joan of Arc.

The 1420's and 1430's witnessed the emergence in France of a new kind of nationalist spirit that eventually set the stage not only for the expulsion of the English but also for the centralized, self-confident, and expansionist state that Louis XI (1461–1483) bequeathed to his successors, most notably Francis I (1515–1547). The "Renaissance" in France owes a great debt to the "waning Middle Ages"—a debt at least as considerable as that contracted with the importation of new values from abroad. Although Rabelais (ca. 1494–1553) was strongly influenced by Italian humanism, he both belongs to and derives from the later medieval traditions of his native France. In consequence, the second and third sections of the present article will focus upon, respectively, (1) the "conservative transformations" characterizing French literary activity from about 1315 to 1420, and (2) the vigorous renewal and innovation that epitomize that activity during the ensuing century.

THE GRAND SIÈCLE

Literary production in France at the close of the twelfth century and during the first decades of the thirteenth differs not so much in kind from what preceded it as in intensity, in scope, and in what I shall call its "immediacy." The genres developed in the vernacular during the eleventh and twelfth centuries—saints' lives, chansons de geste, rhymed chronicles, courtly romance and love lyric, theater—continued to flourish and expand in the period 1190–1220. However, by this time literature in French had gone far toward developing a highly sophisticated self-consciousness of its own. It was one thing to compose courtly romances before Chrétien de Troyes, quite another to do so after him. The opening years of the thirteenth century were a time of poetic questing.

Not only did such texts as Jean Bodel's *Chanson des Saisnes* (or *Chanson des Saxons,* ca. 1198) and *Jeu de saint Nicolas* (ca. 1200), *Aucassin et Nicolette* (ca. 1210–1220), and the Grail continuations (ca. 1190–1215) "grow out" of works preceding them, they also existed coterminously with their models. That is, key texts of the twelfth century survive for the most part in manuscripts or codices copied and assembled during the thirteenth. No manuscript of Chrétien de Troyes or of Marie de France antedates 1200. Nor were twelfth-century texts invariably transmitted in their pure state; scribes usually doctored the works they copied. Textual rearrangement, shortening, lengthening, and recasting are frequent.

Thus, a magnificent Picard codex (Paris, Bibliothèque Nationale, f. fr. 1450), dated from the first half of the thirteenth century, contains, along with the five known romances of Chrétien de Troyes, the texts of Wace's *Brut,* Benoît de Sainte-Maure's *Troie,* and the Seven Sages story *(Dolopathos).* The manuscript opens with *Brut* and continues to the point at which Wace's narrator, commenting on all the tales reported about King Arthur, declares that storytellers have turned truth into fables; at that juncture the scribe transforms himself into the narrator: "You will now, without delay, be able to listen to what Chrétien has to say about Arthur." He thereupon proceeds to transcribe the romances of Chrétien, after which he returns to complete *Brut.* Chrétien's work is thus inserted into that of Wace, whose poem is followed by that of his contemporary (and rival), Benoît. In a sense the thirteenth-century scribe has put together a new and vast poem dealing with the supposed Trojan origins of Britain (as well as Arthur's special place in British "history"), and he has done so by reorganizing the extant twelfth-century texts. Historical material and "truth" become here largely a matter of textual, even codicological, recasting.

Literature, both vernacular and Latin, experienced a set of crises during the period 1190–1220. It might even be said that at that time all forms of discourse were subjected to severe criticism. Whereas, despite struggle and debate, the twelfth century had managed to maintain a spirit of considerable tolerance between the languages of poetry and those of pure thought—the spirit of the Chartrian school and its immediate successors—the later discovery of the "authentic" Aristotle tended to foment a split between those poetic modes of discourse and the mode of the new logicians who increasingly came to occupy important positions at the University of Paris. Little by little the preeminent study of the ancient *auctores* was displaced by that of dialectic. Thus, in a vernacular poem entitled *The Battle of the Seven Arts* (ca. 1230), Henri d'Andeli both amusingly and sadly describes the rout of Grammar's army (poetry and the *auctores,* headquartered at Orléans) by forces led by Dialectic, whose stronghold is Paris—a very early representative of the Battle of the Books genre. Only a rigorously redefined and highly technical language—what would become Scholastic logic, in Latin—could possibly be relied upon to generate true statements; poetry is but ambiguous fable. Analogously, romance tales and courtly songs of love and arms were increasingly subjected to double-pronged attacks, by moralists and churchmen as well as by critics who considered these stories to be historically false. "The matter of Britain," proclaimed Jean Bodel in the forematter to *Saisnes,* "is vain and pleasant," whereas that of the crown of France—stories of Charlemagne and Roland—is "true and noble." The superbly witty *chantefable* called *Aucassin et Nicolette* goes so far as to derive its entire meaning from its systematic overturning of the gamut of earlier narrative, lyric, and dramatic genres; it turns all literature upside down.

Although remaining a primary vehicle for historiography—the "language of record"—and for ecclesiastical communication, Latin became more and more identified with philosophical and theological speculation. Indeed, by the start of the fourteenth century, Dante, in *De vulgari eloquentia* (*ca.* 1303), would consider Latin (*gramatica*) to be the (artificial) language of Scholastic thought. He saw the vernacular as inherently possessing its own "truth," a truth of a more human or naturally immediate sort: it is the speech imbibed with our nurse's milk. Something of Dante's judgment (as well as of his concern for the need to polish rough vernacular speech in order to render it suitable for poetry) pervaded the early thirteenth century in France. By that time vernacular literature had begun to expand greatly, both in scope and in quantity. It was almost as though writers sensed that from then on the vernacular must become the principal repository for the expression of concrete human experience; that, though different from Scholastic Latin and its chancery counterparts, the vernacular was no less authentic or valid. A Latin book might continue to be viewed as the guarantor of its vernacular derivative, but the latter came increasingly to exist on its own terms.

Nevertheless, the vernacular did not escape the crises of the time. Much vernacular literature, especially verse narratives, was perceived as sheer frivolity. Many critics of such verse went a good deal further than Jean Bodel; for some, all verse, not only the matter of Britain, was by definition mendacious. On the one hand, then, verse narrative was linked to fablelike materials, a connection that rendered all such narrative potentially suspect; on the other hand, the constraints of verse—such as rhyme and meter—caused such discourse to be more artificial, less immediately related to the substance of what is being recounted, than prose. The rise of prose narrative (and of certain other genres, such as theater) accompanied, therefore, a feeling of distrust in regard to the principle of mythopoetic construction prevalent during the twelfth century. Proponents of verse were

consequently obliged to rethink their justifications and practices.

Jean Bodel's restating of the popular St. Nicholas legend in dramatic form partakes, then, of the same spirit as that animating the late-twelfth- and early-thirteenth-century recasting into prose of epic legends such as the *Pseudo-Turpin* (*ca.* 1200), translated from a Latin chronicle by Nicolas of Senlis, and of the *roman antique* materials incorporated into the *Histoire ancienne jusqu'à César* and the *Faits des Romains* (*ca.* 1215). For Jean Bodel the immediacy of hagiological truth—its direct impact upon a believing and participating local audience—could best be served by a theatrical presentation involving real-life actors and individualized stock characters, and by eliminating the mediating narrator. The formal transformation thus preserved the essential saintly message; concomitantly it expanded the scope of literary expression by newly defining the possibilities of theater.

Meanwhile, the compilers of the *Histoire ancienne* and the *Faits,* working in prose, sought to preserve what Bodel refered to as the "clerkly wisdom" of the matter of Rome—one medieval version of what today would be tagged "historical truth." Their recastings were designed to encompass the whole of history as well as to explain moralistically the meaning of that history to their noble patrons. The translators claim—in excursuses frequently couched in verse—that their work is absolutely faithful to their Latin sources. Although these claims do not invariably reflect the accurate state of affairs (vernacular sources are also important), they nonetheless place the emphasis squarely on accuracy and truth. This is significant on at least two counts: (1) the translators' emphasis on their fidelity to a book—their French book embodies, quite literally, a Latin book—implies a possible similar assertion of fidelity to events; and (2) their use of prose opens up analogous usages by nonclerks desirous of recording the events they have witnessed or in which they participated.

It is consequently not surprising that the first decades of the thirteenth century saw the completion of accounts of the events of the Fourth Crusade, reported in French prose by the great lord Geoffroi de Villehardouin and his humbler contemporary Robert de Clari. Freed from the constraints of bookish verse, *grand seigneur* and *petit chevalier* alike were able, presumably through dictation, to recount their own experiences; to provide interpretative contexts for their "history" (especially Villehardouin); and to offer these accounts and interpretations as both true and of intrinsic value. Just as lyric song had furnished nonclerks with the possibility of "expressing themselves" in courtly fashion, so prose history, initially of a clerkly type, offered them the opportunity to report their experiences and witness, with a previously impossible immediacy and sense of veracity.

An analogous spirit of "immediacy" pervades other thirteenth-century literary genres. There was a revival of interest in the here-and-now, in observable personal and social experience, as well as in depicting or recording such experience. Thus, whereas the earliest vernacular saints' lives had been devoted to personages remote in time and place (such as Eulalia, Alexis, Nicholas, Mary of Egypt), by the late twelfth century attention increasingly shifted to contemporary holy men or women (such as Thomas Becket) or, of equal importance, to the effect such venerated figures as the Virgin had on the lives of contemporaries. The example of St. Francis of Assisi comes to mind: he was the frequent subject of biographies and paintings from shortly after his death in 1226, and certain long-established genres—such as the troubadour canso during and after the Albigensian Crusade—became imbued with, and were to a considerable degree renewed by, Franciscan spiritual values.

Modern scholars have frequently written of "realistic" trends in thirteenth-century literature—trends they have often linked with the "rise of the bourgeoisie" and with the new importance achieved by urban trading communities. This is an oversimplification, but not entirely inaccurate. Interest in the here-and-now entails paying heed to concrete detail and plausible human behavior. But "realism" is a term at once too vague and too delimited adequately to englobe phenomena as seemingly disparate as, say, the commonly obscene and resolutely anticourtly fabliaux and the tender, devotional poems recounting miracles performed by the Virgin on behalf of repentant sinners. Fabliaux and miracles came into their own in the thirteenth century, and both present a wide range of social and personal types. Both share a propensity for crossing boundaries of social class and for providing examples of recognizable experience—the foibles, the sins, the tears, and the joys of people resembling oneself and one's neighbors. Joseph Bédier referred to the fabliaux as contes à rire, but the laughter is that of recognition. Analogously, stories of the intercession of the Virgin in the lives of many familiar, recognizable types of human beings were surely designed to confirm in their listeners the sense of the immediacy of God's love for his people as well as the understanding of what properly constitutes our service in matters of faith and works.

Neither the fabliaux nor the miracles are abstract, despite the extreme conventionality that characterizes them. Even such "principles" as the "wickedness of women" that is found in many fabliaux, or the "perfidy of the Jews" (a theme developed by Gautier de Coinci [ca. 1177–1236] in his Miracles de la sainte Vierge [ca. 1220]) are either literarily or ideologically immediate—recognizable and present—in the mores of the time. The two genres also illustrate the thirteenth-century penchant for analysis: things and words are not always what they seem. The Virgin redresses many an injustice committed in the name of justice; the juggler's humble gift is more valuable than far costlier presents. Virtuous modesty can be—and often is—carried to ridiculous lengths, as in the case of the hypocritically bashful maid who, in several fabliaux devoted to this theme, cannot bear to hear off-color language but participates lustily in the activities to which that language refers. A kind of philosophic nominalism appears to be at issue here: signs are meaningful only to the degree that we assign meaning to them.

There is something specifically ritualistic about the miracles (one of the reasons they later lent themselves so well to dramatic adaptation), just as the fabliaux are quintessentially entertaining; that is perhaps why both are composed in verse, even though a certain moralizing is detectable in each genre. Neither is solemn, yet in its own fashion each is clerkly—the one, religious; the other, secular—with, however, a shared humanity and distaste for the arbitrary.

Attention to "realistic" detail, comedy, satire, and a certain sardonic playfulness also characterize the poems that grew up during the final quarter of the twelfth century and were continued by numerous contributors until well into the fourteenth. These are the stories of Renard the Fox and his anthropomorphized animal friends, based, like the miracles, on earlier Latin texts (and related to the Aesopic tradition), but which, again like the miracles, rapidly developed a vernacular life of their own. Tibert the Cat, Chanticleer the Cock, Noble the Lion, Isengrin the Wolf, and others are the creatures whom the ever-famished Renard must cajole or dupe in order to make his way in the world and provide for his family. Immensely popular, these figures are found sculpted in stone in churches and cathedrals as well as painted in countless manuscripts.

The world of Renard is junglelike, possessing only the semblance of a society founded on law. Nothing in this world is sacred (a principle that allows several of the poets to make fun of certain cherished mythopoetic constructs, such as Renard's marvelous birth, as recounted in *branche* III).

Quick to take advantage of the plight of those weaker than himself, equally ready to show subservience to the strong, always prepared to trick his adversaries (and occasionally tricked by others), Renard, though not uncourageous, is the perfect antihero, at times odious, at other times amusing and even lovable. His wily character and his compulsions (usually involving immediate material gain, food, power, or sensual gratification) constitute the unifying theme of this vast and disparate textual corpus. Also, like *Aucassin et Nicolette*, the *Renard* poems systematically exploit literary parody and reversal: mock-epic, mock-hagiographic, and mock-courtly dictions pervade the collection and give it a certain unity of tone and of expectation.

Not surprisingly, then, the *Renard* corpus fast assumed an independent existence; at a very early date (by 1190 at the latest) individual stories were seen as belonging to "branches" of a supposedly organic whole. Thus, at the start of *branche* X (ca. 1200) we read: "A priest from La Croix-en-Brie / . . . has applied his energy and understanding / in order to compose [*fere*] a new *branche* / concerning Renard." More than two dozen "branches" (more than 25,000 octosyllabic verses) have survived, either completely or fragmentarily. Many of the authors are anonymous, others are known by name only, and a few (such as Rutebeuf) can be linked to other works. *Renard* consequently straddles the boundary between "poem(s)" and "(sub-)genre." It is a dazzlingly varied, multifaceted, and collective oeuvre, the entirety of which is greater than the sum of its collected parts. Here, then, the idea of wholeness is poetically relevant to what in fact was a piecemeal composition-compilation; *Renard* is an authentic poetic summa.

Along with the spirit of "immediacy," the notion of summa predominates in the most typical, and greatest, literary artifacts of the medieval *grand siècle*: the *Romance of the Rose*, the prose *Lancelot*, the *Grandes chroniques de France,* or the *oeuvre* of Rutebeuf. Also, all these works defend the integrity and value of vernacular literary composition, explicitly or implicitly. Moreover, each constitutes, in idiosyncratic fashion, the recasting or transformation of previous texts.

Despite the accusations of frivolity and mendacity, the production of courtly romances continued unabated during the first half of the thirteenth century and even beyond, though on a reduced scale. Similarly, although much adapted to changed literary tastes, chansons de geste also were composed at this time; romance modes of fantasy, amorous intrigue, and magic were blended into the legendary Carolingian and related epic matter. Jean Bodel's *Saisnes, Huon de Bordeaux* (1216–1229), and the works of Adenet le Roi (*ca.* 1240–after 1297) illustrate these trends.

Of the non-Arthurian romancers Jean Renart (*ca.* 1180–ca. 1250), author of *L'escoufle* (The kite, comprising some 9,100 octosyllabic lines), of *Le roman de la Rose, ou de Guillaume de Dôle* (5,655 octosyllables), in which diverse lyric songs are interpolated into the narrative, and of the beautiful *Lai de l'ombre* (962 octosyllables), is perhaps the most interesting and innovative. The anonymous *Châtelaine de Vergi* (after 1250?), an undisputed masterpiece of 958 lines, narrates the tragedy of a knight and his lady. The knight is forced to reveal a love he had sworn to keep secret; he does this in order to save himself from the consequences of the false accusations brought against him by his duke's wife—a retelling of the biblical story of Joseph and Potiphar's wife. His beloved chatelaine dies of chagrin, he commits suicide (a rare phenomenon in medieval literature), and the wicked duchess is killed by her husband. In reality this text, in typical thirteenth-century fashion, transposes into a narrative mode the dilemmas, or debates, found in the lyric tradition (*jeu parti*). All these non-Arthurian romances take place in a recognizably thirteenth-century setting.

Three very lengthy verse compositions (and an interpolation of some 17,000 verses) "continued" the unfinished *Conte du Graal* of Chrétien de Troyes during the closing years of the twelfth century and on into the thirteenth. In these works adventure is piled on adventure as Gauvain and Perceval pursue their respective quests for the Bleeding Lance and the Grail. The material was Christianized by Robert de Boron (1190's), who sought to impart a thoroughgoing religious and historical significance to the Grail story; he identifies this vessel (which in Chrétien had the shape of a flat soup dish) as having contained the blood of Christ (and therefore as assuming the form of a chalice), and as having passed into the possession of Joseph of Arimathea, who, after being freed from prison by Vespasian, went to Britain, where at Glastonbury he built the first church.

Scholars have found it well-nigh impossible to sort out the ramifications, sources, and interrelations embodied in these various continuations and re-workings. Legends, inconsistencies, and gratuitous invention abound. Yet, these works—and others—led to the immense prose composition (*ca.* 1215–1230), now known as the Vulgate cycle, which re-vitalized the entire matter of Britain and, summalike, countered contemporary attacks on the legitimacy of romance-type narrative.

The Vulgate cycle breaks down into five main sections: the first two—the *Estoire del saint Graal* and the *Estoire de Merlin*—recast and amplify Rob-ert de Boron's *Joseph d'Arimathie* and *Merlin;* the third section, *Lancelot del lac,* treats of that knight's love for Queen Guenevere (reworking Chrétien's *Chevalier de la Charrette*); the fourth section, enti-tled *Queste del saint Graal,* describes how Galaad (Lancelot's bastard son, the perfectly chaste and pure knight), accompanied by Bohort and Perceval, solved the holy mystery of the Grail; finally *Mort Artu* de-picts the destruction of the world of the Round Table and the end of Arthur's kingdom.

These five works differ greatly in tone and pur-port, yet each constitutes a meditation on the totality of Arthurian "romanceness." The *Mort* explores, in essentially secular terms, the tragic consequences of adulterous love and treason (the relationship be-tween Arthur and Lancelot is particularly complex), while the *Queste* provides a spiritual setting of cosmic dimensions for the actions of the Round Table chivalry. What the knights do and how they fare are relentlessly explained by the text (often by knowledgeable hermits) in exegeses that relate be-havior and destiny to matters of Christian judgment and redemption.

Much scholarship has focused on the ideological content of the Vulgate cycle; the *Queste,* for in-stance, has been interpreted as a statement of Cister-cian spirituality—that is, as a condemnation of such secular chivalric values as may be identified with the Arthurian court and the romance tradition. Never-theless, it is not a one-dimensional religious tract. Typical romance-type ambiguities permeate and en-rich the *Queste.* Although the adulterous Lancelot is made to recognize and suffer for his sins, he remains Galaad's father (that is, part of the means through which the mystery will be understood). And Galaad's

last words, immediately preceding his epiphany, are addressed to Bohort (the chief witness of the quest), beseeching him "to greet my lord Lancelot, my fa-ther." In a certain sense Lancelot, the Arthurian world, and perhaps romance narrative itself find jus-tification in the purity and perfection of Lancelot's illegitimate son.

The *Queste* and its congeners constitute, then, a renewal and a profound transformation of Arthurian romance. Couched in prose, the discourse of truth and history, these texts resituate the "vain and pleas-ant" matter of Britain within the meaningful and or-ganic context of a Christianized poetic history; and in so doing, this summa extends the power of ro-mance as genre to the ultimate degree. As adapters of this material (such as Thomas Malory) and the large number of surviving manuscripts testify, the achievements of the Vulgate cycle authors were rec-ognized as extraordinary by many succeeding gen-erations on the Continent and in England. It was es-sentially on the basis of these texts that Dante accorded primacy in narrative to the language of *oïl.*

In several important respects the vernacular *Grandes chroniques de France*—an enterprise begun about 1270 by clerks associated with St. Denis, per-haps at the instigation of Louis IX, and continued until after 1350 by various secular scholars—consti-tutes, along with such antecedents as the *Pseudo-Turpin,* a French response to the Britain-centered Vulgate cycle. Another great prose summa, the *Grandes chroniques,* declares, following Vincent of Beauvais, that the *geste des rois* of France merits being well known because "ceste estoire est mireors de vie" (this [hi]story is the mirror [*speculum,* encyclopedia] of life); it teaches kings and princes to "profit in all things by the examples" of "good and bad, of the beautiful and the ugly, of sense and folly" that it contains. The truth of this narrative is, more-over, guaranteed, inasmuch as it scrupulously fol-lows the "letter and the order [*ordenance*] of the [Latin] chronicles of the Abbey of St Denis."

Certain principles underlie this vast compilation, thereby contributing to its remarkable unity. The first is what has been called the providential view of history. Human history is a function of God's plan of salvation; misfortune is attributable to disobedi-ence or forgetfulness in regard to righteous behav-ior, whereas good fortune is the gift of a God who ever intervenes in man's affairs. These doctrines had become commonplace in medieval Christendom, but in the *Grandes chroniques* they are explicitly for-mulated in terms of the facts and the myths of

"French" history; they underpin the ideology of that history, its meaning.

Second, the *Chroniques* incorporate into their royal genealogy of France the clerkly legend of the Trojan origin of the French (the counterpart to the story of Brutus as the founder of the Britons), with, as a result, the division of that genealogy into three "generations": of "Merovée," of "Pepin," of "Hue Chapet." To each of these "generations" the *Chroniques* devote one "book"; book III culminates in the reign of Philip II Augustus, who is depicted as reuniting "la lignie le grant Challemaine" with that of his Capetian forebears by marrying Isabelle of Hainaut, a descendant of Charlemagne. (St. Louis, their grandson, thus incarnates a special legitimacy within the Capetian dynasty; his existence justifies the struggles and the usurpations that led to the establishment of the modern, and increasingly universalist, French kingdom.)

Third—and this is expressly stated in the prologue (pp. 5ff.)—the *Chroniques* link the process of French history with the same two-part *translatio imperii et studii* (*chevalerie* and *clergie*) found in the forematter to Chrétien de Troyes's *Cligès*. In words exactly reproducing those of Chrétien's romance, the narrator describes the passage of "knightliness" and "clerkliness" from Greece to Rome and at last to France, where "God grant they may endure *longuement.*" However, very significantly, the text of the *Grandes chroniques* associates this transfer with "the glorious martyr and apostle of France, *messires sains Denis,* by whom she was first converted" to the true faith. Chrétien's purely literary utilization of the *translatio* topic is thus both reversed and renewed by the text of the *Grandes chroniques;* it is infused with an authentically historical meaning, a new truth. By the same token, however, the reader senses that the author of this prologue understood Chrétien's amusing mockery of Arthurian historical pretensions in *Cligès* and his glorification of a peculiarly French *clergie.*

Indeed, the ties between the world of the *Grandes chroniques* and that of romance narrative procedures are quite close. There is the same appeal to Latin bookish authority; identical use of rhetorical-poetic devices; and, of course, a proliferation of episodic anecdote. Throughout there is the voice of the clerk-narrator who interprets, and passes judgment on, the events recounted. Examples of "elegant" stylistic effect abound, such as this mixed, but literarily very coherent, metaphor: "la fonteine de clergie, par cui sainte Eglise est sostenue et enluminée, florist à Paris" (the fountainhead of clerkliness, by which the holy church is upheld and illuminated, flourishes in Paris).

A romancelike concern for architectural structure is detectable in these chronicles. Thus, book I is centered on Clovis, while books II and III focus, respectively, on Charlemagne and on Philip Augustus; these reigns constitute the high points of the three "generations." Also—and this contributes weightily to the sense of a universalist French kingdom—a double space-time axis, recalling the *romans antiques,* prevails in the *Grandes chroniques.* On the one hand there is the space-time of the *translatio:* France, as heir to Trojan, Greek, and Roman *chevalerie* and *clergie,* assumes the same worldwide relevance as these civilizations once did. On the other hand, what happens in France is constantly related to what transpires elsewhere (Rome, England, Byzantium, Sicily), with France depicted as the center of everything.

As this historicopoetic summa moves from the remote, legendary past (the times of the *romans antiques*) to the chansons de geste (and *Pseudo-Turpin*) times of the great Charles, down to contemporary, thirteenth-century events, the literary witness becomes increasingly infused with a spirit of ocular and aural testimony. Thus, close to 300 detailed and highly anecdotal pages are devoted to the reign of Philip Augustus; and, equally significant, the French text of the *Grandes chroniques* came to acquire, during the last quarter of the century, an authority at least equal to Latin counterparts composed at that time. By 1300 Latin and French would stand virtually as equals, with French advancing inexorably during subsequent years. Thanks largely to the *Grandes chroniques de France,* direct historical witness in the vernacular came to be especially prized, resulting in the request by Jeanne of Navarre (the consort of Philip IV the Fair) that Jean de Joinville, seneschal of Champagne, compose a book, in French, on the "saintly words and good deeds" of his old friend, the recently canonized St. Louis.

Joinville, who had testified in 1282 on behalf of that canonization, recounts in his *Life of St. Louis* "what he saw and heard" during his long association with Louis IX, particularly at the time of the Seventh Crusade (1248–1254), as well as certain facts gleaned from a *roman* (the *Grandes chroniques*). This masterpiece, dictated to an amanuensis and presented in 1309 tó Philip's son, the future Louis X, is largely autobiographical—that is, the writer's character and sense of values, as well as what befell him during his long life, constitute the prism through which the saintliness, the kingly qualities, and the exemplary morality of Louis IX are refracted. About three-quarters of the work focuses on Joinville; the rest reports what the king said and did. In this sense Joinville's *Life* represents a typical late-thirteenth-century off-shoot of the all-encompassing, general history of the *Grandes chroniques*. The summa, it may be said, engendered in this *Life* a work that at once partakes of its spirit (Joinville's St. Louis possesses all the admirable attributes of the chronicles' Louis IX) and particularizes it, fleshing it out by concentrating on its author's viewpoint and self. By so integrating his work into the system of the *Grandes chroniques,* Joinville frees himself to be himself, and even, on occasion, to criticize his king. To a far greater degree than Villehardouin, Joinville is a master memorialist, a *grand seigneur* whose sense of selfhood and station furnishes the key to what he reports. Joinville's manner foreshadows that of such great sixteenth-century *prosateurs* as Jacques Amyot, Blaise de Monluc, and even Montaigne. With Joinville, French prose reached a high level of individualized, nonclerkly maturity and, it may be added, of extraordinary charm.

There remain two great manifestations of the thirteenth-century propensity for the poetic summa in France: the poetical works of Rutebeuf (*fl. ca.* 1249–1275) and the two-part text of the *Romance of the Rose* (part I, by Guillaume de Lorris, *ca.* 1225–1237, 4,058 octosyllabic lines; part II by Jean de Meun, 1270's, 17,722 lines), arguably the most influential poem in Old French.

No thirteenth-century document mentioning the name of Rutebeuf has survived, though twelve manuscripts of poems ascribed to him (some 14,000 lines in all) have been preserved. From these texts it has been inferred that "Rutebeuf" was born, *ca.* 1230, in Champagne, but that in the early 1250's he took up residence in Paris. He almost certainly frequented the university schools; he knew Latin, and was quite familiar with both the political issues and the many acerbic university disputes occurring during the third quarter of the century. He was well versed in several principal vernacular genres (*Renard,* saints' lives, courtly lyric, the *Miracles* of Gautier de Coinci *et al.*); he knew and imitated the goliardic tradition.

Rutebeuf's modern editors divide his work into five major topical areas: (1) eighteen poems dealing with the church, the mendicant friars, and the controversies afflicting the University of Paris; (2) twelve

crusade poems (advocating the revival of the crusading spirit and of old-style chivalry); (3) eleven poems of personal misfortune (dicing poems, works complaining of an apparently calamitous marriage and of his coming death, a *Renard* poem); (4) eight religious poems, including narratives recounting the life of St. Mary the Egyptian and that of St. Elizabeth of Hungary, and a miracle play about the Faust-like Théophile; (5) seven comic entertainments (*pièces à rire*), one of which is the *fabliau*-like *Pet au vilain* (The churl's fart). On several occasions "Rutebeuf" names himself, at times offering a (perhaps mock) learned etymology explaining his name: "Rustebués," who, like a "*bués* [ox], *rudement oevre*" (labors rudely, in coarse fashion). This name might well have been authentic; it is equally likely, however, that "Rutebeuf" was a kind of school or minstrel nickname, since, with very few exceptions, medieval writers identified themselves by their Christian name, a surname, and/or a name indicating their place of residence or origin.

Four salient features characterize "Rutebeuf's" extant production: (1) its variety of genre and tone, ranging from the bitterly critical and polemical to the hauntingly worshipful; (2) its technical virtuosity (numerous metrical schemes; extensive use of complex figurative devices like paronomasia and annominatio; the chain of thought frequently following the exigencies of, say, rhyme rather than logic); (3) certain constant principles (the poet's unworthiness; his devotion to the Virgin; his hatred of the mendicants, and his love for the traditional university; the sad state of the realm, for which Louis IX is partly to blame); (4) its extraordinary attention to concrete detail and to topicality. Underlying this work in all its diversity is a single, stridently poetic voice or "individuality" that imparts the summalike unity and massiveness that the reader is virtually forced to identify with a "person" called "Rutebeuf," who exists only in regard to his oeuvre.

Essentially Rutebeuf carries the lyric mode to the brink of total transformation. His poems were not meant to be sung, yet the lyric configuration informs even the ostensibly most narrative or theatrical of his compositions. The loving witness that Zozimas, an "unworthy clerk" figure, bears to the beautiful soul of St. Mary constitutes a metamorphosis of the lyric lover-poet's devotion to his lady, and Rutebeuf's own (poetic) devotion to the Egyptian parallels and continues that of Zozimas. And clearly, Théophile, who has sold his soul to the devil for material advancement and who is saved, after his deeply moving prayer of humble repentance, by Our Lady, figuratively represents that clerkly archetype with which the poet, in lyric fashion, identified his own persona.

Rutebeuf exploits these conventions by transmogrifying them. His oeuvre is consequently a typically creative thirteenth-century renewal; but within the spectrum of such renewals Rutebeuf occupies a unique niche, resembling, perhaps, only Marcabru, the great Old Provençal poet who flourished more than a century before him, and François Villon, who lived two centuries later. And in all this we find from time to time examples of poetry of the very highest order, as in the "Griesche d'hiver" (Winter dice game), which contains a moving meditation on chance, free will, sin, the passage of time, redemption, and Christian love, or in such poignant lines as "Savez comment je me demain? / L'esperance de l'endemain, / Ce sont mes festes" (Do you know how I get by? / The hope of tomorrow, / Such are my feast days; "Mariage Rutebeuf," vv. 113ff.).

Rutebeuf's oeuvre celebrates the French vernacular in its literary tradition, in its humaneness—in the people who speak and articulate it—and in its suitability for the expression of both thought and personhood; courtly, uncourtly, coarse, worshipful, strident, lamenting. The effect of this work is centripetal: ostensibly disparate poems acquire their fullest meaning when they are understood in terms of the whole. Interestingly, the *Romance of the Rose* achieves similar results, though it proceeds in an opposite way: here a single, extremely complex poem expresses and contains elements so seemingly irreconcilable as to appear centrifugal with respect to their context.

The *Rose* consists of two parts, the second being the continuation and resolution of the first, which, like Chrétien's *Perceval*, had not brought the story to its full conclusion. As was the case with Rutebeuf's work, the underlying structure of the *Rose* is patterned on the "lyric triangle." First, protagonist and narrator-poet are one and the same person, though with two important distinctions: that the narrator is the Lover some five years after the love experience being recounted and, consequently, that the text, called a *romanz,* adopts the typical romance narrative form of rhyming octosyllabic couplets. Second, the central experience of the poem is that of love: the Lover, in a dream, sees and falls in love with the Rose (the name given to her who "is so worthy of being loved that she must be called Rose"); after a lengthy series of obstacles and hardships, he finally succeeds in consummating his passion (his plucking

of the rose at the end is a thinly veiled metaphor for sexual possession). The third point of the triangle, the idea of song—of lyric craft and diction—and of the truth of poetic coherence constitutes the underpinning of this vast enterprise: the lyric convention of springtime, with the presence of birdsong everywhere; the Lover's courtly rejection of Reason's uncourtly speech; the poem's identity as, first, the very Art of Love and, later, as the Mirror or Encyclopedia for Lovers; the specific linking by Jean de Meun of poetry (in the persons of Ovid, Catullus, Tibullus, Guillaume de Lorris, and Jean himself) with the service of love—all these extol, in almost hyperbolic fashion, the themes and the values of lyric love poetry. Conversely, the poem warns against those who, like Narcissus, have failed to observe the proprieties of love.

The lyric structure of the *Rose* is subsumed into a romancelike poetic architecture. Consequently the *Rose* may be said to renew both the conventional courtly song and the early romance narrative in verse. Thus, at the strategic midpoint of the conjoined texts of Guillaume de Lorris and Jean de Meun—a place where many romances impart a sense of their own, or of their protagonists', identity (compare Chrétien's *Yvain, Lancelot,* and *Cligès*)—Jean causes the God of Love (Amors) to praise the love service, and names both Guillaume—the first thirteenth-century reference to him—and himself as successors to the ancients: after Guillaume's death "Johans Chopinel" will be born, on the banks of the Loire, and he will hold so dear the *roman* that he will continue it and bring it to a perfect end. In this way the doctrines of love will be taught in the schools and at the crossroads, "according to the language of France."

The tightness of this lyric-romance structuring—something any cognizant thirteenth-century reader would immediately grasp—is what poetically contains, and gives order to, the encyclopedically varied and disparate elements. The system of poetic containment operative in this text is bolstered by its classically pristine, romance-style prologue. The work begins with a typical general statement, to the effect that dreams (romances?) are not necessarily mendacious, a judgment supported by an appeal to an ancient authority, Macrobius, the fifth-century author of the immensely influential and mythopoetic *Commentary* on Cicero's *Dream of Scipio*. The narrator proceeds to tell how, one early morning in May some five years previously, he was dreaming; it was the season of love, both for him (he was twenty) and for the calendar year (spring), and he rejoiced in the budding trees, the new flowers, and the concert of birdsong. Without awakening, he rose from his bed as though he were awake and prepared to take a stroll. Following close along a river, he reached an orchard surrounded by high walls painted with images representing Hatred, Villainy, Covetousness, Avarice, and other vices. Romance-style descriptions of these images ensue, imparting to them something of the status of personifications; the reader is tempted to forget that they are paintings and, to boot, emanations of the Lover's dream—that, in fact, the story is taking place in his mind (a *psychomachia*).

Next, with the Lover the reader meets the first talking (and feminine) personification, Oiseuse (the name suggests "leisure," a kind of pleasant and courtly laziness), who lets the Lover into the orchard, where he sees his beloved Rose. Innumerable personifications of the Oiseuse sort populate the romance (Reason, Jealousy, Hypocrisy, the Old Woman, Genius) along with mythological characters either encountered by the Lover (Amors) or referred to more or less lengthily (Pygmalion, Narcissus) and a group of historical, legendary, and fictional personages. The narration of the Lover's quest to possess the Rose is thus laden with commentaries of all sorts—speeches, dialogues, digressions, descriptions—especially in Jean de Meun's part of the work. At times the fiction appears to be overwhelmed by these seemingly disparate commentaries, to be a mere pretext for the discussion of ideas, values, and problems.

Readers have reacted to the *Romance of the Rose* fairly consistently in one of two fundamental ways: poetically or ideologically. For such writers as Dante, Machaut, Froissart, and Chaucer, the *Rose* was essentially a treasure trove of poetic invention, a terrain in—and by—which they found themselves enabled to compose their own poems. These works, to a more or less considerable degree, constituted responses to the *Rose* both as an organic poetic oeuvre and as a compilation of poetic possibilities. The *Rose* acted, then, as a primary governing force in the poetry of the fourteenth and much of the fifteeenth century; it simply could not be ignored. Other readers—and this tradition characterizes most modern (not strictly philological) scholarship—focused on the ideological "content" of the poem, interpreting, it would seem, Guillaume de Lorris' *senefiance* as signifying "ideas" and "viewpoints." As early as the start of the fifteenth century, Christine de Pizan, a

considerable poet in her own right and an impassioned feminist participant in the famous "Quarrel of the *Romance of the Rose*," accused Jean de Meun of misogyny; others, like Pierre Col, "defended" him. Analogously, modern scholars have tended to characterize Guillaume de Lorris as advocating the "doctrines" of "courtly love," and Jean de Meun as systematically opposing them with an almost cynical forthrightness and naturalism. Guillaume, the idealistic courtly poet, is thus contrasted with the "bourgeois rationalist" Jean. (Conversely, for some critics Jean is a profoundly Christian poet who, intent on exposing the fraudulence of an essentially immoral and uncharitable *fin'amors,* makes considerable use of complex techniques of irony: despite what the poem may appear ostensibly to be saying, the Lover is inevitably a silly, immoral, and callow youth.)

The difficulty with any ideological interpretation of the *Rose's senefiance* lies in convincingly establishing a single point of view in the poem—or even in each separate part. It is quite arbitrary to identify any one, or more, of the characters as the author's mouthpiece. Is it wrong for the Lover to reject the amorous advances made to him by Reason, who, though the daughter of God, is smitten with him and, perhaps consequently, wishes to deter him from his "foolish" pursuit of the Rose? She may well be "right," but her motives and rhetoric are decidedly not disinterested. The Lover listens politely to her endless and pedantic tirades; however, he objects to her uttering the word *coiles* (balls, testicles), a term he finds unsuitable in the speech of a young maiden. Eventually she explains, and justifies, her usage: God created *coiles;* the word designating them is as beautiful as his creation. Why bother with euphemism? Steeped in courtly discourse, the Lover is shocked at this rational nominalism (things are naturally and properly designated by the terms plainly applied to them; metaphor, in effect, is by nature improper—Reason is speaking what Dante would call *gramatica*).

The whole passage constitutes a brilliant and very poetic meditation on the nature of language. To say that Reason "represents" Jean de Meun impoverishes this meditation and would imply (erroneously) that Jean is negating the value of poetry. What he is doing, surely, is showing how poetry may be negated, as well as the consequences of such negation (the elimination of *translatio,* of metaphor). The complexity is what counts, the opportunity Jean offers the reader to weigh the matter.

Thus, although it teems with long and short treatises of various kinds (including very Rutebeuf-like diatribes against the mendicants at the University of Paris), the *Rose* is not a treatise, and little is gained by reading it as though it were. In order to understand its *senefiance,* one must attempt to grasp how it functions as a vernacular poetic summa, the greatest of its kind in a *grand siècle* replete with examples of vast and coherent poetic undertakings. To this end, I believe, a reader would do well to borrow a leaf from the fourteenth-century poets who, while recognizing the intellectual seriousness and importance of the *Rose,* nevertheless read it (and "rewrote" it) as a living, indeed archetypal, *translatio*-type poem. For its imitators the *Romance of the Rose* furnished proof that vernacular poetry could rival in truth, profundity, and beauty the learned and great Latin theological summas—tributes to Reason—being produced in Paris by Scholastic thinkers (who, incidentally, belonged overwhelmingly to the Dominican and Franciscan [mendicant] orders and who, for the most part, were not French). There is something theatrical in the *Romance of the Rose:* the Lover's mind and, by extension, the poem itself constitute a stage upon which the major literary and intellectual concerns of the *grand siècle* disport, like characters in a play, speaking to each other and to us with immediacy, verve, humor, and sometimes poignancy.

Authentic dramatic forms in the vernacular also came into their own during the thirteenth century. And in each case the plays were dramatizations of older genres: Bodel's *Jeu de saint Nicolas* transformed hagiographic narrative into play form; Rutebeuf's *Théophile* dramatized the *miracle* tale. The theater, moreover, lies close to the surface of the very playable (and playful) *Aucassin et Nicolette.* The early-thirteenth-century *Courtois d'Arras*—a verse text that combines theater, dramatic monologue, and narrative recital—retells the parable of the Prodigal Son in dramatic terms with the young and foolish Courtois (the Courtly One) as the central character. The play employs a characteristic Picard locale (and dialect), with amusing tavern scenes (a staple in much thirteenth-century comic theater). Transformed in this way, the parable is rendered with recognizable immediacy. *Courtois* blends elements of both "secular" and "sacred" theater so perfectly that one would be hard-pressed to classify it.

The most interesting known playwright of the century is the Artesian (Picard) court poet, musician, and clerk Adam de la Halle (also known as Adam Le Bossu). His *Jeu de Robin et de Marion,* possibly com-

posed for the amusement of the court of Count Robert of Artois, is based on the lyric pastourelle, a genre in which a knight demands the love of a (usually) shy shepherdess (the demand is sometimes accorded, often to the girl's regret, or is refused, in which case the knight either succeeds in violating the girl or is stopped from doing so by the girl's cleverness or the intervention of her shepherd friends). The genre possesses an inherent theatricality: Will he (she) or won't he (she), and how? The setting is bucolic, songs are sung and danced, dialogue is exchanged, class distinctions are explored—all within a highly conventional boy-meets-girl context. Adam's *Robin et Marion* transposes all these conventions into a delightful play, presenting recognizable, even rather nuanced, character types and offering a show of song and dance.

Adam's masterpiece, however, is the *Jeu de la feuillée* (Play of the arbor, 1276), also in verse, a transposition of the lyric congé, the leave-taking genre. At the start the central character, Adam, announces to his Arras compatriots that he is abandoning wife and birthplace in order to return to his studies in Paris. A veritable cross section of the Arras citizenry comes to the fore in order to comment upon this decision and its probable consequences. (It is possible that members of the audience joined the main actors in a to-and-fro movement from spectacle to spectator, eliminating the stage/audience barrier to a considerable degree.) And, as is the case with much of Rutebeuf's poetry, the *jeu* is replete with obscure topical allusiveness. It abounds in puns, wisecracks, and other sorts of wordplay, including very sophisticated literary references. A visit by fairies adds a *Midsummer Night's Dream* quality to the *Jeu,* while characters like the slatternly Dame Douche and the Mad Boy impart auras of earthiness and mystery. The play consists in the highly comic drama of an entire town, with its gossip, its myths, its boisterousness—its life. It ends late at night, with nothing resolved, in a tavern, where a charlatan monk is (justly) tricked into paying for the wine consumed by the very citizens he had tried to bilk with his relics.

This highly original—but very typically thirteenth-century French—chef-d'oeuvre must end our survey of the literary creativity of the medieval *grand siècle.* Needless to say, it has merely glanced at the tops of a few of the more majestic icebergs that dot that vast sea. It is hoped, however, that the chart will provide the novice reader with the means further to explore, with the help of specialized studies, the texts discussed and the many interesting works that have necessarily gone unmentioned (the great prose *Tristan* cycle; *exempla* collections; Bible translations).

THE TERRIBLE YEARS

In the dedication that he composed for his *Life of St. Louis* (1309) and he addressed to Louis le Hutin, king of Navarre and the future Louis X of France, Jean de Joinville made so bold as to state that, in part, he was prompted to write this life in order that "you and your brothers, and others who will hear it read, might profit from [St. Louis's] example, and put [his] examples to work" (sec. 18). One of the most respected lords of the French realm, the aged Joinville—whose reputation was such that the Florentine Francesco de Barberino consulted him on proper chivalric conduct—felt that the successors of Louis IX (especially Philip IV the Fair) had become unworthy of their great forebear (secs. 42, 761), that dishonor and perhaps even divine punishment could well be visited on France.

Thus, only a few years before a strained interpretation of the Salic law led to the accession in 1328 of Philip VI of Valois and the start of the Hundred Years War (1337), Joinville presents not only a sense that the times are out of joint but also an exhortation to return to an earlier, better epoch, when an authentic, God-fearing chivalry prevailed in the kingdom, at the service of a just and devoted monarchy. Factiousness and self-interest have come to characterize the nobility; and, one suspects, Joinville must have increasingly looked askance at the rising power of the new and ever more professionalized royal bureaucracy. Gone are the days when the relationship between king and vassals was frank, open, and based on trust and mutual respect; sycophancy and the pursuit of personal gain have come into their own. Even the currency underwent periodic debasement during the opening decades of the fourteenth century, causing ruin for some and enrichment for others, as debts contracted in earlier times were paid off with cheaper money.

Joinville's concerns (or perceptions) run like an undercurrent through much fourteenth-century literature, even as the greatest writers, for reasons of patronage and position, were obliged to serve the rich and powerful, constantly going from one *grand seigneur* to another, and even shifting allegiance among the different factions: France, England, and, later, Burgundy. However, it was not so much the onset of the war that caused the transformations in literature; rather, those transformations, already visible in the late thirteenth and early fourteenth centuries, paralleled the social, economic, and political developments denounced by Joinville. His *Life of St. Louis* was completed almost four decades after the death of Louis IX: it is a very conservative, even nostalgic, book. Nor was it really a matter of criticizing the institutions of chivalry as such. Those institutions were seen as having been corrupted and, therefore, in need of "restoration." The ideals of chivalry continued to be highly prized, despite—perhaps because of—the corruption to which the practice of chivalry had become subject. "The word *preudomme* [gentleman] is so grand and good, just saying it fills the mouth," or so Joinville quotes Louis IX (sec. 32); and, citing Philip Augustus, "*Preudomme* [is he] whose prowess comes to him as the gift of God" (sec 560). Unlike many modern scholars, Joinville (and most of his contemporaries) did not consider chivalry anachronistic.

The greatest writers of the fourteenth century, working within the context of the terrible years, consequently saw their task as consisting in the restoration and celebration of the great chivalric (and literary) traditions of arms and love. As one scholar has put it, it was the age of the poet and the prince; indeed, it culminated in the figure of Charles of Orléans, who was both poet and prince, and, in many respects, a symbol of the period as it came to an end. Of very high noble station—his father was brother to Charles VI—Charles of Orléans was taken prisoner by the English at Agincourt (1415) and held until 1440. During this time he wrote allegorical love poems and laments on his exile (including the famous *Complainte* urging France to regain her erstwhile grandeur), many of which are pervaded by a sense of sadness and melancholy. He even exchanged ballades with the son of the Burgundian duke who had caused his father to be murdered; this reconciliation helped bring about his release and return to France, and led to his marriage to Marie of Cleves (later the mother of Louis XII). He sponsored numerous poetry competitions at his court at Blois (François Villon participated in one of these).

Though he was not a poet of absolutely the first rank, Charles's example nevertheless proves that poetry continued to merit the high consideration of the very best of French society during the final years of the Hundred Years War. For Charles, poetic activity constituted a superior form of consolation, at once partaking of the chivalric ideal and, when the reality of that ideal fell short, transcending it.

Preservation through transcendence—the shape taken by such fourteenth-century poetic transformation—implies the establishment of complex code systems, a great deal of (at least apparent) paradox and of what might be called reading between the lines. In consequence, when compared with that of the thirteenth century, the literature of the fourteenth is one of increased indirectness. Nowhere is this phenomenon more apparent than in the poetic tradition extending from Guillaume de Machaut to Eustache Deschamps, Jehan Froissart, Christine de Pizan, and Charles of Orléans. This tradition, as suggested above, deals with imaginational categories: ideal chivalry, love, personhood, poetic art, virtues and vices, and intellectual values. It tends to sublimate day-by-day experience, and in so doing it reverses the trends toward concrete detail and direct observation that characterize much of the literary production of the previous century. Yet, for those poets it was as though these ideal categories were somehow more authentic, more lasting, and less subject to the vicissitudes of capricious fate than, say, the truths witnessed sensorially by Joinville, and consequently more adequate for the containment of experience and value. They helped to furnish an order principle—a harmony at once musical and quasi-mathematical—through which the anarchy infecting human events might be dispelled so that these events could take on permanent significance.

Whereas for Joinville the "truth" of St. Louis meshed perfectly and naturally with the events he witnessed and reported, for the fourteenth-century writers treated here the main task was one of forging, through poetry, the necessary harmonies. Thus, a work like Froissart's lengthy Arthurian romance *Méliador* tells of love, of tournaments, and of fighting in such strange lands as "pagan" Ireland; it has the appearance of an old-fashioned throwback to the twelfth century. But, by the same token, Froissart seems to be celebrating the "good old days" when the knights of France and England could join forces against a common danger, and did not fight among themselves in a suicidal civil war.

Small wonder, then, that about 1377 Deschamps applied the ancient title *poete* (which he glossed, carefully and traditionally, as *faiseur*, maker) to the recently deceased Machaut—the first time that noble appellation, hitherto restricted to the ancients, was affixed to a versemaker in the French vernacular. (The precedent, however, had been set by Jean de Meun, who had associated himself and Guillaume de Lorris with the tradition of poetic love service pre-

viously illustrated by Ovid and Catullus.) In his ballade on Machaut's death, Deschamps also refers to his one-time teacher as *cantique* (singer) and enjoins "harps and horns" to weep for the demise of "Machaut, le noble rethorique." Song (music) is the key, both technical and intellectual, to fourteenth-century poetry, whether that poetry, properly speaking, is lyric or narrative or both.

Song and verse had traditionally been associated throughout the history of the medieval lyric, but with Machaut this association acquired new meaning. His work is a far cry from the courtly trouvère manner of Conon de Béthune and others whose *grands chants courtois* were transcribed in variously ordered *chansonniers* (songbooks). First, Machaut was a highly trained intellectual with a degree in theology who, in 1337, was awarded a canonry in the cathedral of Rheims. Second, he was a great innovator as both musician (in secular and sacred modes) and poet. Rejecting the older courtly forms, he refined such folk-type genres as the ballade, the virelay, and the rondeau, and perfected other forms (such as the *chanson royale*) that would set the fashion for close to a century and a half of poetic composition in France. Finally, he was possibly the first major poet to supervise with great care the putting together of codices of his works—regulating the order in which the poems were placed and, quite probably, influencing his illustrators. (During the fourteenth century, French manuscript illustration, especially at Paris, underwent a series of remarkable evolutions, increasingly tending toward "realistic" depiction and portraiture even as the poetic artifacts themselves became, at least on the surface, more stiffly formal and allegorically abstract.)

Thus, to a degree not known in France before his time, Machaut was a thoroughly professional artist whose first and greatest loyalty was to his craft. Manuscripts of his works are true books, in the modern sense of the word. Perhaps for the first time in French literature, the reader witnesses the individualized and conscious elaboration of a vast and sophisticated oeuvre in which each element is related to all the others, to the greater glory of poetry (and music), made incarnate in the person of Machaut *poete*.

Underlying everything is Machaut's response to the uses made of the lyric triangle—I/self, song/craft, love/experience—found in the *Romance of the Rose*. His earliest work, *Le dit dou verger* (The orchard poem), recounts the poet's dream of love in an orchard, beneath a tree in which Amors is perched. The poet is awakened by a cold dew as Amors flies off. However, whereas the *Rose* had made of the lyric triangle an essentially narrative meditation on the nature of poetic language and truth, Machaut "relyricizes" this meditation. This is not to say that Machaut simply returned to the pre-*Rose* courtly song. Rather, he chose to restructure and, in so doing, to reformulate the elements of the *Rose* (dream fiction, allegorical figures, courtly diction) in a series of poems (*dits,* poems or tales) that are set firmly into the context of a specific occasion or matter. Also, along with the octosyllabic rhyming couplets of romance, Machaut employed a variety of stanzaic and metric forms.

The occasions are quite varied. Some constitute developments of explicitly lyric—even technical—situations, like the *jeu parti,* in which a question is explored at length from two opposing viewpoints, as in the *Jugement dou roy de Behaingne* and the *Jugement dou roy de Navarre:* Who deserves more pity, a knight whose beloved is disloyal or a newly widowed lady? (The first poem decides in favor of the knight; the second, in favor of the lady.) The two works are shot through with patterns of Scholastic-type argumentation (such as are found in Jean de Meun)—Machaut was a trained dialectician—but those patterns are strictly governed by the *jeu parti* (lyric) conventions, in that a conclusion, or sentence, is reached that affects Machaut the poet, and therefore the protagonist: for instance, the king of Navarre requires him, as punishment for defending the jilted knight, to write a lay, a rondeau, and a ballade. The inherent drama of each *Jugement* is enhanced by the presence of many voluble allegorical characters (ladies) who argue excitedly, tell stories in support of their contentions, and in general act out "real-life" parts. Although ostensibly quite conventional in their attributes, Machaut's *dits* focus on what might be called factors of performance—something operalike in tone and effect, with characters playing roles, speaking, and singing to one another. The unity imparted to these poems by their structured character allows the poet considerable freedom to include seemingly unrelated digressions (for instance, his description of the plague of 1348–1349 at the start of the second *Jugement*) and other thematically disparate elements, which make up much of the twentieth-century interest of these works.

The authority of Machaut's poems is, thus, indistinguishable from the authority of Machaut as (real or fictional) person—as narrator, singer, participant, and commentator. At times this authority is quick to

assume a doctrinal nature, as in the *Remède de fortune* (4,298 lines, principally octosyllabic, studded with various *formes fixes,* most of which are set to music), a text that recounts a love affair of the poet but, in effect, demonstrates how a love affair is to be treated poetically—that is, integrated into the poet-musician's craft and identified with it in such a manner as to make it true. Other variations on this theme include the *Dit dou lyon* (2,204 octosyllables) and the *Dit de l'alerion* (4,814 octosyllables); the latter, ostensibly treating the poet's noble interest in falconry, actually deals with love. Not surprisingly, then, Machaut tried his hand at other genres: consolation poems like the *Fontaine amoureuse,* and the *Prise d'Alexandrie* (Taking of Alexandria), a kind of verse biography of Pierre de Lusignan, king of Cyprus. Machaut's masterpiece, the *Voir dit* (True story), returns to the twin themes of the poet's love and craft. It consists of a lengthy exchange of prose letters and verse between the aging poet and a precocious young woman who, admiring his poetry, falls in love with him. The *Voir dit* traces the evolution of this affair, which culminates in the lovers' spending the night together (though chastely), their bed enveloped in a cloud conveniently provided by Venus. (The poet's mistress is named in an anagram that has been deciphered as Peronne d'Armentières—perhaps the earliest identification in French poetry of an *amie* by other than a conventional sobriquet.) The *Voir dit,* in addition to prose, contains verse narrative, many fixed forms, and considerable musical notation; it is widely considered to be the first great poetic autobiography in French, although the accuracy of the biographical detail has been much debated.

Perhaps the question is beside the point, for here Machaut's identification of self, craft, and experience is so thorough that it becomes itself a matter for meditation. Peronne falls in love with Guillaume because of, and through, his poetry; yet this love, despite its seeming distinction between the man and the poet (which provokes anxiety felt by Guillaume), is depicted as authentic and deeply sensual. Machaut is both the poet-master and the older man, smitten by the charm, the vivacity, and the poetic intelligence of his young admirer. The ambiguous consummation of their love constitutes a very tender and humane response to the somewhat brutal plucking of the Rose in the *Romance of the Rose.* The *Voir dit* is not only a very subtle and psychologically convincing work; it constantly calls attention, through the absolute mastery of technique that it displays, to its hauntingly lyric beauty. Its technical perfection and the very concept of technical perfection that it embodies constitute the wellspring of its veracity.

The lessons of Guillaume de Machaut were not lost upon his contemporaries and successors. The traditions he renewed were followed by many including Froissart, Chaucer, and Christine de Pizan. Machaut's most earnest disciple (and possibly his nephew) was Eustache Deschamps, poet at the court of Charles V, holder of various offices, and author of more than 80,000 lines of verse, including more than 1,000 ballades). Immensely prolific and, it is said, possessed of an earthiness and matter-of-factness that bordered at times on cynicism, Deschamps, though popular in his own time and a considerable virtuoso, is less interesting today as a poet than for his *Art de dictier* (1392), the first comprehensive poetics in French. The *Art de dictier* codifies in explicit form what Machaut had practiced, though Deschamps goes even further than Machaut in one important respect.

The *Art de dictier* is both a handbook and a treatise. It also situates poetry as a discipline within the framework of the seven liberal arts. Deschamps's attitude toward music is fascinating. Unlike Machaut, he was no composer; indeed, he calls music "artificial music." However, it would not be accurate to dismiss Deschamps as antimusical and, in consequence, oblivious to Machaut's accomplishment. On the contrary, he implies that Machaut's achievement was so completely successful that it is now possible to distinguish between the *musique artificielle* of song and the authentic *musique de bouche* (music of speech) of poetic language. The language of poetry is, in its own right, inherently and naturally musical. Deschamps's theory of poetry is thus grounded solidly in the concept of the lyric triangle: language, or poetic craft, and the poet-as-self are indissolubly linked, and this linkage constitutes the underpinnings of his entire doctrine. Although on one level song is in practice eliminated from serious poetry, the *idea* of music is retained and is infused with new significance. The poet's self, his personal and concrete identity, is inseparable from the authenticity (the *musique de bouche*) of his craft and from the value of that craft as a manifestation of *musique naturelle.*

Deschamps's *Art de dictier* enjoyed considerable influence, particularly during the fifteenth century when theorists and practitioners of poetry came increasingly to focus their attention upon new and intricate kinds of versification and wordplay. The poets known as the *grands rhétoriqueurs* would, for example, indulge in such games of technical virtuosity as palindromes (which read the same backward and forward), inventing new words, and flamboyant *rimes équivoques* (punning rhymes, such as *en place/ample a ce*). Also, the *Art de dictier* may be said to have initiated the very French tradition of the *ars poetica,* later exemplified by Sebillet, du Bellay, Boileau, Gautier, and Verlaine.

Deschamps's *Art de dictier* points, at a time of poetic crisis (Froissart had abandoned poetry by 1375; the Quarrel of the *Romance of the Rose* started in 1400), toward the dominant poetic modes of the following century. The explicit manner in which Deschamps connected the poet's individuality, or persona, and his craft allowed for a considerable expansion of the range of experience deemed suitable for lyric poetry. Thus, in addition to his love poetry, Deschamps himself wrote about bad food and uncomfortable lodgings in Bohemia, being infested with lice or fleas, unpleasant weather, and disgraceful table manners. Everything he saw or experienced could become legitimate grist for his mill, precisely because *he* saw or experienced it, and possessed the craft to write about it. Without Deschamps's example and theories it would be difficult to understand the powerfully lyric, though largely unsonglike, work of François Villon more than half a century later. Both Villon and the *rhétoriqueurs* constitute Deschamps's progeny.

Jehan Froissart, Machaut's most gifted emulator, was the most complex and sophisticated man of letters of the late fourteenth century. Born about 1337 in the county of Hainaut to a bourgeois family, he entered the service of Philippa of Hainaut in England, where he came to know important members of the highest nobility. He was widely traveled and throughout his life served well-placed patrons and *grands seigneurs.* His literary career comprises two fairly distinct, though somewhat overlapping, periods: from his youth to about 1373 he composed occasional verse, *débats,* and a series of lyric-narrative poems *(dittiers)* in the *Rose*-Machaut tradition, of which the most important are, in probable chronological order, *Li orloge amoureus, L'espinette amoureuse, La prison amoureuse,* and *Le joli buisson de Jonece* (1373); during the 1370's he left off writing verse in order to devote himself to his *Chroniques,* a vast prose work recounting mainly the history of the Hundred Years War. (About 1365 a first version of his 30,000-line, octosyllabic Arthurian romance, *Méliador,* was completed; the second version dates from about 1384.)

In some ways Froissart's career and temperament parallel those of Deschamps. He shared his contemporary's obsession with the example of Machaut, and his work reflects a similar predilection for the concrete and the observable. He probably would have subscribed to Deschamps's disdain for *musique artificielle;* his sense of the primacy of the poetic "I" is as strong and acute as that of Deschamps. But he was a greater and a more profound poet and man of letters. The lyric-narrative *dittiers* constitute, on at least two levels, a remarkably coherent autobiography—a poetic autobiography placed under the sign of love. Assuming the traditional role of poet-lover, Froissart on one level explores, with the aid of extraordinarily ramified poetic conceits, certain key and universal facets of noble love. Thus, the *Orloge amoureus* (Amorous clock) minutely compares the mechanism of the lover's heart to that of clockwork: both love and time possess (interrelated) "movements," with their contradictory wheels and the "faces" they present to the world. Like Machaut's *Voir dit,* Froissart's *Prison amoureuse* contains an alternation of letters and verse; like Machaut's consolatory *Remède de fortune,* Froissart's poem conflates the twin notions of art of love and *ars poetica.* But Froissart plays with the texts he emulates: his correspondents—a lover and a clerk—are two men; they are friends, not lovers, a kind of analytic, and somewhat abstract, breakdown of the poet-lover figure. The central experience of the text becomes, rather than love itself, the very writing of the text, with its narrative sections and the insertion of technically flawless *formes fixes.* The *Prison amoureuse* represents a sort of second-generation lyric *roman expérimental,* replete with mythological allusions, allegorical figures, and references to contemporary historical events.

The *Espinette amoureuse* (The amorous hawthorn) and the *Joli buisson de Jonece* (The pretty bush of Youth) illustrate the second of the two levels of poetic autobiography. The interconnected narratives of the *dittiers* recount the story (possibly fiction) of Froissart's personal experience of love; a sequence or progression is at issue here, as is the "history" of Froissart's persona. Written in 1369, by which time Froissart had passed his thirtieth year, the *Espinette* (4,198 mostly octosyllabic lines) first tells of his early youth (at age twelve he would lavish

little gifts on pretty young girls; he loved playing games—except chess; he hated school but devoured romances and love stories). Like Guillaume de Lorris he finally awakens to love in a garden alive with birdsong and budding trees; he forsakes his teacher Mercury for Venus (the astrological motif is important in this symbology of the ages of the growing boy and man), and finally meets the girl he will love (she is reading a romance by Adenet le Roi). Idyllic scenes ensue; his love service is accepted, but then, capriciously, the acceptance is withdrawn: the girl pulls at his hair and abruptly departs. The work ends, somewhat inconclusively, with the poet-lover interpreting this gesture as a token of affection—a closure reminiscent of the unfinished part I of the *Romance of the Rose.*

The *Buisson,* consequently, may be considered Froissart's "continuation" of the *Espinette.* It is presented as the transcription of a dream-adventure that befell the first-person narrator (not thirty-five years old): he visits a time in his past, when he was twenty and came to know the *buisson.* He dialogues with his own thoughts, which at verse 191 are suddenly personified as Philozophie. Philozophie urges the apparently recalcitrant poet-narrator to take up anew the "noble craft" of composing beautiful *dittiers* (these arguments occupy some 900 of the 5,442 lines); he is convinced to do so, and breaks into song (a virelai) when, at Philozophie's suggestion, he opens a coffer in which the portrait of the girl he had loved in the *Espinette* is stored. Ecstatic, he vows to serve not the lady but the portrait; and he dates the night of his contemplation of the portrait (30 November, exactly six months later than May, the lyric time of his—and the *Rose's*—love dream; a complete reversal). Thus, in preferring to serve an immutable and beautiful artifact—the portrait—instead of the capricious, changeable, real-life lady, Froissart, as one critic has convincingly put it, seems to be engaging in a dialogue with his earlier poetic work rather than in a specific love experience. By systematically reversing the patterns he had utilized in the *Espinette,* as well as the conditions initially set by both the *Rose* and Machaut's *Voir dit,* Froissart appears to be rejecting the lyric-amorous world he had inhabited.

In the second half of the *Buisson* the poet-narrator plays essentially the passive role of witness or recorder; he refuses to participate (other than as spectator) in the various games and in the poetry competition led by Jonece. The poet-narrator's progress is also suggested in the explanation Jonece provides, at his request, of the nature of the *buisson:* this bush has seven branches, representing the seven planets responsible for the various ages of man: the Moon, from birth to age four; Mercury, until age fourteen or fifteen; Venus, up to age twenty-five; the sun (worldly honors), until age thirty-five, the poet-narrator's present age. Following the order of this cosmic "clock," the poet is now ready for the tutelage of Mars, the planet of war and public recognition. At any rate, nothing comes of a short final interview he has with his erstwhile beloved, and as Jonece's company goes off to seek Amors in order that he may judge their poetry competition, the poet-narrator awakens from his dream. The world of the *Espinette* has ceased to be; the poet then composes a *Lay de Nostre Dame*—Our Lady, the absolute mediatrix of the only true judgment, that of Judgment Day. Henceforth, Froissart will forsake deeds and thoughts that might cost him salvation. The *buisson* image is transposed from its initial association with his burning desire to a new set of images associated with the Virgin: the burning bush of Moses and the tree of Jesse.

This remarkably subtle and lucid farewell to poetry, though not immediately accessible to the modern reader, constitutes one of the greatest poetic achievements of the French Middle Ages. Its importance as an example of medieval autobiography can hardly be exaggerated—for what, among other things, Froissart is describing in the *Buisson* is his emergence as a prose chronicler, as well as the intentions that inform the chronicle enterprise to which he will dedicate the rest of his life. The *Chroniques* will be no less than the poetic yet truthful record of his century. The *Joli buisson de Jonece* offers an incomparable insight into how a great fourteenth-century *clerc* understood the moral and instructional purposes of his own clerkliness, and of *clergie* in general, within the context of the terrible years of his age. With the *Buisson*, Froissart brought a new dynamics into the *Rose*-Machaut tradition—historicoautobiographical dynamics—and helped to set the stage for the new and expanded historiconational sense that would characterize so much French writing during the fifteenth century. In Froissart we witness the movement from consciousness of self to consciousness of nation, both being predicated on clearly defined, though seemingly intricate, poetic categories.

Modern historians have frequently displayed impatience with Froissart's *Chroniques,* with its early pro-English bias (Froissart was attached to the English court and adopted a pro-Valois stance only later in his career) and its limitless, and fawning, admiration for an "outmoded" chivalry. Perhaps most objectionable of all, to some, is Froissart's "uncritical" acceptance of his sources, his failure to analyze matters in terms of causes and effects. The *Chroniques* are praised chiefly for their extraordinary scope—Froissart seems to have been everywhere and to have talked to everyone, and what he did not see or hear about he learned from books that he subsequently copied, sometimes extensively—and for their brilliant color. In truth, little went on in France and England from 1325 to 1400 that did not find its place in the *Chroniques:* battles, triumphant entries, riots, sieges, pageants, insurrections, repressions, and plagues. The work is a treasure trove of anecdotes, facts, and opinions that translates, with considerable accuracy, what men thought and did (or thought they did) during the period; even Froissart's prejudices are pretty much those of the aristocracy at the time.

But considerable as they are as reportage, the *Chroniques* are more than that. Their underlying principles are closely related to those in the *dittiers.* The *Chroniques* replace the poetic service of love that the *dittiers* celebrated and analyzed with the service of arms. This service, like its love counterpart, is presented as an ideal that transcends mere combat and factiousness. For Froissart the Hundred Years War was a fratricidal evil redeemed only by the exemplary chivalry displayed by both sides (especially by the French). In recording the feats of his aristocratic contemporaries, he provided them with a kind of mirror portrait of what they ought—or believed themselves—to be: worthy defenders of a united Christian kingdom. The fact that such powerful patrons as Gaston III Phœbus welcomed him so warmly indicates that they recognized the best of themselves in his writings.

Instead of studying, say, political relationships or any particular individual Froissart concentrates on an almost supranational chivalry in both defeat and victory. His concept of chivalry (seemingly anachronistic for a period that witnessed the triumph of longbows over armed knights) is essentially poetic and consequently, in fourteenth-century terms, of an exalted moral order. Thus, Froissart's central idea allowed him to indulge in his natural, and very idiosyncratic, penchant for the relating of specific, concrete, and varied events as well as for sketching the careers of numerous personalities. These are all com-

270

ponents of an immense tableau to which Froissart intended to give coherent shape. The general effect of the *Chroniques,* consequently, is one of a large tapestry swarming with a host of detailed and individualized depictions—organized in such a way as to show hope and the possibility of glory for a France in which true chivalry could still be maintained, despite terrible adversity.

As was stated in the discussion of the *Romance of the Rose,* that great work was read ideologically as well as poetically. Many fourteenth-century writers considered it—especially Jean de Meun's continuation—a major compendium of opinions, judgments, and learning characterized by an extraordinary freedom of thought, even by intellectual license and seditiousness. If, at the close of the *Joli buisson de Jonece,* Froissart had announced, in favor of his newly begun *Chroniques,* his renunciation of the *Rose*-Machaut poetic tradition, so, in 1399 and 1400, did France's first well-known woman of letters (and ardent feminist), Christine de Pizan, speak out against poets and moralists (including Jean de Meun) who had slandered and libeled women. Christine's rejection of the *Rose* thus took place on moral and ideological grounds. As the famous Quarrel of the *Romance of the Rose* took shape, especially in 1401–1402, she undertook a remarkable defense of "virtuous ladies" in her monumental *Cité des dames* (City of ladies, 1405).

The fascinating and sympathetic Christine was born at Venice in 1364. Married in 1379 to Étienne du Castel, future secretary to the king, she was widowed in 1389, with three children to support. She lived by her pen, composing a great deal of lyric verse in typical fourteenth-century fashion, at the behest of her patrons, but with frequent, highly personal allusions to her sorrowful state. Talented, well educated—even erudite—Christine also composed several important prose works: the *Cité des dames* is, to a considerable extent, a translation of Boccaccio's *De claris mulieribus;* she compiled a life of Charles V for her patron, Philip the Bold of Burgundy. After the bloody Armagnac-Burgundian massacres of 1418, during which two of her *Rose* adversaries—Jean de Montreuil and Gontier Col—were murdered, she retired to a convent. Before her death, however, she was able to celebrate in verse the exploits of Joan of Arc.

The Quarrel of the *Romance of the Rose* began in earnest in 1401, with analyses of Jean de Meun's poem and several epistolary exchanges. Christine's arguments were countered by Jean de Montreuil (in French and in Latin), who qualified Jean de Meun as *magister noster* and accused Jean's detractors of reading him superficially, out of context (*Ep.* 120), as well as by the brothers Pierre and Gontier Col. Meanwhile, Christine was supported by a powerful ally, John Gerson, chancellor of the University of Paris, perhaps the greatest thinker of the age. Gerson intervened on four occasions in the Quarrel, with sermons, an epistle, and the treatise *Contre Le Ronmant de la Rose* (1402).

As was the case with Christine, Gerson's concerns are moral; he strongly disapproves of Jean de Meun's licentiousness and apparent defense of lechery. Thus, in Chastity's brief of complaint to Justice, Gerson writes: "He [Jean] shoots everywhere a fire more hot and more stinking than Greek fire: a fire of incredibly lecherous, filthy, and forbidden words—sometimes in the name of Venus or of Cupid or of Genius, often in his own name—that burns down my beautiful mansions and lodgings and my holy temples of human souls; and I am cast out from them, villainously." Gerson pulls out all the stops. His quarrel with the *Rose* goes deeper, even, than that of the indignant Christine, and he is often less "polite," less "literary," than his adversaries. Gerson is the profoundly Christian humanist who chooses to identify in the person of Jean de Meun, a—to him—dangerous and freethinking secularism. Person, poet, and poem are, in late-fourteenth-century style, seen as coequal. Jean, a clerk of "subtil engin" and "grande estude," endowed with the gift of "beau parler," is accused by Éloquance Théologienne, Gerson's mouthpiece, of supporting the corrupt cause of Fols Amoureus—that is, depicting sins as being free from shame and of "liberating" young people from any sense of modesty.

Gerson's condemnation of the *Rose* can therefore be read as a passionate and extraordinarily erudite denunciation of what he construes to be its "false eloquence," its poetically intertextual dependence on such "autres livres plussurs" (divers other books) as Ovid, the stories of Abelard and Heloise, Juvenal, the "odious" fables of Venus and Vulcan, of Pygmalion, and of Adonis. Was not Ovid, a "grand clerc et tres ingenieux poette," quite properly exiled for having produced his "miserable" *Art of Love?* And yet, though Ovid, a pagan, was punished by a pagan for this sin, Christians nowadays see fit to praise and defend the doctrines found in the *Rose* as well as the poetically ambiguous structures underpinning them. Gerson does no less than attack the entire mythopoetic structure of the *Rose,* in a rejection that transcends enormously Froissart's earlier farewell to (the *Rose*-Machaut tradition of) poetry, and that far outstrips Christine de Pizan's moral objections to Jean's supposed misogyny. Interestingly, he situates the debate on the terrain of rhetoric (eloquence), not specifically, as the early-thirteenth-century detractors of verse had done, on the terrain of truth versus mendaciousness. The relative merits of verse and prose are not at issue. Gerson clearly admires Jean's learning and technical virtuosity; he denounces all the more vociferously the uses—the poetry—to which this *clergie* had been put. As several scholars have pointed out, this is a characteristically humanist attitude: the way things are said has a "value" of its own, so saying the "wrong" things well is a matter of the highest intellectual and moral concern.

The defeat at Agincourt (and the concomitant loss of faith in chivalry), the imprisonment of Charles of Orléans, and the tribulations suffered by France up to, and after, the martyrdom of St. Joan (1431) mark, in effect, the close of the "terrible years." Nevertheless, the poetic and prose accomplishments of the fourteenth century did much to prepare the way for the fifteenth-century renovations that, in the French nation as well as in its literature, laid the groundwork for the rebirths to come.

RENEWAL AND INNOVATION

French literature from the time of Joan of Arc to that of Rabelais (up to about 1534, the year of the infamous *affaire des placards,* when an enraged Francis I decided to crack down on Protestant dissenters and their sympathizers) is marked by five undisputed masterpieces (not including Rabelais's *Pantagruel* [1532] and *Gargantua* [1534]), each representing a different genre: the *Mystère de la passion* (*ca.* 1450), by Arnoul Greban, an immense theatrical work in the miracle-mystery tradition; the *Farce de maistre Pierre Pathelin* (anonymous; *ca.* 1470), the most perfect of the many comic farces composed during the era; *Jehan de Saintré* (or *Petit Jehan de Saintré; ca.* 1456), a prose fiction written by the widely traveled and experienced courtier Antoine de la Sale, who also produced a number of other texts; the *Grand testament* (*ca.* 1462), by François Villon, a poetic composition (2,023 lines, mostly octosyllabic eight-line stanzas, or *huitains,* interspersed with various set pieces [lais, ballades, rondeaux]), perhaps the best-known medieval French poem; the prose *Mémoires* (in eight books, composed between 1489 and 1498: first, partial edi-

tion, in 1524; first complete edition in 1552) of Philippe de Comines, counselor to Louis XI and, after a period of disgrace, to Charles VIII and Louis XII.

Each of these works represents the tip of an iceberg, and can truly be understood only in terms of the life and works of its author, and/or with respect to the tradition and genre it exemplifies. Furthermore, the variety illustrated by these works, however extraordinary it might seem, does not do justice to other writers and literary currents present at different times during the century. Diversity and invention, both founded on a freewheeling attitude toward tradition, characterize the period. If it is difficult to identify a specific center of gravity proper to the literature of the time, this very disparateness denotes a new sense of growth and of possibility.

Thanks to the invention and spread of the printing press during the closing decades of the fifteenth century, the works of the period and prized earlier works were disseminated, with considerable efficiency, to subsequent centuries. The first edition of Villon's poems was printed in 1489 (during the 1530's and 1540's Clément Marot's corrected version of earlier editions was reissued some ten times); at least fourteen editions of the *Romance of the Rose* appeared between 1481 and 1528 (Lyons and Paris); Comines's *Mémoires* made its first appearance in print. What was known of medieval French literature (except to a very small number of antiquarians and philologists) up to the start of the twentieth century was largely the doing of the fifteenth century. Also, to all intents and purposes Old French, with its two-case declension system, had ceased to be employed in writing before the close of the fourteenth century; the "Middle French" of Villon and Comines is substantially the same language as that of Rabelais and Montaigne.

Although not included in the above list, Alain Chartier (*ca.* 1385–*ca.* 1433) can be said to illustrate trends that would later epitomize fifteenth-century literary activity—in a manner far more typical than, say, Charles of Orléans (who actually survived him by some three decades). Chartier was born in Bayeux, to a well-placed bourgeois family; he received an excellent education based on the Latin classics. He soon became attached to the French royal court at Bourges, appointed notary and secretary to the king. Chartier was a *clerc,* but hardly a professional poet and writer (like Froissart or Deschamps), or a churchman (like Gerson), or, for that matter, a noble poet (in the style of Charles of Orléans); he was a courtier, but not a military man imbued with the notion of *chevalerie.*

No fifteenth-century poet was more esteemed in his own time than Alain Chartier. This was because, although he worked earnestly within the conventions outlined by Deschamps, he struck an innovative note with respect to those conventions. Thus, like Comines at the close of the century, Chartier—subsequent to the disaster at Agincourt—distrusted the chivalric ethos that glorified war. His *Livre des quatre dames* (1415/1416; 3,531 lines), a "judgment" work somewhat in the style of Machaut's two *Jugements,* explores the misfortunes of four ladies (the lover of one has died; another has been taken prisoner; the third is missing; the fourth fled the battlefield): Which lady is most to be pitied? The discussion is merely a pretext allowing the poet to expose the folly of war and of faith in outmoded and inefficacious chivalric mythology. The prose *Quadrilogue invectif* (1422) takes up a similar argument: four characters (representing France, a knight, the people, the clergy) seek to ascribe responsibility for the destructions that have been visited on the realm. The knight accuses the people; the people, with extraordinary vehemence (and the author's obvious sympathy), accuse the knight; the clergy acts as judge. Knighthood is displayed as cowardly, lazy, and rapacious. Only the country, under its rightful king, will restore happiness and prosperity to all. This conclusion, throughout the century, would increasingly impose itself upon the minds and hearts of Frenchmen, and would be acted upon by the likes of St. Joan and Philippe de Comines.

In these works—especially in the *Quadrilogue* but also in the more traditional, or courtly, *Quatre dames*—there is something resembling the moral fervor of Christine de Pizan's and Gerson's invective against Jean de Meun. Ciceronian eloquence and Cato-like moral righteousness prevail. Alain Chartier, I believe, helped to blaze the trail that would be followed by the humanism of the high Renaissance in France, with its emphasis on ethical, spiritual, and political, rather than (as in Italy) aesthetic, concerns.

However, lest an overly one-sided impression be given of Chartier's work, mention must be made of his "La belle dame sans merci" (1424; 800 octosyllables), one of the most popular texts of the fifteenth century. Beautifully crafted, this work exploits the old convention of the lover who, spurned by his lady and, despite his remonstrances, unable to move her, dies, despairing. The poem rises above simple ba-

nality by the perfection of its execution. Indeed, it occasioned poetic debates (particularly among the ladies at court) to which Alain Chartier responded, with much grace and charm, by composing his verse "Excusacion aux dames." Even during the darkest times of the Hundred Years War—perhaps because it *was* so unhappy a time—the games of a refined civilization had to go on.

Despite his impassioned concern for France and her people, Alain Chartier (like the overwhelming majority of the writers who have been discussed) wrote essentially for an aristocratic audience: he was not read by, or to, the "people." Aside from popular song, the one genre to cut across social boundaries in the period from 1325 to about 1550 was the theater; and by the fifteenth century the theater had come to occupy a central position in French national life. Religious theater was represented by the *miracles* (devoted mainly to the Virgin) and the *mystères* (from the Latin *ministerium* [service], not *mysterium* [mystery], though it is probable that eventually the two terms were conflated). Secular theater was confined largely to such comic forms as the didactic *moralité,* the *sottie* (literally, "foolishness"), dramatic monologues, and, above all, the farce; in tone and manner the farce recalls the spirit of the old *fabliau,* with its dim view of the righteousness of human nature and its amusing, often coarse, language. Both secular and religious theater made generous use of earlier popular literature (chansons de geste, hagiography), and incorporated or popularized biblical material, incidents from romance narrative, and devotional writings.

Whereas the *miracles,* like their earlier narrative counterparts, depict the intervention of divine power in the lives of ordinary men and women—usually at a moment of crisis, when the Virgin's or the saint's loving help is sorely needed—the *mystères* focus on the biblical story of the Incarnation as it took—and takes—place in human history and in the church year. The *miracles* dominated religious theater during the fourteenth century; in the final third of that century the *mystères* started to come into their own.

Liturgical drama in French has a lengthy history, reaching well back into the twelfth century. Its earliest function was to illustrate, in dramatic form, the two greatest events of the Christian calendar: the Nativity (or Incarnation) and the Resurrection. In the fourteenth century, however, emphasis was increasingly placed on the Passion and the Crucifixion, almost as though, during those terrible years of war and plague, people saw in Christ's holy suffering an image of their own pain and hurt, as well as the hope of redemption and eventual salvation. The *mystères de la Passion* celebrate the victory of eternal life over misery and death.

By the late 1300's organizations known as *confréries*—societies for the composition and the production of Passion plays and other "saintly" works—had sprung up in several French towns; the Paris *confrères* were officially chartered by Charles VI in 1402, becoming thereby the first institutionalized theatrical company in France. At once clerkly and popular, the *mystères* were spectacularly, lavishly theatrical. Rich costumes, large casts (as many as 200 players), complicated machinery (thanks to which angels could "fly" over the stage), and elaborate scene design characterize these productions. They lasted for hours, even days, and were enormously costly.

In a very real sense, then, the *mystères* represent a collective achievement on the part of the towns that staged them. Surviving illustrated manuscripts underscore the variety and the numbers of those who had a hand in these productions. The texts constitute variations upon one another, almost as though there were one "ideal" *Passion*, of which each individual text was but a slightly idiosyncratic version. Thus, the most famous *Passion*, that of Arnoul Greban (more than 30,000 octosyllables), closely follows that of Eustache Marcadé (*d.* 1440), who successfully introduced into his work lengthy theological debates and other bookishness, in an effort, perhaps, to palliate somewhat the brutality of the many bloody scenes of torture and execution. Played over four days (*journées*), Greban's magnificent text, despite its inevitable longueurs, combines fidelity to the Gospel accounts of the Passion with episodes of horrifying bloodletting and scenes of considerable dramatic poignancy (for instance, when the Virgin touchingly beseeches her son to forgo the worst experiences of the Crucifixion).

Although modern viewers might be repelled by the length and the inclusiveness of the *mystères* (one of these, devoted to the acts of the apostles, contains more than 60,000 lines), this very weightiness and variety contributed to their success in the fifteenth century. The audiences of the *mystères* must have sought total immersion in the overwhelming theatrical experience these dramas provided; the *mystères*, after all, were profoundly felt acts of faith on the part of both their producers and their spectators. (The success of the French Passion plays spread far beyond the borders of the realm; they were imitated and adapted throughout Europe.) Nevertheless, with the transformations that took place in religious sensibility during the Reformation and the Counter-Reformation, the *mystères* came to be judged in France as unworthy and immoral; in November 1548 the Paris *parlement* forbade the *confrères* henceforth to produce "the Mystery of the Passion of Our Savior or other sacred Mysteries." A fascinating chapter in French literary history thus came to a close.

In several respects the farce and other forms of comic theater (which grew in popularity simultaneously with the *miracles* and the *mystères*) constitute the obverse of the French theatrical medal of the time. The origins of this comic drama are impossible to pinpoint, probably because of its improvisational nature and because the plays were not deemed fit to be recorded in writing. However, it would seem likely that the twin traditions of oral literature (such as certain chansons de geste, *dits,* and other jongleur-inspired forms) and of popular amusement (of varying degrees of sophistication, like Adam de la Halle's *Feuillée* or the *fabliaux*) constitute the backdrop for the new comic theater. After all, *fabliau* elements are detectable in many *miracles,* both narrative and dramatic. As was the case with the *mystères, confréries*—such as that of the *Basoche,* founded in the fourteenth century, or the *Enfants sans souci*—were formed to play these comic works; the *confréries* frequently were made up of former law students and clerks, and grew up around the *parlement* and other legal institutions.

Of these comic genres the farce is the most down-to-earth and most like the *fabliau.* (Farces, incidentally, provide the best documentation of the racy colloquial language spoken in the fifteenth and sixteenth centuries.) These entertainments were designed principally to make people laugh. The cuckolded husband, the scheming wife, the astute young lover—the eternal triangle is the very stuff of farce, along with ruses, cheating, and, frequently, splendid wordplay and coarse slapstick. The *Farce de maistre Pierre Pathelin* rises head and shoulders above all other surviving farces. This work of some 1,600 octosyllabic lines tells the following story: A draper is persuaded by Pathelin, an unscrupulous (Renard-like) lawyer, to sell him some cloth and to come later to his house in order to collect payment. The draper does so, only to discover Pathelin in bed, apparently ill and babbling a jargon of unintelligible foreign words; he goes away. Next the draper accuses a shepherd in his employ of stealing sheep; the shepherd engages Pathelin to defend him. The draper is astounded to find a live and well Pathelin in court, and becomes confused. He alternately accuses Pathelin and the shepherd, mixing up the lost cloth with the lost sheep. Try as he may, the judge cannot follow the proceedings. To make matters worse, Pathelin has advised the shepherd to bleat at all the questions put to him. Finally the shepherd, judged to be an idiot, is effectively declared innocent and the case is dismissed. But when Pathelin asks him for his fee, he answers "Bée." Pathelin the trickster is outwitted.

Pathelin, still played today, has given to the French language a word (*patelin,* flattering hypocrite) and an expression (the judge's exasperated "Revenons à ces moutons" [Let's get back to those sheep—that is, to the subject]). Its acute satire of law courts, its clever reversals of plot, and, above all, its artful characterizations demonstrate the anonymous author's sure grasp of the craft of comedy. Pathelin is the very type of the fast-talking, swindling shyster; the draper epitomizes the miserly shopkeeper; the seemingly gullible shepherd (named Aignelet, Little Lamb) turns out to be shrewder than the others; and Pathelin's wife, Guillemette, is her husband's all too willing accomplice. Very much of its own time, *Pathelin* also initiated an ongoing, peculiarly French brand of comic theater that received its highest expression in the work of Molière. *Pathelin* demonstrates that, in the hands of a master, even presumably so base a genre as the late-medieval farce could be utilized in the creation of a new—or renewed— kind of joyful canonical chef d'oeuvre, the popularity and charm of which would endure to this day, and that would therefore transcend both the topicality of its own time and the limitations of simple entertainment.

Like the theater, prose fiction underwent a remarkable renewal during the fifteenth century. The fourteenth-century tradition of verse and prose romance narrative (*Méliador,* the *Voeux du paon,* and the vast compilation known as *Perceforest*) gave way to a new kind of satiric "realism" in the *Quinze joies de mariage* (Fifteen joys of marriage, *ca.* 1400–1410; sometimes attributed, though improbably, to Antoine de la Sale), an acerbically misogynistic and ruthless denunciation of marriage (the joys of which are in reality miseries), replete with cuckolded husbands and vain, pleasure-seeking wives. Marriage is but a source of pain and expense for the poor husband, who is led around by the nose by wife and children (especially daughters). The anonymous author

seems to be siding with Jean de Meun in the *Rose* Quarrel. Similar *fabliau*-type situations prevail in the collection of stories titled *Cent nouvelles nouvelles* (1456–1462), borrowed in part from Boccaccio. Composed by or attributed to a variety of authors (of whom some thirty-five are named), these stories were recited at the court of Philip, duke of Burgundy (mentioned as one of the authors). Many are quite bawdy, full of sexual exploits and deceptions, but unlike the *Quinze joies,* the *Cent nouvelles* are, for the most part, comically, even jokingly, cheerful— redolent of what the French call *l'esprit gaulois,* a kind of earthy, stag-party humor—and laced with amusing, realistic detail in both language and anecdote.

Once again, a single fifteenth-century work appears to have drawn upon all these tendencies—romance narrative, disabused and ironic "realism," as well as the highly pedagogical character of much early humanistic writing—in order to present something new: Antoine de la Sale's *Jehan de Saintré.* Antoine de la Sale (*ca.* 1385–after 1469), born in Provence, served the house of Anjou for some fifty years. He became tutor to the three sons of Louis of Luxembourg in 1448. He traveled extensively, especially in Italy. His writings include *La salade* (*ca.* 1440), a memoir on government; *La salle* (*ca.* 1451), a moral treatise composed for the sons of Louis; and, in addition to *Saintré,* a curious tale recounting a trip he made to the Apennines in 1420 (*Le paradis de la reine Sibylle,* a version of the Tannhäuser legend); and *Le réconfort de Madame de Fresne* (1457), a consolation work describing how two mothers reacted to the deaths of their sons.

Saintré was written when its author was more than seventy. Like Froissart's *Méliador,* though in prose, *Saintré* is a historical fiction, commencing in the reign of John II (1350–1364), son of Philip VI. "Little" Jehan de Saintré is a thirteen-year-old page at court, befriended by a well-born widow identified only as the Dame des Belles Cousines (because the queen refers to her as "Fair Cousin") or, more simply, as "Madame." Madame takes charge of the naive page, at first mocking him gently in public for his callowness, but later instructing him in deportment, letters, and morals. As sixteen years pass, she falls in love with him, and he with her. The time comes for him to take leave of her (with her encouragement) in order to gain worldly fame through tournaments and acts of prowess. Saintré returns in great triumph, but after a period of doing nothing, decides—this time without the permission of either the king or Madame—to go off on his own. Madame is disconsolate; she requests the queen's permission to return home. On her way she stops at an abbey that her ancestors had endowed. There she meets a vigorous, and rather vulgar, young abbot who, after plying her with food and drink, seduces her; a violent passion ensues, as carnal as her former love for Saintré had been idealistic. Saintré returns, finds Madame changed toward him, challenges the abbot (who first defeats him in an unequal, and "unchivalrous," wrestling bout, but whom he vanquishes at arms the following day, running his dagger through his cheeks and tongue), and brings about Madame's disgrace at court. Saintré then goes on to greater knightly glory.

The fiction is very rich; ironies abound. Both Saintré and Madame are to blame for the unhappy end of their love; she is perhaps overly possessive, he never quite grows up. The abbot is an unregenerately disgusting figure, but by the same token, Saintré's devotion to tournaments is depicted as, in some respects, puerile. At times, matters are presented as though the reign of John II was really the "good old days of yore," when knighthood, and not crass materialism, was truly in flower. Yet, knightly fame is potentially as empty as the ideology of love, which, *Saintré* shows, can easily crumble before the onslaught of food, drink, and sex. And even worse than the ideology of love is the sheer power of love (or perhaps lust): apparently no one, and nothing, can withstand it—neither emperors nor popes nor, ostensibly, the most virtuous women can resist its inevitable treachery. Antoine de la Sale, to the end a pedagogue, seems to be saying that only clear, disabused thinking and self-evaluation really count; that, for the most part, human life is but a comedy. Despite its longueurs, then, *Jehan de Saintré* does represent an important milestone in the history of prose fiction, and not least for the ambiguous and complex role in which it casts its author and narrator, who no longer represent the typical medieval clerk figure. It proposes an interesting response to Froissart—both *Méliador* and the *Chroniques*—by incorporating and analyzing that great writer's concept of the ideal (and the limitations) of the chivalric arms and love.

Something in Antoine de la Sale would, I believe, have reacted positively to François Villon's nostalgic and haunting refrain line "Mais ou est le preux Charlemagne?" (But where is the noble Charlemagne?—*Testament*, Rychner and Henry, v. 364). Both the author of *Saintré* and the author of the *Tes-*

tament were aware that a certain noble time—noble despite its glaring defects—had irremediably passed away. But for Villon, the last and perhaps the greatest and most appealing poet of the *Rose*-Machaut tradition, the *Ubi sunt?* theme serves ends more properly those of the lyric poet than those of an inventive prose novelist. Villon invented nothing. Every form, every "idea," every device of his may easily be found in the works of his predecessors. He was a genius at recombining and at reversing—and, consequently, at renewing—what had come before him. That, precisely, is his originality: the effect of the whole of his poem is unlike that of any other.

Perusal of Villon's works (though unreliable) and of archival (especially police) records has permitted the following tentative reconstruction of his life. François de Montcorbier, also known as des Loges, was born at Paris in 1431 or 1432; he would later adopt the name of his benefactor, Guillaume de Villon, chaplain at St. Benoît-le-Bétourné. In 1449 he received the bachelor's degree at the Paris Faculty of Arts; in 1452 he earned his *licence* and the degree of master of Arts. These student years witnessed Villon's first brushes with the law. In 1455 he took part in a brawl that led to his killing a priest, Philippe Sermoise; he was banished from Paris. At the start of the following year he received a pardon for this act of manslaughter, returned to Paris, and, while composing his first major work, *Le lais* (The bequest, a 320-line parody of a last will and testament, written in octosyllabic eight-line stanzas, or *huitains*), he participated (around Christmastime) in the robbery of 500 ecus in gold from the Collège de Navarre. Once again he left Paris, this time for Angers and some four years of wandering about central France. At Blois he entered one of the poetry competitions sponsored by Charles of Orléans.

The summer of 1461 found Villon imprisoned, on the orders of his archenemy, Bishop Thibault d'Aussigny at Meun-sur-Loire; he was freed on the occasion of the newly crowned Louis XI's passing through the town. After a short sojourn in the Bourbonnais, Villon returned to the outskirts of Paris, where early in 1462, it is said that he composed his masterpiece, *Le grand testament*, in which he combined works written earlier with new material. In late 1462 he was again imprisoned, this time in Châtelet, but was released in November against his promise to restore 120 gold ecus to the Collège de Navarre. Arrested once more for brawling and assault, the three-time loser was sentenced to death by hanging. It was then that he composed the beautiful

"Ballade des pendus" (Ballad of the hanged men, also known as the "Épitaphe Villon"). In January 1463 Villon's death sentence was commuted to exile from Paris. There is no further record of him (apart from two—probably spurious—anecdotes recounted by Rabelais); he perhaps led the vagabond life of an itinerant jongleur.

In addition to the above-named works, Villon composed a number of other ballades, verse epistles, requêtes, a rondeau, a debate between the heart and the body, and—though this has been disputed—several jargon or slang poems. This body of work appears slim when compared with the productions of his predecessors.

Many of Villon's modern readers have failed to take sufficient stock of the conventionality of his poetry—his use of traditional topics (such as the Ubi sunt?), of well-known images (for instance, Alexander as the symbol of largess), his constant allusion to such poetic antecedents as the Rose and Charles of Orléans, his repeated utilization of Christian motifs and texts (charitable love versus lust; the Credo; the Bible), his fidelity to the strict forms of the Machaut–seconde rhétorique manner, the references to stock personages in medieval literature (Charlemagne, Helen of Troy, Narcissus), his adoption—and renewal—of certain ageless poetic-rhetorical procedures (for instance, the juxtaposed descriptions of the young and beautiful/old and ugly Heaulmiere who "regrets" her youth; both portraits, in classic medieval style, start with the woman's head and move downward). Consequently, specialist scholars have felt it their duty to point out Villon's lack of "originality," and to caution against applying to Villon the modern equation of poetic creativity and the direct, or "spontaneous," sensorial experience of seeing, hearing, or touching. These scholars are warning—and quite rightly—that Villon's "life" is essentially a fiction, recounted in the traditional bookish terms of his time. His "sincerity" is necessarily something other than the kind associated with certain romantic lyric poets.

But can a written "life," built up with components furnished by literary tradition and infused with a poetically conceived order, be as authentically meaningful as one in which the mediation of "literature" is systematically reduced to a minimum? Villon and the traditions that culminate in him illustrate that the power of writing can—indeed, did—confer meaning on what otherwise might have been an inchoate personal identity; and, I further believe, Villon was extremely conscious of this power.

"François Villon"—"le povre Villon"—is the creation of the Testament; it is also that poem's informing principle. Villon's Testament constitutes perhaps the most perfect explication and utilization of what is creatively tautological in what I have called, in these pages, the "lyric triangle."

Readers have long been fascinated by the multiplicity of identities assumed by the poet-narrator in the Grand testament. Just as the Romance of the Rose imparted through poetry a summalike coherence to an extraordinary multiplicity of ideas, facts, lore, opinions, and science, so, it may be contended, does the Testament give coherent shape to the myriad elements that constitute an "individual" man.

In the oddly incomplete sentence of the first stanza of the Testament, the poet-narrator identifies himself as an "I" who "had drunk all my shames," partly foolish and partly wise, by the time of "my thirtieth year," and as the victim of Thibault d'Assigny. Later he refers to himself in the third person as "le povre Villon." As he tells the story of his misfortunes and (fewer) joys, and as he makes his various comic bequests, he does two interesting things: he reveals himself as, among other things, a scholar, a pauper, a sinner, a penitent, a jailbird, a lecher, a pimp, a victim of love, and a poet (the author, he claims, of the Romance of the Devil's Fart); he witnesses—sometimes taking on the guise of a Peeping Tom—the doings and sayings of an extraordinary number of people. The latter include his contemporaries, historical personages, and characters from books. The Testament swarms with people of all kinds, ages, and walks of life. And they are present because, to one degree or another, they are all affiliated with the poet-narrator.

Just as the poet-narrator is refracted into an "I" and a third-person "povre Villon," so do barriers between him and "others" tend to break down or to be recast. "Villon" is simultaneously "himself"—poet and he-who-experiences—and everyone: all history, all fiction, all society. On occasion his multiplicity of identity attains cosmic proportions, as in the ballade-prayer he describes as having written as a legacy for his "povre" mother in order that she might recite her Creed and pray to Our Lady for the intercession of her Son. The mother, depicted as an unlettered old woman, speaks the words written by Villon, and a curious verbal transformation occurs.

The first stanza could never have been "said" by the ignorant mother; it is replete with pompous Latinisms ("Dame du ciel, regente terrienne,/Emperiere des infernaux palus" [Queen of Heaven, earthly regent,/Empress of the infernal swamps]; vv. 873f.). The second stanza is less ponderous, but it, too, is full of literary allusion ("Pardonne moy comme a l'Egypcienne,/Ou comme il feist au clerc Theophilus" [May he pardon me as he did St. Mary the Egyptian/ Or the cleric Theophilus]; vv. 885f.). The third stanza is entirely colloquial; Villon's words have "become" those of his illiterate mother, as, perhaps, her simple faith has become his own: instead of reading books, she tells the stories she sees painted on the walls of her parish church. The final stanza, or envoi, comprises seven lines; it is written in a style that combines the learnedness of stanza I and the colloquial nature of stanza III, with the roughness of both quite smoothed over: "Vous portastes, digne Vierge, princesse,/Iesus regnant qui n'a ne fin ne cesse" (You carried, worthy Virgin, princess,/Reigning Jesus who is everlasting; vv. 903f.). The wording, almost classical in its simplicity, is plausible for both Villon and his mother. As if to confirm this blending of two voices in a single common denominator of discourse, the initial letters of the lines, read downward, spell VILLONE, the feminine form of his own (assumed) name. Thus, in this poem composed by a son so that his mother might pray to the Mother for the loving intercession of the Son, Villon's poetic persona, through the bookish device of the acrostic, expands to include—to enrich and to be enriched by—the persona of his mother, an illiterate woman whose Christian faith, to him, is exemplary.

It is in this kind of utilization of the traditional resources of medieval poetic art that Villon's genius resides. Many other illustrations of his craft could be adduced. However, it must suffice merely to state what Villon's great poem proves: that, when manipulated by a master, the conventions of medieval literary practice were entirely capable of generating some of the finest and most sympathetic poetry ever known. The *Testament* is an authentic and priceless illustration of the poetic act.

As has been suggested, Villon's *Testament* stands at the end of a tradition (which it nevertheless renews) rather than at the start of anything formally new. Only two poets—Guillaume Coquillart (*ca.* 1450–1510) and Henri Baude (*ca.* 1430–*ca.* 1496), who, like Villon, served a prison term—can be considered his imitators. Nevertheless, features of Villon's verse are discernible in the works of his contemporaries and successors. For example, the tone of much of his writing—even its highly dramatic flavor—seems to echo that of the Basochiens (royal clerks), whose dramatic monologues, *sotties, mo-*

ralités, and farces mix together topical allusion (especially of a low-life sort), coarse diction, and—on occasion—stylistic nobility in a blend very reminiscent of the *Testament*.

Similar concerns characterize the writings of the group of poets that dominated French verse in the years around 1500, the *grands rhétoriqueurs,* or practitioners of the *seconde rhétorique,* who first flourished in the relatively relaxed atmosphere of the court of Burgundy (after 1430 the only true courtly center of literature) up to about 1482, when the duchy was annexed to the French kingdom, and then in Brittany and in France itself. Less touched by the ravages of war than France, and in its own right a significant power center during the fifteenth century, Burgundy offered a haven to men of letters. Chroniclers like Enguerrand de Monstrelet (*d.* 1453), the self-acknowledged continuator of Froissart, poet-chroniclers like Georges Chastellain (*ca.* 1405/1415–1475) and Jean Molinet (1435–1507), and the poet-memorialist Olivier de La Marche (*ca.* 1425–1502) both fitted into, and reflected, the chivalric ceremoniousness and pomp favored at the ducal court.

Just as there was something of playacting in the chivalric activities fostered by the Burgundian court, so the verse of the *rhétoriqueurs* insisted far more on manner than on substance. Whereas in Villon there was a revitalization of the *Rose*-Machaut tradition, in the works of Chastellain and Olivier de la Marche there is a carrying to an extreme of the technical virtuosity prized by certain representatives of that tradition. Molinet's *Art de rhétorique* lists at its beginning some thirty verse forms and rhythms in which the poet was supposed to be proficient. Verbal artifice for its own sake is at issue here; what the poem says, or refers to, appears frequently to be systematically undercut, but without Villon's richly meaningful irony.

Nevertheless, the *rhétoriqueurs* enjoyed immense popularity in nostalgic aristocratic circles as well as among later men of letters (like Octavien de St. Gelais, Guillaume Crétin, and Jean Marot) who represent, in literary history, the transition from the poetry of the Middle Ages to the Italian-influenced poetry of the sixteenth century. Like Eustache Deschamps, the *rhétoriqueurs* defended the dignity and what might be called the "science," or know-how, of poetry. The group produced only one interesting poet, Jean Lemaire de Belges, who combined his training in *rhétorique* with reading in the works of Dante and Petrarch, and who, for this reason, is usually judged to be a precursor of the mid-sixteenth-century poetic school known as the Pléiade; indeed, the Pléiade claimed him as an honored predecessor. However, by and large the *rhétoriqueurs* as such have not enjoyed a good press over the years; their work has often been cited to prove the thesis of a "tired" and "declining" Middle Ages, though this accusation is neither entirely just nor historically accurate.

The Burgundian court was also the stage on which the early period of the career of Philippe de Comines, the last author to be considered here, was played out. Born in Flanders (*ca.* 1447), a Burgundian dominion, he began in 1464 to serve Charles the Bold, who would become duke three years later; he had the rank of squire (*écuyer*). But Comines was temperamentally and intellectually ill-suited for the service of a lord who still held to the (for him) discredited chivalric prejudices of yesteryear. Comines hated war. To him it was wasteful, even foolish, especially when the sovereign might more easily secure his ends by diplomacy and negotiation. (Comines's description of the Battle of Montlhéry [1465] is a masterpiece of irony, for instance, when he depicts a group of armed men cautiously attacking an enemy formation, only to discover that the "foe" is a patch of tall thistles.) He and Louis XI were, quite simply, made for each other. Consequently, during the Normandy campaign of 1472, Comines defected from the Burgundian side and joined the royal forces. The king realized his good fortune; he appointed Comines his counselor, gave him a handsome pension and lands, and arranged his marriage to a rich heiress.

Throughout his reign (1461–1483) Louis recoiled from nothing—cajoling, threats, gifts of money or land, retractions, betrayals, and, when absolutely unavoidable, war—in order to enlarge and consolidate his kingdom; he trusted nobody and was moody, but he was a magnificent administrator, reforming (and of course centralizing) finances as well as the judiciary, inviting foreign and domestic capital investment, creating the first viable postal service. Comines witnessed all this and participated in it. He undertook the composition of his *Mémoires* about 1489, at the suggestion of Angelo Cato, bishop of Vienne, who wished to utilize Comines's testimony in a Latin volume he planned to write on the reign of Louis XI. At the time Comines was in disgrace and was confined to his château at Dreux; previously, on the orders of Charles VIII, he had spent more than a year in one of the iron cages of the castle of Loches. He worked for about a decade on the eight books of the *Mémoires,* with time out for limited periods of further royal service, and died in 1511.

Comines's *Mémoires* constitute a kind of anti-Froissart. He has no use for ideology, chivalric or other, and he shows no inclination to describe, in tableau form, either great battles or any kind of mass event. He is interested in power—in the means of attaining power and of keeping it. For him men are neither innately good nor innately evil; they are motivated by their own interests, as well as by their competence or foolishness—not by ideals (to which, however, they sometimes pay lip service). Yet, Comines was no cynic. In his admiring and very touching portrait of Louis XI, he does not fail to point out the joylessness of the king's life—the portrait is also that of the end of chivalric *joie*—and the suffering he experienced, largely in his soul, because of the suffering he had caused others. Underlying the *Mémoires,* along with what has been called Comines's relentless destruction of the myths of chivalry, there is, however, a profound sense of the grand design—the restoration and, indeed, the rightness of French royal power—to which, in his active life, he had contributed so much. This fact has perhaps not been sufficiently emphasized by modern scholars, who have chosen to see in Comines a kind of "professional" historian obsessed with the analysis of cause and effect within the course of human events.

To be sure, the *Mémoires* are a monumental work of political and historical analysis—the first "modern" work of this kind—but the analysis is anchored, first, in the set of goals to be (or that had been) achieved by Louis XI and, second, in Comines's highly moral sense of the realities of the human potential. Over and over again Comines seems to be saying that what men do, or have done, allows the best determination of what they are capable of doing, and under what conditions. Thus, he contrasts his version of Louis's grand design—its reality, its practicality—with the futility of the chivalric ideal espoused in the past and still mouthed by some contemporaries; but that does not mean that the design, for all its apparently simple practicality, is one whit less grand. Comines's moral sense and his grasp of historical structure transform his work; the *Mémoires* fascinate, regardless of whether the reader cares much about the events of the reign of Louis XI.

Comines claims to have learned neither Greek nor Latin. He means, surely, that he had no systematic literary training (of the sort displayed by the *rhétoriqueurs*). Perhaps, in his view, such training had become merely the equivalent in the intellectual sphere of the gamesmanship he associated with the verbiage of those who claimed to serve knightly ideals. At any rate, like Joinville, he had confidence in what he saw and in what he saw fit to relate. His person—like Villon's persona(s)—shines forth in the *Mémoires*, in the French language, which, because it is what he spoke, was for him an authentic vehicle of plain truth. So, despite what has been said and written, the *Mémoires* truly constitute a celebration: of a mature and universally personal language; of the dignity of prose; and of their subject. Villon made private use of the *Rose*-Machaut tradition, and thereby renewed that tradition; Comines did as much with the prose instrument bequeathed to him by Froissart, Chartier, and the Burgundians, but his renewal constitutes, in the final analysis, a genuine innovation. He is the link between what Joinville had done and, starting with Montaigne, what future honest observers of human events would endeavor to do.

This survey has come to a close. But such is not the case with the subject matter. A discussion of François Rabelais and of others would naturally follow from what has been said. As John Fox has put it, every age is a "middle" age, relating what preceded it to what comes after. The centuries we have dealt with constitute, in reality, a beginning: the story of how men—and women—learned to write and to reconcile what they wrote with what they read (largely in Latin) and with what they experienced. The variety is mind-shattering; their talent, collectively and individually, is breathtaking. Their unique creation is easily the equal of classical Latin antiquity and deserving of consideration as the foundation of what we, in the Western tradition, now feel, believe, say, and write. To use a favorite twelfth-century image, we are the dwarfs perched on their high and broad shoulders. We will be much the poorer if we forget this truth.

BIBLIOGRAPHY

For a summary listing of dictionaries and grammars, anthologies, bibliographies, and general critical works, see the bibliography for French Literature: To 1200.

Studies. Pierre Yves Badel, *Le Roman de la Rose au XIVe siècle: Étude de la réception de l'oeuvre* (1980); Jean Dufournet, *La Destruction des mythes dans les "Mémoires" de Philippe de Commynes* (1966); Janet Ferrier, *French Prose Writers of the 14th and 15th Centuries* (1966); Douglas Kelly, *Medieval Imagination: Rhetoric and the Poetry of Courtly Love* (1978); Daniel Poirion, *Le Poète et le prince, l'évolution du lyrisme courtois de Guillaume de Machaut à Charles d'Orléans* (1965); Jens Ras-mussen, *La prose narrative française du XVe siècle* (1958); Karl D. Uitti, "Vernacularization and Old French Romance Mythopoesis," in Rupert T. Pickens, ed., *The Sower and the Seed* (1983).

Texts and translations. Aucassin et Nicolette: Jean Dufournet, ed. and French trans., *Aucassin et Nicolette* (1973); Eugene Mason, trans., *Aucassin and Nicolette and Other Mediaeval Romances and Legends* (1915). Philippe de Comines: J. Calmette (with G. Durville) ed., *Philippe de Comines (Mémoires)*, 3 vols. (1924–1925); Samuel Kinser, ed., *The Memoires of Philippe de Commynes*, Isabelle Cazeaux, trans., 2 vols. (1969–1973). Fabliaux: Robert Hellman and Richard O'Gorman, trans., *Fabliaux: Ribald Tales from the Old French* (1965); Anatole de Montaiglon and Gaston Raynaud, ed., *Recueil général et complet des fabliaux des XIIIe et XIVe siècles*, 6 vols. (1872–1890). Jean Froissart: Anthime Fourier, ed., *"Dits" et "Debats," Avec en appendice quelques poèmes de Guillaume de Machaut; L'Espinette amoureuse* (1963, 1972); *Le joli buisson de Jonece* (1975); *La prison amoureuse* (1974); Thomas Johnes, ed. and trans., *Chronicles of England, France, Spain . . . by Sir John Froissart*, 2 vols. (1802–1805; latest ed., 1901); Gaston Raynaud *et al.*, *Chroniques de Jean Froissart*, 15 vols. (1869–1975). Jean de Joinville: Margaret Renée Bryers Shaw, trans., *Chronicles of the Crusades* (1963); Natalis de Wailly, ed., *Jean, sire de Joinville. Histoire de saint Louis, Credo, et Lettre à Louis X, texte original, accompagné d'une traduction*, 2nd ed. (1874). Guillaume de Machaut: Ernest Hoepffner, ed., *Œuvres de Guillaume de Machaut*, 3 vols. (1908–1921). Pierre Pathelin: Kate Franks, trans., *Master Peter Patelan: A Fifteenth Century Farce* (1975); Cedric Edward Pickford, ed., *La Farce de maistre Pierre Pathelin* (1967). Christine de Pizan: Christine de Pizan, *The Book of the City of Ladies*, Earl Jeffrey Richards, trans. (1982), an adequate French version of the text is not available at present; Maurice Roy, ed., *Œuvres poétiques de Christine de Pisan* (1886–1896). Renard: Mario Roques, ed., *Le Roman de Renart* (1948–1974). Rhétoriqueurs: Ernest Langlois, ed., *Recueil d'arts de Seconde Rhétorique* (1902). Antoine de la Sale: Irvine Gray, trans., *Little John of Saintré* (1931); Jean Misrahi and Charles Knudson, eds., *Jehan de Saintré* (1965). The Quest of the Holy Grail: Pauline M. Matarasso, *The Quest of the Holy Grail* (1969); Albert Pauphilet, ed., *La Queste del saint Graal; roman du XIIIe siècle* (1967). The Romance of the Rose: Charles Dahlberg, trans., *The Romance of the Rose* (1971); Ernest Langlois, ed., *Le Roman de la Rose*, 5 vols. (1914–1924); Felix Lecoy, ed., *Le Roman de la Rose*, 3 vols. (1970–1974). François Villon: Peter Dale, trans., *The Legacy, the Testament, and Other Poems of François Villon* (1973); Jean Rychner and Albert Henry, eds., *Le testament Villon*, 2 vols. (1974).

KARL D. UITTI

[See also **Adam de la Halle; Anglo-Norman Literature; Arthurian Literature; Aucassin et Nicolette; Bodel, Jean; Cent**

Nouvelles Nouvelles; Charles of Orléans; Chartier, Alain; Christine de Pizan; Chronicles, French; Comines (Commynes), Philippe de; Deschamps, Eustache; Drama, Western European; Fabliau and Comic Tale; France; Froissart, Jehan; Gautier de Coinci; Gerson, John; Grail, Legend of; Grandes Chroniques de France; Guillaume de Lorris; Hundred Years War; Jean de Meun; Joinville, John of; Machaut, Guillaume de; Paris, University of; Passion Plays, French; Quinze Joies de Mariage; Renard the Fox; Rhétoriqueurs; Romance of the Rose; Rutebeuf; Villehardouin, Geoffroi de; Villon, François.]

FRENCH LITERATURE: DIDACTIC

FRENCH LITERATURE: DIDACTIC. Among the principal species of didactic literature in French are the bestiaries, lapidaries, and herbals. Bestiaries are pseudoscientific moral and religious treatises that describe real or fabulous animals, birds, or even stones in order to illustrate Christian moral lessons. Deriving ultimately from the second-century Greek *Physiologus*, French bestiaries of the twelfth through fifteenth centuries include those of Philippe de Thaon, Guillaume le Clerc de Normandie, Gervaise, and (in prose) Pierre de Beauvais. None is remarkable for literary merit, although the first two are perhaps more interesting than the others.

Lapidaries are lists of precious stones or treatises on the virtues or properties of these stones. They were inspired by the Apocalypse (21:19–20) and by the first-century Greek mineral poem of Damigeron, which was translated into Latin as *De lapidibus* by Bishop Marbod of Rennes near the end of the eleventh century. In addition to Damigeron, Marbod's sources also included the *Etymologiae* of Isidore of Seville and Exodus 28:17–21. The first Anglo-Norman prose lapidary was written in the early twelfth century by Philippe de Thaon. The *Lapidary of Modena* and the *Lapidary of Berne* are both continental versions of Marbod's text. A second Anglo-Norman prose lapidary became the source of the continental *Lapidaire chrétien*.

Herbals, pseudoscientific treatises on plants and their alleged properties, are part of a large corpus of medieval *materia medica*. There are many surviving examples (cataloged by Paul Meyer), but they have thus far received little attention from scholars.

BIBLIOGRAPHY

Bestiaries. Editions include Charles Cahier and Arthur Martin, *Mélanges d'archéologie, d'histoire, et de littérature*, II (1851), 85–232, III (1853), 203–288, IV (1856), 57–

87; Edward Ham, "The Cambrai Bestiary," in *Modern Philology* 36 (1938); Max Friedrich Mann, *Der Bestiaire divin des Guillaume le Clerc* (1888); Guy Mermier, *Le Bestiaire de Pierre de Beauvais, version courte* (1977); Paul Meyer, "Le Bestiaire de Gervaise," in *Romania*, 1 (1872); Emmanuel Walberg, *Le Bestiaire de Philippe de Thaün* (1900). See also Florence McCulloch, *Mediaeval Latin and French Bestiaries*, rev. ed. (1962); and Paul Meyer, "Les bestiaires," in *Histoire littéraire de la France*, 34 (1914).

Lapidaries and herbals. Leon Baisier, *The Lapidaire chrétien: Its Composition, Its Influence, Its Source* (diss. Catholic University, 1936); Joan Evans, *Magical Jewels of the Middle Ages and the Renaissance, Particularly in England* (1922); Joan Evans and Mary Serjeantson, *English Medieval Lapidaries* (1932); Paul Meyer, "Recettes médicales en français d'après le ms. B.N. Lat. 8654 B.," in *Romania*, 37 (1908), and "Les plus anciens lapidaires français," in *Romania*, 38 (1909); Louis Mourin, "Les lapidaires attribués à Jean de Mandeville et à Jean à la Barbe," in *Romanica gandensia*, 4 (1955); Leopold Pannier, *Les lapidaires français du moyen âge* (1882); Jean-Baptiste Saint-Lager, *Histoire des herbiers* (1885); Paul Studer and Joan Evans, *Anglo-Norman Lapidaries* (1924); Thomas H. Wright, *Popular Treatises on Sciences Written During the Middle Ages, in Anglo-Saxon, Anglo-Norman, and English* (1841).

GUY MERMIER

[See also **Bestiary; Gems and Jewelry; Herbals, Western European; Marbod of Rennes; Philippe de Thaon.**]

FRENCH LITERATURE: LYRIC

FRENCH LITERATURE: LYRIC. From its twelfth-century beginnings to the late Middle Ages, poetry in the French vernacular was normally conceived as part of an artistic whole, an intimate union of words and melodies, sung (often to instrumental accompaniment on harp, viol, or flute) like medieval Latin verse and troubadour poetry. For much of this literature the tunes survive with the texts in chansonniers. Although interpretations vary as to tempi, rhythm, and word-and-note concordance, it is essential for an understanding of this important genre to realize that much of the literature is wedded to music and widowed without it.

This holds true particularly for the lyric from the thirteenth century onward. Until then, both secular and sacred songs were mainly monodic: set to a single, simple melody, recorded in rather vague notation. For some poems more than one tune is preserved, as in modern hymns. With the thirteenth century came the rise of polyphony: independent melodies sung or played simultaneously. This development culminated in the complex polyphonic vocal music of the fourteenth century, which demanded high virtuosity of both performers and poet-musicians. After Machaut, most poets abandoned the double art. Although some fifteenth-century lyrics were occasionally set to music, this was no longer undertaken by the poets themselves.

With or without music, medieval French lyric, like other contemporary genres, is traditional and conventional rather than original and personal. It is the formal element that dominates. From the beginnings, the trouvères (following the Goliards and the troubadours) assiduously cultivated the technical side of their art; the result was great metrical variety, ingenious rhyme schemes, repetitions, refrains, wordplay, similes, personifications, allegory. Normally, this writing avoids the concrete; the lived experience, the unique event in time or place, the individuality of poet or patron or beloved are relegated to the background, reduced to abstractions. The more conspicuously rhetorical side of verse-making came to characterize a whole school, the late-medieval Grands Rhétoriqueurs; but French lyric was rhetorical from the outset. The manner of the expression carries more weight than the matter communicated; the poet primarily concerns himself with exhibiting not his inner life but rather his talent as an artful arranger of words, lines, and stanzas. He forges verses of infinite variety, rooted in literary precedent and conveying a restricted range of ideas and sentiments.

The subjects are, in the main, love and Christian piety. A few independents, such as Colin Muset, Rutebeuf, Villon, and Christine de Pizan, bring in other, more individual concerns: creature comforts, daily life, popular religion, patriotism, academic and political topics, reflections on marriage and widowhood, the fear of death. Far more common, though, are conventional religious feelings, sometimes in a crusade setting, and conventional passion for a depersonalized beloved. For her the poet alternately hoped and despaired, strove to rise in worth, rejoiced, and sometimes mourned; she represented the highest earthly perfection, and adoration was hers by right. Inexhaustibly, the trouvères sang the cult of the lady.

The reasons for this are to be sought in literary models. Love, even "courtly" love, has long been a favorite theme of lyricism. More immediate antecedents are classical Latin love poetry, medieval Latin secular verse, and Christian Latin hymnody. Oral poetry in the French vernacular is also well attested:

dance songs, satirical songs, crusading songs. Much of this, never written down, has perished; the *chanson de toile* may be one survivor. Sacred and secular, learned and popular, oral and written verse coexisted and inevitably influenced each other. The great bulk of the lyric poetry in the northern *langue d'oïl* that has come down to us consists of the self-conscious, courtly art song of the trouvères; its primary source is the poetry of the troubadours. To them, the first generation of French lyricists is particularly indebted: in themes, in genres, in the care for technical perfection, in metrical and musical inventiveness. Troubadour song, in the *langue d'oc,* was an import into northern France (like the troubadours themselves), a consequence of the increasing cultural contacts between south and north begun with the marriage of Eleanor of Aquitaine to Louis VII in 1137; yet the imitation of this poetry in French began only in the 1160's or 1170's. Much of this voluminous production is anonymous; still some 200 trouvères of the twelfth and thirteenth centuries are known by name. The earliest of them are closest to their southern predecessors and contemporaries; like them, they cultivated the *chanson d'aube,* the *pastourelle,* the *tenson,* the *jeu-parti,* and they sang of love-as-religion.

One of the first trouvères is better known as a romancer: Chrétien de Troyes (*fl. ca.* 1165–1190), a professional writer like his contemporaries Guiot de Provins and Blondel de Nesle. Among the known poets of this generation several were men of rank: Gui de Coucy (a châtelain and crusader), Conon de Béthune (a leader of the Fourth Crusade), Gace Brulé (a petty nobleman), Richard I, the Lionhearted of England. Even these trouvères, adopting the ideology and terminology of troubadour lyric, bestowed on their composition a difference of temperament; cooler, less frankly erotic, they sing of a lady beautiful but remote, ethereal, to be desired but not possessed.

The second generation of French lyricists (of roughly the first half of the thirteenth century) showed even more independence in their treatment of themes and genres. One distinguished poet-musician of this period was a count, Thibaut IV of Champagne, great-grandson of Eleanor. Most outstanding French poets of the time, though, were commoners, professionals like Colin Muset. Many had connections with the prosperous cities of Picardy and Artois, particularly Arras; here Jean Bodel, Pierre Moniot d'Arras, and others were associated with the local Puy (a kind of literary club or academy, which held competitions). Poet-musicians of Arras continued to excel through the century; Adam de la Halle ("le Bossu") ably carried on the tradition of courtly song, which was also perpetuated by many lesser talents. Meanwhile the great Parisian author Rutebeuf (*fl.* 1250–1285) was turning his back on both music and love poetry in favor of religious, didactic, and autobiographic verse.

The fourteenth century saw the triumph of fixed forms (ballade, virelay, rondeau), as brilliantly practiced by Guillaume de Machaut and Eustache Deschamps. In the fifteenth century these forms were much used by Christine de Pizan, Alain Chartier, and Charles of Orléans, all of whom in their different ways perpetuated courtly lyricism; whereas Charles's younger contemporary François Villon, impatient with conventional matter and manner, created an intensely personal oeuvre. The Rhétoriqueurs (Jean Molinet, Olivier de la Marche, Georges Chastellain, and others), historiographers and poets of the Burgundian dukes, packed both fixed and free forms with allegories and verbal acrobatics, and linked the declining Middle Ages to the dawning Renaissance.

BIBLIOGRAPHY

Editions. Friedrich Gennrich, ed., *Altfranzösische Lieder,* 2 vols. (1953–1956); Nigel Wilkins, ed., *One Hundred Ballades, Rondeaux, and Virelais from the Late Middle Ages* (1969); Brian Woledge, ed. and trans., *The Penguin Book of French Verse, I: to the Fifteenth Century* (1961).

Studies. Pierre Bec, *La lyrique française au moyen âge (XIIᵉ–XIIIᵉ siècles),* 2 vols. (1977–1978); Roger Dragonetti, *La technique poétique des trouvères dans la chanson courtoise* (1960); Jean Frappier, *La poésie lyrique en France aux XIIᵉ et XIIIᵉ siècles: Les auteurs et les genres* (1960); Robert Guiette, *D'une poésie formelle en France au moyen âge* (1972); Douglas Kelly, *Medieval Imagination: Rhetoric and the Poetry of Courtly Love* (1978); Moshé Lazar, *Amour courtois et "fin'amors" dans la littérature du XIIᵉ siècle* (1964); Daniel Poirion, *Le poète et le prince: L'évolution du lyrisme courtois de Guillaume de Machaut à Charles d'Orléans* (1965); Hendrik van der Werf, *The Chansons of the Troubadours and Trouvères: A Study of the Melodies and Their Relation to the Poems* (1972); Paul Zumthor, *Langue et techniques poétiques à l'époque romane (XIᵉ–XIIIᵉ siècles)* (1963), and *Le masque et la lumière: La poétique des grands rhétoriqueurs* (1978).

BARBARA NELSON SARGENT-BAUR

[See also **Adam de la Halle; Ballade; Bodel, Jean; Chansonnier; Chansons de Femme; Chansons de Toile; Charles of Orléans; Chartier, Alain; Christine de Pizan; Colin Muset; Conon de Béthune; Courtly Love; Deschamps, Eus-** tache; **Gace Brulé; Machaut, Guillaume de; Music, Popular; Music, Western European; Musical Performance; Pastourelle; Rhétoriqueurs; Richard I the Lionhearted; Rondeau; Rutebeuf; Tenso; Thibaut de Champagne; Troubadours, Trouvères, Trovadores; Villon, François; Virelai.**]

FRENCH LITERATURE: ROMANCES. Romance, as the word is usually used today, appeared in northern France after 1150. It originally combined features drawn from several traditions: vernacular history; classical and medieval Latin literature and poetics; and, to some extent, chansons de geste. Although the twelfth and thirteenth centuries witnessed the most original accomplishments, medieval romances continued to be written, adapted, copied, and eventually printed in significant numbers into the sixteenth century. French romances spread all over Europe, inspiring new and original productions in the major languages.

To Chrétien de Troyes (*fl. ca.* 1165–1190) is usually ascribed the invention of romance. *Roman,* the French word used for romance after Chrétien, originally designated the vernacular language, and subsequently works written in that language. Chrétien makes it refer to narrative, and afterward it tends to be used for what we today call medieval romance.

For Chrétien and his successors, romance narrative at its best is a *conjointure,* that is, a combination that may or may not be "beautiful." Chrétien himself contrasted his *Érec et Énide,* which he calls a "molt bele conjointure" put together from the productions of itinerant storytellers, with the latter's botched failures. Their stories were, to Chrétien, not "beautiful" because they had been dismembered and made incomplete. Chrétien prides himself on achieving just the opposite: bringing together diverse sources in a beautiful, exemplary whole.

THE BEGINNINGS (1135–1170)

The first vernacular literary productions were chansons de geste, hagiography, and chronicles. But chronicles themselves included more than factual records. The two-part history written by the Anglo-Norman Geffrei Gaimar (*fl. ca.* 1140) included the Argonauts, the Trojan War, and Arthur (these parts are now lost), and continued with English history up to Henry I. The earliest known work identified as a romance today—Albéric de Pisancon's *Alexandre,* which dates from 1135 or shortly thereafter—recounts the exploits of Alexander the Great. The legend of Alexander continued to be adapted and expanded throughout the twelfth century and beyond. It contributed to the interest expressed in early romance and chronicle for the links that were believed to exist between the nations and principalities of western Europe and the heroic families of ancient Greece and Rome. At about the same time as Albéric's *Alexandre*, Geoffrey of Monmouth had linked the establishment of the British nation with Troy. The fascination with Trojan settlements in western Europe is apparent in most of the works that appear between 1150 and 1170. The incipient historical sense this suggests encouraged the adaptation of Latin works to French verse (*Thèbes*, *Énéas*, Wace's *Brut*, Benoît de Sainte-Maure's *Troie*, Ovidian adaptations like Chrétien de Troyes's *Philomena*), and the rise of vernacular histories (Wace's *Rou*, Benoît de Sainte-Maure's *Chronique des ducs de Normandie*). The juxtaposition of these works in manuscripts points to the indistinct boundaries between romance and history before Chrétien. But the texts also show that vernacular narrative could express contemporary moral and social values, which was especially important at a time when the great monarchies of France and England were becoming European powers, and when the nobility was establishing itself as a closed caste, conscious of its distinction from the other social orders.

THE GREAT VERSE ROMANCES (1165–1215)

Even before the last of the chronicles and antique romances had been written, a new kind of romance was emerging, one that centered on Celtic themes and subjects. The major works of this period may be divided into Arthurian and non-Arthurian branches, with various subclasses under each head: Round Table, Tristan, and lais under Arthurian; "realist," adventure, and epic under non-Arthurian. The principal distinction among them, according to contemporary evaluations, rested upon their use of the marvelous. Some romances, like *Partonopeu de Blois* (before 1188), were deemed so extraordinary that the audience felt itself transported into a dreamworld. For Jean Bodel (d. 1209–1210), a dramatist and poet, the "matter of Britain," or Arthurian romance, was pleasing, yet vain, empty of meaning or truth. For him only French and Roman romances were true or instructive. Yet the *Huon de Bordeaux* cycle is no less marvelous than *Partonopeu*, although both represent French *matière*. Others inveigh against ro-

mances, alleging that they darken the soul and are morally corrupt. Thus some romancers, notably Gautier d'Arras, set their plots in a more nearly contemporary world, one with adventures and marvelous beauty to be sure, but without the otherworld or dreamlike ambiance typical of the works by most of his contemporaries. Gautier explicitly distinguishes his *Ille et Galeron* from lais and romances that make their audiences feel as if they had been hearing about dreamworlds.

The professed preoccupation of most romancers is the same: to turn sources into a beautiful narrative whole that treats social and emotional concerns of the nobility, especially love and prowess. This preoccupation tends to transform the dreamlike world into an ideal world that reflects, through marvelous adventures, what seemed desirable, yet was absent or imperfect, in the real world of the aristocracy. The fiction expressed truth in an ideal world that one could dream of and even aspire to. The preference among writers even before Chrétien for exclusively noble and clerical audiences fostered the collaboration of knights and clerics, of *chevalerie* and *clergie* (to use the terms of Chrétien's *Cligés*), in the establishment of an aristocratic civilization in France. *Athis et Prophilias*, an adventure romance, evokes the same intention by linking chivalric Rome and learned Athens in the education of young nobility. This civilization is far different from that portrayed in the early chansons de geste. The influence of the troubadours bestowed on the dream of knighthood perhaps its most profound and deeply felt foundation—love for a noble woman, a love best represented by Lancelot and Guenevere as Chrétien invented them for the *Chevalier de la charrette*.

Thus, the romances reflect real social problems and divergent aspirations. Wace suggests in the *Brut* as early as 1155 the potential clash between the old warrior mentality and the new emphasis on courtliness. Other romances, like Raoul de Houdenc's *Méraugis de Portlesguez*, raise questions about the quality of amorous sentiments and the constituents of a noble character. The Tristan and Iseut romances by Béroul and Thomas d'Angleterre, so often referred to in this period, cast a dark shadow over love as an ideal, and show it as irrational, antisocial, even as a kind of madness. Gautier d'Arras's *Eracle* also portrays love in a suspicious light. Such concerns and even anxieties reflect a malaise with regard to love, but a malaise usually sublimated in the verse romances by prowess or marriage. The same is true in the lais contemporary with these romances, especially in the *Lais* by Marie de France (*fl.* 1165–1180). Here too one notes a fascination with love and prowess in dreamlike settings where love is happy or tragic. Many lais were combined in longer romances, so that the distinction between the two is not always sharp. Gautier d'Arras calls his *Ille et Galeron* a lai; and Chrétien probably combined two or more lais for the first part of *Érec et Énide* as the white stag and the sparrow hawk adventures.

Twelfth-century romance was not immune to criticism from those representing religious or moral rigorism, especially in the case of those works that might appear to flaunt established religious, ethical, or social standards, as in the Tristan romances or Chrétien's *Lancelot*. The conflict became especially critical after the emergence of the Grail romances. Chrétien's *Conte du Graal*, or *Perceval*, first projected onto Arthurian romance a strong religious, almost mystical light by linking the humble "grail," a word for a shallow bowl before this romance, and the sacred host to the knight's progress toward atonement for sin. Robert de Boron shortly afterward linked the Grail—a vase for him—to the Last Supper and the Crucifixion, and thus imposed on Arthurian history an eschatological and typological framework (*Roman de l'estoire dou graal*, which included *Joseph d'Arimathie, Merlin,* and probably a *Perceval*). The Grail knight, Perceval, takes a place alongside Gauvain and Lancelot, adding thereby to the ideals of prowess and love that of rectitude. Perceval assumed this role in the various continuations to Chrétien's *Conte du Graal*, especially in the last two by Manessier and Gerbert de Montreuil, and in the early prose adaptations of Robert de Boron.

The Grail romances evince less concern for *bele conjointure*. Because of the often highly disparate, often deliberately additive character of their narratives, one may more properly use the term amalgam to describe their composition. The tendency of scribes, especially in scribal ateliers, literally to sew together diverse works, inserting old manuscripts into newly copied ones, or vice versa—the insertions were called *incidences*—was common. The history of the *Roman d'Alexandre,* from originally brief or discrete versions through various amalgamations to Alexandre de Paris' composite whole, then the subsequent episodic additions in the thirteenth and fourteenth centuries, is a case study of medieval romance amalgamation. There is therefore a formal distinction among works from this period between the whole and complete *conjointures* and the more additive, sometimes open-ended amalgams.

CYCLIC PROSE ROMANCE (1215–1290)

In the thirteenth century, prose gradually replaced verse as the principal vehicle of romance narrative. Various reasons were adduced to justify the change: prose is closer to the truth than verse, which must invent rhymes and thus alter or falsify arbitrarily the truth of the story; increasing literacy in the aristocracy replaced a public of listeners who delighted in wordplay and rhyme with a public of readers more concerned with substance; and the disrepute into which the secular ideals deriving from prowess and love had fallen required a less artificial language to distinguish serious moral concerns from the worldly mentality apparent in most verse romances. Taste also changed to accommodate cyclic narrative, which used interlace to link a great number of more or less discrete narratives, a technique facilitated by multiplying or interweaving quests, as well as by introducing more and more secondary figures to focus the episodic adventures that proliferated during great quests. Succeeding authors and scribes added, subtracted, rearranged, often at will, at times in an effort to clarify or resolve contrasting versions, or to complete what seemed incomplete.

Three principal cycles established themselves, partially overlapping and even coalescing: the Vulgate Arthurian cycle (about 1215–1230) centering on Lancelot and his son Galaad (Galahad), to which were added other cycles, notably the post-Vulgate *Roman du graal* (about 1230–1240), which gives more attention to Arthur, Gauvain's family, and Balain; the Tristan cycle, in two major versions (about 1225–1230 and after 1240); and the Seven Sages of Rome cycle (about 1190–1290).

The beginnings of the Vulgate cycle are apparent early in the thirteenth century. Robert de Boron's verse *Roman de l'estoire dou graal* was turned into prose; among the verse continuations of Chrétien's *Conte du Graal*, there appeared the anonymous *Perlesvaus* in prose. Interlace replaced the amalgam as structural principle, as addition gave way to the elaborate weave of diverse narrative strands. The Vulgate cycle is certainly the work of more than one author, though there were probably a limited number of original authors, perhaps a single original architect who planned out the undertaking, which was completed, with revisions, by others. The work seems to have begun as a Lancelot romance, concluding, as in Chrétien and Robert de Boron, with a Perceval Grail quest. It underwent a remarkable revision when the nearly perfect Galaad replaced the less saintly Perceval as the principal Grail quester, and when the destruction of the Arthurian world (adapted from Wace and Geoffrey of Monmouth) became the somber condemnation of chivalric glory founded on prowess and love. The cyclic romance took on a growing number of adventures and moved back in time to include early Arthurian history (*Merlin*) and Old and New Testament history, especially an apocryphal account of Joseph of Arimathea and the transfer of the Grail to Britain in apostolic times (prose *Estoire del saint graal*)—all of this adapted from Robert de Boron.

Two other cyclic romances grew from or into the Vulgate cycle. The so-called *Roman du graal* elaborated upon features in the prose *Estoire del saint graal,* and then went on to follow Arthur's career and those of his nephews, especially Gauvain. Although its version of the Grail quest is in many ways different from the Vulgate text, it is explicitly linked to it. A subsequent addition is *Palamède,* also called *Guiron le courtois,* which deals with the forefathers to the knights of the Round Table. There were also other compilations and patchwork collections of adventures loosely connected to the earlier cycles about Lancelot, Tristan, and the Grail.

The second major prose cycle is the prose *Tristan.* It was originally an independent cycle, but in a second version it meshed with the Vulgate and post-Vulgate. Tristan becomes a knight of the Round Table, and his love for Iseut is presented more approvingly alongside that of Lancelot and Guenevere, principally because Marc is made to represent a very treacherous king and a major foe of Arthur. Nonetheless, in all these developments, and in the numerous scribal accretions and adaptations apparent in variant manuscripts, the failure of the Grail quest and the destruction of the Arthurian world because of love and arms become increasingly prominent. The romances express a pessimism, even a Pascalian sense of inevitability, of virtual predestination, in human destinies.

The center that holds the Arthurian and Tristan cycles together is the Grail. The prose romances evolved from Robert de Boron's vision of the sacred object and made it at once the goal and the source of meaning for Arthurian history and the marvels and adventures that are its events. The result, eschatological history in which salvation comes through mystical vision of the Grail mysteries, effects the con-

demnation of worldly chivalry, best represented by Lancelot and Gauvain, in favor of divine chivalry as exemplified by Galaad, whose virginity and chastity permit him to replace his father Lancelot as the best knight. The massive failure of the knights of the Round Table in the Grail quest causes the Grail to be withdrawn from them. The ensuing fratricidal and patricidal conflicts betoken self-destruction and bankruptcy of the knighthood without God.

The interlace principle allowed for continual interpolations, rearrangements, and abbreviations, such that it is virtually impossible today to obtain a complete overview of the tradition all three cycles followed. Manuscripts continued to be copied and adapted down to the time of the printing press. Changing tastes and audiences and the very evolution of the French language encouraged adaptations, some happy, some unfortunate, most in need of identification and study today. The prose romances in their cyclic and scribal proliferation stand as a monument to the medieval conception of art as the generation, elaboration, and refinement of an idea by succeeding generations of authors and scribes.

One other major prose cycle appeared in the thirteenth century: that of the Seven Sages of Rome. John of Alta Silva's version of the legend in the twelfth-century *Dolopathos* was rendered into French verse about 1225. But the prose cycle grew from a short, fundamentally misogynist verse romance that was turned to prose shortly before the end of the twelfth century; additional branches were added at irregular intervals, and the harsh misogyny was somewhat mitigated. By and large, the cycle branches out along the lines of a genealogical tree, as the descendants of a Roman emperor expand their rule and activity into all parts of Europe and the Mediterranean world (the *Laurin* even includes Arthur). The cycle brings together features from Arthurian and Roman *matières,* but not always consistently. A deep misogyny in one branch gives way to tender, almost courtly love or conjugal fidelity in others. Heroes and heroines change character as they pass through different branches and different stages in often long and diversified careers. The interlace principle is apparent in the structure of the cycle, and moral rigorism in its themes.

THIRTEENTH-CENTURY VERSE ROMANCE (1190–1300)

Three kinds of verse romance (excluding chansons de geste) were written in the thirteenth century: Arthurian, non-Arthurian, and dream-vision or allegorical. By and large, Arthurian verse romance does not imitate the cyclic narrative of the prose romance, except for the *Perceval* continuations, a few father-son sequences (*Huon de Bordeaux,* Hue de Rotelande's *Ipomedon* and *Protheselaus,* and, perhaps, *Horn*), and romances with multiple quests (*Merveilles de Rigomer, Claris et Laris*). A number of later examples exceed 25,000 lines. There is a clear preference for adventure romance. The quest motif admits of adventures for adventure's sake. Some tend to stereotype chivalric conventions in the face of changing times, others propose new portraits of Arthur and Gauvain. New knights appear at the Round Table, while those who were mere names in earlier romances become prominent: Durmart, Yder, Fergus, Guinglain, Escanor, and others. Occasional doubts are expressed regarding the possibility of preserving the old ideals, but love and the noble marriage, prowess in arms and chivalric service are still held up for admiration and imitation. These works thus avoided or circumvented the great moral issues raised regarding knighthood and love in contemporary prose romance. On the other hand, they seem to have brought attention to matters of more local concern like inheritance, boundaries, feudal obligations, and tournaments. Many Arthurian verse romances seem to have been written for French-speaking audiences in England and Scotland.

The most important non-Arthurian romances are by Jean Renart (*fl.* early thirteenth century), who developed the so-called realistic romance over against Arthurian romance (*Escoufle, Guillaume de Dole*); like Gautier d'Arras, he may also have adapted Breton *matière* to a French context in *Galeran de Bretagne,* and the lai to non-Breton material in the *Lai de l'ombre,* where eloquence and gesture triumph over social and moral constraints in the name of love. Philippe de Remi, lord of Beaumanoir (*ca.* 1250–1296) continues the tradition of "realistic" romance in *Jehan et Blonde* and *La manekine.* The marvelous is still apparent in these works, but as idealization more than as the supernatural. These romances use motifs common in Arthurian romance, but in more nearly contemporary settings (*Amadas et Ydoine, Joufrois de Poitiers, Gui de Warewik,* Jakemes' *Châtelain de Couci,* the *Châtelaine de Vergi,* Gerbert de Montreuil's *Roman de la violette*).

The thirteenth century also witnessed the adaptation of the allegorical mode to romance. Guillaume de Lorris' *Roman de la Rose* (begun in the 1220's) is the most striking example of such romance, but other authors also experimented with al-

legorical narrative to express ideal love (Huon de Mery's *Tournoiement Antechrist*). Allegory, however, was more effective in romance as criticism of aristocratic ideals, for instance in the *Queste del saint graal* in the Vulgate prose, and in Jean de Meun's continuation of the *Roman de la Rose.* Allegorical romance tends to arrange narrative to fit topical progressions, especially the stages for falling in love *(gradus amoris),* in dream visions peopled by personifications of abstract ideals and defects.

LATE ROMANCE (1300–1600)

Verse romance virtually died out in the thirteenth century (Froissart's *Meliador* and Jean Maillart's *Comte d'Anjou* are isolated throwbacks). A number of early verse romances were turned into prose and adapted to new tastes, especially for the court of the dukes of Burgundy in the fifteenth century. The rise of the *nouvelle* paralleled the appearance of short extracts from prose romances. This genre utilized a succinct plot, with a sharp beginning, middle, and surprising ending, and it pointed to the development of the novel through amplifications within the *nouvelle* plot that enhanced its moral or sentimental interest. Cyclic romances continued to be written, often combining Arthurian, French, and other *matières (Perceforest),* or amalgamating various manuscript traditions (Rusticien de Pise, Jehan Vaillant, Michel Gonnot). Late romance was being superseded by the *nouvelle* and by the *roman* as novel, for instance in *Les cent nouvelles nouvelles* (*ca.* 1460) and *Jehan de Saintré* by Antoine de la Sale (1456).

BIBLIOGRAPHY

Robert Bossuat, *Manual bibliographique de la littérature française du moyen âge* (1951), with supplements I (1955) and II (1961); Glyn S. Burgess, *Marie de France: An Analytical Bibliography* (1977); David C. Cabeen, *A Critical Bibliography of French Literature,* I, Urban T. Holmes, Jr., ed., *The Medieval Period* (1952); *Encomia; Bibliographical Bulletin of the International Courtly Literature Society* (1975–); *Grundriss der romanischen Literaturen des Mittelalters,* IV.1, *Le roman jusqu'à la fin du XIIIe siècle* (1978), and VI. 1 and 2, Hans Robert Jauss, *La littérature didactique, allegorique, et satirique* (1968–1970); Douglas Kelly, *Chrétien de Troyes: An Analytic Bibliography* (1976); Otto Klapp, ed., *Bibliographie d'histoire littéraire française/Bibliographie der französischen Literaturwissenschaft* (1956); Henning Krauss, ed., *Europäisches Hochmittelalter* (1981), 217–322, 381–393; Roger Sherman Loomis, ed., *Arthurian Literature in the Middle Ages: A Collaborative History* (1959); Modern Language Association, *International Bibliography* (1921–); Cedric E. Pickford and Rex Last, eds., *The Arthurian Bibliography*, 2 vols. (1981–1983); Hans R. Runte, J. Keith Wikeley, and Anthony J. Farrell, *The Seven Sages of Rome and the Book of Sinbad: An Analytical Bibliography* (1983); David J. Shirt, ed., *Old French Tristan Poems: A Bibliographical Guide* (1980); Société Internationale Arthurienne, *Bulletin bibliographique* (1949–); Société Rencesvals, *Bulletin bibliographique* (1958–), useful for works on relations between romance and chanson de geste; *Year's Work in Modern Language Studies* (1931–).

DOUGLAS KELLY

[See also **Arthurian Literature; Beaumanoir, Philippe de; Chrétien de Troyes; Courtly Love; Gautier d'Arras; Grail, Legend of; Jean de Meun; Robert de Boron; Tristan, Roman de.**]

FRENCH LITERATURE: TRANSLATIONS. The process of transferring Latin texts into the French vernacular was variously designated in medieval French as "metre en romant," "(en)romancier," "metre en françois," "metre en langue françoise," and "translater." However, several centuries before these phrases became current in vernacular texts, the process of translation was already a routine practice, although its practitioners were not yet claiming the title of "translaterres."

The first extant text in French, the *Strasbourg Oaths* (*Serments de Strasbourg*), records an agreement sworn by Louis the German and Charles the Bald, together with their armies, on 14 February 842. For the mutual comprehension of both sides Louis, and Charles' army, used the French language (called "lingua romana" in the text), while Charles, and Louis's army, swore the oaths in German ("lingua teudisca"). This early example of the vernacular is preserved in Nithard's *De dissentionibus filiorum Ludovici Pii* (III, 5), and must inevitably have been a translation, or at least a remodeling, of some Latin original that had originated in the royal chancery.

The second extant text in French, the *Séquence de Ste. Eulalie* (*ca.* 881), was an ecclesiastical product. It too derived from one or several versions of the Latin *Eulalia* sequence, and owed much to these models.

The Council of Tours in 813 authorized the use of French in sermons addressed to laymen. The *Jonas* fragment, preserved in a Valenciennes manuscript from the first half of the tenth century, is an amalgam of French and Latin. Sometimes the two

languages are simply juxtaposed; sometimes Latin phrases are explained by a vernacular translation. Thus the *Jonas* fragment may be regarded as a fossilization of early translation processes in which the bilingual clergy shifted from Latin to French to meet the needs of an uneducated laity. The notes for such sermons probably were composed in Latin. Certainly, few sermons have survived in an original vernacular form, and even the French sermons of the twelfth-century Bernard of Clairvaux are translations of his earlier Latin versions.

There are some exceptions. Two sermons translated from the *Elucidarium* sometime around 1200 contain portions that appear to have been composed directly in French, and four anonymous sermons from the same period in a Cistercian manuscript provide other examples of sermons that apparently dispensed with Latin intermediary versions. Generally speaking, however, the sermons that survive are in the form of a Latin abstract that awaited translation and embellishment, for example, the eleventh- and twelfth-century abstracts of Abelard, Alan of Lille, Anselm, Guibert de Nogent, Hildebert of Mans, and Peter Lombard.

Aside from the many French translations of the Bible and French biblical commentaries, religious works of various sorts constituted the major area of translation from Latin sources in the early Middle Ages. The *Miraculum de conceptione sanctae Mariae* (perhaps by Anselm, abbot of Bury St. Edmunds) and the *Liber de transitu Virginis Mariae* (by Melito) provided the Anglo-Norman Wace with his *Conception Nostre Dame*. The ninth-century Methodius' *Laudatio Sancti Nicolai*, together with John the Deacon's version of that work, was similarly used by Wace for his *Vie de St. Nicolas*. Henry of Salisbury's *De purgatorio Sancti Patricii*, written shortly before 1190, became the basis for several French versions of an *Espurgatoire St. Patriz*, including one by Marie de France (*ca.* 1190) via her intermediary source, Henry of Saltrey's *Tractatus de Purgatorio Sancti Patricii*. A *Vie de St. Gilles* (translated by Guillaume de Berneville) and a *Vie de St. George de Nyssa* (translated by Simund de Freine) provide other examples of Anglo-Norman verse translation of hagiographic works.

Several influential collections of hagiographic legends also served as sources. The lives in the *Vitae patrum*, written by such authors as St. Jerome, John Damascene, and Sulpicius Severus and assembled into collective manuscripts in the sixth century, were translated either singly or in their collective entirety (for example, by Wauchier de Denain for Philippe, marshal of Namur, early in the thirteenth century). Not every collection known as the *Vies des pères* was a translation of the originally compiled *Vitae patrum,* however.

The *Legenda aurea* (Golden legend) had equal success. Written in the thirteenth century by the archbishop of Genoa, Jacobus de Voragine, this collection of hagiographic legends ranged from early Judaic and Christian to contemporary *vitae,* which were ordered according to the festivals of the ecclesiastical calendar. It too was translated several times into French and at the same time was the source for individual *vies.* The *Abbreviatio in gestis et miraculus sanctorum* or *Summa de vitis sanctorum,* in which the saints' lives were ordered according to the saints' days for devotional purposes, was converted into a French prose *légendier.*

In a climate of clerical bilingualism, the translation process was not restricted to the conversion of Latin to French. The reverse process produced a thirteenth-century *Carmen de prodicione Guenonis,* from the *Chanson de Roland,* at least one *Historia septem sapientum* (*ca.* 1330), from a prose version of the *Roman de sept sages,* and two Latin versions of the *Navigatio Sancti Brendani,* from the *Voyage de St. Brendan.*

In general, however, translation was from Latin into French, and such collective items as a *speculum, liber exemplorum, catalogus, summa,* or *alphabetum narrationum* were converted into the vernacular for general use. Thus, the *Composition de la Saincte Escripture,* popularly known as *Ci nous dit,* comprised translated exempla in a collection that has features also of the *Bible moralisée* and of the *doctrinal.* The thirteenth-century Anglo-Norman *Manuel des péchés* employed a similar unembellished style that was ideally suited to the religious instruction of nontheologians. Such works are frequently to be found in the inventories of libraries compiled for the aristocracy.

Another Anglo-Norman, Philippe de Thaon, compiled his *Bestiaire* around 1125, using as his main source a Latin version of the *Physiologus.* The French bestiaries, like their sources, described salient properties of certain animals with a view to Christian allegory. Another edifying translation attributed to Philippe de Thaon is the so-called *Livre de Sibile* (*ca.* 1140), a verse rendering of the Latin *Tiburtine Sibyl.* Its approximate date was 1140.

Bishop Marbod of Rennes's *De lapidibus,* written in the second half of the twelfth century, was the source of several French lapidaries, both rhymed and in prose.

Marie de France translated a collection of Aesop's fables into French octosyllabic couplets (*ca.* 1180). She mistakenly believed that the "Alvrez" who had translated them into English from an unknown Latin source was Alfred the Great, and was unaware of Aesop's authorship and correct identity. Despite her misconceptions, her prologue is useful for its expression of the translator's intent. She there states that it is the responsibility of those who "know letters" (that is, Latin) to apply themselves to the "good books and writings, the examples and sayings which the philosophers have found."

This encyclopedic enthusiasm for ancient philosophy, in its widest sense, and for the propagation of the wisdom of the *auctores* increased throughout the twelfth and thirteenth centuries and beyond. It resulted in vernacular versions of proverbs, fables, herbals, lapidaries, bestiaries, of Cato's *Disticha,* of Petrus Alphonsus' *Disciplina clericalis,* and of Guillaume de Conches's *Moralium dogma philosophorum.* Other such translations included Gossuin de Metz's *Image du monde* (*ca.* 1245), Alart de Cambrai's *Dits et moralités des philosophes* (an adaptation of Guillaume's *Moralium*), Peter of Peckham's verse *Secrets des secrets* and Jofroi de Watreford and Servais Copale's prose *Secrets des secrets* (both translated from the *Secreta secretorum* in the second half of the thirteenth century), and Jehan Bonnet's *Livres des segrez aus philosophes* (also based on the *Moralium* and on the *Secreta secretorum* and the twelfth-century *Imago mundi*).

More particular interests were served by the translation of algorisms and of astronomical treatises and by the conversion of administrative and legal texts into French, for example, Philippe de Novare's *Assises de Jerusalem,* Philippe de Beaumanoir's *Coutumes de Beauvaisis,* and Pierre de Fontaines's *Conseil à un ami* and *Livre de justice et de plaid.* Codes and institutes of Roman law, rhetorical handbooks, military manuals, medical treatises, Ovid's *Ars amatoria,* William of Tyre's *Historia Hierosolimitana,* the Latin chronicles from St. Denis entitled *Abbreviatio de gestis regum Francorum,* and Andreas Capellanus' *De amore* were all converted into the vernacular to enrich the common stock of knowledge.

An important contribution was made by aristocratic patrons whose tastes often determined the translators' choices. For example, the chronicler Lambert d'Ardres recorded that his patron, Baldwin

II, count of Guines, commissioned the following works to be translated during the second half of the twelfth century: *Cantica canticorum* (with commentary), lessons and sermons from the Gospels, and Solinus' *Collectanea rerum memorabilium.* The *Somme le roy,* prepared in 1279 for Philip the Bold by his confessor, contained translations of the Ten Commandments, Credo, the Seven Deadly Sins, the Virtues, and began with a paternoster plus commentary. At the court of Baldwin VIII of Flanders there was strong interest in history and historical legend. Baldwin VIII's sister commissioned a translation of the *Pseudo-Turpin* (a legendary history of France from Charlemagne to Philip Augustus), and two reasons were given in the prologue: a vernacular translation would give wider accessibility to the chronicle ("por ço que teus set de letra qui de latin ne seüst eslire") and would ensure the preservation of the work ("por romanz sera il mielz gardez"). The prologue further explains that the translation is in prose rather than verse because prose is the medium associated with truth ("nus contes rimés n'est verais").

The comment reflected adversely on the highly popular French romances, which had as their primary purpose entertainment rather than edification. Despite their use of classical and other traditional material, they cannot be regarded as translations in the strictest sense. They were, rather, adaptations of an original text that served merely as a "pretext" for the completely new product, the French *romant.*

By the early thirteenth century French translations were demonstrating a new literary awareness. Even though one or two translators continued to work anonymously, their prologues and occasional commentary on the text reveal a pride in the translating art and a consciousness of its responsibilities. The purposes and the practices of translation were gradually changing.

One version of the French *Pseudo-Turpin* claims to have translated that portion of the work which translates the *Vita Ludovici Grossi Regis* without omissions and without additions ("sans riens oster et sanz rien metre de ce que nos trovons an la letre"). Of course, translators continued to regard paraphrase, commentary, and even amplification as legitimate practices when necessary, and it is therefore unlikely that even an approximate "mot et mot" translation was achieved. Nevertheless the aim was in itself revealing.

There were further such statements a few years later in *Li fet des Romains* (ca. 1213), an anonymous translation of various historical texts, principally Caesar's *Commentarii de bello gallico,* Lucan's *Bellum civile,* Sallust's *Catilina,* and Suetonius' *Vitae Caesarum* I. The translator enunciated the principle of faithfulness to the original text when he apologized for including material that might be offensive by Christian standards. He commented that it need not be believed, but that he translated it because Lucan has said it: "qui le veust si l'en croie . . . por itant con Lucans le dist le vos rendons." The comment reveals also that translators were not averse to providing didactic directions. As the prologue of *Li fet des Romains* states, the translation was intended to instruct in "doing good and avoiding evil" with the help of Roman history. This conventional expression of moral didacticism masked another serious purpose, this time political, for *Li fet des Romains* presented Julius Caesar as a model for the young Philip Augustus on the eve of the Battle of Bouvines. Jean de Thuim's prose translation of Lucan, which was done only a few years after *Li fet des Romains,* had more affinities with romance by its expansion of the love interest and its long Ovidian digressions.

Philip the Fair was the patron of Jean de Meun, who was an active translator of classical works. Jean's translation of Vegetius' *Epitoma rei militaris* (which was also translated into verse by Jean Priorat) was completed in 1284 under the title *Li Abregemenz noble honme Vegesce Flave René des establissemenz apartenanz a chevalerie;* it is now more usually known as *L'art de chevalerie.* It too used Latin military *auctoritas* to serve contemporary needs, and was undertaken at the request of Jean de Brienne, count of Eu. Jean de Meun's translation of Boethius, the *Consolation philosophique,* was dedicated to Philip the Fair. Jean was responsible for at least two other major translations: of Abelard's *Historia calamitatum* and of Ovid's *Ars amatoria,* now lost.

By the beginning of the fourteenth century prose was dominant in the many translations—historical, scientific, legal, political, and moralistic—that were enriching the intellectual climate of France. Like Philip the Fair, Louis X, Jean le Bon, and, above all, Charles V enthusiastically encouraged the translation of Latin texts into the vernacular. Some of the resulting works were Pierre Bersuire's *Histoire romaine* (Livy), Jacques Bauchant's *Les voies de Dieu* (St. Elizabeth's visions) and his *Remedes ou confors des maulz de fortune* (Seneca's *De remediis fortuitorum*), Jean Golein's *Livre d'informacion des princes* (Gilles de Rome's *De regimine principum*), Raoul de Presles' *Cité de Dieu* (St. Augustine's *De civitate Dei*), Evrart de Conty's *Problemes* (the pseudo-Aristotelian *Problemata*), Simon de Hesdin's *Anecdotes memorables* (Valerius Maximus' *Factorum ac dictorum memorabilium libri X*), and the anonymous *Li bien universal des mouches a miel* (*Bonum universale de apibus*).

Nicole Oresme (*ca.* 1320–1382) deserves particular mention in this plethora of translators because of his encyclopedic range of knowledge and his linguistic expertise. He translated Aristotle's *De caelo et mundo, Politica*, and *Ethica* into *Livre du ciel et du monde, Livre de politiques*, and *Livre de ethiques* respectively. The pseudo-Aristotelian *Oeconomica* became his *Livre de yconomiques*.

The tradition of patronage continued into the fifteenth century under Jean, duke of Berry, Louis de Bourbon, and Jean d'Orléans, producing, for example, Laurent de Premierfait's translation of Boccaccio's *De casibus virorum et feminarum illustrium* and the *Decameron*, of Cicero's *De amicitia* and *De senectute*, and of Aristotle's *Oeconomica*.

The achievements of medieval French translators are to be gauged also by the fact that Oresme chose to use French for some of his own learned treatises. His *Traetié de la monnoye* is his translation of his own *De mutacionibus monetarum*, and his *Tractié de la divination* was composed directly in French. By this time, therefore, French could compete with Latin as a learned language, thanks to the accumulated heritage of centuries of translation into the vernacular.

BIBLIOGRAPHY

Jeanette M. A. Beer, *A Medieval Caesar* (1976); Jessie Crosland, "Lucan in the Middle Ages," in *Modern Language Review*, **25** (1930); P. H. Delehaye, *Les légendes hagiographiques* (1905); Alex J. Denomy, "The Vocabulary of Jean de Meun's Translation of Boethius's *De consolatione Philosophiae*," in *Mediaeval Studies*, **16** (1954); Georges Doutrepont, *La littérature française à la cour des ducs de Bourgogne* (1909); Ernest Albert Lecoy de la Marche, *La chaire française au moyen âge, spécialement au XIIIᵉ siècle*, 2nd ed. (1886); Robert H. Lucas, "Mediaeval French Translations of the Latin Classics to 1500," in *Speculum*, **45** (1970); Francis Meunier, *Essai sur la vie et les ouvrages de Nicole Oresme* (1857); J. Monfrin, "Humanisme et traductions au moyen âge," in Anthime Fourrier, ed., *L'humanisme médiéval ... du XIIIᵉ au XIVᵉ siècle* (1964), 217–246; Jean Rychner, "Observations sur la traduction de Tite-Live par Pierre Bersuire (1354–1356)," in *Journal des savants* (Oct.–Dec. 1963); A. Thomas, "Traductions françaises de la *Consolatio Philosophiae* de Boece," in *Histoire littéraire*, **27** (1938); Brian Woledge and H. P. Clive, *Répertoire des plus anciens textes en prose française* (1964).

JEANETTE M. A. BEER

[See also **Bible, French; Eulalie, La Séquence de Ste.; Fet des Romains, Li; Jean de Meun; Marie de France; Oresme, Nicole; Pseudo-Turpin; Strasbourg Oaths; Translations and Translators, Western European.**]

FRESCO BUONO, literally "fresh good," the method of painting on damp plaster with water-based pigments so that as the plaster dries a chemical change binds the particles of pigment into the plaster. Cennino Cennini described the process in three parts: first, a heavy layer of plaster (the *arriccio*) was applied to the wall and allowed to dry; second, the composition was sketched on the plaster; third, small areas of thinly applied wet plaster were laid and painted immediately, before the water could evaporate. In practice, the *arriccio* and the second layer of plaster (the *intonaco*) were often equal in depth, and the *intonaco* was frequently applied before the base *arriccio* layer had dried, resulting in a surface that retained its moisture long enough that whole compositions could be painted on damp plaster in one session.

BIBLIOGRAPHY

Cennino Cennini, *The Craftsman's Handbook*, Daniel V. Thompson, Jr., trans. (1961), 42–47; David C. Winfield, "Middle and Later Byzantine Wall Painting Methods: A Comparative Study," in *Dumbarton Oaks Papers*, **22** (1968).

LESLIE BRUBAKER

[See also **Fresco Painting.**]

FRESCO PAINTING (from the Italian for "fresh") is the most permanent form of mural painting because it involves a chemical bond between the paint layer and the wall surface. In true fresco, pigments suspended in water are applied to a moist layer of plaster on a wall. The pigments penetrate the plaster layer and, when dry, fuse with the plaster. Fresco is therefore relatively permanent when not exposed to moisture. Fresco secco involves adhesive-base pigments applied to a dry surface. It is susceptible to flaking over time.

Piero d'Assisi Freed Through the Intercession of St. Francis. Detail of a fresco cycle in the upper church of S. Francesco, Assisi, possibly by Giotto, between 1270 and 1320. ALINARI/ART RESOURCE

The greatest flowering of fresco painting took place in Italy from roughly 1280 to 1400. After a general period of disuse that had lasted from early Christian times, the art of fresco gradually supplanted mosaics as wall decoration. Between 1280 and 1320 Italy experienced a building boom. Every major city established new churches, constructed town halls and hospitals, and built other edifices that required decoration. This building boom coincided with a new attitude toward imagery. The church stressed that religious images could instruct and admonish the illiterate masses in their devotions, as well as provide beautiful decorations. The fresco decorations of early Christian times were viewed with renewed interest, as is evidenced by Pietro Cavallini's restoration of several cycles in Rome. Thus, fresco became the ideal medium to decorate countless chapels, naves, sacristies, and refectories of churches, and the various rooms of secular buildings.

Most fourteenth-century frescoes were painted while the plaster was wet and are therefore considered true (buon) frescoes. Details were often laid in on the dry surface, but the major portion of the mural was completed before the plaster dried. This method required a sure hand, rapid working, and a well-worked-out design.

The design (sinopia) was laid out on a rough lower layer of plaster called the arriccio. Executed in most cases by the shop master, the design was indicated in a reddish wash. Composed directly on the wall surface, the sinopia was first and foremost an accommodation to that wall. It then guided the painter who laid in the fresco. Patches of moist fine plaster called the intonaco were laid over the area of the sinopia to be painted. Only as much intonaco as could be painted in one session was laid. The junctions between patches of intonaco are called giornate. When all the patches of intonaco were applied and painted, the fresco mural was complete and the sinopia was covered.

Today many of the sinopias have been uncovered by a method called stacco, whereby a canvas is glued to the fresco surface and the intonaco is literally peeled off the wall, revealing the arriccio with its sinopia. These uncovered sinopias have given a new understanding of the nature of fresco painting, the process through which frescoes were conceived and executed, and the working methods in medieval painter's workshops.

Following the design of a master, numerous assistants aided in the production of a large mural. Some assistants ground colors, others prepared plaster surfaces, and others laid on colors, using broad brushes. Usually murals covered large walls and required scaf-

The Peaceful City. Ambrogio Lorenzetti, detail of the Allegory of Good and Bad Government, in the Palazzo Pubblico, Siena, first third of the 14th century. SCALA/ART RESOURCE

folding. From what is known, it is assumed that painters started at the top of the wall and worked downward. This method was the most commonly used process for executing murals between 1300 and 1400.

The earliest known works to result from the revived interest in fresco were done for the upper church of S. Francesco at Assisi between roughly 1270 and 1330. Several masters were involved in the various picture cycles, which included the Life of the Virgin, images of the evangelists, and two large *Crucifixions* by Cimabue for the choir and transept; thirty-two scenes of the Old and New Testaments and twenty-eight episodes from the life of St. Francis along the nave, attributed to the S. Cecilia master, Torriti, and the Master of the St. Francis Legend (and/or Giotto). This cycle became a paradigm for later fresco cycles throughout Italy.

Between roughly 1305 and 1310 Giotto painted the next important surviving fresco cycle: the mag-

nificent depiction of the lives of the Virgin and Christ as well as the *Last Judgment* and Virtues and Vices in the Scrovegni (Arena) Chapel in Padua. A consummate piece of wall decoration, the cycle is also a brilliant fusion of narrative and iconographic considerations. It stands as one of the greatest achievements in the history of art.

In 1315 Simone Martini painted his great *Maestà* for the end wall of the great hall of the Palazzo Pubblico in Siena, and by 1330 he probably finished the equestrian portrait of Guidoriccio da Fogliano for the opposite wall. Ambrogio Lorenzetti painted his allegory of Good and Bad Government for the same building at nearly the same time. He and his brother Pietro provided numerous frescoes for Sienese churches and hospitals during the 1320's and 1330's.

Martini and Pietro Lorenzetti were among the artists called to Assisi during those decades to provide murals for the lower church of S. Francesco. Between about 1322 and 1327 Pietro frescoed the south

St. George Saved from the Wheel. Altichiero, detail of a fresco cycle in the Oratorio di S. Giorgio, Padua, *ca.* 1380–1385. ALINARI/ART RESOURCE

transept with scenes from the life of Christ. The vault includes numerous crowded and anecdotal images that function primarily as ornament. The two side walls provide a stark contrast, illustrating the *Deposition* and the *Entombment*. These two frescoes rank as Pietro's greatest surviving works and are among the most moving paintings from the trecento. They clearly demonstrate his profound understanding of the fresco medium. Broadly conceived and painted, their composition is derived from the shape of each vault-crowned wall. The images fuse wall, medium, composition, and narrative into a seamless, unforgettable whole.

Simone Martini's St. Martin Chapel of roughly the same date, also in the lower church of S. Francesco, was similarly conceived. Martini also exploited the setting, taking into consideration the windows, floor, vaults, walls, and subject matter to produce a unified, decorative whole. The narrative flows smoothly from one image to another, while the viewer feels surrounded by sumptuous decoration as well as pictorial action.

Ambrogio Lorenzetti, in his work of about 1330–1340, took fresco painting in new directions. In his *Maestà*, painted for the Chapel of S. Galgano at Monte Siepi, he extended the subject to fill three walls. Thus, the viewer does not simply confront a wall decorated with an isolated image, but is enclosed by and involved with the subject of the image in a new way. Such an involvement, impossible in panel painting, was dependent on and developed from Lorenzetti's brilliant understanding of the possibilities inherent in wall painting. His daring exploitation of setting, medium, and subject was not copied or emulated.

During the 1320's and 1330's other artists experimented with the possibilities of fresco. In Florence the church of S. Croce was decorated with a number of fresco cycles by leading Florentine masters. These cycles were influential, inspiring painters for centuries to come. Giotto's *Life of St. Francis* cycle in the Bardi Chapel and his depiction of the lives of Sts. John the Baptist and John the Evangelist in the Peruzzi Chapel are manifestations of his late style. These cycles enlarged the scale of the figures relative to the picture surface, reduced the anecdotal elements, and broadened the pictorial field to produce a more monumental and expanded effect. Giotto deepened the human quality of his characters and made composition a less obvious, though no less important, element in these quietly moving pictures.

Maso di Banco decorated the nearby Bardi di Vernio Chapel with scenes from the life of St. Sylvester. Inspired by Giotto, he reduced the number of elements in his images and gave his figures a calm, quiet dignity. The interaction between these few startling forms gives a tension to the image, which is echoed in the tension between spatial and compositional elements in the work.

Taddeo Gaddi frescoed the Baroncelli Chapel of S. Croce with scenes from the life of the Virgin that tried (somewhat unsuccessfully) to increase the epic scale of the narrative by increasing the pictorial space and filling it with numerous figures and anecdotal details. This work was influential, however, and his later decorations for the refectory of S. Croce (which probably date from the 1350's) helped establish the tradition for refectory decoration that lasted for two centuries.

In the second half of the fourteenth century there were numerous changes in the style and conception of fresco painting.

Barna da Siena's large and impressive cycle of the *Life of Christ* in the Collegiata of S. Gimignano shows a new understanding of narrative and pictorial composition. Each image is structured so that the composition imposes itself on the viewer's consciousness. The composition is an active rather than passive element of the image, underscoring the dramatic quality of the narrative.

In Pisa the Campo Santo was the site of an ambitious fresco program. The walls of the famous burial ground were decorated mainly by Florentine and Sienese painters in the second half of the trecento. One of the greatest images in the series was probably by a native Pisan, Francesco Traini, whose *Triumph of Death* and *Last Judgment* cycles are brilliant fusions of broad narrative themes and anecdotal details. The Florentine painters Taddeo Gaddi, Andrea da Firenze, and Spinello Aretino also supplied frescoes for the Campo Santo, but the most important Florentine work is that of Antonio Veneziano, who completed the *Life of St. Ranieri* cycle begun by Andrea da Firenze, between roughly 1384 and 1386. Pursuing Giotto's expansive, monumental mural style, Antonio created massive figures and a convincing spatial recession.

In Padua another painter made original contributions to the art of fresco painting, which are still too little appreciated. Between 1370 and 1384 Altichiero provided fresco cycles for the Chapel of S. Giacomo (now S. Felice) and the Oratorio of S. Gior-

The Expulsion from Eden. Masaccio, fresco in the Brancacci Chapel, S. Maria del Carmine, Florence, *ca.* 1425. ALINARI/ART RESOURCE

gio, both in the basilica of S. Antonio in Padua. Illustrating the lives of Sts. James, George, Lucy, and Catherine, the murals are remarkable for their fusion of spatial and compositional considerations. Figures are painted with convincing realism and are surrounded by palpable atmosphere, yet the individual scenes are deftly composed so that realism never dominates the pictorial considerations. Only Altichiero pushed realism to such an extreme yet maintained the compatibility of the mural with the wall through his skillfully ordered compositions. In Florence, Nardo di Cione's *Last Judgment* cycle for the Strozzi Chapel of S. Maria Novella was painted about 1355. It stands as the masterpiece of Florentine fresco in the mid trecento. Uniting the function of the chapel as a burial site with the narrative content of the *Last Judgment,* Nardo's image shows the Strozzi family members arising from floor tombs to join the events taking place. The entire fresco is conceived as a tapestry of figures having a tightly woven configuration that moves the viewer's eye upward to the apex of the story: Christ and the Virgin in majesty. While the figures are real and convincing, they exist in a nonspace, the ephemeral world of the hereafter. Florentine painters after Nardo, with the exception of Antonio Veneziano, appear to have lacked innovative genius and intuitive understanding of the fresco medium. While earlier generations had experimented with diverse spatial, compositional, and narrative approaches to wall painting, between roughly 1380 and 1410, Florentine painters shared similar attitudes toward mural painting.

Spinello Aretino, Agnolo Gaddi, Niccolò di Pietro Gerini, and Cenni de Francesco, the most prolific muralists of the late trecento, crowded their frescoes with innumerable figures, extended their images across the wall, and generally aimed for a decorative effect. Their narrative tended to underplay drama and their styles eschewed eccentricity, giving their murals a neutral, often charming, appearance. Spinello's works at Antella, the Palazzo Pubblico at Siena, and the sacristy of S. Miniato al Monte, all dating from the 1380's and 1390's, are characterized by bright colors, sprightly figures, and a profusion of detail, qualities more strongly emphasized by Cenni di Francesco's murals in the church of S. Francesco at Volterra (1410). Agnolo Gaddi's frescoes in the Castellani Chapel of S. Croce (*ca.* 1385–1388), his *Legend of the True Cross* cycle in the choir of S. Croce (*ca.* 1388–1393), and his *Life of the Virgin* cycle in the cathedral of Prato (1392–1395) demonstrate Gaddi's growing interest in monumentally conceived figures, which are nevertheless placed in settings that give the mural an overall decorative, space-denying effect.

The artist who pushed the tendency toward flat, decorative wall paintings to its greatest extreme was Niccolò di Pietro Gerini. The master of a large and prolific workshop with commissions in Florence, Prato, and Pisa, Gerini conceived of murals as large versions of panel paintings. Every element of his images is rigidly composed, so that no matter how large the mural, symmetry and balance are strictly maintained. Figures are schematically rendered, which gives them a decorative unity with his balanced and completely nonspatial compositions.

The only artist who took this rigid, linear, and decorative mural tradition to a wonderful conclusion was Lorenzo Monaco. His large and stately fresco cycle depicting the life of the Virgin in the Bartolini Chapel of S. Trinità, dating from roughly 1422–1425, maintains Gerini's aloof and nonrealistic style. By relaxing the forms and investing them with an elegant beauty, Monaco gave his murals a grace rarely found in Florentine painting. The easy transitions between groups of figures owes a large debt to Nardo di Cione and the early Sienese tradition.

The early fifteenth century reveals an even greater uniformity of approach to fresco painting. With the exception of Masaccio's remarkable cycle in the Brancacci Chapel of S. Maria del Carmine, and his *Trinity* in S. Maria Novella, Florentine frescoes tended toward a calm narrative, restrained gesture, and idealized settings and figures to produce a harmonious image that is an ornament for its wall. This approach was shared by Masolino, Bicci di Lorenzo, Rosello di Jacopo Franchi, Mariotto di Nardo, Taddeo di Bartolo, and Fra Angelico. Relative to panel painting, fewer frescoes seem to have been painted in the fifteenth century, though fresco remained an important medium well into the sixteenth century.

BIBLIOGRAPHY

Eve Borsook, *The Mural Painters of Tuscany* (1960, 2nd ed. 1981); Enzo Carli, *Pittura pisana del trecento*, II, *La seconda metà del secolo* (1961); Millard Meiss, *Painting in Florence and Siena After the Black Death* (1951), and *The Great Age of Fresco* (1970); John White, *Art and Architecture in Italy, 1250 to 1400* (1966).

ADELHEID M. GEALT

[See also **Altichiero; Andrea da Firenze; Antonio Veneziano; Arena Chapel; Arriccio; Assisi, San Francesco;**

Barna da Siena; Cavallini, Pietro; Cimabue, Cenni di Pepi; Fresco Buono; Fresco Secco; Gaddi, Agnolo; Gaddi, Taddeo; Giotto di Bondone; Intonaco; Lorenzetti, Ambrogio; Lorenzetti, Pietro; Lorenzo Monaco; Martini, Simone; Masaccio, Tommaso Cassai; Maso di Banco; Nardo di Cione; Niccolò di Pietro Gerini; Sinopia; Spinello Aretino; Traini, Francesco.]

FRESCO SECCO, literally "fresh dry," the method of painting on dry plaster in any medium. Because fresco buono did not allow much precise detail, finishing touches were often added *a secco* (that is, after the plaster had dried). Alternatively, a wall could be done entirely in fresco secco.

BIBLIOGRAPHY

Daniel V. Thompson, *The Materials and Techniques of Medieval Painting* (1936), 71–73.

LESLIE BRUBAKER

[See also **Fresco Buono; Fresco Painting.**]

FRESSANT, HERMANN. At the end of the *Märe* "Der Hellerwert Witz," the author identifies himself as Hermann Fressant and indicates that he comes from Augsburg. Very likely he is the person recorded as municipal scribe of Ulm around 1350. His moralistic tale is well written and contains literary allusions. Fressant exemplifies the German scribe with an active interest in literature.

BIBLIOGRAPHY

Hanns Fischer, *Studien zur deutschen Märendichtung*, 2nd ed. (1983).

STEPHEN WAILES

[See also **Mären.**]

FREYR, one of the most prominent gods in the Nordic pantheon. Together with his father Njǫrðr and his twin sister Freyja, he belongs to a group known as the Vanir, primarily important as fertility deities. His name, which means "lord" and was perhaps originally a title rather than an actual name, is frequently invoked together with that of Njǫrðr in the Old Icelandic sources. Freyr is variously designated in the poetry and prose as *veraldar goð* (god of the world), *fólkvaldi goða* (ruler of the gods), and even *ásaiaðarr* (lord of the Æsir). According to the mythological tradition, Freyr is the offspring of a union between Njǫrðr and his sister; he lives in Álfheimr (Elf Home); he possesses the ship *Skíðblaðnir* (Wooden Bladed), which always has a favorable wind, and the boar Gullinborsti (Golden Bristle), which can travel through air and water faster than a horse.

Information about Freyr and his cult is revealed by the records of ancient historians, place-name evidence, and mythological material collected in the texts of medieval Iceland. The cult of Freyr was historically very strong in eastern Sweden, the Oslo region, and along the west coast of Norway, as place-name evidence shows. According to the prologue to the *Prose Edda* and *Ynglinga saga,* Freyr was one of the Æsir who traveled north from Asia with Odin and became the third king of Sweden. Both texts state that he was known as Yngvi and considered to be the founder of the Swedish royal line, the Ynglings. During his reign there was such peace and prosperity that the news of his death was kept from the people for three years. *Ǫgmundar þáttr dytts,* found in the late fourteenth-century *Flateyjarbók,* relates that a young Norwegian named Gunnarr Helmingr went to Sweden where he became part of a procession in which a statue of Freyr accompanied by a young priestess who represented his wife, was carried around on a wagon drawn by oxen. This description parallels in several respects the testimony of Tacitus about the worship of Nerthus. The eleventh-century historian Adam of Bremen mentions in book IV of his *History* a temple at Uppsala containing statues of Odin, Thor, and "Fricco," presumably Freyr. The statue of Fricco was characterized by a large phallus.

The sagas contain references to worship of Freyr. Hrafnkell, the protagonist in *Hrafnkels saga,* is a priest of Freyr and dedicates his horse, Freyfaxi, to the god. In *Víga-Glúms saga* Glúmr slays an enemy on a field sacred to Freyr. The father of the victim, forced off his land by Glúmr, offers an ox to the god, with the prayer that Glúmr eventually be dishonored and chased from his land. Another example is Þorgrímr, who is slain in *Gísla saga.* As priest of Freyr, he holds a yearly sacrificial feast in honor of the god. After his death the saga reports that no snow would stay on his mound because Freyr did not want frost to come between them.

There are also mythical tales about Freyr. The poem *Skírnismál* in the *Poetic Edda* relates the story of how Freyr fell in love with the shining giantess Gerðr and sent his servant Skírnir to woo her for him. For this errand Freyr lent Skírnir his horse and magic sword. Freyr was thus weaponless in his fight against Beli and slew him with a staghorn. Freyr is killed at *Ragnarǫk* by the giant Surtr.

BIBLIOGRAPHY
Henry A. Bellows, trans., *The Poetic Edda* (1923), 107–120; Ólafur Briem, "Vanir og Æsir," in *Studia Islandica,* **21** (1963); Georges Dumézil, *Gods of the Ancient Northmen,* Einar Haugen *et al.,* trans. (1973), 73–79; Gustav Neckel, ed., *Edda. Die Lieder des Codex Regius,* rev. by Hans Kuhn (1962), 69–77; Snorri Sturluson, *The Prose Edda,* Jean I. Young, trans. (1966), 48–62, and *Ynglinga Saga,* in *Heimskringla,* Samuel Laing, trans. (1961); Edward O. G. Turville-Petre, *Myth and Religion of the North* (1964), 165–175; Jan de Vries, *Altgermanische Religionsgeschichte,* II (1970), 177–208.

KAAREN GRIMSTAD

[See also Æsir; Eddic Poetry; Gísla Saga Súrssonar; Hrafnkels Saga; Njǫrðr; Skírnismál; Vanir; Víga-Glúms Saga; Ynglinga Saga.]

FRIARS, members of the mendicant religious orders founded in the thirteenth century. Like the Latin word *frater,* from which it derives, "friar" means simply "brother." The corresponding term for members of religious orders founded in earlier centuries would be "monks." While monks lived in monasteries, friars lived in convents. The main characteristic of a mendicant order was its adherence to the ideal of both corporate and individual poverty.

The principal orders of friars, with their dates of official approbation, are the Order of Friars Minor, or Franciscans (*ca.* 1210); the Order of Preachers, or Dominicans (1216); the Order of Our Lady of Mount Carmel, or Carmelites (1226); and the Order of the Hermits of St. Augustine, or Augustinian Friars (1256). Others included the Order of the Holy Cross, or Crutched Friars (1247); the Order of Penance of Jesus Christ, or Friars of the Sack (1251); the Hermits of St. William, or Williamites (1256); the Order of Friar Servants of St. Mary, or Servites (1256); and the Friars of the Blessed Mary, or Pied Friars (1257).

At the Second Council of Lyons in 1274, an attempt was made to halt the proliferation of mendicant orders. No new ones were to be established, and those already in existence were not to take in novices or set up new convents. An exception was made for the Franciscans and Dominicans. The status of the Carmelites and the Augustinian Friars was left for a later papal determination. (They gained full approval from Boniface VIII in 1298.) The Friars of the Sack and the Pied Friars soon ceased to exist, while the others survived by disavowing mendicancy.

The definition of friars can be made sharper in terms of differences between monks and friars. The individual monk joined a particular monastic community, not the monastic order in general, and was bound by the monastic ideal of stability to remain in that community for the rest of his life. The monk could have no personal possessions, but the community or monastery did. The community was a private and independent corporation with its own endowments, usually of land. Most monastic activity was directed away from an involvement in worldly affairs, including pastoral care. The main focus of monastic spirituality was the liturgy.

The individual friar, on the other hand, joined an order, rather than a particular house or convent. Both the individual and the entire order were to be propertyless. In the early days of the movement started by St. Francis of Assisi, such an ideal was apparently attainable. The friars met each spring at Assisi and then dispersed for the rest of the year. They lived as itinerant hermits, preaching and working or begging in towns by day, and spending the nights in woods and caves outside of towns. Once the Franciscans accepted the gift of a house at Bologna in 1219, the ideal was compromised. Yet the ideal always remained just that, an ideal for the mendicant orders; its mainstay was the legal-theological fiction that everything given the friars became papal property, which the friars were free to use. The main characteristic of mendicant spirituality was the active apostolate to the urban laity. Thus mendicant convents, unlike monasteries, were situated in cities, and individual friars often moved from one convent of their order to another, in keeping with the needs of their ministry.

BIBLIOGRAPHY

Richard W. Emery, "The Friars of the Blessed Mary and the Pied Friars," in *Speculum,* 24 (1949), "The Second Council of Lyons and the Mendicant Orders," in *Catholic Historical Review,* 39 (1953), "The Friars of the Sack," in *Speculum,* 18 (1943), and *The Friars in Medieval France* (1962); David Knowles, *From Pachomius to Ignatius* (1966), 41–58; Jacques Le Goff, "Ordres mendiants et urbanisation dans la France médiévale," in *Annales: Écono-mies, Sociétés, Civilisations,* 25 (1970); Richard W. Southern, *Western Society and the Church* (1970), 214–299.

LESTER K. LITTLE

[See also **Augustinian Friars; Carmelites; Dominicans; Franciscans; Mendicant Orders; Sack, Friars of the.**]

FRIDAY PRAYER (Arabic: *ṣalāt al-jumuᶜa*), a conspicuous and very important form of worship in the Islamic religious community. Performed each Friday afternoon shortly after the sun begins to decline from its zenith, the Friday prayer begins with a *khuṭba* (religious address), which is followed by a congregational prayer consisting of two prayer units (*rakaᶜāt*).

LEGAL STATUS

The majority of Islamic legal scholars have regarded attendance at the Friday prayer to be an individually binding religious obligation (*farḍ ᶜayn*) falling upon all free Muslim males who have attained maturity and are of sound mind and body. They generally do not require attendance of women, children, slaves, travelers, or the sick, although any of these may attend voluntarily. Legal scholars regard the Friday prayer as a manifest symbol (*shiᶜār*) of Islam. Attendance should, ideally, be large so that in addition to being an act of communal worship and orientation, the prayer is also a manifestation of the size and strength of the Muslim community. Indeed, some legal scholars hold that it is not required to hold Friday prayers except in urban communities that can regularly produce substantially large attendance—for example, in urban centers that possess marketplaces or congregational mosques that can accommodate the participants.

During the time of the Friday prayer Islamic law prohibits buying and selling and the making of other types of contracts, such as the contract of marriage, although Islamic legal scholars disagree on whether such transactions and contracts, having been made, remain valid or are to be rendered void. It should be noted, however, that Friday—although the chief weekly day of Muslim worship—never constituted a sabbath for Muslims after the manner of the Jewish and Christian days of rest. On the contrary, the purpose of the prohibition of transactions during the Friday prayer was to free the Muslim community from any preoccupations that might stand in the way of their attendance. Muslims regarded it as permissible to work and to engage in trade and business before and after the prayer. Indeed, many of the earliest Muslim authorities on Islamic law urged Muslims to engage in buying and selling after the Friday prayer and, in the light of the wording of the koranic verses pertaining to Friday prayer (62:9–11), contended that God would bless and amply reward anyone who did so.

THE EXCELLENCE OF FRIDAY

According to Islamic tradition, Friday is the most excellent day of the week, and a large body of *ḥadīth* pertains to its excellence and importance. They state, for example, that Friday is blessed with a special hour during which God will answer the prayer of anyone who calls upon him. Other *ḥadīth* report that God completed the Creation on a Friday, that Adam was created on a Friday, that his entrance into and fall from paradise occurred on a Friday, and that God forgave his disobedience on a Friday. They report that the Day of Judgment will begin on a Friday and that God will manifest himself to the inhabitants of paradise on a Friday; therefore in paradise it will be called *yawm al-mazīd* (the day of increase).

In light of its excellence, Friday is the weekly festival day (*ʿīd*) of the Muslim community, and hence Muslims are to attend the Friday prayer in a happy and festive mood. They are urged not to fast on Fridays or to spend the nights immediately preceding Friday in overly strenuous nocturnal prayer. Muslims are strongly encouraged to bathe each Friday before attending the prayer, to clean their teeth, to wear their best apparel, and to put on scent. Furthermore, Islamic law urges those of whom the prayer is required to attend it regularly; a number of *ḥadīth*, for example, mention harmful spiritual consequences that come to a Muslim who neglects to attend Friday prayers as many as three times because his heart has been hardened, veiled with negligence, or turned to hypocrisy.

HISTORICAL BACKGROUND

The Friday prayer was instituted at Medina somewhat prior to Muḥammad's hegira from Mecca. Islamic sources indicate, however, that Muḥammad, while still in Mecca, directed his community of followers in Medina to conduct this prayer on Friday. The prayer was probably never held in Mecca while the Prophet was there because of the relative weakness of the Muslim community and the hostility it faced from the local majority. Some Islamic religious scholars have held that, when first instituted, Friday prayer was held in a manner similar to *ʿīd* prayers, with the prayer preceding the *khuṭba*. The Friday prayer was probably being conducted in this manner, they continue, when the relevant koranic verses were revealed. At this time many of the Muslims may still not have understood the *khuṭba* to be an obligatory part of the prayer, and thus, as these scholars interpret the koranic passage, on a particular occasion a number of Muḥammad's followers left during the *khuṭba* to receive a caravan of much-needed supplies that had just arrived in Medina. Later, according to these scholars, the structure of the prayer was altered by Muḥammad so that it took its present form, with the *khuṭba* preceding the prayer.

Finally, the origin of the word for Friday—*yawm al-jumuʿa* (occasionally *yawm al-jumʿa* or *al-jumaʿa*, though the first, which is the koranic usage, is preferred)—is not completely clear. The expression means "day of gathering" or "day [the people] gather together," and although it appears to have been used in the pre-Islamic period, it was not the customary pre-Islamic Arab name for Friday. There is consensus among Islamic religious scholars that the customary name for Friday had been *ʿarūba* or *al-ʿarūba*, the former being preferred. Arab philologists, according to al-Shawkānī, generally held that all the pre-Islamic Arabic names of the days of the week, and not just the name for Friday, had been changed with the coming of Islam. Accordingly, *al-jumuʿa* and the other days of the week—whatever pre-Islamic roots they may have had—acquired distinctively Islamic appellations in the Islamic period.

BIBLIOGRAPHY

Solomon D. Goitein, "The Origin and Nature of the Muslim Friday Worship," in *The Muslim World*, **49** (1959), and "Beholding God on Friday," in *Islamic Culture*, **34** (1960); Ignaz Goldziher, "Die Sabbathinstitution im Islam," in M. Brann and F. Rosenthal eds., *Gedenkbuch zur Erinnerungan David Kaufman*, 2 vols. (1969–1970).

UMAR F. ABD-ALLAH

[See also **Law, Islamic; Mosque.**]

FRIDUGISUS OF TOURS (*d.* 834), flourished in the time of Charlemagne and Louis the Pious. He collected laws of Charlemagne and his successors, and wrote the *Epistola de nihilo et tenebris,* in which he tried to prove "nihilum et tenebras esse aliquid" (nothing and darkness are something). A response to the *Epistola* is Agobard's *Contra objectiones Fridugisi.*

BIBLIOGRAPHY

The *Epistola* is in *Patrologia latina,* CV (1864), 751–756; see also Max Manitius, *Geschichte der lateinischen Literatur des Mittelalters,* I (1911), 495.

EDWARD FRUEH

FRIEDRICH VON HAUSEN (*ca.* 1150–1190), member of a noble family that may have had its seat near Kreuznach, not far from Koblenz. A number of documents mention his name between 1171 and 1190. He made his short career as an important member of the Hohenstaufen entourage, went on diplomatic missions to Burgundy and Provence in behalf of Frederick I Barbarossa, campaigned with him in Italy, and was there a second time with Frederick's son, Henry VI. Accompanying Barbarossa on the Third Crusade, Friedrich died when, during the skirmishes near Philomelium, he fell from his horse while pursuing a band of Turks.

Writing at a time when the sophisticated art of the troubadours and trouvères, with its rich variety of poetic forms, had begun to exert its influence on German literature, Friedrich composed seventeen lyrics. They clearly reveal the change from the simple, largely one-strophe writings of the poets identified with the Danube territory to the more form-conscious, more involved, multistrophe lyrics associated with the Rhine region. (That change, a development of the high courtly period, was to reach its apex in the poetry of Walther von der Vogelweide and Reinmar von Hagenau [der Alte].)

Taking a few liberties with his rhymes and using an occasional dialectical form current in his home area, Friedrich wrote courtly love songs in deft language and courtly tone, whether in praise of women or lamenting in reflective manner the state of the egocentrically introspective, troubled lover. In most poems antithetical statements abound, bearing testimony to the intellectuality of the poetic endeavor involved. Behind many a poetic stance lies a cool, detached intellect; it turns these lyrics into pieces of entertainment for a sophisticated audience that is in-

vited to stay abreast of the development of the "plot." In "Ich muoz von schulden sin unfro," for instance, double entendres prevail; subtle irony lies at the heart of this and other lyrics. The irony may be muted, but it clearly makes a game of the persona's delivery to his astute listeners.

Elsewhere there are warmer tones, seemingly based on personal experiences, as when the persona longingly thinks of his far-off beloved and friends ("Mich müet deich von der lieben quam"). Such a tone of genuine feeling and concern comes through also in "Min herze den gelouben hat," which belongs to the genre of the crusade song, as does the epigrammatic "Si welnt dem tode entrunnen sin," which deals with the shirkers who fail to heed the call to the crusade.

Friedrich's most famous poem, "Min herze und min lip diu wellent scheiden," is also a crusade song. In it the persona (the mind) seeks to arbitrate between the body and the heart, which are about to veer in different directions: the former is avid to wage war against the Muslim; the latter clings to the beloved. The lyric is essentially about the threatened destruction of the individual who finds himself in a quandary: since he does not know how to meet the diametrically opposed claims to his loyalty—loyalty to God's cause and loyalty to the lady—the delivery degenerates into a diatribe and causes the persona to flail out in despair against the heart and the lady who commands its devotion. She neither can nor wishes to understand the decision of the mind in favor of the crusade, which will bring about the separation of lovers. There is no indication that genuine spiritual devotion lies at the heart of the persona's problem. Indeed, not even the concept of a knight's service to his lady is fully convincing. Instead, with keen intelligence the poet creates a lyric in which both the heart and the mind are losers: the poetic concern in the end centers on his bereavement rather than on God or the lady.

BIBLIOGRAPHY

Friedrich's lyrics are in the numerous editions of the collection *Des Minnesangs Frühling.* See also Hugo Bekker, *Friedrich von Hausen: Inquiries Into His Poetry* (1977); Friedrich Maurer, "Zu den Liedern Friedrichs von Hausen," in *Neuphilologische Mitteilungen,* 53 (1952); David Mowatt, *Friderich von Husen* (1971).

HUGO BEKKER

[See also **German Literature: Lyric.**]

FRIGG. Together with Freyja, Frigg is one of the two major goddesses in Norse mythology; she is the wife of Odin and mother of Baldr. In *Oddrúnar-grátr* her name and Freyja's are invoked at the birth of children. According to the *Prose Edda,* she is the daughter of an otherwise unidentified Fjǫrgynn, whose name is the masculine form of the noun *fjǫr-gyn,* used in poetic language to designate earth. Her home is Fensalir (Marshy Halls). *Lokasenna* reports that she can foresee the fates of men and gods.

Frigg's existence in the older Germanic culture is well documented. Her name, found in Old High German as Frīja, derives from the Indo-European word *priyā* (beloved). This was the name given to the fifth day of the week in the various Germanic languages as a translation of the Latin *dies Veneris* (day of Venus). Her chief roles in the Old Norse mythological sources are those of mother and wife. As mother, she is a key figure in the myth of the death of Baldr. Frigg tries to protect his life by taking from all things an oath not to harm him; she betrays him, however, by revealing to Loki that she had neglected to include the mistletoe plant in the oath. After Baldr's death Frigg attempts to procure his release from Hel.

In her other role, as wife of Odin, Frigg's image is not as sympathetic. Both *Lokasenna* and Saxo Grammaticus relate that while Odin was away, she was unfaithful to him with his brothers. The prose introduction to *Grímnismál* tells another tale of trickery and deceit. Odin and Frigg argue about the relative merits of their foster sons, Geirrøðr and Agnarr. When Frigg accuses Geirrøðr of being inhospitable and stingy, Odin goes to investigate. Frigg tricks Geirrøðr into capturing and torturing Odin, who comes as a guest under the name Grímnir (The Masked One). In the end Geirrøðr dies and is succeeded by Agnarr.

An interesting analogue to this tale is found in the seventh-century history of the Lombards. In this case Frea tricks her husband, Wodan, into supporting her favorites, the Lombards, in a war against his favorites, the Vandals. Other evidence from continental Europe that verifies Frigg's position in the Scandinavian sources is the Old High German Second Merseburg Charm, dating from 900 or earlier, where her name appears together with that of Wodan and other Germanic deities. Although there is not conclusive place-name evidence of a cult of Frigg, the frequent depictions of *matres* or *matronae* found in the Germanic and Celtic areas during Roman times bear witness to the importance of the worship of goddesses as mothers and wives.

BIBLIOGRAPHY

Henry A. Bellows, trans., *The Poetic Edda* (1923), 84–87, 160–161; Hugo Jungner, "Om Friggproblemet," in *Namn och bygd,* 12 (1924); Gustav Neckel, ed., *Edda. Die Lieder des Codex Regius,* rev. by Hans Kuhn (1962), 56–57, 101–102; Snorri Sturluson, *The Prose Edda,* Jean I. Young, trans. (1966), 37; Edward O. G. Turville-Petre, *Myth and Religion of the North* (1964), 188–189; Jan de Vries, *Altgermanische Religionsgeschichte,* II (1970), 302–307.

KAAREN GRIMSTAD

[See also **Baldr; Charms, Old High German; Grímnismál.**]

FRIK. In the corpus of medieval Armenian literature there are over forty poems that are attributed to a little-known poet by the name of Frik. The name itself is very rarely used in Armenian. According to H. Ačaṙyan, it probably derives from Frederick and also appears once as the name of a scribe. L. Alishan, a nineteenth-century scholar, using an unknown source, states that Frik was the son of Tᶜagvoš and the nephew of Dodonoy. The rest of our information about the poet comes from his poems. From one of these, "Concerning Arhun-Łan and Buła," it is evident that Frik was a contemporary of the Mongol Il-khan Arghūn (1284–1291) and that he lived during the Mongol rule over Transcaucasia. From other poems we learn that the poet was a married man with children, that he was a man of means in the early part of his life, that later in life he lost his worldly possessions and his family, that his son was sold into slavery (which caused him deep grief), and that he devoted the rest of his life to searching for this son.

Unlike the ecclesiastical poets of the period, Frik was, according to his own testimony, unschooled and illiterate. He presumably composed his poems orally and others put them to writing, a practice not unknown in medieval Armenia. His place of origin remains a matter of speculation, but it is clear that the search for his son took him to many lands. One of his characteristic trademarks is mentioning his own name in his work.

The poems, which are written in Middle Armenian, are mostly religious and moral in tone. In some of them he criticizes social injustice. He frequently refers to the plight of the people under the heavy yoke of the Mongols, a situation that is considered to be a God-sent punishment for the sins of Christians. Frik is a highly subjective poet who addresses himself to God to discuss or even complain about social and moral problems that afflict humanity. He uses a variety of meters and writes in a natural but colorful style characteristic of medieval troubadours.

BIBLIOGRAPHY

Frik, *The Divan,* Archbishop Tirayr, ed. (1952), in Armenian. See also Manuk Abełyan, *Hayoc^c hin grakanut^c ean patmut^c iwn,* II (1946).

KRIKOR H. MAKSOUDIAN

[See also **Armenian Literature.**]

FRITHEGOD (**Frithegode, Fridegodus**), English monk, teacher, and poet who flourished around 950. Little is known of his life except that he lived at Canterbury and, according to William of Malmesbury, was tutor to Oswald, the famous Benedictine reformer and future archbishop of York. The only extant work that can with certainty be ascribed to him is the metrical *Life of Saint Wilfrid.* Frithegod wrote at the request of Archbishop Odo, Oswald's uncle, whose preface led many to assign the whole work to him.

Although his poem is a chapter-by-chapter recapitulation of the eighth-century prose biography by Aeddi, Frithegod composed a different work. Where Aeddi gives a straightforward, though partisan, account of the events of Wilfrid's life, Frithegod spins metaphors and draws conclusions in hexameters of lexically obscure Latin occasionally embellished with Grecisms. The result, more a meditation on the significance of Wilfrid's life than a biography, may have been intended to complete rather than replace Aeddi's work.

BIBLIOGRAPHY

For reasons that Douglas C. C. Young makes clear in "Author's Variants and Interpretations in Frithegod," in *Archivum latinitatis medii aevi,* **25** (1955), there is no sound edition of the *Life;* but see James Raine, *The Historians of the Church of York and Its Archbishops,* I (1879), 105–159. See also Max Manitius, *Geschichte der la-*
teinischen Literatur des Mittelalters, II (1923), 497–501; and *Patrologia Latina,* CXXXIII (1853), 978ff.

COLIN CHASE

[See also **Aeddi; Oswald of Ramsey.**]

FROISSART, JEHAN (*ca.* 1337–after 1404), poet, romancer, and chronicler, was born at Valenciennes to a humble bourgeois family. He received a clerical education and entered the service of the counts of Hainaut. In 1361 he went to England to serve Queen Philippa, daughter of the count of Hainaut and wife of Edward III. In his travels to Scotland, France, and Italy, he established numerous social relationships, acquired a distinctly aristocratic outlook, and most important, became a successful and prolific writer who knew how to please his noble protectors. At the death of Philippa in 1369, he returned to Hainaut in search of new patrons. He took holy orders and in 1373 received a benefice in Les Estinnes, near Mons. His two most important benefactors were Guy of Châtillon, later count of Blois (*d.* 1397), who probably encouraged his work on the *Chronicles,* and Wenceslas, duke of Luxembourg and Brabant (*d.* 1383), a poet in his own right, who certainly sponsored his poetry. In 1384 Froissart became a canon at Chimay. He traveled in France and the Low Countries and in 1394–1395 briefly revisited England.

Froissart wrote lyric verse, narrative-didactic poetry, a rhymed romance, and prose chronicles. With the exception of some poems in honor of the Virgin, all of his lyrics celebrate courtly love. His lyric output, composed in fixed forms, is considerable: 13 lais, 6 chansons royaux, 40 ballades, 13 virelais, 107 rondeaux and 20 pastourelles have survived. The last present a special historical interest because the shepherds sometimes make political allusions, and at least six celebrate events that took place between 1364 and 1389. Most of Froissart's lyric and narrative poems were, however, composed before 1373.

Lyric poems were often inserted in the twelve *dits* (or *dittiés* or *trettiés,* that is verse narratives). Some of the *dits* present allegorical dreams, echoing the *Roman de la Rose* and its tradition. In *Le Paradys d'Amour* (1,723 verses) there are not only such traditional figures as Esperance and Doulc Penser but also ancient and Arthurian lovers. *L'espinette amoureuse* (4,192 verses) and *Le joli buisson de Jonece* (5,442 verses) are the most ambitious of Froissart's allegories. Both contain autobiographical details. The principal subject of *La Prison amoureuse* (3,899 verses and 12 prose letters) is a discussion of courtly love by the lover, Rose, and the poet, Flos. There is also an allegorical dream that tells the story of the real captivity of Rose (Wenceslas of Luxembourg) after the Battle of Baesweiler in 1371.

Le temple d'Onnour (1,076 verses) is an allegorical *dit* recounting the marriage of Desire, the son of Honor, to Lady Plaisance; and *Li orloge amoureus* (1,174 verses) systematically compares the poet's love to the movement of a clock (a novelty in Froissart's part of the world). *Le dit dou bleu chevalier* (504 verses), *Le joli mois de may* (464 verses), *Le dittié de la flour de margherite* (192 verses), and *La plaidoirie de la rose et de la violette* (342 verses) have rather thin plots that seem to serve chiefly as excuses for the inserted lyrics. Froissart also wrote two distinctly autobiographical, and quite charming, *dits: Le debat dou cheval et dou levrier* (92 verses) recounts his travels from Scotland seen through the eyes of his horse and his greyhound; *Le dit dou florin* (490 verses) tells of the loss of eighty florins that he received from Gaston Phoebus of Foix in 1389.

If in his lyric and narrative poetry Froissart faithfully followed the literary canons established by Guillaume de Machaut, his verse romance, *Méliador* (more than 30,000 verses), is the conscious return to an earlier tradition. While most late romances were either recastings or continuations, usually in prose, of older works, *Méliador,* composed in traditional octosyllabic couplets, is original. It depicts the Arthurian knights in their youth. While there are many knights-errant who have numerous adventures, the main plot is simple and almost free of the supernatural. Hermondine, daughter of the king of Scotland, is promised to the knight who proves himself most valiant in a series of carefully organized tournaments and adventures. At the end a highly idealized knight, Méliador, son of the duke of Cornwall, wins both the beautiful princess and the Scottish kingdom. *Méliador,* begun in the early 1360's, was not completed until after the death of Wenceslas of Luxembourg in 1383. The duke's seventy-nine lyric poems were incorporated into the romance.

With its frank glorification of chivalry and its evident desire to restore it in his own time, *Méliador* is a link between Froissart's poetry and the main achievement of his life, *Les chroniques de France, d'Engleterre, et des païs voisins,* a history of almost all of western Europe spanning the years between 1325 (just before the accession of Edward III) and 1400 (the death of Richard II). The *Chroniques* are divided into four parts. Book I, cast by the chronicler in four different redactions, relates events up to 1369 (or 1372, or 1377, depending on the redaction). Up to 1361 Froissart's history is a rifacimento of Jean le Bel's *Les vrayes chroniques.* After that year Froissart followed his own observations, hearsay, and, occasionally, some documents. He took some pains to ascertain the facts, interviewing eyewitnesses and participants, and traveling widely to seek out sources. After Book I he wrote the *Chronique de Flandre,* which narrates the Flemish troubles of 1378–1387. The *Chronique* was incorporated into Book II (two redactions), which ends precisely at 1387. Book III, completed in 1390, and Book IV, completed in 1400, exist in only one version.

Froissart's *Chroniques* enjoyed instant and lasting success, particularly in England, and remain a priceless source for fourteenth-century history. But the modern reader should not expect to find penetrating political history or subtle social commentary in them. Froissart was a man of his times. In his chronicles as well as in his poetry, he faithfully, and apparently sincerely, echoed the views and prejudices of his aristocratic patrons. He never understood the aspirations or the growing power of the bourgeoisie; he had nothing but contempt for the French Jacques and for their English counterparts. Like many of his contemporaries, he believed in the values of chivalry and hoped for their restoration. What matters most is that Froissart was a great writer who left behind a distorted but vivid mirror of his epoch.

BIBLIOGRAPHY

Rae S. Baudouin, ed., *Jean Froissart, Ballades et rondeaux* (1978); Geoffrey Brereton, ed. and trans., *Froissart, Chronicles, Selected, Translated and Edited* (1968); George G. Coulton, *The Chronicler of European Chivalry* (1930); Peter F. Dembowski, *Jean Froissart and his Meliador: Context, Craft, and Sense* (1983); Anthime Fourrier, ed., *Jean Froissart, Le joli buisson de jonece* (1975), and *Jean Froissart, La Prison amoureuse* (1974); Auguste Longnon, ed., *Jean Froissart, Méliador,* 3 vols. (1895–1899); William P. Ker, ed., *The Chronicle of Froissart Translated out of French by Sir John Bourchier, Lord Berners, Annis 1523–25,* 6 vols. (1901–1903); Joseph Kervyn de Lettenhove, ed., *Oeuvres de Froissart—Chroniques,* 25 vols. (1870–1877), the only complete ed. of Froissart's chronicles; George C. Macaulay, ed., *Chronicles of Froissart Translated by John Bourchier, Lord Berners, Edited and Reduced into One Volume* (1899); Rob Roy McGregor, Jr., ed., *The Lyric*

Poems of Jean Froissart (1975); Auguste Scheler, ed., *Oeuvres de Froissart—Poésies*, 3 vols. (1870–1872), for *Le Paradis amoureus* and *Li orloge amoureus*; Frederick S. Shears, *Froissart: Chronicler and Poet* (1930).

PETER F. DEMBOWSKI

[See also **Chronicles, French; Dit; French Literature; Historiography, Western European.**]

FROMENT, NICOLAS (*fl. ca.* 1450–*ca.* 1490), French painter. Among his few preserved works the most notable is the Altarpiece of the Burning Bush

Altarpiece of the Burning Bush, central panel. Nicolas Froment, in the cathedral of St. Sauveur, Aix-en-Provence, 1475–1476. GIRAUDON/ART RESOURCE

(1476) in St. Sauveur Cathedral, Aix-en-Provence, a painting of rich iconographical originality commissioned by King René of Anjou. Froment's style reveals influences of Netherlandish, German, and Italian art.

DON DENNY

FROMUND OF TEGERNSEE (*ca.* 960–*ca.* 1008) became a monk at Tegernsee early in life and priest in 1005. A devoted, if limited, scholar, he copied works of Boethius and Priscian, provided them with glosses, and began to write occasional poetry and collections of letters during his brief stay at Feuchtwangen. The letters throw considerable light on contemporary monastic life. The poetry, which shows some acquaintance with Greek, includes poems on specific events, official greetings to high personages, and mere school exercises. It has little technical merit but considerable historical interest.

BIBLIOGRAPHY

Max Manitius, *Geschichte der lateinischen Literatur des Mittelalters*, II (1923), 517–525; Friedrich Seiler, "Froumundi codex und die Gedichte desselben," in *Zeitschrift für deutsche Philologie*, **14** (1882).

W. T. H. JACKSON

FRUCTUOSUS, illuminator of the prayer book written in 1055 for Sancha, consort of Ferdinand I of Castile and León (now in Santiago de Compostela, *Biblioteca de la Universidad*, Res. I). Written exquisitely in traditional Spanish minuscule, its illuminations exhibit new contacts with art outside Spain and represent a first stage in the development of Romanesque style.

BIBLIOGRAPHY

Manuel Gómez-Moreno, *Arte románico español* (1934), 16; John Williams, *Early Spanish Manuscript Illumination* (1977), 29, 109.

JOHN WILLIAMS

[See also **Manuscript Illumination: Western European.**]

King Fernando and Queen Sancha receive the book from the artist. Prayer book written and illuminated by Fructuosus for Sancha, 1055. BIBLIOTECA DEL UNIVERSIDAD DE SANTIAGO DE COMPOSTELA, MS Res. I, fol. 3r

FRUITS AND NUTS. Fruits and nuts formed an important part of the European diet in the Middle Ages. Orchards of fruit trees abounded. Grapes were eaten as a fruit in addition to being made into wine, and in the Mediterranean world both fruit and nut trees were planted between field crops. Mediterranean countries were noted for the rich variety of fruits grown, not only common ones such as peaches, pears, and grapes, but also new varieties, many of which were introduced into Islamic Spain and Sicily by Arab horticulturalists. Among the Arab-introduced fruits were the sour (or Seville) orange (the sweet variety was not known in the medieval Mediterranean world), the fruit of which, sweetened with sugar, was used in preserves and marmalades, while the juice was a popular seasoning; the banana, grown in the south of Spain; and the cultivated watermelon (called *sandía* in Spanish, after its place of origin, the Sind).

Since fruits and nuts were the objects of overseas trade, Mediterranean peoples developed a taste for a wide range of varieties. The city of Valencia, with its irrigated *huerta* (farming district), produced many types of fruits, especially exotics. There Francesc Eiximenis, writing in 1386, noted white and black raisins, figs, almonds, peaches (including the *albèrxica,* the derivation of which from *persica* indicates an originally Persian variety), apples, pears, a number of citrus varieties (including oranges, lemons, and limes), cherries of several kinds, apricots, pomegranates, jujubes, walnuts, hazelnuts, hackberries, loquats, and quince.

Pietro de' Crescenzi, the fourteenth-century Italian agricultural writer, recapitulates in book V of his *Treatise on Agriculture* the specifications of classical Roman agronomists, such as Varro, Cato, and Martial, regarding fruit and nut trees. For both, medical uses of various parts of the fruit are noted, in accordance with the dictates of Galen, Dioscorides, Hippocrates, or Avicenna, and in the case of nut trees the quality and uses of the wood are noted.

Pietro's discussion of nuts is limited to the four major varieties: almonds, hazelnuts, chestnuts, and walnuts. Almonds are either sweet or bitter. The sweet can be used for food; the bitter, for medicinal purposes. The trees bear more fruit when old than when young, and the best nuts are large and round, with a thin shell. Dried, they remain preserved for a long time. From almond branches are made the best walking sticks, the kind nobles use. From the part of the trunk nearest the roots are made strong mallets for splitting wood. Bitter almonds, taken with sugar, are good for asthma and cough. Almond oil, when placed in the ear, helps to alleviate deafness. Hazelnuts are described in a similar vein: the wood is a material for archers' bows and hoops for wine vessels.

Some of the domestic varieties of chestnut have very large fruit, such as those called *marroni* by the citizens of Milan. The wood is best for houses and excellent for outside uses, as in pergolas and vine stakes. As a medicine, chestnut flesh is recommended for stomach ailments, while pulverized shells can be made into a poultice for the treatment of alopecia and swollen breasts. "The walnut *(noce),*" Pietro remarks, "is so called because it is injurious [*nuoce*], its shade being harmful to other trees." From its wood, stools and strong, durable cart wheels are fashioned, the walnut tree providing the best wood for these purposes of all the timber found in Italy. Walnuts yield an oil that is put directly onto food. As medicine it protects the body against poison, if eaten with figs before meals; in a poultice with onions, honey, and salt, it is effective against dog bite.

Of the temperate-climate fruit trees Pietro discusses the cherry, apricot, loquat, pear, plum, and peach, all in similar terms. The cherry cannot sustain much heat and does best in hilly or mountainous regions. The cherry proper is sweet; the sour varieties are called bitter cherry or *marasca* and have physiological effects opposite to those of the sweet cherry. They can be preserved by drying in the sun. There are many different kinds of apple, and "one can learn the advantage [of each] in each region, through experience." They grow in all climates, and wine and vinegar are derived from them (and also from pears). Apples, particularly green ones, are harmful to the stomach, but the juice has the opposite effect. Pietro mentions no way to preserve these fruits except by sun drying. In the case of plums, the dried form is more medicinally valuable than the fresh. The quince can be preserved by being wrapped in fig leaves or immersed in honey or wine.

Three tropical or semitropical fruits are discussed: the pomegranate, the fig, and the date. The pomegranate, or Punic apple, ranges from sweet to sour (with intermediate forms defined by taste) and cannot be grown in cold regions. It produces an easily digestible wine that has many medicinal uses. Pomegranates have four components: skin, flesh, liquor, and seeds. The liquor ranges in taste (from tart to sweet and insipid), and its medicinal uses vary accordingly. The skin itself, when cooked in water, is useful against dysentery and diarrhea. There is a great variety of fig trees, the fruit of which can be preserved by cooking, by sun drying, or by following the technique of the Spaniards: half-drying, to obtain a plumper product. The flesh was highly regarded as a food.

Medical literature is another major source of information on the consumption of fruit and nuts. Book X of Arnald of Villanova's *Regimen sanitatis* is a compendium of prescriptions relating to the ef-

fects of fruits (by which he means both fruits and nuts) on daily dietary regimes. These include specific rules, such as not eating unripe, wormy, or rotten fruit; furthermore, different fruits are not to be eaten at the same time. For example, figs and grapes both soften the belly, but one fruit at a time is enough and, in this case, figs are more beneficial. Two rules pertain to "oily fruits," among which Arnald lists almonds, hazelnuts, walnuts, pinenuts, and pistachios. The first is that raw ones aggravate the belly, but almonds, walnuts, and pistachios do so less (because they are tender) than do the drier hazelnuts and pine nuts. Second, if cooked with honey or sugar, they are less harmful, but such confections are more for the pleasure of the body than for its profit. Finally, Arnald is concerned, as a class, with antidiarrheics (such as quince and loquats) and laxatives (dates and raisins).

A similar source is the section on fruits in Aldobrandino da Siena's thirteenth-century regimen, which is, like Pietro de' Crescenzi's, more explicitly attuned to humoral pathology than is Arnald's more clinical account. Aldobrandino's medical sources are the same as Pietro's (Galen, Avicenna), but he makes specific recommendations, such as praising the nutritive value of raisins, which, after figs, engender "better health and better nourishment than all the other fruits." Raisins, he continues, may be white, black, red, or mixed white and red in color, and have different virtues.

Fruits and nuts are mentioned in other genres of medical literature, such as antidotaries and books of simples. The *Antidotarium* of Nicolaus Salernitanus contains practical recipes and directions for application of medicaments that are unburdened by theoretical considerations; almonds, walnuts, dates, and figs are mentioned, as are the Damascene plum, the citron, cubeb, and tamarind (exotic fruits frequently were mentioned in medical texts before they were widely cultivated or traded). The *Livre des simples médecines* of Matthaeus Platearius, on the other hand, gives more specific information on the medical properties and uses of bitter almonds, cubebs, pomegranates, pine nuts, plums, citrons, raisins, and pistachios.

Both fruits and nuts formed an integral part of medieval cooking. Of more than 200 recipes in the Catalan *Libre del coch* (published in 1520, but representative of Iberian cooking of the late Middle Ages), one third call for almonds: whole, ground, or in the form of "almond milk." Ground almonds were used as a thickening agent in a soup or stew, as flour or cornstarch is used today. Hazelnuts are found in soup and in sauce with almonds having a chicken-broth base; there are sauces of pine nuts and almonds, and of almonds and the juice of oranges or another sour fruit (like the pomegranate), recommended for poultry; and a chicken stuffing of pine nuts and almonds. Apples, both sweet and sour, appear in several forms, including cooked with ginger and cinnamon, and in a mutton soup (together with quince or pears). Pears or quince cooked in broth were the basis of another sauce, and a recipe for quince marmalade is also included. Orange juice, as a convenient souring agent, was the standard garnish for fish dishes; and a sweet sauce or soup, made with lemons, ginger, and chicken broth, was called *limonada*.

Nuts and dried fruits were a prominent component of long-distance trade, as can be appreciated from the *Pratica della mercatura* (Practice of commerce), a mid-fourteenth-century commercial manual by the Florentine Francesco Balducci Pegolotti, in which "fruit" appears as a generic term for nuts and dried fruits. Pegolotti lists them among objects of trade in both the Christian and the Islamic Mediterranean, as well as in northern France, Flanders, and England. The nut most frequently mentioned is the almond, followed by the hazelnut, chestnut, walnut, pistachio, and pine nut. Repeated phrases, such as "fruit, that is, hazelnuts and chestnuts" and "hazelnuts, walnuts, and chestnuts," give the impression that such goods were sold together; dates and figs also appear in lists of nuts. Almonds were sold in the shell, shelled, or crushed. The shelled almond, according to Pegolotti, should be large, fresh, mature, and sold in the year it is harvested. The kernel should be reddish on the outside and white at the core, hard, without fractures, and free of dust. The most popular hazelnuts were those of Naples, which were sold in Constantinople, Acre, Rhodes, and Tunis, and those of Salerno, sold in Naples and Alexandria. The hazelnuts may have been the standard imported nut: in Naples it set the manner of sale for walnuts and chestnuts. Chestnuts were sold in the shell, and Pegolotti also singles out those of Naples. Pistachios were sold mainly in the eastern Mediterranean, but they also appear in specifications for Bruges.

Among dried fruits the most common were dates, figs, and raisins. With regard to dates, Pegolotti specifies that they should be fresh, large, reddish, and, most important, must still be joined to the cap attached to the stalk. With the cap attached, the date will never turn maggotty inside; without it, it will spoil. Dates were sold all over the Mediterranean, with Alexandria mentioned as a frequent place of origin. Figs, mainly from mainland Spain and Majorca, were packed in baskets (as they still are today) and sold all over the Mediterranean, as well as in northern European centers such as Bruges. Raisins appear as exports from various grape-growing regions, including Syria, Italy, and Spain, those from Spain packed in baskets like figs. Pegolotti also mentions currants, oranges, citrons, and carobs. Sour oranges were heavily traded in the fifteenth century, particularly in Sicily, where at least one ship laden with 200,000 of them is documented.

BIBLIOGRAPHY

Aldobrandino da Siena, *Le régime du corps*, Louis Landouzy and Roger Pépin, eds. (1911); Arnald of Villanova, *Obres catalanes,* Miguel Batllori, ed., II, *Escrits mèdics* (1947); Francesco Balducci Pegolotti, *La pratica della mercatura* (1936, repr. 1970); Pietro de' Crescenzi, *Trattato della agricoltura,* 3 vols. (1805); Nicolaus Salernitanus, *L'antidotaire Nicolas,* Paul Dorveaux, trans. (1896); Ruperto de Nola (pseud.?), *Libre del coch* (1977); Matthaeus Platearius, *Le livre des simples médecines* (1913); Andrew M. Watson, *Agricultural Innovation in the Early Islamic World* (1983); Francesc Eiximenis, *Regiment de la cosa publica* (1927).

THOMAS F. GLICK

[See also **Agriculture and Nutrition, II: The Mediterranean Region; Arnald of Villanova; Eiximenis, Francesc.**]

FRUTOLF OF MICHELSBERG (d. 1103), monk of Michelsberg, near Bamberg, compiled a world chronicle covering the period from the Creation to 1099, which is one of the most impressive historiographical achievements of the Middle Ages. Because Frutolf did not mention his own name in the chronicle, historians throughout most of the nineteenth century believed that it was the work of Ekkehard of Aura. It is now known for certain, however, that Ekkehard merely continued Frutolf's chronicle up to 1125.

Frutolf's history is distinguished for its exhaustiveness and concern for accuracy. It relies most heavily in its earliest parts on the world chronicle of St. Jerome, but it also draws on an astonishingly wide array of other sources, including Josephus, Orosius, Jordanes, Isidore of Seville, Bede, Paul the Deacon, Frechulf (or Freuchulf) of Lisieux, Widukind von Korvei, and Richer. For large parts of the tenth and early eleventh centuries it becomes thin because it relies only on a local chronicle of Würzburg; but by the middle of the eleventh century it presents original information, and it becomes a major independent source for the years from 1071 to 1098. Frutolf worked very hard to establish accurate chronologies and to seek the truth wherever his sources disagreed: in such cases he stated his own view but also included the alternatives, to allow the reader to judge.

His style is very restrained and unadorned. When copying other sources he often abbreviated them to present the most essential information. He usually followed the annalistic method of yearly presentation of events, but on a few occasions broke out of this format to give complete accounts of such main developments as the careers of Alexander the Great and Charlemagne. Frutolf was generally more interested in political than ecclesiastical history. When he came to his own age, he devoted much space to the investiture controversy, but he treated it more as a political than as a religious event. His account of the struggle is particularly noteworthy for its avoidance of zealous partisanship, although there is no doubt that Frutolf, who recognized Henry IV's antipope, Guibert of Ravenna, was fully loyal to the imperial cause.

Frutolf's chronicle is a landmark in medieval historiography because there had been no attempt to compile an exhaustive world history for about two centuries before the time he wrote. Considering the materials on which he could draw, he established about the most complete, efficient, and accurate outline of world events possible. Perhaps just because his chronicle was spare and lacked strong opinions or philosophical speculations, it served as an irreplaceable reference work and point of departure for the historical writing of others.

BIBLIOGRAPHY

Sources. Ekkehardi Uraugiensis Chronica, in Georg Waitz, ed., *Monumenta Germaniae historica,* VI (1843), 33–267, the only full edition of Frutolf, includes Ekkehard's and related additions; Franz-Joseph Schmale and Irene Schmale-Ott, *Frutolfs und Ekkehards Chroniken und die Anonyme Kaiserchronik* (1972), German trans. with facing-page Latin of Frutolf for the period starting in 1001, with subsequent additions to 1125 (intro. has best review of recent research).

Studies. Harry Bresslau, "Die Chroniken des Frutolf von Bamberg und des Ekkehard von Aura," in *Neues Archiv der Gesellschaft für ältere deutsche Geschichtskunde,*

21 (1896); Irene Schmale-Ott, "Ekkehard von Aura," in *Die deutsche Literatur des Mittelalters: Verfasserlexikon,* Karl Langosch, ed., V (1955), and "Frutolf von Michelsberg," *ibid.;* Wilhelm Wattenbach and Robert Holtzmann, *Deutschlands Geschichtsquellen im Mittelalter,* rev. ed. by Franz-Joseph Schmale (1967), 491–506.

ROBERT E. LERNER

[See also **Ekkehard of Aura; Historiography, Western European.**]

FUERO (from the Latin *forum,* square, marketplace, place for administering justice, jurisdiction), in medieval Spain generally referred to the legal statute granting privileges to a city or town. Thus, the *fuero municipal* (town charter) was the written expression of the immunities or exemptions from general laws or taxes granted to a place by a king or lord. It reflected the greater or lesser autonomy that the municipality enjoyed.

As early as the ninth and tenth centuries, *fuero* had the meaning of right, exemption, or immunity, and from the eleventh century also that of rent or tax (the *forum* or *fuero* that was paid to the local lord). Thus the word could refer both to a charter of privileges and to the hereditary transfer or use of land. In the thirteenth century it also came to be used in the sense of emphyteutic contract (preserved in the Galician *foro*).

Visigothic law was theoretically still in force in the early Middle Ages, but in practice, since it was not recognized everywhere, custom prevailed as a source of law. In Christian Spain legal practice was governed by ancient customary norms of Germanic origin or by customs derived from more recent socioeconomic conditions. The prevalence of such customs, at first unwritten, led to the development of numerous local legal systems.

In principle the *fueros* were immunities or exemptions granted by the king or by the great lords in order to encourage the rapid colonization and repopulation of lands recently conquered from the Muslims. The present and future inhabitants of a place were given a *carta puebla,* or charter, that listed the exemptions granted to them as well as the laws by which they were to be governed. In this way the inhabitants of many towns obtained a privileged legal position, and some of these powerful frontier towns became almost autonomous entities. The *fuero* was also a unifying force among the inhabitants, for it sanctioned their freedom of residence; freedom from unreasonable search; freedom to will their property to whomever they chose; communal possession and use of waste, pasture lands, forests, and sources of water; and the receipt of payments that were formally the monopoly of the lord.

The oldest local *fueros* appeared in the tenth century and usually contained the immunities granted to a given town, the norms governing the relations between the settlers and the king or lord, and sometimes provisions concerning penal or procedural law. After further elaboration in the eleventh century, the *fueros* achieved their fullest development in the two following centuries, when the previously scattered legal material was compiled and written into statutes. These statutes were based on the original *carta puebla* (if there was one), local customs, and the immunities granted to the place; sometimes new legal provisions or provisions copied from the laws of another town were added. Thus, the later *fueros* set forth in great detail the internal organization and the private, penal, and procedural law of the town.

Many *fueros* were first written in Latin and later translated into the vernacular. Others, however, were originally drafted in the vernacular. Although some of them have a marked popular flavor, reflected in both their rudimentary structure and their language, others, such as the *fuero* of Soria, consist of very careful redactions that reveal the hand of a professional lawyer. Many towns at first had a shorter *fuero* and later a more extensive one. Often the king granted to one locality a *fuero* that was already in force in another place, sometimes with the addition of new legal provisions. For this reason historians of Spanish law have classified the *fueros* in "families" of similar content.

The short Leonese and Castilian *fueros* include the *fuero* of León, granted by Alfonso V to that city (in 1017 or 1020), which greatly influenced such other short *fueros* as those of Pajares and Villavicencio; that granted by Alfonso VI to the Mozarabs, Castilians, and French who settled in Toledo after the reconquest of the city in 1085; and those of Sepúlveda (1076), Oviedo (1145), Guadalajara (1133), and Uclés (1179). In Aragon there is the short *fuero* of Jaca, the prototype of an important family of charters (Estella, S. Sebastián, and others). It contains the oldest use, outside of Catalonia, of the term "burghers" to refer to people engaged in commerce and industry. In Navarre the best-known *fuero* is that of Tudela (1127).

The prototype of the long *fueros* of León and Castile is the *forum Conche* (*fuero* of Cuenca), granted by Alfonso VIII of Castile at the end of the twelfth century. It gave rise to a large family, including Teruel, Morella, Béjar, Plasencia, Cáceres, Sepúlveda, Soria, Alcaraz, Alcázar de S. Juan, Úbeda, and Baeza. In recent years the precise filiation of these charters has been reinvestigated, and their relationship has been questioned. Another important charter, unrelated to that of Cuenca, is the *fuero* of Zamora, which influenced that of Salamanca, that of Madrid (the work of the municipal government), and several Portuguese *fueros*. In Aragon there are the long *fuero* of Teruel and that of Zaragoza (1119); in Catalonia, the *Costums* of Lérida; and in the kingdom of Valencia, the *Costums* of Valencia (1240).

The regional *fueros* appeared later than the local *fueros*. The most ancient of this type are probably legendary: the *fueros* of Sancho Garciá, count of Castile (*d.* 1055), and the Aragonese *fueros* of Sobrarbe. The ancient *fuero* of Aragon was probably redacted to provide a clear statement of the peculiar laws of the kingdom that were to be accepted and respected by the count of Barcelona, Ramon Berenguer IV, upon his accession to the throne of Aragon (1137). Although private copies or digests existed in the twelfth century, the fundamental collections of regional *fueros* were drafted in the thirteenth century: the *fueros* of Castile (1248), the *Siete partidas* of Alfonso X, the *fueros* of Navarre, the *fueros* of Aragon (1247), proclaimed by James (Jaume) I, and the *Furs* of Valencia (originally called *Costums*), ratified by Jaume I in 1261. All of these achieved their maximum development in the fourteenth and fifteenth centuries.

In Aragon and Valencia the regional *fueros* that followed the collections proclaimed by Jaume I were entirely the product of the cortes (parliament), which obtained their ratification through a formal agreement with the reigning sovereign. From then on, in the kingdoms of Aragon and Catalonia *fuero* came to mean any legal provision agreed upon by the three estates that composed the cortes and ratified by the king. As a result the authority of the *fueros* became superior to that of any other law.

In the later Middle Ages the introduction of Roman law into the Iberian Peninsula did not necessarily lead to the rapid extirpation of the ancient local laws, but rather to their gradual supplantation, with both the sovereign and professional lawyers cooperating to that end. Thus, Ferdinand III, respecting the tradition of local *fueros,* granted the Romanized *fuero juzgo,* the old Visigothic code of laws, to the cities he reconquered in Andalusia and Murcia. In 1252 to 1255 Alfonso X, influenced by Roman and Canon law and perhaps inspired by the desire to make the various local Castilian legal systems more uniform, ordered the compilation of a legal code known as the *fuero real.* The nobility and the towns opposed the king in this matter, and the sovereign was compelled to confirm the ancient *fueros* and privileges of some of the cities of his kingdom. By 1300 the Romanized *Código de las siete partidas* had acquired its definitive form; it served to undermine the bases of the older codes of law and to shape the mentality of the new school of professional lawyers.

Despite the failure of the first attempt to standardize the law of the land, common law (Roman-canon) gradually prevailed throughout the peninsula. Because new legal provisions peculiar to a town or region were no longer being created and because judges were unfamiliar with local statutes, local ordinances tended to disappear. In this way the longer *fueros* were reduced to a few specific instances of local law within common law. This change represented a complete reversal of the older legal situation, the diversity of which expressed the social and political fragmentation of Christian Spain.

BIBLIOGRAPHY

Sources. Ramón d'Abadal y Vinyals and Ferrán Valls Taberner, *Usatges de Barcelona* (1913); José Maria Font Rius, *Cartas de población y franquicia de Cataluña* (1969); A. García Gallo, "El fuero de León, su historia, texto y redacciones," in *Anuario de historia del derecho español,* **39** (1969); Hayward Keniston, ed., *El fuero de Guadalajara (1219)* (1924); José Maria Lacarra, *Fueros de Navarra,* I, *Fueros derivados de Jaca* (1969); Real Academia de la Historia, *Colección de fueros y cartas-pueblas de España* (1852), a catalog attributed to Munoz y Romero; Ureña y Smenjaud, *Fuero de Cuenca* (1935).

Studies. Luis García de Valdeavellano, *Curso de historia de las instituciones españolas* (1968); Ernesto Mayer, *Historia de las instituciones sociales y políticas de España y Portugal durante los siglos V al XIV,* 2 vols. (1925–1926); Nicholaas E. Van Kleffens, *Hispanic Law Until the End of the Middle Ages* (1968).

MARIA PILAR APARICIO-LLOPIS

[See also **Law, Spanish.**]

FULBERT OF CHARTRES (*ca.* 970–10 April 1028) was probably born in northern France and was of lowly origin. He apparently studied under Gerbert of Aurillac at Rheims. He was schoolmaster and chancellor of Chartres, had been ordained a deacon there by 1004, and became its bishop two years later. Fulbert was one of the chief leaders in the French church and kingdom, and a steadfast supporter of both episcopal and royal authority. He especially tried to protect the church from the encroachments of the feudal world and to uphold a high standard for the clergy; but at the same time he himself was both feudal lord and vassal, and thus forced to divide his energies between secular and religious tasks. This situation is reflected in his letters. Among his correspondents—and many sought his advice, especially his fellow bishops—were some of the most important churchmen of the time, including Abbo of Fleury and Odilo of Cluny, as well as such great nobles as King Robert II of France, who counted Fulbert among his chief supporters; Duke William V of Aquitaine, who made him treasurer of St. Hilaire at Poitiers and to whom Fulbert wrote a famous letter explaining the feudal oath; and Count Fulk Nerra of Anjou and Count Odo II of Blois.

The school of Chartres was among the best of its day, and Fulbert was a much loved master celebrated not only for his learning but also for the holiness of his life and the soundness of his spiritual guidance. He knew the standard classical and patristic authors, and was especially learned in law and medicine. Although he was abreast of the latest advances in education—some of the astronomical works that had just been translated from Arabic and the new program of dialectical studies that Gerbert had introduced into the curriculum and that was based on the *Logica vetus* and Boethius' writings—Fulbert's intellectual and educational instincts were conservative, particularly in religious matters. Ironically, his best-known student was Berengar of Tours, whose teaching on the Eucharist was so controversial. Fulbert also began the rebuilding of Chartres cathedral, which had been detroyed by fire in 1020; the project was unfinished at the time of his death, and only the crypt remains today.

Fulbert's Latin is unusually clear and precise, and he must be ranked among the best writers of his time. His collected works include his own correspondence as well as that of his closest disciple, Hildegar (in all, 131 letters), 24 poems on religious and school topics, several sermons (mostly aimed at promoting the cult of the Blessed Virgin), an anti-Jewish polemic, and liturgical compositions. They enjoyed a respectable diffusion, primarily in northern France and England, from the mid eleventh to the mid twelfth century; and his letter on the feudal oath and a sermon for the feast of the nativity of the Blessed Virgin achieved the status of minor classics.

BIBLIOGRAPHY

Fulbert's collected works are in *Patrologia Latina,* CXLI (1853), 163ff., now largely superseded by Frederick Behrends, ed., *The Letters and Poems of Fulbert of Chartres* (1976), with full references to manuscripts, earlier editions, and secondary literature. A critical edition of Fulbert's other works also by Behrends, is in progress.

F. BEHRENDS

FULCHER OF CHARTRES (*ca.* 1059–*ca.* 1127), chronicler of the First Crusade and of the Latin principalities of Antioch, Edessa, and Tripoli and the Kingdom of Jerusalem until 1127, when, presumably, he died at Jerusalem. Nothing is known of Fulcher's life except what is explicit or implicit in his *Historia Hierosolymitana* (History of the expedition to Jerusalem), covering the period 1095–1127. Since he is silent on any personal part in the fighting he describes, Fulcher was almost certainly in holy orders and was probably ordained before 1096. Sensitive to the horrors of war, he once wished he were "at Chartres or Orléans" rather than facing the perils of an ambush near Beirut. His report of the Council of Clermont, where Urban II raised the First Crusade, is valuable but not certainly an eyewitness account. Fulcher set out with Stephen, count of Blois and Chartres, probably as his chaplain, and in company with Robert of Normandy and Robert of Flanders. In 1097 he was present at the Battle of Dorylaeum; in the same year he joined Baldwin I, who was to be count of Edessa and, by 1100, king of Jerusalem in succession to Godfrey of Bouillon. Fulcher became canon of the Holy Sepulcher and perhaps prior of Mt. Olivet.

By late 1101 Fulcher began to write the *Historia* and, working with interruptions, apparently brought it down to his own last years. The later portion, recounting events at a distance from Jerusalem, where his age confined him, reflect his concern to question eyewitnesses. Fulcher's use of classical sources has been adjudged to reflect some contact in his youth with the cathedral school at Chartres, but not to show a high level of scholarship. Along with the anonymous *Gesta Francorum et aliorum Hierosolymitanorum* and the *Liber* of Raymond d'Aguilers,

Fulcher's *Historia* is a precious source for the events it recounts.

BIBLIOGRAPHY

Fulcheri Carnotensis, Historia Hierosolymitana (1095–1127), Heinrich Hagenmeyer, ed. (1913); *Fulcher of Chartres: A History of the Expedition to Jerusalem 1095–1127,* Frances R. Ryan, trans., Harold S. Fink, ed. (1969). See also *Anonymi gesta francorum et aliorum Hierosolymitanorum,* Heinrich Hagenmeyer, ed. (1890), trans. by Rosalind Hill as *The Deeds of the Franks and the Other Pilgrims to Jerusalem* (1962); *Historia Francorum qui ceperunt Iherusalem* [by] *Raymond D'Aquilers,* John Hugh Hill and Laurita L. Hill, eds., with English apparatus (1968).

EDWARD A. SYNAN

[See also **Crusades and Crusader States: To 1192; Historiography, Western European.**]

FULDA. Boniface and Sturmi established a community of monks beside the Fulda River on 12 March 743 (or possibly 744). Lying at the intersection of trade routes running east to Erfurt and north to Fritzlar, the monastery became a training center for missionaries. Grants of land and immunities by Carloman were enlarged by later Carolingians and other Frankish families, while Roman ecclesiastical privileges were intended to keep the monks free from interference by bishops of Würzburg and Mainz. Whether formerly rich or poor, each Fulda monk became lord of lands and barns with considerable independence. Abbots were able to avoid most feudal obligations, though other difficulties arose: Sturmi (743–779) was exiled; Baugulf (780–802) and Ratgar (802–817) were forced out of office; Hrabanus Maurus (822–842) retired to avoid political jeopardy; Theoto (856–868) disappeared. After Boniface's death in 754 the presence of his bones brought pilgrims and gifts to Fulda, which grew rapidly and opened priories nearby on the Petersberg, Frauenberg, and Johannesberg, as well as more distant foundations and cells. By 822 there were 134 monks at Fulda itself and about 600 men and women in orders; service personnel and others directly involved with the community probably raised the number to 5,000 persons.

The enormous Salvator basilica (321 by 100 English feet), built mostly under Ratgar and the elderly Eigil (818–822), was modeled on Old St. Peter's in Rome. Its use of modular architecture did not follow the ideal plan apparently derived from Aachen councils of reform, and there is no clear evidence that Benedict of Aniane had any other influence on monastic life at Fulda. The smaller Michaelskirche was also built during this time and is still in use. Crafts of manuscript illumination, wall painting, sculpture, and goldwork flourished in harmony with a penitential system and liturgical pattern that Boniface may have brought from central Italy.

Fulda abbots responded to Charlemagne's emphasis on education by developing their own school and by sending many students to Aachen and Tours, including the architect Einhard, the artist Bruun Candidus, Hrabanus Maurus, abbot Samuel of Lorsch (and bishop of Worms), Recchio Modestus, and abbot Hatto of Fulda (842–856). All returned to Fulda where they taught literature, mathematics, astronomy, singing, biblical exegesis, and theology. They built a great library of about 2,000 books, including Horace, Cicero, Ovid, Pliny, Latin epitomes of Euclid, and a Hipparchan view of the heavens. The school attracted students who later became quite prominent: Walafrid Strabo from Reichenau, the Saxon Gottschalk (later of Orbais), Lupus of Ferrières, Baturich of Regensburg, Otfrid of Weissenburg, Hartmunt and Werinbert of St. Gall, Haimo of Halberstadt, Ermenrich of Ellwangen, Salomon of Constance, Guntram of the imperial chancery, and Bernhard from the royal family and later king of Italy. Its greatest influence was in the missionary areas of Saxony, Thuringia, and Franconia, where legends were transcribed (*Hildebrandslied*) and new writings were stimulated (Otfrid, *Der Krist*) that are among the earliest Old German literature.

Ottonian and Salian politics were detrimental to the piety and learning of Fulda. Its monks were often preferred as bishops, but Henry II placed it under the pluralist abbot Poppo (1014–1018) for reform. Richard (1018–1039) and Sigiward (1039–1043) reestablished the school as well as the liturgy. But continued royal appointments and donations meant an excessive attachment of abbots and monks to interests and personnel of the imperial court. From 1133 the abbots of Fulda were imperial chancellors, and they gained episcopal jurisdiction over their territories and princely status within the empire. The number of monks fell steadily, and the great library did not increase from the mid eleventh century until it was plundered by humanists during the councils of Constance and Basel and again during the Thirty Years War.

BIBLIOGRAPHY

Walter Horn and Ernest Born, *The Plan of St. Gall,* 3 vols. (1979), compare many aspects of Fulda life with those of other monasteries; Raymund Kottje, "Hrabanus Maurus—Praeceptor Germaniae?" in *Deutsches Archiv,* **21** (1975), and "Hrabanus Maurus," in *Die deutsche Literatur des Mittelalters, Verfasserlexikon* IV.1 (1982), useful for the entire first century of Fulda history with excellent bibliographies; Paul Lehmann, "Fulda und die antike Literatur," in Josef Theele, ed., *Aus Fuldas Geistesleben* (1928), valuable concerning the MSS of Fulda and their contents; Karl Schmid *et al., Die Klostergemeinschaft von Fulda,* 3 vols. in 5 (1978), analysis of surviving prayerlists and other sources containing names of Fulda monks, along with other personnel, patrons, and friends; Wesley M. Stevens, "Compotistica et astronomica in the Fulda school," in Wesley M. Stevens and Margot H. King, eds., *Saints, Scholars, and Heroes,* II (1979), includes a large repertoire of sources for monastic scientific studies.

WESLEY M. STEVENS

[See also **Benedictines; Boniface, St.; Hrabanus Maurus.**]

FUNDUQ is the Arabic word used, especially in North Africa, for an urban hostelry. In addition to housing for traveling merchants, a secure depot for merchandise, and stabling for pack animals, the *funduq* also provided space in which merchants could transact business. These functions correspond to those of the urban *khān* (Turkish: *han*) of the eastern Islamic world and the *wakāla* of Egypt, and are similar to those of the caravansaries, or highway hostelries, built along the major trade routes of the Islamic world.

The word *funduq* derives from the Greek *pandocheion,* which, in the medieval period, was a building sometimes attached to a church or synagogue to provide accommodations for needy strangers. In medieval Cairo members of the Jewish community owned several *funduq*s in which tenants paid monthly rent. However, in general *funduq*s were administered by Muslim pious endowments (*waqf*s) that rented space to traders, artisans, or concessionaires. In towns and cities involved with international trade, *funduq*s were occasionally made available to European traders, for whom secure walls and gates offered protection of their wares as well as their persons in case of riot. As early as 1157 the Pisans had a *funduq* in Tunis, and in 1236 the merchants of Marseilles had one in Ceuta.

The typical form of the *funduq* is a rectangular courtyard surrounded by two-story buildings. A single entrance, large enough to admit pack animals, gives access to the courtyard from the street. In the ground-floor rooms facing the court, animals are stabled and merchandise can be stored until the transactions are completed. The second story, reached by stairs, is usually provided with a portico giving access to small rooms for the merchants.

BIBLIOGRAPHY

R. Brunschvig, *La Berbérie orientale sous les Ḥafṣides* (1947), *s.v.* index; Solomon D. Goitein, *A Mediterranean Society,* II (1971), 113–114 and 186–190; Eleanor Sims, "Markets and Caravanserais," in George Michell, ed., *Architecture of the Islamic World* (1978).

JONATHAN M. BLOOM

[See also **Hân; Trade, Islamic; Travel and Transport, Islamic.**]

FURNITURE, ISLAMIC. An examination of the concept of furniture in the Muslim world of the Middle Ages may cast light on some of the most conspicuous features of medieval civilization. Although furniture as such, the usages associated with it, and its various kinds, represent a very narrow and marginal aspect of life, they still illuminate certain matters of great importance in the development of Muslim society.

Most of the data on furniture in medieval Muslim society derives from written sources, but religious (for instance, *ḥadīth*), historical, and geographical literature and belles lettres *(adab)* contain fragmentary data only. Most of the belles-lettres sources reflect everyday life in Baghdad and Cairo and even the Persian regions, though less frequently, whereas Turkish regions are mentioned very rarely, and only in relatively late sources. The name of a bed can be identified from one source; from another we learn that it may have had legs, while in a third source we read something (object, animal) or someone was introduced or crawled beneath the bed, and hence we deduce that this was a bed with legs and of a certain height (not very common in the Muslim world of the Middle Ages, but extant).

This literature is supplemented by documents from the Cairo Genizah, including marriage contracts that specify the dowries of the contracting

Detail of a miniature from a 13th-century manuscript, possibly Syrian, showing a chair. BIBLIOTHÈQUE NATIONALE, MS FONDS ARABE 3465, fol. 83r

parties. This source rounds out our information because most literature deals extensively with the upper classes and sometimes describes poverty, but is deficient in reference to any middle class or lower classes.

Plastic art as an iconographic source is not as rich. Some helpful indications may be derived from the forms of furniture (mainly thrones) hinted at on painted pottery or decorative metalwork. Most useful are the many miniatures dating mainly from the thirteenth century on, for instance the richly illustrated manuscripts of the Iraqi school represented by Bidpay's *Kalīla wa-Dimna* (Paris, Bibliothèque Nationale, MS fonds arabe 3465) and al-Ḥarīrī's *Maqāmāt* (in the Academy of Sciences, Leningrad, MS S-23).

It is also necessary to investigate the language itself. Does the lexical imagery generated by the Arabic language, which was the official literary tongue of the Muslim world, include the concept of furniture? And if Arabic does not express linguistically the concept in the form to which we are accustomed in the West, can furniture be said to exist *functionally* nevertheless?

There is no specific term for furniture in Arabic. Concepts such as "furniture," "tableware," "carpets," "household objects," and "utensils" overlap, and the language frequently resorts to the use of approximate notions and broader categories. These terms include, for example, *farsh* (carpets, bedding, and furniture), *āla* (crockery and household goods), *adāt* (utensils), *athāth* (literally belongings, but also various household objects and, especially in modern Arabic, furniture), and *matāᶜ* (personal property, domestic items). In addition, two of these terms may be used in combination, as with *farsh* and *āla* or *farsh* and *athāth*.

The various linguistic expressions of "furniture" underscore a major difference between "Western style" and "Oriental style" (or, more precisely, what the French call "la mode de vie à l'orientale").

Travelers from the West, and even some orientalists, have often erroneously described the interior of the Muslim household as "uninhabitable" or "empty." But this offhand dismissal fails to consider the various factors that determine how people choose their furniture, such as their way of life, their

taste, and their manner of partaking of food (in this case, it is significant that food is often eaten from a squatting rather than a sitting position).

Life in the medieval Muslim home was lived essentially on ground level. At meals, people squatted in a circle, either directly on the carpet or on "seats" of various thicknesses: a cushion *(wisāda, mirfaqa, tuk'a, miswara, numruq)*, a pillow *(mikhadda)*, a pair of cushions with one on top of the other, or a cushion folded in two. The food was served in a kind of serving dish, with or without legs, the receptacle sometimes separable from its support. Individual plates were not used; rather, those partaking of the meal served themselves directly from the central serving dish, which would be placed on a small, low table *(khuwān, māᵓida, daysaq, fāthūr, mudawwara, muhawwal, muᶜtasamāt,* and *simāt*—most of these terms denote a very small, round table; some, such as *simāt,* signify a low, oblong one). As soon as the meal was over, the serving dish and the table were removed from the room.

Yet not all medieval Arabic furniture was low. There were stools or chairs *(karāsī;* sing., *kursī)*

Baghdadi tables. Detail of a miniature from a 13th-century manuscript. BIBLIOTHÈQUE NATIONALE, MS FONDS ARABE 5847, fol. 47v

with wooden or metal legs, and thronelike seats called *sarīr* and *takht,* but these were not used for meals. Carpenters also built fairly high trestle tables and benches for use outside the home. A high stool indicated elevated status, and might be occupied by a prince, the head of a family, or, sometimes, an ordinary individual to whom honor was due.

Seating levels reflect social categories and class distinctions. Positions range from occupation of a throne or a high stool (indicating supremacy), of two superimposed cushions, of a single cushion folded in two, of just one ordinary cushion, or of the carpet itself, right down to the most humble position of squatting on the ground (a mark of lowliness, abjectness, or mourning). Another indicator of social rank is the range and quality of materials used in furniture; the height of luxury is a bed with legs; not quite as good is the bed without a frame, followed by the *martaba,* a good-quality mattress stuffed with down; simple mattresses laid on the ground and serving as couches by day; ordinary paliasses, sleeping mats, and carpets; piles of rags and heaps of clothing, or lastly, for the very poorest, the bare ground. Again, the slumbering head of the wealthy man would be supported by cushions and pillows both stuffed with and encased in the choicest of fabrics, such as silk, while the lowliest had to make do with rags, or even a stone for a pillow.

In the royal courts, Umayyad art seems to indicate the use of very tall, Western-style thrones, modeled after those of Byzantium. However, scholarship suggests that these images do not mirror conditions in the Syrian court. Medieval texts indicate that a long reclining couch, serving as another kind of throne, was used extensively in the courts of the Umayyads, the Abbasids, and local princes (such as the Ikhshidids in Egypt). Since the sovereign could either recline on his *sarīr* or invite a friend to be seated beside him, the seat must have been fairly long.

In fact, the concepts of mattress, seat, throne, and bed do not admit of clear separation either. The Persian word *takht,* for example, can mean any of the following: board, seat, throne, sofa, bed, calculating tablet, chest, or box. However, this overlap did not prevent the evolution of ceremonial rituals, accompanied by a differentiation of function. Thus a seat or a throne might be used for public or solemn audience, for private audience, or for feasts. The overlap of concepts, moreover, proved no obstacle to the introduction or reintroduction of thrones and narrow seats (of Persian manufacture, for example), as well as longer and more elaborate thrones. Although

certain scholars believed that the bed was unknown in the medieval Muslim world, this is not entirely accurate. The use of the bed with frame for both reclining and sleeping became fashionable in high and middle society toward the end of the ninth century and the beginning of the tenth. More common, however, were mattresses without springs. Documents from the Cairo Genizah frequently indicate that mattresses served as relatively inexpensive beds; as very expensive items, beds with frames figure very rarely in the dowries of young brides. Between these two extremes is the *martaba,* used as a couch by day and a bed by night.

The use of furniture reveals not only distinctions among the various population strata, their living conditions, and their consumer habits, but distinctions between the nomadic life of the majority of Arabs during the pre-Islamic period and the sedentary life after acculturation. For example, *mā'ida, khuwān,* and *sufra* are synonymous in medieval Arabic and denote the small "Eastern" table. Medieval philologists endeavored, quite arbitrarily, it seems, to distinguish between the first two, both of which denote a solid table. The third, and sometimes also *naṭ* and *mā'ida* (exclusively in the context of the Koran and its commentaries and in certain passages of the *ḥadīth* literature) referred to a skin stretched out on the ground and serving various functions in the home and on excursions to the countryside. The *sufra* was used not only among the early Bedouin but also in circles of sedentary Arabs. (In modern colloquial Arabic, *sufra* refers to an ordinary table, and a *sufraji* is a waiter in a restaurant or cafe.)

These terms raise questions of the choices and influences bearing upon sedentary habits. When people had to choose between the relatively higher furniture used in Byzantium, which was less respected outside the metropolis, for instance in Byzantine Syria (because that area had passed through a process of orientalization long before the Muslim conquest, according to some scholars), and the relatively lower furniture common to formerly Persian regions, the influence of Bedouin tradition could play a role in favor of the latter. Medieval lexicographers and commentators (writing on words such as *ṭustkhuwān* and *fāthūr,* for example) imply that it did. This influence was probably not strong enough to prevail among the acculturized Arabs in the sedentary countries, but it had enough strength to influence the choice between the different sedentary traditions and styles.

Although they had no cupboards as such, the medieval Muslims employed a diverse range of chests, cases, and boxes (*ṣundūq, takht, qamṭara, muqaddima, safaṭ*), as well as recesses and racks (*rufūf*).

In surviving examples of medieval wooden furniture, along with certain ceramic objects that imitate them, cavities for storing jugs are sometimes found, which recall the supports-plus-shelves mentioned in the texts. Some are still extant: various Muslim countries separated by great distances offer examples of the *minṣab* (support) or *kursī* (support, small table) with *ṣiniyya* (a round tray). Visual representations also indicate a certain degree of standardization in lifestyle and taste throughout the Muslim world, regional styles notwithstanding, and suggest that household objects were traded from one country to another. Uniformity seems to have prevailed over local modes.

The essential nature of the Eastern way of life was preserved to the very brink of the modern era, as attested by Turkish and Persian miniatures of the seventeenth and eighteenth centuries. The traditional way of life is described by travelers, writers, and orientalist scholars even in the nineteenth and early twentieth centuries, as seen in the writings of Edward R. Lane about Egypt, Louis Lortet about Syria, and Antonin Joseph Jaussen about Palestine. Even though the Mongols introduced the use of a higher type of square table, in certain semiurban areas as late as the early twentieth century the term *franji* (foreign, from "Frankish") can still be found to refer to elements that resemble European furniture, such as beds with frames, and which were introduced from abroad or under foreign influence. European-style furniture, introduced only in the last two centuries, has become popular in our century and has tended to displace the original Eastern way of life that abounded in taste and comfort.

BIBLIOGRAPHY
Solomon D. Goitein, *A Mediterranean Society,* IV, *Daily Life and the Individual* (1983); Oleg Grabar, "Notes sur les cérémonies umayyades," in Myriam Rosen-Ayalon, ed., *Studies in Memory of Gaston Wiet* (1977); Joseph Sadan, "A propos de *martaba*," in *Revue des études islamiques,* **41** (1973), "Meubles et acculturation," in *Annales,* **25,** (1975), and *Le mobilier au Proche-Orient médiéval* (1976); V. Strika, "La formazione dell'iconografia del Califfo nell'arte ommiade," in *Annali, Istituto Universitario Orientali di Napoli,* n.s. **14** (1964).

JOSEPH SADAN

[See also **Cairo Genizah; Kursi; Urbanism, Islamic.**]

FURNITURE, LITURGICAL. Though not as sacrosanct as the altar and altar apparatus with their eucharistic associations, other liturgical furnishings in a medieval church were considered almost as holy. This furniture was to be constructed, used, and destroyed according to specific canonical regulations. It was blessed according to multiple formulas found in pontificals, rituals, and benedictionals. And from late patristic antiquity throughout the Middle Ages, liturgical commentators described in detail various items of this furniture, looked for their origins in the Old and New Testaments, and assigned them spiritual meanings appropriate to the uses to which they were put.

Eucharistic furniture. Related closely to the altar and its apparatus but set apart from the altar were containers used to house the sacred species of bread and wine. In the ancient church the consecrated host might be carried by acolytes and other clerics in *capsae* (reliquaries) and *turres* (tower-shaped vessels) to other churches and to the sick, and even ordinary Christians might carry the Sacrament in containers to their homes for use there. But out of fear of profanation, the maintenance of the consecrated species was later restricted to the church itself and to carrying containers for those in special circumstances. When not kept in hanging pyxes and the like at the altar, the consecrated host might be stored in ambries, or safelike locked cupboards set into the wall of the sanctuary, usually on the Gospel (left) side. During the later Middle Ages enormous sacrament houses were built near the altar and decorated with scenes of the Passion. Some of these were surmounted by gigantic towers and pinnacles reaching high into the vaulting of the church. It was only in the sixteenth century that the tabernacle, covered with its fabric *conopaeum,* came to be placed on the altar itself.

One of the more unusual containers was the structure known as the Easter sepulcher, used to house the consecrated host during the period from the Holy Thursday Mass until the Easter vigil. These might be in the form of an ambry or sacrament house near the main altar or a large, freestanding, round and roofed structure designed to resemble the Basilica of the Anastasis in Jerusalem.

Altar enclosures. Although the ciborium was the most immediate enclosure for the altar, other screening devices set at some distance were common in the ancient and medieval church. Bouyer holds that very early, veils like those used in the Jewish temple were used to screen the altar. Later the chancel area within which the altar lay was enclosed by *cancelli* (balustrades) surmounted by a pergola with its columns and beams, from which might be hung curtains, lamps, votive crowns, and the like. In the High and later Middle Ages the high screen separating the nave and chancel developed into a nearly solid wall, and this was surmounted by a jube or *pulpitum* from which the lessons might be read. On or above the screen might be a rood (large crucifix) on whose sides figures of the Virgin Mary, St. John, and others might be placed.

Liturgical seating. Benches and chairs may be classified broadly as those for the clergy and those for the laity. Even in the ancient church it might have been the case that only one person had seating—the bishop, whose cathedra (throne) symbolized his teaching and judicial roles in the Christian community. In the ancient church and into the Middle Ages, the fixed cathedra might be found in various locations in the church. Until even the ninth century the bishop's cathedra might be in the middle of the nave, but it was more usually placed at the base of the apse, perhaps surrounded by benches for the other clergy. In churches where the altar was at the base of the apse, the bishop's throne could be moved to the Gospel side of the apse, although in some ancient *ordines* it is said to be to the "right" of the altar. In form, the episcopal cathedra was usually a high-backed and armed chair made of wood, stone, metal, or ivory and often richly sculptured, carved, or otherwise decorated. Often it was set on a dais and was covered by a canopy. When the bishop was in the presence of a higher cleric or when he required a movable seat, as at ordinations, he used a faldstool, which consisted of a wood or metal folding chair with armrests but with no back.

For the clergy attending the bishop, a variety of seating arrangements were possible, although until the eleventh century it was possible that all clergy would stand throughout liturgical services. If the bishop's throne was at the apse base, one or more ranks of benches would be placed to either side, and if the throne was freestanding, attending clergy might sit on *scabella* (stools) to either side of him. The priest and, if present, the deacon and subdeacon would sit on sedilia (benches) on the Epistle (right) side of the apse. These benches might be set against or into the wall, be covered with canopies, and might be in the form of a single bench or divided into three compartments, sometimes on different levels denoting the relative dignity of each occupant. Another type of seat for the clergy was the shriv-

ing stool, usually a heavy chair with arms. Until the sixteenth century and the development of the box-like confessional, the confessor sat on this shriving stool in the open church to hear the confession of the penitent.

Lower clergy, canons, and musicians had their own seating arrangements in the so-called schola cantorum and later in the stalls of the choir. The so-called schola could be attached directly to the chancel area or it might be separate from that area and nearer the middle of the nave. The enclosed choir, which became common from the eleventh century, could be attached to the sanctuary, in the middle of the nave, in the west end, or even in the west tribune gallery of the church and would contain rows and perhaps banks of stalls or connected compartmentalized seats facing one another. These stalls might be raised on a dais and have a dorsal (a high back). Made of stone or wood, the stalls could be ornately decorated and carved. Hinged, tip-up seats in the individual stalls frequently had shelflike projections called misericords, often richly and humorously decorated beneath, on which the standing occupant could support himself during long liturgical services.

Until the thirteenth century the laity usually stood, slouched, or supported themselves on sticks during liturgical services, although benches could be placed around the walls for the aged and sick. In some localities in the thirteenth century benches were placed in free areas of the churches, but it was not a general rule to use benches or pews for the laity until the sixteenth century.

Reading furniture. So that ministers chanting or reading the lessons and giving homilies and sermons might easily be heard, special furnishings were constructed. Bouyer points out that, following Jewish practice, early churches had a bema, or platform with lecterns, from which the lector read. These might be in the middle of the church, or when a second solea was used, it might be placed at the entrance to the sanctuary. During the Middle Ages lecterns might be portable or fixed. In the early medieval Spanish churches, for example, it is known from manuscript illuminations that large, movable, decorated wooden lecterns were used, and throughout the Middle Ages such portable lecterns might be moved around the church as needed. These lecterns might have one desk, but for choir use the lectern might have desks on four sides on which enormous choir books could be placed for reading from all sides.

It was the general custom, however, for reading

desks to be set permanently in *ambones* (ambos). There might be one or two of these from which the Epistle and Gospel were read. Rising to twenty feet or more, the ambos could be ornamented with stones, jewels, cosmatesque mosaic tiles, and the like. Particularly impressive are those in southern Italy, from which the deacon read the Exultet at the Easter vigil and over which he unrolled his illuminated text for the congregation to see.

Lessons or sermons could also be given from the jube or *pulpitum*. In the Milanese rite and in the High and later Middle Ages, a pulpit might be placed in the nave of the church next to or attached to the columns, and by the fifteenth century it was frequently surmounted by a canopy or sounding board.

Credence. Within the sanctuary of a church could be a *credentia,* fenestella, or credence. This small table probably developed from a niche or window in the wall of a church's sanctuary into which was placed the piscina, or drain, and on which the bread and wine and eucharistic accessories were placed while not in use. By at least the thirteenth century, tables were substituted for the fenestella, and it was the common practice that such tables be on the Epistle side of the sanctuary. The term credence perhaps derived from the word used to describe any small table on which foods were placed for tasting.

Prie-dieu. Also within the sanctuary could be a litany desk or prie-dieu, called a *genuflexorium* because it was used for kneeling before the altar or the reserved Sacrament, or for other purposes when extended kneeling was required. Such a piece of liturgical furniture was probably in use by at least the eighth century because in the oldest eucharistic rite in the *Ordines romani* it is said that the pope on arriving at the altar prays on an *oratorium.*

Lights. Lights of many types were used in the ancient and medieval church not only for the practical purpose of illumination but also for cultic reasons. Although there was some opposition in the ante-Nicene church to the use of lights for ceremonial purposes because of their connection with pagan celebrations, it appears that by the fourth century they were widely used for a variety of cultic purposes and had come to signify joy, honor, and even such biblical images as the pillar of fire in the wilderness, Christ the light of the world, or the apocalyptic seven lamps before God's throne. Although little distinction was made between the two major types of lights—lamps with their holders, vessels, oil, and wick; and candles with their stands or sticks, wax,

and wick—and although lamps and candles were used indiscriminately for many purposes, it is perhaps appropriate to treat them separately here.

The numbers, sizes, and shapes of lamps and their holders varied enormously in medieval liturgical usage. Hanging chandeliers might take the form of crosses and circular or polygonal *coronae* (crowns). Made of precious or base metals, the crowns holding lamps might have towers at various points symbolizing the splendor of the heavenly Jerusalem. Perhaps the most famous of these chandeliers are that of Pope Adrian I, with its 1,365 lights, and that of Frederick I Barbarossa, given to the cathedral of Aachen in the twelfth century. Lamps might be hung from crossbeams or set on pediculated stands. And cressets of stone or metal might hold one or more lamps and be suspended or placed around the church.

Candles might be set on any of these various types of suspended or standing holders, but much better known are the candlesticks and candelabra that might hold one or more candles. These include standing and processional candlesticks; the trident-shaped hearse (or stand) for the Easter vigil procession; the enormous stationary paschal candlestick, sometimes as high as thirty-five feet and beyond; the multibranched stationary candelabrum reminiscent of the Jewish menorah; and the stationary tenebrae hearse or stand used in the Holy Week office of tenebrae.

Beyond their use for illumination and as part of the altar apparatus, both lamps and candles functioned in a variety of liturgical settings. At baptisms a candle was dipped into the font symbolizing the sanctifying fire of the Holy Spirit. Candles, which were sometimes named, were held by newly baptized persons and, in some places, by all those attending the baptism. At Mass, candles and torches were used in the introit and Gospel processions and, later in the Middle Ages, at the elevation of the Host. During Holy Week from Thursday to Saturday candles or lights were set on the tenebrae hearse, and as the office proceeded they were extinguished, often in groups of threes, until the church lay in darkness. At the Easter vigil ceremony either a candle on a staff with a serpent representing the serpent in the wilderness or three candles on the trident hearse were lit from the new fire and carried in procession to the place where the paschal candle stood. During the singing of the Exultet or *praeconium paschale* by the deacon from his tall ambo, the paschal candle itself, set on its tall stick, incised with a cross, the year, and alpha and omega, bearing grains of incense symbolizing the wounds of Christ, and having appended to it a paschal table or chart with calendric information, would be lit at the words *ignis accendit*. On Candlemas, the Feast of Purification, candles for domestic and liturgical use for the year were blessed and then carried in a penitential procession. In processions with the Sacrament and especially in the later medieval Corpus Christi processions, lights were carried as a mark of honor. At dedications of churches, twelve candles could be placed inside and outside the church. Lamps and candles were hung or set before the shrines of saints, before images and icons, and in the later Middle Ages before the reserved Sacrament. Votive lamps and candles, sometimes cast in the shape of human limbs, were burned in petition for healing or in thanksgiving for blessings received. And finally, in funeral processions, wakes, and the funeral Mass itself candles and torches were burned, at times in ostentatious excess, as at the funeral of the earl of Flanders in 1385 where the hearse had 700 candles and throughout the church 1,226 more were burned.

Textile furnishings. Apart from the textile altar covers and veils, a medieval church could be filled with a miscellany of fabrics. Curtains or veils, often richly decorated, could be hung from the pergola or between the nave and aisles, and there might be a *velum ianuarium* to cover the doors. On festive occasions the hard stone of the floors and covering of straw could be overlaid with carpets, and a miscellany of *parata* (coverlets and canopies) could be placed on the sedilia and over the thrones. Finally, decorated cushions could be placed on thrones, seats, and faldstools for the comfort of the occupant and as a sign of his dignity.

Wall and columnar furnishings. Attached to or standing before the walls and columns in a medieval church could be a variety of furnishings. Besides the biblical, hagiographical, and liturgical scenes in mosaic and fresco, carved or sculpted figures of humans and animals might be attached to the walls or columns as objects of devotion, honor, or instruction. Among these might be crucifixes, figures of saints, patrons, and, in the very late Middle Ages, carved or sculpted stations of the cross depicting scenes from Christ's passion, which with prayers and readings could be followed as a substitution for the way of the cross in Jerusalem.

To honor the faithful departed and patrons, bequest boards and memorial tablets could be appended to the walls and columns of the church, and hatchments with the coat of arms of a deceased person, which had been carried in the funeral procession and kept over the doorway of his house for a period, might then be hung in the church.

Praesepe. In its devotional and instructional aspect the *praesepe* (*presèpio* or crèche) was not unlike the stations of the cross. Following St. Francis' erection of a Christmas crib at Greccio in 1223, the custom of constructing such scenes using sculpted or live figures grew rapidly, and not only were replicas of the Nativity set up in churches, but also scenes depicting other events in Christ's and the saints' lives were made for use at appropriate times in the year.

Processional apparatus. Together with the lights in liturgical processions, other objects might be carried. Crosses were commonly used both inside the church and in outdoor processions. These might be made of precious metals and highly ornamented for festal seasons and days, or they might be of wood and simply painted for penitential seasons. Attached to the cross might be the corpus of Christ, and flowing from its arms might be pennons. Related to these pennons were the vexilla, red streamers attached to processional crosses as early as the seventh century. Although banners were used primarily in secular practice as the battle emblem and identifying standards for military men, they could also be appropriately carried in ecclesiastical processions. Accompanying the candles, crosses, and banners might also be thuribles with their burning incense and small boats with their shovels in which the incense grains were kept.

Umbrellas and canopies, as marks of honor and dignity, were part of the processional apparatus. Canopies on several poles or umbrellas on one were carried over high ecclesiastical dignitaries. And as a mark of respect for the Sacrament, umbrellas were carried over it in the church and canopies or umbrellas in Corpus Christi processions outdoors.

Chests and boxes. Throughout medieval churches a variety of chests, freestanding and set into walls, could be used for liturgical purposes. Ambries set into or attached to the walls of the sanctuary and baptistery were used not only to safeguard the Sacrament but also to hold blessed oils and liturgical books. Freestanding chests were used to keep altar apparatus and books, and presses or closets were set up in sacristies and vestries for liturgical vestments. To receive alms, secured chests were placed in the church, and to hold bread, bought out of bequests and distributed to the poor at the end of Mass, dole cupboards, sometimes highly decorated and with appropriate ventilation holes, were set up in the church or in adjacent rooms and buildings.

Water vessels. Beyond the vessels used for water at the altar, medieval churches contained a miscellany of vessels, fonts, basins, and buckets where water was kept or used in liturgical services. From at least the ninth century, a piscina or sacrarium was set up near the altar or in a niche in the wall with a drain reaching to consecrated earth. It served for the disposal of water and other sacred things that had been used for ritual purposes. By the early thirteenth century it was the custom to have two piscinas, one for the water and wine with which the chalice was cleansed and the other for the water used in the ablution of the priest's hands.

For the washing of liturgical vestments, linens, altar cloths, and feet during the *pedilavium,* basins were used, and canonical legislation regulated the persons and method of washing.

Both portable and fixed containers were used to hold the three types of blessed water. Highly ornamented aspersoria (buckets) were used as early as the ninth century to carry holy water for the little office of the Asperges before Mass. Buckets contained water for sprinkling objects, persons, and animals during benedictions. And so-called Gregorian water—water mixed with salt, ashes, and wine—was carried in buckets and used in the consecration of churches.

Portable buckets with ordinary holy water (exorcised water with salt added) were placed near the entrances of churches for the faithful to dip their fingers in or cross themselves with, but by the eleventh and twelfth centuries these were replaced by fixed stoups set into the wall or by pediculated fonts.

Baptismal water with its oil of catechumens and holy chrism was kept in the baptismal font, which might be placed in a separate baptistery or in the church itself. The font might take several forms: the piscina below floor level for immersion, a font at floor level for immersion or infusion, or one standing above the floor used for infusion. The font itself might have two compartments, one for the blessed water and one for individual baptisms. It might be surmounted by an ornate, heavy cover, often locked so as to prevent profanation of the blessed water within.

Oil vessels. A variety of utensils were used to store and handle the oil of the infirm, oil of catechumens, and holy chrism that had been blessed by the bishop on Maundy Thursday. Ampullae or larger vessels were used to keep diocesan supplies of these three types of oil and might have the letters OI, OS, and CS on them. Parish churches had their own stocks kept secure in ambries. For individual use small chrismatories, appropriately labeled with the type of chrism, held the oil, and this was dispensed either with a spatula or with the priest's thumb.

Funereal furniture. For exequial functions a medieval church maintained a number of liturgical furnishings. When the dead body was carried into the church on its feretory or bier, it was set on a hearse, platform, or stand. Palls belonging to the church or brought by the friends of the deceased were then laid over the body or the *arca* (chest) in which it might be placed. The palls themselves were usually of a somber color, though they could be of gold cloth and adorned with crosses or other symbols in contrasting colors. Over persons of high rank a towering structure known as the *castrum doloris* was raised. This was a lofty arched framework of wood or metal with a number of posts or columns supporting one or more steeply pitched roofs. Fitted into this structure could be prickets for a multitude of candles, which in the case of Sixtus IV (1484) totaled over a thousand. If a funeral service took place without the corpse itself, a catafalque was used resembling the bier with its pall.

Surrounding the bier, *castrum doloris,* or catafalque could be candles on their sticks numbering from a few to as many as two thousand, and these might be taken in procession to the burial site itself.

Musical, signaling, and timing devices. To accompany liturgical services and to signal various points therein, medieval churches were furnished with a number of devices.

Organs are known to have been played in churches as early as the eighth century, and by the tenth century they were used to accompany vocal music. By the thirteenth century they seem to have been common in larger parish churches and universal by the late Middle Ages. At first, organs seem to have been of a small, portable variety, but by the thirteenth century they had become substantial pieces of equipment and thus were fixed in the churches.

Bells are popularly said to have been introduced into Christian worship by Paulinus of Nola (ca. 420), and in evidence thereof it is pointed out that they were called *nola* or *campana* after the town and the region in Italy. There may be a grain of truth in this, but bells also went under the terms *clocca, signa,* and *tintinnabula,* and some of the best brass used in making bells came from the Campania. In any event, bells are mentioned in the writings of Gregory of Tours, and Pope Sabinianus (604–606) is said to have ordered their use in the liturgy of the church. By the eighth century their use was common throughout the church, and special benedictions had been composed for use during their construction and for their consecration or "baptism," when they were anointed with oil and named according to the inscription within them. The thirteenth-century liturgist and bishop Guillaume Durand lists several kinds of bells: *squilla* used in the refectory, *nola* in the church choir, *nonula* (double bell) for the clock, *campana* in the campanile, *signa* for the belfry tower, and *tintinnabula* (little bells). According to the ordination rites for clerics, it was the duty of the *ostiarius* (doorkeeper) to ring the bells. This was done during various parts of the Mass such as the Sanctus, during parts of the Office such as the psalms of compline, during the Angelus, and to signal the beginning of services or to knell the last agony, death, and burial of a Christian.

On Good Friday and Holy Saturday the ringing of bells, with their joyful association, was forbidden, and hence a wooden clapper was used as a signaling device.

A variety of clocks were also used in churches, and an hourglass with the appropriate amount of sand might be hung next to the pulpit to keep an enthusiastic preacher within limits and to mark the time of Scripture reading.

BIBLIOGRAPHY

Louis Bouyer, *Liturgy and Architecture* (1967); David R. Dendy, *The Use of Lights in Christian Worship* (1959); Achim Hubel, *Das Domschatzmuseum Regensburg* (1975); Robert Lesage, *Vestments and Church Furniture*, Fergus Murphy, trans. (1960); John B. O'Connell, *Church Building and Furnishing: A Study in Liturgical Law* (1955); Erwin L. Sadlowski, *Sacred Furnishings of Churches* (1951).

ROGER E. REYNOLDS

[See also **Altar—Altar Apparatus; Ambo; Architecture, Liturgical Aspects; Baldachin; Bells; Bema; Cathedra; Choir; Church, Types of; Ciborium; Exultet Roll; Lighting Devices; Organ; Prie-dieu; Processions; Screen; Screen, Chancel; Sedilia; Solea.**]

FURNITURE, WESTERN EUROPEAN. Very few examples of medieval western European furniture have come down to us, both because the materials used in their construction were easily destroyed and because furniture itself seems to have been a comparatively rare commodity in the Middle Ages.

The attempt to identify the types and usages of furniture in the Middle Ages depends on information gleaned from inventories and allusions in contemporary texts, and on illustrations in illuminated manuscripts. (Although such illustrations may appear to offer only an imaginative perspective rather than realistic evidence, thorough examinations of contemporary inventories imply that manuscript illuminations convey the medieval domestic interior with relative accuracy.) Occasionally, fine carvings, such as may be found in cathedrals or on ivory objects, will provide depictions of furniture.

Consequently, it is not surprising that we have only stray data about furniture before the thirteenth and fourteenth centuries. The Anglo-Saxon epic *Beowulf* refers to a thronelike chair reserved for the overlord; a Carolingian king used a type of gilded bronze stool with curved legs modeled after a Roman variety. The financial and social instability of the age does not appear to have been conducive to the development of an industry designed to refine the standard of living. Similarly, the small percentage of the population able to write or to illuminate manuscripts did not turn its attention to furniture.

Not until the thirteenth century was there sufficient prosperity and stability to permit (or, perhaps, to necessitate) the documentation of furniture. Starting from this period, however, we can begin to form an impression of the furniture of the wealthy. We still cannot approximate the furniture of the poor and of the peasants; some scholars speculate that their living conditions were so primitive that the

Oak chest, the front carved with knights in armor, tilting. Harty Church, Isle of Sheppey, early 15th century. VICTORIA AND ALBERT MUSEUM

Walnut chair with pierced tracery, linenfold panels, and a hinged seat. French, 15th century. METROPOLITAN MUSEUM OF ART, NEG. NO. 139928

poor owned nothing that we today might designate as furniture.

The customs and way of life of the upper classes dictated the development of furniture. In a wealthy or noble household, domestic activity—eating, sleeping, the transacting of business—generally took place in the great hall of the home. The range of functions that the hall served and the numbers of people passing through it required that the furniture be set against the walls, or be readily disassembled.

Moreover, those wealthy enough to own furniture maintained several residences. When they moved among these, they took with them all of their valuable possessions. Furniture had to be either built into the walls of the home or so heavy and massive that it could not be stolen, or else light and easily transportable so that it could be packed and carried.

Folding chairs, tables with heavy but removable tops that rested on folding trestles, and the comparatively generous use of fabrics and cushions characterized the furnishings of even the most affluent. The portability of medieval furniture, perhaps its most striking feature, is an aspect reflected in the French word for furniture, *mobilier*. The practice of routinely moving the household furniture probably developed as protection against invaders; its persistence in peacetime, however, suggests the scarcity and costliness of furniture.

The most fundamental item of furniture was the chest. Originally, the chest was a hollowed log; during the course of the Middle Ages, it evolved into a rectilinear piece. The chest was used for storage and transportation of goods; it was also a seat, a bed, and a table; in the kitchen, it could serve as a hutch first for kneading dough and then for storing bread. A locked chest might house costly goods; with a slotted lid, it became a receptacle for money. Because they often contained valuables and thus invited thievery, chests were sometimes given to churches for safe-keeping.

Oak armoire with linenfold panels. French, 15th century. METROPOLITAN MUSEUM OF ART, NEG. NO. 122036

Many different pieces of furniture evolved from the chest, such as the bench or form (the terms are interchangeable). The bench anchored to a wall may have given rise to the movable form, with or without a paneled back, and with a seat serving as a lid to the chest beneath it. Supplied with an arm at each end, the form with a back became a settle. The settle too could be put to a variety of uses, and like the chest from which it originated, was also used as a bed.

The bed itself was an extremely important piece of furniture. The "best bed" was often the primary bequest made in wills dating from the fourteenth century. Because a medieval hall or castle did not designate separate rooms as bedrooms, beds were designed for privacy and for protection from the inevitable drafts of the hall in which they were commonly placed. From about the twelfth century, a bed was often given a roof and hangings. Closed beds (lits clos), constructed with three wooden walls and a fourth side consisting of curtains, also afforded privacy.

The terms "celure" and "tester" are frequently mentioned in conjunction with beds in medieval documents and refer to the hangings. Although precisely what part of the hangings is meant is uncertain, the words probably indicate the canopy. The fabric used for the canopy and drapery was often luxurious: velvet, satin, silk, and, occasionally, tapestry. The drapery was suspended from valances or from the ceiling. During the day, the drapery would be gathered into bags, also suspended, and the bed could be used as a couch.

A bed would be outfitted with a straw or wool pallet, several feather beds, sheets, blankets, and an embroidered quilt. Fur might adorn or entirely replace the quilt. The bedding, draperies, and valances would be transported when its owner changed residences, but the wood frame would usually be left in place.

Like the bed, the chair was reserved for the most important members of a household. The chair had special significance as a symbol of authority. Rarely did a castle number more than three chairs, and these were for the master, his wife, and a distinguished guest. The modern word "chairman" conveys a sense of the status once conferred by chairs.

The "thrown" or "turned" chair was an early type, with a triangular wooden seat and three legs. It might well have originated in Byzantium, spread to Scandinavia, and been brought to other regions of Europe by the Normans. The popularity of the tripod design is easy to understand; a three-legged chair

did not wobble even if built with less than precise craftsmanship, and even if placed upon uneven floors.

A more regal chair was the chair of estate, set upon a raised platform along a wall of the feudal hall. Elaborate canopies, themselves a mark of status, added height and splendor; a dosser (a backing of tapestry or rich fabric) and a banker (cushion) on the seat provided a touch of luxury. French records indicate that a special leather bouge (trunk) was constructed for each chair to protect it during transport among the owner's various residences.

The curule, whose arms and legs formed an X, was comparatively easy to transport. Having leather or fabric seats and backs, these chairs were lighter and could often be folded. This type of chair was patterned after an ancient Roman model, and probably spread to northern Europe from Italy.

The dresser or dressoir, an open framework of shelves, served to store or display the owner's tableware (usually gold and silver cups and tankards). Re-

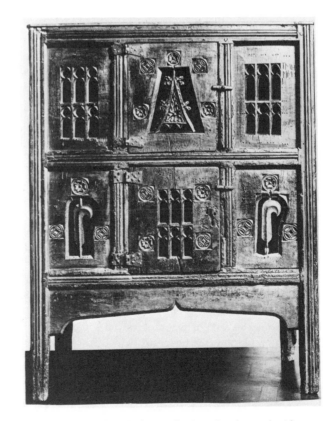

Oak standing cupboard, the panels pierced and carved with tracery; traces of vermilion color are still visible. Probably British, ca. 1500. VICTORIA AND ALBERT MUSEUM

lated to the dresser is a very early piece of furniture known in France as a buffet or buffette, and which could be open, closed, or partially open. Although the design of the buffet varied in complexity, it always included at least one flat space or wide shelf for the storage or display of china, glass, and plate. One type of buffet consisted of superimposed *gradins* (shelves) and was used to display goldware and other finery. Such a buffet would occupy a prominent spot in the medieval home because it offered tangible proof of the owner's prosperity. In France and in the Netherlands, buffets were often exceedingly high and splendid, and sometimes sported elaborate canopies. On a feast day, a type of barrier might be constructed around the buffet to prevent the numerous guests from handling its costly contents.

Several factors may distinguish the buffet from the dresser. First, the buffet seems to have been used to display goods in the hall, while the dresser may have been used to store goods in service quarters. Furthermore, a dresser was, occasionally, only a temporary fixture, erected for a banquet and dismantled thereafter.

What would today be called a cupboard was known as an ambry or aumbry in England and as an armoire in France. In Italy the ambry was almost invariably built into the wall, but in northern Europe this piece was sometimes movable. The ambry consisted of shelves usually enclosed by at least one door, and was used to store arms, housewares, and, especially, food. A food cupboard would be pierced in front to help preserve its contents.

The table was generally a dining table, and of trestle construction. A certain size and weight was essential in order to support the prodigious amounts of food served at banquets. A high table might be set beneath a canopy and upon a dais for the more important members of a household and guests, with the rest of the household seated at side tables placed at right angles to the high table.

A cupboard might double as a side table. A type of side table known as a credenza in Italy and as a credence in France was used as a repository for food about to be served—it was first tasted for poisons at this side table. As this function waned, the credenza developed a back and shelves and was used to display silver.

Medieval furniture was massive and severe. In the northern countries, furniture was generally constructed in oak; the French, Spanish, and Italians also used walnut, and the Alpine countries fir and pine. The forms were generally rectilinear, with emphasis on the vertical (except in Italy, where horizontal lines were more prominent). Only the X-form folding chairs made use of curved lines. Colorful fabrics mitigated the starkness of the furniture. These were not only hung as canopies, but draped over furniture and made into cushions.

North of the Alps, carving was the most popular method of decorating the surface of furniture. With the exception of narrative art depicting scenes from romances, deeds of arms, jousts, and scriptural stories, the decoration was borrowed from Gothic architecture. From about the fourteenth century, arcades of delicate tracery copied from the windows of the cathedrals were extremely popular, and were carved upon cupboard doors, dressers, and chests.

Foliage was another favorite motif, and the forms imitated native plant life, such as maple leaves, parsley, cabbage, and, especially, vine leaves with clusters of grapes. The linenfold motif, however, enjoyed the greatest popularity. This decoration was supposedly patterned after narrow, upright pleats of linen, and may well have originated with the Flemish.

Carved furniture, to the medieval eye, invited bright paint and gilt decoration. Rare extant examples of carved chests bear traces of paint in vivid colors—scarlet, green, and gold. Most furniture, however, was constructed of plain wood, and given a coat of solid, bright paint or covered with fabric.

The use of brilliant color may have compensated for rough construction. Until nearly the middle of the fourteenth century, only carpenters were available to work in wood. At that time, a new technique developed on the Continent that made use of mortise- and-tenon joints and dowel pins or pegs; this was the work of the joiner. By the fifteenth century, the system of paneled framing had been developed in the Netherlands, and this system had great impact on the construction of joined furniture. Before this technique was employed, a joined chest was made of thick boards. With the new development, full walls of uniform thickness were replaced by a system of frames made of uprights and horizontal pieces of thick wood joined with mortise and tenon. The inner edges of the frame had even and deep grooves into which were fitted panels. Set slightly loosely, panels could expand and contract, but would not split, warp, or shrink. These panels might be very thin, since they did not contribute to the support of the structure. Furniture thus joined was lighter and stronger and used less material; accordingly, it was both more economical and more easily transported. Such refinements made possible more detailed con-

Walnut dressoir carved in Flamboyant Gothic tracery. French, late 15th or early 16th century. THE WALLACE COLLECTION, LONDON

struction, such as that involving drawers and compartments.

Furniture seems to have been of fairly uniform style throughout western Europe. As with Gothic architecture, the furniture of France was acknowledged as superior in matters of both design and workmanship. The French were especially noted for precise craftsmanship, an abundance of decoration, and intricately embossed metal fittings. Both the French and the Flemish produced rich yet delicate carving. The English copied or acquired their furniture from the French and the Flemish to such an extent that in 1483 the Guild of Cofferers induced King Richard III to prohibit such trade.

Italy did not conform as completely to the northern styles. It preferred to emphasize horizontal lines in both the design and the decoration of furniture.

For example, the cassone, a variation of the chest, was lower and longer than its northern counterpart. The facade of the cassone bore the most complex decoration, often consisting of intarsia (a kind of inlay work), or pastiglia (a kind of plaster work, usually gilded or painted), or a painted panel set in a pastiglia frame. Classical subjects or scenes from mythology often served as the subjects for such decoration. The Italian interest in horizontality and classical motifs was to inspire and influence the furniture styles of the Renaissance.

BIBLIOGRAPHY

Louise Ade Boger, *The Complete Guide to Furniture Styles,* rev. ed. (1969), 10–65; Penelope Eames, *Medieval Furniture* (1977); Ralph Edwards, *The Shorter Dictionary of English Furniture* (1964); Phyllis Bennett Oates, *The Story of Western Furniture* (1981).

EDITORIAL STAFF

FURS, FUR TRADE

BACKGROUND

There was a great demand for fur during the Middle Ages. Fur coats and fur-lined garments and accessories were often the best source of warmth, and the possession of such garments served as a sign of the wearer's status and wealth. All classes of the population shared in the desire for fur clothes and fur trimmings but, predictably, royalty and aristocrats provided the best market. In medieval England, for example, almost 120,000 squirrel skins were purchased each year for Edward I during the period from 1285 to 1288, and more than 79,000 skins of trimmed *minever* were used by the English royal household in 1344–1345 alone. The fur-lined clothes of the ruling classes required large numbers of pelts: a single *cote* for King John of France was made of 366 skins. Henry IV of England had an outfit or "robe" of 9 garments that used 12,000 squirrel and 80 ermine skins, while Henry VIII had one gown furred with 350 sable skins. When Marie of Savoy was married in 1426, one of the gowns in her trousseau was lined with 618 sable skins.

Rulers were willing to pay dearly for prize furs. At a time when carpenters made around three pence per day, King Richard I of England paid as much as thirteen pounds for one ermine and four sable skins and his brother, King John, spent two pounds on a

FUR TRADE: EASTERN EUROPE

ARCTIC OCEAN

SIBERIA

HALOGALAND

LAPLAND

Kvens

KARELIA

White
Sea

BIARMIA

Pechora R.

Ob R.

Irtush R.

Yūra

Kimāk

Sibir

FINLAND

Lake Onega

Ustiug

Northern
Dvina R.

NORWAY

Lake Ladoga

Beloozero
(White Lake)

Åbo (Turku)

Ves
(Wīsū)

Viatka R.

Kama R.

Helsinki

Gulf of Finland

Neva
R.

Volkhov
R.

Volga

SWEDEN

BALTIC

Reval (Talinn)

Novgorod

R.

Kazan

Volga

Gotland

Dorpat (Tartu)

Pskov

SUZDAL

Kliazma
R.

Mordvins

Bulgār

LIVONIA

Moscow

MORDOVIA

Bulgars

SEA

Riga

Western
Dvina R.

Polotsk

Vitebsk

Lübeck

Danzig

LITHUANIA

Smolensk

PRUSSIA

Dnieper R.

Rus

Burṭas

GERMANY

MAZOVIA

Derevlianians

Don R.

POLAND

Golden

Horde

Nuremberg

Kiev

Cumans

Khazars

Sarai

BOHEMIA

Lvov

PODOLIA

Astrakhan
(Saksin)

Regensburg

AUSTRIA

Tana

Itil

Vienna

HUNGARY

NORTH
PONTIC
STEPPES

On-Ogurs

MOLDAVIA

Venice

TRANSYLVANIA

CROATIA

CRIMEA

Caffa

CAUCASUS

Derbent

CASPIAN SEA

BULGARIA

Cherson
(Sevastopol)

Sudak
(Soldaia, Surozh)

BOSNIA

Dubrovnik (Ragusa)

BLACK SEA

Rome

SERBIA

BYZANTINE
EMPIRE

Constantinople

Baghdad

single sable skin. Al-Mas^cūdī (*ca.* 943) commented that garments made from black *burṭāsī* fox furs were much desired by Arab and Persian rulers, who paid 100 dinars or more per skin. Four centuries later Ibn Baṭṭūṭa noted that an ermine mantle was valued in India at 1,000 dinars and a sable mantle was worth 400 dinars.

Although fur-bearing animals were found throughout most of medieval Europe, nature and fashion combined to favor the animals of northern Europe. In general the most desired furs came from animals taken during the coldest weather; they were normally lighter in color, fuller in texture, and larger in size than those taken from warmer climates or in summer. As a result medieval merchants were inevitably drawn to Scandinavia and the northern parts of eastern Europe, where there was an abundance of highly valued furbearing animals.

The squirrel was the most numerous furbearing animal in central and northern European Russia. Furthermore, squirrel skins from Russia, along with those from Scandinavia, were very highly treasured throughout Europe. Since skinners needed many pelts of exactly the same type to make a garment, Hanseatic merchants developed an elaborate terminology to classify squirrel skins from various parts of Russia and adjoining countries: *schönwerk,* the best and most expensive skins, apparently winter skins from the north; *grauwerk,* winter skins having a bluish-gray back and white belly; *popel,* early summer skins; *ruskyn,* summer skins; *strandling,* autumn skins; *russewerk,* skins from (possibly central) Russia; *clesmes,* skins from the Kliazma region of central Russia; *letowerk,* skins from Lithuania; *onige,* skins from the Lake Onega region; *polanewerk,* skins from Poland; *smolyng,* skins from the Smolensk region; *vair,* furs made from northern winter skins having gray backs and white bellies; *gris,* furs made from the gray backs of northern winter skins; *minever,* furs made from the white bellies of northern winter skins having gray borders; *pured minever,* furs made from the white bellies of northern winter skins having the gray borders cut off.

The most valuable skins came from the weasel family, members of which were found in large numbers throughout central and northern Europe. The black fox, which was highly valued, was found in northern Europe, while white foxes inhabited only the most northern regions. Many otter and beaver were also found along the numerous rivers and streams of Russia. Central and northern Russia thus possessed a great variety of high-quality furs in large

quantities. These areas were unquestionably the most important source of fur in all of Europe.

The medieval Russian fur trade usually involved four basic groups: those who caught the furbearing animals, those who brought the pelts to the major markets of eastern Europe, those who transported the pelts to trading centers scattered from Samarkand to London, and those who sewed and sold the furred garments in local markets outside of European Russia (this last group will not be considered here). The first group remained fairly stable throughout the Middle Ages. It was composed primarily of two distinct people: the Slavic, Baltic, Finnic, and Turkic peasantry who worked arable land in the central regions of European Russia, and the nonagricultural, primarily Finno-Ugrian peoples of northern Russia, most notably the Lapps, who lived beyond the region where farming was possible.

For most of the natives of central and northern Russia the term "trade," applied to the acquisition of furs, was a misnomer. It is true that throughout the Middle Ages they traded some of the pelts of animals they had caught. However, most of the furs sent from these areas were probably obtained by force. At first groups coming from the south and west simply stole the furs. Then these more powerful groups sought to regularize their thefts by calling them "tribute." Among those subject to Turkic-Mongol rulers, it was called *iasak,* the fur tribute. Tribute was often collected by armed bands who visited a region every year or so and took a certain amount of furs. The fur "trade" seldom advanced beyond this stage in northern Russia. In the central regions "tribute" was transformed into "tax" when the Slavic and Turkic-Mongol ruling classes incorporated those lands into their states.

The second group consisted of the tribute and tax collectors, merchants, and raiders who visited the isolated hamlets of central Russia and the inhospitable regions of northern Russia to acquire the furs that they would exchange in the markets of eastern Europe. Most of the people in this group came from the states of European Russia: Kievan Rus and its successor principalities, most notably Novgorod, and the Turkic-Mongol polities that dominated the middle and lower Volga (Khazars, Volga Bulgars, Golden Horde, Kazan khanate). These states provided the great markets of eastern Europe where merchants from all over could purchase the famous Russian furs. To ensure their supply of pelts, almost all of these states attempted to expand their control over central and northern Russia and to convert the natives into tributaries from whom fur could be obtained cheaply.

The Rus and the Turkic-Mongols fought each other for the right to incorporate potential peasant taxpayers along the upper Volga into their states and to transform the inhabitants of northern Russia into their tributaries. Some of the collectors, merchants, and raiders were outsiders, such as the Norwegians, who exploited the Lapps, and the Swedes, who sought to dominate Karelia and the key water route leading from Lake Ladoga to the Gulf of Finland via the Neva River. Novgorod waged a long and fairly successful struggle against these outside threats to its sphere of exploitation. The Rus and Turkic-Mongol states also sought to prevent foreign merchants from trading directly with the natives of central and northern Russia. The prosperity of Novgorod came from its position as chief intermediary in the sale of Russian furs to Westerners such as the Germans of the Hansa, and the Volga Bulgars wanted the same relationship with Muslim merchants.

The third group was composed of the merchants who transported Russian furs and other goods from the markets of eastern Europe to other countries. Most of these merchants were foreigners; they usually came to Russia in groups and received the protection of the local authorities. Rus traders did bring their furs to Constantinople in the tenth and eleventh centuries, and Rus merchants visited Baghdad in the mid ninth century; Novgorodian ships were also active in the Baltic during the first half of the twelfth century. But these were exceptions to the general pattern.

The pelts obtained in European Russia were exported in two general directions: southward to central Asia, the Near East, and Byzantium, and westward to central and western Europe. To understand the medieval Russian fur trade, it is necessary to examine the history of both its western and its southern components.

THE FUR TRADE WITH CENTRAL AND WESTERN EUROPE

The medieval trade in Russian furs with central and western Europe began in the ninth to eleventh centuries. At this time the Vikings developed two main routes to the rich fur lands of central and northern Russia. The northern route led east from the province of Halogaland, in northern Norway, into Lapland. By the second half of the ninth century, the Norwegian kings claimed the right to col-

lect a tribute (the *finnskattr*) from the Lapps, a right they normally delegated to one of their powerful supporters in Halogaland. From this period (*ca.* 880) there is an eyewitness account of a certain Ohthere who sailed from Halogaland to Biarmia, probably the lands along the White Sea coast. Ohthere reports that each Lapp paid tribute according to his means, with the wealthiest paying fifteen marten skins, five reindeer skins, a bear skin, a bear or otter kirtle, and other goods.

Norse sagas such as *Egils Saga, Örvar-Odds Saga,* and the *Heimskringla* describe Norwegian activities in Lapland and Biarmia. While many scholars suspect the historicity of the sagas, their information adds much to an understanding of the northern fur trade. In Ohthere's time the king's agent led a force that might number 100 men or more across the mountains to Lapland during the winter. There the Norsemen not only collected the Lapp tribute but also established a market to trade with the Lapps. In spring the beaver, sable, marten, and other pelts acquired through tribute and trade were brought back to Norway, where the king received his share. Furs obtained from the Lapps were exchanged in countries such as England for wheat, honey, wine, and cloth. In the first quarter of the eleventh century, the king's agent went to Biarmia by boat, accompanied by several merchants. The Norse obtained many gray squirrel, beaver, and sable skins by trading with the natives at a station in the Northern Dvina estuary.

The Norsemen soon found rivals in the quest for northern furs. By Ohthere's time the sagas report that Kylfings from the east (possibly Swedes or Rus) were trading with the Lapps; and the Cwens (or Kvens), who lived north of the Swedes and raided the Lapps, were attacked by the Karelians. The Cwens, according to *Egils Saga,* enlisted Norse aid against the Karelians in return for a share of the booty, which included beaver, sable, and marten skins. According to other sources, the Swedes became active in Lapland and Biarmia, and even collected tribute there. These rivals of the Norse for the furs of Lapland fall into two general groups. The first included the Finnic Cwens and Karelians, who lived just south of the Lapps. The second group included Swedes and Rus, who lived further south and controlled the main fur markets. In the course of time, the Swedes and Rus gained control over the Finnic groups and turned them into intermediaries in the Lapp trade.

The second main Viking fur route led, by way of the eastern Baltic, to central and northern Russia. By the late tenth century Novgorod, located on the Volkhov River south of Lake Ladoga, had emerged as the chief Rus center for the export of Russian fur to the west. Saga stories from the tenth and early eleventh centuries mention Bjorn, nicknamed Fur-Bjorn, who went trading to Novgorod before settling in Iceland; and they tell of Guthleik, a great merchant who often traveled to Russia and, around 1015, journeyed to Novgorod to purchase fine furs and other goods for St. Olaf. These and other reports of Norse merchants who visited Russia leave no doubt that Viking merchants shipped Russian furs to the West from Novgorod. In the course of time, the Baltic route became the chief artery for the export of Russian furs to central and western Europe.

Two changes profoundly altered the Russian fur trade via the Baltic in the twelfth century. Novgorod successfully asserted its independence from the grand prince of Kiev, and the merchants of Gotland, who had succeeded the Vikings as the leading Western traders in Novgorod, slowly lost their place to the merchants from the north German cities. The earliest trade treaty concluded by Novgorod (ca. 1190) was with representatives from Gotland and the north German cities. Early in the thirteenth century the German merchants obtained special privileges for their own center in Novgorod, St. Peter's Yard (the Peterhof). For the next 250 years the bulk of Russia's fur trade with the West was dominated by independent Novgorod and the German merchants who belonged to what became known as the Hansa.

The role of Novgorod in this trade was to provide a regular supply of furs for sale to German merchants. These furs came from two primary sources. The first consisted of the taxes, rents, fees, and fines paid in skins by the Slavic and Slavicized peasantry who worked arable land with the Novgorod domain. The second was the colonial empire of Novgorod in northern Russia, which extended from the Norwegian and Swedish frontiers all the way to western Siberia. Just as the Norwegians asserted a "right" to the Lapp tribute, so Novgorod maintained a "right" to tribute from all peoples of the Russian far north, including the Lapps.

By the late eleventh century Novgorod collected tribute from the Pechera, who dwelt in the basin of the middle Pechora River. A century later Novgorod tax collectors were acquiring sables and other furs among the Iugra, who inhabited the land as far as the west bank of the Ob. This tribute could be collected only by sending a heavily armed expeditionary force, and that small army was in constant danger.

In 1187, for instance, the 100 or so Novgorod tax collectors sent to the Pechera and Iugra were killed.

Novgorod faced internal and external rivals for the furs from its northern empire. Internally, it encountered repeated efforts by the princes of northeastern Rus to expand their influence northward, and either divert the furs into their own territories or levy a tax on the skins being shipped to Novgorod from the Iugra and Pechera lands. In the second half of the twelfth century, Novgorod repulsed the efforts of the princes of Suzdal to extend their control over the northlands. During the fourteenth century Novgorod strongly resisted the attempts by the northern town of Ustiug to interfere with its tribute shipments from the Iugra and Pechera lands.

The most formidable internal danger faced by Novgorod came from the grand princes of Moscow. Ivan I Kalita (1331–1340) tried unsuccessfully to assert his control over these northern lands. From the 1390's on, a sporadic battle was waged between Moscow and Novgorod. Moscow periodically attempted to assert its "rights" in the lands beyond the Northern Dvina, and Novgorod retaliated with raids on Ustiug and other Muscovite areas. The reasons behind this intermittent war were clearly illuminated by the fine that Novgorod imposed on Ustiug in 1425 for raiding its Dvina lands: fifty squirrel skins and six forties of sable. The conquest of Novgorod by Moscow in the 1470's marked the passing of the far northern fur trade into Muscovite hands.

The external threats to Novgorod came from the Swedes and Norwegians. The Swedes' conquest of Finland during the thirteenth century gave them a base from which they sought to dominate Karelia and its fur trade, and to gain control over the water route linking Novgorod with the Baltic. Sweden was not successful in either objective, although it did extend its sphere of influence as far as eastern Finland, with Åbo (modern Turku) becoming a major market for Finnish furs. Norway had abandoned its royal monopoly over Lapland in the thirteenth century, but there were periodic battles with Novgorod in an effort to define their respective spheres of exploitation. Novgorod greatly limited the lands in which Norway could collect the Lapp tribute.

The furs collected from various sources were gathered in Novgorod and exchanged with the German merchants of the Peterhof, who shipped the furs from Novgorod via the Baltic, and distributed them throughout central and western Europe. The Peterhof closely regulated the activities of all German merchants in Novgorod through its written code *(schra).* Trade took place within the Peterhof, and the German merchants rarely ventured out of their compound. The members of the Peterhof were divided into two distinct groups: the winter merchants and the summer merchants. Those who stayed the winter were rewarded with opportunities to buy the choice winter furs. Summer merchants faced less arduous weather but acquired the less valued summer furs. While the figures are far from exact, several hundred German merchants appear to have visited the Peterhof each year during the heyday of Hanseatic trade with Novgorod.

Hansa merchants exported a large number of Russian furs from eastern European cities. Dorpat (modern Tartu), for example, was located along the land route to Novgorod and had very close connections with the Rus town of Pskov. Reval (modern Tallinn) acted as the gathering point for Hansa ships going to and coming from Novgorod. In the early thirteenth century Riga, at the mouth of the Western Dvina, developed an active trade with Rus towns such as Vitebsk and Polotsk on the upper Western Dvina, and even with Smolensk on the upper Dnieper. A 1229 treaty between Smolensk and the merchants from Hansa cities led to the establishment of a German trading center in Smolensk. So many Russian furs were apparently exported to the West by the Western Dvina route that certain squirrels became known as *smolyng,* skins from the area of Smolensk.

In the early fifteenth century two new routes were developed for exporting Russian furs to the West. The merchants from the Prussian towns, who had long faced discrimination at the Peterhof, established an active trade with Lithuania, which then ruled large parts of western Rus. Danzig emerged as a major exporter of furs from Lithuania and Rus, as well as from Mazovia and Podolia in Poland. In addition, south German merchants, primarily from Nuremberg, developed an east–west land route connecting south Germany with Poland. This route gave them direct access to Russian and other east European furs and bypassed the Hansa completely. The land route, however, was never as important as the Baltic maritime routes leading from Novgorod, Riga, Reval, and Danzig.

During the thirteenth through fifteenth centuries, Hanseatic merchants exported a vast number of furs to western Europe. While there are no precise figures and the origin of the furs is not always clear, some isolated but relatively trustworthy data exist. In 1311 Pskov seized 50,000 fur skins belonging to German merchants. Between 1403 and 1415 the brothers Hildebrand and Sievert Veckinchusen exported to Flanders alone more than 300,000 pelts, of which about 30 percent came from Reval, more than 20 percent came from Riga, and about 50 percent came from Danzig. In 1405 three ships owned by 107 Dorpat and Riga merchants left Riga for Bruges with 450,000 pelts. The number of Russian pelts exported to central and western Europe by the Hansa thus totaled in the millions, and the vast majority were from squirrels.

Russian and eastern European furs were sold throughout Europe by Hanseatic merchants. By the thirteenth century German merchants were shipping large quantities of furs to Flanders and England. Furs were also sent to Italy, going first by ship to cities such as Lübeck, from which they were transported south. The most valuable furs—sable, marten, and beaver—were packaged in groups of forty called a *timmer.* Squirrel and cheaper furs went in lots of 250, 500, and 1,000. The prices for eastern European furs varied considerably. In Venice during the early fifteenth century, for example, a sable pelt cost a little over eight-tenths of a ducat; a marten pelt, three-tenths of a ducat; a beaver pelt twelve to fourteen-tenths of a ducat; lynx, otter, and weasel around five-hundredths of a ducat, and an ordinary squirrel skin three- to four-hundredths of a ducat. Despite the great demand for fur throughout Europe, the market could be saturated at times. The correspondence of the Veckinchusen brothers, for instance, contains numerous complaints about the difficulties of selling furs during the early fifteenth century.

In 1494 Grand Prince Ivan III of Moscow closed the Peterhof, arrested its merchants, and seized their goods. Ivan's successor, Vasili III, allowed the Peterhof to reopen in 1514, but it never regained its former importance. The center of the Russian fur trade was shifting to Moscow.

THE FUR TRADE WITH THE NEAR EAST, CENTRAL ASIA, AND BYZANTIUM

Not much is known about the fur trade with the south in the early Middle Ages. Jordanes, writing in the mid sixth century, indicates that the On-Ogurs of the north Pontic steppe traded mouse or marten skins, presumably in Cherson (modern Sevastopol). Finds of Byzantine and Sasanian metalware and silver coins of the sixth and seventh centuries in the basins of the Kama and Viatka rivers suggest that the indigenous inhabitants may well have traded furs for those southern objects. Khwārizmian coins and Sogdian inscriptions found in northern Russia point to a central Asian role in this commerce. Nevertheless, it was only the sharp decline of the Arab–Khazar wars in the Caucasus during the second half of the eighth century that made possible an extensive fur trade between European Russia and the Orient.

Arabic and Persian sources describe in some detail the visits of Muslim merchants to the Volga in the ninth and tenth centuries. There they exchanged their silver coins (dirhams), as well as silks, glassware, fine pottery, and spices, for the furs, wax, honey, and slaves of European Russia. The major centers of this trade were the Khazar capital of Itil, in the lower Volga delta, and the Volga Bulgar lands, at the confluence of the Volga and Kama rivers. The Khazar khagan and the Volga Bulgar ruler derived considerable revenue by exacting a tithe on the goods that passed through their lands.

Rūs merchants were large suppliers of furs to these markets. In fact, several accounts state that the chief occupation of the Rūs was their trade in sables, gray squirrel, and other skins. While the precise identity of the Rūs is a matter of much controversy, they clearly obtained a large number of furs from central and northern Russia. Some of the skins came from their own lands and some were taken from or obtained in trade with the neighboring Saqāliba (peoples of northern and eastern Europe). The furs were then shipped to market. During the second half of the ninth century, Rūs merchants reportedly brought their beaver and black fox skins to the Khazar capital and then sailed across the Caspian Sea to Jurjān (modern Gorgān, Iran), near the southern coast, from where they could travel to Baghdad. In the tenth century the Rūs merchants were known primarily in the markets of the Volga Bulgars and Khazars, where, according to Ibn Faḍlān's eyewitness account (*ca.* 922), they exchanged their sable skins and slave girls for dinars and dirhams. Ibn Rusta and Gardīzī also describe Rūs merchants bartering their sable, ermine, and gray squirrel pelts for silver coins in the Bulgar market.

The Volga Bulgars also played a leading role in the early Russian fur trade with the south. Numerous sable, marten, ermine, gray squirrel, and other furs were sold in their centers; their wealth, according to several sources, consisted of weasel, ermine, and stoat skins, valued at two to two and a half dirhams each, which they used for money. Many of the furs sold in Bulgar markets were brought there by Rūs merchants; many were also obtained within the Volga Bulgar lands. Writing about 1120, the Seljuk

physician Marwazī specifically noted the gray squirrels, sables, and other furbearing animals found in their forests. In addition, the Volga Bulgars acquired many excellent furs from the natives of northern Russia. In the 920's Ibn Faḍlān reported that Bulgar merchants brought back sable and black fox skins from the land of the Wīsū, usually identified as the Ves, who inhabited the area around Beloozero or White Lake. Twelfth-century sources describe Volga Bulgar merchants who in winter journeyed northward twenty days or more on their dog sleds to the Wīsū land, and beyond to the Yūra (probably the Iugra of Rus sources). In one account the Bulgars exchanged clothes, salt, and other goods with the Yūra for their pelts of fine sables and other valuable furs. In another version the Bulgars bartered sword blades with the Wīsū for beaver skins; the Wīsū, in turn, exchanged these blades for sables in the Yūra land and the Region of Darkness near the Arctic Ocean.

Another important source for fur was the land of the Burṭās, situated somewhere between Volga Bulgaria and Khazaria, along the Volga. According to Masᶜūdi the pelts of black *burṭāsī* foxes were very highly valued by Arab and Persian rulers; red fox skins also came from that land. Other sources mention that the wealth of the Burṭās came from marten and weasel or stoat pelts.

Most of the furs collected by the Rūs, Volga Bulgars, Burṭās, and other peoples of European Russia found their way to Khazaria, where they were sold in the international market at Itil. The Khazars, unlike the Volga Bulgars, produced no pelts of their own. Al-Iṣṭakhrī (*ca.* 932) remarks that the furs and other goods sold in Khazaria all came from elsewhere; the beaver skins, for instance, were actually from the Volga Bulgar, Rūs, and other more northern lands. There were two main sources for the furs found at Itil: merchants who brought skins they had acquired in the north and the tribute in fur that the Khazars extracted from the Volga Bulgars (one sable skin per household) and several East Slavic tribes (one white squirrel skin per hearth). So many pelts were sold to Muslim merchants in Khazaria that various furs were known as *khazarī* in the Arabic world.

Many pelts were sent by land from the Bulgars to central Asia. Muqaddasī (*ca.* 980's), for example, lists sable, squirrel, white weasel, ermine, marten, fox, beaver, and hare skins among the goods imported to Khwārizm from Volga Bulgaria. Furs also reached central Asia from western Siberia. For instance, the Kimāk, who at one time lived along the Irtysh River, hunted sables, ermines, martens, foxes, and other animals, then exchanged their pelts for salt. The various furs brought to Khwārizm from European Russia and western Siberia were exported to Iraq and other southern lands.

During the ninth and tenth centuries the Rus of the middle Dnieper developed an active trade with Byzantium. Their major exports to the Black Sea world were furs, wax, honey, and slaves. The Rus rulers of Kiev obtained much of their fur from the tribute they levied upon the East Slavic tribes. In 883, for example, Grand Prince Oleg made the Derevlianians pay one black marten skin apiece. Presumably the tribute of one white squirrel skin per hearth imposed on various East Slavic tribes by the Khazars was collected by the Rus when they replaced the Khazars as overlords of those tribes. Pelts of squirrel and marten composed an important part of the tribute of the early Rus rulers. Many of the furs and other goods obtained by the Rus princes were shipped in merchant convoys down the Dnieper to the Black Sea and Constantinople.

The impression is sometimes created that the trade of European Russia with the south declined sharply or ceased altogether in the two centuries or so preceding the Mongol conquest of 1236 to 1241. Such an impression is misleading, for there is considerable evidence pointing to the existence of a substantial fur trade with the south at this time. Abū Ḥāmid al-Gharnāṭī, for instance, describes a lively fur trade along the Volga on the basis of his trip to this region between about 1130 and about 1150. From the lands of the Wīsū and from the Yūra living along the Sea of Darkness (the Arctic Ocean), Bulgar merchants obtained excellent sable and beaver pelts. The Bulgars also acquired beaver, ermine, and first-class squirrel skins from the area of the Aru (?), and black water sable (?) were caught along the "river of the Slavs." Some of these furs were sold to Muslim merchants; others were shipped to the market at Saksin on the lower Volga, and sold there by Bulgar merchants. Abū Ḥāmid's account leaves no doubt that the Volga fur trade with the south continued after the tenth century.

By the beginning of the thirteenth century, if not earlier, the port of Sudak (Soldaia, Surozh) in the Crimea had become the center of an extensive commerce in furs. Ibn al-Athīr (ca. 1230) reports that Sudak was the town of the Polovtsy (Cumans), who obtained goods there in return for their slaves and the furs of Burṭās, and skins of beavers and squirrels. In the early 1250's William of Rubruck noted that merchants from Russia and the north brought pelts of squirrel, ermine, and other valuable furs to Asia Minor via Sudak.

While the export of Russian furs to the south continued in the period from about 1050 to about 1240, the significance of this trade relative to the western trade did decline. The reasons for this change do not necessarily lie in political and economic developments in the Eurasian steppe, central Asia, and Byzantium. Rather, the southern trade in furs became less important as the massive export of furs to the Baltic from Novgorod and other northwestern Rus cities became more important. Also, some of the furs once shipped from Kiev to Constantinople came to be sent overland to Regensburg. Many of the skins formerly exported to Byzantium, the Near East, and central Asia now were sent to the West.

During the heyday of the Mongol empire, Russian fur trade with the south prospered. The Mongol rulers, like many others, were great consumers of costly fur. Marco Polo noted the abundance of ermine and sable pelts ("the most costly of furs") that lined the tents at the court of Kublai Khan and the use of the same two furs on the clothing of wealthy Mongols. The pelts from the northern regions of Russia and Siberia were still very abundant and the most highly valued. According to Marco Polo, the natives of the Land of Darkness in the very far north were all trappers who caught great quantities of sables, ermines, martens, black foxes, and other animals. Their skins were of better quality and more valuable than the furs from regions inhabited by the Mongols. And in the northern regions of Siberia/Mongolia were huge white bears, big black foxes, and incredible swarms of some member of the weasel family called Pharaoh's mice.

To the south many good-quality furs were still found in the central regions of Russia. William of Rubruck commented, for instance, on the variety of valuable furs brought to the Mongols from Russia, Volga Bulgaria, and adjoining regions. He also mentioned the many fine furs found in the land of the Moxel, apparently the Mordvins or some other people living in the upper Volga basin. Marco Polo also states that large numbers of pelts from ermines, sables, martens, foxes, and other animals were gathered in Russia.

The Mongols obtained some of these fine furs as tribute. John of Plano Carpini (1240's) says, for example, that each person enumerated in the Mongol census of Russia had to pay one skin of each of the following: white bear, black beaver, black sable, black fox, and an animal for which he did not know the Latin name. Nevertheless, large numbers of skins were shipped south every year by merchants. Marco Polo mentions the special dog-sled stations that enabled merchants to reach northern Siberia/Mongolia and notes that the furs from the Land of Darkness were obtained by merchants who made great profits transporting them to countries such as Russia.

Several Muslim sources, such as ᶜAwfī from the thirteenth century and Abūʾl Fidāʾ, Ibn Baṭṭūṭa, and al-ᶜUmarī from the first half of the fourteenth, mention the dumb or silent trade of the Bulgars with peoples of the far north. It is not clear whether these reports reflect contemporary events or simply repeat stories found in older works. Al-ᶜUmarī, however, cites a merchant informant who states that Islamic merchants went only as far as Bulgār; Bulgar merchants went north to the Čūlmān (the Kama River?); and the Čūlmān merchants visited the lands in the very far north. This report suggests that the Bulgar trade with the far north was still active but now used more easterly routes. Presumably this change was due to increased competition with Novgorod and Suzdal-Moscow merchants.

While Bulgār remained an important center for the trade in Russian furs with the south, the Golden Horde capital of Sarai on the lower Volga was probably the major market as long as the Mongols ruled Russia. The furs that reached Sarai from the north as tribute and merchandise were sold there to merchants from numerous countries. Most of the pelts went to the Islamic lands, although a significant number were acquired by Italian merchants and shipped westward from their factories on the northern coast of the Black Sea. In the 1260's the Genoese had obtained trading privileges from the khan of the Golden Horde in the Crimean city of Caffa, and records show that they exported large quantities of ermine and vair from Caffa by 1290. Pegolotti reports in the 1340's that in Tana, at the mouth of the Don, vair and ermine pelts were sold by the thousand, whereas fox, sable, fitch, marten, and deer skins were sold by the piece.

The "Great Troubles" that shook the Golden Horde in the late 1350's initiated the decline of Mongol rule over Russia. By the second quarter of the fifteenth century, the Horde itself began to split up, and the khanates of the Crimea, Kazan, Astrakhan, and Sibir emerged. These circumstances naturally affected the fur trade, the most significant development being the demise of Sarai. New centers and new relationships arose to carry on the tradi-

tional trade in Russian furs with the south. Along the lower Volga, Astrakhan replaced Sarai; Kazan took the place of Bulgār on the middle Volga. Perhaps the biggest change, however, was the growing role of Moscow in the Rus fur trade. Although Moscow obtained some furs from Kazan, substantial quantities came from its growing domain in central and northern Russia. In fact, by the 1480's most of the far northern regions in European Russia were under Muscovite control. At the same time the report of Josafa Barbaro (ca. 1437) suggests that the chief source of Kazan's furs was Mordovia and adjacent lands along the middle Volga ("Zagatai and Moxia"). The best fur lands in European Russia apparently had been lost to Novgorod and Moscow. Kazan's fur trade with the south had not ended, however, and it may even have supplied the skins from Russia and Tatary that Ruy González de Clavijo saw in Samarkand around 1405. But during the fifteenth century Moscow came to rival, and then to surpass, Kazan and Astrakhan.

Many of the furs that Moscow obtained from central and northern Russia were exported to the south. Ambrogio Contarini reported in 1476 that Tatar merchants went by ship from Derbent on the Caspian to Astrakhan in search of furs, and that every year many Tatar merchants traveled from Astrakhan to Moscow to purchase pelts. One part of Moscow's fur trade thus led down the Volga to Astrakhan; from there Russian furs were then exported to all parts of the Islamic world. Another part of Muscovy's southern trade led to Surozh/Sudak and other Italian cities of the Crimea. From 1356 on, the so-called Surozh merchants were very active in this commerce.

Moscow also played an important role in the fur trade with the West. In the 1430's Barbaro noted the furs sent from Moscow to Poland, Prussia, and Flanders. In 1476/1477, Contarini mentioned the many merchants from Germany and Poland who visited Moscow during the winter to buy the skins of foxes, ermines, squirrels, and other animals procured in the far north and sent to Moscow for sale. In Moscow, from the late fifteenth century on, merchants from Europe and the Orient met to compete for the choice Russian furs.

The merchants of Lvov in western Rus exported various goods, including furs, to the south. In the fourteenth century they used the *via Tatarica* leading to Caffa, Tana, and Sarai. By the fifteenth century they were also using the "Moldavian route" to Moldavia, Transylvania, and the Black Sea, a route that continued on to Istanbul after the Ottomans gained control over the Black Sea. When Contarini mentioned the merchant caravans that brought furs from "High Russia" through "Lower Russia," via the Dnieper, on their way to Caffa in the 1470's, he probably referred to the important trade with the south, conducted by Armenian, Jewish, and other merchants centered in western Rus cities such as Lvov.

BIBLIOGRAPHY

Sources. Early Scandinavian trade: *Arrow-Odd: A Medieval Novel,* Paul Edwards and Hermann Pálsson, trans. (1970); *Egils Saga,* C. Fell, trans. (1975); Snorri Sturluson, *Heimskringla,* Lee M. Hollander, trans. (1964); *The Book of Settlements, Landnámabók,* Hermann Pálsson and Paul Edwards, trans. (1972); "The 'Periplus' of Ohthere," trans. and commentary in Omeljan Pritsak, *The Origin of Rus,* I, *Old Scandinavian Sources Other Than Sagas* (1981), 692–699. For comments on fur and the love of furs in the Baltic area before the Hansa, see Adam of Bremen, *History of the Archbishops of Hamburg-Bremen,* F. J. Tschan, trans. (1959).

Rus sources: *The Chronicle of Novgorod, 1016–1471,* Robert Michell and Nevill Forbes, trans. (1914); *The Russian Primary Chronicle: Laurentian Text,* Samuel H. Cross and O. P. Sherbowitz-Wetzor, eds. and trans. (1953). See also George Vernadsky *et al.,* eds., *A Source Book for Russian History from Early Times to 1917,* I, *Early Times to the Late Seventeenth Century* (1972).

Early southern trade: *The Gothic History of Jordanes,* Charles Mierow, trans. (1915, repr. 1960).

Pre-Mongol Islamic trade: *Abū Ḥāmid el Granadino y su relación de viaje por tierras euroasiáticas,* Spanish trans. by César Dubler (1953); H. M. Smyser, "Ibn Faḍlān's Account of the Rūs with Some Commentary and Some Allusions to Beowulf," in Jess B. Bessinger, Jr., and Robert P. Creed, eds., *Franciplegius* (1965); a complete French translation of Ibn Faḍlān is in Marius Canard, "La relation du voyage d'Ibn Fadlân chez les Bulgares de la Volga," in *Annales de l'Institut d'études orientales de l'Université d'Alger,* **16** (1958). There are excerpts from various Muslim authors in Semen Rapoport, "Mohammedan Writers on Slavs and Russians," in *Slavonic Review,* **8** (1929–1930). Complete translations of some of these are in *Ḥudūd al-ʿĀlam,* "The Regions of the World," Vladimir Minorsky, trans., C. E. Bosworth, ed., 2nd ed. (1970); "Gardīzī's Two Chapters on the Turks," A. P. Martinez, trans., in *Archivum Eurasiae medii aevi,* II (1982), 109–217; Vladimir Minorsky, *A History of Sharvān and Darband in the 10th–11th Centuries* (1958), and idem, trans., *Sharaf al-Zamān Ṭāhir Marvazī on China, the Turks and India* (1942); Ibn Rustah, *Les atours précieux,* Gaston Wiet, trans. (1955).

The Mongol era: John of Plano Carpini, "History of the Mongols" and "The Journey of William of Rubruck," in C. Dawson, ed., *The Mongol Mission* (1955); Francesco Balducci Pegolotti, *The Practice of Commerce,* excerpts trans. in Henry Yule, ed., *Cathay and the Way Thither,* III (1914); H. A. R. Gibb, ed., *The Travels of Ibn Battuta,* II (1962); *The Travels of Marco Polo,* Manuel Komroff, trans. (1926).

The post-Mongol southern trade: The best eyewitness accounts come from "Travels of Josafa Barbaro" and "The Travels of the Magnificent M. Ambrosio Contarini," in *Travels to Tana and Persia by Josafa Barbaro and Ambrogio Contarini,* William Thomas and S. A. Roy, trans. (1873). See also *Narrative of the Embassy of Ruy Gonzalez de Clavijo to the Court of Timour at Samarcand, A. D. 1403–1406,* Clements R. Markham, trans. (1859).

Studies. A good introduction to the subject is in Raymond H. Fisher, *The Russian Fur Trade, 1550–1700* (1943). The Viking-age fur trade is discussed by H. R. Ellis Davidson, *The Viking Road to Byzantium* (1976). The fur trade of the eastern Baltic in the post-Viking era is examined in Eric Christiansen, *The Northern Crusades* (1980). For a good overview of the Hansa, see Philippe Dollinger, *The German Hansa* (1970). Perhaps the single best work on the medieval fur trade of northern Europe is Elspeth M. Veale, *The English Fur Trade in the Later Middle Ages* (1966). The creation of the Novgorod colonial empire is discussed in George V. Lantzeff, "Russian Eastward Expansion Before the Mongol Invasion," in *American Slavic and East European Review,* **6** (1947). See also A. L. Khoroshkevich, *Torgovlia velikogo Novgoroda s pribaltikoi i zapadnoi Evropi v XIV–XV vekakh* (1963).

The role of the Khazars in the fur trade and translations of pertinent excerpts from several Muslim sources are in D. M. Dunlop, *The History of the Jewish Khazars* (1954). A new study of the Khazars, including their commerce, with translations of key passages from Muslim sources is Peter B. Golden, *Khazar Studies,* I (1980). For Muqaddasī's account of the fur exports from the Bulgar lands, see Basil A. Collins, *Al-Muqaddasi: The Man and His Work* (1974).

Two recent studies on the southern fur trade in the pre-Mongol era are Élisabeth Bennigsen, "Contribution à l'étude du commerce des fourrures russes: La route de la Volga avant l'invasion mongole et le royaume des Bulghars," in *Cahiers du monde russe et soviétique,* **19** (1978); and Janet Martin, "Trade on the Volga: The Commercial Relations of Bulgar with Central Asia and Iran in the 11th–12th Centuries," in *International Journal of Turkish Studies,* **1** (1980). The fur trade during the Mongol era is discussed in Janet Martin, "The Land of Darkness and the Golden Horde: The Fur Trade Under the Mongols XIII–XIVth Centuries," in *Cahiers du monde russe et soviétique,* **19** (1978). For the commerce of Lvov in the later Middle Ages see Mihnea Berindei, "Contribution à l'étude du commerce ottoman des fourrures moscovites: La route moldavo-polonaise, 1453–1700," in *Cahiers du monde russe et soviétique,* **12** (1971); and Eleonora Nadel-Gulobič, "Armenians and Jews in Medieval Lvov: Their Role in Oriental Trade, 1400–1600," *ibid.,* **20** (1979).

THOMAS S. NOONAN

[See also **Caffa; Hanseatic League; Kievan Rus; Muscovy; Novgorod; Trade.**]

FUSORIS, JEAN (*ca.* 1365–1436), astronomer, mathematician, and maker of clocks and astronomical instruments. After earning master's degrees in the arts and medicine and a bachelor's degree in theology from the University of Paris, Fusoris became a master of medicine at the University in 1396. In 1404 he was appointed canon of Rheims, and subsequently served as canon of Paris and of Nancy, as well as curate of Jouarre-en-Brie.

Fusoris established a workshop that specialized in the production of such astronomical instruments as astrolabes, armillary spheres, sundials, equatoria, and clocks. An astronomical clock commissioned by the chapter of Bourges in 1423 functioned until the nineteenth century.

Fusoris left a body of texts in French and Latin, many of which treat the construction and functions of astronomical instruments. Late in life, Fusoris compiled a trigonometric table as part of a projected establishment of astronomical tables.

BIBLIOGRAPHY

Léon Mirot, "Le procès de maître Jean Fusoris, chanoine de Notre-Dame de Paris, 1415–1416; épisode des négociations franco-anglaises durant la guerre de Cent ans," in *Mémoires de la Société de l'histoire de Paris et de l'Ile-de-France,* 27 (1900); Emmanuel Poulle, *Un constructeur d'instruments astronomiques au XVe siècle* (1963); Antonio Simoni, "Un fortunato rinvenimento," in *La clessidra,* 27 (1971).

EDITORIAL STAFF

FYLGJA (plural *fylgjur*). The concept of the *fylgja*, best translated into English as "fetch," is revealed to us only in Old Norse prose works. The term refers to a supernatural phenomenon representing the essential physical and psychic force of an individual or the guardian spirit of an entire family, which, though normally invisible, can under certain conditions manifest itself in a concrete form. There are two prevailing explanations of its etymology: that it is derived from the verb *fylgja* (to follow) or that it is related to its homonym *fylgja* (afterbirth or caul). In addition to *fylgja*, the sources often use the terms *hugr* (spirit, mind), *vǫrðr* (guardian), and *hamingja* (fortune, guardian spirit) to express the notion of this supernatural force. Most frequently the *fylgja* reveals itself in concrete form while the individual is asleep, drowsy, or at the point of death.

Fylgjur can be divided into two categories, according to their form and function. In the first category is the *fylgja* that manifests itself in animal form and represents the strictly personal physical and psychic force or alter ego of an individual. Generally the animal "fetch" of one person is perceived by another in a dream, as a warning of impending danger. For example, in *Njáls saga* (ch. 62) a number of Gunnarr's enemies have planned an attack against him and his two brothers as they return from a visit. While they are riding along, Gunnarr suddenly becomes very sleepy and must stop to rest. When he awakens, he relates that in a dream he saw a pack of wolves rush out and attack him and his brothers. The three of them fought valiantly, but the wolves managed to kill his brother Hjǫrtr. Shortly thereafter they are ambushed and Hjǫrtr is slain. Occasionally an individual who is wide awake will see his own *fylgja*, an occurrence always interpreted as a death omen. A good example occurs in *Njáls saga* (ch. 41) when the Njálssons' foster father sees a blood-covered goat lying in a hollow. In the sagas *fylgjur* assume a wide variety of animal forms, including bears, wolves, goats, snakes, foxes, and bulls. The type of animal is clearly symbolic of the individual's personality or role within the work. Wolves are usually enemies, while bears represent great heroes. In *Hrólfs saga kraka* (ch. 50) the hero Bjarki sits motionless in his quarters while his *fylgja*, in the shape of a huge bear, fights fiercely against the enemy.

The second and more frequent type of *fylgja* appears in the shape of a woman and is associated with the welfare of an entire family. She remains with the family from one generation to the next, and in each generation she may be primarily attached to the head of the kin. She is sometimes referred to as *fylgjukona* (fetch woman) or *ættarfylgja* (family fetch), and she often makes her appearance when death is near, being seen either by the dying man or by his successor within the family. In *Víga-Glúms saga* (ch. 9) the hero sees a gigantic woman approaching in a dream and understands this to mean that his maternal

335

grandfather has died in Norway and the "fetch" is coming to join the Icelandic branch of the family. According to Else Mundal, the *fylgjukona* represents the protective powers of the family's female ancestors.

The concept of the "fetch" in animal shape seems closely related to the notion frequently encountered in folklore that the physical and psychic force or "soul" of the individual was magical and could be activated to leave the body and be perceived in concrete form by others. The concept of the *fylgjukona,* by contrast, is more probably connected with the belief in *dísir,* which are minor pagan deities, or, in later Christian times, in the guardian angel. An example of how the ideas and terminology of the two belief systems could blend is the statement of Síðu-Hallr in *Njáls saga* (ch. 100) that he wished the archangel Michael to be his *fylgjuengill.*

BIBLIOGRAPHY

Else Mundal, *Fylgjemotiva i norrøn litteratur* (1974); Max Rieger, "Über den nordischen Fylgienglauben," in *Zeitschrift für deutsches Altertum,* **42** (1898); Dag Strömbäck, *Sejd* (1935), 152–159; Edward O. G. Turville-Petre, *Myth and Religion of the North* (1964), 227–230; Jan de Vries, *Altgermanische Religionsgeschichte,* I (1970), 224–228.

KAAREN GRIMSTAD

GABELLE. Various forms of the word "gabelle" were used throughout Mediterranean Europe in the Middle Ages to describe indirect taxes on merchandise resembling what would now be called "value-added taxes." The word has come to be associated almost exclusively with a tax on salt levied by the kings of France. The commerce in salt, like that in other essential and widely traded foodstuffs, was subject to taxes in many parts of medieval Europe. Like other mineral resources, it was also exploited for profit by seigneurs who controlled supplies of it. In some salt-producing regions people had to buy the lord's salt, much as they might be required to use his mill.

Before they obtained regular taxes in the 1360's, the French kings often tried to supplement their revenues by expanding and generalizing existing feudal or seigneurial rights. Philip VI, who possessed salt pans in southwestern France and already collected some taxes on commerce, introduced a general *gabelle du sel* in an ordinance of 16 March 1341. He ordered that all salt in the kingdom be seized, stored in royal warehouses, and then sold for a profit by officials called *gabelliers.* The ordinance aroused bitter opposition in regions where salt had not been taxed or where privileges were threatened. The crown overrode all appeals and subsequently established a more permanent administrative structure in 1343. Knowing that people were much opposed to having the gabelle become permanent, Philip offered to cancel the tax in 1346 if the Estates-General would grant him a substantial war subsidy. Although there is little explicit documentation, it does appear that Philip struck such a bargain with regional assemblies, for by the end of 1347 the gabelle was no longer in evidence.

The Estates-General of Languedoïl, meeting late in 1355, reestablished the gabelle as part of a package of indirect taxes that proved so unpopular they had to be canceled within a few months. The tax next appeared in 1358, when it was imposed in Paris after the government regained that city following a rebellion. It was levied there again two years later, to help finance the first payment of John II's ransom. Meanwhile, in March 1359, the Estates of Languedoc reluctantly authorized the gabelle as a short-term expedient to finance measures against brigandage. It had to be renewed repeatedly in the next twenty years. By the summer of 1359, most of France north of the Loire had revived the salt tax because an English invasion was imminent.

In December 1360 the French crown reestablished the gabelle as one of the general taxes that would pay for the king's ransom. Despite some future interruptions, these taxes became permanent. The gabelle was a 20 percent ad valorem tax until 1367, when complaints and evasions led Charles V to require that his officers appraise all salt, determine a fair price, and add 24 francs per muid (roughly, a wagonload) to that price as a tax. Languedoc purchased exemption from the indirect taxes but continued its own gabelle for defensive measures. In future centuries, as the crown lost and regained provinces, the gabelle became subject to extreme variations from one region to another.

BIBLIOGRAPHY

G. Dupont-Ferrier, *Études sur les institutions financières de la France à la fin du moyen âge,* 2 vols. (1930–1932); John Bell Henneman, *Royal Taxation in Fourteenth Century France: The Development of War Financing, 1322–1356* (1971), and *Royal Taxation in Fourteenth Century France: The Captivity and Ransom of John II, 1356–*

1370 (1976); E. Meynial, "Études sur la gabelle du sel avant le XVIIᵉ siècle en France," in *Tijdschrift voor rechtsgeschiedenis*, 3 (1922); G. Perousse, "Étude sur les origines de la gabelle et sur son organisation jusqu'en 1380," in *Positions des thèses, École des chartes* (1898), 89–98.

JOHN BELL HENNEMAN

[See also **Taxation, French.**]

GABIROL, IBN. See **Solomon ben Judah ibn Gabirol.**

GABRI WARE, lead-glazed earthenware pottery of the eleventh through thirteenth centuries, probably from the Garrus district of Kurdistan. Calligraphic designs or beasts and characters from Persian mythology are depicted in the champlevé technique. Through the name Gabri (fire worshiper) it was erroneously thought to have been connected with the Zoroastrians of pre-Islamic Iran.

BIBLIOGRAPHY

Géza Fehérvári, *Islamic Pottery: A Comprehensive Study Based on the Barlow Collection* (1973); Arthur Lane, *Early Islamic Pottery* (1948).

VENETIA PORTER

[See also **Ceramics, Islamic.**]

Gabri ware. Ceramic bowl, Iranian, late 11th or 12th century. METROPOLITAN MUSEUM OF ART, NEW YORK, NEG. NO. 66476

GABRIEL BIEL. See **Biel, Gabriel.**

GACE BRULÉ (*fl. ca.* 1185–1210), a noble trouvère from Champagne and one of the first Old French lyricists. The name Brulé is from *burelé* (striped), not *bruslé* (burned). His poems are generally of five *coblas unissonans* or six *coblas doblas;* they are occasionally polymetric, and imitate the troubadour style. Many excellent melodies survive. The sixty-nine attributed poems exploit a narrow range of topics: the poet is unsuccessful in love, timid, attacked by slanderers, in pain and without hope; he cannot reasonably expect the superior lady to return his love; yet, submissive to irresistible Amors, he loves without regret.

BIBLIOGRAPHY

Gace Brulé: Trouvère Champenois, éditions des chansons et étude historique, Holger Petersen Dyggve, ed. (1951).

F. R. P. AKEHURST

[See also **French Literature: To 1200.**]

GADDI, AGNOLO (*fl. ca.* 1369, *d.* 1396), Florentine painter, pupil, follower, and son of Taddeo Gaddi. An important muralist, Agnolo's extant frescoes include stories of John the Evangelist in the Castellani Chapel of S. Croce (*ca.* 1380–1388), the *Legend of the True Cross* cycle in the choir of S. Croce (*ca.* 1388–1393), and the *Life of the Virgin* cycle in the cathedral of Prato (1393–1396). Important panels include two wings of an altar in the Munich Alte Pinakothek (late), the crucifix in S. Martino a Sesto, the triptych of *Madonna and Child with Saints* in the Palazzo Pitti of Florence, and two works titled *Coronation of the Virgin,* in the National Gallery of Art, Washington, and National Gallery, London. Gaddi's stylistic development moved away from the rigid hieratic tendencies of late-Trecento Florentine style, and toward a more volumetric, relaxed understanding of form that led the way to the developments of later Renaissance painting.

BIBLIOGRAPHY
Bruce Cole, *Agnolo Gaddi* (1977).

ADELHEID M. GEALT

[See also **Fresco Painting; Gaddi, Gaddo; Gaddi, Taddeo; Giotto di Bondone.**]

GADDI, GADDO (Gaddo di Zanobi, Gherardo di Zanobi) (*ca.* 1260–*ca.* 1333), Florentine painter and mosaicist, registered in the Arte dei Medici e Speziali in 1327. He founded a dynasty of painters that included his son Taddeo Gaddi and his grandson Agnolo Gaddi. No works have been assigned to him with certainty.

BIBLIOGRAPHY
Frank J. Mather, *The Isaac Master: A Reconstruction of the Work of Gaddo Gaddi* (1932); Ulrich Thieme and Felix Becker, eds., *Allgemeines Lexicon der bildenden Künstler*, XIII (1920).

ADELHEID M. GEALT

[See also **Gaddi, Agnolo; Gaddi, Taddeo.**]

GADDI, TADDEO (*ca.* 1300–*ca.* 1366), Florentine painter, pupil and assistant of Giotto, father of Agnolo Gaddi. A major figure whose extant oeuvre is substantial, Taddeo continued Giotto's monumental style well into the decades that saw stylistic alternatives offered by Orcagna and Jacopo di Cione. His greatest gift was a charming and anecdotal narration, as can be seen in his chief surviving fresco cycle, the *Life of the Virgin* (*ca.* 1332–1338, in the Baroncelli Chapel, S. Croce, Florence), which served as a model for subsequent painters. Other frescoes include the *Entombment* in the Bardi di Vernio Chapel, S. Croce, probably based on Maso di Banco's

Meeting of St. Joachim and St. Anne. Detail of a fresco cycle by Taddeo Gaddi in the Baroncelli Chapel, S. Croce, Florence, *ca.* 1332–1338. ALINARI/ART RESOURCE

design; and the refectory frescoes depicting St. Bonaventure's vision of the Crucifixion, in S. Croce. Altarpieces include a portable triptych dated 1334 (Staatliche Museen Preussischer Kulturbesitz, Berlin), a *Madonna and Child with Four Angels* dated 1355 (Uffizi, Florence), and the polyptych done for S. Giovanni Fuorcivitas, Pistoia, dated 1353.

BIBLIOGRAPHY
A. Laddis, *Taddeo Gaddi* (1983).

ADELHEID M. GEALT

[See also **Fresco Painting; Gaddi, Agnolo; Gaddi, Gaddo; Giotto di Bondone.**]

GAELIC. See **Celtic Languages.**

GAGIK I (989–1020) was the seventh king of the main line of the Armenian Bagratid dynasty ruling at Ani. He was the son of Ašot III the Merciful (953–977) and the brother of Smbat II Tiezerakal (977–989). Like his predecessors he bore the title of *šahanšah* (king of kings). Gagik's reign was a prosperous one and is marked by several military successes. He was personally well versed in military matters and organized a permanent army, the *marzpetakan gund*, which consisted of 40,000 men. In the earlier part of his reign Gagik seized several districts and fortresses from the kingdom of Siwnik[c], the petty Armenian principalities of Arc[c]aχ, and Albania. He is described by the contemporary historians as a very powerful and determined ruler who kept the borders of his kingdom intact throughout his thirty years of rule. The peaceful atmosphere made him especially sensitive to the needs of his subjects so that he made frequent largesses and relieved the populace from various taxes. In 998 he allied himself with the curopalate David of Tayk[c] against Mamlān, the emir of Azerbaijan, who was contesting David's occupation of Manazkert and Apahunik[c], which had hitherto been the component parts of a Muslim emirate. The outcome of the contest was favorable to Gagik and David.

In 1000, when the Byzantine emperor Basil II came to Armenia to annex Tayk[c], most of the Georgian and Armenian kings and princes went to greet him and paid homage. Gagik refused to go, considering such an act below his dignity. In general he pursued a very cautious policy toward the Byzantines and remained neutral even at times when the relations were strained between them and the neighboring Georgians.

In 1001 Gagik succeeded in reducing the king of the northern Bagratid kingdom of Tašir-Loṟi to vassal status. He also pacified some of the rebellious principalities in the north and northeast.

His queen, Katramidē, built the renowned cathedral of Ani, founded in the reign of Smbat II. The cathedral was named St. Astuacacin after the Mother of God, and Gagik himself financed the construction of the circular St. Grigor church of Ani (completed in 1000). During the archaeological expedition at Ani in 1906, his statue was discovered in front of the ruins of this church. The king was shown wearing a long Arab tunic and holding a model of the church. Gagik also renovated and built several other churches, monasteries, chapels, and monuments, some of which bear his inscriptions.

BIBLIOGRAPHY

Stepᶜanos Asołik, *Patmutᶜiwn tiezerakan* (1887); French trans., Édouard Dulaurier and Frédéric Macler, *Histoire universelle*, 2 parts (1883–1917), German trans., Heinrich Gelzer and August Burckhardt, *Des Stephanos von Taron Armenische Geschichte* (1909); *Corpus inscriptionum armenicarum*, I, I. A. Orbeli, ed. (1966); Nikolai Iakovlevich Marr, *Ani* (1934), in Russian.

KRIKOR H. MAKSOUDIAN

[See also **Ani, Monuments of; Armenia, History of; Bagratids.**]

GAGIK II, the son of the Bagratid antiking Ašot IV, was the last king of Ani. He ruled from 1041 to 1045. His predecessor, Yovhannēs Smbat, had agreed in 1022/1023 to will his realm to the Byzantine Empire. After his death Emperor Constantine IX Monomachos tried to take over the kingdom of Ani by force but, failing in his effort to stop the Armenians from placing Gagik on the throne, resorted to diplomacy. With the help of the pro-Byzantine party in Armenia, Constantine persuaded Gagik II to go to Constantinople, where he forced the Armenian king to resign. In return for his kingdom Gagik received the cities of Pizu and Kalōn Pełat in Cappadocia. In 1065 he defended the doctrine of the Armenian church in a meeting at Constantinople and wrote a treatise that is preserved in the *Chronicle* of Matthew of Edessa. He was killed in 1079 by the sons of the Greek Mantale at the fortress of Kyzistra.

BIBLIOGRAPHY

Aristakēs Lastivercᶜi, *Patmutᶜiwn* (History), K. N. Yuzbashyan, ed. (1963), French trans. by Marius Canard and Haïg Berberian, *Récit des malheurs de la nation arménienne* (1973); Matthew of Edessa, *Chronicle* (1860, repr. 1898), French trans. by Edouard Dulaurier, *Récit de la première croisade* (1858).

KRIKOR H. MAKSOUDIAN

[See also **Ani; Armenia, History of.**]

GAGIK/XAČᶜIK-GAGIK (879–*ca.* 943), king of Vaspurakan. His father was Grigor-Derenik, the Arcruni prince of Vaspurakan, his mother was the sister of Smbat I Bagratuni, and he was the grandson of King Ašot I Bagratuni. Gagik succeeded his brother Ašot as prince in 904. When his uncle, King Smbat I Bagratuni (890–914), refused to return to the Arcruni the city of Naxcawan, which he had previously given to the prince of Sisakan, Gagik rebelled and joined forces with Yūsuf the Sājid emir of Azerbaijan. In 908 he went to meet Yūsuf, who honored him with gifts and a crown, which provided Gagik with the excuse to declare himself king. Ruling in Vaspurakan during the next three and a half decades, Gagik extended the borders of his kingdom at the expense of the Bagratids and annexed certain districts of the province of Ayrarat.

Gagik did not remain on friendly terms with Yūsuf for long. There is reason to believe that he sided with the Byzantines and that in 921/922 he received the title of *archōn tōn archontōn*, which the Byzantine court had hitherto given to the Bagratid kings of Armenia. He—and not Ašot Erkatᶜ—is presumably the unnamed addressee of letters 101 and 139 of the Byzantine patriarch Nicholas Mystikos that were probably written in 922 and 924/925, for in the 920's Ašot Erkatᶜ was on bad terms with the Byzantines.

Gagik is the author of a long letter in Armenian presumably addressed to the emperor Romanos Lekapenos through the office of the patriarch of Constantinople. Couched in conciliatory terms, it presents the views of the Armenians on controversial christological issues that separated the Armenian and the Byzantine churches. It is difficult to set a specific date to it, but it must have been written after

924/925, since Kat^{c}olikos Yovhannēs Drasχanakertac^{c}i, who died in that year, does not mention it in his *History*.

The historians of the ninth and tenth centuries praise Gagik for his building activities. He is said to have subsidized the construction of several monasteries and churches. Among his greatest accomplishments were the town of Ostan and the royal palace and the cathedral of the Holy Cross, both on the island of Aht^{c}amar in Lake Van. The construction of the church ended about 920. A standing figure of Gagik appears on its west facade.

One of the earliest codices in Armenian was donated by Gagik's wife to the monastery of Varag and according to some scholars may have been commissioned by Gagik himself. This work of art is identified as the Gospel of Queen Mlk^{c}ē, his second wife, and is now in the library of the Mekhitarist congregation of Venice.

There is still controversy about the year of Gagik's death. Earlier historians had accepted 938, but certain modern scholars have now proposed about 943 or even a few years later, and the literary evidence favors the later date.

BIBLIOGRAPHY

T^{c}ovma Arcruni, *Patmut^{c}iwn tann Arcruneac^c* (History of the Arcruni house) (1887); French trans. in Marie F. Brosset, *Collection d'historiens arméniens,* I (1874); Yovhannēs Drasχanakertc^{c}i (John VI Kat^{c}olikos), *Patmut^{c}iwn Hayoc^c* (History of Armenia), various eds. (1853, 1867, 1965); French trans., J. Saint-Martin (1841); English trans., Krikor H. Maksoudian (diss., Columbia Univ., 1973). Studies include R. J. H. Jenkins, "Letter 101 of the Patriarch Nicholas Mysticus," in *Byzantion,* **31** (1961); Steven Runciman, *The Emperor Romanus Lecapenus and His Reign* (1929, repr. 1963); V. M. Vardanyan, *Vaspurakani Arcrunyac^c t^{c}agavorut^{c}yunĕ* (The Arcruni kingdom of Vaspurakan) (1969).

KRIKOR H. MAKSOUDIAN

[See also **Arcrunis; Armenia, History of; Armenian Art; Ašot II Erkat^c; Vaspurakan.**]

GAGIK OF KARS (*d.* 1081), the last king of the Armenian kingdom of Kars. He succeeded his father Abas in 1029 and ruled until 1065, when he handed over his realm to the Byzantine Empire. In return he received Tsamandos, Larissa, Komana, and other towns in the region of present-day Elbistan in Cappadocia. Gagik was a patron of the arts and learning; the library of the Armenian patriarchate of Jerusalem contains the King Gagik Gospel, which was written and illuminated for him. He was the founder of a school in Kars and was recognized as an authority on philosophical and scholarly matters. At his order medical texts were translated from Arabic into Armenian. As a diplomat Gagik succeeded in persuading Emperor Constantine X Doukas to allow the Armenians to elect a new kat^{c}olikos in 1065, thus ensuring the continuity of the Armenian patriarchate.

BIBLIOGRAPHY

Aristakēs Lastiverc^{c}i, *Patmut^{c}iwn* (History), K. N. Yuzbashyan, ed. (1963), French trans. by Marius Canard and Haïg Berberian, *Récit des malheurs de la nation arménienne* (1973); Norayr Bogharian, *Grand Catalogue of St. James Manuscripts,* II (1967), in Armenian; Matthew of Edessa, *Chronicle* (1869, repr. 1898), French trans. by Edouard Dulaurier, *Récit de la première croisade* (1858).

KRIKOR H. MAKSOUDIAN

[See also **Armenia: History of; Kars.**]

GAIMAR, GEFFREI, Anglo-Norman chronicler and cleric who wrote about 1140 for Constance, wife of Ralph FitzGilbert, holder of lands in Lincolnshire and, through his spouse, in Hampshire. Requested by Constance to translate Geoffrey of Monmouth's *Historia regum Britanniae,* Gaimar added to it an *Estoire des Engleis* (6,526 lines in octosyllabic verse) drawn from the Anglo-Saxon Chronicle up to lines 3,583–3,594, and thereafter primarily from unknown sources; it treats English history up to 1100, the year of the death of William II Rufus. As a cleric Gaimar was connected with court life, especially that revolving around the powerful Hugh of Avranches, earl of Chester; he may also have been acquainted with David the Scott, who became bishop of Bangor (1120–1139) upon his return to England from the imperial court in Germany.

Gaimar's design was to trace history from Jason and the Golden Fleece to the death of William Rufus; however, the first part of his work has been supplanted by Wace's *Roman de Brut* and survives (in four manuscripts, immediately following the *Brut*) only from the arrival in England of King Cerdic of Wessex, a relative of Hengist, king of

Kent, in 495; it closes with the death of William Rufus in 1100. Gaimar nevertheless merits literary acclaim in his own right: the story of Haveloc (lines 96–819) is the first known version of the *Lai de Haveloc;* the poignant episode of Buern Bucecarle (lines 2,571–2,720), which is supposed to explain the Danes' conquest of Northumbria in 866, finds a faint echo in the thirteenth-century epic *Anseïs de Cartage;* the narration of the Danish invasion under Gormont (lines 3,239–3,310) differs perceptibly from that found in *Gormont et Isembart* or that of Wace's *Brut;* and the trial of Count Godwine, earl of Wessex (lines 4,861–5,029) reveals a part of Anglo-Norman law that might have been a model for the trial scene in Marie de France's *Lanval.* Gaimar's narrative qualities are uneven: he is gauche when too close to his sources but quite dramatic when he allows himself to indulge in striking episodes.

BIBLIOGRAPHY

Alexander Bell, *L'Estoire des Engleis: By Geffrei Gaimar* (1960), which includes a "Sources and Influences." See also Alexander Bell, "The Epilogue to Gaimar's *Estoire des Engleis,*" in *Modern Language Review,* **25** (1930); Philipp August Becker, *Der gepaarte Achtsilber in der französischen Dichtung,* in *Abhandlungen der Sächsischen Akademie der Wissenschaften, philosophisch-historischen Klasse,* **43,** no. 1 (1934), 40–45; J. S. P. Tatlock, *The Legendary History of Britain* (1950), 452–456.

HANS-ERICH KELLER

[See also **Anglo-Norman Literature; Geoffrey of Monmouth.**]

GALATA. See **Pera-Galata.**

GALERAN DE BRETAGNE (Paris, Bibliothèque Nationale, fonds français, MS 24942), an early-thirteenth-century *roman d'aventure.* Most critics now believe that the author is Renaut, about whom nothing is known, rather than Jean Renart, author of *L'Escoufle* and *Guillaume de Dole.* Set not in the Celtic, Arthurian world but in a more realistic thirteenth-century court, the 7,800-line text is inspired by Marie de France's lai "Fresne." The author demonstrates a sublime confidence in love and nature,

which overcome all obstacles. But, in a marked departure from the courtly tradition, it is in the real world, with its duplicity and complexities, that the lovers, Fresne and Galeran, must find their place.

KATHRYN MARIE TALARICO

GALICIAN-PORTUGUESE POETRY. With more than 2,000 extant texts from the period 1200–1350, Galician-Portuguese rivals in richness of heritage the Provençal lyric tradition from which it borrowed some features. Recent study, however, reveals a lively, pretroubadour indigenous folk poetry with strong thematic ties to the Mozarabic *kharjas* (before 1100) and to the Spanish *villancico.* Onto this native tradition was grafted a courtly tone deriving from the Provençal poetic manner, which traveled the pilgrim route to Santiago and was heard, along with Galician-Portuguese, in the courts of Iberia. Except in Catalonia, all peninsular poets used Galician-Portuguese for lyric song until early in the fourteenth century.

The vast bulk of these poems reposes in three compilations: the *Cancioneiro da Ajuda, Cancioneiro da Vaticana,* and *Cancioneiro da Biblioteca Nacional.* Independent survival of seven songs by Martin Codax was a happy accident. To these secular texts a fourth *cancioneiro* adds more than 400 religious songs, the *Cantigas de Santa Maria* of Alfonso X, whose reign (1252–1284) was the golden age of this lyric school. His songs, plus six by Codax, furnish the sole surviving musical texts.

The secular texts fall mostly into three main types, the best known of which is the *cantiga d'amigo.* A young girl, speaking either to herself or to a confidante (mother, friend, even her lover, the *amigo*), is moved to express a variety of emotions connected with love: longing for the absent lover, impatience with his delayed return, the torment or joy of loving, deception in love, and so forth. Scenes are set at the sea, by rivers or fountains, near shrines, and in the open countryside. Language and thought are simple, description is minimal and symbolic. Repetitions skillfully concentrate the lyric expression, and thematic development is by slight variations.

The least complex form uses a two-line stanza rhyming *AA,* the thought of which is repeated in a second stanza rhyming *BB,* as follows:

Sedia la fremosa seu sirgo torcendo	A
sa voz manselinha fremoso dizendo	A
contigas d'amigo	refrain

Sedia la fremosa seu sirgo lavrando,	B
sa voz manselinha fremoso cantando	B
cantigas d'amigo	refrain

(Estevam Coelho, *Cancioneiro da Vaticana*, 321)

She sat there, the fair maid, her silk strands a-making, her gentle voice lifted, prettily phrasing songs of her lover.

She sat there, the fair maid, her silk strands a-spinning, her gentle voice lifted, prettily singing songs of her lover.

(Author's translation)

Only the rhymes vary; the new ones are usually synonyms, further concentrating the thought and building an incantatory pattern of great expressivity. A poem may continue with sets of double stanzas or, in a brilliant variation, interlock the sets by making the second line of the first pair of stanzas into the first lines of the respective stanzas in the succeeding pair, inventing only new second lines (these are transferred to the next pair and thus may be extended indefinitely).

The *cantigas d'amor* reveal a greater debt, but not a slavish one, to the cultivated love *canso*. Most Galician-Portuguese poets preferred to develop the theme of the sorrows of unrequited love, practically ignoring other themes present in the Provençal models. Many others added refrains characteristic of popular poetry but sprinkled with troubadour conceits.

The more than 400 *cantigas d'escarnho* (witty, ironic satires) *e de maldizer* (personal attacks) give life to a panorama of victims of these poetic barbs: cowardly soldiers, unchaste clerics, tipplers, misers, homosexuals, camp followers, ignoble nobles, hypocrites, and, of course, bad poets.

Galician poetry was absorbed into, and, in the fourteenth century, overshadowed by a vital and dynamic Castilian lyric, a process evident in the *Cancionero de Baena* (1445). Portuguese, which had slowly forged a separate identity, preserved much of the old glories even as it struck out on its own, its past remembered in many of the compositions of the *Cancioneiro geral* (1516).

BIBLIOGRAPHY

Sources. Walter Mettmann, ed., *Cantigas de Santa María*, 4 vols. (1959–1972); José Joaquim Nunes, ed., *Cantigas d'amigo dos trovadores galego-portugueses*, 3 vols. (1926–1928, repr. 1971), and *Cantigas d'amor dos trovadores galego-portuguese* (1932); Manuel Rodrigues-Lapa, ed., *Cantigas d'escarnho e de mal dizer* (1965, 2nd ed. 1970).

Studies. Eugenio Asensio, *Poética y realidad en el cancionero peninsular de la edad media*, 2nd ed. (1970); Jean-Marie d'Heur, *Troubadours d'oc et troubadours galiciens-portugais* (1973); José Filgueira-Valverde, "Lírica medieval gallega y portuguesa," in Guillermo Díaz Plaja, ed., *Historia general de las literaturas hispanicas* (1949); Frede Jensen, *The Earliest Portuguese Lyrics* (1978); Ramón Menéndez-Pidal, *Poesia juglaresca y orígenes de las literaturas románicas* (1957); Joseph T. Snow, *The Poetry of Alfonso X: A Critical Bibliography* (1977).

JOSEPH T. SNOW

[See also **Alfonso X; Cantiga; Cantigas de Amor, Amigo, and Escarnio; Dinis; Mozarabic Kharjas; Portuguese Literature; Provençal Literature: 1200–1500.**]

GALL, ST. (Gallus) (*d. ca.* 650), Irish companion of Columbanus at Luxeuil and Arbon (Switzerland). Good evidence of his career is meager. Jonas, monk of Bobbio, writing in the seventh century, relies on Gall for oral testimony to the life of Columbanus, but says little of Gall himself. Fragments of an eighth-century Life remain. Wettinus and Walafrid Strabo, both monks of Reichenau, use this early life in their own accounts of Gall, adding to it from Jonas and other undetermined sources.

According to this "vulgate" tradition of Gall's life, the saint was born in Ireland not long after 550; he accompanied Columbanus to France and Switzerland (590–612), but refused to follow him into Italy. As a punishment for his refusal, Gall was forbidden to celebrate Mass for the remainder of Columbanus' life. Wettinus and Walafrid emphasize Gall's obedience to this ban: he declined to become bishop of his region without Columbanus' express permission, nor did he assume the title of abbot of the community that he had established. The same hagiographers relate a deathbed forgiveness by Columbanus and a transfer of the great abbot's *cambutta* (crosier) to Gall. Since Gall's hermitage was reestablished as a Benedictine monastery by Otmar in the eighth century, the reconciliation incident appears to have been calculated to legitimize the Abbey of St. Gall as a Columbanian foundation and to ensure that Gall would be regarded as the true patron of the Abbey.

Gall was renowned for his preaching and personal holiness; numerous miracles were ascribed to him. It is now generally agreed that Gall himself contributed little that is tangible to the Abbey's intellectual development, which did not really begin until the early ninth century. Evidence of Gall's own learning is meager. A letter and a sermon attributed to him are almost certainly spurious.

BIBLIOGRAPHY

Bruno Krusch, ed., *Monumenta Germaniae historica, Scriptores rerum Merovingicarum,* IV (1902), provides text and discussion of the lives of St. Gall along with Jonas' life of Columbanus. See also James M. Clark, *The Abbey of St. Gall as a Centre of Literature and Art* (1926); James F. Kenney, *The Sources for the Early History of Ireland: Ecclesiastical* (1966).

MICHAEL HERREN

[See also **Columbanus, St.**]

GALLEGO, FERNANDO, Castilian artist active in Salamanca from about 1466 to 1506, who painted in the Hispano-Flemish style. His works show some influence of Dirk Bouts. Gallego's figures have rustic, expressive, Castilian faces, with the slender, elongated bodies and subtle drapery textures of Bouts. Noteworthy among his works are the personifications of the signs of the zodiac, frescoed on the library ceiling at the University of Salamanca.

BIBLIOGRAPHY

Chandler R. Post, *A History of Spanish Painting,* IV, pt. 1 (1933), 87–150.

MARY GRIZZARD

GALLERY, an architectural term with numerous meanings. As applied to medieval architecture, there are several important ones:

First, a covered story above and as deep as the aisle below and opening into the main vessel of a church through an arcade; if vaulted, a gallery contributes to structural stability, permitting greater height than could be obtained without the gallery or a substitute feature, such as flying buttresses. It is also termed tribune and, incorrectly, triforium.

Second, a similar but normally relatively smaller and narrower construction on the exterior of a church, especially German and Italian churches. It is also termed a loggia or dwarf gallery.

Third, a platform cantilevered from a wall on corbels and, depending on its projection, supported at its outer limits by arches, columns, or piers. In a church or other large space it holds musical instruments (for instance, an organ, hence organ gallery or organ loft) or musicans (hence singers gallery).

CARL F. BARNES, JR.

GALLICAN CHANT, either the ecclesiastical chant of Gaul, suppressed in favor of the Roman by Pepin and Charlemagne in the second half of the eighth century or, less specifically, the chant of a group of non-Roman, Latin liturgies (Iberian, Celtic, Gallic, and north Italian) seen by some liturgists as fundamentally related.

The reasons for the replacement of the local chant were both political and musical. The legitimacy of the Carolingian usurpation was largely based on the authority of the popes, for Stephen II had consented to crown Pepin king of the Franks, and Leo III was to declare Charlemagne emperor in the West. The use of the Roman chant was a continuous reminder of this authority. But, as appears from their subsequent efforts, the Carolingian monarchs were genuinely interested in music, and wished particularly for a uniform practice throughout their kingdom, a uniformity conspicuously lacking before their intervention.

In the days before notation made widespread conformity practical, there were notable differences in the musical practices of churches within the same city. How much greater must have been the diversity between distant ecclesiastical centers of the large Frankish kingdom, some clinging still to the refinements of their imperial Roman legacy; some, scarcely civilized, dominated by barbarian, even tribal, tastes and practices. Gallican chant was not a single, uniform repertory, like the Gregorian or Ambrosian, but a family of such repertories, some well developed, some not, perhaps sharing some of the more important chants of the Mass and Office (these affinities proportional to the proximity of the churches), but with marked local differences.

No Gallican music books survive; and it is unlikely there ever were any. Before the ninth century ecclesiastical chant was everywhere an oral tradition. It is not impossible, however, that some Gallican melodies have survived in manuscripts written long after the suppression. Scholars have claimed to identify a number of such survivors on liturgical evidence, on the basis of textual characteristics, and even on the ground of a distinctive melodic style. Of these criteria the first is the most plausible: melodies found in Frankish copies of Roman chant books, but not in books used in Rome, may be Gallican; and some of these chants can be shown to have unusual melodic characteristics and peculiarities of language. But if they are not Roman, they are not necessarily Gallican; it is as likely, and perhaps more, that most are newer compositions written in Frankish regions as additions to the Roman chant. The production of new chants is well documented north of the Alps in the Carolingian era.

The identified "Gallican" chants are fundamentally similar in forms and styles to the chants of the surviving Latin rites. The various regional repertories used different texts for the same liturgical occasions, and (for all practical purposes) different melodies; but whether Gallican, Iberian or Celtic, Milanese or Roman, these different texts were set, according to the same principles, to many of the same responsorial or antiphonal melody types, which, whatever their ultimate origin, are the unifying feature of the musical repertories that have survived.

BIBLIOGRAPHY

Higini Anglès, "Latin Chant Before St. Gregory," in Dom Anselm Hughes, ed., The New Oxford History of Music, II (1954); Anton Baumstark, Liturgie comparée (1940, 3rd ed. 1953), in English as Comparative Liturgy (1958); Louis Duchesne, Origines du culte chrétien, 5th ed. (1920), in English as Christian Worship, Its Origin and Evolution, M. L. McClure, trans. (1919); Amédée Gastoué, Le chant gallican (1939), contains a list of published transcriptions of melodies claimed as Gallican; Michel Huglo, "Altgallikanische Liturgie," in K. Fellerer, ed., Geschichte der katolischen Kirchenmusik, I (1972); Henri Leclercq, "Gallicane (liturgie)," in Fernand Cabrol, ed., Dictionnaire d'archéologie chrétienne et de liturgie, VI, pt. 1 (1924); William S. Porter, The Gallican Rite (1958); Bruno Stäblein, "Gallikanische Liturgie," in F. Blume, ed., Die Musik in Geschichte und Gegenwart, IV (1955).

TERENCE BAILEY

[See also Gallican Rite; Procession.]

GALLICAN RITE. The term refers here to the liturgical usages in Gaul before adoption of the Roman rite under the Carolingians. It was, along with the Mozarabic and Milanese, one of the three principal non-Roman rites of the early medieval period. It appears to have been less clearly defined than the other two, with a degree of variability from region to region.

Its sources are similarly less satisfactory. On the one hand there are two genuine Gallican lectionaries: an extremely early one from about 500, preserved in the Herzog August Bibliothek at Wolfenbüttel, and the seventh-century Luxeuil Lectionary. On the other hand the sacramentaries are later—from the end of the seventh century and the eighth century—and display Roman influence; they are the Missale Gothicum, and Missale Gallicanum vetus, and the Bobbio Missal. All these sources have been at the disposal of liturgical historians for several centuries, while the Mone Masses, a group of eleven genuine mass formularies from the seventh century, were first published in 1850 by Franz Joseph Mone. As for descriptive sources, reliance must be placed upon scattered references from Caesarius of Arles, St. Gregory of Tours, and the Merovingian church councils; upon comparison with Mozarabic and Milanese sources: and especially upon the Expositio brevis antiquae liturgiae gallicanae, attributed to St. Germanus of Paris.

The Expositio is in the form of two letters: the first gives a detailed description of the Gallican Mass, and the second adds information on liturgical vestments and indicates Lenten variations in antiphon texts. After its first publication by Edmond Martène in 1717, the Expositio was assumed by most to be the authentic work of St. Germanus until in 1924 André Wilmart pointed out, among other things, its apparent dependence on Isidore of Seville's De ecclesiasticis officiis (ca. 620). Since then the consensus has been that it originated about 700 in the area of Autun. In 1962 Alexis van der Mensbrugghe argued vigorously that its authenticity be reacknowledged, a position in which he is seconded by Klaus Gamber. In what follows here, however, the consensus is assumed to be substantially correct.

The Expositio presents a more or less complete outline of the late Gallican Mass, at least as celebrated at Autun. Missing are a number of collects that are known from the sacramentaries and any direct reference to the prayer of consecration, the text of which has not been preserved. The sequence is as follows:

Antiphona ad praelegendum, an entrance chant
*Silentium, the deacon enjoining silence on the people and the bishop greeting them with Dominus vobiscum

Aius, the *Trisagion* sung in Greek and Latin, followed by *Kyrie eleison* sung by three boys

Prophetia, the Canticle of Zachary, *Benedictus*

*Propheta, the Old Testament reading

*Apostolus, the New Testament reading

Hymnum, the song of the three youths, *Benedicite*

Responsorium, presumably a psalm, sung on occasion by boys

Aius ante Evangelium, perhaps in Greek only

*Evangelium, the Gospel, proclaimed from the *tribunal analogii* (an ambon), preceded and followed by a procession

Sanctus post Evangelium, probably the *Aius* in Latin only

*Homiliae, a homily referring to the three readings

*Preces, probably in the form of a litany intoned by the deacon

*Caticuminum, possibly a ceremonial dismissal of catechumens

Sonum, a chant sung during the entrance of bread and wine, possibly derived from the eastern Cherubicon

*Nomina defunctorum, commemoration of the dead and presumably of the living

*Pax, the kiss of peace

*Sursum corda, the preface with concluding Sanctus

*Confractio and *commixtio,* the breaking of the bread and the mingling of the elements, accompanied by the antiphon *Quia [Christo] patiente*

*Oratio dominica, the Lord's Prayer

Benedictio populi, a blessing given by the bishop with texts proper to each feast day

Trecanum, a chant, apparently sung during Communion.

This is clearly a highly developed eucharistic service. As such it renders quite implausible the dominant eighteenth- and nineteenth-century theory of the origin of the Gallican rite: that it was in use at Ephesus during the time of St. John the Apostle and that it was brought intact to Lyons by St. Irenaeus in the second century. During the earlier twentieth century the dominant view was that of Louis Duchesne, who saw the Gallican rite as the transplanted fourth-century Milanese rite, which in turn was imported from the East. However, two considerations render this unlikely. The first, and more specific, is that the late fourth-century Milanese rite now appears to be fundamentally the same as the contemporary Roman rite. Indeed—and this is the second and more general consideration—all eucharistic rites of the time, in both East and West, displayed the same basic character. They shared a series of essential events, most of which are present in St. Justin's description of the second-century Sunday Eucharist (I *Apology,* ch. 67). By the end of the fourth century, a handful

of additional events had become standard, including the opening greeting, the gradual psalm, the Sanctus, and the Communion chant. After this time the various Eastern and Western rites developed their distinctive features.

In the outline of the Gallican Eucharist given above, the presumed fourth-century items are indicated by asterisks. The other items were added in the course of the three centuries leading up to the composition of the *Expositio;* they are mostly importations from the East, especially Syria. The most helpful aids available to follow this complex process and to study the other issues involved with each item, are the essays of William S. Porter, Johannes Quasten, and Aimé-Georges Martimort.

A noteworthy characteristic of Gallican liturgical texts is their prolixity and emotionality of expression, which stand in contrast with the spare and legalistic style of their Roman counterparts.

BIBLIOGRAPHY

Sources. Wolfenbüttel Lectionary: Alban Dold, *Das älteste Liturgiebuch der lateinischen Kirche* (1936). *Luxeuil Lectionary:* Pierre Salmon, *Le lectionnaire de Luxeuil I–II* (1944–1953). *Missale Gothicum:* Leo Cunibert Mohlberg, *Missale Gothicum: (Vat. Regin. lat. 317)* (1961). *Missale Gallicanum vetus:* Leo Cunibert Mohberg, with Leo Eizenhöfer and Peter Siffrin, *Missale Gallicanum vetus* (1958). *Bobbio Missal:* Elias A. Lowe, *The Bobbio Missal, a Gallican Mass Book* (1920). *Mone Masses:* Leo Cunibert Mohlberg, with Leo Eizenhöfer and Peter Siffrin, *Missale Gallicanum vetus* (1958), 74–90; *Expositio antiquae liturgiae Gallicanae* (1971).

Studies. Louis Duchesne, *Christian Worship, Its Origin and Evolution,* 5th ed., trans. from the French by M. L. McClure (1919, repr. 1949 and 1956), 86–105, 151–160, 189–227; Johannes Quasten, "Oriental Influence in the Gallican Liturgy," in *Traditio,* **1** (1943); Aimé-Georges Martimort, "La Liturgie de la messe en Gaule," in *Compagnie de Saint-Sulpice; Bulletin du Comité des études,* **22** (1958); William S. Porter, *The Gallican Rite* (1958); Alexis van der Mensbrugghe, "Pseudo-Germanus Reconsidered," in F. L. Cross, ed., *Studia patristica,* V, pt. 3 (1962); André Wilmart, "Germain de Paris (Lettres attribuées à Saint)," in *Dictionnaire d'archeólogie chrétienne et de liturgie,* VI, pt. 1 (1924).

JAMES W. MCKINNON

[See also **Gallican Chant; Germanus of Paris, St.; Lectionary; Milanese Rite; Mozarabic Rites; Sacramentary.**]

GALLON, a measure of capacity in the British Isles for liquid and dry products. During the Middle Ages it was never defined in cubic capacities or by physical dimensions, but rather by the amount of wheat that it was capable of holding, measured by either the tower or the troy system. By the reign of Elizabeth I, however, standards were promulgated for the following items: ale, 282 cubic inches (4.621 liters), containing 4 quarts or 8 pints and equal to ⅛ ale firkin, ¹⁄₁₆ ale kilderkin, and ¹⁄₃₂ ale barrel; beer, the same as for ale but equal to ⅑ beer firkin, ¹⁄₁₈ beer kilderkin, and ¹⁄₃₆ beer barrel; and grain 268.8 cubic inches (4.404 liters), containing 4 quarts or 8 pints and equal to ½ peck, ⅛ bushel, and ¹⁄₆₄ seam or quarter. Prior to standardization the grain gallon varied from approximately 272.25 to 282 cubic inches. The wine gallon was standardized in 1707 at 231 cubic inches (3.785 liters). Though usually containing 4 quarts or 8 pints and equaling ¹⁄₁₈ rundlet, ¹⁄₄₂ tierce, ¹⁄₆₃ hogshead, ¹⁄₈₄ puncheon, and ¹⁄₂₅₂ tun, its actual capacity varied prior to 1707, with 282 cubic inches and 224 cubic inches being the most common.

There were a significant number of local variations. The Scottish gallon used for both liquid and dry products was considerably larger than the English, being 827.232 cubic inches (about 13.60 liters) or 4 quarts, 8 pints, 16 choppins, 32 mutchkins, or 128 gills. Throughout much of the Middle Ages the gallon was defined in Scottish legislation as a vessel capable of holding 20 pounds, 8 ounces of the clear water of Tay.

BIBLIOGRAPHY

BIBLIOGRAPHY

Ronald Edward Zupko, *A Dictionary of English Weights and Measures* (1968).

RONALD EDWARD ZUPKO

[See also **Weights and Measures, Western European.**]

GALUT (exile) was the fundamental condition of medieval Jewry with a profound and pervasive impact on Jewish law, theology, and psychology. The observance of Judaism was both impoverished and enriched by the reality of exile: a host of laws connected with the land of Israel and the temple in Jerusalem could only be studied wistfully; on the other hand, mourning for the destruction of the temple and the oppression of Israel, calls for revenge, and prayers for redemption became a crucial part of the rituals and liturgy of every medieval Jew.

Exile was essentially viewed as punishment, an interpretation rooted in biblical and rabbinic theodicy, reinforced by the prayer book, indispensable to the work of ethical preachers, and immune to any efforts at total exorcism. Nevertheless, this interpretation raised problems of the most serious kind. Jews were deeply and sincerely persuaded that even a casual glance at medieval realities would establish the moral contrast between themselves and their neighbors; under such conditions God's decision to punish Israel for its sins while leaving gentiles unscathed cried out for explanation.

Under the impact of the crusades, Ashkenazic Jews came to regard the exile as more than simple punishment. The suffering of the Jewish people in exile constituted a sacrifice akin to the binding of Isaac: it was a test of the Jews' faith, an atonement for future generations, and the ultimate sanctification of the name of God. This theme not only permeated the Jewish crusade chronicles but also was made part of the Jewish consciousness by its place in the liturgy of the High Holy Day period. In their exegesis of the "suffering servant" passage in Isaiah 53, some Jews went even further: Jewish suffering was an expiatory sacrifice for the nations of the world. Although this explanation did not achieve prominence in nonexegetical contexts, it is noteworthy for its acceptance of the doctrine of vicarious atonement, which is removed from the Christian messiah and applied instead to the people of Israel.

Judah Halevi, also working with the "suffering servant" passage from Isaiah, produced a striking and influential image: the Jewish people are the heart of all the nations—so central that they are inevitably most sensitive and susceptible to pain. "Only you have I known among all the families of the earth," said the prophet, "therefore I will visit upon you all your iniquities" (Amos 3:2). In one sense the suffering of Israel was an expression of God's mercy, since it assured prompt retaliation and prevented the sort of accumulation of sin that would justify the eventual extermination of a sinful people. In a polemical context Jews did not hesitate to draw the conclusion that the exile endured precisely so that the sins of the gentiles should accumulate to the point of their destruction.

Several Jewish thinkers, including Baḥya ben Asher and Ḥasdai Crescas, saw the dispersion of Israel as part of God's plan to spread religious truth among the nations, while others, like Isaac Pulgar and Solomon ibn Verga, began to consider naturalistic explanations for the Jewish fate. The ancient consoling principle that God shares the exile established itself both in mystical texts and in the Sukkot festival liturgy, while a key liturgical poem of the

Shavuot festival was content to resolve the question of why Jews suffered while gentiles did not with reference to the reversal of roles at the end of days. No explanation of exile could be truly satisfying without the abiding faith in its eschatological liquidation.

BIBLIOGRAPHY

Yitzhak Baer, *Galut* (1947); Joel Rembaum, "The Development of a Jewish Exegetical Tradition Regarding Isaiah 53," in *Harvard Theological Review*, 75 (1982); Shalom Rosenberg, "Exile and Redemption in Jewish Thought in the Sixteenth Century: Contending Conceptions," in Bernard D. Cooperman, ed., *Jewish Thought in the Sixteenth Century* (1983), contains earlier material.

DAVID BERGER

[See also **Exegesis, Jewish; Judah Halevi.**]

GAMES AND PASTIMES. "God has intended that Mankind should enjoy themselves with playing" was the opinion of one of the most enlightened monarchs of the Middle Ages, Alfonso X the Learned, king of Castile and León (1252–1284), set down in the introduction to his *Book of Games*.

Games can roughly be divided into "action games" and "sitting games." Some of the more active "action games," such as bowling and ball-tossing, seem to have bordered on sports. Most of the medieval games survive as children's games, such as blindman's buff, whipping tops, and leapfrog. The playing of games was beneath the notice of most chroniclers. Consequently, one can only guess at the rules of such action games when they are represented in manuscript illustrations (such as the Minnesinger Codex [*ca.* 1320], Heidelberg, Universitätsbibliothek) or as whimsical drolleries on the margins of books (*Roman d'Alexandre* [1334], Oxford; book of hours of Jeanne d'Évreux [*ca.* 1325–1328], New York, the Cloisters).

The medieval version of blindman's buff was hoodman-blind, in which the hood of the player who was "it" was reversed on his head, with the face opening backward. The other players took their hoods off, tied them into a knot, and, holding them by their long tips, struck the blindfolded player. A similar game, only without blindfolding, was frog-in-the-middle. Here the player who was "it" sat on the floor with legs tucked under, while the others tried to touch, pinch, or slap him; whoever got caught in the attempt was the next to be "it."

If this game seems rather rough, it was tame com-

Tournament: Herr Walther von Klingen. *Manesse-Codex,* fol. 52r. UNIVERSITÄTS BIBLIOTHEK HEIDELBERG, CODEX PAL. GERM. 848

pared with a slapping game popular with village swains in which two players sat crosslegged on a bench facing each other. They took turns slapping each other until one fell off the bench. As protection against the main force of the blows they kept their hands palms outward, arms crossed, shielding their faces. In another slapping game, the player who was "it" bent over double and hid his face in the lap of a second, seated player, who made sure that there was no peeking. The others took turns slapping the victim's buttocks; whenever he guessed right, who had just hit him, they had to exchange places. Judging from the illustrations, even girls might participate in this game, which must have become quite ribald as a result.

Mock equestrian battles were fought between pairs of contestants, one boy (or girl) sitting on another's shoulders. A balancing contest was the quintain; two players, each standing on one leg, the soles of their raised feet pressed together, pushed to overturn each other. If one of the players was a girl, she sat on a stool or on the back of a squatting swain, meeting her opponent with one raised foot. More athletic was a wrestling game in which the two players sat on the ground facing each other, feet pressed together. They grasped a stick between them and engaged in a sort of sitting tug-of-war.

Ball games were of rather limited importance during the Middle Ages. This was partly because medieval balls did not bounce (rubber was unknown in Europe before the discovery of America); they were made of leather or fabric stuffed with rags, or were inflated pigs' bladders.

Stickball, a forerunner of baseball, was played with a fist-sized, rag-stuffed ball that was thrown into the air by one player, who then had to hit it with a stick in order to score a run. Exact rules are not preserved; apparently it was a group game that could have any number of players. The same was the case with hurling, a forerunner of field hockey popular in the British Isles (it plays an important role in Irish heroic epics, such as the stories of the First Battle of Moy Tura, and of the boyhood of Cú Chulainn), and with football, a game with a set of rules similar to soccer.

Handball, or fives, was a forerunner of tennis, played by batting the ball with bare hands; the term "tennis" for a game played with racquets is first mentioned in an English ballad of about 1400. Tennis balls were the famous challenge sent by the French to King Henry V that led to the Battle of Agincourt (1415). The first English laws restricting games that might interfere with practicing archery were passed in 1365; the first game named was handball. Football and tennis were banned for working people in 1388, and in 1410 the punishment of six days' imprisonment was established for delinquents.

Bowling was played in two ways: boccie-style, with balls (of wood) only; and as nine pins, with one ball and nine wooden markers. It was an outdoor sport, played on the bowling green.

More exerting sports were stone-tossing, wrestling, and fencing. Stone-tossing was a simple test of strength; both noblemen and peasant lads—at a county fair, for instance—tried to find out who could throw a stone the farthest. Any handy stone would do; there was no standardization of weight as there is in the modern shotput.

In wrestling, basic rules were agreed upon beforehand: whether certain holds were prohibited (as in Greco-Roman style), or whether anything short of gouging and biting was permitted. In northern Europe there was a special type of wrestling in which the participants wore broad belts that afforded the handholds to unbalance an opponent.

Fencing was done with quarterstaffs, swords, or pole arms (such as halberds). Quarterstaff fencing required great skill and alertness, because the staff was used both as weapon of attack and as defense. Both ends of the staff could be used for a blow or thrust, and an unwary fencer could be taken by surprise from an unexpected angle. Sword fencing was done with sword and buckler, a small (not more than about eighteen inches in diameter) circular shield with a central handgrip. Sword strokes were parried by deflecting them with the buckler, as parrying with the sword blade was damaging to the edges and was to be avoided, if possible. Citizens of most medieval communities served in militias and were therefore encouraged to improve their martial arts.

By the fifteenth century most major cities had regular fencing schools where courses could be taken and diplomas ("master of the long sword") earned. By the middle of the fifteenth century, the first fencing handbooks (with illustrations and diagrams) appeared, first as manuscript copies and later in print (Thalhoffer's *Fechtbuch,* 1467). One of the refinements developed in the fencing academies was double fencing, executed with a sword in the right hand and a parrying dagger (instead of a buckler) in the left. By the early sixteenth century, double fencing was fully established (Achille Marozzo's fencing book *Opera nova,* 1536), though conservative fencers continued to use bucklers until the seventeenth and, in isolated cases (such as Scottish clansmen), well into the eighteenth century.

Another competitive martial sport was archery, using either longbows or crossbows. Longbows were preferred in England and in Flanders. Shooting at the butts as a Sunday exercise was required by law in England, as training for the sturdy yeomen archers who were the mainstay of the English army during the Hundred Years War. The burghers of the walled cities of Italy, France, and Germany defended their homes with crossbows from the battlements. Every male citizen had to keep his own arms for the defense of his town. If he failed to do so, he might face a fine, an extra tax, or loss of his voting rights.

Most cities had archers' or crossbowmen's guilds that staged annual shooting contests. These *Schützenfeste* are still popular events in German-speaking countries, and are also preserved in ancient Italian towns (Gubbio, Perugia, Sansepolcro). The targets in these crossbow contests are man-size wooden heral-

Backgammon: Herr Goeli. *Manesse-Codex,* fol. 262v. UNIVERSI-TÄTS BIBLIOTHEK HEIDELBERG, CODEX PAL. GERM. 848

dic eagles with spread wings, hoisted on a tall pole. The bird's individual elements—wings, tail, claws, even single feathers—are loosely doweled together, in order to break off easily when hit. Every part has a point value, and careful score is kept. The best marksman is declared *Schützenkönig* (king of the shooters) for the year (in the Middle Ages he was exempt from local taxes during his "reign"); the worst shot is awarded a suckling pig as a consolation prize. In Flanders, the target for longbow shooting was a wooden popinjay on a pole, or sometimes a live rooster tied to the tip of a wing of a windmill fixed in the upright position.

The most spectacular sport of the Middle Ages was the tournament. Originally it was straightforward battle training of the armored fighters on horseback, the knights, but it gradually became a spectator sport and mass entertainment. As war games and battle training, tournamentlike exercises are mentioned by Roman historians of Germanic tribesmen. As organized events, they are reported in 842 among the Carolingian Franks, and, in the tenth century, the German emperor Henry the Fowler established spear games *(hastiludia)* on a regular basis, complete with a supervisory committee to make sure that the supposedly friendly mock battle stayed friendly.

The tournament was developed in France as a formalized event; the Angevin knight Godefroy de Preuilly is credited with having "invented" *torneamenta* with codified rules in 1062. During the centuries these rules—which soon were believed to have been set up by King Arthur and his knights of the Round Table—were elaborated upon. Their major codifications were the tournament books of King René of Anjou (1452) and Jacques d'Armagnac *(ca. 1470).* The final version was compiled about 1515 by Emperor Maximilian I, who was surnamed "the Last of the Knights."

With the codification of rules came a classification of courses: the joust (the most popular form, in which a pair of combatants on horseback ran at each other with lances); the melee (in which groups of knights fought); the baston course (fought by pairs or groups on horseback, with blunted swords or wooden clubs); and the foot combat (a fencing exhibition with lances and/or swords).

In the tilting courses (joust and melee), the purpose was the unhorsing of the opponent; if both combatants managed to keep their seats, an extra point was awarded to the one who had shattered his lance, because the breaking of the lance proved that he had hit squarely and with the greatest possible force. The lances were fitted with coronals, blunt heads terminating in three or four short prongs, like a little crown. Sharp points were used only in *Rennen,* a more dangerous variant of the joust popular in German-speaking countries.

In the baston course the purpose was to knock the crest off the opponent's helmet. The competitors in this game of fencing skill and horsemanship could use either swords or clubs; morning stars (spiked balls attached to staffs by means of chains) were outlawed, because their strokes were too difficult to control and were likely to go wild.

Originally the tournaments were fought in the same equipment—armor, helmet, and shield—that was used in battle; the offensive weapons were blunted for the sport. By the middle of the fourteenth century, however, reinforcement elements were added to the basic armor for greater safety, and

349

a special tournament shield, the targe, was introduced. It became fashionable for a knight to have a "shield for war" (of the traditional triangular shape) and a "shield of peace" (his tournament targe).

During the fifteenth century tournament armor was developed as a form distinct from battle armor. It became true sports equipment, with large helmets securely bolted to the cuirass, front and back, and a queue to lock the lance into couched position added to the lance rest. Tournament armor was much heavier (up to 120 pounds) than field armor; mounting a horse was therefore done from a mounting block or a short stepladder.

The tournament field was confined by barriers, the lists. Its floor was covered with a thick layer of sand and wood shavings to soften falls. In the fifteenth century, it became customary in the joust to divide the field lengthwise by a rail, to keep the horses from colliding, though in Germany the old-fashioned joust in the open field, without the rail, remained in favor.

Trained attendants (French: *preneurs*) stood by to assist an unhorsed knight and to round up riderless horses. In foot combats the *preneurs* were equipped with quarterstaffs to pry two combatants safely apart, in case they got carried away in the excitement of the fight. Other attendants, selected for their quick-wittedness, were used in crowd control; they were dressed in jesters' costumes, so as not to spoil the holiday mood of the crowd.

Tournaments were often enhanced by parades and pageants, such as "Round Tables," with enactments of stories from Arthurian literature, or "Castles of Love," in which a stage-set castle was "defended" by beautiful damsels and "stormed" by gallant knights using flowers as missiles and weapons. Tournaments with pageants were held on an annual basis as a tourist attraction by rich cities (Joute de l'Épinette at Lille, 1283–1489; Gesellenstechen at Nuremberg, 1445–1561).

Participation in a tournament was strictly limited to knights. Careful checks (*Helmschau*) were made by appointed officials, the heralds, before a contestant was admitted. On the other hand, mock jousts, in which village swains donned tubs, buckets, or baskets instead of armor, were favorite entertainment at county fairs and during Shrovetide revels. In Italy, mock battles with cudgels (*gioco da mazzascudo*) were outlets for local political factions. Guilds of boatmen or fishermen held "jousts" in boats, in which the loser was swept overboard (*Schifferstechen* at Strahlau, near Berlin, still held today).

Training exercises for the joust, such as the quintain and tilting at the ring, became entertainments in their own right. The quintain was a pole with a pivoting crosspiece having a small shield, the target, attached to one end and a club or sandbag attached to the other. The jouster was to hit the target (if he missed, he was in danger of bumping into it), then had to speed out of the way of the other arm swinging around. In Italy, quintain figures were often dressed as Saracens (*gioco di saracino* in Arezzo, still held today; *quintana* in Ascoli Piceno); in Germany they were knights (*Spielroland*).

The horses used by knights for battle and tournament were not huge, lumbering Clydesdales or Percherons, as is generally thought. On the contrary, knightly horses had to be fleet of foot, but also full of stamina to carry the weight of an armored man all day. Throughout the Middle Ages the best horses for a knight were considered to be the Spanish breeds, which still survive as the Andalusian and the Lipizzaner, and also the quarter horse of the American West, descended from the mounts the Spanish conquistadors brought to Mexico in the sixteenth century. Of course, if a true "Castilian" was not available, any local breed would do, as long as the desired qualities were present. As is only natural when large numbers of horses and horsemen gather, horse races were held. Most of them were held at the spur of the moment, as accompaniment of a tournament or a county fair, but some became important annual events, to be held with great ceremony (Palio of Siena).

Other entertainments involving animals were bearbaiting, in which dogs were set upon a bear chained to a post, and cockfights. These "games" involved heavy betting.

At any social gathering, dancing was one of the major entertainments, be it the sedate step dances of the nobility at court, the cheerful round dances of peasants on the greensward, or the boisterously grotesque morris dances, in which the dancers competed for a prize by outdoing each other in inventive contortions. Professional entertainment was provided by jugglers and puppeteers (forerunners of Punch and Judy shows).

The "sitting games" of the Middle Ages consisted of board games, card games, and dicing. Dice were known in Roman times and were the classic gambling game throughout the entire medieval period, innumerable bans and prohibitions by well-meaning city fathers and churchmen intent on saving souls from corruption notwithstanding. The church was

Bowling: Der junge Meissner. *Manesse-Codex,* fol. 339r. UNIVER-SITÄTS BIBLIOTHEK HEIDELBERG, CODEX PAL. GERM. 848

particularly opposed to this kind of gambling, since it could point with a shudder to the soldiers at the Crucifixion throwing dice for Christ's robe at the very foot of the cross.

Board games are probably even older than dice; gaming boards of various types have been found in ancient Egyptian tombs. Among them are boards for morris and *alquerque* games. Nine-men's morris *(merelles, Mühle)* is played on a board with three concentric squares connected by crosslines. Two players have nine game pieces or men each, which are placed—one by one—on the corners of the squares or on the crossing points. A player who has three men in a row may remove one of the opponent's men from the board. Morris boards can be found scratched in the flagstones of cloisters, watch-towers, and castle guardrooms, indicating the popularity of the game for whiling away time.

"Hunt" games of the fox-and-geese type were also favorites. Played on a square or cross-shaped grid, fox and geese requires one player with twelve

to fifteen "geese" to corner a single piece—the "fox" of the opponent. The "fox" may take "geese" by jumping over them. A variant of the game, with sixteen men on one side, and eight men and one "king" on the other, was popular with the Vikings, who called it *hneftafl.* In Spain, the game *alquerque* was played on a similar grid, but with equal numbers (usually twelve men) on either side. Welsh heroic epics tell of a board game called *gwyddbwyll,* which seems to have been similar to checkers. A combination of dice throws and placing (or taking) of men, *backgammon* (French: *trictrac*), was eagerly played in the Middle Ages.

The most prestigious of board games is chess. Invented probably in India during the sixth century, it spread through the Islamic countries to the West. Although it may have received a major impetus through contacts during the crusades, it was known earlier; in 1061 an overzealous cardinal, Peter Damian, gave a penance to the bishop of Florence for indulging in the frivolity of playing chess. This and the ban on playing chess in France imposed by St. Louis (1254) were unusual occurrences, however. Although all sorts of games were banned at one time or another, chess was usually held exempt, as ennobling men's minds instead of corrupting their souls.

Chess is a "war" game, with its men representing the formations of an ancient Indian army: a king, his vizier, war elephants, cavalry, war chariots, and foot soldiers. The moves of the chessmen are styled after actual military tactics, such as the advance with mutual support of the foot soldiers (pawns), the surprise attacks of cavalry (knight's move), or the lumbering charge of war chariots in the straight move of the rooks. Islamic chessmen are of nonfigural, abstract shapes; European ones, by contrast, were often elaborately carved as knights on horseback, enthroned queens, or mitered bishops.

In the movement of the game from India to Europe, some fundamental changes became inevitable, such as the transformation of *alfil,* the war elephant (unknown in Europe), into the bishop, because the two protruding points on top of the *alfil* piece (meant to represent the elephant's tusks) were misinterpreted as the double points of a bishop's miter. War chariots were not used in medieval Europe, but rooks often show finials in the shape of double horses' heads as vestigial remains of the chariot team. By the fifteenth century the rook had assumed the shape of a tower, derived from the fortified howdah of a war elephant, now placed at the flanks of the battle array. (In a thirteenth-century Scandina-

351

vian chess set in the British Museum, the rooks are berserkers!)

The original moves in the Indian game were somewhat different from those used in Europe. Originally the vizier could move only one square diagonally, and thus was the weakest piece on the board. It is a nice indication of the role of ladies in courtly medieval society that the queen became the most powerful piece. The chess game played with living figures in the market square of the north Italian town of Marostica by tradition goes back to a twelfth-century contest for the hand of a fair lady during a period when tournaments were banned by the doge of Venice.

The earliest handbook of chess, *Bonus socius* (Good companion), by Master Nicholas, was written about 1250; the monumental *Libros de acedrex, dados e tablas* (Book of chess, dice, and board games), by Alfonso X of Castile and León, was published in 1283. In the first section of this compendium, Alfonso gives a detailed description of the game of chess, complete with analyses of moves and solutions of problems; in the second, he lists twelve different dice games; and in the third, seven board games, including morris, *alquerque*, draughts (checkers), chess for a ten-by-ten and for a twelve-by-twelve-squares board, chess for four players, and a highly sophisticated astronomical game.

The latest addition to the store of games in the Middle Ages was the card game. Whether playing cards were invented in China or in India is an open question of no importance to the history of the games in Europe. In any case, cards were used in a "war" game like chess that was introduced into Europe late in the fourteenth century. A French edict of 1369 against games of chance does not mention cards, but in 1393 a purchase of three packs of cards from the Parisian Painter Jacquemin Gringonneur for King Charles VI is recorded. The first law against card playing on workdays (by the working people) dates from 1397.

The organization of a suit of cards with a king, a knight (before the queen was taken into the "devil's prayerbook"), a squire (valet), and faceless foot soldiers (the numerals) corresponds to that of a medieval army. The earliest known suit signs—swords, cups (chalices), coins, and staves—were representations of the four classes of medieval society: noblemen, clergy, burghers, and peasants. These suit signs are still preserved in Spanish and Italian decks. The modern French suit signs—spades, hearts, diamonds, and clubs—were introduced in the early fifteenth century, allegedly invented by the French knight Étienne de Vignolles, known as La Hire (The Wrath), the friend and battle companion of Joan of Arc. These suit signs, too, are representations of the four classes: spades (from the Spanish *espada,* sword) for noblemen; hearts for clergy; diamonds (in French *carreau,* the head of a crossbow bolt) for burghers with their archers' guilds; and clubs for peasants.

Interestingly, among the forest-loving Germans the card game was interpreted not as war but as a hunt (*Ambraser Hofjagdspiel, ca.* 1445). German suit signs are therefore acorns, linden leaves, hearts, and hawks' bells. Wild boar, stag, unicorn, and falcon identified the deuces. One of the fifteenth-century German games of chance, *Pochen,* in time developed into poker. In Switzerland, which in the fifteenth and sixteenth centuries was the main supplier of mercenary soldiers (who also were notorious as hardened gamblers), the German suit signs were modified as shields, roses, acorns, and bells. The aces were banners.

The most important special development took place in Italy, with the introduction of the game of *tarocchi* or tarot. In addition to court cards and numerals, the tarot has a third set of cards, the *trionfi* (trumps). Also known as the major arcana, these trumps play an important role in fortune telling. Their use in fortune-telling, however, is an eighteenth-century mystification; the *trionfi* are not an occult code of wisdom going back to the Egyptians, but rather representations of the stages that made up the semireligious pre-Lenten carnival processions held in fourteenth- and fifteenth-century Italy (also celebrated in Petrarch's *Trionfi,* 1340–1344): the triumph of Love over Man, of Chastity over Love, of Death over Chastity, of Fame over Death, of Time over Fame, and of Eternity over Time.

Originally, playing cards were hand-painted—some splendid examples of fifteenth-century cards (tarot by Bonifacio Bembo, *ca.* 1450: *Stuttgarter Spiel, ca.* 1430) are preserved—but after the middle of the fifteenth century printed packs (woodcut and engraving), often designed by famous artists (Andrea Mantegna, Martin Schongauer, Israhel van Meckenem) were mass-produced and, together with handbooks like *Das guldin spil* by Master Ingold (1472), helped the pastime to gain ever-increasing popularity.

BIBLIOGRAPHY

Henri René d'Allemagne, *Les cartes à jouer,* 2 vols. (1906); R. Coltman Clephan, *The Tournament, Its Periods and Phases* (1919); Francis Henry Cripps-Day, *The History of the Tournament in England and France* (1918); Catherine Perry Hargrave, *A History of Playing Cards and a Bibliography of Cards and Gaming* (1930); William Heywood, *Palio and Ponte, an Account of the Sports of Central Italy from the Age of Dante to the XXth Century* (1904); Robert McConville, *The History of Board Games* (1974); James F. Magee, *Good Companion (Bonus Socius)* (1913); Gertrude Moakley, *Tarot Cards Painted by Bonifacio Bembo* ... (1966); H. J. R. Murray, *A History of Chess* (1913); Arnold Steiger, ed., *Alfonso el Sabio, Libros de acedrex, dados e tablas. Das Schachzabelbuch König Alfons des Weisen* (1941); Joseph Strutt, *The Sports and Pastimes of the People of England* (1801); Hans Wichmann and Siegfried Wichmann, *Schach, Ursprung und Umwandlung der Spielfigur in zwölf Jahrhunderten* (1960); Charles K. Wilkinson and Jessie McNab Dennis, *Chess: East and West, Past and Present* (1968).

HELMUT NICKEL

[See also **Alfonso X; Arms and Armor; Bow and Arrow/ Crossbow; Lance, Pike, Spear; Swords and Daggers.**]

GAMES, ISLAMIC. The play instinct must have been as strongly developed in the Islamic world as elsewhere, but the moral and theological attitudes of Islam (following, in many ways, those of some classical Greek authors, such as Aristotle) tended to deprecate games and play as worthy only of women and children, that is, those of weak moral fiber. From earliest Islamic times, games, sport, and the playing of musical instruments were regarded as distractions from the serious business of life and the accumulation of merit for the next world; caliphs such as the Umayyad Yazīd I (680–683) were condemned for their frivolous mode of life and love of diversion, whereas other caliphs such as al-Manṣūr (754–775) displayed their true piety by destroying musical instruments and games equipment. Nevertheless, it is known that children had their games. The Koran refers to the prophet Yūsuf as playing with his brothers; Muḥammad is said to have played as a child; and his favorite wife, ᶜĀᵓisha, had her dolls, although the licitness of dolls for girl children, as a preparation for motherhood, was only reluctantly conceded by Islamic law and ethics, which prohibited representation of living forms.

Specific children's games tend to be mentioned by philologists for their literary interest alone; hence many names of games have come down to us, but rarely their modus operandi. They apparently included the following: games of the *mankala* type, in which counters or pebbles are placed in holes; games of the checkers type, of which the still-popular North African *kharbga* is a representative; games centered on rolling nuts or stones into holes; and those involving a throw of dice or bones. Swings and seesaws seem also to have been in use: ᶜĀᵓisha was seesawing when first seen by the Prophet.

Sporting games included those played with balls, requiring running or jumping, and involving the use of animals, birds, and insects (for racing or fighting, for instance). Rewards and penalties were often involved, bringing an element of gambling into the games. Gambling attracted further disapproval from the purists, since the Koran specifically denounces the pre-Islamic Arabian gambling practice of *maysir*, which involved the drawing of lots by arrows and the slaughtering of a camel. This prohibition was later extended to all gambling *(qimār)*, though the practice flourished at all times in the forms of betting, guessing, and casting of lots.

The general attitude of disapproval toward play meant that all games equipment must have been simple and improvised. Thus, virtually no Islamic toys or games equipment of significant antiquity has survived.

There were also essentially adult games involving intellectual thought and sharpness of wit. The most popular games in the Islamic world were chess *(shaṭranj)* and backgammon or trictrac *(nard, tabula)* which came from the East. Popular Islamic tradition correctly traced chess to an Indian origin, while backgammon was associated in legend with the Sasanian Persian king Ardešīr. Proficiency at these games was regarded as a basic accomplishment of the educated elite; there were chess masters, and blindfold and simultaneous matches were known. Both games could be, and often were, played extensively for stakes; but the official attitude—as expressed, for instance, in some of the Arabic and Persian "Mirrors for Princes" literature—was not entirely disapproving. Since they sharpened the mind, it was conceded that they helped develop the strategic sense of military commanders and princes, and were thus a preparation for actual warfare. There was an extensive discussion of these two games, above all of chess, in medieval Islamic literature.

Field sports for adults were likewise encouraged because of the opportunities they gave for physical exercise and development, and above all for the military training of the mounted archer or lancer who, with the influx of Turkish soldiery into the caliphate

Nushirwan learns chess. Persian miniature in the Shiraz style, late 16th century. INDIA OFFICE LIBRARY, MS W.VIII.47, fol. 463v

A prince hawking. Miniature in the Bukhara style, third quarter of the 16th century. INDIA OFFICE LIBRARY, NO. J.28.2

from the ninth century became the backbone of most medieval Islamic armies. Horse racing was closely linked with gambling, but flight and target shooting with arrows was a basic part of military proficiency as well as a sport. The manuals of war and military training *(furūsīya)*, several of which survive from Ayyubid, Mamluk, and Ottoman periods, stress the importance of activities involving equestrian skill, such as tilting with lances at gourds mounted on poles; in Mamluk Egypt there were special hippodromes and training grounds for such sports. Above all, the game of polo (Persian: *chawgān*, Arabic: *ṣawlajān*), which originated in pre-Islamic Persia and the equipment and procedures of which are well known through their frequent depiction in miniature paintings, was the training par excellence for the cavalryman; a rougher parallel to it survives in the modern Afghan game of *buzkashi*.

BIBLIOGRAPHY

E. W. Lane, *Manners and Customs of the Modern Egyptians* (1954), 355ff.; Adam Mez, *The Renaissance of Islam,* Khuda Bukhsh, trans. (1937), 402–408; H. J. R. Murray, *A History of Chess* (1913), and *A History of Board Games Other Than Chess* (1952); Franz Rosenthal, *Gambling In Islam* (1975), and "Laᶜib," in *Encyclopedia of Islam,* 2nd ed. (1960).

C. E. BOSWORTH

GAMLI KANÓKI (the old canon), whose name and dates are unknown, was, according to *Jóns saga postula* IV, a canon at the Augustinian house at Þykkvabœr in southern Iceland, founded in 1168. He is thought to have composed his *Jónsdrápa* and *Harmsól* in the last decades of the twelfth century, possibly as late as 1200. Only four nonsequential stanzas of *Jónsdrápa* (Lay of John the Apostle) survive. These occur with brief prose links in *Jóns saga.* The poem is in *hrynhent* meter, which was still

354

somewhat unusual in Gamli's day but became increasingly preferred for Christian poems until it dominated those of the fourteenth century.

Harmsól (Sorrow Sun), a verse sermon on repentance, survives complete. This sixty-five-stanza *drápa* is in the more traditional *dróttkvætt* meter and is symmetrically structured: prologue *(upphaf)*, twenty stanzas; refrain section *(stefjabálkr)*, twenty-five stanzas divided equally between two refrains (stanzas 20, 25, 30, and 35, 40, 45), and conclusion *(slœmr)*, twenty stanzas. Gamli begins the prologue by praying that God open up his "fortress of poetry" (breast) and inspire him as he struggles against the inadequacy of human language to his topic. Since Christ commands confession, Gamli enumerates his own sins—pride as a young man, partaking unworthily of eucharistic "flesh and blood," hypocrisy—and speaks of the love shown in the Incarnation.

In the central portion the first refrain subsection *(stefjamél)* deals with the Crucifixion, Resurrection, and Ascension of Christ, and calls attention to the contrast between the two thieves: Gamli puts the mocking challenge of the chief priests into the mouth of the recalcitrant thief; but in unusually simple, direct speech echoing St. Luke's language, the repentant thief asks Christ to remember him. The second *stefjamél* concerns the Last Judgment, an event so terrible that it will cause even the angels to tremble. Gamli urges his audience to remember how uncertain is the hour of death, and to do while young those things usually postponed to old age. The tone seems influenced by the memento mori spirit of Cluniac reform.

In the *slœmr* Gamli recounts exempla of forgiveness and hope: David, Peter, Mary Magdalene. He then addresses prayers for forgiveness to Christ, Mary, and all saints, and names the poem "Sorrow Sun"—the sense of which seems to be the Sun (Christ) who overcomes the sorrow of the repentant sinner—in the penultimate stanza.

Perhaps the most distinctive feature of Gamli's diction is his quest for kennings describing Christ as a cosmic god whose radiant majesty contrasts with the sinner's abjectness: for instance, "bright king of storm hall" (heaven). This kenning type, though not original with Gamli, is effectively varied; Gamli chooses storm compounds when his mood is turbulent but more placid kennings (such as "king of sun canopy") as calmness returns. The consonantal alliterative staves of the first six stanzas seem to be drawn from the title as an incomplete anagram (a device of Latin poetry); only *h, r, m, s, l,* and *v* occur.

BIBLIOGRAPHY

Sources. Finnur Jónsson, ed., *Den norsk-islandske skjaldedigtning* (1908–1915), AI, 561–572 (diplomatic), and BI 547–565 (normalized); a translation is Wolfgang Lange, *Christliche Skaldendichtung* (1958), 30–38.

Studies. Roberta Frank, "Old Norse Court Poetry: The Dróttkvætt Stanza," in *Islandica,* **42** (1978); Jón Helgason, "Til skjaldedigtningen," in *Acta philologica Scandinavica,* 6 (1931–1932) and 10 (1935–1936); Wolfgang Lange, *Studien zur christlichen Dichtung der Nordgermanen 1000–1200,* in Palaestra, CCXXII (1958); Fredrik Paasche, *Kristendom og kvad* (1914), 108–118; E. O. G. Turville-Petre, *Origins of Icelandic Literature* (1953), 161–163.

GEORGE S. TATE

[See also **Skaldic Verse.**]

GANJAK (Modern Armenian: Ganja; Arabic: Janza; Persian: Ganja, treasury; Greek: Kantzakion; Russian: Elisavetpol, now Kirovabad), a city of northeastern Armenia on the Ganja (Ganjachay) River in the old principality of Šakašen (Greek: Sakasenē). Although it was founded in 859 by the Arabs on the Bardhaᶜa–Tbilisi road some 124 miles (200 kilometers) south of Tbilisi, the Persian name seems to indicate that it existed earlier, and there is evidence that it existed in the fifth or sixth century. It rose to prominence, however, only after the sack of Bardhaᶜa by Rus pirates in 944. Its greatest prosperity occurred under the Kurdish Shaddadids (*ca.* 951–1075), who were overthrown by the Seljuk Malik Shāh. Destroyed in 1138/1139 by an earthquake that reportedly killed 100,000 people, the city was sacked by the Georgians shortly afterward. Passing to the Ilduigizids in the thirteenth century, Ganjak became one of the most important and handsome cities of western Asia, a Muslim stronghold and the home of the great poet Niẓāmī (d. 1202/1203). Ganjak was sacked by the Mongols in 1231/1235 and never regained its former importance. Subsequently it passed to the Safavid Persians, then to the Turks (1588), back to the Persians (1606), the Turks (1723), the Persians (under Nādir Shāh, 1735), and finally to the Russians (1804).

From the eleventh to the thirteenth centuries, Old Ganjak was located on both sides of the Ganjachay, which was crossed by three bridges. The town was protected by two walls with large towers at each corner and smaller ones between. The houses were built of brick and stone and supplied with piped water. Besides being a trade center Ganjak manufactured pottery, silk, and other textiles, but the city never regained its former prosperity after the Mongol invasion.

BIBLIOGRAPHY

Guy Le Strange, *Lands of the Eastern Caliphate* (1905, repr. 1966), 178–179; Hakob A. Manandyan, *Trade and Cities of Armenia in Relation to Ancient World Trade*, Nina G. Garsoïan, trans. (1965), 134, 147, 163–164, 169; Vladimir Minorsky, *Studies in Caucasian History* (1953), 1–78.

ROBERT H. HEWSEN

[See also **Albania (Caucasian); Bardha^ca.**]

GANJAK OF ATROPATENE (Greek: Gazaka; Latin: Gazae; Armenian: Ganjak Šahastan; Arabic: Janza), so called to distinguish it from Ganjak in northeastern Armenia. According to Strabo it was the summer capital of the Median kings. As the capital of Media Atropatene it was called Ganzag-ī Shīzīgān (Gazaca). During the Sasanian period (226–*ca.* 636), it became an important Zoroastrian shrine and was known as Shīz.

Ganjak most probably lay on the site of modern Laylān, south of Lake Urmia and Marāgha in northwestern Iran (Azerbaijan). The municipal territory of the city was apparently bounded on the northwest by the Gadarchay River, which in the Roman period separated Atropatene (and hence the Parthian Empire and later the Sasanian Empire) from Arsacid Armenia. Ganjak is possibly to be identified with the otherwise unknown fortress of Zintha (*Gantha?), which marked the southeastern frontier of Armenia according to the Peace of Nisibis (297/298). A Christian bishopric as early as 486, Ganjak was sacked by Emperor Heraklios about 624, and its fire temple of Ādhur-Gushnasp was destroyed in retaliation for the Sasanians' capture of Jerusalem and their abduction of the relics of the True Cross.

BIBLIOGRAPHY

Nikolai Adontz, *Armeniya v epokhu Iustiniana* (1908), trans. by Nina G. Garsoïan as *Armenia in the Period of Justinian* (1970), 8, 176, 225, 374 (n. 1), 436–437 (n. 27), 199*; Joseph Marquart, *Ērānšahr nach der Geographie des Ps. -Moses Xorenac'i* (1901), 108–114; Vladimir Minorsky, "Roman and Byzantine Campaigns in Atropatene," in *BSOAS*, **11** (1944).

ROBERT H. HEWSEN

[See also **Sasanians.**]

GANO DA SIENA, Sienese architect and sculptor, traceable in Siena until 1339. He may be the Fra Galgano di Giovanni who is credited with the plan of the church of S. Geronimo Certosa. Gano signed the 1303 wall tomb of Tommaso d'Andrea (bishop of Pistoia) in the Collegiata of Casole d'Elsa, Siena. His tomb of Ranieri del Porrina, in the same church, is notable for its advanced realism. He is considered the sculptor of the *Virgin and Child Between Saints* on the facade of the cathedral at Cremona.

BIBLIOGRAPHY

Enzo Carli, "Lo scultore Gano da Siena," in *Emporium*, 95 (1942); John Pope-Hennessy, *Italian Gothic Sculpture* (1955).

ADELHEID M. GEALT

[See also **Gothic Art: Sculpture.**]

GAOL DELIVERY. See **Jail Delivery.**

GAON. See **Schools, Jewish.**

GAONIC PERIOD, covering the seventh through eleventh centuries for Babylonia and the twelfth century for more western countries, is named after the leading religious institution of the period, the gaonate (from Hebrew *ga'on* [plural, *ge'onim*], "majesty," the title accorded primarily to the heads of the Jewish academies in Babylonia). The gaonate, in turn, derived its real authority and significance from such individual geonim as Saadiah ben Joseph (*d.* 942) and Samuel ben Ḥofnī (*d.* 1013), men who attempted, with varying success, to impose a uniform leadership upon diverse and often independent-minded Jewish communities. Those communities were spread throughout the Islamic world and beyond, and included primarily the Jews of Babylonia and Persia, Palestine, Egypt, Syria, Yemen, Ifrīqiya (Tunisia), and Spain.

This vast area of the Dār al-Islām (Islamic world) experienced frequent internecine warfare, and it is not surprising that the fortunes of the gaonate reflected the rise and fall of various Islamic dynasties in the period under discussion. The history of the geonim is tied particularly to the Abbasid dynasty in Iraq, as well as to the Fatimid dynasty in Egypt and

Palestine. It was in what is now Iraq, however, long known as Babylonia in Jewish tradition, that the geonim had their greatest success and made their most significant contribution to Jewish history. There, in the academies of Sura and Pumbeditha (both later located in Baghdad), the geonim established themselves in the seventh through eleventh centuries as the heirs to the talmudic tradition and the guarantors of its success within Judaism.

Unlike the Karaites the geonim insisted on the legitimacy and necessity of the oral law in Judaism, and devoted their lives to navigating the "ocean of the Talmud," the vast repository of that law. They thus continued the work of their predecessors in pre-Islamic, Sasanian times—the Amoraim and the less-known Saboraim—in effect canonizing the Talmud as it is known today and assuring its continued use as an object of theoretical study—the very embodiment of God's will—and of practical applicability. Religious authority was located in the Talmud and the Pentateuch, the oral and written laws of Judaism, as interpreted by the geonim in an ongoing process of exegesis and rational inference.

Gaonic judgments usually were not reached unilaterally, though they were proclaimed as such. Each gaon was the principal of an academy (yeshiva) in which the Talmud was studied by a select group of scholars, from among whom the new gaon would normally be chosen, with dynastic considerations often prevailing. Decisions taken in the academy and summaries of its discussions were publicized on various occasions during the year, in both oral and written form. Each academy held a month-long public forum (kallah) in autumn and spring, before the holidays, and throughout the year the geonim responded in writing to legal queries addressed to them from near and far. Copies of these questions and answers (she'elot ve-teshuvot), covering a wide range of Jewish life, were collected in compilations of which portions are extant—for instance, the extensive responsa of Sherira (d. 1006) and his son, Hay (d. 1038). This material has been greatly enhanced in modern times by the discovery of a vast responsa literature in the Cairo Genizah.

The Genizah is also the source, through written material of all kinds that, containing the name of God, could not be destroyed, for much modern detailed knowledge of Jewish society in this period, particularly the latter half. It is thus known that Jews in the gaonic period were increasingly active as merchants and artisans, some achieving great success in mercantile and banking circles. These circles were national and international in character, reflecting the sophistication of commerce and finance in the medieval Islamic world. Jewish merchants traveled widely, establishing contacts (often familial) and founding communities from India to Spain and southern Europe. The wealth amassed in trade gave these people and their families great standing and influence in the Jewish community, and often at court as well, where it was not uncommon to find them engaged by the ruler as statesmen, financiers, and physicians. Two of the most prominent such figures are Ḥasdai ibn Shaprūṭ in tenth-century Umayyad Spain, and Abū Saᶜd Ibrāhīm al-Tustarī in eleventh-century Fatimid Egypt.

Those men were the most striking representatives of a stratum of Jewish society that was well integrated economically and politically in the Islamic world, though less so socially and culturally (in the social and cultural spheres, parallel yet separate patterns developed). Thus the arts and sciences that flourished in Islam were avidly copied and pursued by Jews writing in Hebrew (especially poetry), Arabic, or Judeo-Arabic. Isaac Israeli (Qayrawān, ninth–tenth centuries), Saadiah ben Joseph (Baghdad, tenth century), Judah Halevi (Toledo, twelfth century), Moses Maimonides (Al-Fusṭāṭ/Cairo, twelfth century), and others enriched and enlarged Jewish culture in this period, legitimizing in the process—and not without opposition—aesthetic, philosophical, and scientific concerns formerly regarded as alien to Judaism.

Most Jews in the first few centuries of this period, however, were originally rural villagers and then petit bourgeois townspeople, in either the older communities of the East and Palestine, or the newer centers of Jewish life in North Africa and Spain. The rulers of Islam allowed them a large degree of self-government, presided over by a widely respected figure known in the East as the exilarch and elsewhere as the nagid. Although the Jews thus had their own spiritual and political leaders (occasionally at odds with each other), a special poll tax (jizya) and other discriminatory legislation affected Jews—as well as Christians—adversely. Moreover, anti-Jewish riots and attacks, though infrequent, were not unknown in the Islamic world, some—as in seventh-century Arabia and twelfth-century Spain, affecting large numbers of people.

Threats to physical survival probably spurred mystical and occasionally messianic movements in the gaonic period. These movements, like that of the more ascetically inclined, fundamentalist Karaites, were contained by the rabbis of the time, following the lead of the geonim. The latter strengthened the institutions of rabbinic Judaism, and in addition codified Jewish liturgy and practice, bequeathing to the rabbinic leadership that followed them the spiritual, if not the political, instruments they had perfected.

BIBLIOGRAPHY

For recent studies of the gaonic period, see Solomon D. Goitein, *A Mediterranean Society,* 4 vols. (1967–1983), II, 5–17 and 196–205; Norman A. Stillman, *The Jews of Arab Lands* (1979). Other basic works on the geonim and the period include Simha Assaf, *Tequfat ha-ge'onim ve-sifrutah* (The gaonic period and its literature), (1955); Louis Ginzberg, *Geonica,* 2 vols. (1909, repr. 1968); Jacob Mann, *The Responsa of the Babylonian Geonim as a Source of Jewish History* (1917–1921, repr. 1973).

ALFRED L. IVRY

[See also **Jewish Communal Self-government: Islam; Jews in the Middle East; Sa^cadya ben Joseph; Schools, Jewish; Talmud, Jewish Exegesis and Study of.**]

GARÇON ET L'AVEUGLE, an anonymous thirteenth-century comic play from northern France. It depicts two scoundrels: a blind beggar, who has money hidden away, and his servant, who tricks him out of his hoard. Because of its theme of deceiver deceived, its rapid dialogue, and its slapstick action, the play is considered the oldest surviving French farce.

BIBLIOGRAPHY

Le garçon et l'aveugle, Mario Roques, ed. (1921); *Medieval French Plays,* Richard Axton and John Stevens, trans. (1971), 193–206; Grace Frank, *The Medieval French Drama,* 2nd ed. (1960), 221–224.

ALAN E. KNIGHT

[See also **French Literature: After 1200.**]

GARDENS, EUROPEAN. No medieval European gardens survive today. Although we may know where a garden once existed, and though walls still stand that once enclosed a garden (like the scores of medieval cloisters scattered all over Europe), the plants, and the arrangement of the plants within these areas today, have only the vaguest relationship with what was there in the Middle Ages. Nowhere has unbroken continuity been maintained.

A few literary references to the villa gardens of a Roman kind survive from the late fifth century—one of the last is the letter by the Gallo-Roman Sidonius describing his house and estate in Auvergne, about 460—but there are virtually no further references to "gardens" (as distinct from agriculture) until the very end of the eighth century. Then, in a relatively short space of time, three documents appear that form the basis of any consideration of early medieval gardening.

In 795, or a little later, a collection of regulations was issued concerning the administration of Charlemagne's domains, the *Capitulare de villis vel curtis imperii.* In section 70 of this text, we find a list of seventy-three plants and fruit trees that must be grown in the towns of the empire. There is a full discussion of plants listed in the capitulary in John Harvey, *Medieval Gardens.* Twenty years later, about 816, a detailed plan of a monastery was made, showing the church, the cloister, and the related buildings and gardens. This plan is preserved at the monastery of St. Gall, in Switzerland. Then, some time before his death in 849, the monk Walafrid Strabo, of the abbey of Reichenau near St. Gall, wrote his *Liber de cultura hortorum.* This poem of 444 lines, dedicated to Grimald, abbot of St. Gall, is frequently referred to as the *Hortulus.* Walafrid describes in it the problems he has to face in clearing and planting his small, enclosed area, and lists some thirty plants that he grows, discussing their virtues and properties.

Between them, these documents provide a fair indication of the kinds of garden that were then made, their layout, their content, and the way they were cultivated. In the St. Gall plan several enclosed areas appear that one might class as "gardens"—the two separate regions at either end of the abbey church, marked *paradisus;* the cloister beside the church; the vegetable garden; the physic garden; and the cemetery. Of these, the *paradisus* areas were almost certainly wholly roofed over, and served as ambulatories of an enclosed kind. In this particular instance, therefore, they were not gardens, had nothing planted within them, and probably had no view out to the open air. In contrast the square cloister area appears to have been open toward the center, with a covered ambulatory on each of the four sides. Its shape, as that of earlier and later medieval cloisters, is essentially derived from the Roman atrium. In the St. Gall plan this area was quartered by paths running inward from the middle of each side, meeting in a small central square. Here the word *sauina* could indicate an arbor made with juniper, a plant

Emilia in her garden. From the *Livre du cuer d'amours espris, ca.* 1470. VIENNA, ÖSTERREICHISCHES NATIO-
NALBIBLIOTHEK, CODEX 2617, fol. 53

recommended in the Middle Ages for the construction of long-lasting walks and pergolas in "carpenter's work." What was planted in the four quarters
between the paths is not stated.

The three other gardens on the plan contained
many different plants and trees. Beside the physician's house in the northeastern corner is a square
plot, marked *herbularius,* containing sixteen rectangular beds, each with a named plant; and in the
southeastern section, near to areas designed for
chicken and geese (and possibly including a dove-
cote), is a relatively large rectangular area, with accommodation for the gardener at one end, and a perfectly regular garden *(hortus),* filled with eighteen
beds—two rows of nine, each rectangular and of
equal size. Just to the north of this area is the ceme-

tery, where thirteen groups of trees are planted symmetrically along the walls and among the plots for
graves.

From the details in this plan it is clear that, with
the exception of the cloister, all the garden areas
were firmly utilitarian. Although a few of the plant
names are uncertain, the large majority that can be
read indicate that the physic garden contained small,
shrubby, and aromatic plants of a herbal kind, such
as fennel, lovage, tansy, sage, rue, mint, and rosemary, while the *hortus* contained mainly salads and
vegetables, such as onions, leeks, shallots and garlic,
celery, parsley and chervil, lettuce, radishes, pars-
nips, beetroot, and possibly carrots. The trees in the
cemetery were just as useful—fruit, such as apples,
pears, plums, peaches, and mulberries, and nuts.

359

The foundation of full-scale university botanic gardens was reserved for the period of the Renaissance, beginning at Padua and Pisa in the 1540's. Nonetheless the type of garden designated in the St. Gall plan as *herbularius* was a characteristic feature of the institutional gardens in the Middle Ages for the provision of medicinal herbs. Although no details survive of how these physic gardens were cultivated, their existence and gradually increasing scope and importance is attested by the upsurge of medical studies in the late thirteenth and early fourteenth centuries in southern Italy, and the production of medical treatises and herbals related to the study of herbal medicines. At Salerno, Matthaeus Silvaticus (*fl.* 1280–1320) was known to have his own physic garden, where plants and seeds brought from overseas were tended; another physic garden existed at the medical school in Venice in the same period, and one was established at Prague in 1350.

The plants cultivated by Walafrid Strabo in the *Hortulus* correspond closely with those named in the St. Gall plan and the longer list in Charlemagne's capitulary. What should be noted especially by a modern inquirer is not merely the absence of any plants from the New World (tomatoes, potatoes) but the dearth of plants of an ornamental kind. In Walafrid's poem and in the St. Gall plan, a few flowers are mentioned—roses, flag iris, lilies, poppies. In modern gardens, they appear as ornaments, but in the small and useful gardens of the Middle Ages they had their place because they were valuable, and the *Hortulus* explains this with each plant.

The poppy is *Papaver somniferum*, the opium poppy, essential in medieval medicine; fennel seed is aperient; the lily—*Lillium candidum*—cures snakebite, and the iris quells pains in the bladder and helps starch the wash. Oil of roses, Walafrid explains, has uses beyond number.

Both the St. Gall plan and the *Hortulus* also indicate another dimension of medieval gardens that has become less noticeable in modern times: the symbolic and even religious importance attached to many plants and flowers. The lily is a symbol of purity—particularly that of the Virgin Mary—and the red rose is a symbol of blood, hence of passion, and, in Christian terms, the Passion of Christ and the blood shed by the martyrs of the church. In secular terms, the rose is the flower of love, and in the thirteenth-century *Roman de la Rose* it becomes the mystical goal of the Lover throughout the poem. Likewise, in the St. Gall plan, the thirteen groups of trees in the cemetery are all useful; but their number

is also symbolic, representing Christ and his disciples, with whom the monks may be united when they die. In Walafrid's poem the nourishing, medical, and practical uses of his plants are described—wormwood cures headaches and hangovers, radishes suppress coughing, and gourds provide valuable containers—but the rose leads him to a rapturous account of the beauty and virtues of Christ.

The *Hortulus* is also important for the details of how Walafrid's small garden was cultivated. He had few tools—a rake, a spade, a knife—and needed much manual labor. The patch, when he begins, is untended, and below the surface he finds a web of yellow nettle roots. He clears them, laboriously, and then sows the seed, waters it, and builds up raised beds with planks of wood. This last point is worth comment, for the garden beds of the Middle Ages are almost always raised above the level of the paths. The Roman writer Palladius says that beds should be set higher or lower than the paths, according to the water and drainage available. Walafrid, writing in a northerly climate, knows that drainage is vital; the planks he uses as edging will continue beyond the Middle Ages as a standard feature (the last important garden writer to recommend their use is John Rea in *Flora* [1665]).

After these three documents there is little written directly about gardens for several centuries. Until the appearance of Guillaume de Lorris' *Roman de la Rose* (*ca.* 1225–1230) and the treatise *De vegetabilibus* of Albertus Magnus (*ca.* 1260), references to gardens are brief and tangential, recurring as items in accounts and inventories, or as part of the background for historical, biographical, or fictional events. In the same way, the plants grown in gardens are listed in herbals, medical treatises, and works of an encyclopedic or lexical nature. Between the St. Gall plan and the emergence of lavishly illustrated manuscripts in the fifteenth century there are likewise few diagrams, plans, or illustrations of gardens to supplement the written references.

After the ninth-century documents, the most important medieval texts to deal with gardens are listed below in chronological order:

Guillaume de Lorris, *Le Roman de la Rose, ca.* 1225–1230, translated into English by Geoffrey Chaucer, *ca.* 1380.

Albertus Magnus, "De plantatione viridarium," in *De vegetabilibus, ca.* 1260.

Pietro de Crescenzi (Petrus de Crescentiis), *Ruralium commodorum libri XII, ca.* 1305, with fine illustrations in fifteenth-century versions.

Giovanni Boccaccio, *Il Decamerone,* the "Introduction" to the Third Day and the "Conclusion" to the Sixth Day, *ca.* 1350.

The anonymous *Ménagier de Paris, ca.* 1394.

Jon Gardener, *The Feate of Gardeninge,* before 1450.

The principal influence on gardens in this period, and indeed until the end of the Middle Ages, is biblical and Christian. In the centuries following the St. Gall plan and Walafrid's *Hortulus* much of the factual information and most of the written or illustrative comments concerning gardens come, directly or indirectly, from the activity and teaching of the church. Monastic records—such as the plan (1146) of the water supply and related garden arrangements at the monastery of Christ Church, Canterbury (in the *Eadwine Psalter,* now in Trinity College, Cambridge)—confirm the continuation of the enclosed, ordered, and utilitarian cultivation indicated in the St. Gall plan, while texts and illustrations in manuscripts, sculpture, and stained glass refer obliquely to Eden, the first garden, and to the garden of Gethsemane. God, Adam and Eve, Christ and the disciples are the subject, while the gardens are no more than a background. Early representations, such as the mosaic of Adam and Eve in the Mausoleum of Galla Placidia at Ravenna (fifth century), have only sketchy outlines of the trees, to indicate Eden. In the earliest surviving French play, the *Jeu* (or *Mystère*) *d'Adam* (*ca.* 1150), the Latin stage directions give considerable attention to the deportment and diction of Adam and Eve, while the setting—Paradise—is described most briefly: "Paradise is set up in a high place ... there will be scented flowers and leaves; there are various trees, with fruit hanging from them, so that it appears a most pleasant place [*amenissimus locus*]."

Similarly, the image of Adam in the west window of Canterbury cathedral (*ca.* 1178) shows the details of his face, sheepskin apron, and pointed spade, with a clearly identifiable mattock beside him, hanging on a leafy but rather simple tree. His gardening activity is explicit, but the ground he must dig is simply yet crudely summed up by the billowing green (the grass and turf) and segments of golden brown (the soil that he has already turned).

The garden backgrounds of later religious illustrations are often much more elaborate. The most interesting fourteenth-century depictions of the Garden of Eden are the series by Bartolo di Fredi in the collegiate church at S. Gimignano in Tuscany (1356), where four lunettes show different stages of the story

of Adam and Eve set against a detailed background of plants and flowers—palms, vines, figs, pomegranates, roses—growing in jungly and unordered luxuriance. The nature of the *locus amoenus* has been made explicit. Such attention to the plants, with no hint of arrangement or bedding, is unique until the naturalistic depictions of paradise by the Brueghels in the late sixteenth century.

The religious sense of the enclosed, cruciform garden of a monastery is reinforced by the widespread linking of the virgin bride of Solomon's Song of Songs 4:12 (described in the Vulgate as a *hortus conclusus,* "A garden enclosed is my sister, my spouse; a spring shut up, a fountain sealed") with the Virgin Mary. Many paintings of Mary show her within a garden that is, explicitly or implicitly, enclosed and inward-looking. Around her roses, lilies, columbines (symbolizing the gifts of the Holy Spirit), carnations (divine love), or violets (humility) remind us of aspects of her life or character. From this association comes the idea of the cloister garden as symbolic of the Virgin herself. The best example comes from the *Grimani Breviary* (*ca.* 1510), now in the Biblioteca Nazionale Marciana, Venice. In this picture, the different, realistically depicted parts of the garden and its surroundings are named to indicate their symbolic qualities related to the Virgin. Within the square, enclosed garden, roses and lilies proclaim Christ's Passion and Mary's purity, and a fountain at the center plays four streams of water (the four rivers of paradise) into an enclosing basin ("a fountain sealed").

GARDEN FEATURES

After these general comments, the distinguishing features of gardens in the Middle Ages may be outlined:

Enclosure. With the rarest exceptions, all gardens were enclosed. Within a monastery, a fortification, or a town, the enclosure involved walls, but gardens of a simpler or more modest kind were enclosed with hedges, or fences made of palings, or woven strips of wattle. The "Earthly Paradise" in Jean Corbechon's *Des proprietez des choses* (*ca.* 1415, in the Fitzwilliam Museum, Cambridge) shows Adam and Eve before the Fall within a perfect circle of wattle fencing, while the complex picture of *The Creation and the Fall* in the *Bedford Book of Hours* (*ca.* 1423, in the British Library), shows that Eden, though it may boast a noble stone entrance, still has a competent wattle fence round the back and sides. In the 1440's Fra Angelico painted scenes to do with the

Passion in the monastery of S. Marco in Florence, in which the enclosures of the Garden of Gethsemane are sometimes wattle, sometimes paling fence.

Within the enclosed garden, subdivisions were made with low fences of wattle or latticework, or with higher fences, arches, domes, and arbors of trellis (which we might now call forms of "pergola," but which were then known in English as a "herber" or, from the end of the fifteenth century, as "carpenter's work"). The term "herber" is derived from *herbarium,* and in different contexts can mean either the garden as a whole, or a garden for herbs, of a medicinal or utilitarian kind, or the trelliswork divisions within the garden.

In the *Ruralium commodorum liber* of Pietro de Crescenzi, the section on gardens tells how to prepare a *viridarium* (French: *verger*), either for people of middle status (an area of about 1.5 to 3 acres would be desirable), or for kings and other wealthy noblemen, when the scheme is much more extensive. The royal garden is enclosed by high walls, while the more modest garden is surrounded by ditches and hedges of thorns and roses. The hedges in southern regions will include pomegranates, and in the north there will be nuts, plums, and quinces. Within, "in the most suitable places," trellis arbors will be made in the form of houses, tents, or pavilions. Royal gardens have not only a permanent palace in the southern part, but a palace with rooms and towers "made entirely from growing trees"—both fruit trees and olives, willows, and poplars—where the lord and his lady may enjoy themselves in fair, dry weather. To save time, the work may be done with trellis, covered with vines.

In Boccaccio's *Decameron* the "walled garden" that the joyous fugitives visit on the Third Day is crisscrossed by long, straight paths, "overhung by pergolas of vines," while the paths round the sides of the garden were bordered by tall hedges of white and red roses and jasmine, which provided shade even at midday, and must have had a trellis framework for support.

In the *Très riches heures* illuminated by the Limbourg brothers for the duke of Berry in 1413–1416 (now in the Musée Condé, Chantilly, MS 65), the illustrations for the months of April and June show both outer garden walls of stone or brick, and inner trelliswork grown over with vines. In the picture for June (the royal palace beside the Seine) the trellis is especially gorgeous, rising up above the level of the battlemented wall and involving domes and com-

partments of trellis at either end of a long covered walk.

The inward-looking nature of these enclosed gardens should be stressed. Gardens made within monasteries, most typically the cloister, or within a built-up area in a town would have had little or no view of the surrounding countryside of the kind occasionally demanded by gardening taste in the Renaissance, and then more absolutely in the "landscape gardens" of the eighteenth century. In the Middle Ages, even the garden of a castle, possibly elevated above the surrounding land, would have been unlikely to take advantage of the landscape. Occasional paintings may offer a glimpse of fields or parkland beyond the enclosure of a garden, but the garden, and the people depicted within it, have little or no connection with the prospect.

Raised beds. Inside their enclosure, the gardens of the Middle Ages were mostly subdivided in a four-square, geometrical way, responding both to the transmitted Christian and cruciform tradition and to the practical demands of a small space, constricted within a rectilinear framework.

Whether the garden was religious or secular, this rectilinear subdivision continued, with the individual beds usually raised up above the intersecting paths by means of planks, strips of wattle, or even with a line of bricks. With hardly an exception the plants grown in the beds were as utilitarian in the late fourteenth century as they were in the garden plans of St. Gall. In the *Decameron* the extensive walled garden described in the Introduction to the Third Day has "numerous and varied" shrubs in the beds, set out with great neatness—and they are all "commendable," that is, having their several virtues and uses. In the *Ménagier de Paris* the long section on gardening lists only a handful of plants that are not firmly utilitarian. However, the few flowers named—violets, for example, gillyflowers, paeonies, lilies, and roses—all had medicinal uses as well as their aesthetic attraction, and would also have been used on festal occasions to make garlands and chaplets.

In *The Feate of Gardeninge* by Jon Gardener, a 196-line poem written in the first half of the fifteenth century, nearly a hundred plants are listed, with seasonal advice for their planting and cultivation. Like the text of the *Ménagier,* this short poem says nothing about the shape, size, or situation of the garden, but is intensely practical about the plants, and indicates above all the utilitarian nature of horticulture at this time. In a long list of "herbys," all to be planted in April, the poet includes a few flowers—periwinkle, violet, cowslip, lily, and "Rose ryde, rose whyghte, foxglove and pympernold"—but he has written twenty lines earlier that this list is specifically of "Herbys to make both sawce and sewe [gravy]." These flowers may be "pretty," but they have a culinary or medicinal use as well.

Paths. Within a garden, paths were generally straight, fitting into the rectangular division of the area. Sometimes they were covered with sand or gravel, so that rain would pass quickly through the surface; but in more imaginative gardens they were planted here and there with low-growing, fragrant herbs. In the *Roman de la Rose* the Lover tells how he approached one section of the garden: "Downe by a lytel pathe I fonde, / Of myntes ful, and fenell grene." That is to say, there were herbs to tread on and herbs to brush against as one walked along. The fantasy of the thirteenth-century poem is confirmed as late as 1625 by the practical advice of Francis Bacon, in his essay *Of Gardens,* where he states explicitly that the flowers "which Perfume the Aire most delightfully ... being Troden upon and Crushed, are Three: That is Burnet, Wilde-Time, and Water-Mints. Therefore you are to set whole Allies of them, to have the Pleasure, when you walke or tread."

Topiary. The art of topiary was practiced in Roman gardens, but apart from the training of pliant stems into forms of trelliswork, topiary is not apparent in medieval gardens until the fifteenth century, when occasional illustrations show trees crudely trained, with the central stem supporting two or three flat, clipped platforms of branches and leaves rather like the circular stages of a modern cake stand. Such a tree appears in the miniature of René of Anjou seated in a garden house, with garden outside, in the *Book of Hours of Isabella of Portugal* from about 1480 (in Bibliothèque Royale, Brussels, MS 10308, fol. 1).

Statues. Unlike Roman and Renaissance gardens, medieval gardens contained few statues. In the late fifteenth century, however, the fashion of setting up carved heraldic figures on buildings spread into the garden, where they were erected on wooden posts. Lions, dragons, and other "marvellous beasts" were set up in the gardens at Richmond Palace in 1501 by Henry VII, and the practice was enormously extended in the mid sixteenth century.

Fountains and water jokes. Both for use and for pleasure, medieval gardens would if possible include water, in a stream, a fountain, or a fishpond. In gardens with a religious background the central wellhead or fountain was symbolic of the "four rivers" of Eden and of the "fountainhead of living waters" enclosed within the *hortus conclusus.* The stonework, often elaborately carved, was in the nature of wellheads or founts, rather than "fountains." The water might gush out and down through one or more surrounding basins, but it did not spurt upward. Medieval hydraulics were not sophisticated enough to produce vertical jets of water. The instance in the *Decameron,* "From a figure standing on a column in the center of the fountain, a jet of water, whether natural or artificial I know not, but sufficiently powerful to drive a mill with ease, gushed high into the sky," is likely to be based on fantasy, not fact. The garden jokes involving concealed water jets to wet unwary visitors that are so common in Renaissance gardens, especially after the circulation of the text of Hero of Alexandria's *Pneumatica* from the 1550's onward, are unlikely to have been known in medieval gardens. According to Ernest de Ganay, it is probable that the elaborate sequence of mechanical toys, surprises, and practical jokes created in the park at Hesdin in Artois by the counts of Artois from the end of the thirteenth century were not garden jokes, but devices engineered within various buildings in the park.

Menageries and aviaries. A royal or princely garden might contain an area for strange or exotic beasts or for birds, and both these features are recommended by Crescenzi, together with a group of fishponds. Such enclosures begin with a utilitarian purpose, to provide supplies of fresh food. The beasts and birds listed by Crescenzi are not especially exotic—hares, rabbits, stags, squirrels, and other animals that are not beasts of prey, and pheasants, partridges, nightingales, blackbirds, linnets, goldfinches, and other songbirds. The park, fourteen miles in circumference, established by Henry I at Woodstock in the early twelfth century was said to contain lions, leopards, and other exotic animals, but from its size this was evidently a hunting park, and not a menagerie. The latter is almost exclusively a Renaissance development.

Turf seats. A feature of medieval gardens that has all but disappeared since the seventeenth century is the turf seat—a seat raised up with a wattle, board, or brick surround, and covered with a layer of turf, quite often including small flowers, or consisting of small fragrant herbs, such as camomile. Illustrations often show such seats backed against the enclosing wall or trellis, to allow a view inward to the center of the garden, or backed and partly surrounded by an arbor of trelliswork. One of the earliest writers to mention this feature is Albertus Magnus, who says that a bench of turf must be set up between herb beds and the lawn, with flowers and seats for pleasure and repose. In the anonymous fifteenth-century poem *The Floure and the Leafe*, once attributed to Chaucer, the poet tells of his following a path

> . . . till it me broght
> To right a plesaunt herber well ywroght,
> That benched was, and eke with turfes newe
> Freshly turved, whereof the grene gras,
> So smal, so thikke, so short, so fresh of hewe,
> That most ylike grene wol, I wot, it was.

Much later, in 1516, Sir Thomas More explains in his *Utopia* that, after meeting the traveler Raphael Hythloday in Antwerp, they "adjourned to the garden of [the] hotel, where [they] sat down on a bench covered with a layer of turf, and began to talk more freely." It is on this bench that More will hear the entire account of the island of Utopia.

The most celebrated, flowery, and beautiful of all turf seats is in Shakespeare's *Midsummer Night's Dream* (II.i), where Oberon describes it to Puck:

> I know a bank where the wild thyme blows,
> Where oxlips and the nodding violet grows;
> Quite over-canopied with luscious woodbine,
> With sweet musk-roses, and with eglantine:
> There sleeps Titania sometime of the night.

Lawns. Almost as unfamiliar to modern readers as the turf seat is the character of the medieval lawn, which was formed from turfs of meadow grass laid on the surface of the ground. Two points should be borne in mind—that there were no lawn mowers (the rotary mower was patented by Edwin Beard Budding in 1830) and that fields were still rich with a multitude of wildflowers, since selective weedkillers had not been invented either. As a result medieval lawns inevitably grew tall and coarse—and had therefore to be renewed—and their grass was plentifully mixed with meadow flowers. The process of making a lawn is described fully by Albertus Magnus:

> Nothing refreshes the sight so much as fine short grass. One must clear the space destined for a pleasure garden of all roots, and this can hardly be achieved unless the roots are dug out, the surface is leveled as much as possible, and boiling water is poured over the surface, so that the remaining roots and seeds which lie in the ground are destroyed and cannot germinate.... The ground must then be covered with turfs cut from good

[meadow] grass, and beaten down with wooden mallets, and stamped down well with the feet until they are hardly able to be seen. Then little by little the grass pushes through like fine hair, and covers the surface like a fine cloth.

Later writers from Pietro de Crescenzi until the late sixteenth century repeat this description almost word for word. One variant is the requirement that new turfs should be laid *upside down* and beaten, so that the grass grows, fine and thin, up through the pounded layer of earth and roots.

Albertus prescribes such a lawn within a square enclosure, set with sweet-smelling herbs—rue, sage, basil—and flowers, such as violets, columbines, lilies, roses, and iris. As such, we may imagine it is not unlike that in the miniature of *Emilia in Her Garden* (*ca.* 1470) from the *Livre du cuer d'amours espris* (see illustration). This displays a small, enclosed space, within a high wall, with no outward view. It is square and has a covered arbor of trellis on two sides, grown over with vines. Lesser trelliswork, with sumptuous arcading, supports climbing roses, red and white, while a raised bed in the foreground has low rails on which carnations are trained. Other plants against a lattice fence in the immediate foreground include columbine, mallow, and rosemary. Another raised bed with flowers runs along the rear, outer wall.

The "flowery mede." In the *Roman de la Rose*, the Lover describes the grassy lawn that extends round the streams and pools in the garden. It was, he says, "moche amended" by the flowers that grew there in the grass (lines 1,431–1,438):

> There sprange the vyolet al newe.
> And fresshe perunke, riche of hewe,
> And floures yelowe, white and rede;
> Suche plente grewe there neuer in mede.
> Ful gaye was al the grounde, and queynt,
> And poudred, as men had it peynt,
> With many a fresshe and sondrie floure,
> That casten up ful good savour.

Although this description is ostensibly set within foursquare garden walls, the lawn is given a spaciousness and a variety of flowers that make it more representative of a "flowery mede" than of turf in a small enclosure. The "flowery mede" (or meadow) figures more often in imaginative works than in reality, being a broad, flower-covered grassy expanse of a natural kind. Often it is discovered by chance, when the hero of romance emerges from an oppressive forest into an open clearing, and it may also have magical connections, or be—as is the entire garden in the *Roman de la Rose*—in the framework of a dream. It is untended, it has no gardener.

Another "flowery mede" of a wooded kind is the Valley of the Ladies in the "Conclusion" to the Sixth Day of the *Decameron*. Here, the area, half a mile round, is surrounded by forested hills:

> The plain itself . . . was filled with firs, cypresses, bay-trees, and a number of pines, all of which were so neatly and symmetrically disposed that they looked as if they had been planted by the finest practitioner of the forester's craft. And when the sun was overhead, few or none of its rays penetrated their foliage to the ground beneath, which was one continuous lawn of tiny blades of grass interspersed with flowers, many of them purple in color.

Boccaccio's description earlier stresses the apparent artifice of the region—"the floor of the Valley was perfectly circular in shape, for all the world as if it had been made with compasses." This is a part of its appeal, to seem perfect, though a work not of man but of nature.

Such a natural *locus amoenus* is the background to the series of tapestries depicting the *Lady with the Unicorn* (last quarter of the fifteenth century), now in the Musée Cluny, Paris. The Lady, with attendant unicorn and other animals, is shown in the most profusely leafed and flowery lawn imaginable. Trees grow here and there to give privacy and shade, but it is above all the enmeshed flowers and leaves and grass that characterize the background.

All of these "flowery medes," like medieval gardens as a whole, are still enclosed. Around the garden of the *Roman de la Rose* is a wall; hills rise around the Valley of the Ladies; no open sky, no horizon appears in the tapestries of the *Lady with the Unicorn*. The Middle Ages were not concerned with such an opening-out, such an expansion of gardens into the wider landscape. For this, the Renaissance was responsible, in particular Leone Battista Alberti, whose *De re aedificatoria* (1485) looks for authority in garden matters not to Albertus Magnus or Pietro de Crescenzi, but to Pliny the Younger and other writers of ancient Rome.

BIBLIOGRAPHY

Sources. Albertus Magnus, *De vegetabilibus,* Ernst Meyer and Karl Jessen, eds. (1867); Francis Bacon, "On Gardens," in *The Essayes,* Walter Worrall, ed. (1900); Giovanni Boccaccio, *The Decameron,* G. H. McWilliam, trans. (1972); Pietro de Crescenzi, *Les profits champêtres de Pierre de Crescens,* J. Roubinet, trans. (1965); *The*

Floure and the Leafe, Frederick S. Ellis, ed. (1896); Jon Gardener, *The Feate of Gardeninge,* parallel modern version by M. M. Strachan (1980), also reproduced by A. Amherst, "A Fifteenth-century Treatise on Gardening," in *Archaeologia,* 54 (1894); Benjamin E. C. Guérard, *Explication du Capitulaire de villis* (1853); Walter W. Horn and Ernest Born, *The Plan of St. Gall,* 3 vols. (1979); *Ménagier de Paris,* Georgine E. Brereton and Janet M. Ferrier, eds. (1981), also trans. by Eileen Power as *The Goodman of Paris* (1928); Thomas More, *Utopia,* P. Turner, trans. (1980); *Le Mystère d'Adam,* Paul Studer, ed. (1918); Rutilius T. A. Palladius, *Traité d'agriculture* [*Opus agriculturae*], René Martin, ed. and trans., I (1976), xxxiv, 7; *The Romaunt of the Rose and Le Roman de la Rose: A Parallel-text Edition,* Ronald Sutherland, ed. 1967; Sidonius, *Poems and Letters,* William B. Anderson, trans., I (1936), 416–435; Walafrid Strabo, *Hortulus* [*Liber de culture hortorum*], Richard S. Lambert, trans. (1924), also *Hortulus,* Wilfrid Blunt, ed., Raef Payne, trans. (1966).

Studies. Alice M. Coats, *Flowers and Their Histories* (1956, repr. 1968); Sir Frank Crisp, *Medieval Gardens,* 2 vols. (1924, repr. 1966), with lavish and useful illustrations, but an unreliable text; Ernest de Ganay, *Les jardins de France et leur decor* (1949); John H. Harvey, *Medieval Gardens* (1981), containing a wide-ranging study of plants known to medieval gardeners, with extensive plant lists from about 380 to the 1540's; Dieter Hennebo and Alfred Hoffmann, *Geschichte der deutschen Gartenkunst,* I, Dieter Hennebo, *Gärten des Mittelalters* (1962), which illustrates the history of gardens in Germany, but has a broad European context; Teresa McLean, *Medieval English Gardens* (1980); Derek A. Pearsall and Elizabeth Salter, *Landscapes and Seasons of the Medieval World* (1973); Christopher Thacker, *The History of Gardens* (1979); Eithne Wilkins, *The Rose-garden Game* (1969).

CHRISTOPHER THACKER

[See also **Albertus Magnus; Botany; Herbals, Western European; Romance of the Rose; Walafrid Strabo.**]

GARDENS, ISLAMIC. See **Rauḍa.**

GARGOYLE

GARGOYLE, a spout or hollow, tubelike projection from the gutter of a building or the pier of a buttress, employed to throw rainwater away from the footings of the building. Gargoyles (from Old French *gargoule,* throat) of the Gothic period were frequently given grotesque forms, but the two words are not synonymous, since grotesques did not serve as rainspouts.

Gargoyles. From the south transept of the Cathedral of Milan, early 15th century. PHOTOGRAPH BY WIM SWAAN, COURTESY OF ELEK

BIBLIOGRAPHY

Lester Burbank Bridaham, *Gargoyles, Chimeres, and the Grotesque in French Gothic Sculpture,* 2nd rev. ed (1969).

CARL F. BARNES, JR.

[See also **Gothic Art: Sculpture.**]

GĀTHĀS. The Gāthās (hymns) represent the most ancient section of the Avesta, the sacred scriptures of Zoroastrianism. Believed to have been composed by the prophet Zarathushtra himself, they may be dated as early as about 1000 B.C. The language of the Gāthās is an archaic dialect of Avestan, different from the Younger Avestan in which most of the Avesta was composed. This ancient Gathic dialect is found only in the Gāthās, in four sacred prayers also attributed to Zarathushtra, and in the Yasna Haptānghaiti (the Yasna of the seven chapters).

In the Zoroastrian scriptures the Gāthās were transmitted as a central part of the Yasna, a liturgy of the sacrificial rite codified many centuries after the prophet. Although these hymns are identified in the liturgy as the "five Gāthās," a division seemingly based on meter, they are really seventeen separate hymns.

Since the Gāthās and the sacred prayers are the only surviving records of the teachings of Zarathushtra himself, they are the most often translated section of the Avesta. Translation of the Gāthās, however, is a very exacting task. There are numerous problematic constructions, many lexical items unattested elsewhere in the Avesta, and uncertainty about the meaning of some basic terms. In addition the Gāthās are poetical compositions, with all the layers of meaning characteristic of Indo-Iranian poetry. These uncertainties contribute to substantial disagreements among translators about even the basic thrust of Zarathushtra's teachings.

There is, however, some consensus among Iranists as to the general themes of the Gāthās. A fundamental (one) is the opposition between Good and Evil, Truth and Lie, that seems to lie at the heart of Zarathushtra's teachings. Although this opposition is cosmic, it has consequences in Zarathushtra's personal experiences referred to in the Gāthās. Zarathushtra's initial failure to find a patron among the tribal leaders of eastern Iran is a manifestation of the ability of the Lie and the *daēvas,* gods who have chosen the leadership of the Evil Spirit, Angra Mainyu, to deceive human leaders.

From this ethical opposition flows a doctrine of free will. Human beings can choose the Truth or the Lie in their thoughts, words, and deeds, and each person's choice carries consequences. The concepts of hell and paradise as places where a person receives retribution or reward may have first appeared in Zarathushtra's Gāthās. The doctrine of finite time, in which the forces of evil are made finite and hence vulnerable to the weapons of the Lord Wisdom, Ahurā Mazdā, is implicit in the Gāthās.

The Gāthās should not, however, be construed as an effort at theological explication, even though Zarathushtra was a great theologian. They are hymns of praise to the Lord Wisdom, who engages in cosmic battle with the forces of evil, who brings prosperity to those who choose to do good, who finally provides Zarathushtra with a patron, Kavi (Prince) Vishtāspa. It is the all-encompassing nature of Zarathushtra's vision that in the long run may be the greatest obstacle to modern translators.

GATTAPONI, MATTEO

BIBLIOGRAPHY

An excellent modern translation is by Stanley Insler, *The Gathas of Zarathushtra* (1975), with a bibliography of earlier translations. See also Mary Boyce, *A History of Zoroastrianism,* I (1975), cogent interpretation of Zarathushtra's teachings within the context of the Indo-Iranian tradition.

DALE L. BISHOP

[See also **Avesta; Iranian Literature; Zoroastrianism.**]

GATTAPONI, MATTEO, properly Matteo di Giovanelli Gattaponi da Gubbio (*fl.* 1345–1375), a surveyor *(mensurator, geometra)* and architect, highly esteemed for his urban fortifications. His documented works are the citadel of Spoleto (1362–1370), the Chapel of S. Caterina in S. Francesco, Assisi (1362–1367), and the Collegio di Spagna, Bologna (1365–1369), all for Cardinal Gil Albornoz; and the citadel Portasole in Perugia (1374; destroyed). Attributed works include the Infermeria Nuova in Assisi (1368).

Courtyard of the Collegio di Spagna, Bologna. Matteo Gattaponi, architect, 1365–1370. PHOTOGRAPH BY ANDERSON, ROME, COURTESY OF PENGUIN BOOKS

GAUFRID (GAUDFRED) MALATERRA

BIBLIOGRAPHY

Francesco Filippini, "Matteo Gattaponi da Gubbio architetto del Collegio di Spagna in Bologna," in *Bollettino d'arte,* 2nd ser. **2** (1922–1923); Pietro Toesca, *Il Trecento* (1951), 135–136; John White, *Art and Architecture in Italy, 1250 to 1400* (1966), 330, 352–354.

DALE KINNEY

GAUCHIER DE DOURDAN is the name attributed to the author of the Second Continuation *(Continuation Perceval)* of Chrétien de Troyes's *Conte du Graal.* While the anonymous First Continuation narrates the adventures of Gauvain, the Second Continuation returns to Chrétien's story, recounting Perceval's love for the Lady of the Chessboard and the quest to resolder the Broken Sword. The text ends abruptly after 13,017 verses, furnishing no conclusion to Chrétien's romance.

Gauchier has long been identified as Wauchier de Denain, an early-thirteenth-century author of prose translations of numerous Latin saints' lives, but the assimilation remains unsubstantiated.

BIBLIOGRAPHY

Charles Potvin, *Perceval le Gallois; ou Le conte du Graal,* 6 vols. (1866–1871); William J. Roach, ed., *The Continuations of the Old French Perceval of Chrétien de Troyes,* 4 vols. (1949–1971). See also Guy Vial, "L'auteur de la Deuxième Continuation du *Conte du Graal,*" in *Travaux de linguistique et de littérature publiés par le CPLR de l'Université de Strasbourg,* **16** (1978).

KATHRYN GRAVDAL

[See also **Arthurian Literature; Chrétien de Troyes.**]

GAUFRID (GAUDFRED) MALATERRA (*d.* 1099), a monk of the Order of St. Benedict. Born in Normandy, Gaudfrid was a close associate of Roger I of Sicily, at whose request he wrote a history of Norman rule in England and Apulia. The *Historia Sicula,* consisting of four books, begins with the Norman prince Rollo and ends with events of 1099.

BIBLIOGRAPHY

The *Historia Sicula* may be found in *Patrologia latina,* CXLIX (1882), 1087–1215. See also Max Manitius, *Geschichte der lateinischen Literatur des Mittelalters,* III (1931), 457.

EDWARD FRUEH

GAUTIER D'ARRAS (*d.* 1185), a native of Arras, wrote two verse romances, *Eracle* and *Ille et Galeron,* possibly between 1176 and 1184. *Eracle,* composed for Thibaut V of Blois and Marie of Champagne, introduces contemporary events into a strongly moralistic work combining epic, Byzantine, and courtly elements. *Ille et Galeron,* which proceeds directly from the lai *Eliduc,* goes even more deeply into a psychological and realistic analysis of human sentiments.

BIBLIOGRAPHY

Éracle, Guy Raynaud de Lage, ed. (1976); *Ille et Galeron,* F. A. G. Cowper, ed. (1956). See also William C. Calin, "Structure and Meaning in the *Eracle* by Gautier d'Arras," in *Symposium,* **16** (1962); Anthime Fourrier, *Le courant réaliste dans le roman courtois en France au moyen-âge,* I (1960).

JOHN F. FLINN

GAUTIER DE CHÂTILLON. See Walter of Châtillon.

GAUTIER DE COINCI (*ca.* 1177–1236), a Benedictine prior and prolific author of French lyric and narrative. Piety mingles with playfulness in his songs to the Virgin. His influential and popular major work comprises two books of *Miracles de Nostre Dame* (book I: *ca.* 1218–1224; book II: *ca.* 1227–1233), adapted from Latin originals: fifty-eight verse tales (such as *Théophile* and *La sacristine*) depicting Mary as mediatrix.

BIBLIOGRAPHY

V. Frederick Koenig, ed., *Les miracles de Nostre Dame par Gautier de Coinci,* 4 vols. (1955–1970): vol. I supplements the bibliography in Arlette P. Ducrot-Granderye, *Études sur Les miracles Nostre Dame de Gautier de Coinci* (1932), with bibliography to *ca.* 1931; Gautier de Coinci, *Les chansons à la Vierge,* Jacques Chailley, ed. (1959).

BARBARA NELSON SARGENT-BAUR

GAUTREKS SAGA KONUNGS (The story of King Gautrekr), written in the thirteenth century, though surviving in manuscripts that are of much later date, is an outstanding example of Icelandic legendary fiction. Deeply rooted in ancient tradition, it consists of three episodes, loosely connected but masterfully told.

The story opens with an amusing account of King Gauti of Götaland, who loses his way and his companions on a hunting trip. He stumbles on an isolated family of primitive backwoodsmen, whose bizarre custom it is to leap suicidally over a certain cliff (and be received by Odin in Valhalla) whenever anything out of the ordinary happens to them. The master of the house is so disturbed by the king's visit that he decides to take his wife along to Valhalla, leaving their children to marry incestuously and inherit his property. Gauti spends the night with one of the daughters; as a result she gives birth to a boy, the title hero of the story (he plays only a minor part, mostly in the third episode).

The principal character of the second episode is the tragic hero Starkaðr, whose story is told in much greater detail in Saxo Grammaticus' *Gesta Danorum;* he figures also in *Ynglinga saga* and *Norna-Gests þáttr.* Descended from giants, Starkaðr is taken captive at the age of three and reared by a man called Hrosshárs-Grani (Horsehair Grani), who turns out to be Odin in disguise. In his boyhood Starkaðr is a layabout, sleeping in the ashes by the fire, but at the age of twelve he joins his foster brother King Víkarr and develops into a mighty warrior.

The turning point in his life comes when his destiny is ordained by the gods. Odin bestows on him many blessings, including three life spans, plenty of money, and the art of poetry; Thor counterbalances the blessings with curses: Starkaðr shall commit a foul deed in each of the three life spans, possess neither land nor estates, suffer grievous wounds in every battle, and never remember his poetry after writing it. Starkaðr's first foul deed is the betrayal of King Víkarr, who is sacrificed to Odin. After that the Norwegians hate Starkaðr so much that he is forced to flee to the kings of Sweden, whose berserks make him their laughingstock. In Sweden he reminisces about his misfortunes in a series of verses: "People laugh when they see me; the ugly jaws, the long snout-shaped mouth, the wolf-grey hair and the tree-like arms, the bruised, rough-skinned neck." Both *Skáldatal* and *Landnámabók* refer to Starkaðr as a court poet, and Saxo Grammaticus translates a number of verses attributed to him.

The third episode in *Gautreks saga,* sometimes referred to as *Gjafa-Refs saga,* is about the adventures of another late developer, a farmer's son called

368

Refr, and his benefactor, Earl Neri, who combines great wisdom with exceptional stinginess. Refr presents Neri with a fine gift and in return receives his good counsel, with the result that Refr wins King Gautrekr's daughter and an earldom to boot. Like the first episode, the tale of Refr is written in a humorous vein.

BIBLIOGRAPHY

James Milroy, "The Story of Ætternisstapi in *Gautreks saga*," in *Saga-book of the Viking Society,* **17** (1967–1968); Hermann Pálsson and Paul Edwards, trans., *Gautreks saga and Other Medieval Tales* (1968); E. O. G. Turville-Petre, *Myth and Religion of the North* (1964), 205–211; Wilhelm Ranisch, ed., *Die Gautreks saga in zwei Fassungen* (1900).

HERMANN PÁLSSON

[See also **Fornaldarsögur; Saxo Grammaticus; Starkaðr.**]

GAWAIN AND THE GREEN KNIGHT, SIR, an alliterative Middle English romance, appears in a unique manuscript (British Library, MS Cotton Nero A.x.)—a small quarto volume that also contains *Pearl, Purity* (or *Cleanness*), and *Patience*. Composed in the latter part of the fourteenth century and preserved in an early-fifteenth-century scribal hand, the Cotton Nero poems are customarily attributed to a single anonymous author, possibly a member of an aristocrat's household in the northwest Midlands section of England.

Although the Cotton Nero poems offer varying degrees of complexity in structure and meaning, *Sir Gawain and the Green Knight* is noted particularly for its gamelike tone, its artistic employment of symmetry, and its interwoven motifs, metrical form, symbols, and themes.

While King Arthur and his court revel in Yuletide games, feasts, and gift giving, a huge green stranger rides into the royal hall. Unarmed except for a huge ax, the Green Knight challenges Arthur's court to an exchange of blows, an elaborate type of Christmas game. Once Gawain accepts the challenge and restates the terms of the "beheading game" compact, he decapitates the Knight—who then calmly picks up his severed head and announces that Gawain must receive his blow in turn a year and a day later at the Green Chapel.

Armed for his quest of the Knight, Gawain then leaves the All Saints' Day festivities at Camelot. Buffeted by the chilling blasts of winter and exhausted

by struggles with dragons, trolls, and wild forest creatures, Gawain eventually sights a gleaming castle on the morning of Christmas Eve. After he is welcomed by the lord of the castle, Bercilak de Hautdesert, Gawain is introduced to two women—the lord's beautiful young wife and a crone, subsequently revealed by the Green Knight as Morgan le Fay. Once Bercilak informs him that the Green Chapel is two miles away, Gawain agrees to stay at the castle until New Year's Day to enter into an "exchange of winnings." According to the terms of Bercilak's playful covenant with Gawain, whatever prey is captured by the lord during his hunting expeditions will be exchanged for Gawain's winnings in the castle.

For the next two days (29 and 30 December), as Bercilak revels in the chase, his wife tracks down Gawain in a series of amorous bedroom advances. At the end of each day, Gawain exchanges his castle prizes, the lady's kisses, for the spoils of the lord's hunt. On the third and final day of temptation (31 December), while Bercilak follows the trails of a wily fox, his wife presents Gawain with an alluring gift, an ornamental green and gold girdle *(luf-lace)* that may preserve the knight's life at the Green Chapel. Inasmuch as Gawain promised the lady to conceal the girdle, Gawain offers Bercilak only the three kisses won during the day and receives the lord's fox pelt.

On New Year's Day, entwining the glistening girdle about his waist, Gawain leaves Castle Hautdesert and rides over the desolate terrain near the Green Chapel. Although he expects to find a rustic Christian sanctuary, the Green Chapel is revealed as a hollow mound. The Green Knight then suddenly appears and restates the terms of the Yuletide covenant. Gawain exposes his neck for the blow, and, although the first two strokes of the Knight's ax are feints, the third grazes his flesh, thereby causing his blood to gush forth upon the snow-covered earth.

Following Gawain's triple test, the Green Knight reveals himself as Bercilak and relates the three strokes of the ax at the Green Chapel to Gawain's behavior during the three days of the exchange of winnings at Castle Hautdesert. After Gawain shamefully identifies his faults—cowardice and covetousness—he decides to wear the green girdle as a symbol of his human weakness and as a warning against soldierly pride. With the Knight's revelation that Morgan le Fay created the Challenge in order to test the character of the Round Table, Gawain departs for Camelot. In the presence of Arthur's court, then, a mortified Gawain exhibits the girdle as a token of dishonor. Responding with good-natured laughter, however, each member of Arthur's court agrees to wear a sash of bright green as a sign of the luster of the Round Table.

The narrative structure of *Sir Gawain* highlights the element of game or play—partially serious and partially comic—in the poem. Offering a bewildering variety of festive games—the New Year game involving the use of tokens hidden in the hand (*hondeselle*) as gifts or forfeits, the Christmas *gomen* of exchange of blows, the exchange of winnings, the outdoor hunting games, and Lady Bercilak's indoor game of love—the poet challenges the reader to ascertain what these games mean. Furthermore, through the artful employment of play rules, signalized by legal diction (*twelmonyth and a day, couenaunt,* and *forwarde*), as well as the suspenseful use of ambiguity, the poet toys with his audience, for he often conceals significant information, thereby allowing the reader to seesaw between ignorance and knowledge. Additional evidence reinforcing the concept of game in *Gawain* may be found in elusive color symbols. Although the depiction of Gawain's arming at Camelot contains no allusion to the ambiguous green—a medieval emblem of life, death, the devil, fairies, Otherworld beings, the Green Man, and the Wild Man—three other Yuletide colors (gold, red, and white) attributed to the Green Knight are linked with Gawain. Inasmuch as Gawain gradually reflects the color pattern of the Knight, he assumes the role of unwitting victim in a Christmas game of role-switching. Once Gawain is arrayed in the red coat-armor as well as the green and gold girdle and bares his white flesh for the ax-blow at the Green Chapel, he wears the complete Yuletide livery of his hunter (Green Knight).

The gamelike structure and the tone of *Gawain* are mirrored in an artistic use of symmetry, particularly the elements of parallelism and contrast. The number two, for example, is significant, for there are two New Year's Days, two "beheading games," two courts, two games (indoor and outdoor hunts) at Hautdesert, and two confession scenes. Furthermore, the concluding prayer in *Gawain,* suggesting Christ's earthly suffering and man's desire for eternal joy, echoes the alternation between bliss and trouble (*blysse and blunder*) at the beginning of the poem.

Even more important, perhaps, are the symbolic threes—three prayers and signs of the Cross on Gawain's arrival at Hautdesert, three temptations, three hunts, three cockcrows, three series of kisses, and three strokes of the Green Knight's ax. Thus increasing the sense of the supernatural, the number three is associated with magic in fairy lore and serves as an oblique reminder both of the devil's three temptations of Christ and of Peter's three denials of Christ (three cockcrows and the porter's invocation of Peter at Hautdesert). Finally, this rich panoply of number symbolism includes the gold pentangle, Gawain's heraldic emblem, which appears on his shield. A token of Gawain's truth and fidelity, the pentangle—the "endless knot"—illuminates his five types of fivefold physical, chivalric, and spiritual virtues; such qualities are endlessly interconnected and spiritually conjoined in the Round Table's exemplar of chivalry.

Major decorative patterns in *Gawain,* the gamelike structure and numerical design, are reflected, likewise, in the employment of interlocked motifs, metrical form, symbolism, and themes. Gawain's destiny in the "exchange of blows" contest at the Chapel, for example, is interlaced with his adherence to the rules of the "exchange of winnings" game at Hautdesert. Similarly, each stanza of *Gawain* combines long unrhymed lines, *with lel letteres loken,* and a bob and wheel; the bob (a single line of two syllables) and the wheel (a quatrain containing three-stressed lines) rhyme *a b a b a.* Finally, an ironic reminder of Gawain's five-times-five pentangular merits may be found in the poem's concluding long line (line 2525), an echo of line 1. Tracing the circle of history through the fall of Troy, these lines underscore the concept of worldly vanity as well as the mutability of earthly existence. Furthermore, the most important themes of *Gawain*—pride of life, *untrawpe,* covetousness, and cowardice—are symbolically enmeshed, for Gawain's desire to save his life gradually lures him into a tangle of unknightly actions.

BIBLIOGRAPHY

Sources. William R. J. Barron, ed. and trans., *Sir Gawain and the Green Knight* (1974); Marie Borroff, trans., *Sir Gawain and the Green Knight* (1967); J. R. R. Tolkien and E. V. Gordon, eds., *Sir Gawain and the Green Knight,* 2nd ed. rev. by Norman Davis (1967).

Bibliographies. Robert J. Blanch, *Sir Gawain and the Green Knight: A Reference Guide* (1983); Malcolm Andrew, *The Gawain Poet: An Annotated Bibliography, 1839–1977* (1979).

Studies. William R. J. Barron, *Trawthe and Treason: The Sin of Gawain Reconsidered* (1980); Larry D. Benson, *Art and Tradition in Sir Gawain and the Green Knight*

(1965); Robert J. Blanch, ed., *Sir Gawain and Pearl: Critical Essays* (1966); Marie Borroff, *Sir Gawain and the Green Knight: A Stylistic and Metrical Study* (1962); John A. Burrow, *A Reading of Sir Gawain and the Green Knight* (1965); Denton Fox, ed., *Twentieth-century Interpretations of Sir Gawain and the Green Knight* (1968); Victor Yelverton Haines, *The Fortunate Fall of Sir Gawain: The Typology of Sir Gawain and the Green Knight* (1982); Donald R. Howard and Christian K. Zacher, eds., *Critical Studies of Sir Gawain and the Green Knight* (1968); Laura Hibbard Loomis, "Gawain and the Green Knight," in Roger Sherman Loomis, ed., *Arthurian Literature in the Middle Ages: A Collaborative History* (1959), 528–540; D. D. R. Owen, "Parallel Readings with Sir Gawain and the Green Knight," in R. C. Johnston and D. D. R. Owen, eds., *Two Old French Gauvain Romances* (1972), Part II; Henry L. Savage, *The Gawain-Poet: Studies in His Personality and Background* (1956); Hans Schnyder, *Sir Gawain and the Green Knight: An Essay in Interpretation* (1961).

ROBERT J. BLANCH

[See also **Arthurian Literature; Christmas; Feasts and Festivals, European; Middle English Literature; Pearl, The.**]

GAWIT^C, a large vestibule, a type of structure used in Armenia to serve for religious and secular assemblies and as a burial place for princely families and prominent ecclesiastics. It is a large vaulted hall constructed against the west facade of a church, which is generally smaller; it appears in important monastic complexes built in Armenia in the tenth through fourteenth centuries. Known also as *žamatun,* the *gawit^C* originated in Armenia and was developed from the chambers in Armenian palaces and domestic dwellings with central openings in the ceilings.

In the *gawit^C* original and varied systems of vaulting are used to solve the structural problems of building in stone. Large arches span the structure, supporting the weight of stone vaults and central dome and directing the thrusts. The arches are used in a variety of ways, some similar to those found in later western European architecture. In Armenia the earliest stage of these innovative vaulting systems is found at the Shepherd's Chapel (early eleventh century) before being used in the *gawit^C* structures.

There are three types of *gawit^C*s, the most widespread being the central plan. This form includes examples with four free-standing pillars at the center (the most popular), with two pillars, with vaults resting on pairs of intersecting arches, or with vaults supported directly by external walls.

The first example of the central plan *gawit^C* is found at the Church of St. John (1038), at the monastery of Hoṙomos, near Ani. Four massive pillars support the central drum, which is carved with eight relief panels depicting the Second Coming, crosses, and other motifs. Arches connect the central and wall pillars and divide the interior into nine equal bays.

The central opening of the *gawit^C* can be constructed in a variety of ways, including *muqarna* vaults (for example at Geḷard) and an openwork dome with columns.

BIBLIOGRAPHY

Jurgis Baltrušaitis, *Le problème de l'ogive et l'Arménie* (1936); Varaztad Harouthiounian and Morous Hasrathian, *Monuments of Armenia* (1975); Step^{C}an X. Mnac^{C}akanyan, *Architektura Armjanskich pritvorov* (1952); Sirarpie Der Nersessian, *The Armenians* (1970), and *Armenian Art* (1977 and 1978); Joseph Strzygowski, *Die Baukunst der Armenier und Europa,* 2 vols. (1918); T^{C}oros T^{C}oramanyan, *Nyut^{C}er Haykakan Čartarapetut^{C}yan Patmut^{C}yan,* 2 vols. (1942–1948).

LUCY DER MANUELIAN

[See also **Armenian Art; Geḷard; Hoṙomos.**]

GAYIANĒ, CHURCH OF. The Church of St. Gayianē in Vaḷaršapat was erected by Kat^{C}oḷikos Ezr (630–641) at the site of the martyrdom of the abbess Gayianē by the pagan Armenian King Trdat at the time of the conversion of Armenia to Christianity in the fourth century. The fifth-century Armenian historian Agat^{C}angeḷos reports that St. Gregory the Illuminator erected a martyrium after the site was revealed in a vision. According to the tenth-century historian Kat^{C}oḷikos John, the martyrium was replaced by the present church, a large, longitudinal, cross-in-square structure with four free-standing piers supporting the drum of the central cupola.

BIBLIOGRAPHY

Richard Krautheimer, *Early Christian and Byzantine Architecture* (1965); Sirarpie Der Nersessian, *The Armenians* (1970), and *Armenian Art* (1977 and 1978).

LUCY DER MANUELIAN

GAYRARD, RAYMOND (*d.* 1118), canon of St. Sernin at Toulouse, who supervised the second period of construction of that church, from about

1098, when the choir was completed, until his death. He was responsible for the transept and the eastern bays of the nave. Though termed an *architectus,* Raymond may have been manager of the work rather than its designer-builder.

BIBLIOGRAPHY

Kenneth J. Conant, *Carolingian and Romanesque Architecture, 800–1200* (1959), 98–99.

CARL F. BARNES, JR.

[See also **Toulouse, St. Sernin.**]

GEERTGEN TOT SINT JANS (*d. ca.* 1495), the leading Dutch painter in Haarlem at the end of the fifteenth century, worked for the Knights of St. John. The right wing (now sawed in two) of the *Crucifixion Triptych,* executed for the Church of St. John the Baptist (*ca.* 1485), is now in the Kunsthistorisches Museum, Vienna. On the obverse is *The Lamentation,* and on the reverse, *The Burning of the Bones of St. John the Baptist.* Geertgen excelled in painting lovable Madonnas (*Night Nativity,* National Gallery, London) and in composing unusual devotional panels (*Man of Sorrows,* Aartsbisschoppelijke Museum, Utrecht) that exhibit his strong mystical temperament. He died young, at about the age of twenty-eight.

BIBLIOGRAPHY

Max J. Friedländer, *Early Netherlandish Painting,* V (1969); Erwin Panofsky, *Early Netherlandish Painting* (1953), 324–330.

JAMES SNYDER

[See also **Flemish Painting.**]

GEFFREI GAIMAR. See **Gaimar, Geffrei.**

GEFJON. The goddess Gefjon is central to only one tale in Norse mythology: the origin of the island of Zealand. This story is told by Snorri in both his *Prose Edda (Gylfaginning)* and *Heimskringla (Ynglinga saga,* ch. 5). In each case he cites as his source a verse by the ninth-century Norwegian skald Bragi Boddason the Old in his poem *Ragnarsdrápa,* com-

Nativity. Geertgen tot Sint Jans, Netherlandish, *ca.* 1490. NATIONAL GALLERY, LONDON

posed in honor of a shield given him by Prince Ragnarr Sigurðarson. Several stanzas of the poem are extant; they describe scenes painted on the shield, including one of Gefjon's plowing. The tale relates Odin's journey north from Troy. He establishes himself in Denmark and sends Gefjon to Sweden to reconnoiter. She meets King Gylfi, who in return for her entertainment grants her the amount of land she can plow in one day and night with four oxen. But Gefjon shrewdly yokes up her four oxen sons by a giant and plows away enough land to form the Danish island of Zealand. She drags it over the sea, deposits it in its present site, and settles down there. The hole left in Sweden becomes the great Lake Mälaren, which is supposed to correspond to the contours of Zealand.

The little additional information about Gefjon in the sources seems to link her with Freyja. In *Lokasenna* it is written that, like Freyja, Gefjon owns a necklace that she received in return for sexual favors and that she can foretell the future as well as Odin. Snorri's *Prose Edda* mentions briefly in another passage that Gefjon is a virgin and that unmarried women come to her after death. Her name, which derives from the verb *gefa* (to give) and is related to Gefn, one of Freyja's names, is frequently found in translations as the Old Norse equivalent of Diana.

Names referring to gifts or giving are also associated with the *matres* or *matronae*, statues of female deities (often holding baskets of fruit or cornucopias) found throughout the Germanic area during Roman times. Considering her role in the tale as a plower of land and her evident ties with Freyja, it is tempting to identify Gefjon as a fertility deity of lesser magnitude. Although her special province would seem to be Denmark, there is no certain place-name evidence for a cult.

BIBLIOGRAPHY

Henry A. Bellows, trans., *The Poetic Edda* (1957), 158–159; Gustav Neckel and H. Kuhn, ed., *Edda. Die Lieder des Codex Regius* (1962), 100; Margaret C. Ross, "The Myth of Gefjon and Gylfi and Its Function in *Snorra Edda* and *Heimskringla*," in *Arkiv för nordisk filologi,* **93** (1978); Snorri Sturluson, *Heimskringla,* Samuel Laing, trans. (1844 and later editions), *Ynglinga saga,* ch. 5., and *The Prose Edda,* Jean I. Young, trans. (1964), 29; E. O. G. Turville-Petre, *Myth and Religion of the North* (1964), 187–188.

KAAREN GRIMSTAD

[See also **Bragi Boddason the Old; Scandinavian Mythology; Snorra Edda; Snorri Sturluson.**]

GEISLI. See **Einarr Skúlason.**

GEŁARD (Geghard). The Armenian monastery of Gełard (the lance) of Ayrivank^c (monastery of the cave), located near Garni in the mountains about forty kilometers (twenty-five miles) southeast of Erevan, was one of the most important religious centers and pilgrimage sites of Armenia. Traditionally said to be a foundation of St. Gregory the Illuminator (fourth century), its earliest inscriptions date from the seventh century, and the earliest documentary references are from the tenth century. Sacked and burned by Arabs in the tenth century, the complex was rebuilt in the thirteenth century. Gełard was noted for possessing the Holy Lance, reportedly brought to Armenia by the apostle Thaddeus; for its school and scriptorium; and for the four sculptured chambers expertly carved by Galjag out of the adjacent cliffs.

Monastery of Gełard, main church (1215) and *gawit*^c (1225), view from the southeast. FROM SIRARPIE DER NERSESSIAN, ARMENIAN ART (THAMES AND HUDSON, 1977)

One of a group of splendid monasteries reconstructed after the liberation of Armenia by the Zak^carid princes, Gełard includes two structures commissioned by them: the Kat^colikē (a domed hall-type church, 1215) and its large *gawit*^c (square, with nine bays and a *muqarna* vault, between 1215 and 1225). Human figures, birds, animals, and geometric and floral motifs are carved on these and later structures.

In the 1240's Prince Proš (or Xałbakean), a Zak^carid vassal, purchased Gełard to erect a "place of burial" for his family, and commissioned his first rock-carved church (cruciform, with a *muqarna* vault). Also rock-cut are the second Proš church (cruciform, with figured *khatchk*^c*ars* [crosses] and an elaborately carved cupola), its *gawit*^c (square, with mausoleal niche, carved saints, birds, and animals), both completed by 1283, and the upper *gawit*^c (square, with four massive piers and central cupola), completed in 1288 by his son Babak and daughter-in-law, Ruzuk^can.

Outside the walls are numerous monastic cells, the rock-carved Church of St. Astuacacin (twelfth century), and the cave chamber (*ca.* 1291) of Mxit^car Ayrivanec^ci, one of Gełard's eminent thirteenth-century ecclesiastics.

BIBLIOGRAPHY

G(h)eghard, Documents of Armenian Architecture, VI (1973); Lucy Der Manuelian, "The Monastery of Geghard: A Study of Armenian Architectural Sculpture in the 13th Century" (Ph.D. diss., Boston Univ. 1980); Sirarpie Der Nersessian, The Armenians (1970), and Armenian Art (1977 and 1978), 174, 178–179.

LUCY DER MANUELIAN

[See also **Armenian Art.**]

GELASIUS I, POPE (d. 21 November 496). Deacon and secretary to Felix II (483–492), then pope himself (492–496), Gelasius was, after Leo I, the most influential Roman spokesman of his century. As defender of orthodoxy against the Byzantine emperors during the Acacian schism, he made a distinction between episcopal and secular power that was to define church-state relations for centuries. As pastor he cared for the poor, worked to improve the clergy, and regulated church discipline. Nearly 100 of his letters and treatises have survived, as well as eighteen Mass formulas and the litany known as the *Deprecatio Gelasii*.

BIBLIOGRAPHY

Louis M. O. Duchesne, ed., Le Liber pontificales, I (1886, 2nd ed. 1955), 255–257; Patrologia latina, LIX (1862), and Adalberto Hamman, ed., in Patrologia latina, Supplementum, III (1963), 739–787; Gilbert Pomarès, ed., Lettre contre les Lupercales et dix-huit messes du sacramentaire léonien (1959). See also Walter Ullmann, Gelasius I (492–496). Das Papstum an der Wende der Spätantike zum Mittelalter (1981); Aloysius K. Ziegler, "Pope Gelasius I and His Teaching on the Relation of Church and State," in Catholic Historical Review, 27 (1942).

CLAUDE J. PEIFER, O.S.B.

GELAT^CI. The monastery of Gelat^Ci is located in a valley in western Georgia near Kutaisi. Its construction, begun by King David the Builder in 1106, was completed in 1130. The monastic complex has an irregular circular shape (about 160 meters [525 feet] in diameter) and is surrounded by high walls. Within the monastery and its environs are a number of churches and secular buildings added in the thirteenth and fourteenth centuries. Within the walls of the *mandra* are three churches built of yellowish limestone; in the center is the main church, a cruciform domed building dedicated to the Virgin. In accordance with the architectural tradition of Georgia after the eleventh century, the dome is not supported by four free-standing piers, but only by the western pair of piers; the eastern part of the dome rests on the western ends of the apse walls, thereby increasing the unity of space. The same idea, with minor departures, is reiterated in the Church of St. George, located east of the main church. To the west of the main church is a unique two-story structure, the Church of St. Nicholas.

In the same area are a bell tower and the academy (about 28 by 11 meters [102 by 36 feet]), which played an important role in the spiritual development of Georgia, for Gelat^Ci was not only a monastery but also the center of education. Among the teachers at the academy were numerous men of letters and philosophers, such as Ioane Petric^Ci. The curriculum consisted of both theological and secular subjects: geometry, arithmetic, astronomy, philosophy, grammar, rhetoric, and music.

In the scriptorium of Gelat^Ci numerous original works and translations were written, copied, and illustrated. Most of them are now at the Institute of Manuscripts, Tbilisi.

Some 150 meters (492 feet) northeast of the monastery are the ruins of a *sokhasterion* (a small chapel near the monastery for secluded silent prayer), the hospital, and residences for the elderly. To the south are the ruins of St. Sabas and the repeatedly restored Church of St. Elias. The original gate contains the tomb of David the Builder.

Gelat^Ci is rich in wall decoration. In the Church of the Virgin are paintings executed between the twelfth and seventeenth centuries that permit the study of the development of painting in Georgia. The outstanding work is in the conch, which is completely covered with twelfth-century mosaics of the Virgin and the Christ Child, flanked by the archangels Michael and Gabriel. The accompanying Greek inscriptions and the style of the mosaics suggest a strong Byzantine influence or even the participation of Constantinopolitan mosaicists.

BIBLIOGRAPHY

B. Lominadze, Gelati (1959), in Georgian; Rusudan Mepisashvili and Vakhtang Tsintsadze, The Arts of Ancient Georgia (1979); R. Mepisašvili, Arkhitekturny ansambl Gelati (1966); T. Virsaladze, "Fragment drevnoi freskovoi respisi glavnogo gelatskogo khrama," in Ars Georgica, 5 (1959).

WACHTANG DJOBADZE

[See also **David II (IV) the Builder; Georgian Art and Architecture.**]

GEMISTOS PLETHON, GEORGIOS

GEMISTOS PLETHON, GEORGIOS (*ca.* 1355–1452) was probably the greatest Neoplatonic speculative philosopher produced by Byzantium. He taught at Mistra and in 1438–1439 was a member of the Greek delegation at the Council of Ferrara-Florence, where his informal discourses on Platonism introduced Plato's thought from the original Greek text to the West. That introduction later resulted in Cosimo de' Medici's foundation (1462) of the Platonic Academy in Florence.

BIBLIOGRAPHY

François Masai, *Pléthon et le platonisme de Mistra* (1956).

D. J. GEANAKOPLOS

GEMS AND JEWELRY

SIXTH TO TENTH CENTURIES

It is the splendor of the Byzantine court of Justinian that first comes to mind when thinking of jewelry in the sixth century. This jewelry derived from two very different goldsmith traditions: the Roman and the barbarian. Its hallmark was, however, that it was Christian. Whereas the lavish use of gemstones overpowering the gold background that characterizes a pair of seventh-century bracelets in the Metropolitan Museum of Art proclaims barbarian influence, the majority of the gold bracelets, pendants, necklaces, earrings, and rings derive essentially from Roman jewelry. They are characterized by fine openwork, balanced designs, an abundant use of the rinceau motif, square and round settings (often channeled), beaded borders, and the use of niello on both gold and silver. Pearls on pins or strung on fine wires, sapphires, emeralds, amethysts, and classical intaglios and cameos were the most highly prized stones and jewels. The traditional Roman gold bow fibula was still in vogue. Among the finest pieces of early Byzantine jewelry are the pair of bracelets mentioned above; the necklace now in the Staatliche Museen Preussicher Kulturbesitz, Berlin; and the medallion in the Virginia Museum of Fine Arts, Richmond.

The pectoral cross, either alone or as the central pendant of many, was one of the most popular pieces of jewelry. By the end of the sixth or the beginning of the seventh century, representations of Christ, the apostles, and christological scenes had become popular. Whereas the jewelry of the court and the aristocracy was of gold, silver and silver gilt were used for the more popular jewelry, and gilt bronze for the least expensive.

At this time many Germanic tribes occupied western Europe as a result of the migrations of the Huns. The three most important tribes for the history of jewelry were the Visigoths, the Lombards, and the Franks. All three had close relations with Byzantium. Both the Lombards and the Visigoths imitated the Byzantine imperial regalia, and both received imperial gifts from Byzantium. Thus it is often difficult to distinguish Lombard and Visigothic jewelry from Byzantine work. For example, the cross that is suspended from the votive crown found in Guarazar, Spain, bearing the name (as donor) of Receswinth, king of the Visigoths (and now in the Museo Arqueológico Nacional, Madrid) is now thought to be an imperial gift from Constantinople. Scholars are divided as to whether groups of brooches, earrings, and belt buckles are Lombard or Byzantine. A pair of gold earrings with pearls, amethysts, and plasma in the Walters Art Gallery, Baltimore, was originally thought to be Visigothic because it was allegedly found in the south of Spain with a pair of eagle-shaped Visigothic fibulae, but is now considered to be Byzantine.

Both politically and artistically, the Franks provided the essential link in the West between the fall of the Roman Empire and the establishment of the Carolingian Empire. They achieved political unity largely due to the efforts of King Clovis I and Charlemagne, who, just prior to becoming emperor of the West in 800, assumed the title of king of the Franks and the Lombards.

The Roman aspect of Frankish jewelry is well illustrated by the gold disk fibula from the seventh or eighth century in the Hessisches Landesmuseum in Darmstadt. The central Roman cameo surrounded by a partial wreath of beads, the round and square settings of green paste, the filigree, and the overall balance and symmetry of design are essentially Roman characteristics. Frankish jewelry exemplifies tribal traditions as well. It owes much to Ostrogothic goldsmiths who, after their sojourn on the north shores of the Black Sea in the early third century, either were employed by the Frankish court or carried their style and other influences west from the

GEMS AND JEWELRY

Gold necklace set with pearls, emeralds, and sapphires. Constantinople, early 7th century. STAATLICHE MUSEEN PREUSSISCHER KULTURBESITZ, BERLIN

Gold disk fibula. Frankish, 7th or 8th century. HESSISCHES LANDESMUSEUM, DARMSTADT

Jasper carving with Christ on the obverse and a cross on the reverse. Middle Byzantine, commissioned by Leo VI (866–912). LONDON, VICTORIA AND ALBERT MUSEUM

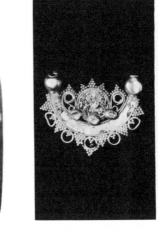

Pair of gold earrings with enameled crescents and roundels showing Christ and the Virgin. Middle Byzantine, 10th century. COURTESY OF THE WALTERS ART GALLERY, BALTIMORE

Gold *kolt* ("temple ring" pendant) with enamel. From the treasure found in the Street of the Three Saints, Kiev. METROPOLITAN MUSEUM OF ART, NEW YORK, GIFT OF J. PIERPONT MORGAN, 1917 (17.190.703)

Black Sea as they migrated. From them the Franks inherited the form of the bow fibula having a semi-circular head plate with projections, the motif of birds' heads, and the predilection for inlaid almandines or red glass, often with gold foil underneath.

Throughout the fifth and sixth centuries the Franks wore bird-shaped, bow, and small cloisonné disk fibulae or brooches in pairs—one on each shoulder—and magnificent belt buckles, rings, and hairpins. In the seventh century the earlier types of fibulae were replaced by the large gold disk fibula worn either singly or in pairs. The gold disk fibula is one of the major contributions of Frankish jewelry to the history of personal adornment in the West; it remained one of the essential articles of dress until the thirteenth century.

As exemplified by the early Carolingian Dorestad fibula, discovered in 1967 (now in the Rijksdienst voor het Oudheidkundig Bodemonderzoek, Amersfoort), the chief difference between the Frankish disk fibulae and Carolingian and Ottonian examples is that the latter are composed entirely of gold, whereas the Frankish examples are made with gold over a bronze core. Although there are not enough extant examples to make any generalizations concerning Carolingian jewelry, there are more pieces of Ottonian jewelry. Ottonian brooches continue the Merovingian traditions of architectural settings, which had been prevalent on pins and on the bezels of rings. However, since Byzantine culture occupied the dominant position in the world at this time, extensive Byzantine influence characterizes Ottonian art. Cloisonné enamel, claw settings, and antique gems are some of the Byzantine characteristics found on Ottonian brooches. Although the treasure of Empress Gisela (late tenth or early eleventh century) was lost during World War II (with the exception of the eagle fibula), it is known from photographs that the large brooch, probably worn to fasten the mantle, had a blue paste in the center of a zone of cloisonné enamel and may have been originally surrounded by pearls. The crescent-shaped earrings from the same treasure also show Byzantine influence.

At the end of the sixth century, the area around the Danube, where the Slavs had been producing great quantities of jewelry, fell under the influence of the Avars, who brought with them a provincial Byzantine culture. During the seventh century the Bulgars, who were hostile to the Avars, moved into the area south of the Danube, cutting off contact between the Slavs and Avars and the centers of Byzantine culture around the Black Sea. Toward the end

of the eighth century, there was a revival of Pontic influences, and the characteristic Avaric strap mounts and belt buckles were once again decorated with abstract plant motifs. The difference was that they were now cast, whereas earlier they had been executed in repoussé. Even after Charlemagne broke the political power of the Avars in the late eighth century, the cast-metal technique of the late Avaric period lingered in many areas, but influence from the West gradually became stronger. Avaric women wore earrings, the most common type having pyramidal clusters of beads on the lower half of the hoop.

Bohemia and Moravia were independent of the Avars. Most typical of the Moravian culture were gold earrings with a "double ear of corn" projecting vertically from the hoop, and spherical buttons of gilt bronze, silver, and occasionally gold. Some of the buttons are decorated with granulation, some with twisted wire, some with bosses, and some with incrustations of blue beads. Still others display repoussé or engraved designs on a punched ground with palmettes, rosettes, or bird motifs. Other types of earrings in gold and silver were variations of the crescent and cluster types. At the end of the ninth century, the products of the Moravian workshops found their way into Bohemia. In the eastern part of central Bohemia, the Stará Kouřim workshop, working in the Moravian tradition, came under the influence of the Arab world by the tenth century, producing silver earrings with chain pendants and animal figures decorated with fine granulation and filigree.

NINTH TO THIRTEENTH CENTURIES

In this period the prestige of Constantinople was acknowledged throughout the world. Cloisonné enamel attained its zenith, as shown in examples of pendant reliquaries, rings, earrings, crowns, and armbands. Although the armbands now in Thessaloniki are the only enameled ones known to date, pictorial representations reveal that armbands were part of the court dress. The Dumbarton Oaks Collection is rich in enameled rings and pendant reliquaries. After the Iconoclast controversy ended in 842, most Byzantine jewelry was marked by religious overtones, and new religious pictorial programs were endorsed by imperial patronage. The enamel medallions on the votive crown of Leo VI the Wise, for example, show the emperor flanked by saints. Small carvings in semiprecious stones were also popular, as were glass paste cameos. Leo VI commissioned a jasper carving with the image of Christ on the obverse and a cross poised on a sphere with an inscription referring to the emperor on the reverse. These two works show the two essential stylistic trends in middle Byzantine art: a return to late antique sources, seen in the humanity, realism, and solidity of the jasper representation of Christ; and a flat, otherworldly approach, characterizing the enamels of the crown.

Unlike the early Byzantine period, when silver was rarely used, at this time silver and niello pectoral crosses and bracelets were common. A cross from the twelfth or thirteenth century, in the Dumbarton Oaks Collection, shows the figure of Christ on the cross and four busts in medallions at the ends of the arms. The bust of the Virgin to the right of Christ is inscribed "Mother of God"; the other inscriptions are not legible. The reverse is inscribed vertically and horizontally "Lord help the wearer." The general form of the cross, in gold, had been extremely popular in the early Byzantine period, as had the inscription "Lord help the wearer" on rings. It was equally popular on gold and silver Middle Byzantine rings, with the difference that the bearer was usually mentioned by name.

A group of silver two-part bracelets that close by hinges may have been inspired by an early Byzantine type. One example from the eleventh or twelfth century, in the Dumbarton Oaks Collection, has niello borders with scrollwork in silver wire enclosing a series of medallions formed by rinceaux, each of which contains a bird, animal, or fantastic creature. The inhabited rinceaux are worked in repoussé and gilded. The early Byzantine prototype, in the British Museum, is also decorated with inhabited rinceaux—these containing birds and issuing from a central vase. It consists of a single openwork band, the hinges of which secure a medallion containing a representation of the Virgin.

Gold earrings were particularly popular in this period, most of them ultimately deriving in shape from the crescent-shaped earrings from about 2500 B.C. found in the royal tombs of Ur. The history of the migration of this shape of earring has been traced throughout the Near East and to Greece via Phoenicia. Consequently the shape was popular in the Islamic world, in Byzantium, and in its tributary states and allies, such as south Russia and the Balkans. The crescent shape with radial projections below, consisting of triangles of granulation alternating with spheres, had its immediate prototype in the Greco-Roman period in Egypt. An Early Chris-

Gold bracelet. Iranian, 10th or 11th century. THE FREER GALLERY OF ART, WASHINGTON, D.C.

tian example of this variant is in the British Museum, and a Middle Byzantine pair from the tenth century, with enameled crescents and roundels above the crescents showing Christ and the Virgin, is in the Walters Art Gallery. An eleventh- or twelfth-century example found in Crete, with an enamel roundel above the crescent showing birds on the front and a Kufic inscription on the reverse, is probably Islamic; it is in the National Archaeological Museum, Athens.

The full crescent shape was perhaps the most common form shared by Islam, Byzantium, and Kiev (predominantly Christian and under Byzantine influence) from the end of the tenth century on. Whereas the Islamic examples are more apt to be made of filigree and granulation and the Constantinopolitan examples are made of two plain sheets of gold decorated with filigree and granulation, the gold Kievan examples always have enamel decoration on the back and the front. The latter usually has birds flanking the Tree of Life, or sirens (occasionally replaced by busts of saints, the Virgin, or Christ); the former has decorative ornamentation. All Kievan pendants, like many of the Islamic ones, have a string of pearls around them. Kiev also produced many silver examples decorated with niello. The treasure found in the Street of the Three Saints in Kiev—most of which is divided between the British Museum and the Metropolitan Museum of Art—contains fine ex-

378

amples of both. These crescent-shaped pendants, generally referred to as *kolty* (temple rings), were suspended from the headdresses of aristocratic men and women. A fourteenth-century fresco in Lesnovo, Yugoslavia, depicts Empress Anna Lyverina dressed as a Byzantine empress with *kolty* suspended from her crown. On a Seljuk lusterware dish from Rayy (near Tehran) of about 1200, now in the Metropolitan Museum of Art, a seated woman is portrayed wearing an elaborate headdress with three crescent-shaped pendants attached to each side, indicating that this fashion was shared by the Muslim world.

Further evidence of Byzantine influence in south Russia is found in bronze cross-shaped pectoral encolpia produced there, which recall the silver Constantinopolitan examples in the Dumbarton Oaks Collection. Byzantine influence was shown in the Balkan countries as well: for example, in a silver twelfth-century, crescent-shaped *kolt* embossed on the front and back with a gilt pair of intertwined birds, and in half of a silver bracelet embossed with animals and mythological beasts, both in the Walters Art Gallery.

In twelfth-century Poland there were many imports from Kiev, including the three-bead type of earring, such as the pair from the Street of the Three Saints now in the British Museum. This form of earring was also popular in twelfth- and thirteenth-century Iraq and Iran.

There are very few datable pieces of jewelry from the Muslim world before the eleventh century. The most important period of Islamic jewelry production encompassed the eleventh through the thirteenth centuries, with the arrival of the Seljuks in eastern Iran in 1038 and the rule of the Fatimid dynasty in North Africa (909–1171). In general, early medieval Islamic jewelry consists principally of filigree and granulation. As has been already noted, the art of the Muslim world drew on the same sources as Middle Byzantine art, especially upon the ancient Near Eastern tradition. The continuation of the latter is well demonstrated by the rows of birds and cones on four Iranian bracelets of the tenth–eleventh centuries in the Metropolitan Museum of Art, the Walters Art Gallery, the Freer Gallery of Art, and the Seattle Art Museum. Repetition of motifs is a hallmark of ancient Near Eastern art, and both birds and cones have a long history of representation in it.

Characteristic types of Islamic jewelry in the early medieval period are bracelets with four hemispheres flanking the clasp and a twisted shank tapering toward the clasp; necklaces with tubular, oval, and

Necklace decorated with filigree, granulation, and cloisonné enamel. Hispano-Mauresque, 14th century. METROPOLITAN MUSEUM OF ART, NEW YORK, GIFT OF J. PIERPONT MORGAN, 1917 (17.190.161)

spherical beads, often enclosing petallike units *à jour* and usually decorated with filigree and granulation; variations of crescent and three-bead earrings; pendants and earrings in shapes of birds and animals in the round and decorated with filigree; and hair ornaments and rings with heavy settings and claws supporting high bezels. Epigraphic and vegetal decoration in niello are common, and the use of cloisonné enamel is frequent.

THIRTEENTH TO FIFTEENTH CENTURIES

During the thirteenth century the focal point in the history of jewelry gradually shifted from the East to the West. The close of the century witnessed the end of the most important period of Islamic jewelry, although the Hispano-Mauresque jewelry of fourteenth-century Nasrid Spain demonstrates the endurance of the magnificent Fatimid tradition. A necklace in the Metropolitan Museum of Art, composed of five boxlike pendant elements decorated with filigree, granulation, and cloisonné enamel, and having gold loops on the circumference for pearls or beads, is an excellent example. The pendants are separated by tubular slides of similar decoration, and the central circular pendant is inscribed "Ave Maria Gracia Plen[a]," indicating that the necklace was made for a Christian patron.

Even after the sack of Constantinople in 1204, Byzantine art lived on, especially in Greece and Russia. Several encolpia with a gem framed by a filigree border often set with precious stones and/or pearls, and frequently engraved on the reverse, bear witness to the survival of Byzantine art in Greece and Russia. A fine example is in the Dumbarton Oaks Collection. As a result of the crusades, Byzantine art was brought to western Europe, where it was incorporated into Western art and influenced its development. Some relics from the crusades went to Ste. Chapelle, and some were given by St. Louis to members of his family as gifts—for example, the thorn from Christ's crown of thorns that the king of Aragon had mounted in a beautiful fourteenth-century setting of gold, amethysts, and translucent enamel (now in the British Museum). A number of ancient engraved semiprecious stones also came to Europe with the crusaders. Some of these, like the Schaffenhausen onyx, were mounted in thirteenth-century plantlike filigree ornamentation with stones in high settings freed from the background. The stones brought by the crusaders served to inspire contemporary gem cutting. By the end of the thirteenth century, the Paris lapidaries had their own guild. Furthermore, jewelry, which had been mainly the product of imperial and monastic workshops, now became the product of independent corporations.

Since in the thirteenth century both men and women wore heavy, long-sleeved, ankle-length woolen clothes, the major items of adornment were the ring brooch and the belt buckle. Both became increasingly ornamented. Because it was the age of chivalry, ring brooches, as well as finger rings, were often enriched with amatory inscriptions and mottoes, usually in niello. Brooches were often set with pearls, rubies, and sapphires, which were believed to have amuletic properties. By the end of the thirteenth century, the new technique of basse-taille enamel was in use in France, Italy, and especially the Rhineland.

The fourteenth century was marked by ever-growing luxury, which reached its zenith in Paris under Charles V and Charles VI (1380–1422). Stronger contacts between Italian trading cities and Eastern marts facilitated the growth in luxury by making precious stones and costly fabrics more available. In the mid fourteenth century fashions changed; women wore fitted dresses of silks and brocades, while men wore thigh-length fitted coats with buttons and padded shoulders, hose, and fanciful hats.

Although the brooch was still the main decoration for the neck, the ring brooch underwent many changes: it was sometimes set with stones in high

Schaffhausen onyx. Augustan cameo in a medieval setting, from the upper Rhine region, *ca.* 1240–1250. ALLERHEILIGENMUSEUM, SCHAFFHAUSEN

collets; the ring was sometimes broken into lobes and projections were added; it appeared as wheel- or heart-shaped. A new form, the cluster brooch, also appeared, and from it the brooch with an image in the center developed. Rings continued to be popular, and gold chains, paternosters, and pomanders were worn by men and women. Fillets and coronals were worn by women on their heads, and pendant crosses and mirrors were suspended from their belts; heraldic hat badges—probably stemming from the tradition of lead pilgrims' badges—were worn by men.

Although the court was the fountainhead of this luxury, the wealthy bourgeoisie shared in it, as did the church. There were also jewels created especially for state and royal occasions. By the end of the fourteenth century, jewelry had become a clear sign of rank, and in most of Europe, laws regulating the wearing of jewels according to status had been introduced.

In the fifteenth century the luxury of the French court spread to the Burgundian court of the Netherlands, which was closely connected with the French crown. The tradition of *émail-en-rondebosse* (enamel in the round), developed in Paris, was continued. At the invitation of Charles the Bold, the knowledge of the method of diamond cutting and of the creation of table-cut diamonds with simple faceting was brought to the court by Louis de Berchem of Bruges. This resulted in the popularity of the diamond in the second half of the fifteenth century and in the table cutting of other stones rather than the traditional simple polishing.

In the first half of the fifteenth century, brooches were still very much in vogue. They were made of gold, pearls, and precious stones, and portrayed figures, animals, and secularized religious subjects with both realism and a tender lyrical quality. The subjects were surrounded by leaves and pointed ornate forms. Probably the most famous example is the Burgundian gold brooch from about 1430–1440 (now in the Kunsthistorisches Museum, Vienna) showing two lovers holding hands in a garden, executed in *émail-en-ronde-bosse* with a diamond, a ruby, and several pearls. In this period cameos with portraits following the Roman tradition were popular, while the jewelry—rings, pendants, hat badges, and emblems—continued Franco-Burgundian techniques.

The chain was the emblem of knightly dignity, and each order had its own badge. Minor aristocracy tried to increase their influence by bestowing house orders. The various jousting societies and religious brotherhoods also had emblems.

In the second half of the fifteenth century, chains with pendants and necklaces replaced the brooch, as a consequence of the steadily falling neckline of ladies' dresses. Pilgrimages were common, and cult relics were greatly treasured. Reliquary pendants were worn around the neck or suspended from the belt. From the latter it was only a small step to the rosary, for which chalcedony and coral were fashionable. By the last quarter of the fifteenth century, burghers had earned the right to assume outward forms of aristocratic display, and goldsmiths consequently adjusted their methods to large-scale demand: silver pendants were cast or worked in repoussé. Some designs were based on Dürer engravings. Pomanders were worn as a safeguard against the plague.

Also in the second half of the fifteenth century, ladies' hair, which had been hidden beneath coifs and wimples, was uncovered. In Italy strands of pearls and precious stones were entwined in the hair, and earrings—especially with pearls—were in fashion. The jewels continued Franco-Burgundian traditions, but established a new monumentality and clarity. From about 1500 on, these Italian styles spread to the rest of Europe.

BIBLIOGRAPHY

John Beckwith, *The Art of Constantinople* (1960); Klement Benda, *Ornament and Jewellery,* I. Irwin, trans. (1967); British Museum, *Jewellery Through 7000 Years* (1976); Katharine Reynolds Brown, "Russo-Byzantine Jewellery in the Metropolitan Museum of Art," in *Apollo* (1980); Etienne Coche de la Ferté, *Collection Hélène Stathatos,* II, *Les objets byzantins et post-byzantins* (1957); O. M. Dalton, *Catalogue of Early Christian Antiquities and Objects from the Christian East* (1901); Joan Evans, *A History of Jewellery 1100–1870* (1953); Stephen Foltiny, "Catalogue of the Morgan Collection," pts. III, IV (unpublished typescript); Jean Heiniger and Ernst A. Heiniger, *The Great Book of Jewels* (1974); Hans Jantzen, *Ottonische Kunst* (1947); Peter Lasko, *The Kingdom of the Franks* (1971); Metropolitan Museum of Art, *Age of Spirituality,* Kurt Weitzmann, ed. (1977); Vera K. Ostoia, "A Ponto-Gothic Fibula," in *The Metropolitan Museum of Art Bulletin,* n.s. **11** (1953); Myriam Rosen-Ayalon, "Four Iranian Bracelets Seen in the Light of Early Islamic Art," in Richard Ettinghausen, ed., *Islamic Art in the Metropolitan Museum of Art* (1972); Marvin C. Ross, "Byzantine Goldsmith-Work" and "Byzantine Enamels," in Council of Europe, *Byzantine Art: An European Art* (1964), *Catalogue of the Byzantine and Early Medieval Antiquities in The Dumbarton Oaks Collection,* II, *Jewelry Enamels and Art of the Migration Period* (1965), and "Jewels of Byzantium," in *Arts in Virginia,* **9** (1968); Helmut Roth, *Kunst der Völkerwanderungszeit* (1979); Wolf Rudolph and Evelyn Rudolph, *Ancient Jewelry from the Collection of Burton Y. Berry* (1973); Erich Steingräber, *Antique Jewelry* (1957); Walters Art Gallery, *Jewelry, Ancient to Modern* (1979).

KATHARINE REYNOLDS BROWN

Gold brooch showing two lovers holding hands in a garden. *Émail-en-ronde-bosse* with a diamond, a ruby, and pearls, Burgundian, *ca.* 1430–1440. KUNSTHISTORISCHES MUSEUM, VIENNA

[See also **Byzantine Minor Arts; Costume, Western European; Enamel; Enamel, Basse-taille; Enamel, Cloisonné; Encolpium; Fibula; Metalsmiths, Gold and Silver.**]

GENESIOS, JOSEPH, a Byzantine writer mentioned in the preface to the chronicle by Skylitzes. He is identified by common opinion with the anonymous author of the *Imperial Histories (Basileiai)* preserved only in the twelfth-century manuscript Codex Lipsiensis I.6 (fols. 248–285), to which Genesios' name was added by a later hand. The facts of Genesios' life remain unknown. The *Imperial Histories* deals with Byzantine history from 813 to 886. Written at the court of Constantine VII, the book had as its aim the whitewashing of Basil I, Constantine's grandfather, and the blackening of Michael III, whose murder he had arranged. The problem of Genesios' sources is complicated: it is still to be decided whether he drew on *Theophanes Continuatus*, whether he was the source for *Theophanes Continuatus*, or whether the works were produced independently, using texts now lost, including military tales. Genesios belonged to the group of tenth-century intellectuals interested in gathering classical heritage; he liked to insert into his text quotations from Homer, learned etymologies, and geographical considerations. In the juxtaposition of Byzantine personages with ancient heroes he consistently stresses the merits of the former.

BIBLIOGRAPHY

Josephi Genesii Regum. Libri quatuor, A. Lesmüller-Werner and I. Thurn, eds. (1978); Herbert Hunger, *Die hochsprachliche profane Literatur der Byzantiner,* I (1978), 351–354; George Huxley, "The Emperor Michael III and the Battle of Bishop's Meadow (A.D. 863)," in *Greek, Roman and Byzantine Studies,* **16** (1975); Patricia Karlin-Hayter, "Études sur les deux histoires du règne de Michael III," in *Byzantion,* **41** (1971); Alexander P. Kazhdan, "Iz istorii vizantiskoi chronographii X v.," in *Vizantiski vremennik,* **21** (1962).

ALEXANDER P. KAZHDAN

[See also **Basil I the Macedonian; Byzantine History (330–1025); Constantine VII Porphyrogenitos; Theophanes Continuatus.**]

GENGHIS KHAN (1155/1167–August 1227), the title of the founder of the Mongol empire (Mongol: *Činggis qaghan* or *Qa'an,* "universal emperor"). He was born as Temüjin of the Borjigid clan of the Mongghol tribe. His father, Yesügei Baghatur, was the nephew of Qutula, the last elected khan of the Mongols. When Temüjin was nine years old, the Tatars poisoned his father. Abandoned by the other Mongol clans, his family barely survived. As he grew older, one clan, the Tayichi'ud, fearing retaliation, captured him. He escaped and made his way to To'oril, ruler of the Kereyid. Allied in some subordinate capacity to this onetime friend of his father, Temüjin soon attracted a following. In 1196 a gathering of some of the most prestigious Mongol clans proclaimed him their overlord (some undoubtedly believing that he would be a convenient figurehead). This marked a formal breach with his *anda* (sworn brother), Jamuqa, who harbored the same imperial ambitions.

In 1198, after restoring To'oril to power, Temüjin and his nominal overlord were allies of the Chin dynasty of northern China against the Tatars. Their success gained them Chinese titles and recognition. Notwithstanding To'oril's cowardly or ambivalent conduct during an 1199 campaign against the Naiman, Temüjin maintained the alliance because he had need of the Kereyid in the war with Jamuqa. Defeating the latter in 1201–1202, the two allies then slaughtered the Tatars. Following this, Temüjin dealt with To'oril (who died in flight from his onetime protégé) and brought the Kereyid under his sole authority in 1203. The next two years witnessed the final defeat and death of old enemies: Jamuqa, the Merkid Toghto'a, and the Naiman ruler Tayang-khan. The latter's son, Küchlüg, fled to the Qara Khitai. Thus, in 1206, at a *quriltai* (congress) on the Onon River, Temüjin was proclaimed the *Činggis qaghan* of all the Mongol tribes and the steppe world at large. The latter, however, remained to be conquered, as did the surrounding sedentary states. Operations against the Chin began in 1211, some two years after the Tangut (Hsi-Hsia) had agreed to pay tribute. Peking fell in 1215.

Pursuit of Küchlüg led to the conquest of the Qara Khitai in eastern Turkistan and brought the Mongols face to face with the unstable state of the khwārizmshāh. The murder of Mongol-dispatched merchants at Otrar and subsequently of Mongol ambassadors (1218–1219) provided a suitable *causus belli.* The khwārizmshāh's resistance crumbled, and the Mongols took Bukhara, Samarkand, and Termez in 1220. A force was sent after Khwārizmshāh Muḥammad (who died in the winter of 1220–1221 on the Caspian island of Abeskun, to which he had fled) and to reconnoiter the western lands. Led by Jebe and Sübedei, its members made their way through northern Iran, Transcaucasia, the north Caucasus, and the Cuman and Rus lands, defeating the Cumano-Rus forces on the Kalka River in 1223.

Upon completing operations against Jalāl al-Dīn Mengübirdi, son of the khwārizmshāh, in Afghanistan and India, the Mongol armies finally turned homeward. Genghis Khan arrived in Mongolia in 1225 and made arrangements for a campaign against the Tanguts in 1226. He died, however, before it was completed.

BIBLIOGRAPHY

Sources. ᶜAlāᵓad-Dīn ᶜAṭāᵓ-Malik Juvainī, *Ta'rīkh-i Jahān Gushā,* M. Qazvīnī, ed., 3 vols. (1937), in English as *The History of the World-conqueror,* John Andrew Boyle, trans., 2 vols. (1958); Juzjānī, *Ṭabaqāt-i Nāsirī,* W. Nassau Lees, Mawlawis Khadim Hosain, and ᶜAbd al-Hai, eds. (1864), in English as *Ṭabaḳāt-i Nāṣirī, a General History of the Muhammadan Dynasties of Asia,* Maj. Henry G. Raverty, trans., 2 vols. (1881–1889); *Mongghol-un Nighucha Tobchiyan/ Yüan Ch'ao Pi-shih: Die geheime Geschichte der Mongolen,* Erich Haenisch, trans. and ed., 2nd ed. (1948), in French as *Histoire secrète des Mongols,* Paul Pelliot, trans. (1949), and in English as *The Secret History of the Mongols and Other Pieces,* Arthur Waley, trans. (1963); *Shêng-wu Ch'in-chêng lu: Histoire des campagnes de Genghis-khan,* Paul Pelliot and Louis Hambis, trans. (1951); *The Secret History of the Mongols,* Francis Woodman Cleaves (1982).

Studies. Emil Bretschneider, *Medieval Researches from Eastern Asiatic Sources,* 2 vols (1910); René Grousset, *L'empire mongol (Iʳᵉ phase)* (1941), and *Conqueror of the World: The Life of Chingis-Khan,* Marian McKellar and Denis Sinor, trans. (1966); Henry Desmond Martin, *The Rise of Chingis Khan and His Conquest of North China* (1950); Paul Ratchnevsky, *Činggis-khan* (1983); Denis Sinor, *Introduction à l'étude de l'Eurasie Centrale* (1963); Boris Iakovlevich Vladimirtsov, *Life of Chingis-Khan,* Prince Mirsky, trans. (1930).

PETER B. GOLDEN

[See also **Mongol Empire**.]

GENIZAH. See **Cairo Genizah**.

GENJA. See **Ganjak**.

GENNADIUS II. See **George Scholarios**.

GENOA. Built on the slopes of the Apennines, Genoa had little space to grow food and expand; but its small natural harbor atop the deepest gulf of the northwestern Mediterranean opened broad African and Asian vistas, and most of Europe was just behind the Apennines. There was potential for greatness, but it was not fully exploited before the late Middle Ages.

Actually, the pre-Roman town already was a "market center of the Ligurians" (according to Strabo), visited by Greeks and Etruscans, but not a prominent one. In the third century B.C. the Romans made it a junction of the *Via Postumia,* which reached Aquileia through the Po valley, and the *Via Aurelia,* which linked Rome with Arles along the coast. About the same time Genoa became a *municipium,* but did not match the importance of Aquileia, Arles, and other ports connected by waterways to their hinterlands. Even along the rocky Ligurian coast Genoa had to compete with Savona and Luni.

Nevertheless, when the Ostrogoths overran Italy in the fifth century, the trade of Genoa had grown enough to support a community of Jews, whom Cassiodorus protected while gently chiding them for their religious beliefs. The Lombard invasion, halted for some seventy years north of the Apennines, gave Genoa a brief chance to emerge, long before Venice, as an outpost of Byzantine civilization; in 569 Honoratus, archbishop of Milan, and many refugees flocked there. But in or about 642 King Rothari of the Lombards conquered the city and virtually reduced it to village status by razing its walls and appointing no major official to govern it; only the episcopal see, established probably in the third century, remained. Virtually isolated by the disrepair of the Roman roads, which caused most of the remaining land traffic to bypass it, and a victim of the general decline of sea trade, Genoa is hardly mentioned in the meager extant sources of the following three centuries.

A charter of 958, by which King Berengar II assured the "inhabitants of the Genoese city" of protection for their goods and respect for their customary laws, dimly reflects a community of freemen relying mainly on agriculture and fishing, and indicates a resumption of local initiative. Indeed, Muslim raids that broke through the Carolingian walls and plundered Genoa with considerable bloodshed between 930 and 935 had shocked the population into action. Rallying around their bishops, led by their urban viscounts and other minor nobles who lived in town, and sustained by a rising demographic tide, the Genoese not only redeveloped their agricultural district but also multiplied and armed their ships for defense, counteroffensive, piracy, and trade. From what must have been a crescendo of private ventures, two joint expeditions by considerable Genoese and Pisan forces (and, in the second expedition, some southern Italians as well) stand out for the quantity of booty and the breakthroughs in profitable directions: in 1015–1016 the Spanish emir al-Mujāhid was beaten at sea and expelled from Sardinia; and in 1088 Al-Mahdīya, the capital of what is present-day Tunisia, was stormed and sacked, the expedition leaving in return for commercial privileges. By that time Genoa, though not yet formally a commune, was practically an independent, self-governing state, and in all probability a more thriving commercial center than it had been in antiquity. Its ships were seen in Syria and Egypt as often as in Provence and Catalonia, "transalpine" merchants came to its market, and no natives appear to have been unfree.

Genoa's medieval peak was reached in the following two centuries; the highlights of its relentless progress are described by the extraordinarily well-informed municipal *Annals,* sponsored by the government and kept up for two centuries by prominent members of the political and economic elite. In 1154 Genoa produced the earliest extant specimen of another invaluable source: notarial minute books, reflecting through thousands of deeds and contracts every aspect and detail of social and individual life. From the thirteenth century there are political and love poems in Provençal, the chronicle and the hagiography of Bishop Jacobus da Voragine (Varazze), the popular poems of an anonymous citizen in love with his town, legal works, navigational maps, and a polyglot dictionary. Genoa was also growing and being beautified; some of its history can be read in extant Romanesque and Gothic churches, fortifications, and private houses.

The *Annals* open with eyewitness accounts of the Genoese participation in the First Crusade, which was substantial (indeed, indispensable in the siege of Jerusalem and the conquest of some seaports) and gave Genoa the first pattern of its colonial system: just enough territory to stop and trade in security and comfort, hardly any agricultural land, mere sections of seaports endowed with autonomy and tariff rebates. At the same time the commune took shape as a consolidation of voluntary associations *(compagne)* open to anyone who had any skill, money, or will to fight to contribute, but ruled by teams of annually elected consuls mostly chosen from old noble families, though nobility was never recognized as a special, privileged status. The bishop preserved only moral authority.

Some original traits persisted throughout the Middle Ages: strong religiousness but no church interference in practical matters, and a combination of irrepressible individualism, family clannishness, and propensity to co-opt any successful or promising newcomer. Commerce was the lifeblood of the community, credit was easily obtained for any business venture, sharing risks and profits was the basic purpose of a great variety of contracts.

By 1099 and for about one century thereafter, the commune of the consuls gave Genoa an unobtrusive yet efficient administration, but the families that almost monopolized the highest offices increasingly indulged in corrupt practices, such as awarding themselves tax farms at prices far below the revenue. They might have gotten away with it if they had not squabbled; but rival families fought one another across narrow streets from the tops of their towers, made truces only to break them, and eventually paralyzed an administration that had otherwise taken good care of the city's political and economic interests, of ordinary justice, and of urban development.

Genoa had extended its authority over virtually the entire Ligurian coast and the key mountain passes, thereby gaining no great resources but precious numbers of skilled sailors and craftsmen, many of whom became residents and citizens of Genoa, and all of whom were subject to draft. The new city walls, built in 1155–1158, enclosed three times the space of the earlier ones; there were open suburbs; and with the contingents of the subject territory Genoa mustered, for an expedition against Almería in 1147–1149, 12,000 infantrymen, plus horsemen and seamen to man 63 galleys and more than 100 other ships. Only Venice and possibly England at that time had the capability of organizing a seaborne expedition of that size or larger.

Although Almeria was sacked and occupied for a while, the main payoff for this and other all-out efforts lay elsewhere: it served notice that it was safer to buy Genoese friendship with commercial concessions than to face Genoese hostility. Thus the Genoese obtained combination inn-storehouses *(fondaci)* and tariff rebates all along the Mediterranean coast from Ceuta to Alexandria and Constantinople.

But the subsiding of clashes with the inhabitants of foreign ports was offset by the flaring up of fiercer conflicts with competitors for the trade of those ports; the chief rivals were the Pisans and the Venetians, who often had a head start on the Genoese. There were no such conflicts between Italian merchants (including the Genoese) who frequented the inland markets of northwestern Europe, such as the Fréjus or the Champagne fairs; travel inland could not be protected by the Italian fleets, and all Italian merchants had to hang together in order not to hang separately.

The demise of the consulship in 1190 was not a social revolution but an attempt to restore law and order by entrusting the supreme executive power to the podestà, an impartial arbiter annually invited from another city. But how could a passing, friendless stranger compel faction leaders to switch from compulsive indiscipline to cooperation? Greeted at first with enthusiasm and supported by drastic punishments of rebels and fugitives, the podestà was gradually undermined and discredited while the alternation of Guelphs and Ghibellines in real power drove prominent members of the losing party into exile and conspiracy with the enemies of the city.

Between 1238 and 1250, while the Guelph government plunged into an all-out war against Frederick II (and simultaneously provided Louis IX with ships and credits for the Egyptian crusade), Ghibelline exiles led imperial fleets on insidious attacks against Genoa and in support of Ligurian ports that had rebelled against it. The Guelphs won the war, readmitted the exiles, and reaped the greatest part of both legitimate and illegal profits in a wave of prosperity that followed. Misgovernment had not arrested economic expansion, especially in relatively new directions and including new immigrants, such as internal trade in western Europe, local and international banking, woolmaking and shipbuilding for export, and other crafts. But a recession that followed the postwar boom precipitated an insurrection of lower- and middle-class elements supported by ambitious Ghibelline nobles. Early in 1257 a rich bourgeois merchant, Guglielmo Boccanegra, was acclaimed "captain of the people" for a term of ten years.

Boccanegra used his extensive powers to clean up the financial mess left by the commune of the podestà, to undertake projects joining aesthetics with usefulness, and to give craft guilds some political leverage. By concluding an alliance with Michael Palaiologos in 1261, on the eve of the reconquest of

Constantinople, he placed the Genoese in the same privileged position the Venetians had enjoyed for centuries. But the Guelph nobility, which had never disarmed, forced him out in 1262. Eight disastrous years of restored podestà government led in 1270 to a new formula: two captains of the people chosen from the two most powerful Ghibelline families (Doria and Spinola) and ruling jointly, with the collaboration of various bodies representing (to some extent) nearly all citizens.

Operative for thirty years, this peculiar hereditary diarchy did not adequately reflect the openness of the Genoese society in an age of accelerated economic growth, but its combination of authority and consent was the best government medieval Genoa had. In 1293 the taxable traffic of wares through the port peaked at an estimated value of nearly 4 million pounds, more than the estimated export traffic of all English ports and more than the revenue of Philip the Fair in the same year. The fall of the crusaders' states had entailed the loss of the oldest Genoese "colonial" footholds, but it was amply compensated by gains in Corsica, Sardinia, the Greek islands, Pera (a suburb of Constantinople), and the Black Sea coasts. Moreover, Genoese ships extended their routes in the Atlantic northward to England, southward to Morocco and the Canary Islands; and they inflicted crushing defeats on their Pisan and Venetian rivals.

Political stability was again broken after 1300 by the insurgency of Guelph nobles (Grimaldi, Fieschi), but private initiative found new, immense outlets as the Mongols changed from dreadful foes to precious friends. From Caffa, Trebizond, and other Black Sea ports the Genoese fanned north into Russia, Romania, and Poland, south into Anatolia and Iran, then east into Turkistan and thence to India and China. Only the greatest merchant families—for instance, the Zaccaria and the Gentile—had enough capital and connections to spread their business throughout the new frontier areas; but the colonial society offered room at the top to daring adventurers, ambitious craftsmen, naturalized foreigners, even emancipated slaves. The groundswell reached Genoa itself: in 1339 a revolution brought to power as doge for life Simone Boccanegra, Guglielmo's grandnephew, and excluded noblemen from eligibility for that office. Unlike the Venetian doge (a nobleman surrounded by noblemen) or the Genoese captains of the people (noblemen expected to be fair to the "people"), the Genoese doge was to be a man of the middle—rich enough not to be intimidated by noblemen, "popular" enough to understand the problems of the poor.

The new arrangement prevailed, with interruptions, until 1527, but can hardly be called a success. Very few doges "for life" died in office; some lasted less than a year, one just a few hours. None was a noble, but soon two popular families, Adorno and Fregoso, monopolized the dogeship, lived like princes, and in their rivalries showed even more propensity than the old noble captains to offer keys and sovereignty of Genoa to a foreign ruler (usually a duke of Milan or a king of France). When this happened, the commune often found itself forced to serve the foreign ruler's political interests, which might run counter to those of Genoa, or else to revolt against him—an action that, even when it succeeded, involved a great expenditure of money and blood.

Nor was a return to independence under a native doge always welcome: the government's irresponsible behavior was forfeiting whatever loyalty and affection the citizens might have felt toward it. More and more accustomed to fend for themselves, the greater noble and popular families in Genoa revived in a modified form the private voluntary associations that had preceded and engendered the commune, filled them with relatives and clients, and used them as political and economic pressure groups. Many Genoese colonies behaved as autonomous members of a federation, sometimes adopting policies opposed to those of the motherland. A growing number of enterprising Genoese accepted service with the rulers of Castile, Portugal, France, England, Hungary, Poland, and even the Ottoman sultan. By the fifteenth century almost the only reliable supporter of the Genoese government was the powerful Banco San Giorgio, formed in 1405 by the creditors of the state and hence committed to its preservation.

Nevertheless, the problems of Genoa must be seen in the light of the overall European depression and incomplete recovery of the late fourteenth and fifteenth centuries: the plagues that turned the demographic tide from flow to ebb, and other ecological troubles; the closing of the eastern frontier owing to the collapse of the Mongols and the advance of the Ottoman Turks; the Hundred Years War and other general conflicts, none of which were under Genoese control. When Simone Boccanegra became doge, business connections of some Genoese merchants stretched from the Thames to the Grand Canal of China; ten years later Asia Minor and southern Russia were the easternmost points accessible, and soon

the Hundred Years War would transform the Atlantic into a battlefield. After eliminating the Pisans as serious competitors in the Battle of Meloria (1284), the Genoese faced the rising power of the Catalans, who, backed by the king of Aragon, wrested Sardinia from them.

In Genoa as elsewhere, trouble had been brewing earlier, but the watershed between growth and decline was in 1346: the city walls were expanded for the last time in the Middle Ages, but the population, which had been close to 100,000, soon afterward tumbled to about half as much; the Guelph rebels were ousted from the Genoese stronghold of Monaco, but they soon came back, and for good; the Mongols of Russia failed to conquer the Genoese stronghold of Caffa, but the defenders caught the plague from the besiegers, and their ships imported it to Genoa. From then on, based at Chios, Pera, and Caffa, the overseas Genoese fought a brave holding war to preserve and extend their eastern European trade; but the Turkish conquest of Constantinople in 1453 entailed the loss of Pera and, in 1475, of Caffa, while Chios, through a heavy tribute, bought a lease on life until 1566. Chronically rebellious Corsica, which was precariously held until 1768, was hardly an asset.

Colonies, however, were not indispensable. Great exporters of alum ever since Benedetto Zaccaria obtained the Phokaia mines from Michael Palaiologos in 1264 and again, when a Genoese private expedition recovered the mines in 1346, the Genoese continued to control that trade after the mines were seized by the Turks. What tended to depress their commerce was not so much the loss of bases of their own or the revocation of fiscal exemptions they had previously enjoyed, as the general depression of markets and shortage of cash. The latter drove them more deeply into a field that they had tended to neglect: banking and exchange. They also gave greater impulsion to the silk industry, started in Genoa when raw silk was easily available from China and Turkistan, and this led the Genoese to develop raw silk production in the kingdom of Granada. Above all, they transferred their investments from the Levant to the Iberian peninsula, an underdeveloped part of the West that responded favorably to their entrepreneurship. Nor was entrepreneurship restricted to the richest merchants and bankers. One young Genoese of a working-class family tried his skills in the Iberian peninsula as a seaman, cartographer, and sugar trader. His name was Cristoforo Colombo.

GENTILE DA FABRIANO

BIBLIOGRAPHY

George Ioan Brătianu, *Recherches sur la commerce génoise dans la Mer Noire au XIIIe siècle* (1929); Teofilo O. de Negri, *Storia di Genova* (1968); Luciano Grossi Bianchi and Ennio Poleggi, *Una città portuale del medioevo: Genova nei secoli X–XVI* (1979); Jacques Heers, *Gênes au XVe siècle* (1961); David Herlihy, Robert S. Lopez, and Vsevolod Slessarev, eds., *Economy, Society, and Government in Medieval Italy; Essays in Memory of Robert L. Reynolds* (1969); Benjamin Z. Kedar, *Merchants in Crisis* (1976); Robert S. Lopez, *Storia delle colonie genovesi nel Mediterraneo* (1938), and *Su e giù per la storia di Genova* (1975); Camilo Manfroni, *Genova* (1929); Harry A. Miskimin, David Herlihy, and Avram L. Udovitch, *The Medieval City* (1977); Società Ligure di Storia Patria, Genova, *Atti* (1858–); Università degli Studi di Genova, Istituto di Paleografia e Storia Medievale, *Fonti e studi* (1958–); Vito Vitale, *Breviario della storia di Genova* (1955).

ROBERT S. LOPEZ

[See also **Guelphs and Ghibellines; Italy in the Fourteenth and Fifteenth Centuries; Pisa; Podestà; Ships and Shipbuilding, Mediterranean; Venice.**]

GENTILE DA FABRIANO (*ca.* 1370/1380–1427) was born Gentile di Niccolò di Massio, at Fabriano; he died at Rome. An esteemed and active painter, Gentile received important commissions in the Marches, Venice, Brescia, Perugia, Fabriano, Siena, and Florence. Established in the Florentine painters' guild by 1422, he dated his *Adoration of the Magi* (now in the Uffizi) May 1423. Although his chronology is difficult to establish, the *Madonna and Child with Sts. Nicholas, Catherine of Alexandria, and a Donor* (Gemäldegaleries, Berlin-Dahlem) and the *Coronation of the Virgin* (in the Brera, Milan) are considered early works. His *Madonna and Child with Sts. Julian and Lawrence* (Frick Collection, New York), surely dated after the Uffizi *Adoration*, and his *Madonna and Child* fresco (now partially destroyed), dated 1425 (the Duomo, Orvieto), are later works. The origins of his style are problematic. Altichiero may have been a source. His later work demonstrates an original and talented mind, absorbing the ideas of Masaccio and Masolino. Throughout his career Gentile maintained a sumptuous and decorative style that found great favor throughout Italy.

BIBLIOGRAPHY

Keith Christiansen, *Gentile da Fabriano* (1981).

ADELHEID M. GEALT

GEOFFREY OF MONMOUTH

Madonna and Child with Two Saints. Gentile da Fabriano, *ca.* 1425. COPYRIGHT THE FRICK COLLECTION, NEW YORK

GEOFFREY OF MONMOUTH (*ca.* 1100–1155) or Galfridus Monemutensis, called Galfridus Arturus in five charters. His birthplace is unknown, but his constant preoccupation with Caerleon-on-Usk, about twenty miles southwest of Monmouth, suggests some family connection there. A member of the secular clergy, he became prior of the Abbey of Monmouth about 1125, an Augustinian canon of St. George's at Oxford, where he was teaching as a *magister* (*ca.* 1129), and in 1152 bishop of St. Asaph (North Wales), where he never resided because the diocese was in the hands of rebellious Welsh. He died in 1155, probably at Llandaff (Glamorganshire, South Wales).

His first work, the *Prophetiae* (or *Libellus*) *Merlini*, written at the request of his superior, Alexander, bishop of Lincoln, was begun by 1130 or shortly thereafter and completed prior to the end of 1135. Although it contains prophecies of the legendary Welsh prophet-wizard Myrddin in which Christian and pagan elements are blended, much of the material in this work appears to be original with Geoffrey, notwithstanding his claim to have translated the prophecies from the Welsh. A residue nevertheless seems to go back to the *Armes Brydein* (The omen of Britain), dated about 930; further evidence of borrowing can be found in the work of Gerald of Wales (Giraldus Cambrensis), though that writer describes two separate Merlins in his *Itinerarium Cambriae* (2.7). Native tradition is also found in a work attributed to John of Cornwall, composed between 1154 and 1156; both he and Geoffrey seem to have drawn independently from a common source.

Geoffrey's *Prophetiae,* originally an independent work, was eventually incorporated into his *Historia regum Britanniae* as book seven. The prophecies were treated as serious history in many countries; Wace rejected them as unintelligible, but three early French translations were subsequently incorporated into some manuscripts of his writings. (Layamon must have had such an inflated manuscript at his disposal since he translates the prophecies, though they are dispersed throughout his work); in addition, the *Prophetiae* were translated into Welsh, and the monk Gunnlaugr Leifsson (*d. ca.* 1218) also translated them into Icelandic under the title *Merlinússpá* (this metric poem was incorporated into the miscellany known as *Hauksbók,* where it appears inserted into the prose translation of the *Historia*). Together with the *Historia,* the prophecies were translated into Middle French by Jean Wauquelin as late as 1444.

Geoffrey's main work, the twelve books that comprise the *Historia regum Britanniae,* was obviously completed very soon after the demise of King Henry I on 1 December 1135, since he dedicated it to Robert, earl of Gloucester, the chief supporter of Matilda, Henry's daughter and designated heir. Yet, on account of the rapidly changing political scene that characterized the following years, the original dedication has been altered in many manuscripts: some contain the names of both Robert and Stephen of Blois, while others omit Robert's name, replacing it with Stephen's. After 1138, when Robert severed ties with Stephen, Geoffrey obviously looked to Stephen for preferment. In all dedications of the work, however, Geoffrey claims that it is merely his Latin translation of "a very old book in the British language"

that had been given to him by Walter, archdeacon of Oxford, by whom he had been befriended.

The *Historia* contains stories of the deeds of all the kings of Britain, from Brutus, the great-grandson of the Trojan Aeneas, to Cadwallader, who, harassed with plague, famine, civil dissension, and never-ending invasion from the Continent, finally abandoned Britain to the Saxons in the seventh century. According to Geoffrey, Walter had brought the book "ex Britannia," a statement that seems to refer to Brittany since he also writes "Armoricum regnum quod nunc Britannia dicitur" ("the kingdom of Armorica, which is now called [Brittany?]"), not to speak of the importance he accords to Caradocus, the legendary founder of Brittany. These considerations all point to the possibility that Geoffrey was of Breton extraction. It is quite possible that Geoffrey had in mind a lost work called *Historia britannica,* which may very well be represented by the fragment of a text written early in the tenth century in the Breton county of Léon that its modern editor has entitled the *Livre des faits d'Arthur.* Some elements of Geoffrey's work are also found in the *Vita Goeznouei* (of which only the rhymed prologue is preserved), dated 1019. Geoffrey's avowed purpose in composing his magnum opus was "to provide the descendants of the Britons with a history of their race dating from the earliest times" (J. S. P. Tatlock). Another point brought out by the work is that all the king's subjects, despite their race, were kindred, since both Celts and French could, like the Romans, trace their lineage to Trojan exiles (Geoffrey conveniently ignores the Anglo-Saxons). This concept applied equally well to the subjects of Henry I, Matilda, or Stephen.

Books 9–11 of Geoffrey's work, containing the stories of Merlin and King Arthur, are the best known. Nennius clearly provided the material for Arthur's battles with the Saxons. Geoffrey also owes to this chronicler a list of British cities, although in the *Historia* this information is dispersed throughout his narrative, as well as the attempt to synchronize events in Britain with those of other lands. In addition, he seems to have exploited the *Annales Cambriae,* a collection of Welsh pedigrees, as well as the work of contemporary historians, especially William of Malmesbury. Geoffrey embellished each story with details not given by other historians, affording additional proof that he had sources of information they did not have at their disposal. The name of Arthur's shield (Pridwen), of his sword (Caliburnus), and of his lance (Ron) were derived from

Welsh sources, especially from *Culhwch and Olwen* and the *Spoils of Annwfn,* while the idea of introducing Modred might have been inspired by the *Annales Cambriae.* It is hard to recall another medieval work of any length containing such foresighted classical symmetry, having the story of Arthur as its high point: this recalls the structure of a good tragedy. Geoffrey conceived of history as a pageant of striking personalities, moving forward to the greatest personality of them all: Arthur, son of Uther Pendragon and Ygerna. With the passing of the great king, Geoffrey's interest seems to die away, as, indeed, does that of the modern reader. Geoffrey employs a plain style with few deviations from classical Latin, though his dedications especially affect a more pompously rhetorical style.

Besides the so-called "Vulgate" text, which is reproduced in most of the more than 200 manuscripts, there exists a "Variant Version" that was clearly written a few years earlier. This is too different from the Vulgate to be a first draft of Geoffrey's *Historia.* Rather, it has to be the work of an anonymous author—perhaps the book that Walter allegedly brought back "ex Britannia," which Geoffrey then greatly exploited. Wace must have seen such a manuscript, since some of his information comes from this text. A second, still unedited Variant Version from the late twelfth century summarizes Geoffrey's text. Yet other versions were made, varying in length from the *Gesta regum Britanniae* (*ca.* 1235), usually credited to Guillaume de Rennes, to brief summaries.

Although the *Historia* was already recognized as historically untrustworthy in the twelfth century, the work had a tremendous success throughout the Middle Ages. It was immediately translated, first into French by Gaimar then, eclipsing the former, by Wace. Even after Wace, it was translated at least five other times: (1) the *Munich Brut* survives in a single excellent manuscript from northern France (after 1200); the text, in a mixed dialect, was probably composed by a resident of England in the second half of the twelfth century. The text runs from *Historia* 1.2 to 2.15 in 2,039 octosyllabic couplets; its abrupt ending seems to suggest that a longer work was intended. (2) The thirteenth-century Harleian MS 1605 (only partially published) is based on the work of a Picard author of the late twelfth century, and covers *Historia* 5.1 to 10.5, including most of Merlin's prophecies. (3) The lost *Bekker-Fragment* (8.9 to 8.12) treated the acquisition and dedication of Stonehenge; the work seems to have been written in

the late twelfth century perhaps by one of the non-Norman French who came to England after the Conquest. (4) The British Museum MS Royal 13.A.xxi (unpublished), by an Anglo-Norman author, dates from the thirteenth or fourteenth century and covers *Historia* 1.3–8.19 in octosyllabic couplets; the fragment may well be from the missing Geoffrey-part of Gaimar's *Estorie des Englés.* (5) The Harleian MS 4733, a late-thirteenth-century fragment of little literary merit, is the work of an Anglo-Norman author of around 1200; its 250 lines cover *Historia* 9.1–4. Furthermore, a translation of the *Historia* forms the first part of an Anglo-Norman chronicle in prose entitled *Le Brut d'Engleter(r)e* or *Les chroniques d'Engleter(r)e* that originally ended with the year 1066, but is continued in the extant manuscripts to 1272, 1307, or even 1133 (all unpublished); most episodes seem to be based on Wace's *Brut,* but some are directly translated from the *Historia.* The chronicle has been adapted into Middle English and medieval Latin.

Wace, on the other hand, was freely (with the *Prophecies*) translated into Middle English by Layamon *ca.* 1200 and even later by another author (anonymous, still unpublished); the fourteenth-century verse chronicle by Robert of Gloucester, as well as works by Thomas Bek of Castleford and Robert Mannyng, are based on Middle English translations of Geoffrey (or Wace) for the earlier parts of their histories. There are also a large number of manuscripts in Welsh, the oldest from *ca.* 1200, of which a copy, the so-called Dingestow Court Manuscript, dates from *ca.* 1300; these manuscripts have been the source of at least five separate translations (often in these manuscripts, the *Brut y Tywysogion* [or *Chronicle of the Princes*] follows the translation). A free rendering into Old Norse under the title of *Breta sǫgur,* with many additions, omissions, and changes, was probably made at the Norwegian court in the mid thirteenth century, or possibly even earlier; Wincentry Kadłubek (bishop of Cracow in 1208) also took Geoffrey as a model for his *Chronica Polonorum,* adapting some material from the *Historia* to his own use, as Shakespeare did much later for his *Cymbeline* and *King Lear.*

Later in his life, Geoffrey composed the *Vita Merlini* (dedicated to Robert de Chesney, who in 1149 became bishop of Lincoln), a poem in 1,529 hexameters about Merlin's power to foretell the future in which the author used some Celtic tales whose exact form eludes modern scholars. The verse in places rises to the level of poetry. The protagonist

Merlin is presented here as an old king, this time with a wife, Guendoloena, a sister, Ganieda, and her husband, Rodarch. The *Vita* survives as a whole in only one manuscript of the thirteenth century and seems to have exercised no great influence on later literature; however, many episodes are found in the *Merlin* by Robert de Boron (after 1200), a poem of which only the first 502 lines are preserved, but which survives in a later prose adaptation. The latter was translated at the end of the thirteenth century into Spanish and at the beginning of the fourteenth into Portuguese, and it was recorded in the fifteenth century in the *Baladro del sabio Merlin*. Around 1450 it was adapted into Middle English. Spenser (*Faerie Queene* 3.3) was inspired by certain elements of this text, and Jacob van Maerlant composed (*ca.* 1260) 10,398 lines of a poem in Middle Dutch based on the French prose version; a continuator added some 26,000 lines, not completing the work until 1326.

BIBLIOGRAPHY

Sources. All three of Geoffrey's works are in Edmond Faral, ed., *La légende arthurienne: Études et documents*, III, *Documents* (1929). See also Acton Griscom, ed., *The "Historia regum Britanniae" of Geoffrey of Monmouth* (1929); and Lewis Thorpe, trans., *The History of the Kings of Britain*, 3rd ed. (1973).

Studies. Brian Blakey, "The Harley *Brut*: An Early French Translation of Geoffrey's *Historia regum Britanniae*," in *Romania*, 82 (1961); James D. Bruce, *The Evolution of Arthurian Romance from the Beginnings down to the Year 1300*, 2nd ed., I (1928), 134–136; Edmund K. Chambers, *Arthur of Britain* (1927), 20–52; Edmond Faral, "Geoffroy de Monmouth: Les faits et les dates de sa biographie," in *Romania*, 53 (1927), and *La légende arthurienne: Études et documents*, II, *Geoffrey de Monmouth*. *La légende arthurienne à Glastonbury* (1929); Robert H. Fletcher, *The Arthurian Material in the Chronicles* (1906, repr. 1966); Acton Griscom, "The Date of Composition of Geoffrey of Monmouth's *Historia*: New Manuscript Evidence," in *Speculum*, 1 (1926); William Leckie, *The Passage of Dominion: Geoffrey of Monmouth and the Periodization of Insular History in the Twelfth Century* (1981); John E. Lloyd, "Geoffrey of Monmouth," in *The English Historical Review*, 57 (1942); Roger Sherman Loomis, ed., *Arthurian Literature in the Middle Ages* (1959); N. Lukman, "The Viking Nations and King Arthur in Geoffrey of Monmouth (–1138)," in *Classica et medievalia*, 20 (1959); John Jay Parry, "The Welsh Texts of Geoffrey of Monmouth's *Historia*," in *Speculum*, 5 (1930); John S. P. Tatlock, *Legendary History of Britain: Geoffrey of Monmouth's "Historia regum Britanniae" and Its Early Vernacular Versions* (1950), contains the best biography, 438–448; Rupert Taylor, *The Political Prophecy in England* (1911); Paul Zumthor, *Merlin le prophète: Un thème de la littérature polémique de l'historiographie et des romans* (1943).

HANS-ERICH KELLER

[See also **Arthurian Literature; Arthurian Literature, Welsh; Breta Sǫgur; Brut, the; Gaimar, Geffrei; Gerald of Wales; Historia Brittonum; Historiography, Western European; Merlínússpá; Wace.**]

GEOFFREY OF NOYERS. Probably of English origin, Geoffrey is mentioned in a thirteenth-century text as the "constructor" of the early Gothic choir of Lincoln Cathedral, begun in 1192. But since another man, a mason, is also mentioned, it is likely that Geoffrey served merely as the overseer for the project and not as the designer.

BIBLIOGRAPHY

Thomas S. R. Boase, *English Art 1100–1216* (1953), 266; James Dimock, ed., *Magna vita S. Hugonis episcopi Lincolniensis* (1864), 336–337, 412*n*; John Harvey, *English Medieval Architects* (1954), 195; James W. F. Hill, *Medieval Lincoln* (1948), 113; J. H. Parker, "On the English Origin of Gothic Architecture," in *Archaeologia*, 43 (1871).

STEPHEN GARDNER

[See also **Architect, Status of; Cathedral; Gothic Architecture.**]

GEOFFREY OF VINSAUF (Galfredus de Vinosalvo, Gaufridus Anglicus), poet and teacher of rhetoric in England in the last quarter of the twelfth and early years of the thirteenth century. Few details of his life are known. He studied in Paris and taught in "Hamton" (probably Northampton). On one occasion he accompanied a mission to Rome in the service of an English king, variously identified in the earliest manuscripts as Richard or John.

Geoffrey is best known as author of the *Poetria nova* (*ca.* 1200), an immensely popular treatise on the art of poetry written in some 2,100 hexameter lines. In it the author discusses and exemplifies techniques of invention (the choice of suitable material, either familiar or new), disposition (the ordering of events in the chosen material, together with methods of amplifying or abbreviating it to accord with the poet's new purpose), style (qualities of clarity, precision, and propriety in adapting diction and tone to the nature of the subject and the poet's intended audience, figures of speech, and modes of metaphor), memorization, and oral delivery.

While recognizing natural ability *(ingenium)* as prerequisite to a poet's success, Geoffrey is concerned more with the practical aspects of a poet's training and a reader's informed appreciation: theoretical understanding of language and composition *(ars),* diligent practice *(usus),* and the reading and imitation of great authors *(imitatio).* The major sources of his doctrine are Cicero's *De inventione,* the pseudo-Ciceronian *Rhetorica ad Herennium,* and Horace's *Ars poetica.*

Two other works on poetic composition are definitely Geoffrey's: *Documentum de modo et arte dictandi et versificandi,* a long prose treatise covering much the same material discussed in the *Poetria nova,* and *Summa de coloribus rhetoricis,* a briefer work concerned primarily with figures of speech. A number of short poems of topical and political interest, almost certainly by Geoffrey, have been published.

The large number of extant manuscripts of the *Poetria nova* (almost 200) and the appearance of several elaborate commentaries on it between the thirteenth and fifteenth centuries testify to Geoffrey's significant influence on the Latin and vernacular literatures of England and western Europe for more than three centuries.

BIBLIOGRAPHY

Sources. The *Poetria nova, Documentum,* and *Summa* are in Edmond Faral, ed., *Les arts poétiques du xiie et xiiie siècles* (1924, repr. 1962). Translations include Ernest Gallo, trans., *The "Poetria nova" and Its Sources in Early Rhetorical Doctrine* (1971); Jane Baltzell Kopp, trans., *Poetria nova,* in James Jerome Murphy, ed., *Three Medieval Rhetorical Arts* (1971); Margaret F. Nims, trans., *Poetria nova of Geoffrey of Vinsauf* (1967); Roger Parr, trans., *Documentum de modo et arte dictandi et versificandi* (1968).

Studies. Edmond Faral, "Le manuscrit 511 du Hunterian Museum," in *Studi medievali,* **9** (1936); Bruce Harbert, *A Thirteenth-century Anthology of Rhetorical Poems* (1975); Douglas Kelly, "The Theory of Composition in Medieval Narrative Poetry and Geoffrey of Vinsauf's *Poetria nova,*" in *Medieval Studies,* **31** (1969); Walter B. Sedgwick, "The Style and Vocabulary of the Latin Arts of Poetry in the Twelfth and Thirteen Centuries," in *Speculum,* **3** (1928).

MARGARET F. NIMS

[See also **Ars Poetica; Latin Literature; Rhetoric, Western European.**]

GEOFFROI D'AINAI (*d.* 1140's) (also found as Geoffroy d'Aignay), a twelfth-century French Cistercian monk of Clairvaux who directed the building of abbeys in France, Flanders, and England. In 1134–1135 he was sent by St. Bernard to England, where he assisted the monks of St. Mary's Abbey, Yorkshire, who had just left the Benedictine order, in designing a suitable Cistercian edifice. The new complex was called Fountains. Geoffroi also worked on the plans of Clairmarais in Flanders, though he did not complete the building program. It is thought that he collaborated with the architect Achard on the restoration of Clairvaux after 1133. Kenneth Conant cites Geoffroi as one of several excellent Cistercian architects working in the twelfth century. Characteristics of his style are orderly planning and a very austere, unadorned adaptation of Burgundian Gothic features. He died at Clairvaux in the 1140's.

BIBLIOGRAPHY

Marcel Aubert, *L'architecture cistercienne en France,* 2 vols. (1947), I, 97, and II, 137; Kenneth J. Conant, *Carolingian and Romanesque Architecture: 800 to 1200* (1974), 225; Marie-Anselme Dimier, *L'art cistercien hors de France* (1971), 14, 299; Sir William H. St. John Hope, *Fountains Abbey, Yorkshire* (1900), 103–117.

JENNIFER E. JONES

[See also **Achard; Architect, Status of; Architecture, Liturgical Aspects; Cathedral; Gothic Architecture.**]

GEOFFROI DE FONTAINES. See **Godfrey of Fontaines.**

GEOGRAPHY AND CARTOGRAPHY, ISLAMIC. Until modern times Islamic geographic works combined aspects of science and literature, for geography was not conceived of as a specific science with well-defined subject matter. The term "Arab" is often applied to these works, for the great majority of them were composed in Arabic, though other nationalities and even non-Muslims made important contributions.

Pre-Islamic Arab geographic knowledge was focused on Arabia and neighboring regions. General concepts and cosmological views can be best perceived from the Koran and the *Hadith,* while some concrete geographical data can be found in pre-Islamic poetry. Scientific geography, begun in Bagh-

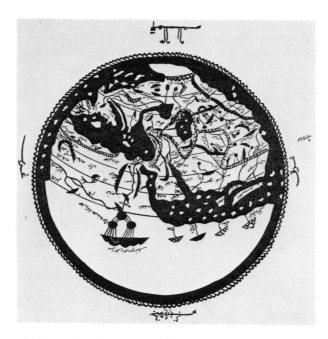

Arabic zonal world map. Copied from al-Idrīsī's map of 1154. OXFORD, BODLEIAN LIBRARY, URI MS 887

dad under the caliph al-Manṣūr (754–775) and particularly encouraged by the caliph al-Maʾmūn (813–833), started with the measurement of the degree of latitude, construction of observatories, production of maps and instruments, and especially the translation and adaptation of Indian, Iranian, and Greek geographical and astronomical treatises.

Among the Indian borrowings were the imaginary Mount Meru, the highest point on dry land directly under the North Pole, the division of the inhabited region of the earth into nine sections, and the calculation of the longitude from Ceylon, the Cupola of the Earth. From the Greeks were borrowed the limitation of the inhabited world to one quarter, the concept of the continents (Europe, Libya, Ethiopia, Scythia), and the idea of the Indian Ocean landlocked between Asia and Africa. In mathematical geography the Arabs accepted the system of seven latitudinal climes (aqālīm; sing., iqlīm) from the equator to the polar circle. Ptolemy's *Geography* was translated repeatedly; particularly influential was the version of al-Khwarizmī (ca. 820). The *Geography* reportedly included maps, but no originals survive. Iranian influences were the strongest in descriptive geography and cartography, including the method of describing the world following the four cardinal directions (beginning in the east) and the di-

vision of the earth into seven *kishwarhā* (equal geometric circles), the central one representing Iran. The lost map of al-Maʾmūn supposedly followed this pattern.

While general geographic data were often included in philosophical, astronomical, historical, and encyclopedic works, the earliest geographical treatises concentrate on such practical needs of government as topography, administrative data, commercial and postal routes, and descriptions of boundaries. In the ninth and tenth centuries this type of work evolved into a special genre called *al-Masālik wa'l-mamālik* (Routes and kingdoms), from the title of the first extant composition of this nature, by Ibn Khurdādhbih.

During the classical period of Islamic geography (ninth to eleventh centuries), two schools of descriptive geography developed. The first was the Iraqi school, so called because it often followed the Iranian system of *kishwarhā* but substituted Iraq for Iran as the center of the Islamic Empire. This school included Ibn Khurdādhbih, al-Yaʿqūbī, Ibn Rusta, Ibn al-Faqīh, and al-Masʿūdī, all of whom wrote world geographies. Al-Yaʿqūbī (d. 897) and al-Masʿūdī (d. 956) traveled extensively, but their personal experiences seem to have had little effect on their geographical concepts.

The second school was that of al-Balkhī (d. 934), whose work does not survive. Among his followers were al-Iṣṭakhrī, Ibn Ḥawqal, and al-Muqaddasī. These geographers focused on the world of Islam and attached central importance to Mecca. They introduced the concept of a country as a geographic unit and enlarged the scope of their science with elements of "human geography," discussing the languages and races of people, their occupations, customs, and religions. Firsthand observation during their travels was an important source of information for these authors, though they borrowed heavily from their predecessors. Al-Muqaddasī, the last and most original representative of this school, created the systematic foundation of Arab geography by discussing its uses and scopes, the geographic terminology, the various methods of division of the earth, and the value of empirical observation.

A distinctive characteristic of this school is its attention to cartography. Texts often seemed to follow the map, and in fact they were usually accompanied by a set of twenty-one maps: one for each of the twenty climes into which they divided Islamic lands, and one world map. Their image of the world conformed to the pre-Islamic concept of the bird-shaped land, with the "head" in China and "tail" in North Africa, surrounded by the Encircling Ocean. The shape of these maps may be round, oval, or oblong, and the orientation is to the south or east. The eastern orientation was a continuation of the old Semitic tradition, which also required placing Jerusalem in the center of the map; the Islamic maps might substitute Mecca or Baghdad at the center. These maps are very similar in character and composed of peculiarly simplified geometric shapes. They show roads and towns but give no indication of coordinates or distances; collectively they are known today as the "Atlas of Islam."

During this period the spirit of exploration and inquiry generated both active travel beyond the better-known areas of the Middle East, India, and Africa, and demand among the reading public for travel accounts. Some of these accounts were reports of authentic journeys, such as Ibn Faḍlān's diplomatic mission to the Volga region (*ca.* 921) and Ibrāhīm ibn Yaᶜqūb's journey from Spain to Germany (*ca.* 965). Others belong to the genre of ᶜajāᵓib (marvels): surviving compositions by Abū Zayd al-Sīrāfī (*ca.* 916) and Buzurg ibn Shahriyār (*ca.* 953) contain, together with factual information, semilegendary stories, including maritime tales; a few found their way into the *Thousand and One Nights* as the stories of Sinbad the Sailor. Yet, although Muslim seafarers knew the Indian Ocean well enough to sail from Malacca to southeast Africa, the formal geographical works say disappointingly little about distant areas. Moreover, the new facts were often overlooked or stubbornly fitted into the old theoretically devised patterns. It was this conservative attitude that forced practice to yield to theory and gradually led to scientific stagnation.

Unique among the late geographers of the classical period is al-Bīrūnī. Apart from his important contribution to regional geography (he described India in detail), he compared and critically evaluated the contributions to geography of the Arabs, Greeks, Indians, and Iranians. An advanced theoretician of geography and astronomy, he was also a bold and undogmatic thinker. For example, he discussed the difference in calendar between the northern and southern hemispheres and argued that, contrary to the prevailing views, life was possible south of the equator; he alone among Muslim geographers conjectured that the Indian Ocean communicated with the Atlantic.

Outside the Arabic tradition of Islamic geography, Persian scholarship, represented by the anonymous *Ḥudūd al-ᶜālam* (Regions of the world, 982), was influenced by the work of al-Iṣṭakhrī, which had been translated into Persian. Some of al-Bīrūnī's works were originally written in, or later translated into, Persian. His contemporary Nāṣir-i Khusraw (*d.* 1060) wrote in Persian, describing his travels in Egypt and Arabia. Generally derivative of Arabic authorities, the works in Persian were produced mainly in Iran, central Asia, and India.

The twelfth to sixteenth centuries represent a period of little conceptual development, with innovation mostly reflected in the emergence of new specialized genres: geographical dictionaries, cosmographies, *ziyārāt,* and maritime literature. The largest and most famous geographical dictionary is that of Yāqūt (*d.* 1229), who presents a great number of place-names, listed alphabetically and accompanied by a wealth of geographical and historical information. This method, and much of his information, were borrowed by the most prominent cosmographer, al-Qazwīnī (*d.* 1283), whose works remain popular even with modern Arab readers. Specifically Islamic variations of the dictionary genre were the guides to religious places or pilgrimage centers, the *ziyārāt;* the most famous of these is by al-Harawī (*d.* 1215). Of course, travel literature continued to appear. Of particular significance for Arabia was the work of Ibn al-Mujāwir (*ca.* 1230); for the Near East, that of Ibn Jubayr (*ca.* 1217); for Europe, Abū Ḥāmid al-Andalusī (*d.* 1170). The most famous traveler was Ibn Baṭṭūṭa, whose journeys took him from his native Maghrib to Arabia, sub-Saharan Africa, Europe, central Asia, Indian, Indonesia, and China.

In the area of world geography the highest achievement was attained by al-Idrīsī, who worked at the Norman court in Sicily and used data produced by the Islamic and European geographers and travelers. His *Nuzhat al-mushtāq fī 'khtirāq al-āfāq* (Entertainment for one who wants to travel the world) was conceived as a description of a large map, each chapter detailing itineraries within one of seventy sections illustrated by a regional map. He innovatively subdivided each of the seven Greek climes into ten longitudinal sections, starting from the west. Although some of the information was incorrect or outdated even at the time, as a universal geography his work remained unsurpassed in the Islamic world, and among mapmakers al-Idrīsī's cartographic tradition survived as late as the sixteenth century. His system influenced Ibn Saᶜīd (*d:* 1274), who supplemented his description with the coordinates of many locations; his map shows the Indian Ocean somewhat realistically for the first time.

Marine geography for the most part remained outside the mainstream of Islamic scholarship. Only works of Aḥmad ibn Mājid (second half of the fifteenth century) and Sulaymān al-Mahrī (first half of the sixteenth century) survive. Among them are sailing manuals and nautical instructions, often in verse, for the Mediterranean and the Red Sea, but particularly for the Indian Ocean, where the Arabs maintained their superiority until the arrival of the Portuguese. A number of astronomical devices were used for navigation; the existence of sea charts is reported, but none remain. It is also often stated, without sufficient justification, that Aḥmad ibn Mājid had been the pilot of Vasco da Gama from East Africa to India.

The development of Ottoman geography began in the fourteenth century. At first it popularized translations of Arab cosmographies; later translations were also made from Persian. After the sixteenth century, Ottoman geography was continuously influenced by European scholarship, especially in cartography. A specifically Ottoman genre was represented by the campaign itineraries of the Turkish sultans.

All the main genres of Islamic geographical literature had been set by the fourteenth century. Although travel accounts and regional studies produced new data, systematic innovation ceased. The new cosmographies, often of inferior quality, simply rehashed outdated information. Use of others' material without credit and indiscriminate compilation prevailed, and pre-Islamic concepts and mythological motifs continued to fascinate the reader. Especially popular among these were the Encircling Ocean surrounding the landmass, and Mount Qāf in turn surrounding the ocean; the Fortunate Isles and the Columns of Hercules as the western boundary of the inhabited earth; the "Wall of Alexander" separating the civilized world from Gog and Magog; the number seven (seven climes, seven kishwarhā, seven seas). The Indian Ocean, so well known to navigators, continued to be perceived as the inner lake, in conformity with the Ptolemaic system, and the lands south of the equator were pronounced too hot for habitation despite evidence to the contrary provided by the numerous travelers.

It is thus obvious that while Islamic geography faithfully preserved ancient and foreign geographical concepts, it failed to produce its own form or to develop a viable synthesis of the old forms with the

new information. Its chief value, then, is not in the field of theory, but in the facts it accumulated, particularly because the total volume of preserved data is very considerable. Its significance goes beyond geography into other areas of knowledge, at least in part because of the prevalence of descriptive geography. Some scholars, such as al-Masʿūdī, treated geography as part of history, and it was also customary to discuss other sciences in the introductions to geographical works. For some parts of the world, or certain periods of their history, medieval Islamic geographers provide major, if not the only, sources of information. Their works are thus invaluable and often indispensable to the study of history and historical ethnography, as well as historical geography and the history of science.

BIBLIOGRAPHY

Studies. S. Maqbul Ahmad, "Djughrāfiyā," in *The Encyclopaedia of Islam,* II (1965), 575–587; Nafis Ahmad, *Muslim Contribution to Geography* (1947); Leo Bagrow, *History of Cartography* (1964); Edgar Blochet, "Contribution à l'étude de la cartographie chez les musulmans," in *Bulletin de l'Académie d'Hippone,* **29** (1898); G. Ferrand, *Introduction à l'astronomie nautique arabe* (1928); Hadi Hasan, *A History of Persian Navigation* (1928); George F. Hourani, *Arab Seafaring* (1951); George H. T. Kimble, *Geography in the Middle Ages* (1968); I. Yu. Krachkovsky, *Arabskaya geograficheskaya literatura* (1957); J. H. Kramers, "Djughrāfiyā," in the *Encyclopaedia of Islam, Supplement* (1934–1938), 63–75, and "Geography and Commerce," in T. W. Arnold and Alfred Guillaume, eds., *The Legacy of Islam* (1943), and "La littérature géographique classique des musulmans," in his *Analecta Orientalia,* I (1954); Konrad Miller, *Mappae arabicae,* 5 vols. (1926–1930); André Miquel, *La géographie humaine du monde musulman jusqu'au milieu du 11ᵉ siècle,* 2 vols. (1967–1975); M. Reinaud, *Introduction générale à la géographie des orientaux* (1848); K. Schoy, "Geography of the Muslims in the Middle Ages," in *Geographical Review,* **14** (1924).

Sources. The following have been selected for the value of the commentary, apparatus, or the general information: S. Maqbul Ahmad, *India and the Neighbouring Territories as Described by the Sharīf al-Idrīsī* (1960); M. Bittner and W. Tomaschek, *Die topographischen Capitel des Indischen Seespiegels Moḥît* (1897); Régis Blachère and Henri Darmaun, *Extraits des principaux géographes arabes* (1957); G. Ferrand, *Relations de voyages et textes géographiques arabes, persans et turks relatifs à l'Extrême-Orient du VIIIᵉ au XVIIIᵉ siècles* (1913–1914); Hamilton A. R. Gibb, trans., *The Travels of Ibn Baṭṭūta,* 3 vols. (1958–1971); Yūsūf Kamāl, *Monumenta cartographica Africae et Aegypti* (1926–1951); A. P. Kovalevsky, *Kniga Ahmeda ibn Fadlana o yego puteshestvii na Volgu v 921–922 gg.*

(1956); T. Lewicki, *Żródła arabskie dó dziejów Słowiańsz-czyzny* (1956–1977); Vladimir Minorsky, *Ḥudūd al-ᶜAlam, 'The regions of the world'; a Persian geography, 372 A.H.–982 A.D.* (1937); T. A. Shumovsky, *Tri neizvest-nye lotsii Aḥmada ibn Mājida* (1957); Gerald R. Tibbets, *Arab Navigation in the Indian Ocean Before the Coming of the Portuguese* (1971); A. Zeki Validi Togan, *Al-Bīrū-nī's Picture of the World* (1941).

M. A. TOLMACHEVA

[See also **Baṭṭūṭa, Ibn; Bīrūnī, al-; Idrīsī, al; Maᶜmūn, al-; Masᶜūdī, al-; Navigation: Indian Ocean, Red Sea; Science, Islamic.**]

GEOGRAPHY AND CARTOGRAPHY, WEST-ERN EUROPEAN.

Although its name did not change, geography in the Middle Ages made the same progression as did alchemy toward chemistry and astrology toward astronomy. An examination of medieval geography is complicated by the necessity of surveying a large area over a long time period, involving divergent cultures and traditions. Moreover, modern interest (which dictates available materials) has concentrated on specific problems and neglected others. What follows is an attempt, within small compass, to survey the whole while stressing aspects that might interest those peering into the Middle Ages from the vantage point of varied disciplines.

Throughout the Middle Ages, the notion of a geocentric universe was generally accepted. Even people who doubted the sphericity of the earth considered the earth focal. To those who believed in a spherical earth and believed that hell was within the

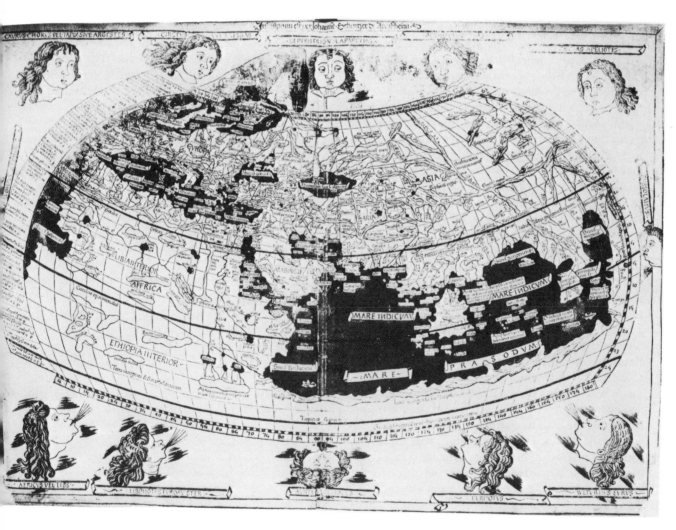

Map of the world. From Claudius Ptolemy's *Cosmographia*, 1482, printed in Ulm. PHOTOGRAPH COURTESY OF THE BRITISH LIBRARY

earth, the universe had to be hell-centered, at least physically.

A thirteenth-century scholar in any of the nascent universities could learn in the pages of *De imagine mundi,* which had been in circulation for at least a century, that the universe was spherical and somewhat analogous to an egg, and that the earth was a small part of the universe, comparable to a drop of grease in the center of the yolk. Although hell, contained within the earth, must have already been rather crowded, there was still much room in heaven. The spherical surface of the earth was usually divided into five climatic zones: two temperate, one torrid, and two frigid. Some savants, however, considered the Latin word *orbis* to signify "wheel" rather than "sphere," and it is not always possible to know which is meant. Similar confusion existed in reference to climatic zones. Isidore of Seville, whose works continued to be used throughout the Middle Ages, conceived of climatic circles placed flat upon the surface of a wheel-shaped flat earth. His confused interpretation of classical texts became rarer in the High Middle Ages, but persisted.

On the whole, the concept of a spherical or wheel-shaped earth and the concomitant concept of encircling climatic zones prevailed and filtered down to an increasingly large number of people, due primarily to the rise of the middle class, many members of which received at least a modicum of schooling. One sign of this broader educational base, apparent by the twelfth century, was the proliferation of handbooks and encyclopedic works in Latin, many with sections devoted to geography. Unfortunately, the most accurate and scholarly works were not always the most popular. Some encyclopedias owed their popularity to being comfortably behind the times. Texts also began to appear in vernacular languages. One of the most notable of these was *L'image du monde,* based on the *De imagine mundi.* Recast, rather than directly translated, into French toward the middle of the thirteenth century, *L'image du monde* upheld the concept of a spherical earth and maintained its popularity in succeeding centuries. In it, the land in one quarter of the sphere (Europe, Asia, Africa, and some islands) was inhabited. The sea ran around and through the land, reappearing as rivers. Salt seawater, in running through the land, became pure, and began its rounds again.

Traditional concepts were increasingly challenged by observation and new instruments. But medieval readers, when furnished with scientifically correct information, frequently accepted it intellec-

tually while ignoring it in their normal thought processes, just as everyday parlance still insists that the sun rises and sets. Some medieval thinkers might try to find a compromise between the scientific and the traditional. Abelard, for example, tried in *Expositio in Hexaemeron* to reconcile a spherical earth with a disk surrounded by the ocean. "Just as any globe," he explained, "may be placed in water so that one part of it rises above the water, even so the globe of the earth rests in the waters so that the sea is in contact with one side of it and pours through its veins, whence springs and rivers take their rise." Alexander Neckam (*d.* 1217), on the other hand, presented the world as a sphere of earth and water in *De naturis rerum,* but also accepted the biblical view that the ocean was the "grave of the waters," enclosed by land. Rivers and streams flowed continually into the ocean. Why, therefore, did the ocean not keep getting higher? Neckam's answer was simple; it did. In fact, it was already higher than the earth, and only the will of God kept back the flood. "The sea is truly higher than the shore line, *ut visus docet.*" His empirical statement might justifiably be translated: "As any fool can plainly see."

Another concept that, to the medieval geographer, demanded considerable adjustment between tradition and observation was the explanation of tides. Various theories were propounded, suggesting as causal Ginnungagap, the abyss, bifurcating equatorial currents, the number seven (following Macrobius), and the influence of the moon. By the thirteenth century, lunar influence was the usual explanation, though there was an undercurrent of suspicion that a deep, breathing abyss was somehow involved. Gerald of Wales, who wrote the *Topographia Hibernica,* includes data indicating that he, or his source, had spent time in observation and had reached the conclusion that the moon was indeed responsible. Long before Gerald, Bede had observed the tides at Jarrow and concluded that the moon was involved.

Whatever its merits, Abelard's floating earth, when applied to cartography, justified placing north at the top, and around 1187 Neckam provided the first undisputed reference to the compass, which also pointed toward a cartographical north. A century later the compass was still looked upon with suspicion. Dante's friend Brunetto Latini visited Roger Bacon at Oxford and, being informed about the properties and function of a compass, was unimpressed, sure that sailors would never trust such an instrument at sea. Yet the compass was quietly transforming practical sailing and cartography. Earlier medieval maps had been oriented by placing east at the top. With the introduction of the compass, Western cartographers took their cue from the needle and placed north at the top. That maps based on the pre-Christian Ptolemy also were north-oriented may explain some of the enthusiasm that greeted their rediscovery. The compass also made possible a more exact science of mapmaking after magnetic deviation was understood. The astrolabe, which was already in service, and the quadrant, which was introduced about 1275, made possible an improved cartographical depiction by making navigation more precise if not more far-flung.

Scholars had to reconcile classical or simply fanciful maps with the new knowledge that sailors were bringing. Roger Bacon, whose opinions are usually cited as influencing Columbus (through Pierre d'Ailly and Aeneas Silvius Piccolomini, later Pope Pius II), was in the vanguard when he recommended an accurate and complete survey of the known world. He designed a world map to accompany his recommendations. This map has been lost, as has a similar map produced by Albertus Magnus. Bacon believed that the inhabited world stretched over more than half of the east-west circumference of the earth. His belief was seemingly confirmed by the Peutinger map (or table), apparently a thirteenth-century copy of an apparently third-century Roman original (which itself may have been a copy). Though not intended to represent the earth's surface graphically, this map emphasized the east-west expanse of the known landmass. It is on a parchment roll over twenty-one feet long and no more than thirteen inches wide. Most maps show little concern for accuracy and the incorporation of new knowledge. The Psalter map, the Hereford map, and the Ebstorf map, all dating from the thirteenth century, have been characterized as "illustrated medieval romances" that do not reveal any advances in geographical knowledge, though they must have influenced the thinking of large numbers of people.

Nor was accuracy helped by maps based on an approach to cartography such as that of Hugh of St. Victor, whose reading of the Bible was combined with mystical projection. The world was a macrocosm of Noah's Ark, which had a rectangular base. There was also biblical reference to the "four corners" of the earth. Hugh drew a rectangle and then an oval around it, touching each of the four corners. The segment of the oval to the east of the rectangle contained paradise; that to the west, the place of universal resurrection. At the Last Judgment the saved would go to the south; the damned, to the north. Hugh's cartography seemed to confirm that the inhabited known world stretched farthest from east to west. There was also increasing talk of landmasses that, though not inhabited, were inhabitable. Hugh provided a use and an explanation for the habitable but unreachable region below the equator. He thought of himself as standing at the end of the world at the end of centuries, and expected that soon the quick and the dead would make their spiritual passage across the Atlantic to the Last Judgment.

O-T maps were similarly inspired. The initial letters of *orbis terrae*, the orb or circle of the earth, were considered to be the key to cartography. The *T* was placed within the *O*, resulting in a map of the world with the east at the top, its simplicity justified by divine truth rather than human observation. Apparently the crossbar of the *T* was gradually lowered to divide the circle at its diameter, enabling the mapmaker to acknowledge that Asia was larger than previously thought and to place Jerusalem at the center. Hugh's ark map and the O-T map seem to have taken a flat earth for granted. The continued popularity of the O-T maps and the mappamundi, such as the Psalter map, which were simply extensions of it, led to the entrenchment of many misconceptions. In the eleventh century, when Adam of Bremen wrote of the Norse discoveries in the Atlantic, he visualized them as on an O-T map, even though elsewhere he paid lip service to sphericity by pointing out that because of it, the sun, in bringing light to one place, leaves another in darkness. In reporting the Norse discoveries, he explains that the ocean flows endlessly around the "orb" of the earth, "having Ireland on the left . . . , on the right the cliffs of Norway, and further off the islands of Iceland and Greenland." The map concept forced Greenland and Vinland to the extreme north of Europe, confusing Vinland, far to the west, with Finland. Adam tried to fit reports of actual voyages into a cartographical concept that took no heed of the actual physical contours of the earth. Others resolved similar problems by insisting that the O-T maps represented the inhabited landmass, which was only a quarter of the global surface.

There was a burgeoning of information from classical sources: some from the Muslim world; some, though preserved in the West, newly discovered or reinterpreted. The encyclopedic *Speculum maius* of Vincent of Beauvais illustrates the variety of sources. It also reveals how much of this material remained to be integrated. There was some lag in communication between regions. Although much would become part of a common fund of information during the next two centuries, in the thirteenth century Europeans were living in northern areas that some southerners still proclaimed uninhabitable. Conversely, in the south Europeans knew of populated regions that their northern colleagues proclaimed too hot for human habitation. The Scandinavian author of the *King's Mirror* (*ca.* 1250) gives a comprehensive view of what northerners knew of their world and of others. The *King's Mirror* remained unknown in the south, though some of the information in it filtered southward. The same is true of Norse saga materials and of the *Heimskringla* (Orb of the world) by Snorri Sturluson. Some manuscript copies of the *Heimskringla* contain an account of Vinland that may have been inserted by Snorri himself. Discoveries in the south were also adding to geographical knowledge. There was a westward penetration into the Atlantic. A Genoese navigator, Lanzarotto Malocello, accompanied by Nicoloso da Recco, visited the Canary Islands in 1336 and 1341. (The islands were known to the ancients as the Fortunate Islands.) His motivation is unknown, though his name, Lanzarotto (Lancelot), may indicate a family interest in King Arthur and western islands. A score of years later the brothers Ugolino and Vadino Vivaldi, also Genoese, reputedly sailed beyond Gibraltar, intending to circumnavigate Africa. They disappeared en route.

The interest of the Vivaldi brothers was shared by Scholastics. Both Ramón Lull and Pietro d'Abano (*d.* 1316) speculated on the possibility of African circumnavigation. The friars William of Rubruck and John of Plano Carpini reported on their eastern travels and found avid readers; William's travels are referred to by Roger Bacon, while John is cited by Vincent of Beauvais. They were, of course, not the only missionaries to trek eastward. Nor was Marco Polo unique as a merchant-traveler, though the book that describes his travels from 1275 to 1295 was eagerly read and justifiably famous. Also stirring Western interest in the East were letters purporting to be from Prester John. According to Alberic of Trois Fontaines (*ca.* 1247), it was in 1165 that "Presbyter Johannes, the Indian King, sent his wonderful letter to various Christian princes."

The possibility of antipodal landmasses was an idea that had never completely died out. Some early Christian scholars thought that such landmasses might exist, but could not be reached by men. By the time of Bede, it was safe to suggest that these antipodes, though unreachable and uninhabited, were inhabitable. Albertus Magnus went even further. Reason, he asserted, demanded that the inhabitable antipodes were inhabited. Those who believed in the antipodes frequently used the walnut as a microcosmic pattern for the world. The shell was the sky; the four sections of nutmeat were the four landmasses. This is probably what Geoffrey of Monmouth had in mind in his *Vita Merlini* when he had Taliesin explain that the sky embraces everything "like the shell surrounding a nut" and that the sea "girds the land in four circles." Other scholars continued to believe that the ocean was surrounded by land. The supposed discovery in the north of land linking Greenland with Europe seemed to provide empirical evidence that the Atlantic was a Mediterranean sea, a concept that flourished in the north. The idea that the coastline of Vinland was an extension of that of Africa also introduced the possibility of sailing south from Vinland and then following the African coastline back to Europe.

Expanding geographic horizons forced the integration of earlier theory with observations based on the personal or vicarious experiences of distant and dramatically different regions. Some scholars deliberately, some seamen heroically, some merchants greedily, and most people unknowingly, with an undercurrent of excitement they could not have explained, began to prepare Europe for the great age of discovery, which was followed by an influx of information and an outpouring of peoples unmatched in the annals of humanity. The horizons of geographical knowledge had been extended in all directions, but present-day information about that geographical knowledge and its implications still has a long way to go. Vast reservoirs of information are still untapped. Some are new; some have been known for so long that they tend to be overlooked. The medieval romances, even familiar ones, such as the *Romance of Tristram and Ysolt* and the *Roman d'Alexandre* have much to yield. So does other literature, such as the Norse and Irish voyaging sagas, the saints' lives, the legends of King Arthur, and even the sculpture on cathedral walls. All of these have been looked at, but few have been systematically studied.

Portolan sailing charts, which played so vital a role in the age of discovery, came into prominence late in the thirteenth century. The oldest examples obviously belong to an established tradition; they are simply the earliest known to have survived. The place of origin of the portolan chart is unknown.

The Scandinavians, the Catalans, the Arabs, the Genoese, the Byzantines, and "ancient sea-kings" all have their champions. Probably no one group was completely responsible. The idea may even have originated at sea, and ships' crews have always tended to be cosmopolitan. Most extant portolans are postmedieval.

Many problems, then and now, stem from attempts to reconcile the Arctic north with the Mediterranean south. Canonical hours went totally askew. Since the grape was not cultivated in the north and trade and outside contact was minimal, beer and other substances frequently had to be found for the sacramental wine. Basic orientation had to be modified. Long before the invention of the compass, King Alfred's north seemed to be 45° off. Once the compass was in common use, magnetic deviation had yet to be understood. The peculiar shape of Greenland on the Zeno map, which like the Yale Vinland map has been considered a hoax, may yet be justified on the basis of magnetic deviation. Many other maritime devices were in use of which the name but not the function is known. The use of cordierite crystals by Norse navigators as "sunstones" to locate the sun on an overcast day has only recently been understood.

BIBLIOGRAPHY

Vincent H. Cassidy, "The Voyage of an Island," in *Speculum*, 38 (1963), "The Location of Ginnungagap," in Carl F. Bayerschmidt and Erik J. Friis, eds., *Scandinavian Studies* (1965), *The Sea Around Them* (1968), and "New Worlds and Everyman: Some Thoughts on the Logic and Logistics of Pre-Columbian Discovery," in *Terrae incognitae*, 10 (1978); Evan Connell, "Vinland: Speculations and Certainties," in *North American Review*, 263 (1978); James Robert Enterline, *Viking America* (1972); Charles H. Hapgood, *Maps of the Ancient Sea Kings* (1956); J. B. Harley and David Woodward, eds., *History of Cartography*, 2 vols. (in press); Jorgen Jensen, "Viking Navigation," in *The Ensign*, 56 (1972); George H. T. Kimble, *Geography in the Middle Ages* (1968); John Horace Parry, *The Discovery of the Sea* (1974); Walter W. Ristow, *Guide to the History of Cartography* (1973); Carl Ortwin Sauer, *Northern Mists* (1968); Jill Tattersall, "Sphere or Disc? Allusions to the Shape of the Earth in Some Twelfth-century and Thirteenth-century Vernacular French Works," in *Modern Language Review*, 76 (1981); John Kirtland Wright, *The Geographical Lore of the Time of the Crusades* (1965).

VINCENT H. CASSIDY

[See also **Exploration by Western Europeans; Mappa Mundi.**]

GEOPONICA, a Byzantine collection of excerpts from ancient works on agriculture compiled by a contemporary of Constantine VII (*d.* 959) on the basis of previous collections, putatively those of Anatolios Ouindanios (Vindanios) of Beirut and of Kassianos Bassos. *Geoponica* contains a preamble in which Constantine is praised for the revival of sciences and arts and for his interest in agriculture; there follow twenty sections on weather, viticulture, olives and fruit, vegetables, cattle breeding, apiculture, game, and fish. It is debatable whether the data of *Geoponica* are applicable to Byzantine agriculture of the tenth century.

BIBLIOGRAPHY

Geoponica; sive Cassiani Bassi scholastici De re rustica eclogae, Henricus Beckh, ed. (1895), Russian trans. by Elena E. Lipshits, *Geoponiki, vizantiyskaya selskokhozyaystvennaya entsiklopedia X veka* (1960).

ALEXANDER P. KAZHDAN

[See also **Agriculture and Nutrition, I: Byzantium.**]

GEORGE KALLIERGIS, fresco painter active in Macedonia during the first quarter of the fourteenth century. With his brothers he painted the Christos Church at Veroia in 1314–1315, then probably painted some of the frescoes at St. Nicholas Orphanos. Kalliergis lived in Thessaloniki, and absorbed the style of the Church of the Holy Apostles (1310–1314) there, but developed his own personal touch. His compositions are unified and have been credited with a "classical calm"; figures are carefully modeled with graduated shadows; and colors are warm and luminous.

BIBLIOGRAPHY

Stylianos M. Pelekanides, *Kallierges oles thettalias aristos zographos* (1973), English summary 123–164.

LESLIE BRUBAKER

GEORGE OF CYPRUS, early Byzantine geographer, the author of the *Descriptio orbis romani*. Heinrich Gelzer placed him in the closing years of the sixth century, whereas Arnold H. M. Jones suggested that he had to have been writing before Justinian's conquest of the western lands, since the *Descriptio* encompasses only eastern provinces.

Nothing is known of George's life; according to an occasional remark in his text, he came originally from the city of Lapithos in Cyprus. Ernst Honigmann regarded his work as a new edition of Hierokles' *Synekdemos*. The discrepancies between *Synekdemos* and George's *Descriptio* demonstrate, according to Jones, that George was closer to the reality of the sixth century: thus George includes the region of Jericho and some others in the Jordan valley, which were omitted by Hierokles.

George's *Descriptio* is preserved as the second part of a private compilation by a certain Basil of Ialimbana (Basil the Armenian), who wrote perhaps between 845 and 869; the first part of the compilation was created by Basil on the basis of ecclesiastical lists, while for the second part he used George's text, despite its secular character.

BIBLIOGRAPHY
Heinrich Gelzer, *Georgii Cyprii Descriptio orbis romani* (1890); Ernst Honigmann, *Le Synekdèmos d'Hiéroklès et l'opuscule géographique de Georges de Chypre* (1939); Arnold H. M. Jones, *The Cities of the Eastern Roman Provinces* (1937, 2nd ed. 1971); Vitalien Laurent, "La 'Notitia' de Basile l'Arménien," in *Echos d'Orient,* **34** (1935).

ALEXANDER P. KAZHDAN

[See also **Hierokles.**]

GEORGE OF PISIDIA (*fl.* 610's–630's), Byzantine poet who wrote mainly in iambic hexameter. Born in Antioch of Pisidia, he became a deacon of Hagia Sophia in Constantinople and held the ecclesiastical offices of *skevophylax* (sacristan), referendary, and perhaps chartophylax of the patriarchate. His poems (most are best known by the Latin titles attributed to them by modern editors) show that he possessed extensive classical knowledge and that he was well aware of the dogmatic, theological, and cosmological problems of his time. Of great importance are his historical epic poems, in which he celebrates—often as an eyewitness—military successes of the Byzantines: *In Heraclium ex Africa redeuntem* (610–611 or perhaps 619–620); *Expeditio Persica* (first Persian campaign of Heraklios, 622); *In Bonum patricium* and *Bellum Avaricum* (salvation of Constantinople from the siege by the Persians and the Avaro-Slavs, 626); *In restitutionem S. Crucis* and *Heraclias* (final victory of Heraklios over Persia, 630).

After 630, George concentrated on theological, cosmological, and moral subjects: *Hexaemeron* (on the creation of the world); on the vanity of life; on human life; on the resurrection of Christ; against the impious Severus (that is, against the Monophysites). He also wrote several minor poems and epigrams. His only preserved prose work is a panegyric on the martyrdom of St. Anastasius the Persian (*d.* 628). In subsequent centuries the Byzantines thought very highly of George and compared him with Euripides.

BIBLIOGRAPHY
Giorgio di Pisidia, *Poemi, I, Panegirici epici,* Agostino Pertusi, ed. (1959). See also Hans-Georg Beck, *Kirche und theologische Literatur im byzantinischen Reich* (1959); Herbert Hunger, *Die hochsprachliche profane Literatur der Byzantiner,* II (1978), 111–113, 159, 167, 232, 269.

NICOLAS OIKONOMIDES

[See also **Byzantine Literature; Heraklios.**]

GEORGE OF TREBIZOND (Georgios Trapezuntios) (4 April 1395–1486) was born in Crete to parents who had fled from their native city of Trebizond. Since Crete was then a Venetian possession, George, who seems to have been well educated, went to Venice about 1417 to take advantage of growing Italian interest in the study of Greek literature. He spent the rest of his life in Italy teaching and translating Greek texts. He taught in Venice, Mantua, and other north Italian towns and served the papal curia as interpreter at the council of Ferrara-Florence (1439), where a union with the Greek Church was planned. George gained the favor of Pope Nicholas V (1447–1455), who was greatly interested in the revival of Greek studies and set him to work translating the Greek fathers. He also translated Aristotle's *Rhetoric,* Plato's *Laws,* and Ptolemy's *Almagest.*

George was a quarrelsome man, and apparently somewhat clumsy in his translations. Cardinal Bessarion criticized his version of the *Laws* and George's counterattack on Bessarion's own work on Plato did him no good. Bessarion was a powerful member of the curia, the one eminent Greek who had accepted papal headship after the Council of Florence, and George eventually found it wise to leave Rome and teach in Naples and Venice. He also managed to quarrel with the humanists Lorenzo Valla and Giovanni Francesco Poggio Bracciolini, claiming that he had really done most of Poggio's translation of Xenophon.

George eventually returned to Rome, but apparently was still eager for a fight. Pope Paul II (1464–1471) imprisoned him briefly for writing offensive statements about earlier popes. George may have attacked the successors of Nicholas V, who were much less friendly to humanists than Nicholas had been. In any case, he seems to have learned his lesson, or perhaps he had less energy for quarrels in his old age. Little is known of his last years.

BIBLIOGRAPHY

There is no one book that gives a full account of the life of George of Trebizond. References to him may be found in Mandell Creighton, *A History of the Papacy from the Great Schism to the Sack of Rome,* III and IV (1919–1923); Deno J. Geanakoplos, *Greek Scholars in Venice* (1962); Jerrold E. Seigel, *Rhetoric and Philosophy in Renaissance Humanism* (1968); John A. Symonds, *Renaissance in Italy,* II (1882, 1920, and many other editions).

JOSEPH R. STRAYER

[See also **Bessarion.**]

GEORGE SCHOLARIOS

GEORGE SCHOLARIOS (*ca.* 1405–*ca.* 1472). A secretary of the Byzantine emperor, John VIII Palaiologos, George Scholarios had attacked the choice of Constantine XI as emperor. Although he had favored union with Rome, he went on to become staunchly opposed to it, even at the price of losing the empire, and under the name of Gennadios II was one of the chief opponents of the attempts to effect such a union. After the fall of the Byzantine Empire to the Ottomans, Gennadios became the first patriarch of Constantinople under Turkish rule, in 1453 or shortly thereafter.

BIBLIOGRAPHY

George Ostrogorsky, *History of the Byzantine State,* Joan Hussey, trans. (1957, rev. ed. 1969).

LINDA ROSE

[See also **Byzantine Empire: History (1204–1453).**]

GEORGE THE MONK

GEORGE THE MONK (Georgios Monachos) (*fl.* mid ninth century), in some manuscripts called also Hamartolos (Sinner), a Byzantine chronicler. The scope of his universal *Brief Chronicle (Chronikon syntomon)* goes from Adam to 842. He wrote in the days of Michael III and completed the chronicle about 866/867. George's biography is unknown, but he was the last representative of monastic literature flourishing in Byzantium from the end of the eighth century to the mid ninth century, when it gave way to the secular trend originating with Photios, a contemporary of George. George's work is a typical monastic chronicle both in its construction and in its interpretation of events. In the preface he determines his subject, contrasting the pagan false teachings (invention of idols, futile ramblings of Hellenic philosophers, myths and marvelous tales, polytheism or atheism of different tribes) with the Christian belief, which he understands above all as monastic order and rule, as a perfect society after the fashion of Christ. He attacks passionately the "raging madness of the Manichaeans," under which name he introduces the Iconoclasts. George consciously rejects artificial embellishment in his narrative, proclaiming that it is better to falter inarticulately in truth than to reach a lying Platonic beauty.

The author's personality finds no place in his narration: in the preface George says that he has no share in external knowledge and that his work is no more than a cheap booklet (*biblidarion*). He neither participates in the events nor dares to express his own opinion, yet he writes in proud assurance that he possesses the sovereign truth. His appreciation of people and events is black and white: the world is divided into heroes and antiheroes, into servants of Christ and supporters of Satan.

Interest in religion dictated the choice of material. George describes Julius Caesar in ten lines and the reign of Augustus in about twenty pages; the latter section is so large because it deals with the Incarnation and with the great amount of biblical and patristic quotations referring to Christ. In the sections on Constantine the Great and Theodosius I attention is drawn first of all to the ecumenical councils; and in the history of Justinian I, to the theological controversies. George's main source for the Byzantine part of his chronicle was Theophanes the Confessor. The section dealing with the period after 813 is based on both oral information and rhetorical texts of the epoch (Ignatius the Deacon's *Vita Nicephori* [Life of Patriarch Nikephoros], the lost speech of Patriarch Nikephoros). The religious controversy forms the core of this section, and the Iconoclasts are presented with a consistent one-sidedness.

George's chronicle was very popular both in Byzantium and among the neighbors of the empire. The Greek text is preserved in many manuscripts of different versions, some of which have a continuation (sometimes under the name of Symeon Logothete) going to 948. George's chronicle was translated into the Slavic and Georgian languages during the Middle Ages.

BIBLIOGRAPHY

The text is available in *Georgii monachi Chronicon,* Carl Gotthard de Boor, ed., 2 vols. (1904). See also Herbert Hunger, *Die hochsprachliche profane Literatur der Byzantiner,* I (1978), 347–351; S. Shestakov, *O proischozhdenii i sostave chroniki Georgiya Monacha (Amartola)* (1891); F. H. Tinnefeld, *Kategorien der Kaiserkritik in der byzantinischen Historiographie* (1971), 81–86.

ALEXANDER P. KAZHDAN

[See also **Byzantine Literature; Historiography, Byzantine; Nikephoros, Patriarch; Theophanes the Confessor.**]

GEORGES CHASTELLAIN. See Rhetoriqueurs.

GEORGES DE LA SONNETTE, French sculptor responsible, with Jean Michel, for the *Entombment of Christ* at Tonnerre, one of the most important examples of monumental sculpture from the Burgundian School following the seminal work of Claus Sluter in the ducal workshop at Dijon. He is mentioned at Tonnerre from 1452 to 1454, when the monument was completed.

BIBLIOGRAPHY

William H. Forsyth, *The Entombment of Christ: French Sculptures of the Fifteenth and Sixteenth Centuries* (1970), 65–69, 188, 200–201; Theodor Müller, *Sculpture in the Netherlands, Germany, France, and Spain 1400 to 1500* (1966), 57; Bernard Prost, "Le Saint Sépulcre de l'hôpital de Tonnere," in *Gazette des beaux-arts,* 3rd ser., 9 (1893).

ANNE M. MORGANSTERN

[See also **Sluter, Claus.**]

GEORGIA: GEOGRAPHY AND ETHNOLOGY. Georgia (Georgian: Sak^{c}art^{c}velo; Armenian: Vrastan; Arabic: Kurj; Persian: Gurjistān; Turkish: Gurçistan; Russian: Gruziya) is located along the Black Sea coast in southwest Caucasia and consists of four geographical regions: the moist, humid, and subtrop-ical Colchian plain, occupying the Black Sea lowlands; the higher and drier Iberian plain to the east; the western half of the Caucasus range, which borders Georgia on the north; and the southern or Moschian Mountains (Lesser Caucasus), which separate Georgia from the Armenian plateau to the south. West Georgia, the valley of the Rioni River (called in classical times the Phasis), is separated from East Georgia, the central valley of the Kura River (Georgian: Mtkvari; Greek: Kyros; Latin: Cyrus; Armenian: Kur), by the Surami or Lixi range, a low-rising spur of the Caucasus linking the main chain with the Lesser Caucasus. The western extension of the Caucasus, which forms northern Georgia, is much moister and more luxuriant than the eastern half, which lies in Azerbaijan; it is subalpine in climate and vegetation on its lower slopes and alpine in its higher reaches. Several peaks in the western Caucasus are higher than any in the Alps; these include Mount Kazbek (16,512 feet/5,033 meters) and Mount Elbrus (18,510 feet/5,633 meters), the highest mountain in Europe.

Rarely united in its history, Georgia has usually comprised two main states, West and East Georgia, corresponding to the natural divisions of the country. West Georgia, originally in Georgian Eg[u]risi (Armenian: Eger; Greek: Ekretike), then from the fifth century, Lazike (Byzantine Lazika), from the eighth, Ap^{c}χazet^{c}i (Byzantine Abasgia), and from the thirteenth Imeret^{c}i (Russian: Imeretiya), is the classical Colchis, the "Land of the Golden Fleece" of Greek mythographers. Its traditional capital was Kut^{c}at^{c}isi, perhaps the Greek Aia, not Kut^{c}aisi. Historically, West Georgia consisted of five divisions: Imeret^{c}i proper, with its capital at Kut^{c}aisi; Ap^{c}χazet^{c}i proper (Abasgia, now Abkhazia), with its capital at C^{c}oχumi (Russian: Sukhumi), inhabited by the Abkhaz, a non-Georgian people related to the Circassians; Svanet^{c}i (Greek: Souania; Russian: Svanetia), with its center at Mestia; Guria, with its center at Ozurget^{c}i (now Makharadze); and Samegrelo (Russian: Mingrelia), with its capital at Zugdidi.

East Georgia, called K^{c}art^{c}li in Georgian (Russian: Kartalinia), the Greek and Latin Iberia or Hiberia (Armenian: Virk^c; Old Persian: Warjan; Middle Persian: Wyrshn; Syriac: Gurzan; Arabic, Turkish, and Modern Persian: Gurjistān), is also divided into two lands: western Iberia (K^{c}art^{c}li proper), with its capital originally at Mc^{c}χet^{c}a, but since the fifth century at Tbilisi (Armenian: Tp^{c}his; Russian: Tiflis); and eastern K^{c}art^{c}li or Kaχet^{c}i, with its capital at Gremi. Eastern Kaχet^{c}i, known as Heret^{c}i, has also

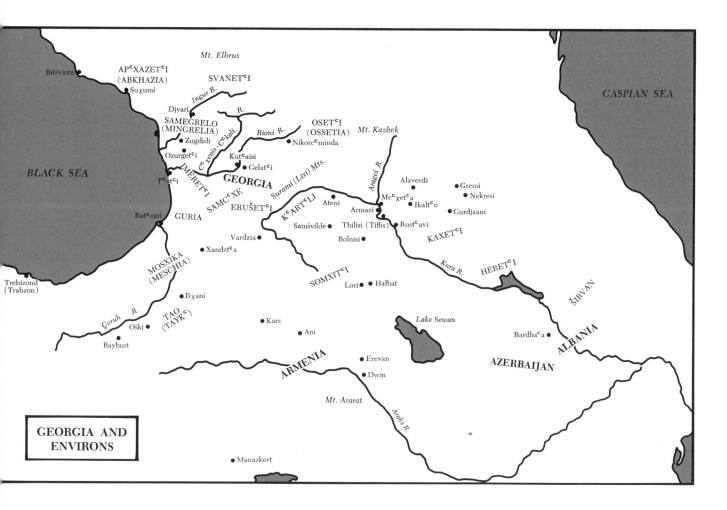

GEORGIA AND
ENVIRONS

been an independent state at certain times in Georgian history. Kᶜartᶜli proper contains the following divisions: inner Iberia (Šida Kᶜartᶜli), which includes south Osetᶜi (Russian: Ossetia); lower Iberia (Kᶜvemo Kᶜartᶜli), later known as Somχitᶜi or Somχetᶜi; and upper Iberia (Zemo Kᶜartᶜli), also known as Mosχika, Mesχetᶜi, or Samcᶜχe (Meschia) in the broad sense of the term. Much of upper Iberia forms a marchland with Armenia, and many of its districts were disputed between the two countries. In the late fifteenth century, most of upper Iberia formed the principality of Samcᶜχe-Saatᶜabago, which passed to Turkish control. Eastern Kᶜartᶜli or Kaχetᶜi is divided into inner Kaχetᶜi; outer Kaχetᶜi; and, on occasion, included the large, far-eastern region of Heretᶜi.

THE GEORGIAN PEOPLE

The Georgians originally called themselves Kᶜartᶜvelni, but their modern self-designation is Kᶜartᶜvelebi; singular, Kᶜartᶜveli (Armenian: Vracᶜi; Turkish: Gürçü; Persian: Gurdzhī; Abkhazian: Akỳrtwa; Russian: Gruziny). On the basis of language, the Georgians are usually divided into four closely related peoples. First, the Georgians proper inhabit Iberia and the eastern parts of West Georgia; they were formerly divided into ten subgroups: Kᶜartᶜlians, Kaχetᶜians, Xevsurs, Pšavs, Tušians, Račᶜans, Mtᶜiuletᶜians, Moχevians, Gurians, and Imeretᶜians. Islamicized Gurians are known as Ačars and are mostly to be found in the Adzhar A.S.S.R., a subdivision of the Georgian S.S.R., and in the extreme northeast of Turkey; the islamicized Kaχetᶜians of Zakatali are known as Ingiloi. Second, the Mingrelians; they call their country Samargalo (Land of the Egrisi) and themselves Margali (People of Egrisi; Georgian: Megreli; Russian: Mingreli; Abkhazian: Aghrwa; Svan: Myzan), and inhabit the plains north of the Rioni River and west of the Cᶜχenis-Cᶜkali, extending north along the

403

Black Sea coast to Očᶜemčᶜiri in the modern districts *(raioni)* of Senaki and Zugdidi. Third, the Svans, who call themselves *Šwan,* singular *Mušwan* or *Mušwni* (Georgian: *Svani;* Greek: *Soanes;* Latin: *Suani;* Old Armenian: *Suankᶜ*; Russian: *Svany* or *Svanety),* inhabit two broad upland valleys located to the south of Mount Elbrus: first, the valley of the upper Ingur River, where in the west they were ruled by the indigenous Dadeškeliani dynasty, while in the east they were free; and second, the valley of the upper Cᶜχenis-Cᶜkali and its tributary, the Xeladula, where they were subjects of the Dadians of Mingrelia until the dynasty was deposed by the Russians in 1864. Finally, the Laz or Čᶜans, who call themselves *Tsani* or *Lazi* (Georgian: *Čᶜani;* Greek: *Sannoi* or *Saniges;* Byzantine: *Tzanoi;* Armenian: *Xaltikᶜ*, later *Laz-er;* Turkish: *Laz;* Abkhazian: *Alas;* Russian: *Lazy),* originally inhabited the Black Sea coast from Atina to Giresun and including the Çoruh valley as far as Bayburt, but are now found in a much more restricted area between Atina and Trabzon (Trebizond), where they are gradually being assimilated to the local Turkish population.

The majority of Georgians follow the Greek Orthodox rite and have their own church organization, but there are Sunni Muslims among them, mainly the Laz and the Ačars. In the past there were also large minorities of Armenians and Muslim Tatars as well as small but significant colonies of Jews and Germans. The Georgians have traditionally been engaged in farming, gardening, viticulture, stock breeding, and the various arts and crafts. The Mingrelians added to these the production of silk; the Svans, apiculture and hunting, and the Laz, fishing and trading.

LANGUAGE

Georgian, Svan, and Mingrelo-Laz together form the South Caucasian language group. Georgian itself *(Kᶜartᶜuli ena)* is divided into two subgroups: West Georgian (Imeretᶜian, Gurian-Ačar, Lečᶜkum, Imerχev, and Račᶜan) and East Georgian (Kᶜartᶜlian, Kaχetᶜian, Pšav, Mtᶜiul, Ingilo, Moχev, Tuš, and Xevsur, the last three often collectively called Pχov). Kᶜartᶜlian, which is the standard literary language as devised in the nineteenth century, has two subdialects, Javaχian and Mesχian. Faraydān, the dialect spoken in a few villages of Georgians in Iran, is the same as Mtᶜiul.

The Svan language comprises four dialects, two of which, Lašχ and Lenteχ, are spoken in the Cᶜχenis-Cᶜkali valley, and two, Upper and Lower Bal, in the

valley of the Ingur. Mingrelian and Laz, two closely related languages, together form the third branch of the South Caucasian language group, which is known as Zan. Since none of these languages or dialects is written except Kᶜartᶜlian (standard Georgian), this language and its alphabet serve as the written language throughout the region.

BIBLIOGRAPHY

William Edward Allen, *A History of the Georgian People* (1932, repr. 1971); *Atlas Gruzinskoi Sovetskoi Sotsialisticheskoi Respubliki* (1964); Bernhard Geiger *et al., Peoples and Languages of the Caucasus* (1959); A. Gugushvili, "Ethnographical and Historical Division of Georgia," in *Georgica,* I.1 (1935); T. Halasi-Kun, "The Caucasus, an Ethno-historical Survey," in *Studia Caucasica,* 1 (1966); Aleksandr N. Dzhavakhishvili and Giorgi Gvelesiani, eds., *Soviet Georgia: Its Geography, History, and Economy* (1964); Cyril Toumanoff, *Studies in Christian Caucasian History* (1963).

Robert Hewsen

[See also **Armenia: Geography; Caucasia; Kura; Kutaisi; Tbilisi.**]

GEORGIA: POLITICAL HISTORY. As the Urartian Empire dissolved under the blows of the Medes in the early sixth century B.C., various tribes speaking Kartvelian languages and living in the Rioni River valley formed a primitive political union known to the Greeks as the "kingdom" of Colchis and later to the Georgians as Egrisi. This West Georgian state, which lasted until the third century B.C. as a semi-independent entity, was known to Xenophon and in time came under the commercial and cultural hegemony of the Greek city-states.

Although its origins properly lie in this little-known state, Georgian political history is usually traced more directly from another tribal formation in eastern Georgia, the kingdom of the Iberoi (Iberians). In the late fourth century B.C. the ruling dynast of Armazi-Mcᶜχetᶜa, P'arnavazi, established his primacy over the other tribal leaders in Iberia (Kᶜartᶜli) and constructed a hierarchical system of government based on royal appointees. The Georgian chronicles, *Kᶜartᶜlis cᶜχovreba* (Life of Georgia), provide the tradition that this first king was a descendant of Kᶜartᶜlosi, the eponymous ancestor of the Georgians, and that he united Georgians of the east with those of Colchis-Egrisi to drive the "Greeks" from Mcᶜχetᶜa. The hegemony of

K^{C}art^{C}li-Iberia over Colchis-Egrisi meant that the Georgian tribes consolidated around the newer state in eastern Georgia, which soon demonstrated greater independence vis-à-vis the major powers in Asia Minor. Georgia was loosely associated with the Seleucid successors of Alexander the Great and benefited from the economic advances of the Hellenistic period.

When, in the second century B.C., Roman legions defeated the Seleucid king of Persia, the Georgians fell under the sway of expansionist Armenian monarchs. Only with the campaigns of Pompey (66–64 B.C.) was Georgia, indeed all of Caucasia, brought under the Pax Romana. From the first century B.C. Georgia and Armenia were the objects of desire and the reason for military confrontation between the rival empires of Rome and Iran. As Cyril Toumanoff put it (1971, p. 114): "Caucasia formed a great natural fortress between the two empires from which each of the rivals could control the delicate frontier-line that lay between them in the south. From it, each could strike at the other's sensitive points, Ctesiphon, the 'Roman Lake,' later Constantinople."

A compromise solution was reached in the Treaty of Rhandeia of A.D. 63, when a Parthian Arsacid was placed on the Armenian throne but was recognized as a vassal of Rome. Similar arrangements were later made with Iberia and Caucasian Albania. But even as the Arsacids came to power in the Caucasian kingdoms, their dynasty was overthrown in its original homeland, Persia, by the Sasanians, who sought to reestablish their claims to Caucasia and to impose the Zoroastrian religion on it. The Arsacid line in K^{C}art^{C}li-Iberia ended in 284, and the Sasanians took advantage of internal strife in the Roman Empire to establish their candidate, Mirian III (Meribanes, 284–361), said to have been the son of the great king of Persia, on the throne of East Georgia. In 298, however, after a major Roman victory, Persia and Rome signed the Peace of Nisibis, and Mirian was recognized as a vassal of Rome. It was in this context of reinforced Roman suzerainty and Persian-Roman conflict that the Georgian king converted to Christianity around 337.

In the late fourth century the Sasanians reestablished their suzerainty over Iberia and part of Armenia, but both newly Christianized peoples resisted the militant efforts of the Persian kings to introduce Zoroastrianism in Caucasia. The Georgian and Armenian alphabets were invented in order to carry out a more intensive propagation of Christianity. The young and vigorous Waχtang I Gurgaslani (ca. 447–

522) broke with his Persian overlord in 482 and allied with Byzantium. Waχtang was driven from Iberia late in his life, and by 532 Byzantium and Persia once again agreed to divide Caucasia between them. Western Georgia and part of Armenia were left in Roman hands, while the larger part of Armenia (Persarmenia) and much of eastern Georgia came under Persian suzerainty.

The dynasts of K^{C}art^{C}li-Iberia had long looked toward the decentralized, tribal empire of Persia for support for their claims to regional power, and in 580, with the acquiescence of the Iberian aristocrats, Persia abolished the monarchy. Within the decade Emperor Maurice retook part of Iberia, but instead of restoring the hereditary monarch he appointed his ally Guaram as curopalate (588–ca. 602). By the Peace of 591 the Persians recognized Byzantine authority in western Iberia while retaining the eastern part as far as Tbilisi. The new Byzantine orientation of the ruling elite of Iberia was reflected in the adherence of Georgia in the first years of the seventh century to the Chalcedonian faith.

Inspired by their new and militant religion, Islam, Arab warriors penetrated Iberia in the 640's. Sasanian claims to Caucasia were now replaced by Islamic ones, and the Arabs soon dominated the area, treating Georgia and Armenia as frontier provinces subject to tribute and governed by an Arab viceroy at Dwin. The Byzantine Empire attempted to subvert the influence of the caliph by encouraging Christian peoples to rebellion, but the defeats of the Georgian and Armenian nobility by the Muslim army were followed by the wholesale extermination of leading landed families. In Georgia, with the extinction of the Guaramids and the near extinction of the Chosroids in the late eighth century, the inheritance of these two royal dynasties was assumed by a branch of the Armenian Bagratids.

Faced by the insurrection of his Arab lieutenants, in Georgia, the caliph decided to rely on the prominent Bagratid family, the heirs of Adarnase I Bagratuni of Klarjet^{C}i-Erušet^{C}i, as protectors of Arab interests in Iberia. Ašot I Bagratuni (813–830) was appointed prince of K^{C}art^{C}li-Iberia by the Arabs and was recognized as curopalate by the Byzantines. The policy was successful enough to be extended to Armenia, where in 862 another Ašot I the Brave became ruling "prince of princes." Within a generation the Arabs permitted him to be crowned king as Ašot I the Great of Armenia (884) and Adarnase IV to become king of K^{C}art^{C}li-Iberia (888). Arab decline combined with Byzantine preoccupation with

405

problems on other frontiers allowed the Bagratid monarchies of Caucasia to develop into relatively powerful and prosperous states in the tenth century, which was marked by a revival of industry, commerce, architecture, and literary expression. But by the late tenth century, Byzantine armies under the so-called Macedonian dynasty were realizing unprecedented successes, and no single monarch in either Georgia or Armenia was strong enough to resist this imperial encroachment or to unify the Caucasian principalities. Georgian rulers included kings in Apᶜχazetᶜi (Abasgia) and Kᶜartᶜli-Iberia, and a prince *(mtᶜavari)* in Kaχetᶜi, as well as the autonomous emir of Tbilisi. Against these tiny states the Byzantine Empire moved relentlessly, threatening in particular a new state rising under Dawitᶜ (David) the Great of Tao (Taykᶜ).

This young Bagratid prince played an extraordinary role in the dynastic politics of Georgia, Armenia, and the Byzantine Empire. When civil war threatened the throne of Basil II between 976 and 979, Dawitᶜ sent 12,000 cavalry troops to help put down the rebels under Bardas Skleros. The emperor rewarded Dawitᶜ with extensive lands on the frontier of Byzantium. As the most powerful ruler in Caucasia, Dawitᶜ sought to preserve his newly won principality by adopting Bagrat, heir to the throne of Kᶜartᶜli-Iberia, as his heir and by securing the throne of Apᶜχazetᶜi for the young prince (978). But Dawitᶜ's plans collapsed when he aided his friend Bardas Phokas against Basil II (987–989), and both were defeated by a Russo-Byzantine army. Dawitᶜ agreed to cede his lands to the empire on his death, which occurred in 1000. Eight years later Bagrat III (978–1014) became the first king of a united Georgia when his own kingdom of Apᶜχazetᶜi was joined to his late father's realm of Kᶜartᶜli-Iberia. A new term, *sakᶜartᶜvelo,* was thereafter used to denote the "country of the Georgians."

While Byzantine expansion still had to be contended with, a new threat appeared from the east, the Seljuk Turks. The united Bagratid kingdom of Georgia stood as a buffer between the Turks and Byzantium and became a haven for defeated Armenian nobles. In 1064 Alp Arslan invaded Georgia, ravaged much of the country in the following years, and took Tbilisi and Rustᶜavi from the Georgians. The "great Turkish troubles" *(didi turkoba)* lasted through the next quarter-century until the energetic and talented King Dawitᶜ II (David, also called David IV by Georgian historians, 1089–1125), known as *almašenebeli* ("the Restorer" or "the Builder"), revitalized

his divided people and began a series of victorious campaigns against the Seljuks. Dawitᶜ annexed Kaχetᶜi-Eretᶜi to his kingdom, limited the autonomy of the dynastic princes, and created a more centralized feudal monarchy. Maintaining peaceful relations with Byzantium, he allied with the Qipchaq Turks to extend his frontiers and create the foundations of a multinational Georgian empire in Transcaucasia. The Seljuks were decisively defeated in 1121 at Didgori, and the next year Tbilisi was retaken by the Georgians, ending nearly 500 years of Muslim control over the Georgian capital.

To his heirs Dawitᶜ bequeathed a renewed and expanded Georgia, as well as a vastly increased royal power and prestige. But Demetre I (1125–1156) and Giorgi III (IV) (1156–1184) were unable to preserve all the territorial gains of their great ancestor. Even more important, the kings of the mid twelfth century were faced by insurrection and opposition from within the dynastic elite that ruled the country. Giorgi III, the younger son of Demetre, not only had to defeat his older brother Dawitᶜ's son to secure the throne but also was required to put down a massive rebellion of the Orbeli and Tᶜoreli nobles (1174–1177). To guarantee the succession for his daughter Tamar, Giorgi had her crowned while he was still alive, and the two reigned as co-rulers. On her father's death, however, Tamar was forced to undergo a second coronation, this time by the nobles of the council *(darbazi),* who by this act reasserted their right to sanction the new monarch.

The medieval Georgian monarchy reached its apogee with Queen Tamar (1184–1212), who was celebrated by Georgia's greatest poet, her contemporary, Šotᶜa Rustᶜaveli. But before the queen was able to expand her realm, she first had to overcome the nobles' resistance to her exercise of power. The *darbazi* had removed advisers loyal to Tamar and her father and required the queen to marry the Russian prince Yuri, son of Andrei Bogoliubskii of Rostov-Suzdal. Only with the death of the inimical Katᶜolikos Mikel was Tamar able to reassert royal power, divorce her unwanted husband, and marry Dawitᶜ Soslan, an Oset prince. Together the queen and her consort successfully routed a rebellion of West Georgian nobles who in 1191 rallied around the scorned Yuri, and Tamar elevated her own supporters, most notably the Armenized Kurdish family of Zakᶜarids (known in Georgia as Mχargrdjeli), to high positions at court. The royal couple launched campaigns against their Muslim enemies, took back Ani, captured Kars, and established their vassals in Širvan.

GEORGIA: POLITICAL HISTORY

Tamar was instrumental in establishing the Komnenian Empire of Trebizond. The prosperity and power of the kingdom remained intact well into the reign of Tamar's son Giorgi IV Lasha ("the Resplendent," 1212–1223), but ended abruptly with the arrival of the Mongols in 1220. The king was killed in battle and succeeded by his sister Rusudan (1223–1245).

The Mongols were sovereign over Transcaucasia through the thirteenth and early fourteenth centuries. Georgia remained autonomous within the Mongol Empire but was required to pay tribute and provide military service. The Mongols supported several co-rulers in Georgia at once, and the country fell into near anarchy. Georgia fragmented into semi-independent principalities (called *samt^{c}avro*), with the consequent rise to power of the class of great nobles *(mtavari)*, especially those favored by the Mongols, and the corresponding decline of monarchical power. Besides the principates of K^{c}art^{c}li and Imeret^{c}i, a third major Georgian political entity arose in this period, Samc^{c}xe. A century after the reign of Tamar, her kingdom was divided and destitute. Royal power had only a symbolic hold over the great princes, and Georgia was entering the twilight of its recent glory.

The fourteenth century marked the last, desperate attempts of the Georgian monarchs to free their kingdom from Mongol rule and reestablish the decaying feudal system. Under Giorgi VI (V) (*ca.* 1314–1346), called "the Brilliant" *(brc^{c}qinvale)*, the Mongols were driven out of Georgia (1327), and the great noble families once again submitted to the king. But the Mongols appeared again in 1386 under Tamerlane, and though Georgia was briefly reunited under Aleksandre I (1412–1442), the country again split into tiny kingdoms and principalities. The brief "feudal" revival of the fourteenth century ended as suddenly as it had begun, and by the fifteenth century Georgian feudalism *(patronqmoba)* was being replaced by the direct rule of the dynastic princes *(t^{c}avadoba)*.

BIBLIOGRAPHY

William E. D. Allen, *A History of the Georgian People*, 2nd ed. (1971); N. A. Berdzenishvili, *Ocherk iz istorii razvitiia feodalnykh otnoshenii v Gruzii* (1938); N. A. Berdzenishvili, V. D. Dondua, M. K. Dumbadze, G. A. Melikishvili, and Sh. A. Meskhia, *Istoriia Gruzii*, I, *S drevneishikh vremen do 60-kh godov XIX veka* (1962); Marie F. Brosset, *Histoire de la Géorgie, depuis l'antiquité jusqu'au XIXe siècle, publiée en géorgien*, I, *Histoire an-*

GEORGIAN ART AND ARCHITECTURE

cienne, jusqu'en 1469 de J.C., 2 vols. (1849–1850); Charles Burney and David Marshall Lang, *The Peoples of the Hills: Ancient Ararat and Caucasus* (1972); Georges Charachidze, *Introduction à l'étude de la féodalité géorgienne* (1971); I. A. Dzavakhov (Javakhishvili), *Gosudarstvenni stroi drevnei Gruzii i drevnei Armenii* (1905), and *Jveti k^{c}art^{c}uli saistorio mcerloba (V–XVIII ss.)* (1921); David Marshall Lang, *The Georgians* (1966); M. D. Lordkipanidze, *Istoriia Gruzii—XI-nachalo XIII veka* (1974); David Magie, *Roman Rule in Asia Minor, to the End of the Third Century After Christ* (1950); H. Manandian, *O torgovle i gorodakh Armenii v svjazi s mirovoj torgovlej drevniykh vremen* (1945); G. A. Melikishvili, *K istorii drevnei Gruzii* (1959); Cyril Toumanoff, *Studies in Christian Caucasian History* (1963), and "Caucasia and Byzantium," in *Traditio*, 27 (1971).

RONALD GRIGOR SUNY

[See also **Ašot I Mec (The Great); Bagratids; Caucasia; Chosroids (Mihranids); David II (IV) the Builder; David of Tao; Giorgi III; Tamar; Tbilisi.**]

GEORGIAN ART AND ARCHITECTURE. The Middle Ages in Georgia began with the adoption of Christianity as the state religion in the first half of the fourth century. Early in the fifth century Arian trends were rejected in favor of orthodoxy as defined by the Council of Nicaea (325). In the course of the sixth and seventh centuries Georgia formally accepted the Orthodox faith in accordance with the distinctions outlined by the Council of Chalcedon (451). The Georgian church remained untouched by the iconoclastic controversy. Despite Arab domina-

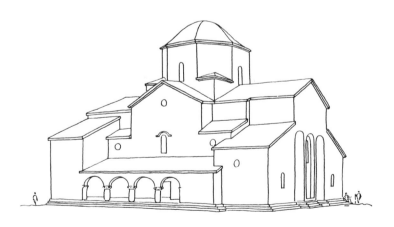

Church of C^{c}romi (Tsromi), view from the southeast, 626–635.
FROM RUSUDAN MEPISASHVILI AND VAKHTANG TSINTSADZE, THE ARTS OF ANCIENT GEORGIA (© 1979)

tion of eastern Georgia after the Muslim conquest, the country continued to develop its artistic forms with little interruption, and although Georgian art shares some common features with the art of Syro-Palestine, Byzantium, and Armenia, it was able to maintain a uniqueness that is based on a deeply rooted national tradition.

Medieval art in Georgia can be divided into four major periods: the early medieval period, extending from the fourth to the seventh century; a transitional period extending from the second half of the seventh to the second half of the tenth century; the High Middle Ages, from the second half of the tenth century to the early fourteenth century; and the late medieval period, from the fourteenth to the eighteenth century.

ARCHITECTURE

In religious architecture of the first period two basic types evolved: the longitudinally oriented traditional basilica and the central-plan, domed church. The former was transmitted to Georgia; the latter can be traced to pre-Christian secular structures native to Georgia—specifically, the *darbazi,* or hall, a rectangular dwelling surmounted by a pyramidal corbeled cupola of hewn logs with an opening at the top for light and air.

With a few exceptions, the circular and octagonal buildings, baptisteries, atriums, and narthexes common to other early Christian architecture never developed in Georgia. Likewise, instead of the timber roofs and columns typical of other church construction, barrel and groin vaults and piers were used. Evenly squared stone blocks with smoothly finished faces were mainly used for construction. They were closely fitted with a minimal amount of mortar, which cannot be seen between the courses.

The earliest churches, ascribed to the second half of the fourth century, are exceptionally small—for example, Nekresi, with exterior dimensions not exceeding 4.6 by 3.8 meters. Its diminutive size, the wide arches in the nave, and the preserved aisle indicate that during the celebration of the liturgy the congregation must have been standing outside the church but was able to observe the service. Apparently Georgian architects did not have a suitable prototype for the celebration of their newly embraced religion. Much more advanced is the large basilica at Bolnisi Seon (or Sioni), built between 478 and 493 by Bishop Dawit[c] (David).

Among the various types of basilical churches in Georgia in the sixth century was the "triple church" or "three-nave basilica," in which the naves are completely separated by walls. The aisles are connected by a door on each side of the middle of each nave and by a gallery at the west end; typical of this plan is the larger church in Nekresi, dated to the seventh century. The "triple church" made it possible to conduct the liturgy simultaneously and independently in all three naves.

The basilical type was short-lived in Georgia. Toward the end of the sixth and early seventh centuries, central-plan, cruciform domed churches emerged, continuing the earlier *darbazi* tradition. The best representative of this type is at Djvari erected on the top of a mountain near the ancient capital of Mc[c]χet[c]a between 586 and 604. Simplified versions of Djvari were built in Dzveli, Šuamt[c]a, Martvili, and Ateni.

New architectural ideas that conditioned the further development of religious architecture in Georgia emerged in the first half of the seventh century. They are exemplified by the church in C[c]romi (626–634), which is of the cross-in-square type. Here the dome is supported not by the walls of the church, as at Djvari (which is the *croix libre* type, with four separate arms), but by four freestanding piers in the middle of the church.

During the Muslim domination, with its subsequent constraint on the economy, building activity in Georgia continued, though at a slower pace, and

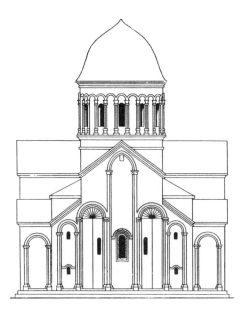

Church of Oški, eastern facade, 963–973. PLAN COURTESY OF THE AUTHOR

408

Cathedral of Išχani, southeastern side of the dome, exterior, 1032.
PHOTOGRAPH BY THE AUTHOR

the quality of craftsmanship declined. At this time a few structurally significant churches were built—the domed church in Samšvilde (759–777), the monastery church of All Saints in Gurdjaani (eighth–ninth centuries), the church at C^{c}irk^{c}oli (ninth century) and Armazi (864). In addition to churches, the course of the eighth and ninth centuries saw the construction of buildings designated for secular use, including palaces, hunting lodges, and educational institutions in Tšeremi, Watšnadziani, and Want^{c}a; however, these are not as well preserved as the religious buildings.

With the reestablishment of Georgian kingdoms in the southwestern provinces of Tao and Klarjet^{c}i, which were not conquered by the Muslims, Georgian monastic life and building activity were revived at Opiza, Xandzt^{c}a, and Doliskana. The most significant innovation began in the second half of the tenth century in the churches of Oški, Xaχuli, Parχali, and Išχani. The majority of Tao-Klarjet^{c}i churches at the end of the first millennium were variants of cruciform domed buildings with boldly accentuated east–west axes, the dome supported by freestanding piers. The tenth-century buildings, such

as those at Oški, are considerably larger and more complex. Not only the apse but also the walls of the entire church were covered with frescoes that required a greater amount of light in order to be seen. That light was supplied by increasing the number of windows, particularly in the dome's drum. The decorative quality of the exterior walls was considerably heightened by the introduction of blind arcades and architectural sculpture consisting of figural as well as diversified plant and geometric motifs. The architectural and decorative concepts developed in Tao-Klarjet^{c}i were soon carried over to other parts of Georgia and became obligatory (for example, at King Bagrat's cathedral in Kut^{c}aisi, Sveti Cχoveli in Mc^{c}χet^{c}a and Alaverdi Cathedral).

In the second half of the tenth century the local basilical plan was revived, as in the church of Ot^{c}χt^c eklesia and at Parχali, but this was only a passing occurrence. It did not influence the development of centrally oriented buildings, which in the High Middle Ages continued to be the main theme in sacral architecture, manifested in the grandiose cathedrals of Sveti Cχoveli, Samt^{c}avro, Alaverdi, and Nikorc^{c}minda (all from the first half of the eleventh century). The number of churches also increased considerably. The continuation of an active building program into the High Middle Ages was accelerated by the increase of political power of the Georgian monarchy and the expansion of monastic centers in Syria, Palestine, Greece, Bulgaria, Cyprus, and Constantinople. Secular buildings, such as the palace in Geguti (tenth to thirteenth centuries), and the academies at Gelat^{c}i (twelfth century) and Ikalt^{c}o (eleventh–twelfth centuries), were erected. The rapid growth of artistic creativity in the High Middle Ages was brought to an end toward the middle of the thirteenth century by the Mongol invasions, and the fifteenth and sixteenth centuries saw a gradual decline in art and architecture.

SCULPTURE

The Middle Ages reveal no evidence of sculpture in the round. However, the earliest examples of reliefs, on the pier capitals of Bolnisi Sioni, vividly depict animals chasing each other or at rest, and on the eastern facade of Djvari are prominent Georgian rulers and the donors of the church in their official costumes.

The end of the tenth and the early eleventh centuries are particularly rich in architectural sculpture, consisting of reliefs both secular and religious in nature, including numerous representations of real and

409

Nikorc^cminda, detail of the tympanum of the west portal, 1010–1014. PHOTOGRAPH BY THE AUTHOR

enth centuries, skillfully carved with intricate geometric patterns and figures of saints and benevolent guardian animals.

METALWORK

Repoussé metalwork in gold and gilded silver flourished in Georgia, but the earliest extant example cannot be dated before the eighth or ninth century. Most common are icons lavishly adorned with precious and semiprecious stones and enamels, such as the one dedicated to the memory of King Leon II (957–967) and a large triptych in Xaχuli adorned with nearly 100 cloisonné enamels deriving from the workshops of Georgia and Constantinople. There are reliably dated gilded book covers, such as the late-twelfth-century work from Opizari, tenth- and eleventh-century pectoral or processional crosses, flabella, chalices, and patens. Besides the repoussé

mythical animals with distinct apotropaic connotations. In some instances (Djvari, Oški) the surfaces of the reliefs were painted in polychrome. As a rule the figures are smaller than lifesize.

ALTAR SCREENS

The great variety of decorative and figural sculpture is preserved on altar screens. The earliest surviving example comes from Cebelda and is dated to the seventh century. Its formal arrangement displays a striking affinity with early Christian ivory diptychs; the style and some of the iconography, however, reveal a definite Sasanian influence, particularly in the costume and headdress of St. Eustathios, shown in the lower register of the closure slab. In the High Middle Ages the closure slab appeared more frequently and was executed with great skill; the character is typically Georgian, with geometric and vegetal patterns as well as scenes from Georgian patristic literature, though in some instances, specifically in the rendering of the human form, Byzantine models are detectable.

In northwestern Georgia (Svanet^ci) there remain several wooden church doors from the tenth or elev-

St. John the Baptist. Detail from the Ančisχat^ci triptych, repoussé silver. Bek^ca Opizari, late 12th century. PHOTOGRAPH BY THE AUTHOR

410

technique, Georgian goldsmiths frequently used engraving, niello, and filigree.

PAINTING

The first examples of Georgian painting are executed in mosaic, such as the floor mosaics in Bitšvinta, dated to the fourth to fifth century, and the floor mosaics containing Georgian inscriptions in a fifth-century monastery near Jerusalem established by a Georgian man of letters, Peter the Iberian (later bishop of Maiuma). Tesserae and other evidence found in the smaller church of Djvari near Mc^{c}χet^{c}a (sixth century) confirm that its conch was covered with mosaics, as was the conch of the apse in C^{c}romi.

From the ninth century on, painted decoration was no longer limited to the conch but covered the entire apse and other parts of the church, as seen with the altar screen at Armazi (864) and the frescoes at Kumurdo (964). After the tenth century al secco painting was commonly used throughout the church. A good example of this is found at Atenis Sioni (1080): in the conch of the apse is the Madonna and Child flanked by the archangels Michael and Gabriel. Below are shown the apostles and church fathers as well as St. Simeon Stylite, a popular figure in Georgia. The squinches are decorated with allegorical representations of the four rivers of paradise.

After the tenth century the close association of Georgian ruling families with the Byzantine court, and the establishment of Georgian monasteries in Antioch, Mt. Athos, Constantinople, and other holy places led to a strong Byzantine influence in the wall paintings. Instructive examples of wall paintings are in the churches of Tao-Klarjet^{c}i and particularly Išχani and Xaχuli, executed in the second half of the tenth century. The domes of these churches contain four hovering angels elevating a cross with widening arms adorned with precious stones. Below, in all cases, are the four chariots of the vision of Zacharia.

The eleventh to thirteenth centuries demonstrate an increasing refinement in the execution of painting (Zemo-Kriχi, Bet^{c}ania, Vardzia), a trend that continued through the fourteenth and fifteenth centuries.

BOOK ILLUSTRATIONS

Illustrated books appeared in Georgia toward the end of the ninth century and during the tenth; surviving examples include the Adiši Gospels (897), the first Djruji Gospels (940), and the Bert^{c}ai Gospels (*ca.* 941–988). The illustrations consist of portraits of the

Sts. Luke and John. Fragment from the Adiši Gospels, Monastery of Šatberdi, 897. PHOTOGRAPH SUPPLIED BY THE AUTHOR

evangelists and canon tables enclosed within architectural frames consisting of arches on columns. The proportions of the evangelists standing against the niches and their plastic rendering betray the Hellenistic stylistic tradition. Iconographically, however, they are closer to Syro-Palestinian and Armenian models. Eleventh-century manuscripts are characterized by an increased decorative vocabulary reflected in elaborate initials and headpieces that are now rectangular instead of semicircular in form. The evangelists have distinct physiognomies, and the illustrations are highly colored. In the twelfth century the number of illustrations multiplied considerably; the second Djruji Gospels, for example, has 359 illustrations; the Four Gospels of Gelat^{c}i has 244. There are some affinities with monumental wall paintings, as seen in the works of Grigor (Gregory) the Theologian. Gradually the linear-style characteristic of early manuscripts copied in the scriptoria of Tao-Klarjet^{c}i replaced the pictorial style featured in the Second Djruji Gospels and the Alaverdi and Gelat^{c}i Gospels.

Although the majority of book illustrations are religious, from the twelfth century on secular subjects were also illustrated. An astronomical treatise of 1188 bears the signs of the zodiac, and representations of the seasons appear in works of Gregory the Theologian.

BIBLIOGRAPHY

General works are Adriano Alpago-Novello, Vakhtang Beridze, *et al., Art and Architecture in Medieval Georgia* (1982); Rusudan Mepisashvili and Vakhtang Tsintsadze, *The Arts of Ancient Georgia* (1979); Giorgi Tshubinashvili, "Georgia, Art of," in *Encyclopedia of World Art,* VI (1971).

On architecture see Wachtang Beridze, "Architecture géorgienne paléochrétienne (IV–VII-s)," in *Corsi di cultura sull'arte ravennate e bizantina* (1973); F. W. Deichmann, "Zur Entwicklung der Pfeilerbasilika: Die Basilica Sion von Bolnisi," in *Second International Symposium on Georgian Art* (1977); N. Djanberidze, *Architectural Monuments of Georgia* (1973); H. Sedlmayer, "Östliche Romanik," in *Erlanger Forschungen,* ser. A, *Geisteswissenschaften,* **20** (1967); Giorgi Tshubinashvili, *Georgische Baukunst,* II, *Die Kirche in Zromi und ihr Mosaik* (1934), and *Pamiatniki tipa Djvari* (1948), with a French summary.

Sculpture is treated in Natela Aladashvili, *Monumentalnaya skulptura Gruzii* (1977), with an English summary; Wachtang Djobadze, "Who Are Represented on the Eastern Facade of the Holy Cross of Mtskheta," in *Oriens Christianus,* **44** (1960) and **45** (1961), and "The Donor Reliefs and the Date of the Church at Oški," in *Byzantinische Zeitschrift,* **69** (1976); Renée Schmerling, *Malye formy v arkhitekture srednevekovoi Gruzii* (1962); David Winfield, "Some Early Medieval Figure Sculpture from Northeast Turkey," in *Journal of the Warburg and Courtauld Institutes,* **31** (1968).

On painting, see Shalva Amiranashvili, *Istoria gruzinskoi monumentalnoi Zhivopisi* (1957); E. L. Privalova, *Pavnisi* (1977), with a French summary; Tina Virsaladze, "Fragmenty drevnei freskovoi rospisi glavnogo Gelatskogo khrama," in *Ars Georgica,* **5** (1959), with a German summary, and "Freskovaia rospis v cerkvi Arkhangelov sela Zemo-Krihi," in *Ars Georgica,* **6** (1963); Aneli Volskaia, *Rospisi srednevekovykh trapeznykh Gruzii* (1974), with a French summary.

Book illustration is treated in Gavane Alibegashvili, *Khudozhestvenni printsip illustrirovania gruzinskoj rukopisnoj knigi 11-nachala 13 vekov* (1973), with a French summary; Shalva Amiranashvili, *Gruzinskaya miniatiura* (1966); R. P. Blake and Sirarpie Der Nersessian, "The Gospels of Bertᶜai: An Old-Georgian Ms. of the Tenth Century," in *Byzantion,* **16** (1942–1943); Renée Schmerling, *Khudozestvennoe oformlenie gruzinskoy rukopisnoy knigi IV–XI vv.* (1979), with a German summary.

Metalwork is the subject of Shalva Amiranashvili, *Medieval Georgian Enamels of Russia* (1964); Wachtang Djobadze, "Notes on Georgian Minor Art of the Post-Byzantine Period," in *Journal of the Walters Art Gallery,* **23** (1960); Tᶜamaz Sanikidze and Guram Abramishvili, *Orfèvrerie géorgienne du VIIᵉ au XIXᵉ siècle* (1979); Giorgi

Tshubinashvili, *Gruzinskoe chekannoe iskusstvo* (1959). On pottery, see Wakhtang Djapᶜaridze, *Kᶜartᶜuli keramikuli cᶜarmoeba XI–XIII ss. sakᶜartᶜvelosi* (1956), with Russian summary.

WACHTANG DJOBADZE

[See also **Atenis Sioni; Bolnisi Seon; David II (IV) the Builder; Djvari; Išχani; Mc ᶜχet ᶜa; Oški; Tsromi; Xaχuli.**]

GEORGIAN CHRONICLE. See **Kᶜartᶜlis Cᶜχovreba.**

GEORGIAN CHURCH AND SAINTS. Medieval Georgia had its own church from the fourth century on, but the identification of the parent-church remains disputed among Antioch, Cappadocia, Armenia, Constantinople, and Jerusalem. The first convert is said to have been St. Nino (*ca.* 338), who would have been dependent on Antioch or Constantinople through her native land of Cappadocia. Under the rule of the Byzantine emperors Zeno and Anastasius I (474–518), who officially endorsed Monophysitism, the Life of the Georgian king Waχtang Gurgasali relates a new autocephalic (Monophysite) church ruled by a katholikos. During this period, the churches of Georgia and Armenia were close enough to claim a common history of conversion by Gregory the Illuminator, and to share a liturgy influenced by Jerusalem, where monasteries of both nations flourished very early. As a result, Nino's legend was inserted in the Armenian history of Pseudo-Movsēs Xorenacᶜi (probably eighth century). Unlike the Armenians, however, the Georgians soon accepted the Chalcedonian religious policy of Emperor Justinian, and the two churches separated in 608. Less isolated by the new Muslim power, Georgia preserved many old Jerusalem traditions, while Armenian church literature was adapted to new conditions. From the ninth and tenth centuries on, as some great Georgian families became influential in Constantinople, Georgian monasteries were founded in Greece, and Byzantine fashion was introduced in Georgia. Georgia remained a strong Christian kingdom from the rule of Dawitᶜ (David) II (IV) the Builder (1073–1125) to the Mongol victory in 1225.

Nearly forty saints or groups of saints are included in the Georgian ecclesiastical calendar. Their Lives reflect the various types that also exist in Byzantine literature; these include historical narratives with hagiographical aim, martyrdoms, lives of ascetics, and lives of prominent founders of great monasteries.

HISTORICAL NARRATIVES

The most complex traditional narrative is certainly the Life of Nino, or the *Conversion of Iberia,* which is attributed to Nino herself, the grand-priest Abiathar, and his daughter Sidonia, and which has been inserted in the Georgian *Annals.* The primary aim of this pseudepigraphical work is to confer on the origins of the Georgian church the symbols of autonomy and celestial conversion that were attributed to Constantine in Roman-Byzantine legend. Thus the discovery of the Lord's Holy Tunic and Elias' mantle in the old city of Mc^c^χet^c^a parallels the finding of the Cross and the Nails by Empress Helena in Jerusalem. The invaluable testimony of Rufinus dated about 400 proves the existence of some historical core for the rule of Mirian III (Meribanes) in the early fourth century. Closer to historiography is the *Martyrdom of St. Šušanik,* written by the priest Jacob of C^c^urt^c^aw not long after her death. Princess Šušanik (Lily), daughter of the Armenian prince Vardan, was married to Vasχen, son of Aršuša, *bdesχ* of C^c^urt^c^aw. After Vasχen urged her to join the Zoroastrian cult and she refused, her husband imprisoned her for seven years with cruel punishments. She became a saint through her asceticism. Her martyrdom is generally dated between 470 and 476, or sometimes 484, according to the testimony of the Armenian historian Łazar P^c^arpec^c^i.

Although King Waχtang Gurgasali is not included in the Georgian calendar, he was surely considered a saint before Justinian's pro-Chalcedonian stance. Waχtang's Life, as it has been preserved by the historian Juanšer, is a difficult source in which history and legend are inextricably intertwined. Nonetheless, the narrative clearly states that Waχtang received the threefold crown of kingdom, prophecy, and martyrdom according to the celestial vision that came to him in a dream while he was attacking the town of Pontus early in his reign, in the mid fifth century. As a prophet he was the founder of the Monophysite church, and according to his Life, he died as a martyr (most probably in 502). His Monophysite role has been censured in the extant Epic.

Of the same period is St. Peter the Iberian, also known as Nabarnugios (Syriac) or Mourvanos (Georgian). He was a direct descendant of the first converted Georgian king. Detained as a hostage in Constantinople during his childhood, he soon devoted himself to monastic life. After several journeys to Palestine, he founded first a Georgian monastery near the Church of Holy Sion. He was chosen and consecrated bishop of Maiuma by the Monophysite bishop of Jerusalem, Theodosius. After a period in Egypt with the Monophysites there, he returned to Maiuma after the publication of the *Henotikon* (edict of union) of Emperor Zeno, and died there in 491. Two Lives are preserved, one Syriac and one Georgian. The Syriac Life, written from the point of view of a Palestinian disciple, is openly Monophysite. The Georgian one, rewritten by a certain Makari and preserved in a fifteenth-century codex, is devoid of any Monophysite features. Makari's testimony that he translated himself the Syriac Life of Peter's disciple Zak^c^arē (Zacharias) is therefore doubtful. His aim is most probably to confirm the orthodoxy of the great prince, monk, and bishop. At one time it was believed that Peter the Iberian and his disciple Iwanē (John) the Eunuch were the authors of the Corpus Areopagiticum (the writings attributed to Dionysus the Areopagite); this hypothesis is generally rejected today, but the debate has not been decisively resolved.

Under the rule of Dawit^c^ II the Builder, Georgia achieved military independence, and a strong ecclesiastical reform took place. Dawit^c^'s fame became so great that he was identified with the mythical Prester John in Western churches. Dawit^c^ has an anonymous Life inserted in the Georgian *Annals.* It is, however, a purely hagiographical work of the Byzantine "High Style."

The most brilliant period of Georgian culture is marked by the rule of Queen Tamar (1184–1212), who was canonized only recently. In the several Lives written about her, she embodies the ideal of the gracious medieval queen. Her hagiographer, Dawit^c^, does not mention her unhappy first marriage with Prince Yuri of Kiev, who attempted to vindicate his rights against Tamar's second husband, the prince of Ossetia, in 1191.

MARTYRDOMS

The literature about the Georgian martyrs is naturally more free of secular history; it includes materials that are essentially historical, those that seem to be more legendary, and those that were only composed with historical records in the eighteenth century. The Martyrdoms of Eustathios of Mc^c^χet^c^a (*ca.* 550) and Abo of Tbilisi (*d.* 786) are among the best genuine compositions, with many archaic features in the classical pattern of a Greek *Martyrium.*

Abo's tetralogy can be compared with that of Step^{c}anos Protomartyr, which is well preserved only in Georgian. Also among the historical narratives are the stories of Dawit^c and Constantin (*d.* 741), King Archil II (eighth century), Constantine Kaχa (ninth century), Michael Gobron (*ca.* 918), King Luarsab (*d.* 1615), Queen Ketevan and her confessor, the Basilian monk Movsēs (*d.* 1624), and Šio Gardjeli (*ca.* 1696). By contrast, the historical background of the *Martyrdom* of Dawit^c and Tiridjan (fourth century) is most uncertain: it seems to serve as the mirror of the execution of Šušanik by the Georgian Vasχen, for here the Georgians are the victims of an Armenian prince. The *Martyrium* of the nine children of Kola, supposedly sixth century, is strongly etiological in character.

Georgian saints' lives were collected by Bessarion Orbelišvili around 1737, and Katholikos Antoni Bagrationi composed the *Martirika* in 1769 in honor of all the Georgian martyrs. The latter work includes five new insertions: St. Ražden (fifth century), whose relics are said to have been obtained by Waχtang Gurgasali; Šalva Mandaturuχuc^{c}essi of Aχalc^{c}iχe (thirteenth century); the 10,000 martyrs of Tbilisi under Genghis Khan (1225), a number probably matching that of the 10,000 martyrs of Ayrarat in Armenian tradition; the martyrs of Kuabtaqev under Tamerlane (1386); and the martyrs of the monastery of Dawid-Garedja (fifteenth century).

ASCETICS

Georgian ascetic monks are represented first of all by the Syrian fathers who settled in Georgia in the sixth century—Iwanē Zedazneli, Ise C^{c}ilkani and his disciple Anthony the Solitary, Iosep (Joseph) Alaverdeli, Šio Młwimeli, Abibos Nekreseli, Dawit^c Garedjeli—as well as, somewhat later, Dodo Garedjeli and Serapion of Zarzma (ninth century), whose narrative is more connected with the promotion of the local dynasty. Kat^{c}ołikos Antoni also adds Neophytos of Urbnisi. All of these names are actually toponyms for the oldest monasteries of Georgia, and the literary genre of those Lives is more akin to the Greek *Paterika*. Among the later Georgian ascetics were Luke of the Convent of the Holy Cross (1260) and Nicholas Dvali in Jerusalem (1314).

FOUNDERS' LIVES

This group includes the three very long Lives of Grigor of Xandzt^{c}a (*d.* 861), Hilarion of Iberia (*d.* 875), and Iwanē and Euthymios (*d.* 1028), who are the founders of the great monasteries of Tao-Klarjeti

(in what is now eastern Turkey), of Georgian monachism in Mount Olympos of Bithynia, and of the great settlement of Mount Athos, respectively. Greek literary parallels are found in the Lives of Athanasius of Mount Athos and Ioannikios of Mount Olympos. It is a quite well-documented story, but one with clear political aim. The Greek Life of Athanasius significantly is silent on the subject of the claims of an older Georgian influence in Mount Athos. Close to these saints are Giorgi Proχore (*d.* 1066), founder of the Convent of the Holy Cross in Jerusalem, and Giorgi Mtac^{c}mindeli (*d.* 1065), one of the great translators of Mount Athos.

BIBLIOGRAPHY

The corpus of Georgian texts is being published as *Jveli K^{c}art^{c}uli agiogra p^{c}iuli jeglebi*, 6 vols. to date (1963–). The best edition of the *Annals* is now that of S. Qaukhcishvili, *K^{c}art^{c}lis tskhovreba*, 2 vols. (1955–1959); see also Cyril Toumanoff, "Medieval Georgian Historical Literature (VIIth–XVth Centuries)," in *Traditio*, **1** (1943), "Christian Caucasia Between Byzantium and Iran," *ibid.*, **10** (1954), and "Caucasia and Byzantine Studies," *ibid.*, **12** (1956). Summaries of the Lives may be found in David Marshall Lang, ed. and trans., *Lives and Legends of the Georgian Saints* (1956). Useful information may also be found in K. Salia, *Histoire de la nation géorgienne* (1980).

MICHEL VAN ESBROECK

[See also **Hagiography, Georgian; Henotikon.**]

GEORGIAN LANGUAGE. Georgian is the only written member of the Kartvelian (South Caucasian) linguistic family. The earliest known examples of written Georgian are mosaic inscriptions from a Georgian monastery near Bethlehem (first half of the fifth century) and the Sioni (Zion) Cathedral inscription from Bolnisi, Georgia (493/494). These were written in the first attested form of the Georgian alphabet, the angular χuc^{c}uri (ecclesiastic) alphabet, which faithfully follows the order of the Greek alphabet in the use of letters as numerals. It is most likely that the χuc^{c}uri was created in Georgia shortly after the adoption of Christianity, about 337. A minuscule form (k^{c}utχovani or nusχuri) developed in the ninth century; from it the contemporary cursive alphabet (mχedruli, "civil") evolved in the eleventh century. Mχedruli does not distinguish between upper and lower cases. The current version consists of thirty-three letters.

The history of the Georgian language is generally

	Labial	Dental	Alveopalatal	Velar	Pharyngeal
Stops	*p ṗ b*	*t ṭ d*		*k ḳ g*	
Affricates	*v*	*c ç j*	*č č̣ ǰ*		
Fricatives		*s z*	*š ž*		*χ q̇ ğ*

divided into two periods: Old Georgian, from the fifth through twelfth centuries, and New Georgian, from the twelfth century on. In its sound system Georgian shares with most of the Caucasian languages a phonemic opposition between voiced stops and glottalized voiceless and aspirated voiceless stops (the subscript period indicates glottalization), as shown in the above table.

In addition there are the nasals *m* and *n,* the liquids *r* and *l,* and the glide *h.* Old Georgian also has the glides *y* and *w* and an aspirated *q.* Both Old and New Georgian have a five-vowel system: *a, e, i, o, u.* The position of the very weak stress is not distinctive for either period of the language. Very common are harmonic clusters, consisting of a labial, dental, or alveopalatal stop or an affricate followed by a velar or pharyngeal, agreeing in articulatory type: for example, *pk, ṗḳ, bg, tk, ṭḳ, dg; ck, çḳ, jg; pχ, ṗq̇, bğ; tχ, ṭq̇, dğ; cχ, çq̇, jğ.*

In Old Georgian there are eight cases for nouns: nominative, absolutive, ergative, dative, genitive, instrumental, adverbial, and vocative; New Georgian lacks the absolutive. In Old Georgian the plural normally has three forms: nominative, vocative, and one form serving for all the remaining cases except the absolutive. In New Georgian the plural is formed from the singular stem with the addition of the suffix *-eb-* before the case ending. In Old Georgian the adjective generally follows the noun it modifies, though the reverse order is also found. Both the adjective and the noun are declined identically, the adjective agreeing in case and number with the noun. There is no grammatical gender. Nouns in the genitive, which usually follow the noun to which they refer, also agree with the noun in case and number: *ṗatron-i saχl-isa-y* (owner [nominative] of the house [genitive plus nominative]), *ṗatron-man saχl-isa-*

man (owner [ergative] of the house [genitive plus ergative]). In New Georgian the adjective generally precedes the noun it modifies and has a special attributive declension if it ends in a consonant; adjectives ending in a vowel are not declined. Genitives precede the noun to which they refer and are not further declined: *saχl-is ṗatron-i* (the house's [genitive] owner [nominative]), *saχl-is ṗatron-ma* (the house's [genitive] owner [ergative]).

The verbal system is extremely complex in both Old and New Georgian. In both, verbs can be classified as transitive (active), passive (including inceptives), middle (generally intransitive active verbs), and *verba sentiendi* (denoting feelings or emotions). There can be three series of forms, each consisting of three sets, one marking a present, one a past, and the third a modal meaning:

Series→	*Present*	*Aorist*	*Perfect*
Present	present	[permansive]	perfect
Past	imperfect	aorist	pluperfect
Modal	conjunctive	optative	[conjunctive perfect]

In New Georgian the permansive and the conjunctive perfect have been lost and a future series has been formed with a future, conditional, and conjunctive future. The verb form itself is capable of marking not only the subject of the sentence but also the person of direct and indirect objects: for example, *maǰlevs* (he gives it to me), *gaǰlevs* (he gives it to you), *maǰlev* (you give it to me), *gaǰlev* (I give it to you), and so on. In Georgian the grammatical subject and objects of the verb vary in case according to verb type and series. For transitive and middle verbs they are as shown below:

Series ↓	*Subject*	*Direct Object*	*Indirect Object*
Present	nominative	dative	dative
Aorist	ergative	nominative	dative
Perfect	dative	nominative	———

With passive verbs the subject is always nominative and any indirect object is dative, while with the *verba sentiendi* the subject is dative and the object is nominative. Indirect objects often have special version markers, indicating most commonly possession or the person for whose benefit an action is performed. In addition to the formation of passives, there is a formation of causatives, from both transitive and intransitive verbs.

The vocabulary of Georgian comes from diverse sources. In addition to the original, inherited Kartvelian roots there are great numbers of loanwords, primarily from Persian, Turkish, Arabic, Greek, Aramaic, and Armenian.

Although many attempts have been made to show a genetic relationship between Georgian and the languages of the North Caucasus (as well as with more distant languages, such as Basque), none can be viewed as successful; and Georgian, along with the unwritten Svan, Mingrelian, and Laz, remains linguistically isolated.

BIBLIOGRAPHY

Howard I. Aronson, *Georgian: A Reading Grammar* (1982); Shota V. Dzidziguri, *The Georgian Language* (1969); Nicolas Marr and Marcel Brière, *La langue géorgienne* (1931); Boris T. Rudenko, *Grammatika gruzinskogo yazyka* (1940); Kita Tschenkéli, *Einführung in die georgische Sprache,* 2 vols. (1958); Hans Vogt, *Grammaire de la langue géorgienne* (1971); Franz Zorell, S.J., *Grammatik zur altgeorgischen Bibelübersetzung mit Textproben und Wörterverzeichnis* (1930); Renée Zwolanek and Julius Assfalg, *Altgeorgische Grammatik* (1976).

HOWARD I. ARONSON

[See also **Alphabets.**]

GEORGIAN LITERATURE. The written literature of Georgia begins in the fifth century of the Christian era. As in neighboring Armenia, the invention of a special script for the national language was the work of ecclesiastical circles, and the first works produced in Georgian were church-oriented—the translation of biblical and liturgical texts. Armenian tradition has it that Maštocᶜ, who invented the Armenian script, also invented the Georgian and Caucasian Albanian scripts, but there is no corroborating evidence. The earliest dated surviving text in Georgian is the inscription of the church of Bolnisi Sion (493). Some of the Georgian inscriptions on mosaic pavements in Palestine have also been dated to the fifth century. Fragments of manuscripts survive that may be dated to the sixth or seventh century, but the earliest precisely dated manuscripts are from the second half of the ninth century.

In the mid fifth century Georgian monks in Palestine were already using the Gospels, Pauline Epistles, and Psalms in their own tongue. The other books of the Old Testament were translated during the next century or so. The first translation of the Gospels and Acts, based on an Armenian text, was later revised against the Greek.

The earliest original composition in Georgian is the *Martyrdom of St. Šušanik* (Susan); the saint was the daughter of the Armenian general Vardan Mamikonean (who was killed in battle against Persia in 451). The *Martyrdom* is attributed to her father confessor, Jacob of Cᶜurtᶜavi. Paul Peeters' conclusion that the text as it exists today is not the work of an eyewitness and that it was not known to Georgian writers until after the separation of the Armenian and Georgian churches at the beginning of the seventh century has not won acceptance in Georgian circles, where the *Martyrdom* is revered as the first mature production of Georgian literature.

Accounts of saints and martyrs, either native Georgians or foreigners, continued to form a significant part of early Georgian literature. Of particular interest for the earlier period are the *Martyrdom of St. Abo of Tbilisi* (end of the eighth century) written by Ioane Sabanisdze, about a Muslim from Baghdad who came to Georgia with Prince Nerses, and the *Life of Grigor of Xandztᶜa* by Giorgi Merčuli, an important source for the history of monasticism in southwest Georgia. Grigor (Gregory) died in 861, and the *Life* dates from the mid tenth century. Only slightly later is the first recension of the *Lives of the Thirteen Syrian Fathers,* which is attributed to Katᶜolikos Arsen II (955–980) and describes the origins of monasticism in sixth-century Georgia.

In addition to early ties with Palestine, which continued after the Muslim occupation and led to numerous translations of Christian texts from Arabic, the Georgians had close political and religious links with Byzantium. Georgian monasteries were established in Greek lands (notably Mount Athos, the site of Iviron ["of the Iberians," as the Greeks called the Georgians]), and an efflorescence of theological and philosophical writing based on Greek models took place in the eleventh and twelfth centuries. Among the earlier translations from Greek, special mention should be made of the *Physiologus* (a collection of animal tales overlaid with Christian symbolism); the Georgian rendering may predate the eighth century.

The foundation of the Georgian monastery on Mount Athos at the end of the tenth century by Ioane, his son Ep^{c}t^{c}me (Euthymios), and Tornikios is described in the *Life of Euthymios* by Giorgi Mt^{c}ac^{c}mindeli (of the holy mountain) the Athonite, an abbot of Iviron (d. 1066). Euthymios' literary career is particularly important. His Greek rendering of the story of Barlaam and Josaphat, the *Balavariani*, is one of the few translations from Georgian into a foreign language. Of greater significance from the Georgian viewpoint was his work on biblical texts: the Apocalypse of John, which he translated for the first time into Georgian, his revision of the Psalms and Gospels, again from Greek texts; his translation of numerous patristic biblical commentaries and of other ascetic, homiletic, and hagiographical works.

Even more significant for the impact of Byzantine liturgical traditions in Georgia were the translations by Giorgi the Athonite of numerous Greek texts including the *Synaxarion*, based on that of Hagia Sophia in Constantinople, and the *Menaia* for the twelve months of the year. From a more strictly literary point of view, the greatest scholar of the eleventh century was Ep^{c}temi Mc^{c}ire (Ephrem the Less), who spent most of his life as a monk on the Black Mountain near Antioch—a monastic center for Greeks, Georgians, Armenians, Syrians, and later for Latins as well. His most important works are commentaries on the Psalms and Pauline Epistles that draw on the great works of Greek patristic exegesis, and translations of ascetic, hagiographical, and homiletic treatises of various authors and the work of Dionysius the Areopagite.

Arsen Iqalt^{c}oeli was Ep^{c}temi's pupil on the Black Mountain. After his master's death Arsen moved to Constantinople, where he translated several texts, including the *Chronicle* of George Hamartolus. In 1114 he returned to Georgia, where he continued Ep^{c}temi's interest in theology and philosophy. The most renowned Georgian philosopher of the medieval period, Ioane Petric^{c}i, studied in Constantinople under Michael Psellos and Johannes Italos. For many years he worked at the monastery of Petric^{c}oni (at Bachkovo in Bulgaria)—hence his name—then returned to Georgia to work at Gelat^{c}i (near Kutaisi), where he founded the most famous medieval Georgian academy. He died about 1125. Ioane's translations cover many fields: history (including the first fifteen books of Josephus' *Antiqui-*

ties), hagiography, astronomy, and, most especially, philosophy. He was responsible for Georgian versions of Nemesius of Emesa's *On the Nature of Man*, Proclus' *Elements of Theology*, and Aristotle's *Topica* and *De interpretatione*. His style is so literal as to be obscure, if not incomprehensible. But his great importance is that he founded a school of Georgian philosophy based on Neoplatonic principles. From then on, the influence of the more strictly religious thought of the monks on Athos declined, and in the following centuries it was secular literature that predominated in Georgia. Indeed, the non-Christian but Neoplatonic ethos of the Georgian epic poem *The Man in the Panther's Skin*, by Shot^{c}a Rust^{c}aveli, would be all the more incomprehensible without this well-established tradition in medieval Georgia.

Theology and philosophy did not exhaust the interests of medieval Georgian scholars. Among the nontheological texts translated from Greek, the *Alexander Romance* of Pseudo-Callisthenes was particularly influential. It was used both as a supposedly historical document and as a source for parallels of a flattering nature—as in a panegyric of King David IV the Builder by the twelfth-century monk Arsen.

Although the Georgians did not produce as many historians in the first centuries of literacy as did the Armenians, there did develop an important historical literature. The earliest such text is the *Conversion of Georgia* by Grigor (Gregory) the Deacon, tentatively dated to the seventh century, though the date has been disputed. To the story of St. Nino (the slave woman with miraculous powers of healing who converted the Georgian king Mirian III *ca.* 337) have been added an account of the legendary invasion of Georgia by Alexander the Great and lists of Georgian kings down to the ninth century. A similar collection, attributed to Leontius Mroveli, makes up the first part of the Georgian *Annals*, the royal histories formally titled K^{c}art^{c}lis c^{c}xovreba (Life of Georgia) and covering the period to the fourteenth century.

Other noteworthy chronicles include the *Dīvān of Kings* by King Bagrat III (d. 1014); a work devoted to the genealogy of the sovereigns of western Georgia, and the *History of the Bagratids*, compiled by Smbat about 1030. A much more elaborate work, the latter gives a legendary origin for the Georgian Bagratid dynasty, tracing it back to King David of Israel and glossing over its Armenian origins. (The Armenian Bagratid claim to a Jewish origin is put forth in the *History of the Armenians* by Movsēs Xorenac^{c}i.) Of the *History of Queen Tamar* (reigned 1184–1212) by her contemporary Basil, only the part down to 1204/1206 has survived. The *History of the Five Reigns* (Demetrius I, David, Giorgi III, Tamar, and Giorgi IV) was written by an anonymous contemporary of Giorgi IV (reigned 1212–1223). The *History of the Invasions of Timur* (Tamerlane) was written in the fifteenth century and then reedited at the time of the compilation of the Georgian *Annals* in the eighteenth century.

Two panegyrical poetic works of the twelfth century are noteworthy: the *Abdulmesiani* (Arabic: ᶜAbd al-Masīḥ, "servant of Christ") written in honor of David the Builder by Ioane Šavteli, enjoyed a high reputation; and the *Tᶜamariani,* composed in honor of queen Tamar and attributed to Šaχruχadze. The latter is in a more stilted style but is interesting for its numerous reminiscences of ancient Greek literature as well as of the romance of *Laylā and Majnūn.* This famous composition by the Persian poet Nizāmī also had a strong influence on Šotᶜa Rustᶜaveli; a Georgian version seems to have been made soon after the Persian original appeared in 1188/1189, and it was translated again in the seventeenth century by King Tᶜeimuraz I. An early version of the collection of animal fables known as *Kalīla wa dimna,* translated from the Persian, was lost, and then the book was retranslated in the early eighteenth century.

Another significant medieval Georgian text, the *Visramiani,* was also a rendering of a Persian tale, the story of Vīs and Rāmīn, put into verse by Gurgānī after 1054. In some places the Georgian adapts the Persian rather than rendering it exactly; in other places there are slight elaborations or contractions, and some references to Christianity have been added. The Georgian translation is traditionally ascribed to Sargis Tᶜmogveli, who is mentioned in the final stanza of the epic by Rustᶜaveli, the *Man in the Panther's Skin,* though this stanza may not be original.

Of equal importance for secular Georgian literature is the *Amiran darejaniani* (Story of Amiran, son of Darejan), a prose tale in twelve sections describing the adventures of Amiran and his friends as they roam the world hunting *dev*s. This original Georgian work is a collection of tales from various sources rather than a single story with a coherent, organized plot. Some of the heroes are mentioned in other sources before the end of the twelfth century, but the date of the final composition is unknown. In the final stanza of Rustᶜaveli's *Man in the Panther's Skin* it is ascribed to a certain Mose Xoneli, of whom

nothing else is known. (This epic by Rustᶜaveli is the most remarkable of all Georgian literary works and is discussed in a separate article, "Šotᶜa Rustᶜaveli.")

Following the great efflorescence of religious and secular prose and poetry in the twelfth and early thirteenth centuries, there was a marked drop in the quality of work produced. The most characteristic compositions of the next 200 years are romantic epics in prose or rhyme, based on Georgian legends or Persian themes, including numerous adaptations and imitations of Firdawsī's epic poem, the *Shāhnāma.* It was only after 1500 that renewed creativity led to the development of lyric poetry and the scholarship of the later Georgian kings.

BIBLIOGRAPHY

Sources. Georgian texts in translation are available in the following: (Geography) Marie F. Brosset, trans., *Description géographique de la Géorgie par le Tsarévitch Wakhoucht* (1842). (Hagiography) Paul Peeters, "Histoires monastiques géorgiennes," in *Analecta Bollandiana,* 36–37 (1917–1919), which contains the lives of Ioane and Euthymios, Giorgi the Athonite, Serapion of Zarzma, and Grigor of Xandztᶜa; David M. Lang, *Lives and Legends of the Georgian Saints* (1956), and *The Balavariani* (1966). (History) Marie F. Brosset, *Histoire de Géorgie,* 4 vols. (1849–1857). (Law) J. Karst, *Le code géorgien de Vakhtang VI,* 2 vols. (1935–1937); and *Corpus juris ibero-caucasici,* 5 vols. (1934–1940). (Secular literature) Marjorie Wardrop, trans., *The Man in the Panther's Skin* (1912, repr. 1966); Robert H. Stevenson, trans., *Amiran-Darejaniani* (1958); Oliver Wardrop, trans., *Visramiani* (1914, repr. 1966); Adolf Endler, ed., *Georgische Poesie aus acht Jahrhunderten* (1971).

Studies. For a brief survey of Georgian literature from the beginnings to the twelfth century, see Gerhard Deeters, "Georgische Literatur," in *Armenisch und Kaukasische Sprachen* (1963). Less up-to-date is J. Karst, *Littérature géorgienne chrétienne,* in the series Bibliothèque catholique des sciences religieuses (1934). Karst and all later surveys depend on K. Kekelidze, *Kᶜartᶜuli literaturis istoria,* 2 vols. (1923–1924, rev. ed. 1958–1960). Vol. I of *Kᶜartᶜuli* forms the basis for the comprehensive study by M. Tarchnišvili, *Geschichte der kirklichen georgischen Literatur* (1955). For brief surveys of *Kᶜartᶜuli* see R. P. Blake, "Georgian Theological Literature," in *Journal of Theological Studies,* 26 (1924), and "Georgian Secular Literature, Epic, Romantic, and Lyric (1100–1800)," in *Harvard Studies and Notes in Philology and Literature,* 15 (1933). For a general survey of Georgian historical literature, see Cyril Toumanoff, "Medieval Georgian Historical Literature, VIIth–XVth Centuries," in *Traditio,* 1 (1943). There is a useful bibliography of theological and liturgical literature in Michel van Esbroeck, *Les plus anciens homéliaires*

418

géorgiens (1975). For Georgian law, see Georges Charachidze, *Introduction à l'étude de la féodalité géorgienne* (1971). The only Western journal devoted to Georgian studies is *Bedi Kartlisa,* published in Paris annually since 1948.

R. W. THOMSON

[See also **Balavariani; Gelat^ci; K^cart^clis C^cχovreba; Hagiography, Georgian; Šot^ca Rust^caveli; Tamar.**]

GEORGIANS (IBERIANS). Although the earliest traditions of the Georgian chronicles (*K^cart^clis c^cχovreba,* Life of Georgia) tell of the giant K^cart^clos and his brothers settling in the valleys of the Kura and Rioni Rivers, the actual ethnogenesis of the Georgian people is not traced by modern scholars from this eponymous hero but from more mundane linguistic, historical, and archaeological evidence. The people who today call themselves *k^cart^cveli* (Georgian) and their country *sak^cart^cvelo* (country of the Georgians) have probably lived in Transcaucasia and eastern Anatolia since the beginning of human evolution. Ancient place-names and the findings of archaeologists do not indicate any great changes in the ethnic composition of the peoples of Caucasia. The languages of the Georgian peoples belong to the southern Caucasian language group known as Kartvelian (*k^cart^cveluri*) and are believed to be descended from an original, proto-Georgian language that began to break into several distinct but related languages about 4,000 years ago. On the basis of language it has been established that the Georgians were made up of three principal tribes—the Karts, the Megrelo-Čans (Zvans), and the Svans—but that there were other Georgian-speaking tribes in Asia Minor, among them the Kaškai (Gashkai), the Muški (Moschi, Mesχi), and the Tibalians (Tibareni).

Signs of primitive peoples living in Georgia have been found dating back to the early Paleolithic, but only in the sixth to fifth centuries B.C. did Georgian-speaking tribes, probably Muški and Tibalians, make their way northeast to settle in the Kura River valley, where they formed the nucleus of the Iberian or East Georgian nation. Their capital was established at Mc^cχet^ca and defended by the fortresses of Armazi on Mount Bagineti and Sevamora on the Aragvi River. Western Georgia, separated from Iberia (K^cart^cli) by the Surami Mountains, was known to the ancient Greeks as Colchis and to the Georgians as Egrisi and later as Ap^cχazet^ci or Imeret^ci. The

Georgians living along the coast and in the Rioni River valley were in close contact with Greek traders and settlers from the sixth century. The cultural influences in Colchis were Hellenic and Hellenistic, while those in Iberia were heavily Persian.

According to Herodotus, the proto-Georgian tribes—the Moschi, Tibareni, Macrones, Mosynoeci, and Mares—made up the nineteenth satrapy of the Achaemenid Empire, but when the Macedonians under Alexander ended the hegemony of the Persians over Asia Minor, these Iberian tribes united under a local dynast, P^carnavazi, and established the first "state" in East Georgia. From the Georgian chronicles and from Strabo it is possible to arrive at a picture of Iberian society's Persian roots. The ruling elite included the king (*mep^ce*) and his closest relatives; the second estate was the pagan priesthood; the third was made up of soldiers and farmers; the fourth was the common people. Over the basic tribal-dynastic structure of Georgian society P^carnavazi imposed a "feudal" hierarchy. A high constable (*spaspeti*) was appointed by the king from among the dynastic aristocracy, and all provincial and local officials were subordinated to him. In each province an *erist^cavi* or *pitiaχš(i)* was appointed as governor, and lesser nobles served as generals, tax collectors, and local administrators. The "feudal" aspects of Georgian society worked to support royal power and keep the country united, while the more ancient tribal-dynastic aspects challenged monarchical authority and encouraged regionalism.

United into a state, the eastern Georgians or K^carts began the gradual assimilation of the various tribes under their sway. The hegemony of Iberia over Colchis-Egrisi and its relative independence from the Seleucid Empire aided in the consolidation of the Kartvelian speakers into a single nationality. The Georgian people were distinguished not only by language and by distinctive aspects of their pagan religion, but also by their sociopolitical formation, which developed along lines more similar to that of the Persians than that of the Greeks and Romans. The king of K^cart^cli-Iberia was a hereditary monarch, like the Persian great king, not an elected or appointed ruler as in the Roman tradition. K^cart^cli early developed a privileged and hereditary nobility based on the land, just as its neighbor to the east had done, and in distinction to Rome-Byzantium, in which the ruling stratum was an imperial officialdom, nonhereditary and largely the creature of the emperor. Yet for all the similarity to Persian society, Georgia early in the fourth century distinguished itself strikingly from the eastern empire and identified in religion with the Byzantines by converting to Christianity.

In the formative period of the fourth to eighth centuries, Georgian society remained divided territorially into "lands" reflecting the ancient tribes and clans that had migrated and merged to form the Georgian people. A tension persisted between efforts of the monarchs to centralize their fragmented kingdom and reinforce a "feudal" hierarchy and the counterefforts of local dynasts to retain their regional authority. The dynasts were prepared to ally with the aristocratic-tribal empire of Persia to thwart royal centralization, while the Georgian kings in general preferred allegiance to Rome-Byzantium with its more monolithic state apparatus. Neither empire was ever consistently or extraordinarily strong enough to dominate Caucasia permanently, and Georgia and Armenia were able to retain a precarious independence between Persia and Byzantium precisely because of the limited military strength of their neighbors. Within Georgia the kings were able to construct a hierarchical governing system (*patronqmoba*), based at first on personal ties and contracts as well as on the granting of benefices. By the eleventh century the relationship between such ties and landed property had been formalized, and in the classical period of Georgian "feudalism" (eleventh to fourteenth centuries) vassal–lord ties based on service were firmly established.

While the Georgian monarchy under Dawit^c (David) II (IV), Giorgi III (IV), and Tamar in the twelfth and thirteenth centuries gained enough strength to wage a successful struggle against Seljuk invaders, their successors proved unable to hold off the Mongols, the Turkomans, and the invasions of Tamerlane in the thirteenth and fourteenth centuries. The effects of Mongol hegemony were to splinter the Georgian kingdom, and despite a brief feudal revival under Giorgi VI (V) the Brilliant (1314–1346), *patronqmoba* dissolved into direct rule by the dynastic princes (*t^cavadoba*). For the next several centuries, until the Russian annexation in 1801, Georgia was divided into several small kingdoms and principalities, with those in the west dominated by the Ottoman Turks and those in the east by the Persians.

BIBLIOGRAPHY

William E. D. Allen, "The Ancient Caucasus and the Origin of the Georgians," in *Asiatic Review* (October 1928), and *A History of the Georgian People*, 2nd ed. (1971); N. A. Berdzenishvili, V. D. Dondua, M. K. Dum-badze, G. A. Melikishvili, and Sh. A. Meskhia, *Istoriia Gruzii*, I, *S drevneishikh vremen do 60-kh godov XIX veka* (1962); Marie F. Brosset, *Histoire de la Géorgie, depuis l'antiquité jusqu'au XIXe siècle, publiée en géorgien*, I, *Histoire ancienne, jusqu'en 1469 de J.C.*, 2 vols. (1849–1850); Charles Burney and David Marshall Lang, *The Peoples of the Hills: Ancient Ararat and Caucasus* (1972); Georges Charachidze, *Le système religieux de la Géorgie paienne, analyse structurale d'une civilisation* (1968); Artur Christensen, *L'Iran sous les Sassanides*, 2nd ed. (1944); I. A. Dzhavakhov (Javakhishvili), *Gosudarstvenni stroi drevnei Gruzii i drevnei Armenii* (1905); David Marshall Lang, *The Georgians* (1966); C. F. Lehmann-Haupt, "On the Origin of the Georgians," in *Georgica*, 1 (1937); Arthur Leist, *Das georgische volk* (1903); G. A. Melikishvili, *K istorii drevnei Gruzii* (1959); S. Qaukhchishvili, ed., *K^cart^clis c^cχovreba: Ana dedopliseuli nusχa* (1942); E. Taqaishvili, ed., *K^cart^clis cχovreba: Mariam dedoplis varianti* (1906); Cyril Toumanoff, *Studies in Christian Caucasian History* (1963).

RONALD GRIGOR SUNY

[See also **Caucasia; David II (IV) the Builder; Giorgi III; K^cart^clis c^cχovreba; Patronqmoba; Tamar.**]

GEORGSLIED, an incomplete Old High German poem about the life of St. George. It is entered at the end of the Heidelberg manuscript of Otfrid's *Evangelienbuch* by a scribe who names himself at the end of the text as Wisolf. It recounts George's trial, imprisonment, torture, death, repeated resurrection, miracles, and preaching under the tyrant Tacianus (that is, Dacianus, or Galerius). Divisible into strophes and employing refrains, it may have been composed at the Abbey of St. George on the Reichenau, where the saint's relics were translated in 896, and intended for processional singing. Wisolf's spelling is highly eccentric, and he breaks off suddenly with the confession "nequeo Vuisolf" ([I] Wisolf am unable).

BIBLIOGRAPHY

John Knight Bostock, *A Handbook of Old High German Literature*, 2nd ed. (1976), 222–234.

DAVID R. MCLINTOCK

[See also **Otfrid von Weissenburg.**]

GERALD OF WALES (Giraldus Cambrensis) (1146–1223), historian, churchman, man of letters. He was born in Manorbier, Pembrokeshire, South Wales, the youngest son of William de Barri, an Anglo-Norman knight, and Angharad, granddaughter of Rhys ap Tewdr, prince of South Wales. Destined for the church, he was educated at St. Peter's, Gloucester, and in Paris. During his first stay in Paris in the 1160's, he studied the arts and taught rhetoric. By 1174 he held benefices in both England and Wales and was serving as legate of Archbishop Richard of Canterbury to the diocese of St. David's (Wales), where he showed himself to be an ardent reformer by zealously enforcing clerical celibacy and the payment of tithes. After suspending an aged archdeacon of Brecon (Brecknock) for refusing to leave his mistress, he was appointed to the archdeaconry by his uncle, David fitz Gerald, bishop of St. David's (1148–1176). It was the highest office he ever held. When his uncle died, Gerald failed in his first bid to become bishop of St. David's and returned to Paris to further his studies in law and theology. He returned to England in 1179 and served as commissary of Peter de Leia, the new bishop of St. David's, administering the diocese during his conflict with the cathedral chapter. In 1184, Gerald was appointed a court chaplain by Henry II; during his ten years in royal service, he became a prolific writer.

Gerald's first two books, the *Topographia Hibernica* and the *Expugnatio Hibernica,* result from his experience as a member of Prince John's expedition to Ireland (1185–1186). After joining Archbishop Baldwin of Canterbury on a five-week journey to Wales to preach the crusade in 1188, he composed his two most popular works: the *Itinerarium Kambriae,* an account of the journey, and the more general *Descriptio Kambriae.* For reasons unknown to us, Gerald retired from the court in 1194 and returned to the schools. Prevented by war from returning to Paris, he spent the next four years in Oxford and Lincoln. When Peter de Leia died in 1198, the chapter of St. David's elected Gerald bishop, but their choice was opposed by Hubert Walter, the archbishop of Canterbury, and by King John. Gerald spent more than four years in litigation and made three trips to Rome trying to secure papal approval of his election and recognition of the metropolitan status of St. David's. In 1203, he accepted defeat; for the remaining twenty years of his life he devoted his time entirely to letters.

Written or revised during these years were a number of works that tell bitterly of the long dispute over St. David's: *De invectionibus, De iure et statu Menevensis Ecclesiae,* the *Speculum duorum,* and the autobiographical *De rebus a se gestis,* in which Gerald attempts to account for his failure. He was also the author of two theological treatises (the *Gemma ecclesiastica* and the *Speculum ecclesiae*), a political tract *(De principis instructione),* and several hagiographical works. Perhaps most representative of the range of his learning, skill as a Latinist, and his vanity and self-justification is the *Symbolum electorum,* a collection of poems, speeches, and short tracts he compiled near the end of his life. These later works remain less well known than Gerald's more original and valuable historical and ethnographical writings on Ireland and Wales. Gerald wrote only in Latin; he did not know the languages of Ireland or Wales.

BIBLIOGRAPHY

Sources. The *Opera* of Giraldus Cambrensis fill eight volumes of the Rolls Series, John S. Brewer, James F. Dimock, and George F. Warner, eds. (1861–1891). The *Speculum duorum* has recently been edited by Yves Lefèvre and R. B. C. Huygens, with translation by Brian Dawson (1974). A new critical edition of the valuable but damaged preface to the *Speculum ecclesiae* has been published by Richard W. Hunt in *Viator,* 8 (1977). Translations include *The Autobiography of Giraldus Cambrensis,* Harold E. Butler, trans. (1937); *The Historical Works of Giraldus Cambrensis,* Thomas Foerster, trans. (1887, repr. 1968); and *The Journey Through Wales and The Description of Wales,* Lewis Thorpe, trans. (1978).

Studies. Robert Bartlett, *Gerald of Wales, 1146–1223* (1982); Frederick M. Powicke, "Gerald of Wales," in *Bulletin of the John Rylands Library,* **12** (1928); Michael Richter, *Giraldus Cambrensis: The Growth of the Welsh Nation* (1972).

S. C. FERRUOLO

[See also **Historiography, Western European; St. David's; Wales; Walter, Hubert.**]

GÉRARD OF CLAIRVAUX, ST., abbot of Clairvaux (1170–1175) who consecrated the Gothic choir of the abbey church there, the so-called Clairvaux III, on 13 October 1174. This choir has been destroyed, but reflections are found at Alcobça in Portugal, Beaulieu in England, Pontigny in France, and elsewhere. Gérard was murdered by a monk at Ivry on 7 December 1175 and is considered a protomartyr of the Cistercian order.

BIBLIOGRAPHY

Anselme Dimier, *Recueil de plans d'églises cisterciennes,* I (1949), 100–101; Archdale A. King, *Cîteaux and Her Elder Daughters* (1954), 252–254.

CARL F. BARNES, JR.

GERARD OF CREMONA (*ca.* 1114–1187), translator of scientific treatises. The twelfth century witnessed a continuous flow of translations, mainly from the Arabic, that revealed unheard-of intellectual riches and at the same time proved strangely disturbing to medieval Europe on account of the unfamiliar ideas and interpretations that they set forth. In these epoch-making labors Gerard of Cremona, a native of an Italian commune and extremely proud of his origins, played the single most eminent and the most durable part.

Gerard seems to have spent some forty years of his life in Spain after his early schooling in Italy. Nourished in his youth on the limited intellectual stock of the Western trivium and quadrivium, he early resolved to come to Toledo for the purpose of making available to his fellow Latin students the principal works of ancient science lost to Europe as well as the rumored wealth of contemporary Arab science.

Gerard arrived in Toledo in 1144 at the latest and immediately set to work. His objective, as declared by biographers writing shortly after his death, was the translation of the *Almagest* of Ptolemy, but he soon found himself involved in a systematic program of translation of entire bodies of science, following the earlier collections of Thābit ibn Qurra and Ḥunayn ibn Isḥāq, the Baghdadi who translated from Greek into Arabic.

For four decades Gerard produced translation after translation, the bulk of them consisting of the "introductory" books in astronomy, mathematics and geometry, and medicine. Although some ancient Greek works were thus recovered by him from the Arabic, the majority of his translations were works of science by Arab authors or Arab commentaries on Greek classics in science.

His landmark translation of the *Almagest,* traditionally assigned to 1175 due to the existence of a transcription of the work bearing this date in its colophon, must have been accomplished some decades earlier. Since Gerard is said by his *socii* (companions) to have come to Toledo with an intense desire to translate the *Almagest,* it scarcely seems credible that he should have waited until 1175, when he was about sixty-one, to achieve his primary goal. That the translation of the *Almagest* is the only work for which Gerard acknowledges the help of a Mozarab translator, Galib (Galippus), offers further evidence that it was an early effort.

Twelfth-century Toledo is often alleged to have been the locale of a school of translators, initiated by Archbishop Raymond (1126–1152) and later flourishing in the times of Gerard's presence there. But there is absolutely no record of this "school." Gerard appears to have worked singly, and according to his own program, for nearly all of his translations. Moreover there is no evidence that he formed any "school" of his own. True, after his death his *socii* drew up a list of his translations as known to them, for they feared that Gerard's excessive humility in habitually not signing his translations could cause the obliteration of his fame. But the list of the *socii* is incomplete, exemplifying the unofficial character of the group, which was not tightly knit and did not have clear records and rules. Certainly no one of them makes any claim to a direct collaboration in translation with Gerard.

Who then were these *socii?* To get an idea of their probable roles in connection with Gerard's activity, we must realize the magnitude of Gerard's enterprise and accomplishments during his more than forty years in Toledo. In addition to producing more than eighty translations, some of which were voluminous, Gerard also gave public lectures on astrology at Toledo. He must have been an extremely active man. Faced with the tasks of tracing, identifying, collecting, and collating the several Arabic manuscripts he was in the habit of requiring for his translations; moreover dictating, copying, verifying the final copies, and so forth, Gerard may have hired a group of helpers—establishing something more like a studio than a formal school in the twelfth-century sense.

Because of the abundance and systematic nature of his production, his thoroughly critical approach to textual tradition, and his faithful adherence to literalness, together with a steady flow of translations produced during the latter half of the twelfth century, Gerard's translations soon came to obtain the preference of Latin scholars through the succeeding centuries. The tremendous upsurge of interest in Arabic and Greek science and philosophy in medieval universities from the start of the thirteenth century owes its stimulation in greater part to the work of Gerard of Cremona.

BIBLIOGRAPHY

My article "Gerard of Cremona" in the *Dictionary of Scientific Biography,* suppl. I (1978), gives a list of Gerard's translations with full bibliography. See also B. Boncompagni, "Della vita e delle opere di Gherardo Cremonese ... " in *Atti dell'Accademia Pontificia dei Nuovi Lincei,* **4** (1851); Sybil D. Wingate, The *Mediaeval Latin Versions of the Aristotelian Scientific Corpus* (1931), 46.

RICHARD LEMAY

[See also **Astronomy; Toledo; Translations and Translators, Western European.**]

GERARD OF CSANÁD, ST. (*d.* 24 Sept. 1046), also known as Gerardo di Venezia, Gerhardus, and (in Hungarian) Gellért. Born near Venice, Gerard was attached to the monastery of S. Giorgio Maggiore, which he left for a pilgrimage to the Holy Land when he was invited to stay at the court of King Stephen I of Hungary in 1015. He may have been the tutor of the king's son, Prince Emeric. In 1023 he retired into a hermitage but in 1030 was called to the missionary bishopric of the recently pacified southeast of Hungary, Marosvár/Csanád. Killed by "pagan" rebels, who rose against the new royal, feudal, and Christian order, he was canonized in 1083. Many of his relics were returned to Venice in 1333, and he is venerated on the day of his martyrdom.

BIBLIOGRAPHY

The *Legenda minor* (eleventh century) and *Legenda maior* (fourteenth century) have been edited by Imre (Emericus) Szentpétery in *Scriptores rerum hungaricarum tempore ducum regumque stirpis Arpadianae gestarum,* II (1938), 461–505. An annotated German translation by Gabriel Silagi is in Thomas von Bogyay, János M. Bak, and Gabriel Silagi, eds., *Die heiligen Könige* (1976), 74–121. See also Jean Leclercq, "San Gerardo di Csanád e il monachesimo," in Vittore Branca, ed., *Venezia e Ungheria nel Rinascimento* (1973), 99–119; Edith Pásztor, "Gerardo, vescovo di Csanád," in *Bibliotheca sanctorum,* 6 (1965); Gabriel Silagi, *Untersuchungen zur "Deliberatio supra Hymnum trium puerorum" des Gerhard von Csanád* (1967).

JÁNOS M. BAK

[See also **Hungary; Stephen, St.**]

GERBERT DE MONTREUIL, French trouvère of the first half of the thirteenth century, who may also have been a monk. He is the author of one of the four continuations of Chrétien de Troyes's unfinished *Conte del graal,* also known as *Perceval.* Gerbert informs us (verses 6,984–6,987) that Chrétien was prevented by death from completing his work. His own contribution to the *Perceval,* some 17,000 lines of octosyllabic verse in rhymed couplets, was composed after 1225, probably between 1226 and 1230. The composition begins and ends with a visit of Perceval to the Grail Castle and recounts the adventures that the hero met while expiating the sin that caused his mother's death. Gerbert is also identified as the author of the *Roman de la Violette* (*ca.* 1227), a *roman d'aventure* dedicated to the countess Marie de Ponthieu. This romance is notable for its lively portrayal of the aristocratic milieu of the period.

BIBLIOGRAPHY

Gerbert de Montreuil, *La Continuation de Perceval,* Mary Williams and Marguerite Oswald, eds., 3 vols. (1922–1975), and *Le Roman de la Violette,* Douglas L. Buffum, ed. (1928); Jean Larmat, "Le Péché de Perceval dans la *continuation* de Gerbert," in *Mélanges Rostaing* (1975); Albert W. Thompson, "Additions to Chrétien's *Perceval—*Prologues and Continuations," in Roger S. Loomis, ed., *Arthurian Literature in the Middle Ages* (1959).

THOMAS E. KELLY

[See also **Arthurian Literature; Chrétien de Troyes.**]

GERBERT OF AURILLAC. See Sylvester II, Pope.

GERHAERT, NIKOLAUS (Nicholas von Leiden) (*fl. ca.* 1460–1473), mysterious sculptor of Dutch origin who spent most of his career in the Germanic regions of Trier, Strasbourg, Constance, Baden, and Vienna. He was the most influential northern fifteenth-century carver. Much of his documented work is lost, but the extant works are characterized by energetic drapery and extreme physical realism. Gerhaert specialized in tombs, altarpieces, and religious carvings.

GERHARD OF AUGSBURG

BIBLIOGRAPHY

Michael Baxandall, *The Limewood Sculptors of Renaissance Germany* (1980), 248–251; G. Eis, "Zum Leben und Werk des Strassburger Bildhauers Nickolaus Gerhaert," in *Archiv für Kulturgeschichte*, **42** (1960); Luise Fischel, *Nicholaus Gerhaert und die Bildhauer der deutschen Spätgotik* (1944); Walter Paatz, "Nicolaus Gerhaerts von Leiden," in *Heidelberger Jahrbücher*, **3** (1959); A. Schädler, "Studien zu Nicolaus Gerhaert von Leiden," in *Jahrbuch der Berliner Museen*, **16** (1974); Otto Wertheimer, *Nikolaus Gerhaert* (1929); E. Zimmerman, "Plastik," in *Spätgotik am Oberrhein 1450–1530* (1970), 69–70.

LARRY SILVER

GERHARD OF AUGSBURG, a tenth-century Augustinian monk, provost of the Cathedral of St. Maria in Augsburg. He wrote a Life of Udalric, Bishop of Augsburg (*d.* 973), who had taught and ordained Gerhard. The *Vita Udalrici* describes primarily the public and private life of Udalric's later years as well as secular and ecclesiastical history. Gerhard's style was criticized for its many grecisms and germanisms.

BIBLIOGRAPHY

Max Manitius, *Geschichte der lateinischen Literatur des Mittelalters,* II (1923), 203–210; the text is in Georg Waitz, ed., *Monumenta Germaniae Historica: Scriptores,* IV (1878), 377–425.

NATHALIE HANLET

GERHARD OF COLOGNE (*fl.* mid thirteenth century), architect of the choir of the Cologne cathedral, begun in 1248; of the Cistercian church at Altenberg, begun in 1255; and possibly of the cathedral of München Gladbach (1256–1275). Whether he was German or French (Galterius can be Gérard as well as Walter), Gerhard knew and consciously employed French ideas from Amiens, Beauvais, and Paris at Cologne.

BIBLIOGRAPHY

Robert Branner, *St. Louis and the Court Style in Gothic Architecture* (1965), 128–134; Paul Frankl, *Gothic Architecture* (1962), 125–127.

CARL F. BARNES, JR.

GERHARD OF SOISSONS (mid tenth century), probably dean of Medardus monastery in Soissons. He wrote a Life of St. Romanus in Latin leonine hexameters at the request of Archbishop Hugo II of Rouen, as well as a Latin prose version. The poem, turgid in style, is concerned with the destruction of the heathen and the miraculous recovery of a sacred oil.

BIBLIOGRAPHY

The text of the poetic version of *Vita Sancti Romani* can be found in *Patrologia latina,* CXXXVIII (1880); for the prose version, see Johanne Carnandet, ed., *Acta Sanctorum* (1868). See also Max Manitius, *Geschichte der lateinischen Literatur des Mittelalters,* II (1923), 495–497.

W. T. H. JACKSON

GERHARDO DI JACOPO STARNINA, Florentine painter mentioned in Florence, 1387; documented in Toledo and Valencia (Spain) between 1398 and 1401. Documents record his now fragmented fresco decoration in the Chapel of S. Jerome, S. Maria del Carmine in Florence, in 1404. In 1409 he executed some frescoes in S. Stefano at Empoli, now destroyed. Though considered an important master by virtue of his commissions, we know very little about Starnina. Various attempts have been made to identify his hand in other paintings, but no attributions are generally accepted.

BIBLIOGRAPHY

Richard Fremantle, *Florentine Gothic Painters from Giotto to Masaccio* (1975); Ugo Procacci, "Gherardo Starnina," in *Rivista d'Arte,* 2nd ser., 5 (April 1933), 7 (October 1935), and 8 (January 1936).

ADELHEID M. GEALT

GERHOH OF REICHERSBERG (1093–27 June 1169), one of the outstanding polemicists during the Investiture Controversy. He left an extensive intellectual heritage of theoretical, historical, and practical writings. A great deal is known about his life, his biography having been compiled soon after his death and included in the Chronicle of Reichersberg by the priest Magnus (*d.* 1195).

Gerhoh's first work, *Opusculum de edificio Dei* (*ca.* 1126), concerned the church. In it he propagated reformist ideas and attacked the simony of the bishops and the clergy, as well as the interference of laymen in church affairs. Later he sent several letters to popes and cardinals, turned his pen against emperors, criticized contemporary conditions, and compiled commentaries on the Psalms (even in these he took up his fight against heretics in the church). Gerhoh wrote theological treatises and studied questions of Christology, morality, liturgy, church discipline, celibacy, and the essence of the Christian faith. Around 1158 he also began the Chronicle of Reichersberg.

Classen lists no less than twenty of Gerhoh's writings, in addition to some dubious ascriptions. Two of them are characteristic of Gerhoh's ideas and preoccupations: *De investigatione Antichristi* and *De quarta vigilia noctis.* In the former, Gerhoh moves beyond general, eschatological speculations and proceeds to an analysis of the events of the historical past and the present, in order to demonstrate the visible activities of the Antichrist. This is particularly striking in the first book. In the second, Gerhoh contrasts the Antichrist with the real Christ, enters into Christological and dogmatic discussions, and turns to the question of contemporary heresies. In the third book he sums up the previous themes and subjects, then embarks on questions of the Christian philosophy of history.

De quarta vigilia noctis, composed of dialogues, is Gerhoh's last significant work. The title refers to the biblical episode of Christ's disciples' being threatened by the storm (Matthew 14:25), which Gerhoh relates to the time of Pope Gregory VII. He emphasizes that avarice dominates the world, unleashing many vices and human sufferings. Gerhoh suggests a form of compromise between the contrasting forces, hoping for a rapprochement through the grace of Christ.

In the past, only part of Gerhoh's work was known and edited. Now there is a better knowledge of his writings, and new editions have appeared with new texts. Classen's book reviews, in an authoritative fashion, all problems related to Gerhoh in a wide historical framework. He analyzes Gerhoh's ideas, dissects his imagery, and demonstrates the historical, logical, and symbolical structures in Gerhoh's writings, ordering them into coherent categories and tables.

Gerhoh's writings are not easily read. His style and presentation are often obscure, his mentality dominated by symbolism. His philosophy of history is expressed with the help of "symbolic constructions" thought to be real categories of events. This is particularly true of his statements concerning eschatology and politics. In this respect he adopts, but forcefully develops, patterns already existing in previous centuries. Although his influence on posterity was limited, he nevertheless laid the foundation for the symbolic and eschatological thinking prevailing, in the wake of Joachim of Fiore, in thirteenth-century Italian spiritual and intellectual life.

BIBLIOGRAPHY

Sources. Gerhohus, *Opera hactenus inedita,* Fr. Scheibelberger, ed. and trans. (1875); *Libelli selecti,* E. Sackur, ed., in *Monumenta Germaniae Historica: Libelli de lite,* III (1897); *Opera inedita I–II,* Damien van den Eynde, Peter Classen, and A. Rijmersdael, eds. (1955–1956); *Letter to Pope Hadrian About the Novelties of the Day,* Nikolaus M. Häring, ed. and trans. (1974).

Studies. W. Beinert, *Die Kirche, Gottes Heil in der Welt* (1973); Peter Classen, *Gerhoch von Reichersberg* (1960); Alois Dempf, *Sacrum imperium* (1962); Damien van den Eynde, *L'oeuvre littéraire de Géroch de Reichersberg* (1957); A. M. Lazzarino Del Grosso, *Società e potere in Germania del XII secolo* (1974); E. Meuthen, "Der Geschichtssymbolismus Gerhohs von Reichersberg," in W. Lammers, ed., *Geschichtsdenken und Geschichtsbild im Mittelalter* (1965).

JOSEF SZÖVÉRFFY

[See also **Investiture and Investiture Controversy.**]

GERMAN LANGUAGE. The designation "German" *(Deutsch),* as it applies to language, has two distinct senses. In a broader sense it is sometimes used to refer to all Germanic dialects (besides Frisian, Danish, and any surviving Gothic) spoken on the European continent after the emigration of the later Anglo-Saxons to England. Thus, in this usage it includes not only the High German dialects of southern Germany but also the northern Low German dialects and even Dutch. This corresponds to the traditionally (and, as we now know, rather simplistically) posited division, on the Germanic family tree *(Stammbaum),* of West Germanic into Anglo-Frisian and Proto-German. It also reflects the distribution of the term *Deutsch* in the late Middle Ages as a designation of one's own language. As a result of a separate national history and the formation of a distinct standard language, however, inhabitants of the Low Countries now distinguish between German *(Duits)* and the variants of their own "Netherlandic" language *(Nederlands, Hollands, Vlaams).*

More narrowly, the designation "German" may be taken to refer to the modern standard language known by that name, and to earlier stages that can reasonably be viewed as ancestors of that standard language. In this usage, then, "German" is roughly equivalent to "High German" (*Hochdeutsch*), and excludes the dialects of northern Germany and their historical antecedents (Old Saxon, Middle Low German).

High German is a geographical and linguistic designation, not an aesthetic judgment. Geographically it refers to dialects spoken on the higher ground of central and southern Germany. Linguistically it is reserved to dialects that have undergone some part of the so-called High German consonant shift (*Zweite, Hochdeutsche Lautverschiebung*), a set of historical changes affecting the West Germanic stop consonants *p*, *t*, and *k*, and, to a lesser extent, *b*, *d*, and *g*. Characteristic of all High German dialects is the change of postvocalic *p*, *t*, and *k* to the fricatives *f(f)*, *ȝ(ȝ)*, and *h(h)*, now usually pronounced as *f*, *s*, and *ch* ([x] or [ç]) (compare German *hoffen, Wasser, machen* with English *hope, water, make*), and initial or postconsonantal *t* to *ts* (usually spelled *z*; compare German *Zoll, Zeit* [time] with English *toll, tide*). Less widespread, but regularly reflected in the standard language, are the change of initial and postconsonantal *p* to *pf* (compare German *Pfund* with English *pound*); *d* to *t* (compare German *Gott, Tochter* with English *god, daughter*); and the geminate (long) stops *bb* and *gg* and *kk* (compare German *Rippe, Rücken* [back] with English *rib*, Dutch *rug*). Found in some dialects, but not in the standard language, are the shift of initial and postconsonantal *k* to *kch* ([kx]) or *ch* ([x]) and the shift of single *b*, *g* to *p*, *k*.

It would be misleading to speak of "a" German language in the Middle Ages; "German" as a unitary concept was quite slow in developing. From about 700 on, there are texts written in dialects that are identifiably High German (as defined above), but that differ markedly in phonology, morphology, and lexicon. Thus it is common practice to refer to the language of these texts by using dialect names (such as Alemannic, Bavarian, East Franconian, South Rhine Franconian, and so on). Only with an eye to the future can a cover term such as "Old High German" reasonably be used as if it named a single thing. With this proviso, however, scholars do indeed use such cover terms, and even attempt to give linguistic criteria for when one cover term should give way to

another. Thus several historical stages in the development of modern standard German can be distinguished: "Old High German" names those High German dialects written and spoken from approximately 700 to 1100. For dialects written and spoken between 1100 and approximately 1350 (for some scholars even 1500) the term "Middle High German" is used. The designation "New High German" must then cover the dialects (and the gradually emerging standard) used from 1350 to the present. Since the latter is a rather long time span, the first three centuries of it (to about 1650) are commonly called "Early New High German."

The further back we go, of course, the fewer texts we find. Thus it is possible, for the older stages at least, to list exhaustively all surviving texts in the language stages in question, and the relatively few that exist generally fall into a limited number of categories. In Old High German times, for example, literary activity was largely confined to monasteries, and the texts show both a preoccupation with religious matters and an understandable orientation toward Latin originals. The "first German book," the *Abrogans* (765–775), is in fact a Latin-German word list, and a number of other Old High German texts are also basically glossaries. One step up in creativity are the "interlinear" translations of Latin originals, of which the Old High German *Tatian* (830) is perhaps the most imposing example. Some translations are much more sensitive to the rules of German (rather than Latin); an early example is the Rhine Franconian *Isidor* (790–800). Later examples can be found in the works of the Alemannic monk Notker Labeo (after 1000). Finally, some texts are clearly free creations; in this group Otfrid's *Evangelienbuch* must be mentioned. This listing is naturally not complete (for the names of other texts, consult works in the bibliography).

By Middle High German times, both the number and the range of texts had increased drastically. Although works with a religious orientation were still plentiful, the classical Middle High German period (1170–1250) saw the rise of several new genres (many under French influence): heroic epics such as the anonymously authored *Nibelungenlied*; courtly epics such as those by Wolfram von Eschenbach, Hartmann von Aue, and Gottfried von Strassburg; and love poetry (*Minnesang*) by great poets like Walther von der Vogelweide. The waning of the classical period saw also an increase in prose writing. Histories, city chronicles, legal codifications, homilies, sermons, and the writings of German mystics added to the growing flood of texts in German.

In neither of these two periods was there anything that can accurately be called a standard language. The German written by poets of the classical Middle High German period comes closest, since their products were meant to be declaimed or read throughout the German-speaking area. But this "standardization" consisted largely of the avoidance of forms or rhymes that would be misunderstood or come out wrong when read in other dialect areas, rather than the creation of normalized phonology and morphology. In any case, with the end of the classical period, even this degree of standardization was abandoned. The creation of a genuine, widely recognized standard language with staying power was to come only during the New High German period, and then only gradually, principally by way of the emerging chancery languages of the imperial and territorial courts.

BIBLIOGRAPHY

Adolf Bach, *Geschichte der deutschen Sprache,* 8th ed. (1965); John Knight Bostock, *A Handbook on Old High German Literature* (1955); Wilhelm Braune, *Althochdeutsche Grammatik,* rev. by Walter Mitzka, 12th ed. (1967); Frans van Coetsem and Herbert Kufner, eds., *Toward a Grammar of Proto-Germanic* (1972), esp. 71–97; Randolph E. Keller, *The German Language* (1978); William Burley Lockwood, *An Informal History of the German Language* (1965); Thomas L. Markey, R. L. Kyes, and Paul T. Robarge, *Germanic and Its Dialects,* III (1977); Hermann Paul, *Mittelhochdeutsche Grammatik,* rev. by Walter Mitzka, 19th ed. (1966); Eduard Prokosch, *A Comparative Germanic Grammar* (1939); Ludwig Erich Schmitt, ed., *Kurzer Grundriss der germanischen Philologie bis 1500,* I (1970); Maurice O'Connell Walshe, *Medieval German Literature* (1962); John T. Waterman, *A History of the German Language* (1966, rev. ed. 1976).

ORRIN W. ROBINSON

[See also **Middle High German Literature; Nibelungenlied; Old High German Literature; Otfrid von Weissenburg.**]

GERMAN LITERATURE. The major genres of German literature are covered here in three sections: **German Literature: Allegory; German Literature: Lyric;** and **German Literature: Romance.** For general surveys of medieval literature in the German-speaking regions, see **Middle High German Literature** and **Old High German Literature.**

GERMAN LITERATURE: ALLEGORY. As in other vernacular literatures, allegories appeared in German literature as parts of works long before they became independent texts. For centuries German writers who used allegory followed in the footsteps of theologians who had developed the allegorical interpretation of the Bible into a highly sophisticated exercise. Since the Bible was the Divine Word, it was considered to contain many hidden meanings. Any biblical mention of Jerusalem, for instance, could be taken as referring to the actual city in Palestine in the literal or historical sense. Allegorically, it could also mean the church of Christ. In the moral or tropological sense, Jerusalem could designate the human soul, and it could mean the Heavenly City in the mystical or anagogical sense (referring to life after death). Besides the Bible, nature as divine creation was later also considered to contain hidden meanings. Whether a mere human being was capable of creating texts that had more than one meaning was a much-debated question. Yet this discussion did not prevent man-made allegories from becoming very popular, especially in the late Middle Ages.

The first to include allegory in a German text was the Alsatian monk Otfrid von Weissenburg, who composed his *Evangelienbuch* in 864–867. It is the first rhymed poem in German and tells the life of Christ, based on the Gospels, in five books. Otfrid often interrupts his narrative with small chapters titled *mystice, moraliter,* or *spiritaliter* that interpret the biblical events allegorically and invite listeners or readers to spiritual meditation.

Over the centuries the Song of Solomon was the book of the Bible that presented the greatest challenge for allegorical commentary. Its highly erotic language and setting cried out to be subdued or enhanced by exegesis. Two basic patterns evolved: the lover and the beloved could either represent Christ and his church, or Christ (the Holy Spirit) and the human soul (or Mary). Both influenced vernacular literature widely and even far beyond the realms of allegory proper. Abbot Williram von Ebersberg chose the exegetical pattern of Christ and the church when he translated and explained the Song of Solomon, in prose that mixed Latin and German, around

1065. Approximately a century later an anonymous writer used Williram's translation but shifted the emphasis of the allegorical exegesis to Christ, Mary, and the pure human soul. This prose text, the *Sankt Trudperter Hohes Lied,* was presumably written for Benedictine nuns. The unique power of its language anticipates later mystical writings.

At least related to this exegetical tradition of the Song of Solomon is the puzzling poem *Die Hochzeit,* which was written around 1160. It is the first independent German allegory for over a century and narrates a simple sequence of events: a powerful lord from a high mountain woos a beautiful noble girl from a deep valley, leads her to his house, and celebrates a splendid wedding feast. The allegorical interpretation of these events is, however, far from simple. Bridegroom and bride represent God and the Virgin as well as God and the individual human being. Yet the events also reflect other aspects of salvation—for instance, Christ's incarnation, passion, and descent into hell as well as the heavenly kingdom and sacraments such as baptism and confession. The poem is far from being a neatly constructed allegory. But then, very few medieval allegories are neatly constructed, and most of them invite, at least at some point, more than one reading.

In the late eleventh and twelfth centuries, another important allegorical tradition took root in German literature: *Physiologus* was adapted and translated into German several times. Of Greek origin, *Physiologus* was widely distributed in Latin prose and translated into many vernacular languages. As the title insufficiently indicates, it is a bestiary that describes a variable series of real or fabulous animals (for instance, the lion and the elephant or the unicorn and the phoenix) and attaches to each an allegorical Christian interpretation, often based on the Bible. The lion, for instance, represents Christ because of his strength and because he is mentioned so often in the Bible. Moreover, since the lion's cub is born dead and comes alive only on the third day after his father breathes on him, according to *Physiologus,* Christ's death and resurrection are here signified.

Many writers of the later Middle Ages drew freely on these beast allegories, which were also quite popular in the visual arts. Despite its wide use, *Physiologus* was far from being the canonical reference work for medieval beast allegory. A particular animal could have more than one significance. Outside the *Physiologus* tradition, for instance, the lion could also stand for the devil, since Samson's fight with the lion was taken to refer to Christ's fight against the devil. There were allegorical conventions that attached a particular meaning to a specific object or being. But they were never standardized to such an extent that these references became entirely predictable and unambiguous. Readers of medieval allegories were therefore presented with an additional challenge.

Allegorical commentary also played a major role in religious visionary texts, especially those of the mystics. Visionaries claimed their revelations to be of divine origin and sometimes wrote them down long after they occurred. Some of these revelations, in which God, the Virgin Mary, saints, or personifications figure prominently and often communicate with the visionary, are actually so straightforward as not to need additional explanations. But other revelations are so hermetic and obscure that they remain inaccessible without commentary. The latter ones are usually accompanied by heavenly voices that elucidate the enigmatic visual images in detail. Even though revelations, by virtue of their divine inspiration, claimed a different and higher spiritual status than man-made allegories, the patterns in which images relate to meaning are very similar in both. The abbess Hildegard of Bingen wrote her powerful *Scivias* (Know the ways) in Latin prose between 1141 and 1153. It contains twenty-six visions of the hermetic kind, each of which is explained in great detail. Some of the early manuscripts even try to capture the visions in pictures that powerfully display a haunting, almost surrealistic world.

A little over a century later, Mechthild von Magdeburg, a Beguine and later a Cistercian nun, recounted her visionary and mystic experiences in a book called *Das fliessende Licht der Gottheit* (The flowing light of the Godhead). She writes an intense vernacular prose that again and again breaks into hymnic verse. Her visions, meditations, and prayers add creatively and spontaneously to the exegetical tradition of the Song of Solomon without being indebted to any specific earlier texts. Mechthild proceeds in her writing less systematically than Hildegard of Bingen. Her visions are also never quite as hermetic, but she takes great care to explain the less self-evident ones in detail. Revelations with or without explications continued to appear in mystical texts throughout the fourteenth century.

Before allegories became independent texts in German literature, they were incorporated into larger narratives. A recurring element in Arthurian romances and heroic epics is the allegorical dream.

Many of these dreams are about animals but do not, however, belong to the *Physiologus* tradition. These dreams are usually interpreted by one of the characters or the narrator, and they either foreshadow future events or give insights into secret relations and facts. Such dreams occur in the *Rolandslied* of Pfaffe Konrad, the *Nibelungenlied*, Wolfram von Eschenbach's *Parzival*, Gottfried von Strassburg's *Tristan*, and the German prose *Lancelot*.

Allegorical episodes appear in only two romances of the great period in German literature (the decades around 1200). The first is considered a borderline case. In Hartmann von Aue's *Erek* (after 1180; based on Chrétien de Troyes's *Erec et Enide*, 1165–1170), the last episode in the hero's quest is the only one in Arthurian verse romance that is explicitly given an abstract title: *Joie de la cort*, or *des hoves vreude*. By fighting with and vanquishing Mabonagrain, Erec frees that character and his beloved lady from their self-inflicted isolation in a magical garden and restores them to courtly society and joy. Thus he recapitulates in reverse what his and Enide's crisis and quest had been all about, and finally recaptures the joy of the court for himself, his wife, and the Round Table. Although this episode contains neither personifications nor even an allegorical location, the title nevertheless serves as an allegorical marker.

The second episode is the cave of lovers in Gottfried von Strassburg's *Tristan* (*ca.* 1210). Again the characters themselves are not allegorical, but Gottfried constructs in elegant detail an allegorical House of Love and then proceeds to interpret it so that every feature corresponds to some aspect of an ideal love relationship. Thus the green marble floor represents constancy; the smooth, straight, white walls, honesty; and the crystal bed, purity and candor in love. The cave or grotto is located far from human society in a landscape reminiscent of paradise. Only tried and true lovers will gain entrance to it, wherever they live on earth (as Gottfried is careful to point out). By letting Tristan and Isolde briefly find refuge in this allegorical house, Gottfried not only raises them to the status of ideal lovers but also creates an allegory of great clarity and cohesiveness. Few later allegories match it in those respects.

Throughout the thirteenth and early fourteenth centuries, allegorical elements were used in narratives for a variety of purposes. Allegorical adventures could initiate a young hero into his quest, as in Johann von Würzburg's *Wilhelm von Österreich* (completed in 1314). A wreath of twelve flowers, representing chivalrous virtues, could function as a pre-

cise code of honor, as in Albrecht's *Jüngerer Titurel* (composed between 1260 and 1275). A description of the winged, blind, naked Cupid and his attributes (arrows, torch, and so on), followed by an item-by-item explication, served again and again as a basic definition of love. As such it turns up not only in narratives but also in lyric poetry and early discourses on love (*Minnereden*).

The early thirteenth century also saw the emergence of a new literary genre, the *bispel*, a sort of parable, the structure of which is allegorical. A *bispel* is a short two-part poem in rhymed couplets. The first part usually contains a brief narrative or description, whereas the second is dedicated to a detailed allegorical interpretation that ends with a summarizing moral. The *bispel* is a particularly flexible genre, since almost any narrative material can be used for its first part (fables were a favorite) and since the interpretation can be religious or secular or a mixture of both. As for so many types of short poems in rhymed couplets, Der Stricker is the early master of the *bispel*, which distinctly, though somewhat modestly, heralds the rise of allegory in the later Middle Ages.

Late medieval German literature contains nothing comparable with Guillaume de Lorris's and Jean de Meun's *Roman de la Rose*, and that pioneer work did not even have much direct influence on German allegories. But by the middle of the thirteenth century, independent allegories began to thrive in Germany as well. They continued to do so for more than two centuries. They can be roughly divided into religious allegories, allegories of the game of chess, and allegories of love. Although each of these types draws variably on a common pool of allegorical elements, they remain fairly distinct, even in structure. Whereas chess allegories and allegories of love flourished in the fourteenth century, religious allegories originated in the thirteenth and continued well into the fifteenth century.

The first independent religious allegories explicate sacred texts or biblical stories. In 1252–1255 the Saxon cleric Heinrich von Kröllwitz wrote a lengthy allegorical interpretation of the Lord's Prayer in rhymed couplets. He concentrates on its beginning, end, and each of the seven petitions separately, and draws occasionally on the *Physiologus* tradition as well as on allegorical gem books (lapidaries). His explicit goal was to make a contribution in the vernacular to a deeper and more sophisticated understanding of this basic prayer.

About two decades later the Magdeburg patrician

Brun von Schönebeck composed the most extensive explication of the Song of Solomon in German (comprising almost 13,000 lines). Using the biblical text freely, Brun first narrates briefly how Solomon woos Pharaoh's daughter and marries her. In the exegesis they represent God and the Virgin Mary as well as God and the human soul. But Brun goes much further and includes large parts of the history of salvation, even the antichrist and the Last Judgment, following for the most part a Latin source. This tendency to cover as much as possible of a particular subject matter is typical of many late-medieval allegories.

Even after allegories had gained independence as texts, they continued to appear within larger works. One example is the poem *Der Streit der vier Töchter Gottes* (The debate of the four daughters of God). Here a life of Christ is preceded by an allegorical dispute. After the Fall two of God's daughters, Truth and Justice, insist that Man be condemned, whereas the two others, Mercy and Peace, plead that he be forgiven. Prudence, personified in Christ, settles the dispute by his incarnation, which means salvation. This debate is a widespread allegorical motif that also surfaces in other religious poems and even in religious drama.

The Viennese doctor Heinrich von Neustadt chose a different allegory to precede a life of Christ and a history of salvation. In his poem *Von Gottes Zukunft* (The coming of God, *ca.* 1310), he narrates allegorically how Nature and the Virtues, assisted by God, create the perfect new human being, who is Mary/Jesus. As Heinrich himself points out, he wanted to introduce Alan of Lille's famous *Anticlaudianus* to his audience. Yet he used an intermediary source rather than the original.

Quite a few of the more extensive and independent religious allegories are concerned with the ways in which the individual human being can lead a decent life and attain God's mercy in the after-life and at the Last Judgment. In most of them, the Seven Deadly Sins figure prominently, fighting against the corresponding Virtues and/or against personifications such as Repentance, Confession, and Penance. The Seven Deadly Sins (Pride, Envy, Wrath, Sloth, Avarice, Gluttony, and Lechery) sometimes fight in big battle formations, as in *Der Sünden Widerstreit* (The battle of the vices, late thirteenth century). They can also serve as a colorful list by themselves or in conjunction with other catalogs (such as the Ten Commandments, the six works of compassion, and others) that help the protagonist—and the reader—recognize and confess his sins, for instance, in Heinrich von Burgeis' (or von Burgus') *Der Seele Rat* (The help [or counsel] for the soul, early fourteenth century).

These sins and their grotesque offspring are also described in vivid detail as they attack and almost defeat the protagonist on his pilgrimage through life toward the heavenly city, as in *Die Pilgerfahrt des träumenden Mönchs* (The pilgrimage of the dreaming monk). This allegory is based on Guillaume de Deguileville's influential and very popular *Pèlerinage de la vie humaine,* for which the *Roman de la Rose* was the model. The *Pèlerinage* itself was adapted twice into German verse (early and mid fifteenth century). All of these poems and many similar ones explore in a great variety of ways man's allegorical quest for salvation.

Allegories of the game of chess pursue more worldly topics and concentrate on how late medieval society should ideally function. The German allegories are all based on the Latin prose treatise *Solatium ludi scaccorum,* written by Jacobus de Cessolis, a Dominican monk from Lombardy, around 1300. He first gives a brief legendary account of how the game originated. Then, and at much greater length, he allegorizes each of the sixteen pieces, its position relative to other pieces, their individual movements, and finally the chessboard itself. Each chessman represents a different class or group in society: the king and queen are the leaders, the bishops are judges, the knights are knights, and the rooks or castles are governors. Each of the eight pawns represents several more or less related crafts or other professions and carries a number of allegorically significant attributes. Only one class or group is conspicuously missing: the clergy. Jacobus demands of each class or group certain virtues or forms of ideal conduct, and castigates its vices. Yet he does not just preach in abstract moral terms. He drives his messages home by quoting many different authorities and by telling exemplary stories, the majority of which derive from classical Roman authors.

If manuscript transmission and the translations or adaptations in many European languages are any indication, Jacobus' treatise was for centuries second in popularity only to the Bible. In German alone there are four adaptations in rhymed couplets from the fourteenth century, and three or four translations into prose. The verse adaptations, in particular, demonstrate how firm yet flexible a framework Jacobus created. None of the adapters changed the basic allegory of the game of chess. But they felt free to add or cut quotations and exemplary stories, and each worked independently of the others.

Two German versions in rhymed couplets stand out for different reasons: Heinrich von Beringen's *Schachgedicht* (*ca.* 1330) and Konrad von Ammenhausen's *Schachzabelbuch* (finished in 1337). Heinrich, who presumably was a cleric at Augsburg and Brixen, tends to cut sententiae and exemplary stories, but he also expands a few of these tales considerably and with much talent for narrative suspense and drama. Like Jacobus de Cessolis and other adapters, Heinrich demands justice, prudence, chastity, compassion, and generosity of the eight "noble" chess figures, whereas he expects the eight "common" ones to be diligent, moderate, and, above all, honest. Konrad was a Benedictine monk and a priest in the small town of Stein am Rhein. He is on the one hand very conscientious in following his main source—so conscientious, in fact, as to mark nearly all of his own digressions from it. On the other hand, he expands it considerably by adding quotations, exemplary stories, and thoughts and advice of his own. He also includes more crafts and professions in the allegorization of individual pawns than Jacobus de Cessolis does. Konrad has a sharp eye for the numerous tricks of the trades to cheat customers, and his work is rich in realistic and colorful detail. Of all the rhymed German chess allegories, his seems to have been the longest-lived and most popular.

Allegories of love explore a third important area of human relationships: the love of man and woman. Comprehensive allegories of love in rhymed couplets flourished in the fourteenth century particularly, while less comprehensive ones continued to be written throughout the fourteenth and fifteenth centuries. The allegorical cave of lovers in Gottfried von Strassburg's *Tristan,* however, is only one of many examples that demonstrate a growing interest in this kind of allegory in narrative and lyrical texts as early as the thirteenth century.

The three major allegories of love were composed between 1330 and 1350. They have two main themes in common: investigating the nature of love and demonstrating how a man should or might win a woman's love and retain it. Each of them approaches these themes in different allegorical ways. In the anonymous East Franconian *Minneburg* (The castle of love), the entering, storming, and defending of a castle serve as the basic model that conveys various allegorical messages. The poem begins with the highly enigmatic account of the narrator's witnessing the conception and birth of a child inside an or-

nate column in the court of the castle. This whole narrative, from the point when the narrator enters the castle to the birth of the child, is later explained in great detail by a sage as revealing the nature and origin of love. Twice in the ensuing narrative, an army of personifications tries to storm the castle while another one defends it. Here no explicit interpretation is given, since the names, attributes, colors, and banners of the personifications speak for themselves (but only to an audience that has some familiarity with allegorical conventions). The first battle allegorizes how to win a woman's love; the second, how two lovers maintain their love and protect it from outside interference. Intermittently and throughout, the narrator laments nonallegorically and ingeniously his own plight of unrequited love. A concluding tribunal of love, over which personifications preside, unites both strands. The *Minneburg* is the most systematic and comprehensive German allegory of love.

The Bavarian nobleman Hadamar von Laber took a different approach in his poem *Die Jagd* (The hunt). His basic allegorical model is the chase, in which the hunter represents the lover and the game the beloved lady. The hunter's hounds stand for virtues, moods, and attitudes of the lover and occasionally also of the beloved. Hadamar thus develops an allegorical framework that is both flexible and expressive and that allows for considerable spontaneity. Hadamar refrains from simply narrating an allegorical hunt. Rather, he narrates only its most dramatic moments, especially the two occasions when the game is surrounded by the hounds and about to be caught or killed. Each time it escapes—the second time forever. For the most part, however, the hunter reflects on the various stages of the hunt, or discusses them with other huntsmen, or shouts spirited commands to his hounds. By these means Hadamar reflects on the nature of love, on the right and wrong ways of wooing a woman, and on the noble suffering of unrequited love from a great variety of angles. Except for an occasional explicit clue, he lets his allegorical meditations and narrative speak mostly for themselves, and in highly suggestive and demanding ways. Like *Minneburg,* Hadamar's *Jagd* is a difficult, at times even hermetic, poem. Yet of all comprehensive German allegories of love, it had the greatest impact on later allegories and discourses on love.

Das Kloster der Minne (The convent of love) is a borderline allegory. There are no personifications. Reflections on the nature of love are not allegorical, and a love relationship develops in simple dialogue and comments on the convent between the narrator and a young woman who acts as his guide. Yet the inhabitants of this convent are perfect lovers and the men, in addition, excellent knights. The area they inhabit is strongly reminiscent of the heavenly city as well as the earthly paradise. This poem is lighter in tone than either the *Minneburg* or Hadamar's *Jagd,* but it is no parody.

Besides these three comprehensive allegories of love, there are numerous shorter ones dating from the late thirteenth to the early sixteenth century. Allegories or allegorical elements are also integrated into many discourses on love. Narrative, discourse, and allegory could be, and were, blended in numerous and often very imaginative ways.

Human salvation, the ideal society, and the love of woman and man were main themes of late-medieval German allegories; but they were not the only ones, and they were also occasionally combined. Allegorical conventions provided writers with a rich arsenal of motifs and devices that could be used freely for individual purposes. Thus Heinrich von Mügeln, a learned poet who found patrons in Bohemia and Austria, composed *Der Meide Kranz* (The Virgin's garland) after 1355. In this poem twelve personified arts appear before Emperor Charles IV and compete for a place of honor in the Virgin's garland. He grants one to each, but the most prominent one to Theology, who is then crowned by Nature in the presence of twelve personified virtues. In the second part of the poem, Theology settles a long debate, whether the twelve Virtues derive from God or from Nature, in favor of God and the Virtues. As this unique poem shows, allegory could be used to discuss demanding conceptual issues.

Less demanding in subject matter, but also unique, is an Alemannic poem, *Des Teufels Netz* (The devil's net, after 1400), which combines elements from religious and chess allegories. In this comprehensive work a hermit and the devil first discuss the Seven Deadly Sins, who are the devil's servants, then violations of the Ten Commandments, and finally, at great length, unacceptable behavior of various social classes and professions. The allegorical leitmotif of the poem is the devil's net, which unfailingly catches all sinners while the righteous escape. This net is woven out of the Seven Deadly Sins, just as, structurally, the poem is. Avarice, for instance, is one of these sins, but it also violates the Ten Commandments and is a dominant vice of many professions and social classes; therefore it is dis-

cussed again and again in different contexts. The same holds true for the other deadly sins. Thus the poem becomes on many different levels an allegory of its title, an achievement unique among late medieval German allegories.

Authors of late medieval German allegories relied much on conventions that must have rendered their work predictable to audiences familiar with these conventions. That apparently was part of the literary game. However, the very diversity and richness of these conventions proved to be a challenge for the individual imagination. Allegory became a perfect medium in which accepted standards and high ideals could be contemplated from ever new perspectives.

BIBLIOGRAPHY

Sources. Brun von Schonebeck, Arwed Fischer, ed. (1893); *Hadamar's von Laber Jagd und drei andere Minnegedichte,* J. A. Schmeller, ed. (1850); Heinrich von Beringen, *Das Schachgedicht,* Paul Zimmermann, ed. (1883); Heinrich von Burgus, *Der Seele Rat,* Hans F. Rosenfeld, ed. (1932); Heinrich von Mügeln, *Der Meide Kranz,* Willy Jahr, ed. (1908); Heinrich von Neustadt, *Apollonius von Tyrland,* Samuel Singer, ed. (1906); Hildegard von Bingen, *Wisse die Wege (Scivias),* Maura Böckeler, trans. (1954); Die Hochzeit, in Albert Waag and Werner Schröder, eds., *Kleinere deutsche Gedichte des 11. und 12. Jahrhunderts,* II (1972); *Das Kloster der Minne,* Maria Schierling, ed. (1980); Konrad von Ammenhausen, *Das Schachzabelbuch,* Ferdinand Vetter, ed. (1892); Mechthild von Magdeburg, *Das fliessende Licht der Gottheit,* P. G. Morel, ed. (1869); *Die Minneburg,* Hans Pyritz, ed. (1950); *Otfrid's Evangelienbuch,* Oskar Erdmann and Ludwig Wolff, eds. (1973); *Physiologus,* in Friedrich Wilhelm, ed., *Denkmäler deutscher Prosa des 11. und 12. Jahrhunderts* (1914); *Die Pilgerfahrt des träumenden Mönchs,* Aloys Bömer, ed. (1915), and Adriaan Meijboom, ed. (1926); *Das St. Trudperter Hohe Lied,* Hermann Menhardt, ed. (1934); *Der Streit der vier Töchter Gottes,* in Karl F. Bartsch, ed., *Die Erlösung* (1858); *Der Sünden Widerstreit,* Victor Zeidler, ed. (1892); *Des Teufels Netz,* Karl Barack, ed. (1863); Williram von Ebersberg, *Exposition in Canticis canticorum,* Willy Sanders, ed. (1971).

Studies. Walter Blank, *Die deutsche Minneallegorie* (1970); Morton W. Bloomfield, *The Seven Deadly Sins* (1952); Ernst Robert Curtius, *European Literature and the Latin Middle Ages,* Willard R. Trask, trans. (1953, repr. 1963); Ingeborg Glier, *Artes amandi: Untersuchung zu Geschichte, Überlieferung, und Typologie der deutschen Minnereden* (1971); Walter Haug, ed., *Formen und Funktionen der Allegorie* (1979), 739–775; Christel Meier, "Überlegungen zum gegenwärtigen Stand der Allegorie-Forschung," in *Frühmittelalterliche Studien,* **10** (1976);

Friedrich Ohly, *Schriften zur mittelalterlichen Bedeutungsforschung* (1977).

INGEBORG GLIER

[See also **Allegory; Bestiary; Gottfried von Strassburg; Hadamar von Laber; Hartmann von Aue; Heinrich von Mügeln; Hildegard of Bingen, St.; Johann von Würzburg; Mechthild von Magdeburg; Otfrid von Weissenburg; Williram von Ebersberg.**]

GERMAN LITERATURE: LYRIC. Written in Middle High German, the language of the "middle" period (*ca.* 1050–1350), medieval German lyric poetry is perhaps best designated "court poetry." While most of it is indeed lyric or love poetry (called minnesong), much of it is didactic, religious, or political verse to which the term "lyric"does not apply. During the two centuries it flourished as a major literary form (*ca.* 1150–*ca.* 1350), its home base was the courts of the gentry. Virtually all of the 170 or so poets whose oeuvres survive either were members of the aristocracy or made their living by singing poems at court.

An alternative designation might be song poetry (*Lieddichtung*), for no matter what their subjects—from tightly reasoned reflections about love to attacks on stingy patrons—all poems came with melodies and were sung. While in Romance languages poems without music began to be written in Dante's time, virtually all German strophic poetry before the seventeenth century (and this can include heroic epics and chronicles) was sung.

More than twenty of the major Middle High German lyric poets are covered by separate articles in this *Dictionary*. For their lives and achievement, these articles should be consulted. The present article is designed as a survey (by topic) of the tradition as a whole and is hence best read as a supplement to the author entries.

INDIGENOUS AND EARLY LOVE LYRICS

An order issued by Charlemagne in March 789, on the founding of convents, forbids nuns (among other things) to "write down or exchange love ditties," using the German term *winileot* (songs of the woman lover) as if referring to an established song type. Such simple indigenous love songs must have had a fairly continuous existence—before 789 and for centuries to come. The court poet Neidhart, writing about 1220–1230, relates how one of his ri-

vals in love, a country bumpkin like the rest, goes trampling through his flower beds while singing, *alta voce,* the love ballads (*wineliedel*) of old. It is perhaps no accident, then, that the oldest surviving German lyric consists of about twenty single strophes in which women speak of their lovers (mainly absent or unfaithful), anonymous laments of the kind perhaps known for centuries as *wineliet*.

Another type of indigenous poetry that must have existed long before the advent of the court lyric were songs chanted by young people dancing in the round (the major form of medieval dance). At Christmas 1020 a group of wayward adolescents in the town of Kölbigk, Saxony, took to dancing in the churchyard. Defying the cease-and-desist order of the local priest (whose daughter was being compromised), they were willed by his curse to continue their wheeling, leaping, and stomping dance for an entire year. First recorded by a monk in Wilton, England (where one palsied victim came to be healed), the story of the "Cursed Daunsers," as Robert Mannyng calls them, also transmits the German ditty chanted at Kölbigk. It consists of a single strophe made up of four long lines with midpoint pauses. This turns out to be the main strophe (Germanic in provenance) used by a group of Austro-Bavarian poets, led by Der von Kürenberg (*fl.* 1150), in composing the oldest known court lyric.

With many of these love lyrics cast in single strophes (*daz liet*), rather than in the polystrophic Romance mode, and with the "lament of the forsaken woman" figuring prominently, it is clear that these first singers (up to Dietmar von Aist) must have raised native ballads to a new form of entertainment, starting at courts along the Danube.

Little of this early Danubian court poetry—reminiscent of the oldest English lyrics, the so-called Harley Lyrics—is preserved. It hardly constituted "adequate fare" for the postclassical collectors compiling manuscripts a century and a half later. It is astonishing, therefore, that among these poems are some of the most evocative love lyrics (such as the "Falcon Song" of Der von Kürenberg) ever written in German. These songs put strong feelings (love, jealousy, loss) into few words and suggest more than they say. Hence they are more accessible to modern readers than much of the minnesong to come. One reason is that—especially with Kürenberg—they present the settings in which the man (a knight) and the woman (a lady of the court) speak: on a castle rampart, at a chamber window, in a bedroom, in the

433

hall, gazing at a wheeling falcon. Such scenery—reminiscent of heroic epics—subsequently disappeared under French influence. In the Romance the gaze is firmly fixed on the inner man, and the singer is a refined courtier, forever serving his lady; in contrast, Der von Kürenberg casts himself as a knight with chain mail and charger who lures a woman the way he does his falcon.

Yet troubadour poetry was, by 1150, too powerful a movement in the rest of Europe to be ignored entirely. Within a decade or two (by 1170), Heinrich von Veldeke, a poet living virtually next door to France (in the county Limburg), started writing graceful airs fully imbued with the courtly love precepts of the troubadours. And some of these themes are in evidence even in the earliest lyrics of the remote southeast (notably those of Dietmar von Aist and Meinloh von Sevelingen): the lover as servant; the lover desirous to protect his lady's "honor," her public reputation (or "face," a central medieval value); the lovers' intimacy threatened by "spies" (merkaere), the guardians (huote) of court morality known to the troubadours as lauzengier; and the lovers engaging a messenger to ward off compromise. This is the stuff of minnesong, now to become the mode and fashion of dozens of poets, spanning six generations, known since the days of Romanticism (Coleridge established the term in England) as minnesingers.

MINNESONG UNDER ROMANCE INFLUENCE: THE POETS AND THEIR WORLD

Like the first troubadour, Duke William IX of Aquitaine, and the first (northern French) trouvère, Bertran de Born, the first minnesingers were members of the upper class, the ruling gentry: Friedrich von Hausen, baron and ministerial councillor (secretarius) to Emperor Frederick I Barbarossa; Rudolf II of Fenis, count of Neuenburg, Burgundy; and King (after 1190 Emperor) Henry VI, son of Frederick I. All were living in areas adjacent to France, along the Rhine and in western Switzerland. The first circle of court poets seems to have constituted itself around the Hohenstaufen emperors, whose political interests (Burgundy, Italy) put them in cultural and linguistic contact with France. Frederick's wife, Beatrix of Burgundy, was venerated by Romance singers, many of whom attended the great knighting festival the emperor held in 1184 at Mainz for his sons, Henry and Philip.

The dependence of the first minnesingers on the poetry of both troubadours (Bernart de Ventadorn, Peire Vidal) and trouvères (Gace Brulé, Conon de Béthune) is evident and extensive. Aside from key images, the German poets took over many strophic forms, known as tunes (dôn, doene), from their French confrères. The most diligent importer was Friedrich von Hausen (his ancestral castle was near Mainz), who used Romance "tunes" for half of his eighteen songs. Closer inspection reveals, however, that the minnesingers (and not just the first generation) were selective in which Romance song types they chose to imitate. They bypassed such popular Western forms as the pastourelle (knight meeting shepherdess), the estampida (dancing song), and the tensone, partimen, and jeu parti (all forms of the debate). Attacks on the high and mighty and appeals to their patrons' largess (largueza), with which the troubadours laced even their love songs, are missing from the German court lyric. Minnesong is devoid of historical references; it has a cautious and refined tone; frustrations are internalized and become the source of intellectual reflection. In the area of metrics, the German poets tended to produce strophes of greater complexity, showing sustained preference for the tripartite stanza (a less standard form in the West).

It is not known whether the poets referred to themselves by the (Middle High German) term minnesinger. The term was known—first used about 1195 by Hartmann von Aue (in a surprisingly derogatory context)—but it does not occur frequently enough to suggest widespread use. In assessing the social estate of the poets (scholars are still too liberal in assigning the designation "knight"), the only distinction that can safely be drawn is between aristocratic "gentlemen-singers" of means (initially in the majority) and poets (like Walther and Neidhart) who earned their living with their art. Poets of the gentry are easier to identify historically because they tend to appear as witnesses in charters. But because the upper classes were fond of passing on first names together with their property, it is often difficult to determine (as in the case of Albrecht von Johansdorf) which member of the family was the poet.

It can be said, in general, that court poetry (like the courtly romance) was entertainment centered at castles of the ruling gentry: the dukes, counts, and barons. It was their territories and their political power that were, around 1200, very much on the increase. They were thus able to "import" Western poetry the way they adopted the entire luxurious lifestyle (from armor to spices) of their brethren in France. It would almost appear that minnesong was considered the special reserve of those not dependent on poetry for a living. Thus, a minor court singer, Der von Buwenburg (quoted by Olive Sayce), can put into the mouth of Lady Love *(Minne)* the complaint that poets who seek cast-off clothes (professional singers, minstrels) are unworthy to sing of love, and bring discredit upon women.

The imperial court of the Hohenstaufen continued to support poetry, but not with the zeal of Frederick I and Henry VI. Both Philip of Swabia and Frederick II engaged the services of Walther von der Vogelweide to promote political causes. A group of Swabian poets (Gottfried von Neifen, Burkhard von Hohenfels, Ulrich von Winterstetten) appears to have gathered in loose association around Henry VII, whom his father, Frederick II, imprisoned after he tried to usurp the crown in 1235. Yet the poetry Frederick II himself wrote was not in German but in the language of his beloved Sicily.

Among the dukes the most prominent patrons were the Babenberg lords of Austria (at Vienna, Klosterneuburg, and Wiener Neustadt): Frederick I (*d.* 1198), the first patron of Walther; Leopold VI the Magnificent (*d.* 1230), who appears to have made Reinmar "minnesinger laureate" over Walther (who left, or was asked to leave, Vienna in 1198); and the last Babenberger, Friedrich II (*d.* 1246), a maker of verses himself, whose free-spending habits drew to the Austrian court minstrels keenly in need of largess *(milte)*: Neidhart, Tannhäuser, Reinmar von Zweter, Bruder Wernher. A particular friend of traveling poets and musicians was Wolfger von Erla, bishop of Passau, a politician of note who lived no less well than his king. In November 1203, mindful that winter had begun, he gave the singer *(cantor)* Walther von der Vogelweide five shillings for the purchase of a fur coat.

The most renowned patron of all was Hermann I, count (landgrave) of Thuringia (plus Hesse and Saxony), favored with a long reign (1190–1217). In 1205, his wealth swelled mightily by political bribes, he began to renovate the old Wartburg castle (near Eisenach) along the lines of palaces *(Pfalzen)* normally reserved for the kings of Germany. While many poets became part of his "family" (Heinrich von Veldeke, Heinrich von Morungen, Wolfram von Eschenbach), Hermann was also fond of surrounding himself with ruffian knights, wine guzzlers all. Walther complains about the party noise they raised, which made reciting poetry a taxing chore. And Wolfram adds (in his *Parzival*) that Hermann could use the services of Sir Kay, the gadfly of King

Arthur's Round Table, to teach his people some manners. Yet Hermann was so fabled a patron that his Thuringian court became the stuff of legend, in the strophic epic *Der Wartburgkrieg* (The singing contest at the Wartburg), written anonymously about 1240 (known today mainly through Richard Wagner's opera *Tannhäuser*).

It would seem likely that princes (such as Hermann) were most in need of poets—and apt to reward them best—at the time of great court festivals. It was hardly an accident that it was the magnificent two-week wedding feast of Duke Leopold VI, in August 1203, that brought Walther von der Vogelweide back to Vienna after he had spent five years in poetic service, mainly to the Hohenstaufen chancery. For the purpose of reciting poetry—as Walther says in his elegy on the death of Reinmar—was to give happiness *(vröude)* to the people at court, for whom festivals (on every conceivable occasion) brought the only bright days in a hard and short life.

At the heart of great court poetry is a sophisticated and subtle use of metrics, or what is known as form. The strophes are polymetric constructs in which rhyme words, repeated and varied in flashing patterns, are placed with the skill of a knife thrower (to use Gottfried von Strassburg's image). Certain rhymes and key words set up aural links between strophes that could be appreciated (heard) only in recital. The poems contain many cross-references, not only to each other but also to the work of other singers, past and present, and even to romances. The analysis of frustration in high minnesong is subtle and requires patience to be savored.

All these characteristics seem to suggest that the poet expected to sing before the initiated, a literate and sensitive audience. There would have been little reason to keep on devising artistic subleties if they were not properly appreciated—and rewarded. It can hardly be assumed that all the ladies and gentlemen listening to the minnesingers were "courtly people" as refined and graceful as those depicted in the great sculpture of the thirteenth century (west choir, Naumburg, Bamberg), but it would take a seasoned cultural pessimist to maintain that the people at court were left entirely untouched by the great verbal and aural art produced in their midst—between 1190 and 1230, at any rate.

The court singer often spoke directly to his listeners, appealing for their sympathies (how much his lady and his rivals make him endure), at times calling for a direct response. About to define for them what constitutes "true love," Walther asks his listeners to shout out "Yes—that's it" when they hear him give the "right answer." Another way of keeping listeners on their toes is to toy with their expectations, using the *revocatio* technique of rhetoric, the "art of persuasion" that constituted a major source of poetic diction. Walther is the master at this game. After having given a description daring for minnesong or having denounced love service, Walther will promptly "take it all back" in the closing verse of the song. The performance must be imagined as a kind of artful parlor game, full of sentiment and wit, with the audience accustomed to having its say, as in the literary cabaret or the folksong café of modern times.

Descriptions of dances found in courtly narrative (*Parzival, Helmbrecht*) indicate that dancers often sang tunes to which they danced. As they moved in group patterns akin to those of modern square dancing, the lead dancer would intone the strophes one by one, to be repeated, in sequel, by the young gentlefolk treading the round. This suggests that courtly lyrics could also be performed as dancing airs, a practice started, most likely, by Walther and Neidhart. If the practice resembled that of the trouvères of northern France, it is reasonable to suppose that "tunes" (*doene*) consisting of shorter verses lent themselves best to dancing.

MANUSCRIPTS, METRICS, MELODIES

Although there are manuscripts of courtly romances (Hartmann's *Iwein*, for instance) written when the author was still alive, the court lyric does not seem to have been committed to vellum (paper was not available to German scribes until about 1300) when it was most in fashion. The first written gathering of courtly lyrics was not made until about 1230–1240, as part of the *Carmina burana* manuscript, the famed collection of Latin songs, anacreontic and otherwise, written (in the south Tyrol) by learned clerics. Yet this gathering constitutes no more than a sampling of typical minnesong, the kind it might have been nice to imitate in Latin, be it the strophe or the melody.

It must be assumed then, that court poetry consisted of song repertoires memorized and sung from memory, either by the author or by another minstrel. Greatly aided by the melodies (musical memory is keener and more permanent), the songs were passed down by having each new generation learn them by heart. The form of "collected poems" arranged by the author himself was unknown in classical court poetry. The only exception is the *Frauendienst* (Service to ladies) of Ulrich von Lichtenstein (postclassical, *ca.* 1255), an Austrian "gentleman-singer" who made his collected poems the basis of a fictional autobiography. Otherwise a poet gathering his own oeuvre for posterity seems to have begun only with Heinrich von Mügeln (*d.* 1372), Oswald von Wolkenstein (*d.* 1445), and Michel Beheim (*d. ca.* 1475–1479; his is the first autograph collection).

Only when court lyrics began to fade as a living art (by 1280 or so) were systematic collections commissioned to preserve the achievement of the "golden age." This was done by collectors, such as the Manesse family of Zurich, who were closely associated with the ruling gentry in Alsace, Swabia, and Switzerland. There are three great collections from this period, beginning with the so-called Smaller Heidelberg Song Manuscript (*A, ca.* 1300), the Weingarten-Stuttgart Manuscript (*B, ca.* 1310–1320), and the Large Heidelberg Song Manuscript, called Manesse-Codex (*C, ca.* 1300–1340). All three are associated with the cities of Constance and Zurich, and—in terms of sources used—with each other. Preserving some 6,000 strophes by 140 poets, the Manesse-Codex (426 folio sheets) is by far the largest and most famous of them. Reproductions of its author portraits (charming, but hardly outstanding examples of book illumination) used to be found on German wall calendars almost as often as quotations from Goethe.

Patterns in the grouping of strophes and text corrections made by the scribes (especially careful in *A*) suggest that all three codices drew on several shorter manuscripts, small booklets, even single folios. It is not known how far back such written sources may have extended. Had the scribal tradition begun more than a decade or two before 1300, some evidence of it should have been expected to survive (manuscript fragments, numerous for courtly narratives). As it stands, the main collections seem one or two steps removed from the living tradition, especially because none of the three—in contrast with the great chansonniers of thirteenth-century France and Spain—contains musical notations for the songs.

The great southwest-German collections—especially *B* and *C*—must be regarded as attempts by aristocratic families to make a record of what they considered their heritage. As has been shown, minnesong was, from its beginnings, the special literary province of the gentry. This explains why the priority sequence of poetic oeuvres in *B* and *C* follows political rank (starting with kings and dukes) and why in the miniatures (137 full pages in C) each poet is given an escutcheon and a helmet crest, signatures of the nobility. Even the gaze of the illustrators is directed toward the past. While the medieval convention in pictorial arts was to present historical figures in the dress and setting of the day, the *B* and *C* illuminators show the poets in outfits courtly people wore around 1250.

After 1350 manuscripts of lyric poetry began to be compiled in greater numbers, facilitated to some extent by the availability of paper. Those written in central Germany and the Rhenish areas, regions not considered "home turf" of court poetry, were now most likely to record the melodies as well. Yet with the exception of Neidhart—whose popular "village songs," with many additions, were handed down in a broad and separate line—the classical court poetry began to recede. What the fifteenth century knew of it was mainly the didactic variety.

Most of the technical terms used in speaking of metrics were borrowed from the meistersingers of the sixteenth century. Only a few of them (such as *dôn,* tune) go back to the Middle High German period. German verses, to begin with the basic unit, are constituted by means of regular alternation of naturally stressed and unstressed syllables, sometimes called lifts and dips. Lines are identified by the number of stresses (lifts) they contain (four-stress, five-stress verse). This is different from Romance poetry, in which a verse has to contain a fixed number of syllables (octosyllabic, decasyllabic verse). A German verse may begin with a stressed or, more commonly, an unstressed syllable, known as anacrusis *(Auftakt);* the ending of a verse, called cadence, normally consisting of the rhyme word, is then of two basic kinds: the final syllable is stressed (masculine cadence) or unstressed (feminine cadence).

Strophes are formed by taking verses containing between two and twelve stresses (lifts) and combining them with end rhyme to form a definite pattern *(diu wort).* Setting them to a melody *(diu wîse)* provides the "tune" *(dôn)* of a given song. The most demanding rule (novel for the time) is that each new song must have a new "tune." Moreover, all strophes of the song must adhere to this tune. In recital, however, slight variations between strophes (metrical, melodic) seem to have been permitted.

The classic strophe, as indicated by its rhyme, consists of two main sections: the *Aufgesang* and the *Abgesang.* The *Aufgesang* is split into two identical halves called *Stollen* and *Gegenstollen,* normally sung to the same melody. A distinctive feature of this tripartite stanza, the canzone strophe, is a pronounced contrast between *Aufgesang* and *Abgesang* (shorter versus longer verses, for instance), underscored by a dramatic shift in the melody. The extant poems most commonly contain—in order of frequency—five, three, or seven strophes. In Italy the canzone later gave rise to the sonnet form.

Part of the achievement of Middle High German court poetry lay in the increasing mastery of form: from assonances and half rhymes of the first two generations to (beginning with Reinmar) rhymes of tonal purity set effortlessly to complex patterns; from the indigenous four-line stanza of the Danubian school, with variable numbers of unstressed syllables between stresses (none or up to three), to lengthy polymetric strophes (up to twelve verses), with rhymes and "key terms" *(Leitwörter)* creating echo effects from strophe to strophe. Still it must be kept in mind that the metrical regularity (strict alternation of stressed and unstressed syllables) informing the texts in modern editions is a philological ideal based on classical Latin verse (as seen by founders of medieval philology like Karl Lachmann). It went unchallenged for a century and a half largely because the melodies, the major means for verifying metrical schemes, have been lost—lost, that is, for classical court poetry. When the texts are checked against melodies for which the notation is extant (beginning with Neidhart), the greater tolerance for metrical irregularity suggested by the manuscript versions is, to some extent, confirmed.

The notations in the Jena MS (*J,* Universitätsbibliothek Jena, Saxony, *ca.* 1340), for instance, show notes entered above syllables that the textbooks have shown as elided. While editors assume that anacrusis must, by definition, consist of one syllable, codex *J* at times has two or more notes above such a "single" syllable. This suggests that modern readers, too, must begin to allow for some irregularities in scanning the strophes.

A final point is the matter of "creative disarray." Where not clearly copied from one another (the *C* collectors were able to draw on prototypes of *A* and *B*), the extant manuscripts tend to contain songs that differ not only textually but also in the number of strophes assigned to a given song and the sequence in which they are arranged. This situation has traditionally been blamed on corruption inherent in the copying process. Yet differences in the order of strophes can to some extent be explained by the non-progressive nature of much love poetry, especially the minne canzone, in which strophes are self-contained variations on a theme and hence "readable" in any sequence. On the whole, this "disarray" may simply mean that poets revised songs in the course of their careers. Prompted by an occasion, such as appearing at a new court, they may have chosen to reorder, drop, or add strophes, thus "updating" some of their songs.

Considering what is extant of the vocal music of France (259 notated melodies for troubadour songs, some 1400 trouvère melodies), the greatest void in Middle High German court poetry lies in the loss of hundreds of melodies. For the entire classical corpus, only two complete (and transcribable) melodies of an authenticity not open to question survive: for the strophe of the didactic poet Spervogel (Jena MS) and for the "Palestine Song" (*Palästinalied*) of Walther von der Vogelweide (Münster Fragment, *Z, ca.* 1350). Although powerful and poignant, even the lone Walther melody turns out to be an adaptation of a May song by the troubadour Jaufré Rudel (*ca.* 1147), who had drawn on a Latin antiphon in praise of the Virgin (*ca.* 1100), which was also known to Walther. Only with Neidhart do manuscripts that record notations permit recovery of the melodies in any number.

It lies in the nature of their craft that philologists do not always take into consideration the difference it makes to hear a poem sung rather than read. The music of court poetry was, to be sure, not that of the German lied, in which the melody plays on key feelings expressed in the text. The Romance tradition would suggest that medieval melodies were largely intended to reinforce—or be counterpoint to—the metrical design of a song. But when working through a Middle High German text on the barren page, it should be kept in mind that much of the minnesingers' art consisted in musical sound.

It is entirely possible that the artistic levels a particular poet reached as versifier and as composer were not of the same height. Comparing the notated songs of Heinrich von Meissen (*d.* 1318) and Wizlaw von Rügen (*fl.* 1300) in codex *J* is an instructive case in point. Famed as an innovative and bold lyricist (with the "florid style"), Heinrich von Meissen (known as Frauenlob) adhered in his melodies to the older form of syllabic monody. Wizlaw, on the other hand, wrote poems conforming to traditional minnesong, while his richly melismatic tunes must be considered progressive. When Gottfried von Strass-

burg and Walther sang the praises of the "nightingale of Hagenau," the great Reinmar, they did so in images suggesting even greater admiration for Reinmar's music (all of it lost) than for his verse.

The aforementioned tune to Walther's "Palestine Song" is the product of a borrowing process (attested for Middle High German poetry by Ulrich von Lichtenstein) known as contrafacture. Guided by metrically identical strophes in songs on similar topics, musicologists have used contrafacture to recover the melodies of a few dozen court lyrics, drawing on both Romance chansonniers and the notated codices of the meistersingers. It remains open to question how authentic, in the historical sense, are such "reconstructed" melodies. There are a host of variables. The very act of contrafacture may have called for some changes; some Romance tunes have come down to modern times in more than one version; by the meistersinger age, long usage had clearly induced substantial alterations.

Evidence from the pictorial arts—when conjoined to descriptions in courtly romances (notably Gottfried's *Tristan*)—suggests that court lyrics were sung to the accompaniment of plucked and bowed string instruments, such as the harp, lyre, fiddle, or vielle (which provided support chords or drone). This cannot be proved conclusively. Perhaps *a capella* recital was common. Yet when lyrics were sung as dancing airs, it would hardly seem possible that some instruments (such as drums or tambourines) were not used to supply a beat. In his *Frauendienst* Ulrich von Lichtenstein states that minstrel-fiddlers thanked him profusely for using high-pitched notes in devising the melody for his new *leich*. Since Ulrich expected this *wîse* (melody) to be played by fiddlers, it can be surmised that other court songs could on occasion (such as a dance) be played as instrumental pieces.

FORMS OF THE MINNESONG

Many poems on the theme of love, to be surveyed in this section, begin with mannered description of a landscape, usually at the forest's edge (trees, grass, flowers, brook, birdsong, breezes). While used by Romance poets, especially in northern France, such nature introductions (*Natureingang*) occurred most frequently in the Latin lyric composed by learned clerics (goliardic poetry). The description sets the mood of the song in a standard and—with the passage of generations—almost mechanical way: It is May, and my lady makes me happy, too; it may be spring outside, but my stern lady makes me sad; it is winter, outside and in my heart; cold winter notwithstanding, serving my lady brings joy. Thus, like much of landscape depiction in Western literature, the *Natureingang* is a device to get from the scene outside to the scene inside, the landscape of the mind. The first poet to make use of nature introduction was Heinrich von Veldeke, the first singer fully receptive to the Romance lyric. As poet of village and countryside (a strange one, to be sure), Neidhart (*fl.* 1210–1237) was its most prolific champion, starting virtually all his songs with either a spring or a winter scene.

At the center of court poetry, from its beginning with the first troubadour, are songs dealing with love in all its varieties, from the bawdy ballad of "menonly" nights to the most cerebral exercises in selfdenial. One of the few types of such love poetry not derived from the West is the exchange *(Wechsel)*, popular with early singers. It features a man and a woman speaking—usually in somber tones—about their love. But because they are apart, they speak to themselves or to a messenger. Often songs of love remembered, these exchanges convey a special blend of intimacy and alienation. The tentative link between the man's strophe and the woman's (they must be imagined as Everyman types) is a reminder that the single self-contained stanza, usually a woman's lament, constituted the basic vessel of indigenous and early love lyric.

The classic form of love poetry is the minne canzone *(minnekanzone)*, the ascetic Song of Songs of the minnesingers. It consists, in its typical form, of five strophes adhering to the tripartite format. Derived from the courtly *canso* of France, minne canzone designates poems on the theme of love, expressing (in Olive Sayce's words) "the lover's grief and the symptoms of his malady, praise of the perfect lady, . . . and pleas addressed to the lady or Love." Because the German minne canzone is (in contrast to its Romance model) devoid of everyday realities of political and court life, it can be said to have constituted a better medium—a laboratory of the soul, as it were—to probe the full range of thoughts associated with desire and denial.

The term *minnesanc*, as first used by Walther von der Vogelweide (*ca.* 1230), suggests that minne canzones were to the court poets a kind of professional obligation. If that was the case, then the all-time professional was Reinmar, the "First One" *(der Alte)*, he was called, or "of Hagenau" (in Alsace), perhaps the place he started out before becoming court poet to the dukes of Austria. In Reinmar's forty-odd songs the poetic "I"—a refined courtier— strives untiringly for the good graces of his lady. His ruminating preoccupation with her is total. Being denied or feeling not worthy of her is the wellspring of his suffering.

Taken over from the troubadours was the convention, followed by Reinmar and others, of expressing this persistent service of the "good one" in the technical vocabulary of medieval feudalism, a network of obligations between lords and vassals. The poet, the "I" persona, is the vassal *(man)*, whose highest duty is to serve his lady *(frouwe)*, whom the troubadours at times address as *midons* (my lord). It is the goal of the court singer to serve a lady of the highest worth. It is a servitude freely entered, but one that must always lead to a peculiar predicament.

To be esteemed, the lady must be the very paragon of virtue; her "good name," her "honor" must remain inviolate. And this requires that she, like one destined for sainthood, keep her distance from all desirous of her—especially from the poet. This raises the powerful contradiction that the poet, by the very act of singing her praises, causes her to become— like the sun rising (the image used by Heinrich von Morungen)—ever more distant from him. Afflicted with yearning beyond attainment, the poets (notably Heinrich von Morungen) tend to view love *(minne)*, the instigating feeling itself, as a magical and demonic force, like the love potion (read "poison") drunk by Tristan and Isolde.

The modern reader might ask who was Reinmar's lady; who were these ladies, both irreproachable and unapproachable, who caused the minnesingers to fall into states of protracted adulation? It is unlikely that they were, as scholars once thought, the "leading ladies" of the court (the duchess of Austria, the countess of Thuringia). Rather, they appear to be projections of the poets themselves: luminous embodiments of virtue, perhaps what the faithful had in mind when they worshiped the Virgin Mary—the "eternal womanly" *(das ewig Weibliche)*, as Goethe called this concept much later.

But if they are projections of the ideal, then their very existence depends on the poet. If he stops singing (as Walther put it so bluntly to Reinmar), the lady is dead. Moreover, worshiping a self-created vision makes every poet a kind of Narcissus, condemned to keep on loving what he cannot possess. In that sense Rilke, a modern minnesinger of sorts, was right when he observed that the minnesinger's worst fear is that his wish (fulfillment) might be granted.

As early as 1195, Hartmann von Aue, invoking the spirit of the crusades, denounced minnesinger's (in the first attested use of the Middle High German term) as artificers of illusion. What was the point of these intellectual exercises of striving and suffering? The answer is given by the poets themselves. Relentless service requires self-discipline and leads to self-improvement. The minne canzone is an exercise in self-analysis and self-cultivation. It makes the singer, in his persona of the refined courtier, a better person, the epitome of the self-disciplined gentleman, and thus a model for the court. In that sense high minnesong—or courtly love in general—is a kind of vernacular religion. The courtier-singer is like the faithful believer who strives to better himself in order to become worthy of the divine.

Like all grand visions, however, high minnesong was a frail creation. It was for no more than three decades that it enjoyed artistic supremacy at the courts. By 1200 or so Walther von der Vogelweide had begun to object to it as a one-sided passion. Taking a stance against Reinmar (perhaps his teacher), he called for songs in praise of reciprocal love. He began to celebrate, in his *Mädchenlieder,* the kind of gracious and generous young woman, devoid of coyness, who had often been the object of affection in Latin love lyrics. She is not the remote lady of the court, but a woman *(wîp)* who loves in return, like the delightful shepherdess of pastoral poetry; a partner in love, whom one addresses with *du* (thou) rather than with the *ir* (you) of the minne canzone.

Walther did not, of course, put an end to the classical minne canzone. He may have written some all along, just as Reinmar, when working a form like the *Wechsel,* was quite capable of speaking of requited love. The modern reader must not expect a medieval poet to have "a consistent outlook" (an ideal most unmedieval). What a poet says is largely governed by the song type he selects. What Walther did, then, was to add a powerful new register to the organ of minnesong. It can be said, however, that the love lyric to come does not contain any thoughts or expressions not found in the classical school as it constituted itself from the beginnings around 1170 (Heinrich von Veldeke, Friedrich von Hausen) to the death of Walther (*ca.* 1230).

What was new in love poetry of the "postclassical" age consisted mainly of counter-forms to the canzone. By 1210 these forms began to be heard at courts in the Austro-Bavarian southeast, in the so-called summer songs and winter songs of Neidhart.

As with parody in general, Neidhart's counter-forms were created by inversion: the lofty lady, immaculate in conduct, is replaced by a free-spirited village lass. In the summer songs she gives full vent to her desires by donning her best dress and scurrying off to join "her knight" (the singer) for a dance under the village linden. The guardian figure *(huote)* of the canzone, charged with protecting the lady's good name, is here replaced by the wanton girl's mother—or her equally uncivil girl friend—whose chaperoning zeal extends to physical violence.

In Neidhart's winter songs the canzone's gentleman-singer, the aesthete of self-cultivation through self-denial, is turned into a village knight, a lascivious bumpkin squire. He too is frustrated, but not because his "lady" is unapproachable—she is very approachable. But, being a village lass, she prefers to dally with peasant lads who—in garb, armor, and weapons—prance about as knights.

Although Neidhart's "village poetry"—the world of minnesong turned topsy-turvy—constituted the most popular counter-form to the canzone, a few others were devised. Most noteworthy, perhaps, are the "harvest songs" or "feasting songs" (*Herbstlieder, Fresslieder*), beginning with Steinmar (*fl.* 1270), in which the blossom time of May and the brittle rewards of courtly love give way to culinary orgies in the harvest kitchen (new wine, freshly slaughtered meat).

It is important to note, however, that such counter-forms did not drive out the classical song types. They represent yet another increase in the number of forms available to court poets. And nothing is more indicative of the craft, as practiced by postclassical generations—and what might be perceived as its detachment from reality—than that a poet (such as Johannes Hadlaub, *fl.* 1300 in Zurich) was capable of producing both lofty minnesongs and their counter-forms.

Much of the achievement of the classical canzone lay in its rich display of metrical virtuosity. In that sense the song type most akin to it is the *leich.* Equivalent to the Romance *descort* or lai, the *leich* was patterned on the sequence of church liturgy involving antiphonal singing by two choirs. With each of many short strophes (versicles) repeated, the *leich* exemplifies the combination of repetition and variation that lies at the heart of court poetry. It thus seems to have served poets as a kind of showpiece. Only after 1250 did they begin to write more than one *leich* each. The first minnesinger, Friedrich von Hausen, was also the first to compose a *leich* (not extant). Its theme, *minne,* was a popular one, though later poets also used the *leich* to call for a crusade (Heinrich von Rugge), to praise the Virgin (Walther), even to create lavish and lengthy dancing airs (Tannhäuser, *fl.* 1230–1250).

In its sensuality the aubade or dawn song (Middle High German: *tageliet*) can be viewed as another kind of antidote to the minne canzone. It consists of a dialogue between two (usually adulterous) lovers who must separate at first light, when their "lookout" (a watchman) sounds a warning. Whether the dawn song (the first German text, *ca.* 1170, is ascribed to Dietmar von Aist) must be derived from its Provençal equivalent, the *alba,* is open to question. For the troubadours the *alba* was a minor form, appearing late (end of twelfth century). Some of its features (jealous husband) are almost never found in the German *tageliet.* Reminiscent of the lament of the "woman forsaken," so popular in the Austro-Bavarian (and indigenous) love lyric, the role of the woman left behind—her pain and words of farewell—are given much more weight in the German dawn songs.

The aubade has been very popular with students of the medieval German lyric, though court poets of the classical period wrote about as few of them as of *leichs.* Only Wolfram von Eschenbach, the master romancer, made aubades the center of his lyric oeuvre (what remains of it). His five dawn songs, graphic in diction, laced with powerful images, take the form through its major variations, including the peaceful awakening of a married couple. The settings of aubades (castle chamber, garden) are evocative, the feelings (anxiety of leave-taking) universal in their appeal. Often odes to "love remembered"—such as Morungen's luminous aubade (two lovers, now separated as in the *Wechsel,* recall their night)—dawn songs strike the modern reader as the most lyrical, most modern form of Middle High German poetry.

Yet the curious figure of the watchman—who from the rampart of his lord's castle shouts out what should be kept secret—serves as a reminder that the dawn song is a convention no less fictional than the canzone. It is, in fact, its patent disregard of reality (would a lady confide in a boorish watchman?) that makes the aubade a target for postclassical parodies. Still, it was just about the only type of court poetry destined to endure. The dawn song found practitioners as late as the fifteenth century, and not in Germany alone. When Romeo and Juliet are awakened (by the lark, "herald of the morn") after spending their night together, Shakespeare has them speak as in a dawn song.

The last type of minnesong to be discussed here, the "crusade song," must be viewed as constituting a form halfway between the love lyric and didactic poetry (*Spruchdichtung*). First used by the troubadour Marcabru (*fl.* 1130–1148), the crusade song (Middle High German: *kriuzliet*) conjoins the theme of *minne* to concerns (invocation of religious obligations, exhortation, chiding, prayer) usually voiced in didactic verse. While imported from the West (Friedrich von Hausen imitates Conon de Béthune, for instance), the *kriuzliet* rose suddenly to the fore with the onset of preparations for the Third Crusade in 1187. Frederick I Barbarossa himself convened a "crusading diet" at Mainz during Lent of 1188. It can be no accident, therefore, that crusade songs were first written by poets associated with his court (Friedrich von Hausen, Heinrich von Rugge).

German poets, ever in search of dilemmas, gave great emphasis to debating the conflicting loyalties between service to the lady and service owed to God. Not that the outcome was unpredictable: no singer ever bids farewell to God. Yet intellectual ruminations, at the heart of high minnesong, flourish most profusely at the moment of decision. And although most poets (in the persona speaking) end by dissolving the bonds to their mistress, not all do. Albrecht von Johansdorf (*fl.* 1205) claims to have praised his lady so ardently that she has become part of him. He has determined to take her along to the Holy Land ("in the casket of his heart"), and the lady will share equally in the blessings awaiting the crusader.

The crusading lyrics of the thirteenth century can be read as a gauge measuring the erosion of faith in this grand enterprise of Christendom. By the time of the Sixth Crusade (1228–1229), Neidhart had written two parodic summer songs that contrast the misery of being on crusade (disease, hostile climate, deadly infidels) with the rustic pleasures of staying home in a "little parish." Others (Freidank, Tannhäuser) soon afterward denounced the political strife between pope and emperor, the plunder campaigns of the knight-crusaders, the grievous perils of the sea crossing. With polemics of this kind, with political and moral invective, the province of didactic poetry had already been entered.

DIDACTIC POETRY (SPRUCHDICHTUNG)

There is a large body of Middle High German verse that—in the modern understanding of the term—cannot be called lyric poetry. Dealing with matters of religion, moral conduct, politics, and polemics (official or personal), it is best designated "instructional" or "didactic" poetry. Although in its form (sung strophic poems) no different from minnesong, it can be characterized as dealing with every subject other than love.

Its intent was social and instructional. Stressing the religious and moral principles of a "good (Christian) life," *Spruchdichtung* was designed to teach people, mostly at the courts, how to make the right decisions. What it does share with *minne* poetry is the premise that wisdom, right and proper conduct (toward the lady, in the world), can be taught. This explains why such didactic poetry, after starting in the twelfth century at the level of proverbial verse, was (with Walther von der Vogelweide) able to gain access to the courts and to become closely associated with the courtly love lyric.

Yet, though recited at court, didactic poetry was not written by people of the court. Virtually none of the many lyric poets belonging to the aristocracy composed didactic verse. The *Spruchdichter* were men of indifferent station: professional singers, usually wandering from court to court in the area bounded by the Rhine, the Elbe, and the Danube. They had to earn a living with their craft. This made them a touchy and defensive lot, none more contentious than the best of them, Walther von der Vogelweide, whose constant references to "personal worth" and "poetic worth" are the clearest indicators that he, too, was not to the landed gentry born.

From early on, the didactic poets adopted professional names. Some attested to the place they came from: Kerling (*fl.* 1140), "He of the Land of Charlemagne" (Lorraine), or Der Meissner (who wrote in the second half of the thirteenth century), "He from the margravate Meissen." Others alluded to their special lot, the nomadic life—Sperling (*fl.* 1190), "The Sparrow"; Rumelant (*fl.* 1260–1290), "Vacator of Lands"; or Der Marner (*ca.* 1231–1267), "The Mariner." As traveling poets they depended on the largess of the courts where they held forth. It is understandable, therefore, that they spent much time praising generous patrons (the dukes of Austria, for instance) and castigating stingy ones (lords in castles along the Rhine). Songsmiths proud of their learning, they were fond of referring to themselves as "masters" (*meister, magistri*), a title passed on, centuries later, to their city offspring, the meistersingers.

Although the rule governing love lyrics that a new "tune" (verse, *wort,* plus melody, *wîse*) must be created for each new song also applied to didactic poetry, it was adhered to less rigidly. The simpler strophic forms were preferred. Few *Spruchdichter* worked in more than a small canon of "tunes." Some—like the early Herger/Spervogel or the celebrated "Second" Reinmar (von Zweter, *fl.* 1230–1250)—made do with a single "tune."

As with indigenous and early lyric, the incipient unit of the *Spruch* is the single strophe (twelfth century), sounding much like a proverb. Walther moved didactic poetry close to the lyric. Hence many of his *Sprüche*—like the "Reichston," the famed "Imperial Tune"—were composed and (more likely) recited as polystrophic songs. Yet some of Walther's thirteen great *Spruchtöne* contain so many strophes (up to nineteen) that the unity of argument or purpose, characteristic of the lyric poem, cannot be said to exist. In fact, the definitive feature of a *Spruchstrophe* is that it can stand by itself, whereas a *Liedstrophe* cannot. It must be assumed that the number of strophes of a given "tune" presented at one recital could vary according to the demands of the occasion.

What political poetry existed in twelfth-century Germany was written by clerical courtiers, like the Archpoet (in service to Rainald of Dassel, archbishop of Cologne and chancellor to Barbarossa), in Latin. Composing the first strophe of his "Imperial Tune" early in 1198, Walther von der Vogelweide was the first to make German poetry an instrument of a political cause. His powerful verses in support of Philip of Swabia (the brother of Emperor Henry VI)—in which he takes the ancient stance of the visionary thinker—mark the start of Walther's lifetime of service to rulers of all kinds, and to their chanceries paying his wages.

With little regard for political (or personal) consistency, Walther was ready, by 1205, to threaten with impeachment by the electors the same Emperor Philip whom he had glorified as the Trinity incarnate at the Magdeburg Christmas diet of 1199. Even before Philip's assassination in 1208, Walther had joined the opposing English-backed Welf camp, and then—to support Emperor Otto IV against Innocent III—wrote some of the most vicious polemics ever directed against the papacy.

Such opportunism may be alarming. Yet the fact remains that Walther's agitational verse was, in his time, so effective that he is still ranked as the most influential political poet of the German language. By 1215 even Thomasin von Zerklaere, an author siding with the papacy, had to admit that Walther succeeded in stirring up "thousands of Germans" against the pope.

Most of the didactic poetry was written in the generations after Walther's death about 1230. Although the courtly love lyric had run its course by the time the great southwest German collections were compiled (1300–1340), the *meister* continued to practice their craft at the courts. In the fourteenth century Heinrich von Mügeln was one of the most learned exponents of didactic poetry. It was only with the prolific Michel Beheim (1416–*ca.* 1475/ 1479) that the last of the breed passed from the scene.

The one universal informing instructional and religious verse after 1250 is that poets derive their authority less from "inspiration" than from learning. Reading the corpus is a bit like reading a late-medieval encyclopedia. The penchant for argumentation and for the logic of detail reminds the modern reader that the *meister* were writing in the age of Scholasticism.

The work of some of these singers—like Konrad von Würzburg (*d.* 1287) and Heinrich von Meissen, called Frauenlob in tribute to his Marian panegyrics—is marked by a desire to make poetry as difficult as possible. They favor the "florid diction" (*geblümte Rede*), derived from the *ornatus difficilis* (heavy ornament) of Latin rhetorical poets. Many poems have the pictorial indirection found elsewhere in Europe only in the court poetry of the Scandinavian skalds.

Yet it might be said that much of later didactic poetry is the daily output of professional versifiers. It lacks vision, imagination, and verbal force. The causes become more narrow and personal, frequently involving the kinds of feuds carried on in modern times by opera singers and politicians. In political verse only the great confrontation, in 1235, between Emperor Frederick II and his rebel son Henry brought forth a measure of polemic fervor (by Bruder Wernher) worthy of Walther's example.

Beginning with Walther, political poetry was informed by an outlook that today is called conservative. "Perversions" of the time were fought by invoking the "golden age." Even with the old feudal order giving way to manufacturing and trade, with a money economy replacing exchange in kind, with cities emerging as cultural centers, the traveling poets continued to side with the aristocracy, the rightful rulers of old. Yet it was in the cities, not the courts, that the last practitioners of didactic poetry,

the meistersingers of the sixteenth and seventeenth centuries, flourished.

What the meistersingers still knew of and admired in classical court poets like Walther, however, was more form than substance. Honoring the great "tunes" of his didactic poetry, they regarded Walther as a "founding master" of their craft, but otherwise had no comprehension of his poetic achievement. By the Reformation the great Middle High German court poetry was largely forgotten. The only exception was Neidhart, whose "village poetry," much imitated, was made into a seminarrative cycle printed as a chapbook as late as 1566. Yet Neidhart was not appreciated as a court poet, but as Knight "Neidhart Fuchs" (the Fox), the Peasant Foe. His poetry had become "his life," a literary legend. Such mythmaking was common to late-medieval generations looking back. Because of his luminous love lyrics, Heinrich von Morungen became known as a notorious *Buhler,* the Don Juan of his age. A similar fate befell Tannhäuser, who was linked to the Venusberg ballad (familiar today through Wagner's opera).

Minnesong lay dormant in manuscripts until the middle of the eighteenth century, when pre-Romantic stirrings rekindled an interest in relics of "ancient poetry." Putting their Swiss German (the dialect still closest to Middle High German) to good use, Johann Jakob Breitinger and Johann Jakob Bodmer published the Manesse-Codex, which they viewed as the proud heritage of their native Zurich. After Romantic poets such as Clemens Brentano and Ludwig Tieck had delighted in the folklike charm and sonorous simplicity of the minnesingers (the term was reestablished) scholarly inquiry began in the 1830's with editions by the founders of medieval philology: Karl Lachmann, Moriz Haupt, Friedrich von der Hagen.

BIBLIOGRAPHY

Sources. Frederick Goldin, trans., *German and Italian Lyrics of the Middle Ages* (1973); Walther Killy, ed., *Epochen der deutschen Lyrik,* I, *Von den Anfängen bis 1300,* Werner Höver and Eva Kiepe, eds. (1978), and II, *Gedichte 1300–1500,* Eva Kiepe and Hansjürgen Kiepe, eds. (1972); Carl von Kraus, ed., *Deutsche Liederdichter des 13. Jahrhunderts,* 2nd ed., rev. by Gisela Kornrumpf, 2 vols. (1978); Karl Lachmann, ed., *Die Gedichte Walthers von der Vogelweide,* 13th ed., rev. by Hugo Kuhn (1965), and *Des Minnesangs Frühling,* 36th ed., 2 vols., rev. by Hugo Moser and Helmut Tervooren (1977); *Neidhart von*

Reuental, Lieder, Helmut Limnitzer, trans. (1966); Olive Sayce, ed., *Poets of the Minnesang* (1967); Günther Schweikle, ed. and trans., *Die mittelhochdeutsche Minnelyrik,* I, *Die frühe Minnelyrik* (1977), with an informative introduction, 1–113.

Studies. Wolfgang Haubrichs, "Deutsche Lyrik," in Henning Krauss, ed., *Europäisches Hochmittelalter,* vol. VII of Klaus von See, ed., *Neues Handbuch der Literaturwissenschaft* (1981); Alfred Karnein, "Die deutsche Lyrik," in Willi Erzagräber, ed., *Europäisches Spätmittelalter,* vol. VIII of von See (1978); Olive Sayce, *The Medieval German Lyric 1150–1300* (1982), now the standard work on the subject; Hans Schottmann, "Mittelhochdeutsche Literatur: Lyrik," in Ludwig Erich Schmitt, ed., *Kurzer Grundriss der germanischen Philologie bis 1500,* II (1971); Helmut Tervooren, *Bibliographie zum Minnesang und zu den Dichtern aus "Des Minnesangs Frühling"* (1969); Max Wehrli, *Geschichte der deutschen Literatur vom frühen Mittelalter bis zum Ende des 16. Jahrhunderts* (1980), 326–391, 420–454, 730–765.

Recordings. German Music of the Middle Ages and Renaissance, Desmar Records, DSM 1015G (1978); *Minnesong and Prosody circa 1200–1320,* Telefunken, Das alte Werk, SAWT 9487-A Ex (1966); *Oswald von Wolkenstein,* Odeon, C 063-30101 (1972).

ECKEHARD SIMON

[See also **Alba; Albrecht von Johansdorf; Aubade; Dietmar von Aist; Frederick II of Sicily; Freidank; Friedrich von Hausen; Gottfried von Neifen; Hartmann von Aue; Heinrich von Meissen; Heinrich von Morungen; Heinrich von Mügeln; Heinrich von Rugge; Heinrich von Veldeke; Johannes Hadlaub; Konrad von Würzburg; Marner, Der; Meinloh von Sevelingen; Minnesingers; Neidhart von Reuental; Oswald von Wolkenstein; Reinmar von Haguenau; Reinmar von Zweter; Spervogel; Steinmar; Tannhäuser, Der; Troubadour, Trouvère, Trovadores; Ulrich von Lichtenstein; Ulrich von Winterstetten; Walther von der Vogelweide; Wolfram von Eschenbach.**]

GERMAN LITERATURE: ROMANCE. The use of the term "romance" as a specialized description of a narrative verse genre of medieval German literature is relatively recent, and even today is by no means universally accepted. The French word *roman* does not, in medieval usage, designate a genre, as such titles as *Roman de la Rose, Roman de Renart,* and *Roman de Troie* make clear. Medieval German authors rarely used the term in describing their work. They were much more likely to employ such general words as *buoch* (book) or *maere* (story),

and there was little attempt to distinguish the various kinds of narrative poetry on generic grounds. German writers did not hesitate to adapt a French chanson de geste into what modern critics would describe as a romance form.

In the absence of even approximate genre indications by medieval writers, it has fallen to modern critics to attempt definitions. In the nineteenth and earlier twentieth centuries, it was customary to divide the longer narrative works into *Volksepos* (such as *Nibelungenlied* and *Kudrun*) and *höfisches Epos* (courtly epic), such as the works of Heinrich von Veldeke, Hartmann von Aue, Wolfram von Eschenbach, and Gottfried von Strassburg. The justification for this division lay in the choice of subject matter. The "popular epics" were based on material that was either historical or purported to be so. Furthermore, it had specifically Germanic origins and numerous collateral stories could be cited in other Germanic literatures, particularly Old Norse. The *Volksepos,* therefore, was seen as a poetic representation of the past of the Germanic peoples, admittedly modified by considerable amounts of folklore, legend, mythology, and epic amplifications but reflecting essentially the characteristics of a people.

The *höfisches Epos,* as its name states, was regarded as a product of the court, written for an aristocratic audience of superior culture and taste. The author frequently makes it clear, in an exordium or an authorial interruption, that he will make special demands on his audience, that analysis and even interpretation will be needed, and that they will be instructed as well as entertained. The material was largely, though by no means exclusively, derived from French sources (in many cases from specific, known French works). The influence of France on the vocabulary can be easily documented. Such words as *bohurt, curtois, turnieren, aventiure,* and *hövisch* are clearly imported from French or are translations of French terms; and they, like such native words as *minne* (love), are used in specialized senses. But the French works are also responsible for the literary use of the court as a center of a special type of civilization with its own mores and conventions. The use of a court as a center of action is, of course, as common in the *Volksepos* as in the *höfisches Epos,* but the conventions are different. In the latter the court is a cultural, not a political, center, a background for individual action, for the romance is private-minded, in contrast with the public-minded epic.

THEMES OF ROMANCES

The subject matter of almost all German romances is drawn from specifically literary antecedents and almost always from written literary works. This is not to argue that there was no influence of orally transmitted material, but to posit that a recognizable written background is either certain or can be assumed from statements made by the author or his contemporaries. It is thus hardly surprising that the origins of romance subject matter are to be sought in the great repositories of written story available to a twelfth-century author: the Latin classical and postclassical writers, both of which groups drew on Greek antecedents; French authors whose work was available in manuscript; possibly, in a few cases, direct knowledge of Celtic and Eastern material; medieval Latin writers who had collected material from various sources, including all those previously mentioned. Few German writers of romance possessed the linguistic skills necessary to make use of all those sources. For the most part they were dependent either on an original written in French or on an earlier German version of the same story—as, for example, Heinrich von Freiberg was on Eilhart von Oberg's *Tristram (Tristrant)*.

The division of narrative material by Jean Bodel into *matière de Rome, matière de France,* and *matière de Bretagne* shows that writers at the beginning of the thirteenth century were aware of groups of subjects set in specific milieus and having certain characteristics in common. The fact that they recognized such groups does not prove that they had a clear definition of the romance or that they necessarily associated any or all of the cycles with the romance. In fact, there are relatively few romances that use the *matière de France*—and with good reason. The characters of the kings—especially Charlemagne and Louis the Pious—were determined by the need to show national leadership or the consequences of the lack of it. In other words, epic, not romance, factors determined the use of the material and the structuring of the poem. Yet the romance is conscious of the fact that it is not national history. The material it uses may be, in the most general sense, historical, but it is composed of events that are not directly connected with the history of western Europe. On the other hand, these events could be manipulated to show certain characteristics and ideals—and even regal lineages—that could be applied to the audience and could reinforce the status of the rulers, major and minor, to whom the poems were addressed. The "historical" events selected for use in romances had already been shaped into literary materials to such a degree that the original occurrences—if they ever happened—are of little significance in comparison with the literary picture that had become part of the Western tradition. The literary-historical events that were used by the romance were the career of Alexander the Great, the Trojan War, the Seven against Thebes, and the kingship of Arthur.

The source of the Western versions of the Alexander romance is largely, though not exclusively, the Latin translation of the Greek text of Pseudo-Callisthenes made by Archpresbyter Leo about 950. A literary tradition is established with a king-hero of youth, culture, and superhuman achievements. There is, however, a marked absence of any dominating love interest, and it is perhaps for this reason that the Alexander romances had to wait for their full flowering until the romance had achieved development on other themes. In German the only important Alexander romance is that of Rudolf von Ems.

The stories of the Trojan War on which the romances were based were those of Dares Phrygius and Dictys Cretensis, which purported to be eyewitness accounts from the Trojan and Greek points of view, respectively. Their works are, in fact, much closer to the Greek romance than they are to history, since they make most of the important events of the war, including the death of Achilles, the result of love in one form or another; and the accounts are much more concerned with exploits of individuals than with any sense of national history. The connection of love and adventure is not made so explicit in Dares (the preferred author because of this Trojan point of view) as it was in medieval romance, but the adaptation was easy and was carried out by Benoît de Sainte-Maure in his *Roman de Troie (ca.* 1165). The material in Dares is amplified, both in the sense that it is much expanded and in the rhetorical sense (the events are illustrated and made more vivid by the use of rhetorical techniques). Individual combat on horseback becomes a central feature, and prowess in it is connected with love.

The treatment of Vergil's *Aeneid* presents perhaps the best example of the way in which classical epic was converted to medieval romance. The work was well known to medieval authors, and there are no "variants" that could have influenced the vernacular authors in their reworking. It must therefore be assumed that the form given to the story in the anonymous French *Roman d'Enéas (ca.* 1160) and the German adaptation of it, Heinrich von Veldeke's *Eneide (Eneit),* was the result of a deliberate attempt to make it into a romance, and that the authors therefore had a clear idea of romance characteristics.

The most obvious feature is the restructuring of the story of Aeneas around his love for two women. The Dido episode is presented in much the same way it appears in the Latin work, with strong emphasis on the irrationality and sensual nature of a love that is essentially disruptive both of society and of individual personality. In Vergil's *Aeneid* it is Aeneas' sense of commitment to his fate and to the future Rome that triumphs. The *Roman d'Enéas* is more concerned with the unfitting nature of this kind of love. In Vergil's work Lavinia is merely a political pawn, and the question of love between her and Aeneas does not arise. In the French work the love between Lavinie and Enéas is central to the development of the poem—indeed, to its whole meaning. The struggle between Enéas and Turnus is due to their love for Lavinie, not to their quest for political domination of Italy.

The first meeting of Enéas and Lavinie follows a pattern that was to become typical of the romance love encounter. She sees him from a tower during a truce. Love is instantaneous; the sight of the beloved is enough to trigger it. Lavinie calls Enéas' attention to herself by having an arrow, with a message wrapped round it, shot near him. He turns his eyes to her and also is instantly in love. This is an essential feature of the romance, the eye-heart mysticism that produces love. Such mysticism is not dependent on close physical proximity; indeed, it flourishes when there is distance, physical in the *Enéas* but sometimes psychological, between the two lovers. The lady in the tower, which must somehow be entered by the lover, is another essential feature.

Other characteristics also appear: the erotic dream; the internal monologue in which each lover debates the possibility of an amorous union; the despair, the hope, and the exaltation brought by love; the denigration, both of the lover and of oneself, that love arouses. Many of these aspects are clearly derived from the works of Ovid, particularly the *Ars amatoria,* but they are carefully made part of the narrative pattern. The defeat of Turnus is thus the event that ensures that Enéas will win Lavinie. The fact that it ensures the existence of a Latin state dominated by Rome is of minor significance.

It should be noted that love in marriage is the object. Love in the romance is not necessarily adulterous—indeed, adulterous relationships are confined to a few groups of stories: those of Tristan and, sometimes, of Lancelot. Love, however, may not be purely sensual. There must be some degree of idealization, of moral elevation, at least for the man. The woman must be capable of inspiring the man to great deeds and not be a mere passive object of his desire. On the other hand, the man must be aware that his relationship to the lady must go beyond a desire for sexual relations with her and that he must prove himself worthy of her love. It is in this last respect that the romances based on material from classical antiquity developed problems. Even though they were literary, not historical, products, the only way in which a warrior could prove himself was in war. Inevitably the lady could not be a direct witness of the warrior's deeds, nor could it be argued that the war was being fought on her behalf. The abduction of Helen may have been the cause of the Trojan War, but the Trojan War romances are hardly built around the attempts of Paris to prove himself worthy of her. The romances of classical antiquity (and also those concerned with the *matière de France*) were thus deficient in one very important feature that is characteristic of the romance genre: the close connection between love and adventure.

The word "adventure" *(aventiure, Abenteuer)* is used in a highly technical sense in both French and German romance. Fortunately a passage is extant in both French and German that defines the meaning in its romance sense. Kalogreant, in the *Yvain* of Chrétien de Troyes *(ca.* 1177–1181) and in its German counterpart, the *Iwein (ca.* 1202) of Hartmann von Aue, meets a giant herdsman, a man of vast strength, who lives in the wild woods. In conversation with him Kalogreant tries to explain what is meant by "knight" and "adventure." Both authors state that Kalogreant is a knight, that it is as a knight that he seeks adventure, and that the purpose of seeking adventure is to give status and improve reputation. In both passages the giant herdsman professes ignorance of such matters, so that it is clear that the concept is not a "natural" one but a product of "civilization."

There are some important differences as well. Chrétien apparently considers *aventure* and *mervoille* to be equally effective in promoting fame, and the trial that awaits Kalogreant partakes of the nature of both. Apart from this, he seems to assume that his audience is fully acquainted with the concept of adventure, and can smile both at and with the

446

giant herdsman's ignorance. Hartmann is more painstaking. He describes exactly what a knight is and makes the very important point that it is only by fighting another knight that he can gain from an adventure. This stress on combat according to rules is one of the major characteristics of the genre. Hartmann's herdsman emphasizes even more strongly than Chrétien's the unnaturalness of adventure—it is the rejection of a pleasant life, and therefore silly.

The passages give real information about the meaning of the term, but they do not point out that while it may be true that in seeking adventure for its own sake, the knights in romance conform to a pattern, many of their combats are not with men of their own class. The matter is worth exploring more deeply, but first the question of the "values of the Arthurian court" should be considered.

ARTHURIAN LEGEND

There is no need to discuss the origins of the Arthurian legend or of the early versions of individual stories. They were not romances. The question that has to be asked is why the court of an obscure Romano-British chieftain, who may not have existed, became celebrated in literature, and even in history, as the center of a quite extraordinary culture and way of life. No clear answer can be given, but it should be noted that Geoffrey of Monmouth devoted no less than one sixth of his *Historia regum Britanniae* (1136) to Arthur's reign, a clear absurdity. It is hard to escape the conclusion that the work was written around Arthur and was intended to endow British history with a dignity hitherto reserved for Troy, Rome, and Charlemagne's empire. Whether in imitation of Geoffrey or for their own reasons, the writers of romance also glorified Arthur's court. None of the early romances, unless we include Wace's *Brut,* a poetic version of Geoffrey, discusses Arthur's deeds or his rule of Britain. They simply present the court as a touchstone of chivalric conduct and assume that its virtues are well known to their audience. It was the very fact that Arthur's court existed only in literature, that it had no verifiable historical basis or clear connection with England's rulers, that enabled the romance writers to ascribe to it those virtues that they thought to be those of an ideal court and that did not necessarily coincide with the qualities of any contemporary court.

It is not difficult to outline the characteristics of Arthur's court, which were later regarded as a standard for all literary courts (and in later centuries for actual courts). The sovereign is wise, kind, and, above all, courteous. It is a "peacetime" court that he rules, and there is rarely mention of wars that he conducts. Similarly, the occupations of his courtiers are those of leisure time—music, dancing, storytelling, and a type of formalized combat with the sole purpose of increasing the honor of those who participate in it. Killing or maiming a worthy opponent is regarded as evil. The only rank that matters for its heroes is that of knighthood, not a rank in the strict sense but a title conferred in recognition of actual or potential prowess and conformity to the standards of the court.

The role of women is of great importance at this court. They are presumed to understand and appreciate the prowess of its male members, and the achievements of the knight with whom a woman is associated reflect a glory on her that she is to recognize. The type of association varies greatly. The knight may be the lady's husband, as he is for much of the narrative of *Erek, Iwein,* and *Parzival;* a lover who seeks the lady in marriage, as Gawain does Orgeluse in *Parzival;* an adulterous lover in the full sense, as Lancelot frequently is to Guinevere, Arthur's wife, and Tristan always is to Isolde, the wife of King Mark. On the other hand, there can be such an innocent relationship as that of Gawain to Obilot, "Little Greensleeves," a young girl full of fanciful notions about having a knight "serve" her.

It is one of the most important conventions of the romance that the deeds performed by a knight are in the service of his lady. Such a convention could, in the Middle Ages, only be a fiction; and it therefore leads to free manipulation and the development of specific game rules for the genre. These rules are designed to provide a framework, deliberately unreal, in which the development of an individual, under the double stress of the desire for recognition by the court on its terms and a desire to attain the highest kind of love from a lady, are studied both as a didactic exercise and as an entertainment for the sophisticated. In spite of the lip service to the idea of feminine predominance, the real interest is in the development of the man and in the tensions that are set up by his overwhelming desire to win the lady and the necessity to prove himself to a masculine, combat-oriented society.

The romances of Chrétien de Troyes seem to have a program to examine the various aspects of this tension. In *Érec,* the earliest extant Arthurian romance, the heroine, Énide, is worthy of love in every sense; the tension arises from the inability of Érec to conceive of love on her terms and her desire not to interfere with his Arthurian responsibilities. Each learns tolerance, but Chrétien's emphasis is on the superiority of natural love. In *Yvain* Chrétien is more interested in the relevance of the concept of adventure to the relation between man and woman, and in the distinction between the useless "service" to a lady who demands it and service to women in need. Chrétien's *Cligès* and *Lancelot* both seem to question seriously the results of putting true power in the hands of women. Fenice shows herself totally immoral in her determination to draw a veil of morality over her illicit relation to Cligès, and Guinevere's spiteful treatment of the devoted Lancelot throws an ironic and questioning light on the whole concept of female dominance.

There are not exact counterparts of these works in German, and German romance in general does not imitate Chrétien's ironic attitudes. Nevertheless, the German works do raise questions about the secularized and specialized morality ascribed to Arthur's court. Hartmann von Aue is deeply concerned about the moral background of his heroes, and both their characterization in the works and his own comments show a closer affiliation to Christian morality than is apparent in Chrétien. The two greatest medieval German romances, Wolfram von Eschenbach's *Parzival* (ca. 1210) and Gottfried von Strassburg's *Tristan und Isolt* (ca. 1210) are both dependent on the form and conventions of the romance established by Chrétien de Troyes, but they move beyond it. Wolfram follows Chrétien in depicting a naïve, even stupid, hero who is exposed suddenly to the conventions of the Arthurian court and to advice that is capricious and inadequate. In Chrétien's, and even more in Wolfram's, work the emphasis is as much on the inadequacy of the conventions as on Perceval's inability to understand them. The contrast is carried further when comparison is made between the Grail company, with its devotion to Christian charity and love in the highest sense, and the court of Arthur, where the concept of love never rises above self-indulgence and the pursuit of worldly glory. The better members of Arthur's court are noble men and by no means to be despised, but they are woefully inadequate for the pursuit of higher Christian concepts.

Gottfried von Strassburg finds the standard romance concepts inadequate on other grounds. The attempt of the romance to answer the difficult question "How shall we treat sexual love?" by saying "By convincing a woman that she is worthy of all service

and dominates our lives," while still seeing everything from the masculine point of view, is rejected by Gottfried. He sees love as an aesthetic, artistic, and moral experience rather than a social one; and, while preserving the form and conventions of the romance, he substitutes a brilliantly educated and sensitive artist for a knight with social graces, and shows the total inadequacy, jealousy, and viciousness of a court dominated by a weak king.

It must be pointed out that in all romances, the Arthurian court shows profound weaknesses. Three characters are invariably present and active—Arthur himself, Gawain, and Kei (also spelled Kay and Deu). Others, such as Guinevere, appear frequently but are not always significant. Arthur rarely exercises true decision, and often his weakness allows a decision by another—Sir Kei, for example—to influence the course of events to a degree incompatible with the ideals of the court. Parzival, for example, kills the Red Knight because Arthur has failed to prevent Kei's irresponsible action in sending him out to fight. Arthur's most notorious weakness is, of course, his failure to protect Guinevere, and he thus contravenes a basic rule of his own court.

Kei represents the lowest aspect of that court. He is entirely sure of his right to dictate conduct. He is jealous, sarcastic, driven by a desire to excel but without the means to do so. In him the Arthurian quest for honor becomes a desire to denigrate the fame of others and to dominate the weak. Kei is the prototype of the seneschal in the romance, but all seneschals are figures to be despised. They invariably show cowardice and lack of a sense of honor—and, equally, exhibit a desire to shine in a manner inconsistent with their station or deserts.

Gawain, the opposite of Kei, is a much more complex figure. He is always the paragon of good manners, the gallant warrior, the perfect lover; but his character is adapted to the romances in which he appears. In most of the early works he is a foil to the hero and is the standard by which others, especially the hero, are to be judged. Both Iwein and Parzival fight against Gawain, without either's knowing who his opponent is; the contest is indecisive, ending with mutual recognition and refusal to continue. The parallel stories of Gawain and Perceval, introduced by Chrétien de Troyes and amplified by Wolfram von Eschenbach, are surely intended to show how the very best of the Arthurian court compares with the Grail hero. Gawain's role is deliberately limited to the pursuit of worldly honor. He is shown as pursuing—and even marrying—different ladies in different romances, and it is clear that there was no such strongly established tradition for him as there was for Tristan. His pursuit of love is part of the quest for honor, and rarely is he subjected to the tension between love and adventure that is characteristic of Erek and Iwein.

A court with these three very different figures at its center gives the authors the opportunity to examine the conduct of their heroes and heroines in relation not only to a code but also to the characters who represent that code. It is, in fact, questionable whether a definite "courtly code of conduct" can be deduced from the romances in anything more than generalities. The behavior of characters like Gawain, who are clearly exemplary, allows the drawing of conclusions, but whether the authors had a "code" in mind is doubtful; and attempts to link a "knightly system of virtues" with Aristotle, Cicero, and the *Moralium dogma* ascribed to William of Conches remain unconvincing. The best description of the qualities of a perfect secular knight is that of the qualities ascribed to *Der arme Heinrich* in Hartmann's poem of that name. In his desire to show the purely secular attitude of his hero, Hartmann names his qualities: no deceit or crude behavior, loyalty and trustworthiness, good manners, generosity to relatives and the needy, skill in love songs, courtliness, and high renown. "Balance" or "moderation" (*mésure, mâze*) has often been said to be the characteristic most admired in the romance, presumably a balance between adventure and love. Such balance is certainly not characteristic of Lancelot or Tristan, and even in Chrétien's *Érec* and *Yvain* its attainment is not clearly demonstrated.

What is most important to note about courts in the romance is that they are never more than places at which individuals act, and places from which they may depart and to which they may return to receive the acclaim of their peers or, sometimes, to realize that they have transcended the courtly values to which they had subscribed. They thus have a structural as well as a cultural significance. The courts are not political, as they are in epic poetry; and their ideas and standards are essentially static and self-centered. It is for this reason that there is a conflict between the court of Arthur and the Grail company. In the work of Wolfram von Eschenbach, the conflict is essentially between two organizations having members dedicated to different aims, and particularly to different forms of service. The pursuit of the Grail, if such it can be called, is carried out only by Parzival, who is predestined to become Grail King.

In the French prose romances, however, the so-called Didot *Perceval* and the Vulgate version of the Arthurian romances (*ca.* 1215–1230), the emphasis shifts to the individual. Wolfram's grail knights conduct their activities "for their sins," but there is little stress on individual salvation. In the prose romances the individual pursuit of the Grail and individual experience of its mystery are the only matters of importance; this stress on individuality leads to the virtual abandonment of Arthur's court by many of his most famous knights and, ultimately, to its breakup. There is a clear shift of values from secular honor to religious experience.

The pursuit of love and adventure makes it inevitable that the structure of romance should conform in some degree to the standard pattern of the narrative tale—the departure of the hero from "home" (the court); his search for a "treasure," with the aid of a "helper," against the obstacles put in his way by opponents; the attainment of the quest. It is possible, however, to be more specific. Rarely does a romance have one quest and one success or failure. Many works, for the most part late in the tradition, offer a seemingly unending series of quests and adventures that are little more than incidents designed to illustrate the hero's character and career. The romances in the tradition of Chrétien tend to follow the pattern of quest-success-return, with the attainment of apparent harmony. A single occurrence breaks the harmony and leads to the undertaking of further quests for reasons very different from those in the first part; these quests lead to a very different harmony.

Such a structure facilitates the careful use of parallelism and contrast, and at its best—in the *Yvain/Iwein* romances and in Wolfram's *Parzival*—produces a tightly controlled and carefully articulated narrative pattern, one that appears to move in a line from incident to incident but is, in fact, more concerned with movement about certain focuses of attention. The knight operates about the court. His actions are determined by it, but his deeds also intersect with the demands, real or imagined, of services to a lady. Return to a starting point is basic to the narrative pattern, but the person who returns is often very different from the one who set out.

EARLY ROMANCES

It is now possible to examine more systematically the German romances that illustrate the general characteristics already noted. Any attempt to present a strictly chronological account is, at least in part, vitiated by the fact that such a chronology is at best approximate and that the works even of major authors cannot, in most instances, be dated exactly. The early version of the Alexander romance by Lamprecht of Trier (*ca.* 1130–1150) may be excluded from consideration because it lacks entirely the characteristics that have been discussed. It is therefore preferable to begin with the *Eneide* of Heinrich von (Hendrik van) Veldeke, who was born about 1140/1150 in the Low German speech area of Maastricht and was related to several noble families in the area. His ability was widely recognized by contemporaries and successor poets. The only one of his works of concern here is *Eneide*. It was written up to line 10,933 by 1174, when it was lent to the countess of Cleves and taken away by a count named Heinrich. The author got his manuscript back after nine years from Hermann von Thüringen and completed the work after 1184 (the year of the Mainz festival to which he refers in lines 13,221–13,252) and before 1190. The romance is based on the French *Roman d'Enéas*. It would, however, be a mistake to think of the German poem as a mere adaptation of the French. Heinrich presents hell in a part-pagan, part-Christian form but does treat it as a place of punishment. Similarly, he treats the pagan gods as independent beings, not merely as devils opposed to Christianity. His strong interest in the details of war and legal process reveal a practical mind. The importance of the work lies in its introduction to Germany of the courtly manner of discussing love and combat—the style and the vocabulary, the love monologue and dialogue, the sense of courtly form. Its popularity is attested by twelve complete or fragmentary manuscripts and its adaptation from its original Limburg dialect to that of Thuringia.

There are no other important German versions of the story of Aeneas in the period under review, but the story of the Trojan War is well represented. Herbort von Fritzlar wrote his *Liet von Troye* (Song of Troy) between 1210 and 1217, dates established by his references to Gottfried's *Tristan* and the death of Hermann of Thuringia. He describes himself as "ein gelarter schuolere" (a learned scholar), and his work bears out the description. His romance is a much shortened version of that of Benoît of Sainte-Maure. He reduces some 30,000 lines of the French poem to about 18,000, and concentrates on narrative rather than on characterization or motivation. There is little attempt at psychological analysis or definition of courtly conduct. The battle scenes are crude, with much gory detail, and the presentation of love gives

little more than a nod in the direction of the new concept of *minne*. The work is clearly designed to present a courtly subject to an audience of somewhat coarser sensibilities.

Otte's *Eraclius* (*ca.* 1210) is based on the *Eracle* of d'Arras. It is the "biography" of the Byzantine emperor Herakleios (610–641) but has been filled out with numerous romantic details, particularly with the story of Athenais and Parides, true lovers who are rescued from the rage of Herakleios' predecessor Phokas. Their story is the only element of true romance in the work, which is essentially a narrative of marvelous events.

Eilhart's *Tristan* (perhaps *ca.* 1180) is the first romance on the subject in German. It is closely associated in spirit and treatment with the Béroul fragments in French but is not based on them. The extant fragments of the original version show that the treatment of the story placed much greater stress on the decline of Tristan as a warrior than on his prowess as a lover. Isolde is merely the object of his love, and that love is ascribed directly and entirely to the love potion. (Mark forgives the lovers when he learns of the potion; and he, like the author, thinks entirely in sensual terms.)

HARTMANN VON AUE

In both *Erek* and *Iwein* by Hartmann von Aue the harmony at Arthur's court is disturbed—in *Erek* by an outsider, in *Iwein* by the abuse of Kei—and a knight of relatively minor significance sets out to prove his honor. Both expeditions lead to an encounter with the central female figure. Erek promises the father of Enide that he will marry her if she is allowed to be the lady whose "honor" he defends at a tournament, where his real object is to defeat the insulting intruder. She is thus a mere pretext for "adventure." Only later is there love in marriage. Iwein fatally wounds the opponent who had dishonored his cousin, then falls madly (in every sense) in love with his widow. Clever argument by Lunete, the widow's lady-in-waiting, brings about marriage. In both cases, therefore, love is the result of adventure undertaken for the recovery of honor as conceived under Arthurian game rules. The love proves fragile. Enide is concerned because Erek's obsession with her leads to his loss of reputation as a knight, but her attitude is interpreted by him as discontent with a failure to seek "adventures" that redound to her honor. Only after painful and tragic encounters, hardly any of which are adventures in the narrow sense, does he realize the depth of her love and reciprocate with a finer love of his own.

Iwein also tries not to neglect adventure. He overstays the leave granted him for the purpose by his wife, Laudine; loses his reason; and for a time leaves the world of man. His cure is effected by a lady whom he subsequently helps but whose love he refuses, and there follows a series of combats in which, under a new identity, he serves women not by adventure but by rescuing them from death and violence. It is in this new identity that he is reconciled to Laudine. Iwein's path to true love is thus very different from Erek's. It is by genuine service to women in danger that he rehabilitates himself in his own eyes, and he is aided in this by his grateful lion, which shows the same "natural" reaction to the absurdities of the rules of Arthurian honor as did the giant herdsman and which interferes to save its master when the odds are unfair.

This question of natural behavior and formal convention is stressed by both Chrétien and Hartmann. The simplicity and sincerity of Enide and her natural reaction to love and honor are hard for Arthurian courtiers to grasp, and the conflicts in the work are largely brought about by the fact that, unlike her cousin in the final adventure, the *Joie de la cort,* she never dreams of exercising female dominance or of exploiting love. Laudine, on the other hand, moves entirely in a formal world of "love service" by a champion and exercises its privileges. It is never clear in Chrétien's work whether she truly loves Yvain or whether they are truly reconciled. Hartmann saw this omission clearly and added a scene in which Laudine declares her love and is reunited with her husband.

This scene is indicative of Hartmann's attitudes. He takes Arthurian morality seriously, for the most part, and attempts to show that it can produce moral men; but he, no more than Chrétien, attempts to see behavior from any but the male point of view. There is much less irony than in Chrétien's poems, and much more detailed treatment and explanation of moral dilemmas. The essentially Christian viewpoint of Hartmann is clear even in works to which Christian morality is not fundamental.

Although the basic structure of repeated departure and return, of harmony disturbed and harmony restored, of apparent success followed by peripeteia, followed by slow progress to true success is to be ascribed to Chrétien, Hartmann's use of it ensured that it would become the norm for most subsequent German romances.

WOLFRAM VON ESCHENBACH AND HIS FOLLOWERS

The relation of the Arthurian ethic to the Christian ethic continued to be a major concern of the German romance. Wolfram von Eschenbach's *Parzival* is perhaps the greatest example of this concern. Chrétien's incomplete poem had already indicated an opposition between the values of the Arthurian court and those of the Christian world. A long series of adventures performed by Gawain, which conform to the Arthurian pattern in every way, contrasts with the early blundering efforts of Perceval to enter that world and with his slow recognition of higher values. But Wolfram goes much further. He postulates a Grail society having an organization not unlike that of the Arthurian court but with motivations and moral values that are totally different. It, too, has a weak king—but his weakness comes from his pursuit of Arthurian love values, which he knew were false and now rejects. He is surrounded by knights who go out on adventures. But these adventures are not purposeless searches for individual combats that will increase the "honor" of the winner; rather, they will aid the weak and oppressed, and at the same time be penance for the sins the knights have committed. Instead of extreme concentration on individual honor, the Grail company seeks the good of its fellow men, and honor comes from that service.

Unlike the knights of Arthur's court, the Grail knights are forbidden to pursue sexual love—on pain of ceasing to be members of the Grail company. Only the Grail King can marry, and the purpose of his marriage is to produce successors in married love. The ranks of the Grail knights are replenished by the marriages of female attendants of the Grail. Wolfram dignifies the female by making her the continuing feature of the Grail pattern, the personification of the spiritual aspects of the Grail. His women are not the ladies of the Arthurian court, exacting love service so that their own honor may be enhanced, but women devoted to spiritual ends and particularly to the task of inspiring their men to noble deeds in the support of others.

Wolfram sets up complicated patterns of male and female relationships to illustrate his point. Sigune, deprived of her lover Schionatulander by the Arthurian values to which she herself had subscribed, learns humility and gains a spiritual crown. Orgeluse, similarly deprived, can think of nothing but revenge, and attempts to use the Arthurian technique of female dominance to destroy Gawain, the greatest representative of Arthurian chivalry. It is thus that Wolfram shows the inferiority of the Arthurian ethic of honor conferred by service to the dominant female to that of service to humanity as inspired by the devoted wife. To him, married love in the service of Christian values is far superior to knightly devotion to a woman's ego. Similarly, combat for adventure is empty. The prowess of a warrior must not be at the behest of a self-centered lady, but at the disposal of those who need help.

Wolfram does not reject Arthurian values. Indeed, it would be possible to argue that his presentation of the higher values of the Grail company is dependent on contrast with those of the Arthurian court, and certainly the effectiveness of the Grail romances is much enhanced by consciousness of Arthurian values in the audience. The Arthurian value is, at least overtly, a-Christian. The romance is concerned with secular values, not with the salvation of the individual soul. Nor does Wolfram stress individual salvation, even though he makes very explicit the connection between the Grail and Christianity. The apparatus of the Arthurian romance is used with great effect to criticize itself, even to the degree of parody. Yet the nobility of Gawain is never denied. Wolfram is intent to show not that Arthurian nobility in its highest manifestations is bad, but that there are values that are far higher. It is in this respect that the dipartite nature of the romance structure developed by Chrétien de Troyes serves Wolfram von Eschenbach in good stead.

The *Titurel* fragment (before 1220) tells the story of Sigune and Schionatulander before the opening of *Parzival*. The work is hardly long enough to do more than confirm Wolfram's attitude toward the Grail company and the Arthurian court. *Willehalm* (*ca.* 1217) is an adaptation of the French chanson de geste based on *Aliscans* and other stories of William of Orange, but its attitudes are more those of the romance. It can be summed up in the aphorism "The pagans fight for love and honor, the Christians for God." In it, as in *Parzival*, Wolfram is intent on showing that the virtues of the Arthurian court can be found as easily among pagans as among Christians, and that both need true faith and humility to rise to the highest good.

Although the general thrust of his views is clear and his differentiation of Arthurian scenes from those in Chrétien's *Perceval* is often very subtle and purposeful, Wolfram's style is far from the "crystal-clear" grace of Hartmann. His obscurity is obviously deliberate and to some degree, at least, intended to parody—and infuriate—such contemporaries as

Gottfried von Strassburg. It is also symptomatic of a bizarre humor that appears throughout his work and gives a sense of distance from, and sometimes distortion of, Arthurian values. Such stylistic peculiarities were easily copied by Wolfram's numerous imitators, but the essence of his work was not.

Typical of Wolfram's successors is Albrecht, identified by Ulrich Füetrer (in his *Buch der Abenteuer*) as Albrecht von Scharfenberg, though there is no other evidence for the identification. The *Jüngere Titurel* can be dated by its references to Richard, earl of Cornwall, and Berthold von Regensburg, both of whom died in 1272. It was long regarded as a work of Wolfram's because of the author's deliberate attempts to imitate his mannerisms and obscurity. Its narrative is typical of later Arthurian romances. A well-established story, that of Schionatulander, is taken from the outlines given by Wolfram and expanded. The Grail family is shown as originating in Troy. Schionatulander goes to the Orient with Gahmuret to prove his love for Sigune, and the cause of his death at the hands of Orilus is a Grail-like (but not Christian) symbol, the *Brackenseil* (Hound leash). Parzival's adventures also are recounted; and it is he, not his half brother Feirefis, who goes to the land of Prester John.

It is clear that the author is totally unaware of the motivation of earlier romance. Adventure and the fabulous are his concern, and he makes full use of the reputation of the Orient to reinforce his point. The exploration of individual motivation and behavior is of little significance, and the social background becomes an end in itself. It can be multiplied into an indefinite series of purposeless adventures, the very thing the great masters despise. Love is the driving force of the characters, but there is no attempt at analysis; and here, as elsewhere, the distinctions between secular success and Christian salvation are blurred. The complicated style reflects the confusion of thought.

Other attempts to reproduce or extend the Grail adventures of Parzival are even more feeble. A good example of this kind of material is the *Neue Parzival* (1331–1336) of Philipp Colin and Claus Wisse, goldsmiths of Strasbourg. The authors state that their work was designed to be inserted into Wolfram's work between Gawain's adventures at the Castle of Marvels and Parzival's encounter with Feirefiz—but it extends to almost 37,000 lines. Much of it is mere translation of the continuations of the *Perceval* of Chrétien de Troyes and is nothing more than a string of adventures. Gawain becomes much more important, partly because of the exploits attributed to him, partly because the authors have no concept of chivalry and none of Wolfram's ideas on its relation to the Grail. The work is only too typical of the popularization of the material of the romance in the century.

Other authors attempted to fill in gaps in Wolfram's work: Ulrich von dem Türlin (*ca.* 1261–1269) tells how Willehalm was looked after as a prisoner by Arabel, a Saracen lady, and how she was converted and married him. The story is derived loosely from the chansons de geste on William of Orange but not based directly on any extant version. Its attempts to imitate Wolfram's manner fail, and it is at its best when simply telling a story. Ulrich von Türheim's *Willehalm* (*ca.* 1250) is a "completion" of Wolfram's poem but in fact tells the story of Rennewart, his giant nephew. In more than 36,000 lines it brings in the motifs of stolen child, reencounter with father in battle, and the warrior as monk.

The discussion of the literary fate of Wolfram's work may be concluded with a mention of *Lohengrin* (*ca.* 1280). The title character was one of Parzival's sons; the basic theme is his rescue, as the Swan Knight, of the duchess of Brabant, but it is clear that the author, described in an acrostic as "the Man from Neuhaus," wanted to use Wolfram's reputation to establish the authenticity of his work, several parts of which are concerned with the deeds (part true, part fabulous) of Emperor Henry I. Wolfram, the writer of romance, has now become so important that both his form and his purpose have been forgotten. His "authorship" is enough to prove that fictional adventures are historical deeds, and he can appear as a character in fictional situations.

GOTTFRIED VON STRASSBURG

The other stream of German romances stems from the work of Eilhart von Oberg and Gottfried von Strassburg, who wrote romances concerning Tristan and Isolde. The source materials they use are slightly different, and the uses they make of their material and the ideas they wish to convey are totally divergent. Eilhart's work, probably written about 1180, is extant only in fragments in a form close to the original, but later reworkings make the story and treatment clear. It conforms to the pattern of romance in the sense that it operates within a framework of artificial courtly values, that it is concerned with the two themes of love and adventure and their interaction, and that it demands of its audience at least some understanding of the rules by which the

romance functions. There is, however, little evidence that Eilhart was aware of the subtler aspects of chivalry. For him the lovers are the victims of a passion that is beyond their control and that they would have preferred to avoid. The love potion is real, and while its effects last, it destroys them.

Eilhart's main concern is less the development of the love affair than the progressive destruction of Tristan the noble warrior, and the conflict of the love affair with conventional morality and religion. Although Tristan does rescue Isolde from the lepers, his prowess as a fighting man does not, in general, have much to do with his love. It may be said that Eilhart feels that Tristan's love is more like that of Eneas for Dido than that of Enéas for Lavinie. The treatment of courtly behavior is often crude. Mark is a vengeful monster and the victim of tricks played by the lovers and their supporters, so that there is no tension between sympathy for him and for Tristan. Eilhart thus uses only the externals of the romance form to tell his story.

Gottfried von Strassburg (*Tristan, ca.* 1210), by contrast, uses the form of the romance and the presumed knowledge of it among his audience with the greatest skill. His mention of Thomas de Bretagne as his source and the statement that only Thomas had told the story correctly probably refer to treatment rather than material. (Exact comparison is impossible, since Gottfried's incomplete poem overlaps hardly at all with the extant fragment of Thomas's work.) Thomas had clearly stressed the special nature of "Tristan-love." Similarly, in a long discussion of some of his contemporaries, Gottfried makes it clear that he was fully conversant with the romance as a form and that he understood its aims. His praise of Hartmann von Aue for his clarity includes some implied criticism of him (and others) that he was content to paint a world in which everything came right in the end and they all lived happily ever after. Gottfried's own intention is to use the romance form to show that love is a mixture of joy and sorrow, and that the two are not always clearly distinguishable.

Gottfried's method is to use all the rules for courtliness that are essential to the romance form and to show their weakness or inadequacy in dealing with the problem of love in society. Arthur does not actually appear, as he does in Eilhart's version, but the courtly rules observed at Mark's and other courts are his. These values are often denigrated in favor of other, more fundamental, virtues. Many critics have pointed out that Gottfried uses religious, and particularly mystical, terminology in his portrayal of love, and that the cave of lovers and its allegorization show clear affinities with the church building and its allegorization. This is true. Gottfried does stress the religious nature of "Tristan-love," but there is more. He also stresses its artistic, intellectual nature and its opposition to the clichés of "eye-heart" instant love and the defense of the lady's honor in combat.

Tristan is not a knight like Gawain or Yvain. He does not win chivalric contests and impress his lady by his prowess. The battles he wins are desperately fought contests, usually won by methods that do not accord with courtly rules, and they are not even remotely connected with love service to Isolde. Yet Tristan does give love service to Isolde: his teachings and music. Courtly values, as represented by Riwalin (Tristan's father), King Mark, Marjodo and other seneschals, and Mark's barons are in various ways and to various degrees condemned. All are seen as either a determination to pursue a male desire to "acquire" a lady or to use the rules of the romance to win her. Equally, Gottfried rejects the artificial idea of the dominant female who has the right to ask total subservience from the male in return for her love, whether within marriage or outside it. The court world of Guinevere and Kei is specifically rejected, and the highest love is seen as a harmonious union of the spirit, achieved in isolation from society. Gottfried thus goes further than Wolfram in rejecting the courtly rules, for he sees little good in them, whereas Wolfram regards them as estimable at their best, though below Christian morality. On the other hand, Gottfried shows love as the greatest force and greatest good, even when it is not within marriage.

Gottfried also brought to the romance a new style, not obscure or deliberately distorted like Wolfram's, but nevertheless highly ambivalent and susceptible to many variations of interpretation and allegorization. It is clear that contemporaries did not grasp his intentions fully, and that his views on the romance form and on the treatment of love between the sexes eluded even those who tried to continue his poem. Ulrich von Türheim completed the work about 1235, using the work of Eilhart as his source and showing more interest in tricks and adventures than in love. The continuation of Heinrich von Freiberg (end of the thirteenth century) is better, if only because the author has some feeling for Gottfried's style and tries, not altogether without success, to imitate it. But the episodes are crude and repetitive, and the depiction of characters and treatment of

love are totally out of harmony with Gottfried's conceptions.

OTHER ROMANCE WRITERS

The influence of Gottfried can best be seen in the work of Konrad von Würzburg (*ca.* 1220/1230–1287), a bourgeois of considerable learning, who admired Gottfried greatly. His short narrative poem *Herzemaere,* though not technically a romance, makes an attempt at a "religion of love" and draws upon Eucharist imagery to describe it. In his *Engelhard* and *Partonopier* Konrad imitates Gottfried's descriptive techniques and centralization of love in different forms, but he lacks Gottfried's lightness of touch, and his rhetoric and moralizing can be deadly. He realizes that he is an imitator, and his romances are overblown confirmations of the fact.

A similar criticism could be made of Konrad's contemporary, Rudolf von Ems, whose activity falls between 1220 and 1254. He belonged to the class of *ministeriales,* who contributed much to courtly culture, but his attitudes anticipate the bourgeois taste of the later Middle Ages. He apparently wrote some conventional (and now lost) romances in his youth and later rejected them as trivial. His extant work lays great stress on instruction and morality; and in the prologues to *Alexander* and *Willehalm von Orlens,* the only two of his works that have any connection with romance, he discusses contemporary authors and the objects of art. He regards literary talent as a gift bestowed by God to promote the truth and lead the author to bliss. Imitation of the masters is the best way to attain it. It is not surprising, therefore, that he uses the techniques of the earlier writers of romance to convey ideas that are essentially conventional Christianity.

There were numerous other writers who imitated the romance form, but their works fall far short of the great masters. Some wrote sentimental love stories with romance trimmings: Konrad Fleck's reworking of the story of Floire and Blanscheflur (perhaps *ca.* 1220), Berthold von Holle's *Demantin* (*ca.* 1260), and particularly Heinrich von Neustadt's *Apollonius von Tyrland* (1312), a reworking of the Greek romance in which an exiled prince wins, loses, and finds again the daughter of the king who receives him. None of these authors investigates the problem of love in anything but the most superficial way. More common are works that take up the other romance theme, adventure. Wirnt von Grafenberg, in *Wigalois* (1204/1209); Der Stricker, in *Dan-*

454

iel von blühenden Tal (*ca.* 1215); Der Pleier, in *Garel vom blühenden Tal* (*ca.* 1260–1280); and Konrad von Stoffeln, in *Gauriel von Muntabel* all try to combine—at great length—the Arthurian background with strings of combats and fantastic adventures that bring in the world of the supernatural and the grotesque. The study of the individual becomes less and less important.

There are, however, a few works that, though far from representing the romance at its best, have merits of their own. Ulrich von Zazikhoven, a Swiss cleric mentioned in a document of St. Gall in 1214, wrote an account of Lancelot very different from that of Chrétien de Troyes. He claims a French source. His work is distinguised by the fact that Lanzelet is not the lover of Queen Guinevere but a prince, brought up by a sea fairy, who wanders in search of adventure and marries one princess after another. The work may legitimately be described as the raw material of romance, for it agglomerates various stories about the hero's prowess without making any real attempt to structure them. The hero is superficially an Arthurian knight, but he has no end in view nor code to live by. There are late prose versions of the story that follow the same pattern.

Moriz von Craûn, almost contemporary with Ulrich's *Lanzelet,* is a fascinating and puzzling work. An unknown author's poem based on a French work no longer extant, it concerns a historical personage, Maurice de Craon. Its interest, however, lies in its handling of romance characteristics. The hero seeks the love of a married woman and performs fantastic feats, including the use of a "land-ship" to impress her, but he falls asleep while waiting for a rendezvous and then scares his lady's husband into a faint when he appears in the bedroom, looking like a knight whom the husband has killed. Although some critics take the story seriously, it is hard to escape the impression that it is a parody of the courtly romance. The lady is cruel—and she is punished by something close to rape. The husband is eliminated by fear, not by deception. Everything is ludicrously exaggerated, but the "standards" are those of the romance. The lady is "served" in the most outrageous fashion; she is presumed to appreciate victory in combat; and in spite of her lover's violence and later rejection of her, she is shown as yearning for his return. It is a poem like this that makes clear the wide understanding and acceptance of romance conventions. It is perhaps significant that there is a French fabliau, "Du chevalier qui recovra l'amor de sa

dame," that uses the same conventions in the same story—but has no consummation and the lovers are reconciled.

This account of the romance may be concluded by mentioning two compilations of romance themes. *Diu Krone* (1215/1220), compiled by Heinrich von dem Türlin, is a long work intended as a crown for noble ladies, with an adventure for each jewel in the crown. The work has Gawain as its central figure and uses many incidents from Wolfram's *Parzival.* Tribute is paid to Hartmann von Aue and the lyric poets, but the confrontation between the good magician Gansguoter and the evil Fimber is characteristic of the work. For the author, connection with famous works, both French and German, is more important than any sense of form or concept of chivalry.

The second compilation is characteristic of its age. Ulrich Füetrer about 1473–1478 brought together most of the courtly adventures in his *Buch der Abenteuer,* at the behest of Duke Albrecht IV of Bavaria. The work is written in the same strophic form as that of the *Jüngerer Titurel* by Albert von Scharfenberg and purports to trace the history of chivalry from the Trojan War and the Aeneas story (with Konrad von Würzburg as a possible source) to the Templars and beyond. The history of the Grail is represented by the story of Merlin according to Albrecht von Scharfenberg, Wolfram's *Titurel* and *Parzival,* and *Diu Krone.* There follows a mass of well-known and less-known Arthurian stories that concludes with a prose *Lanzelet.* Ulrich had little talent for style or motivation. His only purpose was to collect stories from the past and present them as antiquities.

The romance attained its highest point at its beginnings. By taking over an ideal set of values and recognized game rules, the great authors of the late twelfth and early thirteenth centuries were able to explore human conduct in its relation to society, particularly the place of love in society, with a depth of perception that has rarely been equaled.

ROMANCE CRITICISM

In discussing the history of the criticism of the romance, it must be remembered that the great majority of romances were lost for centuries. It was not until after the middle of the eighteenth century that editions began to appear, usually based on one manuscript and often incomplete. They were regarded as curiosities rather than serious literary products. It was the interest of the Romantics that stimulated serious study of the texts. They hoped to find in them confirmation of their views on the superiority of poetry inspired directly by the undisturbed faith of a people untrammeled by "classical" sophistication. Established scholars such as Karl Lachmann and enthusiastic laymen such as Friedrich von der Hagen devoted their attention to research on the authors, and particularly to the production of texts. The great achievement of the nineteenth century lay in the discovery of the great majority of the extant manuscripts and the production of editions, many of which are still in use and all of which are the basis for current editions. There are still a few works for which no adequate editions exist.

Nineteenth-century critics also devoted much time to the realia concerning the romances: their historical background, the biographies of the authors, and the interrelationships of the two. Useful as some of this research was, it diverted attention from more important matters and was at times misleading in its attempts to show the romance as a reflection of contemporary culture. More significant for the evaluation of the works was the study of folklore, mythology, and comparative religion that marked the later nineteenth and early twentieth centuries. The most important result of these studies was the development of the so-called Celtic hypothesis: that the names, incidents, and themes that make up the Arthurian romance are derived almost exclusively from Welsh and Irish mythology and folklore, and that they were transmitted orally, probably by Breton *conteurs*. Although there is undoubtedly some substance to this theory, it took up altogether too much critical effort and is, in the last instance, not of great importance for the evaluation of the romance as a genre.

Criticism since World War II has concentrated on the evaluation of individual works. The influence of religious concepts, particularly mysticism, has received considerable attention and has led to the study of such questions as the relation of the Christian to the Arthurian ethos; the guilt, in several senses, of the heroes of romance; the relationship of courtly love to Christian charity; and the allegorization of the romances as Christian works. Problems of style and structure have also been studied in the light of increased interest in rhetoric, poetics, and the "new" disciplines of semiotics and structuralism.

This concentration on individual works, and only a few of them, has not been entirely beneficial. The neglect of later and lesser-known works that is evi-

dent in the bibliography to the present article has meant that the nature of the genre itself has not been sufficiently studied. It is hard to find an account of its development and decline that is expressed in any but chronological terms.

BIBLIOGRAPHY

There is no specialized bibliography on the medieval German romance. The following general bibliographies give valuable information, and the histories of literature cited below all have bibliographical footnotes or appendixes. Annual bibliographies are *Bulletin bibliographique de la Société internationale arthurienne* (1949–); *Germanistik, Internationales Referatenorgan mit bibliographischen Hinweisen* (1960–); John J. Parry, *A Bibliography of Critical Arthurian Literature*, 2 vols. (1931–1936), continued in *Modern Language Quarterly* annually from 1940 to 1963. Special bibliographies include Joachim Bumke, *Die Wolfram von Eschenbach-Forschung seit 1945. Bericht und Bibliographie* (1970); Henry Kratz, Michael Batts, and George F. Jones, *Handbuch der deutschen Literaturgeschichte*, Abt. 2, *Bibliographien*, 3 vols. (1969–1971); Heinz Küpper, *Bibliographie zur Tristansage* (1941); Hans-Hugo Steinhoff, *Bibliographie zu Gottfried von Strassburg* (1971).

Major reference works. Paul Merker, Wolfgang Stammler, *Reallexikon der deutschen Literaturgeschichte*, 4 vols. (1925–1931, 2nd ed., 1955–); Paul Raabe, *Einführung in die Bücherkunde zur deutschen Literaturwissenschaft*, 3rd ed. (1962); Wolfgang Stammler and Karl Langosch, *Die deutsche Literatur des Mittelalters: Verfasserlexikon*, 5 vols. (1933–1955).

Histories of German literature. Karl Bertau, *Deutsche Literatur im europäischen Mittelalter*, 2 vols. (1972–1973); Helmut de Boor and Richard Newald, eds., *Geschichte der deutschen Literatur*, II, 5th ed. (1962), and III, pts. 1 and 2 (1962–1963); Gustav Ehrismann, *Geschichte der deutschen Literatur bis zum Ausgang des Mittelalters*, II, secs. 1 and 2 (1927–1935); William T. H. Jackson, *The Literature of the Middle Ages* (1960); Bert Nagel, *Staufische Klassik. Deutsche Dichtung um 1200* (1977); Paul Salmon, *Literature in Medieval Germany* (1967); Julius Schwietering, *Die deutsche Dichtung des Mittelalters* (1932, 2nd ed. 1957); Maurice O'Connell Walshe, *Mediaeval German Literature* (1962).

General works. Erich Auerbach, *Mimesis*, Williard R. Trask, trans. (1953); Hans J. Bayer, *Untersuchungen zum Sprachstil weltlicher Epen* (1962); Reto Radulf Bezzola, *Les origines et la formation de la littérature courtoise en Occident (500–1200)*, 3 vols. (1944–1963); Arno Borst, ed., *Das Rittertum in Mittelalter* (1976); Hulde Henriette Braches, *Jenseitsmotive und ihre Verritterlichung in der deutschen Dichtung des Hochmittelalters* (1961); Hennig Brinkmann, *Zu Wesen und Form mittelalterlicher Dichtung* (1928); Joachim Bumke, *Ministerialität und Ritterdichtung* (1976), and *The Concept of Knighthood in the*

Middle Ages, W. T. H. Jackson and Erika Jackson, trans. (1982); Peter Dronke, *Poetic Individuality in the Middle Ages* (1970); Günter Eifler, ed., *Ritterliches Tugendsystem* (1970); Werner Fechter, *Das Publikum der mittelhochdeutschen Dichtung* (1935); Peter F. Ganz and Werner Schröder, eds., *Probleme mittelhochdeutscher Erzählformen* (1972); Günther J. Gerlitzki, *Die Bedeutung der Minne in "Moriz von Craûn"* (1970); Rainer Gruenther, "Zum Problem der Landschaftsdarstellung im höfischen Versroman," in *Euphorion,* 56 (1962).

Peter Haidu, *Aesthetic Distance in Chrétien de Troyes* (1968), and "Approaches to Medieval Romance," in *Yale French Studies,* 51 (1974); Robert W. Hanning, "The Social Significance of Twelfth-century Chivalric Romance," in *Medievalia et humanistica,* 3 (1972), and *The Individual in Twelfth-century Romance* (1977); Hartmut Hoefer, *Typologie im Mittelalter. Zur Übertragbarkeit typologischer Interpretationen auf weltliche Dichtung* (1971); H. R. Jauss, "Theorie der Gattungen und Literatur des Mittelalters," in M. Delbouille, ed., *Grundriss der romanischen Literaturen des Mittelalters,* I (1972); Douglas Kelly, "Theory of Composition in Medieval Narrative Poetry and Geoffrey of Vinsauf's *Poetria nova,*" in *Medieval Studies,* 31 (1969); William P. Ker, *Epic and Romance* (1897, repr. 1957); Erich Köhler, *Ideal und Wirklichkeit in der höfischen Epik* (1956); Erika Kohler, *Liebeskrieg. Zur Bildersprache der höfischen Dichtung des Mittelalters* (1935); Hugo Kuhn, *Text und Theorie* (1969); Moshé Lazar, *Amour courtois et "Fin amors" dans la littérature du XIIᵉ siècle* (1964); Clive S. Lewis, *The Allegory of Love* (1936).

Friedrich Maurer, *Leid. Studien zur Bedeutungs- und Problemgeschichte, besonders in den grossen Epen der staufischen Zeit,* 3rd ed. (1964); Hans Naumann, *Deutsche Kultur im Zeitalter des Rittertums* (1938); Uwe Pörksen, *Der Erzähler im mittelhochdeutschen Epos* (1971); Daniel Rocher, "'Chevalerie' et littérature 'chevaleresque,'" in *Études germaniques,* 21 (1966) and 23 (1968); Dagmar Thoss, *Studien zum Locus Amoenus im Mittelalter* (1972); Eugene Vinaver, *The Rise of Romance* (1971); Emil Walker, *Der Monolog im höfischen Epos. Stil- und literaturgeschichtliche Untersuchungen* (1928); Max Wehrli, *Formen mittelalterlicher Erzählung* (1969); Horst Wenzel, *Frauendienst und Gottesdienst. Studien zur Minne-Ideologie* (1974); Jessie L. Weston, *From Ritual to Romance* (1920).

Arthurian romance. Helen Adolf, *Visio Pacis: Holy City and Grail; an Attempt at an Inner History of the Grail Legend* (1960); Maria Bindschedler, "Die Dichtung um König Artus und seine Ritter," in *Deutsche Vierteljahrsschrift für Literaturwissenschaft und Geistesgeschichte,* 31 (1957); Richard L. Brengle, *Arthur, King of Britain: History, Romance, Chronicle, and Criticism* (1964); Karl Otto Brogsitter, *Artusepik* (1965), a good survey with excellent bibliographical information; James Douglas Bruce, *The Evolution of Arthurian Romance from the Beginnings down to the Year 1300,* 2 vols. (1923–1924; 2nd ed. 1928, repr. 1958); Christoph Cormeau, "Wigalois" und "Die Crône"; zwei Kapitel zur Gattungsgeschichte des nachklassischen Aventiureromans* (1977); Sigurd Eichler, *Studien über die Mâze. Ein Beitrag zur Begriffs- und Geistesgeschichte der höfischen Kultur* (1942); Hildegard Emmel, *Formprobleme des Artusromans und der Graldichtung* (1951).

Gerhild Geil, *Gottfried und Wolfram als literarische Antipoden* (1973); Karin R. Gürttler, *Künec Artûs der guote. Das Artusbild der höfischen Epik des 12. und 13. Jahrhunderts* (1976); Dietrich Homberger, *Gawein. Untersuchungen zur mittelhochdeutschen Artusepik* (1969); Michel Huby, *L'adaption des romans courtois en Allemagne au XIIᵉ et au XIIIᵉ siècle* (1968); Luise Lerner, *Studien zur Komposition des höfischen Romans im 13. Jahrhundert* (1936); Roger S. Loomis, ed., *Arthurian Literature in the Middle Ages* (1959), the best general account in English, though now rather dated, and *The Grail: From Celtic Myth to Christian Symbol* (1963); Douglas D. R. Owen, ed., *Arthurian Romance: Seven Essays* (1970), especially D. H. Green, "Irony and Mediaeval Romance"; Ursula Peters, "Artusroman und Fürstenhof. Darstellung und Kritik neuerer sozialgeschichtlicher Untersuchungen zu Hartmanns 'Erec,'" in *Euphorion,* 69 (1975); Gerhard Schindele, *Tristan. Metamorphose und Tradition* (1971); Walther F. Schirmer, *Die frühen Darstellungen des Arturstoffes* (1958).

W. T. H. JACKSON

[See also **Albrecht von Scharfenberg; Alexander Romances; Arthurian Literature; Berthold von Holle; Chrétien de Troyes; Courtly Love; Eilhart von Oberg; Fleck, Konrad; Gottfried von Strassburg; Hartmann von Aue; Heinrich von Freiberg; Heinrich von Neustadt; Heinrich von Veldeke; Konrad von Stoffeln; Konrad von Würzburg; Pleier, Der; Rudolf von Ems; Stricker, Der; Tristan; Troy Story; Ulrich von Zazikhoven; Wirnt von Grafenberg; Wolfram von Eschenbach.**]

GERMAN TOWNS. The most outstanding characteristic of medieval German towns was their diversity. Each town varied so much from the next, with its own particular status, history, economic role, social configuration, and institutions—differences that burghers of the time cited with pride—that it may not be meaningful to speak generally of "German towns" at all.

Germany was not as highly urbanized as Tuscany or Flanders; the proportion of the population found in true towns was probably never much over 10 percent. Some 2,800 locales did have the legal status of "city" or "town" by the end of the Middle Ages, but

90 percent of them were villages in all but name. There were a few "free cities," some sixty or more relatively autonomous "imperial cities," and many towns under the rule of a prince or bishop. Legal status, however, did not necessarily correspond to political and economic significance. A ducal town like Brunswick, at the crossroads of trade routes and home of significant textile and brass production, with a population of perhaps 10,000, had in practice greater influence on German affairs than a Pfullendorf with 900 souls, even though the latter had the status of an "imperial city." Thus, the many legal "towns" included only about 50 significant urban centers with populations of 2,000 or more.

No single pattern of development characterized these towns. The oldest were Roman foundations on or near the Rhine and Danube, such as Cologne, with roughly 35,000 persons the largest medieval German town. But age was no guarantee of growth: Regensburg (Ratisbon) traced its origins to Roman times, Dortmund to Carolingian; yet in spite of their long commercial importance, neither probably ever exceeded 10,000 in population. In fact, the next largest behind Cologne was probably Lübeck, at around 25,000 persons, and Lübeck was more than 1,000 years younger than Cologne. Some important medieval towns—for example, Kiel and Berlin—arose as late as the thirteenth century. Also, sharp differences existed between one town's economic base and another's, and some towns could achieve substantial prominence largely on one activity. Cologne, like Augsburg, Strasbourg, and Ulm, which all approached 20,000, had a mixed economy including both commerce and textile manufacture; whereas Lübeck was strictly a Baltic seaport and commercial center, making virtually nothing of its own for sale elsewhere. The same was largely true of Danzig (modern Gdańsk; the major port for Polish grain), at around 20,000, Hamburg with 12,000, and the other coastal towns of the Hanseatic League. Nuremberg, with about the same population as Lübeck, had neither sea nor navigable river, yet its vigorous and wide-ranging merchants made it the commercial entrepôt of southern Germany. In all, about fifteen German-speaking towns may have exceeded 10,000 inhabitants in the Middle Ages, including, besides those already mentioned, Basel, Breslau, Erfurt, Frankfurt, Magdeburg, Vienna, and Zurich, each historically and economically distinct in some way.

At least partly because of economic differences, social stratification differed widely as well. The composition of any socioeconomic group—in numbers, proportion of the population, and even the occupations that comprised it—varied considerably from town to town. For example, the weavers' guild was fairly prosperous and politically strong in Cologne, but guilds were illegal in Nuremberg. Property owners from old families apparently held the highest social rank in Ulm, but the wealthiest merchants stood at the top in Hamburg, and some of both, perhaps also including a few craftsmen, seem to have formed a leadership group in Strasbourg.

Each town had its distinctive governing body. By the end of the thirteenth century, most used a *Rat* (council), but these varied widely in composition and function. For instance, Lübeck's council of no fixed size (membership ranged from 17 to 29), all members chosen at large, was hardly the same institution as Brunswick's 103 councillors from specific guilds and sections of town. Moreover, these town councils were coupled with burgomasters or jurymen or aldermen or committees or treasurers, or several of these in bewildering profusion, depending on the town. While certain towns were used as legal models and even as informal points of appeal on interpretation of custom by others—Magdeburg, for example, was the legal "mother" of countless inland towns to the east—in fact each town made its own law. Towns began drawing on Roman law as an alternative source to their own customs only in the later fifteenth century.

Above all, German towns rarely acted in concert as German. Only imagination or a leap of faith can find much "national spirit" in the occasional and, except for the Hansa, mercurial leagues of towns, which usually foundered on local or regional particularism. Not even economic interests clearly united them. The Rhenish and Danubian towns tended toward mixed commercial and industrial economies, and sought politically above all to stop the multiplication of toll stations that the princes of their areas were continually throwing up along the inland routes (the Rhine had fewer than twenty such stations in 1200 but was choked by sixty or more in 1500). The overwhelmingly commercial Hansa towns were tied to the sea lanes, and saw external powers such as Denmark as their major enemies. Competition with other towns was the rule; the independent town ignored or defied the monarchy as often as it supported it.

From a European perspective, however, German towns had more in common than just geography and language. Collectively they were the intermediate example of medieval urban development: not as wealthy or as powerful as northern Italian towns, but stronger and more independent than English, French, or even Flemish towns. No German town had the commercial empire of Venice or the capital accumulation of Florence, nor did the towns together dominate the land to the point where it was effectively divided into city-states. Nevertheless, German economic influence was felt from England to Russia and from the Mediterranean to the Baltic; many towns did control significant portions of the countryside and were independent political forces to be reckoned with. Unlike the English or French monarchs or the dukes of Burgundy in the Low Countries, the German king never used towns as a foundation for his authority, nor, in the eventual parceling out of Germany, did the towns all fall to the princes. The story of medieval German urban diversity is also a tale of partial urban power.

URBAN DEVELOPMENT TO ABOUT 1300

Origins. Hardly anything is more controversial among urban historians than the origins of towns. At the core of the debate is the question of which class provided the driving force in urban development. Did the new bourgeoisie, formed from landless persons *(pauperes),* first collect at fortified places as merchants and then, as trade grew, develop new towns where commerce needed them, as Fritz Rörig (drawing on Henri Pirenne) and others would have it? Or did the impulse rest with established authorities, bishops and princes, who encouraged commerce both as consumers and with new town foundations, and whose ministerials became the leading element, as merchants and landowners, in the growing towns, as Karl Bosl and his school believe?

In fact, the development of the German town required both groups, interacting with each other—and understanding that is more important than trying, from the fragmentary evidence, to determine which came first. The Roman town had been a base of government, and in Italy, where true urban life never quite died, towns remained the natural centers of administration and the seats of the nobility. It was a relatively easy matter for these towns to absorb authority. But in Germany, even though there had been some continuity of settlement at many Roman sites, particularly those that became episcopal, royal, or ducal residences, such as Trier and Regensburg, true towns had to begin again with the revival of commerce in the tenth and eleventh centuries, after the nobility had established itself in and over the countryside. The pattern of interaction between town and

authority was thus more competitive, and German towns always found it more difficult than their Italian counterparts to acquire power and autonomy, and to extend it over the surrounding territory.

Nevertheless, the townsman-noble interaction was not always hostile; in fact, for a successful town, each needed the other. In the ninth century, along the old Roman Rhine and in the upper Danube area, and in the tenth and eleventh centuries beyond that area, embryonic urban communities around a bishop's or emperor's or noble's stronghold became clearly discernible. Such locales provided protection and a supply of consumers for the itinerant merchant, and, of course, there is no reason why local ministerials could not have been merchants, too, with capital at their disposal. Artisans from the countryside or the aristocrat's household also gathered there to sell their wares. In the "suburbs," the market area outside the walls, a permanent settlement frequently developed, and sought recognition through privileges.

The era of expansion. All over Europe the period from about 1050 to 1300 saw population growth, economic revival, and urbanization, all of which meant, in Germany, an explosion of existing and new towns. The basic model of what a German town was to be, physically, legally, and economically—a walled fortress which was a largely self-governing legal jurisdiction and a seat of trade and handicrafts—was worked out in the episcopal towns on the Rhine from about 1050 to 1150 and then imitated elsewhere. In the process of German expansion, however, every town made its own minor or major alterations to the model.

Hans Planitz described the earliest stage of this process as a "communal period": residents of the market settlement banded together, swearing an oath, to win recognition, rights, and eventually independence from the bishop, abbot, or prince. Thus Cologne rose as a commune in 1074 and was recognized between 1106 and 1112, Goslar, by 1107. While this is probably the classic pattern, development actually varied from one town to another and from one region to another, and such revolutionary hostility by townsmen toward feudal authority was by no means always necessary; movements to keep the peace led to many communes, and in some cases princes themselves took the initiative for urban independence.

The same is true for the enormous number of new town foundations, which occurred especially in the twelfth and thirteenth centuries. Some no doubt came from the initiative of merchants who saw a logical stopover or transshipment point, and petitioned a prince for permission to develop a town; others were planned and established by a count or duke, either as a kind of speculation—hoping to attract merchants to the site—or as a way to establish their authority more solidly in a particular area. Freiburg im Breisgau in 1120, under Duke Berthold III of Zähringen, began the trend; Lübeck (1158/1159), where Henry the Lion dispossessed an earlier foundation of his vassal Count Adolf of Schauenburg (Holstein), is another famous example. In both cases the duke obviously worked closely with a consortium of merchants. That scholars can still argue whether the prince or the traders initiated these developments only emphasizes the striking degree of cooperation.

Legal recognition as a town did not necessarily make a town autonomous. Towns that acquired self-government normally achieved it piecemeal, as the community gained privileges and rights from the bishop, duke, or count (slowly in the older Rhenish towns, more rapidly in the new foundations): citizens in key administrative positions, minting and taxing rights, control of fortifications. From each town's precise accumulation of such privileges over time came its degree of independence, and so the status of no town was quite like that of any other. What "town" meant from the beginning, was, in M. M. Postan's phrase, above all an island of urban law in a feudal sea. Out of the law of the marketplace and the merchant came basic concepts of freedom for citizens and equality before the law, of property and investment, and, with autonomy, the right to make more law. With the principle, reflected in the famous slogan "town air brings freedom" and won by many communities, that a serf who lived unchallenged within the walls for a year and a day became legally free, came an important step in the transition from personal law to law tied to the territory in which a person found himself. Since new towns turned to old for their first laws, the basic forms worked out in the Rhenish episcopal towns, notably Cologne, reappeared in codes from the Baltic to Swabia.

Even before the formative stage of the German town was over, towns and their burghers were playing a major role in the expansion of German influence beyond the existing borders, most spectacularly beyond the Elbe and in the lands around the Baltic and North seas. From the mid twelfth to the end of the thirteenth century, for example, some 38 new towns of German law sprang up in the lower Oder region of Pomerania, about 120 towns (and 1,200 villages) in Silesia. This famous *Drang nach Osten,* the German eastward expansion, was by no means undertaken solely by townsmen; in fact a strong case can be made for the peasant settler, clearing forests, draining marshes, and dotting the landscape with German villages, as the most important agent of change in the eastern lands, wiping out smaller West Slav tribes such as the Wends, Vagrians, and Obodrites, and penetrating deeply into Poland and Hungary. The religious order of Teutonic Knights, by turning a movement for the conversion of pagans into territorial conquests from Prussia to Livonia, also clearly had a major part in spreading German power and culture. But both of these groups worked effectively in concert with merchants, who developed new seaports and founded towns as markets for the products of the peasants' villages.

The economic and political forces that culminated, by the fourteenth century, in the Hanseatic League were born in the older German towns, notably those of Westphalia, in the twelfth century. With Cologne's merchants holding a vise grip on the rich trade with Flanders, enterprising and ambitious men turned northeastward, with the concept of the German town as one of their weapons. In the eleventh century the loosely organized, underdeveloped Baltic trade was largely in the hands of Scandinavians who were often part-time peasants. German merchants rose to supremacy in the Baltic in part because their economic, geographic, legal, and political base was the permanent urban community with a resident, full-time merchant population.

Two new town foundations in particular were crucial to the Germans' success. Lübeck, at the southwestern edge of the Baltic, became not only a major port but also a springboard for further expansion; from it left the merchant settlers who established other Baltic seaports, from Wismar, Rostock, and Stralsund around to Reval (modern Tallinn). Wisby, on the island of Gotland, became the seat of a loose association of German merchants from various towns, the nucleus of the later Hansa. These same Germans established the *Kontor* (trading post or factory) for merchants at Novgorod that enabled them to tap the furs and forest products of Russia. With control of these and other staples, such as Scania (Skåne) herring and Lüneburg salt, the Germans were able to make themselves indispensable middlemen in the trade of northern Europe. Lübeck paired with Hamburg as a portage around the Strait of Denmark, and Germans opened "factories" at

Bergen (for Norwegian cod), London, and above all Bruges, where their raw materials could be exchanged for fine Flemish cloth and the other manufactured goods of the West.

The Teutonic Knights worked in partnership with the merchants, and the order was usually in alliance with leading towns. Even the Mongol invasions, which leveled Breslau in 1241, were only a brief interruption in German expansion; in fact, by destroying Kiev, the eastern terminus of the old Regensburg-Prague-Cracow route, in 1240, the Mongols probably helped to shift more east-west trade to Novgorod and the Baltic. With the Scandinavian and Polish monarchies generally in disarray, the merchants of this "Gotland Association" were able to buttress their dominant economic position with extensive privileges from the states they visited, giving them a favored status over natives or anyone else. By the end of the thirteenth century, the German position in the east-west trade of the northern seas seemed unassailable.

The towns and the monarchy. Most of the German-speaking towns lay within the borders of the Holy Roman Empire. Its emperors, the German monarchs, consistently failed to draw on the remarkable energies of the towns to strengthen central government, in spite of apparent possibilities for an alliance against their common enemy, the princes. This failure was probably less the towns' fault than the monarchy's, but it helped to shape the history of both, at once making the crown weaker and giving the towns an opportunity to fill part of the vacuum.

The first great power struggle involving the crown, the papacy, and the princes was the strife over lay investiture in the eleventh century. South of the Alps towns were better developed both economically and politically, and the investiture controversy gave an opening that the Italian city-states could use to increase their authority; it was a major step on their road to dominance. But German towns were not quite strong enough to function either as an independent political force or as a resource for the monarchy, and the outcome tipped the balance of power in Germany in favor of the princes.

Through the twelfth century German towns grew in importance and political potential. Perhaps a skillful and fortunate monarch could have nudged them above their ever-present particularism and used them to help restore royal government to something like its standing before the investiture controversy. But the next crisis was the fight between the papacy and the house of Hohenstaufen, focusing on the

reign of Frederick II (1215–1250). Frederick probably began with some support from towns, inherited from his grandfather Frederick Barbarossa's policies toward them, but he squandered it to keep his throne. For example, Lübeck had fallen under Danish rule, endangering German Baltic expansion; but Frederick II needed his Danish alliance, and so his only aid was a charter making Lübeck an imperial city. A local coalition of towns and princes assembled the forces that drove out the Danes in 1227. Meanwhile, Frederick's concessions of 1220 and 1232 supported the princes against the towns in several important respects. The implication was that towns should defend themselves; they could not count upon the crown. It seems likely that Frederick intended only to buy time with this policy, but the extinction of the dynasty and the confusion of the interregnum (1250–1273) fixed it into a principle. Politically a town had two choices: to achieve effective independence or to fall under the control of a prince.

The concept of the imperial city seems to have taken shape in the same period, the reign of Frederick II and the interregnum. It began with Frederick's language (apparently first used with Lübeck), which clearly made certain towns possessions not of the emperor but of the empire. The effect, over time, was to create a category of towns responsible neither to princes nor to the monarchy, except for occasional tax payments and military aid provided to the latter. Such towns were even invited now and then to be represented at imperial diets, although it was 1486 before their presence was regularly expected. The legal distinctions, however, were never as important as power relationships; given royal weakness and indifference, no "free city" (a classification normally used for former episcopal cities the independence of which had been confirmed by the monarch) or imperial city could hold that position for long without strong resources of its own, while, conversely, any town with strong resources could attempt a considerable degree of independence from a prince. Thus, over the centuries some towns fell from the roll of imperial cities and others were added (or returned).

That the towns had the potential, given a collective focus, to be a major influence in national politics is shown by the Rhenish League of 1254. Founded by Mainz and Worms to keep peace and resist the multiplication of toll stations on the Rhine in the troubled times after the deaths of Frederick and his son Conrad IV, it eventually included some sixty to seventy cities from Aachen to Basel, and was probably the strongest force for effective administration in

Germany during its short life. But its one venture into national politics collapsed, not surprisingly, into particularism and the end of the league. In 1256 the league announced that its members would recognize only a king who had been elected unanimously, but most of them made separate peaces with Richard of Cornwall and accepted him in 1257, one by one. Independence, not centralization, was what towns wanted. Later generations of townsmen indeed protested loyalty to the monarchy, but always in the context of being tied directly to the crown rather than to a prince—less an exercise of "national spirit" than, like the peasants who willingly became serfs of Jesus, a desire to be under a distant lord who was not likely to ask too much. By the mid thirteenth century the political course of the German towns was set: unable to dominate like Italian towns, they would not be a base for the monarchy like French or English towns, and would strive to go their own way, urban powers alongside the princes in a diverse and fragmented Germany.

The emergence of the town council. It is probably no accident that the single most common instrument of German urban government, the town council, first appeared in the era of papal-Hohenstaufen conflict. The earliest certain reference to a German council is at Speyer in 1198. Basel, Lippstadt, Strasbourg, and Worms seem to have had councillors by 1200, and Lübeck in 1201, following which the form spread from town to town with extraordinary rapidity, with some 150 examples by 1250 and perhaps 400 by 1300.

As is true of so many medieval institutions that became important, the origin of the German town council is controversial and shrouded by missing or enigmatic sources. There was nothing new in 1200 about a citizen administrative authority. Several towns had aldermen, jurymen, assessors, or some other organization of leading citizens that was perhaps originally chosen by the overlord but in most cases became effectively a citizen body in the course of the twelfth century. In several towns the council apparently was at first in competition with these earlier groups. In Cologne, for example, both a college of jurymen with various administrative duties and the famous *Richerzeche* (literally, rich man's club), basically a private association, but one that chose the burgomasters and regulated guilds and commerce, existed long before the introduction of a council in 1216; and all three bodies seem to have grappled with each other over lines of authority until the constitutional struggles of the later fourteenth century.

Presumably the concept of the German town council was drawn from the example of the Italian consulate; and from that probable origin and the timing, it can be inferred that councils first appeared to give new urban groups a chance at power: probably pro-Hohenstaufen groups in the earliest examples, or at any rate groups less tied to the existing regime and institutions.

If the conciliar form radiated from a common source, however, like so much else it took on a specific shape in each town. Most frequently it was a body of twelve councillors, but a good many towns had twenty-four, occasionally thirty-six or eighteen; at Osnabrück, Regensburg, and Hamburg sixteen was apparently standard, fifteen at Cologne, thirteen at Metz, ten at Constance, forty for a time at Worms, and in several towns the number was allowed to fluctuate. The length of time a councillor served and the frequency with which councillors were chosen also varied from town to town. One-year terms and annual selections were the most common, but Cologne and Brunswick worked from a three-year rotation, with each councillor sitting for a year and then inactive (though available for consultation) for two years, while in Zurich and Schaffhausen councillors were chosen three times a year, and in Constance quarterly. But most towns had no prohibition against successive terms, and in practice councillors often served for life.

Methods of selection changed over time, and there is evidence that when councils first began, in many towns there was active citizen participation in the choice of councillors. A statute from Bremen in 1246 strongly implies this, and there are further possible examples in Speyer, Trier, Cologne, Constance, Regensburg, Erfurt, Vienna, and elsewhere. However, all that a statute or charter with a vague phrase about councillors being chosen "by the citizens" necessarily meant was that councillors were not chosen by a lord, bishop, or prince. By the end of the thirteenth century, most councils used some form of co-optation, selection of new members either by existing members or, as in Nuremberg, by an electoral board controlled by existing members.

There was, therefore, nothing "democratic" about the council form of government, and in fact the relationship of the council to the citizenry as a whole remained unclear. Not surprisingly, in most towns most councillors tended to come from a circle of certain families. The standard term among historians for this circle is "patriciate," though in Germany the word is anachronistic, not used anywhere before the mid fifteenth century. In fact it is not at all clear whether most towns had a sufficiently defined leadership class to make any term appropriate. Reflecting the debate over town origins, historians argue whether these families came from merchant stock, parlaying wealth gained from commerce into political dominance—which seems likely for Lübeck, Hamburg, and other northern towns—or from noble and especially ministerial lines, carrying prestige from the political order into a commanding position in urban politics—as evidence for Nuremberg and a number of Rhenish towns seems to indicate. In fact the relationship among wealth, social status, and political power probably varied substantially from town to town, and Cologne and many others had leading families of both merchant and ministerial origin. But, at any rate, access to a position on the council was certainly not equally open to all citizens; craftsmen were usually barred or underrepresented, and men with connections to certain families had strong advantages. If the council had been intended as the voice of the citizens, by the turn of the fourteenth century it had become, to a considerable extent, an arm of the wealthy and prestigious.

It seems likely that the early council, as an institution, was no better understood then than now, and that questions about just how much authority a council had and whom it represented remained to be worked out. At any rate, much of the next two or three centuries of German urban history is the story of a two-sided struggle for power by town councils: in national and international politics on the one hand, and against their fellow citizens on the other. In the vacuum left by the shriveling of the monarchy, a council, as a legally recognized body of citizens, was a natural vehicle for the expression of a town's striving for its share of power against lords and princes; and in the early stages of that struggle, at least, townsmen stood solidly behind it. In the process the council, in the name of the town, accumulated rights and privileges (taxing powers, coinage, assembling military forces) and came to control trade routes and territory. In short, it became, like the princes it fought, a governing authority. Yet citizens, for whatever reason—perhaps a memory of communal origins or of an age when councillors had less power and were chosen with citizen participation, perhaps a sense of urban community—were often reluctant to accept a council as an authority over themselves. As late as 1490 the citizens of Speyer brought suit in an imperial court precisely on the issue of whether their council was a government.

Councils had to establish themselves within town walls as well as outside them.

THE PROBLEMS OF POWER, 1300–1500

Councils and the peak of urban authority. For most of the fourteenth century, the town councils expanded their authority with stunning success. Within their own communities, whatever institutions citizens may have possessed to direct, suggest, or even inform council policies tended to melt away. For example, after 1292 no more is heard of Hamburg's *wittigsten,* an advisory board that may have been composed of guild aldermen, and Stralsund's *oldermanni* were phased out between 1328 and 1333. Taxing power was firmly established, and with this income the councils developed effective administration, buying administrative rights, where necessary, from the lord and supplanting his functionaries with their own. With relative autonomy and financial power, the greatest towns began penetrating into the surrounding countryside, acquiring manors and estates and even castles.

Together with private investment in rural land by wealthy citizens—much of it, of course, by council families—the towns assembled territory under urban control that met nobles and even some princes on even terms. Swiss cities such as Zurich, Bern, Basel, and Lucerne are obvious examples, but by the early 1370's even a ducal city like Brunswick controlled some eight or ten castles pawned to it by the Welfs, while citizens acquired hundreds of manors nearby. Nuremberg at its peak ruled a "city-state" of about 25 square miles, and Erfurt more than 200 square miles, including the small town of Sömmerda and eighty-three villages. Ulm, Metz, and Rothenburg also built substantial territories for themselves, and Lübeck was perhaps the most ambitious of all, with rights in at least 240 villages. About one-third of the duchy of Saxony-Lauenburg alone belonged to the town of Lübeck, in addition to castles and bailiwicks in Holstein and Mecklenburg. Some urban acquisitions, of course, helped to guard trade routes; Lübeck in the 1390's built a canal through Lauenburg to the Elbe, creating a navigable channel to both Hamburg and Lüneburg. A territory gave a town a basic supply of food for its citizens and some income from peasants, as well as a zone of land for defense purposes. But no matter why the land was held, with it came power, power taken from nobles and princes, power that would seek expression in the politics of medieval Germany.

It is important to remember that in the fourteenth

century no one knew that the princes would eventually fill most of the vacuum left by the hollowing of the monarchy. The Golden Bull of 1356 was, of course, strikingly favorable to princes; it even prohibited leagues and confederations of towns directed against them. But, strictly speaking, its measures applied only to the seven electors, and other princes spent much of the next two centuries winning the same status for themselves. And, like any other document, time and effective enforcement were necessary to make its words reality. The towns that were strong before it was issued remained strong after it, and in fact the 1370's and early 1380's saw probably the peak of urban power.

Within the various principalities, towns joined with knights and sometimes with bishops in "estates" for defense of their privileges, beginning in the 1340's. In these estates towns held a potentially commanding position. The princes needed money, and the towns had it. Most estates successfully resisted attempts of the princes to establish arbitrary taxing power; in the process estates became an accepted part of the governing process. By the later fourteenth century the estates—claiming to represent the land as a whole and in fact representing the towns' financial and the knights' military resources, without which the prince could not function—held at least as much authority in most lands as the prince did, and wielded it at least as effectively.

In the same period towns—or, rather, town councils—banded together for regional, national, and international political ends, and for a time functioned most impressively. In the 1370's and early 1380's leagues of towns appeared everywhere, and two alliances in particular, the Swabian-Rhenish League in the south and west and the Hansa in the north, held far more power than any prince. The Swabian League began in 1376 when Ulm and Constance, fearing that Charles IV would pawn them away in his efforts to secure the election of his son Wenceslas as his successor, spearheaded an alliance of fourteen imperial cities of Swabia. When Wenceslas' troops failed to put them down, the coalition grew, and in 1381 it joined with a revived league of the towns of the Rhineland. All of these towns shared problems with princes over territory and toll stations, and with the monarch over taxation and other threats to their autonomy. Their struggle became entangled with Luxembourg, Habsburg, and Wittelsbach dynastic politics, but at its peak in 1385, eighty-nine towns, including four Swiss cantons and an Alsatian league, adhered to the Swabian-Rhenish alliance. It

put an army of 10,000 men in the field, and Wenceslas tacitly recognized it in 1387.

The outstanding political achievement of German towns, however, was the Hanseatic League. The "community of German merchants visiting Gotland" of the late twelfth and early thirteenth centuries was precisely that, a loose association of German merchants with strictly economic goals. No test for membership has survived, and apparently any north German or German Baltic trader enjoyed its privileges unless challenged. Merchants elected from among themselves aldermen who directed and protected the others, representing them at foreign courts if necessary. The four great "factories" (trading posts) that developed in the thirteenth century were effectively autonomous. Privileges were granted in the name of the Gotland Association or the community of German merchants (*gemene kopman*) as a whole. The early Hansa was, in fact, a hugely successful commercial self-help society.

From the mid thirteenth to the mid fourteenth century, however, the informal community of merchants gradually became an association of German towns, and, in the absence of a strong monarchy, in effect the great power of the north. Its foundation, of course, remained common economic interests, which over time required stronger measures to defend than merchants alone could provide. Nevertheless, control of the privileges and their use, and domination of the "factories," passed to the councils of the approximately seventy active Hansa towns, and the Hansa became a massive extension of these councils' political authority. The councils of Wisby and Lübeck had jointly supplanted the Gotland Association as protectors of merchants in the Baltic by 1280, and the Gotland Association lost the right to use its seal in 1298. Various regional assemblies finally coalesced in the first full Hanseatic diet in 1356. Over the next twenty years, embassies from diets informed the "factories" that they were now subject to the authority of the combined towns. In 1366 a diet in Lübeck ruled that only citizens of member towns could enjoy the Hanseatic privileges, though in practice about 100 towns beyond those that actively participated in league affairs were usually considered members. That the merchants themselves probably welcomed the legal and military strength that backed them up did not alter the fact that town councils now controlled the great trade of the north.

The new form of community first tested its power from 1358 to 1360, with a successful blockade of Flanders. Aggression by Waldemar IV Atterdag of

Denmark was answered by war: a confederation of Hansa towns, the Teutonic Knights, a few princes, and some Dutch communities swept Waldemar's forces away. The Peace of Stralsund in 1370 recognized the new order: the Hanseatic League won renewal of all privileges on traditional terms, a voice in the Danish succession, and possession of the fortresses that controlled the Sound for fifteen years. Embargoes of England and Flanders in 1388, which ended in acceptance of the Hansa's terms, were icing on the cake. The Hansa, while not a state and so loosely structured that it avoided calling itself a league, nevertheless had carved out a solid place for itself among European powers. Together with the Swabian-Rhenish League, and other associations like the Saxon League, German towns and town councils had demonstrated their strength by the 1380's.

But Germany would not, in the end, be ruled by a confederation of its towns. The same decades had also begun to demonstrate their weaknesses.

Urban economy and society. In 1349 the Black Death began its grim progress down the Rhine valley and across south Germany; it swept across the northern cities in 1350. The death toll seems to have been substantially higher in northern Germany than elsewhere, with reliable figures indicating losses of one-half to two-thirds of the population in all seaport towns, though migration from the countryside may have returned towns to their former size in a generation or less. The economic changes that followed exaggerated and intensified the existing differences between German urban regions. Overall, the Hanseatic area followed the pattern of most of Europe in economic stagnation or decline, but, for reasons not yet fully understood, many southern towns, above all Nuremberg and the towns of the Danube area, experienced something like boom times.

Caution must be exercised when trying to pinpoint a time period for the economic "decline of the Hansa." There are no solid figures for the volume of trade in earlier centuries, and German merchants may have handled as much tonnage as ever through most of the fifteenth century. But slowly, sometimes imperceptibly, from the late fourteenth century on, the league lost its command of northern commerce. Ongoing German settlement of the east had been one engine of Hansa success; with population no longer growing and the towns themselves absorbing the surplus that remained, this slowed to a halt. At the same time English and Dutch merchants began wedging themselves into the monopoly position of the Hansa. First attracted into sailing around Skagen

by the rich Scania herring fisheries, by the mid fourteenth century they had learned to navigate the Sound, opening an all-water alternative to the Lübeck-Hamburg portage. With bulk shipping thus easier and cheaper, the Baltic lands could increase their grain production, and while German merchants shared in this trade, by no means did they dominate it.

More serious than the new merchants were the new products they brought, above all cloth from the fledgling English and Dutch textile industries. The Hanseatic area had developed manufacturing only on its fringes; overwhelmingly the Germans were middlemen dealing in the products of other lands. By the early fifteenth century cloth from England and Holland, North Sea herring, and Bourgneuf salt, selling at lower prices than the Flemish cloth, Scania herring, and Lüneburg salt that the Germans controlled, had broken the Hansa's vise grip on the Baltic.

But the key factor in the slippage, as Philippe Dollinger suggests, was not so much loss of the monopoly as the Hansa's extraordinarily conservative response to that loss. The towns seem to have thought that they could make the English and Dutch go away through measures passed at Hanseatic diets. For a time all foreign merchants were barred from Scania—thus reducing the value of the fairs there and virtually forcing development of the North Sea fisheries—and Hansa merchants were forbidden to invest in any non-Hansa enterprises, including any partnerships with Dutch or English traders.

Thus, while Baltic trade as a whole expanded, the German share of it did not. All privileges were vigorously defended, including the Hansa staple rights at Bruges, in spite of the obvious silting up of its harbor and the gradual shift of most merchant activity to Antwerp. The Germans' attitude was more than merely protectionist; it was an effort to recapture the past. Capital accumulated in commerce by Hansa merchants had never been invested in manufacturing or even banking—an extraordinary portion of it went into the building of individual "treasures" of gold, silver, and jewels, where of course it stimulated no further economic growth—and now, apparently, was no time to start. No new industries developed in Hanseatic towns, and the league went so far as to make sporadic official attacks on credit finance, beginning in 1401; in fact no significant bank appeared in a Hansa town until the Hamburg Wechselbank in 1618.

Nothing could present a stronger contrast than

the reaction of the southern towns to the challenges of the fourteenth century. The council of Nuremberg virtually welcomed foreigners with open arms, practically doing away with limits on length of stay, and Nuremberg merchants were permitted to make trade associations with anyone. At the same time its industries, notably metalworking, were expanded. Above all, the Nuremberg merchants vigorously sought new markets, ranging from Spain and the Low Countries to Italy, Cracow, and Constantinople. Scions of Nuremberg families formed little "colonies" in several important towns, including those of the Hansa. In fact, a significant share of the east-west trade of raw materials for manufactured goods that had been the backbone of the Hansa was now diverted through Nuremberg. Meanwhile, there and elsewhere in the south, merchant capital was moving into industrial production, following the Italian and Flemish example of a "putting-out system" in textiles, where the trader hired craftsmen for weaving and kept ownership of the finished product. Major banking operations grew up in many towns, especially Augsburg, where the Fuggers and Welsers eventually competed on a level with the great Italian houses. As the north stagnated, the southern towns took giant steps on the road to industrial capitalism.

Judging the effects of these economic changes on urban society would be easier if scholars agreed on a single picture of social stratification for the medieval German town. The traditional division of townsmen into "patricians" and "artisans" may work for a few towns in a few times and places, but insofar as it implies a fixed, bipolar social order, it is quite misleading. However, any alternative generalization on the admittedly fragmentary socioeconomic evidence runs into exceptions that may be more significant than the generalization itself. Merchants tended to be wealthier than artisans, but the diversity of wealth within occupations was enormous. The richest draper (merchant in fine cloth) in Brunswick had an estate twenty times the size of the poorest, and three-quarters of the drapers had a net worth below the average for their trade. Guild aldermen usually possessed three to six times the wealth of the average member of their guilds, and some craft fortunes equaled those of the most successful merchants. In Ravensburg fifteen tailors were so poor that they paid no tax at all, but twenty appeared in the highest tax brackets.

Wealth, in short, did not correlate completely with occupation. What mattered first of all, in a preindustrial economy, was economic independence:

anyone with his own commercial concern or his own workplace could, with drive and luck, accumulate a substantial fortune; and if opportunity knocked more often for the merchant, it was still there for the craftsman. Also, men did not have to specialize; prosperous artisans could easily risk ever larger shares of their capital in commerce and eventually shift altogether. In one generation in Hamburg, for example, three tailors and a baker became successful drapers, while a butcher, a tanner, and a cooper joined the Society of Merchants to Scania. But wealth came also to men who simply kept to their craft. A butcher was one of the wealthiest men in Schwäbisch Hall; the ten largest investors in the Hamburg annuity market included a brass pourer; an armorer in Lübeck owned a warehouse, a mansion, and five houses (and married the niece of a councillor).

Wealth studies suggest that as towns differed in economic function, particularly the degree of commerce versus the degree of manufacturing, so they differed in distribution of wealth. As manufacturing increased in importance in a town's economy, so did the size of the lower stratum, which in the fifteenth century included only some 40 percent of the population in a commercial port like Lübeck or Hamburg, 60 percent in the mixed economy of Brunswick, and more than 85 percent in the great textile center of Augsburg. Conversely, the middle stratum in Augsburg was only about 5 percent, but 25 percent in Brunswick and nearly 40 percent in Lübeck. A reasonable conclusion is that the upper stratum in a town consisted primarily of the top merchants, along with some persons living on investments and a few particularly successful artisans; the middle level included most independent craftsmen and the lesser merchants, while dependent craftsmen and servants made up the bulk of the lower stratum. The precise composition in any town depended on the importance of a particular craft or industry in its economy, the opportunities for commerce, and, probably, some individual success stories.

Patterns of association, as far as they can be determined, showed the same diversity. For every town where guilds apparently fitted the classic textbook picture of men working, living, drinking, celebrating festivals, and defending town ramparts together, there were far more where only a few butchers lived on Butcher Street or smiths in Smith Alley, where few or no guildhalls existed, where there were no guild chapels, special saints, or festivals, and where members of the same guild rarely saw each other.

Some guilds combined totally unrelated professions, apparently for political purposes.

While certain elite lineages often were powerful over time, in only a few towns did they form a "closed circle." Research on more than one "patrician" society or drinking club has uncovered the occasional butcher or weaver among the members. Marriages between merchant and artisan families were by no means unheard of, and some elite families in fact had craft branches. Not even political power correlates satisfactorily with either wealth or association. Not all councillors were rich—in fact, remarkable differences in net worth show up, for example, in Brunswick, where a few were 300 percent above the average for a sample of councillors while more than two-thirds were below it, and a full third even below half of it—and far from all rich men were councillors. Every council had its "new men" without connections to the leading families, though the extent of openness varied substantially from town to town.

Given this flexible social order, it is more meaningful and useful to speak of a class of citizens—differentiated within itself into strata, but in several important economic, legal, and social respects one class. The person who had taken citizenship rights was normally an independent merchant or artisan who shared basic obligations of taxation and defense with other citizens, and perhaps interacted socially, first of all, with men closest to himself but generally with other citizens. In an overwhelmingly agrarian, feudal society, this minority group of townsmen who, behind their walls, engaged in commerce or craft production and shared a distinctly urban legal and political status had enough in common with each other to override differences of profession and wealth. Urban society was not a community of equals, but it was, in a very real sense, a community.

It follows that the economic changes of the fourteenth century could only have increased tensions in urban society. The increased emphasis on manufacturing in some towns accentuated the diversity between one town and another, not only economically but also socially. The expansion and precapitalist organization of industries such as textiles in the south tended to increase the number of dependent craftsmen and, presumably, the proportion of the population in the lower stratum. Some of those affected perhaps perceived themselves as falling through the bottom of the community of citizens. At the same time others may have been climbing out at the top. Merchants in any age seek greater security for some

of their capital at the expense of rapid growth—in annuities, houses, and especially land—but the economic uncertainties of the fourteenth century probably accelerated the process. At the same time the agricultural depression following the Black Death had left nobles even shorter of cash than usual, and so made more land available. In any case, from about 1350 members of top urban families, including councillors, apparently invested more heavily in property in general and landed estates in particular.

Two groups of town inhabitants in particular stood, in effect, with one foot outside the community, and faced potential tensions with its citizens. One was the clergy, who belonged to and might identify with one of the great institutions of the larger society outside the town. Even in the fourteenth century towns and their citizens sought to gain greater control over the clergy in their midst, to increase the number and quality of priests, to reform monasteries and intervene in charity and education; and by the end of the fifteenth century many had an effective monopoly over ecclesiastical patronage of priests in parish churches. The Protestant Reformation in such towns, then, continued and expanded a medieval process.

The other group was the body of councillors who had led the towns into a position of power. As their political success allowed them to move an ever greater distance from the rest of the townsmen, as they came to be addressed as "lord," increased the level of taxation, decreased citizen consultation, and otherwise sought to transform their fellow citizens into subjects, they ran the danger of separating themselves from the urban community. This was especially true of councillors with significant landholdings, as they concerned themselves more and more with the administration of their estates and began imitating the way of life of the nobility. To such councillors it was only natural to direct urban policies toward more territorial expansion and more power in German politics. But their fellow citizens, whose wealth was the town's main resource, might disagree.

The limits of urban power. The Swabian-Rhenish League collapsed in 1388. The combined forces of the princes of Swabia and Franconia defeated the Swabian towns' army at Döffingen in August, and the Rhenish towns fell to the count-palatine near Worms in November. The battles did not decide the course of German history—sooner or later the alliance of towns almost certainly would have unraveled through the centrifugal force of urban particularism—but they illustrate it: the political future lay with the princes, not the towns. The Hansa did not go down as quickly or as dramatically, but the later 1380's brought at best a mixed success for it: Denmark regained the fortresses on the Sound in 1385, and only by sparing the Teutonic Order and the Prussian towns from some of the terms could the Hansa agree on the 1388 blockade of Flanders. In retrospect these events were the first signs of a resurgence of Denmark and a splintering of the Hanseatic community. And while the towns, north and south, had been reaching outside their walls for power, within them citizen unrest had been challenging the councils at their foundation. At least twenty-five uprisings shook the towns of the empire between 1365 and 1385, and the disturbances abated only slightly through the fifteenth century. There was no clear turning point, and signs of vigor continued for a long time to overlap hints of decline; but broadly speaking, if up to the 1370's and 1380's councils had been largely developing the potential of urban power, thereafter they were learning its limits.

Towns were restricted outside their walls above all by the rise of territorial states. The trend that in England or France is usually called the development of a stronger central monarchy could not, or at any rate did not, take that form in the empire; but in the last decades of the fourteenth century and through the fifteenth, using many of the same ideas and methods as monarchs elsewhere, the princes began extending their authority effectively through the territory they ruled and consolidating it into something approximating a sovereign state. The most impressive example was on the western fringe of the empire and only partly within it; from 1384 the dukes of Burgundy began assembling from various titles and lordships, notably in the Low Countries, a governed entity that was the envy of many kingdoms. But the Luxembourgs in Bohemia and the Habsburgs in Austria by the end of the fourteenth century, and a whole range of princes by the end of the fifteenth, gradually used the concept of sovereignty and the tools of Roman law to build centralized governments.

This development came only partly from the success of the princes; it was also due to the failure of the estates, which had claimed to represent the land as a whole but in fact used power, when they held it, for their own particular ends. Far too often they had worked not for better government and constitutional taxation but for no central government or taxation at all, or as little as possible. In this process the towns were just as guilty as the knights; once holding territory of their own, towns proved capable of defending local privilege and exploiting peasants as efficiently as any noble ever did, if not more so. There were other factors: the frequent feuds between councils and knights over toll stations, robbery along trade routes, and raids on council or burgher manors strained what was already a tenuous alliance of towns and nobles within the estates. But in the end the towns, by standing for their own particular interests, left wider issues to the princes, and by the close of the fifteenth century the princes, not the estates, governed the land as a whole.

The fall of the estates as an independent power meant the loss of much urban political influence, and it was followed in many cases by loss of independence. The Hohenzollerns were pioneers in this process: in 1442 Elector Frederick II of Brandenburg defeated the federation of Brandenburg cities; deprived its leader, Berlin, of its liberties; took control of its courts; and established a right of confirmation over its council. He then made this status a model for all other towns in his realm, forbidding any leagues of towns without his consent. Each town and each prince followed its own timetable, of course; Mainz was subjugated by 1462, for example, whereas Rostock still had significant independence after the Thirty Years War. Most free and imperial cities kept their status, in a few famous cases (Frankfurt, Hamburg, Lübeck) into the nineteenth or twentieth century. Most towns participated in the *Landtag*, the estates-general of their principality, and so retained some influence over taxation and the expansion of princely authority until the trials of the Reformation and the Thirty Years War shrank the value of even this limited outlet. Towns were still politically important in Germany at the end of the Middle Ages, but the trend was clear: they were on their way down, and time was on the side of the princes.

At the same time, town councils learned that their resources were not unlimited. The pursuit of power was expensive: Lübeck's canal project and territorial expansion in the 1390's, for example, saddled the town with a debt equal to four or five times its annual income in just a dozen years. Efforts of a council to increase existing taxes or develop new taxes almost always met with citizen resistance, and sometimes sparked uprisings against the council.

A great deal of scholarly energy has been expended in trying to make "social movements" of one kind or another out of these uprisings, most of it not very successfully. The traditional term for them is "guild struggles," because so many of them were expressed through guilds and successful ones often obtained seats on the town council for certain guilds. Other historians have suggested even lower social origin for those who would dare challenge council authority. Time and again, however, research shows that the forces behind many uprisings were both craft and commercial—solid, prosperous citizens, with leadership and often the bulk of support from merchant groups—and the men they placed in government were usually as wealthy as other councillors.

No one interpretation will explain all the uprisings—Erich Maschke has identified more than 200 of them from 1300 to 1550, in more than 100 towns. Some, no doubt, were the protests of artisans whose incomes were falling or whose crafts were becoming dependent. But economic and social issues seem far less pertinent to most of them than attitudes about town government and policies. High taxes and financial mismanagement were the major complaints almost everywhere, and some felt they knew why the town was in the red: too many wars and feuds, too much territory. Citizens distrusted these policies, often wondering whether they benefited the town as a whole or just the councillors. The Brunswick uprising of 1374 began with citizen resistance to a tax intended to raise a ransom for troops taken while defending an area in which many councillors held estates; by 1380 a new regime had divested the city of most of the castles that the old council had painfully accumulated. A citizen committee in Rostock in 1409 demanded that men who held landed estates be forbidden to serve on the council.

Less clearly articulated in citizen complaints, but discernible, was a sense that the council had overstepped its authority, set itself above the citizens. In Brunswick the assertion was not just that the tax was bad policy, but that the council had no right to impose a new tax. The proximate cause of the Cologne uprising of 1396 was a refusal of the council to consult with citizens, and the new constitution that resulted from the unrest required citizen consent to any military expedition outside the town and any expenditure in excess of a specified amount. Constitutional changes, then, came not so much to place a social or occupational group on the council as to bring the council back in touch with the citizenry as a whole. To accomplish this, guilds, as an available institution, were often incorporated into government, but occasionally new institutions were created—for example, the citizen committees in Lü-

beck, Hamburg, Rostock, and Wismar in 1408–1410. Cologne's new constitution of 1396 gave selection of councillors to twenty-two occupational *Gaffeln,* at the same time requiring that all citizens join one (they replaced parishes as defense units), thus implicitly transforming them into citizen associations.

The evidence suggests that uprisings focused on taxes and council composition not because the supporters were poor and the taxes a crushing burden, or because they wanted to make councils more "democratic," but because taxes and council composition were the points at which the different concepts of government of council and citizens most clearly and sharply collided. The right to tax without consent was an expression of authority that many citizens believed the councils did not have; some citizen participation in the selection of councillors was a counterstroke that might ensure that citizens were not yet subjects of the council.

Most uprisings, of course, were not successful, and some were bitterly repressed. One result, then, of the waves of unrest was to make town constitutions even more distinctly different from each other then they had been. But whether a council survived untouched or faced new institutional arrangements, the citizens' attitude that the town was one community, to be governed with, not against, its citizens, remained, to erupt again in various towns and various generations. The Reformation was in many ways this kind of citizen movement: many townsmen chose a theology that seemed to express a communal ideal better and often forced their Protestantism on their council.

The political decline of the Hanseatic League illustrates both tendencies: checked by rulers reaching for sovereignty on the one hand, its councils faced citizens unwilling to be subjects on the other. The rise of the stronger princes, and stronger monarchs in areas the Hansa exploited, posed an enormous threat to its privileges. The collection of most of the Low Countries under one ruler made the embargo an increasingly ineffective weapon, since a practical alternative port outside Burgundian jurisdiction became harder and harder to find. The Polish-Lithuanian monarchy blocked the Teutonic Knights and acquired a corridor to Danzig. The electors of Brandenburg forced their towns out of the Hansa beginning in the mid fifteenth century, and other princes proved constant enemies. Above all, a stronger Denmark started to explore anti-Hansa policies.

Under such political pressure on top of economic problems Hansa unity, never strong, was exposed as a facade. Lübeck, the dominant force not only of the Wendish quarter but also of the entire league, had an obvious vested interest in the portage to Hamburg, and could benefit from a war that closed the Strait of Denmark. Danzig and the Prussian and Livonian towns, however, saw increasing profit in sailing the Sound; Cologne and the Rhineland, in overland routes such as Nuremberg was developing. Meanwhile, uprisings shook many of the member towns, most spectacularly in a chain that began at Lübeck in 1408 and included Rostock, Wismar, and Hamburg by 1410. The evidence hints that merchant citizens of many towns had started to wonder whether the Hansa existed for commerce or for the power of councils. Merchants definitely formed the backbone of the uprising in Lübeck, and they not only rejected territorial ambitions but also charged their councillors—the leaders of the Hansa and spokesmen for it in the absence of a diet—with neglecting commercial interests. In response the exiled councillors did not shrink from allying with the league's most dangerous enemy, King Erik VII of Denmark, who interfered with Lübeck's commerce and arrested its merchants.

League arbitration restored peace in Lübeck in 1416, but Erik was aroused, and turned his successful tactics to the entire Hansa. Eventually he imposed higher tolls at Scania and new tolls at the Sound, while favoring more Dutch ships and merchants in the Strait of Denmark and the Baltic. Soon the Hansa went to war, with Denmark from 1426 to 1435 and with the Dutch from 1438 to 1441, with little help from the Rhenish towns and none at all from the Prussian and Livonian. In addition, the war decades were punctuated with uprisings in the Wendish towns. Although both conflicts were technically Hansa victories, calling them ties would be more accurate. Hansa disunity was revealed, Denmark kept the Sound tolls (for more than 400 years), and the Dutch were recognized with reciprocity agreements in Denmark and the Wendish towns. The Baltic would never again be a Hanseatic lake; from this point on, the Dutch increased their share of northern trade while the Hansa's proportion dwindled. Princes and monarchs blocked the councils of the Hansa towns from international power, and their citizens were unwilling to pay for it.

THE MEANING OF MEDIEVAL GERMAN TOWNS

The close of the fifteenth century marks no major turning point in the history of German towns. Although the Hansa's decline had begun, it remained an economic and political force to be reckoned with for several decades, and something of a Hansa staggered on until a last diet in 1669. Elsewhere, in the Rhineland and especially the south, towns were probably just reaching their economic peak in 1500, following the increased demand in far-flung markets for precious metals produced in the empire. To some extent these towns were supplanting Italians in long-distance trade. Textile production and banking were reaching new heights, and with the economic development of eastern Europe, Germans could exploit their position at the crossroads of Europe as never before. With this economic base, artistic and intellectual activities flowered; towns of the south borrowed and made their own contributions to the styles of Italian art and humanism, while the Hansa towns developed a culture based on Flemish influence. Spires on monumental urban churches dominated the landscape; leading councillors of imperial cities began fancying themselves the true elite of the empire.

The basic medieval political trends—above all the three-sided struggle among town councils, princes, and citizens—continued into the Reformation era. The religious disputes were an opportunity for councils to increase their control over church and clergy, for princes to use confessional grounds to bend more towns to their authority, for citizens to use doctrinal movements to escape subjection and draw councils back into the community. On the whole the princes eventually gained the most and citizens the least, but each town had its own distinct outcome.

Although the towns still showed remarkable energies in the early sixteenth century, those energies lacked central direction. Diversity still characterized the towns, and each was committed to its own particular interests. Whether any of the disasters that befell Germany in the period from the Reformation through the seventeenth century could have been avoided if the towns' resources had been devoted to national or regional ends instead of being partly dissipated in conflict is of course impossible to say. Certainly strong medieval towns did not save sixteenth-century Italy from the Habsburg-Valois wars, nor did a functioning monarchy dominating the towns spare sixteenth-century France from its wars of religion. But German towns not only failed to prevent the disasters, they were profoundly affected by them. Beginning in the middle of the sixteenth century, urban economic and political power went into a steep decline that only hit bottom in the devastation of the Thirty Years War. German towns did not regain their significance in the economy of Europe until the mid nineteenth century, and never recaptured as much political importance.

The towns' contributions were by no means lost; above all, the princes borrowed their administrative techniques to consolidate their developing states. Much art, architecture, and literature remained, and some towns preserved a measure of autonomy into modern times. Medieval German towns, for better or worse, had followed their own course, neither wholly ruling nor wholly ruled, and so took their place in later centuries in the particular mosaic that was Germany. If the experiment had not been a complete success, neither was it a complete failure.

BIBLIOGRAPHY

Bibliographic sources. Bibliographie zur Städtege-schichte Deutschlands (1969), 2nd ed. by Wilfried Ehbrecht and Heinz Stoob, in preparation; Paul Guyer, ed., *Bibliographie der Städtegeschichte der Schweiz* (1960); and Erich Keyser, ed., *Deutsches Städtebuch: Handbuch städtischer Geschichte*, 11 vols. (1939–1974).

Studies. Brigitte Berthold, Evamaria Engel, and Adolf Laube, "Die Stellung des Bürgertums in der deutschen Feudalgesellschaft bis zur Mitte des 16. Jhs.," in *Zeitschrift für Geschichtswissenschaft*, 21 (1973); Karl Bosl, *Die Sozialstruktur der mittelalterlichen Residenz- und Fernhandelsstadt Regensburg* (1966), and *Die wirtschaftliche und gesellschaftliche Entwicklung des Augsburger Bürgertums* (1969); Otto Brunner, *Neue Wege der Verfassungs- und Sozialgeschichte*, 2nd ed. (1969), 213–280, 294–334; Philippe Dollinger, "Les villes allemandes au moyen âge," in *Recueils de la Société Jean Bodin*, 6 (1954) and 7 (1956), and *The German Hansa*, D. S. Ault and S. H. Steinberg, trans. (1970); Edit Ennen, *Die europäische Stadt des Mittelalters* (1972), with a bibliography of 952 items; Christopher R. Friedrichs, "Citizens or Subjects? Urban Conflict in Early Modern Germany," in Miriam Usher Chrisman and Otto Gründler, eds., *Social Groups and Religious Ideas in the Sixteenth Century* (1978); Konrad Fritze, *Bürger und Bauern zur Hansezeit* (1976); Erich Maschke, "Verfassung und soziale Kräfte in der deutschen Stadt des späten Mittelalters," in *Vierteljahrsschrift für Sozial- und Wirtschaftsgeschichte*, 46 (1959), and "Deutsche Städte am Ausgang des Mittelalters," in Wilhelm Rausch, ed., *Die Stadt am Ausgang des Mittelalters* (1974); Bernd Moeller, *Imperial Cities and the Reformation*, H. C. Erik Midelfort and Mark U. Edwards, trans. (1972); Hans Planitz, *Die deutsche Stadt im Mittelalter* (1954); Fritz Rörig, *The Medieval Town* (1969), and *Wirtschaftskräfte im Mittelalter*, 2nd ed. (1971); Rhiman A. Rotz, "The Lubeck Uprising of 1408 and the Decline of the Hanseatic League," in *Proceedings of the American Philosophical Society*, 121 (1977); Walter Schlesinger, *Beiträge zur deutschen Verfassungsgeschichte des Mittelalters*, II, *Städte und Territo-rien* (1963); Heinz Stoob, ed., *Altständisches Bürgertum*, 2 vols. (1978), a collection of important articles by various scholars, 1898–1968; Paul Strait, *Cologne in the Twelfth Century* (1974).

RHIMAN A. ROTZ

[See also **Aldermen; Cologne; Commerce; Frederick II of Sicily; Germany: 1254–1493; Germany: Electors; Guilds and Métiers; Hanseatic League; Henry the Lion; Lübeck; Nuremberg; Trade.**]

GERMANOS I, patriarch of Constantinople from 715 to 730. Germanos was deeply involved in the iconoclastic controversy of his time. He had approved the accession of Leo III as emperor and made him swear that he would not change church dogma, but Leo reinstated iconoclasm and called a council of the highest secular and ecclesiastical officials. This council formally denounced images, and when Germanos refused to sign the decree, he was deposed.

BIBLIOGRAPHY

George Ostrogorsky, *History of the Byzantine State,* Joan Hussey trans. (1957, rev. ed. 1969).

LINDA ROSE

[See also **Iconoclasm, Christian.**]

GERMANUS OF AUXERRE, ST. (ca. 375–31 July 446). Born at Auxerre to aristocratic Gallo-Roman parents, Germanus received his secondary education in Gaul and then studied rhetoric and law at Rome. He began his public career as an advocate and eventually rose to the office of dux (military commander), probably in Armorica (Brittany). In 418, still in secular office, he was chosen to succeed St. Amator as bishop of Auxerre. Germanus' first known act as bishop occurred in 429, when he traveled to Britain with Bishop Lupus of Troyes in an attempt to suppress a new outbreak of the Pelagian heresy. After doing so, he led the Britons in their "Alleluia" victory over the Saxons and Picts, who were put to flight merely by the shouts of the Britons.

About 435 Germanus traveled to Arles to obtain tax relief for the people of Auxerre, and in 444 he and his friend Bishop Hilary of Arles assisted in the deposition of Bishop Chelidonius of Besançon. Later in the same year he was recalled to Britain to combat the Pelagians yet again. In 445 the rebellious inhabitants of Armorica appealed to Germanus to mediate between them and the imperial government, and after personally restraining Goar, the leader of the Alani *foederati* sent to quell the rebellion, Germanus journeyed to Ravenna, where he was favorably received by Empress Galla Placidia, Emperor Valentinian, and Peter Chrysogonos. Before his mission could be accomplished, however, he died. His body was returned to Auxerre, where it was interred on 1 October 446.

Germanus' memory was perpetuated by Constantius of Lyons, who composed his biography about 480, at the request of Bishop Patiens of Lyons. During the Middle Ages the work was second only to the Life of St. Martin in popularity among Gallic saints' lives. It was modeled on the Life of Martin in the use of miracles, but it also stressed the saint's usefulness in responding to the necessities of the secular world. As a historical source the Life offers rare insights into conditions in central Gaul and Britain during the period 425–450. It enjoyed great popularity even beyond Gaul, especially in the British Isles, where large sections of it were copied by Bede and where many legends sprang up about Germanus' activities in Britain.

BIBLIOGRAPHY

Texts of the *Vita Germani* are R. Borius, ed., *Vie de saint Germain d'Auxerre* (1965); Wilhelm Levison, ed., *Monumenta Germaniae historica: Scriptores rerum Merovingicarum,* VII (1920), 224–283; a translation is by Frederick R. Hoare in *The Western Fathers* (1954), 284–320. See also Association bourguignonne des sociétés savantes, *Saint-Germain d'Auxerre et son temps* (1950); Wilhelm Levison, "Bischof Germanus von Auxerre und die Quellen zu seiner Geschichte," in *Neues Archiv der Gesellschaft für ältere deutsche Geschichtskunde,* 29 (1904); Ralph Whitney Mathisen, "The Last Year of Saint Germanus of Auxerre," in *Analecta Bollandiana,* 99 (1981).

RALPH WHITNEY MATHISEN

GERMANUS OF PARIS, ST. (ca. 495–28 May 576). Born near Autun to Gallo-Roman aristocrats named Eusebia and Eleutherius, Germanus began his ecclesiastical career as a deacon in his native city. He became a priest (*ca.* 530), and shortly thereafter he was chosen abbot of the monastery of St. Symphorian near Autun. In this position he became known for his care of the poor and for defending church prop-

erty against the Franks in the 540's. Sometime between 562 and 568, in his sixties, Germanus was made bishop of Paris with the support of the Frankish king Childebert I, whose donations to the church included 6,000 solidi for the poor and funds to build the basilicas of St. Vincent and the Holy Cross.

With the approval of King Charibert, Germanus and other bishops met at Tours in 567 to consider matters of ecclesiastical discipline; thereafter Germanus excommunicated the king for irregularities in his marriage. In 573 Germanus presided at a council summoned in Paris by King Guntram at which Promotus, bishop of Chateaudun, was deposed. The resulting civil war was the cause for Germanus' one extant letter, written in 575 to Queen Brunhilde, wife of King Sigebert I, exhorting her to restrain her husband from fratricidal warfare. Germanus died in the following year, and his epitaph was said to have been composed by King Chilperic I.

Germanus is noteworthy for being able to maintain his Roman aristocratic ties at the same time that he was reaching a modus vivendi with the Frankish kings with whom he was so closely associated. The details of his life are known from the frequent occurrence of his name in the works of Gregory of Tours and from his biography, which was composed by Venantius Fortunatus. The Church of St. Germain-des-Prés in Paris, where he was buried, was afterward renamed for him.

BIBLIOGRAPHY

The text of Germanus' letter to Brunhilde is in W. Gundlach, ed., *Monumenta Germaniae historica: Epistolae,* III (1892), 122–124. The text of and commentary on the *Vita Germani episcopi parisiaci,* Bruno Krusch, ed., is in *Monumenta Germaniae historica: Scriptores rerum Merovingicarum,* VII (1920), 337–428.

RALPH WHITNEY MATHISEN

[See also **Brunhild; Merovingians.**]

GERMANY. The history of Germany is covered in three survey articles, **Germany: 843–1137; Germany: 1138–1254;** and **Germany: 1254–1493;** and in five more specific sections, **Germany: Electors; Germany: Idea of Empire; Germany: Imperial Knights; Germany: Principalities;** and **Germany: Stem Duchies.** For the earlier history of this region, see **Carolingians and the Carolingian Empire.**

GERMANY: 843–1137. The East Frankish kingdom, which was assigned to Louis the German at Verdun in 843, stretched from the North Sea to the Alps, and from the Rhine to the Elbe-Saale in the northeast and to what is now western Hungary and northern Yugoslavia in the southeast. It was, compared with Gaul, which had been a Roman province for 500 years, a backward region with little internal unity. The Franks had conquered the Alamanni, Bavarians, Saxons, and Thuringians; but each of these tribes, which were in turn confederations of smaller tribal units, had retained its separate identity. Powerful noble clans with special legal privileges dominated the individual tribes.

The early Carolingians had imposed the Frankish comital structure on their east Rhenish domains; but, in contrast with Gaul, where the county was often the successor of the Roman city-state, large areas of Germany had not been incorporated into the system, and local institutions of justice, such as the Saxon *Gogerichte,* had survived the Frankish conquest. As late as the sixth century, less than 4 percent of the land east of the Rhine had been cleared. Although the monks had introduced cereal production and viticulture as well as Christianity into Germany, and the Carolingians had promoted land reclamation and colonization to strengthen their lordship, vast sections of Germany were still a wilderness in 843 and remained so for centuries thereafter. A few Roman towns, such as Mainz and Regensburg, had

GERMAN EMPIRE IN 1025

473

survived in the Rhine valley and south of the Danube as episcopal sees and/or royal residences; but it was largely a fiction of canon law to classify them as cities. The sparse population lived in relatively overpopulated clearings in the forest.

Unlike Gaul, large parts of Germany, most notably Saxony, had been Christian for only a generation or two in 843. Although Christianity had not been wiped out completely in the extreme west and south during the barbarian invasions, even the Bavarian church had been organized into dioceses by St. Boniface as recently as 739. Charlemagne and Louis the Pious had founded the Saxon bishoprics, and the Stellinga Revolt in Saxony (841–843) was in part a last pagan reaction against Christianity.

The association of the various tribes under a common ruler was the chief factor in the gradual transformation of the East Frankish kingdom into Germany after 843, but even that precarious unity was threatened by the kings' efforts to reunite the empire and by the custom of dividing the kingdom among the kings' sons. When Louis the German died in 876, his three sons divided the realm. Only the early deaths of Carloman (880) and Louis the Younger (882) without legitimate male heirs prevented the permanent partition of the kingdom. The youngest brother, Charles III (sometimes called "the Fat"), who also wore the Italian and West Frankish crowns, was the last Carolingian to govern the united empire. The East Frankish magnates rebelled against his rule in 887 and placed Arnulf of Carinthia, Carloman's illegitimate son, on the throne. They prevented Arnulf from accepting the West Frankish crown the following year and in 889 blocked his plan to establish his two illegitimate sons as subkings.

The events of 887–889 are indicative of the growing power of the nobility in the late ninth century and of an incipient awareness that the East Frankish kingdom, the inhabitants of which were beginning to be called Germans, was a distinct and indivisible entity. Arnulf, the last Carolingian to be crowned emperor, could exercise only a nominal feudal suzerainty over the non-Carolingian kings who had succeeded Charles III in the other parts of the empire. Arnulf's son, Louis the Child (900–911), was the last German Carolingian.

Arnulf, who was paralyzed during the last years of his reign, and the young Louis the Child had been unable to cope with the problems of the kingdom. The Vikings had been raiding the country since Charlemagne's time, and the Magyars were an even greater menace. They had annihilated a Bavarian army at Bratislava in 907 and had established their hegemony east of the Enns. The imperial aristocracy, a select group of Austrasian noble families who had supported the Carolingians in their bid for power and had been rewarded with extensive estates and offices throughout the empire, tended increasingly to coalesce with the local tribal nobility and to adopt the latter's particularistic outlook. Conscious of their innate right to command and reluctant to accept any form of subordination, the nobles were carving out their own lordships in the vast wilderness areas of Germany and arrogating comital rights to themselves. It was a process that was repeated whenever the monarchy was weak. Moreover, the incessant warfare, the gradual shift from the infantry to the cavalry as the chief fighting force, and the communal effort required to grow grain were making the peasantry even more dependent on the large landowners.

Although the early Carolingians had abolished the office of the tribal duke, the duchies had survived in varying degrees as administrative, ecclesiastical, legal, and military entities. This was especially true of Bavaria, the crown land of the East Frankish monarchs and a separate ecclesiastical province, and of Saxony, which no king had visited since 852. Powerful magnates, who had been charged with the defense of a duchy and were related to the Carolingians, were taking advantage of the monarchy's weakness and the need for protection to bring the church, counts, and royal property in their duchy under their direct control. By 911 the Liudolfingians and the Luitpoldingians had established themselves as the dukes of Saxony and Bavaria, respectively, the two duchies most threatened by the invaders. The outcome was still undecided in Franconia and Swabia, but it was conceivable that the kingdom would fragment along tribal lines.

The election of the first non-Carolingian king, Duke Conrad of Franconia, who was anointed with holy oil to sanction his authority, was a tribute to the strength of the monarchal heritage. Only Lorraine, first annexed after Lothar II's death in 869 and still fast in the Carolingian tradition, refused to accept Conrad's election. Supported by the church, Conrad I (911–918) tried to regain Lorraine and to break the power of the dukes; but lacking both a firm base of power and the Carolingians' prestige, he failed miserably. On Conrad's recommendation the Franks and Saxons elected the most powerful duke, Henry of Saxony, as his successor. The election of the first

Saxon monarch symbolized the end of Frankish predominance and the emergence of Saxony as the chief crown land.

Henry I (919–936) and his son, Otto I the Great (936–973), were confronted with three basic problems: halting the invasions, bringing the duchies under royal control, and regulating Germany's relations with the other Carolingian successor states. Henry arranged a nine-year truce with the Magyars in 926, and he used the peace to build castles in Saxony that later formed the nuclei of cities. He defeated the Elbian Slavs in 928/929, and in 933, after refusing to pay the Magyars tribute, he stopped their retaliatory raid at Riade. Thereafter Saxony was safe. While Henry was content to collect tribute from the Slavs, Otto sought to conquer and to convert them. Shortly after his accession he founded the monastery of St. Maurice in Magdeburg as a mission center and entrusted Margraves Hermann Billung and Gero with the task of subduing the Slavic tribes east of the Elbe-Saale. The Slavs had been sufficiently pacified by 948 for bishoprics to be erected in Oldenburg, Brandenburg, and Havelberg. The foundation of the archbishopric of Magdeburg and its suffragan dioceses in 968 was the capstone of Otto's east-Elbian policy. The basic weakness of his program was that little effort was made to promote German settlement in the new lands. As a result, the Elbian Slavs rebelled against the harsh rule of the German kings in 983, after Otto's son, Otto II, had been defeated in Italy. Most of Otto II's conquests, except for the area between the Saale and the upper Elbe, were lost; and it was not until the twelfth century that Christianization and Germanization could begin anew.

Otto I's defeat of the Magyars on the Lechfeld near Augsburg in 955 hastened their pacification and assimilation into Catholic Europe. The victory once again opened up the Danube valley east of the Enns to German settlement. The appointment of the first Babenberg, Leopold I, as the margrave of the newly reestablished Bavarian Danubian mark in 976 marked the birth of Austria.

Henry's and Otto's victories provided them with the personal prestige to deal with the dukes. Henry retained Saxony for himself, forced the dukes to accept his feudal suzerainty, and appointed his own candidate as duke of Swabia. Otto intervened in a similar fashion in Bavaria after the death of Arnulf the Bad in 937. After suppressing a series of revolts between 937 and 939, caused in part by the dukes' discontent with this assertion of royal authority, Otto kept Franconia for himself. Because of its cen-

tral location, which offered access to the other duchies, Franconia was never again conferred on another duke. The combination of Saxony and Franconia made the king more powerful than any of his rivals.

Otto also initiated a policy of appointing his relatives as dukes. The revolt of his oldest son, Duke Liudolf of Swabia, in 953, precipitated by the rivalry between him and his uncle, Duke Henry of Bavaria, revealed the basic weakness of this tactic. Each duke tended to identify with the traditions of his duchy and to use his position for pursuing his own interests. A duke who was a member of a cadet branch of the royal house was an even greater threat than a tribal leader. While Otto and his successors continued to select their kinsmen as dukes, they tried to reduce the size of the duchies. After putting down the revolt of his cousin, Duke Henry the Wrangler of Bavaria, in 976, for example, Otto II separated Carinthia from Bavaria and made it into a duchy. This was not a particularly good solution to the problem, since it increased the number of magnates whom the king had to control.

More important, after the suppression of Liudolf's revolt in 955, the kings relied more than ever on the church as a counterweight to the lay nobility. Henry and Otto had successfully defended their right to nominate the bishops and the abbots of the approximately eighty-five royal monasteries. Instead of selecting candidates from the local church, Otto increasingly chose clerics who had served in the royal chapel and were familiar with his policies. The bishops thus became an important instrument in overcoming tribal loyalties. The Saxon kings enlarged the churches' endowments. This was regarded not as a diminution of the royal estates, since the property of the royal churches was considered to be an appurtenance of the kingdom, but as a device to utilize clerical expertise in administering the land. Moreover, such land usually formed part of an immunity—that is, it was exempt from the count's jurisdiction and directly subject to the king, who appointed an advocate to protect the church's property and to administer justice on the king's behalf. In return the royal churches were required to provision the court on its travels and to supply contingents for military campaigns. The prelates raised three-fourths of the troops, for example, for Otto II's ill-fated Italian war.

Otto I began the practice of enfeoffing bishops with counties. Although the counts were in theory removable royal officials, most counts inherited their offices and were deposed only if they angered the king. The problem of heritability was avoided by the selection of a cleric. This policy reached its climax with Henry II's foundation of Bamberg in 1007, and the division of the Franconian counties between the bishops of Bamberg and Würzburg. This use of the church for secular purposes was not perceived as improper because the king was viewed as God's anointed representative on earth.

After the Saxon kings had restored order in Germany, they turned their attention to the fragmented territory that had been Lothar I's kingdom. Henry I had already regained Lorraine (925) and demonstrated an interest in Burgundy and Italy. Otto the Great's carefully arranged coronation at Aachen, Charlemagne's favorite residence, was a programmatic resumption of the Carolingian inheritance. Following the example of his Carolingian predecessors, Otto intervened in Italy in 951. Margrave Berengar of Ivrea had been crowned king of Italy after the death of his rival Lothar (950), and Berengar had imprisoned Lothar's widow Adelaide, the daughter of King Rudolf II of Burgundy, who had been another claimant to the Lombard throne. Otto assumed the Italian crown at Pavia and then married Adelaide. There were two other reasons besides the Carolingian precedents for Otto's intervention: Berengar's designs on Burgundy, the king of which, Adelaide's brother Conrad, had become Otto's vassal; and the bitter rivalry between Otto's brother Henry and his son Liudolf who, as the dukes of Bavaria and Swabia, respectively, had their own Italian interests and, through their wives, claims to the Lombard crown. Otto's decision has been greatly criticized, but the union of Normandy and England—when a powerful vassal became a king and thus the equal of his nominal lord, the king of France—shows the danger Otto avoided by intervening.

Liudolf's revolt and the subsequent Magyar invasion prevented Otto from decisively defeating Berengar, who was soon causing trouble again in Italy. Summoned by Pope John XII, Otto returned to Italy in 961 and was crowned emperor on 2 February 962. Some members of Otto's court, most notably his brother Archbishop Brun of Cologne, the archetypal Ottonian bishop, had been arguing since the 950's that Otto's victory on the Lechfeld, his possession of the Frankish and Lombard crowns, and his preeminence among the kings of Europe had elevated him to a more than kingly status. Otto rejected this essentially military concept of the imperial dignity and accepted instead the papal contention that only the pope could make an emperor. Otto's coronation did not give him any additional power, except in Rome itself, but it helped to legitimate his control of Burgundy, Italy, and Lorraine, the rulers of which had borne the imperial title in the ninth century. Conrad II assumed direct control of Burgundy after the death of its childless king, Rudolf III, in 1032. It was during Conrad's reign that the term Roman Empire was first used to designate the three kingdoms ruled by the emperor.

Otto's assumption of the emperorship aroused the hostility of Constantinople and entangled him in the internal politics of Rome, and he spent most of the last years of his reign in Italy. After Otto's coronation John XII issued the *Ottonianum,* which required the newly elected pope to swear before his consecration an oath of allegiance to the emperor. When Otto discovered that John was plotting with the emperor's enemies, he obligated the Romans not to elect a pope without his permission. Otto's reduction of the papacy to the status of an imperial bishopric was the logical consequence of his ecclesiastical policies, but it was incompatible with the pope's position as the head of the church.

The emperors' involvement in Italian affairs became even more pronounced during the reigns of Otto's son Otto II (973–983) and young grandson Otto III (983–1002). Otto II, who had married the Byzantine princess Theophano and who adopted the title Emperor Augustus of the Romans, tried to extend his control to southern Italy; but the Arabs annihilated his army at Cape Colonne in Calabria in 982. After attaining his majority Otto III built a palace on the Palatine, adopted Byzantine court ceremonial, and assumed the titles "servant of Jesus Christ" and "servant of the apostles," in a deliberate parallel with the pope's designation as the "servant of the servants of God." These titles expressed Otto's desire to revive the Roman Empire, which he perceived as coterminous with Christendom. More concretely, he hoped by these means to integrate Poland, which had become a papal fief in 990, in order to escape from German domination, into his empire. As the covicar of St. Peter, Otto went to Poland in 1000, elevated Gniezno to the rank of an archbishopric, and designated the Polish duke, Boleslav Chobry (the Brave), as patrician—that is, as imperial representative. The reign of the last member of the Saxon dynasty, Henry II (1002–1024), who belonged to the Bavarian branch of the family, saw a conscious reaction against Otto's imperial and eastern policies.

Henry stressed the German character of his empire and allied with the pagan Ljutizi against Boleslav.

The magnates elected a Salian, Conrad II (1024–1039), a great-grandson of Otto I's daughter but an untitled nobleman, as Henry's successor. The frequent changes in dynasties and the consequent survival of the elective principle have often been blamed for the eventual disintegration of Germany, but in electing Henry II and Conrad the princes paid careful attention to hereditary rights of succession and selected the nearest relative of the dead king. The elective principle became a threat to the monarchy only when it was combined with the canonical concept of suitability for office during the investiture controversy.

Although Conrad retained the basic system of government devised by his predecessors, he appears, as an outsider unexpectedly raised to the kingship, to have perceived its weaknesses. Germany was not a state with even a rudimentary bureaucracy, except for a handful of clerics in the royal chapel, but a confederation, headed by the king, of powerful, interrelated noble clans with entrenched local interests. The system depended on the king's personal prestige and his ability to balance one group of magnates against another. The revolts that greeted each monarch upon his accession were basically a test of his character. The Saxon and Salian kings were capable rulers—perhaps too capable, because their abilities concealed the weaknesses of the system; for while they might depose a rebellious duke or count, they had to select his successor from the same circle of families. The church was not a very effective counterweight to the lay aristocracy since the prelates, recruited from the ranks of the nobility, shared their kinsmen's values and often placed the interests of their clan and of their own bishopric or abbey above the king's.

Conrad II, his son Henry III (1039–1056), and his grandson Henry IV (1056–1106) sought, therefore, an alternative base of power for the German monarchy. Conrad relied in part on the lesser nobility and the counts, but his greatest innovation was his use of the upper stratum of the servile population, the precursors of the later imperial ministerials. The bishops and abbots had already turned to this segment of society to administer their estates and households and to fulfill their military obligations to the crown; Conrad now followed the prelates' example in developing and enlarging the royal domain. He and his successors were especially interested in the area around Goslar, where silver had been discov-

ered in 968 and where the Salians had inherited extensive estates from their predecessors. If the Salians had succeeded in forming a royal domain, administered and defended by servile warriors, in Thuringia and eastern Saxony, comparable with the Capetian Île-de-France, the monarchy's dependence on the nobility would have been greatly reduced.

The Salians' near success in achieving this goal aroused the bitter opposition of the Saxon nobility, whose own territorial ambitions were being thwarted by the kings. Throughout Germany the large noble clans were dividing into distinct lineages, increasingly conscious of their patrilineal descent as officeholding tended to become hereditary, and were seeking to develop their own lordships, just as the Salians were, through an accumulation of counties, advocacies, castles, and alods. The nobles' foundation of family monasteries, often located in strategic places and in areas that needed to be settled, and their adoption of surnames, often the name of the castle that served as the center of their lordship, were the outward manifestations of this change in the structure of the aristocracy. At the same time the ecclesiastical princes were trying to round out their territories in competition with the nobility. The tension was especially acute in Saxony because the Saxons viewed the Frankish Salians, who were so vigorously asserting their own rights in the Harz, as foreigners. When Henry IV reclaimed the royal domains that had been lost during his long minority, he was confronted by a bitter revolt of the Saxon nobility and peasantry, which he crushed with considerable difficulty in 1075.

The nobility's opposition was then subsumed and given religious justification by Henry's conflict with Gregory VII. The German church was probably the best-run church in Europe, and the kings had been actively promoting ecclesiastical reform since the days of Henry II. They had especially favored the Gorze reform movement, emanating from Lorraine, which was compatible with royal control of the monasteries. Henry III, who started the reform of the papacy by appointing four reform-minded German bishops as popes, had been widely hailed by such men as St. Peter Damian as the model of a Christian king. The radical wing among the Roman reformers, led by Cardinals Humbert of Silva Candida and Hildebrand, had utilized Henry IV's minority to free the papacy from imperial domination.

As Pope Gregory VII, Hildebrand sought to free the church from lay control; to subordinate the laity, kings included, to the clergy; and to establish the pope as the effective ruler of the church. His program was a direct attack on the king's quasi-clerical status as the head of Christendom and on an essential source of royal power, the control of the royal churches by the monarchy. Gregory found enthusiastic adherents among those prelates who were genuinely disturbed by Henry's failure to follow his father's example and among the nobles who saw monastic reform as a device to strengthen their own lordships. The Swabian nobility in particular supported the introduction of the Hirsau customs. The Holy See became the proprietor of many of the abbeys that were reformed in this fashion, but the family of the noble founder obtained the hereditary advocacy.

The ensuing fifty-year battle between the king and the pope and his noble allies is known as the investiture controversy (1075–1122), but lay investiture became a major issue only during the reign of Henry's son, Henry V (1106–1125), since it was the one resolvable issue. Henry V surrendered the right to invest bishops with the symbols of their spiritual authority in the Concordat of Worms (1122), but he retained the decisive say in the selection process because the episcopal elections were to occur in the royal presence and the bishop-elect was to be consecrated only after paying homage to the king for the temporal regalia.

Nevertheless, the power of the monarchy had been severely weakened. The bishops had ceased to be royal officials and were becoming instead rulers of their own principalities with divided loyalties between the king and the pope. The nobility utilized the monarchy's weakness and the extinction of numerous noble lineages to acquire additional lands and rights. The duchies and counties had been transformed from vaguely defined districts, in which the dukes and counts exercised specific regalian rights over the free population, into territories where a noble house asserted its lordship based on a combination of ducal, comital, feudal, alodial, and/or advocatory rights. The foundation for Germany's fragmentation into a patchwork of ministates had been laid.

The election of Lothar of Supplinburg (1125–1137), who as duke of Saxony had led the opposition to Henry V, rather than of the late king's nephew and heir, Frederick, the Hohenstaufen duke of Swabia, was symptomatic of the change in the German constitution. It was the princes who chose the king they deemed most suitable for their own interests, rather than the king who selected the princes. Although Lothar rebuilt the royal domain in Saxony, reestablished imperial suzerainty over Germany's northern and eastern neighbors, and even asserted some of the rights guaranteed to him by the Concordat of Worms, he never completely overcame the manner of his selection. He was, in the final analysis, the last of the antikings who had been elected in opposition to the rightful dynasty during the investiture controversy. Although the Hohenstaufen restored the prestige of the monarchy, they did so by accepting the territorialization of Germany.

BIBLIOGRAPHY

Geoffrey Barraclough, *The Origins of Modern Germany,* 2nd ed. (1947, repr. 1962); *idem,* ed. and trans., *Mediaeval Germany, 911–1250,* 2 vols. (1938, repr. 1967); Friedrich C. Dahlmann and Georg Waitz, *Quellenkunde der deutschen Geschichte,* 10th ed., Hermann Heimpel and Herbert Geuss, eds. (1965–); Josef Fleckenstein, *Early Medieval Germany,* Bernard S. Smith, trans. (1978); Bruno Gebhardt, *Handbuch der deutschen Geschichte,* I, 9th ed., Herbert Grundmann, ed. (1970); Karl Hampe, *Germany Under the Salian and Hohenstaufen Emperors,* Ralph Bennett, trans. (1973); Hellmut Kämpf, ed., *Die Entstehung des deutschen Reiches* (1956).

JOHN B. FREED

[See also **Arnulf; Austria; Bavaria; Burgundy, Kingdom of; Carolingians and the Carolingian Empire; County; Germany: Stem Duchies; Gregory VII, Pope; Henry IV of Germany; Investiture and the Investiture Controversy; Otto I the Great; Otto III of Germany; Saxon Dynasty; Saxony, Duchy of; Saxony, Early.**]

GERMANY: 1138–1254. The Hohenstaufen era (1138–1254) was a period of economic and cultural vitality in which the center of Germany shifted to the east. The Hohenstaufen, most notably Frederick I Barbarossa, tried to revive the power of the monarchy by asserting their feudal prerogatives and by building a royal domain; but the opposition of the papacy, the princes, and the Italian cities proved too strong. By the middle of the thirteenth century, Germany was well on its way to being a confederation of principalities and cities ruled by a figurehead king.

The emperor Lothar II's son-in-law, the Welf duke of Bavaria, Henry the Proud (d. 1139), who was also the duke of Saxony and margrave of Tuscany, was the obvious candidate for the crown in 1138; but Henry's overwhelming power made him unacceptable to the other princes. They chose instead Duke

HOLY ROMAN EMPIRE IN 1254

Key

‒ ‒ ‒ Area claimed by the pope

───── Boundary of the Holy Roman Empire

didacy for the crown in 1125, by refusing to recognize Henry as duke of Saxony. Conrad was eventually forced in 1142 to grant Saxony to Henry's young son, Henry the Lion (*d.* 1195); but he conferred Bavaria in 1143 on his Babenberg half brother, Henry II Jasomirgott of Austria. Henry the Lion never accepted the loss.

Nevertheless, some of Conrad's policies foreshadowed Frederick Barbarossa's successful policies. Conrad expanded the royal domain, and his use of the imperial title in his correspondence with the Byzantine emperor was an assertion of the divine origin of royal authority. On balance, however, Conrad must be judged a failure.

For once, the princes, tired of decades of turmoil, elected the best candidate as king, Frederick I Barbarossa (1152–1190), the son of Duke Frederick II of Swabia (*d.* 1147). As the son of a Welf mother, Frederick was in a unique position to end the bitter Hohenstaufen-Welf feud. He immediately demonstrated the strength of his German support by informing the pope of his election rather than asking him, as Lothar and Conrad had done, to confirm it. This was a clear signal that Frederick believed he received his authority directly from God.

This belief in the divine origin of royal power found tangible expression in the adoption by the chancellery of the word *sacrum* (holy) to describe the empire. As God's representative, Frederick viewed himself as the source of justice and peace on earth. While the Hohenstaufen imperial ideology could easily be misinterpreted, then and now, as a claim to the lordship of the world, Frederick and his descendants were basically using this inflated language to assert the autonomy of the secular sphere from papal control. As Roman emperors they were the lords of three kingdoms, and thus the premier monarchs in Europe; but with the possible exception of Henry VI, they regarded the other kings as allies rather than as subordinates. During Frederick's reign the three constituent kingdoms of the empire became more nearly equal, but the balance shifted in favor of Italy under the rule of his son and grandson.

Frederick arranged for his imperial coronation in the Treaty of Constance (1153). Pope Eugenius III promised to crown Frederick and to proceed with ecclesiastical measures against all who injured the honor of the empire, while Frederick agreed not to make peace with the rebellious Romans or the Normans in southern Italy without the pope's consent, to suppress the Roman commune, and to make no territorial concessions in Italy to the Byzantines. The

Frederick II of Swabia's younger brother Conrad, who had been the antiking of the Hohenstaufen party during Lothar's reign. The selection of Conrad III (1138–1152) thus should be seen not as the elevation of the legitimate dynasty to the throne but, rather, as indicative of the princes' preference for a weak monarch.

Historians have judged Conrad's reign harshly. He was the first German king since Otto I not to be crowned as emperor, and he led the Second Crusade to annihilation in Asia Minor (1147). Above all, Conrad revived the Hohenstaufen-Welf feud, which had been started by the Welfs' support of Lothar's can-

implementation of the treaty depended on the restoration of order in Germany.

In 1154 Frederick recognized the claims of his cousin Henry the Lion to Bavaria and granted him the right to invest the bishops of Oldenburg, Ratzeburg, and Mecklenburg. Henry in effect assumed a viceregal position in northern Germany, where he promoted German eastward expansion and built a territorial state in Saxony. In 1156 Frederick compensated his Babenberg uncle, Henry Jasomirgott, for the loss of Bavaria by elevating Austria to the rank of a duchy with extensive authority over lesser nobles.

Frederick's settlement of the Hohenstaufen-Welf feud revealed a key aspect of his German policy: the formation of a small group of princes, who were to be the tenants in chief of the crown and were encouraged to assert their territorial lordship in their spheres of influence. The lay and ecclesiastical princes accomplished this by constructing castles, by forcing lesser nobles to become their vassals or even ministerials, by relying on the ministerials as a counterweight to the nobility, by promoting land clearance and the new religious orders, by founding towns and granting them privileges, and by acquiring the advocacies of the churches located in their domains. Frederick's reorganization of Germany along feudal lines, which was based on an idealized view of the French constitution and was conceptualized in the *Heerschildordnung* (military order of precedence), overlooked the fact that the Capetians ultimately asserted their authority by establishing direct ties with the rear vassals, the group whom Frederick subordinated to the princes.

Adrian IV crowned Frederick as emperor in 1155, but Barbarossa failed to suppress the Roman commune or to proceed against the Normans. The pope was further alarmed by Frederick's first attempts to reassert imperial authority in Lombardy and by the king's initial refusal, at their meeting in Sutri, to hold the stirrup of the pope's horse or to lead it, gestures that could be interpreted as the services of a vassal. The latter incident was another indication that Frederick rejected the curial theory that the empire was a papal fief. Adrian responded by making peace with King William I of Sicily in 1156, a diplomatic reversal that Frederick considered a violation of the Treaty of Constance.

In 1156 Barbarossa married Beatrix, the heiress to the county of Burgundy, in order to create a territorial base for the monarchy in Burgundy. There was another confrontation with the papacy in 1157 at the Diet of Besançon, where Frederick received the homage of the Burgundian magnates. A papal embassy, led by Cardinal Rolando, protested the mistreatment of Eskil, archbishop of Lund, and reminded Frederick of the *beneficia* he had received from the pope. Frederick's chancellor, Rainald of Dassel, who encouraged Frederick in his anticurial policies, translated this ambiguous word as "fiefs," implying that the pope regarded the empire as a papal fief. Frederick and the princes protested, and Adrian eventually settled the dispute by saying that *beneficia* ought to be translated as "favors."

The emperor's second expedition to Italy, in 1158, revived the tension. At the Diet of Roncaglia, Frederick proclaimed that he would resume control of a long list of regalian rights that had been usurped by the Italian communes, unless the holders could prove the legality of their claims. The successful implementation of this decree would have turned Lombardy into a royal province. Milan rebelled, and the pope feared that imperial control of northern Italy would threaten the independence the papacy had gained during the investiture controversy.

The college of cardinals was split at Adrian's death in 1159. The majority elected Cardinal Rolando, the leader of the anti-imperial party, as Pope Alexander III; the minority, with imperial encouragement, chose the antipope Victor IV. While Frederick pretended to be neutral, it was a foregone conclusion that the Council of Pavia, which he summoned to end the schism, would decide in Victor's favor.

For the next two decades Frederick fought Alexander, the Lombard cities, and the kings of Sicily. Most of the German princes, ecclesiastical and lay, backed Barbarossa. Frederick tried to obtain the support of the kings of France and England, but the Western monarchs remained loyal to Alexander. One result of these negotiations was the marriage of Henry the Lion to Matilda, daughter of Henry II of England, which laid the foundation for the subsequent Welf-Plantagenet alliance.

Frederick led his fourth expedition to Italy in 1166 and captured Rome in the summer of 1167. An outbreak of malaria that decimated his army was widely perceived as a divine judgment. The victims included Rainald of Dassel and two of the emperor's cousins: Duke Frederick IV of Swabia, son of Conrad III, and Welf VII, son of Frederick's maternal uncle, Welf VI. The Lombard cities, led by Milan, formed the Lombard League to fight the emperor, who barely escaped from Italy.

This disaster, coupled with Rainald's death, caused Frederick to change his tactics, if not his overall objectives. He led an imperial army to Italy for the fifth time in 1174, and reached a tentative agreement with the Lombards at Montebello in 1175, but the negotiations foundered on Frederick's refusal to make peace with the pope or to recognize the new city of Alessandria as a member of the Lombard League. The Lombards defeated Barbarossa at Legnano on 29 May 1176, and he decided to make peace.

Frederick gained through skillful diplomacy much of what he had failed to achieve by force. He divided his opponents by securing a preliminary agreement with the pope at Anagni. Its terms were modified in the emperor's favor in 1177, in the final Peace of Venice. Frederick was restored to communion and most of the schismatic German bishops retained their offices. The ultimate disposition of the Matildan lands, which Matilda of Tuscany had bequeathed to both the papacy and Henry V, remained unresolved; instead, Frederick was permitted to keep them for fifteen years. In effect this gave Frederick a chance to build a new imperial domain in central Italy. Through the pope's mediation Barbarossa obtained a six-year truce with the Lombards and a fifteen-year armistice with Sicily. The latter was tantamount to a peace treaty.

The long dispute with the Lombards was finally settled in 1183 by the Peace of Constance. Frederick renounced his claims to the regalian rights in exchange for financial compensation. More important, the cities recognized the feudal suzerainty of the empire. All the consuls chosen by the cities were to be invested by the emperor, to whom all major legal disputes could be appealed.

In 1184 Frederick's nineteen-year-old son Henry VI, who had been elected king of the Romans in 1169, was engaged to the thirty-year-old Constance, the aunt of the childless William II of Sicily. While it was not certain that Constance, the heiress presumptive, would eventually inherit the Sicilian throne, the Hohenstaufen may have harbored such hopes; and Henry's marriage sealed the rapprochement with the Norman kingdom.

After the disaster of 1167, Frederick paid more attention to Germany. The deaths of his cousins and the extinction of various noble dynasties provided him with an opportunity to expand the imperial domains in Swabia, Franconia, and Thuringia, and east of the Saale. He promoted the development of such cities as Haguenau, Ulm, and Nuremberg. The imperial ministerials, who supplied most of Frederick's military manpower and reached the height of their influence in the last decades of the twelfth century, were the chief instruments in the execution of this policy. They, along with the ministerials of the princes, gradually formed the new lower nobility that replaced the numerous noble dynasties that died out during the Hohenstaufen period.

This expansion of the Hohenstaufen domains was the chief cause of Frederick's quarrel with Henry the Lion. Their territorial interests clashed at Goslar. When Henry demanded the restoration of Goslar in 1176, in exchange for providing Frederick with military assistance against the Lombards, Frederick refused, and then blamed Henry for his subsequent defeat at Legnano. Henry, in turn, resented Frederick's purchase of the Swabian, Bavarian, and Italian domains of their uncle, Welf VI. Conscious now of the threat that Henry's power posed to the monarchy, Frederick heeded the complaints of the other Saxon princes against Henry, and in complicated legal proceedings Henry was deprived of his duchies and outlawed in 1180. Saxony was divided between the archbishop of Cologne and the Ascanians. Frederick conferred Bavaria, minus Styria, on Otto of Wittelsbach, count-palatine of Bavaria. Styria became a separate duchy, which the Babenbergs acquired in 1192, after the death of Duke Otakar IV. Henry's fall completed the transformation of the stem duchies into territorial entities having a ruler who bore the title of duke, and the formation of a small group of princes who were considered to be the tenants in chief of the crown.

The events of 1180 have often been compared with the destruction of the Angevin empire in 1204, but while Philip II Augustus obtained Normandy, the real victors in 1180 were the German princes, on whose support Frederick depended. It has been argued that German feudal law required Frederick to regrant a vacant fief, the *Leihezwang*. There was no such law, as Frederick II's attempted acquisitions of Austria show; but political reality left Barbarossa with no other choice in 1180, because the princes would have opposed Frederick's own acquisition of Bavaria and Saxony since their addition to the royal domain would have greatly enhanced the power of the monarchy. The fall of Henry the Lion thus revealed both the strength and the weakness of Frederick's position.

Frederick reached the height of his prestige in 1184, at the Diet of Mainz, held in honor of the knighting of his sons. The festivities were the most

481

visible manifestation of the new chivalric culture that had reached Germany from the West. Frederick's policy of building an imperial domain in central Italy created new conflicts with the papacy, but the crisis in the Holy Land after the Battle of Ḥiṭṭīn (1187) made both sides eager for reconciliation. Frederick's death during the Third Crusade was, from the medieval perspective, the crowning glory of a reign that had revived the international standing of the empire.

Henry VI (1190–1197), who had assumed the regency during his father's absence, left for Italy in 1191 to obtain the imperial crown and Constance's Sicilian inheritance. After the death of William II in 1189, a Sicilian national party had placed William's cousin Tancred on the throne with the consent of Pope Clement III, who hoped thus to prevent the unification of Italy under the Hohenstaufen. The summer heat and Henry's illness forced him to abandon the siege of Naples and to return to Germany, which was in a state of turmoil.

Henry the Lion had returned from his English exile and was trying to regain his lost Saxon lands. The emperor's intervention in the disputed episcopal election at Liège deepened the crisis. Henry VI was wrongly suspected of complicity in the murder of the papal candidate, Albert, who was the brother of the duke of Brabant; and the Rhenish princes joined the opposition. The capture of Richard I the Lionhearted, the brother-in-law of Henry the Lion, by Duke Leopold V of Austria in December 1192 saved Henry VI. Leopold turned over his prisoner to the emperor, who used Richard's conflict with his brother John and with Philip II Augustus of France to extort a king's ransom of 150,000 marks. Richard was also required to receive England as a fief from the emperor and to agree to pay an annual tribute of 5,000 pounds before he procured his release in 1194. The reconciliation of the two Henrys was part of the settlement.

Henry VI was now free to take advantage of Tancred's death (1194). The imperial army conquered the Norman kingdom without difficulty, and Henry was crowned king of Sicily on 25 December 1194. The next day Constance gave birth to her only child, the future Frederick II. Henry's eyes were now set on securing the permanent union of Sicily with the empire. He tried to persuade the German princes to accept a hereditary Hohenstaufen monarchy, but they were reluctant to renounce their electoral rights, their most valuable prerogative. Pope Celestine III was even more adamant in his opposition to

a plan that threatened to reduce Rome once again to the status of an imperial bishopric. In the end Henry had to settle for his son's election in December 1196 as king of Germany, an action that appeared to guarantee the personal union of the empire and Sicily for another generation.

Henry had taken the cross in 1195 to pressure the pope and the princes to accept his plans for the transformation of Germany into a hereditary monarchy. His vow may have concealed even greater ambitions. Relations between Barbarossa and the Byzantine emperors had often been tense, and Henry's Norman predecessors in Sicily had long sought to conquer the Eastern Empire. Henry himself enfeoffed the kings of Lesser Armenia and Cyprus with their kingdoms, and his younger brother Philip married Irene, the daughter of the deposed Byzantine emperor, Isaac II Angelos. It is not known whether Henry was really planning to divert the Crusade to Constantinople before he suddenly died on 28 September 1197, but it is certain that the thirty-one-year-old monarch, who had antagonized so many powerful men in his brief reign, was sailing toward shipwreck.

The Hohenstaufen empire collapsed like a house of cards. Constance took Frederick to Sicily, recognized the pope's feudal suzerainty over the kingdom, and, before her own death in 1198, appointed the new pope, Innocent III, as the guardian of her young son. The imperial ministerial, Markward of Anweiler, sought to preserve Hohenstaufen interests in Sicily, but the kingdom plunged into chaos. Innocent seized as many of the disputed territories in central Italy as he could, and thus laid the foundations for the Papal States.

Henry's brother, Philip of Swabia, tried to save the German crown for his nephew, but the machinations of Archbishop Adolf of Cologne forced the Hohenstaufen party to elect Philip as king in March 1198. Adolf had considerable difficulty in finding an antiking, but in June the Welf party finally selected Otto of Brunswick, the second son of Henry the Lion, who had been reared at the court of Richard I of England. Otto's dependence on his uncles, Richard the Lionhearted and John, linked the disputed election to the Plantagenet-Capetian conflict in the West.

Innocent III, however, had the decisive voice. As the weaker candidate, Otto was eager to obtain papal confirmation; but the pope's Italian territorial interests were best served by a prolongation of the discord. Innocent finally decided in Otto's favor in

1201. The pope justified his intervention by arguing that the papacy had transferred the imperial dignity to the Germans, and that as pope he had the right to judge the suitability of the candidate he would crown as emperor. In return, Otto swore to recognize the papal territorial acquisitions and to conduct his relations with Italy and France according to the pope's advice.

Many of the German princes, who were shamelessly bribed by both parties with money, lands, and regalian rights, switched sides repeatedly. At first, fortune appeared to favor Otto, but the collapse of the Angevin empire in 1203–1204 caused many of the princes, including Otto's own brother, to abandon the Welf cause. Innocent was on the verge of recognizing Philip as king when Philip was murdered in a private feud. The Hohenstaufen party then acknowledged Otto as their sovereign.

As the legitimate monarch, Otto IV (1208–1218) behaved no differently than his Hohenstaufen predecessors. He did promise in 1209 to recognize the papal territorial recuperations, to permit free episcopal elections in Germany, and to renounce his rights to the *spolia* (the possessions of a deceased bishop). Otto refused, however, to repeat these concessions at his imperial coronation, as he had sworn, and proceeded to attack Frederick II. The unification of Italy under the Welfs was no more palatable to the pope than Hohenstaufen domination of the peninsula. When Otto crossed the Sicilian border on 18 November 1210, Innocent publicized the emperor's excommunication.

The best way to stop Otto appeared to be the selection of an antiking in Germany, and the pope and Philip Augustus arranged for the election in September 1211 of the only possible candidate, Frederick II. This forced Otto to return home, and Frederick followed him in the autumn of 1212. On 12 July 1213 Frederick issued, with the consent of the princes, the Golden Bull of Eger, in which he ratified the concessions that Otto had made in 1209. The bull legalized Innocent's territorial acquisitions and abrogated the Concordat of Worms. Philip Augustus' defeat of Otto, who had invaded Flanders as an ally of his uncle, John of England, at Bouvines 27 July 1214, decided the German civil war. In a symbolic gesture Philip sent Frederick the golden eagle of the captured imperial standard. Frederick was crowned king of the Germans at Aachen in 1215, and Otto died excommunicate in 1218.

The tragic events of 1197–1215 have often been seen as the decisive turning point in medieval German history. The long battle for the throne destroyed the Hohenstaufen revival of royal authority and left Germany for centuries as the battlefield of foreign powers. The contrast between the political weakness and the cultural vitality of Germany, which was so striking in the age of Goethe, became apparent for the first time in this period.

These years saw the composition of Hartmann von Aue's *Iwein,* Wolfram von Eschenbach's *Parzival,* and Gottfried von Strassburg's *Tristan,* the flowering of Walther von der Vogelweide's lyric genius, the redaction of the *Nibelungenlied,* and the construction of the cathedrals of Bamberg and Naumburg. Ironically, Landgrave Hermann of Thuringia, whose patronage of the arts was celebrated by Richard Wagner in *Tannhäuser,* financed his generosity with the money he gained from his frequent tergiversations in the civil war.

The political chaos threatened, but did not stop, Germany's rapid economic development. Millions of acres were cleared in the Hohenstaufen period—in the Alps and the Black Forest, for instance. Approximately 200 communities were designated as *civitates* in 1200, but by 1400, when the medieval urban network had been completed, there were some 3,500 *civitates* in Germany. While the term *civitas* was applied in Germany to any walled settlement, and not just to the episcopal sees (as was the case in France and England), these statistics speak for themselves. The thirteenth century was the high point in this medieval urbanization. At the end of the century, a Colmar Dominican commented that the two most important Alsatian cities, Basel and Strasbourg, had been insignificant places in 1200 and that such towns as Colmar, Sélestat, Rouffach, and Mulhouse had not existed at all.

The Elbe-Saale, which still formed the eastern border of German settlement at Conrad III's accession, became the central highway of Germany. By 1200 the Germans had colonized Nordalbingia, western Mecklenburg, and the territory between the Saale and the upper Elbe. In the thirteenth century they pushed into eastern Mecklenburg, Pomerania, Brandenburg, Lusatia, Silesia, the Neumark, Prussia, and the Baltic States. Although the German princes employed force in the Wendish crusade of 1147, German eastward expansion, except for the Teutonic Knights' conquest of the eastern Baltic, was generally peaceful. German princes, like the Ascanians in Brandenburg, and Slavic princes, like the Piasts in Silesia, encouraged German monks, peasants, and burghers to settle in their domains. In many cases the Slavic population was granted the more favorable legal status of the German colonists and was gradually Germanized.

Existing settlements were transformed into German cities. The pace of the German advance can be gauged by the so-called foundation dates of various cities or when they were granted a municipal charter, usually modeled after those of Lübeck or Magdeburg: Riga (1201), Rostock (1218), Danzig (now Gdańsk, *ca.* 1224), Wismar (1226), Berlin (1230), Toruń and Chełmno (1233), Stralsund (1234), Szczecin (1243), and Frankfurt an der Oder (1253).

German merchants gradually gained control of much of the trade in the North and Baltic seas. Henry II granted the merchants of Cologne extensive commercial privileges in London in 1157; Henry the Lion procured such rights for the merchants of Lübeck on the island of Gotland in 1161; the Society of German Merchants Traveling to Gotland, the nucleus of the later Hanseatic League, established a *Kontor* (trading station) in Novgorod around 1200; and the Rhenish and Baltic merchants gained common privileges in Bruges in 1252. It was the tragedy of medieval Germany that the monarchy could no longer profit from this vitality.

In 1216 Frederick II promised Innocent III that he would surrender Sicily to his son Henry, who had already been crowned as its king, immediately after his own imperial coronation. The pope hoped thus to prevent the unification of the empire and Sicily under a single monarch. Frederick circumvented this promise by procuring Henry's election as king of Germany in 1220. To obtain the bishops' votes, he promulgated the Confederation with the Ecclesiastical Princes, in which he renounced various regalian rights that the monarchy no longer exercised, and recognized the territorial supremacy (*Landeshoheit*) of the bishops. The privilege did not create the ecclesiastical principalities; it merely legalized their existence. Frederick left for Sicily in 1220 and did not return to Germany for fifteen years. The remaining thirty years of his reign are of only tangential interest to Germany.

Archbishop Engelbert of Cologne (*d.* 1225) served as the regent for Henry VII. Germany remained calm after Pope Gregory IX excommunicated Frederick in 1227 for failing to keep his crusading vow. Only Duke Louis I of Bavaria, who had succeeded Engelbert as regent, was suspected of plotting with the pope against the emperor. The German princes had little to gain from conflict with an absentee ruler; instead, they helped to make peace between pope and emperor in 1230.

Henry had attained his majority, in the meantime, and was eager to excercise his royal authority. He favored the imperial ministerials and burghers, and thus aroused the opposition of the princes. On 1 May 1231 the latter forced him to issue the Statute in Favor of the Princes, which Frederick confirmed in 1232. Like the earlier Confederation with the Ecclesiastical Princes, the statute legalized the existing situation by recognizing the territorial supremacy of the lay princes. It was primarily directed against the cities, which were prohibited, for example, from granting citizenship to the servile dependents of the princes. It is idle to speculate whether it would still have been possible to revive the power of the monarchy with the assistance of the ministerials and burghers, as Henry has been credited with trying; but it is clear that he was too inconsistent in the implementation of such a policy to succeed, and that such a policy was contrary to Frederick's goal of keeping Germany quiet while he tried to conquer the Lombard cities.

Henry was soon at odds with both his father and the pope over their persecution of heretics. The Cathars and Waldensians had made little headway in Germany, but the desire to lead a life of evangelical perfection was strong, especially among women. The church succeeded, on the whole, in channeling such aspirations in orthodox directions in Germany. The friars arrived in Germany around 1220, and by 1300 there were ninety-four Dominican priories, approximately 200 Franciscan friaries, seventy-four Dominican nunneries, and twenty-five houses of Poor Clares.

Misreading the situation, Gregory and Frederick in 1231 launched a campaign against heresy that quickly got out of control. The archbishop of Bremen-Hamburg, for instance, turned his feud with the Stedingers, free peasants who had settled west of the mouth of the Weser and were resisting his attempt to collect tithes and rents from them, into a crusade against heretics. Although the Dominicans were employed as inquisitors, the chief villain was a Premonstratensian, Conrad of Marburg, the former confessor of St. Elizabeth of Hungary. Henry finally intervened, and the campaign came to an abrupt halt after Conrad's murder in 1233. The pope ordered Henry's excommunication, and Frederick planned to go to Germany. To prevent his father from crossing the Alps, Henry committed the unpardonable sin of allying with the Lombards.

Henry obtained the support of the imperial ministerials and a number of bishops, but his revolt collapsed when Frederick appeared in Germany, without an army, in 1235. Henry was deposed and imprisoned for the remainder of his life. At an imperial diet held in Mainz, Frederick ended the Hohenstaufen-Welf feud by turning the alods of Henry the Lion's grandson into the duchy of Brunswick. At the same time the emperor issued a land peace, which prohibited the alienation of the remaining regalian rights and established an imperial justiciar as his permanent judicial representative. Its terms suggest that Frederick may have hoped to revive imperial authority in Germany after he defeated the Lombards.

This became even clearer in Frederick's attempts to acquire Austria and Styria. Duke Frederick II had antagonized his neighbors and subjects; and when he ignored three summonses to appear at the imperial court to respond to their accusations, he was outlawed in 1236 as a contumacious vassal and the emperor took possession of the duchies as vacant imperial fiefs. After Gregory IX excommunicated Frederick for the second time in 1239, he could no longer tolerate the resentment that this increase in the Hohenstaufen domains had caused; and he restored the duchies to the duke. After the childless duke's death in 1246, Frederick extended the administrative structure he had established in northern Italy to the duchies.

At first Frederick's second excommunication had little impact on Germany. Innocent IV aroused an effective opposition in Germany only after the First Council of Lyons deposed the emperor in 1245. The pope ordered the friars to preach a crusade against the Hohenstaufen, appointed papal partisans as bishops, granted dispensations for consanguineous marriages to his supporters, and arranged for the election of two antikings, Landgrave Henry Raspe of Thuringia (1246-1247) and Count William of Holland (1247-1256). They were the creatures of the pope and the Rhenish archbishops. Frederick's son Conrad IV, who had been elected as Henry's successor in 1237, depended on the support of his father-in-law, Duke Otto II of Bavaria. Conrad left Germany after Frederick's death on 13 December 1250. Hohenstaufen rule ended in Germany with Conrad's death in Italy in 1254.

BIBLIOGRAPHY

Geoffrey Barraclough, *The Origins of Modern Germany*, 2nd ed. (1947, repr. 1962); *idem*, ed. and trans., *Mediaeval Germany, 911-1250: Essays by German Historians*, 2 vols. (1938, repr. 1967), and *Eastern and Western Europe in the Middle Ages* (1970); Franz H. Bäuml, *Medieval Civilization in Germany 800-1273* (1969); Friedrich C. Dahlmann and Georg Waitz, *Quellenkunde der deutschen Geschichte*, 10th ed., Hermann Heimpel and Herbert Geuss, eds. (1965-); Bruno Gebhardt, *Handbuch der deutschen Geschichte*, I, 9th ed., Herbert Grundmann, ed. (1973); Karl Hampe, *Germany Under the Salian and Hohenstaufen Emperors*, Ralph Bennett, trans. (1973); Joachim Leuschner, *Germany in the Late Middle Ages*, Sabine MacCormack, trans. (1980); Peter Munz, *Frederick Barbarossa* (1969); James Westfall Thompson, *Feudal Germany*, 2 vols. (1928, repr. 1962); Thomas Curtis Van Cleve, *The Emperor Frederick II of Hohenstaufen* (1972).

JOHN B. FREED

[See also **Adrian IV, Pope; Alexander III, Pope; Austria; Babenberg Family; Bavaria; Frederick I Barbarossa; Frederick II of the Holy Roman Empire, King of Sicily; German Towns; Gregory IX, Pope; Hanseatic League; Heinrich VI; Henry the Lion; Hohenstaufen Dynasty; Innocent III, Pope; Lombard League.**]

GERMANY: 1254-1493. The deaths of Frederick II in 1250 and of his son and heir Conrad IV in 1254 meant not only the removal of the promising Hohenstaufen dynasty from the German throne, but also a period of political confusion that was to last more than two centuries and has sometimes been spoken of as Germany's time of troubles. But the writing of history is a matter of perspective, and depending on where the writer chooses to place the emphasis, the same phenomena reveal signs of either decline or progress. It is true that the institutions of German kingship (the title "emperor" related to the Western empire as a whole; in Germany the emperor was "king") disintegrated, and with them the ability of the monarch to control events. Frederick II had speeded, if not caused, this development by his persistent alienation of royal powers to the nobility, lay and ecclesiastical.

During the interregnum following Conrad's death, the disarray of the monarchy became calamitous. A disputed election in 1257 brought two foreign princes simultaneously to the throne: Richard of Cornwall and Alfonso X of Castile. At the same time the French occupied German territory, and in the south the Swiss began to remove themselves from imperial jurisdiction. The papacy continued its main policy of preventing the creation of a central

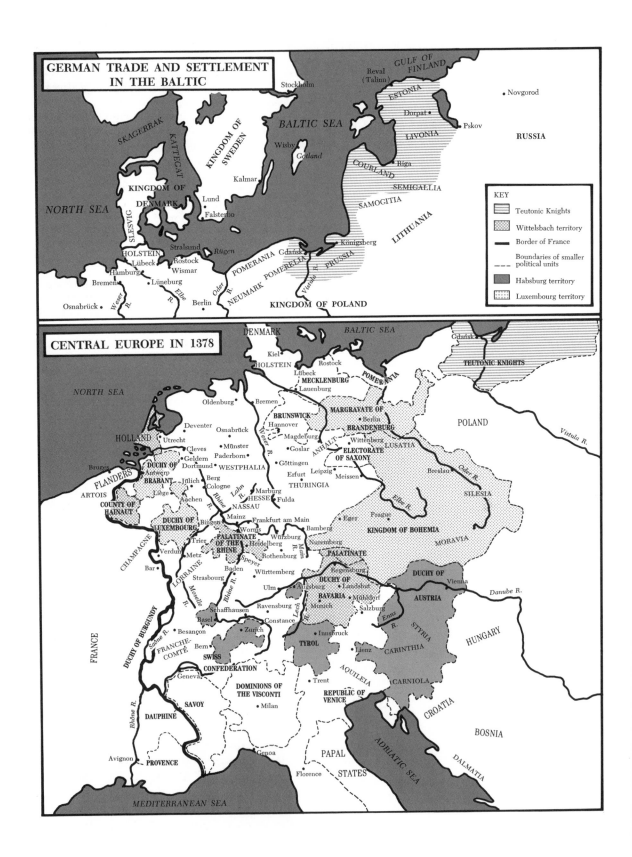

GERMAN TRADE AND SETTLEMENT
IN THE BALTIC

SKAGERRAK

KATTEGAT

KINGDOM OF SWEDEN

BALTIC SEA

GULF OF FINLAND

Stockholm

Reval (Talinn)

ESTONIA

Novgorod

Dorpat

Pskov

LIVONIA

RUSSIA

Wisby

Gotland

Riga

COURLAND

NORTH SEA

Kalmar

SEMIGALLIA

KINGDOM OF DENMARK

Lund

Falsterbo

SAMOGITIA

LITHUANIA

SLESVIG

Stralsund

Rügen

Königsberg

HOLSTEIN

Lübeck

Rostock

Wismar

POMERANIA

Gdansk

PRUSSIA

Hamburg

Lüneburg

NEUMARK POMERELIA

Vistula R.

Bremen

Weser R.

Elbe R.

Berlin

Oder R.

Osnabrück

KINGDOM OF POLAND

KEY

Teutonic Knights

Wittelsbach territory

Border of France

Boundaries of smaller political units

Habsburg territory

Luxembourg territory

CENTRAL EUROPE IN 1378

DENMARK

BALTIC SEA

Kiel

HOLSTEIN

Rostock

Gdansk

NORTH SEA

Lübeck

MECKLENBURG

Lauenburg

POMERANIA

TEUTONIC KNIGHTS

Oldenburg

Bremen

BRUNSWICK

MARGRAVATE OF

Berlin

POLAND

Vistula R.

HOLLAND

Deventer

Osnabrück

Hannover

BRANDENBURG

Utrecht

Weser R.

Magdeburg

ANHALT

Wittenberg

LUSATIA

Cleves

Münster

Goslar

ELECTORATE

Breslau

Oder R.

Bruges

Geldern

Paderborn

WESTPHALIA

Göttingen

OF SAXONY

Antwerp

Dortmund

Leipzig

Meissen

SILESIA

FLANDERS

DUCHY OF

Berg

THURINGIA

Elbe R.

Liège

Cologne

Erfurt

ARTOIS

BRABANT

Jülich

Lohn R.

Marburg

Fulda

Eger

Prague

Aachen

HESSE

COUNTY OF

Rhine R.

Mainz

Frankfurt am Main

Bamberg

KINGDOM OF BOHEMIA

HAINAUT

NASSAU

Bingen

Worms

Nuremberg

MORAVIA

DUCHY OF

Trier

Würzburg

Main R.

LUXEMBOURG

PALATINATE

Heidelberg

PALATINATE

CHAMPAGNE

Verdun

Metz

OF THE RHINE

Rothenburg

DUCHY OF

Speyer

Regensburg

Vienna

Bar

LORRAINE

Baden

Württemberg

Landshut

AUSTRIA

Moselle R.

Strasbourg

Ulm

DUCHY OF

Danube R.

Rhine R.

Ravensburg

Augsburg

Mühldorf

Schaffhausen

Constance

Lech R.

BAVARIA

Munich

Salzburg

STYRIA

Basel

Zurich

Innsbruck

FRANCE

Saône R.

Besançon

FRANCHE-COMTÉ

Bern

SWISS

TYROL

Lienz

CARINTHIA

HUNGARY

DUCHY OF BURGUNDY

CONFEDERATION

AQUILEIA

CARNIOLA

Geneva

DOMINIONS OF

Trent

CROATIA

SAVOY

THE VISCONTI

REPUBLIC OF

Rhône R.

DAUPHINÉ

Milan

VENICE

BOSNIA

ADRIATIC SEA

DALMATIA

Avignon

PROVENCE

Genoa

PAPAL

Florence

STATES

MEDITERRANEAN SEA

power of substance in the empire; to this end it supported Charles of Anjou's seizure of the Hohenstaufen possessions in southern Italy and Sicily, and the elimination by military defeat of Frederick's natural son Manfred in 1266 and of his sixteen-year-old grandson Conradin in 1268. Inside Germany, politically conscious patriots lamented the loss of the international prestige of the empire and the decay of law and order in a Germany lacking a constitutional center and a national sense of direction.

During these decades of confusion, the idea of empire moved from its more or less solid base in Roman history and Christian eschatology to a purely visionary prophetic anticipation of a "new Frederick," who was to appear providentially in the hour of greatest need. The Kyffhäuser legend was the most evocative of these prophecies: Frederick II slumbering deep inside the Thuringian mountain until summoned by God to redeem his nation from internal chaos and foreign domination.

At the same time, a shift of viewpoint yields a very different picture. By far the most important feature of German history in the later Middle Ages is the coming into being of powerful, centrally directed dynastic states in the empire's princely territories, and of large and flourishing cities with prosperous economies and complex societies. For territories such as Bavaria, Austria, Saxony, and Brandenburg, and for city-states like Nuremberg, Augsburg, Hamburg, and Lübeck, the want of a strong monarchical presence in the country meant license to build virtually autonomous polities within their borders. The constitutional history of Germany may be seen, therefore, as moving from the "empire" toward these newly emancipated political units that, as constituent estates, were to become a far more effective guarantee of the survival of the Holy Roman Empire than the posturings of its imperial figureheads.

In the period from 1200 to 1300 the German population increased substantially (following a European trend); this fact explains not only the movement to settle lands along the eastern frontiers during these years, but also the expansion of agricultural areas in the older regions of the country, the significant growth of urban populations, and the foundation of new cities (such as Danzig, now Gdańsk; Berlin; and Königsberg), towns, and villages. In the eastern parts of Germany, silver and copper mines were opened and older ones were enlarged. Meanwhile, a new political force was emerging in the Electoral College, the seven members of which (archbishops of Mainz, Trier, and Cologne;

count-palatine of the Rhine; duke of Saxony; margrave of Brandenburg; and king of Bohemia) were prompted by the political breakdown attendant upon the double election of 1257 to play a leading role in the administration of the kingdom. Such developments as these give German history in the late thirteenth century a generally integrative thrust, and recent scholarship has emphasized this, in distinction to the older nationalistic historiography, which tended to stress the void left by the absence of a strong monarchy.

The election of Rudolf of Habsburg to the German throne in 1273 is a milestone in the nationalistic version of German history because it is thought to have brought the interregnum to an end and to have set the course of German history once again on its proper direction toward unity and strength. In fact, the choice of the first of the Habsburg dynasts did little of the kind. It brought to the throne the head of a vastly ambitious, though relatively new, noble family with ancestral lands on the upper Rhine and the capacity and vision to work diligently for the enlargement of its private might. Rudolf's most notable success was his acquisition of the duchies of Austria, Styria, Carniola, and Carinthia as a result of his victory over King Ottokar of Bohemia (Battle of Dürnkrut, on the Marchfeld, 1278), who had refused to accept the new ruler's authority and was therefore declared forfeit of his possessions. The investment of Rudolf's sons, Albert and Rudolf, with the titles to these conquered areas was the beginning of the *Hausmacht*—the dynastic might—of the house of Habsburg.

But by the end of Rudolf's reign in 1291, the seven electors, in whose hands the choice of a successor now lay, had become so suspicious of Habsburg intentions that they selected not Rudolf's heir, Albert, but Count Adolf of Nassau, a minor noble without dynastic means of wielding power. He was deposed in 1298, when it became clear that he was using his position, as well as liberal subsidies supplied by the kings of France and England, to build a landed power base. In his place the electors raised to the throne Rudolf's son Albert, who showed himself willing to acknowledge the powers of the electors and other leading princes by confirming their privileges.

Albert I's brief reign—he was assassinated by a group including a disgruntled nephew in 1308—was marked by the Battle of Göllheim against the deposed Adolf (who, far from accepting his fate, fought back vigorously), and by unsuccessful attempts to inhibit the development of independent territorial power in his kingdom's principalities. Overshadowing these domestic events was the figure of King Philip IV of France, who employed his wealth and prestige in a bid for domination of German affairs. There was even a plan to make his brother a candidate for election to the German and imperial thrones—a sign of how distant developments in Germany still were from any sort of national objective.

The new German king in 1308, however, was not the French contender, Charles of Valois, but Henry of Luxembourg, whose two most significant undertakings as Henry VII were the acquisition of the kingdom of Bohemia by the marriage of his son John to Elizabeth, the daughter of King Wenceslas (1310), and an ambitious Italian campaign, beginning in 1310, that attempted to revive the imperial designs of the Hohenstaufen. Henry had been called to Italy by Ghibelline and White Guelph supporters there, including the poet Dante, whose ideas concerning the long-awaited restoration of the glorious empire of the ancient Romans were set forth in his political treatise *De monarchia*.

But the independent northern Italian city-states saw things differently. They soon put a stop to Henry's attempt to reactivate the imperial project. He managed to have himself crowned emperor at Rome in 1312 by a few nobles and dissident cardinals, but he died of a fever a year later and the Italian adventure remained a passing episode in the history of the medieval empire. Upon his death the country was treated to another double election (1314) followed by civil war: a Habsburg contender, Frederick the Fair, was favored by some of the electors, while others supported Louis, duke of Bavaria, who was the candidate of the Luxembourg party. The Battle of Mühldorf in 1322 decided the issue for the Bavarian, who ascended the throne as Louis IV.

The reign that followed this victory was scarcely uncontested and peaceful. Louis's great adversary, Pope John XXII (1316–1334), was a Frenchman, a formidable defender of the papacy's ensconcement at Avignon under French protection, a resourceful jurist, and one of the great power politicians in the history of the medieval church. Fearing a repetition of the Italian venture of the preceding reign, the pope refused to recognize Louis as king (hence Louis "the Bavarian"), excommunicated him in 1324, and ruthlessly used the Inquisition and the interdict as weapons against the king's party. Louis, in turn, branded the pope a heretic, in which charge he was vigorously supported by the Franciscan spirituals, who

saw in the Avignon papacy, and in John XXII in particular, the very nadir of the church's fall into corruption.

When the pope placed all Germany under interdict, Louis decided upon a new Italian campaign as a counterthrust. In 1327 he crossed the Alps, demanding the imperial crown not only as successor to Charlemagne but also in the name of the Italian people, of whose wishes Louis now designated himself the instrument. Arguments for this position—a new and revolutionary one in the political thought of the time—were furnished by Marsilius of Padua, Louis's leading theorist and propagandist, whose *Defensor pacis* (1324) cast the emperor in the role of defender of peace and justice against a rapacious church. With Marsilius at his side, the king proceeded to Rome, where an antipapal noble, Sciarra Colonna, crowned him in the name of the Roman populace.

A more concrete result of this political turbulence was the "electoral union" formed by the seven German electors in 1338. They met at Rhens (Rense) and there decided to take measures to protect the empire from foreign, especially papal, troublemaking. Their most important pronouncement declared a properly elected German king to be a truly installed sovereign, without papal confirmation. The emperor extended this principle with his *Licet juris* of the same year, a rule that proclaimed the "imperial dignity and power bestowed by God alone"; a ruler chosen by the electors "is by that very election true king and Roman emperor." The law was meant to end papal interference in German politics. But, as so often in the history of the medieval empire, programmatic announcements had little bearing on actuality.

Having offended the three ecclesiastical electors by dissolving the marriage of Margaret Maultasch and John Henry of Luxembourg, in violation of canon law, Louis was removed from his throne (1346) in favor of the Luxembourg candidate, Charles, son of King John of Bohemia, who was also the favorite of the papacy. Crowned Charles IV in 1347, he proceeded to Rome for his coronation (1355) but otherwise did little to satisfy the "imperial" obligations of his title. Instead he worked systematically and successfully on building a territorial base for his own house and on making his court at Prague one of the leading cultural centers in Europe. Among the other achievements credited to him in this connection is the foundation of the University of Prague in 1348.

Charles also occupies a prominent place in the constitutional history of the empire. The Golden

Bull (from the emperor's golden seal, *bulla*), issued by him in 1356 after prolonged deliberations with the estates, established an orderly procedure for electing a German king by a majority of the seven electors (thus codifying a process customary since the late thirteenth century) in a fixed place, the city of Frankfurt am Main, and according to a precisely delineated ceremonial. The Golden Bull also declared the electors' territories to be indivisible, the electoral title being tied not to the person of the elector but to his land, which was to be passed on according to the rule of primogeniture. Within their own borders the electors were made, by the terms of this bull, practically autonomous rulers. An attack on them was treated as the crime of lèse majesté.

It is commonly said that the Golden Bull of 1356 set the German *Reich* on its path to oligarchy and dualism: the former because the political process was now dominated by an elite of immensely privileged ecclesiastical and lay princes, the latter because national policy now rested in the scales of a fluctuating balance between emperor and estates led by the electors. But the encouragement given to territorial independence was not limited to the lands of the electors. It went on apace in nearly all the empire's principalities and cities, and it forms one of the salient themes in the political history of Germany in the later Middle Ages.

Charles IV was followed in 1378 by his son Wenceslas, an undistinguished monarch whom the electors deposed in 1400 in favor of the similarly unremarkable Count-palatine Rupert (himself one of the electors), who died in 1410. The crown then reverted to the Luxembourg dynasty in the person of Wenceslas' brother Sigismund, who was king of Hungary. Sigismund owes his prominent place in European history to the fact that his reign (1410–1437) coincided with the rise of the conciliar movement, of which he acted as a kind of sponsor. As the driving force behind the Council of Constance (1414–1418), Sigismund came to be associated with progressive tendencies in ecclesiastical and secular politics. In the matter of the *causa unionis*—reuniting the church after its long schism—and in the matter of the *causa reformationis*—improving the condition and image of the church in head as well as members—the council and the conciliar movement generated much hope for the general amelioration of religion and society. For reasons not well known, these hopes came to be associated with the person of Sigismund. Concrete proposals for political, social, and ecclesiastical reforms were attributed to him,

and the most widely read reform tract of the time, the *Reformatio Sigismundi* (written *ca.* 1439, first printed 1476), bore his name in its title, though he was clearly not its author.

In actual accomplishments, however, Sigismund's reign was unimpressive. In Bohemia, where he became king in 1419, he was unable to put an end to the Hussite movement, whose leader, John Hus, had been put to death as a heretic in 1415 by the Council of Constance. Perhaps his most significant act was to designate as successor his son-in-law, Albert II of Habsburg, who was installed on the thrones of Germany and Bohemia-Hungary in 1438, after Sigismund's death in 1437. Though lasting just over a year, Albert's reign was notable for inaugurating the unbroken succession of Habsburg kings and emperors. The Habsburg line lasted from 1438 to the end of the empire in 1806, and in Austria until the close of World War I.

In 1440 the estates chose Albert's cousin Frederick, duke of Styria, who as Frederick III reigned for over half a century of critically important events in the empire and in the domains of the Habsburgs. Frederick showed little interest in, and had little effect upon, imperial affairs. The groundswell for the reform of life and society in Germany—another of the outstanding political issues of German history in the late Middle Ages—received no impetus or support from him, though scarcely a meeting of the *Reichstag* (imperial diet) passed without presentation by the estates of proposals for securing the internal peace and political stability of the empire. Frederick also relinquished what little independence had been gained by the German church in the aftermath of the councils of Constance and Basel. By the terms of the Concordat of Vienna (1448), negotiated between emperor and papacy, the latter took back all the revenues and privileges it had lost in the course of the conciliar movement. From the vantage point of the virulent anti-Roman agitation that characterized the fifteenth century in Germany and led up to the Reformation of the early sixteenth century, this concordat was a significant, though at the time unrecognized, turn of events.

In the private fortunes of Frederick's dynasty, meanwhile, an important shift occurred during his reign. The Habsburg connection with Bohemia and Hungary broke apart as national figures ascended the thrones of these countries against the claims of the nominal Habsburg ruler, Ladislas, posthumous son of Albert II. In 1458, following Ladislas' death, George of Poděbrady, leader of the Utraquist party, became king of Bohemia and was recognized as such by Frederick. In the same year Matthias Corvinus, son of Ladislas' regent, took the crown of Hungary, and in 1469 acquired the throne of Bohemia as well. Frederick, who had been crowned emperor in 1452 (the last emperor to be so acknowledged in Rome), tried to block the tide of Hungarian conquests, but his war against Corvinus ended disastrously as the Hungarian ruler took Vienna in 1485.

To compensate for these losses (later to be recouped by a treaty of inheritance negotiated by Frederick's son, Maximilian, in 1491) the emperor succeeded in tying his house to the duchy of Burgundy, which, under Duke Philip the Good, had emerged as a major political, economic, and cultural presence in the west of Europe, but under Philip's successor, Charles the Bold, overtaxed its resources in a number of destructive conflicts with France, the empire, and the Swiss Confederation. Under these circumstances the marriage of Maximilian to Mary, the heiress of Burgundy, took place. It was a fateful union. When Charles the Bold was killed at the Battle of Nancy in 1477, the Habsburgs fell heir to the congeries of lands precariously grouped in the Burgundian state. But this inheritance meant nothing until it was conquered. It took Maximilian years of costly and bloody campaigning to win acceptance in his wife's domains. More portentously, the Burgundian legacy brought the Habsburgs, and with them the empire, into direct confrontation with France, which had, under Louis XI, advanced to the position of premier power in Europe. Friction occurred wherever the two countries had conflicting interests, from the Netherlands to Italy, and frequently friction resulted in war. This was the situation into which Maximilian came when he took his father's place on the latter's death in 1493.

Within the empire the largely dynastic ambitions of its crowned heads, and their essentially illusory pursuit of the hallowed imperial idea, left a power vacuum that came to be filled by territorial rulers and urban magistrates. As early as the twelfth and thirteenth centuries, important regalian rights had been slowly gathered into the hands of the leading nobles of the stem duchies such as Bavaria (the Wittelsbachs) and Saxony (the Wettins), and of newly created regions such as Brandenburg. This process reached its apogee during the fifteenth century as in each of the many principalities of the empire (seven electoral, about seventy ecclesiastical, and more than twenty-five secular territories) a position of *Landes-*

herrschaft (territorial sovereignty) was created for the reigning prince (duke, landgrave, margrave). This power brought him exclusive rights in his own realm over high justice, coinage, tolls on road and river traffic, and administration.

By consolidating and extending older prerogatives at the expense of lesser nobles and local bodies, the *Fürst* or *princeps* brought into being a kind of state consisting of bureaucratically organized central and local governments, a relatively orderly financial service, a system of law courts, and some control over the church. In each land a *Landesordnung* (territorial constitution) and a codification of civil and criminal laws concluded the process of state building. These enactments reflected the interests of the territorial estates, which in the fourteenth century gained the right to approve tax legislation nearly everywhere. As in the empire at large, therefore, politics in the territorial principalities was a process of deliberations between prince and estates ("dualism"), each party avid for expansion of its own powers and ingenious in devising ways of accomplishing this objective.

At the same time, the empire's eighty or so major cities were able to organize themselves into virtually autonomous political structures. Urban chronicles from the thirteenth, fourteenth, and fifteenth centuries supply the details of this process: the winning by purchase and conquest of a "territory" in the countryside beyond the gates, acquisition of the right to hold markets and issue coins, successive circles of walls to give protection and to accommodate a growing population swelled by immigration, the appearance of splendid public buildings and private dwellings, the evolution of an urban government closely reflecting the city's economic base and trade patterns, the emergence of a communal ethos symbolized by an annual oath pledging each citizen to accept and perform his civic duties. Favored by the emperors, who depended on loans furnished by urban bankers, cities prospered under constitutional privileges renewed in reign after reign. For greater strength they turned to mutual assistance, forming leagues and associations such as the Swabian League of cities in the fourteenth century and the older Hansa. These groups made the city a major factor in the empire's politics and diplomacy. Visitors to Germany (such as the Italian churchman Enea Silvio Piccolomini, later Pope Pius II) praised Cologne, Nuremberg, Augsburg, Lübeck, and Frankfurt as splendid and renowned places. They agreed that whatever the weakness of the empire as a whole, the great metropolises of Germany displayed strength, wealth, and promise in abundance.

BIBLIOGRAPHY

Willy Andreas, *Deutschland vor der Reformation*, 6th ed. (1959); Theo Ludwig Goerliz, *Rudolf von Habsburg* (1961); Ernst Kantorowicz, *Frederick the Second, 1194–1250*, E. O. Lorimer, trans. (1931, repr. 1957); Joachim Leuschner, *Germany in the Late Middle Ages*, Sabine MacCormack, trans. (1980); Hans Friedrich Rosenfeld, *Deutsche Kultur im Spätmittelalter 1250–1500* (1978); Georg Wilhelm Sante, ed., *Geschichte der deutschen Länder* (1964–1971); Ernst Schubert, *König und Reich* (1979); Ferdinand Seibt, *Karl IV* (1978); Lawrence D. Stokes, *Medieval and Reformation Germany: . . . A Select Bibliography* (1972); Bernhard Töpfer *et al., Vom staufischen Imperium bis zum Hausmachtkönigtum (1122–1314)* (1976); Hermann Wiesfleder, *Kaiser Maximilian I*, I, *1459–1593* (1971).

Gerald Strauss

[See also **Conciliar Theory; Elections, Royal; Germany: Electors; Germany: Stem Duchies; Interdict; John XXII, Pope; Marsilius of (Marsiglio) Padua; Maximilian I, Emperor; Philip IV the Fair.**]

GERMANY: ELECTORS. In the late twelfth and the thirteenth centuries the right to choose the German sovereign became the prerogative of a restricted group of princes called *electores* or *Kurfürsten*. In the fourteenth and fifteenth centuries the identity of these princes was set and their privileges reinforced so as to make them a corporation that embodied many of the residual public powers of the empire.

The perennial conflicts between empire and papacy in the eleventh and twelfth centuries and the failure of clear dynastic continuity had the result of stressing the electoral over the hereditary principle in the German monarchy. Canonical standards for the election procedure also increasingly came to be applied, as a result both of the participation of ecclesiastics and of the desire to forestall papal intervention. In a society in which primogeniture was not an accepted practice in ordinary property inheritance and the partition of kingdoms was actively opposed by subjects, the acclamation of one of the several possible rulers had been part of the process for making a king since Carolingian times. The future ruler was acclaimed by "the people," which in East Fran-

cia meant the assembled magnates of one or more of the German duchies. In the twelfth century the application of canonical law to the election process had the result of severely limiting the number of participants to a few members of the class of imperial princes. It was believed that the nobility as a whole elected candidates by a *Wahl*, but that the designation for elevation *(Kur)* could be performed only by a small group of the highest nobility of the empire.

The exact identity of the electors became a matter of continual controversy and special pleading; some argued that the electors should in some manner represent the old tribal duchies, while others held that the office of the emperor, as protector of the Roman church, required that he be chosen only by prelates. The last serious attempt to suppress the election of the German monarch in favor of a hereditary succession on the French or English model was made by Henry VI. Each of the factious elections following Henry VI's death in 1198 brought with it a contentious redefinition of the electoral college.

In his *Sachsenspiegel*, Eike von Repgowe described the electors about 1224 as consisting of the Rhenish archbishops of Mainz, Cologne, and Trier, the count-palatine of the Rhine, the duke of Saxony, the margrave of Brandenburg, and the king of Bohemia. He defined the lay electors in terms of their ceremonial offices at court, since the count-palatine of the Rhine was lord steward, the duke of Saxony lord marshal, the margrave of Brandenburg lord chamberlain, and the king of Bohemia lord butler. Even here the seven princes were seen as capable only of designating a person already acclaimed by the high nobility of the realm ("sollen nicht kiesen nach irme mutwillen; sunder wen swene die vorsten unde alle zu kuninge irwelen, den sollen se aller erst bi namen keisen"; *Sachsenspiegel, Landrecht*, III, 57). Eike doubted that the king of Bohemia could participate in the election, since he was not a German. The reputation of the *Sachsenspiegel* played a major role in establishing the definitive list of electors.

The rights of the three Rhenish archbishops were generally conceded, though doing so excluded several other archbishops. The count-palatine of the Rhine was the chief judge of the royal court, and this made him the ranking lay noble in Germany. The designation of the duke of Saxony, the margrave of Brandenburg, and the king of Bohemia arose from the eastward shift of leadership in Germany around 1200. The performance of their ceremonial offices by the lay electors was a feature of court celebrations, especially following the coronation of the king at Aachen.

The factional elections of the thirteenth century confirmed the persistent ideal, if not the functioning reality, of the seven electors. Papal opinions on the dual elections of 1257 summarized the development of the concept of the college of electors through that time; and the interregnum of 1257–1273 saw the theory of election discussed and elaborated in publicist writings. The election of Rudolf of Habsburg in 1273 followed the guidelines established by papal and canonist opinion; and to avoid giving cause for complaint, the electors designated one of their number to make the *Kur* on behalf of the entire college, an *electio per unum* in keeping with canonical models. During his subsequent reign, Rudolf I sought to invoke the electors as a supreme consultative body, soliciting letters of approval *(Willebriefe)* for alterations in public law. In 1298 the electors deposed Adolf of Nassau; and there were several abortive attempts to set the electors up as a regularly meeting council. The electors came to function on their own, without the preliminary acclamation of a candidate by the nobility demanded by the *Sachsenspiegel:* they had become true creators of the new monarch.

In the late Middle Ages efforts were made to balance the great powers of electing and deposing monarchs with individual and corporate responsibilities. Perennial disputes over the legitimacy of specific elections combined with resentment against papal intervention in German political affairs to precipitate the clarification of electoral procedure. In the wake of the conflict between Pope John XXII and Emperor Louis IV the Bavarian, the electors in 1338 issued a group proclamation, at Rhens, declaring the legal autonomy of a duly elected German monarch. By the middle of the fourteenth century there were also conflicting claims over the possession of electoral rights by specific secular princes; the Wittelsbach family had provided in 1329 that the electoral right should alternate between the Bavarian and palatine branches of the family, and there were disputes over who exercised the electoral powers of Saxony and Brandenburg following partitions of those principalities.

The electoral college was permanently set by the promulgation of the Golden Bull by Emperor Charles IV at Nuremberg on 10 January 1356 and amended at Metz on 25 December 1356. It was the foundation of German constitutional law until the dissolution of the empire in 1806. It specified the procedure for calling and holding the election at Frankfurt am Main, to be followed by the coronation of the Roman king at Aachen. Clauses of the Golden Bull sought to anticipate almost any eventuality, in order to assure an unassailable election. The electors were given new titles and powers. The archbishops, for example, were all named archchancellors of parts of the empire: Mainz for Germany, Cologne for Italy, and Trier for the kingdom of Arles. The archbishop of Mainz, the primate of Germany, was responsible for assembling the electors, but the first vote was cast by the archbishop of Trier. Four votes had to be cast for one candidate in order for that person to be elected, but any majority vote would be proclaimed unanimous.

Secular electors were granted the right of primogeniture and entail for the electoral principality *(Kurland)*. In actual practice this *Kurland* could be a small, designated portion of the principality, so partitions of territories ruled by an elector were not prevented. Electors were granted full regalian rights over coining gold and silver, mining, tolls, and Jews; and secular electors were advised to educate their heirs in the languages of the empire: German, Latin, Italian, and Czech. Electors were to suffer no appeal or evocation to the court of the king save in cases of denial of justice, which made the electors autonomous in legal matters. The count-palatine was to be the regent of the empire during a vacancy, save in areas under Saxon law, where the duke of Saxony would act. Charles IV designated the duke of Saxony-Wittenberg as the Saxon elector. If there should be no heirs in a secular electorate, the monarch could name the new elector, save for the kingdom of Bohemia, which could elect its own ruler.

The Golden Bull foresaw annual meetings of electors with the monarch to discuss matters of public importance, but this plan was never carried out. The Golden Bull regarded a duly elected and crowned German monarch as possessing the full powers of his office without further confirmation or coronation by the pope. (The papacy would not recognize the right of a Roman king to call himself emperor-elect until 1508.)

Although the electors did not meet annually, as the Golden Bull demanded, they constituted a potentially powerful force in the German constitution. In 1400 King Wenceslas of Luxembourg was deposed by the electors; and in 1424 the electors formed an electoral alliance *(Kurverein)* to assert the right of cogovernance with Emperor Sigismund. The electoral college was frequently the focus of efforts to create imperial institutions not dependent on the person of the monarch, most notably in the late 1430's, during the last years of the reign of Emperor Sigismund.

The imperial reform movement led by Archbishop Berthold von Henneberg of Mainz tried to reinforce the rights and privileges of electors over the monarch, as well as over the other estates. Berthold created a true imperial chancery apart from the Habsburg monarch's court; and his plan to create autonomous institutions paid for by a direct tax on individual wealth had the goal of shifting the burden of imperial government from the princes to the population as a whole. The electors became one of the three chambers of the imperial diet, and they named members to the imperial chamber court (Reichskammergericht) in the reform program adopted at Worms in 1495. Since the plan for general direct taxation, the common penny (gemeiner Pfennig), fell through because of the strident opposition of the towns, the taxes to pay for the common institutions of the empire came from the quota list (Matrikel) paid by the princes and towns; the electors were expected to pay more than other princes.

The electors, particularly the Rhenish ones (Mainz, Cologne, Trier, count-palatine), were in the forefront of institutionalizing their principalities, and the Rhenish electors occasionally banded together to pursue common economic projects. The most important of these was the coining of the Rhenish gold guilder (gulden) in 1386 and afterward; it remained the standard German gold currency into the sixteenth century.

The fate of the secular electoral principalities was similar to that of ordinary principalities in the empire in the later Middle Ages, but the possession of the electoral right made their control a matter of general political interest. The count-palatine of the Rhine was a Hohenstaufen cadet through 1214, when the countship was bestowed on a member of the Wittelsbach family. The Golden Bull confirmed that the palatine title adhered to the Rhenish territory with its center at Alzey, later at Heidelberg. The precise location of the Kurland of Saxony led to disputes between the Ascanian dukes at Wittenberg and Lauenburg, but Charles IV fixed the title at Wittenberg. When the Ascanians died out in 1422, the title was bestowed on the Wettiner margrave of Meissen. In 1485 the Wettiners partitioned their holdings, bestowing Wittenberg and the electoral title on the Ernestine line, where it remained until transferred to

the Albertine line in 1547. Brandenburg experienced frequent changes of dynasty in the late Middle Ages after the demise of the Ascanians there in 1320: the Wittelsbachs ruled there with considerable trouble from 1324 to 1373, then the house of Luxembourg from 1373 to 1411; the Hohenzollern were invested with the electorate at the Council of Constance in 1415. Bohemia had its own national history, with the native Přemyslid dynasty ruling through 1306, then the house of Luxembourg from 1306 to 1457, followed by a series of Slavic princes, most notably George of Poděbrady (1458–1471), before the Habsburgs established themselves there in 1526.

In the later fifteenth century there were several mythic explanations for the foundation of the college of electors, but the version most generally accepted held that Pope Gregory V had established it on the death of Otto III in 1002. To most observers in the late Middle Ages, the notion of the German ruler as a king chosen by a regal college of ecclesiastical and lay princes was a special privilege of the German nation and a treasured guarantee of imperial liberties.

BIBLIOGRAPHY

Charles C. Bayley, *The Formation of the German College of Electors in the Mid-Thirteenth Century* (1949); Winfried Becker, *Der Kurfürstenrat* (1973); Wolfgang Fritz, *Die goldene Bulle Karls IV. vom Jahre 1356* (1972); Mario Krammer, *Das Kurfürstenkolleg von seinen Anfängen bis zum Zusammenschluss im Renser Kurverein des Jahres 1338* (1913); Martin Lintzel, *Die Entstehung des Kurfürstenkollegs* (1952, repr. 1967); Heinrich Mitteis, *Die deutsche Königswahl*, 2nd ed. (1944, repr. 1981); Konrad Müller, *Die goldene Bulle Kaiser Karls IV., 1356* (1970); Steven Rowan, "Imperial Taxes and German Politics in the Fifteenth Century: An Outline," in *Central European History*, 13 (1980); Georg Wilhelm Sante, ed., *Geschichte der deutschen Länder. "Territorien-Ploetz,"* I (1964); Gerald Strauss, ed., *Pre-Reformation Germany* (1972), 73–135, 136–161; Karl Zeumer, *Die goldene Bulle Kaiser Karls IV.* (1908); Eduard Ziehen, *Mittelrhein und Reich im Zeitalter der Reichsreform*, 2 vols. (1934–1937).

STEVEN ROWAN

[See also **Eike von Repgowe; Germany: 1138–1254; Germany: 1254–1493; Sachsenspiegel.**]

GERMANY: IDEA OF EMPIRE. The idea of empire is ancient and medieval; its roots are both mythological and historical. While most fully developed in Germany and of the greatest significance to the history of that country, it is a European phenomenon affecting at one time or another every state with ambitions of conquest and hegemony. Compounded of remembered events from the Roman past, deep-seated but elusive religious beliefs, and urgent psychic needs common to men and women everywhere, it grew in the course of the medieval centuries into an ideological force of great consequence in politics and culture, spending itself only gradually in the seventeenth and eighteenth centuries.

The term "empire" is from *imperium*, Latin for "command and the power to issue it," as well as "the area subjected to this power." The German term is *Reich*, related to Latin *regnum*: "rule, government over country and people," which in the Middle Ages meant "kingly rule." From early medieval times, *imperium* and *Reich* were taken as practically synonymous. They were also universalized to signify "worldwide rule," though the extent and limits of the "world" to which this claim related varied considerably from moment to moment. The constant theme was the reference back to imperial Rome, where from the days of Augustus *imperium* had signified "empire." The *Reich* was the *Kaiserreich* (*Kaiser* from Caesar, the paradigmatic Roman ruler); the *imperium* was the *imperium romanum* which, according to the historical theory prevailing throughout the Christian Middle Ages, was expected to last to the end of time. The medieval (German) empire was therefore the successor to, and continuation of, the ancient Roman Empire, the authority and sway of which were guaranteed by Scriptural prophecy to endure until the return of Christ (Dan. 2:31–45).

Since the tenth century a crowned emperor tended to style himself *imperator Romanorum,* while a German sovereign not yet crowned emperor was known as the "Roman king." In the time of the Hohenstaufen dynasty (eleventh through thirteenth centuries), the adjective "holy" was added to "empire," to reflect the claim of a *sacrum imperium* as a divinely instituted ruling authority independent of church and pope and to offer ideological support to emperors engaged in a struggle for power with the *sancta ecclesia.* Thus "Holy Roman Empire" (*sacrum romanum imperium*), a title that endured even when, drastically reduced in area during the late Middle Ages, the empire was further qualified (with a touch of national pride) to be "of the German nation." As the *Heilige römische Reich deutscher Nation,* the empire and the imperial idea persevered

until their official dissolution in the so-called *Reichsdeputationshauptschluss* of 1806.

While the *imperium romanum* of antiquity rested on military conquest and legal fiat, the medieval *Reich* justified its existence with a complex theory of empire. The parts of this theory were assembled in the course of several centuries, and emphasis among them shifted frequently according to political need. Its essential elements were as follows. As the last in the cycle of empires, the *Reich* had taken over from the Romans the rule of the civilized world and the claim to the whole of it. Since its establishment by Augustus, who unwittingly prepared the way for the Pax Christi, and its subsequent Christianization by Constantine, the empire was the stage on which the drama of sacred history was played. Its emperor held authority—symbolized by the worldly sword and the imperial orb said to contain soil from the four corners of the earth—directly from God. His title and power were unique in the world: as there is one God in heaven, so there must be one supreme ruler on earth. In his role as God's secular deputy, the emperor represented the essential unity of Christendom and acted as the chief guardian of church and faith. His highest duty was the achievement and preservation of universal peace and order. In times of trouble, particularly, hopes for a *Friedenskaiser,* a peacebringing emperor, rose high.

This theory, stated most grandiosely by Dante in his *De monarchia (ca.* 1315), led at every point to tensions and conflicts with political competitors inside and outside the empire and, most dramatically, with the emperors' most tenacious rivals for supremacy in the western world, the popes. To a very large extent the history of the medieval empire, and therefore of the imperial idea, is the history of these tensions.

The medieval western empire officially began in Rome on Christmas day of the year 800 when Pope Leo III crowned Charles, king of the Franks—called Charles the Great or Charlemagne—as *a Deo coronatus magnus et pacificus imperator romanum gubernans imperium* (great and peace-bringing emperor crowned by God and governing the Roman Empire). This act, and the title bestowed upon the Frankish monarch, were fraught with significance for the later history of the imperial idea. By 800 Charles had vastly extended his original domains. His kingdom included the lands conquered from the Saxons, the realm of the Lombards in northern and central Italy (from 775 Charles was *rex Francorum et Langobardorum atque patricius Romanorum*), Bavaria in southern Germany, and the border regions wrested from the Avars and the Moors. The mightiest sovereign in the western part of the former Roman Empire, Charles represented a rising power with which the papacy found it prudent to make common cause. Eager to establish his ties to the political realm on a rational and secure basis, the pope decided to shift his allegiance from the distant and declining eastern empire centered on Constantinople to the new Germanic power in the west. It is still a matter of controversy whether coronation and title were the pope's idea or the king's. In any case, Charles found the honor acceptable and ruled thenceforth as both Frankish-Lombard king and Roman emperor.

The union of the two titles lasted for a few generations after Charles's death in 814. But by the tenth century the territorial divisions common in Germanic dynastic custom had reduced the imperial title, and the idea of empire, to insignificance. From this condition they were redeemed in 962 by Otto I, a Saxon who had followed his father in replacing the Frankish rulers on the throne of Germany. Crowned German king in Aachen, a city inseparably associated with Charlemagne's place as sovereign of the Germanic kingdom, Otto made his bid for the imperial title by conquests in the east and successful campaigns in Italy. Despite his resumption of the Carolingian tradition, however, his empire, when the title to it was bestowed on him in St. Peter's Basilica by Pope John XII, was of a very different nature from Charlemagne's. Not only was his kingdom—the only sure source of his real power—much smaller in extent and significance than that of the Frankish ruler; his title was also linked inextricably to the designs of the papacy. There was no immediate disadvantage to this connection. In fact, during the reign of Otto's successor Otto III (crowned 996), empire and papacy worked in harmony on a policy acclaimed in both camps as a *renovatio imperii Romanorum*. This triumphant sense of regeneration became an important ingredient of the idea of empire. As vision, hope, and obligation, it guided (or, as its critics said, deflected) the foreign and domestic politics of succeeding emperors down to the late sixteenth century.

Otto's plan was for a restoration of the empire to its ancient glory, and to this end he prepared to establish his capital in Rome, where Pope Silvester II (the distinguished French scholar Gerbert of Auril-

lac) was ready to join him in the work of renewal. But these plans came to very little, and in the reigns of emperors of the succeeding dynasty, the Hohenstaufen, the union of empire and papacy broke apart—with disastrous consequences for both. The investiture controversy of the eleventh and twelfth centuries—the classic form of church-state conflict in Europe—was a time of chronic instability for the empire and of Pyrrhic victories for the papacy. Frederick I Barbarossa (1122–1190) attempted to reduce his crown's dependence on the popes by legitimizing the empire as an autonomous divine institution (thus *sacrum imperium*) and by developing the Roman law as a source of independent authority for the political order and its rulers.

As imperial law, or *Kaiserrecht,* the Roman law (in its codification achieved under Justinian) was now employed to define and advance the rights and powers of German emperors who claimed direct descent, and therefore legitimacy, from the ancient Caesars. (In the style of late Roman emperors, Frederick I gave his son and successor Henry VI the title "Caesar.") Partially to counteract these devices, the papacy advanced the theory of the *translatio imperii* according to which it had been the popes' exclusive prerogative to transfer the imperial crown from the Greeks and Romans first to the king of the Franks and subsequently to other rulers. This right was now claimed by the popes in perpetuity as a means of preserving a controlling voice in the selection of emperors. In response, certain German writers of the thirteenth century contended that Germans owned the empire by right and by God's will: Germany has the *imperium,* they argued, Italy the *sacerdotium,* France the *studium*—that is, the University of Paris. This assertion was much popularized in Germany, and much attacked elsewhere, in the succeeding centuries.

In the confrontations between Frederick II (Barbarossa's grandson, 1194–1250) and the popes of his time (Innocent III, Honorius III, Gregory IX, Innocent IV) the medieval church-empire conflict reached its culmination. At the time of the emperor's death in 1250, it looked as though the imperial idea had fallen victim to its combined foes and rivals. If one may distinguish between the "real" elements of which the idea was composed—political institutions and legal authority—and "unreal" or "irrational" ones—historical tradition, religious sanctions, hopes, and ideological aspirations—one can conclude that it is the latter that kept the idea of empire alive during the thirteenth and fourteenth centuries and made possible its striking resurgence in the fifteenth. The emperor Sigismund (crowned 1433) in particular became associated with some of the most fervent hopes defining "empire" as a realm of peace, order, and justice. Believed to be the precursor of a *Friedenskaiser* and priest-king named Friedrich (*Fried-Reich,* "realm of peace" or "rich in peace"), Sigismund was linked with most of the grand aspirations of this age of church councils and secular reform projects.

From the late thirteenth century on, a number of "false Fredericks"—pretenders to the legacy of Frederick/Friedrich II—had appeared all over the empire. With the prophecies and promises associated with these claimants, the idea of empire assumes a utopian character. The most famous expression of this, the so-called *Reformation of the Emperor Sigismund*—a sweeping reform tract universally attributed to the emperor but actually written about 1439, some two years after his death—popularized via many printings after 1476 the notions of pacification, order, and justice as the empire's chief mission. The "priest-king" who will come after Sigismund "shall bring peace to the empire and all its lands and regions. . . . His work will go speedily. Though stern at first, his rule will grow mild; he may appear strange to us but will become familiar. Eternal life lies before us. Whoever craves it must join his cause." In these concluding words of the *Reformatio Sigismundi,* the empire's role as the preparer of the way for the Second Coming is clearly indicated.

In the reign of the Habsburg Maximilian I (1493–1519), the imperial idea was again expressed in its universal aspects as that of a worldwide realm based on conquest and hegemony; however, Maximilian failed in nearly all his military and political undertakings and did not even succeed in securing the imperial crown in Rome, taking instead the title *electus Romanorum imperator* (Roman emperor-elect) in 1508. By then the most effective antagonists to imperial rule in Europe were the national sovereigns and the much-strengthened rulers of princely territories in Germany, none of whom was disposed to accept imperial authority in more than an honorific sense, and each of whom claimed, on the basis of an ancient Roman maxim, to be "emperor in his own realm." On the other hand, Maximilian created a far more solid power base for the use of his successors than any previous emperor had done: the dynastic might of the House of Habsburg. When his grandson Charles V came to the German throne in 1519,

he was personal ruler over so large and varied an assemblage of domains that the title "emperor" began once more to ring with a solid sound.

On the universal interests inherent in this title Charles proposed to act. His objective was, in large part at least, the realization of the traditional imperial goal of a world order of unity and peace. Seeing himself as the successor to Charlemagne in this endeavor, Charles took seriously his obligation to church and faith (a position that decisively determined his stand on the Lutheran Reformation), while he strove at the same time to allow his own dynasty to benefit by his undertakings. According to Karl Brandi, his conscious aim was "to leave unimpaired the unity of a world-empire, orthodox in religion and firmly in the hands of his Burgundian dynasty."

But the sixteenth century was too late (or too "modern") a time in which to realize a plan that struck even contemporaries as anachronistic. An empire that consisted of scattered and disparate units, in each of which political particularism was a stronger incentive than a sense of cohesion, proved unsuitable to the fulfillment of an imperial vision born in an age prior to the emergence of such divisive forces as the Reformation, incipient nationalism, and the strains of early capitalism. In the century of religious wars beginning near the end of Charles's reign, the empire was only one among several belligerent forces, and by then it had in the eyes of allies and foes alike been linked inseparably with Roman Catholicism on the one hand and with the dynastic ambitions of the Habsburgs on the other. Toward the end of the seventeenth century the empire was generally scorned or mocked. Samuel Pufendorf's famous seventeenth-century designation of it as a "monstrosity" (meaning that its political character defied classification) came to be widely accepted by theorists and statesmen. Reduced to mere rhetoric and propaganda, the imperial idea seemed played out.

Still, the Holy Roman Empire lasted into the early nineteenth century, and recent scholarship has tried to explain why. Concentrating on functional aspects of the imperial system, historians now tend to say that the empire made possible the survival and coexistence of scores of small political units that would otherwise have been absorbed by expanding states inside and outside the empire. By providing its more than 300 member states and thousands of small urban communities with essential guarantees and services, the empire of the late seventeenth and eighteenth centuries operated—effectively in its way—as a protector of local traditions and peculiarities and a bulwark against the kind of modernizing change always unwelcome to holders of ancient rights and privileges. In its final phase, therefore, the empire stood for tolerance of heterogeneity and of conglomeration. Its guiding spirit was the idea of a permissive political and social milieu that promised to preserve established institutions, hierarchies, values, and conventions. It was therefore not as a rival for world dominance that the Holy Roman Empire succumbed to Napoleon in 1806. Its end came in acknowledgment of the incongruity of its "medieval" character in an age of Enlightenment, revolution, and a new kind of imperialism.

BIBLIOGRAPHY

Geoffrey Barraclough, *The Origins of Modern Germany* (1947), and *The Medieval Empire: Idea and Reality* (1950); Gerhard Benecke, *Society and Politics in Germany 1500–1750* (1974); Karl Brandi, *The Emperor Charles V*, Cicely V. Wedgwood, trans. (1939); John G. Gagliardo, *Reich and Nation: The Holy Roman Empire as Idea and Reality, 1763–1806* (1980); Friedrich Heer, *The Holy Roman Empire*, Janet Sondheimer, trans. (1968); Ernst Kantorowicz, *Frederick the Second 1194–1250*, Emily O. Lorimer, trans. (1931); Ulrich Nonn, "Heiliges römisches Reich deutscher Nation: Zum Nationenbegriff im 15. Jahrhundert," in *Zeitschrift für historische Forschung*, 9 (1982); James A. Vann and Steven W. Rowan, eds., *The Old Reich* (1974); Mack Walker, *Johann Jakob Moser and the Holy Roman Empire of the German Nation* (1981); Jonathan W. Zophy, ed., *The Holy Roman Empire: A Dictionary Handbook* (1980).

GERALD STRAUSS

[See also **Charlemagne; Charles V of France; Frederick I Barbarossa; Frederick II of the Holy Roman Empire, King of Sicily; Otto I the Great; Otto III; Silvester II, Pope.**]

GERMANY: IMPERIAL KNIGHTS. The collapse of the Hohenstaufen imperial system in the mid thirteenth century left a large number of properties, scattered throughout the empire, in the hands of minor nobles and ministerials who had served as local administrators. These crown properties were concentrated in the dissolved duchy of Franconia, in the Hohenstaufen duchy of Swabia, along the Rhine, and in the region around Goslar in the north. In the period after 1257 those nonurban former crown properties that were not absorbed into expanding

principalities strove to assert their identities as distinct estates of the imperial knights. These counts, barons, knights, and squires compensated for the smallness of their holdings through a strong corporate identity and a readiness to band together to protect their rights against attacks from either princes or towns. Many petty nobles within nascent territorial principalities sought to claim the rights and autonomy of imperial knights and achieve recognition as "immediate to the empire" (*Reichsunmittelbar*). The struggles to escape from territorial structures were especially marked in the electorate of Trier and the duchy of Bavaria, but the imperial knights were a model for the aspirations of small nobles throughout Germany.

Rebellions by knights were a regular feature of German life as late as the 1520's. Territorial states that faltered were liable to lose whole regions with noble properties, as when the Kraichgau nobles successfully withdrew from the palatinate. Although the imperial knights were never to obtain formal membership in the imperial diet, they enjoyed the right of standing immediately under the jurisdiction of the sovereign. As a social group the imperial knights provided a disproportionate number of prelates, canons, administrators, judges, and jurists to German public life in the fifteenth century, which meant that their views and prejudices were shared by agents of other authorities in the empire.

Imperial knights were regarded as strong advocates of the ideals of the empire, but this perception of imperial loyalty was born late, when the obsolescence of the knights as warriors reduced them to a chauvinistic gentry. The knights asserted their privilege of feud as a means of asserting their rights until the end of the fifteenth century, and they always opposed paying taxes, claiming that they owed the emperor nothing but military service. Only in the sixteenth century did they come to accept the notion of *subsidia caritativa* (voluntary contributions) in lieu of taxes. In the fifteenth century and after, imperial knights played an important role in the writing and reading of both German and neo-Latin literature.

One response of the independent knights to the demise of the strong imperial state and the rise of territorial governments was the formation of defensive military leagues, most of them contracted for a short term. In the 1370's, however, these leagues began to take on a more lasting character in opposition to large-scale town leagues. In Swabia and Hesse the leagues of knights protested the practice by towns of soliciting knights' subjects as citizens and of asserting economic and legal control over the surrounding countryside *(Bannmeile)*. In 1408, in response to the Swiss challenge in the Lake Constance area at the time of the Appenzell war, knights formed the Swabian Society of the Shield of St. George *(Ritterschaft und Gesellschaft mit St. Jörgenschild in Schwaben)*. Based on the traditions of earlier leagues, it became the dominant association of free knights in the German southwest, though it was frequently disbanded and reorganized. Emperor Sigismund tried to encourage such associations to join with urban leagues to preserve the public peace; and since it was held that such associations had been banned by the Golden Bull of 1356, Sigismund issued a privilege on 13 September 1422 permitting the knights of Germany to organize. In 1431 he added a law for the protection of the imperial nobility from urban harassment.

In 1488 King Maximilian fostered an alliance between the knights of St. George and the towns and princes of Swabia to form the Swabian League. Maximilian humored the imperial knights extensively, though he also subverted their organizations by forcing them to accept members they thought unsuitable. The ban on private warfare proclaimed at Worms in 1495 criminalized the chief tool of noble self-defense, the feud, and forced the knights to rely normally on imperial courts for protection from their enemies. The Swabian League continued to be the basis of public authority in the German southwest until the 1530's, but the imperial knights lost interest when it came to include the very princes whose aggressiveness had led them to band together in the first place: Württemberg and Bavaria. In the fifteenth century, as the mounted knight became less significant in war, there was a tendency for the courts, barons, and lords to join the princes and become petty members of the imperial diet with collective votes *(Curiatstimmen)*. Thus only the smaller noble proprietors continued to participate in associations for imperial knights.

In the mid sixteenth century Charles V encouraged the formation of a separate national corporation of imperial knights set apart from the imperial circles *(Kreise)* that operated as the ordinary regional jurisdictions for the other estates. Although this national league of knights, divided into the circles of Swabia, Franconia, and Rhineland, was believed to be of great antiquity, it was in fact a product of Habsburg policy in the mid sixteenth century. Its effect was to preserve those imperial knights who had managed to survive the ravages of the later Mid-

dle Ages by granting them the full protection of the empire.

BIBLIOGRAPHY

Joseph Bergmann, "Der St. Georgsritterorden vom Jahre 1468–1579," in *Mitteilungen der K. K. Central Commission zur Erforschung und Erhaltung der Baudenkmäler,* **13** (1869); Arno Borst, ed., *Das Rittertum* (1976); Karl Bosl, *Die Reichsministerialität der Salier und Staufer,* 2 pts. (1950–1951); Hellfried Brandl, *Kaiser Maximilian I. und die Ritterschaft* (1970); Otto Brunner, "Friede und Fehde," in *Land und Herrschaft,* 5th ed. (1965); J. S. Burgermeister, *Reichsritterschaftliche Corpus-juris oder Codex diplomaticus* (1707); O. Eberbach, *Die deutsche Reichsritterschaft in ihrer staatsrechtlich-politischen Entwicklung von den Anfängen bis zum Jahre 1495* (1913); William R. Hitchcock, *The Background of the Knights' Revolt, 1522–1523* (1958); Marlene J. LeGates, "The Knights and the Problems of Political Organizing in Sixteenth-century Germany," in *Central European History,* 7 (1974); Hermann Mau, *Die Rittergesellschaften mit St. Jörgenschild in Schwaben,* I (1941); K. O. Müller, "Zur wirtschaftliche Lage des schwäbischen Adels am Ausgang des Mittelalters," in *Zeitschrift für württembergische Landesgeschichte,* 3 (1939); H. Obenaus, *Recht und Verfassung der Gesellschaft mit St. Jörgenschild in Schwaben* (1961); G. Pfeiffer, "Studien zur Geschichte der fränkischen Reichsritterschaft," in *Jahrbuch für fränkische Landesforschung,* 22 (1962); Volker Press, *Karl V., König Ferdinand und die Entstehung der Reichsritterschaft* (1976); Carl Heinrich Eusebius Roth von Schreckenstein, *Die Ritterwürde und der Ritterstand* (1886); Aloys Schulte, *Der Adel und die deutsche Kirche im Mittelalter* (1910).

STEVEN ROWAN

[See also **Class Structure; Germany: 1254–1493; Knights and Knight Service; Swabia, Duchy of.**]

GERMANY: PRINCIPALITIES. German public life in the High and late Middle Ages was marked by a shift from the old Carolingian structure of royal, ducal, and comital authority based on personal ties to one in which noble princes ruled over incipient states of varying size that were defined territorially. These principalities did not encompass all of German society by any means, since a large number of towns, religious houses, knights, and rural communes managed to assert autonomy as imperial entities. Within these principalities, however, urban and rural communities of every sort could be found.

The principality rested in the first instance on the prince, who was a propertied noble or prelate with a title to hierarchical distinction. In 1180 Frederick I Barbarossa recognized the existence of a class of imperial princes *(Reichsfürstenstand)* consisting of those who held a flag fief *(Fähnlehen)* directly from the hand of the sovereign—the ordinary method of enfeoffing royal vassals was through a scepter. The prince was thus defined by his special feudal relation with the ruler and through his possession of a fief of a special quality. It was believed that such a fief could be held by the ruler for only a year and a day before being granted out again *(Leihezwang)*. This practice has been improperly singled out as a major cause of the diminution of royal power, since in fact rulers could divide properties or invest them in members of their own families. One of the greatest of the fiefs, the duchy of Swabia, ceased to exist with the demise of the Hohenstaufen line in 1268, during an interregnum.

Another definition of the hierarchy of German society is found in the *Heerschild* or military shield *(herscild, clipeus militaris),* a common concept in the twelfth century that achieved classic form in the *Sachsenspiegel* (ca. 1224). The *Heerschild* was a feudal pyramid on the top of which was the king, who could not be a vassal. Below him were the ecclesiastical princes in the second rank and the secular princes in the third, both holding of the ruler. It was believed that the sovereign bestowed a shield with an insignia on those who held directly of him. The fourth rank contained barons and counts, who could hold of a prince or princes and who could in turn enfeoff those below them. At the bottom of this pyramid, which could have as many as seven ranks, stood the *einschildig,* those who could serve but could not in turn enfeoff. Whatever reality the system ever had, by the fourteenth century it survived only as a weapon of prejudice against the descendants of ministerials.

Although the imperial diet *(Reichstag)* did not achieve formal organization until 1495 with the recess of the Diet of Worms, the princes were already hierarchically organized in the thirteenth century. The electors were a clearly distinct group consisting of the three Rhenish archbishops of Mainz, Cologne, and Trier, and four secular princes: the count-palatine of the Rhine, the duke of Saxony, the margrave of Brandenburg, and the king of Bohemia. Their rights and privileges were outlined in the Golden Bull issued by Emperor Charles IV in 1356. Briefly, the Golden Bull guaranteed lay electors primogeniture, and at least a portion of the electoral principality was entailed. The elector enjoyed immunity from most interventions and appeals by imperial courts, and he disposed of full regalian rights within his principality.

The secular and ecclesiastical princes formed a special group of the highest nobles of the empire, but their precise function apart from the rest of the nobility is hard to define; eventually, the princes had to share the second chamber of the imperial diet with all but the most petty of the nobility. All bishops of the empire were regarded as princes because of their investiture with the regalia at the hands of the ruler. Abbots of a number of the oldest religious houses were also styled as princes. The secular lords who were clearly princes in the twelfth century were the dukes of Bavaria, Austria, Styria, Carinthia, Lorraine, and Brabant; the margraves of Meissen and Lusatia; the landgraves of Thuringia; and the counts of Anhalt. After 1180 most new princes were created by formal elevation through royal charter and enfeoffment following the approval of the assembled princes. This was the case with the elevation of the counts of Namur (1188), the creation of the dukes of Brunswick (1235), and the elevation of the landgraves of Hesse (1292). The creation of the duchy of Brunswick shows the effect of the creation of the princely fief with the greatest clarity: the Welf lord gave up all his lands and rights, mostly alodial, and received them back from the hand of Emperor Frederick II as a single fief.

In the fourteenth century the dukes of Jülich, Geldern, Mecklenburg, Silesia, Luxembourg, and Berg became princes, as did the margraves of Bar and the counts of Savoy. In the fifteenth century the duchies of Cleves, Holstein, and Württemberg were created, and various French nobles were recognized as princes of the empire either in their own right or as a result of holding a princely fief. Some princes appeared as such without known elevations, such as the dukes of Landsberg, Breslau, and Pomerania, the margraves of Baden, the counts of Henneberg, and the castellans *(Burggrafen)* of Nuremberg. In most cases the princes took the title of duke, margrave, or landgrave, but there were a few "princely counts" *(gefürstete Grafen).*

These princely fiefs could be divided between heirs, or several could be united in one hand, without the need to seek the permission of the sovereign. Only the electoral dignity passed as an indivisible unit, in the same manner as the English peerage. According to an opinion issued by Frederick II at Würzburg in 1216, the sale or alienation of a principality could take place only with the permission of the ruler and the assembled princes and nobles of the empire. The only formal elevations of ecclesiastics to the rank of prince after the late twelfth century were for the grand masters of the Teutonic Knights and the Knights of St. John, and for the provost of Berchtesgaden.

The expansion of the princely class helped to make the group incoherent as a continuing body: elevation to the rank of prince became the ordinary sign that a family had made a success of its pursuit of power, but no family was removed from the rank because of poverty. In the fifteenth century the body that came to represent the empire against the sovereign was neither the princes nor the electors but the corporation of all the substantial estates, the imperial diet. In that century the counts, barons, and lords separated themselves from the petty imperial knights and joined with the princes in the diet, usually satisfying themselves with group votes (*Curiatstimmen*) rather than the individual votes (*Virilstimmen*) held by the princes. In 1521 the definitive tax-quota list named the 7 electors, 50 bishops and archbishops, 31 secular princes, 78 prelates, and 131 counts and petty lords. This number embraced all of the principalities and territorial lordships, leaving only the small holdings of the imperial knights unrepresented.

In the twelfth century a duke or margrave was regarded as free to function as an autonomous lord in developing territories, and this autonomy moved down the noble hierarchy during the subsequent century. The use of feudal relationships to replace the old public offices of the Carolingian and Ottonian eras made the positions of duke, margrave, and count units of property that moved like any other piece of feudal property. The concept that the owning of land bestowed quasi-public authority on its owner (*Grundherrschaft*) combined with the process of feudalization of old public offices to make the erection of territorial lordships possible. Ecclesiastical principalities had the added advantage of immunities from external jurisdiction granted by early German monarchs. When the prelates then became virtually independent of the monarch's control following the investiture conflict, the result was a mass of self-consciously autonomous clerical principalities running along the *Pfaffengasse* (priests' alley) of the Rhine, Main, and Moselle valleys.

The Welf dukes of Bavaria and Saxony had used the traditional "tribal" duchy as a basis for building their own powers through founding towns and villages and clearing land in the middle years of the twelfth century. Henry the Lion's fall in 1180 is usually taken as the beginning of the development of strictly territorial lordships, but that event was more symbolic of changes that were already well under way than significant in itself. Princes located on the eastern frontier built entire new regional structures using immigrants recruited from the interior through offers of free land and immunities from service or taxation. The Hohenstaufens used their ducal powers in Swabia to construct a dense net of castles and small towns controlled by petty nobles and ministerials. They also used their powers to construct imperial territories of smaller scale in Franconia and in the Harz Mountains. The dukes of Zähringen, whose ducal rank derived from an Italian lordship, pursued a career of aggrandizement through clearance and rational settlement in the Black Forest and the Jura, oblivious to the titular regional overlords there. In most cases the traditional counties (*Gaue*) had ceased to function under the impact of population growth in the twelfth century, but those princes seeking to consolidate authority eventually obtained at least the comital rights for their area.

The relatively archaic structure of German public life had begun to produce serious strains as early as the eleventh century, and the increased sensitivity to demands for order led the monarchy and the church to promote the creation of associations to promote public peace (*Landfriede*) in certain areas. The laws to promote public order tended to increase the authority of princely courts and to downgrade the older, more cumbersome courts in the hands of petty nobles, townsmen, or peasants. The public peace courts were empowered to use summary procedures against dangerous persons, which made them more attractive places to bring complaints. The imperial public peace proclaimed at Mainz in 1235 marked the almost complete subordination of the peace mechanism to the princes. After the collapse of the Hohenstaufen state, public peace associations were more regional in scope and developed as a result of bargaining between leagues representing various groups, such as townsmen on the one side and princes on the other. Although all justice derived in theory from the sovereign, the ruler had no regularly constituted court of appeal. Voluntary associations for the public peace occasionally even took on a conspiratorial form, as was the case with the secret *Feme* courts of Westphalia in the fourteenth and fifteenth centuries.

The last major Hohenstaufen ruler in Germany, Emperor Frederick II, recognized the rising power of the German princes by issuing numerous privileges to rid them of irritating competition with imperial agents or with townsmen. The *Confoederatio cum principibus ecclesiasticis* (alliance with the ecclesiastical princes), issued at Frankfurt am Main on 26 April 1220, and the *Statutum in favorem principum* (Statute in favor of the princes), issued at Cividale in May 1232, were the great charters of princely liberties, since they freed the princes from interference in their established rights by agents of the monarch. These two privileges recognized and codified existing realities and placed the sovereign on the side of territorial development. Frederick also assisted in creating unitary lordships through such acts as the elevation of Brunswick to a duchy and principality in 1235 and through the bestowal of sovereign rights on the frontier crusader state of the Teutonic Knights in the Golden Bull of Rimini in 1226. The sovereign's actions were still capable of disrupting the evolution of a particular principality, however, as when Frederick himself dismembered the lordship of the dukes of Zähringen following the death of the last member of the direct male line in 1218.

With the collapse of the Hohenstaufen state in the 1250's, principalities were virtually the only force for public government in Germany. Smaller crown properties such as towns and properties of petty nobles sought to defend themselves against interference through the formation of leagues and alliances. After royal authority was reestablished in 1273, the king might pawn crown properties (including imperial towns) to princes who had cash to lend or needed to be compensated for other services. The king used his office to foster the building of one or more principalities owned by his family, a *Hausmacht*, which remained with the family rather than with the empire. There was thus no difference in principle between the lordship of a king or emperor and one belonging to any other prince.

The entire period from the twelfth to the thirteenth century saw a basic shift in the center of political action in German central Europe toward the east, due both to the shift of population and to the fact that there was a greater potential for uniform development outside the areas of early settlement. The Rhineland, Franconia, and Swabia remained honeycombed with small lordships that were mixed with a variety of imperial entities; and it was politically more difficult to achieve the shift of local princely administration from castle districts run by knights or ministerials to uniform administrative regions, called *Ämter,* run by paid administrators. Expansion of a principality in the west could often take place only through the pawning or purchasing of communities with long-established rights that gave the prince little chance to intervene or increase his income above the traditional level.

The closing of the external and internal frontiers of settlement in Germany in the late thirteenth century meant the end of quick profits from developing virgin territories. In the middle years of the fourteenth century, a collapse of population levels and food prices meant that the profits of land ownership were dramatically depressed. The almost complete reversal of the previous relations between ownership and labor dramatically strained the society, especially in Germany, where relations between social groups had come to be expressed through independent state entities.

In the latter half of the century there was a three-way struggle among the great lords, the petty nobles, and the federated independent towns. The terms of dispute between nobles and towns had already been spelled out in the thirteenth century: nobles resented towns gaining the allegiance of peasant subjects by making them *Pfahlbürger* (external citizens), and they feared competition with lordly monopolies through the erection of competing markets, roads, and mints. Although the Swabian town league was defeated by an alliance of the higher nobles in 1389, arguments between urban and princely representatives continued to be a regular feature of imperial diets during the Hussite wars of the 1420's and 1430's. Towns within weak principalities and lordships often pursued independent policies, particularly in the Hanseatic north, where only a few of the member communities were imperial towns. Most episcopal titular towns became free cities (as distinct from imperial cities) before the thirteenth century, and bishops tended to take up residence in smaller, peripheral towns where the prince did not have to compete with a strong commune.

When princely governments recovered the initiative in the fifteenth century, they sought to reassert control over proprietary urban governments. Despite such pressure, some proprietary towns were able to develop and maintain their own subject territories, contract alliances, and communicate as equals with the imperial towns in the region: Freiburg im Breisgau, for example, was able to control its internal affairs long after becoming a Habsburg town in 1368. The knights living in territorial principalities also tried to emulate the imperial knights in neighboring regions by demanding rights of self-government or total separation from the territory. Much of the progress made in the building of territories in the later fifteenth century came through tightening internal controls, not through actual expansion beyond established borders.

The advantages of expansion and consolidation were often negated by princely mismanagement or by repeated partitions between heirs. The long-term operation of divisible feudal tenure made the use of the feudal bond as a basis for a community of public life increasingly absurd, and groups other than the feudal nobility came to be expected to contribute taxes and participate in government tasks. These tensions resulted in two major institutions typical of the later Middle Ages, estate organization of political life *(Ständestaat)* in the principality itself, and the dynastic ordinance of succession *(Hausordnung)* within the princely house. Both of these institutions formalized and regularized previously private and haphazard developments.

Political estate organization is the middle stage between the feudal state of the High Middle Ages and the bureaucratic or absolutist state of the seventeenth century. Its legal basis was the concept that the levy of extraordinary taxes or the alteration of laws had to be approved by those affected, as embodied in a medieval legal proverb, *Quod omnes tangit, ab omnibus approbetur* (That which touches all must be approved by all). In German public law the precedent was a judgment, pronounced by King Henry VII at Worms on 1 May 1231, that held that neither princes nor others could issue decrees or new laws without the prior consent of the better and greater persons of the territory ("ut neque principes neque alii quilibet constitutiones vel nova iura facere possint, nisi meliorum et maiorum terre consensus primibus habeatur").

The result of this rule was that any expansion of taxation or of the taxpaying population brought with it an extension of the politically active class, so that the old feudal council of the prince soon became a true assembly of estates. The dissipation of the prince's landed endowment made him increasingly dependent on subjects for funds. Revenues came to be centralized and monetarized only at a late date because the usual pattern had been to assign particular sources of income to certain expenditures in perpetuity. Simply unraveling these resources and obligations was a Herculean task for early bureaucrats. Beyond this, the performance of public business in any premodern state called for a great deal of voluntary and unpaid service to undertake surveys or collect taxes, so that any expansion of political activity beyond the feudal class brought with it an alteration of administrative personnel as well. Few German principalities were large or complex enough to have estate organizations consisting of more than two classes of subjects, and members were drawn from a limited number of groups: prelates, petty nobles, towns, administrative officers, or peasant communities. In some territorial principalities, one or two estates might act on behalf of the entire land, though within a particular estate perhaps only a few communities held the franchise for all in that category.

Conflicts between lords and their subjects in the late Middle Ages arose from a fundamental difference in goals and needs. A prince ruled over a complex of territories and lands that were usually perceived by him simply as a source of income, a means to the enjoyment of a style of life in keeping with his status in society. The court of the prince was thus as much a setting for consumption as it was an instrument of governance. The friends and companions of the prince served in groups of greater or lesser formality to get the prince's work done, but formal administrative institutions emerged slowly because of the relatively small size of most estates. The group gathered around the prince might be called a privy council *(Geheimrat),* and there would be a chancery and a treasury of sorts at an early date. But a specialized appeals court usually emerged only after the medieval period. In many cases the prince assigned the functions of an appeals court to the law faculty of a university within his jurisdiction, and this gave a special incentive for the foundation of institutions of higher education in the period after 1345. Since the principality was looked upon by the prince as a source of money, he was often ready to sell, exchange, pawn, or buy properties or entire principalities simply in order to raise cash, without any regard for the needs or desires of his subjects.

The basic unit of the principality was the *Land* or territorial community, a region that had its own law and territorial tradition. The *Land* was the intermediary between the lord and his subjects and the focus of true state life in the principality, since there would rarely be a coherent dialogue between the prince and his subjects on the level of the prince's court. Estates expressed themselves most clearly in the diet *(Landtag* or *Landschaft)* of the territory, where the prince or his representative encountered the *Land* manifested as a group of persons and corporations.

The diet was not the limit of estate participation in political life, since the concept of estates permeated every aspect of premodern administration as well, acting as a perennial corrective to the proprietary interests of the prince. Princes deeply in debt might make concessions to their estates, including estate control over the chancery or privy council. The assessment and collection of taxes granted by estate assemblies legally remained in estate hands, and standing committees managed the state debt and acted as bankers to the rural population. In times of dynastic crisis, estates often insisted on membership in the regency council. The estates represented the interests of the community itself rather than those of the prince, so that they tended to demand a pacific foreign policy, low public expenditures, and restrained public conduct by everyone, including the prince. Estates were earnestly concerned when there was a chance for the partition of the principality, and they cringed when the prince was thought to be squandering his endowment.

Another response to the challenge of instability in late-medieval principalities was the promulgation of dynastic succession ordinances *(Hausordnungen)*. The traditional law of inheritance countenanced the equal division of principalities between male heirs; and the practice of placing younger sons in church livings could not prevent divisions that could eventually produce states too weak to support a princely lifestyle. Further, the increasingly vocal interests of the *Land* made permanent partition of any of the basic building blocks of the principality very hard to carry out. Large dynasties found it hard to reintegrate properties held by collateral branches when these branches died out; and suitable marriages for poor members of great houses called for authoritative regulation. Secular electors enjoyed a special status among princes by having primogeniture, a specific family regency, and entail of at least a portion of the electoral principality guaranteed by the Golden Bull of 1356.

Within a few years of the issuance of the Golden Bull, and in direct emulation of it, Duke Rudolf IV of Austria engineered a forgery of a Habsburg house statute, the *Privilegium maius* (1358–1359), which was elevated into imperial law by Frederick III in 1453. The *Privilegium maius* declared Austria to be an indivisible whole virtually cut off from the rest of the empire and headed by a semiregal personage bearing the novel title of archduke. In case of a plurality of heirs, the house of Austria was to be ruled by all of them in common and unity would be preserved. The practice arose in other houses of having the monarch approve a charter regulating succession within a particular house and controlling partitions. Some partitions were so engineered that the partitioned parts continued to share certain common institutions, so that they would still be interdependent. Some ordinances arranged for the transfer of the heritage of one family to another in the event of the failure of a line, as when the houses of Luxembourg and Habsburg made a hereditary agreement in 1363. The ultimate effect of house ordinances was to assert the principle of solidarity for the scattered elements of large dynasties, such as the Habsburgs, the Wettiner, the Wittelsbachs, the margraves of Baden, and the Hohenzollern.

Despite the examples of the electors and Austria, few princes were able to achieve principalities that were geographically coherent or free from penetration by other jurisdictions. Some princes tried to seal their territories off from other authorities through a royal privilege against appeals or evocations, but appeal was possible in cases of the denial of justice. Other princes seized on hitherto unclaimed common property, such as forests, quarries, or mines, and worked them to assure a steady income. Almost all princes tried to encourage the development of markets and crafts within their borders to undercut the economic power of external towns and merchants.

Still, the inability of individual princes to control their environments adequately encouraged alliances, not just for political ends but also to regulate such public functions as coinage, weights and measures, road building and repair, and fisheries. Despite its variety of states, late-medieval Germany had a surprisingly small number of silver coinage types, and the Rhenish gold guilder (gulden) was a general standard of value from 1386 on. Princes were more reluctant than towns or petty nobles to join permanent alliances, but elaborate short-term alliances of princes did develop in the last years of the fourteenth century in response to the challenge from other groups. Princes were important participants in the Swabian League, founded in 1487 and continuing for almost half a century. Such leagues foreshadowed regional executive organs of the empire, which had been frequently discussed in the fifteenth century but were brought into operation only in the sixteenth century as the imperial circles *(Kreise)*.

In the fifteenth century a rapid process of bureaucratization took place in the German principalities, particularly the larger ones, culminating in the erection of supreme courts of cassation and appeal using Roman law and procedure. The introduction of university-trained jurists to privy councils and superior courts was a gradual process in which the most significant event was the creation of the Imperial Chamber Court *(Reichskammergericht)* in 1495. The adoption of Roman law and procedure in that court forced princes to use scholarly jurists, if only to forestall appeals. In a similar if less dramatic fashion than in civil and criminal courts, princely administration gradually became a closed and specialized field accessible only to trained clerks and jurists. Many of the persons attending the imperial diet as representatives of estates of all sorts were persons who had at least heard law lectures in school; and jurists dominated the committees that drafted the acts of legislation.

The recesses of Worms in 1495 proclaimed a universal and permanent public peace that outlawed private war. This had its greatest impact on the petty nobility, which was thereby deprived of its weapon of feud when its rights were injured. Wars continued to be fought, but recourse was increasingly had to legal process. Most military activity took place as a result of imperial execution orders or public imperial wars. By the end of the fifteenth century, principalities were no longer fluid and dynamic entities, and alteration of frontiers or rights established before that time was supposed to occur only as a result of a public legal act. Princes were the chief actors in public life, but they were both de facto and de jure less than sovereign.

BIBLIOGRAPHY

Heinz Angermeier, *Königtum und Landfriede im deutschen Spätmittelalter* (1966); Hermann Aubin, *Die Entstehung der Landeshoheit nach niederrheinische Quellen* (1920); Karl Siegfried Bader, *Der deutsche Südwesten in seiner territorialstaatlichen Entwicklung* (1950); Peter Blickle, *Landschaften im alten Reich* (1973); Ernst Bock, *Der schwäbische Bund und seine Verfassungen (1488–1534)* (1927); Karl Bosl, "Der wettinische Ständestaat im Rahmen der mittelalterlichen Verfassungsgeschichte," in *Historische Zeitschrift,* 191 (1960); Hans-Stephan Brather, "Administrative Reforms in Electoral Saxony at the End of the Fifteenth Century," in Gerald Strauss, ed., *Pre-Reformation Germany* (1972); Otto Brunner, *Land und Herrschaft. Grundfragen der territorialen Verfassungsgeschichte Österreichs im Mittelalter,* 5th ed. (1965); Francis Ludwig Carsten, *The Origins of Prussia* (1954), and *Princes and Parliaments in Germany* (1959); Henry J. Cohn, *The Government of the Rhine Palatinate in the Fif-teenth Century* (1965); Georg Droege, "Die finanziellen Grundlagen des Territorialstaates im West- und Ostdeutschland an der Wende vom Mittelalter zur Neuzeit," in *Vierteljahrschrift für Sozial- und Wirtschaftsgeschichte,* 53 (1966).

F. R. H. Du Boulay, "Law Enforcement in Medieval Germany," in *History,* 63 (1978); Lawrence G. Duggan, *Bishop and Chapter: The Governance of the Bishopric of Speyer to 1522* (1978); Otto von Dungern, *Der Herrenstand im Mittelalter* (1908), and *Adelsherrschaft im Mittelalter* (1927); Julius von Ficker, *Vom Heerschilde* (1862), and *Vom Reichsfürstenstande,* 2nd ed., 3 vols. (1911–1932); Robert Folz, "Les assemblées d'états dans les principautés allemandes (fin xiiie–début xvie s.), in *Anciens pays et assemblées d'états,* 36 (1965); "Fürstentum," in Hellmuth Rössler and Günther Franz, eds., *Sachwörterbuch zur deutschen Geschichte* (1958); Bruno Gebhardt, ed., *Handbuch der deutschen Geschichte,* 9th ed., I (1970); Dietrich Gerhard, "Regionalismus und ständisches Wesen als ein Grundthema europäischer Geschichte," in *Historische Zeitschrift,* 174 (1952); Werner Goez, *Der Leihezwang* (1962); Herbert Helbig, *Der wettinische Ständestaat,* IV (1955), and "Fürsten und Landstände im Westen des Reiches im Übergang vom Mittelalter zur Neuzeit," in *Rheinische Vierteljahrsblätter,* 29 (1964); Walther Kienast, "Der Herzogstitel in Frankreich und Deutschland (9. bis 12. Jahrhundert)," in *Historische Zeitschrift,* 203 (1966).

Theodor Mayer, *Kaisertum und Herzogsgewalt im Zeitalter Friedrichs I.* (1952), and "The State of the Dukes of Zähringen," in Geoffrey Barraclough, ed. and trans., *Mediaeval Germany, 911–1250,* 2 vols. (1938, repr. 1967), II.175–202; Heinrich Mitteis, *Lehnrecht und Staatsgewalt* (1933, repr. 1974); Werner Näf, "Frühformen des 'modernen Staates' im Spätmittelalter," in *Historische Zeitschrift,* 171 (1951); H. S. Offler, "Aspects of Government in the Late Medieval Empire," in John Hale, Roger Highfield, and Beryl Smalley, eds., *Europe in the Late Middle Ages* (1965); Georg Wilhelm Sante, ed., *Geschichte der deutschen Länder. "Territorien-Ploetz,"* I (1964); Walter Schlesinger, *Die Entstehung der Landesherrschaft,* 3rd ed. (1969); Hermann von Schulze-Gaevenitz, *Das Recht der Erstgeburt in den deutschen Fürstenhäuser und seine Bedeutung für die deutsche Staatsentwicklung* (1851), and *Die Hausgesetze der regierenden deutschen Fürstenhäuser,* 3 vols. (1862–1863); Hans Spangenberg, *Vom Lehnstaat zum Ständestaat* (1912); Gerd Tellenbach, "Vom karolingische Reichsadel zum deutschen Reichsfürstenstand," in Theodor Mayer, ed., *Adel und Bauer im deutschen Staat des Mittelalters* (1943, repr. 1967); D. Willoweit, *Rechtsgrundlagen der Territorialgewalt* (1975).

Steven Rowan

[See also **Carolingians; Frederick I Barbarossa; Germany: 1138–1254; Germany: 1254–1493.**]

GERMANY: STEM DUCHIES. The origins of the newer stem duchies (that is, the post-Carolingian ones) and their dissolution and replacement by the territorial lordships of the nobility and church are among the most controversial problems in medieval German historiography. Indeed, some historians, most notably Karl Ferdinand Werner and Hans-Werner Goetz, have denied that stem duchies existed. At the heart of these controversies are questions about the fundamental nature of the German state. Did the East Frankish monarchy create Germany, as Gerd Tellenbach argues, by its unification of several Germanic tribes; or did the stems unite, as Martin Lintzel and Walter Schlesinger maintain, to form the first German *Reich?* Did particularism destroy the power of a centralized Carolingian state, as nineteenth-century, liberal constitutional historians affirmed? Or has Germany had from its inception, as Theodor Mayer contends, a federal structure? The answers to such questions, explicit or implicit, have provided an ideological justification for the various regimes that have governed Germany since Napoleon. For example, during the Third *Reich,* Tellenbach perceived the dukes as the führers of leaderless folks; and in the era of the Common Market Werner has stressed the common Frankish origin of German and French institutions.

While modern political reality has colored historians' perceptions of the past, the sources themselves offer ample grounds for controversy. The evidence from the sixth to the tenth centuries is far from abundant, and the terminology is often obscure and contradictory. In recent years several scholars have studied the changing meanings of the Latin words *dux* and *ducatus* and their uses in different contexts and sources. The basic meaning of *dux* is leader, and the term could always be employed in this general sense: Jesus, for instance, is called the *dux* of the Christian people. More narrowly, it refers to a military commander; and any general, including an emperor or king, could be designated in this manner.

After Diocletian's reform of the Roman administrative system, *dux* became the title of a specific officeholder: the commander of the troops in a Roman province. Under the Merovingians *dux* could refer to a royal official who commanded the military forces in several counties, the leader of one of the subordinate peoples who had been incorporated into the Frankish realm, or the ruler of a barbarian tribe. Sources from the early Carolingian period employ the term for military leaders; the rulers of barbarian

peoples inside and outside the empire, such as Basques and Slavs; the administrators of large areas; the Carolingian mayors of the palace; and the rulers of the former stem duchies. *Ducatus* could mean leadership in general, a military command, a geographical area, an administrative assignment, or a stem duchy. The problem is to ascertain when the term was used for the ruler of a stem and who was identified in this fashion.

There are some additional complications. Different titles, such as *dux, marchio* (margrave), and *comes* (count), could be employed, often in the same source, for the same individual. Was this usage simply arbitrary, or is there some pattern to these seemingly inconsistent designations? Walther Kienast argues, for instance, that the royal chancelleries were reluctant to dignify the usurpers of royal authority with the title *dux,* while Hans-Werner Goetz perceives a distinction between the comital office and a military function that could be assigned to a count and earn him the additional designation of *marchio* and/or *dux.* Kienast has concentrated on royal charters to obtain the official viewpoint, while Goetz and Herfried Stingl have examined a wider range of sources to ascertain contemporaries' and the magnates' own perceptions of their position. Finally, it is important to remember that these words are translations of Germanic terms. Old High German glosses translated *dux* as *heritogo,* the modern German *Herzog;* but this word also had a broad range of meanings. This fragmentary and confused evidence lends itself to diverse interpretations.

The Germanic tribes that later formed Germany—the Alamanni, Bavarians, Franks, Frisians, and Thuringians—were themselves amalgamations of smaller tribal entities, which had been united during the period of migrations by a process of peaceful alliance and conquest that has largely escaped historical notice. Most of these tribes accepted the overlordship of the Merovingians in the sixth century. The Saxons, who preserved their independence, never had a permanent duke. The highest tribal authority was an annual assembly, composed of the princes and representatives of the three estates from each *Gau* (province, administrative district). In wartime a *dux* would be chosen by lot from among the princes, officials appointed by the assembly; he presided at the *Gau* courts and led the *Gau* contingent into battle. As the dominant people in the Merovingian kingdom, the Franks never established a separate tribal structure.

Such a structure existed, however, among the Alamanni, Bavarians, and Thuringians. The Alamanni had accepted the protection of the Ostrogoths in 506, but after the Byzantine invasion of Italy in 536, they submitted to the overlordship of the Franks. The Merovingians appointed dukes to govern the Alamanni. Like the Merovingians, the Alaholfingians divided the duchy among themselves. Otto Feger argues that the dukes were the descendants of the royal family under whose leadership the Alamanni had been united in the fifth century. While the dukes were royal appointees, Feger maintains that their ancestry and extensive alods gave them an independent source of power.

The Bavarians probably moved from Bohemia to their present homeland after the death of King Theodoric of the Ostrogoths in 526. The Franks utilized the collapse of the Ostrogothic kingdom to extend their power to the eastern Alps and appointed a Bavarian duke. Erich Zöllner maintains that the Agilulfingians were a lineage of Burgundian-Frankish ancestry and that the Alaholfingians were another branch of the same house. The Frankish origin of the dukes is clearest in the case of the Thuringians. The Franks had conquered the Thuringians in 531, and the first known Thuringian duke, Radulf, was a Frankish noble appointed by King Dagobert I (623/629–638).

The decline of the Merovingians after Dagobert's death enabled dukes, Radulf among them, to become virtually independent of Frankish control and to establish ties to the Carolingians' Austrasian opponents. The Carolingian mayors of the palace reasserted Frankish control in the first half of the eighth century. Charles Martel appointed no successor to Heden, the last Frankish duke of Thuringia, after his death around 717. Pepin II had already waged several campaigns against the Alamannic dukes, Gottfried and Willehari, between 709 and 712. After conducting several expeditions against Gottfried's son, Duke Lantfrid, Charles Martel abolished the duchy in 730. The Alamanni rebelled against Charles's sons; but Pepin the Short and Carloman crushed the revolt.

Bavaria resisted the longest. Duke Odilo (737–748), who was married to the sister of Pepin the Short, was the chief opponent of the mayors. He justified his conduct by a profession of loyalty to the Merovingians. Pepin and Carloman defeated Odilo in 743, but permitted him to retain his duchy. After Odilo's death, Pepin and his widowed sister governed Bavaria on behalf of Odilo's son, Tassilo III (748–788). He attained his majority in 757, but was required to swear an oath of fealty to Pepin and his sons. Tassilo broke with his uncle in 763 and allied with the Lombards. Their defeat doomed Tassilo. After a bloodless campaign in 787, Charlemagne deposed Tassilo in 788.

The history of these older stem duchies has been variously interpreted. It is clear that the dukes were not, as was once believed, simply native leaders who utilized the weakness of the Merovingian monarchy to free their peoples from foreign rule, but royal appointees, often of Frankish ancestry, who were related to the leading Frankish lineages and actively involved in the politics of the Frankish realm. Some historians have called them, therefore, official dukes (Amtsherzöge)—that is, men who exercised royal authority on behalf of the king. At the same time the dukes possessed a hereditary right to their office, and their extensive alods and personal ties to the tribal nobility gave them an independent base of power. Ernst Klebel concludes that while the ducal title gave its holder a place in the hierarchy of Merovingian officials, he was, as far as his own people were concerned, a subking.

In contrast, Werner sees these dukes as princes, Frankish officials who, like the Carolingian mayors or the rulers of Aquitaine, assumed in the late seventh century such royal prerogatives as the right to summon a synod of bishops. The internal history of the Frankish realm in the eighth century is thus the story of a struggle for power between rival, Frankish princely dynasties rather than a conflict between the Franks and insubordinate stems. The chief difficulty with Werner's interpretation is that while ruling houses have often been of foreign ancestry, they have also thoroughly identified with their subjects. The modern, British royal family is a case in point. The Frankish ancestry of the dukes does not disprove the tribal element in the opposition to the Carolingians.

The role of the stems in the constitution of the Carolingian Empire after the abolition of the older stem duchies is another controversial topic. Most historians agree that the stems that formed the East Frankish kingdom preserved their separate identities in the ninth century. The Carolingian army was organized in stem contingents. Members of the different tribes spoke distinct dialects. Codifications of tribal law, such as the Lex Baiuvariorum, remained in force. While Charlemagne was careful not to organize the Saxons into a separate ecclesiastical province, Bavaria formed after 798 the archiepiscopal province of Salzburg. Goetz, who has been most critical of the concept of the stem duchies, points out that the tribes did not always fight as units, that they were often divided during the fraternal wars of the Carolingians, that many of the linguistic boundaries reflect later territorial borders, and that the tribal law codes were influenced by Frankish legislation. While Goetz's reservations are well taken, the evidence still favors the prevailing interpretation.

The real question is whether the stems formed administrative units in the ninth century. Nineteenth-century constitutional historians, such as Georg Waitz, argued that the Carolingians sought to prevent the reemergence of the duchies as separate political entities, and could point to such evidence as Charlemagne's abolition of the Saxon tribal assembly and the proposed division of the empire in 806, in which Alamannia and Bavaria south of the Danube were assigned to Pepin's Italian kingdom.

Klebel maintained, in contrast, that the Carolingians paid attention to the existence of the stem duchies. The proposed division of the empire of 839 referred, for instance, to five regions: the *ducatus* of Alsace, Alamannia, Rhaetia, and Thuringia, and a *regnum* of Saxony. These units were governed by royal officials who were variously described in the sources as counts, margraves, prefects, or dukes. While these officials held their own counties, they also exercised a superior judicial and military authority over the other counts in the stem area. At times their place was taken by a Carolingian subking or *missus*. These official dukes became stem dukes around 900, when they assumed the royal right to name counts and bishops and inherited their offices.

Werner has modified Klebel's theory. Instead of talking about stem duchies, he sees the ninth-century Carolingian Empire as being divided into *regna*—for example, the *regnum* of Saxony resulting from the division of 839. These realms formed the subkingdoms of the Carolingians, but were also governed at various times either jointly by a group of counts or by an official who could be called a duke, a prefect, a margrave, or a *missus*. In the second half of the century, these royal appointees gradually made their position hereditary and became the immediate lords of the counts. Like the dukes of the late seventh century, these magnates in both the West and East Frankish kingdoms began to be called princes around 900. In effect, Werner has substituted the words *regnum* and *princeps* for *ducatus* and *dux* in his analysis.

There are two major problems with Klebel's and Werner's views on the internal structure of the East Frankish kingdom. Klebel's duchies and Werner's realms do not correspond to the later stem duchies or principalities. For instance, Alsace, Rhaetia, and Thuringia did not become stem duchies; nor did the subkingdom of Louis the Younger, which consisted of Saxony, Thuringia, and eastern Franconia, develop into a principality. More important, the officials whom Klebel and Werner identified as ninth-century dukes did not have authority over an entire duchy or realm on a continuous basis. This is evident even in the case of Bavaria, the stem character of which was clearly defined and that functioned through much of the ninth century either as a subkingdom or as the royal domain of the East Frankish monarchy. Most historians, including Tellenbach and Stingl, do not believe, therefore, in the existence of the duchies or realms as permanent administrative entities in the ninth century.

The origins of the newer stem duchies must, rather, be sought between 887 and 918, during the turbulent reigns of Arnulf, Louis the Child, and Conrad I. Stingl has defined a stem duke as the permanent leader of a stem, whose authority was based on his personal power, ability, and the consent of the stem folk—that is, the nobility—rather than royal appointment.

Margrave Luitpold, a kinsman of Emperor Arnulf, was the most powerful man in Bavaria after 895 and played a major role in royal politics during the reign of Louis the Child. He held a number of counties, but the area between the Isar and Enns lay in the sphere of other lineages. Although Luitpold led the Bavarians into battle against the Moravians and Magyars, he did not exercise a similar authority in peacetime. He was killed by the Magyars at the battle of Bratislava in 907.

Luitpold's son Arnulf the Bad (*d.* 937) became duke under unknown circumstances after this defeat, but his career suggests that he had support of the nobility. He defeated the Magyars and withstood the attempts of his stepfather, King Conrad I, to remove him. After Conrad's death the Bavarians elected Arnulf king. He recognized Henry I as king in 921, but retained control of the Bavarian church and conducted his own foreign affairs.

Count Liudolf (*d.* 866), the progenitor of the Saxon dynasty and the father-in-law of King Louis III the Younger, was the most powerful man in Saxony in the mid ninth century. He was identified after his death as the duke of the eastern Saxons because he had led them in their battles against the Danes and Slavs. His son Brun (*d.* 880) held a comparable position. Conrad I referred to Brun's brother Otto (*d.*

912), immediately after his death, as a duke; but not all Saxons had accepted Otto's leadership. Otto's son Henry, who was apparently elected duke by the Saxon magnates, extended his authority to Westphalia through his marriage to a Westphalian heiress and gained control of Thuringia. Henry retained the duchy after his election as king in 919.

Two powerful dynasties vied for power in Alamannia. Margrave Burchard of Rhaetia was executed in 911, apparently after he attempted to make himself duke of Swabia. The count-palatine, Erchanger, who had been one of Burchard's opponents, defeated the Magyars in 913. His widowed sister, Kunigunde, the mother of Arnulf of Bavaria, married King Conrad I. Erchanger quarreled with his brother-in-law and, joined by Burchard II, the son of the executed Burchard, defeated the royal forces and was elected duke in 915. Conrad beheaded Erchanger in 917, and Burchard II assumed the leadership of the Alamanni. Burchard defeated King Rudolf II of Burgundy in 919, but submitted later in the year to the new German king, Henry I, who in turn recognized Burchard as duke. Like Arnulf, Burchard conducted his own foreign policy, but could not appoint the Swabian bishops.

Franconia was the site of a bloody feud between the Conradins—who held most of the counties in Rhenish Franconia and Hesse and who enjoyed the support of their kinsman, Louis the Child—and the Babenbergs, whose power was centered in eastern Franconia around Bamberg (Babenberg). The struggle ended with the execution of the last of the Babenbergs in 906. The Conradins did not have sufficient time to consolidate their hold on Franconia before the election of Conrad, the first duke of Franconia, as king in 911. Eberhard inherited his brother's ducal position after Conrad's death in 918, but it is doubtful that Henry I or Otto I ever officially recognized Eberhard as duke, because they viewed Franconia as part of the royal domain. Franconia, which had never been a Merovingian stem duchy or a Carolingian subkingdom, and was not directly threatened by invaders, was, in any case, the weakest stem duchy.

Lorraine was not a stem duchy, but a Carolingian subkingdom named after Lothar II (d. 869) and inhabited by a mixed population of Franks, Frisians, Alamanni, and Gallo-Romans. The West and East Frankish kingdoms contended for possession of Lorraine between 869 and 925, and the nobles often switched allegiances and fought each other. The most powerful native magnates were Count Reginar

(d. 915) and his son Giselbert, who was elected prince in 920. After Henry I gained control of Lorraine in 925, his daughter married Giselbert; subsequently he appointed Giselbert, probably in 928, as duke.

It is possible to draw a number of conclusions about the origins of the newer stem duchies. Tellenbach argues that the reign of Conrad I was the decisive moment in the formation of the duchies, a view that Geoffrey Barraclough's *The Origins of Modern Germany* has made familiar to English-speaking readers. Conrad has been condemned for this reason as a weak king. Stingl points out, however, that Arnulf and Otto established their ducal positions in Bavaria and Saxony, respectively, under Louis the Child, and that Conrad I tried, albeit unsuccessfully, to stop the development of the stem duchies. It is no accident that the dukes of Bavaria and Saxony were the most powerful of the stem dukes. Bavaria and Saxony had preserved their autonomy or independence until the end of the eighth century and were the regions most threatened by invasion at the beginning of the tenth century. The need for effective military leadership, which the kings could no longer supply, was a major factor in the formation of the duchies. The dukes came from the most powerful lineages in their duchies and enjoyed the backing of the stem nobility, but they also belonged to what Tellenbach called the imperial aristocracy. Royal support, often involving family ties to the king, was a major factor in the rise of the ducal lineages.

Historians have often noted the similarity of the formation of the German stem duchies, the Carolingian successor kingdoms, and the French principalities. Although the creators of these new political entities were members of the Carolingian imperial aristocracy, most historians have argued that the stem character of the German duchies distinguished them from the other states.

Kienast and Werner have stressed in recent years the common features of the German duchies and French principalities. Kienast states that only those French princes who ruled over territories with a tribal character, such as Aquitaine or Normandy, were called dukes; but while the German stems formed during the period of migrations, most of the French stems were of more recent origin and consequently had a less developed tribal identity. Henry I and Otto I recognized the existence of the German duchies because they needed the dukes as intermediaries in governing their large kingdom, but the weaker French kings were not faced with this problem and acknowledged the existence of only the duchies of Francia and Burgundy. Like the nonducal French principalities—for example, Anjou—the French duchies were essentially territories united by feudal rather than tribal bonds.

Werner sees no difference between the misnamed German stem duchies and the French ducal and nonducal principalities. These entities were either Carolingian *regna* (Aquitaine or Bavaria), peripheral areas inhabited by a largely non-Frankish population (Brittany), or large counties that emerged from the dissolution of a *regnum* (Anjou). A representative of the king established himself in each of these territories as a prince. The French princes took the lead in establishing effective governmental institutions in the eleventh century, and this enabled the Capetians to absorb the principalities quickly in the twelfth and thirteenth centuries. The Saxon kings' reassertion of royal authority prevented a comparable development in Germany.

Goetz has adapted Werner's thesis in a radical reinterpretation of German history. For Goetz the German principalities were linked to neither the so-called stem duchies nor the Carolingian *regna*, but were simply large noble lordships, the boundaries of which did not coincide with those of the Carolingian provinces. To govern their large kingdom, Henry I and Otto I assigned ducal functions to the most powerful magnates and turned the usurpers of regal authority once again into royal officials. In essence, Goetz has placed the origins of the German princely lordships a century or so earlier than most historians have done, and he has found few followers so far.

There is general agreement that the Saxon kings reasserted royal control over the duchies, however they are perceived. Unlike Conrad I, Henry I accepted the existence of the duchies. As has already been mentioned, Burchard of Swabia and Arnulf of Bavaria submitted to Henry's rule in 919 and 921, respectively, and became Henry's vassals; but they retained extensive control over the church in their duchies and continued to conduct their own foreign affairs. After Burchard's death in 926, Henry strengthened his grip on Swabia by selecting a non-Swabian, Hermann, a cousin of Conrad I, as duke and by assuming direct control over the church. The appointment of the king's son-in-law, Giselbert, as duke of Lorraine tied that duchy more closely to the crown. Henry's success in incorporating the dukes into the constitution of the German kingdom was graphically demonstrated in 936, when the dukes of Lorraine, Franconia, Swabia, and Bavaria served, respectively, as the chamberlain, seneschal, butler, and marshal at Otto I's coronation banquet.

Since the kingdom could be divided among Henry's sons only by depriving the dukes of their duchies, a politically unfeasible act, Henry broke with Carolingian tradition and designated Otto as his sole heir. The establishment of the principle that the kingdom was indivisible was thus a direct consequence of Henry's acceptance of the stem duchies. The dissatisfaction of Otto's brothers with this arrangement and the dukes' resentment of Otto's more rigorous assertion of royal authority—for example, his demand that Arnulf's son, Eberhard, surrender control of the Bavarian church—led to a series of revolts between 937 and 941.

Otto was victorious. In 938 he replaced Eberhard as duke of Bavaria with Arnulf's brother, Berthold, who agreed to Otto's selection of the Bavarian bishops. Eberhard of Franconia and Giselbert of Lorraine were killed in 939, and no new duke was appointed in Eberhard's place. Henceforth, Franconia was part of the royal domain; its central location gave the king direct access to the other duchies.

More important, Otto began a policy of attaching the ducal lineages to the crown through marriage and of providing for royal cadets in this fashion. By 949 Otto's brother Henry was duke of Bavaria; Otto's son Liudolf, duke of Swabia; and Otto's son-in-law, Conrad the Red, duke of Lorraine. All five duchies were thus in the hands of the royal family.

The drawbacks of this policy soon became apparent. Quarrels within the royal family, such as that arising from Liudolf's and Conrad's dislike of Henry of Bavaria, turned into dangerous revolts when a royal duke could count on the assistance of his duchy. Moreover, royal cadets, such as Otto's nephew, Duke Henry the Wrangler of Bavaria, could put forth their own claims to the crown.

Nevertheless, the kings remained convinced that relatives were their most reliable choice as dukes. For fifty-three years between 995 and 1096, either the king, his wife, or his son was duke of Bavaria. Henry III was at his accession in 1039 duke of Bavaria and Swabia, and shortly thereafter he assumed control of Carinthia as well. Henry IV selected his daughter's fiancé, Frederick of Staufen, as duke of Swabia in 1079; and in the twelfth century Swabia became a secundogeniture of the Hohenstaufen dynasty.

Otto and his successors, however, took three measures to limit the threat posed by the dukes. Al-

509

though the dukes belonged to a small number of powerful lineages, often related to the royal family, changes in ducal lineages were frequent; and the kings preferred to select individuals who had no personal ties to their duchy as dukes. This is especially clear in Swabia, where members of eight dynasties, only two of which were of Swabian origin, served as dukes between 926 and 1079. While the king sought the consent of the tribal magnates in making his choice and some attention was paid to hereditary claims, the dukes of Swabia in the Saxon and early Salian periods were essentially royal officials. They had been enfeoffed with royal and church lands, functioned as the king's representative in the duchy, summoned stem assemblies, maintained the peace, and led the stem contingent in wartime; but they had few opportunities to develop their own lordships. The dukes of Swabia were thus at a disadvantage in dealing with powerful native dynasties, like the Welfs and Zähringen, who were developing their own territorial lordships in the eleventh century. The Hohenstaufen's own dynastic holdings in Swabia were comparatively small until Frederick Barbarossa created a Hohenstaufen principality. The identification of Swabia with the Hohenstaufen's domains meant that the duchy ceased to exist in 1268, when the last Hohenstaufen, Conradin, was executed.

Second, the kings reduced the size of the duchies. In 953, during Liudolf's and Conrad the Red's revolt, Otto appointed his brother Archbishop Brun of Cologne as "archduke" of Lorraine. The meaning of this title is not clear, but in 959 Brun chose Count Frederick of Bar as duke of Upper Lorraine. It used to be believed that Brun selected at the same time a Count Godfrey as duke of Lower Lorraine, but Duke Godfrey appears merely to have led the Lotharingian contingent in Italy in 964. The first definite reference to a duke of Lower Lorraine occurs in 977, when Otto II installed a Carolingian, Charles, as duke. The dukes of Upper Lorraine retained the title "duke of Lorraine"; but in the thirteenth century the dukes of Lower Lorraine adopted the designation "duke of Brabant," the name of the territory they actually governed.

Bavaria was treated in a similar fashion. After suppressing the revolt of his cousin, Duke Henry the Wrangler of Bavaria, in 976, Otto II created a separate duchy of Carinthia. There were frequent changes in dynasties in Carinthia, and the dukes never exercised very effective authority. To resolve the Hohenstaufen-Welf-Babenberg feud, Frederick

Barbarossa turned the eastern mark of Bavaria into the duchy of Austria in 1156. After Frederick deprived his cousin, Henry the Lion, of his fiefs in 1180, Frederick elevated Styria to a duchy and enfeoffed the count-palatine of Bavaria, Otto of Wittelsbach, with what remained of Bavaria. *Alt Bayern* of the pre-Napoleonic period developed out of the Wittelsbachs' own noble lordship; but the link to the old stem duchy was a major factor in preserving the separate identity of Bavaria until the twentieth century. The increase in the number of duchies was not a particularly good solution to the problem of the duchies because it increased the number of magnates whom the king had to control.

Finally, as Otto I's selection of Archbishop Brun as "archduke" of Lorraine shows, after the suppression of Liudolf's revolt in 955 the kings relied increasingly on the church as a counterweight to the lay nobility. Otto began the practice of enfeoffing bishops with counties. Henry II applied this policy to Franconia in 1007, when he divided the Franconian counties between the bishops of Würzburg and Bamberg. In effect the bishops took the place of the absent duke as the king's representative in Franconia.

The German bishops, however, often placed the interests of the church ahead of the king's, and, like the lay nobility, gradually turned the complex of royal offices, regalian rights, and church lands into ecclesiastical principalities. Frederick Barbarossa's creation of the duchy of Würzburg in 1168 was symptomatic of the disintegration of the stem duchies into territorial lordships ruled by nobles and prelates.

While the kings took these measures to limit the dukes' power, the large noble clans were dividing into distinct lineages conscious of their agnate ancestry. These noble dynasties sought to develop their own lordships through an accumulation of counties, advocacies, castles, regalian rights, and alods. Theodor Mayer and Walter Schlesinger argued that the nobles possessed an innate right to govern others, but in recent years Michael Mitterauer has attacked the concept of autogenous lordships and demonstrated that the nobles' lordships were based on royal authority, whether formally granted or usurped. The Hohenstaufen duchy of Swabia and the Wittelsbach duchy of Bavaria were such territorial lordships, even though their rulers bore the title of duke.

The Billung duchy of Saxony is another example. The Saxon monarchs did not regrant their duchy after they became kings, but Otto I did appoint Hermann Billung (d. 973) as margrave along the lower Elbe and as his representative during his absences in Italy. This vicariate formed the basis of the Billung duchy of Saxony, the actual authority of which was largely confined to Lower Saxony. After the death of the last Billung duke in 1106, his alods were divided between the Ascanians and the Welfs. Henry V conferred the duchy on Count Lothar of Supplinburg. Lothar's Welf grandson, Henry the Lion, the duke of Saxony from 1142 to 1180, tried to weld this inheritance into a territorial state, but aroused the bitter opposition of other Saxon nobles. After Frederick Barbarossa deprived Henry of Saxony in 1180, he granted Westphalia to the archbishop of Cologne as a duchy and the remainder of the duchy to Count Bernhard of Anhalt, whose actual power was largely confined to the areas around Lauenburg and Wittenberg. Except for its name, the Ascanian duchy of Saxony bore little resemblance to Liudolfingian Saxony.

The downfall of Henry the Lion in 1180 destroyed the last vestiges of the stem duchies. They had been replaced by a patchwork quilt of territorial lordships ruled by nobles and prelates. Frederick Barbarossa organized the most important of these lay and ecclesiastical rulers into the estate of imperial princes that governed Germany until 1918.

BIBLIOGRAPHY

Geoffrey Barraclough, *The Origins of Modern Germany*, 2nd ed. (1947, repr. 1966), and *idem*, ed. and trans., *Mediaeval Germany, 911–1250: Essays by German Historians*, 2 vols. (1938, repr. 1967), I.27–46; Karl Bosl, ed., *Zur Geschichte der Bayern* (1965); Karl Brunner, "Die fränkischen Fürstentitel im neunten und zehnten Jahrhundert," in Herwig Wolfram, ed., *Intitulatio II. Lateinische Herrscher- und Fürstentitel im neunten und zehnten Jahrhundert* (1973); Hans-Joachim Freytag, *Die Herrschaft der Billunger in Sachsen* (1951); Bruno Gebhardt, *Handbuch der deutschen Geschichte*, Herbert Grundmann, ed., 9th ed., I (1970), 747–749; Hans-Werner Goetz, *"Dux" und "Ducatus"* (1977); Hellmut Kämpf, ed., *Die Entstehung des deutschen Reiches (Deutschland um 900)* (1963); Walther Kienast, "Der Herzogstitel in Frankreich und Deutschland (9. bis 12. Jahrhundert)," in *Historische Zeitschrift*, **203** (1966); Walther Lammers, ed., *Entstehung und Verfassung des Sachsenstammes* (1967).

Helmut Maurer, *Der Herzog von Schwaben* (1978); Theodor Mayer, "The Historical Foundations of the German Constitution," in Barraclough, ed. and trans., *op. cit.*, II (1938), and "The State of the Dukes of Zähringen," *ibid.*; Michael Mitterauer, "Formen adeliger Herrschaftsbildung im hochmittelalterlichen Österreich: Zur Frage der 'autogenen Hoheitsrechte,'" in *Mitteilungen des Instituts für österreichische Geschichtsforschung*, **80** (1972); Wolfgang Müller, ed., *Zur Geschichte der Alemannen* (1975); Walter Schlesinger, *Die Entstehung der Landesherrschaft* (1941, repr. 1976); Bernhard Schmeidler, "Franconia's Place in the Structure of Mediaeval Germany," in Barraclough, ed. and trans., *op. cit.*, II (1938); Karl Schmid, "Die Thronfolge Ottos des Grossen," in Eduard Hlawitschka, ed., *Königswahl und Thronfolge in ottonisch-frühdeutscher Zeit* (1971), and "The Structure of the Nobility in the Earlier Middle Ages," in Timothy Reuter, ed. and trans., *The Medieval Nobility* (1978); Max Spindler, ed., *Handbuch der bayerischen Geschichte*, 2nd ed., I (1980); Herfried Stingl, *Die Entstehung der deutschen Stammesherzogtümer am Anfang des 10. Jahrhunderts* (1974); Gerd Tellenbach, *Königtum und Stämme in der Werdezeit des deutschen Reiches* (1939, repr. 1982), and "From the Carolingian Imperial Nobility to the German Estate of Imperial Princes," in Reuter, ed. and trans., *op. cit.*; Karl Ferdinand Werner, "Kingdom and Principality in Twelfth-century France," in Reuter, ed. and trans., *op. cit.*, and *Structures politiques du monde franc (VIᵉ–XIIᵉ siècles)* (1979).

JOHN B. FREED

[See also **Alamanni; Babenberg Family; Bavaria; Billungs; Carolingians and the Carolingian Empire; Duchy; Dux; Germany: 843–1137; Saxony, Duchy of; Swabia, Duchy of.**]

GERSHOM BEN JUDAH (*ca.* 960–1028), one of the most important scholars and leaders of Ashkenazic Jewry in the Middle Ages; he was known from the end of the eleventh century as Me'or ha-Gola (Light of the exile). During his lifetime, and largely because of him, Mainz became a center of scholarship for many Jewish communities in Europe that had formerly been connected with Babylonian yeshivas. From the beginning he granted his yeshiva independence and did not hesitate to take issue with the heads of the Babylonian academies on matters of religious law. Students came to his yeshiva, and questions on religious law were sent to him from Germany, Italy, northern and southern France, and perhaps even from Spain.

Gershom introduced a liberal atmosphere into the system of study at his yeshiva and encouraged his students to put literary works into writing. These students later dispersed among various communities inside and outside of Germany and helped to spread Jewish learning. Less than a century after his death, Rashi, the great scholar of Troyes (*d.* 1105), said of Gershom that "all members of the Ashkenazi diaspora are students of his students."

Gershom's extensive literary work included commentaries on the Talmud, halakhic rulings, responsa, and liturgical poems—some of which still constitute part of Jewish liturgy. He also played an important role in strengthening the authority and procedure of the Jewish communities in Germany. He enacted various regulations in the spheres of public and private life (though not all the provisions that are attributed to him were actually made by him). His most important ones concerned the prohibition of polygamy and of divorcing a wife without her consent. Unanimously accepted by Ashkenazic Jewry, they have exercised a substantial influence on the structure of the Jewish family up to the present day.

As early as the fourteenth century, Asher ben Jehiel, one of the greatest rabbinical scholars, wrote that Gershom's ordinances were "such permanent fixtures that they may well have been handed down on Mount Sinai."

BIBLIOGRAPHY

Irving A. Agus, *Urban Civilization in Pre-Crusade Europe,* I (1965), 38–41; Ze'ev Falk, *Jewish Matrimonial Law in the Middle Ages* (1966); Louis Finklestein, *Jewish Self-Government in the Middle Ages,* 2nd ed. (1964), 20–36, 111–147; Avraham Grossman, Ḥakhme Ashkenaz ha-rishonim (The early sages of Ashkenaz) (1981), 106–174.

AVRAHAM GROSSMAN

[See also **Ashkenaz; Family and Family Law, Jewish; Jews in Europe: After 900.**]

GERSON, JOHN (**Jean Charlier**) (1363–1429), French theologian, reformer, and spiritual writer, was born in Gerson-lès-Barby in the Ardennes region. He entered the University of Paris in 1377, where he resided at the Collège de Navarre. Recipient of the arts degree by 1381, he immediately matriculated in the theological faculty, where, in 1392, under the sponsorship of Pierre d'Ailly, he received the licentiate and doctorate. During his student years, he served, at different times, as proctor of the French nation at the university, court preacher, almoner to the duke of Burgundy, and dean of the collegiate church of St. Donatien at Bruges. In 1395, he succeeded d'Ailly as chancellor of the university.

As chancellor, Gerson played a major role in French deliberations to settle the Western Schism. He early advocated the resignation of both papal contenders and opposed the subtraction of French obedience from the Avignon pope, Benedict XIII, in 1398. In 1399, Gerson made a prolonged visit to St. Donatien in Bruges, where, always desirous of a life of contemplation, he seriously considered resigning the chancellorship. He returned to Paris in 1400 and worked vigorously for the restoration of obedience to Avignon in 1403. A by-product of his stay at Bruges was his plan for the reform of theological studies at Paris.

When the new Roman pope, Gregory XII, expressed his willingness in 1407 to meet with Benedict at Savona concerning the possibility of mutual resignation, Gerson served on the French delegation sent by the king to facilitate the proposed meeting. The failure of Savona greatly disillusioned him and he joined the ranks of those calling for a council to resolve the Schism. Although he did not attend the Council of Pisa in 1409, he wrote several treatises justifying its legitimacy and rejoiced in the election of Alexander V. As did many others, Gerson soon realized that Pisa not only had failed to resolve the Schism but also had introduced a third papal contender. The convocation, therefore, of another council in 1414 at Constance received his strong support and when the Pisan pope, John XXIII, fled the city on 21 March 1415, Gerson, in his famous sermon of 23 March, provided the council with the theological justification for its continued existence. The council accomplished its goal of securing church unity by its election of Martin V in 1417.

Gerson was no less prominent in the realization of the council's second goal, that of eradicating heresy. As chancellor, he frequently reacted against the writings of Wyclif and Hus. At Constance, he served as adviser to his close friend, Pierre d'Ailly, who was a member of the commission that interrogated Hus and ultimately condemned him to death. The case of Jean Petit also attracted Gerson's attention. Petit had justified the Burgundian assassination of the duke of Orléans in 1407 on the basis of tyrannicide. Although Petit was never personally censured by the council, the theory behind his position was formally condemned. Finally, Gerson successfully defended the Brethren of the Common Life against Matthaeus of Grabow, who claimed that they could not aspire to a life of Christian perfection since they did not take the traditional vows of the religious life.

With regard to the council's third goal, that of church reform, Gerson's contribution was less significant. This fact may have been due to his preoccupation with the problems of heresy and tyrannicide. In any case, his view of reform differed considerably from that of Constance. While he supported the council's legislation against abuses in the area of benefices, reservations, taxation, and simony, he strongly felt that institutional renewal, unless accompanied by genuine personal reform, was useless. He called, therefore, for the spiritual renewal of the entire hierarchical order of the church, with special emphasis on the pastoral dimension of the episcopal office. Gerson's approach to church reform did not take root until the Catholic Reformation.

In addition to his contributions in the area of conciliarism and church reform, Gerson was also a leading spiritual teacher and writer. He sought to foster an intensification of the spiritual life on all levels of society. To the professors of Paris, he advocated the reintegration of mystical and speculative theology. With monks he corresponded widely on ascetical matters. He contended with Jan van Ruusbroec on the nature of mystical union. In his numerous works for the laity, he imparted religious guidance appropriate to their state. He was especially conscious of the consequences of the Schism on the spiritual life of his day. The problem of the discernment of spirits also interested him greatly as he sought to eradicate superstition and self-deception in the realm of piety. Closely associated with his interest in spirituality was his concern for the Christian education of the young. His writings in this area are significant for the history of medieval attitudes to children.

Gerson's final days were spent in Lyons. With the close of the Council of Constance in 1418, he was unable to return to Paris since he had incurred the wrath of the duke of Burgundy by his attacks on Jean Petit. After brief stays in Bavaria and Austria, he retired to Lyons, which was under the protection of the dauphin. He resided first in the Celestine monastery there but later moved to the Church of St. Paul. His years in Lyons proved most productive. Through his writings he carried on the cause of church reform and spiritual renewal. He also continued his work with the education of youth. Among his last writings was a defense of Joan of Arc. Gerson was buried in the chapel of St. Lawrent, adjacent to St. Paul's. His tomb, however, was destroyed in 1793 when the forces of the French Revolution invaded and burned the chapel.

BIBLIOGRAPHY

The most recent complete edition of Gerson's works is that of Palémon Glorieux, *Œuvres complètes*, 10 vols. (1960–1973). For an excellent presentation of the times in which Gerson lived and worked, see Étienne Delaruelle, E.-R. Labande, and Paul Ourliac, *L'Église au temps du Grand Schisme et de la crise conciliaire*, 2 vols. (1962–1964). Other important works on Gerson include: André Combes, *La théologie mystique de Gerson*, 2 vols. (1963–1965); James L. Connolly, *John Gerson, Reformer and Mystic* (1928); John B. Morrall, *Gerson and the Great Schism* (1960); Louis Mourin, *Jean Gerson, prédicateur français* (1952); Louis B. Pascoe, *Jean Gerson: Principles of Church Reform* (1973); Guillaume H. M. Posthumus Meyjes, *Jean Gerson: Zijn Kerkpolitiek en Ecclesiologie* (1963); Johann B. Schwab, *Johannes Gerson, Professor der Theologie und Kanzler der Universität Paris* (1858).

LOUIS B. PASCOE

[See also **Ailly, Pierre d'**; **Brethren of the Common Life**; **Conciliar Theory**; **Councils, Western: 1311–1449**; **Devotio Moderna**; **Ruusbroec, Jan van**; **Schism, Great**.]

GERSONIDES. See **Levi ben Gershom**.

GERVASE OF CANTERBURY. As chronicler-historian of Canterbury Cathedral from 1163 to 1210, Gervase wrote an important account of the rebuilding of the chevet in the new Gothic style after the fire of 1174. A significant document for the history of medieval architecture, it chronicles the yearly progress of construction and provides rare insights into how cathedrals were built. As the resident chronicler of the cathedral, Gervase also composed one of the earliest histories of the archbishops of Canterbury.

BIBLIOGRAPHY

Gervase's "Tractatus de combustione et reparatione Cantuariensis ecclesiae" is published in William Stubbs, ed., *Gervasii Cantuariensis opera historica*, I (1879). See also Teresa G. Frisch, *Gothic Art 1140–c. 1450: Sources and Documents* (1971), 14–23; Robert Willis, *The Architectural History of Canterbury Cathedral* (1845); Francis Woodman, *The Architectural History of Canterbury Cathedral* (1981).

STEPHEN GARDNER

[See also **Canterbury Cathedral**.]

GESSO, the Italian word for gypsum, used to designate the painter's mixture of finely ground plaster, water, and glue that is laid over a panel in preparation for the application of paint. Sometimes as many as fifteen separate layers of gesso were applied to a panel before it was considered ready for painting. Each layer was sanded and the final layer scraped down until its surface was smooth and slick. On this well-prepared surface the master laid out the design and applied colors, often with the aid of assistants.

BIBLIOGRAPHY

Cennino Cennini, *Il libro dell'arte. The Craftsman's Handbook,* Daniel V. Thompson, trans. (1933, repr. 1960); Bruce Cole, *The Renaissance Artist at Work* (1983).

ADELHEID M. GEALT

[See also **Panel Painting.**]

GESTA APOLLONII, a tenth-century Latin poem of 792 surviving leonine hexameters set in the form of an eclogue, recounts the first parts of the exploits of Apollonius of Tyre, a story better known in the West in its prose form, the *Historia Apollonii regis Tyri.* The author (probably a monk, possibly from Tegernsee) shows a knowledge of Vergil's *Eclogues,* and the *Gesta* itself may have been composed as an exercise in literary form.

BIBLIOGRAPHY

The text of the *Gesta Apollonii* is in *Monumenta Germaniae historica: Poetae latini aevi Carolini,* II, Ernst Dümmler, ed. (1884), 483–506. See also Max Manitius, *Geschichte der lateinischen Literatur des Mittelalters,* I (1911), 614–616; F. J. E. Raby, *A History of Secular Latin Poetry in the Middle Ages,* 2nd ed. I (1957), 277.

WILLIAM CRAWFORD

[See also **Latin Literature.**]

GESTA FRANCORUM ET ALIORUM HIERO-SOLIMITANORUM narrates the events of the First Crusade from its inception (November 1095) to the Battle of Ascalon (12 August 1099). The identity of its author is unknown, but he was obviously a member, either Norman or Italian, of the contingent of crusaders that Bohemond had recruited in 1096 from the Norman duchy of Apulia. Much of his narration of the journey across Armenia Minor to Jerusalem under the leadership, first, of Bohemond and, subsequently, of Raymond of Toulouse, was

written en route. With the collaboration of a scribe who made occasional clerical or rhetorical interpolations, the anonymous author has thus provided valuable eyewitness information about the crusade from the viewpoint of a knight who was neither a high-ranking leader nor a cleric. He was generally well informed about the leaders' policy decisions, but his greatest historical contribution is undoubtedly his efficient reporting of the daily progress of the crusaders' army (especially his own contingent). He has recorded the tactical successes and failures, the difficult provisioning, the changing moods, the unremitting anti-Greek prejudice, the unself-conscious brutality, and, throughout it all, the simple faith of the ordinary soldier.

From a literary standpoint the anonymous author was to his contemporaries uncultivated and uncouth. Bernard, abbé of Marmoutier, commissioned Robert the Monk of Rheims to rewrite the whole work for literary and historical reasons (the author had neglected to give specific details concerning the Council of Clermont). Baudri of Dol also produced a version of "this rustic little book." However, the influence of the original has persisted. Not only was it constantly plagiarized throughout the Middle Ages, but today it remains one of the most valuable contemporary sources for the First Crusade.

BIBLIOGRAPHY

Sources. The best edition is *Gesta Francorum et aliorum Hierosolimitanorum,* Louis Bréhier, ed. and trans. (1964). Two other important editions are *anonymi Gesta Francorum et aliorum hierosolymitanorum,* Heinrich Hagenmeyer, ed. (1890); and the incorrectly named edition *Tudebodus abbreviatus,* Philippe Le Bas, ed. (1866).

Studies. Jeanette M. A. Beer, *Narrative Conventions of Truth in the Middle Ages* (1981), ch. 2 and app. II; Louis Bréhier, *L'église et l'orient au moyen âge; les croisades,* 4th ed. (1921); Ferdinand Chalandon, *Essai sur le règne d'Alexis Ier Comnène (1081–1118)* (1900); Nicolae Iorga, *Brève histoire des croisades et de leur fondations en Terre Sainte* (1924); Heinrich von Sybel, *Geschichte des ersten Kreuzzugs* (1841, 2nd ed. 1881).

JEANETTE M. A. BEER

[See also **Crusades and Crusader States: To 1192.**]

GHASSANIDS, a South Arabian tribe that after many wanderings in the Arabian peninsula became the client of Byzantium around A.D. 500 and remained in its service until the Arab conquests swept them away in the 630's. A *foedus,* or treaty, governed their relations with Byzantium and made them technically *foederati* or *symmachoi,* allies of the empire, receiving annual subsidies *(annonae foederaticae)* in return for military service. Their chiefs were officially called phylarchs, and in the imperial hierarchy of ranks they were *clarissimi.* Around 530 one of them, al-Ḥārith, son of Jabala, was created supreme phylarch and king, and was put in command of almost all the Arabs in the service of Byzantium in the East.

As *symmachoi* the Ghassanids fought for Byzantium against the nomads of the Arabian peninsula; against the Lakhmids, the Arab clients of the Persians; and against the Persians themselves. Their most illustrious kings in the sixth century were al-Ḥārith (Arethas in Procopius' *History*), son of Jabala (529–569), and his son, al-Mundhir (569–582). The first distinguished himself in the two wars with Persia during Justinian's reign (527–565) and contained the thrust of the Lakhmid offensive against the Byzantine frontier, winning a great victory in 554 near Chalcis in northern Syria, in which the Lakhmid king was killed. The son, al-Mundhir, repeated the exploits of his father against the Lakhmids and even succeeded in capturing and burning Al-Ḥīra, their capital.

The Ghassanids were zealous Christians and brought about the revival of the Monophysite movement in Syria after it was disestablished during the reign of the Chalcedonian emperor Justin I (518–527). It was the Ghassanid king al-Ḥārith who was able, with the help of Empress Theodora, to secure the ordination of two Monophysite bishops, Theodorus and the famous Jacob Baradaeus, after whom the Monophysite church in Syria was called Jacobite. Both al-Ḥārith and his son Mundhir remained throughout their lives staunch supporters of the Monophysite church and its protectors against divisive movements from within, such as the tritheistic heresy of Eugenius and Conon as well as against the attacks of the Chalcedonians.

The Ghassanids are associated with many churches, monasteries, palaces, and castles in Syria. Perhaps the best known is the structure outside Sergiopolis near the Euphrates, which has been identified as either a praetorium or an *ecclesia extra muros.* But most of their structures were erected in the province of Arabia and in the Gaulanitis, where their capital al-Jābiya was located. It was at al-Jābiya that they received such poets of pre-Islamic Arabia as al-Nābigha, who composed splendid panegyrics

and elegies on the Ghassanid princes, and Hassān ibn Thābit, who was to become the Prophet Muḥammad's poet laureate.

The involvement of the Ghassanids in monophysitism, however, brought about their downfall. In the 580's Emperor Tiberius had al-Mundhir arrested and brought to Constantinople, and Emperor Maurice treated his son al-NuC mān similarly; the Ghassanids survived but were considerably weakened. After Heraklios' victory over the Persians, they emerged as the dominant group of Christian Arab allies in the fight against the Muslim Arabs in the 630's. Under their last king, Jabala, they took part in the disastrous battle of Yarmūk (636), in which the fate of Byzantium in Syria, as well as that of the Ghassanids, was decided.

BIBLIOGRAPHY

Sources. The following are important: John of Ephesus, *Historia ecclesiastica,* in CSCO, no. 106 (versio), 90, 129–133, 135–136, 156–170, 212–217, 237, 238; Michael the Syrian, *Chronique,* J.-B. Chabot, trans., II (1901), 245–248, 285, 308–309, 323–325, 344, 345, 349–351, 364–371; Procopius, *History,* 1.17.45–48, 18.26.35–37, 2.1.1–11, 19.12–18, 26–46, and *Anecdota,* 2.23, 28.

Studies. The fundamental work on the Ghassanids is still Theodor Nöldeke, *Die Ghassanischen Fürsten aus dem Hause Gafna's* (1887), which judiciously uses the primary Greek, Syriac, and Arabic sources. More recent studies since Nöldeke's include R. Aigrian, "Arabie," in *Dictionnaire d'histoire et de géographie ecclésiastique,* III, cols. 1200–1219; Jean Sauvaget, "Les Ghassanides de Sergiopolis," in *Byzantion,* **14** (1939); Irfan Shahid (Kawar), "Procopius and Arethas," in *Byzantinische Zeitschrift,* 50 (1957), and "The Patriciate of Arethas," in *Byzantinische Zeitschrift,* 52 (1959).

IRFAN SHAHID

[See also **Lakhmids.**]

GHAZĀLĪ, AL- (Abū Ḥāmid Muḥammad ibn Muḥammad al-Ṭūsī al Ghazālī, 1058–1111), Islamic jurist, theologian, and mystic, is a towering figure in the religious history of medieval Islam. His early training, first in his native city of Ṭūs, then in Jurjān and Nishapur, was in Islamic law. At Nishapur he was introduced to Islamic dialectical theology *(kalām)* by his teacher, the renowned theologian of the AshCarite school, al-Juwaynī (*d.* 1085). In 1091 al-Ghazālī was appointed to the chair of Islamic law in the Niẓāmiyya of Baghdad. The Niẓāmiyya was one of a number of colleges (all bearing this name) established in various Islamic cities by the vizier of the Seljuk sultans, Niẓām al-Mulk, for the teaching of Islamic law according to the school of al-Shāfiᶜī.

The year 1095 saw al-Ghazālī in the throes of a spiritual crisis that resulted in his forsaking his prestigious teaching career in Baghdad for the life of an Islamic mystic, or Sufi. This crisis, as his autobiography suggests, was prompted in part by dissatisfaction with the purely rational and doctrinal aspects of religion. These, he felt, bypassed the heart of the matter, the experiential in religion, the *dhawq* (literally, "taste") of which the Islamic mystics spoke. In July of that year the crisis reached its climax, and for a time al-Ghazālī lost his ability to speak. Shortly thereafter he left Baghdad and for some ten years journeyed in Syria, Palestine (Egypt, according to some accounts), and the Hejaz, leading the life of an ascetic mystic. In 1106 he was persuaded by the Seljuk authorities to resume teaching Islamic law. This he did in Nishapur and then in Ṭūs, where he died.

Al-Ghazālī's numerous writings include works on Islamic law, philosophy, logic, theology, ethics, mysticism, and criticisms of Islamic sects, particularly of Shiism in its Ismaili form. He also wrote a short but poignant autobiography, *al-Munqidh min al-ḍalāl* (The deliverer from error), describing his intellectual quest for certainty and how it led him to mysticism. While teaching at Baghad, he undertook a study of the Islamic philosophers, particularly Ibn Sīnā (Avicenna). During this period he wrote *Maqāṣid al-falāsifa* (The aims of the philosophers), an excellent exposition of Avicennian philosophy (including logic), which was translated into Latin in the twelfth century but erroneously thought by some Scholastics to be an exposition of al-Ghazālī's own philosophy. This work, however, as al-Ghazālī proclaims in the introduction and at its conclusion, was intended as a prelude to his *Tahāfut al-falāsifa* (The incoherence of the philosophers), a brilliant and incisive critique of Islamic philosophy (translated into Latin in 1328). Related to these works are expositions of Ibn Sīnā's logic, which al-Ghazālī argued is a doctrinally neutral tool of knowledge that can be used effectively by Islamic theologians and lawyers. This period also saw his important work on Ashᶜarite theology, *al-Iqtiṣād fī'l-iᶜtiqād* (The golden mean of belief), as well as the critiques of Ismaili Shiism.

It was during the period of his travels (1095–1106) that al-Ghazālī composed his magnum opus, the voluminous and deeply religious *Iḥyāᵓ ᶜulūm al-dīn* (The revivification of the sciences of religion). This work of many dimensions endeavors, among other things, to reconcile traditional Islamic beliefs and practices with Sufism. The reconciliation is achieved in part by the insistence that the mystical experience means closeness to God, not absorption in the divine essence, as some Sufis proclaimed. The work also offers a synthesis of Islamic theological ethical principles, the Aristotelian doctrine of the mean, and the Sufi virtues, the greatest of which is the love of God. Al-Ghazālī's writings after his resumption of the teaching of law include mystical works, such as *Mishkāt al-anwār* (The niche of lights), and a major legal work, *al-Mustaṣfā min uṣūl al-fiqh* (The unadulterated from the principles of jurisprudence).

The work that is of special significance in the history of philosophy is his *Incoherence of the Philosophers*. Though theologically motivated, its arguments are logical. In introducing this work, al-Ghazālī makes it clear that his quarrel is not with the philosophers' mathematics, logic, or theories of natural science that have been "demonstrated." Rather, he is opposed to certain of their theories (largely metaphysical) that contravene the principles of religion. He will prove that, contrary to the claims of the philosophers, these theories (twenty in number) have not been demonstrated. Seventeen of these are innovations that have no proper or explicit basis in scriptural teachings. Three of them, on the other hand, are definitely contrary to Koranic teachings. These three are the theory of the eternity of the world, the Avicennian theory that God knows particulars only "in a universal way," and the theory of the immortality of the individual soul that denies bodily resurrection. To uphold any of these three theories, al-Ghazālī maintained, constitutes infidelity (*kufr*).

Al-Ghazālī's typical method of refuting the philosophers is to present their theory in its strongest form, object to it, raise objections to his objection, answer these, and so on, until he is satisfied that the theory has been refuted. Of special philosophical significance is the seventeenth discussion, devoted to miracles. In it al-Ghazālī voices the Ashᶜarite doctrine that all happenings are directly created by God. The connection between what is habitually regarded as a natural cause and its effect, he argues, is not necessary. No logical contradiction ensues if such a habitual cause is affirmed and the effect denied, or the effect affirmed and the cause denied. Experience proves only concomitance, not necessary causal connection. Nature's uniformity is not necessary in itself, but is a custom or habit decreed arbitrarily by God.

Although al-Ghazālī's attack certainly put Islamic philosophers on the defensive, its consequences were not entirely negative. By explaining and discussing the philosophical theories he criticized, he made them better known in the Islamic world. Moreover, his criticism evoked responses, the most comprehensive of which was the *Tahāfut al-Tahāfut* (The incoherence of The Incoherence) of Ibn Rushd (Averroës), a philosophical classic in its own right that quotes most of al-Ghazālī's work and comments on it paragraph by paragraph.

BIBLIOGRAPHY

Sources. Averroes' Tahafut al-Tahafut (The incoherence of the Incoherence), Simon van den Bergh, trans., 2 vols. (1954); *Al-Ghazali's Tahafut al-Falasifah* (Incoherence of the philosophers), Sabih A. Kamali, trans. (1958); *Al-Munqidh min al-ḍalāl,* F. Jabre, ed. and French trans. (1959), also translated by W. Montgomery Watt in *The Faith and Practice of al-Ghazali* (1953) and by Richard J. McCarthy in *Freedom and Fulfillment* (1980); *The Niche for Lights,* W. H. T. Gairdner, trans. (1924).

Studies. Georges H. Bousquet, *Ih'ya ou Vivification des sciences de la foi* (1953); Maurice Bouyges, *Essai de chronologie des oeuvres d'al-Ghazali (Al-gazel),* M. Allard, ed. (1959); Majid Fakhry, *Islamic Occasionalism* (1958), 56–82; George F. Hourani, "The Chronology of Ghazali's Writings," in *Journal of the American Oriental Society,* 79 (1959), and "Ghazali on Ethical Action," *ibid.,* 91 (1976); F. Jabre, *La notion de la maᶜrifa chez Ghazali* (1958); Duncan B. MacDonald, "The Life of al-Ghazali with Especial Reference to His Opinions," in *Journal of the American Oriental Society,* 20 (1899); George Makdisi, "Muslim Institutions of Learning in Eleventh Century Baghdad," in *Bulletin of the School of Oriental Studies,* 24 (1961); Michael E. Marmura, "Ghazali's Attitude to the Secular Sciences and Logic," in George F. Hourani, ed., *Essays on Islamic Philosophy and Science* (1975); Julian Obermann, *Der philosophische und religiöse Subjektivismus Ghazalis* (1921); Muḥammad A. Sherif, *Ghazali's Theory of Virtue* (1975); W. Montgomery Watt, "The Authenticity of the Work Attributed to al-Ghazali," in *Journal of the Royal Asiatic Society* (1952), and *Muslim Intellectual: A Study of al-Ghazali* (1963); A. J. Wensinck, *La pensée de Ghazali* (1940).

MICHAEL E. MARMURA

[See also **Mysticism, Islamic; Philosophy-Theology, Islamic; Rushd, Ibn; Sīnā, Ibn.**]

GHĀZĀN (KHAN), MAḤMŪD

GHĀZĀN (KHAN), MAḤMŪD (1271–May 1304), Mongol ruler of the Ilkhanids (territorial or subordinate khans) from 1295 to 1304. In his rule over Persia, Iraq, and eastern Anatolia he was theoretically subordinate to the Mongol great khan in Peking, though in fact the bonds with the latter became very relaxed after Kublai's death in 1294.

Ghāzān was the eldest son of the earlier Ilkhanid ruler Arghūn (1284–1291), and during his father's reign he had been provincial governor of the Caspian region and of Khorāsān in eastern Persia. Dispute over the succession arose after Arghūn's death, and Ghāzān finally succeeded after the violent deaths of two ephemeral khans. Whereas Ghāzān had previously been a Buddhist and had erected Buddhist temples, the influence of his general Nawrūz persuaded him to become a Muslim on his accession, the first of his line to follow Islam. It was then that he assumed the Muslim name Maḥmūd.

Ghāzān's foreign policy was dominated by a desire to extend westward into the lands of Syria and Egypt held by the Mamluks of Cairo. In 1299 the Mongol army penetrated to Aleppo and Ḥimṣ, and entered Damascus without striking a blow, but had to withdraw when news came of threats to Syria from central Asia. Ghāzān mounted a second campaign in 1303, having sought support in the previous year from Pope Boniface VIII, presumably in the hope of joining the Christians in an attack on the Mamluks. But the Mongols were decisively defeated by the Mamluks near Damascus and were never able to threaten Syria again.

Ghāzān was the greatest of the Ilkhanids and a very gifted man, reputedly fluent in Middle Eastern and Indian languages, and even in "Frankish" (probably French or Latin). Despite his conversion to Islam, he retained a deep interest in the lore and traditions of his Mongol ancestors, and he encouraged his famous minister Rashīd al-Dīn (1247–1318), a convert to Islam from Judaism, to embark on his world history, the *Jāmiᶜ al-tawārīkh,* the greatest single source for the history of the Mongols. Ghāzān encouraged the sciences, building an observatory at his new capital, Tabriz. After the economic chaos of the years before his accession (when one khan had experimented disastrously with a paper currency, on the Chinese model), a revival of prosperity was encouraged by such measures as a new method of levying the land tax, currency reform, reduction of internal tolls and duties, and abolition of the forced billeting of soldiers and officials on the hapless population. The basic aim was, of course, to increase taxation potential, but there seems to have been some improvement in agriculture and a less arbitrary and tyrannical policy on the part of state officials. Persia certainly appears to have been better governed at this time than it was when, as the fourteenth century progressed, the Ilkhanids declined in power and the region was plunged into political and military chaos.

BIBLIOGRAPHY

Sources. Rashid al-Din, Jami͑ al-tawarikh, Edgar Blochet, ed., 2 vols. (1911), translated into English by John A. Boyle as The Successors of Genghis Khan (1971); Waṣ-ṣāf, Tajziyal al-amṣār wa tazjiyata al-a͑ṣār, published as Geschichte Wassafs, J. von Hammer-Purgstall, ed. and trans. (1856).

Studies. V. V. Barthold and John A. Boyle, "Ghazan," in Encyclopedia of Islam, 2nd ed., II (1968); Cambridge History of Iran, V, John A. Boyle, ed. (1968), 376–397, 491–500; Sir Henry Howorth, History of the Mongols, 4 vols. (1876–1927); Constantin Mouradges d'Ohsson, Histoire des Mongols, 4 vols. (1834–1835); Bertold Spuler, Die Mongolen in Iran, Politik, Verwaltung und Kultur der Il-chanzeit 1220–1350 (1939), 91–105.

C. E. BOSWORTH

[See also **Ilkhanids; Mongol Empire: Foundations; Tabriz.**]

GHĀZĪ, an Islamic term meaning "warrior for the faith." Derived from the Arabic words *ghazā* (to strive . . . make a raid) and *ghazwa* (military expedition), it originally designated one who took part in a razzia. In the Islamic period the *ghazwa* acquired a religious connotation, and the *ghāzī* became "one who wages war for the faith." Organizations of "fighters for the faith" developed on the frontiers of Islam, particularly in central Asia, India, and Anatolia. Their structures ranged from informal groups of volunteers to corporations or chivalric guilds that the central governments sought to control. Thus, Mas͑ūd of Ghazna (1031–1041) set up a *salār-i ghā-ziyān* (commander of *ghāzī*s). The *ghāzī*s were often closely associated with the *futuwwa* (Islamic chivalric orders), deeply influenced by Sufism. Just as the *fityān* ("young men" of the *futuwwa*) could become troublesome urban elements, the *ghāzī*s on the frontier often turned to brigandage when their energies were not directed against the infidel.

The Turkic peoples who had begun to dominate the military life of the caliphate by the mid ninth century also became the predominating element among the Anatolian and central Asian *ghāzī*s. Introduced to Islam in central Asia, they were moved to adopt it not so much by force of arms as by the prestige of the civilization it represented and the charisma of the Sufi mystics who preached to them. These Sufis, possessing many of the characteristics of Turkic shamans, were frequently heterodox. Thus, the movement of Oghuz tribesmen into Anatolia in Seljuk and Mongol times gave the *ghāzī* organizations there a very Turkic and often heterodox character. This popular Islam, little affected by the reforms of the caliph al-Nāsir (1180–1225), survived the breakdown of the Seljuk and Mongol governments and formed the basis upon which the *ghāzī* principalities (*beyliks*) were founded. It was from this milieu that the Ottoman state sprang in the fourteenth century.

BIBLIOGRAPHY

V. V. Barthold, Turkestan Down to the Mongol Invasion, T. Minorsky, trans., 4th ed. (1977); H. A. R. Gibb and H. Bowen, Islamic Society and the West, 2 vols. (1950–1957), I, pt. 2; Mehmed Fuad Köprülü, Les origines de l'empire ottoman (1935), rev. Turkish ed., Osmanlı impar-atorluğunun kuruluşu (1972); F. Taeschner, "Das Fu-tuwwa-Rittertum des islamischen Mittelalters," in Rich-ard Hartmann, ed., Beiträge zur Arabistik, Semitistik und Islamwissenschaft (1944); Paul Wittek, "Deux chapitres de l'histoire des Turcs de Roum," in Byzantion, **11** (1936), and The Rise of the Ottoman Empire (1939, repr. 1958).

PETER B. GOLDEN

GHAZNAVID ART AND ARCHITECTURE was sponsored by the Ghaznavid dynasty, which ruled Afghanistan and eastern Iran from 977 to 1186/1187. Ghaznavid art is known from two sources, archaeological and literary. There are the actual remains, most significantly those found at Ghazni, the Ghaznavid capital and cultural center, and those excavated at Lashkari Bāzār, an extensive palace complex outside the citadel of Bust. There are also numerous and detailed contemporary descriptions of early Ghaznavid monuments, though it is often difficult to relate these literary documents, which give the impression of grandeur and opulence, to the actual preserved monuments.

Ghaznavid architecture and architectural decoration found its primary expression in the palaces of

Minaret of Mas^cud III. Ghazni, 1114–1115. PROPYLÄEN KUNST-GESCHICHTE (© 1973)

the ruler's throne; stylistically the representations seem to be in the tradition of Sogdian and central Asian painting.

The palace of Mas^cūd III (1099–1115) at Ghazni, which like that of Lashkari Bāzār includes a four-*eyvān* plan, features an extensive use of marble panels, carved in low relief. These are decorated with geometric patterns or figural compositions inspired by the activities of court life. The kufic inscriptions from Ghazni, both carved in marble and executed in baked brick, display decorative features, such as foliate devices and plaited letters, which influenced the subsequent development of monumental epigraphy in Iran.

Mas^cūd III also built a minaret that must originally have been associated with a mosque in the vicinity of his palace. Nearby is a second minaret of Bahrām Shāh (1118–*ca.* 1152). All that is left of the two towers are their lower stories, both in the form of an eight-pointed star that once supported a cylindrical shaft. Both minarets were sheathed in a decorative skin of baked brick and carved stucco, though Mas^cūd's minaret bears much more extensive carved stucco decoration than that of Bahrām Shāh.

The excavations of Lashkari Bāzār and Bust have produced a wealth of ceramic objects, which indicate that local ceramic production drew its inspiration first from Samanid and later from Seljuk wares. The numerous examples of metalwork that have been excavated or else purchased in Afghanistan and that are datable to the Ghaznavid period appear to follow contemporary Iranian metalwork, though this material awaits further study.

BIBLIOGRAPHY

General. Frank R. Allchin and Norman Hammond, *The Archaeology of Afghanistan* (1978), 309–330; Clifford E. Bosworth, *The Ghaznavids* (1963), and *The Later Ghaznavids* (1977).

Ghazni. Alessio Bombaci, *The Kūfic Inscription in . . . the Royal Palace of Mas^cūd III at Ghazni* (1966); Alessio Bombaci and Umberto Scerrato, "Summary Report on the Italian Archaeological Mission in Afghanistan," in *East and West,* 10 (1959); S. Flury, "Le décor épigraphique des monuments de Ghazna," in *Syria,* 6 (1925); Janine Sourdel-Thomine, "Deux minarets d'époque seljoukide en Afghanistan," in *Syria,* 30 (1953).

Lashkari Bāzār. In *Mémoires de la délégation archéologique française en Afghanistan,* 18, see the following: Jean Claude Gardin, *Les trouvailles: Céramiques et monnaies de Lashkari Bazar et de Bust* (1963); Daniel Schlumberger, *Lashkari Bāzār: L'architecture* (1978); Janine Sourdel-Thomine, *Lashkari Bāzār: Le décor nonfiguratif et les*

the sultans. Many elements of plan and construction in these monuments were derived from the ninth-century architectural tradition of the Abbasid royal palaces in Iraq. The south palace at Lashkari Bāzār, which is of typical mud-brick construction, dates from the first half of the eleventh century, though it shows considerable evidence of rebuilding. The original nucleus of the structure included a central court with four *eyvāns* (vaulted halls), enclosed within walls buttressed by massive towers. Among the most notable decorations are the frescoes from the audience hall. Executed in tempera on lime plaster, these depict the sultan's bodyguard in a procession toward

inscriptions (1978). Also, Daniel Schlumberger, "Le palais ghaznévide de Lashkari Bazar," in *Syria,* 29 (1952).

LINDA KOMAROFF

[See also **Abbasid Art and Architecture; Eyvān; Minaret.**]

GHAZNAVIDS, an Islamic dynasty that ruled in Afghanistan, northern India, and eastern Persia from 977 to 1186. Originally central Asians who became Turkish slaves, the Ghaznavids had the most powerful military empire known in these regions since the weakening of the Abbasid caliphate in the ninth century.

The founder, Sebüktigin, rose from the slave guard of the Samanid rulers of Transoxiana and Khorāsān to become ruler in Ghazna, in eastern Afghanistan, in 977; the town remained the capital of the empire until its final phase of decline. Sebüktigin began his military expansion within Afghanistan and then moved toward the Indus valley, a policy continued with brilliant success by his son Maḥmūd (998–1030), the greatest figure of the dynasty. Through his conquests as far west as Azerbaijan, northward into Khwarazm in the central Asian steppes, southward to the coast of Baluchistan and the Indus delta, and eastward to the Ganges plain of northern India, Maḥmūd built up an empire of enormous territorial extent.

From his strongly orthodox Sunni religious and diplomatic policies in dealing with other Muslims, and his successes against the pagan Hindus, Maḥmūd achieved a great contemporary reputation as hammer of the infidels, scourge of heretics, and the beau ideal of a despotic ruler in the Perso-Islamic mold; in modern Muslim India, he is generally regarded as a supreme hero of the faith. In fact, his raids into India were primarily for plunder rather than part of a systematic policy of converting the subcontinent to Islam; this last work did not properly get under way until the thirteenth century and the time of the Slave dynasty of Delhi. It is known, for instance, that Maḥmūd was quite happy to employ pagan Indian troops in his India and to use them against Muslims. The treasures of India did, however, provide a steady income to finance the expensive professional army and bureaucracy, as well as to beautify the capital Ghazna and other towns with fine buildings.

Maḥmūd's successor, Masᶜūd I (1030–1041), was less able than his father and lost the Persian prov-

inces to an invading Turkish people from the steppes, the Seljuks, with whom a definitive peace was not made until about 1060. Thereafter, the Ghaznavid Empire, somewhat truncated territorially but still powerful, was essentially oriented toward India and its exploitation. In the early twelfth century, the Ghaznavid sultans came to acknowledge the suzerainty of the Seljuks but were then confronted by a dangerous new power, against whom the Seljuks were powerless to give aid: that of the Ghurid chieftains of central Afghanistan. Ghazna was savagely sacked by the Ghurids in 1150 and never fully recovered. By 1163 the Ghaznavids were forced to abandon it altogether, and until 1186 they were confined to the Punjab and Sind, ruling from a new capital, Lahore. In 1186 the last sultan, Khusraw Malik, was deposed by the Ghurids, who succeeded to what was left of the Ghaznavid heritage.

Culturally, the Ghaznavid sultans were speedily assimilated to the Perso-Islamic tradition; Persian epic and lyrical poetry flourished at their court, and the surviving monuments of Ghaznavid architecture display a vigorous and individual eastern Islamic artistic style.

BIBLIOGRAPHY

Sources. The primary sources are mainly Arabic and Persian chronicles and official memoirs, such as ᶜUtbi's *Kitāb al-Yamīnī,* Gardīzī's *Zayn al-akhbār,* and Bayhaqī's *Ta'rīkh-ī Masᶜūdī,* for the earlier period; these are richer and more nearly contemporary with the events described than the sources for the post-1050 period, for which the main chronicles are Jūzjānī's *Ṭabaqāt-i Nāṣirī* and Ibn al-Athīr's *Kāmil.* All of these works exist in several editions.

Studies. C. E. Bosworth, *The Early Ghaznavids* (1967), *The Islamic Dynasties, a Chronological and Genealogical Handbook* (1967), 181–183, *The Later Ghaznavids* (1977), and *The Medieval History of Iran, Afghanistan and Central Asia* (1977); *Cambridge History of Iran,* IV, Richard N. Frye, ed. (1975), 162–197, and V, John A. Boyle, ed. (1968), 11–23, 50–53, 93–94, 157–166; Muḥammad Nāẓim, *The Life and Times of Sulṭan Maḥmūd of Ghazan* (1931).

C. E. BOSWORTH

[See also **Ghurids.**]

GHENT (Flemish: Gent; French: Gand). One of the five largest cities of modern Belgium and its second largest port, Ghent is an urban agglomeration of approximately 240,000 inhabitants in the 1980's. Located in the province of East Flanders, it was preeminent as a commercial and industrial center even in the tenth century when, along with Ypres and Bruges, it was one of the three leading towns in the county of Flanders. Its name—of Celtic origin, meaning river mouth—was no doubt derived from its strategic location at the confluence of the rivers Schelde and Lys, a location that probably caused it to be inhabited as early as the Roman period and certainly contributed to its becoming the center of a territorial circumscription known as a *pagus* in the Merovingian period (*ca.* 500–750). The area around Ghent, Christianized by the missionary St. Amand early in the seventh century, was the site of the monasteries of St. Bavo and St. Pierre, founded in the 630's. In the later ninth century there was a commercial quarter referred to in a document as a *portus*. This may have been the predecessor of the chief *portus* that developed early in the tenth century beside the new comital castle built on a triangle of land at the intersection of the Schelde and Lys rivers. Arising after Ghent had been pillaged and occupied by the Normans in 853 and again in 879 and 881, this second *portus* became the nucleus of Ghent, which thereafter grew steadily as an urban center. By 1000 it had a yearly fair of St. Bavo (1 October) and a reputation for its fine wool cloth. By 1100 it embraced an area of about 200 acres fortified with a wall and having four new parish churches.

Having undergone extraordinary growth during the twelfth century, Ghent reached its commercial and industrial apogee in the thirteenth. The period from 1100 to 1300 was the high point of exportation of English raw wool to Flanders. By the late twelfth century Ghent replaced Arras as the chief economic center of this area of Europe, and merchants from as far as Italy, Spain, southwestern France, and the Baltic were regular traders. In the second half of the thirteenth century, Ghent fabricated more wool cloth than any other European town. Early in the fourteenth century, however, with the rise of the wool industry in England, Ghent gradually lost its primacy as the wool center of northern Europe.

In the late tenth century the inhabitants of the commercial quarter next to the castle had obtained from the count of Flanders personal freedom with its elementary bourgeois privileges; economic concessions that gave them advantages in selling and buying at the local market as well as the right of owning, selling, and bequeathing property; and legal customs befitting their economic and social status. As a consequence a sharp difference developed between the bourgeois inhabitants of Ghent and the peasants in the surrounding countryside. Until 1127

the inhabitants of Ghent were governed by a comital official, generally the local castellan. When civil war erupted among contenders for the countship after the assassination of Count Charles the Good (1119–1127), Ghent and the other leading towns secured concessions, including the privilege of self-government. Henceforth Ghent had a municipal magistracy, an *échevinage,* that supervised such urban affairs as law enforcement, the courts, trading transactions in the market, taxation, fortifications, and public works. Like Bruges and Ypres, Ghent became a great commune that aspired to, and almost achieved, the political independence of the German free cities along the Rhine and of the city-states of northern Italy.

The twelfth and thirteenth centuries are known as the era of the patricians, those individuals from the bourgeois families who dominated the economic, social, and political life of Ghent as well as of the other Flemish towns. Because they acquired their wealth and position as fabricators and traders in wool cloth, contemporary records refer to them as *drapiers* and *marchands,* but in the Flemish vernacular, the language of Ghent and most of Flanders, they were called *poorters,* a word derived from the Latin *portus.* By the middle of the thirteenth century they not only controlled all the operations essential for the making of wool cloth but also imported wool from England and sold the finished cloth at the fairs of Champagne and throughout Europe. According to estimates this patrician class numbered 1,500–2,000 out of a total population of 60,000 in Ghent in the early fourteenth century.

Having acquired wealth through industry and trade, these patrician entrepreneurs usually purchased land and buildings with their surplus capital and became rentiers, eventually coming to live solely on their landed incomes. As leading members of the merchant guild who had spearheaded the struggle and negotiations for social, economic, legal, and political privileges, they continued to dominate the merchant guild and the magistracy. By the early thirteenth century the merchant guild had become an association limited solely to the patrician entrepreneurs, while the petty merchants, such as the butchers, shoemakers, and craftsmen in the wool industry, had organized themselves into craft guilds. The patricians had thus become capitalists and those they employed, simple wage earners, members of a mushrooming proletarian class. The lines drawn between the two classes were sharp and produced increasing tension.

When Ghent obtained self-government early in the twelfth century, the count of Flanders appointed thirteen men from the leading families to serve as magistrates (*échevins*). The term of office was to be one year, but later in the century they were serving for longer periods and, by usurping the count's power, were nominating their successors, often reappointing themselves. Toward the end of the century the counts forced the *échevins* of most towns to limit their tenure to one year, a condition accepted by Ghent in 1212. In 1214, however, after Count Ferrand (1212–1233) had been defeated at the Battle of Bouvines by his liege lord, King Philip Augustus of France, and taken as a captive to Paris, Ghent acquired more independence. Finally freed by 1228, Ferrand acquiesced to the patricians' demand for more local power. The thirteen *échevins* in office then named five individuals to replace them; they in turn named thirty-four others, among whom could be the original thirteen. The thirty-nine divided themselves into three groups of thirteen. For one year thirteen served as *échevins* on the magistracy, thirteen as councillors, and thirteen as inactive supernumeraries. At the end of the year the *échevins* became the supernumeraries, the supernumeraries the councillors, and the councillors the *échevins*. The following year a similar rotation occurred, with the result that the *échevinage* of thirty-nine retained political power indefinitely. When an *échevin* died, the others co-opted a replacement who invariably came from one of their families or another prominent patrician family. As the century progressed, son succeeded father, with the result that membership became hereditary and even more exclusive because the *échevinage* limited its membership to only a few of the greatest families from a patrician class that comprised at most a fortieth of Ghent's population. By the end of the century the *échevinage* was an oligarchic institution that monopolized local political and economic power without any limitations, and completely excluded the general population from any part in urban government.

Fearful of this powerful group that worked to govern Ghent as though it were an independent city-state, Count Guy de Dampierre (1278–1305) supported the craft guilds in their efforts to restrict the power of the thirty-nine and to acquire some participation in the government. These efforts were seldom successful because the patricians, when feeling threatened, would customarily seek the support of the count's feudal lord, the king of France, who was delighted to intervene in Flemish affairs and thus extend royal power into this rich French fief. To counter the alliance of the patricians with the French king, Guy de Dampierre looked to the English king, Edward I, for support, a natural reaction, given the enmity of the French and English monarchs and the close economic and political ties of England and Flanders since the early twelfth century.

Early in 1297 Guy first threw his support behind popular urban movements in all the Flemish towns, in a desperate bid to displace the patrician regimes that unabashedly regarded Philip the Fair of France as their protector, repudiated his feudal ties with Philip, and concluded a military alliance with Edward I. The patricians cast their lot with Philip while the people supported Guy. Bitter urban tension arose and a struggle erupted. The popular elements took as their standard the banner of the count (the Flemish lion) and called themselves *Clauwaerts* (men of the lion's claw), while referring to the patricians as *Leliaerts* (men of the lilies) because of their collaboration with the French king. In the war that ensued, Guy was defeated and taken as a captive to Paris. Flanders was incorporated into the French kingdom and ruled by a governor whom the Flemish so detested that in 1302 they revolted and threw out the hated French regime and the patricians, who took refuge in France. Although militia from most of the Flemish towns crushed Philip's army at the Battle of Courtrai in July 1302, the Flemish resources were unequal to those of the French. By 1305 the towns had to accede to the Treaty of Athis-sur-Orge, which imposed the return of the hated patricians and heavy indemnities, but nevertheless allowed Flanders to retain its independence.

Back in Ghent the patricians sought to reestablish themselves in power, but found their position so eroded that henceforth they were politically vulnerable. The fourteenth and fifteenth centuries were a time of political, economic, and social troubles ending a kind of golden age for Ghent and inaugurating centuries of stagnation terminated only by the industrial revolution in the late eighteenth century.

Despite their obvious shortcomings the patricians had a civic pride that, prior to the fourteenth century, led them to spend money on such public works as fortifications, paved streets, guild halls, a cloth hall, and canals linking Ghent to the sea. They erected for themselves imposing stone town houses known as *steenen*, such as that of Gerard the Devil, which today houses the provincial archives. They also supported the numerous new parish churches of the thirteenth century as well as leper houses and hospitals operated by religious orders. The Bijloke, the principal hospital of Ghent for seven centuries, was founded by Ermentrude uten Hove, the wife of a rich patrician. Some patricians established elementary lay schools for the basic education of their children. Financially able to aspire to a higher standard of living, the patricians took France as their model for fashion and social behavior. Although their language was Flemish, they learned to speak French, drank French wine rather than beer, dressed like the feudal aristocracy, adopted the title of "seigneur," and contracted marriages with feudal families. Philip the Fair was amazed at the wealth of Ghent and at its size, which embraced 1,600 acres, an extent not reached again until the nineteenth century.

Sometimes known as the "regime of the *métiers*," the two centuries after 1305 witnessed repeated attempts by the large craft guilds of the wool industry, such as that of the weavers, to seize political power in order to better their miserable economic plight, caused by the general European economic contraction of the fourteenth century and the competition of the English wool industry. Popular regimes of the guilds would occasionally seize power for short periods, then lose it to the patricians. The declining wool industry and chronic unemployment were constant economic problems of Ghent in the later Middle Ages. The outbreak of the Hundred Years War in 1337 exacerbated the situation of Ghent because Edward III of England imposed a ban on the export of wool to Flanders, in an attempt to force Count Louis de Nevers (1322–1346) to break his feudal support of the French king and to support England. Louis remained firm, but the desperate Flemish towns, under the leadership of Ghent, concluded a military alliance with Edward III in return for English wool.

Between 1338 and 1345 Jacob van Artevelde, a merchant, dominated the government of Ghent with the support of the craft guilds, and imposed the will of Ghent over all of Flanders. Early in 1340 as captain general of the city, he received Edward III at Ghent, where, in an imposing ceremony, the Flemish towns recognized Edward's claim to the French crown and Edward assumed the title of king of France. With the failure of Edward III's military operations in the Low Countries, however, the weavers turned against Artevelde, killed him, and assumed

power until 1349. At the same time that social and political struggle produced one regime after another within Ghent, there was a contest between Ghent and Count Louis de Mâle (1346–1384) for political control of Flanders. A revolt in 1379 deprived Louis of control and forced him to obtain French military assistance to restore his rule. In 1382 a French army decisively defeated the militia of the Ghent craft guilds led by Jacob van Artevelde's son Philip, who perished on the battlefield of Roosebeke.

In 1384 Louis de Mâle died and the countship passed to Duke Philip the Bold of Burgundy, who had married Louis's daughter and heiress Margaret. The following year Ghent concluded an agreement with Philip that brought an uneasy peace; but it chafed under central princely authority and desired complete political autonomy. In 1436 and again in 1452 Ghent revolted against the powerful Duke Philip the Good (1419–1467). When Philip crushed the stubborn commune in 1453, it was a defeat that forever dashed Ghent's hope for political independence. Nevertheless, it revolted against Charles the Bold (1467–1477), and against his daughter Mary and her husband, Maximilian of Austria. Finally, by the Treaty of Cadzand (1492), Maximilian imposed his will on the recalcitrant town. Until the late eighteenth century Ghent was under the firm control of the Habsburgs.

BIBLIOGRAPHY

Annals of Ghent, Hilda Johnstone, trans. (1951); Patricia Carson, *The Fair Face of Flanders,* rev. 3rd printing (1974); Victor Fris, *L'histoire de Gand,* 2nd ed. (1930); J. A. van Houtte *et al.,* eds., *Algemene Geschiedenis der Nederlanden,* II and III (1950–1951; a 2nd ed. is in process); Henri Pirenne, *Histoire de Belgique,* I, 3rd ed. (1922), and II (1908), *Belgian Democracy: Its Early History* (1915), and *Medieval Cities* (1925); Hans van Werveke, *Jacques van Artevelde* (1943), and *Gand: Esquisse d'histoire sociale* (1946), with an excellent bibliography.

BRYCE LYON

[See also Échevin; Flanders and the Low Countries; Philip IV the Fair; Wool.]

GHENT ALTARPIECE. The Ghent Altarpiece of the Lamb is the masterpiece of fifteenth-century Flemish painting. The huge polyptych consisting of twelve panels painted on both sides (except for the four central pieces) was begun by Hubert van Eyck

Adam and Eve. Two outer panels of the Ghent Altarpiece by Hubert and Jan van Eyck, *ca.* 1425–1432. ARCHIVES CENTRALES ICONOGRAPHIQUES, BRUSSELS

about 1425/1426 and after his death was completed by his brother Jan in 1432. It was commissioned by the local burgher Jodocus Vijd (or Vyd). When opened, the altarpiece displays the panorama of the Adoration of the Lamb by All Saints in Heaven (Rev. 4, 5, 7) in the lower zone, representations of Christ with the Virgin and St. John the Baptist in the center, and music angels, singing and playing instruments, and Adam and Eve in the upper. The two registers of the exterior depict the donor and his wife kneeling before Sts. John the Baptist and Evangelist below and the Annunciation above. The full range

of the Eyckian style is exhibited in the various panels executed with meticulous detail. One panel, the Just Judges, was stolen in 1934 and is replaced by a copy.

BIBLIOGRAPHY
Erwin Panofsky, *Early Netherlandish Painting* (1953); L. Brand Philip, *The Ghent Altarpiece and the Art of Jan van Eyck* (1971).

JAMES SNYDER

[See also **Eyck, Jan van and Hubert van; Flemish Painting.**]

GHIBELLINES. See Guelphs and Ghibellines.

GHIBERTI, LORENZO, Florentine sculptor, artistic entrepreneur, humanist writer, born 1378 or 1381, died 1455. Ghiberti was trained as a goldsmith by his stepfather, Bartolo de Michele, and, according to his autobiography, was influenced by a northern goldsmith named Gusmin.

In 1400 Ghiberti entered the competition to design a second pair of bronze doors for the Florentine Baptistery. Though the youngest of six competitors, he was awarded the commission, which he executed between 1403 and 1424. These doors comprise twenty-eight quatrefoil relief panels illustrating the New Testament, the four evangelists, and the four church fathers. The format recalls Andrea Pisano's doors for the same Baptistery (1330–1336), and the figures in part reflect the International Style in which Ghiberti had been trained. Among the assistants in his extensive workshop during these years were Donatello and Paolo Uccello.

Almost immediately upon the completion of this work Ghiberti was hired to execute the third set of Baptistery doors. He designed ten large square panels, cast in bronze and entirely gilded, illustrating Old Testament scenes. In their shape, size, use of linear perspective, and incorporation of classical imagery, they show the increasing ties between Ghiberti and leading innovators of the early Renaissance. His work continued to reflect, however, the gracefulness and interest in pictorial detail that characterized the International Style. Installed in 1452, the doors came to be known as "the Gates of Para-

Creation of Adam and Eve. Panel from the "Gates of Paradise," gilt bronze doors from the Baptistery, Florence, installed 1452. ALINARI/ART RESOURCE

dise" because of their exceptional beauty. Ghiberti's younger son, Vittorio (ca. 1418–1496), assisted him in the completion of the work.

Ghiberti and his large workshop prepared numerous other works including sculpture for the Or San Michele in Florence and for the Baptismal Font in Siena, as well as stained glass designs for the Cathedral of Florence. His fame as a writer depends on his *Commentarii,* which comprises a history and theory of art composed in accordance with humanist thought.

BIBLIOGRAPHY

Lorenzo Ghiberti, *I Commentari,* Ottavio Morisani, ed. (1947); Richard Krautheimer and Trude Krautheimer-Hess, *Lorenzo Ghiberti* (1956, repr. 1970).

BRUCIA WITTHOFT

[See also **Donatello; Gothic: International Style.**]

GHISLEBERT OF ST. AMAND (also spelled Gislebert) flourished in the late eleventh century as a monk and teacher at St. Amand. He fled the monastery during the fire of 1066, on which he based his long poem *De incendio monasterii sancti Amandi*. Other works include sermons and perhaps a commentary on the Epistles of St. Paul. He died at St. Amand on 7 December 1095.

BIBLIOGRAPHY

De incendio monasterii sancti Amandi, Ludwig K. Bethmann, ed., in *Monumenta Germaniae historica: Scriptores*, XI, 414; Max Manitius, *Geschichte der lateinischen Literatur des Mittelalters*, II (1923), 608–610.

NATHALIE HANLET

GHURIDS, an eastern Iranian dynasty of the twelfth and early thirteenth centuries that built up a powerful military empire in eastern Persia, Afghanistan, and northern India.

The Ghurids arose from the Shansabānī family of petty chiefs in the mountainous and inaccessible province of Ghūr in central Afghanistan, which until a comparatively late date had remained a pagan enclave within the Islamic world. The people of Ghūr must have been of Indo-Iranian stock and language, but it is not now possible to discern exactly to what branch they belonged; there is, however, nothing positive to indicate that they were ancestors of the modern Pushtuns.

Islam was implanted in Ghūr by the first sultans of the Turkish Ghaznavid dynasty, the capital of which was at Ghazna, on the eastern fringes of Afghanistan, and during the eleventh century the Ghaznavids exercised suzerainty over the chiefs of Ghūr. But in the later part of that century, the Shansabānīs were achieving primacy over other local potentates in Ghūr under the leadership of Quṭb al-Dīn Ḥasan; under his son ʿIzz al-Dīn Ḥusayn (1100–1146, known as "Father of Sultans," since four of his sons eventually held power) the Ghurid dynasty emerged as a major force in eastern Islamic history.

By this time the Ghaznavid Empire had lost its western territories and much of its earlier dynamic force. It had been replaced in eastern Persia by the Turkish Seljuks, whose eastern territories were now ruled by the forceful sultan Sanjar (1097–1157). The nascent Ghurid principality thus found itself a buffer state between the Seljuk and Ghaznavid empires, after 1107 paying tribute to the former instead of the latter. Internal disunity and strife over succession within the Shansabānī family limited their military efforts for a while, but a fortified capital was constructed in the heart of Ghūr, on the upper waters of the Heri Rud (at a site not yet exactly identified but perhaps to be equated with that of the still-standing minaret of Jam), and by 1150 ʿAlāʾ al-Dīn Ḥusayn felt ready to launch a campaign against the Ghaznavids, savagely sacking Ghazna and earning for himself the sobriquet *Jihān-sūz* (World Incendiary).

The Ghurids were now an imperial power, for the capture of the Seljuk sultan Sanjar by nomadic Oghuz Turkomans removed pressure on them from the west. The Ghaznavids were eventually compelled to evacuate Ghazna and eastern Afghanistan altogether, and for the final twenty or thirty years of their existence were confined to northern India, with their capital at Lahore, Ghazna having passed to the Ghurids in 1173.

Since the Ghurids had a patrimonial conception of power, their newly constituted empire was not a monolithic unity, but involved a distribution of power among various members of the family; the senior branch ruled over Ghūr from the capital Fīrūzkūh, with other branches ruling from Bāmiyān, over northeastern Afghanistan, and from Ghazna, the latter town providing a base for expansion down to the plains of northern India. Under the brothers Ghiyāth al-Dīn Muḥammad of Ghūr (1163–1203) and Muʿizz al-Dīn Muḥammad of Ghazna (1173–1206), the empire reached its peak of power. Ghiyāth al-Dīn was concerned with expansion westward into eastern Persia or Khorasan, hoping to succeed the Seljuks there. His suzerainty was acknowledged by various local powers of eastern Persia, such as the emir of Sistan and the Turkomans controlling Kermān.

The main obstacle to a Ghurid advance through Khorasan was, nevertheless, the rival imperial power to the northwest of the Turkish khwarizmshahs, who were themselves supported by their suzerains, the Mongol or Tungusic Qara-Khitai. Only after fierce fighting and the death of Khwarizmshah Tekish in 1200 did Ghiyāth al-Dīn extend his authority almost as far west as the Caspian Sea. In this struggle the Ghurids were able to pose as the defenders of Sunni religious orthodoxy and upholders of the caliphal authority, for the Baghdad caliphs feared the expansionist plans of the khwarizmshahs in western Persia. Unfortunately, after Ghiyāth al-Dīn's death, Muʿizz al-Dīn, whose career had been largely spent organizing jihad and plunder raids into India, was unable to stem a revanche by the new khwarizmshah, ᶜAlāᵓ al-Dīn Muḥammad, who was able to take over all of Khorasan except Herat by 1205.

Moreover, within a decade of Muᶜizz al-Dīn's death, the mighty Ghurid empire fell to pieces. There were internal succession disputes, with the Turkish and Ghūrī elements of the army supporting rival candidates, while Ghazna was seized by an ambitious Turkish general, Yildiz. The sultans had to call in their old enemies, the khwarizmshahs, for help, and the latter gradually took power for themselves. In 1215 the shah deposed the last of the Ghurids from Fīrūzkūh, those ruling from Bāmiyān being likewise removed. Thus all the Ghurid possessions save those in India were briefly under Khwarizmian control, until the arrival of the Mongols in the Middle East shortly afterward destroyed the Khwarizmian Empire.

The constituting of a great if transient empire was a remarkable achievement for the chiefs of one of the most backward regions of the eastern Islamic world; thereafter, Ghūr lapsed back into obscurity. But if the Ghurids' achievements in the eastern Persian world were evanescent, their legacy in India was of lasting significance. Muᶜizz al-Dīn expanded into the Punjab, overthrowing the last of the Ghaznavids in 1186 and making Lahore a bastion for further military activity. By the time of his death in 1206, his Turkish slave commanders, such as his lieutenant Quṭb al-Dīn Aybak (d. 1210), had penetrated deep into northern and central India, temporarily capturing Delhi and Gwalior. These conquests, and more, were subsequently consolidated by generals like Shams al-Dīn Iltutmish or, less correctly, Iletmish (d. 1236), the real founder of the independent Muslim sultanate of Delhi and of the line of the Slave dynasty.

BIBLIOGRAPHY

Sources. The chief primary source is Jūzjānī, *Ṭabaqāt-i Nāṣirī,* H. G. Raverty, trans., 2 vols. (1881–1897); it may be supplemented by Ibn al-Athīr, *al-Kāmil,* Carl J. Tornberg, ed., 15 vols. (1867–1877); and by Juwaynī, *Taᵓrīkh-i Jahāngoshā,* M. Qazvīnī, ed., 3 vols (1912–1937), translated by John A. Boyle as *The History of the World-conqueror,* 2 vols. (1958).

Studies. A general survey is given by C. E. Bosworth in "Ghūrids," in *Encyclopedia of Islam,* 2nd ed., II (1968); and in more detail in *Cambridge History of Iran,* V, John A. Boyle, ed. (1968), ch. 1. There is also a historical survey in André Maricq and Gaston Wiet, *Le minaret de Djam, la découverte de la capitale des sultans Ghorides (XIIᵉ– XIIIᵉ siècles)* (1959), 37–54. For the western Ghurid empire, see also Wasily Barthold, *Turkestan down to the Mongol Invasion,* 2nd ed. (1928); and for the eastern, Sir Wolseley Haig, in *Cambridge History of India,* III (1928), ch. 3. For the chronology of the dynasty, see C. E. Bosworth, *The Islamic Dynasties, a Chronological and Genealogical Handbook* (1967), 184–186.

C. E. BOSWORTH

[See also **Ghaznavids; Seljuks.**]

GIACOMO DA CAMPIONE (*d.* 31 October 1398), architect, engineer, and sculptor; native of the Po Valley. His one signed work is a doorway with figural sculpture leading into the north sacristy of Milan Cathedral; he is documented there as "inzignerius" as well (1388–1396). In an architectural capacity he was active also at the Certosa of Pavia (1396–1398).

BIBLIOGRAPHY

Giacomo C. Bascapè and Paolo Mezzanotte, *Il Duomo di Milano* (1965); 12, 13, 15, 17, 18, 84; "Giacomo di Zambonino da Campione," in Ulrich Thieme and Felix Becker, eds., *Allgemeines Lexikon der bildenden Künstler,* XVIII (1925), 290–291; Angiola Maria Romanini, *L'architettura gotica in Lombardia,* II (1964), 312 (index).

DALE KINNEY

GIACOMO DA LENTINO. See **Iacopo da Lentini.**

GIBUIN OF LANGRES (*fl.* late eleventh century), archdeacon of Langres until 1077, then archbishop of Rheims until 1082. A poem attributed to him, "Rithmus domini Gibuini Lingonensis episcopi de paradiso," consists of 120 three-line strophes describing the beauty of paradise in general and containing speculative statements.

BIBLIOGRAPHY

Max Manitius, *Geschichte der lateinischen Literatur des Mittelalters,* II (1923), 492, 618; W. Wattenbach, "Lateinische Gedichte aus Frankreich im elften Jahrhundert," in *Sitzungsberichte der Akademie der Wissenschaften zu Berlin, philosophisch-historischen Klasse* (1891).

EDWARD FRUEH

GILBERT OF POITIERS (Gilbert de la Porrée) (*ca.* 1075–1154) studied at Poitiers and Chartres, and taught at Chartres and, briefly, at Paris. He became bishop of Poitiers in 1142. Possibly influenced by Abelard, he was especially interested in applying logic to problems in theology. Like Abelard, Gilbert was accused of heresy by Bernard of Clairvaux, but was cleared by a council held at Rheims in 1148 and returned to his diocese (as a chronicler reported) "in the fullness of honor." He was considered one of the great masters of theology in the twelfth century, and his commentaries on the theological treatises of Boethius were widely used by later scholars.

BIBLIOGRAPHY

There is a long and interesting report on the trial of Gilbert, written by a contemporary, bishop Otto of Freising, in *The Deeds of Frederick Barbarossa,* Charles C. Mierow and Richard Emery, trans. (1953), 88–101. Nikolaus M. Häring has edited *The Commentaries on Boethius by Gilbert of Poitiers* (1966) and has written a number of useful articles: "The Commentary of Gilbert of Poitiers on Boethius' 'De hebdomadibus,'" in *Traditio,* **9** (1953), "The Commentary of Gilbert, Bishop of Poitiers, on Boethius, *Contra Eutychen et Nestorium,*" in *Archives d'histoire doctrinale et littéraire,* **21** (1954), "The Commentaries of Gilbert, Bishop of Poitiers (1142–1154), on the Two Boethian *Opuscula sacra* on the Holy Trinity," in J. Reginald O'Donnell, ed., *Nine Mediaeval Thinkers* (1955), and "Epitaphs and Necrologies on Bishop Gilbert II of Poitiers," in *Archives d'histoire doctrinale et littéraire du moyen âge* (1969).

JOSEPH R. STRAYER

[See also **Abelard, Peter; Bernard of Clairvaux, St.**]

GILBERTINE RITE. The few extant Gilbertine liturgical manuscripts reflect the Cistercian and Augustinian orientation of Gilbert of Sempringham (*ca.* 1083–1189), the founder of the Gilbertine order: a Cistercian calendar in its form of around 1150 with regional additions; a Cistercian sacramentary and Mass propers of the same period, supplemented with sequences and a few proper formularies; an Augustinian breviary; and an Augustinian ceremonial. This eclectic repertory bears the further stamp of regional particularities (presumably those of Lincolnshire, the chief center of Gilbert's activity). The nuns, who were not allowed to sing, recited their Office in a monotone.

BIBLIOGRAPHY

William Dugdale, ed., "Institutiones beati Giliberti," in *Monasticon Anglicanum,* 2nd ed. (1830), VI, pt. II, *xxix–xcvii; Archdale A. King, *Liturgies of the Religious Orders* (1955), 396–409; Reginald M. Woolley, ed., *The Gilbertine Rite,* 2 vols. (1921–1922).

CHRYSOGONOUS WADDELL, O.C.S.O.

[See also **Cistercian Rite.**]

GILDAS, ST. (*ca.* 500–570). A Briton by birth, Gildas is the principal written source for one of the most turbulent eras in the history of the British Isles. His *De excidio et conquestu Britanniae* provides rare glimpses of the Britons' plight following the end of the Roman occupation. Because they are contemporary or nearly contemporary, his comments on the Britons' resistance to Anglo-Saxon expansion are particularly valuable. Gildas reports that his birth coincided with the year in which the Britons won a stunning victory over the Germanic invaders at Mount Badon (ch. 26). Although the date cannot be fixed precisely, this battle probably took place around 500. The British triumph produced a lengthy period of relative calm during which the Anglo-Saxons were held in check. The peace had lasted for well over a generation at the writing of the *De excidio.* A completion date prior to 550 seems likely, but whether the composition should be placed in the first or second quarter of the sixth century remains uncertain.

Gildas was not a systematic historian; only a very small portion of the *De excidio* can be termed "historical" even in a limited sense. Didactic concerns predominate, and determine the selection of data. The British resurgence had brought comparative peace to the land, but instead of seizing the moment, the Britons had lapsed into indolence and depravity. Nevertheless, the calm gave cause for hope. A chance for significant advance lay at hand, if the Britons would only abandon their profligate ways. Gildas' contemporaries must be made to see both the nature of their folly and the historical ramifications of persistent myopia. To this end he reviews past and present failings, demonstrating a consistent pattern of British weakness and misdeed. Gildas never intended to provide a comprehensive record of contemporary events. The vast preponderance of the *De excidio* is homiletic, and this is especially true of the sections that deal with conditions in his own day.

The *De excidio* does not seem to have been circulated widely during the Middle Ages. Bede drew heavily on the text, thereby ensuring that selected items would become canonical. Later writers repeat the name of Gildas with reverence, but the mistaken attribution of the *Historia Brittonum* to him betrays considerable uncertainty regarding the work upon which his reputation as a historian rested. Very few medieval authors can be shown to have had firsthand familiarity with the text.

Modern scholars have repeatedly called the unity and the authorship of the *De excidio* into question, but their arguments are not convincing. The evidence favors Gildas' authorship of the whole. He appears to have written the *De excidio* before becoming a monk (ch. 65), perhaps as a young deacon. Two Lives of Gildas celebrate his career, one by an anonymous monk of the monastery of St. Gildas-de-Rhuys in Brittany (eleventh century) and the other by Caradog of Llancarfan (twelfth century). The earlier and less fabulous of the biographies plausibly places Gildas' death in 570. Fragments of both a penitential and of some letters also survive, as does a single Latin poem ascribed to Gildas.

BIBLIOGRAPHY

Sources. The *De excidio* was edited by Theodor Mommsen in *Monumenta Germaniae historica: Auctores antiquissimi,* XIII (1898), 1–85, the standard edition of all pertinent Latin texts; see also Hugh Williams, ed. and trans., 1 vol. in 2, Cymmrodorion Record Series, III (1899–1901), facing English trans. for all Latin texts; and Michael Winterbottom, ed. and trans. (1978), which does not include the two Lives of Gildas or the poem.

Studies. Margaret Deanesly, "The Implications of the Term *Sapiens* as Applied to Gildas," in D. J. Gordon, ed., *Fritz Saxl, 1890–1948: A Volume of Memorial Essays* (1957); Robert W. Hanning, *The Vision of History in Early Britain* (1966), 44–62; Kenneth Jackson, "*Varia*: II. Gildas and the Names of the British Princes," in *Cambridge Medieval Celtic Studies,* 3 (1982); F. Kerlouégan, "Le Latin du *De excidio Britanniae* de Gildas," in M. W. Barley and R. P. C. Hanson, eds., *Christianity in Britain, 300–700* (1968); M. Miller, "Bede's Use of Gildas," in *English Historical Review,* 90 (1975), and "Relative and Absolute Publication Dates of Gildas's *De Excidio* in Medieval Scholarship," in *Bulletin of the Board of Celtic Studies,* 26 (1976); Thomas D. O'Sullivan, *The 'De excidio' of Gildas: Its Authenticity and Date* (1978); Patrick Sims-Williams, "Gildas and the Anglo-Saxons," in *Cambridge Medieval Celtic Studies,* 6 (1983); C. E. Stevens, "Gildas Sapiens," in *English Historical Review,* 56 (1941); E. A.

Thompson, "Gildas and the History of Britain," in *Britannia,* 10 (1979) and 11 (1980), the latter being corrigenda.

R. WILLIAM LECKIE, JR.

[See also **Historiography, Western European.**]

GILES OF ROME. See **Egidius Colonna.**

GILIM. See **Kilim.**

GIORGI III (1156–1184). The grandson of David II (IV) the Builder (1089–1125) and the younger son of Demetre I (1125–1155/1156), Giorgi III came to the throne of Georgia after the Orbeli family overthrew and murdered his older brother David (1155) and restored his father, who in turn crowned Giorgi as coruler to assure his succession. Throughout his reign Giorgi was faced by threats to royal authority presented by the most powerful dynastic princes of his kingdom, most notably the Orbeli, who held the supreme military post of *amirspasalar*. In 1174–1177 the Orbeli led a revolt of several noble families to put Prince Demetre, David's son, on the throne, but the king managed to attract other dynasts to his side and defeated the rebels. Demetre was tortured to death, and the Orbeli were replaced as *amirspasalar* by the Kipchak commander Qubasar. Giorgi raised men from the lower classes to high office in order to keep the aristocracy from the center of power. Because he had no direct male heir and because Georgia had no precedent for a female ruler, Giorgi decided in 1178 to crown his daughter Tamar as coruler. A special coin was apparently struck with the names of the two monarchs.

At the same time that Giorgi strengthened his kingdom internally, he embarked on a series of foreign campaigns. The Georgian kings had spent much of the twelfth century in armed struggle with the Seljuks. Giorgi continued the wars of his father and grandfather, winning victories over the Shah-Arman, the Shaddadids, and the atabeg of Azerbaijan. Giorgi ruled a relatively strong kingdom and passed on to his daughter a prospering realm, but the centrifugal tendencies fostered by the dynastic princes remained to plague Queen Tamar (1184–1212).

BIBLIOGRAPHY

William E. D. Allen, *A History of the Georgian People* (1932, repr. 1971); David Marshall Lang, *Studies in the Numismatic History of Georgia in Transcaucasia* (1955); and *The Georgians* (1966); M. D. Lordkipanidze, *Istoriia Gruzii—XI–nachalo XIII veka* (1974); Cyril Toumanoff, "Armenia and Georgia," *Cambridge Medieval History,* IV. 1 (1966), 593–637, 983–1009.

RONALD GRIGOR SUNY

[See also **Amirspasalar; Georgia: Political History.**]

Adoration of the Magi. Giotto, detail of a fresco cycle in the Scrovegni Chapel, Padua, completed by 1305. ALINARI/ART RESOURCE

GIOTTO DI BONDONE (*ca.* 1267–1337), Florentine painter and architect. Giotto is a central figure in the history of Western art. His monumental and naturalistic interpretation of form changed the direction of Italian fourteenth-century painting, and his work had a profound impact on painters of subsequent generations. Famous in his own day, Giotto was the only contemporary artist praised in Dante's *Divine Comedy.*

Only a few documents about Giotto's life have been preserved, but they attest a far-flung and influential career. In 1327 his name was inscribed in the Florentine painters guild, the *Arte dei Medici e Speziali.* By 1328 he was in Naples, and in 1330 he entered the service of King Robert of Anjou, who awarded him an annual pension two years later. In 1334 he was named chief architect of the Florence Cathedral and probably designed its bell tower. In 1336 he was invited by Azzone Visconti to work for him in Milan. Scholars also speculate that he was active in Rimini. His chief surviving fresco cycle is in Padua. Giotto's fame spread over the entire Italian peninsula, and his style affected the syntax if not the whole language of painters.

Giotto's training and the origins of his style are still matters of debate. Tradition places him under Cimabue's tutelage, though scholars discount this connection as legend. Documents mention that Giotto had been in Rome by 1313, leading to speculation that he may have been influenced by the works of Cavallini, though the relative chronology of both artists leaves this question open. No doubt Cimabue's work, as well as the stylistic ferment in the paintings of Cavallini and the sculptures of Nicola Pisano and Arnolfo di Cambio, all active between 1270 and 1300, must have had an impact on Giotto. These artists share a common interest in the heroic, majestic interpretation of form, and in fig-

ures endowed with palpability and enormous volume. They were active in a time when European civilization was ready to witness a profound new understanding of religious art—one that transformed a formal iconic art into a human one in order to communicate with the viewer on a new, more direct level.

Giotto's oeuvre is still disputed, with the greatest controversy centering around his involvement in the fresco cycle depicting the *Life of St. Francis* in the upper church of S. Francesco, at Assisi. Other works such as his half-length *Madonna,* now in the National Gallery in Washington, are also disputed. His three signed works, the *Coronation of the Virgin* in the Baroncelli Chapel of S. Croce in Florence, the *Madonna and Saints* painted for S. Maria degli Angeli in Bologna (now in the Bologna Pinacoteca), and the *St. Francis Receiving the Stigmata* in the Louvre, Paris, are considered shop works.

Among his earliest generally accepted paintings is the fragmented *Madonna and Child,* now in the church of S. Giorgio alla Costa in Florence. This

530

majestic *Madonna* reveals a great affinity for the sculpture of Arnolfo di Cambio in the quiet power and almost mesmerizing reserve that emanates from it. Still demonstrating many elements of dugento prototypes, the S. Giorgio alla Costa *Madonna* already shows the tendency toward volume and gravity in the figures that would later distinguish Giotto's entire body of work.

At roughly the same time, about 1290 to 1300, Giotto must have painted his remarkable *Crucifix,* probably for the church of S. Maria Novella in Florence, where it still hangs. A radical reconception of the traditional crucifix, it transforms an iconic and abstracted conceptualization of a divinity into a startlingly convincing image of a once living, breathing human being who now hangs, heavy and dead, on a cross. Every aspect of human musculature, anatomy, and gesture has been used in this haunting and awesome painting, which is one of the largest surviving painted crucifixes. Its effect on other painters was immediate, and several examples of direct quotations from it are still extant, for example, Deodato Orlandi's S. Miniato al Tedesco *Crucifix* of 1301. The whole development of painted trecento crucifixes owes a great deal to Giotto's image.

Some five years later, about 1305, Giotto completed his magnificent large-scale panel *Madonna* for the Church of Ognissanti in Florence (now in the Uffizi). This painting, a landmark in the history of Western art, realizes all of the tendencies first expressed in Giotto's S. Giorgio alla Costa *Madonna.* Seated within a large gabled throne, which serves to define a fundamentally believable space, the Madonna appears as a superhuman entity, an imposing, inexorable presence. At the same time, this divine being acknowledges our existence as spectators, and her earthly core underscores her role as protectress and sympathetic intercessor for her human subjects. If the development of the painted crucifix was profoundly affected by Giotto's S. Maria Novella cross, then no less can be said for the impact of the Ognissanti *Madonna* painting on subsequent representations of the Madonna.

Giotto's greatest and best preserved achievement in fresco painting is his mural cycle depicting the *Life of Christ,* painted for the Scrovegni family chapel once attached to the now-destroyed Scrovegni palace in Padua. Giotto probably completed the frescoes in 1306; he probably began them sometime after Enrico Scrovegni acquired the land to build the chapel in 1300.

Twenty-two separate scenes narrate the story of Christ's life beginning with the *Expulsion of Joachim from the Temple* on the south wall and ending with the *Pentecost* on the north wall. Personifications of Virtues and Vices adorn the wainscoting. The west wall shows a dramatic depiction of the *Last Judgment.* The east wall depicts God sending Gabriel to tell Mary she will bear Jesus. Intended as a tomb and dedicatory expiation for the sin of usury on the part of Enrico's father, Reginaldo Scrovegni, the fresco cycle achieves the highest possibilities of wall painting as decoration and as pictorial narration. Each image is brilliantly conceived as an individual composition and yet is skillfully and deliberately constructed to relate and contrast with the surrounding images both compositionally and symbolically.

Every element of the fresco—the architecture, figure placement, gesture, color choices, composition type, use and location of solids or voids—is carefully calculated for maximum effect. Each image has myriad associations with those around it, making the Arena chapel cycle an extraordinarily great narrative drama. In order to convey the many meanings and psychological conditions of the characters in his stories, Giotto developed a whole range of expressions, gestures, and poses. His solid, monumental figures and the convincing settings that occupy each frame are endowed with a genial balance between realism and the demands of picture making.

Giotto painted the fresco cycle depicting the *Life of St. Francis* in the Bardi Chapel of S. Croce in Florence. Whitewashed in the eighteenth century, the two walls of frescoes were rediscovered in 1853, restored, and repainted; the repainting was removed in the 1950's. Each wall is divided vertically into three horizontal frames; the subjects illustrated include from top to bottom: *Francis Renouncing His Worldly Goods, The Approval of the Franciscan Rule, The Apparition of St. Francis at Arles, The Trial by Fire, The Death of St. Francis and the Verification of His Stigmata,* and *The Visions of Brother Agostino and Bishop Guido of Assisi.* Generally dated in the 1330's, these frescoes demonstrate a new development of Giotto's style. The narratives are simpler, less anecdotal and more elemental; the movement of his figures, always deliberate, has become at once more varied and slower. The palette, too, is reductive, consisting of a simple range of muted grays, browns, and pinks. The painter's vision is more sparing, but the dramatic impact is no less powerful, since he concentrates on the essential aspects of each story. Probably in response to the tendency found in contemporary painting, such as Simone Martini's 1333 *Annunciation,* there is a new tension between flatness and dimensionality in these images.

Giotto's last known fresco cycle, painted in the adjoining Peruzzi chapel of S. Croce, depicts the lives of SS. John the Baptist (left wall) and John the Evangelist (right wall). These frescoes too were whitewashed and were uncovered in 1841; since they were painted *a secco,* they have suffered more extensively. What is most significant about these broadly conceived frescoes is a new and reciprocal relationship between figures and architecture. The architecture, which set off or underscored figural placement in Giotto's earlier works, is now a convincing and integral part of the setting. The restrained approach found in the Bardi chapel becomes more relaxed in the Peruzzi cycle. The figures are heroic, with incidental details eliminated, but the effect is less concentrated, more haunting, and the image acts more slowly on the viewer. The calm assurance of these images, executed in soft, pastellike colors, are the product of a remarkable late style comparable to that of Titian or Michelangelo. This cycle, which absorbs rather than dominates the viewer, provided inspiration for many later artists, including Donatello, Masaccio, Ghirlandaio, and Michelangelo.

The question of Giotto's involvement in Assisi has challenged scholars for generations. Modern opinions still vary, but most scholars, after analyzing Giotto's sense of pictorial construction, narrative, and figural type, conclude that while Giotto's early style no doubt influenced the painters of the Assisi fresco cycle, Giotto's hand cannot be found with certainty in the paintings themselves.

BIBLIOGRAPHY

Mario Bucci, *Giotto* (1968), translated by Caroline Beamish; Bruce Cole, *Giotto and Florentine Painting, 1290–1375* (1976); *Giotto Bibliografia* (1970–1973); Millard Meiss, *Giotto and Assisi* (1960, 1967); Roberto Salvini, *Giotto, the Scrovegni Chapel in the Arena at Padua* (1953); Alastair Smart, *The Assisi Problem and the Art of Giotto* (1971); James H. Stubblebine, *Giotto: The Arena Chapel Frescoes* (1969); Marvin Trachtenberg, *The Campanile of Florence Cathedral: "Giotto's Tower"* (1971).

ADELHEID M. GEALT

[See also **Assisi, San Francesco; Fresco Painting.**]

GIOVANNI BUON. See **Buon, Giovanni and Bartolomeo.**

GIOVANNI D'AMBROGIO DA FIRENZE (*d.* 1418), Florentine sculptor first documented in 1366. From 1386 to 1387 he worked on the Prudence and Justice reliefs on the Loggia dei Lanzi, Florence, based on designs by Agnolo Gaddi. In 1391 he worked on the Porta della Mandorla of the Cathedral, including reliefs of Hercules. He carved a figure of St. Barnabas (now in the Museo dell'Opera del Duomo) for the Cathedral facade (1395–1396), and was also associated with an Annunciation group for the Porta della Mandorla. He was *capomaestro* of the Cathedral from 1404 to 1407. His name last appears in 1418.

BIBLIOGRAPHY

John Pope-Hennessy, *Italian Gothic Sculpture* (1972); Giulia Brunetti, "Giovanni d'Ambrogio," in *Rivista d'arte,* **14** (1932); Luisa Becherucci and Giulia Brunetti, *Il museo dell'opera del Duomo a Firenze* (1969); Charles Seymour, Jr., "The Younger Masters of the First Campaign of the Porta della Mandorla, 1391–1397," in *Art Bulletin,* **41** (1959).

ADELHEID M. GEALT

GIOVANNI DA CAMPIONE (*fl.* 1346–1363), Lombard in origin, son of the sculptor Ugo da Campione. He worked in Bergamo on the Baptistery (the reliefs of the Virtues on the corners of the building, the figure of St. John the Baptist over the altar, and possibly some reliefs with scenes from the life of Christ) and on S. Maria Maggiore, where he executed the equestrian figure of St. Alexander over the main entrance (1353) and part of the sculptured decoration of the lateral doorway (1360). The reliefs of the Virtues on the Baptistery have been ascribed to both Giovanni da Campione and his father.

BIBLIOGRAPHY

Costantino Baroni, *Scultura gotica lombarda* (1944), and "La scultura gotica," in *Storia di Milano,* (1955), 783–791; René Jullian, "Les persistances romanes dans la sculture gothique italienne," in *Cahiers de civilisation médiévale,* **3** (1960); Angiola M. Romanini, *L'architettura gotica in Lombardia* (1964), 292–295.

SANDRA CANDEE SUSMAN

[See also **Gothic Art: Sculpture.**]

GIOVANNI DA FIESOLE (Fra Angelico) (*ca.* 1400–18 February 1455), Florentine artist and one of the leading painters of his age. Firmly rooted in the traditions of medieval art, Fra Angelico is an important bridge to the Renaissance, and yet his singular vision sets him apart from his Florentine contemporaries. As heir to the rational vision of Masaccio, who helped forge the sturdy realism associated with fifteenth-century Florentine painting, Fra Angelico used these new tools to create images that had an entirely nonrational purpose. Nearly all of Angelico's work was devotional in function, so that the mundane reality first implied in his images gives way to a gentle yet intensely evocative spiritual world. Angelico invented no new themes, but he gave a profoundly personal interpretation to older ones and managed to fuse apparently paradoxical elements into a seamless whole. In his paintings, earthly reality becomes the stage upon which truly holy events take place; recognizable human emotions are chastened and transformed into beatific rapture; the temporal becomes timeless, and ordinary humanity is transformed into a state of the purest innocence. In his remarkable achievements, Fra Angelico remains unequaled in Florentine painting, and his poetic vision has no true parallel in Italian art anywhere except perhaps in the work of Giovanni Bellini.

Fra Angelico was born Guido di Piero. His exact training is unknown, but documents indicate his activity as early as the second decade of the quattrocento. In 1418, for example, a Guido di Piero was paid for an altarpiece for the Gherardini chapel in S. Stefano al Ponte, Florence, a work that does not survive. Shortly thereafter (between 1418 and 1421) he joined the Dominicans and became known as Fra

Annunciation. Giovanni da Fiesole (Fra Angelico), first half of the 15th century. ALINARI/ART RESOURCE

Giovanni da Fiesole, devoting himself exclusively to religious painting. Despite his fame and importance as well as a relatively high survival rate for his work (now concentrated largely at the Museo di S. Marco, Florence), Fra Angelico's career is complex and his artistic development is still the subject of debate. Documents are scarce, especially for his earliest phase, in the late 1410's and 1420's. His earliest surviving documented altarpiece was painted for the Convent of S. Pietro Martire in Florence in 1429. Now in the Museo di S. Marco, it depicts the Virgin with Sts. John the Baptist, Dominic, Peter Martyr, and Thomas Aquinas. Surviving works that may precede this effort include the the S. Domenico di Fiesole altarpiece (the predellas are in London, National Gallery), which probably postdates Masaccio's S. Giovenale triptych of 1422 and Gentile da Fabriano's *Adoration* of 1423 by one or two years. Another work sometimes ascribed to his early career is the *Madonna of Humility,* now in the Museo Nazionale in Pisa, which shows the influence of Antonio Veneziano as well as of Masolino. The *Annunciation,* now in the Prado, Madrid, may have been executed for S. Domenico in Fiesole. If so, it was completed sometime before 1435, though the place of the Prado *Annunciation* in Angelico's oeuvre is still questioned.

Several documented works serve as guideposts for Angelico's activities during the 1430's. In 1433 he received the commission for the triptych to be placed in the guildhall of the Florentine Arte dei Linaiuoli. The frame enclosing the monumental work is based on Ghiberti's design, which suggests that Ghiberti may also have provided models for the figures of standing saints. Connections with Masolino and Masaccio are evident as well. The *Annunciation,* formerly of the Gesù at Cortona and now in the Museo Diocesano there, is also ascribed to this decade. In 1436 Angelico completed the *Lamentation over Christ,* now in the Museo di S. Marco. Commissioned by the confraternity of S. Maria della Croce al Tempio, it may have been done with the aid of assistants. Yet it stands as a masterpiece in its depiction of reverential mourning and its elegiac contrast of figures and landscape.

A polyptych painted for the chapel of St. Nicholas in S. Domenico, Perugia (now in the Galleria Nazionale dell'Umbria) dates from the following year, 1437. This work reflects the gradual maturation of Angelico's style, as he moves away from the monumentality and volumetric dynamism of his earlier works toward a gentler, more delicate, and more cohesive vision. Perhaps shortly earlier is Angelico's altar for the church of S. Domenico at Cortona. Here the spatial energy is still expressed through emphatically stated drapery forms that undulate throughout the picture to carve out a third dimension. The *Coronation of the Virgin,* painted for S. Egidio (S. Maria Nuova), Florence, and now in the Uffizi, is also generally ascribed to this period, as are the frescoes of the *Virgin and Child with Sts. Dominic and Thomas Aquinas* (formerly in the refectory, S. Domenico, Fiesole) and *Christ on the Cross Adored by St. Dominic and the Virgin* (formerly in the refectory, S. Domenico, Fiesole), today in Leningrad and Paris. The frescoes of the *Virgin and Child with Sts. Dominic and Peter Martyr* above the west door of S. Domenico at Cortona are usually dated around 1438.

In 1437 the Dominicans gained title over the ruined convent of S. Marco and began rebuilding with designs by Michelozzo; by 1443 they had completed a total of forty-four cells. Today this complex houses the Museo di S. Marco. In addition to frescoes in forty-three of the cells, the decorative program included *Christ on the Cross Adored by St. Dominic* (ground floor), *Crucifixion with Attendant Saints* (Sala del Capitolo), and a *Crucifixion* (refectory, destroyed in a fire of 1554). The upper-floor frescoes included *Christ on the Cross Adored by St. Dominic,* an *Annunciation,* and a *Virgin and Child with Saints.* Whether they represent Angelico's design alone, or his execution as well, these frescoes constitute one of the most extensive surviving decorative cycles undertaken for a religious order. Angelico also painted a large altarpiece for the convent, to replace Lorenzo Gerini di Niccolo's *Coronation of the Virgin* (1402), which Cosimo de' Medici gave to the church of S. Domenico in Cortona in 1440. It is thought that Angelico painted the high altar in 1437–1438 and then concentrated on the frescoes; he probably continued working on them until he was called to Rome and may have completed some after his return.

Though in poor condition, with its predellas scattered, the high altar for S. Marco stands as a revolutionary work in the history of fifteenth-century Italian painting. A whole new repertoire of pictorial devices (the oriental rug, the wall and row of cypress trees, the arrangement of figures) created spatial cohesion without the artifice of earlier images and expanded the visual vocabulary of future painters. The *Deposition from the Cross* painted for the Strozzi chapel of S. Trinità and now in the Museo di

S. Marco is generally dated to the 1440's, though this dating is not universally accepted. Having inherited a panel (very likely from an unfinished work by Lorenzo Monaco), Angelico imaginatively solved the problem of the tripartite Gothic frame. Using bold and economical compositional devices, he contrasted landscape with figures, unifying them visually without integrating them spatially. This lack of spatial cohesion has led some scholars to suggest an earlier date, though it was quite likely a deliberate choice on the artist's part in the 1440's to concentrate on the actors in this holy tragedy.

The extent of Angelico's activity in Rome is unclear. Vasari reports that Angelico painted various scenes from the life of Christ for the Capella del Sacramento or Chapel of St. Nicholas of Bari (b. 374) for Pope Eugenius IV. However, Vasari also describes portraits whose inclusion in this picture cycle must postdate Angelico's early activity in Rome, making the nature of Angelico's work in the Capella del Sacramento a matter of speculation since the frescoes were torn down by Paul III in the following century. After Eugenius IV died in 1447, his successor Nicolas V commissioned Angelico to decorate his private chapel in the Vatican, now known as the chapel of Nicholas V (however, records indicate that the chapel was founded earlier by Nicholas III). Filling three sides of the chapel, this cycle constitutes Angelico's only surviving Roman work. Payment is recorded in 1447, during which time Angelico and his principal assistant, Benozzo Gozzoli, were also at work in the Cathedral of Orvieto; the Nicholas V chapel was completed in 1448. Depicting the lives of Sts. Stephen and Lawrence, these frescoes are not specifically designed for devotion but as historical narrative. The artist has therefore permitted the rare intrusion of mundane reality into his work. The episodes are sprinkled with incidental details that enrich their specificity and narrative content. Careful of structure and often borrowing compositional devices from Giotto, Angelico forged a new and forward-looking pictorial language in these frescoes, which would profoundly influence the work of Ghirlandaio as well as Benozzo Gozzoli.

In late 1449 or early 1450 Angelico returned to Florence. By June of 1450 he succeeded his brother as prior of S. Domenico at Fiesole. He held the position for two years, during which time he negotiated with Prato Cathedral for the decoration of the choir, a commission ultimately awarded to Fra Filippo Lippi. Thereafter, documentation is scarce. In 1454 his participation in the assessment of frescoes executed in Perugia is noted, and there are hints that he might have returned to Rome in 1453 or 1454. He certainly died there, predeceasing his patron, Nicholas V, by a few weeks. His late works are nearly as difficult to establish as his earliest ones: the altar painted for the Church of S. Buonaventura at Bosco ai Frati (now in the Museo S. Marco) is placed after 1450, as is the *Coronation of the Virgin* now in the Louvre (though this is sometimes given to the 1430's).

All of Fra Angelico's work bears the mark of an artist devoted to his vision not only by training but through faith. He brought to his subjects a reverence born of conviction that endows his images with a purity of sentiment unequaled in the history of art. His influence, which survived by way of his work and his major pupil, Benozzo Gozzoli, was far-reaching, but as a painter of deeply religious art he had no true followers.

BIBLIOGRAPHY

Diane C. Ahl, "Fra Angelico: A New Chronology for the 1420s ... and 1430s," in *Zeitschrift für Kunstgeschichte*, 43–44 (1980–1981); John W. Pope-Hennessy, *Fra Angelico*, 2nd ed. (1974).

ADELHEID M. GEALT

[See also **Florence; Fresco Painting; Gothic Art: Painting and Manuscript Illumination; Italian Painting; Masaccio.**]

GIOVANNI DA MILANO, a Milanese painter documented in Florence between 1346 and 1366 and in Rome in 1369. An extraordinary artistic figure, Giovanni spoke a language of grace, artifice, and sensuality verging on the erotic. His origins are unclear, but his style has a counterpart in the Trecento Sienese painter Barna da Siena, and his ideas were further developed in the fifteenth century by Carlo Crivelli and Matteo di Giovanni (Matteo da Siena). His principal surviving works include the frescoes on the top two tiers of the Rinuccini Chapel of S. Croce, in Florence; his signed *Pietà*, now in the Accademia in Florence (an unusual interpretation of the theme), and five pairs of saints from the high altar of Ognissanti Church, now in the Uffizi, Florence.

BIBLIOGRAPHY

Richard Fremantle, *Florentine Gothic Painters* (1975); Alessandro Marabottini, *Giovanni da Milano* (1950); Pie-

tro Toesca, *La pittura e la miniatura nella Lombardia* (1912).

ADELHEID M. GEALT

[See also **Barna da Siena; Gothic Art: Painting and Manuscript Illumination.**]

GIOVANNI (GIOVANNINO) DE' GRASSI (*d.* 1398), Milanese architect, sculptor, painter, and miniaturist. His distinctive manuscript illuminations, known from the first part of the Visconti Hours (Florence, Biblioteca Nazionale), attributed to him and his workshop during the 1390's, and the Breviary (Milan, Biblioteca Trivulziana) that he executed for Milan Cathedral between 1396 and his death, are marked by detailed figure compositions in naturalistic settings and even more by brightly colored and gilded borders of foliage, figures, and architectural elements. Parts of a sketchbook attributed to Giovanni and depicting detailed renderings of animals survives in Bergamo. Of his prolific and diversified sculptural work, only the relief over the south sacristy lavabo in the Milan cathedral, depicting Christ and the Samaritan woman, remains. Begun in 1391, it was painted and gilded by Giovanni in 1396.

BIBLIOGRAPHY

Millard Meiss and Edith W. Kirsch, *The Visconti Hours* (1972); Paolo Mezzanotte and Giacomo C. Bascapé, *Milano nell'arte e nella storia* (1968); John W. Pope-Hennessy, *Italian Gothic Sculpture* (1972).

ADELHEID M. GEALT

[See also **Gothic, International Style.**]

GIOVANNI DI BALDUCCIO (*ca.* 1290–*ca.* 1350), sculptor, was born in Pisa and employed by its cathedral (1317–1318), where Tino di Camaino was working. Among his works are the high altar of S. Domenico Maggiore, Bologna (*ca.* 1320–1325); the tomb of Guarniero degli Antelminelli in S. Francesco, Sarzana (1327–1328); the pulpit with reliefs of the Annunciation in S. Maria del Prato, S. Casciano (early 1330's); the Baroncelli tomb in S. Croce, Florence (early 1330's); the Baroncelli tomb in S. Croce, Florence (early 1330's); and statuary in S. Maria della Spina, Pisa (after 1318). Giovanni was responsible for the shrine of St. Peter Martyr in S. Eustorgio (1335–

GIOVANNI (NANNI) DI BARTOLO

1339), the tomb of Azzone Visconti (*d.* 1339) in S. Gottardo; the facade of S. Maria de Brera (1347); and the monument of Lanfranco Settala in S. Marco (*ca.* 1349). It is possible that he designed the shrine of St. Augustine in S. Pietro in Ciel d'Oro, Pavia (begun after 1350). Giovanni was an important contributor and gifted member among sculptors of the generation separating Nino from Giovanni Pisano.

BIBLIOGRAPHY
Enzo Carli, "Sculture pisane di Giovanni di Balduccio," in *Emporium,* **97** (1943); Cesare Gnudi, "Un altro frammento dell'altare bolognese di Giovanni di Balduccio," in *Belle arti,* **1** (1946–1948), and "Ancora per l'altare bolognese di Giovanni di Balduccio," in *Critica d'arte,* **8** (1949); Max Seidel, "Studien zu Giovanni di Balduccio und Tino di Camaino," in *Städel-Jahrbuch,* n.s. **5** (1975); Emilio Tolaini, "Alcune sculture della facciata del Camposanto di Pisa," in *Critica d'arte,* n.s. **18** (1956), repr. in *Studi in onore di M. Marangoni* (1957); W. R. Valentiner, "Giovanni Balducci e una scultura di Maso a Firenze," in *L'arte,* n.s. **6** (1935), and "Notes on Giovanni Balducci and Trecento Sculpture in Northern Italy," in *Art Quarterly,* **10** (1947).

SANDRA CANDEE SUSMAN

GIOVANNI (NANNI) DI BARTOLO (*fl.* 1419–1451), called "Il Rosso," a sculptor active in Florence, Venice, Verona, and Tolentino. Between 1419 and 1420 he executed an unidentified sculpture for the facade of the cathedral in Florence; in 1420 or 1421 he completed a marble *Joshua* begun by Ciuffagni (now in the Museo dell'Opera del Duomo). Giovanni assisted Donatello on the *Abraham and Isaac* group for the campanile of the cathedral (now in the Museo dell'Opera del Duomo) in 1421–1422, and in 1422 he produced and signed a marble *Abdias* (Obadiah, also now in the Museo dell'Opera del Duomo) for the campanile. By 1424 he had gone north, where his principal known work is the signed portal of S. Nicola at Tolentino (datable to 1432–1435). The Brenzoni monument in S. Fermo Maggiore, Verona is attributed to him. Giovanni may be the "Rosso" documented in connection with Giovanni and Bartolomeo Buon's work on a wellhead for the Ca' d'Oro in Venice (1427).

BIBLIOGRAPHY
Luisa Becherucci and Giulia Brunetti, eds., *Il Museo dell'Opera del Duomo a Firenze,* I (1969), nos. 149–152;

GIOVANNI DI BENEDETTO DA COMO

John W. Pope-Hennessy, *Italian Gothic Sculpture,* 2nd ed. (1972), 216–217; Charles Seymour, Jr., *Sculpture in Italy, 1400–1500* (1966).

ADELHEID M. GEALT

[See also **Buon, Giovanni and Bartolomeo; Donatello; Gothic Art: Sculpture.**]

GIOVANNI DI BENEDETTO DA COMO, Lombard miniaturist, active in the second half of the fourteenth century. His key work is the signed Book of Hours containing thirty-six miniatures. Painted for Bianca of Savoy, it was executed between 1350 and 1378 and now is located in the Munich Staatsbibliothek (Cod. Lat. 23215). The miniatures are noted for their imaginative use of text.

Miniature from the Book of Hours painted for Bianca of Savoy by Giovanni di Benedetto da Como between 1330 and 1378. MUNICH, BAYERISCHE STAATSBIBLIOTHEK, COD. LAT. 23215, fol. 39v

GIOVANNI DI CECCO

BIBLIOGRAPHY

Mario Salmi, *Italian Miniatures*, Elisabeth Borgese-Mann, trans. (1954), 42–43; Pietro Toesca, *La pittura e la miniatura nella Lombardia, dai più antichi monumenti all metà del quattrocento* (1912), 279ff.

ADELHEID M. GEALT

[See also **Book of Hours; Manuscript Illumination.**]

GIOVANNI DI CECCO (*fl. ca.* 1365–1384), minor sculptor and architect in Siena, also called "Giovannino de la pietra." His documented sculptures are the baptismal font in the Collegiata of S. Gimignano (1379) and the *St. Matthew* for the chapel of the Siena *Campo* (1380–1384). Although he was foreman (*capomaestro*) during completion of the Siena cathedral facade (1377), the facade sculptures are no longer considered his work.

BIBLIOGRAPHY

Enzo Carli, *Il Duomo di Siena* (1979), 26, 28, 59–60; Giovanni Cecchini, *San Gimignano* (1962), 67, 86; Antje Kosegarten, "Einige sienesische Darstellungen der Muttergottes aus dem frühen Trecento," in *Jahrbuch der Berliner Museen*, n.s. 8 (1966); Gaetano Milanesi, *Documenti per la storia dell'arte senese*, I (1854, repr. 1969), nos. 68, 76–80.

DALE KINNEY

[See also **Gothic Art: Sculpture; Siena.**]

GIOVANNI DI PAOLO (*ca.* 1403–1483), Sienese painter. Called a pupil of Paolo di Giovanni Fei, he took much inspiration from his older contemporary Sassetta. Like Sassetta, Giovanni was an expressive, intensely mystical painter who exploited the Sienese tradition to produce paintings that ignored stylistic developments elsewhere. His paintings reach the emotions rather than the rational faculties. Among his most important works are the *Pecci Madonna,* dated 1426, the center panel of which was recently restored; his *Crucifixion,* a polyptych signed and dated 1440 (Siena, Pinacoteca); and the *Branchini Madonna* (1427) (Pasadena, Calif., Norton Simon Museum). His narrative images are exceptional for their visionary, imaginative qualities. Outstanding among them are the four panels depicting Christ's Passion in the Walters Art Gallery, Baltimore, which belong to the dismembered Pecci altar.

GIOVANNI PISANO

BIBLIOGRAPHY

Bernard Berenson, *Italian Pictures of the Renaissance, Central and North Italian Schools*, 2 vols., 2nd ed. (1968); Cesare Brandi, *Giovanni di Paolo* (1947); Bruce Cole, *Sienese Painting in the Age of the Renaissance* (1984); John W. Pope-Hennessy, *Giovanni di Paolo* (1937).

ADELHEID M. GEALT

[See also **Gothic Art: Painting and Manuscript Illumination; Paolo di Giovanni Fei; Sassetta.**]

GIOVANNI PISANO (*fl.* 1265–*ca.* 1314), sculptor and architect, son of Nicola Pisano. His major works are the lower half of the facade of the Cathedral of Siena (*ca.* 1284–1296); the pulpit in S. Andrea, Pistoia (inscribed 1301); the pulpit in the Cathedral of Pisa (1302–1311); and the tomb of Margaret of Luxembourg (*ca.* 1312). He had a minor role in the Siena pulpit of his father, and major ones in the exterior sculpture of the baptistery at Pisa (1270's) and the Fontana Maggiore in Perugia (1278). Giovanni also sculpted a number of Madonnas, including the ivory statuette in Pisa (1298), and a group of wooden crucifixes.

Giovanni was very receptive to the art of the thirteenth-century French sculptors, but this interest led him neither to slavishly imitate their forms nor to reject his father's classicism. It did, however, help him conceive his expressive and highly emotional style, arguably the sculptural counterpart of Giotto's achievement in painting. For the Siena facade Giovanni placed fourteen monumental prophets of the Virgin—including Plato, Aristotle, and a sibyl—at the level of the archivolts of the three large portals. This arrangement owes much to French inspiration, but the result is characteristically unique. The polychromy is, of course, a Tuscan practice, and the figured rinceaux of the colonnettes draw heavily on antique precedents. Of the prophets the sibyl is probably an earlier work; and Mary, the sister of Moses, with her bent neck, outthrust and turned head, a later one.

These distortions continue in the Pistoia pulpit, a hexagon set on steeply pointed, trilobe arches. Around the body of this work are reliefs of the Nativity cycle, the Crucifixion, and the Last Judgment. The iconography is close to Nicola's Siena pulpit, but the style differs. Giovanni links figures by sweeping, scythelike patterns that carry across the corner figures. Below, at the level of the archivolts, are prophets and six ecstatic sibyls.

The later Pisan pulpit is octagonal, but its geometry is complicated by the convexity of the nine reliefs. The usual Nativity segment is supplemented by the infancy of John the Baptist, and the Crucifixion is preceded by Passion scenes. Prophetic figures, including sibyls, are beneath, at the level of the classical consoles. The outstanding feature is the lowest story, which has full-size caryatid figures of the Cardinal Virtues, Ecclesia/Charity, Christ, the evangelists, St. Michael, and Hercules. The text on Christ's scroll paraphrases Psalm 85:12, which suggests that the group symbolizes divine and earthly justice. The

quality of the reliefs and even of certain of the supporting figures is uneven. Some, which tend to be formularized and repetitive, are usually thought to contain much shop participation; others, especially the figures of Christ, the Virtues, and Hercules, are very strong, expressive, and reminiscent of Giovanni's earlier work.

Only dispersed fragments survive from the tomb of Margaret of Luxembourg. A central motif was the resurrection of the empress, which was based on the type of the awakening Virgin known in French sculpture.

Christ carrying the Cross. Giovanni di Paolo, 1426. COURTESY OF THE WALTERS ART GALLERY, BALTIMORE

Strength and Prudence. Detail of the pulpit in Pisa Cathedral.
1302–1311. © PHAIDON PRESS

BIBLIOGRAPHY

Enzo Carli, *Il pergamo del Duomo di Pisa* (1975), and
Giovanni Pisano (1977); Harald Keller, *Giovanni Pisano*
(1942); Antje Kosegarten, "Nicola und Giovanni Pisano
1268–1278," in *Jahrbuch der Berliner Museen,* **11** (1969);
Gian Lorenzo Mellini, *Il pulpito di Giovanni Pisano a Pis-
toia* (1969), and *Giovanni Pisano* (*ca.* 1970); John W. Pope-
Hennessy, *An Introduction to Italian Sculpture,* part 1:
Italian Gothic Sculpture, 2nd ed. (1972), 7–12, 175–180;
Max Seidel, "Das Fragment einer Statue Giovanni Pisanos
im Museo Guarnacci in Volterra," in *Mitteilungen des
Kunsthistorischen Instituts in Florenz,* **15** (1971), *La scultura lignea di Giovanni Pisano* (1971), "Die Berliner Madonna des Giovanni Pisano," in *Pantheon,* **30** (1972), "Die
Elfenbeinmadonna im Domschatz zu Pisa," in *Mitteilung-
en des Kunsthistorischen Instituts in Florenz,* **16** (1972),
and "*Ubera Matris:* Die vielschichtige Bedeutung eines
Symbols in der mittelalterlichen Kunst," in *Städel-Jahrbuch,* **6** (1977).

MICHAEL D. TAYLOR

[See also **Gothic Art: Sculpture; Nicola Pisano.**]

GIRALDUS CAMBRENSIS. See **Gerald of Wales.**

GIRART DE ROUSSILLON, MASTER OF THE.
See **Jean, Dreux.**

GIRAUT DE BORNELH (*ca.* 1140–*ca.* 1200), troubadour, poet, and composer, was born at Excideuil,
near Périgueux. References in his songs indicate that
he traveled extensively through southern France and
northern Spain and participated in the Third Crusade. According to his *vida,* Giraut was a schoolmaster who spent summers at various courts with
two musicians who performed his songs. He thus exemplifies the type of troubadour who was neither nobleman nor professional entertainer. His reputation
was high among court critics, and three of his works
were cited for excellence by Dante in his treatise *De
vulgari eloquentia.* Of Giraut's seventy-seven known
poems, only four have music extant. Among these
four are a *planh* for Richard the Lionhearted and the
alba "Reis glorios."

BIBLIOGRAPHY

Adolf Kolsen, ed., *Sämtliche Lieder des Trobadors Giraut de Bornelh,* 2 vols. (1910–1935, repr. 1976); Arié Ser-
per, "Guiraut de Borneil, le 'gant,' le *trobar clus* et lig-
naure," in '*Revue des langues romanes,* **81** (1974); Hendrik
van der Werf, *The Chansons of the Troubadours and
Trovères* (1972).

MARCIA J. EPSTEIN

[See also **Alba; Provençal Literature; Troubadour, Trouvère, Trovadores.**]

GIRDLED PATRICIAN, a title first given by Emperor Theophilus in 830 to his mother-in-law,
Theoktista, the mother of Empress Theodora II.
Basil II conferred the title on Marie, the widow of
the Bulgarian Czar John Vladislas in 1018. The
holder of this title was the only woman admitted
into the imperial hierarchy and the only woman who
could attend imperial banquets, from which the empress herself was excluded. The girdled patrician
dined at the table of the emperor in the company of
the patriarch, the caesar, the *nobilissimos,* the curopalate, and the basileopator. Her insignia was an

ivory diptych. According to the *Book of Ceremonies* of Constantine VII, there could be more than one at a time, and the girdled patrician occupied the first place among the women of the empress's court.

BIBLIOGRAPHY
Louis Bréhier, *Les institutions de l'empire byzantin* (1949).

LINDA ROSE

GIRK Tᶜ ⱢTᶜOCᶜ (Book of letters), a collection of ninety-eight original and translated documents in the Armenian language, dating from the fifth to the thirteenth centuries, that are for the most part theological works defending the doctrinal position of the Monophysite formula of one nature against the Duophysite formula adopted at the Council of Chalcedon in 451. The first five documents and a few toward the end do not, however, fall into this general category. The earliest manuscript, copied in 1298, has a colophon stating that at the end of the eleventh century the collection contained only the first fifty-six documents. The rest were added after the eleventh century and before 1298.

The older section is well organized and chronologically arranged. It begins with the correspondence between Bishop Sahak of Armenia, and Patriarch Proklos of Constantinople and Bishop Acacius of Melitene (letters I–V). The letters of Proklos and Acacius warn the Armenians about Nestorianism. The Hellenizing style of letters VI and VII, which are against Chalcedonianism, indicates a sixth- or seventh-century origin. The first is attributed to Movsēs Xorenacᶜi. The second is in the name of Archbishop Yovhannēs of Armenia, who is identified with the fifth-century *katᶜolikos* Yovhannēs Mandakuni, but is now believed to belong to Bishop John of Alexandria. These are followed by two letters of *Katᶜolikos* Babgēn (502–508) to the Persian Monophysites (letters VIII–IX); correspondence between *Katᶜolikos* Nersēs II of Bagrewand (548–557) and the Syriac bishop Abdišoy (letters X–XVII); two letters and a treatise of *Katᶜolikos* Yovhannēs Gabełan (XVIII–XX); correspondence between Sormen Stratelates of Byzantine Armenia and Bishop Vrtᶜanēs Kᶜertᶜoł, who was locum tenens of the Armenian patriarchate in the early seventh century; and more than thirty documents that constitute a subunit and are about the Armeno-Georgian schism

of the early seventh century and related events (XXIII–LV). The last document, the "On Faith" of *Katᶜolikos* Komitas (617–622), sets the terminus ad quem for the original compilation, which was probably put together in anticipation of or because of the dialogue with the Byzantines in the 630's on issues of church unity. The name of the editor of the original compilation has not been preserved. Among the suggested candidates are Bishop Movsēs of Cᶜurtaw and, more likely, *Katᶜolikos* Komitas.

The second part of the *Girk Tᶜłtᶜocᶜ* has a disorderly arrangement. Evidently sundry documents, letters, and treatises were added by later editors. Some of these, such as the correspondence between Acacius of Constantinople and Peter of Alexandria (LXI–LXXVIII) and that between Photios and the Armenians (LXXX–LXXXI) are translated spuria. There are also several Armenian spuria attributed to *Katᶜolikos* Yovhannēs of Ōjnecᶜi and *Katᶜolikos* Yovhannēs Mandakuni, among others. Yet, there are many important documents from the eighth to the thirteenth centuries, such as the correspondence between the eighth-century Armenian theologian Bishop Stepᶜanos of Siwnikᶜ and Patriarch Germanos of Constantinople (LXXXIV, LXXXVI). Of great interest is the letter of Bishop Macarius of Jerusalem to Bishop Vrtᶜanēs of Armenia (LXXXIX), which deals with canonical, liturgical, and ritualistic questions; to this day it has not been resolved whether Macarius and Vrtᶜanēs are the bishops who lived in the fourth century or the sixth.

Besides their importance for church historians, the documents in *Girk Tᶜłtᶜocᶜ* are valuable sources for those interested in the political, social, literary, and cultural histories of Armenia and Transcaucasia.

BIBLIOGRAPHY
Girkᶜ Tᶜłtᶜocᶜ (1901). A partial translation is Maurice Tallon, S. J., *Livre des lettres, Iᵉʳ groupe: Documents concernant les relations avec les Grecs* (1955).

KRIKOR H. MAKSOUDIAN

[See also **Armenian Literature.**]

GÍSLA SAGA SÚRSSONAR. The *Saga of Gísli Súrsson* is a classic in the genre of the Icelandic family saga. Tightly constructed and tersely phrased, it tells the story of the tenth-century skald and outlaw Gísli Súrsson against the background of a psychological drama. The introductory chapters cover two generations of family history in Norway prior to Gísli's emigration to Iceland with his sister Þórdís and brother Þorkell. The groundwork for the later tensions is laid when Gísli twice feels compelled by considerations of honor to kill a man who is both his sister's lover and his brother's friend. Once in Iceland, all three marry and the future looks bright. Gísli proposes to bind the clan more closely together with oaths of blood brotherhood, but his sister's husband Þorgrímr refuses to commit himself to Vésteinn, brother of Gísli's wife, and the plan fails. Later it comes to light that Vésteinn is involved with Þorkell's wife and he is subsequently killed during a stormy night, whether by Þorkell or Þorgrímr is not clear. Gísli takes revenge by killing Þorgrímr (his sister's husband and his brother's friend, as in the Norwegian prelude), also under cloak of darkness. The identity of the killer is at first unknown, but Gísli eventually reveals himself in a stanza overheard by Þórdís. She betrays the secret to her new husband, Bǫrkr, and Gísli is outlawed. A series of vengeance expeditions, punctuated by Gísli's narrow escapes, increasingly ominous dreams, and vain appeals to his brother Þorkell, culminates in a memorable last stand in which Gísli kills eight men before succumbing.

Gísla saga is a somber tale of cross purposes. Gísli is a model of rectitude and sees his mission as the preservation of his family's integrity, but this role puts him at odds with Þórdís and Þorkell. Þórdís ultimately betrays him, and Þorkell affords him only nominal support in his outlawry. In one of his stanzas Gísli compares his sister unfavorably with Gudrun, who avenged her brothers; *Gísla saga* is thus in some sense an inversion of the familial drama in the *Poetic Edda*. All the loyalties, animosities, jealousies, ambitions, and temperamental differences that underlie the drama are brought out in a sequence of vivid glimpses. The scenes are brief and sharply etched, the dialogue laconic. The atmosphere is almost oppressively dark, with a preference for night scenes, a persistent use of fatalistic commentary, and little humor. There is no right and no wrong, only a pattern of contradictory perceptions leading to disaster. Gísli is a great hero, but not an apt student of life around him—not, in the saga's language, "a lucky man."

Gísla saga is preserved in two redactions, but the differences are extensive only in the Norwegian prelude. The longer redaction was long held to be a later expansion, but recent studies by Guðni Kolbeinsson, Jónas Kristjánsson, and Alfred Jakobsen

establish that it is primary. The text contains forty skaldic stanzas, almost all attributed to Gísli. Their authenticity is disputed by Peter Foote (113–123). Literary connections with other early sagas place the composition of *Gísla saga* in the first half of the thirteenth century.

BIBLIOGRAPHY

Sources. The Saga of Gisli, George Johnston, trans., with notes and introductory essay by Peter Foote (1963, repr. 1973); Björn K. Þórólfsson and Guðni Jónsson, eds., *Vestfirðinga sögur* (1943), 3–118 (the short redaction); Agnete Loth, ed., *Membrana Regia Deperdita,* vol. 5 (1960), 3–80 (the long redaction).

Studies. Theodore M. Andersson, "Some Ambiguities in *Gísla saga:* A Balance Sheet," in *Bibliography of Old Norse-Icelandic Studies* (1968); Carol J. Clover, "Gísli's Coin," in *Bibliography of Old Norse-Icelandic Studies* (1977); Alfred Jakobsen, "Nytt lys over Gísla saga Súrssonar" and "Noen merknader til Gísla saga Súrssonar," in *Gripla,* 5 (1982); Guðni Kolbeinsson and Jónas Kristjánsson, "Gerðir Gíslasögu," in *Gripla,* 3 (1979).

THEODORE M. ANDERSSON

[See also **Family Sagas, Icelandic; Skaldic Verse.**]

GISLEBERTUS, a Romanesque sculptor known by his signature on the Last Judgment tympanum at S.

God speaking to Cain. Detail of a capital in the Church of St. Lazare, Autun, *ca.* 1125–1135. © TRIANON PRESS

Lazare in Autun, "Gislebertus hoc fecit." He was also responsible for the rest of the sculpture—capitals and north door—in the church (*ca.* 1125–1135). He probably trained at Cluny and seems to have worked at Vézelay before moving to Autun. Gislebertus' style epitomizes the Burgundian Romanesque with its angular, elongated figures and active linear surface pattern, but he was also capable of more three-dimensional forms, as seen on his capitals and, especially, the figure of Eve above the north door.

BIBLIOGRAPHY

Denis Grivot and George Zarnecki, *Gislebertus, Sculptor of Autun* (1961); Otto K. Werkmeister, "The Lintel Fragment Representing Eve from Saint-Lazare, Autun," in *Journal of the Warburg and Courtauld Institutes,* **35** (1972).

LESLIE BRUBAKER

[See also **Romanesque Architecture.**]

GIULIANO DA RIMINI, Riminese painter active from 1307 to before 1346. A follower of Giotto, he is known principally through a signed and dated (1307) dossal depicting a *Madonna and Child Enthroned with Standing Saints,* now in the Isabella Stuart Gardner Museum, Boston.

BIBLIOGRAPHY

Bernhard Berenson, *Italian Pictures of the Renaissance, Central and North Italian Schools,* 3 vols. (1968); Carlo Volpe, *La pittura riminese del Trecento* (1965).

ADELHEID M. GEALT

[See also **Giotto di Bondone.**]

GIUSTO DE MENABUOI (*ca.* 1320/1330–before April 1393), Italian painter born in Florence. He was principally active in Padua between 1367 and 1387, where he developed under the influence of Altichiero and Avanzo as well as Giovanni da Milano. His principal surviving work is a large and elaborate fresco cycle in the vault of the Padua Baptistery; completed by 1376, it depicts Paradise and Old and New Testament scenes.

BIBLIOGRAPHY

Bernhard Berenson, *Italian Pictures of the Renaissance, Central and North Italian Schools,* 3 vols. (1968); S. Bettini,

Le pitture di Giusto de' Menabuoi nel battistero del duomo di Padova (1960).

ADELHEID M. GEALT

[See also **Altichiero; Giovanni da Milano.**]

GLAGOLITIC RITE, the Slavic service in the written vernacular called Glagolitic (from the Slavonic *glagolati,* to speak). The translation of the Latin liturgy into the vernacular had not been a usual practice in the Roman patriarchate before the ninth century because Latin was the principal language in most areas of Europe and, for the most part, was understood by the common people. The situation changed, however, as more and more Slavic peoples were converted to Christianity from the eighth century on. The translation of individual rites into the vernacular, as they are in the tenth-century Freising documents, did not suffice for missionary purposes. Therefore, in the succeeding centuries a more substantial body of translated works appeared.

The first of these were prepared by Cyril and Methodios, Greek brothers sent by the Byzantine emperor Michael III to the Moravian prince Rastislav in 863. Rastislav wanted, it seemed, to break the tie with the Bavarian bishoprics, and for that reason asked Constantinople for Slavic-speaking priests. After several years of missionary work in Moravia, the brothers traveled to Rome via Aquileia and were received by Pope Adrian II (867–872) with great honor. Cyril (named Constantine at birth) was very sick and entered a Greek monastery in Rome, where he died in 869. Methodios was made bishop by the pope and named papal legate to Pannonia.

During their stay in Rome, the question of a translation of the Latin missals into Slavic was discussed. They had already begun this project. According to records, Methodios succeeded in convincing the pope and the bishops of the importance of their work. One thing is certain: from the time of Methodios and Cyril, Slavic (Glagolitic) liturgy books that formerly were used in the missionary territories of Aquileia and Salzburg are found in the missionary territories of Pannonia and Moravia.

Second are the so-called Kiev leaflets (now in the Ukrainian National Library, Kiev), four double leaves with a unified text of a Slavic sacramentary booklet written in a Glagolitic script in the tenth or eleventh century. The first and last sides were covers and remained unused. In addition to two formularies for saints' days (Clement and Felicity), the booklet contains six daily masses as well as a *missa de martyribus* and a *missa de omnibus virtutibus caelestibus*. It represents, true to its exemplar, an excerpt from a Latin sacramentary as it had been used in the Patriarchate of Aquileia. The *canon missae* was not translated. That this translation represents primarily a work of Methodios is shown by a note in the *Conversio Bagoariorum et Carantanorum* (Salzburg, `870): "Usque dum quidam graecus Methodius nomine, noviter inventis sclavinis litteris ... vilescere fecit cuncto populo ex parte (sclavorum) missas et evangelia ecclesiasticumque officum illorum, qui hoc latine celebraverunt" (Until a certain Greek named Methodius, all the people of the territory of the Slavs used to celebrate their masses and [passages of] the Gospels as well as the ecclesiastical Office in Latin, [but] with Slavic letters of his own invention ... he made [the Latin] worthless).

The translator of the prayers into Slavic must have been a priest of the Byzantine rite, for a sentence from the liturgy of St. John Chrysostom has been inserted into the preface of the leaflets.

In the Byzantine rite it has always been a basic principle that the Mass should be celebrated in a language understood by the people—for instance, the Mass had already been translated into Gothic in the fourth century by Ulfilas. Because Methodios came from an area of the Byzantine rite this principle was rather matter-of-factly applied to the Western liturgy.

Third is the Vienna fragment, a document that stems from the eleventh century and is presently in the Österreichische Nationalbibliothek, Vienna (Cod. Slav. 141). It is of a different sort from the Kiev missals; the preface occurs nowhere else. The Latin exemplar can no longer be definitely identified.

Fourth are the Glagolitic missals, which, unlike the sacramentaries, are plenary missals containing hymns for the Mass, readings (Epistle and Gospel), the oration, and the preface. They come from Galatia, where they are still in use. A fragment of such a missal (early fourteenth century) that is now in Wertheim is one of the oldest examples. Missals of this type were used for the last time liturgically in Bohemia.

BIBLIOGRAPHY

L. Cunibert Mohlberg, "Il Messale Glagolitico di Kiew," in *Atti della Pontificia accademia romana de archeologia* (1928).

KLAUS GAMBER

[See also **Byzantine Church; Cyril and Methodios, Sts.; Liturgy, Byzantine Church.**]

GLAJOR. The Armenian monastery of Glajor (Gaylajor) in the province of Siwnik^c was a leading religious, educational, and cultural center noted for its university and school of manuscript painting during its brief existence between about 1291 and 1340.

Praised at the time as a second Athens, the monastery attracted students from many regions of Armenia proper and Cilician Armenia. Its exact location is not known, though excavations indicate it may have been part of the monastery of T^{c}anahat near the village of Vernašen.

Glajor was under the protection of the Prošean and, later, the Orbelean princely families of Siwnik^c. Its eminent scholar-abbots were Nersēs Mšec^{c}i and his successor, Esayi Nč^{c}ec^{c}i.

First page of the book of Genesis. Bible of Esayi Nč^{c}ec^{c}i, painted in the Monastery of Glajor, 1318. FROM SIRARPIE DER NERSESSIAN, ARMENIAN ART (© THAMES AND HUDSON, 1970)

The university housed about 350 students who were trained as *vardapets* (learned doctors) for the religious, educational, and cultural centers of Armenia in a seven- to eight-year course of study including theology, philosophy, grammar, oratory, logic, mathematics, astronomy, geography, and bibliography as well as writing, manuscript painting, and musical notation. Glajor's abbots and monks also played a crucial role in maintaining the independence of the Armenian church during the period of Dominican missions to Armenia.

The Glajor school of manuscript painting, one of the most active and renowned scriptoria in Armenia, synthesized the style and iconography of Armenia, proper, as in the works of its first generation of painters (Yovhannēs, Mattᶜeos), with the ornamental style of Cilician Armenia, particularly in the works of its more notable painters, Tᶜoros Tarōnecᶜi (*Bible of Esayi Nčᶜecᶜi,* Erevan, Matendaran MS 206, dated 1318) and Avag (Erevan, Matenadaran MS 7650, dated 1329). Further characteristics include its distinctive use of color, particularly gold, the expressive faces and lively gestures of its figures, and the introduction of Western themes. Glajor exerted an important influence on the manuscript painting of other centers of Armenia during subsequent centuries.

When the monastery closed, presumably because of political and economic conditions during the period of the Mongol domination of Armenia, Glajor's students moved to the monastery of Tatᶜew.

BIBLIOGRAPHY

Sirarpie Der Nersessian, *Byzantine and Armenian Studies,* II (1973), 519, 615, 629–630, 700, and *Armenian Art* (1977), 220–224; Bezalel Narkiss, ed., *Armenian Art Treasures of Jerusalem* (1979), 75–76.

Lucy Der Manuelian

[See also **Armenian Art; Tᶜoros of Taron.**]

GLANVILLE, RANULF DE (*d.* 1190). Generally recognized as the author of the first text on the English common law known as *Tractatus de legibus et consuetudinibus regni Anglie,* Glanville was typical of those talented, literate, and able professional servants whom Henry II gathered about him and relied upon to achieve his celebrated institutional innovations.

Like most of Henry's officials, Glanville proved himself in varied positions as he moved upward. His first prominent post was sheriff of Yorkshire in 1163. Capturing the king of Scotland in battle in 1174, Glanville thereafter received rapid promotion. He served as an envoy on sensitive missions and became a judge in the common law courts. In 1180 he became justiciar (head of the royal administration and court) of England, an office he held until 1189; he died in 1190 while serving Richard I on the Third Crusade. While holding the most important governmental position in the realm, Glanville had a decisive influence on royal administration and the law. Obviously his service as a judge, both on the central courts and on the judicial circuits, and his proximity to the legal-minded Henry II, prepared him for writing his legal text.

Although the completion date of the text is uncertain, most scholars agree that it was between 1187 and 1190. The treatise was a practical rather than theoretical explanation of the law. Of the revived Roman law Glanville had only a smattering, probably only having read the *Institutes.* The new jurisprudence of the twelfth century did, however, influence Glanville to cast his book in a more logical form and to make the essential distinction between criminal and civil cases and between possessory and proprietary actions. His chief theme is the royal court and its affiliates along with the judicial writs and assizes that were forging the English common law in the twelfth and thirteenth centuries. The text's usefulness for those learning the law was its inclusion of the various writs and assizes to illustrate Glanville's commentary on substance and procedure. An extremely popular book because of its lucidity, it was produced in numerous copies; as late as the middle of the thirteenth century lawyers were still using it and bringing it up to date. It was then superseded by the more comprehensive and sophisticated text by Bracton. That such a book could be written during Henry II's reign demonstrates how far advanced was the legal system of England. Both Germany and France had to wait another seventy-five years before they possessed comparable law books.

A problem that yet concerns scholars is the authorship of this remarkable book, a matter left open by Frederic W. Maitland in the late nineteenth century. Although Maitland favored Glanville, he did not completely rule out Richard fitz Nigel, another trusted official of Henry II. Later it was suggested that a number of royal judges may have collaborated with Glanville and commissioned a clerk to do the writing. More recently another royal judge and official—Geoffrey de Lucy—has been proposed by George D. G. Hall as author of the treatise. But recent study of internal evidence points to a common thread of style and thought that supports Glanville as the author. No one can be certain, any more than was Maitland, but it is premature to uncouple Glanville from *De legibus*.

BIBLIOGRAPHY

Any study of Glanville must begin with Frederick Pollock and Frederic W. Maitland, *The History of English Law Before the Time of Edward I*, 2nd ed., I (1898). For a long time the best edition was by George E. Woodbine (1932); it has now been superseded by the edition and translation of George D. G. Hall, *The Treatise on the Laws and Customs of the Realm of England Commonly called Glanvill* (1965). For more recent commentary on Glanville see Josiah C. Russell, "Ranulf de Glanville," in *Speculum*, **45** (1970), and Doris M. Stenton, *English Justice Between the Norman Conquest and the Great Charter, 1066–1215* (1964).

BRYCE LYON

[See also **Bracton, Henry de; Henry II of England; Law, English Common: To 1272.**]

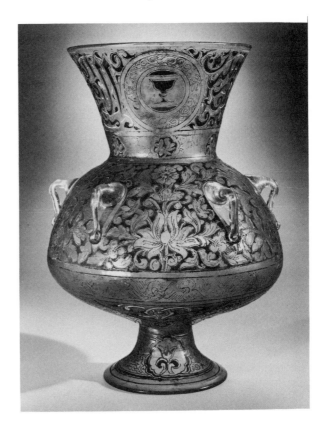

Mosque lamp. Damascus, *ca.* 355. THE CORNING MUSEUM OF GLASS, CORNING, NEW YORK

GLASS, ISLAMIC. Within a century after the death of the prophet Muḥammad (632), the Islamic Empire constituted a vast *koine* with a single faith, language, and legal code. Ideas, styles, and techniques were disseminated rapidly from one region to another, with the result that similar products appeared almost simultaneously in widely separated areas, such as Egypt and Iraq. At the same time, however, vernacular styles survived. These are particularly evident in early Islamic pottery, but glass, too, has regional variants attributable to the survival and development of local traditions.

The Arab armies conquered three regions in which glassmaking was already long established: Syria, Egypt, and Iraq-Iran. In the Hellenistic and Roman periods, Sidon was particularly famous for its glass, and it was probably here, or in some other Syro-Palestinian center, that the use of the blowpipe was invented. This development made mass production possible and brought glass vessels within the reach of even modest households. Blowing into a mold became a popular means of decoration, as were the application of threads and manipulation of the surface. In Egypt, after a long hiatus, glassmaking revived in the Ptolemaic period and centers such as

Alexandria produced luxury items, including gold-sandwich, mosaic, and gold-band vessels. We are well informed about the utility glass of the Roman period, thanks largely to discoveries at Karanis in the Fayyum. In Iraq and Iran, the most sophisticated workshops of the Achaemenid period produced colorless cast and wheel-cut vessels. Later, Iraqi and Iranian craftsmen made blown glass, but the production of cast and wheel-cut objects continued under the Sasanians. At the beginning of the Islamic period, therefore, glass was in common use in Egypt and western Asia, and glassmakers had access to a wide range of techniques, the most common of which were free blowing and blowing into a mold, various methods of applying ornament, manipulation, and cutting.

The first Islamic dynasty, that of the Umayyads, established itself at Damascus in Syria, in 661. Damascus had been a flourishing Roman and Byzantine city, and the earliest Islamic art and architecture of the region shows considerable continuity from earlier times. The mosaics in the mosque of the caliph al-Walid, for example, are in the tradition of Byzantine mosaics in Syria and Palestine. Much of the glass, too, is in the local tradition; indeed it is often impossible to distinguish between "Byzantine" and "Umayyad" products. Thus, lamps fall into well-defined types, which occur both before and after the Arab conquest and were used in churches and mosques alike. Excavations at Jabal Says, an Umayyad palace in the Syrian countryside, revealed a quantity of domestic glassware, none of which is of outstanding quality. Elsewhere, excavations at Ḥamā yielded a wide range of later material, mostly of the period between 1100 and 1400. A large amount of glass has been recovered from excavations in Jerusalem where, according to the geographer al-Muqaddasī, lamps were made in the tenth century.

The second ancient center of glassmaking, Egypt, continued to produce vessels of all qualities in the Islamic period. Excavations at Al-Fusṭāṭ (the forerunner of Cairo, which was founded in 969) have provided an immense quantity of glass, ranging in date from the eighth century to the later Middle Ages. Although proof is lacking, the sheer abundance of the finds indicates that Al-Fusṭāṭ was a center of production. Among the earliest datable objects are coin-like weights, stamped with the names of rulers or government officials. The earliest datable glass weight was made in 708. They came in a variety of colors, among which dark green was particularly popular until about 975, light green and turquoise between about 975 and about 1130, white between about 1130 and 1229, purple between 1229 and about 1315; thereafter, most weights were colorless.

Some of the most sophisticated Egyptian glass vessels were decorated with luster. This shiny, sometimes metallic effect was achieved by painting copper or silver oxide on the surface of the object, which then was fired at a temperature of about 600°C (1112°F.) in reducing conditions. The same technique was used in the decoration of earthenware, not only in Egypt but also in Iraq and Iran. Until recently, controversy raged over the origin of luster painting, but the problem appears to have been solved by the discovery at Al-Fusṭāṭ of a glass cup of local type, inscribed with the name of ᶜAbd al-Samad, governor of Egypt in 771–772. Evidently, Egyptian glass painters were using luster in the eighth century, some time before its appearance in Iraq.

When the Abbasids overthrew the last Umayyad caliph in 750, they decided to move the government from Damascus. In 762, Caliph al-Manṣūr founded a new dynastic capital, Baghdad, on the river Tigris at a point scarcely thirty miles from the Euphrates, where the Khorāsān Road (the western end of the silk route) crossed Iraq. Thanks to its excellent communications, Baghdad flourished, suffering only a brief period of eclipse when another royal city was established at Samarra, farther upstream, between 836 and 883. The presence of the court and other wealthy patrons attracted artists and artisans whose distinctive decorative style now gave greater prominence to Iranian elements. Baghdad, Samarra, and Basra (near the head of the Gulf) all were noted for their glassmakers in the early Abbasid period.

Our knowledge of the early Islamic glass of Iraq and Iran is derived from a handful of excavations, some of which were of indifferent quality. The key site in Iraq—*faute de mieux*—is Samarra, which was excavated in 1912–1913, 1936–1939, and again in the 1970's and 1980's. The chronology of the finds, however, is uncertain. A similar problem surrounds much of the material from Nishapur (Neyshābūr) in Iran. Sīrāf on the Persian Gulf, though carefully excavated, yielded little high-quality glassware.

Under the Abbasids, the Sasanian wheel-cutting technique was revived, and wheel-cut objects are among the finest Islamic glassware. Among the other techniques represented by finds from Samarra, Sīrāf, and other sites are blowing into molds, engraving, and the manufacture of millefiori (mosaic) glass. At the same time, makers produced a wide range of plain utility objects, from window panes to cups and jars for cosmetics.

The wheel-cut glass of Abbasids and their successors may be divided into several styles, the simplest of which features grooves cut in the surface of the vessel. This grooved ornament came to be used by glassmakers all over western Asia, Egypt, and the Maghrib; it is the most common decorative technique, for example, on vessels from the eleventh-century shipwreck at Serçe Liman, near Bodrum in Turkey. The most elaborate Abbasid pieces are decorated in the "beveled" style, in which the outlines are cut on a slant and there is no distinct second plane forming the background. The beveled style was used by craftsmen in many media, including rock crystal, stucco, and wood, and enjoyed widespread popularity. A third style utilizes relief cutting, in which the entire background was removed, leaving the ornament in relief. At its best, this cutting is of extraordinary delicacy. Numerous examples of relief cutting have been found in northern Iran, and scholars usually associate the style with Nishapur in

Khorāsān, which enjoyed wealth and stability under the quasi-autonomous Samanid dynasty (819–1004).

The most puzzling relief-cut vessels are the so-called Hedwig glasses: beakers of colorless glass with a distinctive smoky topaz tinge, which are decorated with lions, griffins, or eagles. The ornament is vigorous, and details are supplied by hatching or cross-hatching. Hedwig glasses are widely believed to be Egyptian and of the twelfth century, but neither the origin nor the date is certain.

A logical extension of wheel-cutting (which again recalls the repertoire of the lapidary) was the cameo technique, in which a layer of glass was applied to all or part of a vessel of a different color. Most of the outer layer then was removed by grinding and cutting, thereby creating relief ornament of a different color from the vessel itself. Cameo cutting had been practiced by Roman glassmakers, first in the period from about 50 B.C. to about A.D. 100, and later in the fourth century, but there is no reason to suppose that production continued into the Islamic period. Indeed, it is much more likely that the technique was reinvented in Iraq or Iran and later imitated in Egypt, where numerous fragments have come to light. Unlike the early Roman cameo glasses, Islamic examples, which belong to the ninth, tenth, and eleventh centuries, have green or blue ornament on a colorless background. The decoration includes both the beveled and the relief-cut styles. The shapes and motifs of the finest vessels recall ewers of rock crystal, some with datable inscriptions that help to establish the chronology of their counterparts in glass.

The latest major group of medieval Islamic glass was decorated with gilding and colored enamels. This ornamentation is found on a wide variety of vessels, including bottles, tumblers, and lamps. It was applied cold and fixed by firing at a low temperature; the same technique was used in the production of enameled metalware and minai pottery. The decorative elements were outlined in red and filled with a variety of colors: white, yellow, green, blue, purple, and pink. A high proportion of this material was made in Syria, the only other center of production being in Egypt.

In 1930, C. J. Lamm divided Islamic gilded and enameled glass into six groups, for which he suggested the following places of manufacture and approximate chronology: (1) Rakka group, 1170–1270; (2) Syro-Frankish group, attributed to the Latin Kingdom of Jerusalem, 1260–1290; (3) Fusṭāṭ group, 1270–1340; (4) Aleppo group, 1250–1265; (5) Damas-

cus group, 1250–1310; (6) "Chinese" group, with Far Eastern motifs copied from the Ilkhans of Mesopotamia and Iran, attributed to Damascus, 1285–1400. Lamm's attributions were largely intuitive, and his chronology leaned heavily on two historical events: the devastation of Rakka and Aleppo by the Mongols in 1259–1260 and the capture of Damascus in 1400 by Tamerlane, who carried off craftsmen, including glassmakers, to Samarkand in central Asia. The vessels attributed to Rakka (for which we have no documentary evidence of glassmaking) often have gilded inscriptions and enameled beading or dots. The Syro-Frankish group is now believed to have been made in the West, perhaps in Venice. The Fusṭāṭ group is small and many of the enameled pieces from this and other sites in Egypt were imported from Syria. Aleppo was mentioned as a glassmaking and decorating center by Yaqūt (d. 1229), Qazvīnī (d. 1283), the poet Saᶜadī (in 1258), and the geographer Ḥāfiẓ-i Abrū (d. 1430). Vessels attributed to Aleppo frequently bear human figures, such as falconers and polo players. From the time of Sultan Baybars (1260–1277), coats of arms, too, were common. Damascus also was described as a glassmaking center by Ibn Baṭṭūṭa (d. 1377) and Niccolò of Poggibonsi, who traveled in the Holy Land in 1345–1346. Lamm assigned two main groups of vessels to Damascus: one decorated with fish placed in herringbone patterns, arabesques, and scenes of revelry, and the other with "Chinese" ornament.

Subsequently, P. J. Riis proposed a modified classification based on finds from excavations at Ḥamā in Syria. He also revised the chronology, basing his estimated dates on stylistic similarities between the ornament of the glass vessels and dated or datable objects of stucco, stone, and metal. Lamm's Rakka group became "Syrian A," believed to have been made between 1185 and 1260. The Aleppo, Damascus, and "Chinese" groups became "Syrian B" (1230–1400). The Fusṭāṭ group was renamed "Egyptian," with the suggested dates 1260–1300. Both Syrian A and Syrian B were subdivided. Apart from refining the chronology, Riis's classification has the merit of dissociating certain products (notably the Rakka group) from places of manufacture that are wholly hypothetical.

The deportation of the glassmakers from Damascus in 1400 is believed to have put an end to the manufacture of gilded and enameled vessels in western Asia. A number of fifteenth-century enameled beakers allegedly found in Syria are thought to be Venetian, as is at least one lamp (bearing the name of

Qāᵓit Bay, ruled 1468–1496) from Egypt. Brascha of Milan, who visited the Holy Land in 1480, tells how the Venetian captain of his ship "sent from Jaffa to Damascus glass vessels from Murano" for one of Qāᵓit Bay's functionaries. The great age of Islamic glassmaking was over.

BIBLIOGRAPHY

Klaus Brisch, "Das Omayyadische Schloss in Usais (II)," in *Mitteilungen des Deutschen Archäologischen Instituts, Abteilung Kairo,* **20** (1965); Grace M. Crowfoot and Donald B. Harden, "Early Byzantine and Later Glass Lamps," in *Journal of Egyptian Archaeology,* **17** (1931); Donald B. Harden, K. S. Painter, Ralph H. Pinder-Wilson, and Hugh Tait, *Masterpieces of Glass* (1968); Carl Johan Lamm, *Das Glas von Samarra* (1928), and *Mittelalterliche Gläser und Steinschnittarbeiten aus dem Nahen Osten* (1929–1930); Prudence Oliver, "Islamic Relief Cut Glass: A Suggested Chronology," in *Journal of Glass Studies,* **3** (1961); Ralph H. Pinder-Wilson and George T. Scanlon, "Glass Finds from Fusṭāṭ: 1964–1971," in *Journal of Glass Studies,* **15** (1973); Poul Jørgen Riis, Vagn Poulsen, and Erling Hammershaimb, *Hama IV.2: Les verreries et poteries médiévales* (1957).

DAVID WHITEHOUSE

[See also **Ceramics, Islamic; Islamic Art; Mamluk Art.**]

GLASS, STAINED. Stained glass is a branch of painting intimately related by iconographic traditions and stylistic developments to works in other media, such as manuscript illumination and wall paintings. In materials and techniques it also resembles champlevé enamel and mosaics. Despite certain limits set by the materials it is an extraordinarily versatile art form. In the Middle Ages it lent itself to the brilliantly colored monumental windows that filled the Gothic cathedrals but it also, by the close of the period, appeared in the form of small panes that resemble translucent prints. Relegated by early art historians to the status of a "minor" or "decorative" art, supposedly dependent on architecture, or to a "craft" because of the complexity of production, stained glass was in fact one of the highest forms of painting in the Gothic period. It might even be argued that the structural innovations of Gothic architecture came about through a consistent desire to provide more window surface for stained glass; it was the dissolution of the wall into a colored membrane that transmitted light, and not the engineering feats of the flying buttress and ribbed vault, that was

the main concern of the patron. Thus, when Abbot Suger had the west end of his church at St. Denis remodeled to include vast windows and then, in 1144, completed the choir with a carefully designed program in stained glass, he had inscribed in the choir: "Bright is the noble edifice that is pervaded by the new light" (Panofsky, ed., 50–51).

The unique province of glass painters is to control with their pigments the transmission of light through colored or uncolored glass, in contrast with painters in other media, who build up masses of color. But in the Middle Ages light was more than a formal component of their art; it also provided an iconographic theme. Light emanated from God, and God was light; the light entering a church through windows with sacred pictures not only illuminated the interior but also enlightened the minds of men;

Prophets Daniel and Hosea. Augsburg Cathedral, *ca.* 1130.
DEUTSCHE VEREIN FÜR KUNSTWISSENSCHAFT

that light could pass through glass without breaking it was a demonstration of the miracles of Christ's immaculate conception and virgin birth.

For Suger the decorations of his choir were more than aids to contemplation; they were a Neoplatonic reflection of divinity that brought about a mystical experience:

> When . . . the loveliness of the many-colored gems has called me away from external cares, . . . then it seems to me that I see myself dwelling, as it were, in some strange region of the universe which neither exists entirely in the slime of the earth nor entirely in the purity of Heaven; and that, by the grace of God, I can be transported from this inferior to that higher world in an anagogical manner. (Panofsky, ed., 62–65)

Images in glass were especially precious, and frequently were rescued from fire and reset in a new building; the "Notre Dame de la belle verrière" of Chartres is the most famous example, evidently made before the fire of 1194 for a small Romanesque window opening and filled out in the thirteenth century to take its place in the new Gothic building. Probably because of their iconic aura, windows tended not to incorporate frivolous or secondary subject matter such as is found in the margins of Gothic manuscripts; it is notable that none of the meaningless or offensive subjects specifically targeted by St. Bernard in his famous treatise addressed to William of St. Thierry abounded in glass.

Glass painting developed as a truly monumental art form only in the context of early Gothic architecture, but the basic techniques had been practiced in northern Europe since at least the ninth century, as evidenced by texts and by scattered archaeological finds, and there were relatively few technical innovations in later centuries. The complex process of design and execution was described by a German monk writing under the pseudonym Theophilus in the first half of the twelfth century; at that time full-scale, detailed designs were drawn on sized trestle tables. In the early thirteenth century, identical borders in the cathedrals of Canterbury and Sens provide evidence that full-scale designs passed from one site to another (though for a single element of a repeating design it would have been possible to use parchment rather than cumbersome board). Some small-scale drawings for stained glass are preserved on parchment. With the use of paper, full-size cartoons were more easily stored and they were reused by more than one generation of painters. Small compositional sketches from the late Gothic period are

Apostle and archbishop surrounded by grisaille. Choir clerestory, Rheims Cathedral, *ca.* 1230–1240. MONUMENTS HISTORIQUES, ARCHIVES PHOTOGRAPHIQUES, PARIS

also known; in the Middle Ages this type of drawing was called a *vidimus*.

In the execution of the window several materials were used, each having a structural and a design function. A rigid iron armature was either riveted onto a wooden frame that was recessed into the stonework (early and high Gothic practice) or slotted into the stone window frame (late Gothic); this armature might be rectilinear or composed of curved bars that form a repeating geometric design. The area between the bars defined the shape and size of the panels of stained glass, which, when assembled, were attached to the armature by a system of lugs, flanges, and keys, and puttied to obtain a watertight seal. The unit of design was sometimes coincidental with the panel, but where large-scale figures were preferred, it was structurally necessary to compose them from two or more panels. As adjuncts to the armature, smaller detachable braces or saddle bars were used.

Glasses, permanently colored by metallic oxides added to the molten frit and therefore known as pot-metal, could be made in any region where silica and potash were readily available. The colors were pure, but restricted in number and essentially nonnaturalistic. They consisted of blue, yellow, green, rose purple, and red; uncolored glass was warm or cool, depending on impurities. The pieces were cut to correspond to the color masses in the design, and details such as the facial features, drapery folds, and modeling were painted with an iron-oxide vitreous enamel and fired on. The pieces were then joined together with cames; these flexible leads, H-shaped in section, both form the outlines of the design and provide resilient structural support. Medieval leads have occasionally survived; they were made in a mold, in contrast to the modern method of extrusion from a mill, and carefully hand-finished.

Some subtle but significant changes took place in the manner of applying paint and in the range of colors available. The painterly techniques described by Theophilus were closely allied to those of the contemporary wall painter or manuscript illuminator; washes of pigment were built up in layers, which were not allowed to fuse into a continuous tonal gradation. Unique to the glass painter, however, was the possibility of exploiting the transparency of the carrier by painting a more distant object on the outer surface, or of strengthening the modeling on the inner side by exterior application of the pigment. Later, this back-painting might take the form of a textile pattern, applied independently of the drapery folds.

Designs in reserve were another specialty of the glass painter; the entire surface of a background, edging, or inscription was covered with a light gray wash and a design picked out with the butt of the brush handle before firing; the contrasts of intensity enliven the flat areas of the design. Somewhat later the same technique was used to create highlights on the face, hair, or draperies. By the fifteenth century a finer instrument, such as a needle, might be used; at the same time the evenly applied washes or smear shadings of the twelfth and thirteenth centuries were replaced by textural brush strokes, often made with a dryish brush of badger hair—hence called badgering. Firm trace lines were softened by continuous gradation of tones; glass painting thus kept pace with current trends in panel painting.

Although the heavy contours of lead were still a necessary part of the design, there was a tendency to use larger pieces of glass. In the early fourteenth century a revolutionary discovery had dispensed with some leads; silver oxide was applied to limited areas of uncolored glass and fired to a rich yellow, allowing an angel's hair or the hem of a mantle to be colored without being separately leaded. Depending on the nature of the glass and the heat of the kiln, this silver stain could vary from pale yellow to orange. It could also be applied to blue glass to make green. Furthermore, although red glass had always been flashed or laminated with uncolored, it was then found that part of the red could be ground away so that the same piece gave both red and uncolored. The only other innovation, before the discovery of enamels, that replaced potmetal in much sixteenth-century glass, was the introduction at the end of the fifteenth century of a hematite or sanguine colorant to give varied flesh tints.

English terminology defines "stained glass" by the use of potmetal, alone or in conjunction with the stains described above; it is thus distinguished from enameled glass, to which the colors were applied much like colored paints so that leading was no longer part of the design. The nineteenth-century term "stained and painted glass" was more accurate; the German *Glasmalerei* (glass painting) is closer to the product of the stained-glass artist. Modern French usage distinguishes *vitrail* or *verrière* (a stained glass panel or window) from *vitrine* (a [plain] glass window). Each modern term has ambiguities and limitations. "Stained glass" can as well apply to Islamic decorative glazing, though it is neither painted nor leaded, but this represents an almost completely separate tradition.

Medieval terminology is equally elusive; *pictor* (painter) does not have any predisposition to any one carrier (panel, parchment, glass, or plastered wall), and whereas *vitrearius* (glazier) was someone who worked exclusively in glass, he may as well have done repairs or made glasses as have designed and painted windows. In fact, comparatively few glass painters are known by name, from documents or signatures, until the late Middle Ages. By the fifteenth century there are guild records, contracts, and accounts for centers such as York that allow the piecing together of a coherent view of the working practices of the artists; by the end of the century it is possible to reconstruct the oeuvre, and to some extent the biography, of glass painters who were famous in their own time, such as Peter Hemmel von Andlau. Nevertheless, the problems of attribution are no less great than for other Renaissance artists. By that period the possibility of designing on paper, and a growing specialization in production, led to a separation of the creative process from the execution, and the relegation of glass painters to a secondary function. Thus, for instance, Albrecht Dürer designed for glass but the work was executed by the Hirsvogel atelier in Nuremberg.

The great works of the twelfth and thirteenth centuries are almost all anonymous, and close examination of styles often indicates more than one painter working in a team; stained glass lends itself to varieties of division of labor. It is all the more extraordinary to see that when it first emerged as monumental decoration, in sequences of preserved windows (as at Augsburg about 1130 or at St. Denis in 1144), the artists were able to balance the intensity of hues, not only in a single panel but throughout a whole window or phalanx of adjacent openings. Complementaries were used in juxtaposition so that the colors retained clarity and brilliance. The artists painted on the uncoloreds and yellows more thickly and on the deep reds more thinly, to counteract the glare of the lighter areas. Scale and chromatic intensity responded to the demands of the patrons and of the architecture. The small lights in the clerestory of Augsburg achieved monumental clarity by the bold outlining of single figures against uncolored grounds; ample light was admitted even through these small windows.

As window openings were enlarged, it became possible to increase the intensity of the colors without losing the luminosity of effect. A decade later, Abbot Suger boasted of using sapphire in his windows, though of course the gems were not real; the limpid *bleu de ciel* grounds there and in the almost contemporary west windows of Chartres cathedral are still legendary. The windows appear like great enameled and jeweled altarpieces. The glowing reds

Ste. Chapelle, Paris, interior facing northeast, 1248. MONUMENTS HISTORIQUES, ARCHIVES PHOTOGRAPHIQUES, PARIS

that were increasingly used in the next century are still referred to as ruby; their special process of manufacture was identical to that then current for making false gemstones. Combined with deeper, cooler blues, they provided the red-blue predominance of the great cathedrals. An empirical approach had led to the use of this saturated blue for the background, thus exploiting the optical illusion of spatial recession that is the result of the shorter wavelength of blue light.

The Ste. Chapelle, completed with its glass by 1248, demonstrates a taste for saturated color and miniaturesque jeweled effects applied throughout the vast window openings; although the building is virtually a glass house, the light is subdued. It has only recently been scientifically demonstrated that such conditions of subdued light increase the perception of certain colors, especially blues. The stained-glass artists of the Ste. Chapelle may have known this empirically, but they also no doubt were concerned, in such a narrow space, not to allow light to stream through the south windows onto the inner side of the north and to kill their brilliance with surface light. They achieved a remarkably even luminosity.

Yet within a generation a new aesthetic had evolved. Saturated colors gave way to greater use of pearly whites in the grounds and greens and yellows in the figures. Clerestory figures in the Rheims and Auxerre cathedrals and narrative panels at St. Urbain in Troyes were set in lightly painted ornamental grounds of uncolored glass, a decorative mode known as grisaille. The interior of St. Urbain is light and airy, departing radically from the gloom and mystery that pervaded Chartres and Bourges. Early in the fourteenth century grisaille suddenly became fashionable in a variety of techniques, from altar hangings to miniatures, but one of the earliest examples—exploiting the newly invented silver stain as the only color—is a panel with the Virgin and other saints that in 1328 replaced the lower part of one of the deeply colored windows of Chartres. In the late-medieval period the taste for uncolored glass may have been encouraged by its lower cost and the need for light by which to read private service books. In southern climates, however, saturated colors continued in use; the fourteenth-century glass of Austria, Switzerland, and Italy employs brilliant hues, though there too the trend was away from deep red and blue toward green, yellow, and purple.

The fifteenth century was also marked by regional diversity, and everywhere by eclecticism. Stained glass was variously influenced by sculpture, architecture, panel painting, and printmaking. A traditional type of window in France, England, and Germany gave monumental figures the semblance of statuary placed in niches under elaborate canopies. Architectural drawings had probably provided models for the glaziers since the thirteenth century in some regions; at first multicolored, these canopies later adopted the grisaille vogue. Thus, by the mid fourteenth century in the choir of Gloucester cathedral this type of design blended harmoniously with adjacent wall areas that were articulated with blind tracery; such canopy windows were very common in the English Perpendicular buildings of the next century.

The Flemish panel painters must have had profound influence on glass painting in their homeland, but little painted glass survived Protestant iconoclasm; their influence can best be seen now in sites as widely dispersed as Bourges from the mid fifteenth century (in the Jacques Coeur window of the cathedral) or Rouen, Cambridge, and Cologne at the turn of the next century. It is thought that two of the glass painters in Cologne were the panel painters

known as the Master of St. Severin and the Master of the Holy Kinship.

In smaller panels or single panes for halls and domestic chapels another mode evolved, consistent with the scale of these buildings. In England even quite large windows, such as those in Richard II's Great Hall at Westminster just before 1400, were glazed with small decorative panes combining lozenges with a design in the center (quarries) with roundels on which subjects were painted. Colored heraldic glass was popular, but other subjects were generally painted on uncolored glass with silver stain as the only colorant. The painters of these square panes or roundels were frequently inspired by prints, and their works may have the severity of woodblocks, but in other cases the availability of a good drawing has to be proposed. Such small panels seem to have had the mobility of panel paintings and earned the name *Kabinettscheiben* (closet panels) in German because of the way they were stored in collections.

As a predominantly monumental art form, stained glass was the vehicle for extended iconographic programs. Few have survived intact, or can be reconstructed from documents. These seem to have been devised ad hoc, depending on the traditions and use of the building and the concerns of its patrons. Upper windows were traditionally filled with large figures, single or paired, seated or standing. They might represent the complete genealogy of Christ, as at Canterbury; apostles and prophets, as at Bourges; or archbishops with apostles (in the choir) and kings (in the nave), as at Rheims. Lower windows lent themselves more readily to narrative or symbolic subjects.

The program devised by Abbot Suger for the choir of St. Denis comprised several esoteric windows in which Latin inscriptions drew attention to the relationship of the Old Testament to the New, as well as lives of saints such as St. Benedict and St. Vincent Martyr and Levite (of Saragossa). The thirteenth-century choir of Bourges combined biblical windows in the ambulatory with the lives of saints in the chapels. At Chartres, on the other hand, it seems that the donors, whether town guilds, noblemen, or ecclesiastics, chose the subject matter of their windows; the barrelmakers favored the story of Noah, the first vine grower, for instance. The result is not so much a program as a medley or compendium of subjects.

It is in narrative cycles of the thirteenth century that stained glass probably made its greatest contri-

GLASS, STAINED

bution to iconography. To fill the windows of Canterbury, Chartres, or the Ste. Chapelle, more scenes had to be created than were apparently available in earlier pictorial recensions, and some were uniquely suited to one site; more than 200 scenes of the miracles of Thomas Becket were placed in windows around his shrine, while St. Louis had the Ste. Chapelle glazed with the story of the crown of thorns that he had brought to Paris and with Old Testament scenes depicting battle heroes and kings to suit his royal crusading image. In Assisi the Franciscan program of the windows is as rich as that of the wall and vault paintings. At Königsfelden in the 1320's, Franciscan iconography was blended with subjects chosen by the Habsburg donors, who appear kneeling at the foot of the windows. One of the most specialized adaptations was made by the Cistercians, who outlawed colored and figural glass from their churches in the twelfth century; they used uncolored glass, cut and leaded into strapwork and other patterns called "blank glazed windows" as well as vegetal designs in grisaille. One of the most complete and famous Cistercian programs is in the cloister of Heiligenkreuz in Austria (ca. 1220–1250). This decorative mode was extremely influential outside the order.

BIBLIOGRAPHY

The study of stained glass is in its infancy; despite the interest of practitioners in the nineteenth century, a second generation of art historians has only just begun to make contributions to the serious study of medieval windows. An international series, published under the title *Corpus vitrearum medii aevi* (here abbreviated as CVMA), offers complete illustrations, including charts showing the replaced pieces in each panel, and critical assessment of problems of date, patronage, authorship, and iconography, but to date only thirty of a projected 100 volumes have been published. For volumes of the CVMA dealing with continental glass, and for many important monographs and articles, the reader is directed to Madeline H. Caviness and Evelyn Staudinger, *Stained Glass Before 1540: An Annotated Bibliography* (1983).

General. Victor Beyer, *Stained Glass Windows,* David Talbot Rice, ed., and trans. from German by R. Gaze (1965); Eva Frodl-Kraft, *Die Glasmalerei. Entwicklung. Technik. Eigenart* (1970); Louis Grodecki, "A Stained Glass *Atelier* of the Thirteenth Century," in *Journal of the Warburg and Courtauld Institutes,* 11 (1948); James Rosser Johnson, *The Radiance of Chartres: Studies in the Early Stained Glass of the Cathedral* (1964, 1965); Roy G. Newton, *The Deterioration and Conservation of Painted Glass: A Critical Bibliography and Three Research Papers,* CVMA Great Britain, Occasional Papers, I (1974); Robert Sowers, *The Lost Art: A Survey of One Thousand Years of Stained Glass* (1954).

Techniques. Edward Liddall Armitage, *Stained Glass: History, Technology and Practice* (1959); John A. Knowles, "The Technique of Glass Painting in Mediaeval and Renaissance Times," in *Journal of the Royal Society of Arts, London,* 62 (1913–1914) and in *Building News,* 106 (1914), and "Mediaeval Cartoons for Stained Glass: How Made and How Used," in *Journal of the American Institute of Architects,* 16 (1927).

France. Madeline H. Caviness, "Suger's Glass at Saint-Denis: The State of Research," in Paula Gerson, ed., *Abbot Suger and Saint-Denis: An International Symposium* (1984); Michael W. Cothren, "The Iconography of Theophilus Windows in the First Half of the Thirteenth Century," in *Speculum,* 59 (1984); Louis Grodecki, "The Jacques Coeur Window at Bourges," in *Magazine of Art,* 42 (1949), and "The Style of the Stained Glass at Saint-Denis," in Paula Gerson, ed., *op. cit.;* Meredith Lillich, "Monastic Stained Glass: Patronage and Style," in Timothy Verdon, ed., *Monasticism and the Arts* (1984), 207–254, and *The Stained Glass of Saint-Père de Chartres* (1978); Musée des arts décoratifs de Paris, *Le vitrail français* (1958); Erwin Panofsky, ed. and trans., *Abbot Suger on the Abbey Church of St.-Denis and Its Art Treasures* (1946; 2nd. ed. 1979), 73–77; Virginia Chieffo Raguin, *Stained Glass in Thirteenth-century Burgundy* (1982); Helen Jackson Zakin, *French Cistercian Grisaille Glass* (1979).

Germany. Hans Wentzel, *Meisterwerke der Glasmalerie* (1951; 2nd enlarged ed. 1954).

Great Britain. John Baker, *English Stained Glass* (1960); Madeline H. Caviness, *The Early Stained Glass of Canterbury Cathedral, circa 1175–1220* (1977), and *The Windows of Christ Church Cathedral Canterbury,* CVMA, Great Britain, II (1981); Jeremy Haselock and David E. O'Connor, "The Stained and Painted Glass," in G. E. Aylmer and Reginald Cant, eds., *A History of York Minster* (1977), 313–393; F. E. Hutchinson, *Medieval Glass at All Souls College* (1949); Nigel J. Morgan, *The Medieval Painted Glass of Lincoln Cathedral,* CVMA, Great Britain, Occasional Paper III (1983); Peter A. Newton and Jill Kerr, *The County of Oxford: A Catalogue of Medieval Stained Glass,* CVMA, Great Britain, I (1979); Gordon McN. Rushforth, "The Great East Window of Gloucester Cathedral," in *Transactions of the Bristol and Gloucestershire Archaeological Society,* 44 (1922), and *Medieval Christian Imagery as Illustrated by the Painted Windows of Great Malvern Priory Church Worcestershire* (1936); Hilary G. Wayment, *The Windows of King's College Chapel, Cambridge,* CVMA, Great Britain, Supplementary vol. I (1972); Christopher Woodforde, *English Stained and Painted Glass* (1954).

Italy. Giuseppe Marchini, *Italian Stained Glass Windows* (1957).

Switzerland. Ellen J. Beer, "Mediaeval Swiss Stained Glass," in *Connoisseur,* **152** (1963); Michael Stettler, *Stained Glass of the Early Fourteenth Century from the Church of Königsfelden* (1949).

MADELINE H. CAVINESS

[See also **Canterbury Cathedral; Chartres Cathedral; Gothic Architecture; Hemmel, Peter; Optics, Western European; Rheims Cathedral; Ste. Chapelle; Suger; Theophilus.**]

GLASS, WESTERN EUROPEAN. The history of medieval glassmaking in western Europe may be said to begin with the breakdown of the Roman Empire and the progressive withdrawal of the Roman presence from Britain, the German areas, and Gaul. In the fifth century the overrunning of Italy itself by the Vandals and Goths, and of Spain by the Vandals and Visigoths, must at least temporarily have disrupted industries settled there, including the glass industry. Glasses found in Lombard graves of the late sixth and seventh centuries show considerable complexity, with applied and combed patterns of opaque-white, -yellow, and -red threads on colored (blue, red, or green) base glass. It is not known where they were made, but though they are distinctive in character, some parallels may be drawn with the combed patterns in opaque-white glass found farther north. These likenesses were probably due to the similar tastes of the Teutonic invaders in both areas.

In Roman times the Rhineland appears to have been the main glassmaking area of northern Europe, with Cologne at its center. Glassmaking sites of Roman date, however, have been found in France, on the territory of modern Belgium, and in Britain itself. With the withdrawal of Roman power, glassmaking probably ceased in Britain. In the Rhineland, however, it appears to have continued in consider-

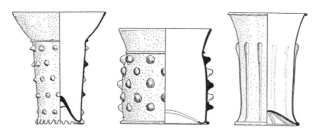

Three glass beakers: colorless, yellowish-green, and pale blue. Corinthian, 11th to mid 12th century. AFTER GLADYS R. DAVIDSON, CORINTH, XII, THE MINOR OBJECTS (1952)

able strength, there being very little break in continuity between the technical character of the glass of the early and late fourth century. Gradually, however, an alien taste asserted itself, and the great range of table glass forms of Roman times was replaced by a limited repertory of mainly drinking vessels—tall beakers in many varieties, and low hemispherical cups being the most common, with occasional bowls and bottles. Clear colorless glass was for the most part superseded by a light- to dark-green or brown "metal" (glass material) owing its coloration to iron-bearing sands and no longer decolorized by the use of antimony or manganese oxide. The material was often bubbled, and the workmanship less sophisticated than in Roman times. The late antique habit of knocking off the rim of a glass without subsequent fire polishing continued, showing perhaps a declining interest in fine craftsmanship.

On the other hand, some types of glass showed a remarkable virtuosity, preeminent among these being the *Rüsselbecher* ("trunk" or "claw" beakers). These get their name from superimposed rows of decorative projections that closely resemble elephants' trunks. They were worked while the vessel was still on the blowing iron, and after it had been decorated with zones of fine spiral threading. The "trunk" was applied in the form of a blob hotter than the body glass, which was melted thereby, whereupon the blower blew the applied glass into a hollow bulb, to be pulled out and manipulated by the servitor so that the lower end adhered to the body. A degree of sophistication also appeared in the use of opaque-white threading, the glass for this being perhaps obtained in cakes or rods from specialized outside glasshouses. Occasionally vessels were made entirely of blue glass.

It used to be assumed that these green glasses were the direct forerunners of the green *Waldglas* (forest glass) of late-medieval Germany, and that the glassmakers must have retreated into the woodlands both for safety and because the woods could supply them with all the fuel and potash they needed to melt their glass. It has now been discovered, however, that until about the turn of the millennium the flux used in the glasses of northern Europe was in fact soda, mainly the produce of plants growing on the Mediterranean littoral, and not potash. In due course, however, the change took place, and the liberation from imported soda meant that the glassmakers could migrate freely from deforested zones to fresh areas that would assure both fuel and flux. A technical penalty had to be paid, however, though it was

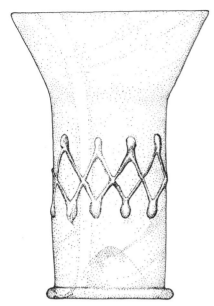

Beaker, made of colorless glass with applied blue threading. Winchester, 14th century. DRAWING SUPPLIED BY THE AUTHOR

not exacted for centuries. Potash glass was not as resistant to attack by climatic conditions as the soda glass had been, and potash glasses buried and excavated are often found reduced to a black or brown powder with a paper-thin glass core, while in window glass the custodians of ecclesiastical stained glass are now often at their wits' end to preserve the treasures in their care.

Whereas in pagan times glasses in northern Europe had been buried with the dead, the coming of Christianity gradually put an end to this custom, and the evidence for glass shapes and styles of decoration after about 700 has to be retrieved in fragmentary form from occupation sites and interpreted in the light of contemporary glasses excavated more or less intact from burials in the pagan Scandinavian north. This evidence shows that the tall cone beaker and the originally hemispherical palm cup were in due course replaced by an even more unstable funnel-shaped beaker that evolved from the palm cup, while the *Rüsselbecher* became taller and thinner, the "claws" being reduced to vestigial, driplike appendages lacking the full-blown form of the sixth and seventh centuries. The vessels of this period often show streaks of red, first found in the post-Roman era. Fragments of similar red-streaked glasses found on a glasshouse site at Cordel, in the Rhineland, suggest that this area was still the main center of production.

In Anglo-Saxon England, too, a period of great richness in burial finds is succeeded by a dearth of intact vessels and a scattering of domestic fragments that can only be fully interpreted from the Scandinavian evidence. In the seventh century, however, the burials of southeastern England, notably Kent, produced one or two types—the bag beaker and squat jar—that do not appear nearly so frequently on the Continent, raising the suspicion that glassmaking may have been transplanted from the Continent at this date, producing variant forms in isolation. If it was, the venture was short-lived, as is suggested by the famous request of Benedict Biscop in 675 for glassmakers *(vitrifactores)* to be brought from Gaul to glaze his conventual church at Monkwearmouth, in Northumberland, such workmen being unknown in England. Even so, his successor Cuthbert had to repeat the request in 758. No glassmaking site has been found in England that can with certainty be referred to this epoch, but a small furnace excavated near Glastonbury Abbey, thought to date from the tenth century, was probably installed to help furnish the abbey church with window glass. Of vessel glass at this date there is very little trace, unless a small, lightly ribbed bowl of somewhat irregular form, found in Shaftesbury Abbey, is of this period: it certainly has medieval analogues on the Continent (Germany and Austria), though these are not as early as the tenth to eleventh century date proposed for the Shaftesbury bowl.

Venice. From the time of these developments in northern Europe come the first intimations of glassmaking in Venice, which later became the undisputed leader in the field. This was toward the end of the tenth century, but it seems unlikely that Italy, the heartland of the Roman Empire, where glassmaking had been at home since at latest the time of Augustus, would entirely have forgotten the art. Indeed, a glasshouse site excavated on the island of Torcello, in the Venetian lagoon, demonstrates that glassmaking was in progress there already in the seventh century. There is indeed evidence to suggest that at a time when Venice was beginning to acquire a dominance in Italian affairs as well as in glassmaking, the art was fairly widespread elsewhere in Italy, notably in Florence and the Ligurian centers of Altare, the glassmakers of which were to play in later times a great part in the diffusion of soda glass manufacture outside Italy. In the thirteenth century there was a scattering of glass making centers across northern Italy (such as Padua, Vicenza, Treviso, Mantua) and no doubt in other areas too. In 1291 the Venetian industry was removed to the island of Murano.

Goblet, made of greenish transparent glass. Nieuwendoorn, Holland, 14th century. DRAWING SUPPLIED BY THE AUTHOR

The first unequivocal mention of a glassmaker in Venice, however, was in 982, when a certain "Domenico Fiolario" (or bottle maker) was witness to a deed of gift of the Church of S. Georgio (Maggiore). Almost exactly a century later, in 1083, one "Petrus Phiolarius" witnessed another deed donating property to the Benedictine abbot of S. Giorgio. The parallel is probably not wholly fortuitous, for there is considerable evidence that the Benedictine order, which deliberately cultivated the crafts, included among them the art of glassmaking. It would be natural enough, therefore, that a glassman should act as witness to a document conferring a benefit on a Benedictine monastery. It is noteworthy, however, that neither Domenico nor Petrus was himself a monk, and it seems likely that an interest, first concentrated on the provision of suitable glass for church windows, and possibly also of opaque colored glass ornaments for book bindings and the like, had spread to embrace such prosaic matters as bottle making, a function doubtless in due course delegated to the laity.

Theophilus. The background to such a development is provided by the books devoted to glassmaking in the dissertation *De diversis artibus,* compiled by the monk Theophilus, probably in the early twelfth century. Theophilus was himself a Benedictine, probably of Cologne, and in his work he not only describes the shapes and functions of glass furnaces, but gives instructions in the making of window glass by the muff technique and in the subsequent processes of making up stained-glass windows. The muff process requires that the glass should be elongated, and Theophilus describes the process of swinging the iron above the glassman's

head to lengthen the parison in making a long-necked bottle, the rim of which was apparently knocked off without further finishing.

Theophilus, however, apart from his hints on coloring glasses for windows, also touches on the subject of opaque glasses, and it is evident that these were prepared not only for manipulation in some of the techniques inherited from the Roman past (for instance, fused mosaic) but also for use in enameling on metal. The products of the former, which seem to have included trailing and combing opaque-white threads on a dark (usually blue) base glass, were mainly jewellike small plaques and cabochons for embellishing bookcovers and liturgical objects. Among the finer kinds of glass alluded to by Theophilus were vessels decorated by enameling and gilding in the "Greek" style, a type that has been identified in a famous bowl in the Treasury of S. Marco, Venice, on the eleventh-century glassmaking site at Corinth, and elsewhere. Fragments decorated in this general way, however, have been found as far north as England, and some of thirteenth-century date show a completely Gothic style, suggesting that this art had moved into western Europe by this time.

SYRO-FRANKISH

The same development seems more and more likely in the case of the more numerous "Syro-Frankish" glasses found in Scandinavia, Germany, Switzerland, Italy, and the British Isles. Though clearly of oriental derivation, their numbers on sites in northwestern Europe, the increasing appearance on them of western themes of decoration, and—most important—the documentary discovery that several glass painters were at work on vessel glass in Venice in the late thirteenth century all combine to

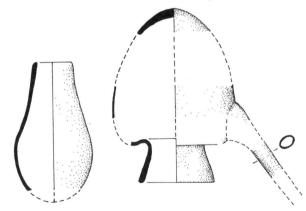

Alembic and cucurbit for distillation, made of green glass. Selborne Priory, Hants., by mid 15th century. DRAWING SUPPLIED BY THE AUTHOR

suggest that many of these glasses were made in western Europe, probably in Venice. This interpretation gives added point to the inscription found on the famous beaker in the British Museum: "Magister Aldrevandin me feci(t)." These glasses are characterized by painting on both sides of the glass in red, blue, white, and yellow enamels, without gilding. The subject matter includes figures of saints, western armorials, and Latin inscriptions, combined with a distinctive type of arcading and pointed foliage.

UTILITARIAN GREEN GLASS

Theophilus' technical recipes seem to depend essentially on the use of potash as a flux. The utilitarian glasses that he mentions as being made from this material were no doubt of a "natural" green color due to the iron impurities in the sand used. In the early Middle Ages, when green was apparently the preferred color, the knowledge of glass decolorizing may have been lost, at least in the north. It is certain that during the High Middle Ages virtually all utilitarian glassware made there was of plain green potash glass. Before these common or garden glasses are discussed in detail, however, it would be appropriate to deal with the fine quality glasses that furnished the tables of royalty and nobility (and later of wealthy commoners) and set the tone for humbler glasswares.

COLORLESS GLASS OF CORINTH, ITALY, AND
SWITZERLAND

It has often been assumed that the making of colorless crystal glass died with the declining Roman Empire, but this was probably not true of the heartlands of the empire and of its successor, the East Roman Empire of Byzantium. All too little, however, is known of early Byzantine glass, though the discovery of glass working sites of the eleventh to twelfth centuries at Corinth has provided capital evidence for its character at this crucial date. Glass of fine quality, some of it virtually colorless, decorated by a number of techniques, was made there; and three forms in particular seem to have had a lasting influence farther west during the thirteenth and fourteenth centuries.

One of these was a tall beaker of almost colorless greenish metal with slightly conical body and everted lip, the change of direction marked by an applied horizontal self-colored thread (of the same material as the body). The beaker had a tall "kick" in the base, which was given further stability by the application of a cordon of glass to form a foot-rim, the metal being pulled out into a series of "toes." The

Green glass lamp. Winchester, early 13th century. WINCHESTER CITY MUSEUM

body is decorated with a diaper of nipplelike applied knobs called prunts. This type of beaker recurs on Apulian sites (southern Italy) of twelfth- to thirteenth-century date, and the suggestion has been made that when the Normans captured Corinth in 1147 they transported glassworkers, as well as other craftsmen, to their south Italian territories. There is no proof of this, however, and no glasshouse sites have been discovered in this area.

The second glass shape found at Corinth (but possibly not manufactured there, since only two fragments occurred), made of a yellowish glass, seems to be a dumpier version of the first, with barrel-shaped, prunted body and a plain foot-ring replacing the pincered "toes." Examples of similar bases and a rim have also been found in Apulia, though not definitely associated with prunted fragments.

The third type of Corinth beaker was cylindrical but slightly waisted, with domed "kick," or indentation, at the base, plain thread foot-ring, vertical ribbing, and normally a blue thread edging the slightly flaring rim. The color could vary from pale blue-green to yellowish, and the rim thread might be self-colored. Beakers of this general type, with blue-thread decoration though without the vertical ribbing, are recorded in south Italy and in England.

Archaeological finds of the 1970's have revealed

that almost colorless glass beakers, generically of the prunted varieties described above, were commonplace in western European countries during the thirteenth, fourteenth, and early fifteenth centuries. Beakers that seem to represent a shortened version of the first Corinth type have been found in Switzerland at Zurich (3), Basel (1), Meiringen (1), and Chur (1); and of the second, barrel-shaped type, at Zurich (1) and Basel (3); while at Schaffhausen a whole series (4), in varying sizes and nuances of manufacture but with "toed" foot-rim, came from a single pit. Where contexts were datable, these Swiss finds seem to belong to the thirteenth century.

BOHEMIA

In Bohemia, beakers similar to the first Corinth type are occasionally found, both excavated and represented in manuscript illuminations, all from the fourteenth or early fifteenth century. The most characteristic Bohemian type, however, running to sixty-five examples, was a very tall, slender glass (up to forty-three centimeters [seventeen inches] high) on a wide foot, decorated with a semé of tiny prunts between trails of self-colored threads below the rim and above the foot. They are dated archaeologically and by manuscript comparisons to the period from about 1340 to the early fifteenth century. A number of variants exist, some shorter, some decorated with notched spiral trails or "wrythen" mold-blown ribbing, some with applied blue threading. The second Corinth type is sparsely represented in Bohemia, but does occur in both excavated examples and book illuminations, dating from approximately the century between 1350 and 1450. All these glasses are in a more or less colorless metal.

YUGOSLAVIA

On the present territory of Yugoslavia a different but analogous situation is found. At Veličani, in Herzegovina, a tomb datable to about 1400 contained a prunted beaker eight centimeters (three inches) high, of fine, slightly yellow-brown glass. Its distinctly cupped mouth, the lower edge delimited by an applied thread, and its relatively squat proportions, suggest the second Corinth type, but its notched foot-ring seems rather to align it with the first, as with the Schaffhausen beakers. It is sparsely prunted, however, though the prunts have the snail-like coiled formation often found in this whole family. This piece stands alone, for all save one of the other colorless goblets with cupped top found in Yugoslavia have vertical ribbing in place of the prunted

zone, thereby recalling the third Corinth type of beaker; while a third specimen, from Stari Kakanj (Bosnia), has mold-blown ribbing from rim to base. Several of these glasses have blue threading, thereby recalling the Corinth prototype, but the notched foot-rims again recall the other tall beaker type.

The second Corinth type of prunted beaker is represented in Yugoslavia by a fragmentary colorless example from the Fortress of Belgrade, and perhaps by prunted fragments from other sites; these seem to belong to the period about 1350–1450. In the second half of the fifteenth century green glass seems to have come into favor as the material for these beakers.

ENGLAND AND FRANCE

This evidence from Bohemia and the Balkans is to some extent confirmed and largely supplemented by recent finds in England. Although no examples of the first Corinth beaker type seem yet to have come to light, the second type is represented by fragments from the Royal Palace of King's Langley, Hertfordshire (1291–1431), and by a more or less complete example from Southampton. Just as the tall types of Corinth beaker were displaced in Bohemia by the very tall and narrow beer glass, and in Yugoslavia by the ribbed beaker with cup top, so in England two fresh vessel types occur, both in colorless glass with blue-threaded decoration. The first of these is a tall goblet on a slender solid stem and wide foot, the bowl decorated by blue-threaded designs and blue and colorless prunts; the second is a low cup of double-ogee profile standing on a pincered foot-rim and decorated with applied blue (and sometimes manganese purple) threads in zigzag patterns of marked angularity. The first of these types (examples from Southampton, *ca.* 1300–1350, and London) has a close analogue in a stemmed goblet found at Lucera in Apulia (fourteenth century), a comparable stem fragment coming from Petrulla, also in the same province. The double-ogee cup (found at Southampton, *ca.* 1330–1350, Nottingham, *ca.* 1300–1350, and Micheldever, Hampshire, fourteenth century) also has Italian parallels, notably in two cups found at Faenza with fourteenth-century material. In addition, England has produced several fragments of colorless beakers with blue threading that may be cousins to the third Corinth type, but without ribbing (Boston, late thirteenth century, and Southampton, *ca.* 1300–1350).

To these shapes, which are common to south Italy and England, may be added a pedestal-stemmed chalicelike goblet, of which an example with ribbed bowl was found at Lucera. Also, examples from about 1400 with vertically ribbed stems and notched bowl threading have been excavated in England (at Knaresborough and Old Sarum), both of these examples made in a curious strong, almost fluorescent, yellow glass that seems peculiar to the fourteenth century. A similar goblet, but in blue glass, has been found at Split (Diocletian's palace, probably fourteenth to fifteenth century) and the fragment apparently of another occurred at La Seube, near Montpellier in Languedoc. A bowl found at Boston, decorated with blue threading and blue and self-colored prunts and standing on a notched foot, is paralleled by fragments of a similar bowl found in Exeter (*ca.* 1300–1350), and a comparable bowl has been found in Italy. All have strong affinities with a bowl excavated at Novo Brdo, Serbia, of about 1400. These examples again tend to connect Italy, England, and the Balkans.

At La Seube special kinds of vessel were found in almost colorless glass with blue thread and blob decoration, though it cannot be absolutely proved that they were made on the site. These finds include several fragments of tall-stemmed goblets with blue details: spreading cups with blue threading and notched feet; and a beaker foot with manganese threading recalling the Southampton cups. Plain conical beakers with blue-trailed rims were also found, a type with parallels at Split and in Italy. A fragmentary bowl had close affinities with the Boston bowl; and an extraordinary dish on three *S*-shaped feet was decorated with a great blue disc in the middle of the foot. The La Seube site also produced fragmentary vessels with combed threaded opaque-white and -red decorations on a dark blue base.

SPAIN

The early history of glassmaking in Spain is almost a blank. Some of the earliest glasses, used for reliquaries *(lipsanotecas),* are evidently Islamic mold-blown flasks cut down for the purpose. The earliest record of glassmaking in Catalonia dates from 1189, but very few medieval glasses have been identified even there. Glass, however, seems to have been made in the thirteenth century in neighboring Roussillon, then part of the kingdom of Aragon, and glasses found at the abbey of Escaladieu (Hautes-Pyrénées) may represent local production. They include colorless glasses with ribbing and blue threading, notably a small spouted ewer or cruet with crested

rim that may anticipate the elaborately pincered glasses later made in Spain (such as the *almorratxa* form).

It seems clear, therefore, that the years between about 1275 and 1425 witnessed an almost Europewide vogue for glass as colorless as the glassman could make it, normally decorated with blue or self-colored threads and prunts. In each territory mentioned, however, there appear to be types that have a peculiar "national" character. In the cases of Bohemia and the Balkans the total absence of stemmed glasses perhaps testifies to differing drinking habits (maybe beer rather than wine). The tall-stemmed goblets of Italy, France, and England may reflect the tastes of wine-drinking people, and are matched by the exceedingly rare surviving fourteenth-century silver goblets with a broad foot and a central knop on the tall, slender stem. The tall-stemmed goblets were also widely copied in green glass in northern Europe, numerous examples being found in Holland, France, and England.

A number of theories have been advanced as to where the colorless glasses were made. The claims of Venice have been strongly advocated and, in the ab-

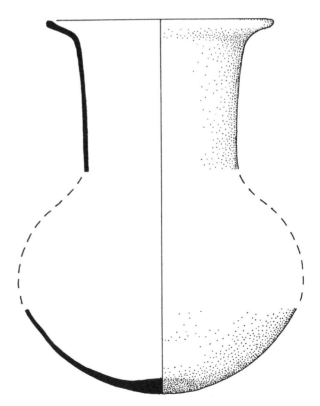

Urinal, made of clear green glass. Winchester, 14th century. DRAWING SUPPLIED BY THE AUTHOR

sence of proof that glass was made in southern Italy, seem very plausible. Bearing in mind that at a later date the Venetians trimmed their style to suit their markets overseas, and that at least as early as the late thirteenth century they are mentioned in the records as making glass for "Romania" (the Byzantine Empire), it is perfectly possible that they made special shapes and types for the Balkan markets. It should also be borne in mind that Ragusa (Dubrovnik) was a glassmaking center, manned by Muranese workmen in the early fourteenth century: its style would presumably be Venetian, but sensitive to the demands of the local market. Within the Bohemian sphere the question is more readily resolved, for the Bohemian glass was a potash-lime material, as opposed to the Mediterranean soda-lime glass, and numerous glasshouses are known in medieval Bohemia. As to England, most of the colorless glass was found in port towns (Southampton, Boston, London, Exeter), of which Southampton and London at least are known to have been important in the Italian trade.

FOURTEENTH- AND FIFTEENTH-CENTURY SHAPES

Apart from the blue-threaded and colorless glasses already described, the fourteenth century saw the development of a simple conical beaker usually decorated with mold-blown patterns of various kinds. Overwhelmingly the most common drinking glass in fifteenth century Italy, it appears constantly in contemporary pictures, often in company with a tall-necked bottle made in one piece with a pushed-in foot with high kick, the neck often spirally ribbed. These two glass types bore the names *moiolo* and *inghistera* in Venice, where innumerable examples were undoubtedly made, and these words probably lay behind the German names *Maigelein* for a small low cup, and *Angster* for a flask with a constricted neck.

GREEN "FOREST GLASS"

With these two types and the prunted beakers already described, almost all the main forms of German green *Waldglas* (forest glass) that developed during the fifteenth century had their prototypes. The change to green potash glass may represent purely a change of taste, or may reflect some economic or technical development not yet understood. Like their presumed Italian prototypes, the German cup forms—the *Maigelein* and the conical beaker with high kick—were mold-blown, sometimes ribbed, sometimes cross-ribbed by blowing a twisted ("wrythen") parison a second time in the same mold.

The peculiarity of the *Angster* or *Kuttrolf* was a neck composed of three or four tubes produced by suction. This technique, already known in late Roman times, reappears in Bohemia (Pilsen) in two examples of about 1400: the intervening stages are at present hidden from us. Later in the fifteenth century, when the Venetian *cristallo* (transparent colorless glass) was established as the supreme deluxe glass of Europe, the Germans copied the distinctive vertically ribbed forms in their own green metal.

Unfortunately, relatively few excavation reports have been published that include early medieval vessel glass from important areas such as France and Germany, but the English evidence is abundant, and since some of the types identified have known analogues in those areas, it may reasonably be assumed that the picture was much the same throughout northwestern Europe. Furthermore, since glassmaking can be documented in England from as early as 1240, and an actual glasshouse site of about 1330 enables us to assess the furnaces used and the types of glass made, we may reasonably conclude that the medieval utilitarian glasses found in England were mostly made there. Unfortunately, owing to the poor durability of potash glass, few whole or reconstructible vessels have survived. Enough remains, however, to give us a general picture of everyday glass in medieval England. This can often be confirmed by manuscript illuminations. The sites concerned are usually monasteries (where lamps and urinals are frequent), castles or manor houses, and the richer dwellings of the towns and cities. The commonest forms are lamps, urinals, flasks, and various types of chemical or alchemical glassware.

The lamps recall the shape so often seen in medieval manuscripts, having a wide and relatively shallow cup top and a tapering stem with solid base, as shown by the only surviving reconstructible example, probably of thirteenth-century date, from Winchester. The solid butts of these lamps survive in scores where the other thinner parts have vanished. It may well be that with time the bowl became deeper and straighter-sided (a reconstructible lamp of this type has been found in a sixteenth-century deposit in Northampton). The shape is echoed in the wood engravings of Martin Schongauer and in the Boulbon altarpiece of the School of Avignon (*ca.* 1400) in the Louvre, and a prolific find of fragments of such lamps (*ca.* 1500), at Bayham Abbey, in Kent, seems to exemplify this evolution. On the other hand, a sole surviving French lamp of allegedly eleventh-century date also shows these proportions, which may also be seen in manuscript illuminations. There may have been a greater variety of shapes than can yet be recognized.

Of as frequent occurence are the urinals. They too have suffered undue fragmentation, an obvious danger when green glass had to be blown thin enough to permit the uroscopist to judge the color and quality of its contents. In consequence, the thickened convex base of the urinal, with its often nipplelike pontil (punty) mark, and after that the wide rim, often with slightly upturned lip, are the most frequent survivals. Two main types appear, one with cylindrical neck and more or less spherical body, the other a pyriform vessel with neck tapering toward the wide, horizontal rim. It seems possible that a third type, of thicker glass, with a wider neck and spreading rim, was used more in the capacity of a chamber pot. With convex rounded bases, all were unstable, needing to be carried about in covered cylindrical cases, often of wicker, with overarching handle.

Of bottles—one of the commonest forms in green forest glass—it is scarcely possible to generalize. Very few examples found in England can be dated before 1400, but the shapes had probably not settled down into standardized types much before then. Examples at Southampton vary from a probably globular-bodied container with wide cylindrical neck, cupped mouth, and slight kick (late thirteenth century) to another with globular but wide-based body with a high kick, tapering neck and slightly outturned lip (ca. 1300–1350). A fine large bottle from Tynemouth Priory is decorated with angular self-colored trails of thirteenth-to fourteenth-century character. Already by about 1300–1350 bottles are decorated with vertical mold-blown ribbing, and this feature continues into the Renaissance period. Seemingly by about 1400 the "standard" English flask has evolved, with slightly sagging globular body, low kick, and tallish neck tapering toward the fairly narrow spreading conical lip, often cut off aslant. This type appears to continue with only slight modifications into the seventeenth century.

In France, some of the earliest bottle forms appear from manuscripts to have had simply spherical bodies and long tapering necks, an example from Bordeaux coming from a supposedly eleventh- to twelfth-century tomb. The type apparently continues into the thirteenth century. A thirteenth-century flask from Poitou, however, has a bulbous ribbed body with a bulge round the base of the longish neck, in a manner recalling some of the flasks at

Corinth; the body of another ribbed bottle came from a twelfth- to thirteenth-century sarcophagus at Bordeaux. Fifteenth-century flasks survive of rather shorter-necked form, one with pronounced ribbing mold-blown on a "second gather," one with flattened body, a feature echoed in a manuscript illumination of about 1410. The rib molding on a second gather is repeated on some almost colorless bottles from Pilsen, in Bohemia (ca. 1400–1450). This "double post" technique did not reach England until the sixteenth century, but was probably established in Germany earlier. Here small flattened flasks with swirled ribbing, sometimes cross-ribbed, echo the technique used on contemporary beakers and provided the models for later English flasks.

WINDOW GLASS

In northern Europe the manufacture of vessel glass was probably always subordinate in economic importance to the manufacture of window glass. In Book II of his *De diversis artibus,* after describing the glassmaker's main furnace and annealing furnace, the monk Theophilus prescribes a third furnace for "spreading out." This relates, though he does not say so, to the final process in making muff window glass. The process itself is not dealt with until chapter 6, where Theophilus describes the gathering, marvering, and repeated blowing until "you see it hanging down like a long bladder." The end of the parison is then reheated so that a hole appears, which must be widened with a wooden tool to match the diameter of the cylinder. Next this rim is pinched together in the middle to produce a figure of eight and the cylinder is detached from the blowing iron, which is then used as a pontil attached to the center of the eight. The cylinder being reheated, the other end is opened up in turn and pinched together, after which the pipe is knocked off and the cylinder carried to the annealing furnace. In due course the cylinders were transferred to the preheated spreading furnace, split open longitudinally with a hot iron, and when soft spread flat with "iron tongs and a smooth, flat piece of wood." The nowflat sheet was next transferred again to the annealing oven until cool and ready for cutting up. This was done (ch. 18) by applying a red-hot iron along the line required by the design, outlined on a wooden table. The rough line could then be adjusted by the "grozing iron," a notched tool by which the glass could be nibbled away gradually to the desired shape. The same technique could clearly be used for secular as well as ecclesiastical buildings, the individual panes being secured by lead cames of *H*-section, or by wooden frames.

This muff technique had been used in Roman times and was probably continuously practiced through the Middle Ages and into the sixteenth century. It was not, however, the only available technique. By at latest the fourth century A.D. glassmakers in the Near East had been making small, circular window panels like flat glass dishes. These were set into plaster or other frames. The technique early passed to Italy (Ravenna, sixth century) and was in use in the Corinth glasshouse (eleventh century). This crown technique has always been associated with Normandy, but its first mention there dates only from the early fourteenth century. The suggestion that it was then a new invention perhaps refers to the making of as large a crown as possible, to be cut up, rather than to the basic process. This consisted of blowing a parison, transferring it to a pontil, opening the hole made by knocking off the blowing iron, reheating, and then spinning the parison until centrifugal force converted it into a wide, flat disk. The Venetians kept these *rui* small and folded their edges, using them leaded up in multiples, with small connecting pieces to fill the spaces between: the Normans split their large discs into various shapes and sizes, including the lozenge-shaped "quarries" that became common for domestic glazing in the fifteenth century. Muff and crown seem to have coexisted in northern Europe from about 1200 onward, the merit of the former being that it provided a single large rectangular sheet, of the latter that it preserved its brilliant fire polish, whereas the surface of the muff was adversely affected by the spreading process.

MIRRORS

Sheet glass was also needed for the making of looking glasses. In antiquity both metal and glass mirrors were used, and small glass mirrors, usually convex, survive from late Roman times, usually set in plaster or other frames. Both types of mirror coexisted until well into the seventeenth century, and words such as *speculum, specchio,* and *miroir* are ambiguous unless qualified by *vitrum, vetro, verre,* and the like. No glass mirrors from the early Middle Ages seem to have survived, and the first verbal reference occurs in the late twelfth century with the mention of *Spiegelglas.* That the first allusion is in German seems significant, for throughout the Middle Ages Germany in general, and Nuremberg in particular, appears to have been the most significant

center of production. In 1215 there is a record of German glass being sent to Genoa for making mirrors, and when in 1317 three Venetians wished to establish the manufacture at Murano, they hired a "certain German master" to be their technician. The Nuremberg guild of mirror makers was established in 1373, and when in 1507 the Venetians again projected a home manufacture, the art was still spoken of as a precious secret known only to certain Germans.

Since the Italians were perfectly capable of making fine glass, the secret perhaps lay in the silvering. The Nuremberg mirror was characteristically convex, and it has been asserted that prior to 1500 the backing was made by blowing into the glass bubble while still hot a metallic mixture with a little resin or salt of tartar (a contemporary Italian writer lists "lead, tin, marcasite of silver, and tartar"). Previously the backing had been of lead. Vincent of Beauvais in his *Speculum historiale* (1250) writes that the best mirrors are made from glass and lead; and Dante in *Paradiso* 2.89–90 (before 1321) refers to "glass backed with lead."

The characteristic convexity, seen in so many fifteenth-century paintings that represent mirrors, and the method of "silvering," together suggest that the glasses were cut from essentially spherical parisons, possibly a technical offshoot of the crown process of making window glass. The essentially northern European development of this technique may partially explain the German dominance of mirror making in the later Middle Ages. The importance of the mirror in medieval imagery requires no stressing, and the glass mirror probably enjoyed a universal European distribution. In England, for instance, John Peckham refers as early as about 1278 to "glass mirrors"; there were "mirrorers" in fourteenth-century London (not necessarily making glass mirrors); and "glasses and Combys" were articles of export from England to Iceland. In 1327 the cargo on a Venetian ship (which does not exclude a German origin) included three dozen mirrors, and the trade must have been widespread.

BIBLIOGRAPHY
General Studies. R. J. Charleston, "Glass of the High Medieval Period (12th–15th Century)," in *Bulletin de l'Association internationale du verre* (1980); Edward Dillon, *Glass* (1907); D. B. Harden, "Medieval Glass in the West," in *Eighth International Congress on Glass, 1968* (1969), "Ancient Glass, III: Post-Roman," in *Archaeological Journal,* **128** (1972), "Table-glass in the Middle Ages," in J. G.

N. Renaud, ed., *Rotterdam Papers*, II (1975), and "Early Medieval Glass," in *Bulletin de l'Association internationale du verre* (1980); Alexander Nesbitt, *Glass* (1878).

The following works are useful on specific topics. Lombard glass: D. B. Harden, "Some Lombard Glasses of the 6th and 7th Centuries," in Vasa Čubrilović, ed., *Verre médiéval aux Balkans* (1975), with a good bibliography. Anglo-Saxon glass: D. B. Harden, "Glass Vessels in Britain and Ireland, A.D. 400–1000," in his *Dark-Age Britain: Studies Presented to E. T. Leeds* (1956), and "Anglo-Saxon and Later Medieval Glass in Britain: Some Recent Developments," in *Medieval Archaeology*, 22 (1978). Cordel (the Rhineland): H. Arbman, *Schweden und das Karolingische Reich* (1937), 26–86; Franz Rademacher, "Fränkische Gläser aus dem Rheinland," in *Bonner Jahrbücher*, 147 (1942); Raymond Chambon and H. Arbman, "Deux fours à verre d'époque Mérovingienne à Macquenoise (Belgique)," in *Kungliga Vetenskapssamfundets i Lund Årsberättelse*, 7 (1951–1952); Clasina Isings, "Glass Finds from Dorestad, Hoogstraat 1," in W. A. Van Es and W. J. H. Verwers, *Excavations at Dorestad*, I (1980). Benedict Biscop: Mary L. Trowbridge, *Philological Studies in Ancient Glass* (1928). Shaftesbury bowl: D. B. Harden, "A Glass Bowl of Dark Age Date and Some Medieval Gravefinds from Shaftesbury Abbey," in *Antiquaries Journal*, 34 (1954).

Torcello: Astone Gasparetto, "A proposito dell'officina vetraria torcellana," in *Journal of Glass Studies*, 9 (1967); E. Tabaczynska, "Remarks on the Origin of the Venetian Glassmaking Center," in R. J. Charleston *et al.*, eds., *Studies in Glass History and Design, Papers Read at the VIIIth International Congress on Glass, 1968* (1970). Florence: Guido Taddei, *L'arte del vetro in Firenze en nel suo dominio* (1954). Altare: Luigi Zecchin, "Sull'origine dell'arte vetraria in Altare," in *Vetro e silicati*, 9 (1965); M. Calegari *et al.*, "La vetreria medievale di Monte Lecco," in *Archeologia medievale*, 2 (1975). Other Italian centers: Luigi Zecchin, "Antiche vetrerie veronesi," in *Giornale economico* (July 1957). Venice: Astone Gasparetto, *Il vetro di Murano* (1958), and "Reperti vitrei medievali della Basilica dei SS. Maria e Donato di Murano," in *Bolletino dei musei civici veneziani*, 1 (1977); Luigi Zecchin, "Vetrerie muranesi dal 1276 al 1300," in *Rivista della Stazione sperimentale del vetro*, 1, no. 4 (1977), "Forestieri nell'arte vetraria muranese (1348–1425)," *ibid.*, 11, no. 1 (1981), "Materie prime e mezzi d'opera dei vetrai nei documenti veneziani dal 1348 al 1438," *ibid.*, 11, no. 2 (1981), "Fornaci muranesi fra il 1279 ed il 1290," in *Journal of Glass Studies*, 12 (1970), and "Nascita del cristallo veneziano," in *Vetro e silicati*, 11 (1967). Théophilus: C. R. Dodwell, trans., *Theophilus: The Various Arts* (1961); John G. Hawthorne and Cyril S. Smith, trans., *On Divers Arts: The Treatise of Theophilus* (1963). Mosaic glass: Rosemary J. Cramp, "Decorated Window-glass and Millefiori from Monkwearmouth," in *Antiquaries Journal*, 50 (1970).

Syro-Frankish enameled glass: John Clark, "Medieval Enamelled Glasses from London," in *Medieval Archaeology*, 27 (1983); C. J. Lamm, *Oriental Glass of Medieval Date Found in Sweden* (1941), 77ff.; Wolfgang Pfeiffer, "Acrische Gläser," in *Journal of Glass Studies*, 12 (1970); Luigi Zecchin, "Un decoratore di vetri a Murano alle fine del Duecento," *ibid.*, 11 (1969).

Colorless glasses with prunts and threading (Byzantine): Gladys R. Davidson, "A Mediaeval Glass-factory at Corinth," in *American Journal of Archaeology*, 44 (1940); Gladys Davidson Weinberg, "A Medieval Mystery: Byzantine Glass Production," in *Journal of Glass Studies*, 17 (1975); Mary R. DeMaine, "The Medieval Glass," in *Diocletian's Palace: Report on Joint Excavations*, III (1979). (General): D. B. Harden, "Some Glass Fragments Mainly of the 12th–13th Century A.D., from Northern Apulia," in *Journal of Glass Studies*, 8 (1966); D. B. Whitehouse, "Ceramiche e vetri medioevali provenienti dal Castello di Lucera," in *Bolletino d'arte*, 3–4 (1966); David Andrews and Denys Pringle, "Vetri, metalli, e reperti minori dell'area sud del Convento di S. Silvestro a Genova," in *Archeologia medievale*, 4 (1977). (England): R. J. Charleston, "Some English Finds of Medieval Glass with Balkan Analogues," in Verena Han, ed., *Medieval Glass in the Balkans* (1975). (Central Europe): Jürg Schneider, "Noppenbecher des 13. Jahrhunderts," in *Zeitschrift für Schweizerische Archäologie und Kunstgeschichte*, 37 (1980). (Balkans): Ljubinka Kojić and Marian Wenzel, "Medieval Glass Found in Yugoslavia," in *Journal of Glass Studies*, 9 (1967); Verena Han, "The Origin and Style of Medieval Glass Found in the Central Balkans," *ibid.*, 17 (1975); Marian Wenzel, "A Reconsideration of Bosnian Medieval Glass," *ibid.*, 19 (1977). (Bohemia): Dagmar Hejdová and Bořivoj Nechvátal, "Late 14th- to Mid-15th-century Medieval Glass from a Well in Plzeň, Western Bohemia," in *Journal of Glass Studies*, 12 (1970); Dagmar Hejdová, "Types of Medieval Glass Vessels in Bohemia," *ibid.*, 17 (1975). (France): James Barrelet, *La verrerie en France* (1953); Nicole Lambert, "La Seube: Témoin de l'art du verre en France méridionale . . ." in *Journal of Glass Studies*, 14 (1972). (Spain): José Gudiol Ricart, *Los vidrios catalanes* (1941); Alice Wilson Frothingham, *Spanish Glass* (1963).

Tall-stemmed glasses in northern Europe: J. G. N. Renaud, "Un verre à boire du 14ᵉ siècle," in *Proceedings of the International Congress on Glass, Brussels, 1965* (1965), and "Das Hohlglas des Mittelalters unter besonderer Berücksichtigung des neuesten in Holland und anderswo gemachten Funde," in *Glastechnische Berichte*, 32K, 8 (1959); Raymond Chambon, "La verrerie entre Rhin et Loire au quatorzième siècle," in *Journal of Glass Studies*, 17 (1975); Michèle Cognioul-Thiry, "Verres du XIVᵉ siècle récemment découverts en Belgique," in *Annales de l'Association internationale du verre*, 7 (1978); Clasina Isings and H. F. Wijnman, "Medieval Glass from Utrecht," in *Journal of Glass Studies*, 19 (1977).

Inghistere and *moioli:* Giovanni Mariacher, "La scoperta di due bottiglie veneziane del secolo XV," in *Journal of Glass Studies,* 6 (1964). *Waldglas:* T. Dexel, *Gebrauchsglas* (1977); Herbert Kühnert, "The Mehlis Glasshouse in the Thüringer Wald," in *Journal of Glass Studies,* 9 (1967); W. Neugebauer, "Die Ausgrabungen in der Alstadt Lübecks," in J. G. N. Renaud, ed., *Rotterdam Papers,* I (1968); Franz Rademacher, *Die deutschen Gläser des Mittelalters* (1933). Sven Schütte, "Mittelalterliches Glas aus Göttingen," in *Zeitschrift für Archäologie des Mittelalters,* 4 (1976). English glassmaking: R. J. Charleston, *English Glass* (1984), 1–108.

Utilitarian glassware: D. B. Harden, "Domestic Window Glass: Roman, Saxon, and Medieval," in E. M. Jope, ed., *Studies in Building History* (1961); I. Noël Hume, "Mediaeval Bottles from London," in *The Connoisseur* (March 1957); Jean Lafond, "Was Crown Glass Discovered in Normandy in 1330?" in *Journal of Glass Studies,* 11 (1969); Stephen Moorhouse, "Medieval Distilling-apparatus of Glass and Pottery," in *Medieval Archaeology,* 16 (1972).

ROBERT J. CHARLESTON

[See also **Glass, Stained; Optics, Western European; Technology, Treatises on; Technology, Western; Theophilus; Venice.**]

GLOBUS CRUCIGER, a spherical globe surmounted by a cross to symbolize Christian dominion over the cosmos. Reserved for rulers and the upper ranks of the celestial hierarchy, such as archangels, the *globus cruciger* appeared on coins shortly after the year 400 and remained widespread throughout the medieval period.

LESLIE BRUBAKER

[See also **Iconography.**]

GLORIA. The first word of a number of different liturgical texts of the Western church, chief among them *Gloria in excelsis Deo* (the *Gloria* of the ordinary of the Mass) and *Gloria Patri,* the so-called lesser doxology (*Gloria Patri, et Filio, et Spiritui Sancto. Sicut erat in principio, et nunc, et semper, et in saecula saeculorum. Amen.*). The *Gloria Patri* was added at the end of psalms when they were chanted in the Divine Office; it was sung to the same formula as that employed for the verses of the psalm, and came just before the return of the antiphon. Thus many liturgical manuscripts, in specifying the ending for the psalm tone in connection with a partic-

ular antiphon, write it out after the antiphon over the letters *e u o u a e* (the vowels of the words *seculorum amen*). When the *Gloria Patri* was added to the introit of the Mass or to an Office responsory (where, however, only the first part of the text was used), it was given a more elaborate setting that matched the verse of the chant. Each Office hymn ended in a paraphrase of the *Gloria Patri;* these were in verse so that they could be sung to the same melody as that employed for the stanzas of the hymn.

BIBLIOGRAPHY

Thomas H. Connolly, "Psalm, II: Latin Monophonic Psalmody," in *The New Grove Dictionary of Music and Musicians* (1980).

RUTH STEINER

[See also **Divine Office.**]

GLOSS (from Greek *glossa,* tongue), specifically, a word or words written in the margin of a text or between the lines to explain or interpret a word or passage; a precursor to the modern footnote. Glosses appear in the earliest extant Latin manuscripts, in medieval and Renaissance texts, and frequently, in early printed books. The gloss in its function as commentary became increasingly important in the interpretation of civil or canon law; the famous glosses on Roman law were begun at Bologna at the start of the twelfth century. By 1400 the gloss became an integral part of the layout and apparatus of a text, along with the rubrics, running titles, paraph marks, and stanza division.

A gloss may translate a word or passage. In the Lindisfarne Gospels, copied at the beginning of the eighth century, the main text is written in Latin with an interlinear Anglo-Saxon gloss or translation. A gloss is sometimes highly abbreviated and is often written in a language different from the text. The glossator of the "Melibee" in the Ellesmere manuscript of the *Canterbury Tales* demonstrates his knowledge of Latin when he glosses "the sentence of Ovide in his book / that cleped is the remedie of love" as "Ovidius de remedio amoris." A gloss may also supply a source reference or identifications. In one mid-fifteenth-century text of Chaucer's *Troilus and Criseyde* (Harley 2392, fol. 64v), the scribe cites parallel passages in Ovid's *Metamorphoses,* including references to specific books. Finally, a gloss may add passages previously omitted from a text.

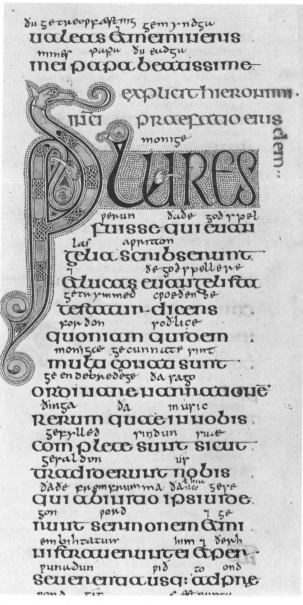

Initial page of St. Jerome's preface to the four Gospels, with Latin text and interlinear glosses in Anglo-Saxon. Lindisfarne Gospels, late 7th century. BRITISH MUSEUM, MS COTTON NERO D.IV, fol. 5v

In its broadest sense, a gloss calls special attention to specific information, and it need not always be verbal. The famous portrait of Chaucer in the Ellesmere manuscript, which occurs just beneath the title "heere bigynneth Chaucers tale of Melibee" is clearly functioning as a pictorial gloss as well as illustration. Likewise, the famous Chaucer portraits in Hoccleve's *The Regement of Princes* effectively gloss the words "I haue heer his lyknesse / do make."

BIBLIOGRAPHY

Elias A. Lowe, *Handwriting: Our Medieval Legacy* (1969), contains many useful plates, including a reproduction of a folio from the Lindisfarne Gospels and another from the Ellesmere manuscript of the *Canterbury Tales.* See also Roger A. B. Mynors, *Durham Cathedral Manuscripts to the End of the Twelfth Century* (1939); Malcolm B. Parkes, *English Cursive Book Hands, 1250–1500* (1969), an introduction to the development of medieval script, with many excellent plates, and his "The Influence of the Concepts of *Ordinatio* and *Compilatio* on the Development of the Book," in Jonathan J. G. Alexander and M. T. Gibson, eds., *Medieval Learning and Literature: Essays Presented to Richard William Hunt* (1976), an exploration of early book layout and apparatus.

MARTHA WESTCOTT DRIVER

[See also **Codicology, Western European; Glossators; Manuscript and Book Production; Paleography, Western European; Translations and Translators, Western European.**]

GLOSSATORS is a term used to designate members of the School of Law at Bologna in its classical period, from its supposed foundation by Irnerius at the very end of the eleventh century to about 1250. This usage, giving the erroneous impression that glossators were the only users of the gloss, a common exegetical tool, bears witness to the impression that these illustrious interpreters of Justinian's *Corpus iuris civilis* created in their own time. For a complex series of motives, these pioneers undertook successfully the task of rendering the ancient laws intelligible and useful to their contemporaries. In their day and to subsequent generations, the achievement seemed so novel and magnificent that legends developed about the rediscovery of the *Pandects (Digest)* at Amalfi after they had been lost for centuries, or about the transfer of the *Corpus iuris* from Rome, prey to the barbarians, to Ravenna and thence to Bologna.

Modern scholarship on the development of Bolognese legal science has stressed the theme of continuity. Roman studies have made clear that the dialectical method was first applied to Roman law at the end of the Republic when it became desirable to extract general definitions and rules from the extant body of customs, leges, and *edicta.* This application of a deductive reasoning, almost but not quite syllogistic in nature, marked the beginning of jurisprudence as a systematic discipline. Throughout the

565

classical period, jurists continued to apply dialectics to the analysis of juridical questions in order to produce a logical interpretation of law.

With the decay of culture in the post-classical period, the task of the jurists became less sublime as they began to compile the bare essentials of classical jurisprudence into practical manuals intended for the use of functionaries, judges, and advocates. Appended to these texts were simple annotations known as glosses or scholia that were intended to elucidate the import of the text by explanations of the meaning of the words. The gloss proved a useful instrument in the creation of new juridical concepts, abstract rules, and definitions. Ironically, Justinian's compilation itself, which reacted against the simplistic and pragmatic character of the juristic work of previous centuries and forbade further definition, was the result of methods characteristic of post-classical thought.

The new methods of interpretation had resulted in a radical change in the manner of legislating: while in the Republican period juridical norms had been created for the solution of particular cases, in the late Empire the norms were increasingly the result of positive legislation, established by the will of the emperor or by codifications made at his command. This change was to condition medieval juridical science as a whole.

Western legal writings from the sixth to the twelfth century share substantial traits with those of the late Empire. This was the natural result of the continuation of Roman traditions, especially in Italy but also in Spain and France, and of the uninterrupted if partial transmission of cultural principles within monastic and city schools by the teaching of the Seven Liberal Arts. Roman law itself was able to survive because of laws, which were accepted in all barbarian states, that allowed the Roman subjects to be judged by Roman law. Moreover, the church always claimed the right to order its affairs in accordance with Roman law. In Italy, this tradition was strengthened by the introduction of Justinian's codification after the Gothic War (533–553). Even there, however, historical conditions did not allow the codification to escape deformation, corruption, and barbarization; this complex body of laws could not be of evident utility to societies that had become predominantly feudal.

Before the activity of the glossators, law had not been separated from the other sciences either theoretically or pedagogically. As a body of rules for life,

it was placed with ethics, a branch of philosophy; as law, its most important mode of expression was a set of words. Therefore it became the object of a form of knowledge to be reduced, in the final analysis, to a semantic interpretation. Thus, the work of the jurist was understood to be part of the trivium and, more specifically, of grammar understood as a logical science. This was a consequence not only of the decay of culture but also of the importance that had been given in the late Empire to rhetorical and dialectical concepts as essential parts of the education of the jurist. Glosses, even if they became purely etymological explanations, continued to be produced throughout this period.

Between the sixth and the twelfth century creative developments occurred only within the sphere of canon law. In this context, norms of positive law were subjected to a critical analysis in order to be brought into line with the ethical and religious principles of the patristic tradition. This evaluation led to a new concept of positive law, namely, the typically medieval view that in order for positive law to be valid, it could not be in contrast with the principles of the church.

The decline of juridical science was halted toward the beginning of the twelfth century; its renewal began with the rise of the method of the glossators who, by their work, established a common basis for European law and produced the techniques that were to shape canon law when adopted by decretists and decretalists. The renaissance of juridical science should be examined in its historical context, if the real merits of the glossators and the contradictions endemic to their work are to be appreciated.

By the end of the eleventh century there were already signs that a reevaluation of Justinian's law had begun at Bologna; the evidence concerning Pepo and his contemporaries makes clear that they were affected by the disputes of the Gregorian reform and that they undertook an active search for the authentic legal texts. The need for a renewal of law to satisfy the exigencies of a changing society was to be met at Bologna.

Because of the lack of adequate information concerning the origins of the Bolognese School, we cannot determine the specific roles played by political movements, individuals, or the intellectual desire to recover a rich heritage that had seemed lost for centuries. All these elements appear to have been at work, and their diversity is reflected in the contradictory aspects of Bolognese doctrine, which was simultaneously bound to the practice of superior tribunals and extraordinarily aware of the philological exigencies implicit in its reliance on texts.

The rise of the School remains wrapped in legend. The gloss, which was the most characteristic instrument of the intellectual activity of its members, testifies to the link between the School and the earlier schools of liberal arts. The principal difference in the new approach is to be found first in the effects of the cultural renaissance in general and that of philosophy and theology in particular on juridical science; second, in the fact that at Bologna law finally became an autonomous discipline of studies. As a consequence, there was a restoration of the complete texts of the *Corpus iuris civilis,* a return to the knowledge of the *Digest,* the attribution of efficacy, of the force of law, to the entire codification of Justinian and especially to the *Codex.*

It must be stressed that Justinian's law had intrinsic authority for the glossators, who made recurring cross-references between it and the proclamations of the Holy Roman emperors. This reassertion of Justinian's voluntaristic conception of law, aside from appearing utopian in relation to the Holy Roman Empire, seemed also to embody a polemical attitude toward the church, especially as the glossators claimed for the civil law those matters it had used to regulate in the sixth century but which the church had made its own since. This appearance of polemicism was further strengthened by the fact that Bolognese doctrine at first seemed unwilling to grant to canon law even the role granted to it by Justinian in his constitutions, namely, that the canons had the same authority as imperial constitutions. The insistence on imperial prerogatives made it difficult for the School, almost to its end, to admit the existence of any other political order—which presented a strange difficulty for citizens of the communes.

The glossators also held that, in Justinian's codification, the principles of justice and equity characteristic of Christianity had been infused with the norms of positive law; it was on this basis that they justified the extension of juridical value to the *Corpus iuris.* From this justifiable view arose their aim to master the juridical texts as completely as possible and their rejection of the possibility of contradiction in them; this body of norms, seen as both equitable and rational, was perceived as a harmonic system of principles. The authoritative character of the texts represented the basic premise of the glossators' methodology, which was basically that of the early

Middle Ages but with the application to legal science of the relationship of received authority to reason, a problem much discussed at the time in biblical exegesis and theology.

Emphasis is usually placed, with some justice, on the close adhesion of the glossators to the words of their texts. This, however, was only the starting point of their exegesis. The aim remained always the achievement of a synthesis of all the norms in the *Corpus iuris.* Passages in the *Corpus* were always examined within their reciprocal relationship. By comparing parallel passages, the glossators investigated the connection of one source to another, attempted to reconcile "apparent" contradictions, and found the reason for a specific norm in the application of a more general principle or as the confirmation or integration of another norm. This was the fixed aim of the glossators despite the variety of literary genres that the vastness of their task and the requirements of teaching made necessary.

The School of Bologna became famous almost immediately for the teaching and writing of its reputed founder, Irnerius, and of the famous Four Doctors who succeeded him, namely, Bulgarus, Martinus Gosia, Jacobus, and Hugo. Important for the immediate influence of Bolognese juridical culture even outside Italy were Rogerius, Vacarius, and Placentinus, through whom Bolognese thought began to show more respect for reality and the possibilities of the application of juridical science to practical problems. Evidence of these new interests was the inclusion within the Bolognese curriculum not only of canon law but also of feudal and Lombard law. Important in this process were Johannes Bassianus and Pillius de Medicina. The new practical turn was shown by many writings on Romano-canonical procedure and the compilation of notarial formularies that incorporated the new doctrine. Thus, in the early thirteenth century, the School produced Corradino da Padova, Raimundo da Perugia, and Salatièle, as well as, toward the middle of the century, Rolandino Passeggieri.

The apogee of Bologna's achievement and of its fame was reached in the mid thirteenth century with Azo and Accursius, who were the most eminent representatives of this pragmatic tendency. Accursius' all-encompassing compilation and creation, the *Glossa ordinaria,* was the consolidation of the exegetic efforts of all the glossators. Thenceforth, this *Glossa* became the basic instrument of all teaching of law and drew the attention and devotion of subsequent jurists to itself rather than to the texts it was supposed to illuminate. The *Glossa* became more than an official interpretation of the *Corpus iuris.* Through it, the value and authority of the work of all the glossators was perpetuated in all European countries in which Roman juridical principles were held in honor.

BIBLIOGRAPHY

Studies on the glossators in English do not abound; as the basic work, one must still refer to Hermann Kantorowicz with William W. Buckland, *Studies in the Glossators of the Roman Law* (1938, repr. with addenda and corrigenda by Peter Weimar 1969). See also *Atti del Convegno internacionale di studi accursiani (Bologna, 1966)* (1968), with many articles on the method and doctrine of the glossators; Francesco Calasso, *Medio evo del diritto,* I, *Le fonti* (1954); Giorgio Cencetti, "Studium fuit Bononie," in *Studi medievali,* 3rd ser. 7 (1966), dealing with the controversial questions of the origins of the School of Bologna; Hermann Kantorowicz and Beryl Smalley, "An English Theologian's View of Roman Law: Pepo, Irnerius, Ralph Niger," in *Medieval and Renaissance Studies,* **1** (1966), also on the origins of the school; Bruno Paradisi, *Storia del diritto italiano: Le fonti del diritto nell'epoca bolognese,* I, *I civilisti fino a Rogerio* (1969); Vincenzo Piano Mortari, "Lineamenti della dogmatica giuridica medievale," in his *Dogmatica e interpretazione: I giuristi medieval* (1976), 1–74, with bibliography.

GIULIO SILANO

[See also **Azo; Bologna, University of; Bulgarus; Corpus iuris civilis; Decretals; Decretists; Hugo; Irnerius; Jacobus; Law, Canon: After Gratian; Law, Schools of; Martinus Gosia; Placentinus; Rogerius; Vacarius.**]

GLOSSATORS, JEWISH. See **Talmud, Jewish Exegesis and Study of.**

GLOUCESTER CATHEDRAL. Originally a Benedictine monastery, St. Peter's at Gloucester achieved episcopal status only in 1541. Large portions of the church begun in 1089 survive, especially in the nave and crypt. The choir was splendidly remodeled shortly after Edward II's burial there in 1327, providing an early example of the Perpendicular style.

BIBLIOGRAPHY

John Britton, *The History and Antiquities of the Abbey and Cathedral Church of Gloucester* (1829); William H. St.

Crypt of Gloucester Cathedral, begun 1089. JEAN ROUBIER

John Hope, "Notes on the Benedictine Abbey of St. Peter at Gloucester," in *Archaeological Journal,* 54 (1902); David Verey, *Gloucestershire,* II, *The Vale and the Forest of Dean* (1970), 198–226.

STEPHEN GARDNER

[See also **Gothic, Perpendicular.**]

GLYKOPHILOUSA (Virgin of Tenderness), an adjectival label for a depiction in which, though the specific type of the Virgin varies, she always holds the Christ Child, who presses his cheek against hers. In older literature, *Glykophilousa* is sometimes used to designate a Virgin Eleousa.

LESLIE BRUBAKER

[See also **Eleousa; Iconography.**]

GNOMIC LITERATURE. The gnome is commonly defined as a concise expression of a general thought. The difficulty of distinguishing between the gnome and other types of pithy saying, such as the proverb, epigram, and maxim, highlights the fact that the gnome may possess characteristics proper to any of these. Thus, a gnome, if widely used, could be regarded as proverbial; if concisely formulated, as epigrammatic. Gnomic literature refers to poetry or prose in which the gnome in itself is cultivated as a form of literary expression, or to anthologies of gnomes; in a looser and wider application the term includes literature that incorporates a significant gnomic element or has a markedly gnomic tone.

The universality and antiquity of gnomic literature is demonstrated by examples from such diverse and ancient literatures as Chinese, Egyptian, Hebrew, and Greek, and by its timeless themes, such as the value of friendship and the inevitability of death. More formally, Hugh M. Chadwick and Nora Kershaw Chadwick distinguish two main types of gnome: those that treat of human actions and choice, often offering instruction as well—for instance, "Better to avenge a friend than to mourn him"—and those founded on observation, which treat of the characteristics of mankind and the properties of the natural world, but without instruction—such as "Fate is strongest." Common stylistic features of gnomic literature are apostrophe, appeal to an authority, personification, use of similes from nature, antithesis, parallelism, the rhetorical question, and logically correlated formulas ("as ... so ..." or "where ... there ...").

The gnomic literature of medieval Europe divides into "early" and "high" categories. The former (600–1100) can be found in the early vernacular literatures of northwest Europe—Irish, English, Welsh, and Norse—which developed outside the cultural domain of the Roman Empire, and therefore were basically of both classical and Christian influence (though the latter became apparent as the period progressed, especially in Old English). The Old Irish, the earliest to be written down, bears striking resemblances to the Indic gnomic tradition, both probably reflecting common elements of their Indo-European heritage. In this group are the aphorisms (Irish: *roscada*) quoted in the law tracts and the gnomes concerned with kingship (for instance, in *Audacht Morainn*). Common to both Irish and Welsh (perhaps a feature of their shared Celtic heritage) are the triadic gnomes, such as "Three deaths better than life: the death of a pig, a salmon, and a robber." Early Welsh gnomes, however, mainly offer observations on nature. Surviving from Old English are the *Exeter Gnomes* (from the *Exeter Book*) and the *Cotton Gnomes* (from British Library, MS Cotton Tiberius B.i); from Old Norse, the *Hávamál* and the *Sigrdrífumál*. Although the two literatures differ

radically in their choice of gnomic type—Old English preferring observation; Old Norse, human actions and choice—stylistic usages such as the *sceal/skal* formula and themes shared by both suggest their common Germanic origin.

With the exception of gnomic collections in medieval Latin from the eleventh century, the greater part of high medieval gnomic literature begins with the emerging vernaculars of the twelfth century: Old French, Provençal, Middle English, Middle High German, Portuguese, and Italian (early thirteenth century). It differs from the earlier gnomic literature in several ways: thematically, in its emphasis on the instructive gnome dealing with human actions (including love); structurally, in its preference for stanzaic forms, usually composed for musical rendition; stylistically, in its more diffuse expression; and culturally, in its basically Christian ethic and its debt to classical literature.

BIBLIOGRAPHY

For a general survey of early European vernacular gnomes, see Hector Munro Chadwick and Nora Kershaw Chadwick, *The Growth of Literature* (1932), ch. 12; for the later vernacular gnomes, Hugo Moser, "Die hochmittelalterliche deutsche 'Spruchdichtung' als übernationale und nationale Erscheinung," in Hugo Moser, ed., *Mittelhochdeutsche Spruchdichtung* (1972). On classical gnomic literature see *The Oxford Classical Dictionary*, 2nd ed. (1970), s. v. "Gnome" and "Sententia"; on medieval Latin, Max Manitius, *Geschichte der lateinischen Literatur des Mittelalters*, 3 vols. (1911–1931), s. v. "Sprichwörter." For individual languages see Kenneth H. Jackson, *Early Welsh Gnomic Poems* (1935); August Knoch, "Die Gnomik der irischen Frühzeit im Lichte der alten indischen Spruchweisheit," in *Zeitschrift für celtische Philologie*, **23** (1943); Blanche C. Williams, *Gnomic Poetry in Anglo-Saxon* (1914).

PÁDRAIG P. Ó NÉILL

[See also **Anglo-Saxon Literature; Hávamál; Irish Literature; Sigrdrífumál; Welsh Literature.**]

GODEFROID OF HUY (Godefroid de Claire) (*fl.* 1143–1177) is designated as a goldsmith and canon in the twelfth-century *obit* (November D° VIII K°) of the register of Neufmoustier Abbey, near Huy. A

Pedestal of a cross made by Godefroid of Huy for the Abbey Church of St. Bertin, second half of the 12th century. MUSÉE DES BEAUX-ARTS, ST. OMER

later entry (dated XIII^med.) calls him a citizen of Huy and a goldsmith of great renown and attributes to him, among other objects, two shrines in the church of Huy. On the basis of a 1274 document, these works have been identified with the shrines of SS. Domitian (1173) and Mangold (1177) in Notre-Dame de Huy. Since these shrines are the only extant documented works that can definitely be assigned to Godefroid, it is unfortunate that they are extensively restored and suggest very little of the artist's style. A similar shrine of St. Vitonus in St. Vanne, Verdun, known only through a 1745 description, was executed between 1143 and 1146 by a "Godefridus" who may be the same artist. There is no evidence to justify the identification of Godefroid with the "aurifex G." who conducted a correspondence with Wibald, abbot of Stavelot, in 1148, or to associate him with the "plures aurifabros Lotharingos" employed by Abbot Suger of St. Denis (1122–1151).

BIBLIOGRAPHY

Comte Joseph de Borchgrave d'Altena, "Les châsses de Saint Domitien et de Saint Mengold de la Collégiale Notre-Dame, à Huy," in *Bulletin de la Société d'art et d'histoire du diocèse de Liège,* **42** (1961); Suzanne Gevaert,

"La note de l'obituaire de l'abbaye de Neufmoustier," in *Bulletin des musées royaux d'art et d'histoire,* **6** (1933); Erwin Panofsky, ed. and trans., *Abbot Suger on the Abbey Church of St.-Denis and Its Art Treasures* (1946), 58; Franz Ronig, "Godefridus von Huy in Verdun," in *Aachener Kunstblätter,* **32** (1966).

GRETEL CHAPMAN

[See also **Enamel; Metalsmiths, Gold and Silver.**]

GODFREY OF FONTAINES (before 1250–29 October 1306/1309), Scholastic philosopher and theologian, was born near Liège. He studied at Paris under Henry of Ghent and was himself a regent master in the faculty of theology there from 1285 until 1297. Canon of Liège, Paris, and Cologne (where he was provost), he resumed his teaching duties at the Sorbonne in 1303 or 1304. Strongly Aristotelian and generally regarded as a Thomist, Godfrey did, however, differ from Aquinas on several important issues: he rejected, for instance, the distinction between essence and existence in finite being. A keen controversialist who actively opposed the privileges of the mendicant orders, he justified the acquisition of private property through labor.

BIBLIOGRAPHY

Godfrey of Fontaines's major works are his fifteen *Quodlibeta,* disputations composed during his regency and published as vols. II–V and XIV of M. De Wulf, A. Pelzer, J. Hoffmans, and O. Lottin, eds., *Les philosophes belges* (1904–1937). See also Robert J. Arway, "A Half Century of Research on Godfrey of Fontaines," in *The New Scholasticism,* **36** (1962); John F. Wippel, *The Metaphysical Thought of Godfrey of Fontaines: A Study in Late Thirteenth-century Philosophy* (1981).

BERNARD CULLEN

[See also **Scholasticism.**]

GODFREY OF RHEIMS (*d.* 1095), scholar and chancellor of the cathedral there. He wrote several Latin poems about contemporaries: *Sompnium Godefridi de Odone Aurelianensi* (Godfrey's dream about Odo of Orléans) describes in 132 distichs the attainments of a friend; *Carmen ad Lingonensem episcopum* (Song to [Hugo] the bishop of Langres) is a dialogue, in 479 leonine hexameters, between the poet and Calliope, muse of epic poetry, on the fall of Troy.

BIBLIOGRAPHY

There are no modern editions of Godfrey's work. For information on early editions, see Max Manitius, *Geschichte der lateinischen Literatur des Mittelalters,* III (1931), 239–240.

W. T. H. JACKSON

GODFREY OF WINCHESTER (*ca.* 1050–1107) was born in Cambrai. He entered the cloister of St. Swithin at Winchester, England, and in 1082 became prior. Godfrey was famous for his epigrams and poetry, which helped to establish a new school of highly representational English poetry. The high point of his work is the 238 epigrams in the *Liber proverbiorum (De moribus et vita instituenda).* The moral character of the epigrams is obvious: gnomes, sententiae, and rules for living appear frequently. Godfrey's primary and declared model is Martial; the influence of Horace is also obvious. The epigrams are in the form of distichs.

BIBLIOGRAPHY

Max Manitius, *Geschichte der lateinischen Literatur des Mittelalters,* III (1931), 769.

EDWARD FRUEH

GODODDIN. See **Welsh Literature: Poetry.**

GODZIN OF MAINZ (also Gozechin or Gozwin) was born in the early eleventh century and studied at Fulda. He was appointed provost of the school at Mainz in 1058. Between 1060 and 1062 he wrote the *Passio Albani* at the request of Sigefrid, abbot of Fulda. Albanus, a critic of the Arian heresy, had settled in Mainz during the reign of emperors Arcadius and Honorius (395–408), and had been martyred by heretics. Also extant is a letter, dated 1065, addressed to Walcher.

BIBLIOGRAPHY

The *Passio Albani* is in *Monumenta Germaniae historica, Scriptores,* XV (1887), 984–990; the letter, "Epistola Gozechini scholastici ad Valcherum," in Jean Mabillon, *Vetera analecta* (1723, repr. 1967), 437–446. See also Max Manitius, *Geschichte der lateinischen Literatur des Mittelalters,* II (1923), 470–478.

NATHALIE HANLET

GOES, HUGO VAN DER (*ca.* 1440–1482). One of the outstanding Flemish painters of the second half of the fifteenth century, Hugo van der Goes was born probably at Ghent, where he remained until 1475 or 1476, when he entered the Roode Klooster (Red Cloister) near Brussels as a *donatus,* or lay brother. He died there at forty-two of an illness brought on by melancholy and madness.

Hugo combined the detailed realism of Jan van Eyck with the monumentality of Rogier van der Weyden, but his paintings often suggest his emotional instability in the eccentric treatment of space and the melancholic expressions of the figures; these features are particularly evident in his last two works, the *Adoration of the Shepherds* (in the Kaiser Friedrich Museum, Berlin) and the *Dormition of the Virgin* (Musée Communal, Bruges), executed about 1480 or 1481. His masterpiece is the Nativity Altarpiece (now in the Uffizi, Florence), a huge triptych painted for the family chapel of Tommaso Portinari in Florence.

Nativity Altarpiece. Central panel of a triptych painted for the Portinari chapel, Florence, by Hugo van der Goes, third quarter of the 15th century. UFFIZI, FLORENCE

BIBLIOGRAPHY
Erwin Panofsky, *Early Netherlandish Painting* (1953); F. Winkler, *Hugo van der Goes* (1964).

JAMES SNYDER

[See also **Flemish Painting.**]

GOFFREDO DA VITERBO (*fl. ca.* 1300–1350), Lombard miniature painter responsible for the notable illustrations of the *Pantheon* made for Azzone Visconti of Milan in 1331 and now in Paris (Bibliothèque Nationale, MS fonds latin 4895). A passional (Milan, Biblioteca Ambrosiana, MS P.165) and 183 folios of a psalter (Berlin, Kupferstichkabinett, MS 78.C.16) follow the same general style.

BIBLIOGRAPHY
Pietro Toesca, *La pittura e la miniatura nella Lombardia* (1912), 201–203, figs. 145–150, pl. IX; Paul Wescher, *Miniaturen-Handschriften und Einzelblätter des Kupferstichkabinetts der Staatlichen Museen Berlin* (1931).

ADELHEID M. GEALT

[See also **Manuscript Illumination: Western European.**]

Birth of Abraham. Goffredo da Viterbo, from his illustrations for the *Pantheon* made for Azzone Visconti, 1331. BIBLIOTHÈQUE NATIONALE, MS FONDS LATIN 4895

GOLD. See **Metalsmiths, Gold and Silver.**

GOLDEMAR. Only a bit more than the first nine strophes of *Goldemar,* composed about 1230 by Albrecht von Kemenaten, remain. A fairy-tale narrative of the Dietrich cycle, the formal elegance of its *Bernerton* strophe and its criticism of heroic narrative according to courtly concepts influenced all subsequent Dietrich epics.

BIBLIOGRAPHY
The text of *Goldemar* is in Julius Zupitza, ed., *Deutsches Heldenbuch,* V (1870, repr. 1968), 203–204. Helmut de Boor and Richard Newald, *Geschichte der deutschen Literatur von den Anfängen bis zur Gegenwart,* III, pt. 1 (1962), 157–158, provides an introduction to *Goldemar* scholarship. Joachim Heinzle, "Albrecht von Kemenaten," in *Die deutsche Literatur des Mittelalters. Verfasserlexikon,* 2nd ed., I (1978), gives a brief outline of the present state of research. The basic guide to the fairy-tale Dietrich epics is Joachim Heinzle, *Mittelhochdeutsche Dietrichepik* (1978)—it does not, however, replace Helmut de Boor, "Albrecht von Kemenaten," in *Unterscheidung und Bewahrung: Festschrift für Hermann Kunisch* (1961), repr. in his *Kleine Schriften,* I (1964).

RUTH H. FIRESTONE

GOLDEN HORDE, a branch of the Mongol dynasty of Chinggis (Genghis) Khan. The name, translated into Russian and other languages from a conjectured Turkic **Altin Orda,* designated the golden (*altin*) tent (*orda/ordu,* khan's abode, subsequently camp or army) of the ruler. According to Turkic color symbolism, it connoted the heartland of the realm. Founded by Genghis Khan's grandson Batu (*d.* 1255), the Golden Horde established capitals on the lower Volga, at Saray and New Saray, and controlled the Qipchaq steppe and much of Rus. Following the disruptions caused by the initial conquest, the new rulers were anxious to revive trade and commerce. Although autonomy was secured under Batu, it was his brother Berke (1257–1267) who, by his conversion to Islam, gave this *ulus* (appanage) a different orientation.

Alienated from his brothers, the great khans Möngke and Qubilai (Kublai), and from his cousin Hulagu (Hülegü), the Ilkhan of Persia, Berke turned to the Qipchaq-Turkic Mamluks, who were co-religionists and the immediate kinsmen of his subjects in the Qipchaq steppe. Warfare between Berke and Hulagu over the Caucasus began in 1261, inducing Berke to conclude a treaty with the Mamluks in 1263. This policy of alliance on the basis of religion created a wedge between the Russian lands, bastions of Orthodox Christianity, and the Turko-Mongolian population of the steppe. Islam, however, furthered the amalgamation of the Mongol elements with the larger mass of Qipchaq Turks to form the Turkic-speaking Tatars.

Möngke Temür (1267–1280), a non-Muslim, effected a limited reconciliation with Kublai Khan without completely divesting himself of the Mamluk connection. The ineptitude of his immediate successors led to the rise of the brilliant major domo Noghay (d. 1299), a grandnephew of Batu. Toqto (or Tokhtu, 1291–1312) eliminated him, but the princely strife that had allowed Noghay to gain so much power remained endemic. Özbeg (1313–1341) restored Islam to its position of supremacy in the khanate. He also reasserted the Golden Horde's authority among the Russian princes, who, profiting from the Tatar civil disturbances, had shown increasing restlessness. In 1328 he granted the grand duchy of Moscow to Ivan Kalita, thereby furthering the rise of Moscow to power.

Özbeg died while en route to a campaign against the Lithuanians, his main competitors for power in eastern Europe. His son, the pro-Christian Tinibeg (1341–1342), was assassinated by his brother Janibeg (1342–1357). The latter achieved his family's longheld goal of conquering Azerbaijan between 1355 and 1357 but died shortly thereafter. The forces of decline now fully asserted themselves. Berdibeg's assassination in 1359 signaled political disintegration from which Lithuania, Moldavia, and Moscow benefited. The 1380 victory of Moscow at Kulikovo over the non-Chinggisid Tatar strongman Mamai ultimately allowed Toqtamish (or Tokhtamysh, d. 1406), a descendant of Orda, to take power with the aid of Timur Leng (Tamerlane). He reestablished Tatar authority over Moscow in 1382. When he then turned on Tamerlane, the latter defeated him and assorted allies (1385–1387, 1391, 1395).

Once again power passed to a strongman, Edigú (or Edigei, d. 1419), who checked Lithuanian ambitions at the Battle of the Vorskla River in 1399. He was unable, however, to arrest the Horde's decline. In 1438 the ever-growing fragmentation produced a division into the "Great Horde" and the khanate of Kazan. Other defections followed: Crimea (ca. 1441) and Astrakhan (1466). The Golden Horde ceased to

exist in 1502 when Mengli Girey, the Crimean khan (and Ottoman vassal) destroyed Saray.

BIBLIOGRAPHY

Sources. ᶜAlāᵓ al-Dīn ᶜAṭā-Malek Joveynī, *Taᵓrīkh-i jahān gushā*, M. Qazvīnī, ed., 3 vols. (1912–1937), trans. by John A. Boyle as *The History of the World-conqueror,* 2 vols. (1958); Juzjānī, *Ṭabaqāt-i Nāṣirī*, W. Nassau Lees, Mawlawis Khadim Hosain, and ᶜAbd al-Hai, eds. (1864), trans. by H. G. Raverty as *Ṭabaḳāt-i Nāṣirī: A General History of the Muhammadan Dynasties of Asia,* 2 vols. (1881–1899); *Kᶜartᶜlis Tsᶜχovreba*, S. Qaukhchᶜishvili, ed., II (1959), older ed., with French trans. by Marie F. Brosset, *Histoire de la Géorgie,* 4 vols. (1849–1858, repr. 1969); *Polnoe sobranie russkikh letopisei* (1841–); Faẓlallāh Rashīd al-Dīn Ṭabīb, *Jāmiᶜ al-tavārīkh*, I, *Taᵓrīkh-i ghāzānī*, Edgar Blochet, ed., 2 vols (1911), trans. by John A. Boyle as *The Successors of Genghis Khan* (1971); al-ᶜUmarī, *Masālik al-Abṣar fī Mamālik al-Amṣar: Das mongolische Weltreich*, Klaus Lech, ed. (1968), with extensive bibliography.

Studies. Armianskie istochniki o mongolakh, A. G. Galstian, trans. (1962): B. D. Grekov and A. Iu. Iakubovskii, *Zolotaia orda i ee padenie* (1950); I. B. Grekov, *Vostochnaia Evropa i upadok Zolotoi Ordy* (1975); A. N. Nasonov, *Mongoly i Rus* (1940); Jaroslav Pelenski, *Russia and Kazan* (1974); M. G. Safargaliev, "Raspad Zolotoi Ordy," in *Uchenye zapiski Mordovskogo Gosudarstvennogo Universiteta,* **11** (1960); Bertold Spuler, *Die Goldene Horde,* 2nd ed. (1965); George Vernadsky, *The Mongols and Russia* (1953); S. Zakirov, *Diplomaticheskie otnosheniia Zolotoi Ordy s Egiptom* (1966).

PETER B. GOLDEN

[See also **Batu; Genghis Khan; Hulagu; Ilkhanids; Mongol Empire; Saray.**]

GOLDEN HORN. A body of water to the north of Constantinople, the Golden Horn is a deep inlet protecting the city. Emperor Constantine built a wall stretching from it to the Sea of Marmara, and subsequent rulers built two additional sets of walls. The great imperial palace at Blachernae was situated at the northwest corner of the Golden Horn. An iron chain across its entrance kept invaders out, and only the Venetians, during the Fourth Crusade (1203–1204), were able to break it. During the Ottoman siege of Constantinople in 1453, Mehmed II, unable to get past the chain, managed to bypass it by transporting his ships overland and, thus, enter the Golden Horn. Galata, an important suburb of Constantinople, where the Genoese had their quarters from 1267, was on the opposite shore of the Golden Horn.

BIBLIOGRAPHY

George Ostrogorsky, *History of the Byzantine State,* Joan Hussey, trans. (1957, rev. ed. 1969).

LINDA ROSE

[See also **Constantinople.**]

GOLDEN HORN WARE, Turkish pottery produced from about 1525 to 1535 at Iznik and Kütahya, misnamed "Golden Horn" ware after fragments excavated in that area of Istanbul. Pieces include dishes, bowls, ewers, and tiles decorated in underglaze blue, turquoise, and olive green, with spiraling patterns derived from manuscript illuminations. A water bottle (British Museum, Godman Collection) is inscribed and dated in Armenian, 1529.

BIBLIOGRAPHY

John Carswell, *Kütahya Tiles and Pottery from the Armenian Cathedral of St James, Jerusalem,* 2 vols. (1972); Arthur Lane, "The Ottoman Pottery of Isnik," in *Ars Orientalis,* **2** (1956), and *Later Islamic Pottery* (1971).

JOHN CARSWELL

[See also **Ceramics, Islamic.**]

GOLDEN LEGEND *(Legenda aurea),* a collection of saints' lives and other pious stories tied to the church calendar and compiled before 1267 by Jacobus de Varagine (Jacopo da Voragine), a Dominican friar who became archbishop of Genoa in 1292. Originally entitled *Legenda sanctorum* (from *legendum, -a:* "reading," "to be read"), the work was intended to inspire devotional living. Jacobus embellished the 182 chapters with marvelous exploits, for which he probably relied on Vincent of Beauvais's *Speculum historiale,* Jean de Mailly's *Abbreviatio in gestis et miraculis sanctorum,* and Bartholomew of Trent's *Liber epilogorum in gesta sanctorum* as sources. Soon translated into vernacular languages, the work enjoyed wide popularity until the sixteenth century. It was one of the first books printed in England (1483), translated by Caxton, whose rendering was frequently reprinted as late as the twentieth century.

BIBLIOGRAPHY

Modern English version by Grangor Ryan and Helmut Ripperger, *The Golden Legend* (1941, repr. 1969). See also Marie-Christine Pouchelle, "Représentations du corps dans la *Légende dorée,*" in *Ethnologie française,* **6** (1976); Ernest C. Richardson, *Materials for a Life of Jacopo da Voragine* (1935); Marguerite de Waresquiel, *Le bienheureux Jacques de Voragine* (1902).

JOHN L. GRIGSBY

[See also **Hagiography, Western European.**]

GOLDEN SECTION, a linear ratio in which the shorter of two lines is related to the longer by the same proportion as the longer is related to the sum of the lengths of both, expressed as $A:B::B:(A + B)$. The mathematical ratio is approximately $0.616:1.000$. The golden section, also called the golden mean, was a widely employed basis of design in medieval architecture and visual arts.

BIBLIOGRAPHY

Charles Bouleau, *The Painter's Secret Geometry* (1963); Garth E. Runion, *The Golden Section and Related Curiosa* (1972).

CARL F. BARNES, JR.

GOLDSMITHS. See **Metalsmiths, Gold and Silver.**

GOLIARDS. The clerical reprobate Golias and his ill-disciplined followers, the goliards, appear as characters in a diverse body of Latin poetry composed by numerous individual authors who have come the be called goliards after the fiction they created. Various etymologies have been proposed to explain the name. Gerald of Wales relates it to *gula,* the Latin word for gluttony: "Item parasitus quidam Golias nomine nostris diebus gulositate pariter et lecacitate famosissimus, qui Gulias melius quia gule et crapule per omnia deditus dici poterit." Modern scholars prefer a derivation from the biblical giant Goliath (Golias in the Vulgate), whom medieval commentators interpreted as a symbol of monstrous wickedness.

The goliards flourished in the twelfth and thirteenth centuries, but their antecedents have been traced as far back as 850–875, when an Irish scholar, Sedulius Scotus, took up residence at the Carolingian court. There he supported himself in the same precarious manner and immortalized it in the same types of verse that would be the hallmarks of the goliardic poets. Although he is credited with the first known reference to a *gens Goliae,* Sedulius did not consider himself a member of the tribe. To him they were not ribald versifiers, but a band of sheep thieves.

After Sedulius there is an unbroken if sparsely represented tradition of poems extolling the pleasures of food, drink, love, and travel. According to the simplest account, the expansion of schools and universities toward the middle of the twelfth century gave rise to a large population of students, trained in Latin composition and not overly pious, who added a dash of shamelessness to this tradition and composed poems in praise of gluttony, drunkenness, lust, and vagrancy. It is these students who gleefully describe themselves as followers of Golias, their bishop, abbot, or mentor. Some of them pretend to membership in an order of goliards, never an actual society but a comic imitation of contemporary monastic orders, complete with a rule that requires its adherents to feast and fornicate.

Parody is one goliardic forte, especially of religious literature and the ceremonies of the church. Trained to write in imitation, students painstakingly mastered the ability to copy the cadence and style of their models. Occasionally they were tempted to burlesque the content. Many of their best effects result from making the slightest possible alteration in a well-known text. It is characteristic of their wit to transform the hymn to the Virgin *Verbum bonum et suave* into the drinker's song *Vinum bonum et suave,* or to make the angels substitute *potatori* (sot) for *peccatori* (sinner) when they descend to beg God's mercy on a dying Goliard with the words "Deus sit propitius huic potatori" (God have mercy on this sot). Nothing was too sacred for such treatment: not the creeds, the Lord's Prayer, the Mass, not even the New Testament, to which was added "The Gospel according to St. Marks of Silver." By the beginning of the thirteenth century, ecclesiastical councils were calling for strict measures against those who sang improper words in church.

The students were but one platoon in the army of Golias. The two poets whose names—or, rather, pseudonyms—have survived did not belong to this youthful cadre. What little is known of them comes from their poems, which describe a life more brutal

than fun. The earlier, Hugh (Primas) of Orléans (*ca.* 1095–*ca.*1160), was a poet of extraordinary verbal facility who wrote metrical or rhythmical verse with equal ease, and who begged a living on the fringes of the schools, threatening to skewer those who refused him with epigrams of unforgettable artistry—and nastiness. Nonetheless, his reputation was such that he became a legendary figure, the winner of a prestigious competition (surely apocryphal) held by the cardinals at Rome, for the shortest summary of the Bible. Hugh captured the essence of sacred history in two lines. Later, he appears as a character in the seventh tale of the First Day of Boccaccio's *Decameron.*

The next generation of goliards produced another master craftsman, the Archpoet (*fl.* 1159–1165), so called from the titles of his patron, Rainald of Dassel, who was archchancellor to Frederick Barbarossa and archbishop of Cologne. The Archpoet occupied the same position in Rainald's household as a minstrel in a secular court. He composed perhaps the most famous of all goliardic poems, the "Confessio Goliae" *(Estuans intrinsecus),* which is both a humorous tour de force filled with parodic allusions (such as the play on "sinner" and "sot" quoted above), and a remarkable psychological study of a character in the grip of vice. Another of his poems contains what might be the motto for the whole troop of goliards: "Tales versus facio, quale vinum bibo" (The lines I write are only as good as the wine I drink). The verbal artistry of Hugh and the Archpoet represent the goliardic contribution to the developments in poetry, vernacular as well as Latin, that were associated with the twelfth-century renaissance of Latin lyric.

At the opposite moral extreme from the poets who wallowed in their own venal excesses, there was a group of serious-minded authors who adopted the persona of Golias to condemn the sins of others. One such work, the "Apocalypse of Golias," is a biting attack on the vices of all kinds of churchmen. Another satire, the "Metamorphosis of Golias," is interesting for its condemnation of the monks who, under the leadership of Bernard of Clairvaux, were trying to limit the speculative freedom of contemporary philosophers, Abelard in particular. It is on account of his satires, similar in perspective to these anonymous works, that Walter of Châtillon (*ca.* 1135–*ca.* 1184), a highly regarded scholar and poet, and by no means a vice-ridden parasite, is often lumped with the unregenerate crew of Golias.

It seems likely, since so few goliardic authors are

known by name, that the fictional company was used to mask the identities of poets who feared that their works, whether parodic, satirical, or just outrageous, would get them into trouble. The authorities were not long fooled. By the mid-thirteenth century anyone who claimed to be a goliard risked being stripped of clerical privileges. Few took the chance. Although the order died out, the word lived on. By Chaucer's time "goliard" was a term of reproach but had not entirely lost its suggestion of verbal skill. Chaucer uses it of the Miller, whose storytelling could scarcely be bettered, whatever the state of his morals.

BIBLIOGRAPHY

James H. Hanford, "The Progenitors of Golias," in *Speculum,* **1** (1926); Boris I. Jarcho, "Die Vorläufer des Golias," in *Speculum,* **3** (1928); Frederic J. E. Raby, *A History of Secular Latin Poetry in the Middle Ages,* 2 vols. (1957, 2nd ed. 1966), esp. II, 171–235; A. G. Rigg, "Golias and Other Pseudonyms," in *Studi medievali,* 3rd ser., **18** (1977), and "Medieval Latin Poetic Anthologies," in *Mediaeval Studies,* **39** (1977), **40** (1978), **41** (1979), and **43** (1981); Helen J. Waddell, *The Wandering Scholars* (1929, 7th ed. repr. 1966); P. G. Walsh, "'Golias' and Goliardic Poetry," in *Medium aevum,* **52** (1983); George F. Whicher, *The Goliard Poets: Medieval Latin Songs and Satires* (1949); Thomas Wright, *The Latin Poems Commonly Attributed to Walter Mapes* (1841).

MARY C. UHL

[See also **Archpoet; Carmina Burana; Gerald of Wales; Hugh (Primas) of Orléans; Latin Literature; Rainald of Dassel; Sedulius Scotus; Walter of Châtillon.**]

GOLOSNIKI (from Russian *Golos,* "voice"), ceramic bowls or jars that were sometimes built into the vaults or walls of medieval Russian churches. They served as acoustical resonators and to lighten the mass of the vaults. *Golosniki* were particularly common in the Novgorod and Suzdal regions of Russia.

GEORGE P. MAJESKA

GǪNGU-HRÓLFS SAGA is an old Norse saga of unknown authorship, probably written in the early fourteenth century, and preserved in several manuscripts from the fifteenth century. The text belongs to the *fornaldarsögur* (legendary sagas).

"Gǫngu-Hrólfr" means "Hrólfr the Walker," so called because he was so big that no normal horse could carry him the whole day. There was a historical person of that name: the son of Rǫgnvald, earl of Mœr; according to Icelandic sources he was the Viking who in 911, under the name of Rollo, became the first duke of Normandy. However, the hero of the saga has nothing in common with the earl's son except the name. Not even the parents are the same, Gǫngu-Hrólfr in the saga being the son of Sturlaugr inn starfsami (the Industrious), the main character in another *fornaldarsaga* and the ruler of Ringerike.

The deceased king Hreggviðr, in search of a champion to defend his daughter Ingigerðr against an unwanted suitor, returns to life in the shape of a swallow and drops one of his daughter's golden tresses in the lap of Earl Þorgnýr of Jutland. Þorgnýr swears to win the hand of the unknown woman, and the hero Hrólfr undertakes the mission on his behalf. Hrólfr sets out for Garðaríki (Russia) in order to win the princess for the earl. In the course of this marriage quest he performs most of the seemingly impossible tasks known from the legendary sagas.

Provided beforehand by his mother with two cloaks that make their wearer invulnerable to iron and poison, Hrólfr is before long given more useful items: a fairy woman gives him a ring that enables him to discern the right direction anywhere, night or day, on sea or land, and that will protect him in all sorts of dangerous quests. After he breaks into Hreggviðr's burial mound, Hreggviðr gives him the sword Hreggviðarnautr. Ingigerðr gives him a special suit of armor and the magic horse Dulcifal, and finally the dwarf Mǫndull gives him a magic visor. Enchanted weapons and invulnerable clothing of one sort or another appear in most of the legendary sagas, but this accumulation clearly marks the text as a late example of the genre. As befits his extraordinary equipment, Hrólfr accomplishes a great many tasks well known from the motif storehouse of the legendary sagas: he defeats berserks and the monster Grímr ægir, son of a sea ogress and a shape shifter of the worst type; he captures a magic stag; and he breaks into a burial mound, thus winning unique weapons and the friendship of the dead inhabitant. Toward the end of the saga Þorgnýr is slain, in Hrólfr's absence, during a surprise raid on Jutland. Hrólfr wins the princess for himself and the kingdom of Garðaríki with her.

Like many heroes of the legendary sagas, Hrólfr is a wanderer and much of the action takes place on his heroic missions. And, like many of the other saga writers, the author pretends that most of the settings are properly defined places in the real world, from Russia in the east to Scotland in the west. In addition to a concise but informative passage on England, there is a geographical description of Denmark containing the names of many towns and islands; this seems to be cribbed from *Knýtlinga saga*. It has been argued that the loan from *Knýtlinga saga* is a copyist's interpolation, but considering the author's remarkable erudition, this seems improbable. Among other things, he refers to wise men who in ancient times told stories that must be understood figuratively, such as "meistari Galterus í Alexandri sögu eða Umeris skáld í Trójumanna sögu" (Master Walter in *Alexanders saga* or the poet Homer in *Trójumanna saga*).

BIBLIOGRAPHY

"Göngu-Hrolfs saga," in Guðni Jónsson, ed., *Fornaldarsögur Norðurlanda,* III (1950), 161–280; *Göngu-Hrolf's Saga: A Viking Romance,* Hermann Pálsson and Paul Edwards, trans. (1981); Halldór Hermannsson, *The Sagas of the Kings (Konunga sögur) and the Mythical-Heroic Sagas (Fornaldar sögur): Two Bibliographical Supplements,* in Islandica, XXVI (1937), 53–54; Hermann Pálsson and Paul Edwards, *Legendary Fiction in Medieval Iceland* (1971).

MARINA MUNDT

[See also **Fornaldarsögur; Knýtlinga Saga.**]

GONSALVES, NUÑO (*fl.* third quarter of the fifteenth century), the most important Portuguese painter of the Hispano-Flemish style. His masterpiece, a large altarpiece for Lisbon Cathedral, is the polyptych *The Veneration of St. Vincent,* painted for Alfonso V between about 1458 and 1462 (now in the Museu Nacional de Arte Antiga, Lisbon). Although his oil technique was less advanced, he is one of the potential sources of training for Bermejo, the important peripatetic artist of the last quarter of the century in Spain.

MARY GRIZZARD

[See also **Bermejo, Bartolomé.**]

GONZÁLEZ DE CLAVIJO, RUY (*d.* 1412), chamberlain of King Henry III of Castile. He was sent by the king, along with two other ambassadors, to the court of Tamerlane and was to report on events in the Levant. The three men left in 1403 and did not return until 1406, having visited many places in the East. Clavijo wrote an account of his travels, *Historia del Gran Tamorlán,* that gives a firsthand view of Persia, across which he traveled, and of the Mongol court at Samarkand, where he was well received and where he stayed for three months in 1404. Also welcomed by the Byzantine emperor, he gives one of the last descriptions of the city of Constantinople as a Christian capital, including indications of the city's diminishing population and general decline.

BIBLIOGRAPHY

Guy Le Strange, trans, *Clavijo: Embassy to Tamerlane* (1928).

LINDA ROSE

GOOD SHEPHERD, Christ as a criophore (standing shepherd bearing a sheep or ram on his shoulders), often accompanied by a small flock. This depiction refers to John 10:1–16, wherein Christ identifies himself as the Good Shepherd who will give his life for his flock and will lead souls to salvation as a shepherd retrieves his sheep. The visual type was derived from the ancient bucolic motif of the criophore, which became a personification of philanthropy in the Greco-Roman period and appeared as an image of salvation on pagan funerary monuments. In the late Roman Empire, the criophore was also identified with Orpheus, and since Orpheus was considered an antetype of Christ by early church writers, Christ as Good Shepherd sometimes wears the Phrygian cap associated with Orpheus. Although a Christian interpretation is usually evident only from the context, the Good Shepherd seems to have been one of the first and most popular images adopted by the early church. It appears in the apse of the Christian baptistery at Dura Europos (*ca.* 232) and innumerable times in the Roman catacombs. Statues of the Good Shepherd were also widespread; the marble figure in the Cleveland Museum of Art from the third quarter of the third century provides an early example.

BIBLIOGRAPHY

Theodore Klauser, "Studien zur Entstehungsgeschichte der christlichen Kunst," in *Jahrbuch für Antike und Chris-*

tentum, **3** (1960), **5** (1962), **7** (1964), **8/9** (1965–1966), and **10** (1967); Kurt Weitzmann, ed., *Age of Spirituality: Late Antique and Early Christian Art, Third to Seventh Century* (1979), 513, 518–521.

LESLIE BRUBAKER

[See also **Early Christian Art; Iconography.**]

GORO DI GREGORIO, Sienese sculptor who signed the white marble shrine of S. Cerbone in the cathedral of Massa Marittima in 1324, and executed the tomb of Bishop Guidotto de' Tabiatis in Messina in 1333. His work exemplifies the delicate, small-scale decorative Gothic style that was adapted from Giovanni Pisano and Tino di Camaiano. He was the son of a sculptor named Goro di Ciuccio Ciuti da Firenze, who was active at Siena in 1272.

BIBLIOGRAPHY
Enzo Carli, *Goro di Gregorio* (1946).

BRUCIA WITTHOFT

Tomb of Bishop Guidotto de' Tabiatis in Messina, 1333. ALINARI/ART RESOURCE

GORZE. The Benedictine monastery of Gorze, located near Metz, was the major center of monastic reform in Lorraine and Germany between the 930's and 1070. The abbey was founded by Bishop Chrodegang of Metz in 749, but declined in the ninth century. Bishop Adalbero of Metz entrusted the reformation of the decayed house in 933 to Einold, archdeacon of Toul. The customs of Gorze were introduced the following year at St. Maximin in Trier, which became the principal center for the dissemination of the Gorze observance in Germany. The Gorze customs were eventually adopted, not always voluntarily, by approximately 160 communities, including St. Emmeram in Regensburg, Niederaltaich, Lorsch, Fulda, St. Alban in Mainz, Einsiedeln, and Reichenau. Emperor Henry II supported the reformation of Reichenau, for instance, because the introduction of the reforms increased the amount of monastic property under the direct control of the abbot, who was required to provide hospitality to the royal court on its travels.

Gorze was long regarded by scholars as a daughter house of Cluny, but there were fundamental differences between the two reform movements, not only in their liturgical practices but also in their constitutional structures. While the Cluniac monasteries sought exemption from the episcopal authorities, the abolition of lay advocacies, and the elimination of the monastic ministerialage, Gorze's acceptance of these institutions made it an integral part of the Ottonian ecclesiastical system. More important, while Cluny tried to retain control of its daughter houses, the monasteries that had been influenced by Gorze were linked only by their common customs. The houses of the Gorze observance were generally imperialist during the investiture controversy and opposed the introduction in their own communities of the Cluniac customs as practiced at Hirsau, Liège, St. Blasien, and Siegburg.

In 1016 Bishop Theoderich II of Metz had placed Gorze under the control of Abbot William of Dijon, who introduced Cluniac customs in the monastery. While William kept charge of the abbey only until 1031, the resulting mixture of Cluniac and Gorze customs, known as the *Junggorze* movement, was introduced into the monastery of Schwarzach am Main in 1046, and spread from there to such important Austrian monasteries as Admont and Melk. Herrand of Ilsenburg propagated the mixed customs in the diocese of Halberstadt after 1070. Unlike the older reform movement associated with Gorze, the

Junggorze houses were generally pro-papal during the investiture controversy.

BIBLIOGRAPHY

Karlotto Bogumil, *Das Bistum Halberstadt im 12. Jahrhundert* (1972), 57–102; Kassius Hallinger, *Gorze-Kluny: Studien zu den monastischen Lebensformen und Gegensätzen im Hochmittelalter*, 2 vols. (1950–1951); A. A. Schacher, "Gorze, Abbey of," in *New Catholic Encyclopedia*, VI (1967).

JOHN B. FREED

[See also **Cluny, Order of; Fulda; Hirsau; Ministerials; Reform, Idea of.**]

GŌSĀN, name given in Parthian times to professional minstrels (Armenian: *gusan;* Georgian: *mgosani*), who comprised both instrumentalists and singers. Some of them were humble wanderers, and some contemporary Armenian sources occasionally refer to them contemptuously as mere entertainers. In reality, however, the *gōsāns* were an indispensable feature of royal and noble courts in Iran, Arsacid Armenia, and Georgia. Since musical training was part of the education of the nobility in the Iranian tradition, some of them may have had distinguished backgrounds, and they played a role of primary importance to the end of the Sasanian period and beyond as the creators and preservers of oral literature. Even such a scholarly historian as Movsēs Xorenac̣i quotes passages of pre-Christian hymns still sung in his own time and cites information from the "songs of [the district of] Gołṭn" in his *History of Armenia*. Much of this oral, epic literature is also imbedded in the Armenian *Epic Histories* attributed to P̣awstos Buzand. With the Christianization of Armenia, the development of written literature, and the Arab conquest of Persia and much of Caucasia, this rich Iranian oral tradition began to die out, and only scattered fragments of it have been preserved.

BIBLIOGRAPHY

Manuk Abełyan, *Istoriia Drevnearmianskoi Literatury,* new ed. (1975), 30–48, 108–134, 226–240; Mary Boyce, "The Parthian *Gōsān* and Iranian Minstrel Tradition," in *Journal of the Royal Asiatic Society* (1957).

NINA G. GARSOÏAN

GOŠAVANK͛. The large Armenian monastery of Gošavank͛ (originally Nor Getik), located north of Lake Sewan, was founded in 1188 by the noted scholar-monk Mχit͛ar Goš, author of the *Book of Laws.* Through its academy and scriptorium, Gošavank͛ became an important religious, educational, and cultural center at which the historian Kirakos Ganjakec͛i and Vanakan Vardapet were trained. The surviving monuments of Gošavank͛ include the domed hall Church of St. Astuacacin (1191–1196) and its columned *gawit͛* (1197–1203); the similarly constructed, smaller Church of St. Gregory (1231); the vaulted, elaborately carved Church of St. Gregory the Illuminator (1237–1241); and a two-story structure with a library below (1241) and, above it, a chapel once surmounted by a lantern (1291); the foundation walls of either a large scriptorium or refectory (1291); and an arcaded passageway between the *gawit͛* and the library.

BIBLIOGRAPHY

Architettura medievale armena, Roma—Palazzo Venezia 10–30 giugno (1968), exhibition catalog; O. Kh. Khalpakhchian, *Architectural Ensembles of Armenia* (1980); A. Khatchatrian, "Nor-Getik," in *Reallexikon zur byzantinischen Kunst,* I (1966); Armen Zarian and Herman Vahramian, *Goshavank* (1974).

LUCY DER MANUELIAN

[See also **Armenian Art.**]

GOSPELBOOK, a collection of the accounts of Christ's life written by Matthew, Mark, Luke, and John that form the first four books of the New Testament. Because these accounts were central to Christianity, the Middle Ages produced more Gospelbooks than any other type of manuscript.

From a very early period, the Gospelbook became an important part of the liturgy and was displayed on the altar; hence large and sumptuous copies are among the oldest of Christian books. Gospelbooks continued to proliferate throughout the Middle Ages, displaying numerous systems of illustration. In the most common system, canon tables, often decorated, precede the four Gospels, each of which is prefaced by a portrait of the author, sometimes accompanied (or replaced) by his symbol. Gospelbooks of the seventh and eighth century from the British Isles add decorated introductory leaves (carpet pages)

St. Mark. Rossano Gospels (Rossano Cathedral Treasury, codex Purpureus, fol. 121r), 6th century. GIRAUDON/ART RESOURCE

to this standard system. Other manuscripts show narrative scenes from the life of Christ, grouped at the beginning of the book (as in the sixth-century Rossano Gospels, housed in the Cathedral treasury in Rossano); dispersed within the text (as in the eleventh-century Gospels in Biblioteca Medicea Laurenziana, Florence, MS Plut. 6.23); or flanking the canon table or author portraits (as in the sixth-century Rabula Gospels and Corpus Christi College Gospels, respectively). In addition to narrative scenes from Christ's life, typological and liturgical imagery often appears, and numerous idiosyncratic systems—one of the most popular of which is an introductory picture of the Fountain of Life—occur in small groups of books. Many examples contain elaborate initial letters and ornamental decoration within the body of the text to emphasize significant passages.

BIBLIOGRAPHY

Florentine Mütherich and Joachim Gaehde, *Carolingian Painting* (1976); Carl Nordenfalk, *Celtic and Anglo-Saxon Painting* (1977); Kurt Weitzmann, "The Narrative and Liturgical Gospel Illustrations," in Merrill M. Parvis and Allen P. Wikgren, eds., *New Testament Manuscript Studies* (1950), repr. in Weitzmann's *Studies in Classical and Byzantine Manuscript Illumination*, Herbert L. Kessler, ed., (1971); Kurt Weitzmann, *Late Antique and Early Christian Book Illumination* (1977).

LESLIE BRUBAKER

[See also **Bible; Canon Table; Carpet Page; Evangeliary; Manuscript Illumination, Western European.**]

GOTHIC ARCHITECTURE

DEFINING THE GOTHIC: THE HISTORICAL SOURCES IN THEIR SOCIOLOGICAL CONTEXT

The term "Gothic" has been applied since the seventeenth century to an architectural phenomenon that developed in the northern Frankish realm of the church province of Gaul and achieved its normative standard ("High Gothic") in the rebuilding of the cathedral of Chartres after a fire in 1194; Earlier buildings are thus popularly called "Early Gothic," and those commenced after the "classic" period of the thirteenth century, "Late Gothic." From its Capetian Frankish area of origin, this architecture was variously disseminated throughout the emerging national states of Europe to become the dominant style of all ecclesiastical building and of significant civic architecture until the fifteenth to seventeenth centuries, when it was displaced, in varying degrees, by the conscious revival of classic Greco-Roman forms, depending on the extent to which the formal tenets of the Italian Renaissance determined regional architectural activity.

The term "Gothic" is thus a misnomer, because it was not applied contemporarily to architecture of any specific style; it does not relate to the nation of the Goths during the time of the migrations but rather, by projection, to the Germanic nations as a whole. Its first uses occur in a thoroughly positive context in early-seventeenth-century Flanders and France (1610, Scribanius: "arcus opere Gotico"; the same year, a Fleming at King's College Chapel, Cambridge: "oeuvre gotique"; 1627, Martellange: "ordre gothique"), reflecting an appreciation of ornamental forms, and, somewhat later, in Germany (1654, by Crombach). Toward the middle of the century it was applied specifically to vaulting techniques (1643, Derand) and subsequently to pre-Renaissance architecture in general.

In Germany toward the end of the seventeenth century (Johann Christoph, 1699), the vaulting again is included in the comprehensive concept of a specific, historically removed style—but one that was

Figure 1. Abbey Church of St. Denis, south ambulatory of the choir seen from the west; vaults and outer walls 1140–1144, glazed triforium, clerestory, and responds added after 1230. JAMES AUSTIN

now intended negatively (1670, Pexenfelder's *Lexikon*), in accordance with Joachim von Sandrart's propagation (1675) of the three-stage historiographic system of the Italian Renaissance, which posited a barbarous interim period between the culture of classical antiquity and the conscious imitation of its outer forms by the Italian architects of the fifteenth and sixteenth centuries. Thus Vasari (1550) reviles the preceding architectural style as "lavoro tedesco" (German mode) and blames the Goths for its invention, but does not apply the term "Gothic." Although the literary tradition of a purported "middle ages" of barbarian ignorance, originating around the mid fourteenth century with Boccaccio and continued by Villani, Ghiberti, Manetti, and Filarete, had by 1518 related the interim period by name to the

Goths (in the circle of Raphael), the adjective is first explicitly applied to architecture in 1622, again by a Fleming, Rubens: "Barbara, ò Gotica," and in 1627, in Villa's description of Milan cathedral.

By contrast, the term "Gothic" continued to indicate a system of positive values in the general usage of northern European humanism, which lacked the negative assumptions necessary to Italian historiography. Rabelais's use of it as a term of abuse, and the isolated contemporary Italianate reflection in statements of Erasmus and Dasypodius, run counter to the broad literary foundation that was conditioned by the major role the Goths played in northern historiography. In fact, in spite of Sandrart, topographical descriptions and travel literature through the middle of the eighteenth century continue to evalu-

581

ate the architectural style positively. While the conscious Renaissance of natural sciences is certainly reflected in the art of painting, recent reevaluation of northern European records of the period to about the end of the seventeenth century contradicts any "Renaissance" notion of an interruption of traditional architectural progress: although antique sources and contemporary Italian building were seen as exemplary, and "modern" forms like the classical orders were incorporated, no single architectural treatise consciously articulates the Italian historical construct. In ecclesiastical building a consistent set of "Gothic" forms continued to be characteristic of a majority of new structures and the pointed arch, the ribbed vault, and tracery were also applied regularly to most significant civic buildings until the middle of the seventeenth century. The meaning of "Gothic" architecture, therefore, cannot be understood solely within the confines of a "Middle Ages."

The erroneous origins of the term "Gothic" have engendered an erroneous definition of the architectural period as such, which perforce has led to misconceptions in regard to the origins of the architectural forms themselves. A correct understanding of the origins of the forms has been obstructed even more by the categorically negative subdivision of history postulated by the Italian humanists.

However, in terms of the origins of the style, Manetti's life of Brunelleschi does provide a constructive insight: it stresses the Frankish *renovatio* (renewal) as an ordering principle in architectural development. This perception is based on implicit recognition of the fact that the Franks did not migrate and invade the Roman Empire as did the other Germanic nations but rather assimilated the northern reaches of Gaul (and subsequently Rome itself in the events of the year 800). What the Renaissance author was incapable of recognizing, however, was the fact that this process occurred in precisely that region of the Roman Empire where Gothic architecture had developed. The surprising tenacity of this consciousness of Frankish leadership in European culture had certainly been fed by the victory of the Capetian Frankish king Philip II Augustus over both the Holy Roman emperor and the English at Bouvines in 1214, and can indeed be related to the style of architecture through one very precise historical document from the "High Gothic" period: Burchard von Hall's chronicle of Wimpfen-im-Tal states that about 1269 the prior "summoned a mason highly skilled in architectural design who came recently from Francia from the city of Paris, and ordered him

to build the church of hewn ashlar in the Frankish manner. ... People flocking from all sides admire the uncommon work, praise its master craftsman." The reference to *opus francigenum* is our first documented indication of conscious discrimination of a specific contemporary style of architecture—to wit, the Frankish manner—as against local traditional forms; furthermore, the source clearly relates this style to the specific talents of an individual master mason, albeit anonymous. This form of organization stands in contrast with earlier ecclesiastical building practices whereby defined groups of monks or lay brothers, also conversi, executed the work under the direction of bishops or other clerics.

Opus francigenum thus provides a contemporary designation for the "High Gothic," the procedure at Wimpfen being further documented by a series of churches that, earlier in the century, already had been commenced beyond the borders of the Frankish realm, often under the direction of named clerics or master masons and in marked contrast with local building traditions: in Spain, the cathedrals of Burgos (begun 1221), Toledo (1224/1227), and León (1255); in the German Empire, including Italy, S. Francesco in Assissi (1228) and St. Elisabeth in Marburg (1235), both subject to monastic orders, Trier, Liebfrauenkirche (1235), the nave of Strasbourg (*ca.* 1235) and the choirs of Doornik (Tournai, 1242) and Cologne (1248) cathedrals; in England, Westminster Abbey (1245). All these examples adhere more or less convincingly to the style of contemporary church building in the Capetian royal domain, initially with a slight retardation but in the latter examples with an immediacy that related them directly to the general development of the style. The greater degree of retardation at earlier churches, such as Avila and Lincoln (late twelfth century), Magdeburg (1209), Limburg an der Lahn (*ca.* 1220), Münster (1221), Vercelli (1219), and Salisbury (1220), is due to the fragmentary dissemination of disparate elements that slowly influenced local building traditions via contiguous regions; the cathedral of Utrecht (1254) provides a closing example of this stage of the development.

The earliest and most important record of this process, and indeed of general building procedures in the preceding century, is provided by the monk Gervase's "treatise on the rebuilding" of the choir of Canterbury Cathedral after a fire in 1174, which records the choice of the Frankish master mason William of Sens to execute the work. (England had traditionally been dependent on continental masons

Figure 2. Ypres, Flanders, cloth hall (13th and 14th centuries) and town hall (16th and 17th centuries). PHOTOGLOB, ZURICH

Figure 3. Chartres Cathedral, ground plan. FROM JAN VAN DER MEULEN, BIOGRAPHIE DER KATHEDRALE (© 1984)

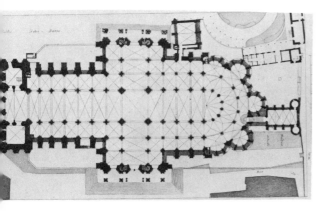

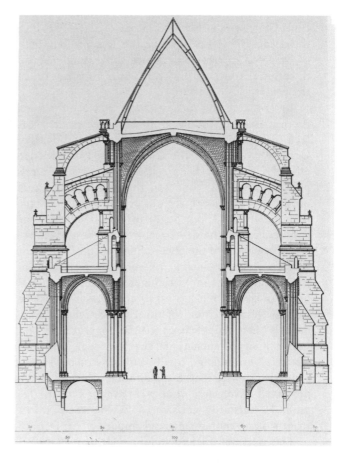

Figure 4. Chartres Cathedral, schematic cross section of the nave, begun 1194. FROM THOMAS H. KING, THE STUDY-BOOK OF MEDIAEVAL ARCHITECTURE AND ART (1868)

and even building material.) It is evident from the contemporary source, however, that there is not yet any question of the master mason creating a new "work of art"; at Canterbury the preserved remains of the original consecrated building conditioned the new work, which amounted to the insertion of a new, vaulted system within the existing outer walls and its extension eastward over the crypt of the Trinity Chapel; even the form and diameter of the old columns were retained, additional drums merely being added to increase their height. These decisions obviously rested with the clerics; the master mason and his English successor are credited by the chronicle with the skills necessary for their execution and with the purely practical expertise as to the condition of the existing masonry. The monastic author, on the other hand, himself displays such extensive knowledge of the technical and aesthetic implications of current vaulting practices, and of the new interior elevation, that few, if any, design prerogatives can be ascribed to the master mason at this time. Gervase not only records personal insights into the monastic supervision of the masons but feels constrained to justify for future generations certain disturbing irregularities (such as the constriction of the central vessel [nave]).

By contrast, the earliest preserved account from the heartland of the Frankish kingdom evidences a lack of any apparent stylistic innovation while, like Gervase, confirming the traditionally retrospective attitudes that had been self-evident in all church building until this time and that were to continue until well into the thirteenth century. Included coincidentally by Abbot Suger in three tracts on the consecration of the western towers (1140) and chevet (1144; see fig. 1) of the abbey church of St. Denis, just north of Paris, are laconic references to technical details of the reconstruction. Suger's fame as a political figure of the church has led to a tendency to ascribe to him the "creation" of the Gothic style. In fact, Suger's "first thought was for the concordance and harmony of the ancient and the new work"; he concentrated on finding "marble columns or the equivalent thereof" to match the antique columns of the preserved nave; since none were available in the region, he seriously considered having them taken from Roman monuments and shipped to St. Denis.

The reuse of ancient building elements (*spolia*) had been a primary characteristic of monumental building activity since the end of the third century, and two documented cases provide obvious Carolingian and Ottonian precedents for Suger's own tra-

Figure 5. Chartres Cathedral nave, central vessel, north wall (1194), from the southeast. FROM JAN VAN DER MEULEN, BIOGRAPHIE DER KATHEDRALE (© 1984)

ditional intentions: both Charlemagne and Otto the Great reused marble columns from Ravenna for their imperial churches at Aachen and Magdeburg, the columns of the latter being reincorporated into the Gothic cathedral after 1220. And this veneration of the consecrated elements of earlier buildings remained in evidence until well after the rebuilding of the east end of St. Denis, for which Suger expresses the determination "to respect the very stones, sacred as they are, as though they were relics." At St. Denis, Christ himself was believed to have consecrated the initial building, of which the ground walls are proved by Merovingian burials to be of late antique origin. A ring passage (annular) crypt had been introduced within the vaulted apse of this building to provide access to the relics of the patron saints, while to the east of it there was a confessio, the outer walls of which are still incorporated into those of the crypt, over which Suger erected his new choir.

Suger's text is at pains to explain the careful incorporation of the earlier vaulted structures in spite of their axial deviations; in fact all existing alignments and dimensions were retained wherever possible, with the minor exception of the windows of the radial chapels, which were evidently increased in size to achieve that wonderful glow of the *lux continua,* or uninterrupted light, that is still evident in the ambulatory today. Although Suger was, thereby, merely continuing an already highly developed tradition in stained glass, he was the first to record the decisive principle of the increased glazed area of the "Gothic" wall. He saw this, however, in terms of the same inestimable splendor of gold and jewels with which he describes the "incomparable luster" of the extant Merovingian church, glowing with great "radiance," and nothing in the text allows us to equate his appreciation of current developments in terms of anything having been invented at St. Denis. Suger maintains silence about the architectural style and provides no concrete information as to archaeological facts.

In summary, the twelfth-century documentary sources indicate that, in accordance with all other intellectual activity (theology, politics, literature), architectural "progress," renovation in its fullest sense, was sought systematically in terms of integral reinterpretation of existing structures. It was the strength of this concept, even during the rise of secular architects in the thirteenth century, that prevented the demolition of the ambulatory vaults and windows of Suger's choir when the upper parts were again renewed around 1231. Significantly, the thirteenth-century sources do not even mention Suger's building activity, stressing rather that the monks had previously not dared to demolish the earlier consecrated masonry and that even the current renovation had required royal counsel.

To understand the origins of Gothic architecture, it is not possible to search for the first "Gothic" building in terms of an "original" work of art, or to project the related concept of architect back into the twelfth century, against all documentary evidence. The well-recorded circumstances of the changes during the twelfth and thirteenth centuries are decisive: the earlier churches, in which the Gothic forms were developed, are the relics of a previous anthropological situation in which liturgical arts were needed to secure the propitious divine presence; religious architecture had been, since Roman times, the physical definition of ritual, but as the causal symbolic meaning became obscured, so the original nature of the buildings was reduced to a formal shell. A church building of the twelfth century could not have been considered as the expression of individualized formal "design" (aesthetic intent).

The forms that were later to be applied by the architects had been generated during the previous history of the church; building could only be subject to the theological concept of the church per se, of that ecclesia, or communion of the saints, established by Christ in the Apostles (Matt. 16:18; John 20:21), founded on him (as "cornerstone," Eph. 2:19–22) and subsisting in its temporal form as a unity of the living congregation of the faithful and the visible ecclesiastical order. It is this church that is the "holy temple of God"—and it is to this theological reality that Suger addresses himself, to this duality of the church itself, not to the mere masonry of the abbey. This orientation is particularly evident where he subjects his account of the actual building of the chevet to the ecclesiologically fundamental passage from Paul's epistle to the Ephesians (*De conscr.* 5); his interpolated stressing of the spiritual and temporal nature of the Holy Temple in the Lord is a theological imperative, not the mark of architectural connoisseurship. The anthropological condition of the pe-

Figure 6. Church of St. Etienne, Nevers, central vessel of the nave, north wall seen from the southeast; reconstructed in the 1060's.
FROM JAN VAN DER MEULEN, BIOGRAPHIE DER KATHEDRALE (© 1984)

riod does not permit the suggestion that Suger could have conceived his primary aim as the genesis of a new style, or that St. Denis was to become the object of the free aesthetic volition of a lay architect.

Correspondingly, the aspects stressed by Suger's own documentation of the building procedure are: alteration of the church's material form (1) compelled by physical conditions but subject to (2) preservation of existing structures and undertaken only with (3) divine concession, Grace, and under (4) ecclesiological deliberation (Panofsky, 27ff.). Of course, it is not the metamorphosis of the building itself that motivates his documentation of the occurrences in the first place, but the consecration and the translation of the relics, that is, the liturgical procedure by which stability is reimposed on the temporal vicissitudes of the mutable physical object.

Church building was generated by its symbolic necessity; it was one aspect of that need for symbolic structure which conditioned all aspects of society. This causal relationship goes beyond the fact that in literary and epigraphic sources from the fourth century on, the church building is referred to as the Heavenly City ("Heavenly Jerusalem" or "Zion") and that since the tenth century it is addressed in the liturgy of both the consecration and the laying of the foundation stone as *Urbs Hierusalem beata,* and represented as such in painted images until well into the thirteenth century. Since classical antiquity, the City, as a metaphor for the essentially sacred State, had been considered holy. The earthly city becomes for St. Augustine "a prophetic shadow and an image" while the City of God "is built of citizens, not of walls"; being consecrated in ritual, humanity is related to divinity, the parts to the whole.

Regardless of the temporal, aesthetic forms taken by the city in the Roman regions where the Gothic developed, the civic entity itself was inherent in the cathedral: metamorphically the Gothic cathedral still reflects the order of the city gate, the colonnaded street *(via sacra),* and the imperial palace in its adherence to (1) the two-towered facade (referred to as city gate in lauds and consecration rites), (2) colonnaded nave (the *cardo* cross-axis of the transept indicating the four corners of the world), and (3) the sanctuary (with the Eucharistic presence of the Lord), respectively (see figs. 3, 13). But etymologically the concept of the imperial palace as royal hall was extended equally to the building as a whole: the built church is addressed as "basilica" (from *basileus,* king) both in Isidore of Seville and in Christian poetry through the thirteenth century. This image cor-

responds to the integration of state and church throughout the period, which still shared with antiquity the certainty that all order was essentially divine, so that its symbols, whether personal or architectural, were, in the end, identical; *palatium, civitas,* and Eucharist were shared in the church. Corresponding to antique tradition, the forms of the temple were applied to the buildings of the temporal hierarchy (as at Sens, Archbishop's Palace).

However, in the course of the thirteenth century, the symbolic quality of church building gradually ceased to be its raison d'être—and, thereby, its social function—to become, instead, its coincidental background, subsidiary to other considerations to such a degree that it required an interpretative apparatus (for example, that of Sicardus, *d.* 1215), which was to become theologically questionable by the time of Guillaume Durand of Mende's allegorical *Rationale divinorum officiorum* (*ca.* 1290). During this period the church building, having become merely an objective image of the heavenly city, could be the ex-

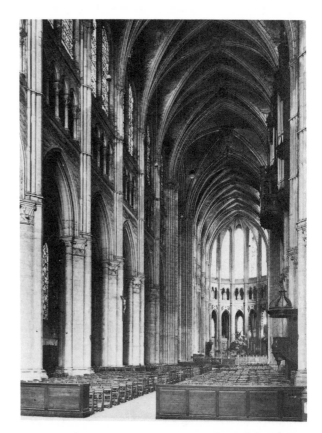

Figure 7. Chartres Cathedral nave, central vessel (1194), view across the transept toward the choir. PHOTOGRAPH BY PIERRE DEVINOY

ercise, or business, of "free" artistic interpretation (as we see in the controversies related to the commissioning of north European architects in 1386 to build the cathedral of Milan), with its forms accordingly usurped by buildings of the nature implied in modern terms of "civic" or "secular": removed from the universal context, individual interests related to commercial profit developed the great cloth halls of Flanders (such as Ieper [Ypres], completed 1304, fig. 2), with dimensions already exceeding those of the cathedrals and towers proclaiming the challenge of the free cities to feudal hierarchy (as at Bruges, second half of thirteenth century). Similar in form and function, the town halls of northeastern Europe (such as Lübeck, 1251; Münster, mid fourteenth century; and Stralsund, 1370) continued that development, while the best examples of the precipitation of ecclesiastic forms down to the domestic level are provided by the north Italian merchants' palaces of the fifteenth century (such as the Ca d'Oro [after 1421] and Ca' Foscari [1452], both in Venice). Conversely, even after the Renaissance was firmly established in secular architecture north of the Alps, post-Gothic forms were considered by lay architects to be the appropriate choice for ecclesiastical design.

The social rudiments of lay architectural activity are tentatively indicated by an incongruent series of drawings of diverse subject matter done by one Villard de Honnecourt; these were later annotated by him and bound into book form, probably before 1240, after which a second owner replaced some of the heterogeneous material with practical instructions for masons. This adaptation has given rise to the misconception that Villard himself was a "distinguished architect." He was, rather, an educated layman whose interest in the crafts as practiced at the church lodges was independent; his work displays no occupational application. His literacy and evident educational background indicate knowledge of the *artes liberales;* thus he cannot have been of low birth. His professionally unrelated activity—genteel dabbling—in the practical *ars mechanica,* or *ars scientiae,* must be seen in relation to the progressive elevation of the socioprofessional status of lay architects. And, indeed, a generation later the memorial tablet of 1263 of Hughes Libergier shows a very aristocratic man holding the model of the church of St. Nicaise in Rheims, designed by him, while the memorial inscription of 1266 to Pierre de Montreuil refers to him as *doctor latomorum,* teacher of masons.

That this indication of social and intellectual status and the corresponding change in the nature of

Figure 8. Laon Cathedral, central vessel, view from northwest toward the flat-ended choir. ELECTA EDITRICE, MILAN

ecclesiastical building activity did not pass unnoticed by the church is confirmed by the respective remarks of Thomas Aquinas and Nicolas de Biard around 1261, to the effect that artificers who call themselves architects (*artifices qui architectones vocantur*) arrogated to themselves the name of sages and that the chief masters of the masons only directed the others by word, but never laid hands to the work themselves. Indeed, after the termination of the cathedrals of Rheims and Amiens toward the end of the thirteenth century, memorial tablets of the responsible architects were integrated into labyrinths in the nave paving; this could only have occurred during or after the suppression of the liturgical function of the labyrinths (as documented for the neighboring archdiocese of Sens as late as the seventeenth century). These cannot have been artisans who had risen through practice, and yet they are not clerics; the respected intellectual abilities of these architects can only have been developed when gentry educated in the liberal arts started to apply themselves to the mechanical arts. This evolution is corroborated by the fact that they appear earlier than the lay organization of the lodges and craft guilds (which they probably infused with intellectual substance—for example, the geometry of rules that was to become the "secret of the lodges"). Their relationship to the practitioners, the master masons and master carpenters, must have amounted to social osmosis and seems to be reflected in the composition of the commissions called to give and receive expertise at Chartres in 1316. In the second half of the century the rise of the Parler family as architects (*Parlier*, literally "spokesman," today *Polier*, "foreman") may indicate a metamorphosis of and usurpation by the artisan-masters.

Only after the masons' "lodges" became detached from the clergy did the necessity arise to regulate their self-jurisdiction. The earliest recorded guild of masons is that of Paris in 1258, which was presumably connected with the development of secular architecture in the city. But although the Strasbourg lodge of "freed masonry" was founded in 1275 "according to the English fashion," the guild at Lincoln was still a religious fraternity in 1313, and the York lodge ordinance dates only from 1370, after York Cathedral was largely finished; thus too at Amiens, where, in 1375, the *maître de la fabrique* was still a canon. It is only with the Regensburg lodge ordinance of 1459 that the full emancipation of the common lodges is finally documented in the wording: to assure good service to owners, including also municipalities wishing to have churches built. No longer is the church the physical manifestation of the Church: it has become a secular object of civic patronage. With the city guild ordinances of Regensburg (1514) and Erfurt (1588), the guilds inherit the maintenance of the post-Gothic style. It is from this late period, between about 1450 and 1516, that model and reference books from the lodges are known to have existed—but they have no relationship to the work of Villard de Honnecourt.

The only standard architectural manual in continuous use from late antiquity through the early Renaissance was the *De architectura* of Vitruvius. Therefore, building activity throughout this period was subject to the conscious continuity of Roman methods. Although the importance of the manual remains unchallenged, past attempts to relate it to the "style" of Gothic architecture have proved futile. The manual's primary intellectual context was determined by the opening phrase, *"Architecti est scientia,"* excluding itself as it were from the higher *artes liberales;* building was a *scientia mechanicae,* and the manual was written for the foreman and works

Figure 9. Abbey Church of Ste. Trinité, Caen, central vessel of the nave from the southwest. The church was consecrated in 1066, but the vaults and secondary system, including wall underlay and triforium, were added to an existing pier arcade, which itself had been introduced within yet older outer walls. FROM ERNST GALL, DIE GOTISCHE BAUKUNST IN FRANKREICH UND DEUTSCHLAND (1955)

manager. It dealt with construction and technical processes generally and was used as such by William of Malmesbury and Vincent of Beauvais.

During the intervening centuries, when all reference to aesthetic systems in architecture was lacking, the use of the term "Roman style" (*romanorum morem*) merely indicated the use of building materials in the Roman manner, not the use of the orders (see the *Epitome* of Faventinus—an abridgment of Vitruvius—of *ca.* A.D. 300). It is only after Poggio that attention has focused upon Vitruvius' exposition of the Greek orders; it was this latter aspect, not the manual itself, that was "discovered" by Poggio in St. Gall in 1416. *Integritas* and *consonantia* could not be applied to the heterogeneous agglomerations of forms that characterize most church building until well into the thirteenth century. Vitruvius' somewhat confusedly traced theories on order, arrangement, and symmetry could not provide builders from late antiquity through the fourteenth century with an effective theoretical system. The iconology of the brilliant Roman development of spatial concepts, and of the complex structures defining their boundaries (the arches and engaged orders of which were to lead to the Gothic cathedral), were not the province of Roman literature but of hieratic oral tradition; the forms of the Pantheon and of the Basilica of Maxentius in Rome were to be generated out of socially self-evident meaning, that is, out of the common functions with which they were imbued by the religious order of everyday existence.

Thus, although discussions of *ordinatio, eurythmia,* and *symmetria* (composition, proportion, and symmetry; Vitruvius, 1.2), applicable to the pictorial, or aspective, arrangement of building masses and facades, disappear completely in the works of Christian authors until the establishment of a lay architectural profession, the architectural categories related to space (which Vitruvius mentions but fails to recognize in their full potential) do reappear in the few Christian sources that have been recorded: *ichnographia*—the *dispositio* of the ground plan, as used by Isidore of Seville (*Etymologiae,* 19.9)—is the abstract intellectual determination (*cogitatio* and *inventio*) of the boundaries of the enclosed space; these boundaries in turn are given form by *distributio,* or *constructio,* and finally receive *decor,* the appropriate corporeal embellishment (which Isidore calls *venustas*). *Dispositio, constructio* (not to be confused with "construction" in the technical sense, but clearly "laterum et altitudinis aedificatio," the articulation of the outer walls in their extent and height), and *venustas* are the principles that suffice for the formal evaluation of architecture, as applied by Isidore and later, identically, Hrabanus Maurus (*De universis,* 21.1–4). In effect, these categories establish architecture as the definition of enclosed space; because it is built, architecture must, then, be understood as the structure of the spatial boundaries.

THE HIGH GOTHIC CATHEDRAL

To this day, the church buildings of the Gothic period nominally serve the same religious cult that was responsible for the exclusively ecclesiastical origins of the style. However, precisely in the region where the Gothic originated, the cult itself was interrupted by the Enlightenment: during the French Revolution, some cathedrals, including Chartres and Strasbourg, were transformed officially into "temples of reason"; others were secularized, sold for nonreligious uses, or demolished for building material. (This systematic demolition was of far more consequence than the iconoclastic destruction of sculptural portal programs and other embellishments dur-

ing the Protestant wars of the sixteenth and seventeenth centuries.) The neo-Gothic restoration of the churches in the course of the nineteenth century (never systematically recorded) was the physical reflection of the restoration of the church as an institution. Yet, the lingering effect of the Enlightenment's intellectual conversion of the ancient sanctuaries has essentially obstructed our understanding of the origins of Gothic architecture.

Almost without exception the Gothic churches are in a dingy state of neglect, corroded down to the dull material structure of their physical core. The present neutralized condition bears no relationship to the original manifestation of the thought that generated them, in the brilliance of vivid primary colors, radiant against the abstract surfaces of the light, white stone. Thus too, paralleling the intellectual neutralization whereby the theological import of complex iconographic programs has been reduced to mere narrative content, the iconology of the abstract structures of the architectural system itself, originally self-evident, has now been lost. Comprehensive study of the neutralizing effect of the interior renovations of the sixteenth through nineteenth centuries is in its infancy; indeed, a certain embarrassed fear of the "barbarian" brilliance of the nineteenth-century restoration of the polychromy at the Ste. Chapelle in Paris called forth facile derogation, as did the recent work at the Cathedral of Limburg an der Lahn.

Our understanding of the buildings is further obstructed by the disengagement of the cathedrals from their environments. Originally, an essential agglomeration of ancillary buildings literally tied into the cathedrals: sacristies, chapels, chapterhouses, chapter closes (partly composed of the houses of the canons), bishops' palaces, hospitals, libraries, administrative buildings, even private dwellings and shops that at various periods nestled up to the very walls of the churches. In recent centuries this overt and fluctuating social integration has been converted by demolition into a sterile presentation, in the nature of works of art in a museum, devoid of their original communal function.

Let no one think that it is possible to experience today a "Gothic" building.

Dispositio: the ground plan (fig. 3). The basic disposition of the Gothic cathedral adheres to that of the great Constantinian martyrium basilica of St. Peter (old St. Peter's), the plan of which had been consciously emulated in the north during the Carolingian *renovatio.* It was through the Carolingian

589

resolve that the Constantinian buildings first came to provide the basis for a new universal architecture, promulgated by the claim of Western imperial authority: the apse, the focus of the ritual presence of the Godhead on the altar, is formally separated from the multivesseled nave by a transept; owing to the spatial unity of the longitudinal axis of the interior, however, this transverse element does not separate the congregation in the central vessel of the nave from its essential communion with the altar. In contrast with the late antique model, growing liturgical needs led to considerable expansion of the sanctuary, or presbyterium, of the Gothic cathedral: not only is the apse separated from the transept by the four bays of a five-vesseled long choir, but the double side aisles of this new element are carried around the apse to form an ambulatory. As a result, the originally centripetal, closed focus of the apse has been transformed, through the apse arcade, into an apparently centrifugal space, which flows out into the spatial envelope of the ambulatory, where it is bounded by the undulating succession of the apsidal outer walls of seven irregular radial chapels.

The transept has also been enlarged by the addition of side aisles, so that some bays are shared with the aisles of the long choir; the spatial interpenetration thus achieved is repeated on the nave side. This apparent expansion of the liturgical areas at the cost of the "ecclesia," the nave as congregational body of the church, is deceptive: in fact the expansion of the initially rather isolated sanctuary represents an extension of the nave side aisles eastward across the transept, in order to make the shrines and relics of

Figure 10. Chartres Cathedral, capital of the main nave arcade, probably sculpted shortly after 1194. FROM WILHELM SCHLINK, DIE KATHEDRALEN FRANKREICHS (© 1978)

the sanctuary freely accessible in spatial and liturgical unity with the western body of the church. The circumambulation of the sanctuary, a Romanesque (Nevers) and Early Gothic (Sens) characteristic, had its antecedents both in a group of Early Christian churches founded by Constantine's family and in the pre-Christian sanctuaries of Gaul where Constantine was raised and came to power; its reappearance in Frankish Gaul is likely due to the consciousness of Capetian imperial pretensions, facilitated by local traditions. Seen from the main axis of the church, the dissolution of what had been the essential closed wall of the antique apse was destined to raise the awareness of the potential dematerialization of the high nave's similarly arcaded spatial boundary in the shadows of ancillary spatial envelopes; however, the change was originally generated by the liturgical function of centripetal circumambulation.

All elements of this aggrandizement of the late antique basilica plan were already established in the Romanesque period and developed in buildings of the Early Gothic that predate St. Denis (such as Noyon). But at Chartres their historical development is uniquely documented by the preservation of the successive stages of the crypt masonry; the disposition of the ground plan is not designed to meet the specific functional requirements of the twelfth-century liturgy (still less to reflect some mystic numerology or secret geometry) but simply reflects the physical reincorporation of existing liturgical traditions and their respective structures, as is the case for both of the foregoing Early Gothic churches for which relevant documentation is available (that is, St. Denis and Canterbury).

The ideal, unified disposition of the first High Gothic building at Chartres is, however, also significantly disturbed by the retention of an earlier heterogeneous western tower complex that prevented the erection of a new, integrally planned west facade. This circumstance must be seen as the final assertion of those traditional ecclesiastical building procedures in which Gothic architecture had its origin. The undeniably decisive architectural synthesis of Chartres, which was to determine the subsequent development of the High Gothic, was itself prevented from achieving the homogeneity of a new "work of art"; instead, the entire new work was subjected to the ancient architectural and theological statement of the main approach facade with its sculptural program. This was not due to economic or other practical considerations, for the change of plan actually resulted in the extension of the transept and the addition of triple portal complexes to the north and south facades. Although transepts were present in northern Europe throughout the foregoing development, in several important churches the transept was absent altogether or else, while fully developed in cross-section, did not extend beyond the outer walls of the nave. The coincidental overaccentuation of the transept at Chartres was imitated at Amiens, Beauvais, and Cologne, whereas the cathedral of Rheims retained the original disposition of what must be considered the ideal High Gothic plan.

Constructio: the structure of the spatial boundaries (the wall and vaulting system). The interior architectural system is determined by its adherence to the basilical cross-section (fig. 4) of late-antique church types. The superelevation of the central vessel above the roofs of the side aisles must be understood—indeed, already in regard to the *dispositio* of the ground plan—as the introduction of an inner wall system within the outer-wall periphery of the ground floor or terrestrial zone. These inner walls of the "high nave," however, being held aloft in a celestial zone by means of a colonnade or arcade that, by allowing free intercommunication, unites the temporal (outer) and celestial (inner) zones. The apparent complexity of the wall structure that determines the spatial boundary of the central vessel, or high nave (figs. 5 and 7) of the Gothic cathedral, on the other hand, adheres in the first instance to the essentially simple dual system of the Romanesque (as at St. Étienne in Nevers, fig. 6) and of the clear restatement of the identical system in new buildings of the Cistercian Order. The "primary system" in the High Gothic cathedral consists of the flat wall of the high nave, illuminated by the brilliant stained glass of the clerestory, spatially articulated by the dark zone of the triforium, and carried by a colonnaded arcade in the tradition of the late-antique basilicas. The individual columns of this arcade are framed by the attenuated engaged shafts of a "secondary system" of independent arcades (as in the central vessel at Chartres) running longitudinally and transversally, those on the longitudinal axes being placed within, or "underneath," the main arcade arches, while those on the transverse axes span across the high central vessel in the vault zone and, by corollary, across the side aisles. (In the following text, the word "arcade" is applied primarily to the detached entity comprised of the arch and its columnar supports, but also, by projection, to the series of arcades that, taken together, form the "arcade" of popular usage.)

This essentially Romanesque detached visual structure of "underposed" arches (see fig. 6)—which is not motivated by structural necessity—remains the most pervasive and consistent architectural statement of Western church architecture until well into the late Gothic period; the resultant bay system with its reticulate compartmentalization of space has long been recognized as a major characteristic. Owing both to the lack of historical information on the construction of the preserved Romanesque churches and to the practice of converting earlier buildings at a later date, it is not known when this dual system was first applied in the West. However, by the sixth century it had emerged in Syria and Armenia as a rational development of the Roman compound wall, which featured an attenuated post-and-lintel construction applied to the arcuated primary system of the wall proper to provide a visual structuring or ordering principle. The symbolic meaning of this visual structure is proved by its application to the interiors of sacred buildings by at least the second century A.D., while throughout the imperial Roman epoch, the symbolism of the arch itself, as the abbreviated universal form of the celestial sphere, is evident in its application to the numinous foci of religious or ceremonial cult buildings, both pagan and Christian. As exemplified in the triforate portico to the aula of Diocletian's palace at Split, in the image on the silver missorium of Emperor Theodosius and in representations of Theodoric's palace in Ravenna, the arch signaled the frame within which celestial, transcendent figures and occurrences or their temporal representatives are manifested, and this tradition demands the presence of the divine to be articulated under the celestial symbol of the "triumphal" arch of the Constantinian and effectively all later Christian basilicas. In fact, the Latin liturgy of the Epiphany, particularly that of Gaul, has to be seen in terms of the Christian transformation of antique epiphany motifs.

It is this symbolically charged architectural motif of the arcade that is applied as a visual structure throughout both the Romanesque and High Gothic buildings, forming the secondary system, or "network," of individual, unitary, arcaded frames, cosmological schemata that determine every space through which the participant progresses toward the place of the eucharistic epiphany in the apse. The literary documents confirm that the building is at one and the same time the place of the epiphany of transcendent spheres and also identical with them. The pointed arch is simply the analogous truncated form

Figure 11. Rheims Cathedral, capital of the main nave arcade, probably first quarter of the 13th century; the frieze interrupts the respond of the transverse arcade. FOTO MARBURG/ART RESOURCE

of the mandorla, equally a cosmological symbol of the Epiphany, but since at least the eleventh century, specifically indicating heaven.

An originally ubiquitous factor in the history of the arch proves to be the most elusive: there is ample evidence for the widespread application of transverse arcades even under the flat ceilings or open roofs of earlier churches. The epithet "diaphragm" arches imperfectly expresses the suspended, or floating (soaring), effect that would have obtained in their original condition. Within the broader symbolic context, these arcades spatially articulated the liturgical hierarchy (as is evidenced on the St. Gall plan of *ca.* 820) and can today be visualized best in the well-known "segregated crossings" of early northern church building, particularly those in combination with transverse nave arcades: for example, at Celles (Hainaut), its duplication at Cerny-en-Laonnais, and in the central subdivision of the naves at Ste. Gertrude (Nivelles) and Villers-St. Paul, near Soissons. Tracing the precise history of the transverse arch, common in Syria in the Early Christian period and in Italy, is impeded in the Latin West by the intense period of building associated with the origins of the Gothic style. But the original high concentration of transverse arcades in the north of France is evidenced by the surprising number that have either been preserved (for example, Jumièges, with regular alternation of pier and column, corresponding to the "quadratic schematism" of Ottonian architecture, but equally prevalent in the "Early Gothic") or else incorporated into the subsequent

vaulting, as at St. Julien-du-Pré (Le Mans) and in two churches at Chalôns-sur-Marne, where the compound piers of both Notre-Dame-en-Vaux and St. Alpin are only slightly varied to express the transverse arcades that were originally present in alternate bays. Similarly, transverse arcades were originally applied to every other bay at Cérisy-la-Forêt (Normandy), Courville (near Rheims), and, in its pre-vaulted condition, at St. Martin-de-Boscherville, though the support system does not alternate at all. At least twelve other churches in the north, including St. Remi, in Rheims, must be mentioned. Although transverse arcades on alternate axes, corresponding to the "quadratic schematism" of earlier churches, are more widely documented, a regular succession in every bay may well have preceded them and was common in Romanesque structures. This will concern us when we return to the vaulting. All transverse arcades are conceived of as intersecting wall systems and usually are articulated as such in the compound piers of the main arcades.

But even where this is not the case, the massive rectilinearity of the compound Romanesque pier (fig. 6) has to be understood as residual wall, in the nature of the original Roman system ("swallowing," as it were, the hidden half of the engaged columns). At Chartres (fig. 5) the primary support is clearly a column, an independent member, with its shaft and capital articulated free of the ancillary shafts of the secondary system, which now form a sort of cage around it: the deep shadow of the acute angle of incidence (fig. 17) sets off the ancillary shafts from the column of the primary system.

Consideration of the column requires a brief historical excursus to analyze the development of this important element of the primary system. The source of what is essentially a restoration of the classic column to the architectural systems of the northern Frankish realm is to be sought in the Carolingian emulation, or *renovatio,* of the imperial forms of the Constantinian and Ravennate basilicas. This reflection of a retrospective attitude, or return to the antique iconic qualities inherent in proportional columns and foliate capitals, was a determinant characteristic of the development of the Gothic cathedral in the Frankish heartland during the rise of the Capetian challenge to the Holy Roman Empire (fig. 8). Tenth-century sources refer to many important buildings as colonnaded basilicas (for example, the cathedrals of Sens and Auxerre and the abbeys of Lobbes and Cluny II). In view of both the persistence of colonnaded naves dated in the eleventh century

Figure 12. Chartres Cathedral, central door of the West (Royal) Portal: Christ in Majesty with the Apostles below, flanked by angel choirs and Elders of the Apocalypse; the jamb statues are unidentified kings, queens, and priests. PHOTOGRAPH BY PIERRE DEVINOY

and the procedural attitude expressed by Suger and Gervase in regard to the earlier columns still extant in St. Denis and Canterbury in the twelfth century, we must assume the probable incorporation of such colonnades (whether in situ, elongated, or reconstituted in other topographical or structural systems) from the immediate, probably unvaulted, forerunners of colonnaded Romanesque or Early Gothic churches, such as St. Julien-le-Pauvre (Paris) and the cathedrals of Paris, Le Mans, Laon (fig. 8), and Mouzon, the choirs of Lillers, St. Germain-des-Prés (Paris), St. Remi in Rheims, and many English examples.

However, the development of Carolingian wall systems cannot be explained solely in regard to the colonnade as such; concurrently, there is evidence of an overriding awareness of the ordering principle of its unitary element—that is, of the inherent symbolic

power, or the traditions, of the individual column. In both the reasonably well-dated buildings to the east of the Rhine and, contiguously west of Aachen, those of the generally undatable Early Gothic, the conciliation of more or less unitary columns with the primary structure of the wall largely determined the subsequent development of wall systems. This occurred in its simplest form by the integration of monolithic antique *spolia*, whereby these distinct elements alternate, either singly or in pairs, with simple "residual wall" piers, as in the paired triforate (from *tri-fores*, triple openings) system of the imperial tribune of the Palace Chapel at Aachen itself (and of its models in Ravenna and Constantinople).

Other, similar triforate Carolingian and Ottonian main arcades raise the question as to whether the monolithic shafts of these churches were not also *spolia*, albeit of granite from the northern Roman provinces instead of marble from Italy; but it is essential to stress that the independent nature of the column is maintained, even when it is constructed of drums, whether *spolia* or not (as at Canterbury), and that this unitary nature is intended even when it is constructed of jointed ashlar, regardless of its lack of Vitruvian proportions. It was this retrospect for the antique that was to assure the Gothic the status of a universal style and elevate it above that of a regional dialect; while the architectural style of the Hohenstaufen Empire sank into oblivion, the Capetian Gothic became the architectural language of a still greater realm. Although both proceeded out of the common Carolingian renewal of Constantinian antiquity, the Capetian regions were compelled by the presence of earlier buildings to subject themselves to that symbolically charged complex wall structure of Gaul discussed above. In all the remaining cathedrals of these regions, and even in the romanized regions of the Germanic Empire, the conciliation of wall and column is, therefore, expressed in diverse terms of alternation between columns and *compound* piers, most frequently in simple alternation (found at Jumièges, above), as in the naves of Noyon, Senlis, Sens, and St. Quentin cathedrals, and in the Soissons south transept, Mantes, St. Leu-d'Esserent and Braine near Soissons, the smaller churches of Agincourt, Nesle-la-Reposte, and Jouy-le-Moutier (Val-d'Oise), and farther afield, for example in St. Pèresous-Vèzelay, but also in England, as at Northampton, Durham, Ely, Norwich, Waltham, and Furness. Less frequently the combination of columns and compound piers takes the form of a triforate nave arcade, popularly termed a "Saxon" alternation of

Figure 13. Amiens Cathedral, view from the southeast; western parts begun after 1220, choir after 1258. PHOTOGRAPH BY JACQUES BOULAS

supports, as at St. Quiriace in Provins and at Mars-sur-Allier in Berry.

It is the incorporation of columns at the tribune (gallery) level that has long been recognized as one of the main elements of ecclesiastical buildings after the Carolingian palace chapel at Aachen in the Rhineland and to the east. The same feature is pervasive in the Capetian realm (fig. 8), where it emulates the four-part interior elevation of Aachen (see the illustration in vol. 1, page 3). At Aachen it was an essential manifestation of imperial theology: the physical screening of an elevated spatial zone by the interposed triforate order of columns expressed the liturgical presence of the emperor in a symbolic sphere (simultaneously a zone of experienced reality) that had previously been reserved for the saints, as in the arcaded niches that ring the intermediate level of the Orthodox Baptistery in Ravenna. In Aachen, the imperial tribune screen is surmounted by a second triforate arcade, articulating a third story, as a visually effective elevated zone, which, being without floor, is insuperable; the physical inaccessibility of

this symbolic upper gallery expresses the presence of a celestial sphere or hierarchy.

There is at Aachen, significantly, no corresponding triforate division on the terrestrial level. Neither is there any such division in the nave arcades of the Capetian churches, although there too it figures prominently on the upper walls. The original triforate demarcation is applied in the nave of the cathedral of the capital, Paris, in Mantes, in St. Leu-d'Esserent, in the south transept of Soissons Cathedral, and in the long choir bay of St. Germer-de-Fly. Far more common, however, is the biforate tribune screen, which appears in most of the remaining Early Gothic churches.

To return to the secondary system of interposed arcaded frames: each bay is confined against the outer wall by the introduction of an extremely attenuated system of wall arcades, thus completing the system. The arcades of the high nave rest on bases above the imposts of the main arcade and rise to frame the huge window medallions that crown the paired lancets of the shimmering clerestory. However, at the crossing piers, where transept and nave intersect (figs. 7, 8), their responds are carried down to the floor, and they are tightly clustered with an augmented group of auxiliary responds that constrict the width of the central vessel to form the linear colossal order of a triumphal arch, entirely truncating the horizontal articulation of the wall. This great arch is repeated beyond, at the entrance to the sanctuary (and toward the transept arms), and the intervening space was initially flooded with light from a lantern tower (Laon, fig. 8, intended but never carried out at Chartres and Rheims), which created the effect of a spatially luminous triumphal arch.

Finally, a third system of arcades is interposed diagonally within the secondary system, its intersecting arches forming the well-known "ribs" that follow the arrises of the groin-vaulted ceiling to define each bay visually in the nature of a ciborium (baldachin) underneath the vaulting. Elevated into the celestial zone in the central vessel, these diagonal arcades have their bases on the imposts of the main colonnade; from this ground level their responds rise high into the clerestory to carry the ribs that frame the high, stilted compartments of the transverse vault (the severies), and thus allow the radiance of the stained glass into the very apex of the vault. This visual structure of illuminated ciborium units within the individual bays of the ancient orthogonal secondary system is clearly articulated as an "inserted,"

594

Figure 14. Parish Church of St. Martin, Landshut, *ca.* 1390. FOTO MARBURG/ART RESOURCE

independent tertiary structure, an effect that reflects both its historical origins and the structural forces inherent in the resultant quadripartite vaulting system.

The historical origins can be determined from many late antique, Romanesque, and Early Gothic examples, where the subsequent insertion of new ceiling systems within much older outer walls is obvious. But in other cases, the new ceilings are integrated so deceptively that the procedure is often thought to be due to a mere change of plan during construction, with the result that scholars erroneously reduce the postulated duration of construction. A significant and incontrovertible example is provided by the imperial cathedral at Speyer, where in the later eleventh century, great groin-vaulted bays were introduced, in emulation of the imperial basilica of "Constantine" in Rome, between the extant earlier Ottonian walls. This technical procedure was also applied—with the significant addition of di-

agonal ciborium arcades—in St. Remi at Rheims and in the cathedral of Le Mans. But it is significantly again in the Capetian archdioceses that the earliest preserved (but as yet undated) consistent examples of integral, original diagonal ciborium arcades were constructed (diagonal socles at St. Étienne, Beauvais, and at St. Germer-de-Fly; see also Sens, Provins, Mantes, and Laon). Many other vaulting systems in these lands retain ambiguous indications of the overpowering tradition of the transverse arches associated with their originally flat-ceiled forerunners, as often indicated by the fact that the compound articulation of the transverse axes of the bays is identical to that of the longitudinal axis of the main arcade. It is quite likely that the original diaphragm arches have been reconstructed within the later vaulted system—or even retained in situ in those cases where the diagonal vaulting "ribs" are footed on responds of which the orthogonal socles (as at Senlis, Noyon, and Paris) render them equally suited to the otherwise intact secondary system of the flat-roofed forerunner.

This procedure explains in turn one of the most typical manifestations of Early Gothic vaulting, the "sexpartite" system, whereby a regular, intersecting barrel vault on an almost square bay is subdivided by an additional transverse arcade (fig. 8). This feature can only be understood in terms of the iconographic imperative to retain a regular succession of the symbolically charged transverse arcade, uninterrupted by the vaulting system; there is no technical explanation for it, as can best be observed in the primitive system that has survived at Ste. Trinité, Caen (fig. 9), where the diaphragm wall does not interrupt the large severy of the intersecting barrel vault at all. It is significant how, in the somewhat later sister church of St. Étienne, the motif is integrated into the severies of the vaulting to form truly sexpartite bays, though the alternation of the main arcade piers clearly indicates that the building originally had transverse arches in an alternating system. However, the rude and divergent forms of the undated Norman vaulting of earlier extant buildings can best be explained historically by their dependence on the consistent development of more advanced forms in the Capetian realm.

Awareness of the historical development of the quadripartite vaulting system facilitates understanding of the second element of work: the structural forces. The Gothic vault may initially be thought of as a barrel vault spanning from wall to wall, but with half of the vault's substance carved out transversely by an interpenetrating barrel vault, as found already in the fourth-century basilica of Constantine; the diagonal arcs of intersection, or "groins," now carry the vault's entire weight, which is therefore concentrated on the four corners of the resultant bay. Technically, the masonry structures (voussoirs) of the diagonal arches can be, and usually are, contained within the webbing of the vault, but in the Gothic cathedral they are expressed visually and provided with the visual support of the responds to form the diagonally placed arcades of the interposed ciborium. The weight and outward thrust of the diagonal "ribs" are in fact carried by the whole of the masonry piers between the windows, where they receive their necessary abutment from exterior masonry and the flying buttresses, which conduct the static forces over the side aisles to the lower level of the exterior walls (fig. 4). But, from the interior, our perception of the vault load and thrust, that is, of the physical ponderosity of the masonry, is translated to the attenuated visual structure of the ciborium arcades and integrated with the arcades of the atectonic secondary system.

The overall dematerialization of the wall mass is a decisive characteristic of the Gothic spatial boundary. It justifies the identification of the High Gothic cathedral as the stylistic synthesis of the earlier buildings of a specific region, and it was to remain the determinant factor both in the future development of the style and in the delimitation of its relative influence. (In this regard, as important as the pointed arch and the ribbed vault were to become for the perception and perseverance of the Gothic style in modern times, neither their structural implications nor their postulated chronology determine the origins of Gothic architecture. Based on misconceptions stemming from the technological pragmatism of the nineteenth century, even recent studies have persisted in identifying as "Gothic" such buildings as the early Cistercian Romanesque churches, the thirteenth-century cathedrals of Bamberg and Naumburg, and the contemporary but consciously mural churches of Florence and Siena.)

First, as mentioned above in regard to the colonnade (fig. 17A), the attenuated elements of the secondary system are sculpted free of the underlying masonry (fig. 17B); in Chartres, as in the Early Gothic, the almost threadlike respond shafts in the upper zone actually were free-standing. But when, in the later development, they were formed as three-quarter round shafts sculpted out of the masonry it-

self, they remained equally set off from the surface by their deep shadows. Similarly the arris, or sharp edge, of the masonry of every intrados curve is replaced by an engaged torus (fig. 18), likewise set off from the wall surface by its shadow (fig. 17B) and preventing any perception of the mass of the ashlar. The limited residual wall areas appear only as taut surfaces, spanning the latticework of tori, and in front of the dark spatial envelopes of the side aisles and triforium. This "diaphanous wall" is then inverted in light in the translucent, flat, chamfered area of the clerestory glass, from which the highest intensity of pure color emanates. These are not windows that allow sunlight into the room, transparent of the unstable natural world outside; rather the light radiates from the translucent colored surface itself or, more correctly, from the abstract patterns of divine content, those mysteries that can be read today with binoculars but which, in their original brilliance, were experienced as immanent but illegible Presence, projected onto and merging with the opposite white surfaces so that, turn where one may, every element of spatially reticulated epiphany was replete with divinity, the luminous equivalent of the aural ritual chant, expectant of the Eucharist.

It must, however, be stressed again that the mysterious dual nature of temporal existence had been expressed in the double-shell spatial boundaries of pagan Roman sacred structures such as the Pantheon, and that its Christian interpretation is better preserved in the compressed, mosaic-encrusted spatial envelopes of the Orthodox Baptistery in Ravenna than in any Gothic cathedral today. But, in comparison with the imperial Roman definition of ritual space that found its final, grandiose expression in the Hagia Sophia in Constantinople, the achievement of the Capetian Franks must be recognized as the sublimation of the additive bay system to become a unified spatial entity, reflecting the laborious *renovatio* of fragments of provincial Roman heritage: by means of consistent plastic development of the corporeal elements of the Roman compound wall, the boundary of the ritual space has been dematerialized—expressed not merely in one final architectural statement, but rather in a succession of huge buildings, each slightly varying the respective articulation of the temporal and celestial spheres (figs. 7, 8), almost as if there were a restless assurance that eventually an appropriate epiphanic structure might be created to accommodate the final Presence.

Although the awareness of the inherent power of the architectural vocabulary must have endured well

Figure 15. Bechin Castle, ground floor; about 1510. WERNER NEUMEISTER

into the thirteenth century (most obviously at Rheims, Amiens, Le Mans choir, Bourges, and Beauvais, even Coutances, Auxerre, Troyes, and Metz), as church building was progressively relinquished to the professional expertise of lay master builders, the history of architectural meaning becomes instead a documented record of the feats of internationally commissioned individual personalities, their sociological function anticipating the Renaissance (for example, Jean des Champs in Clermont-Ferrand, 1248, and in Narbonne, 1272, the forms of the latter influencing Matthew of Arras, commissioned by Charles IV in 1344 for the cathedral of Prague). Competitive achievement led to higher and higher edifices until the spatial proportions became more vertical than those of the Romanesque (Arles or Toulouse, for example), the absolute limit being established at 48 meters (157 feet) by the collapse of the choir of Beauvais in 1284.

The formal terminology applied to the subsequent development by early-nineteenth-century authors lacked any historical bearing. Categories like "Rayonnant," "Flamboyant," "Decorated," and "Perpendicular" reveal more about the social history of scholarship than about its object.

Venustas: sculptural decoration. It is in corporeal embellishment that the personal virtuosity of the new artist/architect first manifested itself.

The specifically Gothic aspect of sculptural ornamentation had been the substitution of exclusively foliate capitals for the earlier forms of historiated and other figural or abstract capitals. Although an overview—or "linear" chronology—of its beginning development is severely complicated by the pervasive reuse of earlier capitals, the decisive stage was reached by the twelfth century with the appearance of the crocket capital (fig. 1). Corresponding to the antique Corinthian system, the foliage is arranged around the clearly articulated bell or "basket" in two superimposed registers, with the lower four leaves set on the cardinal axes, masking the transition to the abacus above, which is supported at the corners by the diagonal arrangement of the upper four leaves; these rise in a taut curve from behind the interstices of the lower corona to end as tightly drawn "buds" that recall the original antique volutes. Additional foliage may variously supplement or obscure the basic system, but this occurs generally within the parameters of Carolingian variations of the antique Corinthian capital as preserved in the early ninth-century church of St. Justinus in Höchst (near Frankfort).

Although ornamental variations of the acanthus leaf itself were propagated by both the Carolingian and Early Gothic builders, it was to be the more abstract, hard-edged, "tongue" forms that developed from the Höchst type to those of Laon (fig. 8), Lisieux, Braine, and Notre Dame in Dijon and, eventually, to the full-fledged crocket capitals of the Noyon apse, Chars, Orbais, the Soissons transept, and the apse arcade of St. Denis.

Already by the end of the twelfth century, the later, progressively more naturalistic development of the specifically Gothic capital is evident: in the earliest nave pier capitals of Chartres Cathedral (fig. 10) intermediate foliage starts to grow out organically from the now full, fleshy stem region of the major crocket leaves—in fact the observation of nature is penetratingly expressed in the presence of twig stubs, as though additional foliage has been broken off. Still iconographically motivated, this naturalism is limited to the column capital, that is, to the lower, terrestrial zone; the gilded star-flames of the adjacent keystones in the celestial sphere of the vault baldachins adhere to a rigidly abstract axial order. In the

Figure 16. Church of the Assumption, Most (Brüx), south wall of the west chapel. WERNER NEUMEISTER

somewhat later execution of the ambulatory keystones, artistic freedom already overrides the inner meaning, and foliate forms encroach in progressively disordered naturalism. Subsequently the crocket buds themselves open and bloom; the foliage starts spreading indiscriminately, as already at Rheims, and thus soon loses any vestige of antique tectonic expression (fig. 11). Once merely decorative, the capitals soon atrophy under the exigencies of the dematerialization of the new architecture, or vacillate between varying degrees of naturalism imposed by the design whims of lay architects.

No other architectural sculpture could be introduced into the interior of the Early and High Gothic churches up to the fifth decade of the thirteenth century (Ste. Chapelle) because the architectural system itself expressed the iconologic intention. The system described above was itself the integral constitutive element of the interior space, and no degree of plastic detachment could justify its being considered mere decor; the system was the architecture, not merely its embellishment.

Similarly it is only with serious reservation that the figural sculpture of the portals may be dealt with in the category of venustas, but it is precisely in sculpture that the effect of the new social circumstances of the architect can most easily be recognized. As long as the building was constituted as an idea, it remained a *Gesamtkunstwerk;* only when theological clarity was dichotomized in the thirteenth century were sculpture and painting emancipated from the intellectual subject, to be presented as objects of individual delectation. Thus, the complex, but obvious, theophanic iconology of all sculpted church portals prior to the thirteenth century reaffirmed the subject (fig. 12): the architectural entrance to the Heavenly Jerusalem was not merely the *porta caeli* but that *ostium,* according to John 10:9, through whom, not through which, the faithful entered the place of participatory experience (in the final inner sheath of the multiple spheres expressed in the interposed arcades of the stepped embrasures). From the tympanum, as in all architectural sculpture since antiquity, the Godhead faces man.

Even in Rheims (fig. 11), where the genial naturalistic sculptors of the foliate capitals of the interior already enjoyed the freedom to introduce unobtrusive figural drollery, the portals were not yet relinquished to artistic innovation but were subjected instead to the restatement of immutable theological truths expressed in the agglomeration of styles among various revised ancient figures. Concurrently,

however, in the Ste. Chapelle in Paris, the self-evidence of earlier ecclesiological symbols is submitted to the need for an interpretative apparatus for emancipated figural sculpture: statues of the apostles are appended to the transverse arcades of the interior (as later in Cologne, St. Ouen [Rouen], and elsewhere). Even the original necessarily neutral concept of the corporeal exterior now gives way to an extreme sculptural decoration of the buttresses, windows, and interpenetrating gables (fig. 13). But, devoid of the essential epiphanic spiritual context of the interior, this richly latticed, venust, exterior image of the Holy City is now presented as a civic object, an ascribed work of art in the modern sense. And by the end of the following century Claus Sluter finally "overcomes the Gothic" in his transformation of the portal of the Chartreuse de Champmol, near Dijon, to a mere stage for the display of his temporal patrons and of his own virtuosity (see illustration to "Gothic Art: Sculpture," below). The church portal had become an essentially disengaged object, to be viewed in its own aesthetic right. The Godhead ignores the observer.

Basic architectural elements were soon to be consumed in similarly individualized design: the symbolic grouping of the clerestory wall at Chartres (fig. 5) was transformed at Rheims into a unified area, subdivided by a corresponding pattern of curving stone mullions. This portentous invention, appropriately called "tracery," is now merely the purview of the draftsman, and many drawings from the thirteenth century and later have been preserved. It not only rapidly develops complex individualized patterns, becoming a major stylistic criterion, but absorbs the triforium, which, once it is glazed, soon loses its identity (St. Denis, nave after 1230, fig. 1; Amiens choir, Strasbourg nave). Furthermore, these linear tendencies correspond to a reduced sculptural plasticity of articulating elements and verticality dominates (Ste. Trinité, Vendôme, 1306–sixteenth century), while the advent of brighter grisaille glazing, casting stronger shadow, enhances the overall graphic effect. Thus after 1330 the walls of the Gloucester Cathedral choir become a linear-patterned, diaphanous sheath extended up into the complex network of vaulting ribs, thereby refining the earlier retrograde English tendency toward anomalous agglomeration into a development that will lead to the final apparent weightlessness of the fan vault with pendent keystones.

But the tracery system at Gloucester is introduced physically between older Romanesque walls; indeed,

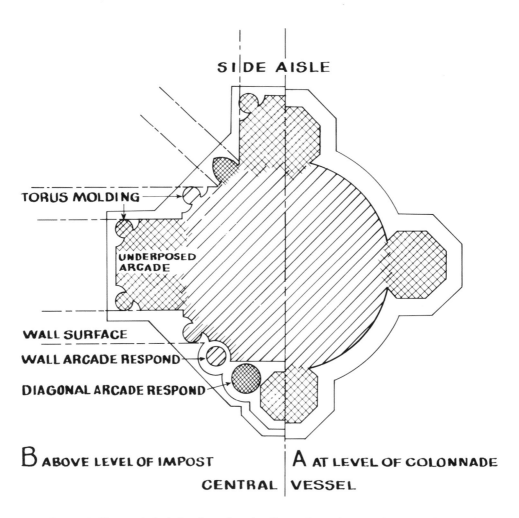

Figure 17. Chartres Cathedral, colonnade and wall articulation, horizontal section schemata. (High nave responds are probably not freestanding as shown.)

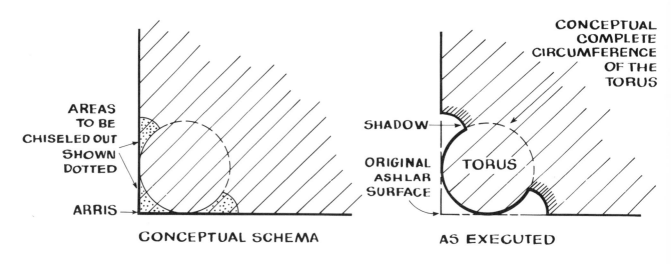

Figure 18. Gothic arris resolved as a torus molding.

600

the process of perpetual resolution and supplementation continues to transform almost every building, even those from the Early and High Gothic, throughout the thirteenth, fourteenth, and fifteenth centuries—but now for the sake of decor more than that of spatial resolution. During the centuries of the Hundred Years War and the Great Schism, it is beyond the periphery of France that the fascination with surface will lead to significant developments of new spatial forms, no longer related to the basic High Gothic vocabulary: when the concepts of light and surface, tentatively developed in the south (Jacobins, Toulouse, 1260–1292; and Palma de Majorca, toward 1300), are applied by Hanns von Burghausen to the flat window walls and prismatic white piers of the simple multivesseled hall church of St. Martin at Landshut at the end of the fourteenth century (fig. 14), the final dematerialization of the Christian church accommodates the subjective mysticism of the Devotio Moderna.

But the restless creativity of a free artistry, beset by its necessary subjection to nature, was eventually to transform the linear vault patterns branching out of smoothly contoured piers into the intertwining branches of Annaberg, after which the vegetal allusions are destined eventually to transform the columns themselves (fig. 15) and to writhe in final naturalistic absurdity out of the very walls (fig. 16), which occasions, perhaps justifiably, the Italian interpretation of the "Gothic" of their contemporary colleagues as the work of ignorant forest dwellers. Generated by this disdain, the urgency to give new birth to now empty classical forms precluded any understanding of forms generated by essential content and therefore obscured the legitimate continuity of late-antique architectural function in the Gothic cathedral.

BIBLIOGRAPHY

Research on Gothic architecture has been distorted from its inception by the irrational nomenclature imposed on it in reaction to building practices of the fifteenth and sixteenth centuries (the late manifestation of the style). Originally conceived of in the sixteenth and seventeenth centuries in ill-defined terms of ethnicity, the word "Gothic" first professed scholarly definition in terms of the architectural design approaches of the nineteenth and twentieth centuries; indeed, the profession of art history was born during the neo-Gothic period. Having been deemed "medieval," the Gothic had been excluded from the Renaissance concept of the individual as artistic genius; the professional history of art, intending to legitimize

the evident genius of the buildings that led up to Chartres, became progressively determined to establish the "birth of the style" in terms of individual artistic creativity. In this regard certain elements of overinterpretation by Erwin Panofsky, in his edition and translation of *Abbot Suger on the Abbey Church of St.-Denis and Its Art Treasures* (1946, 2nd ed. 1979), were criticized by Esmond S. de Beer, "Gothic: Origin and Diffusion of the Term," in *Journal of the Warburg and Courtauld Institutes,* **11** (1948); and by Paul Frankl, *The Gothic: Literary Sources and Interpretation Through Eight Centuries* (1960). Frankl's exemplary survey of the later period was soon supplemented by William D. Robson-Scott, *The Literary Background of the Gothic Revival in Germany* (1965), which provides a convenient English-language introduction to Hermann Hipp, "Studien zur 'Nachgotik' des 16. und 17. Jahrhunderts in Deutschland, Böhmen, Österreich und der Schweiz," 3 vols. (diss. Tübingen, 1979), a mammoth compilation that again exposes the fact that there is no systematic catalog of the Gothic monuments or their sculptural detail. In fact, there is not even a systematic bibliography for any major monument, and there has been no systematic publication of the excavation of any major cathedral that would meet the standards expected by classical archeology—objective diagrams and reports unprejudiced by preconceived chronologies—and even the accessible parts of the buildings have not been measured and reported on. The circumstances for the key monument of Chartres Cathedral are evident from Jan van der Meulen, "Recent Literature on the Chronology of Chartres Cathedral," in *Art Bulletin,* **49** (1967), and "Preliminary Review of Literature Concerning . . . the Pre-Gothic Cathedral Notre-Dame de Chartres," in *Mediaevalia,* **2** (1976). A complete annotated bibliography will be published by Hall, Boston, in 1985 or 1986.

The iconography of the sculptural programs has also been neglected in favor of stylistic studies; thus purely narrative interpretations have hidden the deeper iconologic implications of the images. A complete overview of Chartres Cathedral is provided by Jan van der Meulen and Jürgen Hohmeyer, *Chartres, Biographie der Kathedrale* (1984), which is being translated into English. An introduction to the problem of the iconography is Jan van der Meulen with Nancy Waterman Price, *The West Portals of Chartres Cathedral,* I, *The Iconology of the Creation* (1981). It is, therefore, not surprising that the meanings behind the abstract forms of architecture have been even more difficult to comprehend. Study of this aspect started with Richard Krautheimer, "Introduction to an Iconography of Mediaeval Architecture," in *Journal of the Warburg and Courtauld Institutes,* **5** (1942), and "The Carolingian Revival of Early Christian Architecture," in *Art Bulletin,* **24** (1942). The precepts were expanded by Hans H. Sedlmayr, *Die Entstehung der Kathedrale* (1950, 2nd ed. 1976 with postscript), and several decisive articles reprinted in his *Epochen und Werke: Gesammelte Schriften zur Kunstgeschichte,* 3 vols. (1959–1960 and 1977); reviews by Ernst Gall, Walter Ueberwasser, and Otto S. von Simson, with reply and repartee, all in *Kunstchronik*, **4** (1951); and Louis Grodecki in *Revue générale des publications français et étrangers*, **65** (1952). Further studies of the meanings include Günter Bandmann, *Mittelalterliche Architektur als Bedeutungsträger* (1951); reviewed by Paul Zucker in *Journal of Aesthetics and Art Criticism*, **11** (1953); misunderstood by Robert Branner in *Art Bulletin*, **35** (1953); as well as by Martin Gosebruch in the *Goettingische Gelehrte Anzeigen*, **208** (1954); further developed in Bandmann, *Ikonologie der Architektur* (1969); which is reprinted from *Jahrbuch für Aesthetik und allgemeine Kunstwissenschaft* (1951); and in his article, "Die vorgotische Kirche als Himmelsstadt," in *Frühmittelalterliche Studien*, **6** (1972).

Concurrently with the first studies appeared L. Schürenberg, "Mittelalterlicher Kirchenbau als Ausdruck geistiger Strömungen," in *Wiener Jahrbuch für Kunstgeschichte*, **14** (1950). The first strong support received by iconological scholarship came from Otto G. von Simson, "The Gothic Cathedral: Design and Meaning," in *Journal of the Society of Architectural Historians*, **11** (1952); reprinted in Sylvia Thrupp, ed., *Change in Medieval Society* (1964), 168–187; followed by his book, *The Gothic Cathedral: Origins of Gothic Architecture and the Medieval Concept of Order* (1956, 2nd ed. 1962), which was generally well received. See reviews by Wolfgang Braunfels in *Kunstchronik*, **10** (1957); Sumner McK. Crosby in *Art Bulletin*, **42** (1960); the review by Kenneth J. Conant in *Speculum*, **33** (1958), avoids the central issue altogether. The iconology was confirmed the following year by Laurence H. Stookey, "The Gothic Cathedral as the Heavenly Jerusalem: Liturgical and Theological Sources," in *Gesta*, **8** (1969). Further bibliographical references will be found in *Lexikon der Christlichen Ikonographie* under the entries "Himmel," II (1970), and "Licht," III (1971).

The necessary complementary study of the antique foundations had appeared concurrently with Bandmann in Earl Baldwin Smith, *The Dome: A Study in the History of Ideas* (1950); followed by his *Architectural Symbolism of Imperial Rome and the Middle Ages* (1958, 2nd ed. 1978), the review of which by Conant in *Speculum*, **33** (1958), verges on the absurd in its irrelevance. The further implications with regard to antiquity had already been indicated by Nikolaus Pevsner, "Terms of Architectural Planning in the Middle Ages" in *Journal of the Warburg and Courtauld Institutes* (1942), who provides an introduction to the Vitruvian interpretation later correctly analyzed by Bandmann. The most convenient translation of Vitruvius is by Frank S. Granger, *Vitruvius on Architecture*, 2 vols. (1955–1956). See also Carol H. Krinsky, "Seventy-eight Vitruvius Manuscripts," in *Journal of the Warburg and Courtauld Institutes*, **30** (1967), where earlier literature can be found. The best overview of the spiritual understanding of the temporal city is provided by Lidia Storoni-Mazzolani, *The Idea of the City in Roman Thought* (1970).

See also Carroll W. Westfall's review of Thomas Hall, *Mittelalterliche Stadtgrundrisse* (1978), in *Speculum*, **55** (1980). The historical background against which the relationships of the west Frankish kings to the church must be seen has recently and convincingly been presented by Bernd Schneidmüller, *Karolingische Tradition und frühes französisches Königstum* (1979), reviewed in English by Frederick Behrends in *Speculum*, **57** (1982).

Although our understanding of the symbolism of Gothic architecture is clearly based on liturgical, theological, and political sources of the period, formalistic arguments based merely on contemporary empathy are still brought to bear against it: Willibald Sauerländer, "Abwegige Gedanken über frühgotische Architektur und 'The Renaissance of the Twelfth Century,'" in *Études d'art médiéval offertes à Louis Grodecki* (1981), 167–179. The most recent historical overview of the alternative approaches to Gothic architecture is provided by the introductory chapter of Louis Grodecki, Anne Prache and Roland Recht, *Gothic Architecture* (1976), which has a fairly extensive bibliography up to 1976. However, George Henderson, *Gothic* (1967), could have been added to the general works—and especially also Harald Busch and Bernd Lohse, eds., *Gothic Europe*, with introduction by Kurt Gerstenberg, commentaries by Helmut Domke, translated by P. George (1959), with 200 plates. Grodecki's 440 illustrations are neither annotated nor related to the text; there is no glossary, and the text, translated with serious errors by I. Mark Paris, "offers little for specialists, and it will confuse or prejudice nonspecialists," to quote from the review by Carl F. Barnes, Jr. in *Journal of the Society of Architectural Historians*, **37** (1978). Another volume in the History of World Architecture series deals with the Early Gothic as Romanesque: Hans E. Kubach, *Romanesque Architecture* (1975). The entire formalist approach, locked into a chronological construct, has generated few or no fresh ideas since Ernst Gall, *Die gotische, Baukunst in Frankreich und Deutschland*, I (1925), with the most thorough bibliographical overview; and Hans Jantzen, *Über den gotischen Kirchenraum* (1927); and *Kunst der Gotik* (1957); so that Paul Frankl's *Gothic Architecture* (1962) remains fairly reliable. However, one recent publication provides an objective reevaluation of the self-contradictory state of research into the origins of the Early Gothic and will form the essential basis for future studies: Thomas E. Polk, *Saint-Denis, Noyon, and the Early Gothic Choir: Methodological Considerations for the History of Early Gothic Architecture* (1982).

JAN VAN DER MEULEN

[See also **Aachen, Palace Chapel; Ambulatory; Amiens Cathedral; Apse; Arch; Architect, Status of; Burghausen, Hanns von; Buttress; Canterbury Cathedral; Capital; Cathedral; Chapel; Chartres Cathedral; Chevet; Church, Types of; Ciborium; Clerestory; Construction: Building Materials; Construction: Engineering; Dijon, Chartreuse**

GOTHIC ART: PAINTING AND MANU-SCRIPT ILLUMINATION. Although the Gothic period, at least insofar as architecture is concerned, is usually considered to extend from the building of the choir of St. Denis between 1140 and 1145 to the end of the fifteenth century, painting in a style that can be called "Gothic" did not appear until about 1200. At this time, distinctive changes in figural style, kinds of settings, range of palette, and attitudes toward narration became evident and marked a turning away from the contorted, lively, even ecstatic modes prevalent during the Romanesque period. Nevertheless, generalizations are difficult because distinct differences in style and prevalent medium are evident in various regional centers of artistic activity throughout Europe, and over the three centuries that can be associated with Gothic painting, there are profound stylistic transformations.

The definition of a "Gothic" style of painting is further complicated by imprecise and varying moments of transition from the Romanesque to the Gothic in different regions of Europe: this occurs about 1200 in England and France, perhaps about 1220 in Germany, and not really until the end of the thirteenth century in Italy. Similarly, the transition from the Gothic to the Renaissance is equally variable and vague in different regions of Europe: perhaps in the 1420's in Italy with the work of Masaccio; about 1450 in France with the importation of elements of Italian Renaissance art by Jean Fouquet; and as late as the second and third decades of the sixteenth century in Germany with the assimilation of elements of the Italian Renaissance into some of the works of Albrecht Dürer and Hans Holbein. But none of these artists or their followers completely supplanted pervasive tendencies, first to the courtly

St. Francis. Retable panel in S. Francesco, Pescia, by Bonaventura Berlinghieri, 1235. SCALA/ART RESOURCE

elegance of the International Gothic style, and later to the emotionalism and crowded compositions of the late Gothic period. Moreover, Flemish art of the fifteenth century is difficult to categorize: considered by some, such as Huizinga, as a manifestation of the "waning" Middle Ages, it is signaled by others as evidence of a new direction for a particular form of northern European Renaissance art.

Painting during the Gothic period was practiced in four principal forms, some eclipsing the others in different regions of Europe: frescoes, panel paintings, manuscript illumination, and stained glass. Great cycles of wall paintings in fresco, prevalent in Early Christian and Romanesque churches, continued to be used in southern Europe, where the dematerialized walls of northern Gothic architecture never really found favor. In the north, particularly France, however, stained glass became the main vehicle for pictorial narration in ecclesiastical buildings and remained so until the fifteenth century. Panel paintings became increasingly popular in Italy in the thirteenth century and then in the rest of Eu-

603

rope from about the middle of the fourteenth, becoming in the fifteenth century the dominant form of monumental painting and supplanting even stained glass windows. Conversely, illuminated manuscripts manifest the most complete and continuous stylistic development in northern Europe, but seem to have lagged in importance and innovation behind the more monumental forms of painting in the south. But it should be cautioned that countless examples of wall paintings and panel paintings from the fourteenth and fifteenth centuries may have been lost or destroyed, creating a greater impression of imbalance than may have originally existed. Thus manuscript painting in northern Europe frequently has to serve as the only available indication of the probable nature of the style of monumental painting where no examples have survived.

Thematically, Gothic painting, as in the case of sculpture and stained glass, developed pictorial narrative by amplifying the number of incidents and the amount of internal detail; it further exploited the tendency to expand meanings by depicting typological and historical precedents—devices that were also being used in written commentaries on the Bible such as the *Historia scholastica* of Peter Comestor. The number of incidents of Old and New Testament stories was increased, saints' lives from the *Legenda aurea* of Jacopo da Voragine were depicted, and scenes were derived from pseudo-Gospels or extrabiblical literature such as the *Meditations on the Life of Christ* by the Pseudo-Bonaventura, and the *Revelationes* of St. Bridget of Sweden.

Altarpieces became more complex in the fourteenth and fifteenth centuries, not only in construction, but also in meaning and liturgical usage. Diptychs, triptychs, and polyptychs with hinged wings provided additional surfaces in varying combinations. The Isenheim Altarpiece by Matthias Grünewald (Colmar, Musée d'Unterlinden), with two pairs of wings that fold over each other and cover a sculpted shrine by Nikolaus Hagenauer, presents three different ensembles of paintings intended to be displayed for specific liturgical days.

Basic changes in meaning and effect took place. The Throne of Wisdom (*sedes sapientiae*) Virgin and Child of Romanesque panels inspired by Byzantine icons was transformed into an affectionate motherly image of the Madonna cuddling her infant, often represented as an exquisitely refined and aristocratic young woman. The Coronation of the Virgin became the excuse for depicting assembled saints and martyrs in sumptuous courtly splendor. At

Birth of the Virgin. Altarpiece by Pietro Lorenzetti, 1342. MUSEO DELL'OPERA DEL DUOMO, SIENA

the same time, intense emotionalism was increasingly exploited, whether it was the Virgin recoiling from Gabriel's message in Simone Martini's *Annunciation,* or the depiction of utter despair of Christ's followers in Giotto's *Lamentation* at Padua or the crowded cacophony of a narrative Crucifixion scene in Duccio's *Maestà* altarpiece.

In addition, the growing secularization of life and thought in the Gothic period, occasioned by the growth of cities, the foundation of universities, the flourishing of trade, and the expansion of a mercantile bourgeois class, widened the patronage of the arts from the church and the aristocracy and resulted in the proliferation of paintings and illuminated manuscripts. Increased literacy in this class of society and a growing body of secular literature in the vernacular encouraged the representation of secular themes and even the introduction of secular elements in essentially religious paintings.

These socioeconomic conditions affected the status of the artist during this period. With the growth of cities and commerce, trade guilds were formed and painters were often required to be members of such a guild, frequently the Guild of St. Luke, in order to practice their craft. Their training became highly structured: usually painters were apprenticed to the workshop of a master. Sometimes further training by additional masters in different locales (a tradition that became known as the *wanderjahre* by the late fifteenth century in Germany), and acceptance as a master soon became virtually institutionalized. Thanks to the records of such guilds, as well as the greater number of surviving tax records, contracts for court or civic commissions, and other legal documents, and a growing self-assertiveness on the part of the artists themselves, more artists' names are known to us. The prevailing anonymity of artisans of previous periods gives way before a greater number of works either documented or even signed by known artisans. The ability of artisans was frequently recognized by appointments to court positions (Jean Bondol was made *le peintre du roi* of Charles V of France, and Jan van Eyck, *le varlet de chambre* of Philip the Good, duke of Burgundy).

MONUMENTAL PAINTING

Italy. The survival of the tradition of monumental wall paintings, whether in fresco or mosaic, was particularly strong in Italy because of the only partial acceptance of the dematerialized structures of the Gothic style that were prevalent in the north. In the twelfth and early thirteenth centuries, heavily outlined, earthy-colored, stiffly postured figures continuing the Romanesque style persisted, as in the wall paintings in the lower church of S. Clemente, Rome (early twelfth century) and in the panel paintings of Margaritone of Arezzo, active in the 1260's. Strong Byzantinizing elements were to be found throughout the twelfth century, from the vast mosaic cycles of Sicily, particularly Cefalù (*ca.* 1148) and Monreale Cathedral (1172–1189), to the early-thirteenth-century mosaics at S. Marco, Venice. While these monumental traditions were significant, another major

Detail of frescoes in the Palais des Papes, Avignon, 1343. © PHAIDON

Byzantine contribution not only to Italian art but also, later, to European art in general, may have been the impetus it provided for the dissemination of panel painting. The use of votive and narrative icons had become prevalent in post-iconoclastic Byzantium, and important early icons were painted in the West in emulation of their Byzantine counterparts, such as that of the eighth-century *Virgin and Child with Two Saints* at S. Maria in Trastevere. Painted crosses, executed in tempera on wooden panels coated with gesso, became popular in the early thirteenth century, notably around Pisa and Florence. Those by Berlinghieri Berlinghiero of about 1210 to 1220 show a triumphant Christ, flanked by the Virgin and St. John, in a style that blends the swarthy tonalities and physiognomic types of Byzantium with a sense of three-dimensional form. The dead Christ on the Cross, a frequent theme of the Pisan School, was further developed at the end of the thirteenth century by Cimabue, who added to the Italo-Byzantine formula sinuous line and a compelling sense of pathos. Iconlike images of saints, now usually amplified by narrative scenes of their lives and miracles, were painted on panels in a variety of formats. The principal figures were still stiff and hieratic and the tonalities dark and earthy, but the accompanying scenes became lively and rhythmic in composition, as in the most famous example of *St. Francis* by Bonaventura Berlinghieri, dated 1235 (S. Francesco, Pescia).

Major innovations that led to a distinctive Italian Gothic style were made by Pietro Cavallini in Rome at the end of the thirteenth century in his frescoes for S. Cecilia in Trastevere (see vol. 3, p. 198), where he created softly but emphatically modulated figures swathed in form-defining drapery, perhaps of classical inspiration. Natural postures, ease of action, and softened, humanized visages echo similar characteristics that had appeared in French manuscript illumination almost a century earlier. Jacopo Torriti's apsidal mosaic for S. Maria Maggiore, Rome (*ca.* 1294) combines these features with the persistent hard, angular forms of Byzantine drapery. The most dramatic change was made by Giotto di Bondone, who perhaps in the Isaac and Esau frescoes of the upper church of S. Francesco at Assisi (if they are not by an unknown artist dubbed the Isaac Master), and in the Scrovegni Chapel in Padua (completed by 1306), created massive, simple, strongly modeled figures set within rocky landscapes or cubical architectural ensembles against a blue sky. The number of narrative incidents was increased, and effective use of compositional lines focus on the dramatic and emotional content of the scenes. While the style of Giotto and his followers, such as Taddeo Gaddi, who used a similar figural style but created more crowded compositions, was dominant in Florence during the first half of the fourteenth century, equally dramatic changes were effected by Duccio di Buoninsegna in Siena. His *Maestà* altarpiece of 1308–1311 also amplified the number of narrative scenes, and while retaining the arid, rocky landscapes and gold background of Byzantine painting, introduced elongated, elegant forms and curving lines evocative of the courtly style of France. Like Giotto, he also used the cubical doll's-house constructions. Simone Martini's *Maestà* fresco for the Palazzo Pubblico of Siena (*ca.* 1315) heightened the courtly and secular effect of the scene (a theme elaborated even further by his pupil Lippo Memmi in his *Maestà* for the Collegiate Church of S. Gimignano in 1317), and Martini's scenes of the *Life of St. Martin* in the lower church of S. Francesco, Assisi are filled with details of contemporary costume and settings.

Pietà. Painting attributed to Jean Malouel, commissioned by the duke of Burgundy, *ca.* 1400. MUSÉE DU LOUVRE, PARIS

The innovations of both Siena and Florence are brought together by the Lorenzetti brothers just before the outbreak of the plague in 1348. Pietro Lorenzetti painted starkly emotional scenes of the Crucifixion and Deposition for the lower church at Assisi, and provided a convincing perspective rendering of an architectural setting across all three wings of an altarpiece depicting the birth of the Virgin (Siena, Museo dell'Opera del Duomo). Ambrogio Lorenzetti also achieved an effective spatial interior in his *Presentation of Christ at the Temple* (Florence, Uffizi, 1342), but his greatest accomplishment was the series of allegorical frescoes on the effects of Good and Bad Government in the Palazzo Pubblico of Siena (1337–1340) where his panoramic cityscapes and landscapes and depictions of scenes of everyday life remained unsurpassed until the fifteenth century. Formerly attributed to Francesco Traini after the plague, but now shown to have been painted by an anonymous artist in the early 1340's, the horrific *Triumph of Death* in the Camposanto at Pisa reflects one of the major themes of Gothic art—one that is reflected in similar macabre representations of the *Dance of Death* (fresco at St. Robert, La Chaise-Dieu, *ca.* 1460) or the *Meeting of the Three Quick and the Three Dead* in French art (miniature in the prayer book of Bonne of Luxembourg, New York, Metropolitan Museum, Cloisters Collection).

While the effects of the outbreak of the plague on Italian art may have been exaggerated by some scholars, it is nevertheless true that after 1350 there was a revival of stark, hieratic, sometimes iconlike images such as the Strozzi Altarpiece by Andrea di Cione (called Orcagna; Florence, S. Maria Novella, 1354–1357) and the vast didactic fresco cycle presenting allegorically the *Triumph of the Church* from a specifically Dominican point of view, painted by Andrea da Firenze for the Spanish Chapel at S. Maria Novella between 1366 and 1368. Equally crowded and rigidly composed frescoes of Paradise and Hell were painted by Nardo di Cione for the Strozzi Chapel of S. Maria Novella at about the same time. Meanwhile, in Siena, Barna da Siena adapted Giottesque figures to a highly expressive cycle of frescoes of the *Passion* for the Collegiate Church of S. Gimignano. At the end of the fourteenth century, late reflections of Giotto's style, but more crowded and placed within more intricate Gothic structures, can be seen in the frescoes of Altichiero and his followers in Padua.

By the fifteenth century, northern Italian art had assimilated numerous characteristics from the north, and artists in Lombardy and Tuscany in particular adhered to a sumptuous, elegant, and courtly style that was the Italian manifestation of the International Gothic. Such artists as Lorenzo Monaco and

Gentile da Fabriano were proponents of this last phase of the Gothic at a moment when Masaccio's paintings in the Brancacci Chapel at S. Maria del Carmine and at S. Maria Novella offered the first examples of a truly recognizable Renaissance style. Even Fra Angelico (Giovanni da Fiesole), active in the mid fifteenth century, capitalizing on Renaissance advances in the geometric projection of accurate perspective, nevertheless peopled his paintings with sweet aristocratic personages clothed in brilliantly colored and lavish costumes indicative of the last moment of Gothic painting.

France. Much of the monumental painting in France before the fifteenth century has been lost, but there remain some vestiges that give an indication of the stylistic crosscurrents and achievement of early French painting. Vault frescoes of the *Infancy of Christ* in the chancel of St. Julien des Chartreux at Le Petit-Quevilly, from the first half of the thirteenth century, contain scenes set in vines and medallions that recall the format of contemporary stained glass.

Portrait of Charles VII. Jean Fouquet, *ca.* 1445. MUSÉE DU LOUVRE, PARIS

Wilton Diptych, right panel. Nationality of artist unknown, 1380–1390. NATIONAL GALLERY, LONDON

An early-fourteenth-century fresco of *Christ in Majesty* at the Church of St. Laurent, Auzon reveals Byzantine influences from Italy, while a much damaged *Crucifixion* at St. André, Alet (1333–1355) shows a delicate linear style and refined features that reflect developments in contemporary courtly sculpture in France. A remarkable school of painting patronized by the papal court at Avignon from the 1330's began under Simone Martini and Matteo di Giovanetti da Viterbo, whose well-modeled figures placed within intricate architectural settings, extraordinary perspective renderings of bird cages, and scenes of verdant gardens were almost equal to the achievements of the Lorenzettis. An altarpiece of the *Passion* by Simone Martini found its way to the Chartreuse de Champmol in Dijon, Burgundy before the end of the century, and its compositions were emulated in paintings and manuscript illuminations at the beginning of the fifteenth century.

Surviving panel paintings in France before the middle of the fourteenth century are extremely scarce, the most notable early example being the portrait of John the Good (Paris, Louvre) of about 1360. Artists from Flanders were attracted to the court at Paris, and at the turn of the century important panel paintings were executed for French patrons, including the wings of an altarpiece for the Chartreuse de Champmol by Melchior Broederlam at Ypres, a circular *Pietà* attributed to Jean Malouel from Nijmegen for the duke of Burgundy, and a *Martyrdom of St. Denis* by Jean Malouel that was finished by Henri Bellechose. These and a host of other paintings show a mixture of Flemish, French, and Italian elements that earn them inclusion in the International Gothic style.

The school of Provence continued to flourish in the mid fifteenth century with the stark and deeply emotive *Pietà* of Villeneuve-lès-Avignon (Paris, Louvre) recently attributed to Enguerrand Charonton and paintings of the *Virgin of Mercy* (Chantilly,

Madonna and Child with Pea Blossom. "Master Wilhelm," school of Cologne, *ca.* 1410. MUSEUM WALLRAF-RICHARTZ

608

Musée Condé) and a *Coronation of the Virgin* at Villeneuve-lès-Avignon also by Charonton. Nicolas Froment was strongly influenced by Flemish painting, as manifested by his *Altarpiece of the Burning Bush* in the cathedral of Aix-en-Provence in 1476. This Flemish influence is also evident in the work of the Master of Moulins in his Moulins Triptych of about 1498/1499.

Jean Fouquet, active both as a manuscript illuminator and panel painter, virtually introduced the achievements of the Italian Renaissance to France: his volumetric figures, clear distant landscapes, spatial interiors, and Italianate architectural details are evident in his miniatures for the Hours of Étienne

Chevalier (Chantilly, Musée Condé) as well as in his Melun Diptych (now in Berlin and Antwerp) and monumental portraits of Charles VII and Guillaume Jouvenal des Ursins.

England. Our knowledge of early English painting is severely hampered by the paucity of surviving works, but vestiges of frescoes at Winchester Cathedral of about 1230 and in the Windsor Castle cloisters reveal a delicate, linear style that closely emulates that of the prevalent court style practiced by Matthew Paris in manuscript illumination. A more volumetric drapery style of clothing and elongated, swaying figures dominated East Anglian painting of the fourteenth century, as shown by a Crucifixion

The Miraculous Draught of the Fishes. Detail of the St. Peter Altarpiece by Konrad Witz, 1444. MUSÉE D'ART ET D'HISTOIRE, GENEVA

609

triptych at Thornham Parva in Suffolk and an altarpiece with four scenes from the Life of the Virgin, in the Musée de Cluny, Paris. The most famous painting believed to be of English origin, the Wilton Diptych, painted between 1380 and 1390, contains such a mixture of English, French, and Bohemian stylistic elements that it is sometimes attributed to artists of French or Bohemian origin. Continental influences persist in the few remaining wall paintings of the fifteenth century, particularly in the monochrome frescoes by Gilbert and William Baker in the Chapel of Eton College, painted between 1479 and 1488.

Bohemia and Germany. Strong Italo-Byzantine influences are evident in fourteenth-century paintings of the Bohemian school. The Master of the Hohenfurth (Vyšší Brod) Altar (Prague, National Gallery, *ca.* 1350) placed swarthy figures in luminous draperies on an arid ground plane and against a gold background in the manner of Trecento paintings. The monumental *Glatz Madonna* (Berlin, Staatliche Museen, ca. 1344–1364) appears to combine the Byzantine icon, the Italian architectural setting (in the elaborate throne), and the evolving "soft style" that was to become characteristic of Bohemian painting. Master Theodoric, who painted a vast number of frescoes in the imperial castle of Karlstein under the patronage of Charles IV, further evolved this heavily modeled style and introduced less idealized and more plebeian figure types into his compositions. The Master of the Wittengau (Třeboň) Altar (*ca.* 1380–1390) used more natural skin tonalities and less volumetric draperies, resulting in more slender and graceful figures.

In Germany, large-scale altarpieces had come into vogue by the third quarter of the fourteenth century. In Hamburg, Master Bertram's vast Grabow Altarpiece of 1379–1383 (Hamburg, Kunsthalle) with scenes of the Creation, the story of Isaac, and the first part of the Gospel cycle, appears to combine the soft style similar to that of Master Theodoric with a propensity for extended narration. Master Francke, active in Hamburg between about 1415 and 1424, used compositional groups that he might have learned in France in scenes filled with a new dramatic intensity in his St. Barbara Altarpiece (Helsinki, Nationalmuseum) and the St. Thomas Altarpiece (Hamburg, Kunsthalle, begun 1424). In Westphalia, the multiplication of incidents and personages within scenes, combined with the lavishness and lyricism of the International Gothic style can be found in Konrad von Soest's Niederwildungen Al-

Madonna in a Church. Jan van Eyck, 1425–1427. KAISER FRIEDRICH MUSEUM, BERLIN

tarpiece of about 1403. The "soft style" persists in the School of Cologne, particularly in the sweet and delicate paintings of the *Madonna and Child with Pea Blossom* of about 1410 now in Cologne and Nuremberg, providing a basis for the more firmly modeled and brilliantly colored paintings of Stephan Lochner toward the middle of the century. Influenced by Flemish painting, a harsh new realism in depicting figures and details appears in Lucas Moser's *Magdalen* altarpiece of 1431 at Tiefenbronn, Hans Multscher's Wurzach Altar of 1437 (Berlin, Staatliche Museen), and Konrad Witz's *Speculum of Salvation* altarpiece (Heilsspiegelaltar, of 1434–

1435), but scenes are still placed somewhat incongruously against a gold ground. Witz's St. Peter Altarpiece of 1444 (Geneva, Musée d'Art et d'Histoire), however, contains an identifiable landscape depicted with meticulous detail. Michael Pacher's *St. Wolfgang* altarpiece (1471–1481) contains representations of Gothic architecture seen in perspective in the manner of Italian Renaissance painting, particularly under the influence of Mantegna. With his works and those of Albrecht Dürer between 1495 and 1526, where we find crowded, tumultuous late Gothic representations alternating with calm, stable, spatially conceived ones, and new precepts of Renaissance humanism in his themes, German art turns toward the Renaissance.

Flanders. Very few examples of Flemish painting before the fifteenth century survive, the most notable example being the triptych of the Tanners Guild in the Cathedral of St. Sauveur at Bruges of about 1400, still showing the swaying, rhythmic forms of Gothic art. The Master of Flémalle (now usually identified as Robert Campin) incorporates a heavy sculpturesque style, reminiscent of Claus Sluter, with a new objective realism, placing holy figures in a contem-

porary bourgeois environment, as in his Mérode Altarpiece (New York, Metropolitan Museum, Cloisters Collection; see vol. 3, p. 61). Although his works can be considered the beginning of a new Northern Renaissance style, the heavily charged symbolic value of carefully represented objects, the couching of holy scenes in terms of immediatley comprehensible everyday settings, and the emotive quality of many of these and subsequent Flemish paintings still have a ring of late Gothic sensibilities. Indeed Jan van Eyck's *Madonna in a Church* (Berlin, Staatliche Museen) and some of the figures in the interior of the vast Ghent Altarpiece still appear to be influenced by the International Gothic style, while others on the exterior wings, as well as his portraits, are done in a more sculptural manner and with a searing realism of facial features and textures of materials. Rogier van der Weyden pays similar attention to details, and bourgeois settings, but achieves a quietude of pathos in his *Pietà* in the Prado and *Crucifixion* in Vienna. These tendencies are continued in the second generation of Flemish painters, which extends from Petrus Christus and Dirk Bouts to the paintings of Hans Memling between 1465 and 1494. Gerard David shows a transition from roots in the early-fifteenth-century Flémallesque style to an easy, calm Renaissance style at the end of the century, and Hier-

The Last Supper. Central panel of the Sacrament Altarpiece by Dirk Bouts, 1464–1467. COLLEGIATE CHURCH OF ST. PETER, LOUVAIN

Detail of a fresco at the Monastery of Pedralbes, Spain, by Ferrer Bassa, 1340's. ARCHIVO MÁS

onymus Bosch, a highly individual artist active at the beginning of the sixteenth century, created strange, visionary, moralistic altarpieces filled with grotesques and hybrids that were his heritage from the realm of medieval marginalia.

Spain. Spain enjoyed a long tradition of panel painting in the Gothic style in a variety of regional schools from the thirteenth into the sixteenth century. Early works, such as the tomb painting for Don Sancho Saiz de Carillo from Burgos (Barcelona, Museo de Arte de Cataluña) were executed in flat colors but with a fine linear rendering of faces. In the fourteenth century, a mixture of Italian influences, particularly that of Giotto, resulted in a more monumental and dramatic style, which, combined with Sienese influences, is particularly evident in Ferrer Bassa's frescoes at the monastery of Pedralbes from the 1340's. The International Gothic style permeated the art of Catalonia and Valencia at the end of the fourteenth and beginning of the fifteenth centuries, as exemplified by the colorful paintings of Luis Borrassá. Among the foreigners active in Spain who helped to perpetuate this mix of styles were the German Andrés, Marzal de Sax (1393–1410) in Valencia and Nicolás Francés (*fl.* 1430–1468) at León. Pervasive Flemish influences, resulting in a "Hispano-Flemish" style, began to dominate Spanish painting in the second third of the fifteenth century. Though more inclined to subdued colors, Spanish artists readily adopted the meticulous realism of Northern painting. The *Virgin of the Councillors* by Luis Dalmaú (1443) is an adaptation of motifs found in the Ghent Altarpiece and *van der Paele Madonna* of Jan van Eyck. Rogier van der Weyden, Dirk Bouts, and Hans Memling were closely emulated by the Master of Ávila, Fernando Gallego, and Sancho de Zamora respectively. Pedro Berruguete (*fl.* 1477–1504), trained in Italy, combined the precise detail and microscopic realism of Flemish painting with a new sensitivity for monumental figures in the manner of Italian Renaissance portraiture in his retable of St. Eulalia at Palencia.

MANUSCRIPT ILLUMINATION

The first Gothic style in manuscript illumination emerged in northern Europe with the gradual transformation of Romanesque conventions and a new assimilation of classicizing and Byzantinizing influences. The classicizing tendency may have been sparked by changes in the style of metalwork and sculpture from about the 1180's with the work of Nicholas of Verdun, whose champlevé enamel

plaques for the Klosterneuburg Altarpiece (see vol. 4, frontispiece) manifests increased attention to three-dimensional modeling, normative proportioning of the human figure, and use of looped, channeled drapery folds approximating the effects of classical sculpture. This "hairpin" or *Muldenfaltenstil* drapery appears in manuscript illumination about 1200 in the Ingeborg Psalter (Chantilly, Museé Condé, MS 9 [1695]) and remains a distinctive feature until the mid thirteenth century in France. A much more angular variant persists in German painting and illumination, as the evangeliary from Goslar of about 1235–1240 (Goslar, Rathaus, Städtische Sammlungen). The more natural appearance of human beings, their clothing, their artifacts, and their environment was further encouraged by an increased awareness of and interest in depicting the natural world. To this monumental style were added elements of Byzantine art, particularly the westernized variant found in the mid-twelfth-century mosaics of Norman Sicily, which may have contributed a more humane, less severe image of Christ and a softening of the intense

Virgin of the Councillors. Luis Dalmaú, painted for the Casa de la Ciudad, Barcelona, 1443. ARCHIVO MÁS

Christ in Majesty. From the Westminster Psalter, mid 13th century. LONDON, BRITISH LIBRARY, MS ROYAL 2.A.XXII, fol. 14r

physiognomic expressions of Romanesque art. The result was a style of painting in the early thirteenth century that manifested a calm serenity and monumentality, not only in the Ingeborg Psalter, but also in the drawings of Villard de Honnecourt (Paris, Bibliothèque Nationale, MS fr. 19093), and the *Christ in Majesty* of the Westminster Psalter (London, British Library, MS Royal 2.A.XXII).

By the middle of the thirteenth century, however, this more humane depiction of deity and humanity led to the sweetness of demeanor and aristocratic refinement that dominate manuscript painting in Paris patronized by the court of St. Louis. As a result, figures became less substantial, more elongated, swaying and mincing in posture, and more flat and linear in form. This style was in part engendered by the mass production of stained glass, which was still the dominant pictorial art, for such buildings as the Ste. Chapelle, and its influence can be seen not only in the continued prevalence of red and blue tonalities, but also in the frequent division of miniatures into geometric pictorial fields as in illustrations of the Psalter of Blanche of Castile (Paris, Bibliothèque de l'Arsenal, MS lat. 1186) or in the vertical panels of paired roundels in the copiously illustrated *Bibles moralisées* of this period. Perhaps as a result of the patronage of the court of St. Louis, manuscript illumination became the second most prevalent form of painting in France. Manuscripts such as the Psalter of St. Louis (Paris, Bibliothèque Nationale, MS lat. 10525) contain attenuated, flattened, and linear figures whose features have become repetitive and stereotyped. The palette remains generally in shades of red and blue, and scenes are now placed within architectural frames.

It is not until the 1290's that there is a renewed interest in modulating draperies in terms of light and shade, seen in the illuminations of Master Honoré in the Breviary of Philip the Fair (Paris, Bibliothèque Nationale, MS lat. 1023), though this artist still retains the lively, mincing postures and physiognomic types of the Parisian court school. The most dramatic transformations, building on the innovations of Master Honoré, occur in the illuminations of Jean Pucelle, who depicts fully modeled figures, sometimes painted in *grisaille* as in the Hours of Jeanne d'Évreux (New York, Metropolitan Museum of Art, Cloisters Collection) of the 1320's having the effect of light and shade playing over carved marble or ivory. He was also interested in representing pictorial space, and introduced into Northern art a cubical "doll's house" for architectural interiors, found

Coronation of the Virgin. Illumination by the Master of the Boucicaut Hours, *ca.* 1409. MUSÉE JACQUEMART-ANDRÉ, PARIS, MS 2, fol. 95

in the Hours of Jeanne d'Évreux and in the Belleville Breviary (Paris, Bibliothèque Nationale, MS 10483–84). It is possible that this motif, and the crowded composition of his *Crucifixion* in the Évreux Hours, were in fact derived from a knowledge of Duccio's *Maestà* altarpiece of 1308–1311 in Siena. The influence of Pucelle was to dominate French manuscript illumination and was perhaps responsible for a first wave of Italian Trecento influences almost to the end of the fourteenth century.

Only at that time did an interest in landscape result in the development of exterior pictorial space.

Mary of Burgundy reading in front of a church window. Miniature from a book of hours made for Mary of Burgundy, *ca.* 1480. ÖSTERREICHISCHE NATIONALBIBLIOTHEK, VIENNA

Throughout the thirteenth and well into the fourteenth century, scenes were placed against patterned backgrounds, occasionally with a painted ground line. The Boquetaux Master introduced clumps of diminutive trees *(boquetaux)* into landscapes of arid conical hills, another convention found in Trecento art; but his backgrounds were still patterned. It remained, perhaps, for Jacquemart de Hesdin, a painter employed by Jean, duke of Berry at the turn of the century, to introduce landscapes with a blue sky in the Brussels Hours (Brussels, Bibliothèque Royale, MS 11060–61), and for the Boucicaut Master to further develop the details of a convincing landscape in the Boucicaut Hours (Paris, Musée Jacquemart-André, MS 2) before the Limbourg brothers introduced their detailed and sometimes identifiable landscapes into the calendar scenes of the *Très riches heures* (Chantilly, Musée Condé). In so doing, these illuminators adopted the aesthetic of the panel painting, which at this time was becoming a "window" through which one saw the illusion of a spatial scene, and thereby changed the relationship between

illustrations and the decorated page. The style of these artists and of followers, all of whom were participants in the courtly International Gothic style, dominated French illumination until the mid fifteenth century. At about this time Jean Fouquet introduced a new perception of landscape and architectural space, perhaps based upon knowledge of the accomplishments of Italian Renaissance artists. Jean Colombe, who completed the illuminations for the *Très riches heures,* was an extremely prolific illuminator of books of hours and secular texts toward the end of the century; he continued this tradition of landscape, and introduced heavy Renaissance architectural frames around many of his miniatures. He was followed by Jean Bourdichon, who brought a calm, tranquil Renaissance style to French illumination at the end of the fifteenth century.

During the Gothic period, but particularly in the fifteenth century, books of hours replaced psalters as the principal books used for private devotion. The decoration of these manuscripts, which began as simple branches and leaves painted in the margins during the 1260's, became increasingly intricate and was often filled with drolleries. In the fifteenth century penned branches with gold leaves gave way to flowering naturalistic plants; these in turn gave way, in Flemish illumination, under the lead of the Master of Mary of Burgundy, to illusionistic renderings of flowers casting shadows against a solid-colored or gold ground. Marginal miniatures introduced by the Bedford Master in the 1420's eventually evolved, by the end of the century in both France and Flanders, into pictorial borders completely surrounding another miniature and text. However, with the increased interest in secular texts, some copiously illustrated manuscripts dropped the marginal ornament altogether, thereby paralleling the more austere aesthetic found in the early printed books of the period.

BIBLIOGRAPHY

General. Albert Châtelet, *Les primtifs septentrionaux: La peinture dans l'Europe septentrionale et la péninsule Ibérique au XVe siècle* (1979); Charles D. Cuttler, *Northern Painting from Pucelle to Breugel* (1968); Florens Deuchler, *Gothic Art* (1973); Jacques Dupont and Cesare Gnudi, *Gothic Painting* (1954); Andrew Martindale, *The Rise of the Artist in the Early Middle Ages and Renaissance* (1972); David Robb, *The Art of the Illuminated Manuscript* (1973); Geneviève Souchal, Enzo Carli, and José Gudiol, *Gothic Painting* (1965).

England. Richard Marks and Nigel Morgan, *The Golden Age of English Manuscript Painting 1200–1500*

(1981); Margaret Rickert, *Painting in Britain: The Middle Ages,* 2nd ed. (1965).

Flanders. Shirley Blum, *Early Netherlandish Triptychs: A Study in Patronage* (1969); Max J. Friedlander, *Early Netherlandish Painting* (1967–1976); Barbara G. Lane, *The Altar and the Altarpiece: Sacramental Themes in Early Netherlandish Painting* (1984); Erwin Panofsky, *Early Netherlandish Painting* (1953); Lotte B. Philip, *The Ghent Altarpiece and the Art of Jan van Eyck* (1971).

France. François Avril, *Manuscript Painting at the Court of France: The Fourteenth Century (1310–1380)* (1978); Joan Evans, *Art in Medieval France 987–1498* (1969); Millard Meiss, *French Painting in the Time of Jean de Berry: The Late Fourteenth Century and the Patronage of the Duke; The Boucicaut Master; The Limbourgs and their Contemporaries,* 5 vols. (1967–1974); Jean Porcher, *Medieval French Miniatures* (1959); Grete Ring, *La peinture française du XVe siècle* (1949); Charles Sterling, *La peinture française: Les primitifs* (1938), and *La peinture française: Les peintures du moyen âge* (1942).

Germany and Bohemia. Erich Bachmann, ed., *Gothic Art in Bohemia* (1977); Albert Boeckler, *Deutsche Buchmalerei. Der Gotik* (1959); Antonín Matějček and Jaroslav Pešina, *Gothic Painting in Bohemia 1350–1450,* 4th ed. (1956); Hanspeter Landolt, *German Painting, the Late Middle Ages (1350–1500)* (1968); Alfred Stange, *Deutsche Malerei der Gotik* (1934–1961); Wilhelm Worringer, *Die Anfänge der Tafelmalerei in Deutschland* (1924).

Italy. Frederick Antal, *Florentine Painting and Its Social Background* (1948); Eve Borsook, *The Mural Painters of Tuscany* (1960); Enzo Carli, *Italian Primitives: Panel Painting of the Twelfth and Thirteenth Centuries* (1965); Frederick Hartt, *History of Italian Renaissance Art,* 2nd ed. (1974); Millard Meiss, *Painting in Florence and Siena After the Black Death* (1951), and *Giotto and Assisi* (1960); Robert Oertel, *Early Italian Painting to 1400* (1968); Mario Salmi, *Italian Miniatures,* 2nd ed. (1957); Alistair Smart, *The Dawn of Italian Painting 1250–1400* (1978); James Stubblebine, ed., *Giotto: The Arena Chapel Frescoes* (1969); Pietro Toesca, *Storia dell'arte italiana,* I, *Il Medioevo* (1927), and II, *Il Trecento* (1951); Raimond van Marle, *The Development of the Italian Schools of Painting,* 19 vols. (1923–1938); John White, *Art and Architecture in Italy 1250–1400* (1966).

Spain. José Gudiol Ricart, *Pintura Gótica* (1955); Chandler R. Post, *A History of Spanish Painting,* I–XI (1930–1953, repr. 1970).

ROBERT G. CALKINS

[See also **Bible Moralisée; Book of Hours; Byzantine Art; Flemish Painting; Fresco Painting; Glass, Stained; Gothic Architecture; Gothic, International Style; Guilds of Artists; Icons, Manufacture of; Manuscript Illumination: Western European; Psalter;** and individual artists.]

GOTHIC ART: SCULPTURE

FRANCE

The Gothic style in sculpture was born around 1150 in the Île-de-France. From there it spread across Europe, transforming local Romanesque styles until, by the late thirteenth century, it had become an international idiom. The greatest cathedral projects were concentrated in northern France, so that this area maintained its artistic hegemony throughout the twelfth and thirteenth centuries.

French Gothic sculpture differs from the Romanesque, which preceded it, in the degree of naturalism of form, the comprehensiveness of iconographic schemes, and the rigorous organization of portal and facade. Individual figures are rendered more naturalistically in volume, proportion, and texture. Drapery patterns help to define the position of the body or to establish the weight and texture of the material, whereas in the Romanesque a single pattern might unify all the elements of a field. On the other hand, as if to counteract the exploration of the corporeal and the particular, the thematic content of the

Chartres Cathedral, right door of the Western (Royal) Portal, *ca.* 1145. PHOTOGRAPH COURTESY OF W. S. STODDARD

Gothic portal is more lofty and universal, lacking the narrative detail or popular anecdote of Romanesque examples. In a Gothic Last Judgment, for example, the concern is the redemption of the soul; representations of the virtuous life and the Intercessors are as important as the final division of the blessed and damned.

The sophistication of Gothic iconographic programs reflects the new rigor of Scholastic argument, which set out theses in logical order from the most essential or general to the particular or merely illustrative. In the portal the ordered relationship of architectural parts allows such a temporal sequence to be translated into visual terms. The center of attention, over the door, is the tympanum, which contains the dominant theme. The archivolts, the concentric frames around the tympanum, contain figures that are subordinate to the tympanum in size and marginal placement. The closer to the tympanum, the more important is the class of archivolt figures. The jamb figures, in the setbacks from the exterior surface of the wall to the portal, are subordinate to the tympanum because they are in diagonal positions, like flanking courtiers. The small console figures and basement reliefs serve to identify the jamb figures above them or to narrow their significance. A Romanesque portal could harbor diverse scenes from many different sources, not always rigorously related to the central theme, but the vast reaches of the Gothic portal had to be strictly ordered, and the elements had to be familiar in order to be understood. Only on the west facade of Rheims do the jamb figures turn completely freely toward one another and away from the door, for there are no tympana to which they must defer.

At the beginning of the twelfth century the Île-de-France had no sculptural tradition; therefore the sculptors of the revolutionary west facades of St. Denis (*ca.* 1140) and Chartres (*ca.* 1145) had to be found in other regions, primarily Burgundy, to judge from the floral ornament and drapery style. But the slender figures addossed to columns are a new invention. They bear only the most superficial resemblance to the niche figures of Provence or the relief

Virgin being raised from her tomb by angels. Detail of the lintel of the central portal on the west facade of the Cathedral of Notre Dame, Senlis, *ca.* 1170. PHOTOGRAPH COURTESY OF JAMES AUSTIN

figures of Languedoc, and these statue-columns are integrated into a new portal design. Because of their diagonal or splayed position, the jambs with their statues, as well as the archivolts, are subordinated to the tympanum. French sculptors grasped the indivisibility of this composition and adopted the whole rather than borrowing parts.

The west facade of Chartres was the model for a generation of sculptors. Comparing this central tympanum with the Romanesque tympanum from Moissac (*ca.* 1115), also representing the Apocalyptic Vision, reveals the new order of the Gothic form. The dramatic and spiritual excitement of the earlier work is considerably reduced. The figures are severely regimented at the same time that they are more naturalistically rendered, even to fur and feathers on the apocalyptic beasts that symbolize the Evangelists. At Moissac all forms share the same overlapping ribbon motif, which contributes to the visual excitement. Following the Gospel text, the twenty-four Elders are seated around the figure of Christ. At Chartres the Elders are relegated to the archivolts, while the

Apostles, mentioned in Matthew's description of the Last Judgment (24:31), line up on the lintel. Whereas judgment had only been implied in the apocalyptic vision of John, it is made specific at Chartres with the addition of the Apostles.

Such levels of allusion and significance typify the Gothic program. In the right portal at Chartres the Nativity of Christ and the Presentation in the Temple are arranged so as to underscore the sacrificial significance of the Incarnation, both liturgical (Christ offered upon the altar) and symbolic (Christ in the manger offered to the faithful, the ox and ass). As Adolf Katzenellenbogen has shown, even the statue-columns refer both to Old Testament kings, queens, and priests and to their medieval counterparts.

The force of structural logic, felt in the clear division of lintel and tympanum and in the rolled form of the archivolt with its discrete voussoir units, is most clearly illustrated by the statue-columns. The delicately garbed figures with their finely modeled,

Detail of the Last Judgment pier, Strasbourg Cathedral, *ca.* 1230. FOTO MARBURG/ART RESOURCE

Jamb figures. Detail of the central portal on the west facade of Amiens Cathedral, begun 1220. FOTO MARBURG/ART RESOURCE

618

expressive heads are still obedient to the form and site of the columns; their hands are aligned on the vertical axis; their contours are closed; their verticality is exaggerated through elongation. Even in the freestanding figures of the thirteenth century, the echo of the structural column will be felt in the solidity, repetition, and closed contour of the forms. Only occasionally will a pose or gesture threaten this calm order. The long tradition of architectural sculpture had a conservative influence on the jamb figure and on relief sculpture in France, but this formal discipline was also the basis of its strength.

Gothic sculpture changes very rapidly from 1140 to 1260, taking a new direction about every twenty years. Around 1170 an emphatically naturalistic style, stressing the articulation of the figures, developed and spread across Europe. A portal celebrating the Virgin, north of Paris at Senlis (*ca.* 1170), provides an early example. The lintel portrays her Death and Assumption while the tympanum illustrates a new scene, Christ crowning the Virgin in heaven. Without Gospel authority and with only the most poetic model in the Song of Solomon, this invention immediately gained acceptance because it reflected popular devotion to the Virgin while embodying the ecclesiastical idea of the establishment of the church in heaven. As the earthly monarchies grew stronger, the church reasserted the supremacy of the heavenly king and queen with this reflection of the worldly ritual of coronation.

Yet at Senlis theological abstraction is bodied forth in passionately human forms, none more winning than the flurry of angels, sleeves rolled up, lifting the Virgin's body heavenward. The breath of drama enlivens the jamb statues: Abraham raises his knife to sacrifice his son, and St. John baptizes a figure kneeling at his feet. The jamb figures, which also include Samuel, Moses, David, Isaiah, Jeremiah, and Simeon, were the most prominent prototypes of Christ, but their actions here particularly prefigure the sacraments of the church such as the Eucharistic sacrifice and baptism. In the archivolts the genealogical ancestors of Christ and the Virgin are entwined in a vinelike Tree of Jesse. This preoccupation with legitimacy of bloodline is also evident in contemporary chronicles of the Capetians, uneasy successors to the Carolingians. Even as the Gothic program seems to become more systematically theological, it reflects the political concerns of the period.

While Senlis still owes a debt to Chartres in having drapery patterned all over with pencil-thin folds, it may be placed in the so-called "Style 1200" phase

Joseph. Detail of the Presentation Portal, Rheims Cathedral, *ca.* 1230. PHOTOGRAPH COURTESY OF JAMES AUSTIN

because of the rigorous definition of the body and the extreme actions. Such a proud display of the understanding of the body presupposes some fresh contact with the classical tradition through contemporary Byzantine works such as the mosaics of Norman Sicily or portable icons. The latter may have served as inspiration for the metalworkers of the Meuse and Rhine valleys: the shrines of Nicholas of Verdun (from the 1180's) demonstrate a striking understanding of classical drapery, facial types, and even iconographical motifs. But the translation of two-dimensional and often miniature forms into large-scale sculpture was an even more challenging task. At Laon (*ca.* 1195) the drapery, more varied than at Senlis, has smooth areas where the limbs press against the cloth, fine folds of uneven width, and bunches caught about the limbs. At Paris a torso from the central portal of Notre Dame (now in the Musée de Cluny) looks like a provincial Roman work, especially as the depressions between the folds resemble those made with a running drill, a tool favored in late antiquity.

The transepts of Chartres (1194–1225) comprise the largest French project in this style, having three portals on each transept. The Last Judgment tym-

Detail of commemorative tomb for the Capetian kings, St. Denis, *ca.* 1240. JEAN ROUBIER

panum on the south is again calm and orderly. The Intercessors, the Virgin and St. John the Evangelist, sit flanking Christ and turned toward him, their full, rounded forms revealed through the thin drapery. The difference in scale is reduced in the interest of naturalism. Below, the Elect and Damned march off in orderly fashion to their respective rewards, the assymmetrical nature of which is mitigated by relegating the particulars of heaven and hell to the archivolts. While the Romanesque Last Judgment (see Conques or Autun) had portrayed the momentous drama of the Last Day in imaginative detail, the Gothic portal emphasized the Way to Eternal Life as taught and lived by the Apostles, who serve as examples rather than judges. Virtues and Vices and Martyrs and Confessors provide further lessons. In particular it is the presence of the Intercessors that signals the new meaning, reminding the beholder of the Crucifixion (as does Christ, who shows his wounds rather than condemn) and promising redemption to the penitent. Rather than merely contemplating in terror the mysterious ways of God, the beholder is encouraged to seek the good offices of the church and to study the models offered him.

The Last Judgment was transformed into a didactic program on the theme of salvation at the same time that the Coronation of the Virgin (the central portal of the north transept) was introduced to symbolize the establishment of the Eternal Church, the Intercessor, in heaven. These two scenes become canonical, signifying in their totality the Era under the Law (the prophets), the beginning of the Era of Grace (the Assumption of the Virgin), and its end with the Last Judgment.

The most recent additions to Chartres, the transept porches, were decorated with some of its most appealing figures: St. Modeste (north transept), who turns about her freestanding pier in one long and sensuous flow, and St. Roland (or Theodore, south transept), who stands with his weight on one leg and has the texture of his stubble beard, chain mail, and soft, linen tunic marvelously rendered. It is this late style of Chartres that immediately turns up at Strasbourg (*ca.* 1230) with a peculiarly Germanic intensity and an even more emphatic naturalism. The Death of the Virgin, inserted into a round Romanesque arch, is isolated, with little theological apparatus, as a touching human drama told through the tragic expressions and gestures of the Apostles, the broken contour of the Virgin's body, and the excited play of drapery. The large figures of Ecclesia and Synagoga, unlike French jamb figures, were placed

Elizabeth. From the choir of Bamberg Cathedral, after 1225. STAATLICHE BILDSTELLE, BERLIN

Crucifixion. Detail of the choir screen in Naumburg Cathedral, *ca.* 1250. STAATLICHE BILDSTELLE, BERLIN

on pedestals rather than before columns. While resembling St. Modeste at Chartres, they move more freely. The instability of Synagoga, her feet too close together, her broken spear echoing her bowed head, is contrasted with the firmly supported, confident Ecclesia. The clinging drapery, heavy coils of hair, and soft flesh are rendered illusionistically as though the last veil of stone, still present at Chartres, were lifted (see vol. 4, p. 371). The lively and sensuous quality of these particular personifications may seem anomalous, but the sculptor (likely German and trained at Chartres) and presumably his clerical adviser apparently were not much interested in the abstruse or exegetical approach to themes. No better example of the divergence from the French approach may be found than the Last Judgment pier inside the church at Strasbourg, where the figures of Apostles, angels, and Christ emerge from the column in an entirely quixotic fashion. Such tampering with a central theme and with a traditionally structural element would be unthinkable in France.

At the moment that the naturalistic style was being adopted in many artistic centers in Europe, a new style, ideal and abstract, was created in Paris, which had only recently become the permanent seat of the French monarchy. It is tempting to call this a "court style," to see the abstract forms and remote and elegant physiognomies as expressions of aristocratic taste, but the Capetians were not the chief patrons of Notre Dame nor was this style dominant at the cathedral. The recent discovery of some twenty-two heads from the statues of the kings' gallery along with fragments from several portals reveals the great diversity of talent working there in the first quarter of the thirteenth century. Sculptors from Sens were responsible for some of the intensely soulful heads as well as the dado reliefs of the west facade (central and left portals) with their fluid forms, among the most engaging products of the Style 1200. The style of the Coronation Portal tympanum over the left doorway (*ca.* 1210), however, is totally different. The heads, almost identical, are impassive.

The outlines of the bodies are stiffly rectangular, and the skirts fall in harsh pleats that stress the stone. Each figure is controlled by its position in the design rather than by its role in a scene. Any ambiguity in the significance of the tympanum is banished by conflating the Death and Assumption into one scene so that the body of the Virgin, the Ark of the New Covenant, is placed directly above the Ark of the Old Covenant flanked by kings and prophets of the Old Testament. The tympanum is now self-sufficient.

Although the jamb figures were destroyed in the Revolution, the Paris archivolt figures survive and closely resemble the jamb figures of Amiens, begun in 1220, so that we may presume that the Paris shop moved to that site. The Amiens figures stand upon flat platforms rather than narrow, humped bases, the repetitive pleats of their garments emphasizing the rotundity of their forms as do the flutes of Doric columns. These are the first jamb figures to appear truly detached and rounded, but the sculptors set them free very cautiously, stressing stability, verticality, and stoniness, especially in the Apostles of the cen-

tral portal. The jamb figures of the Coronation Portal, however, enact the Annunciation, Visitation, and Presentation almost without disturbing the columnar order. Old Testament prophets stand against the projecting buttresses so that the three portals are linked by the continuous line of large-scale figures.

One of the Amiens masters next appears at Rheims, where he executed an Annunciation as well as the Virgin and Simeon of the Presentation for the west facade central portal. The artists of Rheims eagerly adopted his innovations, the independent stance and the volume, while rejecting his severely stony rendering. To judge the impact of his figures, one may compare the Visitation Master's works made before and after the Amiens Master's arrival. Peter and Paul from the north transept Judgment portal (*ca.* 1225) and the Virgin and Elizabeth from the central portal (*ca.* 1230) are distinguished by the same dazzling virtuosity in their classical drapery and heads, but the earlier pair, frontal and relieflike, teeter on narrow bases, while the latter stand or turn quite independent of the wall, their movements and their bulk underscored by the wrapping of the mantles.

Facade of the Cathedral of Siena, after 1280. ALINARI/ART RESOURCE

Head of a prophet. From the west facade of Strasbourg Cathedral, begun 1277. FOTO MARBURG/ART RESOURCE

The daring break of the Visitation figures from the restrictions of the column was surpassed during the same campaign by the twisting, pivoting figure of Joseph from the Presentation. The great, fanning bowl-like folds of the mantle represent the movement of the concealed body. The delicate balance between rational body and expressive drapery has been relinquished here in the interests of a full spatial movement.

Rheims is the most intriguing of all the great cathedrals. Amiens appears quite homogeneous in style and consistent in program; it is often cited as a kind of canon with its three west portals dedicated to the Last Judgment, Coronation, and local saints. The Chartres transepts are somewhat more complex because changes were made in structure and program during the construction, and several distinct shop styles may be identified. Rheims, however, seems to have been created by a great number of mature masters, each working at the top of his form as if inspired by the competition rather than conforming to the ideas of a headmaster. There is little conventional or derivative work even in the archivolts of the upper story. The inner west facade (*ca.* 1250) alone contains a variety of approaches to the figure in the niche: the silhouette, the volume in space, and the flickering light and dark image.

After Rheims there is a retrenchment. The experiments in movement, for example, threatening the traditional structural logic of the portal, do not persist for long. The Apostles of the Ste. Chapelle (*ca.* 1241), which resemble the Joseph in their puffy slanted eyes and elegantly curled beards, are muffled in drapery whose large hollows and peaks no longer signify the movement of the body. The broad surfaces were suitable for brightly painted patterns and were visible in the dim interior light. The single-story chapel, all glass and paint and mosaic, was a monumental reliquary for the newly acquired Crown of Thorns, the jewel of Louis IX's kingdom. The precious quality of these figures appears appropriate in this setting.

Another group of Apostles from Ste. Chapelle, now in the Musée de Cluny, represents a totally different stylistic direction, reasserting the balance between body and drapery and between stone and the texture represented. This style, called "classical" by César Gnudi, persists for a generation. Found first in the environs of Paris, in the south transept of St. Denis (*ca.* 1240), the tomb of Dagobert in the choir of the same church (*ca.* 1245), and the Bourges choir screen (*ca.* 1260), it is distinguished by rather sub-

Virgin and Child. Detail of a portal by Claus Sluter of the Chartreuse de Champmol, Dijon, late 14th century. FOTO MARBURG/ART RESOURCE

dued movements and studied gestures and, in reliefs, by drapery patterns that extend across several figures. In the commemorative tomb campaigns at St. Denis (1264) the Capetian tombs represent the last of the "classical" style while the Carolingian tombs reveal the first signs of a petrification of the formula.

GERMANY

German sculptors adopted French ideas with such understanding that it seems likely that some had worked on French cathedrals rather than merely having sketched statues in the shops. From 1225 on at Bamberg the impact of Rheims is found everywhere, but it is modified by the local tradition represented by the prophet figures in the large choir reliefs with their prominent, fleshy features and ropelike loops of drapery. The Virgin of the Visitation, clearly modeled upon her counterpart at Rheims, still has the dimpled cheek and long nose of the prophets. The Elizabeth ventures far beyond the Rheims model in the haunting, prophetic expression and in the dramatic waterfall of her mantle. These great German works are in no way diminished by the fact of their French inspiration.

The Master of the Naumburg cathedral choir screen (*ca.* 1250) defies comparison; like Giotto, he seems to have interpreted the Passion completely afresh, to have found gestures and expressions for each of the five scenes on the choir partition as though none had been depicted before. The stage space of the Last Supper, moreover, is unique in its continuous planes knit together by the varied poses. In the west choir of Naumburg the twelve lifesize figures of long-dead donors astonish the observer with their varied facial types and repertory of expressions. The heavy drapery, while inspired by certain forms from Rheims, is here made to enhance the strong expressive gestures signifying inner torment, fear, complaisance, foolishness. Little wonder that German sculptors elevated the Wise and Foolish Virgins and the Virtues from their subordinate place in French portals to prominence in the jambs as at Magdeburg or at Strasbourg on the west facade. The rift between German and French sculpture widened at mid-century as the German artists sought emotional intensity and the French explored formal patterns.

ITALY

Italian sculptors were less dependent upon French ideas in the Gothic period because classical sculpture provided them with an immediate and congenial source of inspiration. In the period around 1220 to 1250 Emperor Frederick II Hohenstaufen commissioned astonishingly competent adaptations of Roman busts, figures, and capitals for his castles and gates in Campania and Apulia. Nicola Pisano (*fl.* 1258–1278), called "da Apulia" in documents of 1266, may have worked for Frederick, a thesis supported by his thorough understanding of classical sarcophagi. His first known work, the Pisa Baptistery pulpit, completed in 1269, is his most classicizing with its temple fronts, heavy and noble figures, and remarkable nude Hercules personifying Fortitude. His next work, the Siena pulpit (1265), is already modified by French elements such as hipshot poses, certain drapery designs, such as arabesque hems and fanning tube folds, and softer treatment of

forms. John White has suggested that Nicola found these Gothic forms more powerfully expressive and more appropriate to the contemporary interpretation of the New Testament themes than his heroic classicizing style, and certainly this seems a more satisfactory reason for the change than the theory that his very young son, Giovanni, introduced the new spirit. Nicola's adoption of Gothic forms did not mean that he denied his training, however, for his figures retain their individuality and independence. The authority of the frame or wall plane is never as strong as it is in France. Nicola's special talent, later exploited by his son, lies in the creation of figures that move freely in several planes. As in third-century sarcophagi, background figures are represented slightly above the foreground figures but projected forward so that almost all have the same prominence.

Nicola's immensely gifted son, Giovanni Pisano (*ca.* 1250–after 1314), also produced marble pulpits, but his are marked by elongated, intensely passionate figures, and by deep undercutting, variously textured surfaces, and great hollows between figures, which give emotional color to the scenes. Where Nicola's figures are massive and noble, Giovanni's are eaters of shadows. The cathedral of Siena, designed by Giovanni in the last twenty years of the thirteenth century, may be compared with a contemporary French program, the transepts of Rouen Cathedral. At Siena the large-scale sculptures, confined to areas outside the portal embrasures and above the level of the lintel, represent sibyls and classical figures and prophets who prophesied the birth of the Virgin or Christ. These figures lean out from their shallow niches as if to speak across the spaces of the facade or to peer around corners. Deep undercutting and large movements allow one to grasp individual characterization even in glaring sun and at a great distance. At Rouen deep niches confine the figures and make a homogeneous pattern of light and dark across towers and walls. Even the small jamb figures are set in niches, while the basement zone, now extending high up the wall, is covered with innumerable reliefs in quatrefoils. The crowded tympana represent the Last Judgment and the Passion in many small scenes. The decorative and miniature style of the sculpture seems appropriate to the narrative garrulity of the scenes. Siena, in comparison, harks back to the early-thirteenth-century cathedrals in its monumental scale and single-minded theme while differing from these in the placement of the figures and their large movements.

LATE GOTHIC FORMS

For some 140 years France had exported the latest word on style while allowing few importations. German sculptors might work at Rheims, but their work did not affect their French colleagues, immune to the strong expressions and intense naturalism. Eventually the creative ferment that produced such various works as Paris, Chartres, and Amiens all in the same few years, or the marvels of Rheims over a forty-year period, was bound to slow down, lacking a new reactive agent. There are other reasons, including the diminished patronage of church and court and the greater importance of interior sculpture such as choir screens and votive images, which, smaller in scale and more brightly painted, demanded less of the sculptor. Without large projects to draw them together, sculptors became isolated and often specialized.

It is not surprising, then, that we notice less reliance on French models abroad. In France itself the forty-year-old portal of the south transept of Paris was copied quite exactly at Meaux in 1300. In Germany the west facade of the cathedral of Strasbourg (begun 1277) breaks away from the contemporary French conventions to carry on in the direction the Joseph Master of Rheims had indicated. The Virtues and Prophets lean out of their niches, their bold gestures accentuated by the broadly drawn drapery. Their expressions are emphasized to the point of caricature. The Apostles and Virgin in the choir of Cologne Cathedral (*ca.* 1290), while more elegant, nonetheless share this strong spatial movement and expressiveness. The Germans, moreover, invented a new image for the age, that of the terribly tortured Crucified Christ, sometimes so scarred as to appear stricken with the Black Death (see the frontispiece to this volume). In response to the demand for votive images the Germans produced individual groups like the Visitation, the Pietà, and Christ with St. John from the Last Supper. As in France in the fourteenth century, church furniture, tombs, and choir screens or retables provided the bulk of sculptural commissions; as a result the few architectural programs have the scale and busy quality of interior works.

ENGLAND

If we mention England only now, it is because that country's sculpture was for the most part confined to decorative elements, such as capitals and corbels, and to tombs. Cistercian iconoclasm may be in part to blame for the lack of a continuous monumental tradition. Intermittent challenges, such as the vast program for Wells Cathedral (begun around 1200), suffer from this lack of experience; the great columnar statues of Amiens have inspired thin, planar figures of uneven quality, buried in deep niches. The decoration of Westminster Abbey in 1245 called forth the best artists King Henry III could find in a task that was more congenial. In the little that remains the angels with fluttering draperies in the spandrels of the south transept as well as the Annunciation of the Chapter House reveal a delicate linearity heretofore associated with English manuscript illumination. While much of the monumental sculpture suffers fron uneven treatment or from conservative dependence upon old French models, the tombs are frequently original and of high quality, whether produced by the Purbeck marblers of London or by the competent provincial shops. The knightly effigies with crossed legs and lively gestures comprise some of the most dramatic figures in the English repertory. But by the late thirteenth century the elaborate foliage, cusped arches, and finials on tabernacles and baldachinos begin to swamp the small-scale figures and invade all parts of the architectural structure. As Lawrence Stone points out, the decorator has triumphed over the architect.

In France in the fourteenth century the most important works, while carved for interiors, remain large in scale. The fine series of saints carved for Enguerran de Marigny, counselor to Philip IV the Fair, for his church at Ecouis, the choir screen for Notre Dame in Paris, and the endless series of variations on the Apostles of the Ste. Chapelle, all have a largeness of design suggesting that the grand, monumental spirit was still alive. Around mid-century the ravages of the Hundred Years War restricted sculptural production to a few tombs, but the reign of Charles V (1364–1380) saw a revival of monumental sculpture whose quality makes up for the limited quantity. A series of statues representing Charles V and his counselors (*ca.* 1376), high on a buttress of Amiens, is notable for the sensitive portraits as well as the fashionable hats and mantles whose lines are a welcome relief from the stereotyped wrappings of holy figures. The moving portraits of Charles V and his queen, Jeanne of Bourbon, in the Louvre may once have flanked an entrance to the old Louvre palace. At the end of the century Jean de Marville and Claus Sluter turned the portal of the Chartreuse de Champmol at Dijon into a stage. In the embrasures the kneeling duke and duchess of Burgundy are presented by their patron saints to the Virgin and Child on the trumeau. The complete and deliberate undermining of structural logic is revolutionary, both in the broad, swaying movement of the Virgin in her key position against the support of the lintel, and in the kneeling and bending figures who no longer recall their genesis as columns.

Gothic sculpture encompasses much more than architectural sculpture, but in France it was born on the wall and its development was influenced by this genesis. The advent of the Dutch Sluter and other sculptors who had acquired a foreign taste for verism or naturalism signals the end of this influence.

BIBLIOGRAPHY

France. Françoise Baron, "Le décor sculpté et peint de l'hôpital Saint-Jacques-aux-Pélerins," in *Bulletin monumental,* **109** (1951); Kurt Bauch, *Das mittelalterliche Grabbild: figürliche Grabmäler des 11. bis 15. Jahrhunderts in Europa* (1976); Alain Erlande-Brandenburg, *Les sculptures de Notre-Dame de Paris au musée de Cluny* (1982); *Les Fastes du Gothique: Le siècle de Charles V,* Paris: Exposition au Grand Palais (1981); César Gnudi, "Le jubé de Bourges et l'apogée du 'classicisme' dans la sculpture de l'Île-de-France au milieu du 13ᵉ siècle," in *Revue de l'art,* **3** (1969); Adolf Katzenellenbogen, *The Sculptural Programs of Chartres Cathedral* (1959); Hartmut Krohm, "Die Skulptur der Querhausfassaden an der Kathedrale von Rouen," in *Aachener Kunstblätter,* **40** (1971); Louise (Pillion) Lefrançois and Jean Lafond, *L'art du XIVe siècle en France* (1954); Emile Mâle, *L'art religieux de la fin du moyen âge en France,* 4th ed. (1931), and *The Gothic Image: Religious Art in France of the Thirteenth Century,* Dora Nussey, trans. (1958); Hans Reinhardt, *La cathédrale de Reims* (1963); Willibald Sauerländer, *Gothic Sculpture in France, 1140–1270,* Janet Sondheimer, trans. (1972); *The Year 1200: A Symposium,* 2 vols. (New York, 1975).

Germany. Reiner Hausherr, "Der Kölner Domchor und seine Ausstattung. Bericht über ein Colloquium in Köln. 2.–3. Nov. 1978," in *Kunstchronik,* **32** (1979); Erwin Panofsky, *Die deutsche Plastik des XI. bis XIII. Jahrhunderts,* 2 vols. (1924); Wilhelm Pinder, *Die deutsche Plastik des XIV. Jahrhunderts* (1925), and *Die deutsche Plastik des XV. Jahrhunderts* (1924); Willibald Sauerländer, "Reims und Bamberg," in *Zeitschrift für Kunstgeschichte,* **39** (1976).

Italy. John Pope-Hennessy, *Italian Gothic Sculpture* (1955); Charles Seymour, Jr., "Invention and Revival in Nicola Pisano's 'Heroic Style,'" in *Studies in Western Art, Acts of the XX International Congress of the History of Art,* I (1963), 207–226; John White, *Art and Architecture in Italy, 1250 to 1400* (1966).

England. T. S. R. Boase, *English Art 1100–1216* (1953); Peter Brieger, *English Art 1216–1307* (1957); Joan Evans, *English Art, 1307–1461* (1949); Lawrence Stone, *Sculpture in Britain: The Middle Ages* (1955).

GEORGIA SOMMERS WRIGHT

[See also **Amiens Cathedral; Archivolt; Chartres Cathedral; Column Figure; Dijon, Chartreuse de Champmol; Ecclesia and Synagoga; Gargoyle; Giovanni Pisano; Guilds of Artists; Iconography; Moissac, Church of St. Pierre; Nicola Pisano; Notre Dame, Paris, Cathedral of; Rheims Cathedral; Romanesque Art; Sainte Chapelle, Paris; Sluter, Claus; Strasbourg Cathedral; Tympanum; Westminster Abbey.**]

GOTHIC, DECORATED, an influential English architectural style that developed about 1285 in response to Rayonnant and was supplanted by Perpendicular Gothic in the 1330's. The Decorated Style has been subdivided into a geometric phase, characterized by continuous gridlike tracery and an enriched surface linearity (as in the St. Etheldreda Chapel in Ely Place in Holborn, *ca.* 1285), and a curvilinear phase, initiated by the crosses erected to commemorate the death of Queen Eleanor in 1290 and dominant by about 1310. Curvilinear Decorated Gothic relies on the ogee arch, flowing curvilinear tracery, walls patterned with ornamental motifs, and curved or polygonal surfaces. The Lady Chapel at Wells (begun by 1315) provides a fine example. Other hallmarks of the Decorated Style include the use of heraldic shields as a decorative device, crenellated cornices, and a variety of multilinear vaulting systems, particularly the tierceron, lierne, and net vault.

Star vault of the Lady Chapel, Wells Cathedral, 1315. PHOTOGRAPH BY HERBERT FELTON

626

BIBLIOGRAPHY
Jean Bony, *The English Decorated Style* (1979).

LESLIE BRUBAKER

GOTHIC, FLAMBOYANT (*cf.* French *flamboyant,* flaming), the French response to the English Decorated Style, prevalent between 1370 and 1400 but lingering through the fifteenth century. Flamboyant differs from Decorated in its retention of such Rayonnant features as a stress on verticality and a clear bay structure. Flamelike tracery is a characteristic detail. A notable example is the facade of Rouen Cathedral, begun in 1386.

BIBLIOGRAPHY
Harry Bober, "A Reappraisal of Rayonnant Architecture," in Francis Lee Utley, ed., *The Forward Movement of the Thirteenth Century* (1961); Camille Enlart, "Origine anglaise du style flamboyant," in *Bulletin monumental,* **70** (1906), and in *Archaeological Journal,* **63** (1906); Roland Sanfaçon, *L'architecture flamboyante en France* (1971); Max M. Tamir, "The English Origin of the Flamboyant Style," in *Gazette des beaux-arts,* 6th ser., **29** (1946).

LESLIE BRUBAKER

GOTHIC, INTERNATIONAL STYLE, a term (*courant international*) first articulated by Louis Courajod at the end of the nineteenth century to describe late Gothic art of the period from about 1360 to 1430. Used at first in pointing out the French and Flemish contributions to Florentine sculpture, it was soon adopted by other art historians to refer to pervasive affinities, in spite of regional and individual variations, among the arts of France, England, the Netherlands, Flanders, Germany, Austria, Bohemia, northern Italy, Tuscany, and northern Spain. The art of this period was the subject of two major exhibitions in 1962, one at the Kunsthistorisches Museum in Vienna, the other at the Walters Art Gallery in Baltimore.

While some scholars question the validity of this term, it remains a useful one to suggest the close interrelationships between artistic centers and the major aristocratic families that patronized the arts at the turn of the fifteenth century. These connections and the increased mobility of artists resulted in a constant interchange of motifs, compositions, icon-

ographical innovations, and stylistic characteristics that justify the use of the term "international." The difficulties art historians have had in determining the place of origin of many works confirms the international homogeneity of the arts of the period.

The breakdown of distinctly identifiable regional styles received considerable impetus even before the blossoming of the International Gothic style with the establishment of the papal court at Avignon (1309–1377). Simone Martini was attracted to this milieu and brought with him a Sienese Gothic style already imbued with the delicate refinement at least equivalent to that found in French Gothic art, if not influenced by it. Such later Italian painters as Matteo di Giovanetti (*fl.* 1343–1366) associated with French artists in this milieu and developed not only a new degree of sumptuousness but also a new sense of landscape detail and effective illusionistic perspective that rivaled the paintings by the Lorenzetti brothers in Siena. From Avignon some artists went farther west to Catalonia, where Italian influences had already been present in the works of Ferrer Bassa in the 1340's and where additional French elements permeated the work of Luís Borrassá (*fl. ca.* 1380–1424) and of the Master of the Bañolas Altar in the fifteenth century.

At the Bohemian court, continuous contacts were maintained with the court at Avignon through the chancellor to the House of Luxembourg, John of Neumarkt. Thus Italian and French influences via Avignon were recombined with Trecento and Italo-Byzantine influences directly from Bologna and Venice in the paintings by the Master of Hohenfurth (Vyšší Brod) and the illuminated manuscripts made for the Bohemian court. Bohemian sculptors were developing a style of refined, sweet-faced statues, particularly Madonnas (*Schöne Madonnen*) enveloped with voluminous, curvilinear folds of drapery. This "soft style" (*schöner Stil* or *weicher Stil*) was disseminated throughout Bohemia, Austria, and the Rhineland, in part through the widespread influence of the Parler family of architects and sculptors, active at the end of the fourteenth century. In France this style was reflected in the sculptures of André Beauneveu (*fl.* 1363–1404) for the duke of Berry, and it served as a point of departure for the intense, psychologically powerful statues of Claus Sluter for the Chartreuse de Champmol near Dijon. The soft style permeated painting as well and appears in the panels by Master Theodoric for Karlstein Castle in Bohemia. It also dominates the paintings of the Cologne

School, culminating in the tender refinement and sumptuous color of Stefan Lochner in the 1440's.

In England, connections between the court and Bohemia were established by the marriage of Richard II with Anne of Bohemia in 1382. The Wilton Diptych (London, National Gallery), which depicts Richard II before the Virgin Mary, manifests such a mixture of English and Bohemian, as well as French, elements that specialists have continuously questioned the origins of its painter. Continental influences from Germany and the Netherlands were also brought into England by Herman Scheere, who established an influential school of illuminators there.

In Lombardy, the court of the Visconti patronized artists who combined the elegant refinement of the French Gothic style with a new sensitivity for objective reality. Giovannino de' Grassi and Michelino da Besozzo made convincingly accurate studies of birds, animals, and plants but used them as exotic motifs in lavish miniatures and in the borders of books of hours. In Verona, Antonio Pisanello (*ca.* 1395–1455) made similar sketches and also relegated them to the role of mere detail, as in his fresco of St. George and the Princess for the church of Sant'Anastasia. Stefano da Zevio (*ca.* 1374/1375–after 1438), also active in Verona, included a myriad of accurately observed flowers in his elegant, tapestrylike painting of the Virgin in a Rose Garden.

Milan under the Visconti became an international meeting ground, attracting architects and sculptors from Germany and France for the planning and construction of Milan Cathedral. Many of these artists, such as Jacques Coene from Bruges, undoubtedly returned to the north with new repertoires of Italian-inspired motifs. Under the Visconti the International Gothic style flourished until after the middle of the fifteenth century around Milan, where Belbello da Pavia (*fl. ca.* 1434–1462), the Zavattari (*fl.* 1404–1479), and Bonifacio Bembo (*fl. ca.* 1420–1489) continued to produce brilliantly decorative paintings imbued with fantasy and filled with courtly personages.

In fifteenth-century Siena the art of Sassetta (*ca.* 1392–1450) retained the lyrical quality that had been introduced by Duccio di Buoninsegna and refined by Simone Martini. In Florence, while Masaccio and Donatello were introducing powerful representations of objective reality in the new style later termed "Renaissance," Masolino da Panicale (1383–1440/1447), Lorenzo Monaco (1370/1371–1425/1426), and Gentile da Fabriano (*ca.* 1370–1427) continued to use the lilting figures, flowing line, and sense of

pageantry found in much of the International Gothic style. Lorenzo Ghiberti (1331–1455) manifests a transition from this lyrical, late Gothic style to strongly expressive figures and experimentation with modes of perspective in the new Renaissance manner in his sculptures for the Or San Michele and reliefs for the north and east doors of the Baptistery in Florence.

The courts of the Valois in Paris and of the duke of Burgundy at Dijon were major centers for the intermingling of foreign artisans. Jean Bondol (*fl.* 1368–1381), court painter for Charles V, was from Bruges. He introduced a capability to render accurate portraits combined with the current penchant for emphatically and smoothly modeled figures. Jean Malouel (*fl. ca.* 1390–1415) from Guelders continued this heavily modeled style in his intensely religious paintings such as the tondo of the Trinitarian Pietà (Paris, Louvre). Melchior Broederlam (*fl.* 1381–1395) at Ypres in northern France employed the conical hills and stylized diminutive buildings of Trecento Italian landscapes in his wings for the altarpiece at the Chartreuse de Champmol, but gave the rocks and foliage of his landscapes a greater effect of actuality. Jacquemart de Hesdin (*fl. ca.* 1384–1409) from Flanders also used the Trecento formula for landscapes, adding blue sky and rendering them with specifically northern details and with a subdued tonal unity. Jacques Coene (*fl.* 1398–1404), also from Bruges, probably introduced Italian elements as a result of a trip to Milan. If he is in fact the Master of the Hours of the Maréchal de Boucicaut, he continued the development of objectively rendered details and introduced a new sense of atmospheric perspective into some of his landscapes. The Boucicaut Master's architectural scenes are rendered with an intuitive but effective use of diagonals to indicate space in perspective, though mitigated by the bright color patterns that restate the decorative surface of his miniatures.

The three Limbourg brothers from Guelders carried these developments to their ultimate manifestation in the miniatures of the *Très riches heures* executed for the duke of Berry between 1413 and 1416. In addition to creating convincingly naturalistic details and effective landscape space, they depicted portraits of identifiable buildings. The Limbourgs also introduced Italian and classical motifs and compositions into these miniatures. In the hunting scenes of the calendar, they achieved, together with their heightened perception of reality, an equally heightened sense of courtly pageantry and aristocratic languor juxtaposed with accurate observations of contemporary peasant life. The presence of an Italian illuminator in Paris, the Master of the Brussels Initials (sometimes identified as Zebo da Firenze), who brought with him a repertoire of motifs from the frescoes of Altichiero in Padua, the swarthily modeled figures of Niccolò da Bologna, and a brilliant palette, may have been also responsible for the further mixing of Italian and French motifs.

While Italian and Northern artists were influencing the development of French art in the first decade of the fifteenth century, artists in Paris were in turn influencing German art. Meister Francke from Hamburg was apparently trained in the circle of the Master of 1402 and the Boucicaut Master's atelier, and he shows knowledge of some of their compositions in his St. Barbara and St. Thomas altarpieces (Helsinki and Hamburg). He also manifests a dramatic intensity in gestures and expressions, a tendency that is also present in the work of the Austrian Master of Heiligenkreuz (*fl. ca.* 1410) and that erupts with expressionistic vibrancy in the work of the Master of the Rohan Hours of Louis of Anjou (Paris, Bibliothèque Nationale, MS fonds latin 9471), believed by some scholars to be of Germanic, and by others of Catalonian or Netherlandish, origin.

Concurrent with the intermingling of styles and influences was also a mixture of diverse and contrasting themes. The International Gothic style encompassed both fantasy and realism, decorative planarity and experimentation in the rendition of space, lyrical courtliness and harsh emotionalism, and fervent mysticism and heightened secularism. Such themes mirror the concurrent and complex developments of attitudes toward art, of changing religious needs and concerns, and of late-medieval society in a period of transition.

The pervasive courtliness of much of this art was largely a result of its aristocratic patronage: the nobility was therefore idealized, dressed in lavish costumes, endowed with exquisitely refined features and mannered postures, and shown participating in festive activities. The elegance of these representations matched a new interest in art as a secular artifact. The extensive collections of Charles V and of his brother Jean, duke of Berry, reveal as much an interest in the preciousness and lavishness of bindings and illuminations of manuscripts as in the contents of the texts. The love of the rare and exotic was also reflected in the collection of animals. The Visconti and the dukes of Burgundy maintained zoos and exchanged unusual animals, some of which undoubt-

edly served as live models for the drawings of Giovannino de' Grassi (*d.* 1398), but these, in turn, merely reverted to manifestations of exotic splendor appropriate for gatherings of nobles in finished paintings.

The increased secularization of the purpose and destination of art was therefore accompanied by an intensified awareness of reality. Portraits, nature studies, botanical representations, and sketches of varied physiognomic types and drapery folds show that such artists as Pisanello and Jacques Daliwes turned increasingly to recording images from direct observation. Perhaps stemming in part from this tradition, Matteo di Giovanetti's garden scenes at Avignon, an unknown Italian artist's frescoes of the Labors of the Months at the Torre Aquila in Trento, and finally the Boucicaut Master and the Limbourg brothers in manuscript illumination placed accurately observed details into a larger context in their landscapes, even though high horizon lines, elements of fantasy, and decorative, tapestrylike patterning often prevailed.

In contrast to the courtly art and to the glimpses of objective reality found within it were strong mystical and emotive strains. The ethereal images of the Master of Wittingau (*fl. ca.* 1380) in Bohemia and the harsh emotionalism of the Rohan Master in France were accompanied by a proliferation of images of pathos: the Throne of Grace Trinity, the Man of Sorrows, depictions of the wounds of Christ (arma Christi), and the Pietà. Increased emphasis on private devotion, on more immediate and meaningful religious experiences such as were provided by the Devotio Moderna, reflected the heightened spiritual needs of a society in transition. By the first decades of the fifteenth century the conventions of the aristocratic feudal society were subjected to the continuing stresses of peasant and bourgeois revolts, the grim realities of the continuing Hundred Years War with the defeat of France at the Battle of Agincourt in 1415, outbreaks of epidemics such as the one in which the Limbourgs and their patron, Jean of Berry, died in 1416, and the increasingly materialistic values of a growing mercantile society and economy. The tensions caused by these events and the resulting change in attitudes undoubtedly helped to imbue the International Gothic style with its quality of romantic poignancy.

BIBLIOGRAPHY
Exhibition catalogs. Baltimore, Walters Art Gallery, *The International Style: The Arts in Europe Around 1400*

(1962); Cologne, Kunsthalle, *Die Parler und der schöne Stil 1350–1400: Europäische Kunst unter den Luxemburgern,* 5 vols. (1978–1980); Frankfurt am Main, Liebieghaus Museum alter Plastik, *Kunst um 1400 am Mittelrhein: Ein Teil der Wirklichkeit* (1976); Hamburg, Kunsthalle, *Meister Francke und die Kunst um 1400* (1969); Vienna, Kunsthistorisches Museum, *European Art Around 1400* (1962).

Studies. Liana Castelfranchi Vegas, *International Gothic Art in Italy,* B. D. Phillipps, trans. (1966); Albert Châtelet, *Les primitifs septentrionaux: La peinture dans l'Europe septentrionale et la péninsule Ibérique au XVe siècle* (1979), 23–46; Louis Courajod, *Leçons professées à l'École du Louvre 1887–1896,* II (1901); Max Dvořák, "Die Illuminatoren des Johann von Neumarkt," in *Jahrbuch der kunsthistorischen Sammlungen des allerhöchsten Kaiserhauses,* **22** (1901); Bella Martens, *Meister Francke,* 2 vols. (1929); Erwin Panofsky, *Early Netherlandish Painting* (1953), 51–74; Eleanor P. Spencer, "The International Style and Fifteenth Century Illuminations," in *Parnassus,* **12,** no. 3 (1940); Pietro Toesca, *La pittura e la miniatura nella Lombardia* (1912), 453ff.

ROBERT G. CALKINS

[See also **Avignon; Gothic Art: Painting and Manuscript Illumination; Manuscript Illumination: Western European; Patronage; Très Riches Heures;** and names of individual artists.]

GOTHIC, MANUELINE, a national style of architecture and sculptural decoration in Portugal named after Manuel I (1495–1521), during whose reign it reached its greatest popularity, although hybridizations of the style continued well into the late sixteenth century.

Architecture and sculpture in the Manueline style demonstrate a predilection for heightened relief, robust curves, and dramatic spatial volumes while maintaining clarity of line. Their designs boast a plethora of fanciful features, such as twisted columns and variegated silhouettes. The style draws on a number of traditions: Gothic, northern European, and the Portuguese interest in nautical forms that reflects contemporary exploration activities. Typical buildings include the unfinished chapels and royal church at Belém in Lisbon (begun 1502) and the Church of Jesus at Setúbal (1489–1498), both involving the work of Diogo Boytac (or Boutaca); the nave and chapter house of the Monastery of Christ at Tomar (1510–1514) by Diogo Arruda, and the tower at Belém on the Tagus River (1515–1520) by Francisco de Arruda. Major sculptors include Diogo Pires

Vault of the Capela Mór of the Church of Jesus, Setúbal, by Diogo Boytac, 1492–1498. FROM REYNALDO DOS SANTOS, *O ESTILO MANUELINO* (1952)

the Younger (*fl.* 1511–1535) and Nicholas Chanterene (*fl.* 1517–1551).

BIBLIOGRAPHY

Reynaldo dos Santos, *O estilo manuelino* (1952) and *L'art portugais* (1953); George Kubler and Martin Soria, *Art and Architecture in Spain and Portugal and Their American Dominions, 1500 to 1800* (1959).

JENNIFER E. JONES

[See also **Gothic Architecture.**]

GOTHIC, PERPENDICULAR, an English architectural style that emerged along with Decorated Gothic from the French Rayonnant. The style was formulated in the lower story of St. Stephen's Chapel at Westminster Palace (1292–1297) but only came

Henry VII's chapel at Westminster Abbey, 1503–1509. PHOTO-
GRAPH BY HERBERT FELTON, COURTESY OF B. T. BATSFORD

GOTHIC, RAYONNANT ("radiating" Gothic), a term derived from the vast, spoked rose windows characteristic of the style; also known as the Court Style of St. Louis since it began early in Louis IX's reign (1226–1270). Rayonnant introduced no innovative structural features, but treated older systems in a new way. Interiors such as that of the rebuilt St. Denis (*ca.* 1235) give an impression of linear and skeletal weightlessness; the Ste. Chapelle, dedicated in 1248, looks like an insubstantial and jeweled glass reliquary. These effects are due to a unification of the interior space through an overall surface pattern, the introduction of the compound pier with its hierarchic arrangement of slender shafts connecting all levels of the elevation like a filigree net, and the victory of void over solid forms, achieved by glazing the triforium and integrating it with the clerestory. Exteriors became increasingly structurally unrelated to interiors, and also succumbed to the passion for surface treatment; the gabled motif proliferated from the 1240's and external decoration became progressively more brittle and complex, as exemplified by the upper parts of the chevet at Cologne Cathedral (*ca.* 1270–1320).

BIBLIOGRAPHY

Robert Branner, *St. Louis and the Court Style in Gothic Architecture* (1965); Jean Bony, *French Gothic Architecture of the 12th & 13th Centuries* (1983), 357–423.

LESLIE BRUBAKER

[See also **Cathedral; Gothic Architecture; Sainte Chapelle, Paris; St. Denis, Abbey Church; Tracery.**]

GOTHS. See **Ostrogoths; Visigoths.**

fully into its own in 1332 with William Ramsey's Chapter House for Old St. Paul's in London. The style differs from Decorated Gothic in its retention of such Rayonnant features as vertical attenuation and its rejection of curvilinear for rectilinear forms, a shift particularly obvious in the tracery. By the 1360's and 1370's Perpendicular Gothic had matured; it continued to dominate English architecture until the mid sixteenth century. Characteristic features include rows or tiers of cusped arches set against a blank wall and fan vaults, as in Henry VII's Chapel at Westminster Abbey.

BIBLIOGRAPHY

John H. Harvey, "St. Stephen's Chapel and the Origin of the Perpendicular Style," in *Burlington Magazine,* **88** (1946); Maurice Hastings, *St Stephen's Chapel and Its Place in the Development of Perpendicular Style in England* (1955).

LESLIE BRUBAKER

[See also **Ramsey, William.**]

GOTLAND is a Baltic Sea island (between 57° and 58° N. latitude) about fifty miles from the mainland of Sweden, of which country it has been a formal part since the seventeenth century. The island is seventy-seven miles long by about thirty miles wide. Its importance in the Middle Ages derived from its location astride major trade routes and the wealth accumulated by its inhabitants. Archaeological (especially numismatic) evidence provides ample testimony to the volume, variety, and extent of its commerce.

While the archaeological record of the economic life of Gotland stretches back to the Bronze Age (before 800 B.C.), it is not until the prime of the Roman Empire that its "subterranean archive" becomes significant to medievalists. Coin hoards of the Roman period abound; more than 5,000 Roman coins have been found in Gotland's soil. The coins suggest that strong cultural and economic ties to the Roman Empire had developed prior to A.D. 400. The wealth of the island undoubtedly attracted robbers and other enemies to Gotland in the Migration Period.

The political history of the island before 900 is unknown. According to tradition, it became subject to the Swedish kings at Uppsala about a century earlier. Generally speaking, throughout the Late Iron Age (400–800) Gotland was more closely allied with the Baltic islands of Öland and Bornholm than with the Swedish mainland. Similarities between settlement sites, methods of building construction, deposits of treasure, fortifications, and above all burial customs and grave goods show that the inhabitants of the three islands shared the same cultural traditions, and may have been a single people.

No towns existed on Gotland prior to the twelfth century. The commerce of the island, based on agricultural products and the transshipment of luxury imported goods, was undertaken by local farmer-merchants rather than by foreign visitors. This is proved by the widespread distribution of coin hoards of all periods. The absence of islandwide political unity may be inferred from the presence of sanctuary-fortresses (*tilflugtsborge*), which seem to have served only a temporary, defensive purpose rather than an offensive role, or to have been erected by an individual for his personal retinue.

The meaning of the coin hoards on Gotland has been much discussed. They do not necessarily indicate an era of violence or represent religious traditions. An example of the latter would be the need to present votive offerings to deities in the form of treasure. However, the period of greatest activity in the burial of hoards on Gotland, shortly after 550, corresponds to similar activity on Öland (where most hoards were deposited about 480–500) and Bornholm (around 500), as well as to a period of intense fortress building on the Swedish mainland, especially in central Sweden around Lake Mälaren (Uppland). This would seem to confirm that most hoards were buried in time of war, but does not explain the deposit of all of them.

Another significant feature of the archaeological record of Gotland in the pre-Christian centuries (before 1050) is the carved pictorial stones (*Bildsteine*), which date mostly to the period 400–800. They are commemorative in nature but were not (or almost never) placed over graves. At least 250 examples, averaging six feet in height, are known. They are basically phallic in shape. The stones are ornamented with spiral-and-interlace and geometric designs, but their chief importance is their representation of the mythology and religion of pagan Scandinavia. As pictorial art they constitute a rare survival, since most pre-Christian Scandinavian art that exists today is abstract ornament.

Gold is particularly common in the treasure hoards of the Migration Period. The finds include bracteates (thin gold disks stamped on one side only); gold fogies (thin rectangular plates the size of a watch fob); and Byzantine lightweight gold solidi, minted largely in the period 408–518 and apparently deposited around 550. More than 200 examples of such solidi have been found on Gotland.

Beginning in the early ninth century, the treasure hoards of Gotland are largely of silver, and the silver coins found in such hoards are almost entirely Kufic (Islamic). The number of western European and Byzantine coins is quite small. In the first half of the ninth century, the number of coins in each hoard is modest, but there are at least 32 such hoards from Gotland, with a total of more than 4,000 coins. There is a particular concentration of coins deposited around 860. In the tenth century an unusually large number of deposits was made in the decade after 940. The individual hoards increase greatly in size, with six Gotland hoards containing more than 1,000 coins each. In the late tenth century (after 970) there is a remarkable decline in the number and size of the hoards for about thirty years, but the first half of the eleventh century witnessed the deposit of the greatest number and largest hoards of any period in Gotland's history. This may have been a most troubled time for the island—probably related to the domination of the Baltic by Cnut the Great of Denmark and the establishment of a Danish sea empire; to the activities of the Jomsvikings and their possible interruption of Gotland's commerce; to efforts at Christianization and the cupidity of rapacious missionaries; and above all to the establishment of trade routes to the newly founded principality of the Rus.

In 1143 Adolf II of Holstein founded the town of Lübeck as a terminus for Baltic trade with Scandinavia. He granted privileges to the Gotland merchants who might frequent the new town. As a quid pro quo, the Gotland merchants agreed to allow similar privileges, including extraterritoriality (the right to be judged by the Germans' own laws and customs) to the merchants of Lübeck who might visit Gotland. As a result of this arrangement the town of Visby was established on the western coast of the island. In the next 200 years Visby became one of the greatest cities of the Hanseatic League. But the town was inhabited mostly by foreigners, who also came to dominate the island's trade. In fact, two distinct communities, one of foreigners living within the formidable walls of Visby and one composed of locals dwelling in "suburbs" surrounding the walls, came into being. Evidence of the dual nature of the population can be found in the *Sea Laws of Visby*, a collection of enactments that, upon examination of their text, may be seen to be drawn largely from the maritime law of Amsterdam.

In 1361 the Danish king Waldemar IV Atterdag, in an effort to reestablish the preeminence of Denmark in Baltic affairs and to strengthen his kingdom after a century of weak kingship, embarked upon the conquest of Gotland. The native Gotlanders were defeated in a great battle outside the walls of Visby and buried in a mass grave (excavated in the 1940's, it has provided an important record of medieval armament). The Danish attack and conquest of the island, Denmark's renewed political power, the recurring Black Death, and the shift of trade routes to Skåne brought about Gotland's economic decline. The island became part of the Kalmar Union with Denmark and Norway in 1397. When Sweden broke from the Union in 1523, the island remained in Danish hands. It became a permanent part of the Swedish kingdom when ceded by the Danes through the Treaty of Brömsebro in 1645.

BIBLIOGRAPHY

There are a number of monographs dealing with the prehistory of Gotland that should be examined by the student. Birger Nerman, *Die Völkerwanderungszeit Gotlands* (1935); and Mårten K. H. Stenberger, *Die Schatzfunde Gotlands der Wikingerzeit*, 2 vols. (1938–1947), are most important. For the *Sea Laws of Visby*, see Jean Marie Pardessus, *Collection de lois maritimes antérieures au XVIIIᶜ siècle*, I (1828), ch. 11. More general accounts are in Holger Arbman, *Svear i österviking* (1955); Sune Lindqvist, *Svenskt forntidsliv* (1944); P. H. Sawyer, *The Age of the Vikings*, 2nd ed. (1971); Martin Spencer, *Gotland* (1974), and Mårten Stenberger, *Sweden*, Alan Binns, trans. (1962).

SIDNEY L. COHEN

[See also **Denmark; Hanseatic League; Mints and Money; Sweden; Trade, European.**]

GOTTFRIED VON NEIFEN (*fl.* 1234–1255). The roughly fifty songs ascribed to Gottfried von Neifen, a Swabian baron at the court of King Henry VII, the son of Frederick II, are predominantly courtly lyrics in praise of love and the lady (and, to a lesser extent, ardent pleas and laments). Elaborate patterns of internal rhyme, rich rhyme, and grammatical rhyme, as well as anaphora, annominatio, alliteration, antithesis, parallelism, repetition, and other rhetorical figures are profusely conjoined with static commonplaces. Ubiquitous nature introductions and frequent addresses to the lady and/or her rose-red mouth characterize the formally intricate songs. The replies are postulated in the subjunctive, and there are scarcely any references to a social setting, to an audience, or to a performance situation. Thoughts and imagery are seldom developed.

In addition to the ornate songs there are about as many other songs that are far simpler in form. Of this group, Carl von Kraus considered almost twenty to be spurious. Many of them present narrative elements in the tradition of the pastourelle, and a variety of roles appear. Scholars generally agreed that von Kraus went too far with his atheteses, as well as in his textual reconstructions. Although there are clear differences between the two types, there is also a remarkable degree of overlap; Neifen seems to have delighted in introducing a trace of crudity into a polished courtly work and a trace of rhetorical polish into songs of almost inane simplicity.

The songs seem to presuppose an audience interested in technical virtuosity and entertainment to the exclusion of ethical deliberations and/or definitions. They lack the didacticism characteristic of Walther von der Vogelweide and his peers, even of Neidhart von Reuental and, to a lesser degree, of Ulrich von Liechtenstein and Tannhäuser, as well as a sense of audience involvement. Kuhn remarks convincingly that Neifen's formalistic petrification of the conventions of *Minnesang* was an active attempt to restructure old traditions in order to make them appropriate to a new reality.

Neifen's influence was considerable. Ulrich von Winterstetten emulated him, as did numerous others, especially among the Swiss. His predecessors are less clear, though he obviously learned from Walther and Neidhart. Whether and how he was influenced by medieval Latin, Provençal, and French traditions remains a subject of debate. It has been suggested that his dialogues and narratives may derive from Romance and German noncourtly traditions, but the details of this derivation remain nebulous.

BIBLIOGRAPHY

Carl von Kraus (and Hugo Kuhn), *Deutsche Lieder-dichter des 13. Jahrhunderts,* I (1951), 82–127, and II (1958), 84–162; Hugo Kuhn, *Minnesangs Wende,* 2nd ed. (1967); Silvia Ranawake, *Höfische Strophenkunst: Vergleichende Untersuchungen zur Formentypologie von Minnesang und Trouvèrelied* (1976); Anthonius H. Touber, *Rhetorik und Form im deutschen Minnesang* (1965).

HUBERT HEINEN

[See also **German Literature: Lyric; Middle High German Literature; Walther von der Vogelweide.**]

GOTTFRIED VON STRASSBURG (*fl.* early thirteenth century). Nothing factual is known about the life of Gottfried von Strassburg. He is named as the author of the unfinished romance *Tristan und Isolt,* written in Middle High German, by two men who wrote continuations of it, Ulrich von Türheim and Heinrich von Freiberg. According to their statements and those of two other thirteenth-century authors, Konrad von Würzburg and Rudolf von Ems, Gottfried lived in Strasbourg and was prevented by death from finishing his poem. Three lyrics in the collection known as Heidelberg manuscript *C* are attributed to "Meister Gottfried von Strassburg." That title caused the author of the *Tristan* to be regarded as a bourgeois by earlier critics, but it is more likely to mean that he was a *dominus* or *magister,* a person of considerable education but not a priest. His work shows a knowledge of classical and contemporary French literature superior to that of any other medieval author writing in German, and he is clearly proud of his erudition and sense of form.

No documents mention Gottfried, and the date given for the last work on his poem, 1210, depends on his references to contemporary poets and on theirs to him. Gottfried and Wolfram von Eschen-bach allude to each other, although never by name, and each was acquainted with at least some part of the other's work. The date of Wolfram's *Parzival,* set by probable references to historical events as 1210, thus provides a terminus ante quem. The date remains an approximation.

Virtually all critics agree that the three lyrics in Heidelberg *C* are not Gottfried's work, but some are inclined to attribute to him two short moralizing works appearing in the same manuscript under the name of Ulrich von Liechtenstein but said by Rudolf von Ems to be Gottfried's work. They are of little significance.

Gottfried's *Tristan* consists of 19,548 lines of four-beat rhyming couplets. In spite of its incomplete state, it is the finest of all realizations of the Tristan theme. Eleven manuscripts of the complete text are extant, as well as numerous fragments, some recently discovered. Two of the complete manuscripts are from the thirteenth century and four from the fourteenth, and it seems likely that one of the former group, *M,* as well as some fragments, were written before 1250 in a Strasbourg scriptorium. There is thus a strong association with Gottfried's city in the manuscript tradition. Establishment of a good text presents few problems.

In his preface Gottfried declares that Thomas de Bretagne (of Britain or Brittany) was the only author who had told the Tristan story correctly. It has been generally assumed that the reference is to subject matter, and it is true that Thomas' version does differ from others in some incidents. It is far more likely, however, that Gottfried is referring to Thomas' treatment of the theme, which differs markedly from that of Eilhart von Oberg and Béroul. They stress the corruption of Tristan the warrior and the conflict between the honor of a knight and a love that has strong elements of magic to reinforce its sensuality. In Thomas, love is idealized and brought into conformity with the principles exemplified in the French *Roman d'Énéas* and the works of Chrétien de Troyes. It is a force more important than the fabric of the society in which it operates.

The extant fragments of Thomas' poem overlap hardly at all with Gottfried's work, since only the last third of Thomas' poem is represented. Direct comparison is therefore impossible. There exists a complete version of the French poem written in Old Norse by Brother Robert (1226), but it is unreliable as a representative of the French work. It is therefore hard to say how original Gottfried's treatment is.

GOTTFRIED VON STRASSBURG

His views of love and of its relation to society seem to go beyond those of his predecessor.

The outlines of the Tristan story were well established by the middle of the twelfth century, and the subject had been made into a poem by Eilhart von Oberg. Gottfried owes little to the work of his German predecessor, though he appears to have known it. Many of the themes in the story are undoubtedly of Celtic origin, but this fact is of little significance for the interpretation of Gottfried's poem. Riwalin, a young lord of Parmenie, while visiting the court of King Mark of Cornwall to learn its high standards of courtliness, loves Blanscheflur, Mark's sister, and Tristan is conceived. They go to Parmenie without Mark's knowledge and marry. Riwalin is killed in a battle against his overlord, Duke Morgan, and Blanscheflur dies giving birth to Tristan. Riwalin's retainer, Rual li Foitenant, brings up Tristan as his son to save him from Morgan.

At fourteen, handsome and brilliantly educated in languages and music, Tristan is kidnapped by merchants, escapes, and finds himself in Cornwall. His skills endear him to Mark even before Rual arrives and reveals his origin. He avenges his father after being knighted and frees Cornwall from tribute by killing Morolt of Ireland, at the cost of a wound that can be cured only by Morolt's sister, Queen Isolde of Ireland. He obtains this cure by teaching her daughter, Isolde the Fair, his skills in the arts, posing as the minstrel Tantris. On his return to Cornwall, Tristan's enthusiastic praise of his pupil causes Mark's barons, now jealous of his power over Mark, to urge the king to send him to win Isolde the Fair as queen. Isolde has been promised to any nobleman who kills a dragon ravaging the kingdom. Tristan does this but is poisoned by its tongue, which he keeps as proof. The two Isoldes find him half dead and keep him as evidence against a seneschal who has falsely claimed the kill. Isolde the Fair, attracted to him, is looking at his weapons when she finds a notch in his sword that corresponds with a fragment embedded in Morolt's skull and thus identifies "Tantris" as the Irish champion's killer. She rushes to kill Tristan but cannot do so, and in the end the offer to make her queen of Cornwall is accepted.

On the voyage Tristan and Isolde accidentally drink a love potion prepared by Queen Isolde for the wedding night, and are indissolubly united in love. Brangaene, Isolde's lady-in-waiting, substitutes for Isolde on the wedding night, but from then on, the lovers are engaged in a long struggle to deceive Mark—and even more the steward Marjodo and the dwarf Melot, who are bent on their destruction. One trap set for them leads to Isolde's false oath: she arranges for the exiled Tristan to disguise himself as a pilgrim, carry her from a ship, and fall with her, so that she can swear that no man has lain with her except the pilgrim and her husband. Their obvious affection later leads to their banishment and life in the cave of lovers, the high point of the poem. Tristan's final exile comes when they are discovered sleeping together in an orchard. He goes to the court of his friend Kaedin, for whom he had earlier killed the giant Urgan, and there meets Isolde of the White Hands, Kaedin's sister. The poem breaks off as he tries to resolve the contradictions caused by his loneliness, yearning for Isolde the Fair, and physical attraction to the third Isolde.

Gottfried sets forth his intentions in an elaborate prologue. The first part is a series of rhymed quatrains principally concerned with the relation of author to audience that indicate, with deliberate ambiguity, the need for the audience to attune itself to the author's intention. The first letters of the quatrains spell out "G DIETRICH," presumably Gottfried and a patron or friend, then "TI IT." At intervals in the poem there are other quatrains beginning with the letters necessary to spell "Tristan" and "Isolde." The names would have been complete had the poem been finished. In the second part of the prologue, Gottfried reveals his source and his intended audience, the *edele herzen* (lofty spirits) who alone can appreciate "Tristan love." For them the poem will provide spiritual sustenance akin to that given to Christians by the word of God and the Eucharist. This is the first occurrence of a major feature of the poem, the use of religious, and particularly mystical, symbolism and terminology to describe "Tristan love."

Gottfried does not intend to indicate that this love is Christian in the sense of being spiritual and nonsensual. Indeed, the episode of the drinking of the love potion may represent the triumph of sensuality, and certainly all the episodes in which the lovers deceive Mark show them attempting to sleep together. This is not the only element, however, as it is in many versions, since it is made clear that the first attraction between the two comes from Tristan's instruction of Isolde in the arts, particularly in music. The harmony established between them at this level, and realized in its highest form in the love grotto, undoubtedly partakes of the true Christian harmony of love, but it is entirely secular in its manifestations. Gottfried sets the lovers in contexts in which it is clear that more than mere sexual encounter is involved. Of these, by far the most important is the stay in the love grotto.

An incident in which the lovers, expelled from court, spend some time in the forest, is common to all versions, but in most it is a time of misery, and they return gladly to court when permitted to do so. Gottfried shows them escaping from a hostile environment at court and moving into a lovers' paradise. The grotto had been a resort of love since pre-Christian times. In Gottfried all the elements of the ideal landscape, the literary milieu for love, are present, but another element is added. The grotto is fashioned so that it has many of the characteristics of a Christian church. In particular, the place of the high altar is taken by a crystalline bed. More important still, Gottfried allegorizes the grotto in terms like those used by Christian writers to allegorize the church building: as the building and its component parts represent Christ's church and its qualities, so the grotto represents "Tristan love" and its characteristics. By implication, the lovers are priests or, as some argue, martyrs of this love-faith. Gottfried thus heightens his concept of love by using the methods of Christian exegesis—an allegory of an allegory.

One other aspect of Gottfried's attitude to Christianity should be mentioned. When Isolde agrees to testify to her chastity by undergoing the ordeal of the hot iron, she indeed prays for divine help, but her plan to fall with Tristan is designed to trick God as well as Mark. Either God agrees with the verbal accuracy of the oath or he condones her adultery, for she is unscathed. Gottfried comments that this proves that Christ is as manipulable as a windblown sleeve. Does he mean that Christ will agree to any conduct if the correct motions are made? Or that to determine God's will by such methods is ludicrous? What seems certain is that "Tristan love" is outside Christianity, even though the images by which the two are manifested may have much in common.

Gottfried's *Tristan* is a romance in the tradition of Chrétien de Troyes and Hartmann von Aue. It makes use of the chivalric trappings, the courtly ethic, the literary *topoi* that distinguish the romance as a genre. In the comments he associates with Tristan's knighting, Gottfried discusses the state of German poetry; praises Hartmann von Aue, Heinrich von Veldeke, Reinmar von Haguenau, and Walther von der Vogelweide; and he condemns Wolfram von Eschenbach, though not by name. At the root of his

discussion, however, is the question of what would be the best literary means of realizing his new concept of the love of Tristan and Isolde. He seems to come to the reluctant conclusion that lyric and other poetical forms must be rejected in favor of the romance, but of a romance with a difference. His hero may look like a knight, but his real character is to be sought beneath the exterior trappings. Even the victories he wins as a knight are attained by highly unchivalric means.

Tristan survives because he uses intelligence ruthlessly. He is educated in languages, in rhetoric, in music—in other words, as an artist, not a warrior. He is much more the role player, the minstrel, the man of words and cunning than a man of action like Yvain or Érec. Isolde, too, is intellectually far above her romance sisters and is ruthless in her pursuit of love, even to the point of plotting the death of the faithful Brangaene. Her appreciation of the mutual nature of love and of its power sets her far above the court ladies of the romance.

In essence Gottfried rejects the courtly ethic of his predecessors. Several courts appear in the work. Little can be said of that of Morgan, and at the court in Dublin it is clear that there is little culture before the arrival of Tristan. Mark's court, to which Tristan's father had gone to improve himself, is overwhelmed by the abilities of the young Tristan, but its courtiers reveal themselves as a cowardly and jealous group of timeservers when they are faced with danger. They are afraid to challenge Morolt, they try to send Tristan to his death in Ireland, and their representatives Marjodo and Melot seek the destruction of the lovers from jealousy rather than from love of Mark.

There is no Gawain at Mark's court; and Gottfried, unlike other authors, does not bring Arthur's court into his work, though he does mention it. The portrait of the Irish seneschal who claims to have killed the dragon in order to win Isolde makes even Kay, the seneschal at Arthur's court, look like a noble gentleman. Mark, the sovereign of this Cornish court, is a feeble ruler. Though personally kind and humane, he is incapable of decision or leadership. It is typical that he tamely allows the Irish minstrel Gandin to take away Isolde, after being tricked into granting him an unspecified boon, and that he never brings himself to accept fully the evidence of Isolde's adultery. He loves her in his own way, but that way is shallow sensuality, and he shows repeatedly how unworthy he is of her. He and his court represent the darker side of Arthurian chivalry, and

Gottfried is at pains to show that love cannot flourish in such an environment. He may well have believed that the whole "courtly" solution to the problem of love in society was not viable.

Gottfried does not pretend that his lovers are moral in any conventional sense. Indeed, only two persons in the poem stand out in their unselfishness: Tristan's foster father Rual li Foitenant and his wife Floraete. Loyalty and domestic affection motivate their conduct, and they do not spare themselves. Typically, they are not members of such courts as Mark's or Arthur's but simple country gentry.

Like all writers of romance, Gottfried is less concerned with the presentation of character than with exemplary figures. The twelfth-century romance had been developed to present sexual love in an idealized society where its attainment could be linked to service by the lover, which took the form of combat for honor against one's peers or on behalf of the weak. Recognition of this service by the lady led to acceptance of the lover. Tristan's parents conform very largely to this pattern, though they are treated with some irony. In presenting "Tristan love," however, Gottfried abandons the idea of love-service altogether. There is no link between the combats that occur in the work and the love that develops. Nor does Tristan fall in love with Isolde when he first sees her, as Yvain does with Laudine. The service that Tristan performs for her is to teach her his understanding of true love and to exemplify it in his conduct toward her. She in her turn complements his love and forms it into a unified whole. He has no need to perform deeds "in her honor," since their mutual love is their sole goal. The best expression of their love, apart from its practice, is in verse and song, and it is thus that they express themselves in the grotto. Such love is beyond the grasp of the courts, but it is comprehensible to the *edele herzen*, the audience for the poem.

Gottfried's stress on the artistic and intellectual qualities of his lovers, on their sense of form and harmony, is reflected in his own style. He has little interest in the mere narration of events, preferring careful depiction of motivation, of state of mind, and of psychological attitude through complex images, wordplay, and allusion. He occasionally uses authorial intervention, such as his statement that he, too, has visited the grotto of love, in order to point the way to the correct interpretation of his poem, but more frequently he uses complex images to make his point. He is particularly fond of playing variations on those images that had become part of the conventions of courtly romance, and thus indicating his utilization of the form and his departure from its meaning. In the *Tristan* such well-worn images as the war of love and the wound and cure of love take on totally new meanings as a physical wound is cured by incurring a deep and internal spiritual wound. The common puns on *la mer* (sea), *l'amer* (love), and *l'amer* (bitterness) are used to show the lovers groping for the solution to the problem of their sudden pain. Although Gottfried uses the rhetorical techniques of his time in masterly fashion, the principal interest of his style lies in his variations of them, in particular his use of antithesis and contrasting and reinforcing pairs of words to show the tensions of the lovers and the court.

Although Gottfried implicitly rejects much of the ethic developed in twelfth-century romance, especially the idea of chivalric combat in service to a lady, his work is incomprehensible without the background of that romance. He plays upon his audience's knowledge of romance conventions as he does on their feelings of religion to present his own views of the nature of love and its relation to society. In doing so he offers one of the greatest of all love poems, not a pleasant story of love and adventure but a penetrating analysis of human emotions.

BIBLIOGRAPHY

Sources. Karl Marold, ed., *Tristan,* rev. by Werner Schröder (1969); Reinhold Bechstein, ed., *Tristan und Isolde,* 5th ed. rev. by Peter Ganz, 2 vols. (1978); Friedrich Ranke, ed., *Tristan und Isold,* rev. by Eduard Studer (1958); Gottfried Weber, ed., *Tristan* (1967), with prose summary and explanation of terms. See also *Tristan,* Arthur T. Hatto, trans. (1960), including fragments of Thomas of Britain.

Studies. Hans-Hugo Steinhoff, *Bibliographie zu Gottfried von Strassburg* (1975), is virtually complete up to 1971. See also the bibliography under "Gottfried von Strassburg" in *Dizionario critico della letteratura tedesca* (1978). Following are a few major works that, for various reasons, do not appear in the bibliographies: Joan M. Ferrante, *The Conflict of Love and Honor: The Medieval Tristan Legend in France, Germany, and Italy* (1973); C. Stephen Jaeger, *Medieval Humanism in Gottfried von Strassburg's Tristan and Isolde* (1977); Ruth Goldschmidt Kunzer, *The Tristan of Gottfried von Strassburg: An Ironic Perspective* (1973); Gottfried Weber, *Gottfried von Strassburg,* 4th ed. (1973).

W. T. H. JACKSON

[See also **Arthurian Literature; Courtly Love; German Literature: Romances; Heinrich von Freiberg; Middle High**

German Literature; Tristrams Saga; Tristan: Eilhart von Oberg's; Tristan, Legend of; Tristan, Roman de; Ulrich von Türheim.]

GOTTSCHALK OF ORBAIS (*ca.* 803–867/869) was a Benedictine monk whose ideas about predestination incited a controversy. The son of Berno, a Saxon nobleman, Gottschalk as a child was pledged as an oblate to the monastery at Fulda, where he spent most of his early life except for a short stay, sometime between 824 and 827, at Reichenau. In 829, at a church synod held at Mainz, Gottschalk asked to be released from his monastic vows, claiming that the abbot of Fulda, Hrabanus Maurus, had held him against his will, and that the oath binding him to monastic life had not been sworn before Saxon witnesses and was hence invalid. He also demanded the return of his inheritance, which his father had turned over to the monastery.

The synod offered Gottschalk release from his vows with compensation for time spent at the monastery, but did not offer to return his inheritance. Hrabanus Maurus appealed this decision at another synod at Worms, winning a reversal that sent Gottschalk to Orbais, where he remained until about 838 except for some time that he spent at Corbie. Both at Corbie, under Ratramnus, and at Orbais, Gottschalk studied St. Augustine's writings at length, and at Orbais he developed a reputation as a successful teacher of these writings. Toward the end of his stay at Orbais, Gottschalk was ordained a priest (but this ordination was nullified in 848 because the local bishop had not given his consent beforehand).

Some scholars believe that between 829 and 838 Gottschalk wrote the poetry that is noteworthy for its unmistakable lyricism and the then innovative use of rhyming stanzas to support that lyricism; however, at present no consensus exists as to when any of his seventeen extant poems were actually composed.

Sometime after 838, Gottschalk left Orbais, traveling and preaching in Italy, Dalmatia, and Hungary. During these travels he began to teach a doctrine of double predestination, asserting that before the advent of time, God had irrevocably predestined both the elect and the damned, according to his foreknowledge of their deeds. Hrabanus Maurus and other prominent churchmen pronounced Gottschalk's teachings both dangerous and heretical. Hrabanus used his influence to have Gottschalk thrown out of the household of Count Eberhard of Friuli in northern Italy, where he had been staying.

In 848 Gottschalk returned to Mainz to defend his ideas before a church synod, but he was condemned. That same year, at a synod at Quiercy-sur-Oise, he was not only reviled but also whipped, forced to burn his writings, expelled from the priesthood, and imprisoned for life at the monastery of Hautvillers. These harsh punishments were not imposed solely on account of his ideas concerning predestination, however. The apparent irregularities in his ordination at Orbais, the fact that he had left Orbais without permission, and his reportedly caustic personality all influenced his sentence. During his imprisonment at Hautvillers, Gottschalk continued to write about predestination and other theological controversies.

Sometime between about 850 and 860, Gottschalk's ideas on predestination were severely upbraided in writings by John Scottus Eriugena, Amalarius of Metz, and Hincmar of Rheims. Yet other respected theologians, such as Ratramnus of Corbie, Prudentius of Troyes, and Florus of Lyons, wrote tracts generally supportive of double predestination.

For eleven years after Gottschalk's condemnation at Quiercy, numerous church synods and councils debated the question of predestination. The question was never really settled, but in a document attributed to a church council at Toucy (860), the attending clerics representing both sides of the controversy accepted a document worded vaguely enough to satisfy everyone. In 866 Guntbert, one of his friends from Hautvillers, attempted to present some of Gottschalk's writings on predestination to Pope Nicholas I at Rome. No evidence exists that the writings ever reached Rome, and Nicholas died within the year. Consequently, the debate about predestination ended until the Reformation. Gottschalk never left Hautvillers after his imprisonment.

Gottschalk's ideas about predestination were not original. They were interpretations of St. Augustine's postulations, which had been written more than four centuries earlier. Gottschalk's doctrine of a double predestination maintained that one group of people was saved because God gave them a gift of grace; the other group was damned because God withheld the gift of grace from them and judged them worthy of damnation because of their evil, which he had foreseen before the Creation. This doctrine implied that since God from before the Creation had predestined some people irrevocably to damnation, he sacrificed Jesus on the cross only for those he had already determined to save—not for those predestined to damnation. Even sacraments such as baptism and communion supposedly benefited only those predestined to salvation, since the spiritual cleansing resulting from participation in a sacrament could have no real effect on one who was predestined to damnation. Predestination, then, according to Gottschalk, placed limitations on free will, since the damned had no free will to do good, only a will to do evil; the elect had a free will to do good only as a consequence of having received God's gift of grace.

Gottschalk also wrote a long treatise on grammar and several concerning other theological subjects, including one on the origin of the soul in which he reviews various theories on the subject but does not arrive at any specific conclusion. In another work Gottschalk speculates about Christ's presence in the Eucharist in terms similar to those used by his friend Ratramnus of Corbie against Paschasius Radbertus. He also wrote two short works on the Trinity in which he used his own grammatical arguments, as well as theological arguments culled from Augustine and other church authorities, to affirm that God is one spirit, not three, and that the Father, Son, and Holy Ghost are inseparable.

BIBLIOGRAPHY

Sources. The poems are in *Monumenta Germaniae historica: Poetae latini aevi carolini,* III, Ludwig Traube, ed. (1896), 707–738; IV, Karl Strecker, ed. (1923), 934–936; and VI, Karl Strecker, ed. (1951), 86–106. The prose writings are in Cyril Lambot, ed., *Oeuvres théologiques et grammaticales de Godescalc d'Orbais* (1945), and "Lettre inédite de Godescalc d'Orbais," in *Revue bénédictine* (1958).

Studies. Eleanor Shipley Duckett, *Carolingian Portraits* (1962), 153–159, 196–200, 258–264; Jean Jolivet, "L'enjeu de la grammaire pour Godescalc," in René Roques, ed., *Jean Scot Érigène et l'histoire de la philosophie, Colloques internationaux du Centre national de la recherche scientifique,* 561 (1977); Walter Kagerah, *Gottschalk der Sachse* (1936); Max Ludwig Laistner, *Thought and Letters in Western Europe, A.D. 500 to 900* (1931), 243–246, 287–289; Max Manitius, *Geschichte der lateinishen Literatur des Mittelalters,* I (1911), 568–574; Peter von Moos, "Gottschalks Gedicht *O mi custos*—eine confessio," in *Frühmittelalterliche Studien,* 4–5 (1970–1971); Klaus Vielhaver, *Gottschalk der Sachse* (1956).

TIMOTHY R. ROBERTS

[See also **Augustinism; Carolingian Latin Poetry; Heresies, Western European; Hrabanus Maurus; Latin Meter; Philosophy and Theology, Western European.**]

GOWER, JOHN (*ca.* 1330–1408). In his own lifetime and for more than a century after his death, the English poet John Gower enjoyed a reputation nearly equal to the fame of his great contemporary and friend Geoffrey Chaucer. In the closing lines of his *Troilus and Criseyde,* Chaucer submitted his work to the judgment of "moral Gower," and the epithet was repeated as a term of respect by Gavin Douglas in *The Palice of Honour* (1501) and by Stephen Hawes in the *Passetyme of Pleasure* (1509). Gower himself evidently conceived his duty as poet in similar terms. The Latin colophon in many manuscripts of his works describes his three major poems as "three works of instruction *(doctrine)*" written in order to share with others whatever God-given insights he may possess.

The *Speculum Meditantis* (Mirror of man reflecting), or *Speculum Hominis* (Mirror of man), as the first major work is called in the earliest versions of the colophon, is described as "a book written in the Gallic language . . . it discusses the vices and virtues as well as the various classes of society and it attempts to teach the right path by which a sinner should return to knowledge of his creator." This work, long believed lost, was identified in 1895 by George C. Macaulay as the *Mirour de l'Omme* (Mirror of man), a poem originally consisting of some 31,000 lines in octosyllabic twelve-line stanzas, written in a late, corrupt form of Anglo-Norman that is perhaps better called Anglo-French. The unique extant manuscript of the poem (Cambridge, University Library, MS Add. 3035) was dated by Macaulay in the latter half of the fourteenth century; the correctness of the text persuaded him that it had been copied under the direction of Gower himself.

Although the manuscript was missing several leaves and offered no indication of its author, Macaulay was able to identify it with Gower's *Speculum Meditantis* because so many of its lines were paralleled in Gower's other works and because the plan of the work fit so closely the description in the colophon. The first part (lines 1–18,420) is an account of the vices and virtues; the second (lines 18,421–27,360) is a satire on the vices of the various classes of society; and the conclusion (lines 27,361–29,945) is a life of the Virgin Mary.

The first part resembles discussions of the vices and virtues in works like the *Somme le roi* of Lorens d'Orléans and its English adaptations. In this tradition the vices are commonly portrayed as branches of a tree; Gower, however, portrays the Seven Deadly Sins as the offspring of a liaison between the

Devil and his daughter Sin, and the five vices associated with each sin as offspring of a subsequent union between the Seven Deadly Sins and the World. Similarly, the virtues that provide remedies for the vices are portrayed as offspring of a union between Reason and the Seven Cardinal Virtues.

The second part belongs to the tradition of estates satire and follows this tradition in basing many of the examples of vice on contemporary practices of the various classes. The topical allusions in this section led Macaulay to date the work from about 1376–1379. For example, Gower comments on the Great Schism of 1378 (lines 18,829ff.), criticizes the king for taxing the clergy to support the war with France (lines 22,297ff.), and denounces a king who would allow a woman to usurp his power (lines 22,807ff.), probably a reference to the power of Alice Perrers in the last years of Edward III's reign. Although Gower attacks all classes as guilty of vice, he also defends various groups against charges traditionally made against them; perhaps most notable are his account of the divinely appointed role of merchants (lines 25,192ff.), his defense of legitimate mercantile profits (lines 25,201ff.), and his memorable celebration of the wool trade (lines 25,369ff.).

As a work designed to popularize Latin learning, the *Mirour* draws on a variety of Latin sources. In addition to the Vulgate Bible, Gower quotes extensively from the Latin fathers Jerome, Augustine, Gregory, Bernard, and Ambrose, and from the Stoic moralist Seneca; quotations from a variety of other authors were probably drawn from florilegia. Like Gower's other works, the *Mirour* is also a compendium of proverbs, illustrations from natural history, and bits of folklore. As its title suggests, the *Mirour* is influenced by the medieval tradition of encyclopedic works having titles that begin with speculum (mirror).

In Macaulay's view, Chaucer's "moral Gower" most probably refers to the *Mirour,* but the work does not seem to have been widely known by Gower's contemporaries. The allegory of Sin and Death and the parliament of the Devil and his followers are similar to Milton's treatment of these subjects in *Paradise Lost,* but there is no other evidence that Milton knew the *Mirour.* For modern readers, as a compendium of traditional lore on the vices and virtues and the life of Mary, combined with a wealth of detailed social criticism based on fourteenth-century English society, the *Mirour* is a valuable mirror of the views of an educated layman in the period.

The *Vox Clamantis* (Voice of one crying out), the second of Gower's major works, elaborates further on the kind of social criticism offered in the *Mirour,* in 10,265 lines of Latin elegiac verse divided into seven books. Books III and IV describe the vices of the clergy, and book V is divided equally between a description of the vices of the knighthood and the vices of the common people, including the merchants and artisans. The estates satire in this part of the work has less topical reference and circumstantial detail than the corresponding section of the *Mirour;* the main emphasis in the *Vox* is on the violation of basic moral principles, the foundation of law and order, by all estates. Book VI emphasizes Gower's views on the importance of law, first by focusing on the perversions of law by the legal profession and then by addressing a letter of counsel to the king as the ultimate safeguard of law in society.

This critical examination of law and order in society is preceded by a general discussion (book II) of the causes of the decline of England as lying in the sinful nature of man. Book VII makes a similar point in more universal terms: not only England but also the entire world gives increasing evidence of corruption and decay, and the source of this corruption is the corrupt nature of man. The only safeguard for society or the individual is obedience to the law of God. As social order depends on the rule of a good king, so individual well-being depends on virtuous self-rule: "Every good man who governs his actions well is king over himself."

In most manuscripts of the *Vox,* a dream vision recounting the events of the Peasants' Revolt of 1381 appears as book I. Gower describes how he sees the peasants transformed into bands of animals who march on London. The main events of the revolt in London—the riots, the attack on John of Gaunt's London house (the Savoy), the storming of the Tower of London, and the murder of Simon Sudbury, archbishop of Canterbury—are described in terms recalling the fall of ancient Troy. Gower then describes his flight to a ship that is assailed by storms and sea monsters until it is saved by Mayor William Walworth, who strikes down Wat Tyler, leader of the rebels. Macaulay believes that this vision was written shortly after the revolt, when the rest of the *Vox* was already complete. The addition of the vision reinforces the main points of the *Vox:* for Gower the revolt is a symbol of the anarchy that results when the principle of moral law is overthrown.

Another of Gower's convictions emerges from his use in the *Vox* of a large number of lines borrowed or adapted from other works, most notably the works of Ovid and the *Aurora,* a versified Bible by Peter Riga. Gower describes the *Vox* as based on quotations from a variety of authorities, just as "the honeycomb is gathered from the buds of various flowers." As a collection of *sententiae,* the *Vox* expresses Gower's view that "from writings of the past come examples for the future." So the fall of Troy is a type of the fall of London threatened by the Peasants' Revolt, and both falls are types of the approaching end of the world, which takes its origin ultimately in the fall of Man.

The *Vox Clamantis,* surviving in eleven manuscripts, evidently reached a wider audience than the *Mirour,* for reasons that may be political as much as literary. Some manuscripts of the *Vox* are revised so as to link the work with the *Cronica tripertita,* the Latin chronicle of 1,062 leonine hexameters that Gower wrote in 1399–1400 to justify the deposition of Richard II and the accession of Henry IV. The *Cronica* begins with an interpretation of the events leading up to what is now called the Merciless Parliament (1388) as a plot by Richard II against those who criticized his government: the lords appellant, led by Warwick, Gloucester, and Arundel. In Gower's view, from 1387, when Richard consulted with judges in order to extend the definition of treason to include accroaching the royal prerogative, to 1397, when Richard invoked the definition of treason to take reprisals against the lords appellant, and finally to the last years of his reign, when he forced his subjects to sign blank charters, Richard II's reign was punctuated by a series of perversions of the rule of law; his deposition was a triumph of the forces of law over lawless tyranny. As a historical record, the *Cronica* is too biased to be of great value but, taken as a continuation of the *Vox Clamantis,* it does present Gower's conviction that failure to uphold the law is tyranny, whatever form it takes, whether it be the revolt of peasants or the increasingly absolutist rule of a king.

Gower's third major work is the *Confessio Amantis* (The lover's confession), a poem of some 30,000 lines in English octosyllabic couplets, divided into eight books, with a lengthy prologue to the whole. The *Confessio* combines the traditions and themes of the *Mirour* and the *Vox* in what Gower himself calls a "newe thing," new both in form and in content.

The framing narrative of the poem is the lover's confession to which the title refers; as in the *Mirour,* Gower draws on the tradition of the Seven Deadly Sins, devoting one book of the poem to each sin. The

discussion of the sins, however, is adapted not to any of the traditional social classes but to the psychological condition of a lover. The priest who instructs the lover Amans, moreover, is no traditional confessor but the allegorical figure Genius, who in the *Roman de la Rose* had appeared as a priest to hear the confession of Nature and preach a sermon to advance the cause of Venus. In the *Confessio,* Genius is a priest in the service of Venus who administers her command that Amans confess his sins as a way of proving that he deserves a reward for his service in the court of love.

The conclusion of this confession is as unorthodox as its beginning. Amans feels no contrition and rejects his confessor's view that he is guilty of sin. For her part, Venus refuses Amans any reward, regardless of his deserts, because, after a lifetime of service in her court, he is now too old for love. The injustice of this conclusion illustrates Gower's point that "loves lawe is oute of reule," that Love rules in human hearts like a tyrant who refuses to acknowledge the rule of law. The poem ends when Amans, dismissed from the service of love, is restored to himself as the poet Gower, an old man who intends to devote the rest of his life to God.

The framing story of the lover's confession is surrounded by a second frame, a prologue and conclusion that recall the kind of social analysis found in the *Vox.* The prologue discusses the progressively corrupt ages of the world and denounces the absence of virtuous love, law, and order in contemporary society. The long digression on the education of Alexander the Great that fills book VII is a mirror for princes that offers, as a remedy for disorder, the ideal of a king who is himself ruled by the love of virtue. The social analysis of this second frame serves as a corrective for the image of misrule given in the lover's distorted confession. The moral advice given to rulers in book VII is useful for all men, especially those who have become the slaves of passion.

This double framework surrounds a collection of more than 100 tales, told as *exempla* to illustrate the vices and virtues about which the priest interrogates the penitent. The tales are taken from a variety of sources: Ovid, the Bible, the story of Troy as recounted by Guido delle Colonne and Benoît de Sainte-Maure, the story of Alexander as recounted by a variety of writers, and history, fables, and folklore from many sources. As a framed collection of tales, the *Confessio* combines features found in works like *Handlying Synne* by Robert Mannyng as well as the *Canterbury Tales* of Chaucer. Gower's collection is noteworthy for its distinctive combination of complexity in the double framework and simplicity in the tales. Each tale is designed to illustrate one of the vices or virtues in its relation to love or good rule, and many tales are susceptible to several kinds of applications. The profusion of rhetorical devices that characterizes Gower's Latin verse is notably reduced in his English tales; they are marked by sparing but effective use of visual detail and a straightforward narrative line, uninterrupted by digressions or by intrusions of the narrator.

The *Confessio Amantis* was Gower's most popular work. It survives in 49 manuscripts and was first printed by Caxton in 1483. A prose translation into Spanish, the *Confisión del Amante* (*ca.* 1400) by Juan de Cuenca, refers to an earlier translation into Portuguese. Berthelette's edition in the sixteenth century presents Gower as "a model of pure English," and Ben Jonson's *English Grammar* takes 30 of its 130 quotations from the *Confessio*. In *Pericles*, Shakespeare brings Gower on stage for the opening of each act, and in Robert Greene's *Vision* (1592), Gower and Chaucer appear to debate the relative merits of their styles of poetry.

Gower's modern reputation is based primarily on his abilities as a teller of tales in the *Confessio*. In his modern edition of the poem, Macaulay dismisses the carefully constructed double framework as mere "machinery," and the epithet "moral Gower" has further served to discourage readers for whom didactic poetry holds little interest. More recent scholarship by Maria Wickert, Patrick Gallacher, John Fisher, and Russell Peck has directed attention to the coherence of Gower's moral views and has argued in favor of reading his major works as he intended them, as a coherent oeuvre designed to bear witness to his times.

In addition to his major works, Gower wrote shorter poems in French, Latin, and English. An English poem, "In Praise of Peace" (*ca.* 1399), appears together with a selection of shorter Latin poems on good governance and related topics in the Trentham manuscript (*ca.* 1400), apparently designed for presentation to Henry IV shortly after his accession to the throne. The Trentham manuscript is also the unique source of the *Cinkante balades*, a sequence of Anglo-French ballades on the subject of love in a variety of situations. If, as Fisher argues, the *Balades* were originally written before 1374, the poem is one of the earliest ballade sequences written. A second sequence, of eighteen ballades, probably of a later date, entitled *Traitié ... pour essampler les amantz marietz* (Treatise ... to give examples to married lovers), treats the moral value of married love, drawing on a variety of exempla, including many of those used in the *Confessio Amantis*. Gower seems to have regarded the *Traitié* as something of an appendix to the *Confessio;* seven of the ten surviving manuscripts of the *Traitié* appear following the *Confessio,* linked by a note in Anglo-French prose. In these manuscripts the *Confessio,* with its main text in English, with Latin elegiacs as epigraphs for each of its main sections, and with a coda of ballades in Anglo-French, is fully representative of Gower's uncommon position as a poet in three languages.

Apart from the evidence provided by his works, historical records of Gower are scarce. Fisher's careful analysis of the available evidence yields several records of real estate transactions, suggesting that Gower was a man of some means and perhaps connected in some way with the legal profession. He was, as his epitaph records, a substantial benefactor of the priory of St. Mary Overie in Southwark, where he lived during the latter part of his life, making use of its library and perhaps also establishing there a scriptorium for the production of manuscripts of his works. There is a record of his marriage to Agnes Groundolf in 1398.

Gower's friendship with Geoffrey Chaucer is one of the few known details of his personal life. When Chaucer traveled to the Continent in 1378, he left Gower with power of attorney. The conclusion of the first version of the *Confessio* (1390) includes a flattering greeting from Venus to Chaucer, "mi disciple and mi poete," and a reference to Chaucer's poems, known throughout the land. In addition to the direct reference to "moral Gower" in the *Troilus,* Chaucer gives to the Man of Law in the *Canterbury Tales* a speech referring to the tales of Canace and Apollonius, two stories from the *Confessio*. The disparaging tone of the Man of Law's comments, together with the removal of the reference to Chaucer in most, but not all, manuscripts of the later versions of the *Confessio,* have led to the conjecture that their friendship ended in the 1390's, but no clear evidence exists to support this view.

Sometime around 1400, Gower became blind, and he wrote little after this date. The effigy on his tomb in Southwark cathedral, though much restored, preserves his image as he wished; it portrays a man lying in repose, a collar of *S*'s with a swan pendant (insignia of Henry IV) around his neck, and his head resting on three volumes bearing the titles *Vox Clamantis, Speculum Meditantis,* and *Confessio Amantis.*

BIBLIOGRAPHY

The standard edition is *The Complete Works of John Gower,* George C. Macaulay, ed., 4 vols. (1899–1902), vols. II and III repr. as *The English Works of John Gower* (1900–1901). Translations include *The Major Latin Works of John Gower,* Eric W. Stockton, trans. (1962).

Studies include J. A. W. Bennett, "Gower's 'Honeste Love,'" in John Lawlor, ed., *Patterns of Love and Courtesy* (1966); Arthur B. Ferguson, *The Articulate Citizen and the English Renaissance* (1965), 13–23, 44–63; John H. Fisher, *John Gower: Moral Philosopher and Friend of Chaucer* (1964); Patrick J. Gallacher, *Love, the Word, and Mercury: A Reading of John Gower's "Confessio Amantis"* (1975); C. S. Lewis, *The Allegory of Love* (1936), 198–227; Derek Pearsall, "Gower's Narrative Art," in *PMLA,* **81** (1966); Russell A. Peck, *Kingship and Common Profit in Gower's "Confessio Amantis"* (1978); Maria Wickert, *Studien zu John Gower* (1953), trans. by Robert J. Meindl as *Studies in Gower* (1981); Robert F. Yeager, *John Gower Materials: A Bibliography Through 1979* (1981).

PATRICIA J. EBERLE

[See also **Anglo-Norman Literature; Latin Literature; Middle English Literature; Peasants' Revolt.**]

GOZBERTUS, a name known only from a signature on an incense burner now in the Trier Cathedral treasury. While it is generally accepted that Gozbertus is the artist, the name might more readily refer to the donor of the object. Joseph Braun has placed the censer in the twelfth century on typological grounds, but there is little external evidence of date. Some writers have identified this "Gozbertus" with a monk of Trier mentioned in several letters to Egbert, archbishop of Trier (990–996), as having performed valuable services for Gerbert, archbishop of Rheims, but nothing further is known about this individual or his work. A bronze fountain signed by "Frater Gozbertus" (since destroyed) formerly stood in the cloister of St. Maximin, Trier. Known only through two seventeenth-century descriptions and a drawing, it provides an inadequate basis for stylistic comparison. Iconographical evidence, however, suggests a twelfth-century date. In effect, there may have been several different artists with the name Gozbertus, living at widely different periods but all associated more or less closely with the city of Trier. The linkage between extant monuments and the artist (or artists) of this name is not firmly established.

BIBLIOGRAPHY

Stephan Beissel, "Erzbischof Egbert von Trier und die byzantinische Frage," in *Stimmen aus Maria-Laach,* **27** (1884); Hermann Bunjes, Nikolaus Irsch, *et al., Die kirchlichen Denkmäler der Stadt Trier* (1938), 318–319, fig. 218; Otto von Falke and Erich Meyer, *Bronzegeräte des Mittelalters,* I, *Romanische Leuchter und Gefässe; Giessgefässe der Gotik* (1935), fig. 179; Nikolaus Irsch, *Der Dom zu Trier* (1931), no. 34, 341–343, figs. 223–225; Hermann Schnitzler, *Rheinische Schatzkammer,* II, *Die Romanik* (1959), no. 2, pls. 6–7.

GRETEL CHAPMAN

GRADUAL, the second of the proper chants of the Gregorian Mass. Also, a book containing Mass chants. The name for the chant derives from *responsorium grad[u]ale,* a designation found in the earliest Gregorian manuscripts (*ca.* 800), and refers, evidently, to the position of the singer on the steps (*gradus*) of the ambo.

At the time of St. Augustine (*ca.* 400) the gradual appears to have been a whole psalm sung in response to the first lesson of Mass. It seems likely that the performance of this psalm became increasingly elaborate, and that this elaboration led to the abridgment of the early practice. In any case, by the beginning of the ninth century, the gradual normally consisted of a single psalm verse, preceded and followed by a choral refrain; and by the beginning of the tenth, the time of the oldest neumed examples, the verse and refrain were both elaborately melismatic. A further abridgment, by shortening the second and any subsequent occurrences of the refrain, is frequently indicated.

For about one in ten of the graduals found in the oldest sources, the text of the refrain or verse is not drawn from the psalms or canticles. These chants are likely later additions to the repertory. It is clear from the earliest ordinals that the verses were sung solo. However, sometime after the adoption of Gregorian chant in Frankish regions, the choir was given more to sing and the cantor less, his part reduced to its practical minimum: the singing of the first few syllables, to get the choir started properly.

Much of the music of the graduals is shared, and the majority can, on this account, be assigned to one or other of three or four groups, the most cohesive of which employ what are virtually standard melodies.

In its second sense *(liber gradualis)* the title "gradual" was applied originally to books containing only the solo chants of the Mass. The designation derives, obviously, from the *responsorium grad[u]ale,* the first of such items. This narrow usage (which is adhered to by certain modern writers) and the Frankish origin of the term are attested to (*ca.* 830) by Amalarius of Metz: "quod dicimus gradale illi vocant cantatorium" (what we call gradual, they [the Romans] call cantatorium). By the beginning of the tenth century, however, the title "gradual" was used more generally for a book that contained the Mass music.

The early graduals (using the term in its wider sense) usually include only the proper chants of the Mass; introits, graduals, alleluias, tracts, offertories, and communions, not all of them assigned to occasions. Later graduals are more specific, and often contain such items as the chants of the ordinary, processional pieces, tropes, and sequences.

The contents of the Gregorian gradual are largely Roman and fixed, but even the earliest copies incorporate Frankish elements, and even the latest may include local variations.

BIBLIOGRAPHY

Willi Apel, *Gregorian Chant* (1958, 3rd ed. 1966); Helmut Hucke and Michel Huglo, "Gradual," in the *New Grove Dictionary of Music and Musicians,* VII (1980); Peter Wagner, *Origins and Development of the Forms of the Liturgical Chant* (1901).

TERENCE BAILEY

[See also **Gregorian Chant.**]

GRAF RUDOLF is a Middle High German verse narrative that survives in fourteen fragments totaling less than 1,400 lines from a single twelfth-century manuscript. Reconstruction of the text must rely on early transcriptions, since the use in the nineteenth century of chemical reagents meant to improve legibility has instead severely obscured the

original script. The dialect of the work is either Thuringian or Hessian. It was composed between 1170 and 1185 and is based on a French source, though not *Boeve (Beuves) de Haumtone* as was long believed. The anonymous poet was probably a layman, judging by the worldly and realistic tone, the marked lack of theological commentary in crusading episodes, and the emphasis on luxuries of contemporary courtly life.

The beginning and end of the work are missing; what survives may be divided into two sets of fragments, one involving a crusading story and the other a tale of love and abduction or *Brautwerbungsgeschichte.* In response to the pope's call for a crusade, Graf Rudolf sets off for Jerusalem, where he is well received by the Christian King Gilot. When the Christians hear of a pagan king at Ascalon, they lay siege to the city with startling brutality, slaughtering "women and children like cattle." The pagan King Halap learns of these atrocities and prepares for battle at the urging of his counselor Girabobe. Hostilities last for more than six months: almost all of Rudolf's army is destroyed and the pagans are reduced to putting women on the battlements in men's clothing. Girabobe arranges a truce, and Gilot, trying to emulate the emperor, holds a great festival. Rudolf, the model of courtliness, outlines the proper training of a young man.

An important part of the story is missing at this point. Rudolf next appears as an ally of the pagans, accused of treachery by Gilot. When Halap refuses to surrender Rudolf, the Christians declare war. Rudolf fights brilliantly for the pagan army. He woos a pagan princess (generally assumed to be Halap's daughter), and the two enjoy a night of love while a servant stands guard. After Rudolf returns to battle, the princess has herself baptized and takes the name Irmengart. She gives alms freely so that God will spare Rudolf. He escapes from prison, manages to rejoin Irmengart, and the two abscond with gold and jewels. Rudolf's servant Bonifait dies defending him.

This important fragment is especially perplexing in its treatment of the crusading theme. It begins with a call to a crusade that advances all the contemporary justifications and promises of spiritual reward, only to end with the hero fighting for the pagans. The Christians are repeatedly depicted as inexplicably cruel, and several pagans are praised without qualification. Girabobe is even characterized as the archetypal good counselor and Rudolf's equal in courtliness. Neither Rudolf nor the poet entertains any scruples about a Christian's courtship of a pagan, nor is Irmengart's conversion accompanied by any reference to its religious significance. The absence of Christian bias throughout makes it doubtful that the missing parts of the narrative adhered to a more traditional attitude. *Graf Rudolf* is not mentioned by later poets, and its influence appears to have been limited.

BIBLIOGRAPHY

Graf Rudolf, Peter F. Ganz, ed. (1964); Georges Zink, "Graf Rudolf: Essai de présentation," in *Études germaniques*, **20** (1965).

BONNIE BUETTNER

[See also **German Literature: Romance; Middle High German Literature.**]

GRAIL, LEGEND OF. The quest for the Holy Grail, the cup of the Last Supper and the chalice of the first Mass, became the predestined mission of Arthur's Round Table in the continuations of Chrétien de Troyes's *Conte du Graal.* Supposedly brought to Britain by Joseph of Arimathea, it was guarded by a succession of Grail kings at Castle Corbenic. Galahad and others beheld the Grail miracle, a literal enactment of transubstantiation, then healed the maimed Grail keeper and restored the Waste Land. The favored theory of its origin is that the legend is a Christianization of an ancient Celtic tale concerning a magic feeding vessel.

BIBLIOGRAPHY

Helen Adolf, *Visio pacis: Holy City and Grail* (1960), treats the Grail as the "fruit of the crusades"; Jean Frappier, *Chrétien de Troyes et le mythe du Graal* (1972); Urban T. Holmes, Jr., and Sister Amelia M. Klenke, *Chrétien, Troyes, and the Grail* (1959), giving a Judaeo-Christian theory of origins; Roger Sherman Loomis, *The Grail: From Celtic Myth to Christian Symbol* (1963); Jean Marx, *La légende arthurienne et le Graal* (1952); Helaine Newstead, *Bran the Blessed in Arthurian Romance* (1939), treating the contributions of Welsh and Irish legends.

ROBERT W. ACKERMAN

[See also **Arthurian Literature; Chrétien de Troyes; Eucharist; French Literature; Malory, Sir Thomas; Matter of Britain; Welsh Literature; Wolfram von Eschenbach.**]

GRAIN CROPS, WESTERN EUROPEAN

BARLEY

Introduced into Europe from the Near East by Neolithic farmers, barley (*Hordeum vulgare* L.) was probably the dominant cereal of most of Europe in the early Middle Ages. The scanty and often inconsistent textual and archaeological evidence suggests that barley declined in relative importance during the period of agricultural expansion around 1000–1300 and became more important again with the depopulation that followed. Because of its short growing season, barley is the most adaptable of the grains and can be grown at the fringes of agriculture, at high latitudes and elevations as well as in regions of scanty rainfall. It is the most tolerant of cereals to dry heat, drought, and saline and chalky soils, and in the Middle Ages consistently outyielded other grains.

Most of the races in medieval times were six-rowed and covered, but wherever barley was important in the human diet, naked sorts were grown to some extent. Barley makes a poor sort of bread and was usually eaten as porridge or in soups and stews. It was the preferred cereal for brewing into beer and was a major livestock feed. From central France northward and at upper elevations, barley was spring-sown. In Mediterranean regions of winter rainfall and summer drought, all cereals except the millets were fall-sown.

THE WHEATS

Several distinct species and subspecies (*Triticum* spp.) were grown. The grains of the glume wheats are mostly enclosed within the glumes of the spikelets after threshing and winnowing, and further processing in a mill or mortar is required to free them. The naked wheats are free-threshing. The several species are quite distinct, but common names are not always discriminating. "Spelt" or *Spelz* can refer to glume wheats as a class and is frequently confounded with emmer or even einkorn in the literature. "Emmer," *Amelkorn* (German), *far* (Latin), *amidonnier* (French), and similar derivatives always referred to the tetraploid glume wheat, but "spelt," *Spelz*, and sometimes *Dinkel* could be either emmer or spelt—resulting in much confusion. The free-threshing wheats were also frequently confounded in common usage.

Einkorn, introduced from the Near East in Neolithic times, was widespread over Europe but never a major cereal, and was a relict crop by the early Middle Ages.

Emmer, with a similar origin, was much more successful and was the dominant wheat of Europe throughout the Neolithic and Bronze ages. It was the sacred *far adoreum* of the Romans but was largely replaced by bread wheat in Mediterranean lands during Roman times. In the north, spelt, oats, rye, and bread wheat all increased at the expense of emmer, to the point that it had become a minor crop by the early Middle Ages and a relict crop by the end of the period. It was usually spring-sown in the north and fall-sown in the south.

Spelt has a history that is still not clear, but recent evidence suggests that it reached central and northern Europe by a route different from that of other wheats. Migrating northward from the Caucasus and across the Dnieper and Don valleys, it reached what is now Czechoslovakia in the Hallstatt epoch of the Iron Age, spread to Denmark and Gotland in the Bronze Age, and reached Britain in the early Iron Age. By the early Middle Ages it had declined in importance in England and Scandinavia, but was much grown in Carolingian times in northern France and western Germany. Spelt was especially popular among some of the Germanic tribes and, though it is a primitive wheat requiring special processing, it lingered on in some districts into the twentieth century. It is not much grown now, but the area sown to spelt exceeded that of bread wheat in Württemberg, Swabia, Bavaria, Baden, and other regions of southern Germany down to the end of the nineteenth century. Elsewhere in Europe spelt declined in the later Middle Ages, being replaced largely by rye in northern Europe. Spelt is resistant to cold and diseases, and was especially appreciated in mountainous regions.

English or rivet wheat, despite its name, was grown primarily in Mediterranean lands. It was grown in southern England, west, central, and southern France, and parts of Spain in the early Middle Ages. Though productive and tolerant of high rainfall, it gradually gave way to bread wheat.

Durum wheat is the "hard" wheat especially well suited for pasta products. Characteristically a Mediterranean wheat, its introduction is closely associated with the Islamic invasion of southern Europe.

Bread wheat is now the dominant wheat of Europe and of the world, but it is doubtful that this was so in the early Middle Ages, when it was competing not only with barley and rye but also with the other wheats. It was the preferred cereal of the Romans,

but the Germanic tribes adopted it slowly. There is evidence that it was gaining in importance during the agricultural expansion of the eleventh through thirteenth centuries, but declined with the disasters of the fourteenth.

OATS

This cereal (*Avena sativa* L.) is largely a product of the Middle Ages. It is known archaeologically in the early Iron Age, but the early finds seem to represent weeds. Oats were grown in Roman Britain and became a major crop in Saxon England. By Carolingian times they were an important crop in northern France and in Germany. The wild progenitor (*Avena sterilis* L.) is a native of the Near East and Mediterranean lands. It contributed weed races that infested Neolithic barley and emmer fields. It is thought that the cultivated oat was selected from the weed oats of northern Europe. Indeed, oats continued to be grown as a mixture with wheat or barley throughout the Middle Ages. Such mixtures were called "dredge" or "drage" in English and were listed separately in Winchester manor records. The most common dredge mixture was oats and barley, probably because both were spring-sown in much of Europe, whereas wheat and rye were fall-sown. Oats were eaten in bread and porridge, but were also much grown as horse feed. As horses became more popular during the High Middle Ages, oats flourished accordingly.

RYE

Rye (*Secale cereale* L.) has a similar history; the wild progenitor is also found in the Near East, but at higher elevations than the wild oats. It moved as an admixture of wheat into Europe, where it began to become important as a crop in the early Middle Ages. Tolerant of cold and well adapted to sandy soils, it replaced much of the emmer and spelt in northern Europe. It was also grown in mixtures— usually with wheat, since the two were commonly fall-sown. Maslin or mancorn, *méteil*, and *Mengkorn* were common names for wheat-rye mixtures. Rye flour makes a very heavy black bread, but lighter breads can be made using maslin or by mixing with wheat flour.

THE MILLETS

The importance of millets is often underestimated because of social prejudice. They were considered "coarse" foods and fit only for the lowest classes of society. Quite often, however, the rural poor were sustained by millet while they were selling wheat for cash. The millets were not demanding, could be grown on poor soils, had a short growing season, and could be used as a catch crop if other cereals failed. Above all, they were dependable. They differ fundamentally from the cereals described above in that they are "warm season" species and must be grown in summer. They are not well suited to the winter rainfall belt.

Common (or proso) millet (*Panicum miliaceum* L.), introduced from the Asian steppes in Neolithic times, was widely grown in Europe throughout the Middle Ages. It was usually eaten as porridge but could be ground into flour and made into a flat bread.

Italian (or foxtail) millet (*Setaria italica* L.), also introduced from the Asian steppes, was largely confined south of the Alps until after the Middle Ages.

Sorghum (*Sorghum bicolor* [L.] Moench), according to Pliny, was introduced from India into Italy in his lifetime. By the early Middle Ages it had become fairly important in northern Italy and southern France.

Bluthirse or crabgrass (*Digitaria sanguinalis* [L.] Scop.) was never fully domesticated, but was cultivated and harvested as a cereal in central and southern Europe. The cereal form is only slightly different from the common weed of lawns and gardens. The German name derives from the red color of the plant at maturity.

CHANGES IN GRAIN GROWING

During the climatic warming of the Middle Ages, oats and barley were grown in Iceland, wheat in southeast Greenland, and barley as far north as 70° N. in Norway. While warm, dry summers helped agriculture in the north, severe droughts were common in the south. Farming retreated in Scandinavia after 1200, but most of western Europe enjoyed an agricultural expansion from about 1000 to about 1300. Forests were cleared, swamps drained, polders reclaimed, and lands east of the Elbe were settled by farmers. Windmills and water mills became common, and a wheeled moldboard plow with a coulter was popularized, making it possible to exploit heavy clays and wet land. Horses began to supplement or replace oxen for traction, and a three-field system (winter grain, summer grain, hay/fallow) replaced a two-field system (grain, hay/fallow) over much of Europe north of the Loire, increasing the amount of land devoted to cereals.

During the expansion, bread was eaten more and

porridge less, and grains were shipped in increasing amounts. The valleys of the Seine and the Somme were granaries supplying communities of the Low Countries and Scandinavia that could not meet their own needs. England exported grain in good years, sending much of it to Gascony in exchange for wine. Germanic colonization east of the Elbe brought in vast new production, and East German and Polish rye and *Mengkorn* flowed west from Baltic ports.

The fourteenth century was disastrous, with the great famine of 1314–1317, the result of too much rain, especially devastating all over Europe. The depopulation resulting from the Black Death was made worse by adverse climate. With worsening conditions and abandonment of farmlands, there was a trend for barley, rye, and the millets to increase at the expense of wheat. Conditions improved at the close of the Middle Ages, and the area devoted to wheat increased again.

YIELDS

Statistics were customarily given in terms of amount of grain harvested for a given amount sown. Since it is seldom stated how much was sown, only estimates are possible, but these are uniformly low. Returns of 3–5 to 1 were common, with 10 to 1 in very good years and less than 1 to 1 in very bad years. Actual yield and price data have been calculated from heriot records of the Winchester manors of England covering the period 1209–1350. With more than 2,000 calculations (each manor reported on several fields most years) for each cereal, the highest yields for the period were only 14 bushels per acre for wheat, 16 for oats, 17 for mancorn, and 27.6 for barley. Data from seven shires over the period 1325–1349 show average yields for wheat and oats of about 10 bushels per acre and of 17.7 for barley. Data from France, Holland, and Germany were similar. Average yields of wheat, spelt, rye, or barley were on the order of 600–700 kilograms per hectare, with 1,000 kilograms in a good year and 300 kilograms in a poor year; complete crop failures occurred occasionally. Famines were common even during the period of expansion. Increased mortality due to famine was reflected in the Winchester heriot records. In England the price of wheat (about 5 shillings in 1313) quadrupled in 1315 to 20 shillings and rose to 40 shillings in 1316 as the result of two consecutive crop failures. The long-term price trend was upward from the early Middle Ages until the fourteenth century, when prices were generally depressed, except for the enormous deflection just mentioned. The fifteenth century saw considerable improvements in the agricultural economy of western Europe.

BIBLIOGRAPHY

Lord Beveridge, "The Yield and Price of Corn in the Middle Ages," in Eleanora M. Carus-Wilson, ed., *Essays in Economic History,* I (1954, repr. 1966); Georges Duby, ed., *L'Europe au moyen âge,* II (1969); Herbert P. R. Finberg, ed., *The Agrarian History of England and Wales* (1972), 420–422; Augustin Fliche, *Histoire du moyen âge,* II (1939); Guy Fourquin, "Le premier moyen âge," in Georges Duby, ed., *Histoire de la France rurale,* I (1975), and "Le temps de la croissance," *ibid.;* Robert Gradmann, *Der Getreidebau im deutschen und römischen Altertum* (1909); Hans Helbaek, "Early Crops in Southern England," in *Proceedings of the Prehistorical Society,* **18** (1952), and "Spelt (*Triticum spelta* L.) in Bronze Age Denmark," in *Acta Archaeologica,* **23** (1952); Karl Jessen and Hans Helbaek, "Cereals in Great Britain and Ireland in Prehistoric and Early Historic Times," in *Kongelige Danske Videnskabernes Selskat, Biologiske Skrifter,* **3** (1944); Harold H. Lamb, *Climate: Present, Past and Future,* II (1977); G. N. Lisitsina, "Main Types of Ancient Farming on the Caucasus—on the Basis of Palaeoethnobotanical Research," in *Berichte der Deutschen botanische Gesellschaft,* **91** (1978); Henry S. Lucas, "The Great European Famine of 1315, 1316, and 1317," in Eleanora M. Carus-Wilson, ed., *Essays in Economic History,* II (1962); Charles Parain, "The Evolution of Agricultural Technique," in Michael M. Postan and H. J. Habakkuk, eds., *Cambridge Economic History of Europe,* I, *The Agrarian Life of the Middle Ages,* 2nd ed., I (1966); John Percival, *The Wheat Plant* (1921); Michael M. Postan, *Essays on Medieval Agriculture and General Problems of the Medieval Economy* (1973); Jergen Schultze-Motel and J. Kruse, "Neue Daten zur Verbreitung des Spelzes (*Triticum spelta* L.) in prähistorischer Zeit," in *Monatsberichte der Deutschen Akademie der Wissenschaften zu Berlin* (1964); Bernard H. Slicher van Bath, *Yield Ratios, 810–1820* (1963); J. Z. Titow, *Winchester Yields: A Study in Medieval Agricultural Productivity* (1972); Nikolai I. Vavilov, *Studies on the Origin of Cultivated Plants* (1926).

JACK R. HARLAN

[See also **Agriculture and Nutrition; Famine in Western Europe.**]

GRAMADEGAU'R   PENCEIRDDIAID. See **Bardic Grammars (Irish, Welsh).**

GRAMMAR. The teaching of grammar established itself firmly within medieval education. In western Europe from the earliest years of the Middle Ages medieval scholarship was the continuation of classical scholarship under changed and changing circumstances, notably the rise to doctrinal and secular dominance of the Roman church and the replacement of the once-unified western Roman Empire by independent kingdoms.

As a joint consequence of the classical Latin heritage and the authority of the church, the official language of which was Latin, the language of Rome was, and remained throughout the Middle Ages in the West, the language of education, erudition, law, and international communication and commerce. Latin was the universal second language, and to learn Latin boys had to be taught Latin grammar; by the middle of the first millennium the Romance vernaculars were already on the way to becoming different langauges from each other and from literary Latin, and for the Germanic tribes Latin had always been a foreign tongue.

Apart, however, from the necessity of studying Latin grammar as an indispensable tool for education at all, grammar was enshrined as an essential component of the school and university syllabus, the Seven Liberal Arts. This system of education drew on an earlier, no longer extant encyclopedic compilation of Varro (first century B.C.), the *Disciplinae.* The seven arts were divided into the trivium (grammar, dialectic, rhetoric) and the quadrivium (music, arithmetic, geometry, astronomy).

Latin grammar had been codified by a number of writers, collectively known as the Late Latin grammarians, since about A.D. 100. The most famous and the most used were Donatus (fourth century) and Priscian (*ca.* 500), and in this subject Priscian can be regarded as a Janus-figure looking backward and forward between antiquity and the Middle Ages. Donatus' *Ars grammatica* was brief and concise, and in part already cast in that favorite teaching mode of the Middle Ages, the catechism ("Partes orationis quot sunt? Octo. Quae? Nomen, pronomen, verbum, adverbium, participium, coniunctio, praepositio, interiectio"). It occupies fifty pages of modern print. Priscian's *Institutiones grammaticae,* by contrast, is immensely long, very full of detail, some of its statements being justified by theoretical argument, and throughout it is enriched by numerous quotations from classical authors. It was in truth a reference grammar and the source of most grammatical teaching and grammatical scholarship throughout the Middle Ages. Several hundred manuscript copies are known to have existed.

Unlike Donatus' *Ars,* Priscian's *Institutiones* was far too long to serve as a school text, or even as a teacher's handbook. Most grammatical teaching made use of abridgments or summaries and commentaries on specific topics. Writers of these commentaries, known as *glossatores,* constitute one of the vital links maintaining Latin learning and scholarship through the early years of the Middle Ages and into the more settled conditions of the Carolingian Empire and the high Scholastic age.

Several authors of didactic Latin grammars are known, and numerous manuscripts testify to their popularity and importance. A method for the systematic and ordered teaching of Latin had been established as early as the first century A.D. in Quintilian's *Institutio oratoria;* it was reinforced by the primer by Donatus, and in the eighth century, as part of the Carolingian renaissance, the teaching of Latin grammar was further strengthened by Charlemagne's educational reforms and his encouragement of teachers of Latin like Alcuin, who was appointed head of the school attached to the imperial court.

The teaching program comprised orthography and syllable structure (though little attention seems to have been paid to actual pronunciation), the parts of speech and their morphological paradigms, and syntax, together with warnings against errors both in incorrect sentence construction and in deviant word forms. Priscian's *Partitiones,* exercises in the grammatical analysis of twelve lines of Vergil's *Aeneid,* provided a pattern for teaching practice, and classical authors and the patristic writers were used for grammatical exemplification and as models.

In the first few centuries after Priscian, his commentators confined themselves largely to simplifying and expounding, but from around 1100 a gradual change began to take place. This was partly the product of the rise of the medieval universities, especially the University of Paris, but more particularly it resulted from the rediscovery of much of Aristotle's philosophical writing, formerly lost after the breakup of the Roman Empire, and to the incorporation of scholarly studies at university level into Aristotelian philosophy as understood and ordered by the church. This fusion of Aristotelianism and Christian dogma constitutes the main characteristic of Scholasticism, the principal authority of which was the scholar-churchman St. Thomas Aquinas.

This incorporation of grammar, along with other components of the Seven Liberal Arts, into the university curriculum had a profound, though gradual, effect on the study and teaching of Latin grammar.

The earlier commentators were criticized for merely restating Priscian without explaining (that is, justifying philosophically) the form and structure of his grammar; and a division arose between mere pedagogical grammar and philosophical or speculative grammar, this latter being the province of the philosopher, who "diligently considering the true nature of things discovers grammar" (Thurot, 1869, 124). A large number of such speculative grammars were written between the twelfth and the fourteenth centuries; they were highly theoretical and were directed at university education rather than school teaching. School grammars continued to be written and greatly used; one of the best was the *Doctrinale* of Alexander of Villedieu, written about 1200 in verse, no doubt for ease of memorization. It remained in use throughout the medieval period. But in general grammatical pedagogy was looked down on by the writers of philosophical grammars ("As the fool is to the wise man, so is the grammarian ignorant of logic to one skilled in logic": Thurot, 1869, xi–xii).

Not only in this respect did the Scholastic grammarians distance themselves from the earlier Priscianic tradition (though they preserved the details of his description of Latin almost slavishly). Seeing grammar as occupying its proper place in Scholastic philosophy and theology, they no longer related their teaching to classical, pagan, literature. Priscian's grammar was illustrated by quotations from Cicero, Terence, and Vergil, along with Homer when comparison to Greek grammar was being made. Scholastic grammarians contented themselves with merely formulaic sentences to exemplify constructions without regard to literature or context; "Socrates percutit Platonem" (Socrates hits Plato) and "Socrates albus currit bene" (White Socrates runs well) are just two typical examples.

Such an abandonment of the delights of ancient literature did not go unchallenged. While Paris was the center of Scholastic philosophical grammar, Orléans remained the champion of grammar within the study of classical literature. The academic hostility between these two attitudes toward the teaching of the subject is the theme of Henri d'Andeli's famous allegorical poem *La bataille des sept arts* (1236): Priscian, the traditional grammarian, along with Homer and the other classical authors, goes forth from Orléans to challenge the stronghold of Aristotle and his followers in Paris; their attack is beaten back and they retire, vowing that their day will come and that literature will regain its proper place in education and its control over the teaching of grammar. In fact this did come to pass. One aspect of Renaissance linguistic studies was the rejection of Scholastic grammar and its allegedly barbarous medieval Latin, and a reawakened enthusiasm for the teaching of classical Latin and Greek as the language of the great authors and the material of a glorious civilization to which, across the years between, Renaissance man now proudly stretched his hands.

In western Europe the teaching of grammar throughout the Middle Ages was predominantly the teaching of Latin grammar. The regular and universal teaching of European vernacular languages was a feature of Renaissance Europe rather than of medieval Europe, though some noteworthy work was done in this field in medieval times. This occurred mainly in the context of independent scholarship centered on vernacular literature, and most importantly in the bardic and monastic schools of medieval Ireland. There the *Auraicept na nÉces* (The scholars' primer), the oldest part of which probably belongs to the eighth century, was followed by a number of didactic writings in a tradition derived jointly from native sources and the Latin grammars of Donatus and Priscian. A similar tradition provided the matrix for Welsh grammatical teaching; the texts for this language belong mostly to the fifteenth century, though they probably derive from earlier work in Welsh monastic communities.

The first known Latin grammar written in Old Enligh (*ca.* 1000) was the work of Aelfric, abbot of Eynsham, designed for English schoolboys. Based on the Donatus-Priscian model, it was accompanied by a Latin conversation manual, the *Colloquy,* and a Latin-English dictionary (the first of its kind). Its significance in vernacular grammar teaching lies in the author's recommendation that it would serve not only for its prime task of teaching Latin but also as an introduction to the study of English grammar, so initiating a long line of Latin-based grammars of the English language, the emancipation from which involved the continuing efforts of successive English grammarians from the seventeenth to the twentieth century.

Another area in which a grammatical tradition developed in the later Middle Ages was Iceland, then more closely linked with the rest of Europe than it subsequently was until the nineteenth century. A number of treatises on the language of the time, Old Icelandic, deriving their method of presentation from the grammars of Donatus and Priscian, survived in manuscript form. The best known of them

was the so-called *First grammatical treatise,* dating from the twelfth century, in effect a well-thought-out and systematic project for spelling reform on the lines of modern phonological principles. This treatise clearly belongs to, and is evidence of, an established and advanced tradition for the study and teaching of Icelandic grammar in this period.

While the teaching of Latin grammar, at all levels, dominated the schools of western Europe, the teaching of Arabic grammar took an important place in the Islamic world after the vigorous geographic expansion of Arab power during and after the seventh century; and Greek grammar played a comparable part in the Byzantine Empire, broadly the continuation of the Greek-speaking half of the once-unitary Roman Empire.

From Persia in the east to the Arabic domains in Spain in the west, secular, literary, and religious requirements motivated the production and use of teaching manuals of classical Arabic. In particular, in the Middle Ages as in the present day, the Koran could only be studied properly in its original, and Arabic grammatical instruction was closely linked with instruction in the Islamic faith.

Sībawayhi's *Al-kitāb* (eighth century), the first authoritative grammar of the language, was the basis for teaching, though, like Priscian's work, it was too copious and difficult to be a teaching book in itself, and much effort was devoted to the production of abridgments and summary presentations for verbal instruction. At the theoretical level two main school centers emerged, at Basra and at Al-Kufa, where somewhat different attitudes toward the standard of correct Arabic and the principles of grammar were maintained.

Medieval grammatical scholarship among the Arabs was also influential in the development of medieval studies in Hebrew grammar, facilitated by the geographical propinquity and the structural affinities of the two languages.

In the Byzantine Empire, Greek continued to be the language of education and literature and the official language of the church, and it extended its influence in neighboring territories in the wake of missionary activity from the church in Constantinople. In a situation similar to that faced by western teachers, the classical Greek language, the works of classical Greek authors, the Bible, and contemporary ecclesiastical writings had to be taught to populations that spoke non-Greek languages or forms of Greek that were becoming more and more unlike classical Greek.

Under these conditions the teaching of classical Greek grammar took up much time and effort in schools and universities. Numerous summaries and presentations of classical syntax and morphology were composed, all based on the authoritative and copious grammatical writings of Apollonios Dyskolos (second century A.D.), himself taken as a model by the Latin grammarian Priscian. Many of these Byzantine grammars were directly related to schoolroom use, with the familiar catechisms, paradigms, and formalized methods of grammatical and lexical explication (*schedographia*), criticized by some contemporaries as mechanical and uninspiring. Modern scholars too have dismissed the greater part of Byzantine grammatical writing as elementary textbook production, of little theoretical interest. This is not wholly justified, as some important developments in grammatical theory took place, but in any case these grammars and the didactic tradition that they represented and sustained for a period of a thousand years provided the indispensable foundation, in material and in living scholars, for the revival of Greek learning in Italy and beyond, in the western European Renaissance.

BIBLIOGRAPHY

Sources. Donatus, *Ars Grammatica,* in H. Keil, ed., *Grammatici latini,* IV (1864), 353–402; Priscian, *Institutiones grammaticae* and *Partitiones, ibid.,* II–III (1855–1858), 1–377, 457–515.

Studies. R. R. Bolgar, *The Classical Heritage and Its Beneficiaries* (1954); William Boyd and Edmund J. King, *The History of Western Education,* 9th ed. (1968), chs. 3, 4, 5; G. L. Bursill-Hall, *Speculative Grammars of the Middle Ages* (1971), and *The Middle Ages* (1975), 179–230, has bibliography and manuscript bibliography; Anwar G. Chejne, *The Arabic Language: Its Role in History* (1969), chs. 3, 4; Hartwig Hirschfeld, *Literary History of Hebrew Grammarians and Lexicographers* (1926); Richard W. Hunt, *The History of Grammar in the Middle Ages* (1980); Karl Krumbacher, *Geschichte der byzantinischen Literatur,* in Iwan von Müller, ed., *Handbuch der Altertumswissenschaft,* IX, pt. 1 (1897), 499–604, with full bibliographical references; Louis J. Paetow, *The Arts Course at Mediaeval Universities, with Special Reference to Grammar and Rhetoric* (1910); C. Thurot, *Notices et extraits de divers manuscrits latins pour servir à l'histoire des doctrines grammaticales au moyen âge* (1868, repr. 1964).

R. H. ROBINS

[See also **Aelfric; Arabic Language; Auraicept na nÉces; Bardic Grammars; Greek Language, Byzantine; Hebrew Language, Study of; Latin Language; Priscian; Trivium; Universities.**]

GRANADA, the capital of the former Muslim kingdom of that name and one of the major cities of Muslim Andalusia. Located at the foot of the Sierra Nevada some 689 meters (2,260 feet) above sea level, the city was built on three hills, two of which are separated by a deep ravine through which the Darro River (Arabic: Ḥadārru) flows, covered for much of its length by broad, tunnellike bridges.

Built on the site of successive Iberian, Roman, and Vandal settlements, Granada owes its name to that of the neighboring village of Gharnāṭa, itself possibly derived from the Berber place-name Kernāṭa (perhaps hill of strangers) or the Romance form *granata* (pomegranate, a common local fruit found on the coat of arms of the city). The three major sections of the city are the Antequeruela (named after refugees from Antequeruela who settled there in 1410), which is enclosed by the Darro River, with the Alhambra to the west; the Albaicín (from *rabaḍ albayazīn,* or falconers' quarter, though one tradition connects the name with refugees from Baeza who fled there in 1245, after Christians captured their town), which is the oldest quarter, much favored by Muslim nobles, located to the northwest, on the other side of the Darro; and Granada proper.

Granada's illustrious past is inextricably linked with the Arabs. Following the Muslim conquest in the early eighth century, it was governed by the Umayyad caliphate at Damascus and later came to be known as the Damascus of the West. After 1031 the Zirid ruler Zāwī established an independent kingdom here—the name of the royal palace, Dār Dīk al-Riḥ (House of the Weathervane), is recorded—but it fell to the Almoravids in 1090. A series of Almoravid rulers sent by the central government at Marrakesh held the city against increasing Almohad pressure until 1156.

In the Albaicín area are the remains of the old, partly Zirid Alcazaba (citadel), the fragmentary northwest walls of which include the gates known as Cieda, al-Bonaida, Monaita, Nueva, and the crenellated Elvira (from the Roman Illiberis); further north the outer walls enclosed the later suburbs and contained the Bib Bayezin (Falconers' Gate) and Bib Fajjallauza (Almond Ravine Gate, from the Arabic Bāb Fajj al-Lawza). The gates and walls of southern Granada have disappeared, but by the close of the twelfth century, at the latest, the city had elaborate fortifications; within a century there were twenty towers to protect its environs, and by 1492 it had a double ring of encircling walls with more than 1,000 towers.

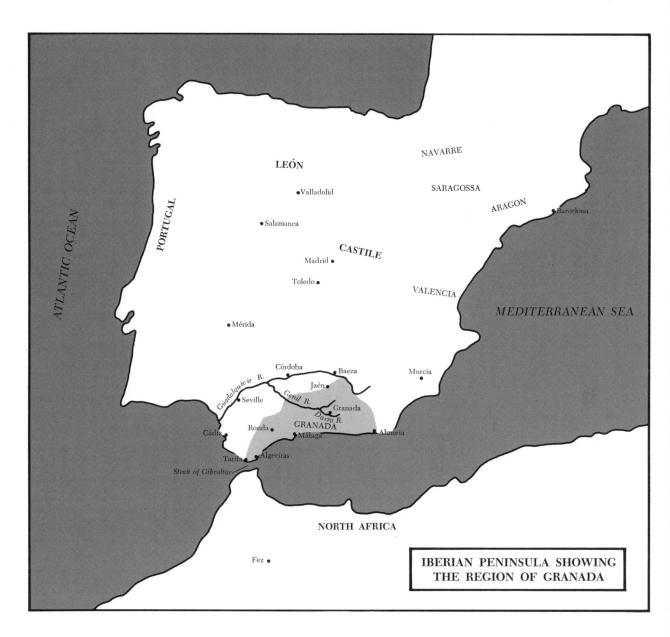

IBERIAN PENINSULA SHOWING
THE REGION OF GRANADA

The increasing prosperity of Granada under Al-mohad rule made it, by about 1200, the fifth largest city in Spain, with a population of Arab, Spanish, and Berber Muslims, Spanish Christians, and Jews living in separate quarters. A brief period of insur-rection between 1229 and 1238 brought a scion of the Banū Ḥūd from Saragossa to power. He ruled Granada as part of a larger kingdom stretching from Algeciras to Almería, but he was defeated by Mu-ḥammad ibn al-Aḥmar, prince of Jaén, who with the support of the Banu'l-Ashqīlūla seized the city and founded the Nasrid dynasty there in 1248, becoming lord of Málaga and Almería at the same time.

This Muḥammad was the first of an unbroken line of twenty-one Nasrid sovereigns who, against all odds, contrived to maintain the independence of their diminutive state for some 250 years. For most of that time they represented the sole surviving Mus-lim power in Spain. Muḥammad ibn al-Aḥmar set the tone for this achievement by becoming a vassal of Ferdinand I of Castile, contracting to pay him a large annual tribute, and even helping him to con-quer the Muslim principality of Seville.

Muḥammad's immediate successors rang the changes on this policy by forming an alliance with the Marinid sultans of Morocco. From 1273 this allowed Granada some respite from Christian pressure—indeed, in the course of four forays across the Strait of Gibraltar, Marinid armies twice defeated the Castilians. Eventually the princes of Granada had at their disposal a corps of Moroccan troops, the *ghuzāt,* commanded by a Marinid sheikh. The Moroccan kingdom exacted a heavy price for this support, taking Algeciras, Tarifa, and Ronda from the Nasrids. However, Fez (and, for that matter, Tunis) was a secure asylum for deposed Nasrid sultans or disaffected officials. Granada in its turn provided refuge for Muslims expelled from Spanish Christian territory, such as Valencia and Almería, and these refugees in time doubled the size of the city, besides increasing the luster of its civilization.

Granada thus rendered a useful service to its Christian neighbors; this and its natural impregnability go far to explain its long survival. Indeed, it enjoyed a unique position athwart Christian Spain and the Muslim Maghrib. The historian Ibn Khaldūn, the philologist Abū Ḥayyān, the globe-trotting geographer Ibn Baṭṭūṭa, and the vizier-cum-*littérateur* Ibn al-Khaṭīb frequented this court. Besides their patronage of the arts, literature, and science, the Nasrid sultans cultivated a consciously Islamic civilization. Arabic was the only language used in the city, and in the later stages of Nasrid rule there were no Mozarabic Christians there. Jurists of unimpeachable orthodoxy, representatives of the traditionalist Mālikī law school, wielded much power.

The second reign of Muḥammad V (1362–1391) witnessed the apogee of Nasrid culture in Granada. Much of the Alhambra was built; silks and other textiles of unsurpassed quality were widely exported; irrigation and agriculture flourished as never before. Estimates of the population of the city, though no doubt exaggerated, reach as high as 400,000. An Arabic saying goes to the heart of the matter: "Paradise is that part of the heavens which is above Granada."

A few traces of this splendor survive. The Cuarto Real de Santo Domingo is a bijou thirteenth-century villa set in beautiful gardens; the Alcázar de Genil was built in the mid fourteenth century as a palace for the Nasrid queens. Several other examples of Nasrid domestic architecture survive. The Casa del Cabildo Antigua has as its core a fourteenth-century college founded by Yūsuf I, and beneath the modern restorations of the Corral del Carbón may be discerned a Muslim inn, Alhondiga gedida (*al-funduq-al-jadīd,* the new inn). Some of the nine original Arab bridges over the Darro were incorporated into the urban fabric when the river was partially cov-

ered; the best-preserved of them is the Puente del Genil (*qanṭarat Shanīl).* The Church of S. Maria occupies the site of the Great Mosque, the Church of S. Ana was also originally a mosque, and the towers of the churches of S. José and S. Juan de los Reyes utilize minarets. The covered market now known as Alcaiceria *(al-qaysarīya)* was burned down in 1843 but was rebuilt using the ancient pillars. The street of El Zacatin, the name of which preserves *al-saqqāṭīn* (the junk-dealers [street]), is still full of second-hand shops. Nearby is the Bibarrambla Plaza (*raḥbat Bāb al-Ramla,* "Sand Gate"), which in medieval times was the scene of tournaments, feuds, and a form of bullfighting. There are even two Arab baths, including the "Nut-tree Bath," Baño del Nogal, near the eleventh-century Puente del Alcalde (*qanṭarat al-qāḍī,* "Bridge of the Judge").

The later history of the Nasrid dynasty and of the city has to be gleaned principally from hostile Christian sources. They recount how the kingdom fell prey to bitter feuds between the leading noble families, notably the Banū Sarrāj and the Zegris, and to harem intrigues. The Muslims compounded these disasters by refusing to pay tribute and at the same time engaging in prolonged disputes about the succession. They were no match for the war of attrition waged from 1481 on by the newly united kingdom of Aragon and Castile, jointly ruled by Ferdinand and Isabella. After a six-month siege Granada surrendered on 2 January 1492, and its ruler, Abū ᶜAbd Allāh Muḥammad XI—the Boabdil of European writers—departed to a penurious exile in Morocco.

ROBERT HILLENBRAND

[See also **Alhambra; Islamic Architecture; Spain, Muslim Kingdoms of.**]

GRANDES CHRONIQUES DE FRANCE, the largest corpus of vernacular historiography devoted to the history of a single country ever produced in medieval Europe. They were written at the royal abbey of St. Denis near Paris between 1274 and 1461. The first part, completed by Hugh (Primas) of Orléans in 1274, covered all French history through the reign of Philip Augustus (1179–1223). It is formed exclusively of translations of previous Latin works that had been preserved in the monastic library, including Aimoin de Fleury's *Historia Francorum* and the *Liber historiae, Chronographia,* and *Vita Sigi-*

berti III of Sigebert of Gembloux for the Merovingian period; the *Annales* and *Vita Caroli Magni* of Einhard, the chronicle of *Pseudo-Turpin,* and Hugh of Fleury's *Historia Francorum* for the Carolingians; and the continuations of Aimoin, Hugh of Fleury, and Guillaume de Jumièges' *Historia Normannorum ducum* for the Capetians.

The next identifiable stage in the redaction of the *Grandes chroniques* is that of an integral text containing French translations of the Latin *Lives* of St. Louis (1226–1270) and Philip III (1270–1285) by Guillaume de Nangis, a monk of St. Denis. These *Lives,* preceded by the brief relation of the reign of Louis VIII (1223–1226), form a bridge between the first and remaining parts of the *Chroniques.*

From 1285 on, the nature of the sources for the *Chroniques* changes. For the reigns of Philip the Fair and his successors (1285–1340), regnal histories in Latin were lacking. Instead, the monks relied on Guillaume de Nangis' universal *Chronicon* and its continuations, then being produced at St. Denis, as well as the continuations of the universal chronicle of Geraud de Frachet, which were also written at the abbey.

From 1340 to the death of Philip VI of Valois in 1350, the narration becomes completely original, though it is still the work of a monk of St. Denis who wrote, apparently, before the battle of Poitiers (1356). The next installment, covering the reigns of Jean II and Charles V (1350–1380), however, is usually attributed to Pierre d'Orgement, Charles V's chancellor.

Under Charles VI (1380–1422) and Charles VII (1422–1461) the abbey of St. Denis once again possessed the office of royal historiographer and returned to the tradition of producing both Latin and French versions of the *Chroniques.* The account of the reign of Charles VI is the work of Jean Jouvenel des Ursins, archbishop of Rheims, who wrote about 1430, basing his text on the official Latin history of Michel Pintoin, chanter of St. Denis from 1411 to 1421. For the reign of Charles VII, the *Grandes chroniques* include Jean Chartier's *Chronique de Charles VII,* a revised translation of his Latin text, with a continuation covering the last decade of the reign. With Chartier, the *Chroniques* come to a close.

From the twelfth to the fifteenth century, the monks of St. Denis continually recorded the history of French kings. In so doing, they framed a context in which the changing nature of the French monarchy could be understood. Their version of French history remained an essential foundation of historical knowledge about the medieval past of France for many centuries, and the royal myth that the monks of St. Denis helped foster contributed to the formation of French national identity.

BIBLIOGRAPHY

The text is edited by Jules Viard, *Les grandes chroniques de France,* 10 vols. (1920–1958).

See also François Bethune, "Les Écoles historiques de Saint-Denis et Saint-Germain-des-Prés dans leurs rapports avec la composition des *Grandes chroniques de France,*" in *Revue d'Histoire Ecclésiastique,* **4** (1903); Henri-François Delaborde, "La vraie chronique du religieux de Saint-Denis," in *Bibliothèque de l'École des chartes,* **51** (1890); Auguste Molinier, "Les *Grandes chroniques de France* aux XIIIᵉ siècle," in *Études d'histoire du moyen âge dédiées à Gabriel Monod* (1896), 307–316; Gabrielle M. Spiegel, *The Chronicle Tradition of Saint-Denis: A Survey* (1978), and "The Cult of Saint Denis and Capetian Kingship," in *Journal of Medieval History,* **1** (1975).

GABRIELLE M. SPIEGEL

[See also **Aimoin de Fleury; Einhard; Chronicles, French; French Literature: After 1200; Historiography, Western European; Hugh of Fleury; Pseudo-Turpin; Sigebert of Gembloux.**]

GRANDMONT, ORDER OF, a manifestation of the eleventh-century monastic reform movement. Contradictory evidence in the sources and the lack of constitutions during its first seventy-five years make the early history of the order obscure. The Italian travels of St. Stephen of Muret (*ca.* 1046–1124), son of the viscount of Thiers in the Auvergne, brought him in contact with the goals of the Gregorian reform movement and with the new eremitical ideals within monasticism. Desiring to introduce these into his own region, in 1076 Stephen withdrew to Muret, a forested area in the mountains north of Limoges (present department of Haute-Vienne). His spiritual precepts of absolute poverty, strict silence, severe fasting, and total abstinence from meat, together with the practical aims of complete renunciation of lands, animals, revenues, parishes, novices' dowries, and the customary financial incidents of manorialism—all of which Stephen feared might involve litigation—represent the ideal of the apostolic life in eleventh- and twelfth-century reformed monasticism. Grandmont is often considered the most extreme example of these principles, and the severity of its regulations caused the bitter controversies with which its history is filled.

The priory attracted many recruits and won the official approval of Pope Gregory VII. The first monks lived in individual cells on the Carthusian model, reflecting Stephen's eremitical inclinations, but growth in numbers led to the construction of simple conventual buildings along Cistercian lines. The original habit was a brown tunic with scapular and hood; a black habit was later adopted, over which choir monks wore an elegant rochet with biretta. Stephen developed no rule, his sole precept being "There is no rule save the gospel." Immediately after his death in 1124 disagreement with nearby Benedictine monks in Limoges over the ownership of the land of Muret led to the community's move to the nearby desertlike area of Grandmont (25 June 1125). Pope Clement III issued the bull of Stephen's canonization in 1189.

Between 1150 and 1160, Stephen of Liciac (1139–1163), the fourth prior, compiled from Stephen's precepts the order's rule. It shows the influences of the rules of Sts. Augustine, Basil, and Benedict with perceptible Cistercian and Carthusian traces. The Grandmontine Rule stressed simplicity of life and the monk's avoidance of all secular interests and contacts. They were never to leave the enclosure. The admission of houses of women was forbidden, though four small houses of nuns were subsequently founded in the diocese of Limoges. In 1188 Pope Clement III approved the rule. Grandmont's reputation for austerity, its proximity to the pilgrimage routes to the shrines at Rocamadour and Santiago de Compostela, and especially the generous patronage of Kings Henry II of England and Louis VII of France led to the rapid expansion of the order, first in the French lands of the English king, then throughout France. Two houses were established in Spain, three in England: Alberbury, Craswall, and Grosmont. By 1200, when the order's prestige reached a peak, the "bon hommes," as the Grandmontines were called, possessed perhaps 140 monasteries and numbered about 1,200 monks.

The order initially laid greatest emphasis on material poverty. Taking John the Baptist as model, Stephen intended that his monks live "as hermits" in the "desert," while the manual and administrative work of lay brothers preserved seclusion. The exclusive authority given lay brothers over property distinguishes the Grandmontines from all other contemporary monastic institutes. As the ideal of absolute poverty waned in the later twelfth century

and possessions accumulated, the power of the lay brothers increased. Their control over temporalities, their large numbers in proportion to the choir monks, and their ill-defined constitutional position led to violent disputes. In 1185 the lay brothers of Grandmont revolted and expelled the prior and many monks. Comparable scandals recurred in 1219 and again in 1244, when the papal threat to unite Grandmont with Cîteaux, and the expulsion of many monks, brought temporary peace. Relaxation of the constitutions on such matters as abstinence from eating meat and total silence, however, led to a decline in observance.

Disagreements continued and a serious schism among the monks provoked Pope John XXII in 1317 to impose drastic reforms. He consolidated the houses, reducing the number from about 149 to 39. Grandmont was erected as an abbey, the abbot to be chosen by its monks, rather than as formerly by electors from daughter houses; the superiors of those dependent monasteries became priors. The pope required that Grandmont be inspected annually by four visitators and established an annual general chapter of all superiors for the maintenance of discipline throughout the order. These measures produced a temporary revival. In the fifteenth century, the papal practice of appointing commendatory abbots of Grandmont, together with the disorders accompanying the Hundred Years War, aggravated old problems and brought fresh ones. The Calvinists occupied the abbey for a time in the late sixteenth century, and the foundation in 1643 of a branch called the Strict Observance of the Order of Grandmont represents the beginning of yet another Grandmontine revival. In 1768 the Commission des Réguliers of France suppressed the order and in 1780 the monks were dispersed. Grandmont itself was destroyed in the early nineteenth century.

Scholars have yet to investigate the contributions that Grandmontine houses made to the economic development of their particular areas; the lay brothers probably were involved in the reclamation of waste and forest land. Grandmont produced no spiritual writers of significance, though the various late-twelfth-century Lives of St. Stephen, which emphasized his insistence that each person develop an individual method of prayer aiming at the growth of "interiority" (the complete giving of the self to Christ), made a contribution to the Christian humanism of the period. Grandmontine church architecture was characterized by choirs and smaller, aisleless naves, reflecting the fact that they had no parochial responsibilities. Apses at the east end were broader than the rest of the building, suggesting the large number of priest-monks.

BIBLIOGRAPHY

Jean Becquet, "Les institutions de l'ordre de Grandmont au moyen âge," in *Revue Mabillon*, **42** (1952), "La règle de Grandmont," in *Bulletin de la Société archéologique et historique du Limousin*, **87** (1958), "La première crise de l'Ordre de Grandmont," *ibid.*, **87** (1960), and *Scriptores ordinis Grandimontensis* (1968), an invaluable collection of documents; Rose Graham, "The Order of Grandmont and its Houses in England," in her *English Ecclesiastical Studies* (1929), 209–246.

BENNETT D. HILL

[See also **Gregory VII, Pope; Monasticism, Origins; Reform, Idea of.**]

Dancer in the hall of the old Rathaus in Munich. Erasmus Grasser, wood carving, 1480. FROM P. M. HALM, ERASMUS GRASSER (1928)

GRASSER, ERASMUS. Leading sculptor in Munich during the early sixteenth century (active 1474–1518), Grasser developed an energetic yet natural figure style based on the works of Nicholas Gerhaerts. He worked mainly in wood, and is best known for the twisting, grotesque *Morris Dancers* (1480) in the Munich Town Hall, oak choirstalls at the cathedral of Munich (with workshop, *ca.* 1502), and the high altar at Reichersdorf (1502–1506).

BIBLIOGRAPHY

Michael Baxandall, *The Limewood Sculptors of Renaissance Germany, 1475–1525* (1980), 277; Philipp M. Halm, *Erasmus Grasser* (1928); Theodor Müller, *Alte baierische Bildhauer* (1950), 40.

LARRY SILVER

[See also **Gerhaert, Nikolaus.**]

GRATIAN, a twelfth-century ecclesiastical lawyer. Only one secure fact is known about this elusive figure: he compiled a collection of ecclesiastical (canon) law entitled the *Concordia discordantium canonum* (Concord of discordant canons), later always referred to as the *Decretum*. It became the most important law book from the twelfth century. Gratian was an Italian who worked and most likely taught canon law at Bologna from about 1130 to 1140. Due in large part to the success of his collection and, probably, to his teaching, canon law was established as a partner to Roman law in the law schools by the end of the twelfth century. Gratian worked on the *Decretum* over a long period of time, finishing it about 1140. He incorporated the canons of the Second Lateran Council (1139) into his collection, but since he often did not fully integrate them into his discussions, it seems likely that he wrote the bulk of the *Decretum* before 1139. There are only a few other pieces of information on Gratian's life. While teaching in Bologna, he may have lived at the monastery of SS. Felice and Nabor. Since monks were not permitted to study or practice law, the tradition that he was a monk must be treated cautiously. He may have served as a legal consultant to a papal judge holding court at Venice in 1143. He had died by the 1160's, since Rufinus, a Bolognese canonist, refers to him as of *ille magne memorie* (he of pious memory).

The title of the *Decretum* describes Gratian's purpose and methodology. He gathered together almost 4,000 chapters taken from papal decretals (letters), the decrees of councils, and the writings of the church fathers. His sources covered the entire history of the Christian church from its beginnings to the twelfth century. He relied on earlier collections of canon law for his texts, particularly those of Anselm of Lucca, Burchard of Worms, and Ivo of Chartres, but, unlike them, he attempted to reconcile the contradictions of doctrine and law embedded in this material. He applied the dialectical methodology of the twelfth-century Schoolmen, particularly that of the great logician Peter Abelard, to his legal texts, adding a commentary to his collection in which he pointed to problems, raised questions, and often provided answers (the "Concord" of his title).

Earlier canonical collections had systematically arranged their authorities according to subject matter. Gratian eschewed their organizational plan of dividing a work into books with each book treating related topics. Instead, he organized the *Decretum* in two parts. In all the manuscripts and the printed editions, the first part consists of 101 *distinctiones* (distinctions). However, some scholars have argued that since Gratian referred to the various sections of the first part as *tractatus* (tractates), he must not have been responsible for these divisions. The first twenty distinctions introduce the types, origin, and definitions of law. The remaining eighty-one distinctions discuss ecclesiastical government and discipline. For example, distinctions 31 to 36 treat the morals of the clergy; 60 to 63, ecclesiastical elections; 64 and 65, episcopal ordination; 77 and 78, the age of ordination; 95 and 96, secular and ecclesiastical authority.

Gratian divided the second part into thirty-six *causae* (cases) and subdivided each *causa* into *quaestiones* (questions). He began each *causa* with a short, imaginary case, followed by a series of questions. Since he mentions them in his commentary, the *causae* were part of Gratian's original plan. Like the distinctions, some *causae* treat a single subject, while groups of *causae* sometimes form treatises on areas of law. Thus *causa* 1 discusses simony. *Causae* 2 through 7 deal with procedure; 16 to 20, monks; 23, war; 27 to 36, marriage. Two important parts of the *Decretum* were probably added shortly after Gratian completed it: a treatise on penance *(De penitentia)* was added to *causa* 33, and a long tract on the sacraments *(De consecratione)* was appended to *causa* 36. The methodology, the structure, and the earliest manuscripts indicate that these two sections may not have been Gratian's work.

Numerous smaller additions were made to the *Decretum*. For reasons that are not entirely clear, Gratian did not include texts taken directly from Roman law in his original draft of the *Decretum*. The remaining 200 fragments of Roman law later incorporated into the *Decretum* were added by Gratian himself in later reworkings of his text or by others. The canonists also added many canonical texts, called *paleae* (literally "chaff"). Even canonists who wrote shortly after Gratian were no longer certain of this word's original meaning. By the end of the thirteenth century as many as 147 chapters of the *Decretum* were designated *paleae*. These additions were clearly part of the law schools' efforts to modify the collection in order to fill lacunae. This practice was not unusual; other canonical collections were also similarly altered in the twelfth and thirteenth centuries.

Gratian's *Decretum* established the study of canon law at Bologna and became the standard introductory textbook in European law schools. Although the papacy never officially approved or authenticated the collection, it became the first part of the body of canon law *(Corpus iuris canonici)* in the law curriculum. Pope Gregory XIII finally ratified the customary status of the *Decretum* when he issued the Roman edition of 1582, the first official printed *Corpus iuris canonici*.

The *Decretum* was not only taught, but it was also commented upon, generating a substantial literature through which canon law was given more precision and sophistication. Huguccio of Pisa (*ca.* 1191) was the most influential commentator of the twelfth century. He wrote an enormous *Summa* on the *Decretum* that was cited and copied until the sixteenth century. In the first half of the thirteenth century, Johannes Teutonicus (*ca.* 1215–1218) wrote a gloss that was accepted as the standard commentary on the *Decretum* (Ordinary gloss) in the schools. Later, Bartholomaeus Brixiensis revised Johannes' gloss (*ca.* 1245), and this version was copied into most manuscripts and printed in all late-fifteenth-, sixteenth-, and most seventeenth-century editions. Gratian's *Decretum* remained one of the standard texts of canon law until it was replaced by the Codex of 1917.

BIBLIOGRAPHY

There were many printed editions of the *Decretum* from the fifteenth to nineteenth centuries. The last, and most convenient, is Emil Friedberg's *Concordia discordantium canonum* (1879, repr. 1959). Titus Lenherr, "Arbeiten mit Gratians Dekret," in *Archiv für Katholisches*

Kirchenrecht, **151** (1982), discusses the text of Friedberg's edition.

Two articles examine Gratian's biography: C. Mesini, "Postille sulla biografia de 'Magister Gratianus,' padre del diritto canonico," in *Apollinaris,* **54** (1981); and John T. Noonan, "Gratian Slept Here: The Changing Identity of the Father of the Systematic Study of Canon Law," in *Traditio,* **35** (1979). See also Stanley Chodorow, *Christian Political Theory and Church Politics in the Mid-twelfth Century: The Ecclesiology of Gratian's Decretum* (1972); and Stephan Kuttner, *Gratian and the Schools of Law, 1140–1234* (1983), a volume of collected essays.

KENNETH PENNINGTON

[See also **Huguccio; Johannes Teutonicus; Law, Canon.**]

GREAT (or OLD) MORAVIA. The name Moravia is the latinized form of a Slavic political formation that existed in the ninth century. Traditionally associated with Moravia on the Morava River north of Vienna, Great Moravia has now been identified instead with the burg of Morava on the Sava River, as attested in a variety of sources.

Part of the larger patrimonial realm known as Slavonia, Moravia extended from Belgrade toward the Dalmatian coast and at times claimed parts of Upper Pannonia. The name Moravia first appears in sources in 822; the formation ceased to exist about 900 as a result of successive Frankish invasions (occurring in 864, 869, 871, 892, 893, 898, and 900), with occasional support from the Hungarians. In fact, "Great Moravia" is an unfortunate modern translation of the term *megale Moravia* used by the emperor-historian Constantine VII Porphyrogenitos about 950 for "Old Moravia" after the burg had been destroyed by the Hungarians. In that period the terms *megas, magnus,* and *great* carried the connotation of being removed by one generation, as in *grand*father, *Magna* Germania, or *Magna* Graecia.

Moravia achieved prominence under princes Mojmar (830–846), Rastislav (846–870), and Sventopolk (870–894)—frequently referred to in historiography as Mojmír, Rostislav, and Svatopluk. Once the Slavonian realm had been emancipated from Avar control (*ca.* 800), the leaders of Moravia sought support against Frankish tutelage from Rome and Constantinople. Independence from Frankish rule, they believed, could be achieved only if the realm of Slavonia acquired its own archbishop. A Slavonian church province was feasible because Rastislav (846–870) controlled Sirmium, a former archiepiscopal see

located on the Sava River across from the burg of Morava. Failing to gain support in Rome, Rastislav and other princes of the realm turned to Constantinople in 863, and Emperor Michael III responded by sending Constantine the Philosopher (later known as Cyril), a diplomat versed in church affairs, to Rastislav. Michael was murdered and Patriach Photios deposed in 867. As a result, Constantine placed his mission under the protection of the papacy. After Constantine died during a visit to Rome in 869, his brother and companion, Methodios, became a priest and was subsequently appointed archbishop of Sirmium. Before he could reach his post, however, he was detained by the bishops of Bavaria, who claimed jurisdiction over the former church province of Sirmium. Released from detention in 873, Methodios assumed his duties as archbishop, thus strengthening the autonomy of Moravia under the papacy.

Sventopolk succeeded Rastislav in 871 and, according to South Slavic sources, even gained the title of king under papal and Byzantine auspices about 880. After his realm was devastated by the Hungarians, Sventopolk, who was related to the Frankish ruling house, received Bohemia as a fief from Arnulf, the East Frankish king, in 890. Supported by the Czechs, Sventopolk conquered large territories northeast and east of Bohemia, but his revolt against Arnulf subsequently ended in defeat and the loss of Bohemia proper. After Sventopolk's death in 894, his retainers remained in control of the valleys of the northern Morava River and the upper Vistula. Remnants of his realm in the south, controlled by his sons, were occupied by the Hungarians after 895.

Great Moravia's history is associated with the introduction of Slavonic as a new liturgical language by Constantine and Methodios, and its use alongside Greek and Latin constituted a unique privilege among the nations of the Roman church. The Glagolitic alphabet, created by Constantine for the translation of liturgical texts, provided a basis for the Croats, Bulgarians, Serbs, and Russians to develop vernacular literatures from the tenth century on. The Glagolitic alphabet remained in use in parts of Croatia till modern times (the first printed book in Croatia was Glagolitic). In the other nations that used Slavonic in liturgy the Glagolitic has been replaced by the Greek alphabet with some letters retained from the Glagolitic.

BIBLIOGRAPHY

Sources for the study of Great Moravia have been edited by Lubomír Hav'ík, *Magnae Moraviae fontes histo-*

rici, 5 vols. (1966–1976), and analyzed by Imre Boba, *Moravia's History Reconsidered* (1971). These works provide bibliographies of earlier studies, though monographs listed there are fraught with confusion concerning the exact location of Great Moravia. Multilingual collections have appeared under the titles *Vel'ká Morava* (1963), *Magna Moravia* (1965), and *Grossmähren* (1966). Studies in English include Zdenek Radslav Dittrich, *Christianity in Great-Moravia* (1962); Francis Dvornik, *The Making of Central and Eastern Europe* (1949), and *The Slavs, Their Early History and Civilization* (1956).

IMRE BOBA

[See also **Bohemia-Moravia; Cyril and Methodios, Sts.; Glagolitic Rite; Moravia.**]

GREATER ARMENIA. See **Armenia: Geography.**

GRÉBAN, ARNOUL (*fl.* 1450–1460), dramatist of Le Mans. Gréban spent a number of productive years in Paris, where he was organist and choirmaster of Notre Dame while studying theology and writing the *Mystère de la Passion* (*ca.* 1450). Contained in numerous manuscripts, the play is considered to be the model for many late-fifteenth- and early-sixteenth-century French *mystères.* Gréban follows Mercadé's division into four days (a total of over 34,425 lines), but whereas Gréban, like his predecessor, restricts the play to Christ's history, he also adds a *creacion abregée,* or shortened version of some Old Testament elements contained in early Passions. The play contains complex versification, extensive musical directions, and considerable literary quality, incorporating many lyrical forms into the dialogue. In addition to theological erudition, Gréban's *Passion* displays a marked sympathy for the Virgin and a new degree of concern for realistic detail. Arnoul Gréban also collaborated with his brother Simon on a mystery play about the Acts of the Apostles.

BIBLIOGRAPHY

Arnoul Gréban, *Le mystère de la Passion,* Omer Jodogne, ed. (1959). See also Maurice Accarie, *Le théâtre sacré de la fin du moyen âge: Étude sur le sens moral de la Passion de Jean Michel* (1979); Omer Jodogne, "La tonalité des mystères français," in *Studi in onore di Italo Siciliano,* I (1966), 581–592; Émile Roy, *Le mystère de la Passion en France du XIVe au XVIe siècle: Étude sur les* sources et le classement des mystères de la Passion (1903–1904, repr. 1974).

T. S. FAUNCE

[See also **Drama, French; Drama, Western European; French Literature: After 1200; Mercadé (Marcadé), Eustache; Passion Cycle.**]

GREEK CROSS. See **Cross, Forms of.**

GREEK FIRE, one of the Byzantines' most effective weapons, was discovered, probably about 673, by Callinicus, a Greek architect from Heliopolis (Baalbek) in Syria. The formula was a carefully guarded secret, and it is likely that only the imperial fleet stationed at Constantinople was equipped with it, except in times of emergency, when the thematic fleets also received it. The exact composition is still unknown, but it was probably a combination of naphtha, sulfur, and quicklime, which was combustible in water and exploded on contact with it. It was fired through siphons or lances with high-velocity nozzles; the *siphonarios* stood in the bow of the ship and armed the mouth of the siphon. It could also be used in hand grenades, which were made of earthenware vessels. Greek fire was used most notably against the Arabs, especially in repelling the Arab sieges of Constantinople in 674–678 and 717–718, but it was also used against the Russians in 941 and was still being used against the Venetians during the Fourth Crusade.

BIBLIOGRAPHY

W. H. Spears, Jr., *Greek Fire: The Fabulous Secret Weapon That Saved Europe* (1969).

LINDA ROSE

[See also **Technology, Byzantine; Warfare, Byzantine.**]

GREEK LANGUAGE, BYZANTINE. The Byzantine Empire was always a polyethnic and multilingual society, and especially so before the Arab conquests of the mid seventh century. But Greek was always the language of the dominant culture. A person knowing only Syriac or Armenian might play a limited and local role, but Greek language and culture alone gave access to leading positions in state and church. Upward social mobility often involved hellenization, as with the sixth-century Syrian Romanos, whose religious poetry is in Greek; with the many Armenians in the middle Byzantine period who adopted the Greek language and Orthodox Christianity; or with the Slavs Niketas and Ioannikios, who in the eighth century became, respectively, patriarch and saint.

Throughout the Byzantine period the Greek language was marked by an internal bilingualism or diglossia inherited from the Greek culture of the Roman Empire. On the one hand there was the Greek used by all classes in daily life; on the other, an archaizing Greek based on imitation of classical models and used in writing or formal speech. The spoken language was subject to gradual change; in late antiquity and the early Middle Ages it underwent radical structural changes that foreshadowed modern Greek. The literary language was in theory changeless. The spoken language was learned in childhood. The literary language was acquired through long study of grammar and rhetoric. The spoken language, in somewhat stylized form, had been the normal vehicle of prose literature in the Hellenistic age but thereafter was confined to technical writing and the internal communication of minority groups such as the early Christians. From the first century of the Christian era the literary language became a mark not only of intellectual attainment but also of social status.

As Christianity spread among the urban upper classes, it abandoned the language of the New Testament in favor of the prestigious and classicizing learned tongue. The great church fathers of the fourth and fifth centuries, men of education and social distinction, wrote in literary Greek. Only the best would do for the service of the Lord. Therefore, in Byzantine eyes literary Greek enjoyed a double prestige, as the vehicle both of classical wisdom and of Christian doctrine.

Active command of literary Greek was always restricted to a small intellectual elite, concentrated largely in Constantinople. But knowledge of it was never a clerical monopoly, as was knowledge of Latin in many parts of western Europe. Passive understanding of literary Greek was more widespread; it was not a foreign language, and was familiar to all from its use in the liturgy.

Up to the ninth century some literature was written in a language that owed little to classical models and showed some of the morphological, syntactical,

and lexical innovations of the spoken tongue. It consisted mainly of lives of holy men and naïve world chronicles, and was often of provincial origin. More serious literature was composed in classicizing Greek. Technical writing often followed a middle course, neither archaizing nor popular. As the Byzantine Empire turned from defense to expansion at the end of the ninth century, and once again became the dominant power in Europe and much of the Near East, a new consciousness of superiority found its expression in more profound study of classical literature and more rigorous imitation of its language and style. The old popular saints' lives were rewritten for liturgical use in inflated classicizing Greek. World chronicles, state papers, and private letters were replete with archaic words culled from dictionaries and obsolete grammatical forms like the dual and the optative.

Any departure from rigorous classicism called for an excuse: that the subject matter was technical, that the text was of a private nature, or that the writer had not studied grammar. Some writers, such as Michael Psellos and Niketas Choniates, handling the literary language with flexibility and expressiveness, made full use of its rich vocabulary and its opportunities for literary allusion. For others, like Photios or Anna Komnena, anxiety over the form hindered free self-expression. Perceptive men of letters in the twelfth century (among them Theodore Prodromos and Eustathios) were sometimes interested in everyday language, drew upon it to explain features of classical Greek, and even imitated it in satirical genre pieces.

The destruction of the Byzantine Empire by the crusaders in 1204 interrupted the educational tradition that was the support of the classicizing literary language. But the tradition was revived, first by the government in exile in Nicaea and then by the restored Byzantine Empire after 1261, as part of its assertion of legitimacy and the new Byzantine self-identification. The hated Westerners might have military power, but they were considered barbarians, since they lacked direct access to classical learning and Christian revelation that only Greek culture could give. Classicism became part of patriotism. Late Byzantine serious literature is uncompromisingly archaizing and imitative in language. Some specimens of it were long believed to be works of classical antiquity.

At the same time a new bourgeoisie was beginning to emerge in the cities, and some members of the ruling class were growing disillusioned with the sterility of much late Byzantine culture. A new reading public that cared little for imitation of the past arose. Texts written in the learned tongue were occasionally paraphrased in simpler language. From about 1300 written poetry began to approximate the spoken tongue. It comprised mainly ballads of chivalry, some of which were adapted from Western models, romanticized history, and satirical caricatures of Byzantine life. This development seems to have begun in the upper ranks of metropolitan society rather than at a popular or provincial level.

The new vernacular writing was confined to "light" literature and belonged to the domain of entertainment. All serious work, and much that was pretentious rather than serious, continued to be written in the learned language, the prestige of which remained undimininished. The fourteenth-century breakthrough of vernacular Greek into literature was a false dawn. For lack of a Greek Dante to make the language of the people a universal medium, fit for the most lofty purposes, the Byzantines bequeathed to post-Byzantine Greek society a divisive heritage of internal bilingualism that has lasted to the present day.

BIBLIOGRAPHY

Gertrudis Böhlig, "Das Verhältnis von Volkssprache und Reinsprache im griechischen Mittelalter," in *Aus der byzantinistischen Arbeit der Deutschen Demokratischen Republik,* **1** (1951); Robert Browning, *Medieval and Modern Greek* (1969, 2nd ed. 1983), and "The Language of Byzantine Literature," in Speros Vryonis, Jr., ed., *The "Past" in Medieval and Modern Greek Culture* (1978); M. J. Jeffreys, "The Literary Emergence of Vernacular Greek," in *Mosaic,* 8 (1975); S. G. Kapsomenos, "Die griechische Sprache zwischen Koine und Neugriechisch," in *Berichte zum XI. Internationalen Byzantinisten-Kongress* (1958), II.i.

ROBERT BROWNING

GREEK ORTHODOX. See **Byzantine Church; Russian Church.**

GREGORIAN CHANT (also known as "plainchant"), broadly, the musics attached to the five major Latin liturgies of the Western church—the Ambrosian, Celtic, Gallican, Mozarabic, and Roman rites. Inherently the term is an anachronism for it

tends to perpetuate a pious legend, which gained wide acclaim after the mid ninth century, that Gregory the Great (590–604) received this music directly from the Holy Spirit and gave it to the church. In actuality the testimony of primary sources, such as the *Liber pontificalis* and *Ordo romanus I,* is excruciatingly terse about papal involvement in the formation and codification of a musical liturgy from Damasus (366–384) to Vitalian (657–672). Within this historical framework Gregory's role, like that of his predecessors, is limited to specific reforms and pastoral admonitions, not to the invention of religious song.

Of the five Western rites three fell by the wayside during the Middle Ages. Celtic chant from Scotland, Ireland, Wales, northwest England, and Brittany, and Gallican chant from Merovingian Gaul were effectively suppressed during the seventh and eighth centuries before systems of written musical notations evolved. Only a few melodies are thought to survive from these liturgical uses. The corpus of Mozarabic chant, by contrast, has come down to us remarkably intact in about forty full manuscripts and fragments. Unfortunately, this liturgical music, which was used by Christians living among the Muslims in medieval Spain until the year 1085, is difficult to understand because the melodies are preserved in two types of musical notation that cannot be deciphered. Attempts to restore this liturgy and chant in Toledo shortly after 1500 by Cardinal Ximénez de Cisneros were well-intentioned, but futile. Thus, only two repertoires of Western chant still flourish: the music that is used throughout the Roman Catholic Church today, and Ambrosian, or Milanese chant, which is confined largely to the diocese of Milan.

Intrinsically, Gregorian chant is sacred music. It functions to sanctify traditional forms in Christian worship and it places communal expressions of belief in the mystery of man's salvation on an elevated psychological and artistic level. When chant is removed from its natural devotional and ceremonial setting within the liturgy to the concert hall, classroom, or phonograph recording much of its internal spiritual meaning, at least in aesthetic and theological terms, is negated.

The historical origins of Gregorian chant, its social development within the institution of the early church, and its dispersion to many regions of Europe before the beginning of the tenth century are shrouded in obscurity. Essentially this is due to a single cause: except for less than three dozen scant examples from the ninth century, we lack any liturgical book containing a substantial number of melodies written down in a musical notation dating before 890–925. Prior to this time the sacred music of the church was performed from memory. When musical notations did emerge around the year 900, from twelve to fifteen (depending on the criteria used) distinct types of notation from different geographical zones in Europe are discernible. From a twentieth-century perspective these families, even the diastematic (intervallic) types, were all imperfect, because none could express simultaneously and with precision the inherent qualities of melody, pitch, and rhythm.

This absence of direct musical evidence has compelled scholars to reconstruct the early development of chant from an assortment of historical, apologetic, liturgical, legal, and exegetical writings. Interpretation of these secondary sources frequently presents problems because the literal meaning of words is a source of confusion. There are, for example, numerous allusions to sacred music in the writings of the early ecclesiastical fathers and popes, the proceedings of church councils, the rules of early monastic orders, and various chronicles. But what may appear to be obvious Latin musical terms, may, in fact, be phrased in imagery and have little direct bearing on actual musical use.

Medieval chant is marked by a singular paradox—abundance and anonymity. It is evident that the dynamic process of composing liturgical music continued vigorously throughout the Middle Ages both in the writing of new compositions and in the adaptation and restructuring of older melodic prototypes and formulas to different texts. Despite this prolixity, few composers—at least in the modern sense of a Bach, Chopin, or Stravinsky—are known, so that in most cases the origin and date of individual chants can be deduced only from flimsy evidence. The approximate number of extant melodies is a matter of conjecture. At present, our best practical guide to the repertoire is the Bryden and Hughes *Index of Gregorian Chant*, which lists over 11,000 tunes and texts compiled from nineteen publications and sources.

There are two orders of liturgy with chants, the Mass and the Divine Office. The Mass, from a theological standpoint, is most sacred, because it represents the Eucharistic sacrament, the daily reenactment of the Last Supper. In contrast, the Divine Office is an intricate set of eight nonsacramental prayer services scheduled throughout the day: matins, which is divided into three nocturnes (3:00 A.M.); lauds (daybreak); prime (6:00 A.M.); terce (9:00 A.M.); sext (noon); none (3:00 P.M.); vespers (at dusk); and compline (before retiring).

Each day of the ecclesiastical year, a period that extends from early December until late November, has its own Mass and Office. This liturgical calendar is divided into two commemorative cycles—the fixed feasts of the Proper of the Saints (sanctorale) and the movable feasts of the Proper of the Time (temporale). For example, the Mass and Office for 9 October recall the life and pious works of the martyr St. Denis, the first bishop of Paris. Conversely, Septuagesima Sunday, which anticipates the penitential season of Lent in its liturgy, may fall on any Sunday during late January or February depending on the date of Easter. Festivals from the two cycles are ranked by their relative importance, and in the event of a conflict on any given day a table of occurrences determines which feast takes precedence.

The daily Masses and Offices are constructed of specific prayers that are either sung, recited aloud, or read silently in a prescribed order and manner by the celebrant, his assistant, the choir, the soloist, or the congregation. Chants or prayers that are repeated each day belong to the Ordinary of the Mass or Office, while those that vary with each service belong to the Proper. During the Middle Ages the texts of the Ordinary were set to many melodies. Martin Schildbach, for example, has identified 267 settings of the Agnus Dei. Proper texts, on the other hand, are normally associated with one melody. The incidence of melodic cross-fertilization, the adaptation of texts to pre-existent tunes, is much greater among metrical and poetic forms than among those that are entirely in prose.

The principal musical formularies of the Roman Mass are the introit, gradual, alleluia, tract, offertory, communion, Kyrie eleison, Gloria in excelsis, Credo, Sanctus, and Agnus Dei. Those of the Roman Divine Office are the invitatory, antiphon, hymn, psalm, canticle, versicle, and the great and short responsories. The chart accompanying the article "Divine Office" (vol. 4, pp. 226–228) demonstrates the complex internal arrangement of the Offices for both monastic and secular clergy.

In the early ninth century a third class of chant, the paraliturgical forms, which were essentially textual and musical accretions to the standard Mass and Office chants, began to enter the liturgy and persisted until the reforms of the Council of Trent in the late sixteenth century. The important types are the sequence (or prosa), prosula, sequentia, trope, and processional antiphon. Some tropes and sequences became so assimilated into the regular liturgy by popular use and decree during the Middle Ages that, for all practical purposes, they assumed the status of traditional Gregorian music. For example, this eleventh-century Italian trope was interpolated into the ancient dismissal acclamation of the Mass:

Ite, laudantes Deum atque Dominum semper *missa est.*
Deo, reddentes suis ac fidelibus cunctis *gratias.*
(*Analecta hymnica,* **47** [1905], 409)

These elaborate musical liturgies of the Mass and the Divine Office were transmitted throughout Europe during the Middle Ages, including Norway, Sweden, Poland, Hungary, Bohemia, and northern Yugoslavia, in a variety of liturgical books. Most were hand-copied and decorated by trained scribes and illuminators; this bookmaking craft did not die out until the eighteenth century, more than 300 years after the first printed chant book, the so-called "Constance Gradual," was published about 1473.

There are four general classes of chant manuscripts. Chants of the Mass are contained in the gradual, notated missal, Kyriale, and the cantatorium, while those of the Divine Office appear in the antiphonal and the notated breviary. Most frequently the paraliturgical chants were incorporated into the Mass and Office books, but when collected into anthologies, these books were known as tropers, prosers, and processionals. Finally, there are two types of practical manuals that aided the singers in the proper instruction and selection of their music, the tonary and the ordinal. Among the modern scholarly editions of medieval chant books three deserve particular attention. René J. Hesbert edited the texts of six late-eighth- and ninth-century graduals (they contain no music) in *Antiphonale missarum sextuplex* (1935) and twelve antiphonals in *Corpus antiphonalium officii* (1963–1979). The most important series of photographic facsimile editions is *Paléographie musicale* (1889–).

Since the publication of the first modern history of Gregorian chant, Martin Gerbert's *De cantu et musica sacra* (1774), theorists and historians have attempted to formulate systematic typologies of the repertoire. For purposes of definition certain classifications and stylistic characteristics can be enumerated, though it should be cautioned that this music, which has embellished the liturgy of the Western church for at least 1600 years, has been subjected to countless reforms and modifications.

Unlike the polyphonic music that began to find wide acceptance in church services after 1100, Gregorian chant is monodic music; it consists of a single melodic line. Many liturgical texts sung as chants are passages from the Latin Bible, the Vulgate. Ordinarily, Gregorian chant is thought of as strictly vocal music sung in unison by a choir, but other venerable, short-lived traditions of adapting instrumental accompaniments to the melodies, as the organ and serpent, have come and gone. Most chants exhibit an internal structural form that can be analyzed and classified. Willi Apel divides the repertoire into three classes—recitation, repetition, and free forms. The most easily recognized formal arrangements are the strophic verses of the hymn, the paired lines of the sequence, and the psalmodic reciting tones. Each Gregorian melody conforms to one of the eight church modes, a medieval scale of seven degrees with characteristic melodic ranges (ambitus) and internal and final cadences. During the Middle Ages an extensive literature of speculative and theoretical treatises developed explaining the chants of the Mass and the Divine Office, particularly the nature of the modal scales and the function of the psalm and intonation formulas.

Chant melodies are frequently grouped into three categories according to their melodic ornateness. The scriptural pericopes, collects, litanies, passions, Glorias, creeds, paternosters, psalms, antiphons, invitatories, short responsories, hymns, doxologies, and salutations are syllabic chants, that is, each text syllable is usually set to a single musical note. A second class, the neumatic chants, include the introits, communions, tropes, Sanctus, and Agnus Deis; here, small clusters of notes from several to more than a dozen may accompany a syllable. Melismatic chants, as the Kyries, alleluias, tracts, offertories, and great responsories contain very florid passages; a single vowel can be set to as many as 200 notes.

The question of whether or not Gregorian chant was sung rhythmically, that is, to note values of unequal short and long durations, remains a matter of sharp dispute. Except for about a dozen tenth- and eleventh-century manuscripts from the region of St. Gall, Switzerland, which display an abundance of rhythmic cues, most medieval chant melodies are notated without rhythmic indications. Orthodox performance practice in the church today is dominated by the so-called "Solesmes method," an aesthetically satisfying, free-flowing, virtually nonrhythmic style of singing. To a marked degree this mode of performance is based on elaborate theories of rhythmic motion promulgated by three influential scholars from the Benedictine Abbey of Solesmes in France, Dom Joseph Pothier (1835–1923), Dom André Mocquereau (1849–1930), and Dom Joseph Gajard (1885–1972). Those who hold that chant was sung to some kind of measured rhythm (they are called "mensuralists") have had virtually no impact on prevailing use.

The matter of what constitutes an "authentic" Gregorian melody is a thorny issue that touches upon many current studies. Considering the repertoire as a whole, comparatively few tunes survive as unica; rather, most are transmitted in from several to hundreds of manuscripts in variant forms. These melodic variants—some subtle, others very complex—can appear as different graphic representations of neumatic groupings, as tonal variants of individual notes, and as omitted or added notes. The most elaborate study of variants among the Mass melodies is *Le graduel romain,* a survey of 371 manuscripts.

Modern attempts to restore "authentic" Gregorian song to liturgical services by ecclesiastical authority are invariably associated with decrees issued by the Council of Trent (1545–1563), and their implementation by three popes: Pius V (1566–1572), Sixtus V (1585–1590), and Urban VIII (1623–1644). Unfortunately, the process of standardization begun at Trent is often misunderstood. For one thing, the terms "Tridentine Mass" and "Tridentine Office" are misleading. No new liturgy was set forth, but rather religious establishments throughout Europe were mandated to follow "prescribed customs and normative usage" and "corrected" liturgical books; it was a conservative movement in the true sense of the word, as Hayburn documents it. Further, in strictly musical terms, the sought-for reforms were completely illusionary, for, despite an official imprimatur that was affixed to most chant books—"Ex decreto Sacrosancti Concilii Tridentini restituti"—a bewildering diversity of chant melodies flourished for another 300 years.

It was not until the last quarter of the nineteenth century, when the scholarly disciplines of musicology and paleography reached a point of sufficient technical sophistication, that uniform melodic use was achieved. Three Vatican publications issued under the auspices of Pius X (1903–1914) stand as monuments to this turn-of-the-century scholarship, the *Kyriale* (1905), the *Graduale sacrosanctae romanae ecclesiae* (1908), and the *Antiphonale sacrosanctae romanae ecclesiae* (1912). Uniform use, however, should not be confused with "authentic" restoration. Twentieth-century chant books are functional compilations destined for practical use, and lack critical commentaries and manuscript sources.

BIBLIOGRAPHY

Analecta hymnica medii aevi, Guido M. Dreves, Clemens Blume, and Henry M. Bannister, eds., 55 vols. (1886–1922, repr. 1961), and *Analecta hymnica medii aevi, Register,* Max Lütolf, ed., 3 vols. (1978); Willi Apel, *Gregorian Chant* (1958), 529; Terence Bailey, *The Intonation Formulas of Western Chant* (1974); Clyde W. Brockett, "Antiphons, Responsories, and Other Chants of the Mozarabic Rite," in *Musicological Studies,* 15 (1968); John R. Bryden and David C. Hughes, *An Index of Gregorian Chant,* 2 vols. (1969); John Caldwell, *Medieval Music* (1978), 11–93; Solange Corbin, "Die Neumen," in *Paleographie der Musik,* I, *Die einstimmige Musik des Mittelalters,* III (1977), 230; Richard L. Crocker, *The Early Medieval Sequence* (1977), 470; John A. Emerson, "Plainchant," in the *New Grove Dictionary of Music and Musicians,* XIV (1980), 805–844 (with a bibliography of over 800 items); Paul Evans, "The Early Trope Repertory of Saint Martial de Limoges," in *Princeton Studies in Music,* 2 (1970); Karl G. Fellerer, ed., *Geschichte der katholischen Kirchenmusik,* 2 vols. (1972–1976); *Le graduel romain: Édition critique par les moines de Solesmes,* 3 vols. (1957–1962); Robert F. Hayburn, *Papal Legislation of Sacred Music 95 A.D. to 1977 A.D.* (1979); René J. Hesbert, *Antiphonale missarum sextuplex* (1935); *Corpus antiphonalium officii,* in Rerum ecclesiasticarum documenta, ser. major, *Fontes,* vii–xii, 6 vols. (1963–1979); Andrew Hughes, *Medieval Music: The Sixth Liberal Art,* in Toronto Medieval Bibliographies, IV (1975, rev. 1980), with an extensive annotated bibliography; Heinrich Husmann, *Tropen- und Sequenzenhandschriften,* in Repertoire international des sources musicales, ser. *B,* V.1 (1964), 236; *Monumenta monodica medii aevi,* Bruno Stäblein, ed., 5 vols. (1956–); *Paléographie musicale: Les principaux manuscrits du chant grégorien, ambrosien, mozarabe, gallican,* 21 vols. in two series (1889–); John Rayburn, *Gregorian Chant: A History of the Controversy Concerning Its Rhythm* (1964), 90; Martin Schildbach, *Das einstimmige Agnus Dei und seine handschriftliche Überlieferung vom 10. bis zum 16. Jahrhundert* (1967), 205; Robert A. Skeris, *Musical Imagery in the Ecclesiastical Writers of the First Three Centuries* (1976), 252; Bruno Stäblein, "Schriftbild der einstimmigen Musik," in *Musikgeschichte in Bildern,* Lfg. 4, 4 (1975), 260; Gregory M. Suñol, *Introduction à la paléographie musicale grégorienne* (1935; Catalan ed., 1925), 660.

JOHN A. EMERSON

[See also **Antiphonal; Divine Office; Gradual; Hymns; Kyriale; Mass; Melisma; Mode; Monophony; Music, Liturgical; Plainsong Sources; Psalm Tones; Responsory; Sequence (Prosa); Solesmes; Tropes (to the Proper of the Mass); Tropes (to the Mass Ordinary).**]

GREGORIDS, an Armenian noble family descended from St. Gregory the Illuminator, whose members were patriarchs of Armenia from the early fourth century to the death of its last male member, St. Sahak I, in 437/439. The known members of the family in addition to St. Gregory are his younger son Aristakēs, the coadjutor and successor of his father, who probably represented Greater Armenia at the Council of Nicaea in 325; his elder son, Vrt^c^anēs (*ca.* 333–341), successor of Aristakēs; Vrt^c^anēs' sons Yusik (*ca.* 341–347/348) and Grigoris, whose evangelization of the Iberians and Albanians led to his martyrdom; Yusik's sons Pap and At^c^anakinēs, both of whom refused the perilous dignity of patriarch after their father's murder; Yusik's grandson, St. Nersēs I (353–373); Yusik's great-grandson, St. Sahak I (387–428, 432–437/439), who left one daughter, Sahakanuyš.

Both the family name of the Gregorid house, Part^c^ew, and Armenian tradition derive the origin of the family from the great Iranian house of the Sūrēn, and the medieval Armenian writer Movsēs Xorenac^c^i asserts in his *History of Armenia* (3.51) that St. Sahak's honorable reception at the Sasanian court was due to his noble lineage. The domain of the family appears to have been in western Armenia, in the provinces of Ekełeac^c^ and Daranałik^c^, where the members of the family were taken for burial, and they also possessed estates in Tarōn. In accordance with the early Armenian tradition of hereditary offices, the Gregorids were considered to be the legitimate patriarchs of Armenia, and contemporary sources insist that only members of this family were the true holders of that dignity, though other bishops were occasionally appointed by the Armenian kings or the Persians.

The great Gregorid patriarchs, especially Nersēs I and his son Sahak I, guided the foundation of the Armenian church, presiding over early councils, developing the native liturgy, and creating monastic and charitable institutions. Despite their position as heads of the national church, the Gregorids often pursued a generally hellenizing policy, steering Ar-

menian Christianity away from its Syrian origins. Until the death of Nersēs I they were consecrated at Caesarea in Cappadocia. The Gregorids' opposition to the Arianizing policies of the contemporary Arsacid kings of Armenia and their support of the Mamikonean house often brought them into conflict with the Armenian crown and resulted in the murders of Yusik and Nersēs I. The opposition of Sahak I to the policy of the Sasanians after the end of the Armenian kingdom brought about his deposition by the Persians in 427/428. After Sahak I's death, his daughter Sahakanuyš carried the Gregorid domains into the family of her husband, Hamazasp Mamikonean, and the patriarchate of Armenia ceased to be a hereditary office.

BIBLIOGRAPHY

Nikolai Adontz, *Armenia in the Period of Justinian,* Nina G. Garsoïan, trans. (1970), 100, 273–275, 286–287; Gérard Garitte, *La Narratio de rebus Armeniae* (1952), 53–54, 56–58, 61–62, 74–75, 87–88, 91–94, 402, 406, 415–417, 421; Nina G. Garsoïan, "Politique ou orthodoxie? L'Arménie au quatrième siècle," in *Revue des études arméniennes,* n.s. 4 (1967), and "Prolegomena to a Study of the Iranian Aspects in Arsacid Armenia," in *Handēs amsoriya,* 90 (1976), cols. 180–181, 182–183, 197–198 n. 28, 213–214 n. 45; Josef Markwart, *Die Entstehung der armenischen Bistümer* (1932), 152–233; Malachia Ormanean, *Azgapatum* (1912), I, 117–326; Cyril Toumanoff, *Studies in Christian Caucasian History* (1963), 138–139, 207–208n, 236, 218.

NINA G. GARSOÏAN

[See also **Armenia: History of; Gregory the Illuminator, St.**]

GREGORIUS. See Bar Hebraeus.

GREGORY OF NAREK, ST. See **Grigor Narekac^c^i, St.**

GREGORY OF NAZIANZUS, ST. (*ca.* 330–389/390), one of the three Cappadocian fathers of the church, celebrated as the classical Greek interpreter of the Trinitarian doctrine, and known in Greek usage as "the Theologian."

Son of a Christian bishop, Gregory was born near Arianzum, in Cappadocia. After studying rhetoric and philosophy in several centers of Hellenistic learning, including Athens, he became a close friend of Basil the Great, who, as bishop of Caesarea in Cappadocia, became one of the major fathers of Eastern Christendom. Together they studied Origen and, as young men, became fascinated with the early Christian monastic movement.

Gregory was ordained a priest by his father in 362, and in 371 was convinced by his friend Basil, who needed help in his struggle with the Arians, to accept consecration as bishop of Sasima. He never occupied his see, however; after administering the church of Nazianzus for a short time, he was invited to head the small Orthodox congregation in Arian-dominated Constantinople (379). It is there, in the house-church of the Anastasia (Resurrection) that he delivered his famous *Theological Orations* on the Trinity.

After the restoration of Orthodoxy in the capital by Emperor Theodosius I (380), Gregory occupied the archiepiscopal throne. However, unable to reconcile the parties of bishops, who struggled at the Council of Constantinople (381), and challenged by the Alexandrians, who, supported by Rome, had consecrated a competing archbishop of Constantinople, Maximus the Cynic, Gregory withdrew first to Nazianzus and then to a monastic retreat. He died in 389 or 390.

Surnamed "the Theologian" for the accuracy of his Trinitarian definitions, Gregory left a total of 45 orations, a series of poems, and a collection of 244 letters.

In his Trinitarian theology, together with the other Cappadocians (Basil the Great and Gregory of Nyssa), Gregory insisted not only on the unity of a consubstantial Godhead, in accordance with the definition of the Council of Nicaea (325), but also on the doctrine of the three distinct hypostases. This "neo-Nicene" doctrine made possible a wider acceptance of Nicene orthodoxy in the East.

BIBLIOGRAPHY

The writings of Gregory are published in *Patrologia graeca,* XXXV–XXXVIII; the five *Theological Discourses* with commentary by J. Barbel (1963); and the *Letters* are edited by P. Gallay, 2 vols. (1964–1967). See also J. Plagnieux, *S. Gregoire de Nazianze, théologien* (1951).

JOHN MEYENDORFF

[See also **Gregory of Nyssa, St.**]

GREGORY OF NYSSA, ST. (*ca.* 335–*ca.* 394), a brother of Basil the Great and one of the three Cappadocian fathers whose intellectual and spiritual leadership dominated Greek theology in the later part of the fourth century.

Gregory received training as a rhetorician, married, and planned a secular career. However, under the influence of his brother Basil and his friend Gregory of Nazianzus, he eventually opted for the church and in 371 was consecrated bishop of Nyssa. In 376 he was deposed in absentia by a synod of Arian bishops. He later took an active part in restoring Nicene Orthodoxy in Constantinople when, in 381, under Theodosius I, he became a member of the Second Ecumenical Council. Since Basil had died in 379 and Gregory of Nazianzus had retired from active life in 381, Gregory of Nyssa became the main spokesman of neo-Nicene Orthodoxy and a close theological adviser of the imperial court.

In his numerous writings Gregory showed himself to be a creative and sometimes speculative theologian, extending his investigations beyond the necessary aspects of anti-Arian polemics to the fields of anthropology and cosmology. He was also a major exponent of what is often called mystical theology, the knowledge of God through "spiritual senses."

Gregory's writings include the twelve-book *Against Eunomius,* which contains his polemics against that extreme Arian theologian, who had been Basil's adversary. His treatise *To Ablabius, That There Are Not Three Gods* is particularly important for an understanding of the Cappadocian doctrine of the three hypostases. His *Great Catechetical Oration* is a short but general introduction to Christian theology. Gregory also devoted much attention to exegesis, which he understood, following Origen, as an exercise in a spiritual interpretation of biblical texts. Thus, in his *Life of Moses,* he describes the human ascent to God, using as a model the story of Moses according to Exodus and Numbers. Gregory's anthropology is contained primarily in his treatise *On the Creation of Man.* His ascetic and spiritual doctrine is further expanded in his homilies on the Song of Songs and the beatitudes, as well as in his short treatises *On Virginity* and *On Christian Life (De instituto Christiano).*

There is a very close connection between the thought of Gregory of Nyssa and contemporary Neoplatonism. While overcoming some Neoplatonic categories (as in his doctrine of the absolute transcendence of God, who can be perceived only through *epektasis*—an eternal progress "from glory to glory"), Gregory seems to accept the doctrine of the *apokatastasis,* or ultimate restoration of all things in God.

BIBLIOGRAPHY

There is a full critical ed. of Gregory's work in process of publication by Werner Jaeger *et al.,* I–IX (1921–1967); see also Johannes Quasten, *Patrology,* III, *The Golden Age of Greek Patristic Literature* (1960), 254–296. Secondary literature includes Ekkehard Mühlenberg, *Die Unendlichkeit Gottes bei Gregor v. Nyssa* (1966); Maria-Barbara von Stritzky, *Zum Problem der Erkenntnis bei Gregor von Nyssa* (1973).

JOHN MEYENDORFF

[See also **Gregory of Nazianzus, St.**]

GREGORY OF TOURS, ST. (30 November 538/539–17 November 594/595), was born Georgius Florentius in Avernus (modern Clermont-Ferrand). His family was an ancient Gallo-Roman one that, on his father's side, could trace its roots to a Christian named Vectius Epagatus who was martyred in 177. During the tumultuous sixth century, when rival Frankish factions fought for control of Gaul, six of its members served as bishops of Langres, Clermont, Tours, and Lyons. When Georgius Florentius was called to the bishopric of Tours in 573 to succeed his uncle, Bishop Euphronius, he began to use the name Gregorius, apparently in honor of his sainted relative, Bishop Gregorius of Langres (506/507–539/540).

The see of Tours was no sinecure. It was fought over and pillaged several times during Gregory's pontificate. Gregory traveled both frequently and in high circles to defend the people and property of his see. His role as eyewitness to and participant in the major events of his time prepared him to record its history. Gregory, however, was no academic historian. His perceptions of his world, and consequently his writings, were deeply influenced by his religion. Tours, in addition to its political importance, was renowned as one of the most celebrated Christian sites in the Frankish realm, possessing the remains of St. Martin, Gregory's fourth-century predecessor as bishop and noted miracle worker both during and after his life. The afflicted who visited Martin's tomb in the sixth century and obtained miraculous cures provided testimony to the validity of Gregory's Christian beliefs.

Encouraged by his mother, Gregory recorded the lives, and especially the miracles, of Martin and of many other Gallic saints. Some modern scholars, on the evidence of several manuscripts, prefer the title *The Ecclesiastical Histories* to the more generally accepted *The History of the Franks* for Gregory's major historical work. The former title would seem to capture better the spirit of all of Gregory's work, for he wrote as a Christian bishop firmly committed to documenting the growth of his religion in his time and to illustrating the rewards and punishments that history shows await the good and the evil.

Gregory's *History* and his saints' lives were immensely influential. The *History* was used by Marius of Avenches while Gregory was still alive, and it remains the most important literary source for the history of the Franks in the sixth century. His saints' lives helped to define that genre in the Middle Ages and were copied many times over. They and the *History* are rich in information on politics, Christian practices and spirituality, place-names, the Latin language, and early medieval education and culture. A commentary on the Psalms has been lost. A work on the wonders of the world, discovered in 1853, appears not to have circulated very widely or to have been known beyond the sixth century.

BIBLIOGRAPHY

Sources. H. L. Bordier, ed., *Les livres des miracles et autres opuscules de Georges Florent Grégoire, éveque de Tours,* 4 vols. (1857–1864), with French trans.; Bruno Krusch and Wilhelm Levison, eds., *Monumenta Germaniae historica: Scriptores rerum Merovingicarum,* I (1951). See also: F. S. Haase, ed., *Liber ineditus de cursu stellarum* (1853). English translations are Ernest Brehaut, trans., *History of the Franks: Selections* (1916, repr. 1969); Lewis Thorpe, trans., *The History of the Franks* (1974); William C. McDermott, ed., *Selections from the Minor Works* (1949), which is reprinted in Edward Peters, ed., *Monks, Bishops, and Pagans* (1975), 117–218.

Studies. Paul Antin, "Notes sur le style de saint Grégoire de Tours," in *Latomus,* 22 (1963); Helmut Beumann, "Gregor von Tours und der Sermo rusticus," in Konrad Repgen and Stephan Skalweit, eds., *Spiegel der Geschichte* (1964), 64–98; François L. Ganshof, "L'historiographie dans la monarchie franque sous les Mérovingiens et les Carolingiens," in *La storiografia altomedievale,* II (1970), 631–685; Pierre Riché, *Education and Culture in the Barbarian West from the Sixth Through the Eighth Century,* John J. Contreni, trans. (1978); John M. Wallace-Hadrill, "The Work of Gregory of Tours in Light of Modern Research," in his *The Long-haired Kings* (1962).

JOHN J. CONTRENI

[See also **Historiography, Western European; Merovingians.**]

GREGORY THE ILLUMINATOR, ST.

GREGORY THE ILLUMINATOR, ST. (ca. 240–ca. 332, Armenian: Grigor Lusaworičᶜ, the "enlightener"), converted King Trdat III/IV of Armenia (ca. 298–330) and the Armenian people to Christianity. The Greek ecclesiastical historians of the fourth and fifth centuries do not mention his name. The main sources on him are the *History* of Agatᶜangełos and the lost *Life of Gregory* (fifth century), which has survived only in Greek and a number of other languages. According to the latter, Gregory was a Christian missionary of Cappadocian Greek origin. Agatᶜangełos, on the other hand, states that he was the son of a Parthian prince named Anak, who had assassinated King Xusrō (Xosrov) I of Armenia, the father of Trdat. According to the same source, Gregory was raised as a Christian and educated in Caesarea Mazaca (in Cappadocia); he was married and had two children. He entered the service of King Trdat to atone for his father's sin. When he refused to offer sacrifice to the statue of the goddess Anahit in Erēz and openly declared his Christian faith, the king had him tortured and condemned him to the *nerkᶜin* or χor virap (deep dungeon or pit) of Artašat, where he remained for thirteen years among poisonous reptiles. On the order of Trdat's sister, Princess Xosroviduχt, he was released in order to cure the king of an ailment that had turned him into the likeness of a boar.

After Gregory cured him, the king, followed by his court and the army, became Christians. Soon thereafter Gregory was sent to Caesarea, where he was ordained bishop by Bishop Leontius. Returning to Armenia, he undertook the task of proselytizing the people, appointed bishops, wiped out idolatry, and built churches and martyria. He accompanied King Trdat to Rome and met the emperor Constantine. Upon his retirement Gregory was succeeded by his younger son, Aṙistakēs, and spent the rest of his life in solitude at *Maneay ayrkᶜ* (Caves of Manē) in the district of Daranałikᶜ.

The historicity of the above account is difficult to establish. The conversion of Trdat as the result of "a marvelous Divine sign which was wrought in his own house" is well known from Sozomen (2.8); so is the name of Leontius, the metropolitan bishop of Caesarea (314–325). Peter, one of Gregory's attendants, who is mentioned in the Greek and Arabic versions of the *Life*, is also a historical personality; he was the bishop of Sebastia (303–320). The references of Agatᶜangełos and the *Life* to a council in Caesarea soon after Gregory's consecration also agree with historical reality: a council of the Cappadocian bishops actually met in 314. The fact that Gregory, his two sons, and their descendants occupied the throne of chief bishop of Armenia is also known from various fifth- and sixth-century sources. The cult of St. Gregory and the veneration of his relics since the mid fifth century are well attested by the late-fifth-century historian Łazar Pᶜarpecᶜi. These and similar indications have convinced most scholars that the historical core of the *Life* and Agatᶜangełos' account of Gregory's mission in Armenia may be authentic and that Gregory was indeed responsible for the conversion of Armenia. Hakob Manandyan, however, has conclusively shown that Trdat and Gregory's visit to Rome is an anachronism that echoes the trip of Trdat I in A.D. 66.

Later tradition ascribed to Gregory canons, sermons under the title *Yačaχapatum,* and liturgical works. Modern scholarship has shown these to be from later periods.

BIBLIOGRAPHY

Agathangelos, *History of the Armenians,* translation and commentary by R. W. Thomson (1976); P. Paolo Ananian, "La data e le circostanze della consecrazione di S. Gregorio Illuminatore," in *Le muséon,* 74 (1961); Gérard Garitte, *Documents pour l'étude du livre d'Agathange* (1946).

KRIKOR H. MAKSOUDIAN

[See also **Agatᶜangełos; Armenian Saints.**]

GREGORY I THE GREAT, POPE

GREGORY I THE GREAT, POPE (ca. 540–604). Pope from 590 to 604, popularly acclaimed a saint, named "the Great," and regarded as one of the four doctors of the Western church since the eighth century, Gregory was the architect of the medieval papacy and the most influential bridge between the ancient world and the Middle Ages.

Born of a prominent Roman family, Gregory received a good classical education and probably studied law, but he did not know Greek. He held the important post of prefect of the city in 573, as did his younger brother Palatinus in 590. About 574 Gregory founded six monasteries on family properties in Sicily and another, St. Andrew, on the Coelian, where he himself became a monk. But in 579 he was made deacon and sent by Pelagius II to Constantinople as papal ambassador. There he lived the monastic life with the Latin monks who accompanied him. After returning about 586, he again resided at St. Andrew, but served Pelagius as deacon. In 590 he unwillingly left his monastic solitude when summoned by the clergy and people to assume the heavy burden of the papacy in troubled times.

Italy had suffered from the Lombard invasion since 568, and the Byzantine exarch at Ravenna was almost powerless, despite persistent pleas to the emperor for help. War, famine, plague, and floods had devastated much of Italy. Gregory efficiently reorganized the administration of the church's estates and fed the poor with their produce. He tirelessly defended the weak from the depredations of the powerful and sought peace with the Lombards in order to restore normalcy.

By filling the vacuum that resulted from imperial impotence, Gregory vastly increased the power and prestige of the Holy See and laid the foundations for the medieval papacy. However, his purpose in undertaking political and administrative functions was solely to enable him to exercise his pastoral mission. In spite of miserable health, he devoted himself untiringly to his flock. He was concerned to obtain worthy bishops for each diocese, to combat heresy and schism, to have the Gospel preached to the people, to improve the quality of the clergy, and to promote the monastic life. He sent monks to faraway England to convert the Anglo-Saxons.

The 854 letters of Gregory's Register are the primary historical source for this period. He also left a collection of homilies (forty on the Gospels and twenty-two on Ezekiel). His commentaries on the Song of Songs and on 1 Kings, as well as his longest and most mystical work, the *Morals on Job,* were directed to monks. The *Pastoral Care* is a directory for bishops and priests; the *Dialogues* a collection of popular edifying stories about Italian saints. The latter two books were especially influential in the Middle Ages.

Intent upon pastoral goals, Gregory was always practical and moralizing. He was not an original theologian, but he capably absorbed the teaching of the Fathers and transmitted a simplified Augustinism to posterity in a form that was attractive to the medieval mind.

BIBLIOGRAPHY

Sources. Complete works of Gregory can be found in *Patrologia latina,* LXXV–LXXIX (1849), but better editions are now available: *Registrum epistularum,* Dag Norberg, ed., 2 vols. (1982); *Expositiones in Canticum canticorum, in librum primum regum,* Patricius Verbraken, ed. (1963); *Homiliae in Hiezechihelem prophetam,* Marcus Adriaen, ed. (1971); *Moralia in Iob,* Marcus Adriaen, ed., 2 vols. (1979); *Dialogues,* Adalbert de Vogüé, ed., 3 vols. (1978–1980). English translations are: *Pastoral Care and Selected Letters,* James Barmby, trans. (1895); *Pastoral Care,* Henry Davis, trans. (1950); *Dialogues,* Odo John Zimmerman, trans. (1959).

Studies. Claude Dagens, *Saint Grégoire le Grand: Culture et expérience chrétienne* (1977); Frederick Homes Dudden, *Gregory the Great: His Place in History and Thought,* 2 vols. (1905, repr. 1967); Jeffrey Richards, *Consul of God: The Life and Times of Gregory the Great* (1980).

CLAUDE J. PEIFER, O.S.B.

[See also **Doctors of the Church; Papacy, Origins and Development of.**]

GREGORY VII, POPE (*ca.* 1020–1085), one of the most important and influential popes in the history of the papacy. Born in Tuscany of an obscure family, Hildebrand, as he was called before assuming the papal office, gravitated very early in his life to Rome, where he seems to have become a monk (probably of St. Mary's on the Aventine). Nothing else is known of his early career except that before late 1046 he entered the service of the first reforming pope, Gregory VI. From 1047 to 1049 Hildebrand was in northern Europe, having first accompanied the deposed Gregory VI into German exile, and then, on Gregory's death, becoming associated with a party of northern church reformers. In 1049 he returned to Rome with one of these reformers, who recently had been raised to the papacy as Leo IX, and thereafter served Leo and four succeeding reform popes in a variety of leading capacities. By the time of Alexander II (1061–1073), Hildebrand had become the foremost of papal advisers. On Alexander's death he was so obviously the heir apparent that he was enthroned as pope by a tumultuous Roman crowd without the formality of a canonical election.

What distinguished Gregory VII's pontificate from those of all his reforming predecessors was his determination to use the papal office to create a regime of "justice" or righteousness in all of Christian society. Whereas the preceding popes had concentrated on asserting the primacy of the pope within the government of the church and on trying to reform the morals of the clergy by legislating against the buying of clerical offices and clerical marriage, Gregory enthusiastically pursued these policies but also went far beyond them. For him, the pope as "vicar of Peter" had the power to "bind and loose" on earth as well as in heaven, which meant that the pope could demand obedience from all mortals toward the goal of achieving right order in the world. Rather than merely asking, as his reforming predecessors had, that ecclesiastical offices be freed from the control of temporal lordship, Gregory insisted that the priesthood be recognized as superior to the laity and that the pope as the head of the ecclesiastical hierarchy be recognized as the preeminent authority within the entire Christian community, with the power to marshall all secular rulers under the banner of St. Peter to serve him in whatever way he might deem fit. Accordingly, Gregory VII's papacy began a trend in Western Christendom away from the ascetic ideal of withdrawal from society toward an activist one in which the priesthood and papacy would confront the world and try to guide it.

Gregory's goals were bound to lead him into conflict with Henry IV of Germany, the mightiest secular power of the day, but even before this happened Gregory stated some of his first principles in a document of March 1075 known as the *Dictatus papae.* Among other things, this declared that the pope alone may use the insignia of the Roman Empire, that he alone should have his feet kissed by all princes, that he may depose emperors, that he can be judged by no one, and that he may absolve subjects from their allegiance to unjust rulers. Although most of these statements had some canonical precedents, hardly any had ever been put into effect. Taken together they constituted a document of revolutionary implications, especially when compared with the reality of papal weakness that had previously prevailed. Since Gregory, and most of the popes after him throughout the High Middle Ages, proceeded to act with determination on the principles enunciated in the *Dictatus papae,* it seems warranted to compare it with Magna Carta, the Declaration of Independence, and the Communist Manifesto as one of the most influential programs of action ever to lay its imprint on the history of the Western world.

The struggle between Gregory and Henry IV broke out over the conflicting attempts of both to assert control over the archbishopric of Milan and soon became a test of whether king or pope would gain dominance one over the other. When Gregory in a scathing letter of December 1075 criticized Henry for supporting a rival candidate in preference to the papally sponsored archbishop of Milan, Henry promptly responded in January of 1076 by convening a council of German bishops, which declared Gregory to be deposed. Unintimidated, the pope at the head of his own council lived up to the *Dictatus papae* a month later by excommunicating Henry, declaring him deposed, and releasing all his subjects from their obedience. With the contest so clearly joined, Gregory first gained the advantage because he won the support of many German princes who were delighted to seize upon the pretext of piety to rid themselves of an overly strong ruler. The princes' declaration that they would agree to depose their king if he did not soon gain papal absolution led Henry to cross the Alps in the midst of the severe winter of 1076–1077 to make his humiliating penance before the pope at the north Italian castle of Canossa.

The royal submission at Canossa was an enormous moral and symbolic victory for Gregory VII, but in the short term it provided a tactical victory for Henry because by forcing Gregory to lift his excommunication it deprived the pope and the princes of their initiative. The more intransigent princes went ahead and elected a rival king in March of 1077, but Henry regained enough support in Germany to win the ensuing civil war in 1080. Although Gregory excommunicated and deposed Henry in 1080 for a second time, his actions now had much less effect. Instead of fearing for his crown, Henry named his own antipope and carried the war into Italy. In 1084 he besieged Rome itself, and Gregory had to call on the brutal Normans of southern Italy for aid. After the Normans looted the city in the course of driving off Henry's troops (the worst sack of Rome since the fifth century), Gregory retired with them to the south and died in Salerno in May of 1085.

At the time of Gregory's death it seemed as if the Gregorian cause was on the verge of utter defeat, but appearances were deceiving. Successor popes would carry on the struggle against Henry IV to victory, and the medieval German Empire would never again become as strong as it had been before 1075. An even greater Gregorian victory was the triumph of the First Crusade (1095–1099), called by a Gregorian pope, Urban II, to help spread right order in the world by rallying secular powers in support of Christian principles. Finally, and above all, the papacy in the course of the twelfth and thirteenth centuries built up the government of the church along centralized, monarchical lines and came to exert a greater influence on lay society throughout all of western Europe than Gregory VII himself might ever have imagined possible.

BIBLIOGRAPHY

Translations of GregoryVII's letters are in *The Correspondence of Pope Gregory VII,* Ephraim Emerton, trans. (1932), and *The Epistolae Vagantes of Pope Gregory VII,* Herbert E. J. Cowdrey, ed. and trans. (1972). See also Carl Erdmann, *The Origin of the Idea of Crusade,* Marshall W. Baldwin and Walter Goffart, trans. (1977); Allan J. Macdonald, *Hildebrand: A Life of Gregory VII* (1932); Gerd Tellenbach, *Church, State and Christian Society at the Time of the Investiture Contest,* Ralph F. Bennett, trans. (1940); James P. Whitney, *Hildebrandine Essays* (1932); Schafer Williams, ed., *The Gregorian Epoch* (1964).

ROBERT E. LERNER

[See also **Canossa; Dictatus Papae; Henry IV of Germany; Investiture and Investiture Conflict; Papacy, Origins and Development of.**]

GREGORY IX, POPE (*ca.* 1170–22 August 1241). Ugolino dei Conti was a relative of Innocent III. He studied at the universities of Paris and Bologna and was appointed cardinal bishop of Ostia and Velletri. He served numerous times as papal legate and displayed great interest in the work of St. Dominic and St. Francis of Assisi. As the first protector of the Franciscans, he organized the order so as to enable the thousands of Franciscans to maintain an orderly life of preaching and poverty.

Once elected pope in March of 1227, Gregory continued to support the new mendicant orders. He founded convents of the Poor Clares in northern and central Italy and also assisted in the reform and spread of the Carmelites, Cistercians, Camaldolese, Premonstratensians, and the Teutonic Order.

Gregory lent his organizing hand to the defense against heresy, an area hitherto handled by individual bishops and secular rulers. In February 1231 he issued the constitution *Excommunicamus et anathematisamus,* which decreed death for the obstinate, and life imprisonment for the unrepentant heretic; it was the birth of the Inquisition. Elsewhere, Gregory commissioned the Dominican Raymond of Peñafort

to collect systematically the constitutions enacted by previous popes and councils—a codification of canon law known as the Decretals, which remained in effect until 1917.

Gregory continued the great struggle with the Holy Roman emperors. Frederick II had long delayed fulfilling a vow to go on crusade, and Gregory finally excommunicated him (29 September 1227). In defiance, however, Frederick sailed to the Holy Land, where he succeeded in negotiating the reacquisition of Jerusalem. At the same time, imperial forces invaded the Papal States. The conflict continued sporadically through the 1230's, until Gregory called a general church council to meet in Rome to depose the emperor. Frederick, for his part, waylaid a convoy of prelates sailing to the council, and then marched on Rome. At this point, Gregory, still resisting, died.

BIBLIOGRAPHY

Gregory IX's bulls are in *Registre de Grégoire IX,* Lucien H. L. Auvray, ed., 4 vols. (1890–1955). See also Pietro Balan, *Storia di Gregori IX e dei suoi tempi,* 2 vols. (1872–1873); Ernst Brem, *Papst Gregor IX* (1911); Augustin Fliche and Victor Martin, eds., *Histoire de l'église depuis les origines jusqu'à nos jours,* X (1968), 217–426; James M. Powell, "Frederick II and the Church: A Revisionist View," in *Catholic Historical Review,* **48** (1963); Christine Thouzellier, "La légation en Lombardie du cardinal Hugolin," in *Revue d'histoire ecclésiastique,* **45** (1950).

PAUL R. THIBAULT

[See also **Franciscans; Frederick II of Sicily; Inquisition.**]

GREGORY OF AKANC. See **Grigor Aknerc͓i.**

GREGORY OF RIMINI (*ca.* 1300–1358), Augustinian theologian and philosopher. Born at Rimini, Gregory joined the Hermits of St. Augustine (O.E.S.A.). His studies took him to Paris during the years 1323 to 1329. He taught at Bologna until 1338, then at Padua and Perugia. In 1342 he was back in Paris, where he lectured on the *Sentences* of Peter Lombard during 1343 and 1344. By 1345 he was known as *magister cathedraticus,* and by 1347 he was teaching once again at Padua. In 1351 he became the master of the house of studies and then prior of the Augustinian house recently established at Rimini, where he remained until his election as prior general of his order in 1357. He died the following year in Vienna. In addition to his lectures on the *Sentences,* he has left behind his register as prior general and a number of theological tracts.

Like nearly all the theologians of his day, Gregory stressed the omnipotence of God *(potentia absoluta)* and the radical contingency of the created order, as a response to the deterministic tendencies of the Aristotelian view of the cosmos. He tempered the potential skepticism of this approach with his faithfulness to the teachings of Augustine.

Gregory was best known for his teaching on predestination. He taught that God predestined not only the elect but also the damned (double predestination). He rejected any suggestion that the human creature can take any initiative on the path to salvation. In short he understood free will as sin and good works as the signs of grace.

Gregory's nominalism led to a simplified view of the divine attributes, the Trinity, and the human soul. His opinion that all reality is individual reinforced the empiricism in the natural sciences, which was gaining ground in his day.

Finally, Gregory made no claims for theology as a science.

BIBLIOGRAPHY

Sources. A. de Meijer, ed., *Gregorii de Arimino O.S.A. Registrum generalatus 1357–1358* (1976); A. D. Trapp *et al.,* eds., *Gregorii Ariminensis O.E.S.A. Lectura super primum et secundum Sententiarum,* I (1981), IV–V (1979), VI (1980).

Studies. W. Eckerman, *Wort und Wirklichkeit* (1978), with good bibliography; E. García Lescún, *La teología trinitaria de Gregorio de Rímini* (1970); Gordon Leff, *Gregory of Rimini* (1961); A. D. Trapp, "Gregory of Rimini: Manuscripts, Editions and Additions," in *Augustiniana,* 8 (1958).

MARK A. ZIER

[See also **Augustinian Friars.**]

GREGORY PALAMAS

GREGORY PALAMAS (1296–14 November 1359), archbishop of Thessaloniki and eminent theologian of the late Byzantine period; his stand on behalf of the hesychast or mystical tradition of Eastern Christian monasticism led to important theological and cultural developments in Eastern Orthodoxy.

Gregory was born in Constantinople. His father died while Gregory was young and, with other members of his family, the boy embraced the monastic life at Mt. Athos. After his ordination (1326) he lived in several Athonite communities and gained notoriety as a hagiographer and spiritual writer.

Around 1337, Gregory began a correspondence with an Italo-Greek philosopher, Barlaam the Calabrian, on the problem of the knowledge of God. Barlaam, insisting on divine transcendence, tended to reduce such knowledge to symbolism, whereas Gregory, agreeing with his opponent on the point of the absolute transcendence of the divine essence, defended the full reality of communion with God through the Incarnation, the sacraments, and mystical experience—in other words, according to the Greek patristic notion of "deification" *(theosis)* of human beings. The debate led Gregory to the formulation of a theological distinction, particularly characteristic of his thought, between the transcendent essence of God and his energies, through which God enters into communion with creatures. Since the debate touched on the spiritual experience of contemplative (hesychast) monks, whom Barlaam tended to ridicule, Gregory published his nine treatises (Triads) *For the Defense of the Holy Hesychasts,* which constitute his major theological writing.

Gregory's theology was upheld by a council meeting in Constantinople in 1341. However, in the midst of a civil war that raged in Byzantium between 1341 and 1347, he had to face the active theological opposition led by Gregory Akindynos. After the victory of John VI Kantakouzenos (r. 1347–1354), he was upheld again by conciliar decisions, taken in 1347 and 1351, that sanctioned the victory of the monastic or hesychast party in Byzantium. However, this victory of "Palamism" continued to be opposed by representatives of Byzantine humanism, such as Nikephoros Gregoras. Some anti-Palamites also adopted the views of the Western Thomistic school.

During these events Gregory published a number of theological treatises, letters, and homilies. In 1347 he was consecrated archbishop of Thessaloniki. In 1354–1355 he was a prisoner of the Turks in Asia Minor; his description of his stay there is an interesting historical document. He was formally canonized as a saint in 1368 by his disciple and friend, patriarch Philotheos Kokkinos.

BIBLIOGRAPHY

Editions of Gregory's writings are *Palamas syngrammata* (Writings of Palamas), Pangiotes Khrestou, ed., 3 vols. (1962–); *Défense des saints hésychastes,* John Meyendorff, ed., 2 vols., 2nd ed. (1973). For a partial English trans., see Gregory Palamas, *The Triads*, John Meyendorff, ed., Nichola Gendle, trans. (1983). See also John Meyendorff, *A Study of Gregory Palamas*, George Lawrence, trans., 2nd ed. (1974); D. Stiernon, "Bulletin sur le palamisme," in *Revue des études byzantines*, **30** (1972).

JOHN MEYENDORFF

[See also **Barlaam of Calabria; Hesychasm; Historiography, Byzantine.**]

GRETTIS SAGA ÁSMUNDARSONAR was probably written in the first quarter of the fourteenth century. Four vellum and two paper manuscripts provide a relatively stable text. The chief variations concern the number of verses cited as Grettir's, and some passages inserted by the scribe of the *A*-group original.

Several kinds of narrative tradition are united in this story. Folktale material plays a prominent role: Grettir fights a barrow dweller, a bear, berserks, trolls, and revenants. (Two of these fights are close analogues to Beowulf's with Grendel and his dam.) European narrative influence is also apparent: the fabliau interlude of Grettir and the serving girl may be related to Boccaccio's *Decameron* (day three, tale one); the *Spesar þáttr,* a biography of Grettir's avenger, is a reworking of the Tristan story. A third influence is that of the native Icelandic saga tradition: the author alludes to characters and events found scattered through some seventeen other sagas. Although one or two of these sagas may be the borrowers rather than the sources, the author was clearly a widely read man. He may even have used a written Icelandic source for his story. Sigurður Nordal, following Árni Magnússon and others, argues that Sturla Þórðarson (*d.* 1284) wrote an account of Grettir's life.

The saga is characterized by its way of combining these disparate narrative elements into an effective whole. Its late date of composition reflects its peculiar makeup: the ethically mixed portrait of Grettir as outlaw, poet, bully, hero, and man of ill luck is classic; the monster fights are flamboyantly romantic. Grettir's boyhood as "male Cinderella" is vivid beyond the usual power of that gambit because of the classically dispassionate description of his vicious tricks.

Grettir is best known for having spent some nineteen years as an outlaw. Expelled from an agrarian, Christian society, he subsists on its inhospitable fringes by stealing sheep. To the farmers he is as much a scourge as the revenants he exterminates, but when the farmers finally kill Grettir—aided by witchcraft, treachery, and Grettir's infected leg wound—they destroy something irreplaceable: a man who, whatever his faults, was greater than they could ever be.

Grettis saga includes a larger amount of obviously fictional material than do most family sagas. Scholars have, however, gradually discovered that more and more of the apparently objective episodes styled in the classical manner are also fictive. An outlaw named Grettir did live from about 996 to 1031, but what more is true is not known. Even the verses attributed to him in the text date from later centuries, and cannot, in their present form, be his. Despite the unusual combination of realistic and fantastic elements, *Grettis saga* is generally accounted one of the supreme literary achievements of medieval Iceland, along with *Egils saga, Njáls saga,* and *Laxdœla saga.*

BIBLIOGRAPHY

Sources. Grettis saga Ásmundarsonar, Guðni Jónsson, ed. (1936, repr. 1964); *The Saga of Grettir the Strong,* George A. Hight, trans., ed. with intro. and notes by Peter Foote (1965); *Grettir's Saga,* Denton Fox and Hermann Pálsson, trans. (1974).

Studies. Robert J. Glendinning, "Grettis Saga and European Literature in the Late Middle Ages," in *Mosaic,* **4.2** (1970); Kathryn Hume, "The Thematic Design of *Grettis saga,*" in *Journal of English and Germanic Philology,* **73** (1974); Halldór Kiljan Laxness, "Lítil samantekt um útilegumenn," in *Tímarit Máls og Menningar,* **10** (1949); Sigurður J. Nordal, *Sturla Þórðarson og Grettis saga* (1938); Hermann Pálsson, "Drög að siðfræði Grettis sögu," in *Tímarit Máls og Menningar,* **30** (1969).

KATHRYN HUME

[See also **Sturla Þórðarson.**]

GRIGOR AKNERCᶜI (Gregory of Akancᶜ). Very little is known about the author of the *History of the Nation of the Archers* (the Mongols), a work that treats the forty-four-year period from 1229/1230 to 1273. He is presumed to have been born in Cilicia around 1250, to have been the abbot of Akner monastery in Cilicia around 1312/1313, and to have died in 1335.

Grigor's *History,* completed in 1271/1272, has certain shortcomings. First, as the product of a Cilician author who was in his early twenties when the work was finished, this work lacks the immediacy found in the compilations of accounts of eastern Armenian eyewitnesses to the Mongol conquest and domination. Grigor was not a well-educated individual, and his frequent lapses into fantasy jeopardize the credibility of other information for which he is the only source. Among the sources used by Grigor were oral accounts of events provided by Armenian visitors to Akner monastery who were either from Greater Armenia or had traveled there. It was from such informed individuals that Grigor learned the meanings of the large number of Mongolian military and juridical terms that he incorporated into the *History*. He also appears to have used some written sources: the *Chronography* of Michael the Syrian, a colophon of Vardan Arewelc^ci, and perhaps Vanakan Vardapet's now-lost *History*.

The *History of the Nation of the Archers* provides a biblical genealogy of the Mongols (ch. 1) and an original account of the illumination of Genghis Khan in which he comes to realize that he is destined to become ruler of the world (ch. 2). Chapters 3 through 6 narrate the Mongol invasions and conquests of the Caucasus and of eastern Asia Minor. Chapters 7, 10, and 14 contain valuable information on Cilician-Mongol and Cilician-Mamluk relations. Accounts of the Caucasian princes' rebellion against the Mongols (1249/1250, ch. 9), the Mongol capture of Baghdad (1258, ch. 11), the reign of Hulagu (ch. 12), the rebellion of Tegüder (ch. 16), and the reign of Abaqa (ch. 17) contain details not found elsewhere. While Grigor is guilty of chronological inaccuracies in the early section of his work, for the post-1249 period he is generally reliable.

BIBLIOGRAPHY

The classical Armenian text of the *History* was first published in Jerusalem in 1870, based on thirteenth- and seventeenth-century MSS. An independent edition based on another seventeeth-century MS was published the same year in St. Petersburg by Keropé Patkanean, who published a Russian translation in 1871. The work had previously been translated into French by Marie Brosset, in *Additions et éclaircissements à l'Histoire de la Géorgie* (1851), 438–467. A critical edition with an English translation by Robert Blake was published in the *Harvard Journal of Asiatic Studies*, **12** (1949), along with Francis Woodman Cleaves's important article, "The Mongolian Names and Terms in the *History of the Nation of the Archers* by Grigor of Akanc^c." These two articles were reprinted as *History of the Nation of the Archers* (1954). Blake's translation has a number of inaccuracies, on which see Robert Bedrosian, *The Turco-Mongol Invasions and the Lords of Armenia in the 13–14th Centuries* (Ph.D. diss., Columbia Univ., 1979), 41–42, n.3. All publications prior to Blake's incorrectly named a certain Małak^cia the monk as the author.

ROBERT BEDROSIAN

[See also **Armenia: History of; Mongol Empire.**]

GRIGOR MAGISTROS (*ca.* 990–*ca.* 1058) was the son of Prince Vasak Pahlawuni, Lord of Bǰni. He received his education at Ani, the capital of Bagratid Armenia, and became well versed in Greek and Greek classical learning. As a statesman he played an active role in the political life of Armenia from the 1030's until his death. He also participated in military enterprises, since the office of commander in chief was hereditary in his family. Even though the Pahlawuni and Grigor himself were loyal to the Bagratid kings, he had a serious conflict with the young king Gagik II (1042–1045), who was probably under the influence of the party opposed to that of Grigor. In 1045 Grigor accompanied Gagik and several Armenian princes to Constantinople, where the Armenian king was forced to agree to the annexation of the kingdom of Ani to the Byzantine Empire. Grigor also agreed to hand over his lands at Bǰni to the emperor, from whom he received in return lands in southern Armenia and northern Mesopotamia. He was given the honorary title of *magistros,* and in 1048 he was appointed *dux* of the Byzantine province of Mesopotamia, which included his territories in southern Armenia.

Grigor is better known for his cultural work. He financed the construction of several churches and chapels at Bǰni, Keč^caṙoyk^c, Hawuc^c T^caṙ, and Muš. He spent most of his life in the pursuit of intellectual interests, corresponded with the important intellectual figures of Armenia, taught science and philosophy, and wrote. More than eighty of his letters have survived and bear testimony to his erudition. They provide a glimpse of the cultural temper of Bagratid Armenia. Among the recipients of these letters were Kat^coḷikos Petros, several prelates, learned priors, the Jacobite patriarch, and various princes. The subject matter varies from the sciences to philosophy, theology, and politics. During four days in Constantinople, Grigor wrote a long epitome of the story of the Bible in verse; it is the first rhymed poem of such length in Armenian (more than 1,000 lines). In addition, he produced a commentary on the grammar of Dionysius Thrax and several poems written in a very difficult style. Grigor is renowned as the translator of the *Elements* of Euclid and some dialogues of Plato.

BIBLIOGRAPHY

The writings of Gregory are published as *Talasacᶜutᶜiwnkᶜ Grigori Magistrosi Pahlawunwoy* (Poems of Grigor Magistros Pahlawuni) (1868) and *Grigor Magistrosi tᶜltᶜerě* (The letters of Grigor Magistros) (1910). See also Manuk Abełyan, *Hayocᶜ hin grakanutᶜyan patmutᶜyun* (History of ancient Armenian literature), II (1946); V. Langlois, "Mémoire sur la vie et les écrits du prince Grégoire Magistros," in *Journal asiatique*, 6th ser., 13 (1869); M. Leroy, "Grégoire Magistros et les traductions arméniennes d'auteurs grecs," in *Annuaire de l'Institut de philologie et d'histoire orientales et slaves*, 3 (1935).

KRIKOR H. MAKSOUDIAN

[See also **Armenia: History of; Armenian Literature; Bagratids, Armenian; Gagik II; Pahlawuni.**]

GRIGOR NAREKACᶜI, ST. (Gregory of Narek)

(*ca.* 951–27 February 1003), Armenian mystical poet. His father was the scholar Xosrov, bishop of Anjewacᶜikᶜ; he was educated by his uncle, Anania Narekacᶜi, a philosopher known for his antiheretical writings. Grigor lived at Narek monastery, and refers to himself in a manuscript dated 977 as a *kᶜahanay* (priest). He appears to have been accused of heresy and to have acquitted himself of this charge by the working of miracles. Numerous legends surrounding Grigor's later life as a cave-dwelling anchorite on the shores of Lake Van survive in Armenian literature, and copies of his *Book of Lamentation* are prized as talismans.

Grigor composed some twenty-five hymns, which are notable for their alliterative quality. The finest example is found in the Canticle of the Nativity (*Meledi cnndean*): *ačᶜkᶜn cov i cov cičalaxit cawalanayr yaṙawawtun* (Laughing eyes dilated, sea into sea, in the morning). He wrote a letter against the Tᶜondrakite heresy, a commentary on the Song of Songs, and various panegyrics, but he is best known for his *Book of Lamentation* (Armenian: *Matean ołbergutᶜean*), a collection of ninety-five meditations, "conversation with God from the depths of the heart."

The poet perceives God as "inaccessibly distant and inseparably near." Although he believes "with single-minded hope, taking refuge in the powerful

Hand, not only in attaining to atonement, but in seeing [God] Himself" (XII), he confesses that "none is as sinful as I" (LXXII) and rebukes his own delight in sin: "Your heart returns ever to Egypt" (II). Grigor worries about the remoteness of God, crying, "Will you ignore your lovingkindness, O provident one?" but he affirms his belief in a wholly good God: "There is no part of darkness in you" (L). One achieves mystical enlightenment through refining the divine essence in the human heart, "a residue of shining light . . . asleep in the watery abysses" (XI), which is met and drawn upward by the redemptive power of Grace.

BIBLIOGRAPHY

Sources. Grigor Narekacᶜi, *Matenagrutᶜiwnkᶜ* (Writings) (1840); *Narek: Matean ołbergutᶜean*, Garegin, bishop of Trebizond, trans. (1948); *Le livre de prières*, Isaac Kéchichian, trans. (1961); *Grigor Narekatsi: Kniga skorbi*, Naum Grebnev, trans. (1977).

Studies. Manuk Abełyan, *Erker* (Works), III (1968), 567–629; Varag Aṙakᶜelyan, *Grigor Narekacᶜu lezun ev oča* (The language and style of Gregory of Narek) (1975); M. Mkryan, *Grigor Narekacᶜi* (1955); Ṙubēn Ragupean, *Grigor Narekacᶜi* (1939).

JAMES R. RUSSELL

[See also **Armenian Literature.**]

GRIGOR II VKAYASĒR (*d.* 1105), *katᶜolikos* of

Armenia from 1065 to 1105, was the son of Prince Grigor Magistros Pahlawuni. His baptismal name was Vahram, and he was educated in the classics under the supervision of his learned father. In his youth he was married and assisted his father, who was in the service of the Byzantine Empire. In 1059 Vahram succeeded his father as *dux* of Mesopotamia. Soon thereafter he resigned his office, withdrew from the world, and applied himself to religious studies. In 1065 he was the only person acceptable to the Byzantines as a candidate for the Armenian patriarchal see. There is no specific reference to his ecclesiastical status prior to his ordination as *katᶜolikos;* he may have been raised to that rank from a lay status. He was named Grigor at the time of his ordination.

Grigor's pontificate coincided with the turbulent period of Seljuk penetration into Armenia and Asia Minor. At a time of a complete breakdown of political and ecclesiastical authority, Grigor succeeded in keeping the Armenian patriarchate a vibrant force.

The dispersed state of the Armenian people, Grigor's own interest, and his concern for church discipline prompted him to spend most of his early years traveling, and he never maintained a permanent residence. In 1073 he went to Ani, and in 1074 he visited Constantinople, then went on to Rome and Egypt. He visited Egypt again in 1085 and was in Jerusalem when the crusaders conquered the town in 1099.

Grigor was called Vkayasēr (Martyrophile) because of his great interest in hagiographical literature. He commissioned, edited, and translated several saints' lives from Greek and Syriac with the aid of associates. Grigor edited the Armenian synaxarion and revised the lectionary, into which he introduced new readings for some forty days. Grigor is the first of the Pahlawuni patriarchs, who held the position of katᶜolikos of Armenia until 1203.

BIBLIOGRAPHY

Matthew of Edessa, *Chronicle* (1869, 1898), French trans. by Edouard Dulaurier (1858); Malachia Ormanian, *The Church of Armenia*, 2nd ed. (1955); H. F. Tournabize, *Histoire politique et religieuse de l'Arménie* (1910).

KRIKOR H. MAKSOUDIAN

[See also **Armenian Saints; Grigor Magistros.**]

GRÍMNISMÁL (Words of Grímnir) are one of the mythological poems of the *Poetic Edda*; they are the fourth poem in Codex Regius 2365 4°; they also appear in the Codex Arnamagnaeanus 748 4° (*Poetic Edda* fragment), and some twenty-four strophes (several only partial) are in the *Snorra Edda*. The meter is *ljóðaháttr* in the large majority of the strophes, but metric irregularity is frequent, particularly in the sections consisting of listed material (*þulur*). The Neckel and Kuhn edition reads fifty-four strophes (thirty-nine regular *ljóðaháttr*, five *ljóðaháttr* with an extra long and an extra short line, the rest with greater irregularity) preceded by a prose introduction of some 350 words and followed by a prose epilogue of some 60 words.

The introduction provides the narrative frame: King Hrauðungr has two sons, Agnarr and Geirroðr, whose boat is driven out to sea by a storm. The goddess Frigg takes the elder, Agnarr (aged ten), as her protégé; Odin fosters the younger, Geirroðr (aged eight). Just before their departure Odin gives Geirroðr secret advice. On landing in their home-

land, Geirroðr sends his brother back to sea by means of a charm and succeeds his deceased father as king. Later Odin teases Frigg over the fate of her protégé; she responds by slandering Geirroðr as a stingy host. A wager results; in order to win, Frigg sends a false warning to Geirroðr to beware a stranger skilled in magic. This trick succeeds in that Geirroðr shows Odin a harsh welcome; the god, under the cover name Grímnir, is seated between two fires to be forced to admit his intentions. After eight nights of deprivation, Geirroðr's son Agnarr finally brings Odin a horn of drink and criticizes his father's treatment of the guest.

In response Odin recites a poem. It begins with his complaints against Geirroðr and praise of Agnarr's kindness, which will be rewarded splendidly (strophes 1–3). There follows a list of the heavenly dwellings of the gods (4–16), culminating in the eighth strophe, Odin's Valhalla, then a list of the god's wolves and ravens, the food and drink served to the heroes assembled in the hall, and so on (17–25). The subject shifts from Valhalla via the goat Heiðrún—which stands on its roof, eating the leaves of Læraðr (Yggdrasill)—to other, mostly destructive animals associated with the world ash (26–35), concluding with Níðhǫggr, then to several ominous strophes related to the eschatology (36–39). It changes again to the cosmogony (Ymir as the protomatter) and the attributes of the gods (40–44). The conclusion of the poem consists of Odin's apotheosis: the god begins with a list of some forty of his many names, follows with incriminations and threats directed at Geirroðr, and concludes by naming himself as Odin.

The prose epilogue tells how Geirroðr rises to rush to his previous protector, falls on his sword "by accident," and is succeeded by his son Agnarr, who then rules long as king.

The *Grímnismál* are generally considered to be among the older Eddic poems, and considerable weight is given to the mythological material contained, much of which is unique. Controversy centers on the relative age of the narrative frame (the prose and, obviously, strophes 1–3 and 51–53, which are directly involved in that content). Even more worthy of skepticism is the questionable homogeneity of the mythological section; it seems more likely—as is accepted to be the case with the *Hávamál*—that a large amount of accretion swelled the content. Individual bits of information—for instance, that Odin's only sustenance is wine (strophe

19)—are quite remarkable in and of themselves; much discussion has centered on Valhalla's 540 doors, through which the 800 warriors exit at *Ragnarǫk* (fate of the gods), and the archaic mathematics (Indic, Akkadian, Sumerian, pre-Sumerian) suggested by the resulting product and its symbolism. It is also of interest that Odin favors the younger Geirroðr just as he helps the youngest son, Konr, in *Rígsþula,* and Freyja assists the young Óttarr in *Hyndluljóð*—all by supplying numinous/magical instruction—in their competition with their elders for an inherited kingship.

BIBLIOGRAPHY

Sources. A text edition in *Edda. Die Lieder des Codex Regius nebst verwandten Denkmälern,* Gustav Neckel, ed., 4th ed. by Hans Kuhn, I (1962). Translations are *The Poetic Edda,* Henry Adam Bellows, trans. (1923, repr. 1969) and *The Poetic Edda,* Lee M. Hollander, trans., 3rd ed. (1962).

Studies. Hans Bekker-Nielsen and Thorkil Damsgaard Olsen, eds., *Bibliography of Old Norse-Icelandic Studies* (1964–); Hugo Gering and Barend Sijmons, eds., *Die Lieder der Edda,* III, *Kommentar zu den Liedern der Edda,* 2 pts. (1927–1931); Jóhann S. Hannesson, *Bibliography of the Eddas* (1955); Halldór Hermannsson, *Bibliography of the Eddas* (1920). There are annual bibliographies in *Arkiv för nordisk filologi* (1927–1962) and *Acta philologica scandinavica* (1926/1927–).

JERE FLECK

[See also **Eddic Meters; Eddic Poetry; Frigg; Odin.**]

GRÍMS SAGA LOÐINKINNA. The brief saga of Grímr loðinkinni (hairy cheek) belongs to the *fornaldarsögur* or legendary sagas, fictional prose narratives in Old Norse that take place in the early heroic age of Scandinavia, before the settlement of Iceland.

The childhood of Grímr, son of Ketil hæng (salmon) and the giantess Hrafnhild, is described briefly in the saga of his father. In *Gríms saga,* the hero is introduced when he is about to be married. His fiancée, Lopthæna, disappears shortly before the wedding, and Grímr sets off to find her. He overhears a family of trolls in a cavern talking about Lopthæna and her whereabouts, but he kills them before they are able to say much. After defeating twelve men in a fight over a stranded whale, Grímr lies bleeding profusely and waiting for death. He is rescued and healed by a hideous troll woman, who offers to restore him to health if he will accept life from her, kiss her, and share her bed. Grímr accepts with the greatest reluctance, and awakes the following morning to find his lost fiancée sleeping next to him. She had been turned into a troll by the sorcery of her stepmother, and was fated not to regain her own form unless a man agreed to the conditions she offered Grímr. The couple are married and the stepmother is stoned to death. Grímr and Lopthæna have a daughter. The hero and his friend Ingjald fight twelve men to keep Grímr's daughter from marrying against her will. The saga ends with a series of genealogies connecting Grímr and his sister Hrafnhild to historical and semihistorical Icelanders. It is stated that Grímr also fathered, with another wife, the hero of a more famous *fornaldarsaga,* Örvar-Oddr.

Grímr loðinkinni is mentioned in all versions of the *Landnámabók* (Book of settlements), as well as in *Egils saga Skallagrímssonar,* as one of the men of Hrafnista and the ancestor of many historical settlers of Iceland.

The thick hair on his cheek, from which the hero derives his name, shows the influence on the saga of a widespread folktale pattern known as the Bear's Son tale. The hairy cheek is a sign of mixed parentage, which in the folktale points to a nonhuman (animal or supernatural) parent. Most elements of the pattern are found, in their traditional sequence, in the account of Grímr's rescue of his fiancée, the end of which blends with the equally familiar motif of the loathly lady.

The saga contains a *senna* (a match of invective in verse), here between Grímr and two troll women, as well as two loose stanzas recited by Grímr after his fight with twelve men. *Senna* and stanzas are in the simpler Eddic meter and diction.

The saga of Grímr and that of his father Ketil hæng are preserved together in three fifteenth-century vellum manuscripts in the Arnamagnaean collection (Copenhagen, Universitets Bibliotek): AM 343a 4°, AM 471 4°, and AM 576 4°.

BIBLIOGRAPHY

The standard edition is in Guðni Jónsson and Bjarni Vilhjálmsson, eds., *Fornaldar sögur norðurlanda,* I (1943), 267–280. See also Andreas Heusler and Wilhelm Ranisch, eds., *Eddica minora. Dichtungen eddischer Art aus den Fornaldarsögur und anderen Prosawerken* (1903), lxix–lxxv; Peter A. Jorgensen, "The Two-troll Variant of the

Bear's Son Folktale in *Halfdanar saga Brönufóstra* and *Gríms saga loðinkinna*," in *Arv*, **31** (1975); Joaquín Martínez-Pizarro, "Transformations of the Bear's Son Tale in the Sagas of the Hrafnistumenn," *ibid.*, **32–33** (1976–1977).

JOAQUÍN MARTÍNEZ-PIZARRO

[See also **Egils Saga Skallagrímssonar; Ketils Saga Hængs; Landnámabók; Örvar-Odds Saga.**]

GRÍPISSPÁ (The prophecy of Grípir) is the first in a group of Eddic poems centering on the legend of Sigurd and Brynhild. It is transmitted in Codex Regius 2365, 4°, and comprises fifty-three stanzas in pedestrian *fornyrðislag*. Sigurd comes to the hall of his maternal uncle Grípir and inquires into his future. In a sequence of questions and answers Grípir prophesies his nephew's avenging the death of his father, his killing of Reginn and Fáfnir and seizure of Fáfnir's treasure, his release of the Valkyrie Sigrdrífa, his betrothal to Brynhild, the potion of forgetfulness administered to him by Grimhild, his oaths of brotherhood with Gunnarr and Högni, his proxy wooing of Brynhild on Gunnarr's behalf, the subsequent double wedding joining him to Gudrun and Gunnarr to Brynhild, Brynhild's plotting of his murder, and Gudrun's grief.

Grípisspá is generally conceded to be a late and secondary piece. It is based on the poems dealing with Sigurd's vengeance and winning of Fáfnir's treasure (combined in the Eddic *Reginsmál-Fáfnismál*), on the poem that relates Sigurd's encounter with the Valkyrie Sigrdrífa (partially preserved in the Eddic *Sigrdrífumál*), and especially on the fullest of the Eddic poems dealing with Sigurd and Brynhild, the lost *Sigurðarkviða in meiri*. Dependence on *Sigurðarkviða in meiri* is shown not only by features in *Grípisspá* that run counter to the preserved Sigurd poems, but also by verbal correspondences with the portions of *Völsunga saga* taken over from *Meiri* before it was lost. The proximity to *Meiri* is clearest in the common motif of a prior betrothal between Brynhild and Sigurd, a theme not developed in any other Eddic poem. The poet's reliance on *Meiri* makes it possible to use *Grípisspá* as an important key to the contents of this lost poem. Andreas Heusler speculated that *Grípisspá* was composed as an introduction to a small poetic biography of Sigurd comprising the vengeance and treasure poems, the

awakening of Sigrdrífa, and *Meiri*. This hypothetical collection, which Heusler called the *Sigurdliederheft*, was subsequently absorbed into the *Poetic Edda*.

The late date assigned to *Grípisspá* is justified by its derivation from the latest and most highly developed of the Eddic poems about Sigurd and Brynhild, a poem that is unlikely to have been composed before the end of the twelfth or the beginning of the thirteenth century. In addition, there are verbal correspondences with the poem *Merlínússpá* (Prophecy of Merlin), adapted by Gunnlaugr Leifsson from Geoffrey of Monmouth's *Historia regum Britanniae*. It has been assumed that Gunnlaugr borrowed from *Grípisspá*, but the reverse may be true. Gunnlaugr died in 1218/1219, and his poem presumably would not have been available for imitation until the early thirteenth century.

BIBLIOGRAPHY

The poem can be found in *Edda. Die Lieder des Codex Regius nebst verwandten Denkmälern*, Gustav Neckel, ed., 4th ed. by Hans Kuhn, I (1962). Translations are *The Poetic Edda*, Henry Adam Bellows, trans. (1923, repr. 1969), and *The Poetic Edda*, Lee M. Hollander, trans., 2nd ed. (1962). See also Theodore M. Andersson, *The Legend of Brynhild* (1980); and Andreas Heusler, "Die Lieder der Lücke in Codex Regius der Edda,"in *Germanistische Abhandlungen, Hermann Paul dargebracht* (1902), 1–98, repr. in his *Kleine Schriften*, II (1969).

THEODORE M. ANDERSSON

[See also **Reginsmál-Fáfnismál; Sigrdrífumál; Sigurðarkviða in Meiri.**]

GRISAILLE, a painting done entirely in monochrome, properly—as the name implies—in a series of neutral grays. In practice, monochromatic painting of any hue is often loosely referred to as grisaille. Both grisaille proper and monochromatic painting were popularized by the Romans, who were possibly inspired by earlier Greek examples, and continued to be produced sporadically throughout the Middle Ages, particularly in Palaiologan frescoes and late Gothic manuscripts. Later painters such as Pucelle, Giotto, and Jan van Eyck used the technique to emphasize the sculptural solidity of their figures or to simulate sculpture. The term also describes a

Grisaille painted on silk. Center portion of the Narbonne altar-frontal, *ca.* 1374–1378. MUSÉE DU LOUVRE, PARIS

particular technique of stained-glass painting in monochrome.

LESLIE BRUBAKER

[See also **Glass, Stained.**]

GROAT (French: *gros;* German: *Groschen;* Italian: *grosso*), a coin of high silver content and weight that served as the multiple of the penny throughout Latin Europe from the thirteenth through the fifteenth centuries and into the modern period.

From the time of Charlemagne's monetary reforms at the end of the eighth century, only a single denomination of coinage was minted in Latin Europe: the penny (along with its half, the *obole*). Originally of pure silver and weighing about 1.7 grams, the penny declined in both weight and fineness in most regions of medieval Europe from the ninth

through the twelfth centuries. By the year 1200 the commercial centers of Europe felt the need for a coin of higher value than the base penny.

The first silver multiple coin appears to have been the *grosso* of Venice of 1202, though claims of precedence have been made for Genoa, Pisa, and Milan. The *grosso* of Venice (also known as the *matapan*

Gros tournois, after 1266. PHOTOGRAPHS SUPPLIED BY THE AUTHOR

and *ducatus argenti*) was of generally Byzantine appearance, though based on no specific Byzantine prototype. Weighing about 2.18 grams and 96.5 percent pure silver, it was issued as the equivalent of twenty-four of the contemporary base coins of Venice; its exchange value quickly rose even higher. The issuance of large silver multiple coins was taken up in the succeeding decades by various towns of Lombardy and Tuscany. In 1253 the Roman senate issued an even heavier silver *grosso* weighing 3.5 grams and valued at twelve Roman *provisini* pennies.

In 1266, as part of a general reform of coinage, Louis IX of France created the *gros tournois,* which was to become the basis for most of the succeeding multiple silver coins. With 4.2 grams of 96 percent pure silver, the *gros tournois* was originally valued at 12 *tournois* pennies, but, as with the Venetian *grosso,* its exchange value rose continually after its issue. Charles of Anjou, brother of Louis IX, brought the standard of the *gros tournois* to his possessions in Provence and Italy. This standard was also followed in the *gros* of Montpellier initiated by James I of Majorca in 1272, and the *croat* of Barcelona of Peter II the Great in 1284. The same standard was followed in the *groots* minted by the rulers of Flanders, Brabant, and Holland.

In Hainaut, Margaret of Constantinople introduced a multiple silver coin in the late thirteenth century that was the equivalent of two-thirds of the *gros tournois* and twice the English sterling penny; as the *cavalier* or *ridder* this denomination found favor in many other principalities of the Low Countries. In Tyrol, Meinhard II issued two silver multiples of lighter weight than the *gros tournois;* his *grosso aquilino* was adopted as the standard for the Ghibelline towns of northern Italy, and his *Kreuzer* was widely imitated in southern Germany.

In 1300 Wenceslas II of Bohemia used the newly discovered silver mines in his realm as the source for his *Prager Groschen,* which followed the standards of the *gros tournois.* This coin circulated widely in the neighboring regions of Germany and was imitated in the multiple coins of such mints as Meissen, Hesse, and Cracow.

England, with its fine sterling penny maintained throughout the later Middle Ages, was the last major European country to adopt a silver multiple. An overvalued groat was introduced in 1279 as part of a general coinage reform of Edward I but was soon abandoned; it was not until 1351 that a groat, valued at four pennies, was established in England.

BIBLIOGRAPHY

"Les commencements de la grosse monnaie et de la monnaie d'or en Europe centrale (1250–1350)," in *Numismatický sborník,* **12** (1973); Arthur Engel and Raymond Serrure, *Traité de numismatique du moyen âge,* III (1905); John Porteous, *Coins in History* (1969), 83–139.

ALAN M. STAHL

[See also **Mints and Money; Penny.**]

GROENLENDINGA SAGA. See Vinland Sagas.

GROINED VAULT. See Vault.

GROOTE, GEERT (October 1340–20 August 1384), Dutch reformer born in Deventer of wealthy parents, began his studies in Paris at fifteen and received the master of arts degree in less than three years. He remained in Paris for ten years, studying canon law and collecting manuscripts. On his return to the Netherlands, he led a worldly life supported by two prebends, but in 1374 he gave up these offices, turned his family home over to a group of women who subsequently became the first Sisters of the Common Life, and retired for nearly three years to the Carthusian monastery of Monnikhuizen, near Arnhem. At about this time he was in contact with the famous Flemish mystic Jan van Ruusbroec and translated his *Adornment of the Spiritual Wedding* into Latin. After being ordained a deacon in 1379, Groote preached with overwhelming success throughout Holland, exhorting men "of good will" to join together in leading lives of deep spirituality and simple poverty, and criticizing the worldliness of churchmen—until a ban on preaching by deacons aimed at silencing Groote was pronounced in 1383.

The church forbade the founding of new religious orders but not of brotherhoods, which did not require their members to take vows. Thus, in accordance with the desires of his followers, Groote established the Brethren of the Common Life, perhaps at the urging of Florens Radewijns, who later inherited the leadership of the community. Groote died of the plague at the age of forty-three. On his deathbed he advised his followers to join the order of the Augustinian Canons Regular because their rules were much like those of the Brethren.

Among Groote's works are *Conclusa et preposita, non vota,* a seminal work laying out many of his basic ideas, and *Contra turrim traiectensem,* a tract protesting the building of the great tower of the Utrecht cathedral because of the worldliness of the endeavor. His translations of a breviary and seven psalms into Dutch were extremely popular.

BIBLIOGRAPHY

Jean M. E. Dols, *Bibliografie der Moderne Devotie,* 2 vols. (1936–1937); Georgette Épiney-Burgard, *Gérard Grote (1340–1384) et les débuts de la dévotion moderne* (1970); Albert Hyma, *The Brethren of the Common Life* (1950); Regnerus R. Post, *The Modern Devotion* (1968); Thomas P. van Zijl, *Gerard Groote: Ascetic and Reformer* (1963).

MARY-JO ARN

[See also **Brethren of the Common Life; Devotio Moderna; Ruusbroec, Jan van.**]